Collins COBUILD

International Business English Dictionary

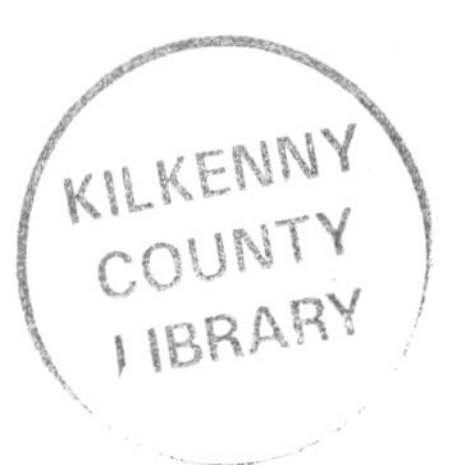

HarperCollins Publishers
Westerhill Road
Bishopbriggs
Glasgow
G64 2QT

First edition 2011

Reprint 10 9 8 7 6 5 4 3 2 1 0

ISBN 978-0-00-741911-1

www.collinslanguage.com
www.collinselt.com

A catalogue record for this book is available from the British Library

Typeset by Davidson Publishing Solutions, Glasgow

Printed and bound in Italy, by LEGO SpA, Lavis (Trento)

Senior Editor
Ian Brookes

Project Manager
Lisa Sutherland

Contributors
Sandra Anderson
Carol Braham
Barbara Campbell
Penny Hands
Kate Mohideen
Enid Pearsons
Jane Solomon
Elizabeth Walter
Kate Wild

For the publisher
Lucy Cooper
Kerry Ferguson
Elaine Higgleton

The publisher would like to thank Nick Brieger for his contribution to the dictionary.

Contents

About COBUILD

When the first COBUILD dictionary was published in 1987, it revolutionized dictionaries for learners. It was the first of a new generation of language reference materials that were based on actual evidence of how English was used, rather than lexicographer intuition.

Collins and the University of Birmingham, led by the linguist John Sinclair, developed an electronic corpus in the 1980s, called the Collins Birmingham University International Language Database (COBUILD). This corpus, which for several years was known as the Bank of English™, became the largest collection of English data in the world. COBUILD dictionary editors use the Collins Corpus to analyze the way that people really use the language.

The Collins Corpus now contains 4.5 billion words taken from websites, newspapers, magazines, and books published around the world, and from spoken material from radio, TV, and everyday conversations. New data is added to the corpus every month, to help COBUILD editors identify new words, grammatical structures, and meanings from the moment they are first used.

All COBUILD language reference books are based on the information our editors find in the Collins Corpus. Because the corpus is so large, our editors can look at lots of examples of how people really use the language. The data tells us how the language is used; the function of different structures; which words are used together; and how often these words and structures are used.

All of the examples in COBUILD language materials are examples of real English, taken from the corpus. The examples have been carefully chosen to demonstrate typical grammatical patterns, typical vocabulary, and typical contexts.

For the *Collins COBUILD International Business English Dictionary*, a special subset of the corpus was created, called the Collins Business Corpus. This contains only texts that relate to the world of business. Collins editors and researchers were able to use this business corpus to establish which words and expressions were the most important to include in the dictionary.

The Collins Corpus lies at the heart of COBUILD, and you can be confident that COBUILD will show you what you need to know to be able to communicate easily and accurately in English.

If you would like to learn more about the Collins Corpus, or to sign up for our online corpus service, please go to **www.collinslanguage.com/wordbanks**.

If you would like to learn more about how Collins can help you improve your international business English skills, go to **www.collinselt.com**.

Introduction

English is the international language of business, and anyone who works with customers, clients, or suppliers in another country needs to be able to use the language effectively. Knowledge of the words and phrases that occur frequently in business will prevent misunderstandings, improve working relationships, and ultimately improve the success of a business. *Collins COBUILD International Business English Dictionary* is therefore a valuable tool for improving business performance.

The dictionary includes all of the up-to-date business words that you may need, including words from economics, finance, business administration, e-commerce, and marketing. Each word is explained with a **definition** that is easy to understand. Where helpful, words are also illustrated with **examples** of natural English, which are taken from the Collins Corpus, and reflect the way that the word is likely to be used in business. As well as definitions and examples, key entries include additional information about **collocations** and **phrases** to help you put the vocabulary into practice.

Besides specialized business terms, the dictionary also includes a wide selection of general vocabulary that you may need when traveling in the English-speaking world. The book will not only help you with the language you encounter during a business meeting, but will also provide the language you will need on the journey to and from the meeting, and when building relationships with your colleagues.

The book is designed for all areas of the world where English is spoken. Where there is variation between American and British English, the word-forms preferred in American English are used. However, where an equivalent British word exists, this has also been included and cross-referred to the standard American word.

The dictionary also includes practical help that will be invaluable to anyone who has to use English for business. An extensive **writing guide** contains advice on writing emails, business letters, and reports. There is also guidance on how to give successful business **presentations**, including useful phrases and practical tips. A further section lists **important phrases** that you may need to use or understand in meetings, telephone calls, and business negotiations. Finally, a series of short articles on **cultural awareness** explains some of the different attitudes you may encounter around the world and helps you to be prepared for these.

We hope that *Collins COBUILD International Business English Dictionary* provides the answers to any problems you may encounter with the English language and so contributes to the success and growth of your business.

Guide to dictionary entries

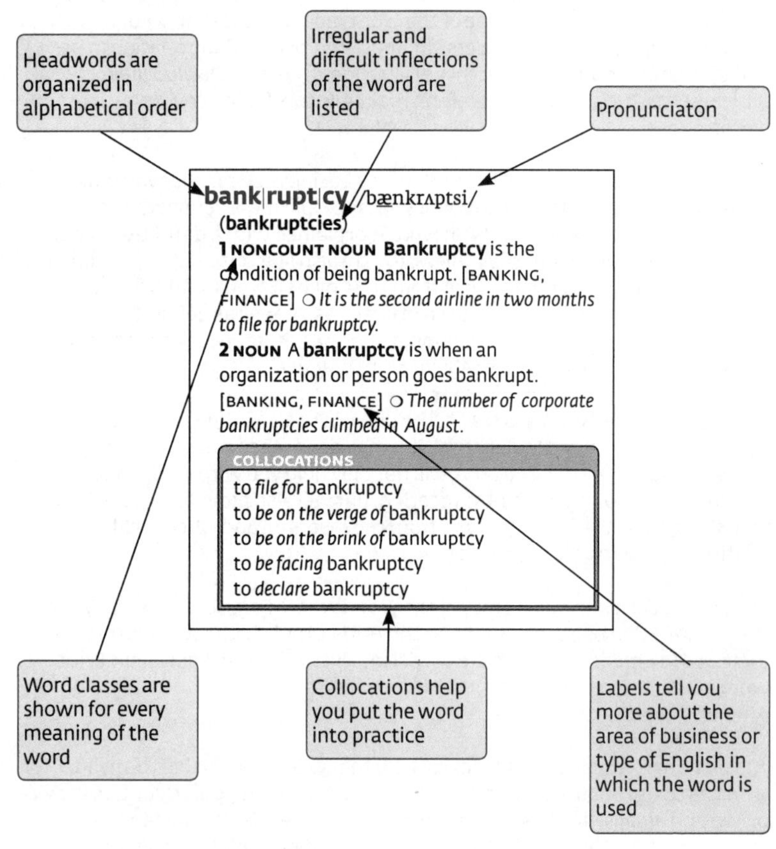
Headwords are organized in alphabetical order
Irregular and difficult inflections of the word are listed
Pronunciaton
bank|rupt|cy /bæŋkrʌptsi/
(bankruptcies)
1 NONCOUNT NOUN Bankruptcy is the condition of being bankrupt. [BANKING, FINANCE] ○ It is the second airline in two months to file for bankruptcy.
2 NOUN A bankruptcy is when an organization or person goes bankrupt. [BANKING, FINANCE] ○ The number of corporate bankruptcies climbed in August.
COLLOCATIONS
to file for bankruptcy
to be on the verge of bankruptcy
to be on the brink of bankruptcy
to be facing bankruptcy
to declare bankruptcy
Word classes are shown for every meaning of the word
Collocations help you put the word into practice
Labels tell you more about the area of business or type of English in which the word is used

Definitions explain what the word means in simple language

British forms are cross-referred to American forms

casual|ise /kæʒuəlaɪz/ [BRIT] → **casualize**

casual|ize /kæʒuəlaɪz/ (**casualizes, casualizing, casualized**) VERB If a business **casualizes** its employees or **casualizes** their labor, it replaces employees with permanent contracts and full rights with employees with temporary contracts and few rights. [ECONOMICS] ○ *a casualized workforce*

● **casual|iza|tion** /kæʒuəlɪzeɪʃən/ NONCOUNT NOUN ○ *the casualization of employment*

Related words are listed without a definition when the meaning is easy to understand from the headword

Examples show how the word is used in context

Guide to labels

Grammatical labels

All the words in the dictionary have grammar information given about them. For each word, its word class is shown after the headword. The sections below show more information about each word class:

ADJ

An **adjective** is a word that is used for telling you more about a person or thing. You would use an adjective to talk about appearance, color, size, or other qualities, e.g. *Anna was absent from the meeting.*

ADV

An **adverb** is a word that gives more information about when, how, or where something happens, e.g. *He described it quite accurately.*

ARTICLE

An **article** is one of the words *a, an,* or *the* that is used before a noun. It shows whether you are talking about a particular thing or a general example of something, e.g. *He started eating an apple.*

AUX

An **auxiliary verb** is a verb that is used with another verb to show its tense, to form questions, or to form the passive. The main auxiliary verbs in English are *be, have,* and *do*, e.g. *He was driving to work when the accident happened.*

CONJ

A **conjunction** is a word such as *and, but, if,* and *since.* Conjunctions are used for linking two words or two parts of a sentence together, e.g. *I waved goodbye and went down the steps.*

EXCLAM

An **exclamation** is a word or phrase that is spoken suddenly or loudly in order to express a strong emotion, e.g. *"Oh!" Kenny said. "Has everyone gone?"*

MODAL

A **modal verb** is a verb such as *may, must,* or *would.* A modal verb is used before the infinitive form of a verb, e.g. *I can access the figures you need.*

NONCOUNT NOUN

A **noncount noun** is used for talking about things that are not normally counted, or that we do not think of as single items. Noncount nouns do not have a plural form, and they are used with a singular verb, e.g. *Thank you for your help.*

NOUN

A **noun** is a word that refers to a person, a thing, or a quality. In this book, the label *noun* is given to all count nouns. A count noun is used for talking about things that can be counted, and that have both singular and plural forms, e.g. *Gold is traditionally a hedge against inflation, Her talk highlighted the problems we face.*

PHRASAL VERB	A **phrasal verb** consists of a verb and one or more particles, e.g. *The quickest way of getting the cash was to jack up interest rates.*
PL NOUN	A **plural noun** is always plural, and it is used with plural verbs, e.g. *My private affairs are no one's business but my own.*
PREP	A **preposition** is a word such as *by*, *with*, or *from* that is always followed by a noun group or the *-ing* form of a verb, e.g. *It rained heavily throughout the game.*
PRON	A **pronoun** is a word that you use instead of a noun, when you do not need or want to name someone or something directly, e.g. *I need someone to help me.*
VERB	A **verb** is a word that is used for saying what someone or something does, or what happens to them, or to give information about them, e.g. *So far, the strategy appears to be working.*

Subject labels

The following labels are used when a word or phrase relates to a particular profession or area of business:

ADMINISTRATION
BANKING
BUSINESS MANAGEMENT
E-COMMERCE
ECONOMICS
FINANCE
HR (= HUMAN RESOURCES)
LEGAL
LOGISTICS AND DISTRIBUTION
MARKETING AND SALES
PRODUCTION
PURCHASING
R & D (= RESEARCH AND DEVELOPMENT)
TECHNOLOGY

Labels

The following labels are used to provide more information about a word:

BRIT	British English
FORMAL	used mainly in formal situations, and not usually in everyday conversation
INFORMAL	used mainly in informal situations with people at work who you know well, but not in official, formal situations
OLD-FASHIONED	no longer used in English
SPOKEN	used mainly in speech, but not usually in writing
WRITTEN	used mainly in writing, but not usually in speech

Pronunciation guide

IPA symbols

Vowel	Sounds
ɑ	calm, ah
æ	act, mass
aɪ	dive, cry
aʊ	out, down
ɛ	met, lend, pen
eɪ	say, weight
ɪ	fit, win
i	feed, me
ɒ	lot, spot
oʊ	note, coat
ɔ	claw, more
ɔɪ	boy, joint
ʊ	could, stood
u	you, use
ʌ	fund, must
ə	the first vowel in about
i	second vowel in very
u	second vowel in actual

Notes

Stress is shown by a line below the stressed syllable. For example, in the word *accomplish*, /əkɒmplɪʃ/, the second syllable is stressed.

Consonant	Sounds
b	bed, rub
d	done, red
f	fit, if
g	good, dog
h	hat, horse
k	king, pick
l	lip, bill
ᵊl	handle, panel
m	mat, ram
n	not, tin
ᵊn	hidden, written
p	pay, lip
r	run, read
s	soon, bus
t	talk, bet
v	van, love
w	win, wool
x	loch
y	yellow, you
z	zoo, buzz
ʃ	ship, wish
ʒ	measure, leisure
ŋ	sing, working
tʃ	cheap, witch
θ	thin, myth
ð	then, bathe
dʒ	joy, bridge

Business Dictionary A–Z

Aa

a /ə, STRONG eɪ/ or **an** /ən, STRONG æn/
1 ARTICLE The word **a** is called the "indefinite article." You use it before a singular noun or to avoid saying exactly which person or thing you mean. ❍ *A waiter came in with a glass of water.* ❍ *He started eating an apple.*
2 ARTICLE every or each ❍ *She goes to London three times a month.*

aban|don /əbændən/ **VERB** If you **abandon** someone or something, you leave them, especially when you should not. ❍ *The system was abandoned in 1987.* ● **aban|doned ADJ** ❍ *They found an abandoned car.*

ab|bre|via|tion /əbriviejʃən/ **NOUN** a short form of a word or phrase ❍ *The abbreviation for Managing Director is MD.*

abil|ity /əbɪlɪti/ (**abilities**) **NOUN** a quality or skill needed to do something ❍ *the company's ability to compete in global markets* ❍ *information-processing abilities*

able /eɪbᵊl/ (**abler** /eɪblər/, **ablest** /eɪblɪst/) If you **are able to** do something, you can do it. ❍ *Only larger firms will be able to afford the increasing costs.*

ab|nor|mal /æbnɔrmᵊl/ **ADJ** unusual, in a way that is a problem ❍ *an abnormal heartbeat*

aboard /əbɔrd/ **PREP** or **ADV** on a ship or plane ❍ *He invited us aboard his boat.* ❍ *It took two hours to get all the people aboard.*

abol|ish /əbɒlɪʃ/ (**abolishes, abolishing, abolished**) **VERB** If someone **abolishes** a system or practice, they officially end it. ❍ *arguments for abolishing corporate tax*

about /əbaʊt/
1 PREP used to introduce a particular subject ❍ *She knew a lot about tax law.*
2 ADV used in front of a number to show that the number is not exact ❍ *The firm was about eight years old.*
3 If you are **about to** do something, you are going to do it very soon. ❍ *He's about to leave.*

above /əbʌv/
1 PREP over or higher than ❍ *He lifted his hands above his head.* ❍ *Their apartment was above a clothing store.*
2 PREP greater than a particular level ❍ *The temperature rose to just above 40 degrees.*

above-the-line ADJ In an **above-the-line** advertising campaign, a company employs an advertising agency to use newspapers, television, the Internet and posters. Compare with **below-the-line**. [MARKETING AND SALES] ❍ *We've launched new products and put money into above-the-line advertising.*

above-the-line pro|mo|tion (**above-the-line promotions**) **NOUN** **Above-the-line promotion** is the use of promotional methods that cannot be directly controlled by the company, such as advertisements in magazines or on television. Compare with **below-the-line promotion**. [MARKETING AND SALES] ❍ *Most of our above-the-line promotion is conducted through magazines.*

abroad /əbrɔd/ **ADV** If you go **abroad**, you go to a foreign country. ❍ *Many students go abroad to work for the summer.*

ab|rupt /əbrʌpt/ **ADJ** very sudden ❍ *His career came to an abrupt end in 1998.*
● **ab|rupt|ly ADV** ❍ *Demand stopped abruptly.*

ab|sence /æbsᵊns/ **NOUN** Someone's **absence** from a place is the fact that they are not there. ❍ *Her absence from work is becoming a problem.*

ab|sent /æbsᵊnt/ **ADJ** not at a particular place ❍ *Anna was absent from the meeting.*

ab|sen|tee|ism /æbsᵊntiɪzəm/ **NONCOUNT NOUN** **Absenteeism** is the habit of frequently being away from work, usually without a good reason. [HR] ❍ *We need to tackle the high rate of absenteeism.*

A

ab|so|lute /æbsəlut/ **ADJ** total and complete ❍ *absolute certainty*

ab|so|lute|ly /æbsəlutli/
1 ADV totally and completely ❍ *You're absolutely right.*
2 ADV a way of saying yes or of agreeing with someone strongly ❍ *"Do you think I should call him?"—"Absolutely."*

ab|sorb /əbsɔrb, -zɔrb/
1 VERB To **absorb** a liquid or gas is to take it in. ❍ *The carbon filter absorbs the air pollutants.* ● **ab|sorb|ent** /əbsɔrbənt, -zɔrb-/ **ADJ** ❍ *an absorbent material*
2 VERB To **absorb** changes, effects, or costs is to deal with them without being badly affected. ❍ *Manufacturers are absorbing higher production costs rather than passing them on to consumers.*

ab|sorb|ing /əbsɔrbɪŋ, -zɔrb-/ **ADJ** very interesting ❍ *an absorbing book*

ab|stract /æbstrækt/
1 ADJ based on general ideas rather than on real things ❍ *abstract thought*
2 ADJ **Abstract** art uses shapes and patterns rather than showing people or things. ❍ *abstract paintings*

abuse (**abuses, abusing, abused**)

> Pronounce the noun /əbyus/. Pronounce the verb /əbyuz/.

1 NONCOUNT NOUN **Abuse** is cruel treatment of someone. ❍ *child abuse*
2 NONCOUNT NOUN **Abuse** is rude and unkind remarks directed towards someone. ❍ *I shouted abuse as the car drove away.*
3 NOUN The **abuse** of something is the use of it in the wrong way. ❍ *drug abuse*
4 VERB If someone **is abused**, they are treated cruelly. ❍ *Other employees were physically and verbally abused.*

a/c also **A/C**
1 a/c is a written abbreviation of **account**. [FINANCE, BANKING]
2 a/c is a written abbreviation of **current account**. [FINANCE, BANKING]

aca|dem|ic /ækədɛmɪk/ **ADJ** relating to the work done in schools, colleges, and universities ❍ *academic standards*

acc. **acc.** is a written abbreviation of **account**. [FINANCE, BANKING]

ac|cel|er|ate /æksɛləreɪt/ (**accelerates, accelerating, accelerated**) **VERB** If something **accelerates**, it gets faster. ❍ *Suddenly the car accelerated.* ❍ *Inflation will begin to accelerate.*

ac|cent /æksɛnt/
1 NOUN a way of pronouncing a language ❍ *He had a slight Southern accent.*
2 NOUN a mark written above a letter to show how it is pronounced ❍ *The word "café" has an accent on the "e."*

ac|cept /æksɛpt/
1 VERB If you **accept** something, you agree to take it. ❍ *The company may not accept my offer.*
2 VERB If you **accept** a situation, you realize that it cannot be changed. ❍ *Investors have to accept the possibility of a slowdown in economic activity.*
3 VERB If you **accept** responsibility for something, you agree that you are responsible for it. ❍ *The company accepted responsibility for the damage.*

ac|cept|able /æksɛptəbᵊl/ **ADJ** If something is **acceptable**, people consider it to be normal or good enough. ❍ *Asking people for money is not acceptable behavior.* ❍ *This deal looks acceptable.* ● **ac|cept|ably** **ADV** ❍ *capping profits at an acceptably low level*

ac|cept|ance /æksɛptəns/
1 NOUN the act of agreeing to an offer or proposal ❍ *The committee recommended acceptance of the proposal.* ❍ *his acceptance speech for the Nobel Peace Prize*
2 NONCOUNT NOUN If there is **acceptance** of something, most people agree with it or approve of it. ❍ *a theory that is steadily gaining acceptance* ❍ *We are very pleased with consumer acceptance of our new products.*
3 NOUN a formal agreement by a debtor to pay a bill [LEGAL]

ac|cess /æksɛs/ (**accesses, accessing, accessed**)

1 NONCOUNT NOUN If you have **access to** a building or other place, you are allowed to go into it. ❍ *The general public does not have access to the White House.*
2 NONCOUNT NOUN If you have **access to** information or equipment, you are allowed to use it. ❍ *Patients have access to their medical records.*
3 VERB If you **access** information on a computer, you find it. ❍ *Parents can see which sites their children have accessed.*

ac|ces|sible /æksɛsɪbᵊl/ **ADJ** easy for people to reach or enter ❍ *Most rooms are accessible for wheelchairs.*

ac|ces|so|ry /æksɛsəri/ (**accessories**) **NOUN** **Accessories** are things such as belts and scarves. ❍ *We shopped for handbags, scarves, and other accessories.*

ac|ci|dent /æksɪdənt/
1 NOUN an unexpected event in which something bad happens ❍ *There were 14 highway accidents yesterday afternoon.*
2 If something happens **by accident**, it happens by chance. ❍ *We met by accident.*

ac|ci|den|tal /æksɪdɛntᵊl/ **ADJ** happening by chance ❍ *accidental death* ● **ac|ci|den|tal|ly** /æksɪdɛntli/ **ADV** ❍ *They accidentally removed the names from the computer.*

ac|ci|dent in|sur|ance **NONCOUNT NOUN** **Accident insurance** is insurance that pays money if someone is injured in an accident. [BANKING] ❍ *Workers are entitled to accident insurance.*

ac|com|mo|date /əkɒmədeɪt/ (**accommodates, accommodating, accommodated**) **VERB** If a building or space can **accommodate** someone or something, it has enough space for them. ❍ *Ports are to get longer piers to accommodate all the containers.*

ac|com|mo|da|tion /əkɒmədeɪʃən/ **NOUN** **Accommodations** are buildings or rooms where people live or stay. ❍ *luxury accommodations*

ac|com|pa|ny /əkʌmpəni/ (**accompanies, accompanying, accompanied**)
1 VERB If you **accompany** someone, you go somewhere with them. [FORMAL] ❍ *Ken agreed to accompany me on a trip to Africa.*
2 VERB If you **accompany** a singer or a musician, you play one part of a piece of music while they sing or play the main tune. ❍ *Her singing teacher accompanied her on the piano.*

ac|com|plish /əkɒmplɪʃ/ (**accomplishes, accomplishing, accomplished**) **VERB** If you **accomplish** something, you succeed in doing it. ❍ *We accomplished our goal.*

ac|com|plish|ment /əkɒmplɪʃmənt/ **NOUN** something special that someone has achieved by working very hard ❍ *appreciation for each person's special efforts and accomplishments*

ac|cord|ing /əkɔrdɪŋ/
1 If something is true **according to** a particular person, that is where the information comes from. ❍ *According to police reports, they then drove away in a white van.*
2 If something is done **according to** a set of rules or a plan, it is done in a way that agrees with these rules or this plan. ❍ *If everything goes according to plan, the building should be finished by March.*

ac|count /əkaʊnt/
1 NOUN If you have an **account** with a bank, you leave your money there and take some out when you need it. [BANKING] ❍ *I have $3,000 in my bank account.*
2 NOUN an arrangement to do regular work for another company [BUSINESS MANAGEMENT] ❍ *Our priority is to win the British Airways account.*
3 PL NOUN **Accounts** are records of all the money that a person or business gets and spends. [FINANCE] ❍ *They kept detailed accounts.*
4 NOUN an arrangement you have with a company to use a service they provide ❍ *an email account*
5 NOUN a report of something that has happened ❍ *a detailed account of events*
▸ **account for** If you **account for** something, you explain it. ❍ *How do you account for these differences?*

ac|count|an|cy /əkaʊntənsi/ [FINANCE, BRIT] → **accounting**

a

A

ac|count|ant /əkauntənt/ **NOUN** a person whose job is to keep financial accounts [FINANCE, ADMINISTRATION] ❍ *He's an accountant with a big law firm.*

ac|count ex|ecu|tive (**account executives**) **NOUN** an executive who works in advertising and deals with regular customers [MARKETING AND SALES, ADMINISTRATION] ❍ *She is an account executive in marketing for IBM.*

ac|count|ing /əkauntɪŋ/ **NONCOUNT NOUN** **Accounting** is the activity of keeping financial records. [FINANCE] ❍ *the accounting firm of Leventhal & Horwath*

ac|count pay|able (**accounts payable**) **NOUN** an account that shows how much a firm owes to suppliers [FINANCE, BANKING] ❍ *Accounts payable were approximately $20 million that year.*

ac|count re|ceiv|able /əkaunt rɪsivəbᵊl/ (**accounts receivable**) **NOUN** an account that shows how much a firm is owed by customers [FINANCE, BANKING] ❍ *Accounts receivable are unpaid customer invoices, and any other money owed to you by customers.*

ac|cru|al /əkruəl/
1 NOUN the adding together of something such as interest or investments over a period of time [FINANCE] ❍ *After an employee has 25 years of service, there is no further accrual of benefits.* ❍ *the accrual of funds used during construction*
2 NOUN an amount of money owed in one accounting period that has not been paid by the end of it [FINANCE]

ac|crue /əkru/ (**accrues, accruing, accrued**)
1 VERB If money or interest **accrues**, it gradually increases in amount over a period of time. [FINANCE] ❍ *I owed $5,000 – part of this was accrued interest.* ❍ *If you do not pay within 28 days, interest will accrue.*
2 VERB If things such as profits **accrue to** someone, they are given to that person over a period of time. [FORMAL] ❍ *Most of the benefits accrue to the shareholders.*

ac|cu|mu|late /əkyumyəleɪt/ (**accumulates, accumulating, accumulated**) **VERB** When you **accumulate** things or when things **accumulate**, they collect or are gathered over a period of time. ❍ *He accumulated $42,000 in 6 years.*
● **ac|cu|mu|la|tion** /əkyumyəleɪʃən/ **NOUN** ❍ *the accumulation of wealth* ❍ *an accumulation of experience and knowledge*

ac|cu|rate /ækyərɪt/
1 ADJ **Accurate** information is correct. ❍ *an accurate description* ● **ac|cu|ra|cy** **NONCOUNT NOUN** ❍ *the accuracy of financial forecasts* ● **ac|cu|rate|ly** **ADV** ❍ *He described it quite accurately.*
2 ADJ A person or machine that is **accurate** is able to do something without making a mistake. ❍ *an accurate watch* ● **ac|cu|ra|cy** **NONCOUNT NOUN** ❍ *the accuracy of the firm's deliveries* ● **ac|cu|rate|ly** **ADV** ❍ *Both print heads deposit their materials accurately.*

ac|cuse /əkyuz/ (**accuses, accusing, accused**) **VERB** If you **accuse** someone **of** something bad, you say that they did it. ❍ *They accused her of lying.*

ace /eɪs/
1 NOUN a very skillful and famous sports player ❍ *former tennis ace John McEnroe*
2 ADJ **Ace** is also an adjective. ❍ *ace film producer Lawrence Woolsey*
3 NOUN in tennis, a serve (= a hit) that is so fast that the other player cannot return the ball ❍ *Federer served three aces in the final set.*

ache /eɪk/ (**aches, aching, ached**)
1 VERB If a part of your body **aches**, you feel a continuous dull pain there. ❍ *My legs ache after all that running.*
2 NOUN **Ache** is also a noun. ❍ *aches and pains*

achieve /ətʃiv/ (**achieves, achieving, achieved**) **VERB** If you **achieve** something, you succeed in doing it, usually after a lot of effort. ❍ *He worked hard to achieve his goals.*

achieve|ment /ətʃivmənt/ **NOUN** something that you succeed in doing, especially after a lot of effort ❍ *The government's economic achievements of the past year.*

acid /æsɪd/ **NOUN** a chemical liquid that can burn your skin and cause damage to other substances ❍ *sulphuric acid*

ac|knowl|edge /æknɒlɪdʒ/ (**acknowledges, acknowledging, acknowledged**) VERB If you **acknowledge** a fact or a situation, you agree that it is true or that it exists. [FORMAL] ❍ *He acknowledged that he was wrong.* ❍ *At last, the government has acknowledged the problem.*

ac|quaint|ance /əkweɪntəns/ NOUN someone you know slightly but not well ❍ *He's an old acquaintance of mine.*

ac|quire /əkwaɪər/ (**acquires, acquiring, acquired**)
1 VERB If you **acquire** something, you get it. [FINANCE, BUSINESS MANAGEMENT, FORMAL] ❍ *Chugai recently acquired 100,000 shares in Vicon.*
2 VERB If you **acquire** a skill or a habit, you learn it or develop it. ❍ *Employees who complete this training course will acquire a wide range of skills.*

ac|quir|er /əkwaɪərər/ NOUN a company or person who buys another company [FINANCE, BUSINESS MANAGEMENT] ❍ *the ability of corporate acquirers to finance large takeovers*

ac|qui|si|tion /ækwɪzɪʃən/ NOUN the act of buying another company or part of a company [FINANCE, BUSINESS MANAGEMENT] ❍ *the acquisition of a profitable paper recycling company* ❍ *the number of mergers and acquisitions made by Europe's 1,000 leading firms*

ac|qui|si|tion ac|count|ing NONCOUNT NOUN **Acquisition accounting** is an accounting procedure in which assets are transferred from their book value to the market value when a company has recently been taken over. [FINANCE, BUSINESS MANAGEMENT]

acre /eɪkər/ NOUN An acre is a unit for measuring areas of land. One acre is equal to 4840 square yards or about 4047 square meters. ❍ *He rented three acres of land.*

across /əkrɔs/
1 PREP If someone goes **across** a place, they go from one side of it to the other. ❍ *Mrs. Segal's job requires substantial travel across Michigan.*
2 ADV **Across** is also an adverb. ❍ *He stood up and walked across to the window.*
3 PREP If something is **across** something else, it goes from one side of it to the other. ❍ *The bridge across the river was closed.*

act /ækt/
1 VERB When you **act**, you do something for a particular purpose. ❍ *Companies have acted to improve their cash-flow positions.*
2 VERB If someone **acts** in a particular way, they behave in that way. ❍ *The youths were acting suspiciously.* ❍ *He acts as if I'm not there.*
3 VERB If you **act** in a play or film, you have a part in it. ❍ *He acted in many films, including "Reds."*
4 NOUN a single thing that someone does ❍ *an act of kindness*
5 NOUN An **Act** is a law passed by a government. ❍ *an Act of Congress*
6 NOUN one of the main parts that a play is divided into ❍ *Act two has a really funny scene.*

act|ing /æktɪŋ/ NONCOUNT NOUN **Acting** is the activity or job of performing in plays or films. ❍ *I'd like to do some acting some day.*

ac|tion /ækʃən/
1 NONCOUNT NOUN **Action** is the process of doing something for a particular purpose. ❍ *The government must now take action.*
2 NOUN something that you do on a particular occasion ❍ *He couldn't explain his actions.*
3 VERB If you **action** something that needs to be done, you make sure that it happens. ❍ *Documents can be actioned, or filed immediately.*

ac|tive /æktɪv/
1 ADJ Someone who is **active** moves around a lot or does a lot of things. ❍ *At 75, she's still very active.*
2 NOUN In grammar, **the active** is the form of a verb that you use to show that the subject performs the action. For example, in "I saw him," the verb **see** is in the active. Compare with **passive**.
3 ADJ producing profit or being used to produce profit [BANKING] ❍ *active balances*
4 ADJ **Active** stocks and shares have been bought and sold recently. [FINANCE] ❍ *Out of 183 active stocks traded during the day, 118 losers led the scene.*

ac|tiv|ity /æktɪvɪti/ (**activities**)
1 NONCOUNT NOUN **Activity** is all the things

that people do ❍ *periods of high economic activity*

2 NOUN something that you do for pleasure ❍ *sport and leisure activities*

A

ac|tor /æktər/ **NOUN** someone whose job is acting in plays or movies ❍ *a famous actor*

ac|tress /æktrɪs/ (**actresses**) **NOUN** a woman whose job is acting in plays or movies ❍ *a British actress*

ac|tual /æktʃuəl/ **ADJ** real or exact and not imagined or guessed ❍ *The characters in the book are based on actual people.* ❍ *I could give you an approximate number but I don't know the actual figure.*

ac|tu|al|ly /æktʃuəli/ **ADV** used for saying that something surprising really is true ❍ *The judge actually fell asleep during the trial.*

ac|tu|ary /æktʃuɛri/ (**actuaries**) **NOUN** a person who is employed by insurance companies to calculate how much they should charge their clients for insurance [BANKING]

acute /əkyut/ **ADJ** An **acute** situation or feeling is very severe or serious. ❍ *He was in acute pain.* ❍ *an acute shortage of nurses*

ad /æd/ **NOUN** an advertisement [MARKETING AND SALES, INFORMAL] ❍ *I placed an ad in the newspaper.*

AD /eɪ di/ also **A.D.** **AD** is used in dates to show the number of years that have passed since the year in which Jesus Christ was born. Compare with **BC**. ❍ *The church was built in 600 AD.*

a|dapt /ədæpt/

1 VERB If you **adapt to** a new situation, you change your ideas or behavior in order to deal with it. ❍ *We had to adapt to the new culture.*

2 VERB If you **adapt** something, you change it so that you can use it in a different way. ❍ *They adapted the library for use as an office.*

add /æd/

1 VERB If you **add** one thing **to** another thing, you put it with the other thing. ❍ *Barclays added $233 million to Third World debt provisions.*

2 VERB If you **add** numbers or amounts **together**, you calculate their total. ❍ *Add all the numbers together, and divide by three.*

3 VERB If you **add** something when you are speaking, you say something more. ❍ *"And he's not happy," she added.*

▸ **add up** If you **add up** numbers or amounts, you calculate their total. ❍ *Add up the number of hours you spent on the task.*

add|ed value **NONCOUNT NOUN** **Added value** is something that makes a product more appealing to customers. ❍ *We can create significant added value by upgrading the standard of product design.*

ad|dict /ædɪkt/

1 NOUN someone who cannot stop taking harmful drugs ❍ *a drug addict*

2 NOUN someone who likes a particular activity very much and does that activity too often ❍ *a TV addict*

ad|dict|ed /ədɪktɪd/ **ADJ** Someone who is **addicted to** a harmful drug cannot stop taking it. ❍ *Many of the women are addicted to heroin.*

ad|dic|tion /ədɪkʃən/

1 NOUN the condition of not being able to stop taking drugs or alcohol ❍ *She helped him fight his drug addiction.*

2 NOUN a strong need to do a particular activity for as much time as possible ❍ *his addiction to computer games*

ad|di|tion /ədɪʃən/

1 NONCOUNT NOUN **Addition** is the process of calculating the total of two or more numbers. ❍ *She can count to 100, and do simple addition problems.* ● **ad|di|tion|al** /ədɪʃənᵊl/ **ADJ** ❍ *an additional 2.1 million shares*

2 You use **in addition** when you want to mention another thing relating to the subject you are discussing. ❍ *recoverable reserves of 428 million barrels, in addition to natural gas*

add-on **NOUN** something that can be added to a piece of equipment to improve its performance ❍ *To use this software, you don't need a CD-ROM drive or any expensive add-ons for your computer.* ❍ *The store sells ringtones and other add-ons for its phones.*

ad|dress (**addresses, addressing, addressed**)

> Pronounce the noun /ədrɛs/ or /ædrɛs/. Pronounce the verb /ədrɛs/.

1 NOUN the number of the building where you live, together with the name of the street and the city or state ❍ *The address is 2025 M Street NW, Washington, DC 20036.*
2 NOUN a group of letters, numbers, and symbols that allows you to find a particular website on the Internet, for example, http://www.heinle.com, or that allows you to send an email to someone [TECHNOLOGY] ❍ *a website address* ❍ *an email address*
3 VERB If something **is addressed to** you, your name and address have been written on it. ❍ *The letter was addressed to me.*
4 VERB If you **address** a group of people, you speak to them formally. ❍ *He addressed the crowd of 17,000 people.*
5 NOUN Address is also a noun. ❍ *Judge Richardson began his address to the jury.*
6 VERB If a ship or its cargo is **addressed**, it is handed over to a person who is going to sell it.

ad|dress book
1 NOUN a book in which you write people's names and addresses
2 NOUN a computer program that you use to record people's email addresses and telephone numbers [TECHNOLOGY]

ad|equate /ædɪkwɪt/ **ADJ** If something is **adequate**, there is enough of it or it is good enough. ❍ *One in four people worldwide do not have adequate homes.*

ad|ja|cent /ədʒeɪsᵊnt/ **ADJ** If two things are **adjacent**, they are next to each other. ❍ *adjacent rooms*

ad|jec|tive /ædʒɪktɪv/ **NOUN** An **adjective** is a word such as "big," or "beautiful" that describes a person or thing. Adjectives usually come before nouns or after verbs like "be" or "feel."

ad|just /ədʒʌst/ **VERB** If you **adjust** something, you make a small change to it. ❍ *You can adjust the height of the table.*

ad|min /ædmɪn/ **Admin** is an abbreviation of **administrative** or **administration**. [ADMINISTRATION] ❍ *admin costs*

ad|min|is|tra|tion /ædmɪnɪstreɪʃən/
1 NONCOUNT NOUN Administration is the work of organizing and managing an organization. ❍ *A private company took over the administration of the local jail.*
2 NOUN The administration is the government of a country. ❍ *the Obama administration*

ad|min|is|tra|tive /ædmɪnɪstreɪtɪv/ **ADJ** relating to the work of managing a business or organization ❍ *Administrative costs were high.*

ad|min|is|tra|tive as|sist|ant (**administrative assistants**) **NOUN** a person who helps to supervise the way that an organization functions

ad|min|is|tra|tor /ædmɪnɪstreɪtər/ **NOUN** a person whose job is to supervise the way that an organization functions [ADMINISTRATION] ❍ *On Friday the company's administrators received permission from the court to keep operating.*

ad|mire /ədmaɪər/ (**admires, admiring, admired**) **VERB** If you **admire** someone or something, you like and respect them. ❍ *I admired the way she dealt with the situation.*
● **ad|mir|er NOUN** ❍ *He was an admirer of the company.*

ad|mis|sion /ædmɪʃən/
1 NONCOUNT NOUN Admission is permission given to a person to enter a place. ❍ *He was refused admission to the building.*
2 NOUN a statement admitting that you have done something wrong ❍ *Mr. Dennis is by his own admission "not always easy to get on with."*
3 NONCOUNT NOUN Admission at a park, museum, or other place is the amount of money that you pay to enter it. ❍ *Admission is free.*

ad|mit /ædmɪt/ (**admits, admitting, admitted**)
1 VERB If you **admit** that you have done something wrong, you agree that you did it. ❍ *I am willing to admit that I made a mistake.*
2 VERB If someone **is admitted to** a place or organization, they are allowed to enter it or

join it. ❍ *She was admitted to law school.* ❍ *Security officers refused to admit him.*

A

ado|les|cent /æd^əlɛs^ənt/
1 ADJ used for describing young people who are no longer children but who are not yet adults ❍ *adolescent girls*
2 NOUN An **adolescent** is an adolescent boy or girl. ❍ *Adolescents don't like being treated like children.* ● **ado|les|cence** /æd^əlɛs^əns/ **NONCOUNT NOUN** ❍ *Adolescence is often a difficult period for young people.*

adopt /ədɒpt/
1 VERB If you **adopt** a new idea or way of behaving, you begin to have it. ❍ *She needs to adopt a more positive attitude.*
2 VERB If you **adopt** someone else's child, you take him or her into your own family and make them legally your son or daughter. ❍ *She was adopted.* ● **adop|tion NONCOUNT NOUN** ❍ *They gave their babies up for adoption.*
3 VERB If you **adopt** a system, process or product, you accept it and start to use it. ❍ *The directors adopted an anti-takeover plan, similar to those adopted by a number of companies.* ● **adopt|er NOUN** ❍ *In the 1990s Americans and Scandinavians were early adopters of cellphones.*

adore /ədɔr/ (**adores, adoring, adored**)
VERB If you **adore** someone or something, you love or like them very much. ❍ *She adored her parents.* ❍ *I adore cooking.*

adult /ədʌlt/
1 NOUN a fully grown person or animal ❍ *Tickets cost $20 for adults and $10 for children.*
2 ADJ **Adult** is also an adjective. ❍ *I am the mother of two adult sons.*

ad va|lorem /æd vəlɔrəm/
1 ADJ An **ad valorem** tax is charged at the estimated value of the goods being taxed. [FINANCE] ❍ *They are liable to duties at ad valorem rates.*
2 ADV in proportion to the estimated value of the goods taxed [FINANCE] ❍ *The customs officer decided to charge 20% ad valorem.*

ad|vance /ædvæns/ (**advances, advancing, advanced**)
1 VERB To **advance** means to move forward, often in order to attack someone. ❍ *Soldiers were advancing toward the capital.*
2 VERB To **advance** means to make progress, especially in your knowledge of something. ❍ *Science has advanced greatly in the last 100 years.*
3 NOUN a movement forward, usually as part of a military operation ❍ *Hitler's army began its advance on Moscow in June 1941.*
4 NOUN progress in understanding a subject or activity ❍ *There have been many advances in medicine and public health.*
5 NOUN The **advance** of goods is when they are supplied before they are paid for. The goods supplied in this way can be called an **advance**.
6 NOUN The **advance** of a sum of money is when it is paid before the thing it is to pay for has been received. The money supplied in this way can be called an **advance**.
7 If you do something **in advance**, you do it before a particular date or event. ❍ *The theater sells tickets in advance.*

ad|vanced /ædvænst/ **ADJ** modern and using the most recent knowledge and methods ❍ *advanced technology*

ad|van|tage /ædvæntɪdʒ/
1 NOUN a benefit that puts you in a better position than others ❍ *Being small gives our company an advantage.*
2 NOUN a way in which one thing is better than another ❍ *the advantage of Web advertising over the traditional variety*
3 If you **take advantage of** something good, you get a benefit from it while you can. ❍ *People are taking advantage of lower prices.*
4 If someone **takes advantage of** you, they treat you badly in order to get something good from you. ❍ *She's very generous and I think he takes advantage of her.*

ad|ven|ture /ædvɛntʃər/ **NOUN** an experience that is unusual, exciting, and sometimes dangerous ❍ *his Arctic adventures* ❍ *an adventure story*

ad|verb /ædvɜrb/ **NOUN** a word such as "slowly," "now," "very," or "happily" that adds information about an action, event, or situation

ad|vert /ædvɜrt/ **NOUN** **Advert** is an abbreviation of **advertisement**. [MARKETING AND SALES, BRIT]

ad|ver|tise /ædvərtaɪz/ (**advertises, advertising, advertised**) **VERB** If you **advertise** something, you tell people about it in newspapers, on television, on signs, or on the Internet. [MARKETING AND SALES] ❍ *They are advertising houses for sale.* ❍ *We advertise on radio stations.*

ad|ver|tise|ment /ædvərtaɪzmənt/ **NOUN** an announcement in a newspaper, on television, on a sign or on the Internet about something such as a product, event, or job [MARKETING AND SALES, FORMAL] ❍ *an advertisement for a new movie* ❍ *They saw an advertisement for a job on a farm.*

ad|ver|tis|ing /ædvərtaɪzɪŋ/ **NONCOUNT NOUN** **Advertising** is the business of creating films, pictures, and articles that persuade people to buy things. [MARKETING AND SALES] ❍ *I work in advertising.* ❍ *a well-known advertising slogan*

ad|ver|tis|ing agen|cy (**advertising agencies**) **NOUN** a company whose business is to create advertisements for other companies or organizations [MARKETING AND SALES] ❍ *Several big advertising agencies report that ad spending this year is lower than expectations.*

ad|ver|tis|ing cam|paign **NOUN** a planned series of advertisements [MARKETING AND SALES] ❍ *The Government has launched a mass advertising campaign to reduce the nation's electricity consumption.*

ad|ver|tis|ing stand|ards **PL NOUN** **Advertising standards** are the levels of truthfulness, honesty, and decency that advertisements are expected to follow. [MARKETING AND SALES, LEGAL] ❍ *Agencies must conform to global advertising standards.*

Ad|ver|tis|ing Stand|ards Author|ity **NOUN** In Britain, the **Advertising Standards Authority** is an organization that ensures that advertisements are honest and decent. [MARKETING AND SALES, LEGAL] ❍ *The Advertising Standards Authority has reprimanded two companies for the way they portrayed women in their advertisements.*

ad|ver|tor|ial /ædvərtɔriəl/ **NOUN** an advertisement that is presented as if it was editorial material [MARKETING AND SALES] ❍ *They published an eight-page advertorial in a leading fashion magazine.*

ad|vice /ædvaɪs/ **NONCOUNT NOUN** If you give someone **advice**, you tell them what you think they should do. ❍ *Can I give you a piece of advice?* ❍ *My advice is to read the small print carefully.*

ad|vise /ædvaɪz/ (**advises, advising, advised**) **VERB** If you **advise** someone **to** do something, you tell them what you think they should do. ❍ *Passengers are advised to check in two hours before their flight.*

ad|vis|er /ædvaɪzər/ also **advisor** **NOUN** an expert whose job is to give advice ❍ *a financial adviser*

ad|vo|cate (**advocates, advocating, advocated**)

Pronounce the verb /ædvəkeɪt/. Pronounce the noun /ædvəkɪt/.

1 VERB If you **advocate** a particular action, you say that it should be done. [FORMAL] ❍ *The report advocates a national program to educate the public.*
2 NOUN An **advocate of** a particular action is someone who says it should be done. [FORMAL] ❍ *He was a great advocate of free trade.*

aer|ial /ɛəriəl/ [mainly BRIT] → **antenna 2**

aero|plane /ɛərəpleɪn/ [BRIT] → **airplane**

aes|thet|ic /ɛsθɛtɪk/ [BRIT] → **esthetic**

af|fair /əfɛər/
1 NOUN an event or a group of related events ❍ *She has handled the whole affair badly.*
2 NOUN a sexual relationship between two people, usually when one of them is in a relationship with someone else ❍ *He had an affair with his secretary.*
3 PL NOUN Your **affairs** are things in your life that you consider to be private. ❍ *My private affairs are no one's business but my own.*

A

af|fect /əfɛkt/ **VERB** If something **affects** a person or thing, it causes them to change in some way. ❍ *This problem affects all of us.* ❍ *This area was badly affected by the earthquake.*

af|fec|tion /əfɛkʃən/ **NONCOUNT NOUN** If you feel **affection** for someone, you love or like them a lot. ❍ *He never shows her any affection.*

af|firma|tive ac|tion /əfɜrmətɪv ækʃən/ **NONCOUNT NOUN** **Affirmative action** means making sure that people such as women, members of smaller racial groups, and disabled people get a fair share of the opportunities available. [HR]

af|ford /əfɔrd/ **VERB** If you **can afford** something, you have enough money to pay for it. ❍ *I can't afford a new computer.*

afloat /əfloʊt/
1 ADV remaining partly above the surface of water and not sinking ❍ *They tried to keep the ship afloat.*
2 ADV having just enough money to pay your debts and continue operating [FINANCE] ❍ *A number of efforts were being made to keep the company afloat.* ❍ *Many firms are finding it hard to stay afloat.*

afraid /əfreɪd/
1 ADJ anxious because you think something bad might happen ❍ *The founder is afraid to relinquish control of the business.*
2 ADJ frightened ❍ *She's afraid of spiders.* ❍ *Don't be afraid, no one's going to hurt you.*

af|ter /æftər/
1 PREP later than a particular time, date, or event ❍ *The company's sales have recovered after a fall of almost 20%.* ❍ *She left after the meeting.*
2 CONJ **After** is also a conjunction. ❍ *The phone rang two seconds after we arrived.*
3 PREP If you go **after** someone, you follow or chase them. ❍ *They ran after him.*
4 PREP **After** is used when you are telling the time. If it is **ten after six**, for example, the time is ten minutes past six.

after|care /æftərkeər/ also **after-care** **NONCOUNT NOUN** **Aftercare** is the maintenance of a product after it has been sold. [MARKETING AND SALES, BUSINESS MANAGEMENT] ❍ *All aspects of Rolls-Royce ownership will be catered for with a comprehensive aftercare program.*

after|market /æftərmarkɪt/
1 NOUN all the related products that are sold after an item has been bought [MARKETING AND SALES] ❍ *All sectors of the automobile aftermarket are growing.*
2 NOUN **The aftermarket** is the buying and selling of stocks and bonds after they have been issued. [FINANCE] ❍ *They continued to offer bonds in the aftermarket.*

after|noon /æftərnun/ **NOUN** the part of the day between 12 noon and about six o'clock ❍ *He's arriving this afternoon.* ❍ *He stayed in his office all afternoon.*

after-sales ser|vice (**after-sales services**) **NOUN** all the help and information that a company provides to customers after they have bought a product [MARKETING AND SALES, BUSINESS MANAGEMENT] ❍ *a local retailer who offers a good after-sales service*

after|ward /æftərwərd/ also **afterwards** **ADV** after an event or time ❍ *Shortly afterward, the police arrived.*

AG /eɪ dʒi/ In German-speaking countries **AG** is used after the names of large business corporations. **AG** is short for "Aktiengesellschaft." [ADMINISTRATION, BUSINESS MANAGEMENT] ❍ *Stena Holdings AG*

again /əgɛn, əgeɪn/
1 ADV used for saying that something happens another time ❍ *The share price fell again.*
2 ADV used for saying that something is now in the same state it was in before ❍ *He opened his case, took out a folder, then closed it again.*

against /əgɛnst, əgeɪnst/
1 PREP touching and leaning on ❍ *She leaned against him.*
2 PREP having the opinion that something is wrong or bad ❍ *He was against the merger.*
3 ADV **Against** is also an adverb. ❍ *66 people voted in favor of the decision and 34 voted against.*
4 PREP competing with someone ❍ *a legal battle against a large corporation*
5 PREP trying to harm someone ❍ *Security*

forces are still using violence against opponents of the government.

6 PREP If you do something **against** someone's wishes or advice, you do not obey them. ❍ *The government cut interest rates against the Bank's advice.*

7 PREP If something is **against** the law or **against** the rules, there is a law or a rule that says you must not do that thing. ❍ *It is against the law to help other people to kill themselves.*

age /eɪdʒ/ (**ages, aging** or **ageing, aged**)

1 NOUN the number of years that you have lived ❍ *Diana left school at the age of 16.* ❍ *They have two children: Julia, age 8, and Jackie, age 10.*

2 NONCOUNT NOUN Age is the state of being old. ❍ *He refuses to let age slow him down.*

3 VERB When someone **ages**, or when something **ages** them, they seem much older. ❍ *Worry has aged him.*

4 NOUN a period in history ❍ *the Iron Age*

age dis|crimi|na|tion NONCOUNT NOUN **Age discrimination** is the practice of treating older people less fairly than other people. [HR] ❍ *The government published a code of conduct to combat age discrimination.*

agen|cy /eɪdʒənsi/ (**agencies**) **NOUN** a business that provides a service ❍ *an advertising agency*

agen|da /ədʒɛndə/

1 NOUN a set of things that someone wants to do ❍ *They support the president's education agenda.*

2 NOUN a list of subjects to be discussed at a meeting [BUSINESS MANAGEMENT] ❍ *I'll add it to the agenda for Monday's meeting.*

agent /eɪdʒənt/

1 NOUN a person whose job is to do business for another person or company [BUSINESS MANAGEMENT, ADMINISTRATION] ❍ *I am buying direct, not through an agent.*

2 NOUN a person who works for a particular government department ❍ *FBI agents*

ag|gre|gate /ægrɪgɪt/ **ADJ** An **aggregate** amount or score is made up of several smaller amounts or scores. ❍ *TeleVideo has had aggregate net losses of about $64.5 million.*

ag|gres|sive /əgrɛsɪv/ **ADJ** An aggressive person or animal behaves in an angry or violent way toward others. ❍ *The man became aggressive when the flight attendant asked him to sit down* ● **ag|gres|sive|ly ADV** ❍ *He reacted aggressively.*

> **BUSINESS ETIQUETTE**
> Before you travel abroad for business, make sure you know a little about the culture of the people you are visiting. The history and religion of the area will often affect the behaviour and beliefs of the people who live there.

agio /ædʒioʊ/ **NOUN** the difference between the nominal and actual values of a currency [ECONOMICS]

AGM /eɪ dʒi ɛm/ **NOUN AGM** is an abbreviation of **annual general meeting**. [BUSINESS MANAGEMENT, ADMINISTRATION] ❍ *The CCBA is holding its AGM at 3pm on January 8.*

ago /əgoʊ/ **ADV** in the past ❍ *Earnings were unchanged from a year ago.*

ago|ny /ægəni/ **NONCOUNT NOUN Agony** is great physical or mental pain. ❍ *She screamed in agony.*

agree /əgri/ (**agrees, agreeing, agreed**)

1 VERB If people **agree with** each other about something, they have the same opinion about it. ❍ *I agree with you.* ❍ *Do we agree that there's a problem?*

2 VERB If you **agree to** do something, you say that you will do it and if you **agree to** a plan, you accept it. ❍ *He agreed to pay the fine.* ❍ *She agreed to the terms of the contract.*

3 VERB If one thing **agrees with** another, or two things **agree**, they are consistent. If you **agree** one thing **with** another, you make them consistent. ❍ *The two statements do not agree.* ❍ *They agreed the balance sheet with the records by making some adjustments.*

agree|ment /əgrimənt/ **NOUN** a plan or a decision that two or more people have made ❍ *After two hours' discussion, they finally reached an agreement.*

ag|ri|busi|ness /ægribɪznɪs/ **NONCOUNT NOUN** **Agribusiness** is the businesses that produce, sell, and distribute farm products on a large scale. [BUSINESS MANAGEMENT] ❍ *Half of Mississippi's employment depends on agribusiness.*

ag|ri|cul|ture /ægrɪkʌltʃər/ **NONCOUNT NOUN** **Agriculture** is the business or activity of farming. ● **ag|ri|cul|tur|al** /ægrɪkʌltʃərəl/ **ADJ** ❍ *agricultural land*

ag|ri|tour|ism /ægrɪtʊərɪzəm/ or **agrotourism** **NONCOUNT NOUN** **Agritourism** is a type of tourism in which people stay on working farms during their travels. [BUSINESS MANAGEMENT, MARKETING AND SALES] ❍ *Agritourism is starting to flourish.*

agro|nom|ics /ægrənɒmɪks/ **NONCOUNT NOUN** **Agronomics** is the study of the distribution, management, and productivity of land. [BUSINESS MANAGEMENT, ECONOMICS]

ahead /əhɛd/

1 ADV in front ❍ *The road ahead was blocked.* ❍ *Brett looked straight ahead.*

2 ADV winning ❍ *Mr. Koizumi has surged ahead in opinion polls.*

3 ADV in the future ❍ *There are exciting times ahead.*

4 You say **go ahead**, when you are giving someone permission to do something. ❍ *"Can I borrow your copy of the report?"—"Sure, go ahead."*

5 If someone is **ahead of** you, they are in front of you. ❍ *I saw a man thirty yards ahead of me.*

6 If something happens **ahead of** a planned time, it happens earlier than you expected. ❍ *We finished a week ahead of schedule.*

aid /eɪd/ **NONCOUNT NOUN** **Aid** is money, equipment, or services that are given to people who do not have enough money. ❍ *They have promised billions of dollars in aid.*

AIDA /eɪ aɪ di eɪ/ **NONCOUNT NOUN** **AIDA** describes the way that advertisements should work by making people pay attention to a product, become interested in it, want it, and buy it. **AIDA** is short for "Attention, interest, desire, action." [MARKETING AND SALES]

AIDS /eɪdz/ **NONCOUNT NOUN** **AIDS** is a disease that destroys the body's system of protection against other diseases. ❍ *AIDS sufferers*

ail|ing /eɪlɪŋ/ **ADJ** performing poorly [ECONOMICS] ❍ *The rise in overseas sales is good news for the ailing American economy.*

aim /eɪm/

1 VERB If you **aim** to do something, you plan and hope to do it. ❍ *We aim to improve the quality of young people's services in the area.*

2 VERB If you **aim** a weapon or object **at** something or someone, you point it toward them. ❍ *He was aiming the rifle at Wright.*

3 NOUN the purpose of something ❍ *The aim of the meeting is to thrash out an agreement.*

AIM /eɪm/ **AIM** is an abbreviation of **Alternative Investment Market**. [ECONOMICS, BANKING]

air /ɛər/

1 NONCOUNT NOUN **Air** is the mixture of gases all around us that we breathe. ❍ *fresh air*

2 NONCOUNT NOUN **Air** is used for talking about travel in aircraft. ❍ *air travel*

3 NONCOUNT NOUN **The air** is the space around things or above the ground. ❍ *He was waving his arms in the air.*

air-conditioned **ADJ** If a room or a vehicle is **air-conditioned**, a special piece of equipment makes the air in it colder.

air-condition|ing **NONCOUNT NOUN** **Air-conditioning** is a system for keeping the air cool and dry in a building or vehicle.

air|craft /ɛərkræft/ (**aircraft**) **NOUN** an airplane or other vehicle that can fly ❍ *The aircraft landed safely.*

air|line /ɛərlaɪn/ **NOUN** a company that carries people or goods in airplanes ❍ *low-cost airlines*

air|mail /ɛərmeɪl/ **NONCOUNT NOUN** **Airmail** is the system of sending letters, packages, and goods by air. ❍ *an airmail letter*

Air Miles **PL NOUN** **Air Miles** are points that you can collect by buying plane tickets, and use to pay for other flights. [MARKETING AND SALES, BUSINESS MANAGEMENT, mainly BRIT,

TRADEMARK] ❍ *A return flight from Manchester to Paris requires only 500 Air Miles.*

air|plane /ɛərpleɪn/ **NOUN** a vehicle with wings that can fly through the air

air|port /ɛərpɔrt/ **NOUN** a place where airplanes come and go, with buildings and services for passengers ❍ *Heathrow Airport*

air way|bill /ɛər wɛɪbɪl/ **NOUN** a receipt for goods that are transported by air [FINANCE, LOGISTICS AND DISTRIBUTION]

aisle /aɪl/ **NOUN** a long narrow passage where people can walk between rows of seats or shelves ❍ *the frozen food aisle of a supermarket*

alarm /əlɑrm/

1 NOUN a piece of equipment that warns you of danger, for example, by making a noise ❍ *a fire alarm*

2 NOUN an **alarm clock** ❍ *She set the alarm for eight the next day.*

alarm clock (**alarm clocks**) **NOUN** a clock that makes a noise to wake you up ❍ *I set my alarm clock for 4:30.*

al|co|hol /ælkəhɔl/

1 NONCOUNT NOUN Alcohol is drink that can make people drunk. ❍ *She doesn't drink alcohol.*

2 NONCOUNT NOUN Alcohol is a liquid that is found in drinks such as beer and wine, that is also used as a chemical for cleaning things. ❍ *Clean the wound with alcohol.*

al|co|hol|ic /ælkəhɔlɪk/

1 NOUN someone who drinks alcohol too often and who cannot stop drinking it ❍ *He admitted that he is an alcoholic.*

2 ADJ containing alcohol ❍ *alcoholic drinks*

alert /əlɜrt/

1 ADJ paying full attention to what is happening and ready to deal with problems ❍ *The financial manager must stay alert to conflicts of interest.*

2 VERB If you **alert** someone **to** a dangerous situation, you tell them about it. ❍ *He wanted to alert people to the danger.*

al|ien /eɪliən/

1 NOUN someone who lives in a country where they are not a legal citizen ❍ *an illegal alien*

2 NOUN a creature from another planet ❍ *aliens from outer space*

align /əlaɪn/ **VERB** If a company **aligns** its products **with** a particular market, it presents them in a way that suggests they are suitable for that market. ❍ *The firm needs to align its huge array of products with today's consumer tastes.*

alike /əlaɪk/

1 ADJ If two or more things are **alike**, they are similar in some way. ❍ *The companies are very alike.*

2 ADV in a similar way ❍ *the principle that all income should be taxed alike*

alive /əlaɪv/ **ADJ** living ❍ *Is her father still alive?*

all /ɔl/

1 the whole of something ❍ *He works hard all day.* ❍ *Did you read all of it?*

2 everyone or everything of a particular type ❍ *Hugh and all his co-workers came to the party.*

3 ADV completely ❍ *I went away and left her all alone.*

4 You use **at all** to make negative sentences stronger. ❍ *She didn't look at all happy.*

Allah /ɑlə, ælə, ɑlɑ/ **NOUN Allah** is the name of God in Islam. ❍ *We thank Allah that the boy is safe.*

all-cash deal (**all-cash deals**) **NOUN** a financial transaction in which the payment is made entirely in money [FINANCE, ECONOMICS] ❍ *Shareholders are entitled to demand an all-cash deal.*

al|ler|gic /əlɜrdʒɪk/ **ADJ** If you are **allergic to** something, you become sick when you eat it or touch it, or breathe it in. ❍ *patients who are allergic to penicillin*

al|ler|gy /ælərdʒi/ (**allergies**) **NOUN** a medical condition in which you become sick if you eat or touch something or you breathe something in ❍ *a nut allergy*

al|ley /æli/ **NOUN** a narrow street between the backs of buildings

al|li|ga|tor /ælɪgeɪtər/ **NOUN** a long animal with rough skin, big teeth, and short legs ❍ *Do not feed the alligators.*

A

al|lo|ca|tion /æləkeɪʃən/
1 NOUN an amount of money that is given to a particular person or used for a particular purpose ❍ *The training allocation is still under review.*
2 NONCOUNT NOUN The **allocation** of something is the decision that it should be given to a particular person or used for a particular purpose. ❍ *They need to agree on the best allocation of resources.*

al|low /əlaʊ/
1 VERB If someone **is allowed to** do something, they have permission to do it. ❍ *The winners were allowed to keep their prizes.*
2 VERB If something is **allowed**, you have permission to do it, have it or use it. ❍ *Dogs are not allowed in the park.* ❍ *Cellphone use is not allowed.*

al|low|able /əlaʊəbᵊl/
1 ADJ If people decide that something is **allowable**, they let it happen. ❍ *Capital punishment is allowable only under exceptional circumstances.*
2 ADJ Allowable costs or expenses are amounts of money that you do not have to pay tax on. ❍ *Her expenses were allowable deductions.*

al|low|ance /əlaʊəns/
1 NOUN an amount of money that is given regularly to someone ❍ *Amy gets a weekly allowance of $5 from her parents.* ❍ *an annual living allowance of $250,000*
2 If you **make allowances for** something, you consider it when you are making a decision or plan. ❍ *We do not make allowances for sudden adverse events like an interest rate rise or a belated tax bill.*
3 If you **make allowances for** someone, you accept their behavior because you understand why they are behaving in that way. ❍ *He's tired so I'll make allowances for him.*

all right
1 ADJ acceptable ❍ *I'll come later if it's all right with you.*
2 ADJ well or safe ❍ *Are you all right?*
3 You say "**all right**" when you are agreeing to something. ❍ *"I think you should go now."— "All right."*

ally /ælaɪ/ (**allies**) **NOUN** a person or country that supports another person or country when there is trouble ❍ *the Western allies* ❍ *He is a close ally of the president.*

al|most /ɔlmoʊst/ **ADV** nearly but not completely ❍ *We have been in business for almost three years.* ❍ *He caught flu, which almost killed him.*

alone /əloʊn/
1 ADJ not with any other people ❍ *She wanted to be alone.* ❍ *We were alone together.*
2 ADV Alone is also an adverb. ❍ *He lives alone.*
3 ADV without help from other people ❍ *Competing alone against the industry's giants is very difficult.*

along /əlɔŋ/
1 PREP moving from one end of a road or other place to the other ❍ *He was walking along the street.*
2 PREP in or next to a long, narrow place ❍ *Cellular call boxes have been set up along the freeways to aid motorists.*
3 ADV moving forward ❍ *He was talking as they walked along.*
4 ADV If you take or bring someone or something **along**, you take them with you. ❍ *Johnson brought along the newest member of his team.*

along|side /əlɔŋsaɪd/
1 PREP next to ❍ *He crossed the street and walked alongside Central Park.*
2 ADV Alongside is also an adverb. ❍ *He waited for a car to stop alongside.*
3 PREP together with ❍ *He worked alongside Frank and Mark.*

aloud /əlaʊd/ **ADV** When you speak, read, or laugh **aloud**, you speak, or laugh so that other people can hear you. ❍ *The clerk read aloud from the official report.*

al|pha|bet /ælfəbɛt, -bɪt/ **NOUN** a set of letters that is used for writing words ❍ *the modern Russian alphabet*

al|pha|beti|cal /ælfəbɛtɪkᵊl/ **ADJ** in the normal order of the letters in the alphabet ❍ *The books are arranged in alphabetical order.*

al|ready /ɔlrɛdi/ **ADV** If something has **already** happened, it has happened before the present time or earlier than expected. ❍ *She's already left.* ❍ *The meeting had already finished when we arrived.*

al|right /ɔlraɪt/ [BRIT] → **all right**

also /ɔlsoʊ/ **ADV** in addition to something that has already been mentioned ❍ *The book also includes an index of all U.S. presidents.* ❍ *Two other workers were also hurt.*

al|ter /ɔltər/ **VERB** If something **alters**, or if you **alter** something, it changes. ❍ *World War II altered American life in many ways.*

al|ter|nate (**alternates, alternating, alternated**)

Pronounce the verb /ɔltərneɪt/. Pronounce the adjective /ɔltɜrnɪt/.

1 VERB When you **alternate between** two things, you do one thing and then the other. ❍ *Investors have been alternating between buying and selling stocks.*

2 VERB When one thing **alternates with** another, the first thing happens, then the second thing, then the first thing again. ❍ *Rain alternated with snow.*

3 ADJ If something happens on **alternate** days, weeks, or years, for example, it happens on one, then it happens on every second one after that. ❍ *Drivers can only use their vehicles on alternate days.*

4 ADJ used to describe an available plan or system that is different from the one that is being used now ❍ *an alternate route*

al|ter|na|tive /ɔltɜrnətɪv/

1 NOUN If one thing is an **alternative to** another, the first can be used or done instead of the second. ❍ *The new treatment may provide an alternative to painkillers.*

2 ADJ used to describe an available plan or system that is different from the one that is being used now ❍ *alternative methods of travel*

3 ADJ not traditional, being different from the usual thing ❍ *Have you considered alternative health care?*

Al|ter|na|tive In|vest|ment Mar|ket (**Alternative Investment Markets**) **NOUN** a market for smaller companies on the London Stock Exchange [ECONOMICS, BANKING]

al|though /ɔlðoʊ/

1 CONJ used for introducing a surprising idea ❍ *Their system worked, although no one knew how.* ❍ *Although income has been growing, many people aren't any better off.*

2 CONJ used for introducing information that slightly changes what you have already said ❍ *They are all managers, although of different companies.*

al|to|geth|er /ɔltəgɛðər/ **ADV** in total ❍ *There were eleven of us altogether.*

alu|min|ium /æljumɪniəm/ [BRIT] → **aluminum**

alu|mi|num /əluːmɪnəm/ **NONCOUNT NOUN Aluminum** is a light metal used for making things such as cans for food and drink. ❍ *aluminum cans*

al|ways /ɔlweɪz/

1 ADV all the time ❍ *He's always late for work.* ❍ *She always remains calm.* ❍ *Why are you always interrupting me?*

2 ADV forever ❍ *There will always be new things to learn.*

a.m. /eɪ ɛm/ also **am** You use **a.m.** after a number when you are talking about a time between midnight and noon. Compare with **p.m.** ❍ *The program starts at 9 a.m.*

am /əm, STRONG æm/ **Am** is a form of the verb **be**. ❍ *I am French.*

amal|gam|ate /əmælgəmeɪt/ (**amalgamates, amalgamating, amalgamated**) **VERB** When two companies or organizations **amalgamate**, they join together to form a single company or organization. [ADMINISTRATION, BUSINESS MANAGEMENT] ❍ *The chemical companies had amalgamated into a vast conglomerate.* ● **amal|gama|tion** /əmælgəmeɪʃən/ **NOUN** ❍ *Cement Major was formed by an amalgamation of ten smaller cement companies.*

ama|teur /æmətʃər, -tʃʊər/ **NOUN** someone who does something as a hobby and not as a job ❍ *an amateur investor*

amaze /əmeɪz/ (**amazes, amazing, amazed**) **VERB** If something **amazes** you, it surprises you very much. ❍ *He amazed us with his knowledge of our work.*

A

amaze|ment /əmeɪzmənt/ **NONCOUNT NOUN** **Amazement** is the feeling you have when something surprises you very much. ❍ *I looked at her in amazement.*

amaz|ing /əmeɪzɪŋ/ **ADJ** very surprising, often in a good way ❍ *I saw it as an amazing opportunity.* ● **amaz|ing|ly** **ADV** ❍ *They learned amazingly fast.*

am|bas|sa|dor /æmbæsədər/ **NOUN** an important official person who lives in a foreign country and represents his or her own country there ❍ *We met the ambassador to Poland.*

am|bigu|ous /æmbɪgyuəs/ **ADJ** not clear, and able to be understood in more than one way ❍ *an ambiguous statement*
● **am|bigu|ous|ly** **ADV** ❍ *She answered his questions ambiguously.*

am|bi|tion /æmbɪʃən/
1 NOUN If you have an **ambition to** do something, you want very much to do it. ❍ *His only ambition is to get a better job.*
2 NONCOUNT NOUN **Ambition** is the desire to be successful, rich, or powerful. ❍ *These young people have hopes for the future and great ambition.*

am|bi|tious /æmbɪʃəs/
1 ADJ Someone who is **ambitious** very much wants to be successful, rich, or powerful. ❍ *Chris is very ambitious.*
2 ADJ An **ambitious** idea or plan is a large one that needs a lot of work or money. ❍ *He has ambitious plans for the firm.*

am|bu|lance /æmbyələns/ **NOUN** a vehicle for taking people to a hospital

Ameri|can /əmɛrɪkən/
1 ADJ belonging to or coming from the United States of America ❍ *the American ambassador*
2 ADJ coming from North America, South America, or the Caribbean
3 NOUN someone who is from the United States of America ❍ *He's an American living in Israel.*
4 NOUN someone who is from North America, South America, or the Caribbean

among /əmʌŋ/
1 PREP surrounded by a group of things or people ❍ *He was sitting among a crowd of women.* ❍ *There was a building among the trees.*
2 PREP happening within or felt by a group ❍ *We discussed it among ourselves.* ❍ *The feeling among staff is that the offer isn't high enough.*
3 PREP between more than two ❍ *Any money will be shared among the union members.*

amor|tise /æmərtaɪz/ [BRIT] → **amortize**

amor|tize /æmərtaɪz/ (**amortizes, amortizing, amortized**) **VERB** If you **amortize** a debt, you pay it back in regular payments. [FINANCE] ❍ *There's little advantage to amortizing the loan, especially on a 30 or 40-year basis.* ● **amor|ti|za|tion** /æmərtɪzeɪʃən, əmɔr-/ **NONCOUNT NOUN** ❍ *The period of amortization should not exceed 40 years.*

amount /əmaʊnt/
1 NOUN The **amount of** something is how much of it there is. ❍ *He needs that amount of money to live.* ❍ *I still do a certain amount of work for them.*
2 VERB If something **amounts to** a particular total, all the parts of it add up to that total. ❍ *The payment amounted to $42 billion.*

amt **amt** is a written abbreviation of **amount**. [FINANCE]

amuse /əmyuz/ (**amuses, amusing, amused**)
1 VERB If something **amuses** you, it makes you laugh or smile. ❍ *The thought amused him.*
2 VERB If you **amuse yourself**, you do something in order to not become bored. ❍ *I did a crossword to amuse myself while I was waiting.*

amuse|ment /əmyuzmənt/
1 NONCOUNT NOUN **Amusement** is the feeling that you have when you think that something is funny. ❍ *Tom watched them with amusement.*
2 NOUN something that you do for pleasure ❍ *People did not have many amusements to choose from in those days.*

amus|ing /əmyuzɪŋ/ **ADJ** funny ❍ *an amusing story*

an /ən, STRONG æn/ **ARTICLE** used instead of "a" before words that begin with vowel sounds

analog /ænəlɔg/ **ADJ** An **analog** clock or watch shows the time using hands (= the long parts that move around and show the time) instead of numbers. Compare with **digital**.

anal|ogy /ənælədʒi/ (**analogies**) **NOUN** a comparison between two similar things ❍ *She made an analogy between the human mind and a computer.* ● **analo|gous** /ənæləgəs/ **ADJ** [FORMAL] ❍ *The two situations are not analogous.*

ana|lyse /ænəlaɪz/ [BRIT] → **analyze**

analy|sis /ənælɪsɪs/ (**analyses** /ənælɪsiz/) **NOUN** the process of considering or looking at something carefully in order to understand it or find out what is in it ❍ *data analysis* ❍ *They collect blood samples for analysis.*

ana|lyze /ænəlaɪz/ (**analyzes, analyzing, analyzed**) **VERB** If you **analyze** something, you consider or look at it carefully in order to understand it or to find out what it is made of. ❍ *We need to analyze the data.* ❍ *They haven't analyzed the samples yet.*

an|ces|tor /ænsɛstər/ **NOUN** Your **ancestors** are the people in your family who lived a long time ago. ❍ *Our daily lives are so different from those of our ancestors.*

an|chor /æŋkər/ **NOUN** a heavy object that you drop into the water from a boat to stop it moving away

an|cient /eɪnʃənt/ **ADJ** very old, or from a long time ago ❍ *ancient Jewish traditions*

and /ənd, STRONG ænd/

1 CONJ used to connect two or more words or phrases ❍ *I met Mark and Amy.* ❍ *I'm tired and hungry.*

2 CONJ used to connect two words that are the same, in order to make the meaning stronger ❍ *Learning becomes more and more difficult as we get older.* ❍ *We have seen this happen again and again.*

3 CONJ used to show that one event happens after another ❍ *I waved goodbye and went down the steps.*

4 CONJ used to show that two numbers are added together ❍ *Two and two makes four.*

an|gel /eɪndʒəl/

1 NOUN a spirit that some people believe can bring messages from God, shown in pictures with wings

2 NOUN a very kind, good person ❍ *Thank you so much, you're an angel!*

3 NOUN An **angel** or **angel investor** is someone who provides money for a business venture. [BANKING] ❍ *He obtained funding from angel investors and technology partners.*

an|ger /æŋgər/

1 NONCOUNT NOUN Anger is the strong, bad emotion that you feel when you think that someone has behaved badly or has treated you unfairly. ❍ *He felt such anger toward her.*

2 VERB If something **angers** you, it makes you feel angry. ❍ *The decision angered some Californians.*

an|gle /æŋgəl/

1 NOUN the space between two lines or surfaces that meet in one place, measured in degrees ❍ *a 30 degree angle*

2 If something is **at an angle**, it is leaning so that it is not straight. ❍ *He wore his hat at an angle.*

an|gry /æŋgri/ (**angrier, angriest**) **ADJ** very annoyed ❍ *We are very angry about the decision to close the plant.* ❍ *An angry crowd gathered.*

ani|mal /ænɪməl/

1 NOUN a creature such as a dog or a cat, but not a bird, fish, insect, or human ❍ *wild animals*

2 NOUN any living creature, including a bird, fish, insect, or human

ani|ma|tion /ænɪmeɪʃən/ **NONCOUNT NOUN** the process of making films in which drawings appear to move ❍ *computer animation*

an|kle /æŋkəl/ **NOUN** the joint where your foot joins your leg ❍ *John twisted his ankle badly.*

an|ni|ver|sa|ry /ænɪvɜrsəri/ (**anniversaries**) **NOUN** a date that is remembered because something special happened on that day in an earlier year ❍ *They just celebrated their fiftieth wedding anniversary.*

a

A

an|nounce /ənaʊns/ (**announces, announcing, announced**) VERB If you **announce** something, you tell people about it officially. ❍ *He has just announced his resignation.*

an|nounce|ment /ənaʊnsmənt/ NOUN something that is told to a lot of people officially and gives information ❍ *The president is expected to make an announcement about his future today.*

an|noy /ənɔɪ/ VERB If someone or something **annoys** you, they make you angry. ❍ *It annoyed me that she didn't apologize.*

an|noyed /ənɔɪd/ ADJ angry about something ❍ *She was annoyed that Sasha was late.*

an|noy|ing /ənɔɪɪŋ/ ADJ making you feel angry ❍ *It's very annoying when this happens.*

an|nual /ænyuəl/

1 ADJ happening once every year ❍ *They held their annual meeting May 20.* ● **an|nual|ly** ADV ❍ *The prize is awarded annually.*

2 ADJ **Annual** amounts or rates are for a period of one year. ❍ *The company has annual sales of about $80 million.* ● **an|nual|ly** ADV ❍ *El Salvador produces 100,000 tons of copper annually.*

an|nual gen|er|al meet|ing [BUSINESS MANAGEMENT, ADMINISTRATION, BRIT] → **annual meeting**

an|nual meet|ing (**annual meetings**) or **annual stockholders' meeting** NOUN a meeting that an organization holds once a year in order to discuss the previous year's activities and accounts [BUSINESS MANAGEMENT, ADMINISTRATION] ❍ *The firm has its annual meeting at the end of this month.*

an|nual per|cent|age rate (**annual percentage rates**) NOUN the rate of interest that a borrower has to pay on a loan [FINANCE] ❍ *They are advertising a personal loan with an annual percentage rate of 8 percent.*

an|nual re|port (**annual reports**) NOUN a report that the directors of a company present to its stockholders each year [FINANCE, BUSINESS MANAGEMENT] ❍ *The financial statement section of our most recent annual report is 32 pages long.*

an|nu|ity /ənuɪti/ (**annuities**) NOUN an investment or insurance policy that pays someone a fixed sum of money each year [BANKING] ❍ *He received a small annuity of $100.*

anony|mous /ənɒnɪməs/ ADJ not saying your name or letting anyone know who you are ❍ *Someone had made an anonymous complaint.* ● **anony|mous|ly** ADV ❍ *The photographs were sent anonymously to the magazine's offices.*

an|oth|er /ənʌðər/

1 ADJ one more ❍ *The figures won't be available for another month.*

2 PRON **Another** is also a pronoun. ❍ *"These cookies are delicious."—"Would you like another?"*

3 ADJ used to describe a different person or thing ❍ *I'll deal with this problem another time.*

4 PRON **Another** is also a pronoun. ❍ *He said one thing but did another.*

5 PRON You use **one another** to show that each member of a group does something to or for the other members. ❍ *We all help one another.*

an|swer /ænsər/

1 VERB When you **answer**, you say something back to someone who has asked you something. ❍ *I asked him but he didn't answer.*

2 VERB When you **answer** the telephone, you pick it up when it rings. ❍ *Why didn't you answer my calls?*

3 VERB When you **answer** the door, you open it when you hear a knock or the bell.

4 NOUN **Answer** is also a noun. ❍ *I knocked at the front door and there was no answer.*

5 VERB When you **answer** a question on a test, you write or say what you think is correct. ❍ *Did you answer all the questions?*

6 NOUN **Answer** is also a noun. ❍ *I got three answers wrong.*

ant /ænt/ NOUN a very small insect that lives in a large group

an|ten|na /æntɛnə/ (**antennae** /æntɛni/ or **antennas**)

> **Antennas** is the usual plural form for meaning **2**.

1 NOUN one of two long, thin parts on the head of an insect that the insect uses for feeling things
2 NOUN a piece of equipment that sends and receives television or radio signals

anti|bi|ot|ic /æntibaɪɒtɪk, æntaɪ-/ **NOUN** a drug that is used for killing bacteria and curing infections ❍ *These infections are treated with antibiotics.*

an|tici|pate /æntɪsɪpeɪt/ (**anticipates, anticipating, anticipated**) **VERB** If you **anticipate** an event, you think about it and prepare for it before it happens. ❍ *Organizers anticipate an even bigger crowd this year.*

an|tici|pa|tion /æntɪsɪpeɪʃən/
1 NONCOUNT NOUN Anticipation is a feeling of excitement about something that you know is going to happen. ❍ *There was all the anticipation of a Hollywood opening.*
2 If you do something **in anticipation of** an event, you do it because you believe that event is going to happen. ❍ *Users postponed purchases in anticipation of lower prices.*

anti-inflationary /æntiɪnfleɪʃənɛri, æntaɪ-/ **ADJ** relating to methods that are designed to reduce the effects of inflation [ECONOMICS] ❍ *The government is introducing a tough anti-inflationary policy.*

an|tique /æntik/ **NOUN** an old object that is valuable because of its beauty or because of the way it was made ❍ *Jill collects antiques.*

anti|so|cial /æntisoʊʃəl, æntaɪ-/ **ADJ** not friendly toward other people or showing no care for other people ❍ *antisocial behavior*

anti|trust /æntitrʌst, æntaɪ-/ **ADJ** In the United States, **antitrust** laws are intended to stop big companies interfering with free competition. [BUSINESS MANAGEMENT, LEGAL] ❍ *The firm had violated antitrust laws.*

anti-virus also **antivirus** /æntivaɪrəs/ **ADJ Anti-virus** software protects computers from attack by viruses (= programs that enter computers and stop them from working).

anxi|ety /æŋzaɪɪti/ **NONCOUNT NOUN Anxiety** is a feeling of being nervous and worried. ❍ *Her voice was full of anxiety.*

anx|ious /æŋkʃəs/ **ADJ** feeling nervous or worried about something ❍ *He appeared anxious to end the conversation.* ● **anx|ious|ly ADV** ❍ *They are waiting anxiously for news.*

any /ɛni/
1 ADJ used in negative sentences to show that no person or thing is involved ❍ *I don't have any plans yet.* ❍ *I didn't get any help.*
2 PRON Any is also a pronoun. ❍ *The children needed new clothes and we couldn't afford any.*
3 ADJ used in questions to ask if there is some of a particular thing ❍ *Do you speak any other languages?*
4 PRON Any is also a pronoun. ❍ *I'll answer questions if there are any.*
5 ADJ used in positive sentences when you want to say that it does not matter which person or thing you choose ❍ *I'll take any offers.*
6 If something does not happen **any longer** or **any more**, it has stopped happening. ❍ *She doesn't come here any more.*

any|body /ɛnibɒdi, -bʌdi/ **PRON Anybody** means the same as **anyone**.

any|how /ɛnihaʊ/ **ADV Anyhow** means the same as **anyway**.

any|more /ɛnimɔr/ also **any more ADV** If something does not happen or is not true **anymore**, it has stopped happening or is not now true. ❍ *I couldn't trust him anymore.*

any|one /ɛniwʌn/

You can also say **anybody**.

1 PRON used in negative statements and questions instead of "someone" or "somebody" ❍ *Don't tell anyone.* ❍ *Why would anyone do that?*
2 PRON used to talk about someone when the exact person is not important or to mean all people ❍ *Anyone who comes late won't get in.* ❍ *Anyone could do what I'm doing.*

any|thing /ɛnɪθɪŋ/
1 PRON used in negative statements and questions instead of "something" ❍ *I didn't eat anything.* ❍ *Did you find anything?*
2 PRON used to talk about something when the exact thing is not important ❍ *He could sell anything.* ❍ *More than anything else, he wanted to teach.*

any|time /ɛnitaɪm/ **ADV** used to mean a point in time that is not fixed ❍ *He can leave anytime he wants.*

any|way /ɛniweɪ/

You can also say **anyhow**.

ADV used to suggest that something is true despite other things that have been said ❍ *She wondered if it was wrong, but she went ahead anyway.*

any|where /ɛniwɛər/

1 ADV used in negative statements and questions instead of "somewhere" ❍ *Did you try to get help from anywhere?* ❍ *technologies you don't see anywhere else*

2 ADV used to talk about a place, when the exact place is not important ❍ *I can meet you anywhere you want.*

apart /əpɑrt/

1 ADV When people or things are **apart**, they are some distance from each other. ❍ *The two institutions are about 25 miles apart.*

2 ADV If you take something **apart**, you separate it into parts. ❍ *He likes taking bikes apart and putting them together again.*

apart|ment /əpɑrtmənt/ **NOUN** a group of rooms where someone lives in a large building ❍ *Christina has her own apartment.*

ape /eɪp/ **NOUN** a type of animal like a monkey that lives among trees and has long, strong arms and no tail ❍ *wild animals such as monkeys and apes*

apol|ogies /əpɒlədʒiz/ **PL NOUN** **Apologies** are a statement from someone that they cannot attend a meeting. [BRIT] ❍ *Johnson and McPherson could not make it to the meeting, but they sent their apologies and reports.*

apolo|gise /əpɒlədʒaɪz/ [BRIT] → **apologize**

apolo|gize /əpɒlədʒaɪz/ (**apologizes, apologizing, apologized**) **VERB** When you **apologize**, you say that you are sorry. ❍ *He apologized for being late.* ❍ *I spelled your name wrong – I do apologize!*

apol|ogy /əpɒlədʒi/ (**apologies**) **NOUN** something that you say or write in order to tell someone that you are sorry ❍ *I didn't get an apology.* ❍ *a letter of apology*

apos|tro|phe /əpɒstrəfi/ **NOUN** the mark (') that shows that one or more letters have been removed from a word, and that is also added to nouns to show possession

ap|par|ent /əpærənt/ **ADJ** clear and obvious ❍ *Everyone left the room for no apparent reason.*

ap|par|ent|ly /əpærəntli/ **ADV** used to talk about something that you have heard is true but do not know for sure ❍ *Apparently, they're leaving Portland.*

ap|peal /əpil/

1 VERB If something **appeals to** you, you find it attractive or interesting. ❍ *The idea appealed to him.*

2 VERB If you **appeal to** people, you ask them for something in a serious and urgent way. ❍ *Police have appealed to the public for help.*

3 NOUN a serious and urgent request ❍ *The police made an urgent appeal for help.*

ap|peal|ing /əpilɪŋ/ **ADJ** pleasant and attractive ❍ *The restaurant serves an appealing mix of Asian dishes.*

ap|pear /əpɪər/

1 VERB When someone or something **appears**, it becomes possible to see them. ❍ *A woman appeared at the far end of the street.* ❍ *The charges will appear on a customer's monthly statement.*

2 VERB If someone or something **appears to** be the way you describe it, it seems that way. ❍ *So far, the strategy appears to be working.*

ap|pear|ance /əpɪərəns/ **NOUN** Someone's or something's **appearance** is the way that they look. ❍ *stores that are similar in their appearance*

ap|pe|tite /æpɪtaɪt/ **NOUN** your desire and ability to eat ❍ *He has a huge appetite.*

ap|plaud /əplɔd/ **VERB** When people **applaud**, they clap their hands together many times to show that they like something. ❍ *The audience laughed and applauded.*

ap|plause /əplɔz/ **NONCOUNT NOUN** **Applause** is the noise that a group of people make when they all clap their hands together to show that they like something. ❍ *loud applause*

ap|ple /æpᵊl/ **NOUN** a firm round fruit with green, red, or yellow skin ❍ *I always have an apple in my packed lunch.*

ap|pli|ance /əplaɪəns/ **NOUN** a machine that you use to do a job in your home [FORMAL] ❍ *domestic appliances*

ap|pli|cant /æplɪkənt/ **NOUN** someone who formally asks to be considered for a job or course [HR] ❍ *job applicants* ❍ *The firm recently had fifty applicants for one job.*

ap|pli|ca|tion /æplɪkeɪʃən/
1 NOUN a written request to be considered for a job or course [HR] ❍ *a job application*
2 NOUN In computing, an **application** is a piece of software that is designed to do a particular task.

ap|pli|ca|tion form (**application forms**) **NOUN** a written list of questions that you have to answer when you apply for a job [HR] ❍ *I enclose my completed application form for the post of Administrative Assistant.*

ap|ply /əplaɪ/ (**applies, applying, applied**)
1 VERB If you **apply for** a job, you write a letter or write on a form in order to ask for it. [HR] ❍ *I am applying for a new job.*
2 VERB If a rule or a statement **applies to** a person or a situation, it is about them. ❍ *This rule does not apply to you.*

ap|point /əpɔɪnt/ **VERB** If you **appoint** someone **to** a job or a position, you choose them for it. [HR] ❍ *The bank appointed Conley as manager of its office in Aurora.*

ap|point|ment /əpɔɪntmənt/
1 NOUN an arrangement to see someone at a particular time ❍ *a doctor's appointment*
2 NOUN a job or a position of responsibility ❍ *I decided to accept the appointment as director.*

ap|prais|al /əpreɪzᵊl/ or **appraisement**
1 NOUN If you make an **appraisal of** something, you consider it carefully and form an opinion about it. ❍ *What is needed in such cases is a calm appraisal of the situation.*
2 NONCOUNT NOUN the formal assessment of the strengths and weaknesses of employees [HR] ❍ *Performance appraisal is used as way of identifying training needs.*
3 NOUN a judgement that someone makes about how much money something is worth ❍ *It may be necessary to get a new appraisal of the property.*

ap|praise /əpreɪz/ (**appraises, appraising, appraised**)
1 VERB If you **appraise** something or someone, you consider them carefully and form an opinion about them. [HR, FORMAL] ❍ *This caused many employers to appraise their recruitment policies.*
2 VERB When experts **appraise** something, they decide how much money it is worth. ❍ *His estate is now appraised at a figure near $1,000,000.*

ap|pre|ci|ate /əpriʃieɪt/ (**appreciates, appreciating, appreciated**)
1 VERB If you **appreciate** something, you like it. ❍ *Everyone can appreciate this kind of achievement.*
2 VERB If you **appreciate** something that someone has done for you, you are grateful. ❍ *Peter helped me so much. I really appreciate that.* ● **ap|pre|cia|tion NONCOUNT NOUN** ❍ *He wants to show his appreciation for her support.*

ap|pren|tice /əprɛntɪs/ **NOUN** a young person who works for someone in order to learn their skill [HR, ADMINISTRATION] ❍ *I started off as an apprentice and worked my way up.* ❍ *an apprentice woodworker*

ap|pren|tice|ship /əprɛntɪsʃɪp/ **NOUN** the system of learning a skill by working for someone who has that skill [HR, ADMINISTRATION] ❍ *After serving his apprenticeship as a toolmaker, he became a manager.*

ap|proach /əproʊtʃ/ (**approaches, approaching, approached**)
1 VERB When you **approach** something or someone, you move closer to them. ❍ *He approached the front door.* ❍ *When I approached, the girls stopped talking.*
2 VERB When you **approach** a task, problem, or situation in a particular way, you deal with

it in that way. ❍ *The bank has approached the situation in a practical way.*

3 NOUN a way of dealing with a situation ❍ *He was very professional in his approach.*

ap|pro|pri|ate /əproʊpriɪt/ **ADJ** right for a particular situation ❍ *an appropriate response* ❍ *Wear clothes that are appropriate to the job.* • **ap|pro|pri|ate|ly ADV** ❍ *He behaved appropriately.*

ap|pro|pria|tion /əproʊprieɪʃən/ **NOUN** a sum of money that is set apart for a specific purpose [ECONOMICS] ❍ *Democrats are hoping for an appropriation of $500 million for a jobs program.*

ap|prov|al /əpruvᵊl/

1 NONCOUNT NOUN Approval is formal agreement that is given to a plan or request. ❍ *The chairman gave his approval for an investigation.*

2 NONCOUNT NOUN If someone or something has your **approval**, you like and admire them. ❍ *She badly wanted her co-workers' approval.*

3 If you have goods **on approval**, you are given them to examine in order to decide whether to buy them.

ap|prove /əpruv/ (**approves, approving, approved**)

1 VERB If you **approve of** someone or something, you like them or think they are good. ❍ *Just over 50% of respondents in polls approve of him personally.* ❍ *They say they approve of the job the president is doing.*

2 VERB If someone in a position of authority **approves** a plan, they formally agree to it. ❍ *The directors have approved the proposal.*

ap|proxi|mate /əprɒksɪmət/ **ADJ** not exact but near ❍ *The approximate value of the apartment is $300,000.* • **ap|proxi|mate|ly ADV** ❍ *They've spent approximately $150 million.*

APR /eɪ pi ɑr/ **NOUN APR** is an abbreviation of **annual percentage rate**. [ECONOMICS, FINANCE] ❍ *Shoppers with store credit cards could be paying an APR of as much as 30%.*

apri|cot /æprɪkɒt, eɪp-/ **NOUN** a small, soft, round fruit with yellow flesh and a large seed inside ❍ *dried apricots*

April /eɪprɪl/ **NOUN** the fourth month of the year ❍ *The new store is due to open in April.*

ap|ti|tude /æptɪtud/ **NOUN** an ability to learn a particular kind of work or activity quickly and to do it well ❍ *He discovered an aptitude for working with accounts.*

ap|ti|tude test (**aptitude tests**) **NOUN** a test that is designed to find out how well you can do something [HR] ❍ *Most insurance companies use aptitude tests to select potentially successful agents.*

ar|bi|trage /ɑrbɪtrɑʒ/ **NONCOUNT NOUN Arbitrage** is the activity of buying securities or currency in one financial market and selling it at a profit in another. [BANKING, BUSINESS MANAGEMENT] ❍ *Whenever there is an arbitrage opportunity, we'll take it.*

ar|bi|tra|ger /ɑrbɪtrɑʒər/ or **arbitrageur NOUN** someone who buys securities or currency in one financial market to sells at a profit in another market [BANKING, BUSINESS MANAGEMENT]

ar|bi|trary /ɑrbɪtrɛri/ **ADJ** not based on any principle or system and seeming unfair because of this ❍ *The judges' decisions often seemed arbitrary.*

ar|bi|tra|tion /ɑrbɪtreɪʃən/ **NONCOUNT NOUN Arbitration** is the act of officially judging a dispute between people or groups. [LEGAL, BUSINESS MANAGEMENT] ❍ *The matter is likely to go to arbitration.*

arch /ɑrtʃ/ (**arches**) **NOUN** a structure that is curved at the top and is supported on either side ❍ *The bridge is 65 feet at the top of the main arch.*

archi|tect /ɑrkɪtɛkt/

1 NOUN a person whose job is to design buildings

2 NOUN a person who plans or creates something ❍ *Eaton, one of the architects of the merger, became chairman.*

archi|tec|ture /ɑrkɪtɛktʃər/ **NONCOUNT NOUN Architecture** is the art of designing buildings. ❍ *He studied architecture in Rome.* ❍ *modern architecture*

are /ər, STRONG ɑr/ **Are** is a form of the verb **be**. ❍ *You are right.*

area /ɛəriə/
1 NOUN a particular part of a place, country, or the world ❍ *a poor area of the city*
2 NOUN a piece of land or part of a building that is used for a particular activity ❍ *a rest area*
3 NOUN The **area** of a surface is the amount of flat space that it covers, measured in square units. ❍ *The reps cover a total area of 400 square miles.*

arena /ərinə/ **NOUN** a place where sports or entertainments take place ❍ *an indoor sports arena*

aren't /ɑrnt, ɑrənt/ short for "are not"

ar|gue /ɑrgyu/ (**argues, arguing, argued**)
1 VERB If you **argue with** someone, you disagree with them about something. ❍ *I didn't argue with him.*
2 VERB If you **argue that** something is true, you give the reasons why you think it is true. ❍ *Employers argue that the law should be changed.*

ar|gu|ment /ɑrgyəmənt/
1 NOUN a conversation in which people disagree with each other ❍ *Annie had an argument with one of the other girls.*
2 NOUN a reason for having a particular opinion ❍ *This is a strong argument against nuclear power.*

arise /əraɪz/ (**arises, arising, arose, arisen** /ərɪzən/) **VERB** If a situation or problem **arises**, it begins to exist. ❍ *When the opportunity finally arose, thousands of workers left.*

arm /ɑrm/
1 NOUN Your **arms** are the two parts of your body between your shoulders and your hands. ❍ *She stretched her arms out.*
2 NOUN The **arm** of a chair is the part on which you rest your arm when you are sitting.
3 NOUN the part of a piece of clothing that covers your arm ❍ *The coat was short in the arms.*
4 PL NOUN **Arms** are weapons, especially bombs and guns. ❍ *illegal arms*
5 VERB If you **arm** someone **with** a weapon, you provide them with a weapon. ❍ *She armed herself with a rifle.*

arm|chair /ɑrmtʃɛər/ **NOUN** a big comfortable chair that supports your arms ❍ *She was sitting in an armchair.*

armed /ɑrmd/ **ADJ** carrying a weapon, usually a gun ❍ *armed guards*

army /ɑrmi/ (**armies**) **NOUN** a large group of soldiers who are trained to fight battles on land ❍ *Perkins joined the Army in 1990.*

around /əraʊnd/
1 PREP Things or people that are **around** a place or object surround it. ❍ *She looked at the people around her.*
2 PREP If you move **around** a place, you go along its edge, and back to the point where you started. ❍ *We went for a walk around the block.*
3 ADV **Around** is also an adverb. ❍ *They live in a little village with hills all around.*
4 PREP If you move **around** something, you move to the other side of it. ❍ *The man turned back and hurried around the corner.*
5 PREP If you look **around** something, you look to see what is on the other side. ❍ *I looked around the door but the room was empty.*
6 PREP or **ADV** You use **around** to say that something happens in different parts of a place or area. ❍ *Other retailers around the country report the same.* ❍ *Why are you following me around?*
7 ADV If you move things **around**, you move them so that they are in different places. ❍ *I've moved the furniture around.*
8 ADV If someone or something is **around**, they are in a place. ❍ *Have you seen Mr. Jones anywhere around?*
9 ADV **Around** means approximately. ❍ *My salary was around $45,000.*
10 PREP **Around** is also a preposition. ❍ *We're leaving around May 15.*

ar|range /əreɪndʒ/ (**arranges, arranging, arranged**)
1 VERB If you **arrange** an event, you make plans for it to happen. ❍ *She arranged an appointment for Friday afternoon.* ❍ *I've arranged to see him Thursday.*
2 VERB If you **arrange** things somewhere, you carefully place them in a particular position. ❍ *She enjoys arranging dried flowers.*

A

ar|range|ment /əreɪndʒmənt/
1 NOUN a plan that you make so that something can happen ❍ *travel arrangements*
2 NOUN a group of things that have been placed in a particular position ❍ *a flower arrangement*

ar|rears /ərɪərz/
1 PL NOUN **Arrears** are amounts of money that you owe. [FINANCE] ❍ *They have promised to pay the arrears over the next five years.*
2 If someone is **in arrears with** their payments, they have not paid the regular amounts of money that they should have paid. [FINANCE] ❍ *Thousands of households are more than six months in arrears with their mortgages.*
3 If sums of money are paid **in arrears**, they are paid at the end of a period of time. [FINANCE] ❍ *Interest is paid in arrears after you use the money.*

ar|rest /ərɛst/
1 VERB If the police **arrest** you, they take you to a police station, because they believe you may have broken the law. ❍ *Police arrested five young men in the city.*
2 NOUN **Arrest** is also a noun. ❍ *Police later made two arrests.*

ar|ri|val /əraɪvᵊl/ **NOUN** the act or time of arriving ❍ *his late arrival*

ar|rive /əraɪv/ (**arrives, arriving, arrived**) **VERB** When a person or vehicle **arrives** at a place, they come to it from somewhere else. ❍ *Their train arrived on time.* ❍ *After a couple of hours, we arrived at the airport.*

ar|ro|gant /ærəgənt/ **ADJ** behaving in an unpleasant way toward other people because you believe that you are better than them
❍ *I found him rather arrogant.* ● **ar|ro|gance** **NONCOUNT NOUN** ❍ *He shows none of the arrogance that often goes with money.*

ar|row /æroʊ/
1 NOUN a long thin weapon that is sharp and pointed at one end ❍ *a bow and arrow*
2 NOUN a written sign that points in a particular direction ❍ *The arrow pointed down to the bottom of the page.*

art /ɑrt/
1 NONCOUNT NOUN the activity of creating pictures or objects for people to look at, or the pictures or objects themselves ❍ *She decided she wanted to study art.* ❍ *modern American art*
2 PL NOUN **The arts** are activities such as music, painting, literature, film, theater, and dance. ❍ *a career in the arts*

ar|tery /ɑrtəri/ (**arteries**) **NOUN** An **artery** is a tube in your body that carries blood from your heart to the rest of your body. Compare with **vein**. ❍ *blocked arteries*

ar|ti|cle /ɑrtɪkᵊl/
1 NOUN a piece of writing in a newspaper or magazine ❍ *a newspaper article*
2 NOUN in grammar, one of the words "a," "an," or "the," which show whether you are talking about a particular thing or things in general

ar|ti|fi|cial /ɑrtɪfɪʃᵊl/ **ADJ** made by people, instead of nature ❍ *an artificial lake* ❍ *artificial additives in the diet* ● **ar|ti|fi|cial|ly** **ADV** ❍ *artificially sweetened lemonade*

art|ist /ɑrtɪst/
1 NOUN someone who draws, paints, or creates other works of art ❍ *Each painting is signed by the artist.*
2 NOUN a performer such as a musician, an actor, or a dancer ❍ *He was a popular artist, who sold millions of records.*

ar|tis|tic /ɑrtɪstɪk/ **ADJ** good at drawing or painting ❍ *He was sensitive and artistic.*

as /əz, STRONG æz/
1 CONJ at the same time that ❍ *He was leaving as we arrived.*
2 CONJ used to say how something happens or is done ❍ *Today, as usual, he was late.*
3 CONJ because ❍ *As I was so young, I didn't have to pay.*
4 PREP used to describe someone's job ❍ *She works as a nurse.*
5 PREP used to describe the purpose of something ❍ *The fourth bedroom is used as a study.*
6 You use **as ... as** when you are comparing things, or saying how large or small something is. ❍ *It's not as easy as I expected.* ❍ *I'm nearly as old as you!*

7 You use **as if** when you are saying how something seems to be. ❍ *Anne stopped, as if she didn't know what to say next.*

ASB /eɪ ɛs bi/ **NOUN** The **ASB** is the British organization that regulates standards in accounting. **ASB** is an abbreviation for "Accounting Standards Board." [FINANCE]

ash /æʃ/ (**ashes**) **NOUN** **Ash** is the gray powder that remains after something is burned. You can also call this substance **ashes**. ❍ *cigarette ash*

ashamed /əʃeɪmd/ **ADJ** If you are **ashamed** of someone or something, you feel embarrassed or guilty because of them. ❍ *I felt so ashamed of myself for getting angry.*

ash|tray /æʃtreɪ/ **NOUN** a small dish for cigarette ash

aside /əsaɪd/

1 ADV If you move something **aside**, you move it to one side of you. ❍ *Sarah closed the book and put it aside.*

2 ADV If you move **aside**, you move so that someone can pass you. ❍ *She stepped aside to let them pass.*

ask /æsk/

1 VERB If you **ask** someone something, you say something to them in the form of a question. ❍ *"How is Frank?" he asked.* ❍ *I asked him his name.* ❍ *She asked me if I understood.*

2 VERB If you **ask** someone **to** do something, you tell them that you want them to do it. ❍ *We politely asked him to leave.*

3 VERB If you **ask for** something, you say that you would like to know it or have it. ❍ *She asked for a raise.*

4 VERB If you **ask** someone **to** an event or place, you invite them to go there. ❍ *I asked Juan to join the company.*

ask|ing price **NOUN** the price that someone says that they want for something they are selling [PURCHASING] ❍ *Offers 15% below the asking price are unlikely to be accepted.*

asleep /əslip/

1 ADJ sleeping ❍ *They never seem to stop talking except when they are asleep.*

2 When you **fall asleep**, you start sleeping. ❍ *Sam soon fell asleep.*

as|pect /æspɛkt/ **NOUN** An **aspect** of something is a quality or a part of it. ❍ *He was interested in all aspects of the work here.*

as|pi|rin /æspərɪn, -prɪn/ **NOUN** a mild drug that reduces pain and fever

as|sas|si|nate /əsæsɪneɪt/ (**assassinates, assassinating, assassinated**) **VERB** When someone important **is assassinated**, they are murdered, often for political reasons. ❍ *Robert Kennedy was assassinated in 1968.*
● **as|sas|si|na|tion** /əsæsɪneɪʃən/ **NOUN** ❍ *Pope John Paul survived an assassination attempt in 1981.*

as|sault /əsɔlt/

1 NOUN a physical attack on a person ❍ *a serious assault*

2 VERB To **assault** someone means to physically attack them. ❍ *The gang assaulted him with baseball bats.*

as|sem|ble /əsɛmbəl/ (**assembles, assembling, assembled**)

1 VERB When people **assemble**, they come together in a group. ❍ *There was nowhere for students to assemble between classes.*

2 VERB To **assemble** something means to collect it together or to fit the different parts of it together. ❍ *They assemble airplanes.*

as|sem|bly line /əsɛmbli laɪn/ (**assembly lines**) **NOUN** an arrangement of workers and machines in a factory, where the product passes from one worker to another until it is finished [PRODUCTION] ❍ *He works on an assembly line.*

as|sess /əsɛs/ **VERB** When you **assess** a person, thing, or situation, you consider them in order to make a judgment about them. ❍ *I looked around and assessed the situation.* ❍ *They should be able to assess whether they are getting value for money.*

as|sess|ment /əsɛsmənt/ **NOUN** the process of considering a person, thing, or situation in order to make a judgment about them ❍ *We carry out an annual assessment of senior managers.*

as|ses|sor /əsɛsər/ **NOUN** a person who is employed to calculate the value of something [BANKING] ❍ *Assessors estimate* *that damage to local industry amounts to $1.2 billion.*

A

as|set /æsɛt/
1 NOUN something or someone that is considered to be useful or valuable ❍ *He is a great asset to the company.*
2 NOUN something that is owned by a company or person [FINANCE] ❍ *The group had assets of 3.5 billion euros.*

asset-stripping NONCOUNT NOUN **Asset-stripping** is the act of buying companies cheaply, selling their assets to make a profit, and then closing the companies down. [FINANCE] ❍ *The firm was accused of asset-stripping.*

as|set value NOUN the value of a share in a company [FINANCE] ❍ *The asset value of the fund dropped 4.5%.*

as|sign /əsaɪn/
1 VERB If you **assign** a piece of work **to** someone, you give them the work. ❍ *The group was assigned the task of designing a plan.*
2 VERB If someone **is assigned to** a particular place, they are sent to work there. ❍ *He was assigned to the Chicago office.*

as|sign|ment /əsaɪnmənt/ NOUN a task that you are given to do, especially as part of your studies ❍ *a written assignment*

as|sist /əsɪst/ VERB If someone or something **assists** you, they help you. ❍ *He was assisting elderly passengers with their baggage.*

as|sis|tance /əsɪstəns/ NONCOUNT NOUN **Assistance** is help ❍ *Please let us know if you need any assistance.*

as|sis|tant /əsɪstənt/ NOUN someone whose job is to help another person in their work ❍ *Kalan asked his assistant to answer the phone while he went out.*

as|so|ci|ate (**associates, associating, associated**)

> Pronounce the verb /əsoʊʃieɪt, -sieɪt/.
> Pronounce the noun /əsoʊʃiɪt, -siɪt/.

1 VERB If you **associate** someone or something **with** another thing, you connect them in some way. ❍ *Some people associate money with happiness.*
2 NOUN someone that you spend a lot of time with, especially at work ❍ *business associates*

as|so|ci|ate com|pa|ny (**associate companies**) NOUN or **associated company** a company in which between 20% and 50% of the shares are owned by another company or group [ADMINISTRATION] ❍ *A large stockholding should provide considerable influence over the associate company.*

as|so|cia|tion /əsoʊʃieɪʃən, -sieɪ-/ NOUN an official group of people who have the same job, purpose, or interest ❍ *the Hong Kong Tourist Association*

as|sort|ment /əsɔrtmənt/ NOUN a group of things that are all different from each other ❍ *There was an assortment of books on the shelf.*

as|sume /əsum/ (**assumes, assuming, assumed**) VERB If you **assume that** something is true, you suppose that it is true. ❍ *I assumed it was an accident.*

as|sur|ance /əʃʊərəns/
1 NOUN a statement that something is definitely true or will definitely happen ❍ *They want an assurance that jobs will be protected.*
2 NONCOUNT NOUN Assurance is insurance that pays money to someone's family when they die. [BANKING, BRIT] ❍ *a life assurance policy*

as|sure /əʃʊər/ (**assures, assuring, assured**) VERB If you **assure** someone **that** something is true or will happen, you tell them that it is definitely true or will definitely happen. ❍ *He assured me that there was nothing wrong.*

asth|ma /æzmə/ NONCOUNT NOUN **Asthma** is a lung condition that makes breathing difficult.

aston|ish /əstɒnɪʃ/ (**astonishes, astonishing, astonished**) VERB If something or someone **astonishes** you, they surprise you very much. ❍ *The news astonished them.*
● **aston|ished** ADJ ❍ *I was astonished to read your article.*

aston|ish|ing /əstɒnɪʃɪŋ/ ADJ very surprising ❍ *astonishing news*
● **aston|ish|ing|ly** ADV ❍ *The venture was astonishingly successful.*

as|tro|naut /æstrənɔt/ **NOUN** a person who is trained for traveling in space

at /ət, STRONG æt/

1 PREP used to say where someone or something is ❍ *He will be at the airport to meet her.* ❍ *I like working at home.*

2 PREP used to say when something happens ❍ *The meeting will take place this afternoon at 3:00.* ❍ *Workers were expected to leave at age 55.*

3 PREP used to give information about speed or quantity ❍ *I drove back down the highway at normal speed.* ❍ *There were only two apartments at that price.*

4 PREP used to show that an action is directed toward someone ❍ *He looked at Michael and laughed.*

5 PREP used to say that someone or something is in a particular state or condition ❍ *The two nations are at war.*

6 PREP used to say what someone is reacting to ❍ *He told me that he was still angry at how he'd been treated.*

ate /eɪt/ **Ate** is a form of the verb **eat**.

ath|lete /æθlit/ **NOUN** a person who is good at any type of physical sports or games, especially in competitions ❍ *Jesse Owens was one of the greatest athletes of the twentieth century.*

ath|let|ic /æθlɛtɪk/ **ADJ** relating to athletes and athletics ❍ *He comes from an athletic family.*

ATM /eɪ tiː ɛm/ **NOUN ATM** is an abbreviation of **automated teller machine**. [BANKING]

at|mos|phere /ætməsfɪər/

1 NOUN the layer of air or other gases around a planet ❍ *the Earth's atmosphere* • **at|mos|pher|ic** /ætməsfɛrɪk/ **ADJ** ❍ *atmospheric gases*

2 NOUN the general feeling in a place ❍ *The rooms are warm and the atmosphere is welcoming.*

atom /ætəm/ **NOUN** the very smallest part of something

atom|ic /ətɒmɪk/ **ADJ** relating to atoms or to power that is produced by splitting atoms ❍ *atomic energy*

at|tach /ətætʃ/ (**attaches, attaching, attached**)

1 VERB If something is **attached to** an object, it is fastened to it. ❍ *There is usually a label with instructions attached to the product.* ❍ *Please use the form attached to this letter.*

2 VERB If you **attach** a file **to** an email, you send it with the message. ❍ *I'm attaching the document to this email.*

at|tached /ətætʃt/ **ADJ** liking someone very much ❍ *She is very attached to her secretary.*

at|tach|ment /ətætʃmənt/ **NOUN** a file that is attached to an email message and sent with it ❍ *an email attachment*

at|tack /ətæk/

1 VERB To **attack** a person or place means to try to hurt or damage them. ❍ *I thought he was going to attack me.* ❍ *He was in the yard when the dog attacked.*

2 NOUN Attack is also a noun. ❍ *There have been several attacks on police officers.*

3 VERB To **attack** a person, belief, or idea is to criticize them strongly. ❍ *At the time, the French deal was widely attacked.*

4 NOUN Attack is also a noun. ❍ *Mr. Lamont launched an attack on the bank for failing to lower its interest rates.*

5 NOUN a time when you suffer badly from an illness ❍ *an asthma attack*

at|tain /əteɪn/ **VERB** If you **attain** something, you get it or achieve it, often after a lot of effort. [FORMAL] ❍ *That year he attained his pilot's license.* • **at|tain|ment NONCOUNT NOUN** ❍ *the attainment of independence*

at|tempt /ətɛmpt/

1 VERB If you **attempt to** do something, you try to do it. ❍ *I attempted to explain the situation.*

2 NOUN an act of trying to do something ❍ *a takeover attempt*

at|tend /ətɛnd/

1 VERB If you **attend** an event, you are present at it. ❍ *I was unable to attend the meeting.*

2 VERB If you **attend** a school, college, or church, you go there regularly. ❍ *They attended college together.* • **at|tend|ance NONCOUNT NOUN** ❍ *Attendance at the school is always high.*

A

at|tend|ant /ətɛndənt/ **NOUN** someone whose job is to serve people in a public place ❍ *a parking lot attendant*

at|ten|tion /ətɛnʃən/

1 NONCOUNT NOUN If you give someone or something your **attention**, you look at them, listen to them, or think about them carefully. ❍ *Can I have your attention?*

2 NONCOUNT NOUN If someone or something is getting **attention**, someone is dealing with them or caring for them. ❍ *medical attention*

3 If you **pay attention**, you watch and listen carefully. ❍ *Are you paying attention to what I'm saying?*

at|tic /ætɪk/ **NOUN** a room at the top of a house just under the roof

at|ti|tude /ætɪtud/ **NOUN** Your **attitude to** something is the way that you think and feel about it. ❍ *attitudes to labor, technology, and training*

at|tor|ney /ətɜrni/ **NOUN** In the United States, an **attorney** is a lawyer. [LEGAL] ❍ *a prosecuting attorney*

at|tor|ney gen|er|al (**attorneys general** or **attorney generals**) **NOUN** the chief law officer of a government [LEGAL]

at|tract /ətrækt/

1 VERB If you are **attracted to** someone or something, you like them, and you are interested in knowing more about them. ❍ *Working women and housewives are attracted to online shopping.*

2 VERB If something **attracts** people or animals, they want to see or visit it. ❍ *The museum attracts thousands of visitors every month.*

3 VERB If one object **attracts** another object, it causes the second object to move towards it. ❍ *Opposite ends of a magnet attract each other.*

at|trac|tion /ətrækʃən/

1 NONCOUNT NOUN **Attraction** is a feeling of liking someone. ❍ *mutual attraction*

2 NOUN something that people can visit for interest or enjoyment ❍ *a tourist attraction*

at|trac|tive /ətræktɪv/ **ADJ** pleasant to look at or imagine ❍ *The apartment was small but attractive.* ❍ *We think it's a very attractive deal.*

at|trib|ute (**attributes, attributing, attributed**)

The verb is pronounced /ətrɪbyut/. The noun is pronounced /ætrɪbyut/.

1 VERB If you **attribute** something **to** a particular situation or action, you think that it was caused by that situation or action. ❍ *She attributes her success to hard work.*

2 VERB If a piece of writing, a work of art, or a remark **is attributed to** someone, people say that they wrote it, created it, or said it. ❍ *For a long time the painting was attributed to Rembrandt.*

3 NOUN a quality or feature of someone or something ❍ *He had all the attributes of a really great manager.*

at|tri|tion /ətrɪʃən/ **NONCOUNT NOUN** **Attrition** is a decrease in the number of employees in a company, caused by people leaving and not being replaced. [HR] ❍ *The company cut its workforce through natural attrition.*

auc|tion /ɔkʃən/

1 NOUN a public sale where items are sold to the person who offers the most money ❍ *The painting sold for $400,000 at auction.*

2 VERB If something **is auctioned**, it is sold in an auction. ❍ *Eight drawings by the artist will be auctioned next week.*

auc|tion|eer /ɔkʃənɪər/ **NOUN** a person or company in charge of an auction [BANKING] ❍ *eBay, the online auctioneer*

audi|ence /ɔdiəns/

1 NOUN the people who are watching or listening to a performance, movie, or television program ❍ *There was a TV audience of 35 million.*

2 NOUN the people that an advertising campaign is directed at ❍ *Discount clothes are becoming more acceptable for a wider audience.*

audio /ɔdioʊ/ **ADJ** **Audio** equipment is used for recording and producing sound. ❍ *audio and video files*

audit /ɔdɪt/

1 VERB When an accountant **audits** accounts, he or she examines them officially in order to

make sure that they are correct. [FINANCE, BUSINESS MANAGEMENT] ❍ *Each year they audit our accounts and certify them as being true and fair.*
2 NOUN Audit is also a noun. ❍ *The bank first learned of the problem when it carried out an internal audit.*

audi|tion /ɔdɪʃən/ **NOUN** a short performance that an actor, dancer, or musician gives so that someone can decide if they are good enough to be in a play, film, or orchestra ❍ *She went to an audition for a Broadway musical.*

audi|tor /ɔdɪtər/ **NOUN** an accountant who officially examines the accounts of organizations [FINANCE, ADMINISTRATION] ❍ *An inquiry by the company's auditors revealed a series of incorrect accounting entries over several years.*

Audi|tor Gen|er|al (**Auditors General**) **NOUN** an official in Canada or Scotland who is responsible for auditing government departments [FINANCE, ADMINISTRATION] ❍ *An auditor general's report showed the target is not being met.*

August /ɔgəst/ **NOUN** the eighth month of the year ❍ *The movie comes out in August.*

aunt /ænt, ɑnt/ **NOUN** the sister of someone's mother or father, or the wife of their uncle ❍ *She wrote to her aunt in Alabama.* ❍ *Aunt Margaret is coming to visit next week.*

aus|ter|ity /ɔstɛrɪti/ **NONCOUNT NOUN Austerity** is a situation in which people's living standards are reduced because of economic difficulties. [ECONOMICS] ❍ *the years of austerity that followed the war*

authen|tic /ɔθɛntɪk/ **ADJ** real and not false ❍ *They serve authentic Italian food.*

author /ɔθər/ **NOUN** a person who has written a book ❍ *a best-selling author*

author|ise /ɔθəraɪz/ [BRIT] → **authorize**

authori|tar|ian /əθɔrɪtɛəriən/ **ADJ** controlling, and not letting people decide things for themselves [BUSINESS MANAGEMENT] ❍ *Authoritarian regimes should be encouraged to reform.*

author|ity /əθɔrɪti/ (**authorities**)
1 NONCOUNT NOUN Authority is the power to control other people. ❍ *Only the police have the authority to close roads.* ❍ *a position of authority*
2 PL NOUN The authorities are the people who are in charge of everyone else. ❍ *The authorities are investigating the attack.*
3 NOUN an official organization or government department ❍ *the Philadelphia Parking Authority*

author|ize /ɔθəraɪz/ (**authorizes, authorizing, authorized**) **VERB** If someone **authorizes** something, they give their permission for it to happen. ❍ *Only the president could authorize its use.*
● **authori|za|tion** /ɔθərɪzeɪʃən/ **NONCOUNT NOUN** ❍ *We didn't have authorization to enter.*

auto|bi|og|ra|phy /ɔtəbaɪɒgrəfi/ (**autobiographies**) **NOUN** the story of someone's life, written by them ❍ *He published his autobiography last fall.*

auto|crat|ic /ɔtəkrætɪk/ **ADJ** having complete power and making decisions without asking anyone else's advice [BUSINESS MANAGEMENT] ❍ *They criticized Weston's autocratic management style.*

auto|graph /ɔtəgræf/ **NOUN** the signature of someone famous ❍ *He asked for her autograph.*

auto|mat|ed /ɔtəmeɪtɪd/ **ADJ** using machines instead of people to do work [TECHNOLOGY] ❍ *The equipment was made on highly automated production lines.*

auto|mat|ed tell|er ma|chine (**automated teller machines**) **NOUN** a machine that allows people to take money from their bank account, using a special card [BANKING]

auto|mat|ic /ɔtəmætɪk/
1 ADJ used to describe a machine that can continue to work when no one is operating it ❍ *an automatic door*
2 ADJ used to describe an action that you do without thinking about it ❍ *an automatic response* ● **auto|mati|cal|ly** /ɔtəmætɪkli/ **ADV** ❍ *Checks will be paid automatically four times a year.*

auto|ma|tion /ɔtəmeɪʃən/ NONCOUNT NOUN **Automation** is the use of machines to do work that was previously done by people. [TECHNOLOGY] ❍ *Automation has reduced the work force here by half.*

auto|mo|bile /ɔtəməbil/ NOUN a car ❍ *the automobile industry*

autumn /ɔtəm/ NOUN the season between summer and winter when the weather becomes cooler and the leaves fall off the trees

aux|ilia|ry /ɔgzɪlyəri, -zɪləri/ (**auxiliaries**) NOUN In grammar, an **auxiliary** or **auxiliary verb** is a verb that you can combine with another verb to change its meaning slightly. In English, "be," "have," and "do" are auxiliary verbs.

avail|abil|ity of la|bor /əveɪləbɪlɪti əv leɪbər/ NONCOUNT NOUN The **availability of labor** for a particular task is whether or not there are enough workers available to do that task. ❍ *The benefits of producing in this country are low labor costs and the availability of labor.*

avail|able /əveɪləbᵊl/

1 ADJ Something that is **available** can be obtained. ❍ *The color and black-and-white model will be available in January.*

2 ADJ Someone who is **available** is not busy and is free to do something. ❍ *He was not available for interviews today.*

av|a|tar /ævətɑr/ NOUN an image that you can use to represent yourself on the Internet ❍ *This site will create your avatar from any photo.*

AVC /eɪ vi si/ NOUN An **AVC** is an extra amount of money paid into a pension fund. **AVC** is an abbreviation of "additional voluntary contribution." [FINANCE, BANKING, BRIT]

av|enue /ævɪnyu, -nu/

1 NOUN **Avenue** is sometimes used in the names of streets. ❍ *They live on Park Avenue.*

2 NOUN a straight road, especially one with trees on either side

av|er|age /ævərɪdʒ, ævrɪdʒ/

1 NOUN the result that you get when you add two or more amounts together and divide the total by the number of amounts you added together ❍ *Add the figures together and find the average.*

2 ADJ **Average** is also an adjective. ❍ *The average price of goods went up by just 2.2%.*

3 NOUN the normal amount or quality for a particular group of people or things ❍ *Productivity has grown at twice the average rate for all American manufacturing.*

4 ADJ **Average** is also an adjective. ❍ *The average adult man burns 1,500 to 2,000 calories per day.*

5 ADJ **Average** means ordinary. ❍ *He seemed like a pleasant, average guy.*

avoid /əvɔɪd/

1 VERB If you **avoid** something unpleasant, you do something to stop it from happening. ❍ *It was a last-minute attempt to avoid a disaster.*

2 VERB If you **avoid** doing something, you choose not to do it. ❍ *I avoid working in public places.*

3 VERB If you **avoid** a person or thing, you keep away from them. ❍ *She went to the women's restroom to avoid him.*

awake /əweɪk/ ADJ not sleeping ❍ *I stayed awake until midnight.*

award /əwɔrd/

1 NOUN a prize that a person is given for doing something well ❍ *a National Quality Award for service from the Commerce Department*

2 VERB If someone **is awarded** a prize, it is given to them. ❍ *She was awarded the prize for both films.*

aware /əwɛər/ ADJ If you are **aware of** something, you know about it. ❍ *They are well aware of the danger.* ● **aware|ness** NONCOUNT NOUN ❍ *We are trying to raise awareness of the issue.*

away /əweɪ/

1 ADV moving from a place ❍ *He turned and walked away.*

2 ADV not at home, school or work ❍ *Jason is away for a few days.*

3 ADV When a sports team plays **away**, it goes to its opponents' ground to play. Compare with **home**. ❍ *Canada's Davis Cup team will play away against the Netherlands in February.*

4 ADJ **Away** is also an adjective. ❍ *Charlton are about to play an important away match.*

5 ADV If you put something **away**, you put it

where it should be. ❍ *I put the file away and went home.*

6 ADV If an event is an amount of time **away**, it will happen after that time. ❍ *Christmas is now only two weeks away.*

7 If something is a particular distance **away from** a person or place, it is not near that person or place. ❍ *Remember to stay a safe distance away from the car in front.*

awe|some /ɔsəm/

1 ADJ very powerful or frightening ❍ *the awesome power of the ocean waves*

2 ADJ very good or special [INFORMAL] ❍ *You remember their awesome commercial!*

aw|ful /ɔfəl/ **ADJ** very bad ❍ *The food was awful.* ❍ *That was an awful plan.*

awhile /əwaɪl/ **ADV** for a short time ❍ *I waited awhile.*

awk|ward /ɔkwərd/

1 ADJ embarrassing and difficult to deal with ❍ *He kept asking awkward questions.*

● **awk|ward|ly ADV** ❍ *There was an awkwardly long silence.*

2 ADJ difficult to use or carry because of the design ❍ *The package was small but awkward to carry.*

3 ADJ An **awkward** movement or position looks strange or uncomfortable. ❍ *Amy made an awkward movement with her hands.*

● **awk|ward|ly ADV** ❍ *He fell awkwardly.*

awoke /əwoʊk/ **Awoke** is a form of the verb **awake**.

ax /æks/ (**axes, axing, axed**)

1 NOUN a tool used for cutting wood

2 VERB If something **is axed**, it is ended suddenly and without discussion. ❍ *Community projects are being axed by social services departments.* ❍ *Over 900 jobs will be axed at the factory next month.*

axe /æks/ [BRIT] → **ax**

a

Bb

B2B /bi̲ tə bi̲/ **B2B** is an abbreviation for **business-to-business**. [BUSINESS MANAGEMENT] ❍ *American analysts have been somewhat cautious in estimating the size of the B2B market.*

B2C /bi̲ tə si̲/ **B2C** is an abbreviation for **business-to-consumer**. [BUSINESS MANAGEMENT] ❍ *B2C companies look particularly vulnerable with 19 percent of them now worth little more than the cash on their balance sheets.*

B2G /bi̲ tu dʒi̲/ **B2G** is the selling of goods and services by businesses to government agencies using the Internet. **B2G** is an abbreviation for "business-to-government." [BUSINESS MANAGEMENT]

baby /beɪ̲bi/ (**babies**) **NOUN** a child in the first year or two of its life ❍ *She was holding a baby.*

baby|sit /beɪ̲bisɪt/ (**babysits, babysitting, babysat**) **VERB** If you **babysit for** someone, you look after their children while they are not at home. ❍ *I promised to babysit for Julia.*

baby|sitter /beɪ̲bisɪtər/ **NOUN** a person who looks after a child while the child's parents are not at home ❍ *We need a babysitter for Friday night.*

bach|elor /bæ̲tʃələr/ **NOUN** a man who has never been married

back
❶ ADVERB USES
❷ OPPOSITE OF FRONT; NOUN AND ADJECTIVE USES
❸ VERB USES

❶ **back** /bæ̲k/

1 ADV in the direction that is behind you ❍ *She stepped back into the room.*

2 ADV returning to where you were before ❍ *I went back to my office.* ❍ *I'll be back as soon as I can.*

3 ADV returning something to the place where it was before ❍ *Put the book back on the shelf.*

4 ADV doing something to someone that they have done to you ❍ *I'll call you back after lunch.*

5 If someone moves **back and forth**, they move in one direction and then in the opposite direction, many times. ❍ *He paced back and forth.*

❷ **back** /bæ̲k/

1 NOUN the part of your body from your neck to your bottom that is on the opposite side to your chest ❍ *He was lying on his back.*

2 NOUN The **back of** something is the side or part of it that is farthest from the front. ❍ *She was in a room at the back of the store.*

3 ADJ used for describing the side or part of something that is farthest from the front ❍ *the back door* ❍ *the back seat of a car*

4 If you say something **behind** someone's **back**, you say it when they are not there. ❍ *She'd been criticizing me behind my back.*

❸ **back** /bæ̲k/

1 VERB When you **back** a vehicle somewhere, you move it backward. ❍ *He backed his car out of the space.*

2 VERB If you **back** someone, you support them. ❍ *She backed the President in the recent debate.*

3 VERB If you **back** a business enterprise, you provide money for it.

▸ **back away** If you **back away**, you move away, often because you are frightened. ❍ *James stood up, but the girl backed away.*

▸ **back off** If you **back off**, you move away in order to avoid problems. ❍ *When I approached him he backed off.*

▸**back out** If you **back out**, you decide not to do something that you agreed to do. ❍ *They've backed out of the project.*

▸**back up**

1 To **back up** a statement means to give proof that it is true. ❍ *He didn't have any evidence to back up his theory.*

2 If you **back up** a computer file, you make a copy of it that you can use if the original file is lost. ❍ *Make sure you back up your files every day.*

back|bone /bækboun/ **NOUN** the line of bones down the middle of your back

back|date /bækdeɪt/ (**backdates, backdating, backdated**) also **back-date** **VERB** If a document or an arrangement **is backdated**, its effect starts from a date before the date when it is completed or signed. [BANKING, FINANCE] ❍ *The contract that was signed on Thursday morning was backdated to March 11.*

back-end load (**back-end loads**) **NOUN** A **back-end load** is a charge that an investor pays when they sell shares in a mutual fund, or when they cancel a life insurance policy. Compare with **front-end load**. [FINANCE] ❍ *A back-end load can amount to as much as 5 or 6 percent of the investment.*

back|er /bækər/ **NOUN** someone who helps or supports a project, organization, or person, often by giving money [FINANCE] ❍ *I was looking for a backer to assist me in the attempted buyout.*

back|ground /bækgraʊnd/

1 NOUN a person's family, education, or work experience ❍ *He came from a very poor background.* ❍ *His background was in engineering.*

2 NOUN **The background** is faint sounds that you can hear that are not the main thing you are listening to. ❍ *I could hear some music in the background.*

3 NOUN **The background** of a picture is the part behind the main things or people. Compare with **foreground**. ❍ *She was in the background of the photograph.*

back|hand|er /bækhændər/ **NOUN** A **backhander** is the same as a **bribe**. [FINANCE, ECONOMICS, mainly BRIT, INFORMAL]

back|ing /bækɪŋ/

1 NONCOUNT NOUN If someone has the **backing of** an organization or an important person, they receive support or money in order to do something. [BANKING, FINANCE] ❍ *The small company needed his advice to get financial backing and legal assistance.*

2 NOUN a layer of something such as cloth that is put onto the back of something in order to strengthen or protect it ❍ *The table mats and coasters have a nonslip, soft green backing.*

back|log /bæklɔg/ **NOUN** a number of things that have not yet been done but that need to be done [PRODUCTION] ❍ *Tektronix said it had started the quarter with an unusually small backlog of orders.*

back of|fice (**back offices**)

1 NOUN The **back office** of a financial institution is the administrative, accounting, and computing departments. [ADMINISTRATION] ❍ *He has invented a new retail-banking strategy and overhauled the back office.* ❍ *Back offices of financial service businesses are discovering that automation can replace large numbers of people.*

2 ADJ **Back-office** is also an adjective. ❍ *They can secure cost reductions by centralizing their back-office operations.*

back|pack /bækpæk/ **NOUN** a large bag that you carry on your back

back pay **NONCOUNT NOUN** **Back pay** is money that an employer owes an employee for work that he or she did in the past. [FINANCE] ❍ *He will receive $6,000 in back pay.*

back shift [BRIT] → **swing shift**

back|up /bækʌp/ also **back-up**

1 NONCOUNT NOUN **Backup** is extra help that you can get if you need it. ❍ *If you need backup, just call me.*

2 NOUN a copy of a computer file that you can use if the original file is lost ❍ *Always make backups of your data.*

back|ward /bækwərd/

1 ADJ directed behind you ❍ *He walked away without a backward glance.*

2 ADV in the direction that is behind you ❍ *He took two steps backward.*

B

3 ADV in the opposite way to the usual way ❍ *Kate counted backward from ten to zero.*
4 If someone or something moves **backward and forward**, they keep moving in one direction and then in the opposite direction. ❍ *The driver's seat has backward and forward adjustment.*

back|war|da|tion /bækwərdeɪʃən/ NONCOUNT NOUN **Backwardation** is when a seller postpones delivery of securities on the London Stock Exchange. The seller must pay a fee to the buyer. [FINANCE]

back|wards /bækwərdz/ [BRIT] → **backward 2**

back|yard /bækyɑrd/ also **back yard** NOUN the land at the back of a house ❍ *The house has a large backyard.*

ba|con /beɪkən/ NONCOUNT NOUN **Bacon** is thin pieces of salted or smoked meat from a pig. ❍ *We had bacon and eggs for breakfast.*

BACS /bæks/ NONCOUNT NOUN **BACS** is a method of making payments directly to a person's bank without using a check. **BACS** is an abbreviation for "Bankers' Automated Clearing Services." [FINANCE] ❍ *BACS payments avoid the problems of postal delays and loss.* [BRIT]

bac|te|ria /bæktɪəriə/ PL NOUN **Bacteria** are very small living things that can make people sick. ❍ *There were high levels of dangerous bacteria in the water.* ● **bac|te|rial** ADJ ❍ *a bacterial infection*

bad /bæd/ (**worse, worst**)
1 ADJ not good, being unpleasant or harmful ❍ *bad weather* ❍ *bad news* ❍ *Too much coffee is bad for you.* ❍ *He's in a bad mood.*
2 ADJ of poor quality ❍ *a really bad product*
3 ADJ having no skill in a particular activity ❍ *a bad driver*
4 ADJ If you **feel bad** about something, you feel guilty about it. ❍ *I feel bad that he's doing most of the work.*
5 ADJ used for describing a part of the body that causes pain or does not work well ❍ *Joe has a bad back.*
6 ADJ **Bad** language contains rude or offensive words. ❍ *He uses a lot of bad language.*

bad debt (**bad debts**) NOUN a sum of money that a person or firm owes but is not likely to pay back [BANKING, FINANCE] ❍ *The bank set aside 1.1 billion dollars to cover bad debts from business failures.*

badge /bædʒ/ NOUN a small piece of metal or plastic that you wear on your clothes to show people who you are ❍ *He showed me his police badge.*

bad|ly /bædli/ (**worse, worst**)
1 ADV in a way that is not successful or effective ❍ *whether stocks will perform well or badly in the next six months* ❍ *The whole project was badly managed.*
2 ADV If someone or something is **badly** hurt or **badly** affected, they are seriously hurt or affected. ❍ *The fire badly damaged a church.* ❍ *One man was killed and another was badly injured.*
3 ADV If you want or need something **badly**, you want or need it very much. ❍ *a country that badly needs to attract foreign investment*

bag /bæg/ NOUN a container for carrying things ❍ *a shopping bag*

bag|gage /bægɪdʒ/ NONCOUNT NOUN Your **baggage** is all the bags that you take with you when you travel. ❍ *baggage reclaim*

baht /bɑt/ NOUN the basic unit of money that is used in Thailand [ECONOMICS]

bake /beɪk/ (**bakes, baking, baked**) VERB When you **bake** food, you cook it in an oven. ❍ *freshly baked French bread*

bak|er /beɪkər/ NOUN a person whose job is to make and sell bread and cakes

bak|ery /beɪkəri, beɪkri/ (**bakeries**) NOUN a place where bread and cakes are baked or sold ❍ *The town has two bakeries.*

bal|ance /bæləns/ (**balances, balancing, balanced**)
1 VERB If someone or something **balances**, they stay steady and do not fall, and if you balance something, you put it in a position where it stays steady and does not fall. ❍ *I balanced on the top of the ladder.* ❍ *She balanced the chair on top of the table.*
2 NONCOUNT NOUN **Balance** is the state of

being steady and in a position where you will not fall. ❍ *Dan lost his balance and fell on the ice.*
3 VERB If you **balance** one thing **with** something else, you make sure you give both things enough time and energy. ❍ *You have to balance the demands of your work with the needs of your family.*
4 NOUN the amount of money you have in your bank account [BANKING] ❍ *I'll need to check my bank balance first.*
5 NOUN an amount of money that is still owed when part of an amount has been paid [FINANCE] ❍ *Let me have the balance of what you owe me.*
6 NOUN In accounting, a **balance** is the difference between the credit and debit totals. [BANKING]
7 An account is **in balance** when the credit and debit totals are equal. [BANKING]

bal|anced /bælənst/
1 ADJ A **balanced** way of considering things is fair and reasonable. ❍ *Journalists should present balanced reports.*
2 ADJ A **balanced** diet has the right amounts of different foods to keep your body healthy. ❍ *Eat a healthy, balanced diet and get regular exercise.*

bal|ance of pay|ments **NONCOUNT NOUN** A country's **balance of payments** is the difference between what it pays to buy goods and services from other countries and the money it earns from selling goods and services to other countries. [BANKING, ECONOMICS] ❍ *The country claimed it ran a surplus in its balance of payments in 1988.*

bal|ance of trade **NONCOUNT NOUN** A country's **balance of trade** is the difference in value between the goods it buys from other countries and the goods it sells to other countries. [BANKING, ECONOMICS] ❍ *As other nations grow and spend more money on American products, the balance of trade should even out.*

bal|ance sheet (**balance sheets**)
1 NOUN a statement of the amount of money and property that a firm has and the amount of money that it owes [FINANCE] ❍ *Rolls-Royce needed to produce a strong balance sheet.*
2 NOUN the general financial state of a firm [FINANCE] ❍ *The strong currency has helped the balance sheets of Brazilian companies with international aspirations.*

bal|co|ny /bælkəni/ (**balconies**)
1 NOUN a place where you can stand or sit on the outside of a building, above the ground
2 NOUN In a theater, **the balcony** is the seats upstairs.

bald /bɔld/ **ADJ** having no hair or very little hair on your head ❍ *He went bald in his thirties.*

ball /bɔl/
1 NOUN a round object that is used in games such as tennis and soccer, or an object with this shape ❍ *Michael was kicking a soccer ball against the wall.* ❍ *a ball of string*
2 NOUN a large, formal party where people dance ❍ *a New Year's ball*

bal|let /bæleɪ/ **NONCOUNT NOUN** **Ballet** is a type of dancing that needs a lot of skill and in which there are many carefully controlled movements. ❍ *a ballet dancer*

bal|loon /bəlun/ **NOUN** a round, brightly-colored rubber object that is filled with air or gas

bal|loon mort|gage (**balloon mortgages**) **NOUN** a mortgage in which you make small payments over a period of time and repay the balance in one large final payment [BANKING, FINANCE]

bal|loon pay|ment (**balloon payments**) **NOUN** a large final payment of a loan [BANKING, FINANCE] ❍ *At the end of the five years, the loan will be due and payable, and the investor will have a balloon payment to make.*

bal|lot /bælət/ (**ballots, balloting, balloted**)
1 NOUN a secret vote in which people choose a candidate in an election, or express their opinion about something ❍ *The result of the ballot will not be known for two weeks.*
2 VERB If you **ballot** a group of people, you find out what they think about a subject by organizing a secret vote. [BUSINESS MANAGEMENT, HR, mainly BRIT] ❍ *The union said they will ballot members on whether to strike.*

bam|boo /bæmbu/ **NONCOUNT NOUN** **Bamboo** is a tall, tropical plant that has hard,

B

hollow stems that are sometimes used for making furniture. ❍ *a bamboo hut*

ban /bæn/ (**bans, banning, banned**)
1 VERB If someone **bans** something, they say that it is not allowed. ❍ *Ireland was the first country to ban smoking in all workplaces.*
2 NOUN an official order saying that something is not allowed ❍ *The report proposes a ban on plastic bags.*

ba|na|na /bənænə/ **NOUN** a long, curved fruit with a yellow skin ❍ *a bunch of bananas*

banc|as|sur|ance /bæŋkəʃʊərəns/ **NONCOUNT NOUN** **Bancassurance** is the selling of insurance products by a bank to its customers. [BANKING] ❍ *Not many life insurance companies are looking at bancassurance in a big way, since face-to-face interaction works better here.*

band /bænd/
1 NOUN a group of people who play music together ❍ *a rock band*
2 NOUN a narrow piece of material that you wear around your head or wrists, or that is part of a piece of clothing ❍ *She had a band in her hair.*
3 NOUN a narrow circle of rubber or metal that holds many things together ❍ *a rubber band*

band|age /bændɪdʒ/ (**bandages, bandaging, bandaged**)
1 NOUN a long, narrow piece of cloth that is wrapped around an injured part of the body ❍ *We put a bandage on John's knee.*
2 VERB If you **bandage** a part of someone's body, you tie a bandage around it. ❍ *We bandaged her hand.*

Band-Aid (**Band-Aids**) also **band-aid** **NOUN** a small piece of sticky material that you use to cover small cuts on your body [TRADEMARK] ❍ *She had a Band-Aid on her knee.*

bang /bæŋ/
1 NOUN a sudden loud noise ❍ *I heard four or five loud bangs.*
2 VERB If you **bang** something or **bang on** something, you hit it hard, making a loud noise. ❍ *Lucy banged on the table with her fist.*
3 PL NOUN **Bangs** are hair that is cut shorter at the front so it forms a line above your eyes. ❍ *Both of them had blond bangs.*

bank /bæŋk/
1 NOUN a place or organization that looks after people's money [BANKING] ❍ *He had just $14 in the bank when he died.*
2 NOUN a raised area of ground along the edge of a river ❍ *We walked along the east bank of the river.*
▸ **bank on** If you **bank on** someone or something, you depend on them. ❍ *In 1972 most consumers were banking on cheap oil for ever.*

bank|able /bæŋkəbəl/ **ADJ** In the entertainment industry, someone or something that is described as **bankable** is very popular and therefore likely to be very profitable. [BANKING, BUSINESS MANAGEMENT] ❍ *This movie made him the most bankable star in Hollywood.*

bank ac|count (**bank accounts**) **NOUN** an arrangement with a bank that allows you to keep your money in the bank and to take some out when you need it [BANKING] ❍ *Paul had at least 17 different bank accounts.*

bank bill (**bank bills**) or **banker's bill**
1 NOUN A **bank bill** is the same as a **banknote**. [BANKING]
2 NOUN A **bank bill** is the same as a **bank draft**. [BANKING]

bank card (**bank cards**) or **ATM card** **NOUN** a plastic card that you use to get money from your bank account [BANKING]

bank clerk (**bank clerks**) [BANKING, ADMINISTRATION, BRIT] → **teller**

bank draft (**bank drafts**) **NOUN** a check that is written by one bank against its account in another bank and is payable to a particular person or company [BANKING]

bank|er /bæŋkər/ **NOUN** someone who works in banking at a senior level [BANKING, ADMINISTRATION] ❍ *The slowdown in Hong Kong has its good side, according to some local bankers.*

bank|er's or|der (**banker's orders**) [BANKING, BRIT] → **standing order**

bank holi|day (**bank holidays**) [BRIT] → **national holiday**

bank|ing /bæŋkɪŋ/ **NONCOUNT NOUN** **Banking** is the business activity of banks and similar institutions. [BANKING] ○ *the online banking revolution*

bank loan (**bank loans**) **NOUN** a loan from a bank that you have to repay with interest [BANKING]

bank man|ag|er (**bank managers**) **NOUN** someone who is in charge of a particular branch of a bank [BANKING, ADMINISTRATION] ○ *The bank manager must minimize risk by acquiring assets that have a low rate of default.*

bank|note /bæŋknoʊt/ (**banknotes**) also **bank note** **NOUN** a piece of paper money [BANKING, ECONOMICS] ○ *a shopping bag full of banknotes*

Bank of Eng|land /bæŋk əv ɪŋglənd/ **NONCOUNT NOUN** The **Bank of England** is the central bank of the United Kingdom, which acts as banker to the government and the commercial banks. It is responsible for managing the government's debt and for setting interest rates. [BANKING, ECONOMICS] ○ *The Bank of England left rates unchanged at 4% last week.*

bank rate (**bank rates**) **NOUN** the rate of interest at which a country's central bank lends money to other banks [BANKING] ○ *The United States reduced its bank rate ten days ago.*

bank|roll /bæŋkroʊl/ **VERB** To **bankroll** a person, organization, or project means to provide the money that they need. [BANKING, ECONOMICS, INFORMAL] ○ *The company has bankrolled a couple of local movies.*

bank|rupt /bæŋkrʌpt/

1 ADJ People or organizations that go **bankrupt** do not have enough money to pay their debts. They can be forced by law to close down their business and sell their assets. [BANKING, FINANCE] ○ *If a company cannot sell its products, it will go bankrupt.*

2 VERB If you **bankrupt** a person or organization, you make them bankrupt. [BANKING, FINANCE] ○ *The move to the market nearly bankrupted the firm and its director.* ○ *Uninsured people can be bankrupted by big medical bills.*

3 NOUN a person or organization that has been declared bankrupt by a court of law [BANKING, FINANCE]

COLLOCATIONS
to *go* bankrupt
to *be declared* bankrupt

bank|rupt|cy /bæŋkrʌptsi/ (**bankruptcies**)

1 NONCOUNT NOUN **Bankruptcy** is the condition of being bankrupt. [BANKING, FINANCE] ○ *It is the second airline in two months to file for bankruptcy.*

2 NOUN A **bankruptcy** is when an organization or person goes bankrupt. [BANKING, FINANCE] ○ *The number of corporate bankruptcies climbed in August.*

COLLOCATIONS
to *file for* bankruptcy
to *be on the verge of* bankruptcy
to *be on the brink of* bankruptcy
to *be facing* bankruptcy
to *declare* bankruptcy

bank state|ment (**bank statements**) **NOUN** a document showing all the money paid into and taken out of your bank account during a particular period of time [BANKING] ○ *All transactions must appear on the next bank statement.*

ban|ner /bænər/ **NOUN** a long, narrow piece of cloth or plastic with something written on it ○ *The crowd waved banners.*

ban|ner ad (**banner ads**) **NOUN** an advertisement on a website that appears across the top or along the side of the page [MARKETING AND SALES] ○ *A survey of 1,000 Americans found that only 1% of web surfers click on banner ads.*

bar /bɑr/

1 NOUN a long, straight piece of metal ○ *There were bars on all of the windows.*

2 NOUN a small block of something ○ *What is your favorite chocolate bar?*

3 NOUN a place where you can buy and drink alcoholic drinks ○ *We met at a local bar.*

B

bar|becue /bɑrbɪkyu/ (**barbecues, barbecuing, barbecued**) also **barbeque, BBQ**
1 NOUN a piece of equipment that you use for cooking outdoors, or an outdoor party where you eat food cooked on this ❍ *We had a barbecue on the beach.*
2 VERB If you **barbecue** food, you cook it on a barbecue. ❍ *The fish can be grilled, fried, or barbecued.*

bar|ber /bɑrbər/ **NOUN** a person whose job is to cut men's hair

bar code (**bar codes**) also **barcode NOUN** an arrangement of numbers and lines that is printed on a product that can be read by a computer in order to get information about the product [MARKETING AND SALES, TECHNOLOGY] ❍ *Although all bar codes contain some common information, such as a general description of the product, they have space for only so much detail.*

bare /bɛər/ (**barer, barest**)
1 ADJ If a part of your body is **bare**, it is not covered by clothes. ❍ *bare feet*
2 ADJ A **bare** surface is not covered or decorated with anything. ❍ *bare wooden floors*
3 ADJ If a room, cupboard, or shelf is **bare**, it is empty. ❍ *His refrigerator was bare.*

bare|ly /bɛərli/
1 ADV only just ❍ *Spending on services and goods such as food and clothing barely grew.*
2 ADV used for emphasizing how quickly one action or event followed another ❍ *She had barely sat down when her name was called.*

bar|gain /bɑrgɪn/
1 NOUN something that is being sold at a lower price than usual [MARKETING AND SALES] ❍ *At this price, the dress is a real bargain.* ❍ *Some are starting to offer wines at bargain prices.*
2 NOUN an agreement in which two or more people promise to give or perform something ❍ *UN negotiators had struck a last-minute bargain in New York.*
3 VERB When people **bargain**, they try to persuade other people to pay them more money or to provide better conditions for them. ❍ *The workers have the right to bargain for better pay.* ❍ *We use personal selling efforts to negotiate and bargain with customers.*

bar|gain base|ment also **bargain-basement ADJ** cheap and not very good [MARKETING AND SALES] ❍ *a bargain basement rock musical*

bar|gain|ing agent (**bargaining agents**) **NOUN** a labor union that represents a group of workers in talks with an employer [MARKETING AND SALES, ADMINISTRATION]

bark /bɑrk/
1 VERB When a dog **barks**, it makes a short, loud noise. ❍ *I could hear a dog barking.*
2 NOUN Bark is also a noun. ❍ *a dog's bark*
3 NONCOUNT NOUN Bark is the rough surface of a tree.

barn /bɑrn/ **NOUN** a building on a farm where animals and crops are kept

bar|on /bærən/
1 NOUN In Britain, a **baron** is a man who is a member of the lowest rank of the nobility. ❍ *their stepfather, Baron Michael Distemple*
2 NOUN someone who controls a large part of a particular industry or activity and who is therefore extremely powerful [ECONOMICS] ❍ *the battle against the drug barons*

bar|rel /bærəl/
1 NOUN a large container with curved sides and flat ends, used for storing liquids ❍ *barrels of oil*
2 NOUN the long metal part of a gun

bar|ri|er /bæriər/ **NOUN** a fence or a wall that prevents people or things from moving from one area to another ❍ *A police barrier blocked the road.*

bar|tender /bɑrtɛndər/ **NOUN** a person who makes and serves drinks in a bar

base /beɪs/ (**bases, basing, based**)
1 NOUN the lowest part of something ❍ *They planted flowers around the base of the tree.*
2 NOUN something from which something else can be developed ❍ *The post will give him a powerful political base from which to challenge the Kremlin.*
3 VERB If one thing is **based on** another thing, it is developed from it. ❍ *The film is based on*

a novel by Alexander Trocchi.
4 NOUN a place where soldiers live and work ❍ *a military base*
5 NOUN A **base** is a group of people or things that supports and forms an important part of something. A firm's customer **base** is the group of regular customers that the firm gets most of its income from. ❍ *This path roughly tracks the transition of a country from an agricultural to an industrial base.*
6 NOUN a place where a certain activity can be done ❍ *The general manager says the building is an excellent base for the worldwide export business.*

base|ball /beɪsbɔl/ **NONCOUNT NOUN** **Baseball** is a team game played on a large field in which players score by hitting a ball with a bat and running around four bases.

base|ment /beɪsmənt/ **NOUN** a floor of a building that is below ground level ❍ *They put the old files in the basement.*

base pay **NONCOUNT NOUN** Your **base pay** is the amount of money you earn at your job, not including overtime and bonuses. [HR]

base rate (**base rates**)
1 NOUN In Britain, the **base rate** is the interest rate set by the Bank of England. The **base rate** controls the interest rates charged throughout the banking system. [BANKING, ECONOMICS] ❍ *Bank base rates of 7 percent are too high.*
2 [BANKING, ECONOMICS, BRIT] → **prime rate**

ba|sic /beɪsɪk/ **ADJ** of the simplest and most important type ❍ *the basic skills of reading and writing* ❍ *There were shortages of the most basic foods.*

ba|si|cal|ly /beɪsɪkli/ **ADV** used for talking about a situation in a general way ❍ *Basically, he is a nice man.*

ba|sic in|dus|try (**basic industries**) **NOUN** an industry that is very important in a country's economy [PRODUCTION]

ba|sic rate **NONCOUNT NOUN** In Britain, the **basic rate** is the standard percentage of income that most people have to pay in tax. [FINANCE] ❍ *The basic rate is 20 percent and the higher rate is 40 percent.*

ba|sic wage (**basic wages**)
1 NOUN Your **basic wage** is the same as your **base pay**. [HR]
2 NOUN The **basic wage** is the same as the **minimum wage**. [ECONOMICS]

ba|sis /beɪsɪs/ (**bases** /beɪsiz/)
1 NOUN If something happens **on a** particular **basis**, it happens in that way. ❍ *We meet for lunch on a regular basis.*
2 NOUN the most important part of something that other things can develop from ❍ *The UN plan is a possible basis for peace talks.*

ba|sis point (**basis points**) **NOUN** one hundredth of a percent [ECONOMICS, FINANCE] ❍ *The dollar climbed about 30 basis points during the morning session.*

bas|ket /bæskɪt/
1 NOUN a container that you use for carrying things, made from thin pieces of wood or metal that are crossed under and over each other ❍ *a picnic basket*
2 NOUN the net that you throw the ball through in the game of basketball
3 NOUN A **basket of** currencies or a **basket of** goods is the average or total value of a number of different currencies or goods. [ECONOMICS] ❍ *The pound's value against a basket of currencies hit a new low of 76.9.* ❍ *An inflation measure that gauges the price of a fixed basket of goods and services was revised down slightly for the second straight month.*

basket|ball /bæskɪtbɔl/ **NONCOUNT NOUN** **Basketball** is a game in which two teams of five players each try to throw a large ball through a round net hanging from a high metal ring.

bass /beɪs/ **ADJ** A **bass** drum or guitar is one that makes a deep sound. ❍ *He plays bass guitar.*

bat /bæt/ (**bats, batting, batted**)
1 NOUN a long piece of wood that is used for hitting the ball in games such as baseball ❍ *a baseball bat*
2 VERB When you **bat**, you hit the ball with a bat in a game such as baseball. ❍ *Paxton hurt his elbow while he was batting.*

3 NOUN a small animal that flies at night and looks like a mouse with wings

batch /bætʃ/ (**batches**) **NOUN** a group of things or people of the same kind, especially a group that is dealt with at the same time

B

batch pro|duc|tion NONCOUNT NOUN **Batch production** is a method of producing goods in a factory in which a large number of goods are produced for several customers. Compare with **flow production**, **job production**. [PRODUCTION]

bath /bæθ/ **NOUN** When you take a **bath**, you sit or lie in a bathtub (=long container) filled with water, and wash your body. ❍ *He took a bath before he went to bed.*

bath|room /bæθrum/ **NOUN** a room that contains a toilet ❍ *She asked if she could use the bathroom.*

bath|tub /bæθtʌb/ **NOUN** a long container that you fill with water and sit or lie in to wash your body ❍ *She was lying in a huge pink bathtub.*

bat|tery /bætəri/ (**batteries**) **NOUN** a device for storing or producing electricity, for example in a radio or a car ❍ *The game requires two AA batteries.*

bat|tle /bætᵊl/ (**battles, battling, battled**)
1 NOUN a violent fight between groups of people, especially between armies during a war ❍ *the battle of Gettysburg*
2 NOUN a struggle for success or control over something ❍ *The union is likely to influence any takeover battle.*
3 VERB If you **battle**, you try very hard to do something although it is extremely difficult. ❍ *Doctors battled all night to save her life.* ❍ *He spent the next 23 years battling the big oil companies that were determined to shut him down.*

bay /beɪ/ **NOUN** a part of a coast where the land goes in and forms a curve ❍ *We sailed across the bay in the morning.*

ba|zaar or **bazar** /bəzɑr/
1 NOUN a place where there are many small stores, especially in areas such as the Middle East and India [MARKETING AND SALES, ECONOMICS] ❍ *Kamal was a vendor in Cairo's open-air bazaar.*
2 NOUN a sale to raise money for charity ❍ *a church bazaar*

BC /bi si/ also **B.C.** You use **BC** to refer to a date before the year in which Jesus Christ is believed to have been born. Compare with **AD**. ❍ *He probably lived in the fourth century BC.*

be
❶ AUXILIARY VERB USES
❷ OTHER VERB USES

❶ **be** /bi, STRONG bi/ (**am, are, is, being, was, were, been**)
1 AUX You use **be** with a present participle to form the continuous tense. ❍ *She is coming.* ❍ *He was driving to work when the accident happened.*
2 AUX You use **be** with another verb to form the passive. ❍ *The deal was done quickly.*
3 AUX You use **be** with an infinitive to show that something is planned to happen. ❍ *The talks are to begin tomorrow.*

❷ **be** /bi, STRONG bi/ (**am, are, is, being, was, were, been**)
1 VERB You use **be** to introduce more information about a subject. ❍ *She's my boss.* ❍ *He is very efficient.* ❍ *He's about fifty.* ❍ *The packaging was black.*
2 VERB You use **be** with "it" when you are giving your opinion on a situation. ❍ *It was too cold for swimming.* ❍ *It is important to be able to say no.* ❍ *It's nice having friends to talk to.*
3 VERB You use **be** in expressions like **there is** and **there are** to say that something exists. ❍ *There are very few cars on this street.*

beach /bitʃ/ (**beaches**) **NOUN** an area of sand or stones next to a lake or ocean ❍ *a beautiful sandy beach*

bead /bid/ **NOUN** a small piece of colored glass, wood, or plastic that is used for making jewelry

beak /bik/ **NOUN** the hard, pointed part of a bird's mouth ❍ *a black bird with a yellow beak*

beam /bim/
1 VERB If someone **is beaming**, they are

smiling a lot because they are very happy. ❍ *Frances was beaming after she got the news.*
2 NOUN A **beam** of light is a line of light that shines from something bright.
3 NOUN a long thick bar of wood or metal that supports the roof of a building ❍ *The ceilings are supported by oak beams.*

bean /bin/ **NOUN** a seed of a climbing plant or the part of the plant that contains the seeds, eaten as a vegetable ❍ *green beans*

bean-counter **(bean-counters)** also **bean counter** **NOUN** an employee whose job involves controlling costs and increasing profits [BUSINESS MANAGEMENT, INFORMAL] ❍ *Chrysler's bean counters were arguing that the $80 million investment would be better spent elsewhere.*

bear /bɛər/ **(bears, bearing, bore, borne)**
1 VERB If you **bear** an unpleasant experience, you accept it. ❍ *The loneliness was hard to bear.*
2 VERB If you **can't bear** someone or something, you dislike them very much. ❍ *I can't bear her voice.*
3 VERB If something **bears your weight**, it is able to support it. ❍ *The ice wasn't thick enough to bear their weight.*
4 VERB If someone **bears** the cost of something, they pay for it. ❍ *Patients should not have to bear the costs of their own treatment.*
5 VERB If something such as a bank account or an investment **bears** interest, interest is paid on it. [BANKING] ❍ *The eight-year bond will bear annual interest of 10.5%.*
6 NOUN a large, strong wild animal with thick fur and sharp claws
7 NOUN **Bears** are people who sell shares of stock when they expect the price to drop, hoping to make a profit by buying the shares again after a short time. Compare with **bull**. [FINANCE, ECONOMICS]

beard /bɪərd/ **NOUN** hair growing on a man's chin and sometimes cheeks ❍ *He had a long white beard.*

bear|er /bɛərər/ **NOUN** The **bearer** of a piece of paper used instead of money is the person who presents it for payment. [BANKING] ❍ *A former manager was charged with stealing $30,000 in bearer bonds.* ❍ *As long as it is payable to "order" or to "bearer," the holder may sell this note or use it as security for a loan.*

bear|ish /bɛərɪʃ/ **ADJ** In the stock market, if there is a **bearish** mood, prices are expected to fall. Compare with **bullish**. [FINANCE, ECONOMICS] ❍ *Dealers said investors remain bearish.* ❍ *We've been bearish on gold for the past two years.*

bear mar|ket **(bear markets)** **NOUN** A **bear market** is when people are selling a lot of shares of stock because they expect the price to drop. Then they make a profit by buying the shares again after a short time. Compare with **bull market**. [FINANCE, ECONOMICS] ❍ *Is the bear market in equities over?*

bear raid **(bear raids)** **NOUN** an attempt to force down the price of a stock by selling many shares or by spreading a negative rumor about the firm [FINANCE, ECONOMICS]

beast /bist/ **NOUN** a large, wild animal ❍ *There were wild beasts in the woods.*

beat /bit/ **(beats, beating, beat, beaten)**
1 VERB To **beat** someone or something means to hit them hard and repeatedly. ❍ *They beat him, and left him on the ground.* ❍ *We could hear the rain beating against the windows.*
2 VERB When your heart **beats**, it makes a regular sound and movement. ❍ *I felt my heart beating faster.*
3 NOUN **Beat** is also a noun. ❍ *He could hear the beat of his heart.*
4 NOUN the rhythm of a piece of music ❍ *Play some music with a steady beat.*
5 VERB If you **beat** someone in a competition or election, you defeat them. ❍ *The Red Sox beat the Yankees 5-2 last night.*

beau|ti|ful /byutɪfəl/ **ADJ** very attractive ❍ *a beautiful woman* ❍ *It's a beautiful city.*
• **beau|ti|ful|ly** /byutɪfli/ **ADV** ❍ *Karin sings beautifully.*

beau|ty /byuti/ **NONCOUNT NOUN** **Beauty** is the quality of being beautiful. ❍ *The hotel is in an area of natural beauty.*

be|came /bɪkeɪm/ **Became** is a form of the verb **become**.

be|cause /bɪkɔz, -kɒz/
1 CONJ used for giving the reason for something ○ *I went home because I was tired.* ○ *Export prices fell because of lower prices for basic metals.*
2 If an event or situation happens **because of** something, that thing is the reason or cause. ○ *He's retiring because of ill health.*

be|come /bɪkʌm/ (**becomes, becoming, became, become**) **VERB** If someone or something **becomes** a particular thing, they start to be that thing. ○ *He became seriously ill because of stress.* ○ *It has become a very popular tourist destination.*

bed /bɛd/
1 NOUN a piece of furniture that you lie on when you sleep ○ *We went to bed at about 10 p.m.* ○ *Nina was already in bed.*
2 NOUN The ocean **bed** or a river **bed** is the ground at the bottom of the ocean or of a river.

bed|room /bɛdrum/ **NOUN** a room that is used for sleeping in

bee /bi/ **NOUN** a flying insect that has yellow and black stripes on its body and makes honey ○ *Bees were buzzing in the flowers.*

beef /bif/ **NONCOUNT NOUN Beef** is meat from a cow. ○ *beef importers*

been /bɪn/
1 Been is a form of the verb **be**.
2 VERB If you have **been** to a place, you have gone to it before. ○ *Have you ever been to Paris?*

beep /bip/
1 NOUN a short, high sound ○ *Please leave a message after the beep.*
2 VERB If a piece of electronic equipment **beeps**, it makes a short, high sound. ○ *My cellphone beeps when I receive a text message.*
3 NOUN a short, loud sound made by a car horn
4 VERB If a horn **beeps**, or if you **beep** it, it makes a short, loud sound. ○ *He beeped the horn and waved.*

beer /bɪər/ **NONCOUNT NOUN Beer** is an alcoholic drink made from grain. ○ *a cool glass of beer*

beet /bit/ **NOUN** a dark red root that is eaten, often cold, as a vegetable ○ *Harvesting of the beets starts this month.*

be|fore /bɪfɔr/
1 PREP earlier than a particular time ○ *A decision will be made before next Monday.* ○ *He arrived before me.*
2 CONJ Before is also a conjunction. ○ *People rushed to buy things before prices rose in April.*
3 ADV at a time in the past ○ *Have you been to Athens before?* ○ *I had met Professor Lown before.*

before|hand /bɪfɔrhænd/ **ADV** before a particular event ○ *How did she know beforehand that I was going to go out?*

beg /bɛg/ (**begs, begging, begged**)
1 VERB If you **beg** someone **to** do something, you ask them in a way that shows that you very much want them to do it. ○ *I begged him to come to New York with me.* ○ *I begged for help but no one listened.*
2 VERB If someone **is begging**, they are asking people to give them food or money because they are very poor. ○ *Homeless people were begging on the streets.*

be|gan /bɪgæn/ **Began** is a form of the verb **begin**.

beg|gar /bɛgər/ **NOUN** someone who lives by asking people they do not know for money or food ○ *There are no beggars on the streets in Vienna.*

be|gin /bɪgɪn/ (**begins, beginning, began, begun**)
1 VERB If you **begin to** do something or **begin doing** something, you start to do it. ○ *David began to look angry.* ○ *Stocks began falling sharply yesterday afternoon.*
2 VERB When something **begins** or when you **begin** it, it starts to happen. ○ *The problems began last November.* ○ *He has just begun his second year at college.*

be|gin|ner /bɪgɪnər/ **NOUN** someone who has just started learning to do something ○ *a course for beginners*

be|gin|ning /bɪgɪnɪŋ/ **NOUN** the first part of something ○ *This was the beginning of her career.* ○ *The conference is at the beginning of May.*

be|gun /bɪgʌn/ **Begun** is a form of the verb **begin**.

be|half /bɪhæf/ If you do something **on** someone's **behalf**, you do it for that person. ❍ *She thanked us all on her son's behalf.*

be|have /bɪheɪv/ (**behaves, behaving, behaved**)
1 VERB If you **behave** in a particular way, you act in that way. ❍ *He'd behaved so badly.*
2 VERB If you **behave** or **behave yourself**, you are polite and do nothing to upset other people. ❍ *Did the kids behave themselves?*

be|hav|ior /bɪheɪvyər/ **NONCOUNT NOUN** A person's or animal's **behavior** is the way that they behave. ❍ *You should always reward good behavior.*

be|hav|iour /bɪheɪvyər/ [BRIT] → **behavior**

BUSINESS ETIQUETTE
Before you travel abroad for business, make sure you are aware of the table manners and eating etiquette that are associated with the country you are visiting.

be|hind /bɪhaɪnd/
1 PREP at the back of something or someone ❍ *I put a cushion behind his head.* ❍ *We parked behind a truck.*
2 PREP following someone ❍ *Keith walked along behind them.*
3 ADV Behind is also an adverb. ❍ *The other police officers followed behind in a second vehicle.*
4 PREP late in doing a piece of work ❍ *We're already 4 weeks behind schedule.*
5 ADV If you leave something or someone **behind**, you do not take them with you when you go. ❍ *He went, leaving behind both his home and an unpaid mortgage.*

be|ing /biɪŋ/
1 Being is a form of the verb **be**.
2 NOUN a living creature, either real or imaginary ❍ *beings from another planet*

be|lief /bɪlif/ **NOUN Belief** is a powerful feeling that something is real or true. ❍ *my belief in God*

be|lieve /bɪliv/ (**believes, believing, believed**)
1 VERB If you **believe** that something is true, you think that it is true. [FORMAL] ❍ *Scientists believe that life began around 4 billion years ago.*
2 VERB If you **believe** someone, you feel sure that they are telling the truth. ❍ *Many people will not believe him, just because of who he is.*
3 VERB If you **believe in** something, you feel sure that it exists. ❍ *I don't believe in ghosts.*

bell /bɛl/
1 NOUN a device that makes a ringing sound and is used to attract attention ❍ *I rang the door bell.*
2 NOUN a hollow metal object with a loose piece hanging inside it that hits the sides and makes a sound ❍ *The church bells were ringing.*

bel|ly /bɛli/ (**bellies**) **NOUN** a stomach ❍ *She put her hands on her swollen belly.*

be|long /bɪlɔŋ/
1 VERB If something **belongs to** you, you own it. ❍ *The land belongs to the federal government.*
2 VERB If you **belong to** a group, you are a member of it. ❍ *workers at private firms who belong to unions*
3 VERB If something or someone **belongs** somewhere, that is the right place for them to be. ❍ *Henry Ford knew that he belonged in engineering and manufacturing.*

be|long|ings /bɪlɔŋɪŋz/ **PL NOUN** Your **belongings** are the things that you own. ❍ *I gathered my belongings and left.*

be|low /bɪloʊ/
1 PREP in a lower position than something else ❍ *He came out of the apartment below Leonard's.* ❍ *We watched the sun sink below the horizon.*
2 ADV Below is also an adverb. ❍ *I could see the street below.*
3 PREP less than an amount, rate, or level ❍ *Interest rates fell below 10% for the first time.*
4 ADV Below is also an adverb. ❍ *Daytime temperatures were at zero or below.*

below-the-line **ADJ** In a **below-the-line** advertising campaign, a company does not employ an advertising agency in order to sell its products. Compare with **above-the line**. [MARKETING AND SALES] ❍ *The company is* *plowing $7 million into sponsorship and other below-the-line activity.*

below-the-line pro|mo|tion (**below-the-line promotions**)
1 NONCOUNT NOUN Below-the-line promotion is the use of sales and marketing methods that can be controlled by the firm. Compare with **above-the-line promotion**. [MARKETING AND SALES] ❍ *below-the-line promotion such as direct mailing and in-store displays*
2 NOUN Below-the-line promotions are sales and marketing methods that can be controlled by the firm. [MARKETING AND SALES] ❍ *Multicom can build innovative elements into below-the-line promotions so that they automatically catch the attention of the media.*

belt /bɛlt/ **NOUN** a long, narrow piece of leather or cloth that you fasten around your waist ❍ *He wore a belt with a large brass buckle.*

bench /bɛntʃ/ (**benches**) **NOUN** a long seat made of wood or metal ❍ *a park bench*

bench|mark /bɛntʃmɑrk/ **NOUN** something that is used to assess whether performance has been successful [PRODUCTION, BUSINESS MANAGEMENT] ❍ *The truck industry is a benchmark for the economy.*

bench|mark|ing /bɛntʃmɑrkɪŋ/ **NONCOUNT NOUN Benchmarking** is when a firm compares its products and methods with those of the most successful firms in its field, in order to try to improve its own performance. [PRODUCTION, BUSINESS MANAGEMENT]

bend /bɛnd/ (**bends, bending, bent**)
1 VERB When you **bend**, you move the top part of your body down and forward. ❍ *I bent over and signed the letter.* ❍ *She bent down and picked up the note.*
2 VERB When you **bend** a part of your body, you change its position so that it is no longer straight. ❍ *Remember to bend your legs when you do this exercise.*
3 VERB When something straight **bends**, it changes direction to form a curve. ❍ *The road bends slightly to the right.*
4 NOUN A **bend** in a road or a pipe is a curve or angle in it. ❍ *The accident happened on a sharp bend in the road.*

be|neath /bɪniθ/ **PREP** under something ❍ *He sat in the conference room beneath a huge photograph of himself.*

ben|efit /bɛnɪfɪt/
1 NOUN an advantage that you get from something ❍ *the benefits of exercise*
2 PL NOUN Benefits are extra things that some people get from their job in addition to their salary. [HR] ❍ *The parents were employed at jobs that paid little and did not provide benefits.*
3 VERB If you **benefit from** something, it helps you in some way. ❍ *You would benefit from a change in your diet.*

ben|efit so|ci|ety (**benefit societies**) **NOUN** a group of people who pay into a fund, from which benefits are paid to members in need [HR, ECONOMICS]

ben|efits pack|age (**benefits packages**) **NOUN** a set of benefits that some people get from their job in addition to their salary [HR] ❍ *New West Consultants has an excellent benefits package.* ❍ *They offered a benefits package that included maternity leave, part-time work, and job sharing.*

bent /bɛnt/
1 Bent is a form of the verb **bend**.
2 ADJ not straight ❍ *Keep your knees slightly bent.*

ber|ry /bɛri/ (**berries**) **NOUN** a small, round fruit that grows on a bush or a tree

be|side /bɪsaɪd/ **PREP** next to ❍ *Can I sit beside you?*

be|sides /bɪsaɪdz/
1 PREP in addition to something ❍ *They have investments in a whole variety of businesses besides manufacturing.*
2 ADV used for giving another reason for something ❍ *The house is too expensive. Besides, I don't want to leave our little apartment.*

best /bɛst/
1 ADJ a form of the adjective **good**, meaning "better than any other" ❍ *my best friend* ❍ *Drink regularly through the day—water is best.*

2 ADV a form of the adverb **well**, meaning "more than any other" ❍ *I like all the ideas you had but I liked the first one best.* ❍ *He is best known as a former minister, spokesman, and trouble-shooter.*
3 NOUN If someone or something is **the best**, they are better than all other people or things. ❍ *We offer only the best to our clients.*
4 NOUN If you **do your best**, you try very hard to do something well. ❍ *If you do your best, no one can criticize you.*

best prac|tice
1 NONCOUNT NOUN Best practice is an agreed process for getting something done in the most efficient way. [BUSINESS MANAGEMENT] ❍ *a place where people can meet to swap ideas and develop best practice*
2 PL NOUN Best practices are the best methods to get something done or to accomplish a goal. [BUSINESS MANAGEMENT] ❍ *As natural-resource funds proliferate, they will have more opportunities to share expertise and best practices.*

best-seller (**best-sellers**) or **bestseller**
NOUN a product that is very popular and that many people buy [MARKETING AND SALES] ❍ *The best-sellers are electronic toys.* ❍ *Every book featured on Oprah's monthly book club has made the New York Times best-seller list.* ● **best-selling ADJ** ❍ *Astrology magazines and booklets are among the best-selling publications at supermarket checkouts.*

bet /bɛt/ (**bets, betting, bet**)
1 VERB If you **bet on** the result of a race or sports game, you give someone money that they give you back with extra money if the result is what you said it would be. ❍ *I bet $20 on a horse called Bright Boy.*
2 NOUN Bet is also a noun. ❍ *Did you make a bet on the horse race?* ● **bet|ting NONCOUNT NOUN** ❍ *Betting is illegal in many countries.*
3 You say "**I bet**" to show that you are sure something is true. [INFORMAL] ❍ *I bet the market will be up 50 points on Monday.*

bet|ter /bɛtər/
1 ADJ a form of the adjective **good**, meaning "of a higher quality" ❍ *This machine is much better.*
2 ADV a form the adverb **well**, meaning "more" or "in a way that is more successful" ❍ *You know her better than me.* ❍ *Carlo did better than me in his exams.*
3 ADJ If you are **better** after an illness or injury, you are well again. ❍ *Are you feeling better today?*
4 You use **had better** when you are saying what should happen. ❍ *We had better think about it.*

be|tween /bɪtwin/
1 PREP in the middle of two things or people ❍ *Nicole was standing between the two men.*
2 PREP from one place to another and back again ❍ *I spend a lot of time traveling between Waco and El Paso.*
3 PREP more than one amount and less than another amount ❍ *Between 250 and 300 insurance claims are filed each year.*
4 PREP after one time and before another time ❍ *The house was built between 1793 and 1797.*
5 PREP shared between a number of people ❍ *The profit was shared between him and his business partners.*

bev|er|age /bɛvərɪdʒ, bɛvrɪdʒ/ **NOUN** a drink [FORMAL] ❍ *hot beverages*

be|ware /bɪwɛər/ **VERB** If you tell someone to **beware** of a person or thing, you are telling them to be careful because the person or thing is dangerous. ❍ *Beware of the dog.*

be|yond /bɪyɒnd/
1 PREP on the other side of a place ❍ *On his right was a garden and beyond it a large house.*
2 ADV Beyond is also an adverb. ❍ *The house had a fabulous view out to the ocean beyond.*

B/F also **b/f B/F** is used in an account book to describe an amount of money that was transferred from one page or column to the next page or column. **B/F** is short for "brought forward." [BANKING] ❍ *Balance b/f: $100*

bias /baɪəs/ (**biases**) **NOUN** a tendency to prefer one person or thing to another, and to favor that person or thing ❍ *The study concluded there was "a bias toward the publication of positive results."*

Bible /baɪbəl/ **NOUN The Bible** is the holy book of the Christian and Jewish religions.

bi|cy|cle /baɪsɪkᵊl/ NOUN a vehicle with two wheels which you ride by sitting on it and using your legs to make the wheels turn

bid /bɪd/ (**bids, bidding, bid**)

1 NOUN If you make a **bid** for something that is being sold, you say that you will pay a certain amount of money for it. ❍ *We made the winning $620 bid for the statue.*

2 VERB If you **bid** for something that is being sold, you say that you will pay a certain amount of money for it. ❍ *An American company may be preparing to bid for the group.*

bid price (**bid prices**) NOUN The **bid price** is the price that investors are willing to pay for a particular security. Compare with **offer price**. [MARKETING AND SALES, FINANCE] ❍ *Investors feel that the bid price undervalues the company.*

big /bɪg/ (**bigger, biggest**)

1 ADJ large in size ❍ *Australia is a big country.* ❍ *They have a very big house.*

2 ADJ important or serious ❍ *It's a big problem for us.* ❍ *You're making a big mistake.*

3 ADJ A **big sister/brother** is a child's older sister or brother. ❍ *I lived with my dad and my big brother, John.*

Big Bang (**Big Bangs**)

1 NOUN a sudden forceful beginning or major change ❍ *The drag of tradition may yet cause the Soviet Union's big bang to collapse back on itself.*

2 NOUN In financial markets, a **Big Bang** is a major set of changes in rules or practices. **The Big Bang** was the particular set of changes that took place on the London Stock Exchange in 1986. [BANKING, ECONOMICS] ❍ *Johannesburg's Big Bang echoes London's in 1986.*

Big Board

1 NONCOUNT NOUN The **Big Board** is a listing of the securities that are bought and sold on the New York Stock Exchange. [ECONOMICS, FINANCE]

2 NONCOUNT NOUN The **Big Board** is a name for the New York Stock Exchange. [ECONOMICS, FINANCE, INFORMAL] ❍ *Big Board volume was 179,270,000 shares.*

big busi|ness

1 NONCOUNT NOUN **Big business** is business that involves very large companies and very large sums of money. [BUSINESS MANAGEMENT] ❍ *Big business will never let petty nationalism get in the way of a good deal.*

2 NONCOUNT NOUN Something that is **big business** is something that people spend a lot of money on, and that has become an important commercial activity. ❍ *Online dating is big business in the United States.*

bike /baɪk/ NOUN a bicycle or a motorcycle [INFORMAL] ❍ *When you ride a bike, you exercise all your leg muscles.*

bi|lat|er|al trade /baɪlætərəl treɪd/ NONCOUNT NOUN **Bilateral trade** is a system of trading between two countries in which each country attempts to balance its trade with that of the other. [ECONOMICS] ❍ *This year America's bilateral trade deficit with Japan will be less than half of what it was five years ago.*

bill /bɪl/

1 NOUN a piece of paper that shows how much money you must pay for something ❍ *They couldn't afford to pay their bills.*

2 VERB If you **bill** someone **for** goods or services, you send them a bill stating how much money they owe you. [PURCHASING] ❍ *Are you going to bill me for this?*

3 NOUN a piece of paper money [BANKING] ❍ *The case contained a large quantity of U.S. dollar bills.*

4 NOUN in government, a written document that contains a suggestion for a new law ❍ *The bill was approved by a large majority.*

5 NOUN [BRIT] → **check 4**

bill|able /bɪləbᵊl/ ADJ **Billable** hours are the hours that a professional spends doing work for clients and for which the clients will have to pay. [FINANCE] ❍ *Most law firms expect at least forty billable hours a week.*

bill|board /bɪlbɔrd/ NOUN a very large board for advertisements that is placed at the side of the road [MARKETING AND SALES]

bill|ing /bɪlɪŋ/ NONCOUNT NOUN **Billing** is the process of preparing and sending someone a bill for goods or services. [PURCHASING] ❍ *More customers have been asking for itemized billing.*

bil|lion /bɪlyən/

> The plural form is **billion** after a number.

the number 1,000,000,000 ❍ *The country's debt has risen to 3 billion dollars.* ❍ *The ceremony was watched by billions of people around the world.*

bil|lion|aire /bɪlyənɛər/ NOUN an extremely rich person who has money or property worth at least a billion dollars

bill of ex|change (**bills of exchange**) NOUN a document ordering someone to pay someone else a stated sum of money at a future date [BANKING, FINANCE]

bill of lad|ing /bɪl əv leɪdɪŋ/ (**bills of lading**) NOUN a document containing full details of the goods that are being shipped [LOGISTICS AND DISTRIBUTION, ECONOMICS] ❍ *There were bills of lading from a steel mill in Indiana.*

bin /bɪn/ NOUN a container that you keep things in ❍ *a plastic storage bin*

bind /baɪnd/ (**binds, binding, bound**)
1 VERB If you **bind** something, you tie rope or string around it to hold it firmly. ❍ *They bound his hands behind his back.*
2 VERB Is someone **is bound by** an agreement, they are forced to act in a certain way by it. ❍ *New residents are required to sign the lease and be bound by its terms.* ● **bind|ing** ADJ ❍ *The company has no binding contracts with either of them.*

bin|ocu|lars /bɪnɒkyələrz/ PL NOUN **Binoculars** are special glasses that you use to look at things that are a long distance away.

bio|data /baɪoʊdeɪtə, -dætə/ PL NOUN **Biodata** is information about a person's education and work experience that appears on their job application. [HR] ❍ *Careful research is necessary if biodata are to prove useful as predictors of managerial success.*

bi|og|ra|phy /baɪɒgrəfi/ (**biographies**) NOUN the story of someone's life, written by someone else ❍ *a biography of Franklin D. Roosevelt*

bio|logi|cal /baɪəlɒdʒɪkᵊl/ ADJ happening in the bodies and cells of living things ❍ *biological processes such as reproduction and growth*

bi|ol|ogy /baɪɒlədʒi/ NONCOUNT NOUN **Biology** is the scientific study of living things. ● **bi|olo|gist** /baɪɒlədʒɪst/ NOUN ❍ *a marine biologist*

bird /bɜrd/ NOUN an animal with feathers and wings ❍ *a bird's nest* ❍ *The bird flew away as I came near.*

birth /bɜrθ/
1 NOUN the occasion when a baby is born ❍ *They are celebrating the birth of their first child.* ❍ *Alice weighed 5 lbs 7 oz at birth.*
2 When a woman **gives birth**, a baby comes out of her body. ❍ *She's just given birth to a baby girl.*

birth|day /bɜrθdeɪ, -di/ NOUN the day of the year that you were born ❍ *Mom always sends David a present on his birthday.*

BIS /bi aɪ ɛs/ NONCOUNT NOUN The **BIS** is an institution that promotes international financial cooperation and serves as a bank for all central banks. **BIS** is short for "Bank for International Settlements." [ECONOMICS, FINANCE] ❍ *The BIS standards will require banks to have capital roughly equal to 8% of their total assets.*

bish|op /bɪʃəp/ NOUN a leader in the Christian church whose job is to look after all the churches in an area

bit /bɪt/
1 NOUN a unit of information that can be stored on a computer [TECHNOLOGY]
2 A bit of something is a small amount of it, or a small part of it. ❍ *I do a bit of work at my children's school sometimes.* ❍ *Only a bit of the cake was left.*
3 A bit means a little. ❍ *She was a bit strange.* ❍ *I think he's a bit happier now.*
4 Quite a bit means quite a lot. [INFORMAL] ❍ *Things have changed quite a bit.*
5 If you do something **a bit** or **for a bit**, you do it for a short time. ❍ *Let's wait a bit.*
6 Bit is a form of the verb **bite**.

bite /baɪt/ (**bites, biting, bit, bitten**)
1 VERB If you **bite** something, you use your teeth to cut into it or through it. ❍ *William bit*

into his sandwich.

2 NOUN a small piece of food that you cut into with your teeth ❍ *Dan took another bite of apple.*

B

3 VERB If a snake or an insect **bites** or **bites** you, it makes a mark or a hole in your skin with a sharp part of its body. ❍ *Do these flies bite?*

4 NOUN a painful mark on your body where an animal, a snake, or an insect has bitten you ❍ *a dog bite*

bit|ter /bɪtər/

1 ADJ tasting unpleasantly sharp and sour ❍ *The medicine tasted bitter.*

2 ADJ feeling very angry and upset about something that has happened to you ❍ *She's very bitter about the way she lost her job.*

● **bit|ter|ly ADV** ❍ *"And he didn't even try to help us," Grant said bitterly.* ● **bit|ter|ness NONCOUNT NOUN** ❍ *He says, with some bitterness, that the president ignored his letter.*

3 ADJ **Bitter** weather is extremely cold. ❍ *A bitter east wind was blowing.* ● **bit|ter|ly ADV** ❍ *It's bitterly cold here in Moscow.*

bi|zarre /bɪzɑr/ **ADJ** very strange ❍ *bizarre behavior*

black /blæk/

1 ADJ being the color of the sky at night ❍ *a black coat* ❍ *He had thick black hair.*

2 NOUN **Black** is also a noun. ❍ *She was wearing black.*

3 ADJ belonging to a race of people with dark skins, especially a race originally from Africa ❍ *He worked for the rights of black people.*

4 NOUN Black people are sometimes called **blacks**, especially when comparing different groups of people. Other uses of the word could cause offense. ❍ *There are about 31 million blacks in the U.S.*

5 ADJ **Black** coffee has no milk in it. ❍ *a cup of black coffee*

6 If you are **in the black**, you do not owe any money. [BANKING] ❍ *It is one of the few European computer firms that stayed in the black last year.*

black and white also **black-and-white ADJ** In a **black and white** photograph or film, everything is shown in black, white, and gray. ❍ *old black and white films*

black|berry /blækbɛri/ (**blackberries**)

1 NOUN a small, soft black or dark purple fruit

2 NOUN a small computer that can be used for receiving and sending email, and sometimes making phone calls [TRADEMARK]

black|board /blækbɔrd/ **NOUN** a big, dark-colored board for writing on in a classroom

black econo|my (**black economies**) **NOUN** the portion of a country's income from the sale of goods and services that is not officially reported [BANKING, ECONOMICS] ❍ *The black economy is very pronounced where tax levels are high.* ❍ *Greece, Italy, and Spain have the biggest black economies in the industrial world.*

black knight (**black knights**) **NOUN** A **black knight** is a person or firm that makes an unfriendly takeover bid for another firm. Compare with **white knight**. [BANKING]

black|mail /blækmeɪl/

1 NONCOUNT NOUN **Blackmail** is saying that you will say something bad about someone if they do not do what you tell them to do. ❍ *He was accused of blackmail.*

2 VERB If one person **blackmails** another person, they use blackmail against them. ❍ *Jeff suddenly realized that Linda was blackmailing him.*

black mar|ket (**black markets**) **NOUN** If something is bought or sold **on the black market**, it is bought or sold illegally. Compare with **gray market**. [BANKING, ECONOMICS] ❍ *There is a plentiful supply of arms on the black market.*

black mon|ey

1 NONCOUNT NOUN **Black money** is the portion of a country's income that relates to its black economy. [BANKING, ECONOMICS] ❍ *The main form of black money is probably undeclared capital gains.*

2 NONCOUNT NOUN **Black money** is any money that a person or organization acquires illegally. ❍ *He only made matters worse by declaring that "depositors were largely crooks with black money who got what they deserved."*

3 NONCOUNT NOUN **Black money** is money to

fund a government project that is concealed in the cost of some other project. [BANKING, ECONOMICS]

blade /bleɪd/ **NOUN** the flat, sharp edge of a knife or other cutting device ❍ *The cigar cutter has extremely sharp replaceable stainless steel blades.*

blame /bleɪm/ (**blames, blaming, blamed**)
1 VERB If you **blame** someone or something **for** something bad, you say that they caused it. ❍ *The director blamed the airlines for causing the delays.*
2 NONCOUNT NOUN If you get or take the **blame for** something bad that has happened, people say that you caused it. ❍ *I'm not going to take the blame for a mistake he made.*

blank /blæŋk/
1 ADJ Something that is **blank** has nothing on it. ❍ *a blank page*
2 ADJ If you look **blank**, your face shows no reaction. ❍ *Albert looked blank. "I don't know him, sir."* ● **blank|ly ADV** ❍ *Ellie stared at him blankly.*

blank check/ (**blank checks**) **NOUN** a signed check on which the amount of money has not been written yet [BANKING]

blan|ket /blæŋkɪt/ **NOUN** a large, thick piece of cloth that you put on a bed to keep you warm

blast /blæst/ **NOUN** a big explosion, especially one caused by a bomb ❍ *250 people were killed in the blast.*

blaze /bleɪz/ (**blazes, blazing, blazed**)
1 VERB When a fire **blazes**, it burns strongly and brightly. ❍ *Three people died as the building blazed.*
2 NOUN a large fire that destroys a lot of things ❍ *More than 4,000 firefighters are currently battling the blaze.*

BUSINESS ETIQUETTE
Remember that public holidays can vary widely between countries around the world. Keep a note of days when your business associates abroad will be unavailable to respond to your emails or answer your calls.

blaz|er /bleɪzər/ **NOUN** a type of light jacket for men or women

bleed /blid/ (**bleeds, bleeding, bled**) **VERB** When part of your body **bleeds**, you lose blood from it. ❍ *Ian's lip was bleeding.* ● **bleed|ing NONCOUNT NOUN** ❍ *We tried to stop the bleeding from the cut on his arm.*

blend /blɛnd/
1 VERB If you **blend** substances together, you mix them together. ❍ *Yogurt, jam, and pie makers sometimes blend wild berries with cultivated blueberries.*
2 NOUN a mixture of two or more things ❍ *They will begin filling their cars with a blend of petrol and biofuel.*
3 VERB When different things **blend**, they combine well. ❍ *All the colors blend perfectly together.*

bless /blɛs/ (**blesses, blessing, blessed**)
1 VERB When a priest **blesses** people or things, he or she asks for God's protection for them. ❍ *The pope blessed the crowd.*
2 You can say "**bless you**" to someone when they sneeze. [SPOKEN]

blew /blu/ **Blew** is a form of the verb **blow**.

blind /blaɪnd/
1 ADJ unable to see ❍ *My grandfather is going blind.*
2 PL NOUN The blind are people who are blind. ● **blind|ness NONCOUNT NOUN** ❍ *Early treatment can often prevent blindness.*
3 PL NOUN Blinds are a piece of cloth or other material that you can pull down over a window to cover it. ❍ *Susan pulled the blinds up to let the sunlight into the room.*

blind|fold /blaɪndfoʊld/
1 NOUN a piece of cloth that is tied over someone's eyes so that they cannot see
2 VERB If you **blindfold** someone, you tie a blindfold over their eyes. ❍ *Mr. Li was handcuffed and blindfolded.*

blind trust (**blind trusts**) **NOUN** a financial arrangement in which someone's investments are managed without the person knowing where the money is invested [BANKING, FINANCE] ❍ *Yang transferred the stocks into a blind trust earlier this week.*

bling /blɪŋ/ or **bling-bling** NONCOUNT NOUN **Bling** is expensive or fancy jewelry. [INFORMAL] ❍ *Famous jewelers want celebrities to wear their bling.*

B

blink /blɪŋk/ VERB When you **blink**, you shut your eyes and very quickly open them again. ❍ *I stood blinking in the bright light.*

blip|vert /blɪpvɜrt/ NOUN a very short television advertisement [MARKETING AND SALES, mainly BRIT] ❍ *There's this belief that young people can only concentrate on 30-second blipverts, or their heads will explode from boredom.*

blis|ter /blɪstər/ NOUN a raised area of skin filled with a clear liquid ❍ *I get blisters when I wear these shoes.*

blis|ter pack (**blister packs**) NOUN a package in which a small item is sold, consisting of a curved plastic cover attached to cardboard [MARKETING AND SALES]

block /blɒk/

1 NOUN a large, solid piece of a substance that has straight sides ❍ *a block of wood*

2 NOUN in a town or city, a group of buildings with streets on all sides, or the distance between each group of buildings ❍ *He walked around the block three times.* ❍ *She walked four blocks down High Street.*

3 VERB If someone or something **blocks** a road, it prevents things from passing along it. ❍ *The police blocked a highway through the center of the city.* ❍ *A tree fell down and blocked the road.*

4 VERB If someone or something **blocks** a proposed action, it prevents it from happening. ❍ *The government should block the proposed takeover.* ❍ *a court order blocking the deal*

blog /blɒg/ NOUN a website that describes the daily life of the person who writes it, and also their thoughts and ideas ❍ *His blog was later published as a book.*

blog|ger /blɒgər/ NOUN someone who writes a blog ❍ *Loewenstein is a freelance author, blogger, and journalist.* ● **blog|ging** NONCOUNT NOUN ❍ *Blogging is huge.*

bloke /bloʊk/ [BRIT] → **guy**

blonde /blɒnd/ (**blonder, blondest**)

1 ADJ **Blonde** hair is pale-colored. ❍ *My sister has blonde hair.*

2 ADJ Someone who is **blonde** has blonde hair. ❍ *Miss Young is clever, capable, glamorous, and blonde.*

blood /blʌd/ NONCOUNT NOUN **Blood** is the red liquid that flows inside your body. ❍ *His shirt was covered in blood.*

bloom /blum/ VERB When a plant or tree **blooms**, it grows flowers on it. When a flower **blooms**, it opens. ❍ *This plant blooms between May and June.*

blos|som /blɒsəm/

1 NONCOUNT NOUN **Blossom** is the flowers that appear on a fruit tree. ❍ *Cherry blossom lasts only a few days.*

2 VERB When a tree **blossoms**, it produces blossom. ❍ *The peach trees will blossom soon.*

blouse /blaʊs/ NOUN a shirt for a girl or woman

blow /bloʊ/ (**blows, blowing, blew, blown**)

1 VERB When the wind **blows**, the air moves. ❍ *A cold wind was blowing.*

2 VERB If the wind **blows** something somewhere, it moves it there. ❍ *The wind blew her hair back from her forehead.*

3 VERB If you **blow**, you send out air from your mouth. ❍ *Danny blew on his fingers to warm them.*

4 VERB When someone **blows** a whistle, they make a sound by blowing into it. ❍ *The referee blew his whistle.*

5 VERB When you **blow** your nose, you force air out of it in order to clear it. ❍ *He took out a handkerchief and blew his nose.*

6 NOUN a hard hit with something ❍ *He went to the hospital after a blow to the face.*

7 NOUN something that makes you very unhappy or disappointed ❍ *The increase in tax was a blow to the industry.*

▸ **blow out** If you **blow out** a flame, you blow at it so that it stops burning. ❍ *I blew out the candle.*

▸ **blow up**

1 If someone **blows** something **up** they destroy it with an explosion. ❍ *He was jailed for trying to blow up a plane.*

2 If something **blows up** it is destroyed in an explosion. ❍ *A truck packed with explosives blew up outside the main offices.*
3 PL NOUN If you **blow** something **up**, you fill it with air. ❍ *He was blowing up balloons for the party.*

blue /blu/ (**bluer, bluest, blues**)
1 ADJ being the color of the sky on a sunny day ❍ *a blue sky* ❍ *She has pale blue eyes.*
2 NOUN **Blue** is also a noun. ❍ *The paths through the store are shown in blue.*
3 PL NOUN **The blues** is a type of slow, sad music that developed among African American musicians in the southern United States. ❍ *I grew up singing the blues at home with my mom.*

blue chip (**blue chips**) **NOUN** a stock that is considered fairly safe to invest in while also being profitable [BUSINESS MANAGEMENT] ❍ *Blue chip issues were sharply higher, but the rest of the market actually declined slightly by the end of the day.*

blue-collar **ADJ** **Blue-collar** workers work in industry, doing physical work, rather than in offices. [HR, BUSINESS MANAGEMENT] ❍ *It wasn't just the blue-collar workers who lost their jobs, it was everyone.*

blue-sky law (**blue-sky laws**) **NOUN** a state law regulating the sale of securities and intended to protect investors from fraud [LEGAL]

Blue|tooth /blutuθ/ **NONCOUNT NOUN** **Bluetooth** is a type of technology that allows computers, the Internet, and cellphones to communicate with each other. [TRADEMARK] ❍ *the latest Bluetooth technology*

blunt /blʌnt/
1 ADJ saying exactly what you think and not trying to be polite ❍ *She can be a bit blunt.*
2 ADJ not sharp or pointed ❍ *a blunt pencil*

blush /blʌʃ/ **VERB** When you **blush**, your face becomes red because you are ashamed or embarrassed. ❍ *"Hello, Maria," he said, and she blushed again.*

board /bɔrd/
1 NOUN a flat, thin piece of wood ❍ *There were wooden boards over the doors and windows.*
2 NOUN a flat piece of wood or plastic that you use for a special purpose ❍ *the staff bulletin board* ❍ *a wooden chopping board*
3 NOUN the group of people in a firm who organize it and make decisions about it [ADMINISTRATION, LEGAL] ❍ *The board will announce its decision tomorrow.* ❍ *Here is the agenda for the September 12 board meeting.*
4 VERB When you **board** a train, a ship, or an aircraft, you get into it to travel somewhere. [FORMAL] ❍ *I boarded the plane to Boston.*
5 If something happens or exists **across the board**, it affects everyone or everything in a group. ❍ *Shares fell across the board yesterday.* ❍ *The president promised across-the-board cuts.*
6 When you are **on board** a train, a ship, or an aircraft, you are on it. ❍ *All 25 people on board the plane were killed.*

board of di|rec|tors (**boards of directors**) **NOUN** the group of people elected by a firm's shareholders to manage the firm [ADMINISTRATION, HR] ❍ *The board of directors has approved the decision unanimously.*

board of trade (**boards of trade**) **NOUN** A **board of trade** is the same as a **chamber of commerce**. [ECONOMICS]

board|room /bɔrdrum/ also **board room** **NOUN** a room where the board of a firm meets [ADMINISTRATION, BUSINESS MANAGEMENT] ❍ *Everyone had already assembled in the boardroom for the 9:00 a.m. session.*

boast /boʊst/ **VERB** If you **boast**, you annoy people by proudly saying that you have something or have done something. ❍ *He boasted that the police would never catch him.* ❍ *Carol was boasting about her new job.*

boat /boʊt/ **NOUN** a small ship ❍ *a fishing boat*

body /bɒdi/ (**bodies**)
1 NOUN Your **body** is all of you, from your head to your feet. ❍ *Yoga creates a healthy mind in a healthy body.*
2 NOUN Your **body** is the main part of you, but not your arms, head, and legs. ❍ *Gently pull your leg to your body.*
3 NOUN a dead person ❍ *A body was pulled from the water.*

b

4 NOUN an organized group of people who deal with something in an official way ❍ *They should check the planners' filings with regulatory bodies, such as the Securities and Exchange Commission.*

B

COLLOCATIONS
a *review* body
a *regulatory* body
an *independent* body

body|guard /bɒdigɑrd/ **NOUN** a person whose job is to protect someone important ❍ *the President's bodyguards*

BOGOF /bɒgɒf/ (**BOGOFs**) also **bogof** **NOUN** **BOGOF** is the practice of giving customers an extra free item of the same type when they buy something. **BOGOF** is an abbreviation for "buy one, get one free." [MARKETING AND SALES] ❍ *The major theme of the sector over the past year has been BOGOF.* ❍ *bogof promotions*

boil /bɔɪl/
1 VERB When a hot liquid **boils**, bubbles appear in it and it starts to change into steam. ❍ *I'm waiting for the water to boil.* ❍ *They have now been advised not to eat fish and to boil water.*
2 VERB When you **boil** food, you cook it in boiling water. ❍ *The president consulted his advisers over boiled eggs at breakfast.* ❍ *I put the potatoes in a pot to boil.*

boil|er|plate /bɔɪlərpleɪt/ **NOUN** a contract that can easily be changed to fit different situations [TECHNOLOGY, LEGAL] ❍ *We just looked at a boilerplate standard contract.*

bold /boʊld/
1 ADJ brave and confident ❍ *I wasn't bold enough to ask.*
2 ADJ bright and clear ❍ *bold colors* ❍ *a bold design*

bo|lí|var /bɒləvər, bəlivɑr/ **NOUN** the basic unit of money that is used in Venezuela [ECONOMICS]

bolt /boʊlt/
1 NOUN a long piece of metal that you use with a piece of metal with a hole in it (= a nut) to fasten things together ❍ *The bolts are all tight enough.*
2 NOUN on a door, a piece of metal that you move across to lock the door
3 VERB When you **bolt** a door, you move the bolt across to lock it. ❍ *He locked and bolted the door.*

bolt-on **ADJ** **Bolt-on** buys are purchases of other firms that a firm makes in order to add them to its existing business. [FINANCE] ❍ *He said the firm would make further bolt-on acquisitions in the U.S.*

bomb /bɒm/
1 NOUN a weapon that explodes and destroys things that are near to it ❍ *Bombs went off at two London train stations.*
2 VERB When people **bomb** a place, they attack it with bombs. ❍ *Military airplanes bombed the airport.* ● **bomb|ing** **NOUN** ❍ *the bombing of the capital*

bond /bɒnd/
1 NOUN A **bond between** people is a strong feeling of friendship, love, or shared beliefs. ❍ *The experience created a special bond between us.*
2 VERB When people **bond with** each other, they form a relationship based on love or shared beliefs and experiences. ❍ *Belinda quickly bonded with her new baby.*
3 NOUN a certificate issued to investors when a government or firm borrows money from them [BANKING, FINANCE] ❍ *Most of it will be financed by government bonds.* ❍ *the recent sharp decline in bond prices*

bond|ed /bɒndɪd/ **ADJ** A **bonded** company has entered into a legal agreement that offers its customers some protection if the company does not fulfill its contract with them. [FINANCE] ❍ *They are a fully bonded and licensed company.*

bond|ed ware|house (**bonded warehouses**) **NOUN** a warehouse in which goods are stored until duty is paid or the goods are cleared for export [LOGISTICS AND DISTRIBUTION, FINANCE] ❍ *It is worth paying extra for your wine to be stored in a bonded warehouse, because you avoid duty while it is in storage.*

bond|holder /bɒndhoʊldər/ also **bond holder** NOUN a person who owns one or more investment bonds [BANKING, FINANCE]

bone /boʊn/ NOUN one of the many hard, white parts that form the structure of the body ❍ *a broken bone*

bon|fire /bɒnfaɪər/ NOUN a large fire that you make outside ❍ *Bonfires are not allowed in many areas.*

bon|net /bɒnɪt/
1 NOUN a hat with ribbons that are tied under the chin
2 NOUN [BRIT] → **hood 2**

bo|nus /boʊnəs/ (**bonuses**)
1 NOUN an extra amount of money that is added to your usual pay [HR, FINANCE] ❍ *Each member of staff received a $100 bonus.*
2 NOUN something good that you get in addition to something else ❍ *The view from the hotel was an added bonus.*
3 NOUN a sum of money that an insurance firm pays to its policyholders, for example a percentage of the firm's profits [HR, FINANCE] ❍ *These returns will not be enough to meet the payment of annual bonuses to policyholders.*

COLLOCATIONS
an *annual* bonus
to *receive* a bonus

bo|nus is|sue (**bonus issues**) NOUN the distribution of free shares of stock (called **bonus shares**) among existing shareholders, based on the number of shares they own [HR, FINANCE] ❍ *A bonus issue does not really add to shareholder wealth, but is merely an indicator of potential performance.*

book /bʊk/
1 NOUN a number of pages, usually with writing on them, held together inside a cover ❍ *I just read the new book by Rosella Brown.*
2 VERB When you **book** a hotel room or a ticket, you arrange to have it or use it at a particular time. ❍ *Laurie booked a flight home.* ❍ *Three-star restaurants are normally booked for months in advance.*
3 PL NOUN A firm's **books** are its financial records. [ADMINISTRATION] ❍ *For the most part, he left the books to his managers and accountants.*
4 PL NOUN If someone is **on the books** of a firm or an organization, their name appears in the official records. ❍ *Around 12 percent of the people on our books are in the computing industry.*

book|case /bʊkkeɪs/ NOUN a piece of furniture with shelves that you keep books on

book|keeper /bʊkkipər/ also **book-keeper** NOUN a person whose job is to keep an accurate record of the money that is spent and received by a business [FINANCE, ADMINISTRATION]

book|keeping /bʊkkipɪŋ/ also **book-keeping** NONCOUNT NOUN **Bookkeeping** is the job or activity of keeping an accurate record of the money that is spent and received by a business or other organization. [FINANCE, ADMINISTRATION]

book|let /bʊklɪt/ NOUN a very thin book that gives you information about something ❍ *the manufacturers' instruction booklet*

book|mark /bʊkmɑrk/
1 NOUN in computing, the address of a website that you add to a list on your computer so that you can return to it easily ❍ *Use bookmarks to give you quick links to your favorite websites.*
2 VERB **Bookmark** is also a verb. ❍ *I've bookmarked the page.*

book|store /bʊkstɔr/ NOUN a store where books are sold

book value (**book values**)
1 NOUN the value of a business asset as shown on the firm's account books [FINANCE] ❍ *The book value may understate current value or replacement cost.*
2 NOUN the value of a firm as shown on its account books, after subtracting what it owes from what it owns [FINANCE] ❍ *He thinks this will produce a large gain in the company's stated book value for the December quarter.*
3 NOUN the value of a single share of stock, calculated by dividing the value of the firm by the number of shares it has issued [FINANCE] ❍ *The buyback price was 38% below the stock's book value.*

B

boom /bu̲m/

1 NOUN a big increase in the number of things that people are buying and the amount of profit that is being made [ECONOMICS, FINANCE] ❍ *The country's economic boom has produced a growing hunger for energy that only foreign supplies can satisfy.*

2 VERB When something or someone **booms**, they make a loud, deep sound. ❍ *"Ladies," boomed Helena, "We all know why we're here tonight."*

3 NOUN Boom is also a noun. ❍ *We heard a loud boom.*

COLLOCATIONS

a *consumer* boom
an *economic* boom
a *market* boom
boom *years*
boom *time*

bo̲o̲m-bu̲st cy|cle (**boom-bust cycles**)
NOUN a series of events in which a rapid increase in business activity in the economy is followed by a rapid decrease in business activity [ECONOMICS, FINANCE] ❍ *We must avoid the damaging boom-bust cycles which characterized the 1980s.*

boom|ing /bu̲mɪŋ/ **ADJ** If a market is **booming**, the amount of things being bought or sold in that market is increasing quickly. [ECONOMICS] ❍ *For U.S. manufacturers, there's a growing realization that to fuel growth, they must take advantage of booming markets in Europe and the Far East.* ❍ *It has a booming tourist industry.*

boost /bu̲st/

1 VERB If one thing **boosts** another, it causes it to increase or improve. ❍ *Lower prices will boost sales.*

2 NOUN Boost is also a noun. ❍ *The event would give the economy the boost that it needs.*

3 VERB If something **boosts** your confidence, it improves it. ❍ *If the team wins, it will boost their confidence.*

4 NOUN Boost is also a noun. ❍ *closing that deal gave me a real boost.*

boost|er|ism /bu̲stərɪzəm/ **NONCOUNT NOUN Boosterism** is the active promotion of a city or region and its local businesses. [MARKETING AND SALES] ❍ *They decided some civic boosterism was in order and they invented the Seafair summer celebration.*

boot /bu̲t/

1 NOUN a type of shoe that covers your whole foot and the lower part of your leg

2 VERB If you **boot** a computer, you make it ready to start working. ❍ *Put the CD into the drive and boot the machine.*

3 Boot up means the same as **boot**. ❍ *Wait while I boot it up.*

4 NOUN The **boot** of a car is the same as the **trunk**. [BRIT]

boot|strap /bu̲tstræp/ (**bootstraps, bootstrapping, bootstrapped**)

1 NOUN an offer to purchase a controlling share in a firm [FINANCE] ❍ *Leveraged buyouts, as bootstrap deals came to be known, began as a kind of aid to the elderly.*

2 VERB If a business **bootstraps** itself, or if it **bootstraps** an activity, it achieves success with limited resources. [FINANCE] ❍ *Each kicked in $15,000 of their own money to bootstrap the project for six months.*

3 ADJ depending only on your own hard work and limited resources [FINANCE] ❍ *Until now, the venture has been a bootstrap operation, financed by the programmer and his family.*

4 If you have **pulled** yourself **up by** your **bootstraps**, you have overcome difficulties and achieved success through your own hard work.

bor|der /bɔ̲rdər/

1 NOUN the dividing line between two countries ❍ *They drove across the border.*

2 NOUN a decoration around the edge of something ❍ *The curtains were white with a red border.*

bore /bɔ̲r/ (**bores, boring, bored**) **VERB** If someone **bores** you, they make you feel tired and annoyed, usually by saying things that are not interesting. ❍ *Dick bored me with stories of his vacation.*

bored /bɔ̲rd/ **ADJ** tired and annoyed because something does not interest you ❍ *Trainees will learn little if they are bored, tired, or fed up.*

bor|ing /bɔrɪŋ/ **ADJ** not interesting or enjoyable ❍ *a boring meeting*

born /bɔrn/

1 VERB When a baby **is born**, it comes out of its mother's body. ❍ *She was born in Milan on April 29, 1923.*

2 ADJ used for describing someone who has a natural ability to do a particular activity or job ❍ *Jack was a born teacher.*

borne /bɔrn/ **Borne** is a form of the verb **bear**.

bor|row /bɒroʊ/

1 VERB If you **borrow** something that belongs to someone else, you use it for a period of time and then return it. ❍ *Can I borrow a pen please?*

2 VERB If you **borrow** money **from** someone or **from** a bank, they give it to you and you agree to pay it back at some time in the future. [BANKING] ❍ *Morgan borrowed £5,000 from his father to form the company 20 years ago.* ❍ *It's so expensive to borrow from finance companies.*

bor|row|er /bɒroʊər/ **NOUN** a person or organization that borrows money [BANKING] ❍ *Borrowers with a big mortgage should go for a fixed rate.*

bor|row|ing /bɒroʊɪŋ/ **NONCOUNT NOUN** **Borrowing** is the activity of borrowing money. [BANKING] ❍ *We have allowed spending and borrowing to rise in this recession.*

boss /bɔs/ (**bosses**) **NOUN** the person in charge of you at the place where you work [HR, ADMINISTRATION] ❍ *He likes his new boss.*

Bos|ton ma|trix /bɔstən meɪtrɪks, bɒs-/ **NONCOUNT NOUN** The **Boston matrix** is a chart that is used by large companies to plan their business strategy by dividing business units or products into various categories. [BUSINESS MANAGEMENT]

both /boʊθ/

1 ADJ used for saying that something is true about two people or things ❍ *Stand up straight with both arms at your sides.* ❍ *Both men were transferred.*

2 PRON **Both** is also a pronoun. ❍ *Dan and Mike are both from Brooklyn.* ❍ *They both worked at Harvard University.*

3 ADJ used for showing that you are talking about two people or things ❍ *Both of these people are very good at their work.* ❍ *Both of them were there.*

4 You use **both ... and ...** to show that each of two facts is true. ❍ *Now women work both before and after having their children.*

b

both|er /bɒðər/

1 VERB If you do not **bother to** do something, you do not do it because you think it is not necessary. ❍ *Lots of people don't bother to get married these days.*

2 VERB If something **bothers** you, it makes you feel worried or angry. ❍ *Is something bothering you?*

3 VERB If someone **bothers** you, they try to talk to you when you are busy. ❍ *I'm sorry to bother you, but there's someone here to speak to you.*

bot|tle /bɒtᵊl/ **NOUN** a glass or plastic container in which drinks and other liquids are kept, or the amount contained in a bottle ❍ *an empty water bottle* ❍ *She drank half a bottle of apple juice.*

bottle|neck /bɒtᵊlnɛk/

1 NOUN a place where a road becomes narrow or where it meets another road so that the traffic slows down or stops, often causing traffic jams

2 NOUN a situation that stops a process or activity from progressing [PRODUCTION] ❍ *He pushed everyone full speed ahead until production hit a bottleneck.*

bot|tom /bɒtəm/

1 NOUN the lowest part of something ❍ *He sat at the bottom of the stairs.* ❍ *Answers can be found at the bottom of page 8.*

2 ADJ being the lowest of many ❍ *There are pencils in the bottom drawer of the desk.*

3 NOUN If you say that **the bottom** has **dropped** or **fallen out of** a market or industry, you mean that people have stopped buying the products it sells. ❍ *The bottom had fallen out of the city's property market.*

4 NOUN **The bottom of** an organization or career structure is the lowest level in it, where new employees often start. ❍ *He has worked in the theater for many years, starting at the bottom.* ❍ *She is a researcher at the bottom of the pay scale.*

▶**bottom out** If a trend such as a fall in prices **bottoms out**, it stops getting worse or decreasing. ❍ *He expects the recession to bottom out.* ❍ *House prices have bottomed out.*

B

bot|tom fish|ing NONCOUNT NOUN **Bottom fishing** is when you invest in low-priced securities in the hope of making a profit. [FINANCE] • **bot|tom fish|er** (**bottom fishers**) NOUN ❍ *Bargain hunters and bottom fishers, investors who thrive on troubled securities, were scouring the junk market yesterday.*

bot|tom line (**bottom lines**)
1 NOUN **The bottom line** in a decision or situation is the most important factor that you have to consider. ❍ *The bottom line is that it's not profitable.*
2 NOUN Your **bottom line** in a business deal is the least amount of money that you are willing to accept. [BUSINESS MANAGEMENT] ❍ *She says $95,000 is her bottom line.*
3 NOUN The **bottom line** is the total amount of money that a firm has made or lost over a particular period of time. [FINANCE] ❍ *The threat was enough to force chief executives to look beyond the next quarter's bottom line.*

bottom-up ADJ from the lower levels of an organization to the top level [BUSINESS MANAGEMENT] ❍ *a bottom-up approach to corporate decision-making*

bought /bɔt/ **Bought** is a form of the verb **buy**.

bounce /baʊns/ (**bounces, bouncing, bounced**)
1 VERB When an object such as a ball **bounces**, it hits a surface and immediately moves away from it again. ❍ *The ball bounced across the floor.* ❍ *Matthew came in bouncing a rubber ball.*
2 VERB If you **bounce** on a soft surface, you jump up and down on it. ❍ *Leila was bouncing on the trampoline.*
3 VERB If an email **bounces**, it is returned to the person who sent it, often because the address was wrong.

bound /baʊnd/
1 Bound is a form of the verb **bind**.
2 If something **is bound to** happen, it is certain to happen. ❍ *There are bound to be price increases next year.*
3 VERB If a person or animal **bounds** somewhere, they move quickly with large steps or jumps. ❍ *He bounded up the steps.*

bounda|ry /baʊndəri, -dri/ (**boundaries**) NOUN an imaginary line that separates one area of land from another ❍ *The river forms the western boundary of the farm.*

bou|quet /boʊkeɪ, bu-/ NOUN a bunch of flowers that have been cut ❍ *They gave her a bouquet of roses.*

Bourse /bʊərs/ also **bourse** NOUN the stock exchange of Paris and some other European cities [BANKING]

bou|tique /butik/ NOUN a small store that sells fashionable clothes, shoes, or jewelry

bow
❶ BENDING
❷ OBJECTS

❶ **bow** /baʊ/
1 VERB When you **bow to** someone, you bend your head or body toward them as a formal way of greeting them or showing respect. ❍ *He stood and bowed to the crowded court.*
2 NOUN **Bow** is also a noun. ❍ *a theatrical bow*

❷ **bow** /boʊ/
1 NOUN a knot with two round parts and two loose ends ❍ *a ribbon tied in a bow*
2 NOUN a wooden structure used for shooting arrows ❍ *a bow and arrows*
3 NOUN a long thin piece of wood with threads stretched along it that you move across the strings of a violin or similar instrument

bowl /boʊl/
1 NOUN a round container that is used for mixing and serving food ❍ *a soup bowl*
2 VERB In a sport such as bowling, when a bowler **bowls**, he or she rolls the ball down a narrow track.

bowl|ing /boʊlɪŋ/ NONCOUNT NOUN **Bowling** is a game in which you roll a heavy ball down a narrow track toward a group of wooden objects and try to knock them down. ❍ *We go bowling every Saturday afternoon.*

box /bɒks/ (**boxes, boxing, boxed**)
1 NOUN a container with a hard bottom and sides, and usually a lid ❍ *a cardboard box* ❍ *a box of chocolates*
2 NOUN a square space on a form that you have to write something in ❍ *Check the appropriate box.*
3 VERB To **box** means to fight in the sport of boxing. ❍ *At school I boxed and played baseball.*

box|ing /bɒksɪŋ/ **NONCOUNT NOUN Boxing** is a sport in which two people wearing gloves hit each other with their fists.

boy /bɔɪ/ **NOUN** a male child ❍ *Fred's four boys grew up around the family business.*

boy|friend /bɔɪfrɛnd/ **NOUN** a man or boy that a girl or woman is having a romantic relationship with ❍ *Brenda came with her boyfriend, Anthony.*

BPR /bi pi ɑr/ **BPR** is short for **business process reengineering**. [BUSINESS MANAGEMENT]

brace|let /breɪslɪt/ **NOUN** a piece of jewelry that you wear around your wrist

brack|et /brækɪt/ **NOUN Brackets** are curved ( ) or square [ ] marks that you can place around words, letters, or numbers when you are writing. ❍ *There's a telephone number in brackets under his name.*

brag /bræg/ (**brags, bragging, bragged**)
VERB If you **brag**, you annoy people by proudly saying that you have something or have done something. ❍ *He's always bragging about winning the gold medal.*

brain /breɪn/ **NOUN** the organ inside the head that controls the body's activities and allows someone to think and to feel things ❍ *You have to use your brain in this sort of work.* ❍ *a brain tumor*

brake /breɪk/ (**brakes, braking, braked**)
1 NOUN Brakes are the parts in a vehicle that make it go slower or stop. ❍ *He stepped on the brakes as the light turned red.*
2 VERB When the driver of a vehicle **brakes**, he or she makes it slow down or stop. ❍ *The driver braked to avoid an accident.*

branch /bræntʃ/ (**branches, branching, branched**)
1 NOUN one of the parts of a tree that grow out from the main trunk ❍ *the upper branches of a tree*
2 NOUN A **branch of** a business or other organization is one of its offices, stores, or groups that are located in different places. ❍ *The local branch of Bank of America is handling the accounts.*
3 NOUN A **branch of** an organization is a department that has a particular function. ❍ *Senate employees could take their employment grievances to another branch of government.* ❍ *He had a fascination for submarines and joined this branch of the service.*
▸ **branch out** If a person or an organization **branches out**, they do something that is different from their normal activities or work. ❍ *ASEAN has branched out into the security business.*

brand /brænd/ **NOUN** the name of a product that a particular firm makes [MARKETING AND SALES] ❍ *I bought my favorite brand of cookies.* ❍ *Planters is the leading brand with 50% of the salted-nut business.*

brand aware|ness NONCOUNT NOUN Brand awareness is how much people know about a particular product or service, and the ideas they have about it. [MARKETING AND SALES] ❍ *The challenge for the company is increasing brand awareness with a tiny marketing budget.*

brand con|tami|na|tion /brænd kəntæmɪneɪʃən/ **NONCOUNT NOUN Brand contamination** is when the reputation of a particular product is hurt by bad publicity or by association with a different product. [MARKETING AND SALES] ❍ *Some analysts have questioned the wisdom of supermarkets moving into financial services, saying they risk brand contamination if mistakes are made.*

brand|ed /brændɪd/ **ADJ** A **branded** product is one that is made by a well-known manufacturer and has the manufacturer's label on it. [MARKETING AND SALES] ❍ *Supermarket lines are often cheaper than branded goods.*

b

B

brand ex|ten|sion NONCOUNT NOUN **Brand extension** is when a firm uses a well-known brand name to sell a new product. They think that people who buy the existing products with that brand name will also buy the new ones. [MARKETING AND SALES] ❍ *Topman opened in 1978, as a brand extension to its established 10-year-old sister, Topshop.*

brand im|age (**brand images**) NOUN the opinion or impression that people have about a particular brand of a product [MARKETING AND SALES] ❍ *Few products have brand images anywhere near as strong as Levi's.*

brand|ing /brændɪŋ/ NONCOUNT NOUN The **branding** of a product is the presentation of it to the public in a way that makes it easy for people to recognize or identify. [MARKETING AND SALES] ❍ *Local companies find the sites and build the theme parks, while we will look after the branding.*

COLLOCATIONS

a branding *strategy*
corporate branding
global branding

brand loy|al|ty NONCOUNT NOUN **Brand loyalty** is the way some people always buy a particular brand of a product, and are not likely to start buying a different brand. [MARKETING AND SALES] ❍ *Perfume is becoming an everyday purchase and buyers are no longer showing brand loyalty.*

brand name (**brand names**) NOUN the name that a manufacturer gives to a product that it sells [MARKETING AND SALES] ❍ *The drug is marketed under the brand name Viramune.*

brand-new ADJ completely new ❍ *a brand-new car*

brand re|cog|ni|tion NONCOUNT NOUN **Brand recognition** is when a person knows what a product is or knows something about it as soon as they see it or hear its name. [MARKETING AND SALES] ❍ *The strategic linchpin of Sun-Rype's marketing plans is the strong brand recognition enjoyed by their products.*

brand stretch|ing NONCOUNT NOUN **Brand stretching** is the same as **brand extension**. [MARKETING AND SALES] ❍ *The Government will limit the indirect brand stretching of tobacco products with the marketing of fashion goods under the same name.*

bran|dy /brændi/ (**brandies**) NOUN strong alcoholic drink that is made from wine

brass /bræs/ NONCOUNT NOUN **Brass** is a yellow-colored metal. ❍ *a shiny brass door knocker*

brave /breɪv/ (**braver, bravest**) ADJ willing to do things that are dangerous and not showing fear ❍ *I tell my colleagues to be brave and not be afraid of risks.* • **brave|ly** ADV ❍ *The army fought bravely.*

bread /brɛd/ NONCOUNT NOUN **Bread** is a food made from flour and baked in an oven. ❍ *a loaf of bread* ❍ *bread and butter*

break /breɪk/ (**breaks, breaking, broke, broken**)

1 VERB When an object **breaks** or when you break it, it becomes damaged or separates into pieces. ❍ *The plane broke into three pieces.* ❍ *I'm sorry. I broke a glass.*

2 VERB If you **break** a part of your body, a bone cracks in it. ❍ *She broke her leg in a skiing accident.*

3 VERB If a machine **breaks**, it stops working, and if you break a machine, you cause it to stop working. ❍ *Who broke the toaster?*

4 NOUN a short period of time when you can rest ❍ *At work we get a 15-minute coffee break.*

5 VERB If you **break** a rule or the law, you do something that you should not do. ❍ *We didn't know we were breaking the law.*

▸ **break down**

1 If a machine or a vehicle **breaks down**, it stops working. ❍ *Their car broke down.*

2 If someone **breaks down**, they start crying. ❍ *I broke down and cried.*

▸ **break even** If a business or person **breaks even**, they earn as much money as they spend but they do not make a profit. [FINANCE, ECONOMICS] ❍ *The airline hopes to break even next year and return to profit the following year.*

▸ **break in** If someone **breaks in**, they get into a building by force. ❍ *The robbers broke in and stole $8,000.*

▸ **break into** If someone **breaks into** a building, they get into it by force. ❍ *They caught him trying to break into the house.*
▸ **break off** If you **break** a part of something **off**, you remove it by breaking it. ❍ *Grace broke off a large piece of bread.*
▸ **break out** If something **breaks out**, it begins suddenly. ❍ *He was 29 when war broke out.*
▸ **break up** If you **break up with** someone, your relationship with that person ends. ❍ *My girlfriend has broken up with me.*

break|age /breɪkɪdʒ/
1 NONCOUNT NOUN Breakage is when you break something. [FINANCE] ❍ *Check that your insurance policy covers breakage and damage when moving.*
2 NOUN A **breakage** is something that has been broken. ❍ *We arrived to find the staff cleaning up some breakages, and they asked us where we had been when the earthquake hit.*

break|down /breɪkdaʊn/
1 NOUN the failure and ending of a relationship, plan, or discussion ❍ *Newspapers reported the breakdown of talks between the two countries.* ❍ *a marriage breakdown*
2 NOUN a situation in which a car or a piece of machinery stops working ❍ *You should be prepared for breakdowns and accidents.*

break|even chart /breɪkivən tʃɑrt/ (**breakeven charts**) also **break-even chart NOUN** A **breakeven chart** is a graph that shows the relationship between a firm's earnings and costs and the number of units it sells. The point on the graph where earnings and costs cross each other is the breakeven point. [FINANCE, ECONOMICS]

break|even fig|ure /breɪkivən fɪgyər/ also **break-even figure NOUN** the number of units of a product that a firm must sell in order to equal the amount of money the firm has spent [FINANCE, ECONOMICS]

break|even point /breɪkivən pɔɪnt/ (**breakeven points**) also **break-even point** or **breakeven NOUN** the point at which the money a firm makes from the sale of goods or services is equal to the money it has spent [FINANCE, ECONOMICS] ❍ *"Terminator 2" finally made $200 million, the breakeven point for the movie.* ❍ *The bank announced in the final quarter of last year that it had reached breakeven.*

break|fast /brɛkfəst/ **NOUN** the first meal of the day ❍ *Would you like eggs for breakfast?*

break-out group (**break-out groups**) **NOUN** a group of people who separate themselves from a larger group or meeting in order to hold separate discussions [BUSINESS MANAGEMENT] ❍ *There was discussion in small interactive break-out groups to permit participants sufficient opportunity to develop recommendations.*

break|through /breɪkθru/ **NOUN** an important discovery that is made after a lot of hard work ❍ *a breakthrough in cancer treatment*

break|up value /breɪkʌp vælyu/ (**breakup values**) also **break-up value**
1 NOUN the value of a firm if its individual assets and divisions were sold separately and all its debts were paid
2 NOUN the value of one share of stock in a firm based only on the value of the firm's assets [FINANCE]

breath /brɛθ/
1 NONCOUNT NOUN Your **breath** is the air that you let out through your mouth when you breathe. ❍ *His breath smelled of onion.*
2 NOUN When you take a **breath**, you breathe in once. ❍ *He took a deep breath, and knocked on the door.*
3 If you are **out of breath**, you are breathing very quickly because your body has been working hard. ❍ *She was out of breath from running.*

breathe /brið/ (**breathes, breathing, breathed**) **VERB** When people or animals **breathe**, they take air into their lungs and let it out again. ❍ *He was breathing fast.*
• **breath|ing NONCOUNT NOUN** ❍ *Her breathing became slow.*

breed /brid/ (**breeds, breeding, bred**)
1 NOUN a particular type of a horse, dog, cow or other animal ❍ *There are about 300 breeds of horse.*

2 VERB If you **breed** animals or plants, you produce more animals or plants with the same qualities. ❍ *The breeding of snakes is serious business in America.*

3 VERB When animals **breed**, they produce babies. ❍ *Birds usually breed in the spring.*

B

breeze /briz/ **NOUN** a gentle wind ❍ *a cool summer breeze*

bribe /braɪb/ (**bribes, bribing, bribed**)

1 NOUN money or another gift that one person offers to another in order to persuade them to do something [ECONOMICS, BUSINESS MANAGEMENT] ❍ *It is said that the police took bribes from criminals.*

2 VERB If one person **bribes** another, they offer them money or another gift in order to persuade them to do something. [ECONOMICS, BUSINESS MANAGEMENT] ❍ *He was accused of bribing a bank official.*

brick /brɪk/ **NOUN** a hard rectangular block used in building ❍ *a brick wall*

bricks and clicks also **bricks-and-clicks** **NONCOUNT NOUN** **Bricks and clicks** is a combination of business that is carried out in stores and offices and business that is carried out on the Internet. [E-COMMERCE, TECHNOLOGY] ❍ *ICICI hopes to convert bricks-and-clicks into earnings.*

bricks and mor|tar /brɪks ən mɔrtər/ also **bricks-and-mortar**

1 NONCOUNT NOUN **Bricks and mortar** is a building or buildings that are considered in terms of their value. [E-COMMERCE, ECONOMICS] ❍ *He invested in bricks and mortar rather than stocks.*

2 ADJ **Bricks-and-mortar** is also an adjective. ❍ *Their strategy was so successful that soon they were sucking deposits away from bricks-and-mortar banks across Europe.*

BRICs /brɪks/ **PL NOUN** The **BRICs** are Brazil, Russia, India, and China, countries which are seen as having large, important, and fast-growing economies. [ECONOMICS] ❍ *This year, sales of cars in the BRICs should overtake those in America.*

bride /braɪd/ **NOUN** a woman who is getting married ❍ *the bride and groom*

bridge /brɪdʒ/ **NOUN** a structure that is built over a river or road so that people or vehicles can cross from one side to the other ❍ *A small increase in highway and bridge construction is expected.*

bridge loan (**bridge loans**) **NOUN** money that a bank lends you for a short time, for example so that you can buy a new house before you have sold the one you already own [BANKING, FINANCE]

bridg|ing loan /brɪdʒɪŋ loʊn/ (**bridging loans**) [BANKING, FINANCE, BRIT] → **bridge loan**

brief /brif/ (**briefer, briefest, briefs**)

1 ADJ lasting only for a short time ❍ *She once made a brief appearance on television.*

2 ADJ in only a few words ❍ *The book begins with a brief description of his career.*

3 PL NOUN **Briefs** are men's or women's underpants. ❍ *a pair of briefs*

brief|case /brifkeɪs/ **NOUN** a small case for carrying business papers in

brief|ly /brifli/ **ADV** lasting only for a very short time ❍ *He smiled briefly.*

bright /braɪt/

1 ADJ having a strong, light color that is very noticeable ❍ *She wore a bright red dress.*

2 ADJ shining strongly or with a lot of light ❍ *the bright lights of a TV studio* ❍ *a nice bright room* ● **bright|ly** **ADV** ❍ *The sun shone brightly in the sky.*

3 ADJ able to learn things quickly ❍ *a bright student*

bright|en /braɪtᵊn/

1 VERB If someone **brightens**, they suddenly look happier. ❍ *Seeing him, she seemed to brighten a little.*

2 VERB If someone or something **brightens** a place, they make it more colorful and attractive. ❍ *Flowers brighten a room.*

bril|liant /brɪlyənt/

1 ADJ extremely clever or skillful ❍ *She had a brilliant mind.* ● **bril|liant|ly** **ADV** ❍ *Bob has handled the extraordinary growth of the company quite brilliantly.* ● **bril|liance** **NONCOUNT NOUN** ❍ *Mozart showed his brilliance at an early age.*

2 ADJ A **brilliant** light or color is extremely bright. ❍ *brilliant green eyes*

brim /brɪm/ **NOUN** the part of a hat that sticks out around the bottom

bring /brɪŋ/ (**brings, bringing, brought**)
1 VERB If you **bring** someone or something **with** you when you come to a place, you have them with you. ❍ *Remember to bring a comfortable pair of shoes.* ❍ *Can I bring Susie to the party?*
2 VERB If you **bring** something that someone wants, you get it for them. ❍ *He poured a glass of milk for Dena and brought it to her.*
▶ **bring back** When you **bring** something **back**, you return it. ❍ *I've brought back your books.*
▶ **bring in** If someone or something **brings in** money, they earn it. ❍ *My job brings in about $24,000 a year.*
▶ **bring up**
1 When someone **brings up** a child, they take care of it until it is an adult. ❍ *She brought up four children.* ❍ *He was brought up in Nebraska.*
2 If you **bring up** a particular subject, you introduce it into a conversation. ❍ *Her mother brought up the subject of going back to work.*

brisk /brɪsk/
1 ADJ A **brisk** activity or action is done quickly and with energy. ❍ *a brisk handshake*
• **brisk|ly ADV** ❍ *Eve walked briskly through the park.*
2 ADJ If trade or business is **brisk**, things are being sold very quickly and a lot of money is being made. ❍ *Vendors were doing a brisk trade in souvenirs.* ❍ *Its sales had been brisk since July.*
• **brisk|ly ADV** ❍ *A trader said gold sold briskly on the local market.*

broad /brɔd/
1 ADJ wide ❍ *broad shoulders*
2 ADJ including a large number of different things ❍ *a broad range of books*

broad|band /brɔdbænd/ **NONCOUNT NOUN** **Broadband** is a method of sending many electronic messages at the same time over the Internet. [TECHNOLOGY] ❍ *broadband customers*

broad|cast /brɔdkæst/ (**broadcasts, broadcasting, broadcast**)
1 NOUN a program, a performance, or a speech on the radio or on television ❍ *a live television broadcast of the game*
2 VERB To **broadcast** a program means to send it out so that it can be heard on the radio or seen on television. ❍ *The concert will be broadcast live on television and radio.* ❍ *CNN also broadcasts in Europe.*

bro|chure /broʊʃʊər/ **NOUN** a thin magazine with pictures that gives you information about a product or a service [MARKETING AND SALES] ❍ *travel brochures*

broke /broʊk/
1 Broke is a form of the verb **break**.
2 ADJ having no money [INFORMAL] ❍ *I don't have a job, and I'm broke.*

bro|ken /broʊkən/
1 Broken is a form of the verb **break**.
2 ADJ damaged and in pieces ❍ *a broken window*

bro|ker /broʊkər/
1 NOUN a person whose job is to buy and sell securities, foreign money, real estate, or goods for other people [BANKING] ❍ *Reports from insurance brokers indicate that insured losses could amount to $1 billion.*
2 VERB If you **broker** an agreement, you try to negotiate or arrange it. ❍ *The United Nations brokered a peace deal in Mogadishu at the end of March.*

bro|ker|age /broʊkərɪdʒ/ **NOUN** a firm of brokers [BANKING] ❍ *Japan's four biggest brokerages*

broker-dealer (**broker-dealers**) **NOUN** A **broker-dealer** is the same as a **stockbroker**. [BANKING]

bro|ker|ing /broʊkərɪŋ/
1 NONCOUNT NOUN Brokering is the business of a broker. [BANKING] ❍ *The group provides a comprehensive range of financial services, which include investment services and insurance brokering.*
2 ADJ Brokering is also an adjective. ❍ *Rothschild collected a $400,000 brokering fee, according to copies of checks and bank wire transfers.*

b

B

bronze /brɒnz/
1 NONCOUNT NOUN Bronze is a yellowish-brown metal that is a mixture of copper and tin. ❍ *a bronze statue of a ballet dancer*
2 ADJ being yellowish-brown in color

brooch /broʊtʃ/ (**brooches**) **NOUN** a piece of jewelry that has a pin on the back so that it can be fastened on to your clothes

brood /brud/ **VERB** If someone **broods** over something, they feel sad about it or they worry about it a lot. ❍ *She constantly broods about her failures.*

broom /brum/ **NOUN** a type of brush with a long handle that is used for sweeping the floor

Bros. Bros. is used as part of the name of a firm as a written abbreviation for "Brothers." [ADMINISTRATION] ❍ *a Warner Bros. film*

broth|er /brʌðər/ **NOUN** a boy or a man who has the same parents as you ❍ *That's Peter's brother.*

brother-in-law (**brothers-in-law**) **NOUN** the brother of someone's husband or wife, or the man who is married to their sister

brought /brɔt/ **Brought** is a form of the verb **bring**.

brow /braʊ/ **NOUN** the part of your face that is above your eyes ❍ *He wiped his brow with the back of his hand.*

brown /braʊn/ (**browner, brownest**)
1 ADJ being the color of earth or wood ❍ *brown eyes*
2 NOUN Brown is also a noun. ❍ *She wears a lot of black and brown.*

brown|field /braʊnfild/ or **brownfield site NOUN** an area of land that was once used for industry [BUSINESS MANAGEMENT, PRODUCTION] ❍ *a brownfield project involving five industrial sites*

brown goods PL NOUN Brown goods are consumer goods such as televisions, radios, or videos. Compare with **white goods**. [MARKETING AND SALES, PRODUCTION]

browse /braʊz/ (**browses, browsing, browsed**)
1 VERB If you **browse** in a store, you look at things in it. ❍ *I stopped in several bookstores to browse.*
2 VERB If you **browse through** a book or a magazine, you look through it in a relaxed way. ❍ *She was sitting on the sofa browsing through a magazine.*
3 VERB If you **browse** the Internet, you search for information there. [TECHNOLOGY] ❍ *The software allows you to browse the Internet on your cellphone.*

brows|er /braʊzər/ **NOUN** a piece of computer software that allows you to search for information on the Internet [TECHNOLOGY] ❍ *a Web browser*

bruise /bruz/ (**bruises, bruising, bruised**)
1 NOUN an injury that appears as a purple mark on your body ❍ *How did you get that bruise on your arm?*
2 VERB If you **bruise** a part of your body, a bruise appears on it because you injured it. ❍ *I bruised my knee on a desk drawer.* • **bruised ADJ** ❍ *a bruised knee*

brush /brʌʃ/ (**brushes, brushing, brushed**)
1 NOUN an object with many short, thick hairs which you use for painting, cleaning things, and for making your hair neat ❍ *a hair brush* ❍ *a scrubbing brush*
2 VERB If you **brush** something, you clean it or make it neat using a brush. ❍ *Have you brushed your teeth?* ❍ *Brush your hair, Taylor.*
3 VERB If you **brush** something away or off, you remove it with movements of your hands. ❍ *He brushed the snow off his suit.*
4 VERB If you brush something or you **brush against** something, you touch it lightly while passing. ❍ *Something brushed against her leg.*

bru|tal /brutᵊl/ **ADJ** cruel and violent ❍ *a brutal military dictator* ❍ *a brutal attack*
• **bru|tal|ly ADV** ❍ *Her parents were brutally murdered.*

BTW short for "by the way," often used in email ❍ *BTW, the new car is amazing.*

bub|ble /bʌbᵊl/ (**bubbles, bubbling, bubbled**)
1 NOUN a small ball of air or gas in a liquid ❍ *Air bubbles rise to the surface.*

2 NOUN a ball with a very thin outer layer of soap ❍ *soap bubbles*
3 VERB When a liquid **bubbles**, bubbles move in it, for example, because it is boiling. ❍ *Heat the soup until it is bubbling.*
4 NOUN a situation in which there is a large increase in economic activity [BUSINESS MANAGEMENT] ❍ *These hi-tech companies look like the focus of a speculative bubble.*

buck /bʌk/ **NOUN** a U.S. or Australian dollar [ECONOMICS, INFORMAL] ❍ *The food cost about fifty bucks.* ❍ *Why don't you spend a few bucks on a new scanner?*

buck|et /bʌkɪt/ **NOUN** a round metal or plastic container with a handle that is used for carrying water ❍ *She threw a bucket of water on the fire.*

buck|le /bʌkəl/ (**buckles, buckling, buckled**)
1 NOUN a piece of metal or plastic on one end of a belt or strap that is used for fastening it ❍ *He wore a belt with a large silver buckle.*
2 VERB When you **buckle** something, you fasten it with a buckle. ❍ *She sat down to buckle her shoes.*

bud /bʌd/ **NOUN** a new growth on a tree or plant that develops into a leaf or flower ❍ *Small pink buds were beginning to form on the bushes.*

Bud|dhism /budɪzəm, bʊd-/ **NONCOUNT NOUN** **Buddhism** is a religion that teaches that the way to end suffering is by controlling your desires.

Bud|dhist /budɪst, bʊd-/
1 NOUN a person whose religion is Buddhism
2 ADJ relating or belonging to Buddhism ❍ *Buddhist monks*

budg|et /bʌdʒɪt/
1 NOUN the amount of money that you have available to spend [FINANCE, MARKETING AND SALES] ❍ *She will design a new kitchen for you within your budget.* ❍ *a low budget film*
2 VERB If you **budget** a certain amount of money for something, you decide that you can spend that amount. [FINANCE, MARKETING AND SALES] ❍ *The company has budgeted $10 million for advertising.*
3 NOUN **The budget** is a statement from the government about a country's financial situation, giving details such as changes to taxes. [FINANCE]

COLLOCATIONS
a budget *deficit*
budget *cuts*
the budget *for* something
a *balanced* budget

buf|fet /bʊfeɪ/ **NOUN** a meal at which people serve themselves ❍ *a cold buffet*

bug /bʌg/
1 NOUN an insect [INFORMAL]
2 NOUN a slight illness that you get from other people [INFORMAL] ❍ *a stomach bug*
3 NOUN a small mistake in a computer program that causes problems in the way that it works [TECHNOLOGY] ❍ *There is a bug in the software.*

build /bɪld/ (**builds, building, built**)
1 VERB If you **build** something such as a house, you make it by joining parts together. ❍ *They're building a hotel.* ❍ *The house was built in the early 19th century.*
2 NONCOUNT NOUN Someone's **build** is the shape of their body. ❍ *He's six feet tall and of medium build.*

build|ing /bɪldɪŋ/ **NOUN** a structure that has a roof and walls ❍ *The building was designed to resemble a French chateau.*

build|ing and loan as|so|cia|tion (**building and loan associations**) **NOUN** A **building and loan association** is the same as a **savings and loan**. [BANKING]

build|ing so|ci|e|ty (**building societies**) [BANKING, BRIT] → **savings and loan**

built /bɪlt/ **Built** is a form of the verb **build**.

bulb /bʌlb/
1 NOUN the glass part of an electric lamp which gives out light ❍ *A single bulb hangs from the ceiling.*
2 NOUN a root of a flower or plant ❍ *tulip bulbs*

bulk /bʌlk/
1 The **bulk of** something is most of it. ❍ *The bulk of the money will go to the children's hospital in Dublin.*

2 If you buy or sell something **in bulk**, you buy or sell large amounts of it. [PURCHASING] ❍ *It is cheaper to buy supplies in bulk.*

bulk buy|ing NONCOUNT NOUN **Bulk buying** is the purchase at one time of a large quantity of a particular product. [PURCHASING] ❍ *Supermarkets use their bulk buying power to drive down prices.*

B

bull /bʊl/
1 NOUN a male of some animals, especially cows
2 NOUN **Bulls** are people who buy shares of stock when they expect the price to rise in order to make a profit by selling the shares again after a short time. Compare with **bear**. [FINANCE, ECONOMICS]

bull|doz|er /bʊldoʊzər/ NOUN a large vehicle with a wide blade at the front that is used for moving large amounts of earth

bul|let /bʊlɪt/
1 NOUN a small piece of metal that is shot out of a gun
2 NOUN a final payment of a loan which consists of the whole amount of the loan, where previous payments were interest only [FINANCE]

bul|letin /bʊlɪtɪn/ NOUN a short news report on the radio or television ❍ *We heard the early morning news bulletin.*

bul|letin board
1 NOUN a board on a wall for notices giving information ❍ *Her telephone number was pinned to the bulletin board.*
2 NOUN in computing, a system that allows users to send and receive messages

bull|ish /bʊlɪʃ/ ADJ In the stock market, if there is a **bullish** mood, prices are expected to rise. Compare with **bearish**. [FINANCE, ECONOMICS] ❍ *The market opened in a bullish mood.*

bull mar|ket (**bull markets**) NOUN A **bull market** is when people are buying a lot of shares of stock because they expect the price to increase. Compare with **bear market**. [FINANCE, ECONOMICS] ❍ *There was a decline in prices after the bull market peaked in April 2000.*

bul|ly /bʊli/ (**bullies, bullying, bullied**)
1 NOUN someone who uses their strength or power to frighten other people ❍ *One employee complained that his supervisor was a bully.*
2 VERB If someone **bullies** you, they use their strength or power to frighten you. ❍ *I wasn't going to let him bully me.*

bump /bʌmp/
1 VERB If you **bump** something or **bump** into something or someone, you accidentally hit them while you are moving. ❍ *They stopped walking and I almost bumped into them.* ❍ *She bumped her head on a low shelf.*
2 NOUN an injury that you get if you hit something or if something hits you ❍ *She fell over and got a large bump on her head.*

bump|er /bʌmpər/ NOUN a heavy bar at the front or back of a vehicle that protects the vehicle if it hits something ❍ *I felt something hit the rear bumper of my car.*

bun /bʌn/ NOUN a small round cake ❍ *He had a cinnamon bun and a glass of milk.*

bunch /bʌntʃ/ (**bunches**)
1 NOUN a group of people [INFORMAL] ❍ *a bunch of absolute idiots* ❍ *They're a nice bunch.*
2 NOUN a number of cut flowers with their stems held together ❍ *He left a huge bunch of flowers in her office.*
3 NOUN a group of bananas or grapes growing together
4 A **bunch of** things is a number of things. [INFORMAL] ❍ *You're spending all your time on a bunch of insignificant details.*

bun|dle /bʌndəl/ (**bundles, bundling, bundled**)
1 NOUN a number of things that are tied or wrapped together so that they can be carried ❍ *He left a bundle of papers on the floor.*
2 VERB If computer software or hardware **is bundled**, it is sold in a package with another product. [MARKETING AND SALES, PURCHASING] ❍ *They had a 1.8-gigahertz chip bundled with a motherboard on offer for $49.*

buoy /bui/ NOUN an object floating in a lake or an ocean that shows boats where they can go

bur|den /bɜrdᵊn/ **NOUN** something that causes people a lot of worry or hard work ❍ *I don't want to become a burden on my family when I get old.*

bu|reau /byʊəroʊ/ (**bureaus**)
1 NOUN an office, an organization, or a government department [ADMINISTRATION] ❍ *the Federal Bureau of Investigation*
2 NOUN a piece of furniture with drawers in which you keep clothes or other things
3 NOUN an office of a firm or organization that has its main office in another city or country [ADMINISTRATION] ❍ *the Wall Street Journal's Washington bureau*

bu|reau|cra|cy /byʊrɒkrəsi/ (**bureaucracies**)
1 NOUN a system of government based on organization into many departments that are managed by a large number of officials ❍ *State bureaucracies can tend to stifle enterprise and initiative.*
2 NONCOUNT NOUN Bureaucracy is all the rules and procedures followed by government departments and similar organizations, especially when you think that these are complicated and cause long delays. [ADMINISTRATION] ❍ *People usually complain about too much bureaucracy.*

bu|reau|crat|ic /byʊərəkrætɪk/ **ADJ** involving complicated rules and procedures that can cause long delays [ADMINISTRATION] ❍ *Efforts to computerize health records tend to run into bureaucratic, technical, and ethical problems.*

bu|reau de change /byʊəroʊ də ʃanʒ, byʊəroʊ/ (**bureaux de change**) **NOUN** an office where you can exchange foreign money [BANKING]

burg|er /bɜrgər/ **NOUN** meat pressed into in a flat, round shape that is eaten between two pieces of bread ❍ *a burger and fries*

bur|glar /bɜrglər/ **NOUN** someone who enters a building by force in order to steal things ❍ *A burglar stole some money and securities from an unlocked safe.*

bur|gla|ry /bɜrgləri/ (**burglaries**) **NOUN** an occasion when someone enters a building by force and steals things ❍ *The policy covers the loss of personal property from a burglary or robbery.*

burn /bɜrn/ (**burns, burning, burned** or **burnt**)
1 VERB If you **burn** something, you destroy or damage it with fire. ❍ *Supporters burned buses, cars, and shops and attacked police stations.*
2 VERB If you **burn** part of your body, or **burn yourself**, you are injured by fire or by something very hot. ❍ *Take care not to burn your fingers.*
3 NOUN Burn is also a noun. ❍ *She suffered burns to her back.*
4 VERB If something is **burning**, it is on fire. ❍ *Forty forest fires were burning in Alberta yesterday.*
5 VERB If you **burn** a CD, you copy something onto it. [TECHNOLOGY] ❍ *I have the equipment to burn audio CDs.*

burst /bɜrst/ (**bursts, bursting, burst**) **VERB** If something **bursts**, it suddenly breaks open and the air or other substance inside it comes out. ❍ *The driver lost control of his car when a tire burst.*
▸ **burst out** If someone **bursts out** laughing or crying, they suddenly start laughing or crying. ❍ *The whole class burst out laughing.*

bury /bɛri/ (**buries, burying, buried**)
1 VERB If you **bury** something, you put it in a hole in the ground and cover it up. ❍ *Some animals bury nuts and seeds.*
2 VERB If you **bury** a dead person, you put their body into a grave and cover it with earth. ❍ *Soldiers helped to bury the dead.*

bus /bʌs/ (**buses**) **NOUN** a large motor vehicle that carries many passengers ❍ *He missed his last bus home.*

bush /bʊʃ/ (**bushes**)
1 NOUN The bush is an area in a hot country that is far from cities and where few people live. ❍ *the Australian bush*
2 NOUN a short, thick plant with many thin branches ❍ *a rose bush*

busi|ness /bɪznɪs/ (**businesses**)
1 NONCOUNT NOUN Business is work that is

related to producing, buying, and selling things. ❍ *He had a successful career in business.* ❍ *She attended Harvard Business School.* ❍ *Jennifer has an impressive academic and business background.* ❍ *business trips.*
2 NOUN an organization that produces and sells goods or that provides a service ❍ *The bakery is a family business.*
3 NONCOUNT NOUN Business is how many products or services a company is able to sell. ❍ *They worried that German companies would lose business.* ❍ *Business is booming.*
4 NONCOUNT NOUN Business is work or some other activity that you do as part of your job and not for pleasure. ❍ *I'm here on business.*
5 If a company **goes out of business**, it stops trading. [FINANCE] ❍ *50,000 companies have gone out of business.*

COLLOCATIONS
a business *fails*
a business *goes bust*
a business *goes under*
the business *community*

busi|ness an|gel (**business angels**) **NOUN** a person who invests in a business without being involved in its management [BANKING, FINANCE]

busi|ness an|gle (**business angles**) **NOUN** a plan or a way of thinking about something that involves earning money ❍ *I don't do anything that doesn't have a business angle.*

busi|ness cy|cle (**business cycles**) **NOUN** the periods of growth, depression, and recovery that occur over and over again in the economic activity of a country [ECONOMICS]

busi|ness eth|ics PL NOUN Business ethics are the moral beliefs and rules about right and wrong that are involved in business. [HR, BUSINESS MANAGEMENT] ❍ *Business ethics are coming to the forefront of the agenda.*

busi|ness|man /bɪznɪsmæn/ (**businessmen**) **NOUN** a man who works in business ❍ *a rich businessman*

busi|ness mod|el (**business models**) **NOUN** the structure of a business, including the relationships between the different parts of the business [BUSINESS MANAGEMENT] ❍ *the entirely new business models made possible by the Internet* ❍ *There are inefficiencies in traditional business models.*

busi|ness ob|jec|tive (**business objectives**) **NOUN** something that a company is trying to achieve [BUSINESS MANAGEMENT] ❍ *The key business objectives of commercial and charitable organizations are to bring in as much money as possible and to make the most effective use of available resources.*

busi|ness plan (**business plans**) **NOUN** a detailed plan for setting up or developing a business [FINANCE] ❍ *She learned how to write a business plan for the catering business she wanted to launch.*

busi|ness pro|cess re|en|gi|neer|ing /bɪznɪs prɒsɛs riɛndʒɪnɪərɪŋ/ **NONCOUNT NOUN Business process reengineering** is when an organization changes its procedures and structure in order to make itself more efficient. [BUSINESS MANAGEMENT]

business-to-business ADJ Business-to-business refers to selling goods and services by one firm to another using the Internet. The abbreviation **B2B** is often used. [BUSINESS MANAGEMENT]

business-to-consumer ADJ Business-to-consumer refers to selling goods and services by businesses to consumers using the Internet. The abbreviation **B2C** is often used. [BUSINESS MANAGEMENT]

bust /bʌst/ (**busts, busting, busted** or **bust**)
1 VERB If you **bust** something, you break it or damage it so badly that it cannot be used. [INFORMAL] ❍ *They will have to bust the door to get him out.*
2 VERB If someone **is busted**, the police arrest them. [INFORMAL] ❍ *They were busted for possession of cannabis.*
3 VERB If police **bust** a place, they go to it in order to arrest people who are doing something illegal. [INFORMAL] ❍ *Police busted an underground network of illegal sports gambling.*

4 NOUN Bust is also a noun. ❍ *Six tons of cocaine were seized last week in Panama's biggest drug bust.*

5 ADJ A firm or fund that is **bust** has no money left and has been forced to close down. [FINANCE, INFORMAL] ❍ *It is taxpayers who will pay most of the bill for bailing out bust banks.*

6 If a firm **goes bust**, it loses so much money that it is forced to close down. [FINANCE, INFORMAL] ❍ *a Swiss company that went bust last May*

7 NOUN A **bust** is a statue of the head and shoulders of a person. ❍ *a bronze bust of Thomas Jefferson*

8 NOUN You can use **bust** to refer to a woman's breasts, especially when you are describing their size. ❍ *Good posture helps your bust look bigger.*

busy /bɪzi/ (**busier, busiest**)

1 ADJ working hard and not free to do anything else ❍ *I can't come - I'm busy.* ❍ *They are busy preparing for the opening on Saturday.*

2 ADJ A **busy** place is full of people who are doing things. ❍ *We walked along a busy city street.*

3 ADJ When a telephone line is **busy**, you cannot make your call because the line is already being used by someone else. ❍ *I tried to reach him, but the line was busy.*

but /bət, STRONG bʌt/

1 CONJ used for introducing something that is different than what you have just said ❍ *I've enjoyed my vacation, but now it's time to get back to work.* ❍ *Nobody likes the deal, but we feel it is the best we will get.*

2 PREP except ❍ *You've done nothing but complain all day.*

butch|er /bʊtʃər/ **NOUN** someone who cuts up and sells meat

but|ter /bʌtər/ **NONCOUNT NOUN Butter** is a soft yellow food made from cream that you spread on bread. ❍ *bread and butter*

butter|fly /bʌtərflaɪ/ (**butterflies**) **NOUN** an insect with large colored wings ❍ *Butterflies are attracted to the wild flowers.*

but|ton /bʌtᵊn/

1 NOUN a small hard object that you push through a hole in order to fasten a piece of clothing ❍ *He wore a blue jacket with silver buttons.*

2 VERB If you **button** a piece of clothing, you fasten it using buttons. ❍ *Ferguson stood up and buttoned his coat.*

3 NOUN a small object on a piece of equipment that you press to operate it ❍ *He put in a DVD and pressed the "play" button.*

buy /baɪ/ (**buys, buying, bought**) **VERB** If you **buy** something, you get it by paying money for it. [PURCHASING] ❍ *He could not afford to buy a house.* ❍ *Lizzie bought herself a bike.*

▸ **buy out**

1 When a firm **buys out** another firm, they purchase all of the stock of that firm. [PURCHASING, FINANCE]

2 If you **buy** someone **out**, you buy their share of a firm or piece of property that you previously owned together. [PURCHASING, FINANCE] ❍ *The bank had to pay to buy out most of the 200 former partners.* ❍ *He bought his brother out for $17 million.*

▸ **buy up**

1 If you **buy up** land, property, or a product, you buy large amounts of it, or all that is available. [PURCHASING] ❍ *The mention of price increases sent citizens out to their stores to buy up as much as they could.* ❍ *The tickets will be on sale from somewhere else because the agencies have bought them up.*

2 [PURCHASING] When a firm **buys up** another firm, it purchases most of the stock of that firm.

buy|back **NOUN** A **buyback** is when a firm purchases some or all of its shares of stock from an investor who put capital into the firm when it was formed. [PURCHASING] ❍ *The company announced a buyback of 18% of its 5.8 million shares.* ❍ *a share buyback program*

buy|er /baɪr/

1 NOUN a person who is buying something or who intends to buy it [PURCHASING] ❍ *Car buyers are more interested in safety and reliability than speed.*

2 NOUN a person who works for a large store

deciding what goods will be bought from manufacturers to be sold in the store [PURCHASING] ❍ *Diana is a buyer for a chain of furniture stores.*

B

buy|er's mar|ket (**buyer's markets**) **NOUN** When there is a **buyer's market** for a particular product, there are more of the products for sale than there are people who want to buy them. In a **buyer's market**, buyers have a lot of choice and can make prices come down. [PURCHASING] ❍ *Real estate remains a buyer's market.*

buy|ing de|part|ment (**buying departments**) [PURCHASING, ADMINISTRATION, BRIT] → **purchasing department**

buy|out /baɪaʊt/ **NOUN** the buying of a firm by its managers or employees [PURCHASING] ❍ *It is thought that a management buyout is one option.*

buy-to-let **ADJ** In a **buy-to-let** property market, people are buying properties to let to tenants rather than to live in themselves. [BUSINESS MANAGEMENT, BRIT] ❍ *the buy-to-let boom* ❍ *Only 1.1 percent of buy-to-let loans were three months or more in arrears.*

by /baɪ/

1 PREP used for showing who or what has done something ❍ *All the artwork was made by the children.* ❍ *She was interrupted by a loud noise in the street.* ❍ *a presentation by the CEO*

2 PREP used for saying how something is done ❍ *We usually travel by car.*

3 PREP next to ❍ *Jack stood by the door, ready to leave.*

4 PREP moving past you without stopping ❍ *A few cars passed close by me.*

5 ADV **By** is also an adverb. ❍ *People waved and smiled as she went by.*

6 PREP before ❍ *I'll be home by eight o'clock.*

bye /baɪ/ or **bye-bye** **Bye** and **bye-bye** are informal ways of saying goodbye. ❍ *Bye, guys.*

Cc

CA /si̲ eɪ/
1 NOUN **CA** is an abbreviation for **chartered accountant**. [FINANCE, BRIT]
2 NOUN **CA** is an abbreviation for "chief accountant." [FINANCE]

cab /kæ̲b/ **NOUN** a taxi ❍ *I'll call a cab.*

cab|bage /kæ̲bɪdʒ/ **NOUN** a large, round vegetable with green or white leaves

cab|in /kæ̲bɪn/
1 NOUN a small wooden house in the woods or mountains ❍ *a log cabin*
2 NOUN a room in a ship where a passenger sleeps
3 NOUN the part of an airplane where the passengers sit

cabi|net /kæ̲bɪnɪt/
1 NOUN a piece of furniture with shelves, used for storing things in ❍ *a medicine cabinet*
2 NOUN **The cabinet** is a group of members of the government who advise the leader, and who are responsible for its plans and actions.

ca|ble /ke̲ɪbᵊl/
1 NOUN a very strong, thick rope, made of metal
2 NOUN a thick wire that carries electricity ❍ *underground power cables*

ca̲|ble te̲le|vi|sion **NONCOUNT NOUN** **Cable television** is a television system in which signals travel along wires.

CAD /kæ̲d/ **NONCOUNT NOUN** **CAD** refers to the use of computer software in the design of things such as cars, buildings, and machines. **CAD** is an abbreviation for "computer-aided design." Compare with **CAM**. [TECHNOLOGY] ❍ *CAD software*

café /kæfe̲ɪ/ also **cafe** **NOUN** a place where you can buy drinks and small meals

caf|eteria /kæ̲fɪtɪ̲əriə/ **NOUN** in places such as hospitals and offices, a restaurant where you buy a meal and carry it to the table yourself

caf|feine /kæfi̲n/ **NONCOUNT NOUN** **Caffeine** is a chemical in coffee and tea that makes you more active.

cage /ke̲ɪdʒ/ **NOUN** a structure made of metal bars where you keep birds or animals ❍ *I hate to see birds in cages.*

cake /ke̲ɪk/ **NOUN** a sweet food made by mixing and then baking flour, eggs, sugar, and butter ❍ *a piece of chocolate cake* ❍ *a birthday cake*

cal|cu|late /kæ̲lkyəleɪt/ (**calculates, calculating, calculated**) **VERB** If you **calculate** an amount, you find it out by using numbers. ❍ *Have you calculated the cost of the advertising campaign?*

cal|cu|la|tion /kæ̲lkyəle̲ɪʃən/ **NOUN** You make a **calculation** when you find out a number or amount by using mathematics. ❍ *Staff had done some calculations based on previous orders.*

cal|cu|la|tor /kæ̲lkyəleɪtər/ **NOUN** a small electronic machine that you use to calculate numbers ❍ *a pocket calculator*

cal|en|dar /kæ̲lɪndər/ **NOUN** a list of days, weeks, and months for a particular year ❍ *There was a calendar on the wall.*

calf /kæ̲f/ (**calves** /kæ̲vz/)
1 NOUN a young cow
2 NOUN the thick part at the back of your leg, between your ankle and your knee

call /kɔ̲l/
1 VERB If you **call** someone a particular name, you give them that name. ❍ *Her secretary is called Charlotte.*
2 VERB If you **call** something, you say it in a loud voice. ❍ *Someone called his name.*
3 VERB If you **call** someone, you telephone them. ❍ *I'll call you tomorrow.*

4 VERB If you **call** somewhere, you make a short visit there. ❍ *A salesman called at the house.*
5 NOUN **Call** is also a noun. ❍ *The engineer was out on a call.*
6 NOUN When you make a telephone **call**, you telephone someone and when you get a call, someone telephones you. ❍ *I made a phone call to my boss.*
7 VERB If you **call** a meeting, you arrange it. ❍ *Bergandi called a meeting of his top managers.*
8 VERB If you **call** something such as a loan or a bond, you demand payment for it. [FINANCE]
9 NOUN A **call** or a **call option** is an option to buy an agreed amount of securities at an agreed price during an agreed period. [FINANCE]
10 If someone such as a doctor or an engineer is **on call**, they are available to work at a time that is not in their normal working hours.
▸**call back** If you **call** someone **back**, you telephone someone who telephoned you before. ❍ *I'll call you back.*
▸**call off** If you **call off** an event that has been planned, you cancel it. ❍ *He called off the trip.*
▸**call on** If you **call on** someone, you visit them for a short time. ❍ *I thought I might call on my accountant.*
▸**call up** If you **call** someone **up**, you telephone them. ❍ *When I'm in Pittsburgh, I'll call him up.*

call cen|ter (**call centers**) **NOUN** an office where people work answering or making telephone calls for a particular firm

call|er /kɔlər/ **NOUN** a person who is making a telephone call ❍ *The firm was flooded by callers wanting to place an order.*

call loan (**call loans**) **NOUN** A **call loan** is the same as a **demand loan**. [BANKING]

calm /kɑm/ (**calmer, calmest**)
1 ADJ quiet and relaxed, not showing anxiety, anger, or excitement ❍ *a calm, patient woman* ❍ *Try to keep calm.* ● **calm|ly ADV** ❍ *Alan said calmly, "I don't believe you."*
2 ADJ If water is **calm**, it is not moving. ❍ *The ocean looked calm.*
3 ADJ with little wind ❍ *It was a fine, calm day.*
▸**calm down** If you **calm down**, you become less angry, upset, or excited, and if you calm someone down, you make them less angry, upset, or excited. ❍ *Calm down and listen to me.* ❍ *I'll try to calm him down.*

calo|rie /kæləri/ **NOUN** a unit used for measuring the amount of energy in food ❍ *These sweet drinks have a lot of calories in them.*

CAM /kæm/ **NONCOUNT NOUN** **CAM** is the use of computer software to manufacture products. **CAM** is an abbreviation for "computer-aided manufacture." Compare with **CAD**. [TECHNOLOGY] ❍ *Components could be assembled in a unique way via CAM.*

came /keɪm/ **Came** is a form of the verb **come**.

cam|era /kæmrə/ **NOUN** a piece of equipment for taking photographs or making movies ❍ *a digital camera*

camp /kæmp/
1 NOUN a place where people live or stay in tents ❍ *an army camp*
2 NOUN a place in the countryside where children are looked after during the summer and activities are provided ❍ *a summer camp*
3 VERB If you **camp** somewhere, you stay there in a tent. ❍ *We camped near the beach.*
● **camp|ing NONCOUNT NOUN** ❍ *They went camping in Colorado.*

cam|paign /kæmpeɪn/
1 NOUN a set of actions that is intended to get a particular result ❍ *a sales campaign*
2 VERB If you **campaign**, you do a set of actions over a period of time in order to get a particular result. ❍ *We are campaigning for better wages.*

can
❶ MODAL USES
❷ CONTAINER

❶ **can** /kən, STRONG kæn/

> Use the form **cannot** in negative statements. When you are speaking, you can use the short form **can't**, pronounced /kænt/.

1 MODAL If you **can** do something, you have

the ability to do it. ❍ *I can access the figures you need.* ❍ *Can you open these files?*
2 MODAL You use **can** to show that something is sometimes true. ❍ *Too much debt can be dangerous.*
3 MODAL You use **can** before words like "smell," "see," and "hear." ❍ *I can smell smoke.*
4 MODAL If you **can** do something, you are allowed to do it. ❍ *Can I come to the meeting?* ❍ *Sorry. We can't answer any questions.*
5 MODAL You use **can** to make requests or offers. ❍ *Can I have a look at the sales figures?* ❍ *Can I help you?*

❷ **can** /kæn/ **NOUN** a metal container for food, drink, or paint ❍ *a can of tomato soup*

ca|nal /kənæl/ **NOUN** a river that people have made ❍ *the Eerie Canal*

can|cel /kænsəl/ (**cancels, canceling** or **cancelling, canceled** or **cancelled**) **VERB** If you **cancel** something that has been planned, you stop it from happening. ❍ *We canceled our trip to Washington.* ● **can|cel|la|tion** /kænsəleɪʃən/ **NOUN** ❍ *the cancellation of his visit*

can|cer /kænsər/ **NOUN** **Cancer** is a serious disease that makes groups of cells in the body grow when they should not. ❍ *lung cancer*

can|di|date /kændɪdeɪt/ **NOUN** someone who is trying to get a particular job, or trying to win a political position [HR] ❍ *He is a candidate for governor of Illinois.*

can|dle /kændəl/ **NOUN** a long stick of wax with a piece of string through the middle, that you burn to give you light ❍ *She lit the candle.*

can|dy /kændi/ (**candies**) **NOUN** a sweet food such as chocolate that people do not usually eat as part of a meal ❍ *a piece of candy*

can|ni|bal|ise /kænɪbəlaɪz/ [BRIT] → **cannibalize**

can|ni|bal|ize /kænɪbəlaɪz/ (**cannibalizes, cannibalizing, cannibalized**)
1 VERB If you **cannibalize** something, you take it to pieces and use it to make something else. ❍ *They cannibalized damaged planes for the parts.*
2 VERB If one of a firm's products **cannibalizes** the firm's sales, people buy it instead of any of the firm's other products. [MARKETING AND SALES] ❍ *Placing the chain restaurants so closely together can cannibalize sales.*

can|not /kænɒt, kənɒt/ the negative form of **can**

can't /kænt/ short for **cannot**

can|teen /kæntin/ [BRIT] → **cafeteria**

cap /kæp/
1 NOUN a soft, flat hat with a curved part at the front ❍ *a baseball cap*
2 NOUN the lid of a bottle ❍ *She took the cap off her water bottle and drank.*
3 NOUN an upper financial limit [ECONOMICS] ❍ *The estimated cost of the proposal exceeds the $870 million cap the government put on disaster relief.*

cap. /kæp/ **cap.** is an abbreviation of **capital** or **capitalization**.

ca|pable /keɪpəbəl/
1 ADJ If you are **capable of** doing something, you are able to do it. ❍ *We are still capable of winning big orders.*
2 ADJ good at doing a job ❍ *She's a very capable team leader.*

ca|pac|ity /kəpæsɪti/ (**capacities**)
1 NOUN your ability to do something ❍ *Every human being has the capacity for love.*
2 NOUN the highest number or amount that can go in something ❍ *The stadium has a capacity of 50,000.*
3 If a factory or industry is working at **full capacity**, it is using all its available resources. [PRODUCTION] ❍ *Bread factories are working at full capacity.*

capi|tal /kæpɪtəl/
1 NOUN the most important city in a country where its government meets ❍ *Berlin is the capital of Germany.*
2 NOUN the large letter that you use at the beginning of sentences and names ❍ *He wrote his name in capitals.* ❍ *Print your occupation in capital letters.*
3 NONCOUNT NOUN **Capital** is money that you use to start a business. [FINANCE, ECONOMICS] ❍ *They provide capital for small businesses.*

capi|tal ac|count (**capital accounts**) **NOUN** a financial statement showing the net value of a firm [FINANCE, ECONOMICS]

capi|tal al|low|ance (**capital allowances**) **NOUN** an amount of money that can be taken off the profits of a firm before they are taxed [FINANCE, ECONOMICS]

C

capi|tal as|sets **PL NOUN** **Capital assets** are the same as **fixed assets**. [FINANCE, ECONOMICS]

capi|tal em|ployed **NONCOUNT NOUN** **Capital employed** is the value of a firm's assets minus its liabilities. It represents the investment required to enable a business to operate. [FINANCE, ECONOMICS] ○ *Our marketing business continues to make less than acceptable returns on capital employed.*

capi|tal ex|pendi|ture **NONCOUNT NOUN** In accounting, **capital expenditure** is money that is spent on buying or improving fixed assets. [FINANCE, ECONOMICS] ○ *He plans to cope with the fall in sales by drastically reducing capital expenditure and cutting staff.*

capi|tal gains **PL NOUN** **Capital gains** are the profits that you make when you buy something and then sell it again at a higher price. [FINANCE, ECONOMICS] ○ *Higher capital gains and investment income are offset by increased reserves.*

capi|tal gains tax (**capital gains taxes**) **NOUN** a tax on the profit made from the sale of an asset [FINANCE, ECONOMICS]

capi|tal goods **PL NOUN** **Capital goods** are used to make other products. Compare with **consumer goods**. [ECONOMICS] ○ *Most imports into Korea are raw materials and capital goods.*

capi|tal in|flow **NONCOUNT NOUN** In economics, **capital inflow** is the amount of capital coming into a country, for example in the form of foreign investment. [ECONOMICS] ○ *a large drop in the capital inflow into America*

capital-intensive **ADJ** **Capital-intensive** industries and businesses need the investment of large sums of money. Compare with **labor-intensive**. [ECONOMICS] ○ *highly capital-intensive industries like auto manufacturing*

capi|tal|ise /kæpɪtəlaɪz/ [BRIT] → **capitalize**

capi|tal|ism /kæpɪtəlɪzəm/ **NONCOUNT NOUN** **Capitalism** is an economic and political system in which businesses and industry are owned by private companies and not by the government.

capi|tal|ist /kæpɪtəlɪst/

1 NOUN someone who believes in and supports the principles of capitalism ○ *Lenin had hoped to even have a working relationship with the capitalists.*

2 ADJ **Capitalist** is also an adjective. ○ *Capitalist production, trade, and commerce were able to grow very rapidly during this period.*

3 NOUN someone who owns a business that they run in order to make a profit [FINANCE, ECONOMICS] ○ *They argue that only private capitalists can remake Poland's economy.*

capi|tal|iza|tion is|sue (**capitalization issues**) **NOUN** A **capitalization issue** is the same as a **rights issue**. [ECONOMICS]

capi|tal|ize /kæpɪtəlaɪz/ (**capitalizes, capitalizing, capitalized**)

1 VERB If you **capitalize on** a situation, you use it to gain some advantage for yourself. ○ *Car dealers are capitalizing on the expected price increases to generate more showroom traffic.*

2 VERB In business, if you **capitalize** something that belongs to you, you sell it to make money. [ECONOMICS] ○ *Our intention is to capitalize the company by any means we can.*

● **cap|ital|iza|tion** **NONCOUNT NOUN** ○ *Its market capitalization has fallen from $650 million to less than $60 million.*

capi|tal mar|ket (**capital markets**) **NOUN** A **capital market** is the financial institutions that deal with medium-term and long-term capital loans. Compare with **money market**. [BANKING, ECONOMICS]

capi|tal stock **NONCOUNT NOUN** A firm's **capital stock** is the money that stockholders invest in order to start or expand the business. [FINANCE, ECONOMICS] ○ *The bank has a capital stock of almost 100 million dollars.*

cap|tain /kæptɪn/
1 NOUN in the army or navy, an officer of middle rank ❍ *He was a captain in the army.*
2 NOUN the leader of a sports team
3 NOUN the person who is in charge of an airplane or ship

cap|tion /kæpʃən/ **NOUN** a piece of writing next to a picture, that tells you something about the picture ❍ *The photo had the caption "Tyneside factory, 1967."*

cap|tive mar|ket /kæptɪv mɑrkɪt/ (**captive markets**) **NOUN** a group of consumers who give a supplier a monopoly because they are obliged to buy a particular product [MARKETING AND SALES] ❍ *Airlines consider business travelers a captive market.*

cap|tiv|ity /kæptɪvɪti/ **NONCOUNT NOUN** **Captivity** is when you are kept in a place and you cannot leave. ❍ *animals kept in captivity*

cap|ture /kæptʃər/ (**captures, capturing, captured**) **VERB** If you **capture** someone or something, you catch them and keep them somewhere so that they cannot leave. ❍ *The airplane was shot down and the pilot captured.*

car /kɑr/ **NOUN** a motor vehicle with space for about 5 people ❍ *They came by car.*

cara|van /kærəvæn/ [BRIT] → **trailer**

car|bo|hy|drate /kɑrboʊhaɪdreɪt/ **NOUN** a substance in food that gives the body energy, or a food containing this substance ❍ *carbohydrates such as bread and pasta*

car|bon /kɑrbən/ **NONCOUNT NOUN** **Carbon** is a chemical element that diamonds and coal are made of.

car|bon foot|print (**carbon footprints**) **NOUN** Your **carbon footprint** is the amount of energy that you use, for example by heating your home or by traveling by airplane. ❍ *We all need to look for ways to reduce our carbon footprint.*

car|bon neu|tral **ADJ** not causing an increase in the amount of carbon dioxide in the atmosphere ❍ *a carbon neutral company*

car|bon trad|ing **NONCOUNT NOUN** **Carbon trading** is the practice of buying and selling the right to produce carbon dioxide emissions. [TECHNOLOGY]

card /kɑrd/
1 NOUN a piece of stiff paper with a picture and a message, that you give someone on a special occasion ❍ *a birthday card*
2 NOUN a small piece of cardboard or plastic that has information about you written on it ❍ *an identity card*
3 NOUN a small piece of plastic that you use to pay for things ❍ *a credit card*

card|board /kɑrdbɔrd/ **NONCOUNT NOUN** **Cardboard** is thick, stiff paper that is used for making boxes. ❍ *a cardboard box*

card|holder /kɑrdhoʊldər/ **NOUN** someone who has a credit card or debit card [BANKING] ❍ *The average cardholder today carries three to four bank cards.*

care /kɛər/ (**cares, caring, cared**)
1 VERB If you **care** about someone or something, you are interested in them, or you think they are important. ❍ *He doesn't care about his staff.*
2 VERB If you **care for** someone, you like or love them. ❍ *I still care for you.*
3 VERB If you **care for** someone, you look after them. ❍ *A nurse cares for David in his home.*
4 NONCOUNT NOUN If you do something **with care**, you do it very carefully so that you do not make any mistakes. ❍ *He chose his words with care.*
5 NONCOUNT NOUN Care of someone is treatment for them or help and support for them. ❍ *the care of the elderly*
6 If you **take care of** someone or something, you look after them or deal with them. ❍ *The company takes care of its former workers.* ❍ *Malcolm will take care of the arrangements.*

ca|reer /kərɪər/ **NOUN** a job, or the years of your life that you spend working ❍ *She had a long career in advertising.*

ca|reer break (**career breaks**) **NOUN** If someone **takes** a **career break**, they stop working in their particular profession for a period of time, with the intention of returning to it later. [HR] ❍ *Many women still take career breaks to bring up children.*

C

care|ful /kɛərfəl/ ADJ paying close attention to what you are doing so that you do not make mistakes ❍ *Be careful – it's hot!* ● **care|ful|ly** ADV ❍ *Check your figures carefully!*

care|less /kɛərlɪs/ ADJ not giving enough attention to what you are doing, so that you make mistakes ❍ *careless mistakes*

care|taker /kɛərteɪkər/ NOUN someone who looks after a building and the area around it

car|go /kɑrgoʊ/ (**cargoes**) NOUN the goods that a ship or airplane is carrying ❍ *a cargo of bananas*

car park (**car parks**) also **carpark** [BRIT] → **parking lot**

car|pen|ter /kɑrpɪntər/ NOUN a person whose job is to make and repair wooden things

car|pet /kɑrpɪt/ NOUN a thick, soft covering for the floor

car pool (**car pools, car pooling, car pooled**) also **carpool, car-pool**
1 NOUN an arrangement where a group of people take turns driving each other to work, or driving each other's children to school ❍ *He drives the children to school in the car pool.*
2 VERB **car pool** is also a verb. ❍ *Fewer Americans are carpooling to work.* ● **car pool|ing** NONCOUNT NOUN ❍ *The government should encourage car pooling to cut the number of one-passenger cars on the roads.*
3 NOUN a number of cars that are owned by a firm or organization for the use of its employees or members

car|ri|er /kæriər/
1 NOUN a firm that provides telecommunications services, such as telephone and Internet services [TECHNOLOGY] ❍ *Japan's top wireless carrier* ❍ *Regional carriers get paid for calls that pass through their switches.*
2 NOUN a passenger airline ❍ *American Airlines is the third-largest carrier at Denver International Airport.*
3 NOUN a firm that transports goods from one place to another by truck [LOGISTICS AND DISTRIBUTION] ❍ *The Colorado Motor Carriers Association represents 450 trucking companies across the state.*

car|rot /kærət/ NOUN a long, thin, orange-colored vegetable

car|ry /kæri/ (**carries, carrying, carried**)
1 VERB If you **carry** something, you hold it and take it somewhere. ❍ *He was carrying a briefcase.*
2 VERB To **carry** someone or something means to move them from one place to a different place. ❍ *Trucks carrying food and medicine arrived yesterday.*
3 VERB If you **carry** or **carry over** an amount of money, you transfer it to the following year's account. [FINANCE, BANKING]
▶ **carry back** In accounting, if you **carry back** an amount, you apply a loss or credit to the taxable income of a previous year in order to spread a tax bill more evenly. [FINANCE, BANKING] ❍ *The ability to carry back a contribution is still available.*
▶ **carry forward**
1 In accounting, if you **carry forward** a number, you transfer it to the next page or column of accounts. [FINANCE, BANKING] ❍ *Carry forward the figure from box 1.1 on page 4.*
2 In accounting, if you **carry forward** an amount, you apply a loss or credit to the taxable income of following years in order to spread a tax bill more evenly. [FINANCE, BANKING] ❍ *Tax breaks allow them to carry forward losses between financial years.*
▶ **carry on** If you **carry on** doing something, you continue to do it. ❍ *The economy carried on growing.*
▶ **carry out** If you **carry** something **out**, you do it. ❍ *A management team carried out the takeover.*
▶ **carry over** In accounting, to **carry over** is the same as to **carry forward**. [FINANCE, BANKING]

car|ry|back /kæribæk/ also **carry-back** NONCOUNT NOUN In accounting, **carryback** is when a loss or credit is applied to a previous tax year. [FINANCE, BANKING]

carry-forward NONCOUNT NOUN In accounting, **carry-forward** is when an amount is carried forward to the next tax year.

[FINANCE, BANKING] ❍ *They will lose their budget carry-forward.*

car|ry|over /kæriouvər/ also **carry-over**
1 NOUN In accounting, a **carryover** is a sum or balance that is carried forward. [FINANCE, BANKING] ❍ *This rule does not apply to carry-overs of investment interest.*
2 NONCOUNT NOUN In accounting, **carryover** is the same as **carry-forward**. [FINANCE, BANKING]

cart /kart/
1 NOUN an old-fashioned wooden vehicle that is pulled by a horse
2 NOUN A **cart** or a **shopping cart** is a large metal basket on wheels that a customer uses in a supermarket.

car|tel /kartɛl/ **NOUN** an association of similar firms or businesses that have grouped together in order to prevent competition and to control prices [ECONOMICS, BUSINESS MANAGEMENT] ❍ *a drug cartel*

car|ton /kartᵊn/ **NOUN** a plastic or cardboard container, or the amount contained in a carton ❍ *bulk cartons of office supplies* ❍ *a carton of milk*

car|toon /kartun/
1 NOUN a funny drawing, often in a magazine or newspaper ❍ *cartoon characters*
2 NOUN a film that uses drawings for all the characters and scenes instead of real people or objects ❍ *We watched children's cartoons on TV.*

car|tridge /kartrɪdʒ/ **NOUN** a container for ink that you put in a printer or pen ❍ *You need to change the cartridge.*

carve /karv/ (**carves, carving, carved**)
1 VERB If you **carve** an object, you cut it out of wood or stone. ❍ *He carved the statue from one piece of rock.*
2 VERB If you **carve** meat, you cut slices from it. ❍ *Andrew carved the chicken.*

case /keɪs/
1 NOUN a particular situation that you are using as an example ❍ *In some cases, it can be very difficult.*
2 NOUN a crime that police or lawyers are working on [LEGAL] ❍ *a copyright infringement case*
3 NOUN a container that holds and protects something ❍ *a glasses case*
4 You say **in any case** when you are adding another reason for something. ❍ *The concert was sold out, and in any case, I couldn't afford a ticket.*
5 You say **in case** to explain something that you do because a particular thing might happen. ❍ *I've brought some food in case we get hungry.*
6 In that case means if that is the situation. ❍ *"Max will be there."—"Oh, in that case I'll come too."* ❍ *The plumber might also owe the bank money in the form of a loan, in which case the bank is also a creditor of this business.*

cash /kæʃ/ (**cashes, cashing, cashed**)
1 NONCOUNT NOUN Cash is money in the form of bills and coins. [FINANCE] ❍ *two thousand dollars in cash*
2 VERB If you **cash** a check, you take it to a bank and get money for it. [BANKING]

cash-and-carry (**cash-and-carries**) **NOUN** a large store where you can buy goods in larger quantities and at lower prices than in ordinary stores [MARKETING AND SALES]

cash|back /kæʃbæk/
1 NONCOUNT NOUN Cashback is a service provided by some supermarkets in which customers who pay by debit card can pay extra and ask for cash in return. [FINANCE] ❍ *They take most types of credit and debit cards, and they also offer cashback.*
2 NONCOUNT NOUN Cashback is a payment made by a lender, such as a bank, to a new borrower when they take out a mortgage. [MARKETING AND SALES, FINANCE] ❍ *Many first-time buyers find the idea of cashback mortgages appealing.*

cash card (**cash cards**) **NOUN** A **cash card** is the same as a **debit card**. [BANKING]

cash cow (**cash cows**) **NOUN** a product or investment that continues to be profitable for a long time [BUSINESS MANAGEMENT, E-COMMERCE] ❍ *The units have been a cash cow for the firm, contributing 42% of the firm's profit last year.*

cash crop (**cash crops**) NOUN a crop that is grown in order to be sold [ECONOMICS] ❍ *Cranberries are a major cash crop in New Jersey.*

cash desk (**cash desks**) [MARKETING AND SALES, BRIT] → **checkout**

C

cash dis|count (**cash discounts**) NOUN a discount given to a purchaser who pays before a specific date [FINANCE]

cash dis|pens|er (**cash dispensers**) NOUN [BANKING, BRIT] → **automated teller machine**

cash flow also **cash-flow** NONCOUNT NOUN The **cash flow** of a firm or business is the movement of money into and out of it. [FINANCE] ❍ *The company ran into cash-flow problems and faced liquidation.*

COLLOCATIONS
operating cash flow
negative cash flow
positive cash flow
cash flow *problems*

cash|ier /kæʃɪər/ NOUN a person who customers pay money to or get money from in places such as stores or banks [BANKING, ADMINISTRATION]

cash|less /kæʃlɪs/ ADJ A **cashless** system uses credit cards or electronic transfer of funds instead of bills or coins. [BANKING] ❍ *cashless shopping*

cash ma|chine (**cash machines**) NOUN A **cash machine** is the same as an **automated teller machine**. [BANKING]

cash on de|liv|ery NONCOUNT NOUN **Cash on delivery** is a system where the carrier is paid cash when the merchandise is delivered. [BANKING] ❍ *People were given an option of paying cash on delivery or by credit card.*

cash|point /kæʃpɔɪnt/ [BANKING, BRIT] → **automated teller machine**

cash reg|is|ter (**cash registers**) NOUN a machine in a store, bar, or restaurant that is used to add up and record how much money people pay [FINANCE]

cash-starved ADJ not having enough money to operate properly, usually because another organization is not giving them the money that they need [ECONOMICS] ❍ *We are heading for a crisis with cash-starved organizations forced to cut back on vital community services.*

ca|si|no /kəsinoʊ/ NOUN a place where people gamble by playing games

cast /kæst/

1 NOUN all the people who act in a play or movie ❍ *a very strong cast*

2 NOUN a hard cover for protecting a broken arm or leg ❍ *His arm is in a cast.*

cas|tle /kæsᵊl/ NOUN a large building with thick, high walls that was built in the past to protect people during battles

cas|ual /kæʒuəl/

1 ADJ relaxed and not worried about what is happening ❍ *She tried to sound casual, but she was frightened.* ● **casu|al|ly** ADV ❍ *"No need to hurry," Ben said casually.*

2 ADJ **Casual** clothes are clothes that you normally wear at home or on vacation, and not on formal occasions. ● **casu|al|ly** ADV ❍ *casually dressed*

casual|ise /kæʒuəlaɪz/ [BRIT] → **casualize**

casual|ize /kæʒuəlaɪz/ (**casualizes, casualizing, casualized**) VERB If a business **casualizes** its employees or **casualizes** their labor, it replaces employees with permanent contracts and full rights with employees with temporary contracts and few rights. [ECONOMICS] ❍ *a casualized workforce* ● **casual|iza|tion** /kæʒuəlɪzeɪʃən/ NONCOUNT NOUN ❍ *the casualization of employment*

casu|al|ty /kæʒuəlti/ (**casualties**)

1 NOUN a person who is injured or killed in a war or in an accident ❍ *Helicopters bombed the town, causing many casualties.*

2 NONCOUNT NOUN **Casualty** is the same as **emergency room**. [BRIT]

cat /kæt/ NOUN a small animal covered with fur ❍ *The cat sat on my lap, purring.*

cata|log /kætᵊlɒg/ NOUN a list of things such as the goods you can buy from a particular company, the objects in a museum, or the books in a library [MARKETING AND SALES] ❍ *the world's biggest seed catalog*

cata|logue /kæt^əlɒg/ [MARKETING AND SALES, BRIT] → **catalog**

ca|tas|tro|phe /kətæstrəfi/ NOUN a very bad event that causes a lot of suffering or damage ❍ *Many financial catastrophes have been caused by selling options.*

cata|stroph|ic /kætəstrɒfɪk/ ADJ extremely bad, causing a lot of suffering or damage ❍ *catastrophic losses*

catch /kætʃ/ (**catches, catching, caught**)
1 VERB If you **catch** a person or animal, you find them and hold them. ❍ *His killer was never caught.* ❍ *Where did you catch the fish?*
2 VERB If you **catch** an object that is moving through the air, you take hold of it with your hands. ❍ *I jumped up to catch the ball.*
3 NOUN **Catch** is also a noun. ❍ *That was a great catch.*
4 VERB If you **catch** part of your body somewhere, it accidentally gets stuck there. ❍ *I caught my finger in the car door.*
5 VERB When you **catch** a bus, train, or airplane, you get on it in order to travel somewhere. ❍ *We caught the bus on the corner of the street.*
6 VERB If you **catch** someone doing something wrong, you see or find them doing it. ❍ *He caught me reading his emails.*
7 VERB If you **catch** an illness, you become ill with it. ❍ *I've caught a cold.*
▸**catch up**
1 If you **catch up with** someone, you reach them by walking faster than they are walking. ❍ *I stopped and waited for her to catch up.*
2 To **catch up** means to reach the same level as someone else. ❍ *You'll have to work hard to catch up.*

cat|ego|ry /kætɪgɔri/ (**categories**) NOUN a set of things or people of a similar type ❍ *The product became the leading brand in its category.*

cat|ego|ry man|age|ment NONCOUNT NOUN In marketing, **category management** is the promotion of a range of related products in a way that is designed to increase sales of all of the products. [MARKETING AND SALES] ❍ *Retailers must implement category-management techniques to ensure continued profitability.*

ca|ter /keɪtər/ VERB If someone **caters for** a party, they provide the food for it. ❍ *We can cater for birthday parties of any size.*

ca|thedral /kəθidrəl/ NOUN a very large and important church ❍ *Chartres Cathedral*

Catho|lic /kæθlɪk/
1 ADJ belonging to the Roman Catholic Church ❍ *a Catholic priest*
2 NOUN a member of the Roman Catholic Church ❍ *His parents are Catholics.*

cat|tle /kæt^əl/ PL NOUN **Cattle** are cows that are kept for their milk or meat.

caught /kɔt/ **Caught** is a form of the verb **catch**.

cau|li|flow|er /kɔliflaʊər/ NOUN a large, round, white vegetable surrounded by green leaves

cause /kɔz/ (**causes, causing, caused**)
1 NOUN The **cause of** an event is the thing that makes it happen. ❍ *The report identifies several causes of waste and inefficiency.*
2 NOUN an aim that a group of people support or fight for ❍ *A strong leader will help our cause.*
3 VERB To **cause** something means to make it happen. ❍ *The company's losses were caused by interest payments on debt.*

cau|tion /kɔʃən/ NONCOUNT NOUN **Caution** is great care to avoid danger. ❍ *There is continued caution among consumers.*

cau|tious /kɔʃəs/ ADJ very careful to avoid danger ❍ *Investors remain cautious about this market.* ● **cau|tious|ly** ADV ❍ *Some foreign businessmen are cautiously returning to the country.*

cave /keɪv/ NOUN a large hole in the side of a hill or under the ground

ca|veat emp|tor /kæviɑt ɛmptɔr/ NONCOUNT NOUN **Caveat emptor** means "let the buyer beware," and is a warning to someone buying something that it is their responsibility to identify and accept any faults in it. [LEGAL, FORMAL]

CC /si si/ **cc** is used at the beginning of emails or at the end of a business letter to show that a copy is being sent to another person. ❍ *cc j.jones@harpercollins.co.uk.*

CD /si di/ (**CDs**) **NOUN** A **CD** is a disk for storing music or computer information. **CD** is short for **compact disc**.

C

CD burn|er /si di bɜrnər/ (**CD burners**) **NOUN** a piece of computer equipment that you use for copying information or music from a computer onto a CD [TECHNOLOGY]

CD play|er (**CD players**) **NOUN** a machine that plays CDs

CD-ROM /si di rɒm/ (**CD-ROMs**) **NOUN** a CD that stores a very large amount of information that you can read using a computer [TECHNOLOGY]

cease /sis/ (**ceases, ceasing, ceased**) **VERB** When something **ceases**, it stops. [FORMAL] ❍ *Our corn exports will probably cease soon.*

cedi /seɪdi/ **PL NOUN** the standard monetary unit of Ghana [ECONOMICS]

ceil|ing /silɪŋ/
1 NOUN the top inside surface of a room ❍ *high ceilings*
2 NOUN an upper limit, for example on prices or wages ❍ *Both bills would set a $100,000 ceiling on disaster payments to individual farmers.*

cel|ebrate /sɛlɪbreɪt/ (**celebrates, celebrating, celebrated**) **VERB** If you **celebrate** or **celebrate** something, you do something enjoyable for a special reason. ❍ *The fall in fuel prices is something to celebrate.* ❍ *The company celebrates its 100th anniversary next year.*

cel|ebra|tion /sɛlɪbreɪʃən/ **NOUN** a special event that is organized in order to celebrate something ❍ *The company is organizing a weekend of celebrations.*

ce|leb|rity /sɪlɛbrɪti/ (**celebrities**) **NOUN** a famous person ❍ *Warren Buffet will be our celebrity guest.*

cel|ery /sɛləri/ **NONCOUNT NOUN** a vegetable that consists of long, pale-green sticks

cell /sɛl/
1 NOUN the smallest part of an animal or plant ❍ *blood cells*
2 NOUN a small room with a lock in a prison or a police station ❍ *How many prisoners were in the cell?*

cel|lar /sɛlər/ **NOUN** a room under a building ❍ *He kept the boxes in the cellar.*

cell|phone /sɛlfoʊn/ **NOUN** a telephone that you carry around with you ❍ *The woman called the police on her cellphone.*

Celsius /sɛlsiəs/ **NONCOUNT NOUN** **Celsius** is a way of measuring temperature. Water freezes at 0° Celsius and boils at 100° Celsius. ❍ *11° Celsius is 52° Fahrenheit.*

ce|ment /sɪmɛnt/ **NONCOUNT NOUN** **Cement** is a gray powder that you mix with sand and water to make concrete.

cem|etery /sɛmətɛri/ (**cemeteries**) **NOUN** a place where dead people are buried

cent /sɛnt/ **NOUN** A **cent** is a coin. There are one hundred cents in a dollar. ❍ *The book cost six dollars and fifty cents.*

cen|ter /sɛntər/
1 NOUN the middle of something ❍ *We sat in the center of the room.*
2 NOUN a place where people can take part in a particular activity, or get help ❍ *a health center*

cen|ti|me|ter /sɛntɪmitər/ **NOUN** A **centimeter** is a unit for measuring length. There are ten millimeters in a centimeter. ❍ *This tiny plant is only a few centimeters high.*

cen|ti|me|tre /sɛntɪmitər/ [BRIT] → **centimeter**

cen|tral /sɛntrəl/ **ADJ** in or near the middle part of a place or object ❍ *Central America*

cen|tral bank (**central banks**) also **Central Bank** **NOUN** a national bank that does business mainly with a government and with other banks [BANKING] ❍ *Coins are issued by the Central Bank.*

cen|tral heat|ing **NONCOUNT NOUN** **Central heating** is a heating system that uses hot air or water to make every part of a building warm.

cen|tre /sɛntər/ [BRIT] → **center**

cen|tu|ry /sɛntʃəri/ (**centuries**) **NOUN** one hundred years ❍ *The labor movement began with the industrial revolution of the nineteenth century.*

CEO /si i oʊ/ (**CEOs**) **NOUN** **CEO** is an abbreviation for **chief executive officer**. [ADMINISTRATION]

ce|ram|ic /sɪræmɪk/ **NONCOUNT NOUN** **Ceramic** is clay that has been heated to a very high temperature so that it becomes hard. ❍ *ceramic tiles*

ce|real /sɪəriəl/
1 NONCOUNT NOUN **Cereal** is a food made from grain, that you can mix with milk and eat for breakfast. ❍ *I have a bowl of cereal every morning.*
2 NOUN a plant that produces grain for food ❍ *cereals such as corn and wheat*

cer|emo|ny /sɛrɪmoʊni/ (**ceremonies**) **NOUN** a formal event such as a wedding or funeral ❍ *a wedding ceremony*

cer|tain /sɜrtᵊn/
1 ADJ definite and with no doubt at all ❍ *These share options are certain to pay out.* ❍ *No-one is certain how the contract would be enforced.*
2 If you know something **for certain**, you have no doubt at all about it. ❍ *Nobody knows for certain which firms will survive.*

cer|tain|ly /sɜrtᵊnli/
1 ADV without doubt ❍ *This year's profits will certainly be down.*
2 ADV used for agreeing or disagreeing strongly with what someone has said ❍ *"Can you supply such a large order?"—"Certainly."* ❍ *"Perhaps I should go now."—"Certainly not!"*

cer|tifi|cate /sərtɪfɪkɪt/
1 NOUN an official document that proves that the facts on it are true [ADMINISTRATION] ❍ *a birth certificate*
2 NOUN an official document that you receive when you have completed a course of study or training ❍ *To the right of the fireplace are various framed certificates.* ❍ *a Post-Graduate Certificate of Education.*

cer|tifi|cate of ori|gin (**certificates of origin**) **NOUN** a document stating the name of the country that produced a particular shipment of goods [ADMINISTRATION, PRODUCTION] ❍ *Argentina started to require certificates of origin for imported toys in May 1998.*

cer|ti|fied ac|count|ant (**certified accountants**) **NOUN** In Britain, a **certified accountant** is a member of the Chartered Association of Certified Accountants, who is officially allowed to check company accounts. Compare with **chartered accountant**. [FINANCE, BRIT] ❍ *The company's accounts must be audited annually by a chartered or certified accountant.*

BUSINESS ETIQUETTE
Before you travel abroad for business, it is a good idea to find out about the type of gift that would be appropriate, and when you should give it. In some cultures, gift-giving in a business context is not considered good practice.

cer|ti|fied pub|lic ac|count|ant (**certified public accountants**) **NOUN** A **certified public accountant** is someone who has received a certificate stating that he or she is qualified to work as an accountant within a particular state. The abbreviation **CPA** is also used. [FINANCE]

cer|ti|fy /sɜrtɪfaɪ/ (**certifies, certifying, certified**) **VERB** If someone **certifies** something, they officially say that it is true. ❍ *Each year they audit our accounts and certify them as being true and fair.*

c/f **c/f** is a written abbreviation for **carry forward**. [FINANCE, BANKING]

CFO /si ɛf oʊ/ **CFO** is an abbreviation of **chief financial officer**. [FINANCE]

chae|bol /dʒeɪbəl, tʃeɪ-/ **NOUN** a large business group in South Korea that is usually family-owned [BUSINESS MANAGEMENT]

chain /tʃeɪn/
1 NOUN a line of metal rings that are connected together ❍ *He wore a gold chain around his neck.*
2 VERB If a person or thing **is chained to** something, they are attached to it with a chain. ❍ *The dogs were chained to a fence.*

3 NOUN a number of businesses such as stores or hotels that are owned by the same company [BUSINESS MANAGEMENT] ❍ *a supermarket chain*
4 NOUN a series of related processes [ECONOMICS] ❍ *the distribution chain*
5 NOUN a series of deals in which each buyer must sell something before they can buy the thing they want [PURCHASING] ❍ *The house is for sale with no upward chain.*

chain of pro|duc|tion NONCOUNT NOUN The **chain of production** is all the stages of production that a product passes through before it is passed to a consumer. [PRODUCTION] ❍ *There are other environmental costs attached to washing powders, earlier in the chain of production.*

chain store (**chain stores**) NOUN A **chain store** is one of several similar stores that are owned by the same person or company that sells a variety of things. [BUSINESS MANAGEMENT]

chair /tʃɛər/
1 NOUN a piece of furniture for one person to sit on, with a back and four legs ❍ *He suddenly got up from his chair.*
2 VERB If you **chair** a meeting, you are the person who controls it. [ADMINISTRATION, BUSINESS MANAGEMENT] ❍ *She chaired the committee meeting.*

chair|man /tʃɛərmən/ (**chairmen**) NOUN the person who controls a meeting or organization [ADMINISTRATION, BUSINESS MANAGEMENT] ❍ *He is chairman of the committee that wrote the report.*

chair|person /tʃɛərpɜrsᵊn/ (**chairpeople**) NOUN the person who controls a meeting or organization [ADMINISTRATION, BUSINESS MANAGEMENT] ❍ *She's the chairperson of the planning committee.*

chair|woman /tʃɛərwʊmən/ (**chairwomen**) NOUN the woman who controls a meeting or organization [ADMINISTRATION, BUSINESS MANAGEMENT] ❍ *the chairwoman of the Socialist Party*

chalk /tʃɔk/ NONCOUNT NOUN **Chalk** is a soft white rock.

chalk|board /tʃɔkbɔrd/ NOUN a dark-colored board that you write on with chalk

chal|lenge /tʃælɪndʒ/ (**challenges, challenging, challenged**)
1 NOUN something that is difficult to do ❍ *Our company must be able to respond to new challenges.*
2 VERB If you **challenge** someone, you invite them to compete with you or do something difficult. ❍ *They are being challenged by rival manufacturing firms.*

cham|ber of com|merce /tʃeɪmbər əv kɒmɜrs/ (**chambers of commerce**) NOUN an organization of businesspeople that promotes local commercial interests [BUSINESS MANAGEMENT]

cham|pagne /ʃæmpeɪn/ NONCOUNT NOUN **Champagne** is an expensive French white wine with bubbles in it.

cham|pi|on /tʃæmpiən/ NOUN the winner of a competition ❍ *He was an Olympic champion twice.*

cham|pi|on|ship /tʃæmpiənʃɪp/ NOUN a competition to find the best player or team in a particular sport ❍ *the world chess championship*

chance /tʃæns/
1 NOUN If there is a **chance** that something will happen, it is possible that it will happen. ❍ *There is a good chance that gold will hold its value.*
2 NOUN If you have a **chance to** do something, there is a time when you can do it. ❍ *Everyone gets a chance to contribute to the meeting.*
3 Something that happens **by chance** happens unexpectedly. ❍ *Things happened to this industry by chance, not design.*

change /tʃeɪndʒ/ (**changes, changing, changed**)
1 NOUN If there is a **change**, something becomes different. ❍ *There will soon be some big changes in our company.*
2 VERB When something **changes** or when you **change** it, it becomes different. ❍ *Skill requirements have changed drastically.* ❍ *The company has no plans to change the way it*

markets its products.
3 VERB To **change** something means to replace it with something new or different. ❍ *They decided to change the name of the product.*
4 VERB When you **change** your clothes, you put on different ones. ❍ *Ben changed his shirt.*
5 NONCOUNT NOUN Your **change** is the money that you get back when you pay with more money than something costs. ❍ *She gave him his change.*
6 NONCOUNT NOUN **Change** is coins. ❍ *"I need 36 cents. Do you have any change?"*
7 NONCOUNT NOUN **Change** is money given in exchange for the same amount in coins or bills of larger values. ❍ *Do you have change for a $10 bill?*

change man|age|ment **NONCOUNT NOUN** **Change management** is a style of management that aims to encourage organizations and individuals to deal effectively with the changes taking place in their work. [HR] ❍ *She is hoping to go into change management or IT management when she graduates.*

chan|nel /tʃænᵊl/
1 NOUN a television station
2 NOUN a narrow passage that water can flow along ❍ *a shipping channel*

chan|nel of dis|tri|bu|tion **(channels of distribution)** **NOUN** the people and organizations involved in overseeing all steps of the production of a product [LOGISTICS AND DISTRIBUTION, PRODUCTION] ❍ *The middle person in a channel of distribution between producers and consumers plays the important role of breaking the bulk of what is produced by the manufacturers.*

chant /tʃænt/
1 NOUN a word or group of words that is repeated again and again ❍ *Then the crowd started the chant of "U-S-A!"*
2 VERB If you **chant** something, you repeat the same words again and again. ❍ *The crowd chanted "We are with you."*

cha|os /keɪɒs/ **NONCOUNT NOUN** **Chaos** is when there is no order or organization. ❍ *The economy was in chaos.*

cha|ot|ic /keɪɒtɪk/ **ADJ** completely confused and without order ❍ *The company's management has been chaotic.*

chap|el /tʃæpᵊl/ **NOUN** a room or part of a church that people pray in

chap|ter /tʃæptər/ **NOUN** one of the parts that a book is divided into ❍ *For more information, see Chapter 4.*

char|ac|ter /kærɪktər/
1 NOUN all the qualities that make one person or place different from another person or place ❍ *There's a gentler side to his character.*
2 NOUN one of the people in a story ❍ *Collard himself plays the main character.*

char|ac|ter|is|tic /kærɪktərɪstɪk/ **NOUN** a quality that is typical of someone or something ❍ *The firm has two main characteristics that make it attractive to investors.*

charge /tʃɑrdʒ/ (**charges, charging, charged**)
1 VERB If you **charge** someone, you ask them to pay money for something. ❍ *How much do you charge for printing photos?*
2 NOUN **charge** is also a noun. ❍ *There was no charge.*
3 VERB If you **charge** something or **charge** something **to** a credit card, you use a credit card to buy it. [BANKING] ❍ *I'll charge it to my Visa.*
4 VERB When the police **charge** someone, they formally tell them that they have done something wrong. ❍ *They have enough evidence to charge him.*
5 VERB To **charge** a battery means to put electricity into it. ❍ *Alex forgot to charge his cellphone.*
6 If you are **in charge of** someone or something, you have responsibility for them. [ADMINISTRATION] ❍ *He was named managing partner of this accounting and consulting firm's New York office in charge of the client practice.*
7 If a person or thing is **in** someone's **charge**, they are under their care. ❍ *Managers need to be able to think through the limits on social responsibility set by their duty to the performance capacity of the enterprises in their charge.*

charge|able as|set /tʃɑrdʒəbᵊl æsɛt/ (**chargeable assets**) NOUN any asset that can give rise to assessment for capital gains tax when you sell it [ECONOMICS]

charge ac|count (**charge accounts**) NOUN a credit system where a customer obtains goods at one time and pays for them later [BANKING]

charge card (**charge cards**)
1 NOUN a plastic card that you use to buy goods on credit from a particular store or group of stores [BANKING]
2 NOUN A **charge card** is the same as a **credit card**. [BANKING]

char|ity /tʃærɪti/ (**charities**) NOUN an organization that collects money for people who need help ❍ *a children's charity*

charm /tʃɑrm/ NONCOUNT NOUN **Charm** is the quality of being pleasant and attractive. ❍ *This hotel has real charm.*

charm|ing /tʃɑrmɪŋ/ ADJ very pleasant and attractive ❍ *a very charming man*

chart /tʃɑrt/ NOUN a diagram or graph that shows information ❍ *See the chart on the next page for more details.*

char|ter /tʃɑrtər/ NOUN a formal document that describes the rights or principles of an organization ❍ *the United Nations Charter*

char|tered /tʃɑrtərd/ ADJ used to indicate that someone, such as an accountant or a surveyor, has formally qualified in their profession [BRIT]

char|tered ac|count|ant (**chartered accountants**) NOUN A **chartered accountant** is an accountant who has passed the examinations of a professional body in the United Kingdom. Compare with **certified accountant**. [FINANCE, BRIT] ❍ *He qualified as a chartered accountant and soon became a director of a Swiss-based finance firm.*

chase /tʃeɪs/ (**chases, chasing, chased**)
1 VERB If you **chase** someone, you run after them in order to catch them. ❍ *She chased the boys for 100 yards.*
2 NOUN **Chase** is also a noun. ❍ *The chase ended at about 10:30 p.m. on Highway 522.*

chat /tʃæt/ (**chats, chatting, chatted**)
1 VERB When people **chat**, they talk in an informal, friendly way. ❍ *I was chatting to him the other day.*
2 NOUN **Chat** is also a noun. ❍ *I had a chat with John.*

chat room (**chat rooms**) also **chatroom** NOUN a website where people can exchange messages

chat|ter /tʃætər/
1 VERB If you **chatter**, you talk quickly about unimportant things. ❍ *Erica chattered about her work.*
2 NONCOUNT NOUN **Chatter** is also a noun. ❍ *noisy chatter*
3 VERB If your teeth **chatter**, they keep knocking together because you are cold.

cheap /tʃip/ (**cheaper, cheapest**) ADJ costing little money ❍ *cheap fuel* ❍ *The raw materials were quite cheap.* • **cheap|ly** ADV ❍ *You can deliver more food more cheaply by ship.*

cheat /tʃit/
1 VERB If someone **cheats**, they do not obey the rules in a game or exam. ❍ *If the firm cheats, the value of investments goes rapidly to zero.*
2 NOUN **Cheat** is also a noun. ❍ *Are you calling me a cheat?* • **cheat|ing** NONCOUNT NOUN ❍ *The company was accused of cheating.*

check /tʃɛk/
1 VERB If you **check** something, you make sure that it is correct. ❍ *Check the meanings of the words in a dictionary.* ❍ *I think there is an age limit, but I'll check.*
2 NOUN **Check** is also a noun. ❍ *We need to do some quick checks before the plane leaves.*
3 VERB If you **check** something that is written on a piece of paper, you put a mark like this ✔ next to it. ❍ *Please check the box below.*
4 VERB When you **check** your luggage at an airport, you give it to the airline so that it can go on your plane. ❍ *We checked our luggage early.*
5 NOUN in a restaurant, a piece of paper with the cost of a meal on it
6 NOUN a printed form from a bank that you write on and use to pay for things [BANKING] ❍ *He handed me a check for $1,500.*

▸**check in** When you **check in** at an airport or a hotel, you tell the person at the desk that you have arrived. ❍ *He checked in at Amsterdam's Schiphol airport for a flight to Atlanta.*
▸**check out** When you **check out of** a hotel, you pay the bill and leave. ❍ *They packed and checked out of the hotel.*
▸**check off**
1 When you **check off** something **from** a list, you mark it to show it has been done. ❍ *They're all checked off your list.*
2 When an employer **checks off** money from a paycheck, the employer deducts union contributions directly from an employee's paycheck.

check|book /tʃɛkbʊk/ **NOUN** a book of checks

check box (**check boxes**) **NOUN** a square on a form where someone puts a mark to indicate agreement

check-in (**check-ins**) **NOUN** at an airport, a desk where you tell someone that you have arrived

check|ing ac|count (**checking accounts**) **NOUN** a bank account that you can take money out of by writing a check [BANKING] ❍ *I have a checking account and a savings account.*

check mark (**check marks**) **NOUN** a written mark like this ✔ that you use to show that something is correct or done

check|out /tʃɛkaʊt/ **NOUN** the place in a store where you pay for the things you are buying [PURCHASING]

cheek /tʃik/ **NOUN** Your **cheeks** are the sides of your face below your eyes. ❍ *The tears started rolling down my cheeks.*

cheer /tʃɪər/
1 VERB When people **cheer**, they shout loudly to show they are pleased or to encourage someone. ❍ *We cheered as the annual profits were announced.*
2 NOUN **Cheer** is also a noun. ❍ *The audience gave him a loud cheer.*
▸**cheer up** When you **cheer up** or **cheer** someone **up**, you become happier or you make someone feel happier. ❍ *Cheer up. Life could be worse.* ❍ *Stop trying to cheer me up.*

cheer|ful /tʃɪərfəl/ **ADJ** seeming happy ❍ *Paddy was always smiling and cheerful.*
● **cheer|ful|ly ADV** ❍ *"We've got several new orders," Pat said cheerfully.* ● **cheer|ful|ness NONCOUNT NOUN** ❍ *I liked his natural cheerfulness.*

C

cheer|leader /tʃɪərlidər/ **NOUN** one of a group of people who encourage the crowd to shout support for their team at a sports event

cheese /tʃiz/ **NOUN** a solid, white or yellow food made from milk ❍ *We had bread and cheese for lunch.* ❍ *French cheeses*

chef /ʃɛf/ **NOUN** a cook in a restaurant

chemi|cal /kɛmɪkᵊl/
1 ADJ involved in chemistry or using chemicals ❍ *a chemical reaction* ❍ *chemical weapons*
2 NOUN **Chemicals** are substances made by the use of chemistry. ❍ *the use of chemicals in farming*

chem|ist /kɛmɪst/
1 NOUN a scientist who studies chemistry
2 NOUN A **chemist** is the same as a **pharmacy** or a **pharmacist**. [BRIT]

chem|is|try /kɛmɪstri/ **NONCOUNT NOUN** **Chemistry** is the scientific study of substances and the ways in which they change when they are combined.

cheque /tʃɛk/ [BANKING, BRIT] → **check 6**

cheque ac|count or **chequing account** [BANKING, BRIT] → **checking account**

cher|ry /tʃɛri/ (**cherries**) **NOUN** a small, round fruit with a red or black skin and a stone in the middle

chess /tʃɛs/ **NONCOUNT NOUN** **Chess** is a game for two people, played on a black and white board using different shaped pieces.

chest /tʃɛst/
1 NOUN the top part of the front of your body
2 NOUN a large, strong box for storing things

chew /tʃu/ **VERB** When you **chew** or **chew** food, you break food up in your mouth with your teeth. ❍ *Always chew your food well.*

C

chick|en /tʃɪkɪn/
1 NOUN a bird that is kept on a farm for its eggs and meat
2 NONCOUNT NOUN **Chicken** is the meat of this bird. ❍ *chicken sandwiches*

chief /tʃif/
1 NOUN the leader of a group ❍ *Industry chiefs have said very little.*
2 ADJ main or most important ❍ *New laws on pensions were the chief topic of conversation.*

chief ex|ecu|tive of|fic|er (**chief executive officers**) **NOUN** The **chief executive officer** of a firm is the person who has overall responsibility for the management of that firm. The abbreviation **CEO** is often used. [ADMINISTRATION, BUSINESS MANAGEMENT]

chief fi|nan|cial of|fic|er (**chief financial officers**) **NOUN** The **chief financial officer** of a firm is the person who has responsibility for the financial arrangements of that firm. The abbreviation **CFO** is often used. [FINANCE, ADMINISTRATION]

child /tʃaɪld/ (**children**)
1 NOUN a boy or girl who is not yet an adult ❍ *When I was a child I lived in a village.* ❍ *The show is free for children age 6 and under.*
2 NOUN a son or daughter ❍ *They have three young children.*

child|hood /tʃaɪldhʊd/ **NOUN** the period of time when you are a child ❍ *She had a happy childhood.*

child|ish /tʃaɪldɪʃ/ **ADJ** silly, like the behavior of a small child ❍ *I thought it was very childish of him to refuse to go.*

child la|bor **NONCOUNT NOUN** **Child labor** is the use of children as workers in industry. [HR, BUSINESS MANAGEMENT] ❍ *a boycott of goods made with child labor*

chil|dren /tʃɪldrən/ **Children** is the plural of **child**.

chili /tʃɪli/ (**chilies** or **chilis**) **NOUN** a small red or green vegetable that tastes very hot

chill /tʃɪl/ **VERB** To **chill** something means to make it cold. ❍ *We specialize in transporting chilled foodstuffs.*

▶ **chill out** To **chill out** means to relax. [INFORMAL] ❍ *After work, we chill out and watch TV.*

chil|ly /tʃɪli/ (**chillier, chilliest**) **ADJ** slightly cold ❍ *It was a chilly afternoon.*

chim|ney /tʃɪmni/ **NOUN** a pipe above a fire that lets the smoke travel up and out of the building ❍ *Smoke from chimneys polluted the skies.*

chim|pan|zee /tʃɪmpænzi/ **NOUN** a type of small African ape

chin /tʃɪn/ **NOUN** the part of your face below your mouth

Chin|dia /tʃɪndiə/ **NOUN** China and India considered together in economic and strategic terms [BUSINESS MANAGEMENT]

Chi|nese wall /tʃaɪniz wɔl/ (**Chinese walls**) **NOUN** an imaginary barrier between the parts of a business, across which no information should pass ❍ *There's a Chinese wall between the computer's applications and its operating system.*

chip /tʃɪp/ (**chips, chipping, chipped**)
1 NOUN **Chips** or **potato chips** are very thin slices of fried potato. ❍ *a bag of potato chips*
2 NOUN a very small part that controls a piece of electronic equipment [TECHNOLOGY] ❍ *a computer chip*
3 NOUN a small piece that has been broken off something ❍ *chocolate chip cookies*
4 VERB If you **chip** something, you break a small piece off it. ❍ *I chipped my tooth.*
● **chipped** **ADJ** ❍ *a chipped plate*

chip and PIN **NONCOUNT NOUN** **Chip and PIN** is a method of paying for goods you have bought by using both a bank card and a PIN number. [BANKING, mainly BRIT]

chit /tʃɪt/ **NOUN** a short official note, such as a receipt or a memo, usually signed by someone in authority ❍ *He initialed the chit for the barman.*

choco|late /tʃɔkəlɪt, tʃɔklɪt/
1 NONCOUNT NOUN **Chocolate** is a sweet brown food that you usually buy in a block. ❍ *a bar of chocolate*
2 NONCOUNT NOUN **Chocolate** or **hot**

chocolate is a hot drink made from chocolate.
3 NOUN a small candy covered in chocolate ❍ *a box of chocolates*

choice /tʃɔɪs/
1 NOUN a range of different things that are available to choose from ❍ *It comes in a choice of colors.* ❍ *Customers are demanding a wider choice.*
2 NOUN something that you choose ❍ *The group is at risk if its choice of investments fails.*
3 If you **have no choice**, you cannot choose to do something else. ❍ *We had to agree - we had no choice.*

choir /kwaɪər/ **NOUN** a group of people who regularly sing together ❍ *a church choir*

choke /tʃoʊk/ (**chokes, choking, choked**) **VERB** If you **choke**, you cannot breathe because there is not enough air, or because something is blocking your throat. ❍ *A small child may choke on nuts.*

cho|les|ter|ol /kəlɛstərɔl/ **NONCOUNT NOUN** **Cholesterol** is a substance in your blood that can cause heart disease in large amounts. ❍ *cholesterol levels*

choose /tʃuz/ (**chooses, choosing, chose, chosen**)
1 VERB If you **choose** someone or something, you decide to have that person or thing. ❍ *The first Indian company to venture overseas chose Africa as its destination.* ❍ *You can choose from several different products.*
2 VERB If you **choose to** do something, you do it because you want to. ❍ *She chose to invest in oil.*

chop /tʃɒp/ (**chops, chopping, chopped**) **VERB** If you **chop** something, you cut it into pieces with a knife or other sharp tool. ❍ *Chop the pepper into small pieces.* ❍ *We started chopping wood for a fire.*
▸ **chop down** If you **chop down** a tree, you cut through its trunk (= the thick part that grows up from the ground). ❍ *Sometimes they chop down a tree for firewood.*
▸ **chop off** To **chop** something **off** means to cut it off. ❍ *Chop off the fish's heads and tails.*

chop|stick /tʃɒpstɪk/ **NOUN** one of two thin sticks that people in East Asia use for eating food

chord /kɔrd/ **NOUN** a number of musical notes played or sung at the same time ❍ *I can play a few chords on the guitar.*

cho|rus /kɔrəs/ (**choruses**) **NOUN** the part of a song that you repeat several times ❍ *Join in with the chorus.*

chose /tʃoʊz/ **Chose** is a form of the verb **choose**.

cho|sen /tʃoʊzᵊn/ **Chosen** is a form of the verb **choose**.

chris|ten /krɪsᵊn/ **VERB** When a baby **is christened**, he or she is given a name during a Christian ceremony.

Christian /krɪstʃən/
1 NOUN someone who believes in Jesus Christ, and follows what he taught
2 ADJ relating to Christians ❍ *the Christian Church*

Chris|ti|an|ity /krɪstʃiænɪti/ **NONCOUNT NOUN** **Christianity** is a religion that believes in Jesus Christ and follows what he taught.

Christian name (**Christian names**) [mainly BRIT] → **first name**

Christ|mas /krɪsməs/ (**Christmases**) **NOUN** the period around the 25th of December, when Christians celebrate the birth of Jesus Christ ❍ *"Merry Christmas!"* ❍ *the Christmas holidays*

Christ|mas Day **NONCOUNT NOUN** **Christmas Day** is the 25th of December, when Christians celebrate the day that Jesus Christ was born.

Christ|mas Eve **NONCOUNT NOUN** **Christmas Eve** is the 24th of December, the day before Christmas Day.

chub|by /tʃʌbi/ (**chubbier, chubbiest**) **ADJ** slightly fat ❍ *a little boy with chubby cheeks*

chunk /tʃʌŋk/ **NOUN** a thick, solid piece of something ❍ *Large chunks of ice floated past us.*

church /tʃɜrtʃ/ (**churches**) **NOUN** a building where Christians go to pray ❍ *We got married in Coburn United Methodist Church.* ❍ *They've gone to church.*

c.i.f. /si aɪ ɛf/ or **CIF** **c.i.f.** is an abbreviation for "cost, insurance, and freight." [LOGISTICS

AND DISTRIBUTION, FINANCE] ❍ *the CIF value of imported capital goods*

ci|gar /sɪgɑr/ NOUN a roll of dried tobacco leaves that some people smoke

ciga|rette /sɪgərɛt/ NOUN a small tube of paper containing dried leaves (= tobacco) that some people smoke

C

CIM /si aɪ ɛm/ NONCOUNT NOUN **CIM** is a manufacturing method that uses computers to improve the speed and efficiency of the production process. **CIM** is short for "computer-integrated manufacture." [BUSINESS MANAGEMENT, PRODUCTION] ❍ *CIM allows manufacturers to make customized products in small batches, at costs close to those of mass-produced goods.*

cin|ema /sɪnɪmə/ NOUN a building where people go to watch movies ❍ *a multiplex cinema*

cir|cle /sɜrkᵊl/ NOUN a round shape ❍ *The company logo is a white square with a red circle in the center.*

cir|cuit /sɜrkɪt/

1 NOUN a track that cars race around ❍ *the grand prix circuit*

2 NOUN An electrical **circuit** is a complete path that electricity can flow around.

cir|cu|lar /sɜrkyələr/ ADJ shaped like a circle ❍ *a circular building*

cir|cu|late /sɜrkyəleɪt/ (**circulates, circulating, circulated**) VERB When something **circulates**, it moves easily and freely in a place. ❍ *The blood circulates through the body.*

cir|cu|la|tion /sɜrkyəleɪʃən/

1 NONCOUNT NOUN **Circulation** is the movement of blood through your body. ❍ *Regular exercise is good for the circulation.*

2 NONCOUNT NOUN **Circulation** is the free movement of something, such as money or air, around a place. [ECONOMICS] ❍ *This ensures the circulation of air within the building.* ❍ *The broadest measure of the money supply includes deposits of most major financial institutions and currency in circulation.*

cir|cum|stance /sɜrkəmstæns/ NOUN **Circumstances** are the facts about a particular situation. ❍ *The marketing systems of most firms are influenced by external economic circumstances.* ❍ *Under normal circumstances, this process would only take about 20 minutes.*

cir|cus /sɜrkəs/ (**circuses**) NOUN a group of people and animals that travels around to different places and performs shows ❍ *circus clowns*

citi|zen /sɪtɪzᵊn/

1 NOUN someone who legally belongs to a particular country ❍ *We are proud to be American citizens.*

2 NOUN someone who lives in a particular town or city ❍ *the citizens of Buenos Aires*

city /sɪti/ (**cities**) NOUN a large town ❍ *We visited the city of Los Angeles.*

City /sɪti/ NOUN **The City** is the area of London that contains the main financial institutions. [BANKING] ❍ *Rumors in the City sent the share price tumbling.*

civ|il /sɪvᵊl/

1 ADJ connected with the people of a country and their activities ❍ *civil unrest*

2 ADJ connected with the state, and not with the army or the church ❍ *We had a civil wedding in the town hall.*

3 ADJ polite, although not friendly [FORMAL] ❍ *Try to at least be civil to him.*

ci|vil|ian /sɪvɪlyən/ NOUN a person who is not a member of a military organization ❍ *The soldiers were not shooting at civilians.*

civi|li|sa|tion /sɪvɪlɪzeɪʃən/ [BRIT] → **civilization**

civi|lised /sɪvɪlaɪzd/ [BRIT] → **civilized**

civi|li|za|tion /sɪvɪlɪzeɪʃən/ NOUN a group of people with their own social organization and culture ❍ *the ancient civilizations of Greece*

civi|lized /sɪvɪlaɪzd/

1 ADJ A **civilized** country or society is very advanced in its laws and organization, its education, and culture. ❍ *Boxing should be illegal in a civilized society.*

2 ADJ polite and reasonable ❍ *We discussed the matter in a civilized manner.*

civ|il war (**civil wars**) NOUN a war between different groups of people who live in the same country ❍ *the American Civil War*

claim /kleɪm/

1 VERB If someone **claims** something, they say that it is true. ❍ *The firm claims to have continued operations through the war.* ❍ *He had claimed to be very rich.*

2 NOUN something that someone says is true ❍ *Most people just don't believe their claims.*

3 VERB If you **claim** something, you say that it belongs to you. ❍ *If nobody claims the money, you can keep it.*

4 NOUN something that you ask for because you think you should have it ❍ *an insurance claim*

claims ad|just|er (**claims adjusters**) also **claims adjustor** **NOUN** someone who is employed by an insurance company to decide how much money a person making a claim should receive [BANKING, ADMINISTRATION]

clamp /klæmp/

1 NOUN a piece of equipment that holds two things together

2 VERB When you **clamp** one thing **to** another, you fasten the two things together with a clamp. ❍ *Clamp the microphone to the stand.*

clap /klæp/ (**claps, clapping, clapped**) **VERB** When you **clap**, you hit your hands together, usually to show that you like something. ❍ *The audience clapped.* ❍ *Margaret clapped her hands.*

clari|fy /klærɪfaɪ/ (**clarifies, clarifying, clarified**) **VERB** To **clarify** something means to make it easier to understand, usually by explaining it. [FORMAL] ❍ *I would like to clarify those remarks I made.*

clar|ity /klærɪti/ **NONCOUNT NOUN** **Clarity** is the quality of being clear and easy to understand. ❍ *This new law will bring some clarity to the situation.*

clash /klæʃ/ (**clashes, clashing, clashed**)

1 VERB When people **clash**, they fight or argue with each other. ❍ *He often clashed with his staff.*

2 NOUN **Clash** is also a noun. ❍ *Management clashes between merged companies were blamed.*

3 VERB If one color **clashes with** another, they do not look nice together. ❍ *His pink shirt clashed with his red hair.*

class /klæs/ (**classes**)

1 NOUN a group of students who learn at school together ❍ *He spent six months in a class with younger students.*

2 NOUN a period of time when you learn something at school ❍ *Classes start at 9 o'clock.* ❍ *We do lots of reading in class.*

3 NOUN a group of things that are the same in some way ❍ *You may only exchange between the same class of shares.*

4 NOUN one of the social groups into which people are divided ❍ *the relationship between different social classes*

clas|sic /klæsɪk/

1 ADJ A **classic** movie or piece of writing is very good, and has been popular for a long time. ❍ *Fleming directed the classic movie "The Wizard of Oz."*

2 NOUN **Classic** is also a noun. ❍ *"Jailhouse Rock" is one of the classics of modern popular music.*

3 NONCOUNT NOUN **Classics** is the study of the languages, literature, and cultures of ancient Greece and Rome.

clas|si|cal /klæsɪkᵊl/ **ADJ** used for describing music that is traditional in form, style, or content ❍ *I like listening to classical music and reading.*

clas|si|fy /klæsɪfaɪ/ (**classifies, classifying, classified**) **VERB** To **classify** things means to divide them into groups or types. ❍ *They are classified as limited liability companies.*

class|mate /klæsmeɪt/ **NOUN** a student who is in the same class as you at school

class|room /klæsrum/ **NOUN** a room in a school where lessons take place

clause /klɔz/ **NOUN** in grammar, a group of words that contains a verb

claw /klɔ/ **NOUN** one of the thin, pointed parts at the end of the foot of a bird or animal ❍ *Kittens have very sharp claws and teeth.*

clay /kleɪ/ **NONCOUNT NOUN** **Clay** is a type of earth that is soft when it is wet and hard when it is dry, and is used for making things such as pots and bricks. ❍ *a clay pot*

C

clean /klin/ (**cleaner, cleanest**)
1 ADJ free from dirt ❍ *Are your hands clean?* ❍ *clean clothes*
2 VERB If you **clean** something, you remove the dirt from it. ❍ *He cleaned the windows.*
▸ **clean up**
1 If you **clean up** a place, you clean it completely. ❍ *Hundreds of workers are cleaning up the beaches.*
2 If you **clean up** dirt, you remove it from a place. ❍ *Who is going to clean up this mess?*

clean|er /klinər/ NOUN a substance or a piece of equipment used for cleaning things ❍ *an oven cleaner*

clear /klɪər/ (**clearer, clearest**)
1 ADJ easy to understand, see, or hear ❍ *clear instructions* ❍ *This camera takes very clear pictures.*
2 ADJ obvious ❍ *It is clear that things will have to change.* ● **clear|ly** ADV ❍ *Sport has clearly become a global business.*
3 ADJ without color and easy to see through ❍ *clear glass*
4 ADJ not having anything blocking the way ❍ *The runway is clear—you can land.*
5 ADJ with no clouds ❍ *a clear blue sky*
6 VERB When you **clear** a place, you remove things from it. ❍ *Can someone clear the table, please?*
7 VERB When the sky **clears**, the clouds disappear. ❍ *The sky cleared and the sun came out.*
▸ **clear away** When you **clear** things **away**, you put away the things that you have been using. ❍ *The waitress cleared away the plates.*
▸ **clear out** If you **clear out** a closet or a place, you make it neat and throw away the things in it that you no longer want. ❍ *I cleared out my desk before I left.*
▸ **clear up** When you **clear up**, you make things neat and put them away. ❍ *The children played while I cleared up.*

clear|ance /klɪərəns/
1 NONCOUNT NOUN **Clearance** is the process by which a check is paid by one bank to another. [BANKING] ❍ *The report said that check clearance was too slow.*
2 NOUN If you get **clearance to** do or have something, you get official approval or permission to do or have it. ❍ *He has a security clearance that allows him access to classified information.*

clear|ing bank (**clearing banks**) NOUN one of the main banks in Britain [BANKING, BRIT]

clear|ing house (**clearing houses**) or **clearinghouse** NOUN a central bank that deals with all the business between the banks that use its services [BANKING]

clerk /klɜrk/
1 NOUN a person whose job is to work with numbers or documents in an office [ADMINISTRATION] ❍ *She works as a clerk in a travel agency.*
2 NOUN someone who sells things to customers in a store, or who works behind the main desk in a hotel [ADMINISTRATION] ❍ *Thomas was working as a clerk in a shoe store.*

clev|er /klɛvər/ (**cleverer, cleverest**) ADJ very intelligent ❍ *He's a very clever man.* ● **clev|er|ly** ADV ❍ *The firm has reacted cleverly by cutting its own prices.*

click /klɪk/
1 VERB If something **clicks** or if you **click** it, it makes a short, sharp sound. ❍ *Hundreds of cameras clicked as she stepped out of the car.*
2 NOUN **Click** is also a noun. ❍ *I heard a click and then her recorded voice.*
3 VERB If you **click** on a part of a computer screen, you press one of the buttons on the mouse in order to make something happen on the screen. ❍ *I clicked on a link.*
4 NOUN **Click** is also a noun. ❍ *You can access this information with a click of your mouse.*

clicks-and-mortar ADJ A **clicks-and-mortar** business makes use of traditional trading methods in conjunction with Internet trading. [ECONOMICS]

click|stream /klɪkstrim/ NOUN a record of the path taken by users through a website [TECHNOLOGY]

cli|ent /klaɪənt/ NOUN a person who pays someone for a service ❍ *A lawyer and his client were sitting at the next table.*

COLLOCATIONS
client *service*
client *list*

cli|ent base (**client bases**) NOUN A business's **client base** is the same as its **customer base**. [MARKETING AND SALES] ○ *a client base of more than 2,000 organizations worldwide* ○ *the group has struggled to expand its client base*

cliff /klɪf/ NOUN a high area of land with a very steep side ○ *The car rolled over the edge of a cliff.*

cli|mate /klaɪmɪt/ NONCOUNT NOUN The **climate** of a place is the normal weather there. ○ *She loves the hot and humid climate of Florida.*

cli|max /klaɪmæks/ (**climaxes**) NOUN the most exciting or important moment of something, usually near the end ○ *the climax of the dotcom boom*

climb /klaɪm/
1 VERB If you **climb** or **climb up** something, you move toward the top of it. ○ *Climbing the hill took half an hour.* ○ *Climb up the steps onto the bridge.*
2 NOUN **Climb** is also a noun. ○ *It was a hard climb to the top of the mountain.*
3 VERB If you **climb** somewhere, you move into or out of a small space. ○ *He climbed into the car and drove off.*

climb|er /klaɪmər/ NOUN a person who climbs rocks or mountains ○ *a mountain climber*

cling /klɪŋ/ (**clings, clinging, clung**) VERB If you **cling to** someone or something, you hold them tightly. ○ *He was found clinging to the boat.*

clin|ic /klɪnɪk/ NOUN a place where people receive medical advice or treatment

clip /klɪp/ (**clips, clipping, clipped**)
1 NOUN a small object for holding things together ○ *She took the clip out of her hair.*
2 NOUN a short piece from a movie ○ *They showed a film clip of the Apollo moon landing.*
3 VERB When you **clip** things together, you fasten them using a clip. ○ *Clip the rope onto the ring.*

clock /klɒk/ NOUN a device that shows what time of day it is ○ *He could hear a clock ticking.*

clock-watcher (**clock-watchers**) NOUN an employee who checks the time in anticipation of a break of the end of the working day

clock|wise /klɒkwaɪz/
1 ADV moving in a circle in the same direction as the hands on a clock ○ *The children started moving clockwise around the room.*
2 ADJ **Clockwise** is also an adjective. ○ *in a clockwise direction*

close
❶ SHUTTING
❷ NEARNESS

❶ **close** /kloʊz/ (**closes, closing, closed**)
1 VERB When something such as a door **closes**, it moves so that it is no longer open and when you **close** something such as a door, you move it so that it is no longer open. ○ *If you get cold, close the window.* ○ *The door closed behind her.*
2 VERB If a store **closes** at a certain time, people cannot use it after that time. If a store is **closed** on a certain day, people cannot use it on that day. ○ *The store closes at noon.* ○ *The store closes on public holidays.*
3 VERB If a stock exchange **closes** at a certain time, people cannot trade after that time. [FINANCE] ○ *Floor trading closes at 4:30pm.*
4 VERB If you **close** a bank account, you take all your money out of it and inform the bank that you will no longer be using the account. [BANKING] ○ *He had closed his account with the bank five years earlier.*
▸ **close down** If a business **closes down**, all work stops there, usually for ever. ○ *That store closed down years ago.*

❷ **close** /kloʊs/
1 ADJ near to something else ○ *Is the apartment close to the beach?* ○ *He moved closer.*
2 ADJ People who are **close** like each other very much and know each other well. ○ *She was very close to her sister.* ○ *close friends*
3 ADJ careful and complete ○ *Let's have a closer look.*

C

4 ADJ won by only a small amount ❍ *It was a close contest for a Senate seat.*

closed /kloʊzd/ **ADJ** When a store or business is **closed**, it is not open and you cannot buy or do anything there. ❍ *The office was closed when we got there.*

C

closed shop (**closed shops**) **NOUN** If a factory, store, or other business is a **closed shop**, the employees must be members of a particular trade union. [HR] ❍ *the trade union which they are required to join under the closed shop agreement*

clos|et /klɒzɪt/ **NOUN** a very small room for storing things, especially clothes ❍ *My closet is full of clothes that I never wear.*

clos|ing price (**closing prices**) **NOUN** the price of a share at the end of a day's business on the stock exchange [ECONOMICS] ❍ *The price is slightly above yesterday's closing price.*

cloth /klɔθ/

1 NONCOUNT NOUN **Cloth** is material that is used for making clothing. ❍ *a piece of cloth*

2 NOUN a piece of material that you use for cleaning or drying things ❍ *Clean the surface with a damp cloth.*

clothes /kloʊz, kloʊðz/ **PL NOUN** **Clothes** are the things that people wear, such as shirts and dresses. ❍ *Milly went upstairs to change her clothes.*

cloth|ing /kloʊðɪŋ/ **NONCOUNT NOUN** **Clothing** is the things that people wear. ❍ *a women's clothing store*

cloud /klaʊd/

1 NOUN a white or gray mass in the sky that contains drops of water ❍ *rain clouds*

2 NOUN A **cloud of** smoke or dust is an amount of it floating in the air. ❍ *A cloud of black smoke spread across the sky.*

cloudy /klaʊdi/ (**cloudier, cloudiest**) **ADJ** with a lot of clouds in the sky ❍ *a cloudy sky*

clown /klaʊn/ **NOUN** a performer who wears funny clothes and make-up, and does silly things to make people laugh

club /klʌb/

1 NOUN an organization of people with a particular interest who meet regularly, or the place where they meet ❍ *He joined the local golf club.* ❍ *I stopped at the club for a drink.*

2 NOUN A **club** is the same as a **nightclub**. ❍ *The streets are full of bars, clubs, and restaurants.*

3 NOUN a long, thin, metal stick that you use to hit the ball in the game of golf ❍ *a set of golf clubs*

4 NOUN a thick, heavy stick that is used as a weapon ❍ *The men were carrying knives and clubs.*

clue /klu/ **NOUN** a piece of information that helps you to find an answer ❍ *Unsold gold gives clues about the direction of the economy.*

clum|sy /klʌmzi/ (**clumsier, clumsiest**) **ADJ** not moving in an easy way and often breaking things ❍ *As a child she was very clumsy.*

clung /klʌŋ/ **Clung** is a form of the verb **cling**.

clutch /klʌtʃ/ (**clutches, clutching, clutched**)

1 VERB If you **clutch** something, you hold it very tightly. ❍ *Michelle clutched my arm.*

2 NOUN in a vehicle, the part that you press with your foot before you change gears

cm **cm** is short for **centimeter** or **centimeters**.

c/o You write **c/o** before an address on an envelope when you are sending it to someone who is staying or working at that address, often for only a short time. **c/o** is an abbreviation for "care of."

Co. /koʊ/ **Co.** is an abbreviation for **company**. [BUSINESS MANAGEMENT] ❍ *Telephone & Telegraph Co.*

coach /koʊtʃ/ (**coaches, coaching, coached**)

1 NOUN someone who is in charge of teaching a person or a sports team ❍ *She's the women's soccer coach at Rowan University.*

2 VERB If you **coach** someone, you help them to become better at a particular sport or skill. ❍ *She coached a golf team in San José.*

coachee /koʊtʃi/ **NOUN** a person who receives training from a coach in business or office practice [HR]

coal /koʊl/ **NONCOUNT NOUN** **Coal** is a hard black substance that comes from under the ground and is burned to give heat. ❍ *The area's timber and coal industries are in decline.*

coast /koʊst/ **NOUN** the edge of the land where it meets the ocean ❍ *They are planning to build a pipeline to the west coast.* ● **coast|al** /koʊstᵊl/ **ADJ** ❍ *Coastal areas have been flooded.*

coat /koʊt/
1 NOUN a piece of clothing with long sleeves that you wear over other clothes ❍ *He put on his coat and walked out.*
2 NOUN An animal's **coat** is its fur or hair.
3 NOUN A **coat of** paint is a thin layer of it. ❍ *The front door needs a new coat of paint.*
4 VERB If you **coat** something **with** a substance, you cover it with a thin layer of it. ❍ *The probe is a piece of optical fiber coated in aluminum.*

cock|tail /kɒkteɪl/
1 NOUN an alcoholic drink that is a mixture of several drinks ❍ *a champagne cocktail*
2 NOUN a mixture of a number of different things ❍ *a cocktail of chemicals*

coco|nut /koʊkənʌt/ **NOUN** a very large nut with a hairy shell that grows on trees in warm countries, or the white flesh of this nut ❍ *Add two cups of grated coconut.*

COD /sɪ oʊ di/ **COD** is an abbreviation for **cash on delivery**. [PURCHASING]

code /koʊd/
1 NOUN a secret way to replace the words in a message with other words or symbols, so that some people will not understand the message ❍ *They sent messages using codes.*
2 NOUN a group of numbers or letters that gives information about something ❍ *The area code for western Pennsylvania is 412.*

code of prac|tice (**codes of practice**) **NOUN** a set of written rules that explains how people working in a particular profession should behave [BUSINESS MANAGEMENT] ❍ *The auctioneers are violating a code of practice by dealing in stolen goods.*

code-sharing **NONCOUNT NOUN** **Code-sharing** is a commercial agreement between two airlines that allows passengers to use a ticket from one airline to travel on another. ❍ *American carriers are making their own code-sharing arrangements with overseas airlines.*

cof|fee /kɔfi/ **NONCOUNT NOUN** **Coffee** is the beans (= seeds) of the coffee plant, made into a powder, or a hot drink made with this powder. ❍ *Would you like some coffee?*

cof|fin /kɔfɪn/ **NOUN** a box that you put a dead person in when you bury them

COGS /si oʊ dʒi ɛs/ **COGS** is an abbreviation for "cost of goods sold." [FINANCE] ❍ *We have achieved $60 million in COGS productivity improvements.*

co|her|ent /koʊhɪərənt, -hɛrənt/ **ADJ** clear, sensible, and able to be understood ❍ *We need a coherent marketing strategy.* ❍ *He wasn't capable of holding a coherent conversation.* ● **co|her|ence** /koʊhɪərəns, -hɛrəns/ **NONCOUNT NOUN** ❍ *I thought the business plan lacked coherence.* ● **co|her|ent|ly** **ADV** ❍ *He can't even express himself coherently.*

coin /kɔɪn/ **NOUN** a small round piece of metal money ❍ *She put the coins in her pocket.*

co|in|cide /koʊɪnsaɪd/ (**coincides, coinciding, coincided**) **VERB** If one event **coincides with** another, they happen at the same time. ❍ *The launch coincides with the European Computer Trade show.*

co|in|ci|dence /koʊɪnsɪdəns/ **NOUN** a situation in which two or more things occur at the same time by chance ❍ *It was just a coincidence that they arrived at the same time.*

COLA /koʊlə/
1 COLA is an increase in benefit payments according to the rate of inflation. **COLA** is short for "cost of living adjustment." [ECONOMICS]
2 COLA is extra money paid to workers in areas where the cost of living is more expensive. **COLA** is short for "cost of living allowance." [ECONOMICS]

cold /koʊld/
1 ADJ Someone or something that is cold has a low temperature. ❍ *cold water* ❍ *It's cold outside.* ❍ *Put on a sweater if you're cold.*
2 ADJ not showing emotion and not friendly

○ *His boss was a cold, unfeeling woman.*
3 NOUN a slight illness that makes liquid flow from your nose and makes you cough ○ *She has a bad cold.*
4 ADJ **Cold** business practices involve contacting customers who have not been contacted before and have shown no interest in a product. ○ *cold mailing*
5 If you **catch cold**, or **catch a cold**, you become ill with a cold.

cold call (**cold calls, cold calling, cold called**) also **cold-call**
1 NOUN If someone makes a **cold call**, they telephone or visit someone they have never contacted, without making an appointment, in order to try and sell something. [MARKETING AND SALES] ○ *She had worked as a call center operator making cold calls for time-share vacations.*
2 VERB **Cold call** is also a verb. ○ *You should refuse to meet anyone who cold-calls you with an offer of financial advice.* ● **cold calling** **NONCOUNT NOUN** ○ *Spam allows unethical businesses to target many more potential investors than cold calling or mass mailing.*

col|lapse /kəlæps/ (**collapses, collapsing, collapsed**)
1 VERB If a structure or a person **collapses**, they fall down very suddenly. ○ *A bridge had collapsed in the storm.* ○ *He collapsed at his home last night.*
2 NONCOUNT NOUN **Collapse** is also a noun. ○ *A few days after his collapse he was sitting up in bed.*

col|lar /kɒlər/
1 NOUN the part of a shirt or coat that goes around the neck and is usually folded over ○ *He pulled up his jacket collar in the cold wind.*
2 NOUN a band of leather or plastic that you put around the neck of a dog or cat

col|lat|er|al /kəlætərəl/ **NONCOUNT NOUN** **Collateral** is money or property that is used as a guarantee that someone will repay a loan. [BANKING, ECONOMICS, FORMAL] ○ *Many people use personal assets as collateral for small business loans.*

col|league /kɒlig/ **NOUN** a person that you work with ○ *friends and colleagues*

col|lect /kəlɛkt/
1 VERB If you **collect** things, you bring them together from several places or several people. ○ *The Commerce Department has many roles, such as collecting economic statistics.*
2 VERB If you **collect** things, you get them and save them over a period of time because you like them. ○ *I collect stamps.*

col|lec|tion /kəlɛkʃən/
1 NOUN a group of similar or related things ○ *He has a large collection of paintings.*
2 NONCOUNT NOUN **Collection** is the process of bringing many things together from several places or people. ○ *the collection of data*

col|lec|tive /kəlɛktɪv/
1 ADJ **Collective** actions, situations, or feelings involve or are shared by every member of a group of people. ○ *It was a collective decision.* ● **col|lec|tive|ly** **ADV** ○ *They collectively decided to recognize the changed situation.*
2 ADJ A **collective** amount of something is the total obtained by adding together the amounts that each person or thing in a group has. ○ *Their collective volume wasn't very large.* ● **col|lec|tive|ly** **ADV** ○ *In 1968 the states collectively spent $2 billion on it.*
3 NOUN a business or farm that is run, and often owned, by a group of people [BUSINESS MANAGEMENT] ○ *He will see that he is participating in all the decisions of the collective.*

col|lec|tive agree|ment (**collective agreements**) **NOUN** a negotiated agreement between an employer and employees' representatives covering rates of pay or terms and conditions of employment [HR, LEGAL] ○ *The greater variation of jobs in the workforce has made it harder to implement collective agreements.*

col|lec|tive bar|gain|ing **NONCOUNT NOUN** When a labor union engages in **collective bargaining**, it has talks with an employer about its members' pay and working conditions. [LEGAL] ○ *a new collective-bargaining agreement*

col|lege /kɒlɪdʒ/ **NOUN** a place where students study after they leave high school ○ *Lauren is attending a local college.* ○ *I have one son in college.*

col|lide /kəlaɪd/ (**collides, colliding, collided**) VERB If people or vehicles **collide**, they hit each other. ❍ *The two cars collided.*

col|li|sion /kəlɪʒᵊn/ NOUN an accident in which two moving objects hit each other ❍ *Fifty-three passengers were killed in the collision.*

col|lude /kəlud/ (**colludes, colluding, colluded**) VERB If one person **colludes with** another, they cooperate with them secretly or illegally. ❍ *Several local officials are in jail on charges of colluding with the Mafia.* ❍ *We all colluded in the myth of him as the swanky businessman.* ● **col|lu|sion** NONCOUNT NOUN ❍ *Some stockbrokers, in collusion with bank officials, obtained large sums of money for speculation.*

colo|ny /kɒləni/ (**colonies**) NOUN an area or a group of people that is controlled by another country ❍ *Massachusetts was a British colony.*

col|or /kʌlər/ NOUN red, blue, green, pink, etc. ❍ *"What color is the car?"—"It's red."* ❍ *The products are available in a range of colors.*

col|or|ful /kʌlərfəl/ ADJ having many bright colors ❍ *colorful clothes*

col|our /kʌlər/ [BRIT] → **color**

col|our|ful /kʌlərfəl/ [BRIT] → **colorful**

col|umn /kɒləm/

1 NOUN a tall, solid structure that supports part of a building ❍ *The house has six white columns across the front.*

2 NOUN a group of short lines of words or numbers on a page ❍ *In the left column you'll see a list of names.*

coma /koʊmə/ NOUN If someone is **in** a **coma**, they are not conscious for a long time. ❍ *She was in a coma for seven weeks.*

> **BUSINESS ETIQUETTE**
> There are many parts of the world where people regularly drink alcohol as a way of building relationships. In contrast, other cultures strongly disapprove of drinking. Before you travel abroad on business, find out whether drinking alcohol is acceptable there.

comb /koʊm/

1 NOUN a flat object with long, thin pointed parts that you use for making your hair neat

2 VERB When you **comb** your hair, you make it neat using a comb. ❍ *He combed his hair.*

com|bat (**combats, combating** or **combatting, combated** or **combatted**)

> Pronounce the noun /kɒmbæt/.
> Pronounce the verb /kəmbæt/.

1 NONCOUNT NOUN **Combat** is fighting during a war. ❍ *More than 16 million men died in combat.*

2 VERB If people in authority try to **combat** something, they try to stop it from happening. ❍ *Stimulus packages were announced to combat the economic downturn.*

com|bi|na|tion /kɒmbɪneɪʃən/ NOUN a mixture of things ❍ *Pay can be based on skill, position, length of service, or some combination of these factors.*

com|bine /kəmbaɪn/ (**combines, combining, combined**) VERB If you **combine** two or more things, you join them together, and if things **combine** they join together. ❍ *The merged firm can combine its effort, perhaps to launch a joint brand.* ❍ *Growing trade, increased efficiency, and investment may combine to produce higher growth rates.*

come /kʌm/ (**comes, coming, came, come**)

1 VERB You use **come** to say that someone or something arrives somewhere, or moves toward you. ❍ *Several employees came into the room.* ❍ *Our finance director came to see me this morning.* ❍ *Come here, Tom.*

2 VERB When an event or time **comes**, it happens. ❍ *The announcement came after an emergency board meeting.*

3 VERB If someone or something **comes from** a particular place, that place is where they started. ❍ *She comes from Spain.* ❍ *Most of Germany's oil comes from the North Sea.*

4 VERB If someone or something **comes** first, next, or last, they are first, next, or last. ❍ *I came last in the race.*

▶ **come across** If you **come across** something or someone, you find them or meet them by chance. ❍ *I came across this article in a magazine.*

C

▶**come back** If someone **comes back** to a place, they return to it. ❍ *He came back to Washington.*

▶**come in** If someone **comes in**, they enter a place. ❍ *Come in and sit down.*

▶**come on** You say **"Come on"** to someone to encourage them to do something or to be quicker. [SPOKEN] ❍ *Come on, or we'll be late.*

▶**come out** When the sun **comes out**, it appears in the sky because the clouds have moved away.

▶**come up**

1 If something **comes up** in a conversation, someone mentions it. ❍ *The subject came up at work.*

2 When the sun **comes up**, it rises. ❍ *We watched the sun come up.*

com|edy /kɒmədi/ (**comedies**) NOUN a play, a movie, or a television program that is intended to make people laugh ❍ *a romantic comedy*

com|fort /kʌmfərt/

1 NONCOUNT NOUN **Comfort** is the state of being relaxed, and having no pain. ❍ *You can sit in comfort while you watch the show.*

2 VERB If you **comfort** someone, you make them feel less worried or unhappy. ❍ *They were somewhat comforted by the latest sales figures.*

com|fort|able /kʌmftəbᵊl, -fərtəbᵊl/

1 ADJ making you feel physically relaxed ❍ *a comfortable chair*

2 ADJ feeling physically relaxed and having no pain ❍ *Sit down and make yourself comfortable.*

● **com|fort|ably** ADV ❍ *Are you sitting comfortably?*

com|ic /kɒmɪk/ ADJ intended to make you laugh ❍ *a comic film*

comi|cal /kɒmɪkᵊl/ ADJ If something is **comical**, it makes you want to laugh because it is funny or silly. ❍ *She had a slightly comical look on her face.*

com|ma /kɒmə/ NOUN the punctuation mark ,

com|mand /kəmænd/

1 NOUN an official instruction to do something ❍ *He shouted commands at his staff.* ❍ *He obeyed the command.*

2 NOUN an instruction that you give to a computer

3 VERB If someone **commands** you to do something, they tell you that you must do it. ❍ *He commanded his soldiers to attack.*

com|mand econo|my (**command economies**) NOUN an economy in which business activities and the use of resources are decided by the government, and not by market forces [ECONOMICS] ❍ *the Czech Republic's transition from a command economy to a market system*

com|ment /kɒmɛnt/

1 VERB If you **comment on** something, you give your opinion or say something about it. ❍ *He has not commented on these reports.*

2 NOUN something that you say about a person or a situation ❍ *She made a few comments on what I'd written.*

com|merce /kɒmɜrs/ NONCOUNT NOUN **Commerce** is the buying and selling of large amounts of goods. [ECONOMICS] ❍ *international commerce* ❍ *They have made their fortunes from industry and commerce.*

com|mer|cial /kəmɜrʃᵊl/

1 ADJ concerned with making money and profits [ECONOMICS] ❍ *New York is a center of commercial activity.*

2 ADJ relating to the buying and selling of goods [ECONOMICS] ❍ *Whether the project will be a commercial success is still uncertain.*

3 NOUN an advertisement on television or radio

com|mer|cial art|ist (**commercial artists**) NOUN a person who creates art for advertising and product packaging [MARKETING AND SALES]

com|mer|cial bank (**commercial banks**) NOUN a bank that makes short-term loans using money from money deposited in current accounts [BANKING]

com|mer|cial|ise /kəmɜrʃəlaɪz/ [MARKETING AND SALES, BRIT] → **commercialize**

com|mer|cial|ize /kəmɜrʃəlaɪz/ (**commercializes, commercializing, commercialized**) VERB If something **is**

commercialized, it is used or changed in such a way that it makes money, often in a way that people disapprove of. [MARKETING AND SALES] ❍ *It seems such a pity that a distinguished and honored name should be commercialized in this way.* ● **com|mer|cial|ized** ADJ ❍ *Rock'n'roll has become so commercialized and safe since punk.* ● **com|mer|ciali|za|tion** /kəmɜrʃəlɪzeɪʃən/ NONCOUNT NOUN ❍ *the commercialization of Christmas*

com|mis|sion /kəmɪʃən/ (**commissions, commissioning, commissioned**)
1 VERB If you **commission** something or **commission** someone **to** do something, you formally arrange for someone to do a piece of work for you. ❍ *The Department of Agriculture commissioned a study into organic farming.* ❍ *You can commission them to paint something especially for you.*
2 NOUN **Commission** is also a noun. ❍ *Our pottery can be bought off the shelf or by commission.*
3 NONCOUNT NOUN **Commission** is money paid to a salesperson for every sale that he or she makes. If salespeople are paid **on commission**, the amount they receive depends on the amount they sell. [ECONOMICS] ❍ *The salespeople work on commission only.*
4 NONCOUNT NOUN If a bank or other company charges **commission**, they charge a fee for providing a service, for example for exchanging money or issuing an insurance policy. [ECONOMICS] ❍ *Travel agents charge 1 percent commission on tickets.*

com|mit /kəmɪt/
1 VERB If someone **commits** a crime, they do something illegal. ❍ *I have never committed a crime.*
2 VERB If you **commit** to something such as a purchase or an agreement, you say that you will definitely buy it or agree to it. ❍ *You don't have to commit to anything over the phone.* ❍ *Banks and retailers committed themselves to launching smartcards by the end of the year.*

com|mit|ment /kəmɪtmənt/
1 NONCOUNT NOUN **Commitment** is when you work hard at something that you think is important. ❍ *Increasing competition from abroad weakened their commitment to free trade.*
2 NOUN If you make a **commitment to** do something, you promise to do it. ❍ *They made a commitment to lower interest rates.*

com|mit|tee /kəmɪti/ NOUN a group of people who meet to make decisions or plans for a larger group ❍ *He chaired an eight-member committee of outside directors.*

com|mod|ity /kəmɒdɪti/ (**commodities**) NOUN something that is sold for money [BUSINESS MANAGEMENT] ❍ *Prices went up on several basic commodities like bread and meat.*

com|mon /kɒmən/
1 ADJ existing in large numbers or happening often ❍ *This practice is common in the car industry.* ❍ *a common cause of staff dissatisfaction* ● **com|mon|ly** ADV ❍ *These chemicals were commonly used in the grain industry.*
2 ADJ shared by two or more people or groups ❍ *Three characteristics are common to many of today's takeover transactions.*
3 If people or things have something **in common**, they have similar qualities or interests. ❍ *He had nothing in common with his colleagues.*

com|mon car|rier (**common carriers**) NOUN a person or firm in the business of transporting goods or passengers [LOGISTICS AND DISTRIBUTION] ❍ *Deliveries are made by common carrier.*

com|mon mar|ket (**common markets**)
1 NOUN an organization of countries who have agreed to trade freely with each other and make common decisions about industry and agriculture [ECONOMICS] ❍ *the Central American Common Market*
2 NOUN **The Common Market** is the former name of the **European Union**. [ECONOMICS]

com|mon sense also **commonsense** NONCOUNT NOUN **Common sense** is the ability to make good judgments and to be sensible. ❍ *Use common sense: don't use obvious passwords.*

com|mon stock NONCOUNT NOUN **Common stock** refers to the shares in a company that are owned by people who have a right to vote at the company's meetings and to receive part of the company's profits after the holders of preferred stock have been paid. Compare with **preferred stock**. [ECONOMICS, FINANCE] ○ *The company priced its offering of 2.7 million shares of common stock at 20 cents a share.*

C

com|mu|ni|cate /kəmyu̲nɪkeɪt/ (**communicates, communicating, communicated**) VERB If you **communicate with** other people, you share information with them, for example by speaking or writing. ○ *They communicate regularly by email.*

com|mu|ni|ca|tion /kəmyu̲nɪke̲ɪʃən/
1 NONCOUNT NOUN **Communication** is the process by which people or animals exchange information. ○ *Good communication is vital in business.*
2 PL NOUN **Communications** are ways of sending or receiving information. ○ *a communications satellite*

com|mun|ism /kɒ̲myənɪzəm/ also **Communism** NONCOUNT NOUN **Communism** is the political belief that people should not own private property and workers should control how things are produced.
• **com|mun|ist** also **Communist** /kɒ̲myənɪst/ NOUN ○ *a committed communist* ○ *the Communist Party*

com|mu|nity /kəmyu̲nɪti/ (**communities**)
1 NOUN all the people living in a particular area ○ *the local community*
2 NOUN a particular group within a society ○ *the business community*

com|mute /kəmyu̲t/ (**commutes, commuting, commuted**) VERB If you **commute**, you travel to work or school. ○ *Mike commutes to Miami every day.*

com|mut|er /kəmyu̲tər/ NOUN someone who regularly travels to work ○ *In Tokyo, most commuters travel to work on trains.*

com|pact /kəmpæ̲kt/ ADJ small and taking up little space ○ *a compact camera*

com|pact disc /kəmpæ̲kt dɪ̲sk/ (**compact discs**) NOUN A **compact disc** is a small disk on which sound, especially music, is recorded. The short form **CD** is also used.

com|pan|ion /kəmpæ̲nyən/ NOUN someone who you spend time with or who you travel with ○ *my traveling companion*

com|pa|ny /kʌ̲mpəni/ (**companies**)
1 NOUN a business that sells goods or services ○ *an insurance company*
2 NONCOUNT NOUN **Company** is having another person or other people with you. ○ *I always enjoy Nick's company.*
3 If you **keep** someone **company**, you spend time with them and stop them from feeling lonely or bored. ○ *I'll stay here and keep Emma company.*

com|pa|ny car (**company cars**) NOUN a car that an employer gives to an employee to use as their own, usually as a benefit of having a particular job, or because their job involves a lot of driving ○ *changes to tax laws for company cars*

com|pany doc|tor (**company doctors**)
1 NOUN a businessperson or accountant who specializes in turning poorly performing companies into profitable enterprises [ADMINISTRATION]
2 NOUN a physician employed by a company to advise its employees on health matters [ADMINISTRATION]

com|pany sec|re|tary (**company secretaries**) [ADMINISTRATION, mainly BRIT] → **corporate secretary**

com|pany union (**company unions**) NOUN an unaffiliated union of workers usually restricted to a single business enterprise [ADMINISTRATION]

com|pa|rable /kɒ̲mpərəbᵊl/ ADJ similar and able to be compared ○ *No other company can provide comparable goods or services.*

com|para|tive /kəmpæ̲rətɪv/ NOUN In grammar, the **comparative** is the form of an adjective or adverb that shows that one thing has more of a particular quality than something else has. For example, "bigger" is the comparative form of "big." Compare with **superlative**.

com|para|tive ad|ver|tis|ing NONCOUNT NOUN **Comparative advertising** is a form of advertising in which a company's product is compared favorably with similar products made by other companies. [MARKETING AND SALES] ❍ *The Japanese believe companies should pitch products on their own merits rather than relying on comparative advertising.*

com|pare /kəmpɛər/ (**compares, comparing, compared**) VERB When you **compare** things, you consider how they are different and how they are similar. ❍ *I use the Internet to compare prices.*

com|pari|son /kəmpærɪsən/ NOUN When you make a **comparison**, you consider two things together and see in what ways they are similar or different. ❍ *The information helps investors to make comparisons between share options.*

com|part|ment /kəmpɑrtmənt/
1 NOUN a separate part inside a box or a bag where you keep things ❍ *The case has a separate compartment for camera accessories.*
2 NOUN one of the separate spaces of a railroad car ❍ *the first-class compartment*

com|pas|sion|ate leave /kəmpæʃənɪt liv/ NONCOUNT NOUN **Compassionate leave** is time away from your work that your employer allows you when a member of your family dies or is seriously ill. [HR, BRIT]

com|pat|ible /kəmpætɪbəl/
1 ADJ able to work successfully together ❍ *Is your MP3 player compatible with your computer?*
2 ADJ having similar opinions and interests to someone else and so able to have a good relationship with them ❍ *They soon saw that the country wasn't a compatible business partner.*

com|pen|sate /kɒmpənseɪt/ (**compensates, compensating, compensated**)
1 VERB To **compensate** someone **for** money or things that they have lost means to pay them money to replace what they have lost. ❍ *We have to compensate investors for their losses.*
2 VERB If something good **compensates for** something bad, the good thing makes the bad thing seem less unpleasant. ❍ *Her energy and enthusiasm compensate for her lack of experience.*

com|pen|sa|tion /kɒmpənseɪʃən/ NONCOUNT NOUN **Compensation** is money that someone who has had a bad experience claims from the person or organization who caused it. [HR] ❍ *He has to pay $6,960 compensation for the damage he caused.*

com|pete /kəmpit/ (**competes, competing, competed**)
1 VERB If you **compete** in a contest or a game, you try to win it, along with other people. ❍ *He will compete in the 10k road race again this year.*
2 VERB When one firm or country **competes** with another, it tries to get people to buy its own goods in preference to those of the other firm or country. [BUSINESS MANAGEMENT] ❍ *The stores will inevitably end up competing with each other in their push for increased market shares.* ❍ *the American economy and its ability to compete abroad*

COLLOCATIONS
to compete *successfully*
to compete *fiercely*
to compete *effectively*

com|pe|tence /kɒmpɪtəns/ NONCOUNT NOUN **Competence** is the ability to do something well. ❍ *No one doubts his competence.*

com|pe|tent /kɒmpɪtənt/ ADJ able to do something well ❍ *a competent manager*

com|pe|ti|tion /kɒmpɪtɪʃən/
1 NOUN an event in which people try to show that they are best at an activity ❍ *The two boys entered a surfing competition.*
2 NONCOUNT NOUN **Competition** is activity involving two or more companies, in which each company tries to get people to buy its own goods in preference to the other company's goods. [BUSINESS MANAGEMENT] ❍ *This has put the telecommunications company in direct competition with firms that already offered limited DSL and cable-modem access.* ❍ *The farmers have been seeking higher prices as better protection from foreign competition.*

C

compet̲ition-based pric̲|ing NONCOUNT NOUN **Competition-based pricing** is the policy of setting a price for goods or services based on the price charged by other companies for similar goods or services. Compare with **cost-based pricing**, **market-oriented pricing**, and **penetration pricing**. [MARKETING AND SALES]

com|peti|tive /kəmpɛ̲tɪtɪv/
1 ADJ always wanting to or able to be more successful than other people ❍ *He's always been very competitive.*
2 ADJ sufficiently low in price or high in quality to be successful against commercial rivals [BUSINESS MANAGEMENT] ❍ *Japan has a highly competitive market system.*

com|pe̲ti|tive ad|va̲n|tage (**competitive advantages**) NOUN something that makes one particular firm or economy more likely to succeed than others [BUSINESS MANAGEMENT, MARKETING AND SALES] ❍ *a general shift towards using IT systems to gain competitive advantage*

com|pe̲ti|tive e̲dge (**competitive edges**) NOUN an advantage that makes a person or organization more likely to be successful than its competitors [BUSINESS MANAGEMENT, MARKETING AND SALES] ❍ *Quality of service is becoming an increasingly important consideration in maintaining a competitive edge in all markets.*

com|peti|tor /kəmpɛ̲tɪtər/
1 NOUN a person who takes part in a competition ❍ *One of the oldest competitors won the silver medal.*
2 NOUN A company's **competitors** are companies who are trying to sell similar goods or services to the same people. [BUSINESS MANAGEMENT] ❍ *The bank isn't performing as well as some of its competitors.*

COLLOCATIONS
a *major* competitor
to *lose ground* to a competitor
to *see off* a competitor
a *direct* competitor
a *close* competitor

com|pile /kəmpa̲ɪl/ (**compiles, compiling, compiled**) VERB When you **compile** a book or list, you produce it by collecting and putting together pieces of information. ❍ *The book took 10 years to compile.*

com|plain /kəmple̲ɪn/
1 VERB If you **complain about** something or someone, you say that you are not satisfied with them. ❍ *We complained about the poor service.* ❍ *"It's too expensive," he complained.*
2 VERB If you **complain of** a pain or an illness, you say that you have it. ❍ *He went to the hospital, complaining of chest pains.*

com|plaint /kəmple̲ɪnt/ NOUN a statement in which you say that you are not satisfied with something ❍ *a complaint about abusive behavior from a business rival*

com|ple|ment

Pronounce the verb /kɒ̲mplɪmɛnt/.
Pronounce the noun /kɒ̲mplɪmənt/.

1 VERB If people or things **complement** each other, they have different qualities or features that go together well. ❍ *We use on-line resources to complement formal training.*
2 NOUN Something that is a **complement to** something else goes well with it. ❍ *Intervention is a complement to monetary policy, not a substitute.*
3 NOUN In grammar, a **complement** of a link verb is a word or phrase that comes after the verb and gives information about the subject. For example, in the sentence "They felt very tired," "very tired" is the complement.

com|plete /kəmpli̲t/ (**completes, completing, completed**)
1 ADJ in every way ❍ *The announcement didn't come as a complete surprise.* ● **com|plete|ly** ADV ❍ *High technology is a completely different sector.*
2 ADJ If a job is **complete**, it is finished. ❍ *The project is not yet complete.*
3 VERB If you **complete** a task, you finish it. ❍ *We hope to complete the project by January.*
4 VERB If you **complete** a form, you write the necessary information on it. ❍ *Complete the first part of the application form.*

com|plex (**complexes**)

> Pronounce the adjective /kəmplɛks/ or sometimes /kɒmplɛks/. Pronounce the noun /kɒmplɛks/.

1 ADJ having many parts and difficult to understand ❍ *Crime is a very complex problem.*
2 NOUN a group of buildings used for a particular purpose ❍ *They are based in an industrial complex just north of the city.*

com|plex|ion /kəmplɛkʃən/ **NOUN** the quality or color of the skin on your face ❍ *She had a pale complexion.*

com|pli|cate /kɒmplɪkeɪt/ (**complicates, complicating, complicated**) **VERB** To **complicate** something means to make it more difficult to understand or deal with. ❍ *Please don't complicate the situation.*

com|pli|cat|ed /kɒmplɪkeɪtɪd/ **ADJ** having many parts and difficult to understand ❍ *The situation is very complicated.*

com|pli|ca|tion /kɒmplɪkeɪʃən/ **NOUN** a problem or difficulty ❍ *There were a number of complications.*

com|pli|ment

> Pronounce the verb /kɒmplɪmɛnt/. Pronounce the noun /kɒmplɪmənt/.

1 NOUN something nice that you say to someone, for example about their appearance ❍ *He paid me several compliments.*
2 VERB If you **compliment** someone, you say something nice to them, for example about their appearance. ❍ *They complimented me on the way I managed the team.*

com|po|nent /kəmpoʊnənt/ **NOUN** one of the parts of something [PRODUCTION] ❍ *The plan has four main components.*

com|pose /kəmpoʊz/ (**composes, composing, composed**)
1 VERB If something is **composed of** particular parts or people, they are its parts or members. ❍ *They used an audit team composed of outside directors.*
2 VERB When someone **composes** a piece of music, a speech, or a letter, they write it. ❍ *Vivaldi composed a large number of concertos.*

com|pos|er /kəmpoʊzər/ **NOUN** a person who writes music ❍ *great composers, such as Mozart and Beethoven*

com|po|si|tion /kɒmpəzɪʃən/
1 NOUN a piece of music or writing
2 NONCOUNT NOUN The **composition** of something is its parts or members. ❍ *The background of the chief executive determines the composition of a firm's board.*

com|pound /kɒmpaʊnd/
1 NOUN in chemistry, a substance that is made from two or more elements ❍ *Dioxins are chemical compounds that are produced when material is burned.*
2 ADJ In grammar, a **compound** verb, noun, or adjective is a word that is made from two or more other words.
3 VERB If you **compound** interest, you pay it on both the original amount of money and the interest that has already been paid on it. [FINANCE]

com|pound an|nual re|turn (**compound annual returns**) **NOUN** the total return available from an investment, including the interest earned as well as the capital [BANKING]

com|pound in|ter|est **NONCOUNT NOUN** **Compound interest** is interest that is paid both on an original sum of money and on interest that has already been paid on that sum. Compare with **simple interest** [BANKING]

com|pre|hend /kɒmprɪhɛnd/ **VERB** If you **comprehend** or you **comprehend** something, you understand it. [FORMAL] ❍ *I don't think you fully comprehend what's happening.*

com|pre|hen|sion /kɒmprɪhɛnʃən/ **NONCOUNT NOUN** **Comprehension** is the ability to understand something. [FORMAL] ❍ *a reading comprehension test*

com|pre|hen|sive /kɒmprɪhɛnsɪv/ **ADJ** including everything that is needed or related ❍ *a comprehensive guide to the region*
• **com|pre|hen|sive|ly** **ADV** ❍ *The book is comprehensively illustrated.*

com|prise /kəmpraɪz/ (**comprises, comprising, comprised**) **VERB** If something

C

comprises or **is comprised of** a number of things or people, it has them as its parts or members. [FORMAL] ❍ *The group comprises eight operating divisions.* ❍ *The 500 Stock Index is comprised of industrial, transportation, public utilities, and financial stocks.*

C

com|pro|mise /kɒmprəmaɪz/ **NOUN** a situation in which people accept something slightly different from what they really want ❍ *In the end they reached a compromise.*

comp|trol|ler /kəntroʊlər, kɒmp-/ **NOUN** someone who is in charge of the accounts of a business or a government department [FINANCE, ADMINISTRATION] ❍ *Robert Clarke, U.S. Comptroller of the Currency*

com|pul|so|ry /kəmpʌlsəri/ **ADJ** If something is **compulsory**, you must do it. ❍ *a compulsory retirement system*

com|pute /kəmpyut/ (**computes, computing, computed**) **VERB** To **compute** a number means to calculate it. ❍ *Compute your scores by adding or subtracting your scores for each item.*

com|put|er /kəmpyutər/ **NOUN** an electronic machine that can store and deal with large amounts of information ❍ *He was working on the computer.*

com|put|er chip (**computer chips**) **NOUN** a tiny integrated circuit that is used in the manufacture of electronic devices [TECHNOLOGY]

com|put|ing /kəmpyutɪŋ/ **NONCOUNT NOUN** **Computing** is the activity of using a computer and writing programs for it. ❍ *They offer a course in business and computing.*

con|ceal /kənsil/ **VERB** To **conceal** something means to hide it or keep it secret. ❍ *Exceptionally high investment rates concealed inefficiencies in the allocation of investment funds.* ❍ *He could not conceal his disgust.*

con|ceive /kənsiv/ (**conceives, conceiving, conceived**)
1 VERB If you cannot **conceive of** something, you cannot imagine it or believe it. ❍ *I can't even conceive of that amount of money.*
2 VERB When a woman or a couple **conceives**, the woman becomes pregnant. ❍ *They had been trying to conceive for three years.*

con|cen|trate /kɒnsəntreɪt/ (**concentrates, concentrating, concentrated**) **VERB** If you **concentrate on** something, you give it all your attention. ❍ *They are concentrating on introducing new technology into the business.*

con|cen|tra|tion /kɒnsəntreɪʃən/ **NONCOUNT NOUN** **Concentration** is the process of giving something all your attention. ❍ *Ed kept interrupting, breaking my concentration.*

con|cept /kɒnsɛpt/ **NOUN** a general idea about something ❍ *I want you to understand the concept of diversification.*

con|cern /kənsɜrn/ (**concerns, concerning, concerned**)
1 NONCOUNT NOUN **Concern** is worry about something or someone. ❍ *She expressed concern about my grandfather's health.*
2 NOUN something that you consider to be important ❍ *Owning stock encourages directors to identify far more closely with the concerns of shareholders.*
3 VERB If something **concerns** you, it worries you. ❍ *It concerns me that she hasn't called.* ● **con|cerned** **ADJ** ❍ *a bit concerned about her state of mind.*
4 VERB If a book or a piece of information **concerns** a particular subject, it is about that subject. ❍ *The book concerns the artist's two children.* ● **con|cerned** **ADJ** ❍ *Randolph's work is concerned with the effects of pollution.*

COLLOCATIONS
concern *with*
concern *for*

con|cern|ing /kənsɜrnɪŋ/ **PREP** relating to [FORMAL] ❍ *He raised questions about the accuracy of disclosures concerning the company's business operations.*

con|cert /kɒnsərt/ **NOUN** a performance of music ❍ *The weekend began with an outdoor rock concert.*

con|ces|sion /kənsɛʃən/
1 NOUN If you make a **concession to**

someone, you agree to let them do or have something in order to end an argument or conflict. ❍ *We made too many concessions and we got too little in return.*

2 NOUN an arrangement where someone is given the right to sell a product or to run a business, especially in a building belonging to another business [BUSINESS MANAGEMENT] ❍ *the man who ran the catering concession at the Rob Roy Links in Palominas*

con|ces|sion|aire /kənsɛʃənɛər/ **NOUN** a person or firm that has the right to sell a product or to run a business in a building belonging to another business [BUSINESS MANAGEMENT] ❍ *Concessionaires and shop owners report retail sales are up.*

con|ces|sion|er /kənsɛʃənər/ **NOUN** A **concessioner** is the same as a **concessionaire**. [BUSINESS MANAGEMENT]

con|cili|ation /kənsɪlieɪʃən/ **NONCOUNT NOUN** **Conciliation** is willingness to end a disagreement or the process of ending a disagreement. [HR] ❍ *Resolving the dispute will require a mood of conciliation on both sides.*

con|clude /kənklud/ (**concludes, concluding, concluded**)

1 VERB If you **conclude** something, you make a judgment after thinking about a subject carefully. ❍ *The report concluded that financial regulation had been inadequate.* ❍ *So what can we conclude from this experiment?*

2 VERB When something **concludes**, it ends. [FORMAL] ❍ *The meeting concluded with a presentation from the chief executive.*

con|clu|sion /kənkluʒᵊn/

1 NOUN a judgment that you make after thinking carefully about something ❍ *They came to the conclusion that they would have to compete on price.*

2 NONCOUNT NOUN the end of something [FORMAL] ❍ *He called for a swift conclusion to the negotiations.*

con|crete /kɒŋkrit/ **NONCOUNT NOUN** **Concrete** is a hard building material made by mixing cement with sand and water. ❍ *The hotel is constructed from steel and concrete.*

con|demn /kəndɛm/

1 VERB If you **condemn** something, you say that it is not acceptable. ❍ *Managers have condemned the strikes.*

2 VERB If someone **is condemned to** a punishment, they are given that punishment. ❍ *He was condemned to life in prison.*

C

con|di|tion /kəndɪʃən/

1 NOUN the state that someone or something is in ❍ *Investors must adjust to the economic conditions.* ❍ *The building is in good condition.*

2 PL NOUN The **conditions** in which people live or work are the things that affect their comfort and safety. ❍ *People are working in terrible conditions.*

3 NOUN an illness or medical problem ❍ *a heart condition*

con|do|min|ium /kɒndəmɪniəm/

1 NOUN an apartment building in which each apartment is owned by the person who lives there

2 NOUN an apartment in a condominium

con|duct

Pronounce the verb /kəndʌkt/. Pronounce the noun /kɒndʌkt/.

1 VERB When you **conduct** an activity or a task, you organize it and do it. ❍ *They conducted an in-depth consumer survey.*

2 VERB If you **conduct** yourself in a particular way, you behave in that way. [FORMAL] ❍ *The way he conducts himself embarrasses his colleagues.*

3 VERB If something **conducts** heat or electricity, heat or electricity can pass through it.

4 VERB When someone **conducts** musicians, they stand in front and direct the performance. ❍ *The new musical work was composed and conducted by Leonard Bernstein.*

5 NONCOUNT NOUN Someone's **conduct** is the way they behave. ❍ *A report concluded that the directors' conduct fell below that to be expected.*

con|duc|tor /kəndʌktər/

1 NOUN a person who stands in front of a group of musicians and directs their performance

2 NOUN on a train, a person whose job is to help passengers and check tickets

cone /koʊn/
1 NOUN a solid shape with one flat round end and one pointed end ❍ *orange traffic cones*
2 NOUN a thin cookie in the shape of a cone that you put ice cream into and eat ❍ *an ice-cream cone*

con|fer|ence /kɒnfərəns, -frəns/ **NOUN** a long meeting about a particular subject that many people attend ❍ *a conference on sales techniques*

con|fer|ence call (**conference calls**) **NOUN** a phone call with more than two people ❍ *There are daily conference calls with Washington.*

con|fess /kənfɛs/ **VERB** When you **confess**, you admit that you did something wrong. ❍ *He confessed to selling arms illegally.* ❍ *Directors confessed that they were worried about these investments.*

con|fes|sion /kənfɛʃən/ **NOUN** a statement in which someone admits that they have done something wrong ❍ *I have a confession to make. I lied about my age.*

con|fi|dence /kɒnfɪdəns/
1 NONCOUNT NOUN If you have **confidence in** someone, you are certain of their abilities and know that you can trust them. ❍ *You need to have confidence in the management.*
2 NONCOUNT NOUN If you have **confidence**, you feel sure about your own abilities and ideas. ❍ *He certainly doesn't lack confidence.*

con|fi|dent /kɒnfɪdənt/
1 ADJ certain that something will happen the way that you want it to ❍ *I am confident that we'll succeed.*
2 ADJ sure about your own abilities and ideas ❍ *In time he became more confident and relaxed.*
● **con|fi|dent|ly ADV** ❍ *She walked confidently into the boss's office.*

con|fi|den|tial /kɒnfɪdɛnʃəl/ **ADJ** Information that is **confidential** must be kept secret. ❍ *Discussions in the board room are confidential.* ● **con|fi|den|ti|al|ity** /kɒnfɪdɛnʃiælɪti/ **NONCOUNT NOUN** ❍ *the confidentiality of the client-attorney relationship*
● **con|fi|den|tial|ly ADV** ❍ *Any information will be treated confidentially.*

con|fine /kənfaɪn/ (**confines, confining, confined**) **VERB** If a person or an animal **is confined** in a particular place, they cannot leave it. ❍ *The animals are confined in tiny cages.*

con|firm /kənfɜrm/
1 VERB When someone **confirms** something, they say that it is true. ❍ *The doctor confirmed that the bone was broken.*
2 VERB If you **confirm** an arrangement, you say that it will definitely happen. ❍ *He called at seven to confirm our appointment.*
● **con|fir|ma|tion NONCOUNT NOUN** ❍ *You will receive confirmation of your order by email.*

con|flict

> Pronounce the noun /kɒnflɪkt/.
> Pronounce the verb /kənflɪkt/.

1 NOUN Conflict is fighting or arguments between people or countries. ❍ *conflict between workers and management*
2 VERB If ideas or plans **conflict**, they are very different from each other. ❍ *The law may also conflict with intellectual-property rights.*

con|front /kənfrʌnt/
1 VERB If you **confront** someone, you move close to them and start to fight or argue with them. ❍ *She confronted him face to face.*
2 VERB If you **confront** someone **with** a fact, you tell them it in order to accuse them of something. ❍ *She decided to confront her boss with the truth.*

con|fuse /kənfyuz/ (**confuses, confusing, confused**)
1 VERB If you **confuse** two things, by mistake, you think that one of them is the other one. ❍ *I always confuse my left with my right.*
2 VERB To **confuse** someone means to prevent them from understanding something. ❍ *You're just confusing me!*

con|fused /kənfyuzd/ **ADJ** not able to understand something because information is not clear ❍ *Consumers can become confused about the type of life insurance to buy.*

con|fus|ing /kənfyuzɪŋ/ **ADJ** difficult to understand because information is not clear ❍ *The financial regulations are really confusing.*

con|fu|sion /kənfyu̲ʒᵊn/
1 NONCOUNT NOUN If there is **confusion** about something, people do not understand something because information is not clear. ❍ *There's still confusion about the scale of their debts.*
2 NONCOUNT NOUN Confusion is a situation in which a lot of things are happening in a badly organized way. ❍ *In the confusion, he managed to escape.*

con|glom|er|ate /kənglɒ̲mərɪt/ **NOUN** a large business firm consisting of several different companies [ADMINISTRATION] ❍ *the world's second-largest media conglomerate*

con|gratu|late /kəngræ̲tʃəleɪt/ (**congratulates, congratulating, congratulated**) **VERB** If you **congratulate** someone, you express pleasure about something good that has happened to them. ❍ *She congratulated him on his company's impressive results.*

con|gratu|la|tions /kəngræ̲tʃəle̲ɪʃənz/ You say "**Congratulations**" to someone in order to congratulate them. ❍ *Congratulations on your new job!*

Con|gress /kɒ̲ŋgrɪs/ **NOUN** the part of the government in the United States that makes laws ❍ *Members of Congress are elected by the people.*

con|junc|tion /kəndʒʌ̲ŋkʃən/ **NOUN** a word that joins together parts of sentences, for example, "and" and "or"

con|nect /kənɛ̲kt/
1 VERB If you **connect** one thing **to** another, you join them together. ❍ *Next, connect the printer to your computer.*
2 VERB If one train, airplane, or boat **connects with** another form of transportation, passengers can change from one to the other in order to continue their trip. ❍ *The train connects with an airplane to Ireland.*

con|nec|tion /kənɛ̲kʃən/
1 NOUN a relationship between two things, people, or groups ❍ *There is almost no connection between grower and consumer.* ❍ *He denied that there was any connection between the union and the vandalism.*
2 NOUN a way of communicating using the telephone or a computer ❍ *a fast Internet connection*
3 NOUN a train, bus, or airplane that allows you to continue your trip by changing from one to another ❍ *My flight was late and I missed the connection.*

con|quer /kɒ̲ŋkər/ **VERB** If one country or group of people **conquers** another, they take complete control of their land. ❍ *They had been conquered by the neighboring country the century before.*

con|science /kɒ̲nʃəns/ **NOUN** the part of your mind that tells you if what you are doing is wrong ❍ *My conscience wouldn't allow me to treat employees that way.* ❍ *I had a guilty conscience over the money that I'd taken.*

con|scious /kɒ̲nʃəs/
1 ADJ If you are **conscious of** something, you are aware of it. ❍ *We have to be conscious of rising oil prices.*
2 ADJ awake, and not asleep or unconscious ❍ *She was fully conscious an hour after the operation.*

con|sen|sus /kənsɛ̲nsəs/ **NOUN** general agreement among a group of people ❍ *The consensus among the world's scientists is that the world is likely to warm up over the next few decades.*

con|sent /kənsɛ̲nt/
1 NONCOUNT NOUN Consent is permission to do something. [FORMAL] ❍ *Nothing can be done without the shareholders' consent.*
2 VERB If you **consent to** something, you agree to do it or to allow it to happen. [FORMAL] ❍ *He finally consented to the deal.*

con|se|quence /kɒ̲nsɪkwɛns, -kwəns/ **NOUN** a result or effect of something that has happened ❍ *They are suffering the fiscal consequences of the slowdown.*

con|se|quent|ly /kɒ̲nsɪkwɛntli, -kwəntli/ **ADV** as a result [FORMAL] ❍ *Consequently, demand for part-time workers is growing.*

con|ser|va|tion /kɒ̲nsərve̲ɪʃən/ **NONCOUNT NOUN Conservation** is actions that are done to protect nature and the environment. ❍ *wildlife conservation*

C

con|serva|tive /kənsɜrvətɪv/ **ADJ** not liking change or new ideas ❍ *People often become more conservative as they get older.*

con|serve /kənsɜrv/ (**conserves, conserving, conserved**)
1 VERB If you **conserve** energy or water, you deliberately use less of it. ❍ *Factories have closed for the weekend to conserve energy.*
2 VERB If you **conserve** land, oceans, or other areas of the environment, you take action to protect them. ❍ *World leaders have agreed to work together to conserve the forests.*

con|sid|er /kənsɪdər/
1 VERB If you **consider** a person or a thing **to** be a particular way, that is your opinion of them. ❍ *Health insurance is not considered to be a taxable benefit.*
2 VERB If you **consider** something, you think about it carefully. ❍ *The firm is considering selling its headquarters in Geneva.* ❍ *He never stops to consider other people's feelings.*

con|sid|er|able /kənsɪdərəbᵊl/ **ADJ** great or large [FORMAL] ❍ *The land cost a considerable amount of money.* ● **con|sid|er|ably ADV** ❍ *The growth of the economy slowed considerably in the second quarter.*

con|sid|er|ate /kənsɪdərɪt/ **ADJ** always thinking and caring about the feelings of other people ❍ *He's the most considerate man I know.*

con|sid|era|tion /kənsɪdəreɪʃən/
1 NONCOUNT NOUN If you show **consideration**, you think about and care about the feelings of other people. ❍ *Show some consideration for your neighbors.*
2 NONCOUNT NOUN Consideration is careful thought that you give to something. ❍ *After careful consideration, we have decided not to go ahead with the project.*

con|signee /kɒnsaɪni, kənsaɪ-/ **NOUN** a person, agent, or organization to which merchandise is handed over and entrusted [LOGISTICS AND DISTRIBUTION]

con|sign|ment /kənsaɪnmənt/
1 NOUN a load of goods that is being delivered to a place or person [LOGISTICS AND DISTRIBUTION] ❍ *The first consignment of food was flown in yesterday.*
2 If goods are sold **on consignment**, the owner is given a percentage of the price once they are sold. [LOGISTICS AND DISTRIBUTION] ❍ *She sold clothes on consignment to benefit homeless people.*

con|sist /kənsɪst/ **VERB** Something that **consists of** particular things or people is made up of them. ❍ *The offer consists of $410.5 million in cash and the rest in notes.*

con|sist|ent /kənsɪstənt/ **ADJ** always showing the same qualities or behavior, and never changing ❍ *The fund has been a more consistent performer than other funds.*
● **con|sist|en|cy NONCOUNT NOUN** ❍ *There's no consistency in her performance.*
● **con|sist|ent|ly ADV** ❍ *The airline consistently wins awards for its service.*

con|sole (**consoles, consoling, consoled**)

Pronounce the verb /kənsoʊl/. Pronounce the noun /kɒnsoʊl/.

1 VERB If you **console** someone who is unhappy, you try to make them feel happier. ❍ *She started to cry and I tried to console her.*
2 NOUN a device with switches or buttons that allows you to operate a piece of electronic equipment [TECHNOLOGY] ❍ *a games console*

con|soli|da|tion loan /kənsɒlɪdeɪʃən loʊn/ (**consolidation loans**) **NOUN** a single loan that is taken out to pay off several separate loans [BANKING]

con|sor|tium /kənsɔrʃiəm, -ti-/ (**consortia** /kənsɔrʃiə, -ti-/ or **consortiums**) **NOUN** a group of people or firms who have agreed to cooperate with each other [ADMINISTRATION, FORMAL] ❍ *The consortium includes some of the biggest building contractors in North America.*

con|stant /kɒnstənt/ **ADJ** happening all the time or always there ❍ *She is in constant pain.* ❍ *Earnings have remained constant despite the strength of the dollar.* ● **con|stant|ly ADV** ❍ *The direction of the wind is constantly changing.*

con|sti|tute /kɒnstɪtut/ (**constitutes, constituting, constituted**)

1 VERB If something **constitutes** a particular thing, it can be considered as being that thing. ❍ *Testing patients without their consent would constitute a legal offense.*
2 VERB If a number of things or people **constitute** something, they are the parts or members that form it. ❍ *These payments constitute 31.5 percent of the current expenditures.*

con|sti|tu|tion /kɒnstɪtuʃən/ **NOUN** a set of laws and rights of the people belonging to a country or organization ❍ *the American Constitution*

con|struct /kənstrʌkt/ **VERB** If you **construct** something, you build it. ❍ *His company constructed an office building in Denver.*

con|struc|tion /kənstrʌkʃən/
1 NONCOUNT NOUN Construction is the work of building things. ❍ *Who will finance the construction of these new schools?*
2 NOUN something that has been built ❍ *The new theater is an impressive steel and glass construction.*

con|struc|tive dis|charge /kənstrʌktɪv dɪstʃardʒ/ **NONCOUNT NOUN** If an employee claims **constructive discharge**, they begin a legal action against their employer in which they claim that they were forced to leave their job because of the behavior of their employer. [LEGAL, HR] ❍ *The woman claims she was the victim of constructive discharge after being demoted.*

con|struc|tive dis|miss|al /kənstrʌktɪv dɪsmɪsᵊl/ [LEGAL, HR, mainly BRIT] → **constructive discharge**

con|sult /kənsʌlt/ **VERB** If you **consult** someone you ask them for their advice. ❍ *Perhaps you should consult an attorney.*

con|sult|ant /kənsʌltənt/
1 NOUN someone who gives expert advice on a subject ❍ *a management consultant*
2 NOUN In medicine, a **consultant** is the same as a **specialist**. [BRIT]

con|sul|ta|tion /kɒnsəlteɪʃən/
1 NOUN a meeting with a doctor or expert to discuss a particular problem and get his or her advice ❍ *A personal diet plan is devised after a consultation with a nutritionist.*

con|sum|able /kənsuməbᵊl/
1 ADJ intended to be bought, used, and then replaced [PRODUCTION] ❍ *demand for consumable articles*
2 NOUN Consumable is also a noun. [PRODUCTION] ❍ *Suppliers add computer consumables, office equipment, and furniture to their product range.*

con|sume /kənsum/ (**consumes, consuming, consumed**)
1 VERB If you **consume** something, you eat or drink it. [FORMAL] ❍ *Martha consumed a box of cookies every day.*
2 VERB Something that **consumes** fuel, energy, or time, uses it. ❍ *Airlines consume huge amounts of fuel every day.*

con|sum|er /kənsumər/ **NOUN** a person who buys something or uses a service [BUSINESS MANAGEMENT] ❍ *consumer rights*

COLLOCATIONS
consumer *confidence*
consumer *demand*
consumer *goods*
consumer *protection*
consumer *spending*

con|sum|er be|hav|ior **NONCOUNT NOUN Consumer behavior** is the way that groups of consumers typically behave. [MARKETING AND SALES] ❍ *Developments in materials, marketing, and styling have all had an effect on consumer behavior.*

con|sum|er choice **NONCOUNT NOUN Consumer choice** is the number of different products or services that are available for people to buy. [MARKETING AND SALES] ❍ *The experts say health service reform means higher taxes and less consumer choice.*

con|sum|er du|rables [MARKETING AND SALES, BRIT] → **durable goods**

con|sum|er goods **PL NOUN Consumer goods** are items bought by people for their own use, rather than by businesses. Compare with **capital goods**. [MARKETING AND SALES] ❍ *The choice of consumer goods available in local stores is small.*

con|sum|er|ism /kənsumərɪzəm/
1 NONCOUNT NOUN Consumerism is the belief

that it is good to buy and use a lot of goods. [ECONOMICS] ❍ *They have clearly embraced Western consumerism.*

2 NONCOUNT NOUN Consumerism is the protection of the rights and interests of consumers. [ECONOMICS]

C

con|sum|er|ist /kənsuːmərɪst/ **ADJ** consuming a lot of goods [ECONOMICS] ❍ *a rootless, consumerist twenty-something*

con|sum|er laws PL NOUN Consumer laws are laws designed to protect people's rights when they buy something. [MARKETING AND SALES, LEGAL]

con|sum|er pan|el (consumer panels) NOUN a specially selected group of people who are intended to represent the likely users of a particular product or service [MARKETING AND SALES]

con|sum|er price in|dex (consumer price indexes) NOUN a list of the prices of typical goods that shows how much the cost of living changes from one month to the next [ECONOMICS] ❍ *The consumer price index for September is expected to show inflation edging up to about 10.8 percent.*

con|sum|er pro|tec|tion NONCOUNT NOUN Consumer protection is the protection provided to consumers by laws. [MARKETING AND SALES, LEGAL] ❍ *Many consumer groups welcomed the move, saying it would enhance consumer protection.*

con|sum|er rights PL NOUN Consumer rights are the legal rights that people have when they buy something. [MARKETING AND SALES, LEGAL] ❍ *an organization campaigning for consumer rights*

con|sump|tion /kənsʌmpʃən/

1 NONCOUNT NOUN The **consumption** of fuel or natural resources is the act of using them or the amount used. ❍ *The laws have led to a reduction in fuel consumption in the U.S.*

2 NONCOUNT NOUN The **consumption** of food or drink is the act of eating or drinking something, or the amount eaten or drunk. [FORMAL] ❍ *Most of the wine was unfit for human consumption.*

3 NONCOUNT NOUN Consumption is the act of buying and using things. [ECONOMICS] ❍ *Recycling the waste from our increased consumption is better than burning it.*

con|tact /kɒntækt/

1 NONCOUNT NOUN Contact is communication between people, either spoken or written. ❍ *I'm still in contact with my former colleagues.* ❍ *I don't have much contact with the sales team.* ❍ *There are many ways to make contact with potential customers.*

2 VERB If you **contact** someone, you telephone them or send them a message or a letter. ❍ *Thomson has been contacted by 11 potential buyers.*

con|tact cen|tre (contact centres) [BRIT] → **call center**

con|tact lens (contact lenses) NOUN a small, very thin piece of plastic that you put on your eye to help you see better

con|tain /kənteɪn/ **(contains, containing, contained) VERB** If one thing **contains** other things, those things are inside it. ❍ *The envelope contained an agenda for the meeting.*

con|tain|er /kənteɪnər/

1 NOUN something such as a box or bottle that you keep things in ❍ *They have ordered hundreds of large-capacity containers.*

2 NOUN a very large metal box, used for transporting goods [LOGISTICS AND DISTRIBUTION] ❍ *a container ship*

con|tain|er|ise /kənteɪnəraɪz/ [LOGISTICS AND DISTRIBUTION, BRIT] → **containerize**

con|tain|er|ize /kənteɪnəraɪz/ **(containerizes, containerizing, containerized) VERB** When you **containerize** something you put it in standard-sized containers for shipping. [LOGISTICS AND DISTRIBUTION] ❍ *containerized cargo*

content

❶ NOUN USES
❷ ADJECTIVE USES

❶ **con|tent** /kɒntɛnt/

1 PL NOUN The **contents** of a container are the things inside it. ❍ *Empty the contents of the can into a bowl.*

2 PL NOUN The **contents** of a book are its different chapters and sections. ❍ *a table of contents*

❷ **con|tent** /kəntɛnt/ **ADJ** happy and satisfied ❍ *She seems quite content with her life.*

con|test /kɒntɛst/ **NOUN** a competition or game ❍ *It was an exciting contest.*

con|test|ant /kəntɛstənt/ **NOUN** a person who takes part in a competition or a game ❍ *Contestants on the TV show have to answer six questions correctly.*

con|text /kɒntɛkst/

1 NOUN The **context of** an event is the situation in which it happens. ❍ *You have to see these events in their historical context.*

2 NOUN The **context** of a word or a sentence is the words and sentences that come before and after it, that help you to understand its meaning.

con|ti|nent /kɒntɪnənt/ **NOUN** a very large area of land, such as Africa or Asia

con|ti|nen|tal /kɒntɪnɛntəl/ **ADJ** The **continental** United States is all the states that are on the main continent of North America, and not Hawaii or the Virgin Islands. ❍ *Pikes Peak is the highest mountain in the continental United States.*

con|tinu|ation /kəntɪnyueɪʃən/ **NONCOUNT NOUN** The **continuation of** something is the fact that it continues to happen or to exist. ❍ *Investors are hoping for a continuation of Monday's 41-point rally.*

con|tinue /kəntɪnyu/ (**continues, continuing, continued**)

1 VERB If something **continues**, it does not stop. ❍ *Production of coal continued for another four years.*

2 VERB If you **continue to** do something or **continue** doing something, you do not stop doing it. ❍ *Nine out of ten workers continue to have jobs.* ❍ *She is determined to continue working.*

3 VERB If someone or something **continues**, they start again after stopping. ❍ *The trial continues today.* ❍ *She looked up for a minute and then continued working.*

con|tinu|ous /kəntɪnyuəs/

1 ADJ happening over a long time without stopping ❍ *This is a research arm for their continuous innovation in consumer goods.*
● **con|tinu|ous|ly ADV** ❍ *The system pushes workers to improve productivity continuously.*

2 ADJ A **continuous** line has no spaces in it. ❍ *There was a continuous line of cars outside in the street.*

3 ADJ In English grammar, the **continuous** form is made using the auxiliary "be" and the present participle of a verb, as in "I'm going on vacation."

con|tinu|ous im|prove|ment NONCOUNT NOUN The **continuous improvement** of products by a firm is a continual effort to improve the quality of those products by that firm. [PRODUCTION] ❍ *Its manufacturing techniques and culture of continuous improvement were the envy of the business world.*

con|tract /kɒntrækt/

1 NOUN an official agreement between two companies or two people [LEGAL] ❍ *He signed a contract to play for the team for two years.*

2 PHRASE If you are **under contract to** someone, you have signed a contract agreeing to work for them during a fixed period of time. [LEGAL] ❍ *The director wanted to cast an actress, then under contract to Warner Brothers.*

con|tract of em|ploy|ment (**contracts of employment**) **NOUN** a written legal agreement between an employer and an employee that states the terms of employment [LEGAL, HR] ❍ *Overtime is the period of time worked by employees over and above what is agreed to be a standard working week in their contract of employment.*

con|trac|tor /kɒntræktər, kəntræk-/ **NOUN** a person or firm that does work for other people or organizations [ADMINISTRATION] ❍ *We told the building contractor that we wanted a garage big enough for two cars.*

con|tract rate (**contract rates**) **NOUN** a reduced price that is available because you agree to use a service on a regular basis

[LEGAL, FINANCE] ❍ *If the hotel does not honor the contract rate, ask to speak to the hotel manager.*

contra|dict /kɒntrədɪkt/ **VERB** If you **contradict** someone, you say that what they have just said is wrong. ❍ *She looked surprised, but she didn't contradict him.*

C

con|trast

Pronounce the noun /kɒntræst/.
Pronounce the verb /kəntræst/.

1 NOUN a clear difference between two or more people or things ❍ *The contrast between their management styles is quite striking.*
2 VERB If you **contrast** things, you show the differences between them. ❍ *In this section we contrast four different ideas.*

con|trib|ute /kəntrɪbyut/ (**contributes, contributing, contributed**) **VERB** If you **contribute** something or **contribute to** something, you give something such as money or time to it. ❍ *The U.S. is contributing $4 billion to the project.* ❍ *I'd like to contribute to her leaving present.* ● **con|tribu|tor** /kəntrɪbyətər/ **NOUN** ❍ *The financial services industry is a major contributor to the economy.*

con|tri|bu|tion /kɒntrɪbyuʃən/ **NOUN** If you make a **contribution**, you give money to help to pay for something. ❍ *He made a $5,000 contribution to the charity.*

con|trol /kəntroʊl/ (**controls, controlling, controlled**)
1 NONCOUNT NOUN Control of something is the power to make all the important decisions about it. ❍ *He took control of every situation.*
2 If you are **in control of** something, you have the power to make all the important decisions about it. ❍ *She feels that she's in control of the business again.*
3 VERB If someone **controls** something, they have the power to make all the important decisions about it. ❍ *He controls the largest company in California.*
4 VERB If you **control** a person or a machine, you are able to make them do what you want them to do. ❍ *A computer system controls the lighting.* ❍ *His manager couldn't control him.*
5 NONCOUNT NOUN Control is also a noun. ❍ *Garcia never lost control of the trust or the funds.*
6 If something is **out of control**, people cannot deal with it. ❍ *Inflation was out of control.*
7 If something is **under control**, people can deal with it. ❍ *The situation is under control.*
8 NOUN a switch that you use in order to operate a machine ❍ *the volume control*
9 VERB If you **control** financial accounts, you examine them and check that they are correct. [FINANCE, ADMINISTRATION]

con|trol|ler /kəntroʊlər/
1 NOUN a person who has responsibility for a particular organization or for a particular part of an organization [mainly BRIT] ❍ *the job of controller of BBC1*
2 NOUN A **controller** is the same as a **comptroller**. [FINANCE, ADMINISTRATION]

con|trol|ling in|ter|est (**controlling interests**) **NOUN** a quantity of shares in a business that is enough to ensure control over the direction of the business [ADMINISTRATION, BUSINESS MANAGEMENT] ❍ *The group may seek to acquire a controlling interest in the motor company.*

con|tro|ver|sial /kɒntrəvɜrʃᵊl/ **ADJ** Something that is **controversial** causes arguments because many people disapprove of it. ❍ *I tried to stay away from controversial subjects.* ❍ *a controversial decision*

con|tro|ver|sy /kɒntrəvɜrsi/ **NONCOUNT NOUN Controversy** is when many people argue about something, or disapprove of it. ❍ *The company caused controversy when it sacked half its workforce.*

con|veni|ence /kənvinyəns/
1 NONCOUNT NOUN Convenience is the condition of being easy and quick to do and of not needing extra effort or time. ❍ *Customers get the convenience of being able to make a single payment.* ❍ *I use a credit card for convenience.*
2 NOUN a piece of equipment that is designed to make your life easier ❍ *There were all the modern conveniences that you would expect in such an apartment.*

con|ven|i|ence store (**convenience stores**) NOUN a small store that sells mainly food and that is usually open until late at night [ECONOMICS] ○ *The convenience store sells only a few items, with little or no choice of brands.*

con|veni|ent /kənvinyənt/
1 ADJ easy to use or making something easy to do ○ *American businesses have found it convenient to make deposits locally.*
• **con|veni|ent|ly** ADV ○ *The office is conveniently located close to the railroad station.*
2 ADJ A **convenient** time is a time when you are available to do something. ○ *She will try to arrange a convenient time.*

con|ven|tion|al /kənvɛnʃənᵊl/ ADJ traditional and considered normal by most people ○ *My parents were very conventional.*

con|ver|sa|tion /kɒnvərseɪʃən/ NOUN an occasion when two or more people talk to each other ○ *I had an interesting conversation with one of our suppliers this morning.*

con|vert /kənvɜrt/ VERB If you **convert** one thing **into** another thing, you change it into a different form. ○ *He wants to convert the building into a hotel.*

con|vert|ible /kənvɜrtɪbᵊl/
1 NOUN a car with a soft roof that can be folded down or removed
2 ADJ easily exchanged for other forms of investments or money [ECONOMICS] ○ *the introduction of a convertible currency*
• **con|vert|ibil|ity** /kənvɜrtɪbɪlɪti/ NONCOUNT NOUN ○ *the convertibility of the peso* ○ *rapid export growth based on currency convertibility*

con|vict /kənvɪkt/ VERB If someone **is convicted of** a crime, they are found guilty of it in a court of law. ○ *He was convicted of fraud.*

con|vince /kənvɪns/ (**convinces, convincing, convinced**)
1 VERB If someone or something **convinces** you **to** do something, they persuade you to do it. ○ *Mr. Schlesinger's victory could convince other consumers to sue telemarketers.*
2 VERB If someone or something **convinces** you **of** something, they make you believe that it is true or that it exists. ○ *He must convince the markets that he can maintain this success.*
• **con|vinced** ADJ ○ *She was convinced that interest rates would go up.*

COO /si oʊ oʊ/ **COO** is an abbreviation for "chief operating officer." [PRODUCTION]

cook /kʊk/
1 VERB When you **cook** or **cook** food, you prepare food for eating by heating it. ○ *I have to go and cook dinner.* ○ *I never learned to cook.*
2 NOUN a person who prepares and cooks food ○ *I'm a terrible cook.*

cook|er /kʊkər/ [BRIT] → **stove**

cook|ery /kʊkəri/ NONCOUNT NOUN **Cookery** is the activity of preparing and cooking food. [mainly BRIT]

cookie /kʊki/ NOUN a small, flat, sweet cake ○ *chocolate chip cookies*

cook|ing /kʊkɪŋ/
1 NONCOUNT NOUN **Cooking** is the activity of preparing food. ○ *He did the cooking and cleaning.*
2 NONCOUNT NOUN **Cooking** is food that is cooked in a particular way. ○ *Italian cooking*

cool /kul/ (**cooler, coolest**)
1 ADJ slightly cold, often in a way that is enjoyable ○ *I felt the cool air on my neck.* ○ *a nice cool drink*
2 ADJ calm ○ *You have to remain cool in very difficult situations.*
3 ADJ fashionable and interesting [INFORMAL] ○ *I met some really cool people there.* ○ *She had really cool boots.*
4 VERB When something **cools**, it becomes lower in temperature and when you **cool** something, you make it become lower in temperature. ○ *Take the meat from the oven and allow it to cool.*
▸ **cool down**
1 To **cool down** means the same as to **cool**. ○ *Let the cake cool down before you take it out of the tin.*
2 If someone **cools down**, they become less angry. ○ *He has had time to cool down.*

cool hunt|er (**cool hunters**) NOUN a person who is employed to identify future marketing trends, especially in fashion or the media [TECHNOLOGY, INFORMAL] ○ *In New York, the*

C

corporate "cool hunters" head down to the basketball courts of Brooklyn to check out the latest street fashion.

co-op /koʊɒp/ NOUN **Co-op** is an abbreviation for **co-operative**. [BUSINESS MANAGEMENT, INFORMAL] ❍ *The co-op sells the art work at exhibitions.*

co|oper|ate /koʊɒpəreɪt/ (**cooperates, cooperating, cooperated**) or **co-operate** VERB If you **cooperate with** someone, you work with them or help them. ❍ *He finally agreed to cooperate with the police.* ● **co|opera|tive** /koʊɒpərətɪv/ ADJ ❍ *I made an effort to be cooperative.* ● **co|opera|tion** /koʊɒpəreɪʃən/ NONCOUNT NOUN ❍ *Thank you for your cooperation.*

co-operative /koʊɒpərətɪv/ or **cooperative, cooperative society** NOUN a business or organization run by the people who work for it, or owned by the people who use it [BUSINESS MANAGEMENT] ❍ *Oxfam aids small farming co-operatives to improve their yields significantly.*

COLLOCATIONS

a *housing* co-operative
a *workers'* co-operative
a co-operative *society*
a co-operative *movement*

co|or|di|nate /koʊɔrdᵊneɪt/ (**coordinates, coordinating, coordinated**)
1 VERB When you **coordinate** an activity, you organize it. ❍ *She coordinated their marketing campaign.*
2 VERB If you **coordinate** the parts of your body, you make them work together well. ❍ *She finds it hard to coordinate her eye and hand movements.* ● **co|or|di|na|tion** NONCOUNT NOUN ❍ *You need great hand-eye coordination to hit the ball.*

cop /kɒp/ NOUN a policeman or policewoman [INFORMAL] ❍ *The cops know where to find him.*

cope /koʊp/ (**copes, coping, coped**) VERB If you **cope with** a problem or task, you deal with it in a successful way. ❍ *The centers were started over a decade ago to help America cope with its trade problem.*

cop|per /kɒpər/ NONCOUNT NOUN **Copper** is a soft reddish-brown metal.

copy /kɒpi/ (**copies, copying, copied**)
1 NOUN a form of something that is exactly like the original ❍ *I made a copy of the agenda.*
2 NOUN a single book or newspaper ❍ *I've got a copy I could lend you.*
3 VERB If you **copy** something, you make or write something that is exactly like the original thing. ❍ *Copy files from your old computer to your new one.*
4 VERB If you **copy** a person, you try to behave as they do. ❍ *They have tended to copy or improve on other companies' developments.*

copy|right /kɒpiraɪt/ NOUN a legal right that makes it illegal to reproduce or perform it a piece of writing or music without the creator's permission [LEGAL] ❍ *Who owns the copyright on this movie?*

copy|writer /kɒpiraɪtər/ NOUN a person whose job is to write the words for advertisements [LEGAL, ADMINISTRATION]

cord /kɔrd/
1 NONCOUNT NOUN **Cord** is a strong, thick string. ❍ *She was carrying a package tied with heavy cord.*
2 NOUN an electrical wire covered in rubber or plastic ❍ *Place all electrical cords out of children's reach.*

core /kɔr/
1 NOUN the central part of a fruit that contains the seeds ❍ *an apple core*
2 NOUN The Earth's **core** is its central part.

core sec|tor (**core sectors**) NOUN the most important or most profitable areas of a firm or industry [ECONOMICS] ❍ *We have neglected production as a core sector, subsequently losing in world trade terms to Germany, Japan, and Korea.*

core values PL NOUN A group or organization's **core values** are the things they believe in and consider to be most important. [HR] ❍ *With all that change going on, one of my most important jobs is keeping the company focused on our core values.*

cork /kɔrk/ NOUN an object that you push into the top of a bottle to close it ❍ *He took the cork out of the bottle.*

cork|screw /kɔrkskru/ NOUN a tool for pulling corks out of bottles

corn /kɔrn/ NONCOUNT NOUN **Corn** is a tall plant that produces long vegetables covered with yellow seeds, or the seeds of this plant. ❍ *sacks of corn*

cor|ner /kɔrnər/

1 NOUN a point where two sides of something meet, or where a road meets another road ❍ *There was a table in the corner of the room.* ❍ *He stood on the street corner, waiting for a taxi.*

2 VERB If a firm or place **corners** an area of trade, they gain control over it so that no one else can have any success in that area. ❍ *This restaurant has cornered the Madrid market for specialist paellas.* ❍ *Zurich's affluence came initially from cornering a sizeable chunk of the silk trade.*

3 PHRASE If you **cut corners**, you do something quickly by doing it in a less thorough way than you should. ❍ *Take your time, don't cut corners, and follow instructions to the letter.*

Corp. **Corp.** is a written abbreviation for **corporation**. [ADMINISTRATION] ❍ *Sony Corp. of Japan*

cor|po|rate /kɔrpərɪt, -prɪt/ ADJ relating to large companies [ADMINISTRATION] ❍ *Our city apartments are popular with private and corporate customers.*

COLLOCATIONS
- corporate *clients*
- corporate *culture*
- corporate *lawyer*
- corporate *sector*
- corporate *structure*

cor|po|rate ad|ver|tis|ing NONCOUNT NOUN **Corporate advertising** is advertising that aims to promote a firm's name and image rather than a particular product. [MARKETING AND SALES] ❍ *a massive corporate advertising campaign*

cor|po|rate cul|ture (**corporate cultures**) NOUN the set of values and attitudes within a firm or organization that influences the general behavior of its employees [BUSINESS MANAGEMENT] ❍ *The entire corporate culture must embrace diversity.*

cor|po|rate gov|ern|ance /kɔrpərɪt gʌvərnəns, kɔrprɪt/ NONCOUNT NOUN **Corporate governance** is the balance of control between the stakeholders, managers, and directors of an organization. [BUSINESS MANAGEMENT] ❍ *He has made corporate governance a priority at his recent ventures, appointing truly independent directors.*

cor|po|rate hos|pi|tal|ity /kɔrpərɪt hɒspɪtælɪti, kɔrprɪt/ NONCOUNT NOUN **Corporate hospitality** is the entertainment that a firm offers to its most valued clients. [MARKETING AND SALES] ❍ *a corporate hospitality tent*

cor|po|rate i|den|tity (**corporate identities**) or **corporate image** NOUN the way a firm presents itself to its members and the public [BUSINESS MANAGEMENT] ❍ *A good corporate identity should permeate the whole organization.*

cor|po|rate lo|go /kɔrpərɪt loʊgoʊ, kɔrprɪt/ (**corporate logos**) NOUN a graphic image that represents the brand of a firm [MARKETING AND SALES] ❍ *promotional items imprinted with corporate logos and names*

cor|po|rate raid|er (**corporate raiders**) NOUN a person or organization that tries to take control of a firm by buying a large number of its shares [ECONOMICS] ❍ *Your present company could be taken over by corporate raiders.*

cor|po|rate re|spon|si|bil|ity NONCOUNT NOUN the sense of responsibility that a firm considers it has towards things such as the local community and the environment [BUSINESS MANAGEMENT] ❍ *a plan for corporate responsibility designed to create a framework to combine profit generation with social accountability*

cor|po|rate re|struc|tur|ing NONCOUNT NOUN **Corporate restructuring** is the process by which an organization changes its business strategy in order to increase its long-term profitability. [BUSINESS MANAGEMENT] ❍ *Further corporate restructuring has been promised in September.*

cor|po|rate sec|re|tary (**corporate secretaries**) **NOUN** a person whose job is to look after the administration, accounts, and legal affairs of a firm [BUSINESS MANAGEMENT]

cor|po|rate sec|tor (**corporate sectors**) **NOUN** The **corporate sector** of industry consists of businesses that supply goods and services. [BUSINESS MANAGEMENT]

cor|po|rate val|ues **PL NOUN** The **corporate values** of a firm are its attitudes and goals in relation to such things as its workforce, its customers, and society in general. [BUSINESS MANAGEMENT] ❍ *They have noticed changes in traditional corporate values, particularly in relation to environmental and social performance.*

cor|po|rate ven|tur|ing **NONCOUNT NOUN** **Corporate venturing** is when one firm provides venture capital for another firm in order take steps toward acquiring it. [FINANCE]

cor|po|rate vil|lage (**corporate villages**) **NOUN** an area close to the workplace where many everyday facilities are provided for a firm's workers

cor|po|ra|tion /kɔrpəreɪʃən/ **NOUN** a large business or firm [ADMINISTRATION] ❍ *He works for a big corporation.*

cor|po|ra|tion tax **NONCOUNT NOUN** **Corporation tax** is a tax that firms have to pay on the profits they make. [FINANCE]

corpse /kɔrps/ **NOUN** a dead body ❍ *Police found the corpse in a nearby river.*

cor|rect /kərɛkt/

1 ADJ right or true ❍ *the correct answer*

• **cor|rect|ly** **ADV** ❍ *Did I pronounce your name correctly?*

2 VERB If you **correct** a problem or a mistake you make it right. ❍ *There should be some sort of procedure for correcting errors.*

cor|rec|tion /kərɛkʃən/ **NOUN** a change that you make to a mistake, in order to make it right ❍ *You may make corrections to your figures.*

cor|re|spond /kɔrɪspɒnd/

1 VERB If one thing **corresponds to** another, they are very similar or connected. ❍ *The rise in food prices corresponds closely to rises in oil prices.*

2 VERB If you **correspond with** someone, you write letters to them. ❍ *She still corresponds with her American friends.*

cor|re|spond|ent /kɔrɪspɒndənt/

1 NOUN a newspaper or television journalist ❍ *As our Diplomatic Correspondent Mark Brayne reports, the president was given a sympathetic hearing.*

2 NOUN a person or firm that has regular business relations with another firm in a foreign country

cor|rupt /kərʌpt/

1 ADJ behaving in a dishonest way in order to gain money or power ❍ *corrupt officials*

• **cor|rup|tion** /kərʌpʃən/ **NONCOUNT NOUN** ❍ *The president faces charges of corruption.*

2 VERB If a computer file or program **is corrupted**, it starts to have mistakes in it that stop it from working as it should. [TECHNOLOGY] ❍ *The files were corrupted by a virus.*

cos|met|ic /kɒzmɛtɪk/ **NOUN** **Cosmetics** are make-up products. [TECHNOLOGY] ❍ *nail polish and other cosmetics*

cost /kɔst/ (**costs, costing, cost**)

1 NOUN the amount of money you need in order to buy, do, or make something ❍ *the cost of a loaf of bread* ❍ *There will be an increase in the cost of mailing a letter.*

2 VERB If something **costs** an amount of money, you have to pay that amount in order to buy, do, or make it. ❍ *This class costs $150 per person.* ❍ *It will cost us over $100,000 to buy new trucks.*

3 PL NOUN A company's **costs** are the total amount of money involved in operating the business. [FINANCE] ❍ *Costs have been reduced and work practices are changing to meet the demands of a much more competitive environment.*

COLLOCATIONS
low-cost
cost-*cutting*
cost-*effective*
cost *savings*
to *cut* costs
to *reduce* costs
to *incur* costs
rising costs
fixed costs

cost ac|count|ing NONCOUNT NOUN **Cost accounting** is the recording and analysis of all the various costs of running a business. [FINANCE]

cost-based pric|ing NONCOUNT NOUN **Cost-based pricing** is the policy of setting a price for goods or services based on how much it costs to produce, distribute, and market them. Compare with **competition-based pricing**, **market-oriented pricing**, and **penetration pricing**. [FINANCE, PURCHASING] ❍ *A cost-based pricing strategy had caused this company to lose orders it should have won.*

cost-benefit ADJ A **cost-benefit** analysis takes into account a project's costs and benefits to society as well as the revenue it generates. [ECONOMICS, FINANCE]

cost cen|ter (**cost centers**) NOUN a department in a firm that analyzes costs of a firm but does not bring the firm direct profit [FINANCE] ❍ *They took what was historically a cost center and converted it into an independent and profitable entity.*

cost-effective ADJ saving or making a lot of money in comparison with the costs involved [BUSINESS MANAGEMENT] ❍ *The bank must be run in a cost-effective way.* ● **cost-effectively** ADV ❍ *The management tries to produce the magazine as cost-effectively as possible.* ● **cost-effectiveness** NONCOUNT NOUN ❍ *A report has raised doubts about the cost-effectiveness of the proposals.*

cost|ing /kɔstɪŋ/ NOUN an estimate of all the costs involved in a project or a business venture [FINANCE] ❍ *We'll put together a proposal, including detailed costings, free of charge.*

cost|ly /kɔstli/ (**costlier, costliest**) ADJ expensive ❍ *We must try to avoid such costly mistakes.*

cost of liv|ing NONCOUNT NOUN The **cost of living** is the average amount of money that people in a particular place need to afford basic food, housing, and clothing. [ECONOMICS] ❍ *The cost of living has increased dramatically.*

cost-plus ADJ If you agree a contract on a **cost-plus** basis, the buyer agrees to pay all the cost for work to be done plus a profit. [FINANCE] ❍ *All vessels were to be built on a cost-plus basis.*

cost-push in|fla|tion NONCOUNT NOUN **Cost-push inflation** is an increase in prices caused by an increase in the cost of producing goods. Compare with **demand-pull inflation**. [FINANCE]

cost struc|ture (**cost structures**) NOUN an organization's different costs and the way these costs relate to and affect each other [FINANCE] ❍ *The company needs to change their entire cost structure to cope with the rising minimum wage.*

cos|tume /kɒstum/ NOUN a set of special clothes that someone wears in a performance ❍ *The costumes and scenery were designed by Robert Rauschenberg.*

cosy /koʊzi/ [BRIT] → **cozy**

cot /kɒt/
1 NOUN a narrow bed that you can fold and store in a small space
2 NOUN A **cot** is the same as a **crib**. [BRIT]

cot|tage /kɒtɪdʒ/ NOUN a small house, usually in the country ❍ *She lived in a little white cottage in the woods.*

cot|tage in|dus|try (**cottage industries**) NOUN a small business that is run from someone's home, especially one that involves a craft such as knitting or pottery [BUSINESS MANAGEMENT] ❍ *Bookbinding is largely a cottage industry.*

cot|ton /kɒtᵊn/
1 NONCOUNT NOUN **Cotton** is cloth or thread that is made from the cotton plant. ❍ *He's wearing a cotton shirt.* ❍ *a reel of cotton*

C

2 NONCOUNT NOUN **Cotton** is a plant that is used for making cloth. ❍ *a cotton plantation*
3 NONCOUNT NOUN **Cotton** is a soft mass of this substance that you use for cleaning your skin. ❍ *Take the cream off with cotton balls.*

couch /kaʊtʃ/ (**couches**) NOUN a long, comfortable seat for two or three people

cough /kɔf/
1 VERB When you **cough**, you suddenly force air out of your throat with a noise. ❍ *James began to cough violently.*
2 NOUN **Cough** is also a noun. ❍ *cough medicine* • **cough|ing** NONCOUNT NOUN ❍ *We could hear loud coughing in the background.*
3 NOUN an illness that makes you cough ❍ *I had a cough for over a month.*

could /kəd, STRONG kʊd/
1 MODAL If you **could** do something, you were able to do it. ❍ *I could see that something was wrong.* ❍ *The firm faced bankruptcy if it could not find a quick buyer.*
2 MODAL You use **could** to show that something is possibly true, or that it may possibly happen. ❍ *Recessions leave a huge gap between an economy's output and what it could potentially produce.* ❍ *"Where's Jack?"—"I'm not sure; he could be in a meeting."*
3 MODAL You use **could** in questions to make polite requests. ❍ *Could you help me with this report, please?*

couldn't /kʊdᵊnt/ **Couldn't** is short for "could not."

could've /kʊdəv/ **Could've** is short for "could have."

coun|cil /kaʊnsᵊl/ NOUN a group of people who are chosen to control a particular area ❍ *The city council has decided to build a new school.*

coun|se|lor /kaʊnsələr/
1 NOUN a young person who takes care of children at a summer camp ❍ *Hicks worked as a camp counselor in the summer vacation.*
2 NOUN someone whose job is to give people advice and help them with problems ❍ *a careers counselor*

count /kaʊnt/
1 VERB When you **count**, you say all the numbers in order. ❍ *Nancy counted slowly to five.*
2 VERB If you **count** all the things in a group, you see how many there are. ❍ *He counted the dollar bills.* ❍ *I counted 34 workmen doing nothing.*
3 VERB If someone or something **counts**, they are important. ❍ *Every penny counts when your profit margins are so low.*
4 ADJ A **count** noun is a noun that has a plural.
5 If you **keep count of** a number of things, you know how many have occurred. ❍ *Keep count of the number of hours you work.*
6 If you **lose count of** a number of things, you cannot remember how many there have been. ❍ *I lost count of the number of times she called.*
▶ **count on** If you **count on** someone or something, you feel sure they will help you. ❍ *You can count on our support.*

coun|ter /kaʊntər/ NOUN in a store or café, a long flat surface where customers are served ❍ *That guy works behind the counter at the DVD rental store.*

counter|offer /kaʊntərɔfər/ (**counteroffers**) NOUN an offer that someone makes, for example, for a house or business, in response to an offer by another person or group ❍ *Many would welcome a counteroffer from a foreign bidder.*

coun|try /kʌntri/ (**countries**)
1 NOUN an area of the world with its own government and people ❍ *This is the greatest country in the world.* ❍ *We crossed the border between the two countries.*
2 NOUN **The country** is land that is away from cities and towns. ❍ *She lived alone in a small house in the country.* ❍ *a country road*
3 NONCOUNT NOUN **Country** or **country music** is a style of popular music from the southern United States.

country|side /kʌntrisaɪd/ NONCOUNT NOUN **The countryside** is land that is away from cities and towns. ❍ *I've always loved the English countryside.*

country-specific /kʌntrispəsɪfɪk/ ADJ relating to a particular country ❍ *country-specific economic, political, and social events*

coun|ty /kaʊnti/ (**counties**) **NOUN** a part of a state or country ❍ *Palm Beach County*

cou|ple /kʌpᵊl/

1 NOUN two or a very small number ❍ *I'm meeting a couple of friends.* ❍ *Things should get better in a couple of days.* ❍ *Out of 750 customers, there may be a couple that are unhappy.*

2 NOUN two people who are married or who are having a romantic relationship ❍ *The couple had no children.*

cou|pon /kupɒn, kyu-/ **NOUN** a piece of paper that allows you to pay less money than usual for a product, or to get it free ❍ *Cut out the coupon on page 2 and take it to your local supermarket.*

cour|age /kɜrɪdʒ/ **NONCOUNT NOUN** **Courage** is the quality of being brave and not showing that you are afraid. ❍ *The girl had the courage to tell the police.*

cou|ra|geous /kəreɪdʒəs/ **ADJ** brave ❍ *a courageous decision*

course /kɔrs/

1 NOUN a series of lessons on a particular subject ❍ *I'm taking a course in business administration.*

2 NOUN one part of a meal ❍ *Lunch was excellent, especially the first course.*

3 NOUN in sports, an area of land for racing, or for playing golf ❍ *a golf course*

court /kɔrt/ **NOUN** a place where a judge and a jury decide if someone has done something wrong [LEGAL] ❍ *The man will appear in court later this month.*

cour|teous /kɜrtiəs/ **ADJ** polite and respectful to other people ❍ *He was a kind and courteous man.* ● **cour|teous|ly** **ADV** ❍ *He nodded courteously to me.*

cour|tesy /kɜrtɪsi/ **NONCOUNT NOUN** **Courtesy** is polite behavior that shows that you consider other people's feelings. [FORMAL] ❍ *Showing courtesy to your colleagues costs nothing.*

cous|in /kʌzᵊn/ **NOUN** the child of your uncle or your aunt ❍ *Do you know my cousin Alex?*

cov|er /kʌvər/

1 VERB If you **cover** something, you put something over it to protect or hide it. ❍ *Cover the dish with a heavy lid.*

2 VERB If one thing **covers** another, it forms a layer over its surface. ❍ *Snow covered the city.* ❍ *The desk was covered with papers.*

3 NOUN something that is put over an object to protect it ❍ *Keep a plastic cover on your computer when you are not using it.*

4 NOUN the outside part of a book or magazine ❍ *She appeared on the cover of last week's "Zoo" magazine.*

cov|er|age /kʌvərɪdʒ/ **NONCOUNT NOUN** The **coverage** of something in the news is the reporting of it. ❍ *Now a special TV network gives live coverage of most races.*

cov|er let|ter (**cover letters**) **NOUN** a letter that you send with a package or with another letter in order to provide extra information ❍ *Your cover letter creates the employer's first impression of you.*

cov|er|mount /kʌvərmaʊnt/

1 NOUN an item attached to the front of a magazine or newspaper as a gift [mainly BRIT] ❍ *In most magazine markets, covermounts have become big business.*

2 VERB When a publisher **covermounts** an item, it attaches a free gift to the front of a magazine or newspaper. [mainly BRIT] ❍ *Cycle Sport magazine comes complete with a free, covermounted 60-minute DVD featuring "Great Moments in Cycling."*

cow /kaʊ/ **NOUN** a large female animal that is kept on farms for its milk ❍ *Dad went out to milk the cows.*

cow|ard /kaʊərd/ **NOUN** someone who is easily frightened and avoids dangerous or difficult situations ❍ *They called him a coward because he refused to fight.*

co-worker /koʊwɜrkər/ **NOUN** a person who works alongside another ❍ *A co-worker of mine mentioned that the deadline was moved back a week.*

cozy /koʊzi/ (**cozier, coziest**) **ADJ** comfortable and warm ❍ *You can relax in the cozy hotel lounge.*

CPA /si pi eɪ/ (**CPAs**) **NOUN** **CPA** is an abbreviation for **certified public accountant**.

[FINANCE] ❍ *He is a CPA in both New York and New Jersey.*

cr.
1 cr. is a written abbreviation for **credit**. [FINANCE, BANKING]
2 cr. is a written abbreviation for **creditor**. [FINANCE, BANKING]

C

crab /kræb/
1 NOUN an ocean animal that moves sideways and has a shell and five pairs of legs
2 NONCOUNT NOUN Crab is the meat of this animal. ❍ *a crab salad*

crack /kræk/
1 VERB If something hard **cracks**, it becomes slightly broken, with lines appearing on its surface, and if you **crack** something, you break it in this way. ❍ *The plane's windshield had cracked.* ❍ *I cracked a tooth as I fell.*
2 NOUN a very narrow gap between two things ❍ *Kathryn saw him through a crack in the curtains.*
3 NOUN a line that appears on the surface of something when it is slightly broken ❍ *The plate had a crack in it.*
4 NOUN a sharp sound, like the sound of a piece of wood breaking ❍ *Suddenly there was a loud crack.*

craft /kræft/ **NOUN** an activity that involves making things skillfully with your hands ❍ *We want to teach our children about native crafts and culture.*

crash /kræʃ/ (**crashes, crashing, crashed**)
1 NOUN an accident in which a vehicle hits something ❍ *His son was killed in a car crash.*
2 VERB Crash is also a verb. ❍ *Her car crashed into the back of a truck.*
3 NOUN a sudden loud noise ❍ *There was a loud crash behind me.*
4 VERB If a computer or a computer program **crashes**, it suddenly stops working.
5 VERB If a business or financial system **crashes**, it fails suddenly, often with serious effects. ❍ *When the market crashed, they assumed the deal would be canceled.*
6 NOUN Crash is also a noun. ❍ *He predicted correctly that there was going to be a stock market crash.*

crate /kreɪt/ **NOUN** a large box for moving or storing things ❍ *wooden crates*

crawl /krɔl/
1 VERB When you **crawl**, you move on your hands and knees. ❍ *I began to crawl toward the door.*
2 NONCOUNT NOUN Crawl is a way of swimming in which you lie on your front and move your arms over your head, while kicking your legs.

crawl|ing peg (**crawling pegs**) **NOUN** a method of stabilizing exchange rates or prices by maintaining a fixed level for a specified period before any change can occur [ECONOMICS]

cra|zy /kreɪzi/ (**crazier, craziest**)
1 ADJ very strange or stupid [INFORMAL] ❍ *People thought we were crazy spending all that money.* ● **cra|zi|ly ADV** ❍ *He ran crazily around in circles.*
2 ADJ Someone who is going **crazy** is extremely bored or upset, or feels they cannot wait for something any longer. [INFORMAL] ❍ *Annie thought she might go crazy if she didn't find out soon.*
3 ADJ If you are **crazy about** someone or something, you like them very much. [INFORMAL] ❍ *Infotech and pharma are sectors that punters today are crazy about.*

cream /krim/
1 NONCOUNT NOUN Cream is a thick, yellowish-white liquid that comes from milk. ❍ *strawberries and cream*
2 NOUN a substance that you rub into your skin ❍ *hand cream*
3 ADJ yellowish-white in color ❍ *a cream silk shirt*

crease /kris/ (**creases, creasing, creased**)
1 NOUN a line that appears in cloth or paper when it has been folded or pressed ❍ *pants with sharp creases*
2 VERB If cloth **creases** or if you **crease** it, lines appear on it after being folded or pressed. ❍ *Most clothes crease a bit when you're traveling.* ● **creased ADJ** ❍ *a creased linen jacket*

cre|ate /krieɪt/ (**creates, creating, created**)
VERB To **create** something means to make it

happen or exist. ❍ *Creating green jobs is a sensible aspiration for the government.* ❍ *Could this solution create problems for us in the future?*
● **crea|tor** NOUN ❍ *Matt Groening, creator of The Simpsons*

crea|tion /kriеɪʃən/ NOUN something that someone has made or produced ❍ *a great comic creation*

crea|tive /kriеɪtɪv/ ADJ good at inventing things and having new ideas ❍ *When you don't have much money, you have to be creative.*

creat|ive ten|sion NONCOUNT NOUN **Creative tension** is a situation where disagreement or discord ultimately produces good ideas or outcomes. ❍ *Reform can work well when squabbling advisers generate creative tension.*

crea|ture /kritʃər/ NOUN a living thing that is not a plant ❍ *Like all living creatures, birds need plenty of water.*

cred|it /krɛdɪt/
1 NONCOUNT NOUN **Credit** is a system in which you pay for goods after you have received them. [FINANCE, BANKING] ❍ *They buy everything on credit.*
2 NONCOUNT NOUN **Credit** is praise for something you have done. ❍ *I can't take all the credit myself.*
3 NOUN one part of a course at a school or a college ❍ *He doesn't have enough credits to graduate.*
4 VERB When a sum of money **is credited** to an account, the bank adds that sum of money to the total in the account. Compare with **debit**. [BANKING] ❍ *She noticed that only $80,000 had been credited to her account.*
5 NOUN A **credit** is a record of the money paid into your bank account. Compare with **debit**. [BANKING]

cred|it card (**credit cards**) NOUN a card that you use to buy something and pay for it later [BANKING] ❍ *Call this number to order by credit card.*

cred|it crunch (**credit crunches**) NOUN or **credit squeeze** a period during which there is a sudden reduction in the availability of credit from banks and other lenders [BANKING, ECONOMICS, INFORMAL] ❍ *The credit crunch means the company will have to turn to existing assets for working capital.*

cred|it line (**credit lines**) NOUN the amount of debt a person or firm is allowed by their credit card firm [BANKING] ❍ *The amount of your credit line will depend on your home's value.*

cred|itor /krɛdɪtər/ NOUN someone who people owe money to [BANKING, ADMINISTRATION] ❍ *The company said it would pay in full all its creditors.*

cred|it rat|ing (**credit ratings**) NOUN a judgment of how likely someone is to pay money back if they borrow it or buy things on credit [BANKING] ❍ *Your overdraft rate depends on your credit rating.*

credit-reference agen|cy (**credit-reference agencies**) NOUN an agency that provides credit ratings for people and organizations [BANKING, BUSINESS MANAGEMENT]

cred|it stand|ing (**credit standings**) NOUN a person or firm's reputation for fulfilling financial obligations [BANKING] ❍ *Wall Street's biggest players are struggling to maintain the stellar credit standing required to finance their activities.*

cred|it trans|fer (**credit transfer**) [BANKING, BRIT] → **wire transfer**

cred|it un|ion (**credit unions**) NOUN a financial institution that offers its members low-interest loans [BANKING] ❍ *All the money that we have is tied up in a credit union.*

credit|worthy /krɛdɪtwɜrði/ also **credit-worthy** ADJ judged able to be lent money or allowed to have goods on credit [BANKING] ❍ *The Fed wants banks to continue to lend to creditworthy borrowers.*
● **credit|worthi|ness** NONCOUNT NOUN ❍ *They now take extra steps to verify the creditworthiness of customers.*

creep /krip/ (**creeps, creeping, crept**) VERB If you **creep** somewhere, you move there quietly and slowly. ❍ *He crept up the stairs.*

cre|mate /krimeɪt/ (**cremates, cremating, cremated**) VERB When someone

C

is cremated, their dead body is burned, usually as part of a funeral service. ❍ *She wants Jim to be cremated.*

crew /kru/ NOUN the people who work on a ship or aircraft ❍ *the crew of the space shuttle*

C

crib /krɪb/ NOUN a bed with high sides for a baby

crick|et /krɪkɪt/ NOUN a small jumping insect that produces short, loud sounds by rubbing its wings together

crime /kraɪm/ NOUN an illegal act, or illegal acts generally ❍ *Police are searching the scene of the crime.* ❍ *violent crime*

crimi|nal /krɪmɪnᵊl/ NOUN a person who does something illegal ❍ *dangerous criminals*

cri|sis /kraɪsɪs/ (**crises** /kraɪsiz/) NOUN a situation that is very serious or dangerous ❍ *This is a worldwide crisis that affects us all.*

cri|sis man|age|ment NONCOUNT NOUN **Crisis management** is a management style that solves the immediate problems occurring in a business rather than looking for long-term solutions. ❍ *The business is overcome by day-to-day crisis management.* ❍ *a crisis-management team*

crisp /krɪsp/ ADJ Food that is **crisp** is pleasantly hard. ❍ *a nice crisp apple*

cri|teri|on /kraɪtɪəriən/ (**criteria** /kraɪtɪəriə/) NOUN a factor on which you judge or decide something ❍ *The most important criterion for entry is that applicants must design and make their own work.*

> **COLLOCATIONS**
> *selection* criteria
> *performance* criteria
> to *meet* a criterion *for* something
> to *set* a criterion *for* something

crit|ic /krɪtɪk/ NOUN a person who writes and gives their opinion about books, movies, music, or art ❍ *a film critic*

criti|cal /krɪtɪkᵊl/

1 ADJ serious and dangerous ❍ *The economic situation may soon become critical.*

• **criti|cal|ly** ADV ❍ *Food supplies are critically low.*

2 ADJ expressing disapproval of a person or a thing ❍ *His report is critical of the judge.*

criti|cise /krɪtɪsaɪz/ [BRIT] → **criticize**

criti|cism /krɪtɪsɪzəm/

1 NONCOUNT NOUN **Criticism** is when someone expresses disapproval of someone or something. ❍ *The president faced strong criticism for his remarks.*

2 NOUN a statement that expresses disapproval ❍ *Managers should say something positive before making a criticism.*

criti|cize /krɪtɪsaɪz/ (**criticizes, criticizing, criticized**) VERB If you **criticize** someone or something, you express your disapproval of them. ❍ *His staff rarely criticized him.*

CRM /si ɑr ɛm/ **CRM** is an abbreviation for **customer relationship management**. [MARKETING AND SALES]

crook|ed /krʊkɪd/ ADJ not straight ❍ *He has crooked teeth.*

crop /krɒp/ NOUN a plant that is grown for food, such as wheat or potato ❍ *Rice farmers here still plant their crops by hand.*

> **cross**
> ❶ MOVING ACROSS
> ❷ ANGRY

❶ **cross** /krɔs/ (**crosses, crossing, crossed**)

1 VERB If you **cross** a place, you move from one side of it to the other. ❍ *She crossed the road without looking.*

2 VERB In sports, if you **cross** the ball, you hit it or kick it from one side of the field to a person on the other side. ❍ *Ronaldinho crossed the ball into the penalty area.*

3 NOUN in sports, the act of hitting or kicking the ball from one side of a field to a person on the other side

4 VERB If you **cross** your arms, legs, or fingers, you put one of them on top of the other. ❍ *She crossed her legs.*

5 NOUN a line going downwards with a shorter horizontal line across it, or any object shaped like this, especially one which is a Christian symbol ❍ *She wore a cross around her neck.*

6 NOUN a written mark in the shape of an X ❍ *Put a cross next to those activities you like.*
▶**cross out** If you **cross out** words, you draw a line through them. ❍ *He crossed out her name and added his own.*

❷ **cross** /krɔs/ (**crosser, crossest**) **ADJ** angry ❍ *Don't get cross with me.* ● **cross\|ly ADV** ❍ *"No, no, no," Morris said crossly.*

cross\|walk /krɔswɔk/ **NOUN** a place where drivers must stop to let people walk across a street

crouch /kraʊtʃ/ (**crouches, crouching, crouched**) **VERB** If you **crouch**, you bend your legs so that you are close to the ground. ❍ *We crouched in the bushes to hide.*

crowd /kraʊd/
1 NOUN a large group of people who have gathered together ❍ *A huge crowd gathered in the town square.*
2 VERB When people **crowd around** someone or something, they move closely together around them. ❍ *The children crowded around him.*
3 VERB If a lot of people **crowd into** a place, they enter it so that it becomes very full. ❍ *Thousands of people crowded into the city center to see the president.*

crowd\|ed /kraʊdɪd/ **ADJ** full of people ❍ *He tried to find her in the crowded room.*

crown /kraʊn/
1 NOUN a gold or silver circle that a king or a queen wears on their head
2 VERB When a king or a queen **is crowned**, they officially become king or queen, and a crown is put on their head. ❍ *Two days later, Juan Carlos was crowned king.*

cru\|cial /kruʃᵊl/ **ADJ** extremely important ❍ *a crucial decision* ● **cru\|cial\|ly ADV** ❍ *These systems are crucially important to an organization's strategic capability.*

crude /krud/ (**cruder, crudest**)
1 ADJ simple and rough ❍ *Demographics are a very crude mechanism of targeting.* ● **crude\|ly ADV** ❍ *It is important to obtain some impression, however crudely derived.*
2 ADJ rude or offensive ❍ *The men were telling crude jokes.*

cru\|el /kruəl/ (**crueler, cruelest**) **ADJ** Someone who is **cruel** deliberately causes suffering. ❍ *These working practices are very cruel.* ● **cru\|el\|ly ADV** ❍ *He was treated cruelly by his employers.*

cru\|el\|ty /kruəlti/ **NONCOUNT NOUN** **Cruelty** is behavior that deliberately causes suffering. ❍ *There are laws against cruelty to animals.*

cruise /kruz/ (**cruises, cruising, cruised**)
1 NOUN a vacation that you spend on a ship or boat ❍ *He and his wife went on a world cruise.*
2 VERB If a car, a ship, or an aircraft **cruises** somewhere, it moves at a steady comfortable speed. ❍ *A black and white police car cruised past.*

crumb /krʌm/ **NOUN** one of many small pieces that fall when you break food such as bread or cake ❍ *I stood up, brushing crumbs from my pants.*

crum\|ble /krʌmbᵊl/ (**crumbles, crumbling, crumbled**) **VERB** If something **crumbles** or you **crumble** something, it breaks into small pieces. ❍ *The stone wall was crumbling away in places.*

crunch /krʌntʃ/ (**crunches, crunching, crunched**)
1 VERB If something **crunches** it makes a breaking or crushing noise. ❍ *The gravel crunched under his boots.*
2 NOUN Crunch is also a noun. ❍ *We heard the crunch of tires on the road up to the house.*
3 VERB If you **crunch** something, you noisily break it into small pieces between your teeth. ❍ *She crunched an ice cube loudly.*
4 To **crunch numbers** means to do a lot of calculations using a calculator or computer. ❍ *I pored over the books with great enthusiasm, often crunching the numbers until 1:00 a.m.*

crush /krʌʃ/ (**crushes, crushing, crushed**) **VERB** If you **crush** something, you press it very hard so that it breaks or loses its shape. ❍ *Andrew crushed his empty can.* ❍ *The drinks were full of crushed ice.*

crust /krʌst/
1 NOUN the hard outer part of bread ❍ *Cut the crusts off the bread.*

2 NOUN The Earth's **crust** is its outer layer. ❍ *Earthquakes damage the Earth's crust.*

crutch /krʌtʃ/ (**crutches**) **NOUN** a long stick that you put under your arm and use to help yourself walk when you are injured ❍ *I can walk without crutches now.*

C

cry /kraɪ/ (**cries, crying, cried**)
1 VERB When you **cry**, tears come from your eyes. ❍ *I hung up the phone and started to cry.*
2 VERB If you **cry** something, you say it very loudly. ❍ *"See you soon!" she cried.*
3 Cry out means the same as **cry**. ❍ *"You're wrong, you're all wrong!" Henry cried out.*
4 NOUN a loud, high sound that you make when you feel a strong emotion ❍ *She saw the spider and let out a cry of horror.*
5 NOUN the loud, high sound that a bird or animal makes ❍ *the cry of a strange bird*

crys|tal /krɪstᵊl/
1 NOUN a small, hard piece of a natural substance such as salt or ice ❍ *salt crystals*
2 NONCOUNT NOUN a transparent rock used in jewelry ❍ *a crystal necklace*

CSR /si ɛs ɑr/ (**CSRs**)
1 NOUN CSR is an abbreviation for "customer service representative." [MARKETING AND SALES]
2 NONCOUNT NOUN CSR is an abbreviation for "corporate social responsibility." [BUSINESS MANAGEMENT]

cube /kyub/ **NOUN** a solid object with six square surfaces ❍ *a tray of ice cubes* ❍ *sugar cubes*

cu|cum|ber /kyukʌmbər/ **NOUN** a long dark-green vegetable that you eat raw ❍ *cheese and cucumber sandwiches*

cul|ti|vate /kʌltɪveɪt/ (**cultivates, cultivating, cultivated**) **VERB** If you **cultivate** land, you grow plants on it. ❍ *She had cultivated a small garden of her own.*

cul|tur|al /kʌltʃərəl/ **ADJ** relating to the arts ❍ *We've organized a range of sports and cultural events.*

cul|tur|al awa|re|ness NONCOUNT NOUN Someone's **cultural awareness** is their understanding of the differences in attitudes and values between themselves and people from other countries or other backgrounds. [BUSINESS MANAGEMENT] ❍ *programs to promote diversity and cultural awareness within the industry*

cul|ture /kʌltʃər/
1 NONCOUNT NOUN Culture is activities such as art, music, literature, and theater. ❍ *Movies are part of our popular culture.*
2 NOUN the way of life, the traditions, and beliefs of a particular group of people ❍ *Peru has created a culture of fiscal propriety.*

cum div|idend /kʌm dɪvɪdɛnd, kʊm/ **ADJ** Investors who buy a share **cum dividend** are entitled to keep the dividend if they receive it. The short form **cum div.** is sometimes used. [FINANCE]

cu|mu|la|tive /kyumyələtɪv/ **ADJ** If a series of events have a **cumulative** effect, each event makes the effect greater. ❍ *It is simple pleasures, such as a walk on a sunny day, which have a cumulative effect on our mood.*
● **cu|mu|la|tive|ly ADV** ❍ *His administration was plagued by one petty scandal after another which was cumulatively very damaging.*

cun|ning /kʌnɪŋ/ **ADJ** clever and dishonest ❍ *a cunning ploy*

cup /kʌp/
1 NOUN a small round container that you drink from ❍ *Let's have a cup of coffee.*
2 NOUN a measure of 16 tablespoons or 8 fluid ounces ❍ *Gradually add 1 cup of milk.* ❍ *Add half a cup of sugar, and mix.*
3 NOUN a large round metal container that is given as a prize to the winner of a competition ❍ *I think New Zealand will win the cup.*

cup|board /kʌbərd/ **NOUN** a piece of furniture with doors and shelves for storing food or dishes ❍ *The kitchen cupboard was full of cans of soup.*

curb /kɜrb/ **NOUN** the edge of a sidewalk next to the road ❍ *I pulled over to the curb.*

curb ap|peal NONCOUNT NOUN If a house has **curb appeal**, it is attractive to potential buyers when they look at it from the road. [MARKETING AND SALES] ❍ *Prospective buyers will often drive past your home before viewing,* *so it needs curb appeal. Give the front door a fresh coat of paint.*

cure /kyʊər/ (**cures, curing, cured**)
1 VERB If a doctor or a treatment **cures** someone or their illness, the person becomes well again. ❍ *The new medicine had cured her headaches.* ❍ *Almost overnight, I was cured.*
2 NOUN A **cure for** an illness is a treatment that makes the person well again. ❍ *There is still no cure for a cold.*

cu|ri|os|ity /kyʊəriɒsɪti/ **NONCOUNT NOUN** **Curiosity** is a desire to know about something. ❍ *The scale of their foreign investments may arouse curiosity and concern.*

cu|ri|ous /kyʊəriəs/ **ADJ** wanting to know more about something ❍ *I'm curious about his background.* ● **cu|ri|ous|ly ADV** ❍ *She looked at them curiously.*

curl /kɜrl/
1 NOUN a piece of hair shaped in a tight curve or circle ❍ *a little girl with blonde curls*
2 VERB If your hair **curls**, it forms curved shapes and if you curl your hair, you make it form curved shapes. ❍ *Her hair curled around her shoulders.* ❍ *Maria curled her hair for the party.*
▸ **curl up** If you **curl up**, you move your head, arms, and legs close to your body. ❍ *She curled up next to him.*

curly /kɜrli/ (**curlier, curliest**) **ADJ** **Curly** hair is shaped in curves. ❍ *I've got naturally curly hair.*

cur|ren|cy /kɜrənsi/ (**currencies**) **NOUN** the money that is used in a particular country [ECONOMICS] ❍ *The plans were for a single European currency.*

cur|rent /kɜrənt/
1 NOUN a steady flow of water, air, or energy ❍ *The fish move with the ocean currents.* ❍ *an electric current*
2 ADJ happening now ❍ *Current expenditure exceeds the original estimate.* ● **cur|rent|ly ADV** ❍ *He is currently unemployed.*

cur|rent ac|count (**current accounts**) [BANKING, FINANCE, BRIT] → **checking account**

cur|rent af|fairs or **current events PL NOUN** **Current affairs** are political events that are discussed on television, in newspapers, and on the Internet.

cur|rent as|sets PL NOUN **Current assets** are assets that a firm does not use on a continuous basis, such as stocks and debts, but that can be converted into cash within one year. [FINANCE] ❍ *The company lists its current assets at $56.9 million.*

current-cost ac|count|ing NONCOUNT NOUN **Current-cost accounting** is a method of accounting that records the value of assets according to how much it would cost to replace them, rather than their original cost. [FINANCE] ❍ *Current-cost accounting attempts to capture the effect of inflation on asset values.*

cur|rent ex|pen|ses PL NOUN In accounting, **current expenses** are the everyday costs that are necessary to run a business. [FINANCE] ❍ *They deduct current expenses when calculating profit but do not deduct capital expenses.*

cur|rent lia|bil|ities PL NOUN In accounting, **current liabilities** are the sums of money a business has to pay out during the current tax year. [FINANCE] ❍ *Graham liked companies whose current assets were at least twice their current liabilities.*

cur|ricu|lum /kərɪkyələm/ (**curriculums** or **curricula**) /kərɪkyələ/ **NOUN** all the courses of study that are taught in a school or college ❍ *Business skills should be part of the school curriculum.*

cur|ricu|lum vitae /kərɪkyələm vaɪti/ (**curriculum vitae**) **NOUN** A **curriculum vitae** is the same as a **CV**. [HR]

cur|ry /kɜri/ **NONCOUNT NOUN** **Curry** is a dish, originally from Asia, that is cooked with hot spices. ❍ *vegetable curry*

curse /kɜrs/ (**curses, cursing, cursed**)
1 VERB If you **curse**, you use very rude or offensive language. [FORMAL] ❍ *Jake nodded, but he was cursing silently.*
2 NOUN **Curse** is also a noun. ❍ *Shouts and curses came from all directions.*
3 NOUN a strange power that seems to cause unpleasant things to happen to someone

❍ *He believed that an evil spirit put a curse on his business.*

cur|sor /kɜrsər/ **NOUN** on a computer screen, the small line that shows where you are working ❍ *He moved the cursor and clicked the mouse.*

C

cur|tain /kɜrtᵊn/
1 NOUN one of two pieces of material that hang from the top of a window ❍ *She closed her bedroom curtains.*
2 NOUN In a theater, **the curtain** is the large piece of material that hangs at the front of the stage until a performance begins. ❍ *The curtain fell, and the audience stood and applauded.*

curve /kɜrv/ (**curves, curving, curved**)
1 NOUN a smooth, gradually bending line ❍ *the curve of his lips*
2 VERB If something **curves**, it has the shape of a curve or moves in a curve. ❍ *Her spine curved forward.* ❍ *The ball curved through the air.*
• **curved ADJ** ❍ *curved lines*

cush|ion /kʊʃən/ **NOUN** a soft object that you put on a seat to make it more comfortable ❍ *The cat lay on a velvet cushion.*

cus|to|dian /kʌstoʊdiən/ **NOUN** a person whose job is to take care of an office or a school and the ground around it ❍ *He worked as a school custodian for 20 years.*

cus|tom /kʌstəm/ **NOUN** something that is usual or traditional among a particular group of people ❍ *This is an ancient Japanese custom.* ❍ *It was the custom to give presents.*

cus|tom|er /kʌstəmər/ **NOUN** someone who buys something ❍ *a satisfied customer*

COLLOCATIONS
customer *satisfaction*
customer *service*
to attract customers
to gain customers
to lose customers *to somebody*

cus|tom|er base (**customer bases**) **NOUN** all a business' regular customers, considered as a group [BUSINESS MANAGEMENT] ❍ *a customer base of 21 million people*

cus|tom|er care NONCOUNT NOUN **Customer care** refers to the way that firms behave toward their customers. [MARKETING AND SALES] ❍ *very low standards of customer care* ❍ *What has happened to our reputation for customer care and good service?*

cus|tom|er da|ta NONCOUNT NOUN **Customer data** is information about customers' shopping habits that a firm stores in a database. [BUSINESS MANAGEMENT] ❍ *IT allows networks of car dealers to collect, store, and analyze customer data.*

cus|tom|er loy|al|ty NONCOUNT NOUN If a business has high **customer loyalty**, many of its customers use its products or services again and again. [MARKETING AND SALES] ❍ *Frequent-shopper programs are marketed to retailers as a way of increasing customer loyalty.*

cus|tom|er pro|file (**customer profiles**) **NOUN** a description of the typical sort of customer who is regarded as likely to buy a particular product [MARKETING AND SALES] ❍ *They plan to move from an older customer profile to a younger market.*

cus|tom|er re|la|tions
1 PL NOUN **Customer relations** are the relationships that a business has with its customers and the way in which it treats them. [MARKETING AND SALES, BUSINESS MANAGEMENT] ❍ *Good customer relations require courtesy, professionalism, and effective response.*
2 NONCOUNT NOUN **Customer relations** is the department within a company that deals with complaints from customers. [MARKETING AND SALES, BUSINESS MANAGEMENT] ❍ *Tucson Electric's customer-relations department*

cus|tom|er re|la|tion|ship man|age|ment NONCOUNT NOUN **Customer relationship management** is the practice of building a strong relationship between a business and its customers. [MARKETING AND SALES, BUSINESS MANAGEMENT] ❍ *The agency views customer relationship management as a key feature of any marketing strategy.*

cus|tom|er sat|is|fac|tion NONCOUNT NOUN When customers are pleased with the goods or services they have bought, you can refer to this as **customer satisfaction**. [MARKETING AND SALES, BUSINESS MANAGEMENT] ❍ *I really believe that it is possible to both improve customer satisfaction and reduce costs.* ❍ *Customer satisfaction with their service runs at more than 90 percent.*

cus|tom|er ser|vice NONCOUNT NOUN **Customer service** refers to the way that firms behave toward their customers. [MARKETING AND SALES, BUSINESS MANAGEMENT] ❍ *a mail-order business with a strong reputation for customer service* ❍ *The firm has an excellent customer service department.*

COLLOCATIONS
to *provide* customer service
to *improve* customer service
a customer service *representative*
a customer service *center*

cus|tom|ise /kʌstəmaɪz/ [BRIT] → **customize**

cus|tom|ize /kʌstəmaɪz/ (**customizes, customizing, customized**) VERB If you **customize** something, you change its appearance or features to suit your tastes or needs. ❍ *a control that allows photographers to customize the camera's basic settings*

cus|toms /kʌstəmz/
1 NOUN the official organization responsible for collecting taxes on goods coming into a country and preventing illegal goods from being brought in [FINANCE] ❍ *What right does Customs have to search my car?*
2 NONCOUNT NOUN **Customs** is the place where people arriving from a foreign country have to declare goods that they bring with them. ❍ *He walked through customs.*

cus|toms duty (**customs duties**) NOUN taxes that people pay for importing and exporting goods [FINANCE] ❍ *Foreign investors can now import and export goods without paying customs duties.* ❍ *Customs duty on cotton is being removed to ensure cheaper availability of raw material.*

cus|toms un|ion (**customs unions**) NOUN an association of nations that promotes free trade within the union and establishes common tariffs on trade with other nations [FINANCE]

cut /kʌt/ (**cuts, cutting, cut**)
1 VERB If you **cut** something, you use something sharp to remove part of it, or to break it. ❍ *Cut the tomatoes in half.* ❍ *You had your hair cut, it looks great.*
2 NOUN **Cut** is also a noun. ❍ *Carefully make a cut in the fabric.*
3 VERB If you **cut yourself**, you accidentally injure yourself on a sharp object so that you bleed. ❍ *I cut my finger while chopping the vegetables.*
4 NOUN **Cut** is also a noun. ❍ *He had a cut on his left eyebrow.*
5 VERB If you **cut** something, you reduce it. ❍ *We need to cut costs.*
6 NOUN **Cut** is also a noun. ❍ *The government announced a 2% cut in interest rates.*

▶ **cut down**
1 If you **cut down on** something, you use or do less of it. ❍ *He cut down on coffee.*
2 If you **cut down** a tree, you cut through it so that it falls to the ground. ❍ *They cut down several trees.*

▶ **cut off** If you **cut** something **off** or **cut** something **out**, you remove it using scissors or a knife. ❍ *She cut off a large piece of meat.* ❍ *I cut the picture out and stuck it on my wall.*

▶ **cut up** If you **cut** something **up**, you cut it into several pieces. ❍ *Cut up the tomatoes.*

cut and paste (**cuts and pastes, cutting and pasting, cut and pasted**) VERB When you **cut and paste** words or pictures on a computer, you remove them from one place and copy them to another place. ❍ *She had cut and pasted the entire paragraph.*

cute /kyut/ (**cuter, cutest**) ADJ pretty or attractive [INFORMAL] ❍ *Oh, look at that dog! He's so cute.* ❍ *Your sister's cute.*

cut-price [MARKETING AND SALES, ECONOMICS, BRIT] → **cut-rate**

cut-rate ADJ cheaper than usual [MARKETING AND SALES, ECONOMICS] ❍ *cut-rate auto insurance*

CV /si vi/ (**CVs**) [BRIT] → **résumé**

C

CWO /si dʌbᵊlyu oʊ/ also **C.W.O. CWO** is an abbreviation for "cash with order." [FINANCE, PURCHASING]

cy|ber|space /saɪbərspeɪs/ **NONCOUNT NOUN Cyberspace** is the imaginary place where electronic communications take place. [TECHNOLOGY] ❍ *cyberspace communications*

cy|ber|squat|ting /saɪbərskwɒtɪŋ/ **NONCOUNT NOUN Cybersquatting** involves buying an Internet domain name that might be wanted by another person, business, or organization with the intention of selling it to them and making a profit. [TECHNOLOGY] ● **cy|ber|squatter NOUN** ❍ *The old official club website address has been taken over by cybersquatters.*

cy|cle /saɪkᵊl/ (**cycles, cycling, cycled**)
1 NOUN a process that is repeated again and again ❍ *We had to put an end to the damaging cycle of boom and bust.*
2 VERB If you **cycle**, you ride a bicycle. ❍ *He cycles to school every day.* ● **cy|cling NONCOUNT NOUN** ❍ *The quiet country roads are ideal for cycling.*
3 NOUN A **cycle** is the same as a **bicycle**. [mainly BRIT]

cyc|li|cal un|em|ploy|ment /sɪklɪkᵊl ʌnɛmplɔɪmənt, saɪklɪ-/ **NONCOUNT NOUN Cyclical unemployment** is unemployment caused by fluctuations in the level of economic activity in trade cycles. [ECONOMICS]

cy|clist /saɪklɪst/ **NOUN** someone who rides a bicycle ❍ *a keen cyclist*

cyni|cal /sɪnɪkᵊl/ **ADJ** believing that people are usually bad or dishonest ❍ *He has a cynical view of the world.* ● **cyni|cal|ly ADV** ❍ *They are cynically taking advantage of the crisis.*

Dd

dad /dæd/ **NOUN** Your **dad** is your father. [INFORMAL] ○ *My dad was a doctor.*

dai|ly /deɪli/
1 ADV happening every day ○ *The website is updated daily.*
2 ADJ **Daily** is also an adjective. ○ *a daily newspaper*

dairy /dɛəri/ (**dairies**)
1 NOUN a place where milk, and food made from milk, such as butter, cream, and cheese are produced
2 ADJ used for describing foods such as butter and cheese that are made from milk ○ *dairy products*

dam /dæm/ **NOUN** a wall that is built across a river in order to make a lake ○ *Before the dam was built, the Campbell River often flooded.*

dam|age /dæmɪdʒ/ (**damages, damaging, damaged**)
1 VERB To **damage** something means to break it or harm it. ○ *Hurricanes have severely damaged crops.* ○ *The new tax will badly damage Australian industries.* ● **dam|ag|ing ADJ** ○ *We can see the damaging effects of pollution in cities.*
2 NONCOUNT NOUN **Damage** is physical harm that happens to an object. ○ *The explosion caused a lot of damage to the factory.*

damp /dæmp/ (**damper, dampest**) **ADJ** slightly wet ○ *Timber swells when it is damp.* ○ *Crops are often stored in damp and warm conditions.*

dance /dæns/ (**dances, dancing, danced**)
1 VERB When you **dance**, you move your body to music. ○ *She turned on the radio and danced around the room.* ○ *Let's dance.* ● **danc|ing NONCOUNT NOUN** ○ *Let's go dancing tonight.*
2 NOUN a particular series of movements that you usually do in time to music ○ *a traditional Scottish dance*
3 NOUN a party where people dance with each other ○ *the Christmas dance*

danc|er /dænsər/ **NOUN** a person who earns money by dancing, or a person who is dancing ○ *She's a dancer with the New York City Ballet.*

dan|ger /deɪndʒər/
1 NONCOUNT NOUN **Danger** is the possibility that someone or something may be harmed or badly affected. ○ *I'm worried that she's in danger.* ○ *The economy is in danger of collapse.*
2 NOUN something or someone that can cause harm ○ *the dangers posed by toxic waste*

dan|ger mon|ey NONCOUNT NOUN **Danger money** is extra money that is paid to someone who does a dangerous job. [mainly BRIT]

dan|ger|ous /deɪndʒərəs, deɪndʒrəs/ **ADJ** likely to harm you ○ *We're in a very dangerous situation.* ○ *a dangerous breed of dog* ● **dan|ger|ous|ly ADV** ○ *We are dangerously close to a recession.*

dare /dɛər/ (**dares, daring, dared**)
1 VERB If you **dare to** do something, you are brave enough to do it. ○ *I wouldn't dare to disagree with him.*
2 MODAL **Dare** is also a modal verb. ○ *They dare not change the product in case they lose customers.*
3 VERB If you **dare** someone **to** do something, you ask them if they will do it in order to see if they are brave enough. ○ *We dared him to ask Mr. Roberts for a promotion.*
4 You say "**how dare you**" to someone when you are very angry about something that they have done. [SPOKEN] ○ *How dare you say that about me!*

dar|ing /dɛərɪŋ/ **ADJ** brave ○ *Mr. McGee had daring plans to triple the size of the airline's fleet.*

dark /dɑrk/ (**darker, darkest**)
1 ADJ When it is **dark**, there is not much light. ❍ *It was too dark to see much.* ❍ *It's getting dark – we'd better go.* ● **dark|ness** NONCOUNT NOUN ❍ *The light went out, and we were in total darkness.*
2 ADJ Something **dark** is black or a color close to black. ❍ *He wore a dark suit.* ❍ *a dark blue dress*
3 ADJ If someone has **dark** hair, eyes, or skin, they have brown or black hair, eyes, or skin. ❍ *He had dark, curly hair.*
4 NONCOUNT NOUN **The dark** is the lack of light in a place. ❍ *We drove to the airport in the dark.*

dar|ling /dɑrlɪŋ/ NOUN You call someone **darling** if you love them or like them very much. ❍ *Thank you, darling.*

dart /dɑrt/
1 VERB If a person or animal **darts** somewhere, they move there suddenly and quickly. ❍ *Ingrid darted across the street.*
2 NOUN a small, narrow object with a sharp point that you can throw or shoot
3 NONCOUNT NOUN **Darts** is a game in which you throw darts at a round board that has numbers on it.

dash /dæʃ/ (**dashes, dashing, dashed**)
1 VERB If you **dash** somewhere, you go there quickly and suddenly. ❍ *She dashed off to the meeting.*
2 NOUN If you **make** a **dash** for a place, you go there quickly and suddenly. ❍ *We made a dash for the door.*
3 NOUN a short, straight, horizontal line (—) that you use in writing

dash|board /dæʃbɔrd/ NOUN in a car, the area in front of the driver where most of the controls are ❍ *The clock on the dashboard showed two o'clock.*

da|ta /deɪtə, dætə/
1 PL NOUN **Data** is information, especially in the form of facts or numbers. ❍ *Government data show that unemployment is going up.*
2 NONCOUNT NOUN **Data** is information that can be used by a computer program. [TECHNOLOGY] ❍ *The new format holds huge amounts of data.*

data|base /deɪtəbeɪs, dætə-/ also **data base** NOUN a collection of data that is stored in a computer and that can easily be used and added to [TECHNOLOGY] ❍ *There is a database of names of people who are allowed to vote.*

Da|ta Pro|tec|tion Act NONCOUNT NOUN In Britain, the **Data Protection Act** is a law that gives rules about how information about people that is stored on a computer can be used. [LEGAL] ❍ *Using names from a computer without permission breaches the Data Protection Act.*

date /deɪt/ (**dates, dating, dated**)
1 NOUN a particular day and month or a particular year ❍ *"What's the date today?"— "July 23."*
2 NOUN an arrangement to meet a boyfriend or a girlfriend ❍ *I have a date tonight.*
3 VERB If you **are dating** someone, you go out with them regularly because you are having a romantic relationship with them. ❍ *I dated a woman who was a teacher.*
4 NOUN a small, dark-brown, sticky fruit with a stone inside

dat|ed /deɪtɪd/ ADJ old-fashioned ❍ *Many of his ideas have value, but some are dated and others are plain wrong.*

daugh|ter /dɔtər/ NOUN Someone's **daughter** is their female child. ❍ *We met Flora and her daughter, Catherine.* ❍ *She's the daughter of a university professor.*

daughter-in-law (**daughters-in-law**) NOUN Someone's **daughter-in-law** is the wife of their son.

dawn /dɔn/ NOUN the time in the morning when the sky becomes light ❍ *I have to leave at dawn tomorrow.*

dawn raid (**dawn raids**) NOUN If a person or firm carries out a **dawn raid**, they try to buy a large number of a firm's shares at the start of a day's trading. [ECONOMICS] ❍ *Southern acquired 11.2 percent of Sweb in a dawn raid on Monday.*

day /deɪ/
1 NOUN one of the seven 24-hour periods of time in a week ❍ *They'll be back in three days.* ❍ *We had meetings every day last week.*
2 NOUN The **day** is the time when it is light

outside. ❍ *We spent the day discussing the new proposal.* ❍ *The streets are busy during the day.*
3 One day or **some day** means at some time in the future. ❍ *We hope to move our headquarters to Dallas some day.* ❍ *Restrictions may change one day.*

day|book /deɪbʊk/ **NOUN** In bookkeeping, a **daybook** is a book in which the sales and purchases for each day are recorded. [ECONOMICS]

day la|bor|er (**day laborers**) **NOUN** an unskilled worker who is hired by the day [HR, ECONOMICS] ❍ *Many peasants were forced to abandon their independent farming and become day laborers in agriculture.*

day|light /deɪlaɪt/ **NONCOUNT NOUN** **Daylight** is the natural light that there is during the day. ❍ *A little daylight came through a crack in the wall.*

day shift (**day shifts**)
1 NOUN a group of workers who work during the daytime in a place where other workers work at night [HR]
2 NOUN the period of time worked by these workers [HR] ❍ *Instead of working a normal day shift, employees work either 6 till 2 or 2 till 10.*

day|time /deɪtaɪm/ **NOUN** **The daytime** is the part of a day between the time when it gets light and the time when it gets dark. ❍ *He rarely went anywhere in the daytime.*

day trad|er (**day traders**) **NOUN** In the stock market, **day traders** are traders who buy and sell particular securities on the same day. [ECONOMICS] ❍ *Unlike the day traders, they tended to hold on to stocks for days and weeks, sometimes even months.*

day trad|ing **NONCOUNT NOUN** **Day trading** is the practice of buying and selling particular securities on the same day to try to make a quick profit. [ECONOMICS]

DD also **dd** /di di/ **DD** is an abbreviation for **direct debit**. [BANKING]

dead /dɛd/
1 ADJ no longer living ❍ *She told me her husband was dead.*
2 PL NOUN **The dead** are people who have died. ❍ *Two soldiers were among the dead.*
3 ADJ A piece of electrical equipment that is **dead** has stopped working. ❍ *a dead battery*

dead-cat bounce (**dead-cat bounces**) **NOUN** a temporary improvement in share prices following a big fall in their value that happens just before a firm fails completely [ECONOMICS]

dead|line /dɛdlaɪn/ **NOUN** a time or date before which a piece of work must be finished ❍ *Unfortunately, we missed the deadline.*

dead|ly /dɛdli/ (**deadlier, deadliest**) **ADJ** likely or able to kill someone ❍ *a deadly disease*

deaf /dɛf/ (**deafer, deafest**)
1 ADJ unable to hear anything, or unable to hear well ❍ *She was born deaf.* ❍ *I'm a little deaf in my left ear.*
2 PL NOUN **The deaf** are people who are deaf. ❍ *Marianne works as a part-time teacher for the deaf.*

deal /dil/ (**deals, dealing, dealt**)
1 NOUN an agreement or arrangement, especially in business ❍ *They made a deal to share the money between them.*
2 VERB If a firm **deals in** a type of goods, it buys or sells those goods. ❍ *They deal in antiques.* ● **deal|er** **NOUN** ❍ *an antique dealer*
3 If you have **a great deal of** a particular thing, you have a lot of it. ❍ *You can earn a great deal of money in this job.*
▸ **deal with**
1 When you **deal with** something or someone, you do what is needed for them. ❍ *Could you deal with this customer, please?*
2 If you **deal with** another firm, you do business with them. ❍ *The firm deals with many overseas suppliers.*

deal|ing room (**dealing rooms**) **NOUN** a place where shares, currencies, or commodities are bought and sold [ECONOMICS]

deal|ings /dilɪŋz/ **PL NOUN** Someone's **dealings with** a person or organization are the relations that they have with them or the business that they do with them. ❍ *He has learned little in his dealings with the international community.*

dear /dɪər/ (**dearer, dearest**)
1 ADJ much loved ❍ *She's a very dear friend of mine.*
2 ADJ written at the beginning of a letter or an email, followed by the name of the person you are writing to ❍ *Dear Mr. Roberts* ❍ *Dear Sir or Madam*

D

death /dɛθ/ NOUN the end of the life of a person or animal ❍ *It's the thirtieth anniversary of her death.* ❍ *Companies must report any malfunctions which result in death or injury.*

death duty (**death duties**) NOUN In Britain, **death duty** is the former name for a tax paid on things that you inherit. [ECONOMICS, FINANCE] ❍ *When he died, his family was allowed to keep the remaining pieces in his collection and avoid paying death duties.*

death fu|tures PL NOUN **Death futures** are the insurance policies of dying people, bought by firms so that they collect the insurance money when that person dies. [BANKING]

de|bate /dɪbeɪt/ (**debates, debating, debated**)
1 NOUN a long discussion or argument ❍ *The debate will continue until they vote on Thursday.* ❍ *There has been a lot of debate among managers about this subject.*
2 VERB If people **debate** a subject, they discuss it. ❍ *The committee will debate the issue today.* ❍ *They were debating which product would be more profitable.*

de|ben|ture /dɪbɛntʃər/
1 NOUN a type of savings bond that offers a fixed rate of interest over a long period, issued by a firm or the government [BANKING]
2 NOUN an official document that shows that someone owes someone else a particular sum of money [BANKING]
3 NOUN an official document that shows that someone is entitled to a refund of excise or import duty [FINANCE]

deb|it /dɛbɪt/
1 VERB When your bank **debits** your account, money is taken from it and paid to someone else. Compare with **credit**. [BANKING] ❍ *We will always confirm the revised amount to you in writing before debiting your account.*
2 NOUN A **debit** is a record of the money taken from your bank account, for example, when you write a check. Compare with **credit**. [BANKING] ❍ *The total of debits must balance the total of credits.*

deb|it card (**debit cards**) NOUN a bank card that you can use to pay for things [BANKING]

debt /dɛt/
1 NOUN an amount of money that you owe someone [ECONOMICS] ❍ *He's still paying off his debts.*
2 If you are **in debt**, you owe money and if you **get into debt**, you start to owe money. [ECONOMICS] ❍ *Many students get into debt.*
3 If you are **out of debt** or get **out of debt**, you succeed in paying all the money that you owe. [ECONOMICS] ❍ *Once you are out of debt it is good to keep unwanted expenses to a minimum.*

debt bur|den (**debt burdens**) NOUN a large amount of money that one country or organization owes to another and that they find very difficult to repay [ECONOMICS] ❍ *The massive debt burden of the Third World has become a crucial issue for many leaders of poorer countries.*

debt|or /dɛtər/ NOUN a country, organization, or person that owes money [ECONOMICS] ❍ *important improvements in the situation of debtor countries*

debt re|sched|ul|ing NONCOUNT NOUN **Debt rescheduling** is when the date on which the payment of a debt must be made is changed. [BANKING, FINANCE] ❍ *Pressure on the external sector was temporarily eased by debt rescheduling.*

debt re|struc|tur|ing /dɛt ristrʌktʃərɪŋ/ NONCOUNT NOUN **Debt restructuring** is a method of organizing a firm's debts in a different way in order to make the firm more likely to be able to pay them. [BANKING, FINANCE] ❍ *The firm finally announced a debt restructuring agreement with its banks.*

debt swap (**debt swaps**) NOUN a legal agreement where two people or companies exchange their debts, often where one has a fixed interest rate and one does not [LEGAL, FINANCE]

dec|ade /dɛkeɪd/ **NOUN** a period of ten years ❍ *The country's debt has risen steadily in the last two decades.*

de|cay /dɪkeɪ/ (**decays, decaying, decayed**)
1 VERB When something **decays**, it is gradually destroyed by a natural process. ❍ *The bodies had started to decay.*
2 NONCOUNT NOUN Decay is also a noun. ❍ *tooth decay*

de|ceive /dɪsiv/ (**deceives, deceiving, deceived**) **VERB** If you **deceive** someone, you make them believe something that is not true. ❍ *She accused the government of trying to deceive the public.*

De|cem|ber /dɪsɛmbər/ **NOUN** the twelfth and last month of the year ❍ *The conference is in December.*

de|cent /disᵊnt/
1 ADJ acceptable or good enough ❍ *Clients expect a decent return on their investment.*
• **de|cent|ly ADV** ❍ *They treated their prisoners decently.*
2 ADJ honest and morally good ❍ *a decent man*

de|cep|tive /dɪsɛptɪv/ **ADJ** making you believe something that is not true ❍ *The organizers claimed that deals worth $1.4 billion had been made, but those figures are deceptive.*
• **de|cep|tive|ly ADV** ❍ *It is a deceptively simple proposal.*

de|cide /dɪsaɪd/ (**decides, deciding, decided**)
1 VERB If you **decide** to do something, you choose to do it after thinking about it. ❍ *In the end I decided to call him.* ❍ *I can't decide whether to go or not.*
2 VERB If a person or group of people **decides** something, they choose what something should be like after careful consideration. ❍ *We need to decide how much of our budget to spend on training.*

deci|mal /dɛsɪmᵊl/
1 NOUN a part of a number that is written in the form of a dot followed by one or more numbers ❍ *The interest rate is shown as a decimal, such as 0.10, which means 10%.*
2 ADJ A **decimal** system involves counting in units of ten.

deci|mal cur|ren|cy (**decimal currencies**) **NOUN** a currency in which the units are based on the number ten [ECONOMICS]

de|ci|sion /dɪsɪʒᵊn/ **NOUN** a choice or judgment that you make about something ❍ *I think I made the right decision.*

decision-making NONCOUNT NOUN **Decision-making** is the process of reaching decisions, especially in a large organization or in government. [BUSINESS MANAGEMENT] ❍ *She wants to see more women involved in decision-making.*

deck /dɛk/
1 NOUN a lower or upper level on a vehicle such as a bus or ship ❍ *a passenger deck*
2 NOUN a flat wooden area attached to a house, where people can sit
3 NOUN A **deck** of cards is a complete set of playing cards.

> **BUSINESS ETIQUETTE**
> Remember that there are many parts of the world where visitors are required to remove their shoes on entering certain buildings, such as mosques and people's homes. It is a good idea, therefore, to make sure that you wear shoes that are easy to remove and put on again.

dec|la|ra|tion /dɛklərеɪʃən/ **NOUN** an official statement about something that has happened or will happen ❍ *a declaration of war*

de|clare /dɪklɛər/ (**declares, declaring, declared**)
1 VERB If you **declare** something, you give information, often about what you intend to do, in a firm, clear way. ❍ *The company publicly declared that it would continue to fund the project.*
2 VERB If you **declare** something, you officially state that it is true or happening. ❍ *Three days later, war was declared.* ❍ *The judges declared Mr. Stevens innocent.*
3 VERB If you **declare** goods that you have bought in another country, you say how much you have bought so that you can pay tax on it. ❍ *Please declare all food, plants, and animal products.*

de|cline /dɪkla͟ɪn/ (**declines, declining, declined**)

1 VERB If something **declines**, it becomes less in amount or importance. ❍ *The local population is declining.*

2 VERB If you **decline** something, you politely refuse to accept it. [FORMAL] ❍ *He declined their invitation.*

3 NOUN If there is a **decline in** something, it becomes less in quantity, importance, or quality. ❍ *The decline in sales means that advisers are completing on only a handful of endowments each year.*

deco|rate /dɛ͟kəreɪt/ (**decorates, decorating, decorated**)

1 VERB If you **decorate** something, you make it more attractive by adding things to it. ❍ *They decorated the room with Picasso prints.*

2 VERB If you **decorate** a room or the inside of a building, you put new paint or paper on the walls and the ceiling. ❍ *They are decorating the new offices.* ● **deco|rat|ing** NONCOUNT NOUN ❍ *money spent on repairs, painting, and decorating*

deco|ra|tion /dɛ͟kəre͟ɪʃən/

1 NOUN Decorations are things that are used for making something look more attractive. ❍ *Colorful paper decorations were hanging from the ceiling.*

2 NONCOUNT NOUN The **decoration** of a room is its furniture and the paint or paper on the walls. ❍ *The decoration was practical for a family home.*

deco|ra|tive /dɛ͟kərətɪv, -əreɪtɪv/ **ADJ** intended to look attractive ❍ *The drapes are only decorative – they don't open or close.*

de|crease (**decreases, decreasing, decreased**)

> Pronounce the verb /dɪkri͟s/. Pronounce the noun /di͟kris/ or /dɪkri͟s/.

1 VERB If something **decreases** or if you **decrease** something, it becomes less or smaller. ❍ *The average price decreased from $134,000 to $126,000.*

2 NOUN a reduction in the amount or size of something ❍ *There has been a decrease in the number of people without a job.*

> **COLLOCATIONS**
> to decrease *sharply*
> a *marked* decrease
> to *significantly* decrease
> a *dramatic* decrease
> a *significant* decrease

dedi|cate /dɛ͟dɪkeɪt/ (**dedicates, dedicating, dedicated**) **VERB** If someone **dedicates** a book, a play, or a piece of music **to** you, they say on the first page that they have written it for you. ❍ *She dedicated her first book to her sons.* ● **dedi|ca|tion NOUN** ❍ *I read the dedication at the beginning of the book.*

de|duct /dɪdʌ͟kt/ **VERB** When you **deduct** an amount from a total, you make the total smaller by that amount. ❍ *The company deducted the money from his wages.*

de|duct|ible /dɪdʌ͟ktɪbəl/

1 ADJ Deductible is the same as **tax-deductible**. [FINANCE] ❍ *Part of the auto-loan interest is deductible as a business expense.*

2 NOUN a sum of money that you have to pay toward the cost of an insurance claim when the insurance company pays the rest [FINANCE] ❍ *Each time they go to a hospital, they have to pay a deductible of $628.*

de|duc|tion /dɪdʌ͟kʃən/

1 NOUN an amount that has been subtracted from a total ❍ *Most homeowners can get a federal income tax deduction on interest payments to a home equity loan.*

deep /di͟p/

1 ADJ If something is **deep**, it goes down a long way. ❍ *The water is very deep.* ❍ *a deep hole*

2 ADV Deep is also an adverb. ❍ *She put her hands deep into her pockets.*

3 ADJ strongly felt ❍ *He expressed his deep sympathy to the family.* ❍ *his deep love of his country* ● **deep|ly ADV** ❍ *He loved her deeply.*

4 ADJ A **deep** sound is low and usually strong. ❍ *He spoke in a deep, warm voice.*

5 ADJ used for describing colors that are strong and dark ❍ *The sky was deep blue and starry.*

6 ADJ taking a lot of air into your body or breathing a lot of air out of your body

❍ *Cal took a long, deep breath.* ● **deep|ly** ADV ❍ *She sighed deeply.*

deep|en /dipən/ VERB If an emotion or a feeling **deepens**, it becomes stronger or more noticeable. ❍ *Her feelings for him had deepened in recent months.* ❍ *the deepening conflict in the region*

deer /dɪər/ (**deer**) NOUN a large wild animal, the male of which usually has large horns that look like branches

de|fault /dɪfɔlt/

1 NONCOUNT NOUN The **default** is the way that something will be done if you do not give any other instruction. ❍ *The default setting on the printer is for color.*

2 NOUN a failure to pay money that is owed [BANKING, FINANCE] ❍ *Investors should ask whether it makes sense to insure against a default on Treasury bonds.*

3 VERB If a person or organization **defaults on** a payment, they fail to pay an amount they owe. [BANKING, FINANCE] ❍ *Purchasers of bonds need to know whether a corporation is likely to default on its bonds.* ● **de|fault|er** NOUN ❍ *Denmark's legal system makes it easy for banks to seize the homes of defaulters.*

de|feat /dɪfit/

1 VERB If you **defeat** someone, you beat them in a battle, a game, or a competition. ❍ *They defeated the French army in 1954.*

2 NOUN **Defeat** is the experience of being beaten in a battle, a game, or a competition ❍ *He didn't want to accept defeat.* ❍ *The firm has conceded defeat to its two rivals.*

de|fect /difɛkt/ NOUN a fault or imperfection ❍ *A report has pointed out the defects of the present system.*

de|fec|tive /dɪfɛktɪv/ ADJ with faults and not working properly ❍ *defective equipment*

de|fence /dɪfɛns/ [BRIT] → **defense**

de|fend /dɪfɛnd/

1 VERB If you **defend** someone or something, you take action in order to protect them. ❍ *The army must be able to defend its own country against attack.*

2 VERB In sports, if you are **defending**, you are trying to stop the other team from getting points.

3 VERB If you **defend** a decision, you argue in support of it. ❍ *The president defended his decision to go to war.*

4 VERB When a lawyer **defends** a person in a court, they argue that the person is not guilty of a particular crime. ❍ *He has hired a lawyer to defend him in court.*

de|fend|er /dɪfɛndər/ NOUN a player in a game whose main task is to stop the other side from scoring ❍ *Lewis was the team's top defender.*

de|fense /difɛns/

Pronounce **defense** /difɛns/ in meaning **3**.

1 NONCOUNT NOUN **Defense** is action to protect someone or something against attack. ❍ *The land was flat, which made defense difficult.*

2 NONCOUNT NOUN **Defense** is the organization of a country's armies and weapons, and their use to protect the country. ❍ *Twenty-eight percent of the country's money is spent on defense.* ❍ *the U.S. Defense Secretary*

3 NOUN in games such as soccer or hockey, the players in a team who try to stop the opposing team from scoring a goal or a point ❍ *a weak defense*

de|fen|sive /dɪfɛnsɪv/ ADJ in games such as soccer or hockey, used for describing the things that are done to prevent the opposing team from scoring ❍ *strong defensive play*

deferred /dɪfɜrd/

1 ADJ delayed until a later time ❍ *deferred payments*

2 ADJ **Deferred** shares are ones where dividends are paid only after ordinary shareholders have been paid.

de|ferred an|nu|ity (**deferred annuities**) NOUN an annuity that starts not less than a year after the final amount has been paid for it [BANKING]

de|fi|cien|cy /dɪfɪʃənsi/ (**deficiencies**)

1 NONCOUNT NOUN **Deficiency in** something, especially something that your body needs, is not having enough of it. ❍ *They did blood tests on him for signs of vitamin deficiency.*

2 NOUN a fault in someone or something [FORMAL] ❍ *The most serious deficiency in NATO's* *air defense is the lack of an identification system to distinguish friend from foe.*

3 NOUN A **deficiency** is the same as a **deficit**.

defi|cit /dɛfəsɪt/ **NOUN** an amount by which something is less than the amount that is needed ❍ *The state budget showed a deficit of five billion dollars.*

D

deficit fi|nanc|ing or **deficit spending** **NONCOUNT NOUN** **Deficit financing** is paying for government spending through borrowing rather than revenue. [ECONOMICS] ❍ *The overriding problem is the continuing deficit financing of the federal government.*

de|fine /dɪfaɪn/ (**defines, defining, defined**) **VERB** If you **define** something, you say clearly what it is and what it means. ❍ *The government defines a household as "a group of people who live in the same house."*

defi|nite /dɛfɪnɪt/

1 ADJ firm and clear and not likely to change ❍ *I need to make definite arrangements.*

2 ADJ certainly true and not just guessed ❍ *We didn't have any definite proof.*

defi|nite|ly /dɛfɪnɪtli/ **ADV** certainly ❍ *Growth is definitely going to be slower next quarter.*

defi|ni|tion /dɛfɪnɪʃən/ **NOUN** a statement that explains the meaning of a word or expression, especially in a dictionary ❍ *We need to agree on a definition of 'organic'.*

de|fla|tion /dɪfleɪʃən/ **NONCOUNT NOUN** **Deflation** is a reduction in economic activity that leads to lower levels of production, employment, investment, trade, profits, and prices. [ECONOMICS] ❍ *Deflation is beginning to take hold in the clothing industry.*

● **de|fla|tion|ary** **ADJ** ❍ *the government's refusal to implement deflationary measures*

de|fray /dɪfreɪ/ **VERB** If you **defray** someone's costs or expenses, you give them money to pay for them. [FORMAL] ❍ *The government has committed billions toward defraying the costs of the war.*

defy /dɪfaɪ/ (**defies, defying, defied**) **VERB** If you **defy** someone or something, you refuse to obey them. ❍ *Supermarkets are defying the ban.*

de|gree /dɪgri/

1 NOUN a unit for measuring temperatures, often written as °, for example, 70° ❍ *It's over 80 degrees outside.*

2 NOUN a unit for measuring angles, often written as °, for example, 90° ❍ *It was pointing outward at an angle of 45 degrees.*

3 NOUN a qualification that you receive when you have successfully completed a course of study at a college or university ❍ *He has an engineering degree.*

de|in|dust|rial|ise /diɪndʌstriəlaɪz/ [ECONOMICS, BRIT] → **deindustrialize**

de|in|dust|rial|ize /diɪndʌstriəlaɪz/ (**deindustrializes, deindustrializing, deindustrialized**) **VERB** If a country or a region **is deindustrialized** or if it **deindustrializes**, it loses industries that produce things. [ECONOMICS]

● **de|in|dust|ri|ali|za|tion** /diɪndʌstriələzeɪʃən/ **NONCOUNT NOUN** ❍ *The extent of deindustrialization in the UK was even more marked in the early 1980s.*

de|lay /dɪleɪ/

1 VERB If you **delay** doing something, you do not do it until a later time. ❍ *We have decided to delay the launch of the new model until January.*

2 VERB To **delay** someone or something means to make them late. ❍ *Passengers were delayed at the airport for five hours.*

3 NOUN a situation in which something happens at a later time than planned ❍ *He apologized for the delay.*

de|lay|er /dileɪər/ **VERB** If a firm or organization **is delayered**, the number of managers is cut by reducing the number of levels of management. [BUSINESS MANAGEMENT] ● **de|lay|er|ing** **NONCOUNT NOUN** ❍ *downsizing, delayering, and other cost cutting measures*

del|egate (**delegates, delegating, delegated**)

Pronounce the noun /dɛlɪgɪt/. Pronounce the verb /dɛlɪgeɪt/.

1 NOUN a person who is chosen to vote or

make decisions on behalf of a group of other people at a conference or a meeting [BUSINESS MANAGEMENT] ❍ *The Canadian delegate offered no reply.*

2 VERB If you **delegate** duties, responsibilities, or power **to** someone, you give them those duties, those responsibilities, or that power so that they can act on your behalf. [BUSINESS MANAGEMENT] ❍ *He talks of traveling less, and delegating more authority to his deputies.*

3 VERB If you **are delegated to** do something, you are given the duty of doing that thing. [BUSINESS MANAGEMENT] ❍ *Officials have now been delegated to start work on a draft settlement.*

del|ega|tion /dɛlɪgeɪʃən/

1 NOUN a group of people who have been sent somewhere to have talks with other people on behalf of a larger group of people [BUSINESS MANAGEMENT] ❍ *the German delegation to the UN talks in New York*

2 NONCOUNT NOUN Delegation is the act of giving your duties to other people. [BUSINESS MANAGEMENT] ❍ *A key factor in running a business is the delegation of responsibility.*

de|lete /dɪlit/ (**deletes, deleting, deleted**) **VERB** If you **delete** something that has been written down or stored in a computer, you put a line through it or remove it. ❍ *He deleted the files from the computer.*

de|lib|er|ate /dɪlɪbərɪt/ **ADJ** A **deliberate** action is one that you intended. ❍ *They told deliberate lies in order to sell newspapers.*
• **de|lib|er|ate|ly ADV** ❍ *They were accused of deliberately misleading clients.*

deli|cate /dɛlɪkɪt/

1 ADJ easily damaged or broken ❍ *delicate glassware* ❍ *Do not rub the delicate skin around the eyes.*

2 ADJ A **delicate** color, taste, or smell is pleasant and light. ❍ *The beans have a delicate flavor.*

de|li|cious /dɪlɪʃəs/ **ADJ** tasting very good ❍ *We had a delicious meal there.*

de|light /dɪlaɪt/ **NONCOUNT NOUN Delight** is a feeling of great pleasure. ❍ *He expressed delight at the news.* ❍ *Andrew laughed with delight.*

de|list /dilɪst/ **VERB** If a company **delists** or if its shares **are delisted**, its shares are removed from the official list of shares that can be traded on the stock market. [ECONOMICS] ❍ *The company's stock was delisted from the Nasdaq market in July 2000.*

de|liv|er /dɪlɪvər/ **VERB** If you **deliver** something somewhere, you take it there. ❍ *Only 90% of first-class mail is delivered on time.*

de|liv|ery /dɪlɪvəri/ (**deliveries**)

1 NONCOUNT NOUN Delivery is when someone brings letters, packages, or other goods to an arranged place. ❍ *Please allow 28 days for delivery.*

2 NOUN an occasion when goods or mail are delivered ❍ *We are waiting for a delivery of new parts.*

de|mand /dɪmænd/

1 VERB If you **demand** information or action, you ask for it in a very firm way. ❍ *Workers are demanding pay rises.*

2 NOUN a firm request for something ❍ *There were demands for better services.*

3 If someone or something is **in demand** or **in great demand**, they are very popular and a lot of people want them. ❍ *Imported toys are in great demand.*

4 NONCOUNT NOUN Demand is the amount of a product or service that customers want to buy. Compare with **supply**. ❍ *Demand for gas is likely to rise.*

de|mand bill (**demand bills**) or **demand draft NOUN** a bill of exchange that is payable on demand [BANKING]

de|mand de|pos|it (**demand deposits**) **NOUN** A **demand deposit** is a bank deposit from which money may be withdrawn at any time. Compare with **time deposit**. [BANKING]

de|mand|ing /dɪmændɪŋ/

1 ADJ A **demanding** job or task requires a lot of your time, energy, or attention. ❍ *He tried to return to work, but found he could no longer cope with his demanding job.*

2 ADJ People who are **demanding** are not easily satisfied or pleased. ❍ *Ricky was a very demanding child.*

de|mand loan (**demand loans**) NOUN a loan that is payable on demand [BANKING]

demand-pull in|fla|tion NONCOUNT NOUN **Demand-pull inflation** is an increase in prices caused by an increase in the demand for goods. Compare with **cost-push inflation**.

D

de|mar|ca|tion /dimarkeɪʃən/ also **demarkation**

1 NONCOUNT NOUN **Demarcation** is the establishment of boundaries or limits separating two areas, groups, or things. [FORMAL] ○ *Talks were continuing about the demarcation of the border between the two countries.*

2 NONCOUNT NOUN **Demarcation** is the strict separation of work between workers of different types. ○ *a demarcation dispute*

de|mar|ket /dimarkɪt/ VERB If a company **demarkets** a product, they try to persuade people not to buy it. [MARKETING AND SALES]

de|merge /dimɜrdʒ/ (**demerges, demerging, demerged**) VERB If a large company **is demerged** or if it **demerges**, it is broken down into several smaller companies. [ADMINISTRATION, BRIT] ○ *Zeneca was at last demerged from its parent firm, ICI.*

de|mer|ger /dimɜrdʒər/ NOUN the separation of a large company into several smaller companies [ADMINISTRATION, BRIT] ○ *After ICI announced its demerger plans on Thursday, its share price jumped by 12%.*

demo /dɛmoʊ/

1 NOUN an event where people march to show their opposition to something or their support for something [INFORMAL] ○ *They did not join a nearby demo in which political activists were dispersed by police.*

2 NOUN a demonstration of something [INFORMAL] ○ *Download free demos of our newest products and upgrades.*

3 NOUN an example of a product, for example a car, that a customer can use before deciding whether or not to buy one [INFORMAL]

de|moc|ra|cy /dɪmɒkrəsi/ (**democracies**)

1 NONCOUNT NOUN **Democracy** is a system of government in which people choose their leaders by voting for them in elections. ○ *the spread of democracy*

2 NOUN a country in which the people choose their government by voting for it ○ *a modern democracy such as ours*

demo|crat /dɛməkræt/

1 NOUN A **Democrat** is a supporter of a political party that has the word "democrat" or "democratic" in its title, for example, the Democratic Party in the United States. ○ *Democrats voted against the plan.*

2 NOUN A **democrat** is a person who believes in and wants democracy. ○ *This is the time for democrats and not dictators.*

demo|crat|ic /dɛməkrætɪk/

1 ADJ A **democratic** country, government, or political system has leaders who are elected by the people that they govern. ○ *Bolivia returned to democratic rule in 1982.*

2 ADJ based on the idea that everyone has equal rights and should be involved in making important decisions ○ *Education is the basis of a democratic society.*

de|mo|graph|ic /dɛməgræfɪk/

1 NOUN a group of people in a society, especially people in a particular age group [ECONOMICS] ○ *The station has won more listeners in the 25-39 demographic.*

2 PL NOUN The **demographics** of a place or society are the statistics relating to the people who live there. [ECONOMICS] ○ *the changing demographics of the United States*

de|mol|ish /dɪmɒlɪʃ/ (**demolishes, demolishing, demolished**) VERB To **demolish** a building means to destroy it completely. ○ *Both factories were demolished and the site redeveloped.* • **demo|li|tion** /dɛməlɪʃən/ NONCOUNT NOUN ○ *the demolition of the old bridge*

dem|on|strate /dɛmənstreɪt/ (**demonstrates, demonstrating, demonstrated**)

1 VERB If you **demonstrate** something, you show people how it works or how to do it. ○ *Several companies were demonstrating their new products.*

2 VERB When people **demonstrate**, they march or gather somewhere to show that they oppose or support something. ❍ *200,000 people demonstrated against the war.* • **de|mon|stra|tor** NOUN ❍ *Police were dealing with a crowd of demonstrators.*

dem|on|stra|tion /dɛmənstreɪʃən/
1 NOUN a show of how something works or how to do something ❍ *We watched a demonstration of the new program.*
2 NOUN a gathering of people who show that they oppose or support something ❍ *Soldiers broke up an anti-government demonstration.*

de|mon|stra|tor /dɛmənstreɪtər/
1 NOUN a person who is marching or gathering somewhere to show their opposition to something or their support for something ❍ *I saw the police using tear gas to try and break up a crowd of demonstrators.*
2 NOUN a person who shows people how something works or how to do something ❍ *a demonstrator in a department store*
3 NOUN an example of a product, for example a car, that a customer can use before deciding whether or not to buy one

de|mu|tu|alise /dimyutʃuəlaɪz/ [BRIT] → **demutualize**

de|mu|tu|alize /dimyutʃuəlaɪz/ (**demutualizes, demutualizing, demutualized**) VERB If a financial company **demutualizes**, it gives up its mutual status and becomes a different kind of company. [BUSINESS MANAGEMENT] ❍ *The group won the support of 97 percent of its members for plans to demutualize.* • **de|mu|tu|ali|za|tion** /dimyutʃuəlɪzeɪʃən/ NONCOUNT NOUN ❍ *The 503,000 policyholders who voted for demutualization should be represented.*

denar /dɛnɑr/ NOUN the monetary unit of Macedonia [ECONOMICS]

de|na|tion|al|ise /dinæʃənəlaɪz/ [BRIT] → **denationalize**

de|na|tion|al|ize /dinæʃənəlaɪz/ (**denationalizes, denationalizing, denationalized**) VERB To **denationalize** an industry or business means to put it into private ownership so that it is no longer owned and controlled by the state. [ECONOMICS, OLD-FASHIONED] ❍ *The government started to denationalize financial institutions.* • **de|na|tion|ali|za|tion** /dinæʃənᵊlɪzeɪʃən/ NONCOUNT NOUN ❍ *the denationalization of industry*

de|ni|al /dɪnaɪəl/ NOUN a statement saying that something is not true, or that something does not exist ❍ *There have been many official denials of the government's involvement.*

de|nomi|na|tion /dɪnɒmɪneɪʃən/ NOUN The **denomination** of a banknote or coin is its official value. [ECONOMICS] ❍ *She paid in cash, in bills of large denominations.*

dense /dɛns/ (**denser, densest**)
1 ADJ containing a lot of things or people in a small area ❍ *a dense forest* • **dense|ly** ADV ❍ *Java is a densely populated island.*
2 ADJ thick and difficult to see through ❍ *dense fog*
3 ADJ In science, a **dense** substance is very heavy for its size. ❍ *Ice is less dense than water, and so it floats.*

den|sity /dɛnsɪti/ (**densities**) NOUN In science, the **density** of a substance or object is how heavy it is for its size. ❍ *Jupiter's moon Io has a density of 3.5 grams per cubic centimeter.*

dent /dɛnt/
1 VERB If you **dent** the surface of something, you make a hollow area in it by hitting it. ❍ *The stone dented the car's fender.*
2 NOUN a hollow in the surface of something that has been hit or pressed too hard ❍ *There was a dent in the car door.*

den|tal /dɛntᵊl/ ADJ relating to teeth ❍ *dental care*

den|tist /dɛntɪst/ NOUN a person whose job is to examine and treat people's teeth ❍ *Visit your dentist twice a year for a check-up.*

deny /dɪnaɪ/ (**denies, denying, denied**) VERB When you **deny** something, you state that it is not true. ❍ *The company denied owning any of the bonds.* ❍ *He denied that he was involved in the crime.*

de|odor|ant /dioʊdərənt/ NONCOUNT NOUN a substance that you put on your skin to hide or prevent bad smells

de|part /dɪpɑrt/ **VERB** When something or someone **departs**, they leave. [FORMAL] ❍ *Flight 43 will depart from Denver at 11:45 a.m.*

de|part|ment /dɪpɑrtmənt/
1 NOUN one part of an organization such as a government, a business, or a university [ADMINISTRATION] ❍ *She works for the U.S. Department of Health and Human Services.*
2 NOUN one part of a large store, selling a particular thing [MARKETING AND SALES] ❍ *the shoe department*

D

de|part|ment head (**department heads**) **NOUN** the most senior person in a particular department ❍ *All a small store needs is one manager and a few department heads who actually manage on the selling floor.*

de|part|ment store (**department stores**) **NOUN** a large store that sells many different types of goods [MARKETING AND SALES] ❍ *Hudson's Bay, based in Toronto, is Canada's largest department store operator.*

de|par|ture /dɪpɑrtʃər/ **NOUN** the act of leaving somewhere ❍ *Illness delayed the president's departure for Helsinki.*

de|pend /dɪpɛnd/
1 VERB If one thing **depends on** another, the first thing will be affected by the second thing. ❍ *The amount of stock purchases will depend on market conditions.*
2 VERB If you **depend on** someone or something, you need them in order to do something. ❍ *Manipur depends on imported rice from Punjab.*
3 VERB If you can **depend on** someone or something, you know that they will support you or help you when you need them. ❍ *"You can depend on me," I assured him.*

de|pend|ent /dɪpɛndənt/ also **dependant**
1 ADJ If you are **dependent on** something or someone, you need them in order to succeed or to be able to survive. ❍ *The company is heavily dependent on international flights for its revenue.* ● **de|pend|ence** **NONCOUNT NOUN** ❍ *We discussed the city's dependence on tourism.*
2 NOUN Your **dependents** are the people you support financially, such as your children. ❍ *He's a single man with no dependents.*

de|pos|it /dɪpɒzɪt/
1 NOUN a sum of money that you give as part of the payment for goods or services [FINANCE] ❍ *He paid a $500 deposit for the car.*
2 VERB If you **deposit** money as part of the payment for goods or services, you give someone a sum of money for that purpose. [FINANCE]
3 NOUN an amount of a substance that has been left somewhere as a result of a chemical or geological process ❍ *underground deposits of gold*
4 NOUN an amount of money that you put into a bank account [BANKING] ❍ *I made a deposit every week.*
5 VERB If you **deposit** money in a bank account, you put it there. [BANKING] ❍ *They arranged for the money to be deposited in a bank in Andorra.*
6 NOUN If you make a **deposit** of valuable goods at a bank, you leave them there to be looked after. [BANKING]
7 NOUN a sum of money that you give to someone in case you lose or damage something that you have hired from them, and which is given back to you if you return that thing in good condition [FINANCE]

de|pos|it ac|count (**deposit accounts**) [BANKING, BRIT] → **savings account**

de|posi|tor /dɪpɒzɪtər/ **NOUN** a person who has an account with a bank [BANKING]

de|pot /dipoʊ/
1 NOUN a bus station or train station ❍ *She was reunited with her boyfriend in the bus depot of Ozark, Alabama.*
2 NOUN a large building where things are kept until they are needed [LOGISTICS AND DISTRIBUTION] ❍ *food depots*

de|pre|ci|able /dɪpriʃiəbᵊl/
1 ADJ If something you use for your business is **depreciable**, its loss in value over time will count toward reducing your tax. [FINANCE] ❍ *They acquired property consisting of land and depreciable improvements.*
2 ADJ losing value as it gets older [FINANCE]

de|pre|ci|ate /dɪpriʃieɪt/ (**depreciates, depreciating, depreciated**) VERB If something **depreciates** or if something **depreciates** it, it loses value. [FINANCE] ❍ *Inflation is rising rapidly; the yuan is depreciating.*

de|pre|cia|tion /dɪpriʃieɪʃən/
1 NONCOUNT NOUN **Depreciation** is when the value of something falls because of its age or how much it has been used. [FINANCE]
2 NONCOUNT NOUN In accounting, **depreciation** is a sum of money deducted from the gross profit of a firm because of assets which have lost value. [FINANCE] ❍ *Depreciation is deducted to get net investment.*
3 NONCOUNT NOUN **Depreciation** is the decrease in the exchange value of one currency against another currency. [FINANCE] ❍ *Dollar depreciation raised the cost of U.S. imports.*

de|pressed /dɪprɛst/
1 ADJ feeling sad and without hope for a period of time ❍ *She was very depressed after her mother died.*
2 ADJ A **depressed** area is one with an economy that is not successful. [ECONOMICS] ❍ *Any foreigner willing to invest at least a quarter of a million dollars in an economically depressed area would be awarded an immediate visa.*
3 ADJ A **depressed** economy or market is one that is not successful. [ECONOMICS] ❍ *Accommodating the exiled Kuwaitis has given a boost to the depressed property market.*

de|pres|sion /dɪprɛʃən/
1 NONCOUNT NOUN **Depression** is a state of mind in which you are sad and without hope for a period of time. ❍ *David suffers from depression.*
2 NOUN a time when there is very little economic activity, causing a lot of unemployment and social problems [ECONOMICS]
3 NOUN **The Depression** or **The Great Depression** was a period in the U.S. during the 1920s and 1930s when there were very few jobs because the economy was in a bad state. [ECONOMICS]

de|prive /dɪpraɪv/ (**deprives, depriving, deprived**) VERB If you **deprive** someone **of** something, you take it away from them, or you prevent them from having it. ❍ *They were deprived of fuel to heat their homes.*
● **dep|ri|va|tion** /dɛprɪveɪʃən/ NONCOUNT NOUN ❍ *Many CEOs suffer from stress and sleep deprivation.* ● **de|prived** ADJ ❍ *These are some of the most deprived children in the country.*

d

depth /dɛpθ/
1 NOUN The **depth** of something is how deep it is. ❍ *The average depth of the ocean is 4000 meters.*
2 If you deal with a subject **in depth**, you deal with it in a very detailed way. ❍ *We will discuss these three areas in depth.*

depu|ty /dɛpyəti/ (**deputies**)
1 NOUN the second most important person in an organization ❍ *Dr. Thomas is a former deputy director of NASA's astronaut office.*
2 NOUN a police officer

de|regu|late /dirɛgyəleɪt/ (**deregulates, deregulating, deregulated**) VERB To **deregulate** something means to remove controls and regulations from it. [BUSINESS MANAGEMENT, LEGAL] ❍ *the need to deregulate the U.S. airline industry*

de|regu|la|tion /dirɛgyəleɪʃən/ NONCOUNT NOUN **Deregulation** is the removal of controls and regulations in a particular area of business. [BUSINESS MANAGEMENT, LEGAL] ❍ *Since deregulation, banks are permitted to set their own interest rates.*

de|riva|tive /dɪrɪvətɪv/ NOUN a financial product, the value of which is dependent on the value of another financial product to which it is linked [BANKING] ❍ *Only 10% of the UK derivatives market is in the hands of private investors.*

de|rive /dɪraɪv/ (**derives, deriving, derived**) VERB If you **derive** pleasure or a benefit **from** someone or something, you get it from them. [FORMAL] ❍ *The company derived significant benefits from the merger.*

de|scend /dɪsɛnd/ VERB If you **descend**, you move down from a higher level to a lower level. [FORMAL] ❍ *We descended to the basement.*

de|scribe /dɪskraɪb/ (**describes, describing, described**) VERB If you **describe** someone or something, you say what they are like. ❍ *What does he look like? Describe him.* ❍ *The document describes the proposed product.*

de|scrip|tion /dɪskrɪpʃən/ NOUN an explanation of what someone looks like, or what something is ❍ *Police have given a description of the man.* ❍ *He gave a detailed description of how the new system will work.*

de|se|lect /disɪlɛkt/ VERB If someone is **deselected** during their period of training for a job, they are told that they cannot continue with that job. [HR]

des|ert

Pronounce the noun /dɛzərt/. Pronounce the verb /dɪzɜrt/.

1 NOUN a large area of land where there is almost no water, trees, or plants ❍ *the Sahara Desert*
2 VERB If people **desert** a place, they leave it and it becomes empty. ❍ *Poor farmers are deserting their fields and coming to the cities to find jobs.* ● **de|sert|ed** ADJ ❍ *a deserted street*

de|serve /dɪzɜrv/ (**deserves, deserving, deserved**) VERB If someone **deserves** something, they should receive it because of their actions or qualities. ❍ *He works hard – he deserves a promotion.*

de|sign /dɪzaɪn/
1 VERB If you **design** something new, you plan what it will be like. ❍ *Who designed the costumes?*
2 NOUN a drawing that shows how something should be built or made ❍ *his design for the new house*
3 NOUN a pattern of lines, colors, or shapes ❍ *The tablecloths come in three different designs.*

de|sign|er /dɪzaɪnər/
1 NOUN a person whose job is to design things by making drawings of them ❍ *a fashion designer*
2 ADJ **Designer** goods are designed by well-known designers and are usually expensive. ❍ *designer jeans*

de|sir|able /dɪzaɪərəbəl/ ADJ If something is **desirable**, you want to have it or do it because it is useful or attractive. ❍ *a desirable neighborhood*

de|sire /dɪzaɪər/ (**desires, desiring, desired**)
1 NOUN a strong wish to do or have something ❍ *customer needs and desires*
2 VERB If you **desire** something, you want it. [FORMAL] ❍ *goods and services desired by the consumer* ● **de|sired** ADJ ❍ *This will produce the desired effect.*

desk /dɛsk/
1 NOUN a table that you sit at to write or work
2 NOUN a place in a public building where you can get information ❍ *Ask at the reception desk.*

desk clerk (**desk clerks**) NOUN someone who works at the main desk in a hotel [ADMINISTRATION]

de|skill /diskɪl/
1 VERB If workers **are deskilled**, they no longer need special skills to do their work, usually because of new machinery or other technology. [BUSINESS MANAGEMENT] ❍ *Administrative staff may be deskilled through increased automation and efficiency.*
2 VERB If workers **are deskilled**, they are made to do jobs which do not use the skills they have. [BUSINESS MANAGEMENT]

desk re|search NONCOUNT NOUN **Desk research** is research that can be done from a desk, for example reading reports or looking on the Internet. Compare with **field research**. [R & D] ❍ *Desk research cannot fulfill the field research role of putting the supplier in direct touch with the consumer.*

desk|top /dɛsktɒp/ also **desk-top**
1 ADJ **Desktop** computers are a convenient size for using on a desk or a table.
2 NOUN the images that you see on the screen of a computer, when the computer is ready to use ❍ *You can rearrange the icons on the desktop.*

des|pair /dɪspɛər/
1 NONCOUNT NOUN **Despair** is a hopeless feeling about a situation, when you feel that everything is wrong and that nothing will improve. ❍ *I looked at Johnson in despair.*
2 VERB If you **despair**, you feel that everything

is wrong and that nothing will improve. ❍ *"Oh, I despair sometimes," she said when we told her about the results.*

des|per|ate /dɛspərɪt/
1 ADJ If you are **desperate**, you are extremely unhappy or worried and willing to try anything to change your situation. ❍ *He was desperate to get back to the city.* ❍ *There were hundreds of patients desperate for his help.*
● **des|per|ate|ly** ADV ❍ *Thousands of people are desperately trying to leave the country.*
2 ADJ A **desperate** situation is very difficult, serious, or dangerous. ❍ *Conditions in the hospitals are desperate.*

de|spite /dɪspaɪt/ PREP used for introducing a fact that makes the other part of a sentence surprising ❍ *The film was a commercial success, despite mixed reviews.*

des|sert /dɪzɜrt/ NOUN a sweet dish that you eat at the end of a meal ❍ *She had ice cream for dessert.*

de|sta|bi|lise /disteɪbəlaɪz/ [BRIT] → **destabilize**

de|sta|bi|lize /disteɪbəlaɪz/ (**destabilizes, destabilizing, destabilized**) VERB To **destabilize** something such as a government or an economy means to do something to make it weaker. ❍ *Their sole aim is to destabilize the Indian government.*

des|ti|na|tion /dɛstɪneɪʃən/ NOUN Your **destination** is the place you are going to. ❍ *He wanted to arrive at his destination before dark.* ❍ *a popular tourist destination*

des|ti|ny /dɛstɪni/ (**destinies**) NOUN A person or group's **destiny** is everything that happens to them during their life, including what will happen in the future. ❍ *Eastman split into two companies, reflecting the need for each to pursue its own destiny.*

de|stock /distɒk/ VERB If a company **destocks**, it reduces the amount of stock it holds. [ECONOMICS]

de|stroy /dɪstrɔɪ/ VERB To **destroy** something means to damage it so much that it is completely ruined. ❍ *The factory was destroyed by fire.* ● **de|struc|tion** /dɪstrʌkʃən/ NONCOUNT NOUN ❍ *We must stop the destruction of our forests.*

de|struc|tive /dɪstrʌktɪv/ ADJ causing great damage ❍ *a destructive storm*

de|tail /diteɪl/
1 NOUN one of many small parts of or facts about something ❍ *We discussed the details of the agreement.*
2 PL NOUN **Details** are information. ❍ *See the bottom of this page for details of how to apply for this offer.*
3 If you discuss a situation or examine something **in detail**, you talk about many different facts or parts of it. ❍ *She didn't explain the proposal in detail.* ● **de|tailed** ADJ ❍ *The report gives a detailed description of the new merchandise.*

de|tect /dɪtɛkt/ VERB If you **detect** something, you find it or notice it. ❍ *the bank's efforts to detect fraud*

de|tec|tive /dɪtɛktɪv/ NOUN someone whose job is to discover what has happened in a crime, and to find the people who did it ❍ *Detectives are still searching for the four men.*

de|ter /dɪtɜr/ (**deters, deterring, deterred**) VERB To **deter** someone **from** doing something means to make them not want to do it or continue doing it. ❍ *High prices deter people from buying.*

de|terio|rate /dɪtɪəriəreɪt/ (**deteriorates, deteriorating, deteriorated**) VERB If something **deteriorates**, it becomes worse. ❍ *The quality of sales is deteriorating.*
● **de|terio|ra|tion** /dɪtɪəriəreɪʃən/ NOUN ❍ *There has been continued deterioration of economic conditions.*

de|ter|mi|na|tion /dɪtɜrmɪneɪʃən/ NONCOUNT NOUN **Determination** is the quality of wanting very much to do something and not letting problems prevent you from doing it. ❍ *Her determination to succeed is impressive.*

de|ter|mine /dɪtɜrmɪn/ (**determines, determining, determined**)
1 VERB If something **determines** what will happen, it controls it. [FORMAL] ❍ *Rates are determined by the difference between the two levels.*

2 VERB To **determine** a fact means to discover it. [FORMAL] ❍ *Police are still trying to determine exactly what happened.*

de|ter|mined /dɪtɜrmɪnd/ **ADJ** If you are **determined to** do something, you want very much to do it and will not let problems prevent you from doing it. ❍ *He is determined to boost profits.*

D

de|valua|tion /divælyueɪʃən/
1 NOUN a deliberate decrease in the exchange value of a currency against another currency that is made by a government [ECONOMICS, FINANCE] ❍ *It will lead to devaluation of a number of currencies.*
2 NOUN a decrease in the value, status, or importance of something

de|value /divælyu/ (**devalues, devaluing, devalued**) or **devaluate**
1 VERB To **devalue** something means to cause it to be thought less valuable or important. ❍ *They spread tales about her in an attempt to devalue her work.*
2 VERB To **devalue** the currency of a country means to reduce its value in relation to other currencies. [ECONOMICS, FINANCE] ❍ *India has devalued the rupee by about eleven percent.*

dev|as|tate /dɛvəsteɪt/ (**devastates, devastating, devastated**) **VERB** If something **devastates** an area or a place, it damages it very badly or destroys it completely. ❍ *The earthquake devastated parts of Indonesia.*
• **dev|as|ta|tion** /dɛvəsteɪʃən/ **NONCOUNT NOUN** ❍ *The war brought massive devastation to the area.*

de|vel|op /dɪvɛləp/
1 VERB When a person or thing **develops**, they grow or change over a period of time. ❍ *As children develop, their needs change.*
2 VERB If a problem **develops**, it begins to happen. ❍ *A problem developed aboard the space shuttle.*
3 VERB If someone **develops** a new product, they design it and produce it. ❍ *Scientists have developed a car paint that changes color.*

de|vel|oped /dɪvɛləpt/ **ADJ** A **developed** country or region is rich and has a lot of industries. ❍ *the developed nations*

de|vel|op|er /dɪvɛləpər/
1 NOUN a person or a firm that buys land and builds on it, or buys existing buildings and makes them more modern ❍ *common land which would have a high commercial value if sold to developers*
2 NOUN someone who develops something such as an idea, a design, or a product ❍ *John Bardeen was also co-developer of the theory of superconductivity.*

de|vel|op|ing /dɪvɛləpɪŋ/ **ADJ** **Developing** countries or the **developing** world are the countries or the parts of the world that are poor and have few industries. [ECONOMICS] ❍ *In the developing world cigarette consumption is increasing.*

de|vel|op|ment /dɪvɛləpmənt/
1 NONCOUNT NOUN **Development** is gradual growth or change over a period of time. ❍ *the development of language*
2 NONCOUNT NOUN **Development** is the growth of a business or an industry. [R&D] ❍ *Our business is the development of new technology.*
3 NONCOUNT NOUN **Development** is the process or result of making a basic design gradually better and more advanced. ❍ *the development of new and innovative telephone services*
4 NOUN an event that has recently happened and has an effect on an existing situation ❍ *Police say this is an important development in the investigation.*

de|vel|op|ment area (**development areas**) **NOUN** a poor area that is given government help to establish more industries [ECONOMICS, BRIT]

de|vel|op|ment bank (**development banks**) **NOUN** a bank that provides money for projects in poor countries or areas [BANKING, ECONOMICS] ❍ *the Asian development bank*

de|vice /dɪvaɪs/ **NOUN** an object that has been invented for a particular purpose ❍ *He used an electronic device to measure the rooms.*

dev|il /dɛvᵊl/ **NOUN** In many religions, **the devil** is a very powerful evil spirit that makes bad things happen.

de|vise /dɪvaɪz/ (**devises, devising, devised**) VERB If you **devise** a plan, you have the idea for it. ❍ *We devised a strategy to protect profits.*

de|vote /dɪvoʊt/ (**devotes, devoting, devoted**) VERB If you **devote** yourself, your time, or your energy **to** something, you spend all of your time or energy on it. ❍ *He devoted the rest of his life to science.*

de|vot|ed /dɪvoʊtɪd/ ADJ loving someone very much ❍ *He was devoted to his wife.*

DG /di dʒi/ (**DGs**) NOUN **DG** is an abbreviation for **director-general**. [ADMINISTRATION]

di|ag|no|sis /daɪəgnoʊsɪs/ (**diagnoses**) NOUN **Diagnosis** is when a doctor discovers what is wrong with someone who is ill. ❍ *I had a second test to confirm the diagnosis.*

dia|gram /daɪəgræm/ NOUN a simple drawing of lines that is used, for example, to explain how a machine works ❍ *He showed us a diagram of the inside of a computer.*

dial /daɪəl/

1 NOUN a part of a machine or a piece of equipment that shows you the time or a measurement ❍ *The dial on the clock showed five minutes to seven.*

2 NOUN a small wheel on a piece of equipment that you move in order to control the way it works ❍ *He turned the dial on the radio.*

3 VERB If you **dial** or if you **dial** a number, you press the buttons on a telephone in order to call someone. ❍ *Dial the number, followed by the "#" sign.*

dia|lect /daɪəlɛkt/ NOUN a form of a language that people speak in a particular area ❍ *They were speaking in the local dialect.*

dia|log box /daɪəlɔg bɒks/ (**dialog boxes**) NOUN a small area that appears on a computer screen, containing information or questions for the user

dia|logue /daɪəlɔg/ also **dialog** NOUN a conversation between two people in a book, a movie, or a play ❍ *He writes great dialogues.* ❍ *The movie contains some very funny dialogue.*

dial-up ADJ A **dial-up** connection to the Internet uses a normal telephone line.

dia|mond /daɪmənd, daɪə-/

1 NOUN a hard, clear stone that is very expensive, and is used for making jewelry ❍ *a pair of diamond earrings*

2 NOUN the shape ♦

dia|ry /daɪəri/ (**diaries**) NOUN a book for writing things in, with a separate space for each day of the year ❍ *I read the entry from his diary for July 10, 1940.*

dice /daɪs/ (**dice**) NOUN a small block of wood or plastic with spots on its sides, used for playing games ❍ *I threw both dice and got a double 6.*

dic|tate /dɪkteɪt, dɪkteɪt/ (**dictates, dictating, dictated**) VERB If you **dictate** something, you say it or record it onto a machine, so that someone else can write it down. ❍ *He dictated a letter to his secretary.*

dic|ta|tion /dɪkteɪʃən/ NONCOUNT NOUN **Dictation** is when one person speaks and someone else writes down what they are saying.

dic|ta|tor /dɪkteɪtər/ NOUN a ruler who has complete power in a country ❍ *The country was ruled by a dictator for more than twenty years.*

dic|tion|ary /dɪkʃənɛri/ (**dictionaries**) NOUN a book in which the words and phrases of a language are listed, together with their meanings ❍ *We checked the spelling in the dictionary.*

did /dɪd/ **Did** is a form of the verb **do**.

didn't /dɪdᵊnt/ **Didn't** is short for "did not."

die /daɪ/ (**dies, dying, died**)

1 VERB When people, animals, or plants **die**, they stop living. ❍ *My dog died last week.* ❍ *His mother died of cancer.*

2 VERB If you **are dying for** something or **dying to** do something, you want it very much. [INFORMAL] ❍ *I'm dying for some fresh air.* ❍ *I'm dying to see him.*

diet /daɪɪt/

1 NOUN the type of food that you regularly eat ❍ *It's never too late to improve your diet.*

2 NOUN a plan for eating less food than usual

because you are trying to become thinner ❍ *Have you been on a diet? You've lost weight.*
3 VERB If you **are dieting**, you are eating less food than usual in order to become thinner. ❍ *Many women diet after the birth of a child.*

dif|fer /dɪfər/ **VERB** If two or more things **differ**, they are different from each other. ❍ *Our policies differ markedly from those of our rivals.*

D

dif|fer|ence /dɪfərəns, dɪfrəns/
1 NOUN a way in which one person or thing is not like another ❍ *There are many differences between the two firms.*
2 NOUN the amount by which one quantity is more or less than another ❍ *Compare the prices and you'll notice quite a difference.*
3 If something **makes** a **difference**, it has a noticeable, usually good, effect on you. ❍ *A good training programme makes a difference to the organization.*

dif|fer|ent /dɪfərənt, dɪfrənt/
1 ADJ If people or things are **different**, they are not like each other. ❍ *London was different from most European capital cities.* ❍ *The products are very different.* ● **dif|fer|ent|ly ADV** ❍ *Other buyers may respond differently.*
2 ADJ used for showing that you are talking about two or more separate things of the same type ❍ *Different countries export different products.*

dif|fer|en|tial /dɪfərɛnʃᵊl/ **NOUN** In mathematics and economics, a **differential** is a difference between two values in a scale. ❍ *the wage differential between blue-collar and white-collar workers*

dif|fer|en|ti|ate /dɪfərɛnʃieɪt/ (**differentiates, differentiating, differentiated**)
1 VERB If you **differentiate between** things or if you **differentiate** one thing **from** another, you see or show the difference between them. ❍ *Packaging helped to differentiate the brand from the competition.*
2 VERB A quality or feature that **differentiates** one thing **from** another makes the two things different. ❍ *This policy differentiates the Democrats from all other political parties.*

dif|fi|cult /dɪfɪkʌlt, -kəlt/
1 ADJ not easy to do, understand, or deal with ❍ *The task was too difficult for us.* ❍ *It was a very difficult decision to make.*
2 ADJ behaving in a way that is not reasonable or helpful ❍ *a difficult child*

dif|fi|cul|ty /dɪfɪkʌlti, -kəlti/ (**difficulties**)
1 NOUN a problem ❍ *The main difficulty is getting information.*
2 NONCOUNT NOUN If you have **difficulty** doing something, you are not able to do it easily. ❍ *The company is having difficulty financing its offer.*

dig /dɪg/ (**digs, digging, dug**) **VERB** If people or animals **dig**, they make a hole in the ground. ❍ *I grabbed the shovel and started digging.* ❍ *First, dig a large hole in the ground.*

digi|tal /dɪdʒɪtᵊl/
1 ADJ sending information in the form of thousands of very small signals ❍ *digital television*
2 ADJ **Digital** equipment gives information in the form of numbers. Compare with **analog**. ❍ *a digital watch*

dig|nity /dɪgnɪti/ **NONCOUNT NOUN** **Dignity** is the quality of being serious, calm, and controlled. ❍ *She received the news with quiet dignity.*

di|lem|ma /dɪlɛmə/ **NOUN** a difficult situation in which you have to make a choice between two things ❍ *the dilemma that increased automation might lead to increased unemployment but also increased profitability*

di|lute /daɪlut/ (**dilutes, diluting, diluted**) **VERB** If you **dilute** a liquid, you add water or another liquid to it. ❍ *Could you dilute the juice with water, please?*

dim /dɪm/ (**dimmer, dimmest, dims, dimming, dimmed**)
1 ADJ not bright or not easy to see ❍ *The lights were dim.* ● **dim|ly ADV** ❍ *Two lamps burned dimly.*
2 VERB If you **dim** a light or it dims, it becomes less bright. ❍ *Could someone dim the lights, please?*

dime /daɪm/ **NOUN** a U.S. coin worth ten cents [ECONOMICS] ❍ *The penny meters are* *slowly being replaced by electronic ones that take nickels, dimes, and quarters.*

di|men|sions /dɪmɛnʃənz, daɪ-/ **PL NOUN** The **dimensions** of something are its measurements. ❍ *We don't yet know the exact dimensions of the room.*

di|min|ish /dɪmɪnɪʃ/ (**diminishes, diminishing, diminished**) **VERB** When something **diminishes**, or when something **diminishes** it, it becomes less. ❍ *The threat of war has now diminished.* ❍ *These practices may diminish the quality of services.*

di|min|ish|ing re|turns **PL NOUN** In economics, **diminishing returns** is a situation in which production, profits, or benefits increase less and less as more money is spent or more effort made. [FINANCE, ECONOMICS]

di|nar /dinɑr/ **NOUN** the monetary unit of some Balkan, North African, and Middle Eastern countries [ECONOMICS]

dine /daɪn/ (**dines, dining, dined**) **VERB** When you **dine**, you have dinner. [FORMAL] ❍ *We dined in a French restaurant.*

din|ing room (**dining rooms**) **NOUN** a room where people eat their meals

din|ner /dɪnər/

1 NOUN the main meal of the day, usually eaten in the evening ❍ *Let's discuss this over dinner.*

2 NOUN a formal social event in the evening at which a meal is served ❍ *a series of official dinners*

dip /dɪp/ (**dips, dipping, dipped**)

1 VERB If you **dip** something **in** a liquid, you put it in and then quickly take it out again. ❍ *Dip each apple in the syrup.*

2 NOUN a thick sauce that you dip pieces of food into before eating them ❍ *a plate of chips and dips*

di|plo|ma /dɪploʊmə/ **NOUN** a qualification that a student who has completed a course of study may receive ❍ *He was awarded a diploma in social work.*

dip|lo|mat /dɪpləmæt/ **NOUN** a senior official whose job is to discuss international affairs with officials from other countries

dip|lo|mat|ic /dɪpləmætɪk/

1 ADJ relating to diplomacy and diplomats ❍ *The two countries enjoy good diplomatic relations.*

2 ADJ careful not to upset or offend people ❍ *She's very direct, but I prefer a more diplomatic approach.*

di|rect /dɪrɛkt, daɪ-/

1 ADJ going somewhere in a straight line or by the shortest route ❍ *They took a direct flight to Athens.*

2 ADV **Direct** is also an adverb. ❍ *You can fly direct from Seattle to London.*

3 ADJ with nothing else in between ❍ *employees who have direct contact with customers*

4 ADV **Direct** is also an adverb. ❍ *More farms are selling direct to consumers.*

5 ADJ honest and saying exactly what you mean ❍ *He avoided giving a direct answer.*

6 VERB When someone **directs** a project or a group of people, they are responsible for organizing them. ❍ *Christopher will direct everyday operations.*

7 VERB When someone **directs** a movie, play, or television program, they are responsible for the way in which it is performed. ❍ *Branagh himself will direct the movie.*

> **BUSINESS ETIQUETTE**
> In China, Japan, and India, you should present and receive business cards with both hands. If someone gives you a business card, you should examine it carefully, and put it away in a special card case, as a show of respect.

di|rect ac|tion **NONCOUNT NOUN** **Direct action** involves doing something such as going on strike or demonstrating in order to make an employer or government to do what you want, instead of trying to talk to them.

di|rect costs **PL NOUN** **Direct costs** are amounts of money spent on particular projects or pieces of work. Compare with **indirect costs**. [FINANCE] ❍ *Their direct costs include raw materials, direct labor, and subcontract costs.*

d

di|rect deb|it (**direct debits**) NOUN A **direct debit** is an order given to a bank to pay a particular person or company any sum of money they ask for. Compare with **standing order**. [FINANCE, BANKING] ❍ *More people are being encouraged to pay their bills automatically by standing order or direct debit.*

di|rec|tion /dɪrɛkʃən, daɪ-/
1 NOUN the general line that someone or something is moving or pointing in ❍ *The nearest town was ten miles in the opposite direction.* ❍ *He started driving in the direction of the airport.*
2 PL NOUN **Directions** are instructions that tell you what to do, how to do something, or how to get somewhere. ❍ *She stopped the car to ask for directions.*

di|rect la|bor NONCOUNT NOUN **Direct labor** is the people who work directly on a project or piece of work, for example people who make things. Compare with **indirect labor**. [ECONOMICS] ❍ *Direct labor may account for only a tiny fraction of production costs but often attracts the lion's share of management time.*

di|rect|ly /dɪrɛktli, daɪ-/
1 ADV exactly ❍ *Never look directly at the sun.*
2 ADV with no other person or thing involved ❍ *It's best to deal directly with the manager of the organization.*
3 ADV in a way that is clear and honest ❍ *Explain simply and directly what you hope to achieve.*

di|rect mail NONCOUNT NOUN **Direct mail** is a method of marketing that involves firms sending advertising material directly to people who they think may be interested in their products. [MARKETING AND SALES, BUSINESS MANAGEMENT] ❍ *efforts to solicit new customers by direct mail and television advertising*

direct-mail shot (**direct-mail shots**) NOUN the mailing of advertising material directly to people who may be interested in a product or service [MARKETING AND SALES, mainly BRIT] ❍ *The initiative will feature a direct-mail shot to tens of thousands of opinion-formers around the world.*

di|rect mar|ket|ing NONCOUNT NOUN **Direct marketing** is the same as **direct mail**. [MARKETING AND SALES, BUSINESS MANAGEMENT] ❍ *The direct marketing industry has become adept at packaging special offers.*

di|rec|tor /dɪrɛktər, daɪ-/
1 NOUN one of the people that controls a firm or an organization [BUSINESS MANAGEMENT, ADMINISTRATION] ❍ *We wrote to the directors of the bank.*
2 NOUN The **director** of a play, movie, or television program is the person who tells the actors and technical staff what to do.

di|rec|to|rate /dɪrɛktərɪt, daɪ-/
1 NOUN a board of directors in a firm or organization [ADMINISTRATION] ❍ *The bank will be managed by a directorate of around five professional bankers.*
2 NOUN a part of a government department that is responsible for one particular thing [ADMINISTRATION] ❍ *the CIA's intelligence directorate*

director-general (**director-generals**) NOUN the head of a large organization such as the CIA or the BBC [BUSINESS MANAGEMENT, ADMINISTRATION]

di|rec|tor|ship /dɪrɛktərʃɪp, daɪ-/ NOUN the job or position of a company director [BUSINESS MANAGEMENT, ADMINISTRATION] ❍ *Barry resigned his directorship in December 2003.*

di|rec|tory /dɪrɛktəri, daɪ-/ (**directories**) NOUN a book containing a list of people's names, addresses, and telephone numbers ❍ *a telephone directory*

di|rect sales chan|nel (**direct sales channels**) NOUN something such as a website where you can buy things directly from a firm [MARKETING AND SALES, BUSINESS MANAGEMENT] ❍ *A higher portion of total sales came through direct sales channels, which have lower margins than retail sales.*

di|rect sell|ing NONCOUNT NOUN **Direct selling** is the same as **direct mail**. [MARKETING AND SALES, BUSINESS MANAGEMENT] ❍ *Direct selling became big business in the early 1980s.*

di|rect tax (**direct taxes**) NOUN A **direct tax** is a tax such as income tax which a person or organization pays directly to the government. Compare with **indirect tax**. [FINANCE] ❍ *What people had to pay in direct and indirect taxes had not gone up since 1979.*

dirham /dɪəræm/ **NOUN** the monetary unit several North African and Middle Eastern countries [ECONOMICS]

dirt /dɜrt/ **NONCOUNT NOUN** If there is **dirt** on something, there is dust or mud on it. ❍ *I started to clean the dirt off my hands.*

dirty /dɜrti/ (**dirtier, dirtiest**) **ADJ** not clean ❍ *dirty boots*

dis|abil|ity /dɪsəbɪlɪti/ (**disabilities**) **NOUN** a permanent injury or condition that means you cannot use a part of your body or brain in the way that most people can [HR] ❍ *We're building a new classroom for people with disabilities.*

dis|abled /dɪseɪbᵊld/ **ADJ** unable to use a part of your body or brain in the way that most people can ❍ *parents of disabled children*

dis|ad|vant|age /dɪsədvæntɪdʒ/
1 NOUN something that makes things more difficult for you ❍ *The big disadvantage of this computer is its size.*
2 If you are **at a disadvantage**, you have a difficulty that many other people do not have. ❍ *This puts foreign companies at a disadvantage.*

dis|agree /dɪsəgri/ (**disagrees, disagreeing, disagreed**)
1 VERB If you **disagree with** someone, you have a different opinion from theirs. ❍ *I really have to disagree with you here.*
2 VERB If you **disagree with** an action or decision, you disapprove of it. ❍ *I respect the president but I disagree with his decision.*

dis|agree|ment /dɪsəgrimənt/ **NOUN** **Disagreement** is when people do not agree with something. ❍ *Britain and France have expressed disagreement with the plan.*

dis|ap|pear /dɪsəpɪər/ **VERB** If someone or something **disappears**, they go away and you cannot see them. ❍ *His daughter disappeared thirteen years ago.* ❍ *The sun disappeared behind the clouds.* ● **dis|ap|pear|ance NOUN** ❍ *Her disappearance remains a mystery to this day.*

dis|ap|point /dɪsəpɔɪnt/ **VERB** If something **disappoints** you, it is not as good as you hoped. ❍ *The new proposal is likely to disappoint some banks.* ● **dis|ap|point|ing ADJ** ❍ *Sales have been disappointing.*

dis|ap|point|ed /dɪsəpɔɪntɪd/ **ADJ** slightly sad because something has not happened or because something is not as good as you hoped ❍ *We were disappointed by the low figures.*

dis|ap|point|ment /dɪsəpɔɪntmənt/
1 NONCOUNT NOUN **Disappointment** is the feeling of being slightly sad because something has not happened or because something is not as good as you hoped. ❍ *Business leaders have expressed disappointment with the slow pace of progress.*
2 NOUN something that is not as good as you hoped ❍ *Last year's performance was a big disappointment.*

dis|ap|prove /dɪsəpruv/ (**disapproves, disapproving, disapproved**) **VERB** If you **disapprove of** something or someone, you do not like them, or do not approve of them. ❍ *He disapproved of the way they dealt with the situation.*

dis|as|ter /dɪzæstər/
1 NOUN a very bad accident or event that kills or hurts many people ❍ *an air disaster*
2 NOUN a complete failure ❍ *The launch was a total disaster.*

dis|as|trous /dɪzæstrəs/ **ADJ** causing great problems ❍ *The country suffered a disastrous earthquake in July.*

dis|be|lief /dɪsbɪlif/ **NONCOUNT NOUN** **Disbelief** is a feeling of shock and the feeling of not believing something. ❍ *She looked at him in disbelief.*

dis|charge (**discharges, discharging, discharged**)

> Pronounce the verb /dɪstʃɑrdʒ/. Pronounce the noun /dɪstʃɑrdʒ/.

1 VERB When someone **is discharged from** a somewhere, they are officially allowed to leave, or told that they must leave. ❍ *He has a broken nose but may be discharged from the hospital today.*

2 NOUN Discharge is also a noun. ❍ *He was given a conditional discharge and ordered to pay Miss Smith $500 compensation.*

3 VERB If someone **discharges** their duties or responsibilities, they do everything that needs to be done in order to complete them. [FORMAL] ❍ *the quiet competence with which he discharged his duties*

4 VERB If something **is discharged** from inside a place, it comes out. [FORMAL] ❍ *The resulting salty water will be discharged at sea.*

dis|ci|pline /dɪsɪplɪn/

1 NONCOUNT NOUN Discipline is the practice of making people obey rules. ❍ *The manager needs to impose discipline in order to get better performance.*

2 NONCOUNT NOUN Discipline is the quality of being able to obey particular rules and standards. ❍ *He was impressed by the team's effectiveness and discipline.*

dis|con|nect /dɪskənɛkt/ **VERB** If you **disconnect** a piece of equipment, you stop electricity or water from going into it. ❍ *Try disconnecting the modem for a while.*

dis|count /dɪskaʊnt/

1 NOUN a reduction in the usual price of something [MARKETING AND SALES] ❍ *All staff get a 20% discount.*

2 VERB If a store or firm **discounts** a product, they take an amount off the usual price. [MARKETING AND SALES] ❍ *This has forced airlines to discount fares heavily in order to spur demand.* ● **dis|count|ing NONCOUNT NOUN** ❍ *heavy discounting of football shirts*

dis|count house (**discount houses**)

1 NOUN A **discount house** is the same as a **discount store**. [MARKETING AND SALES]

2 NOUN a financial organization that buys and sells bills before they mature, often at a reduced rate [BANKING, ECONOMICS]

dis|count rate (**discount rates**) **NOUN** the rate of interest at which the Federal Reserve Bank lends money to other banks [BANKING, ECONOMICS]

dis|count store (**discount stores**) **NOUN** a store that sells goods at lower prices than usual [MARKETING AND SALES] ❍ *A growing number of shoppers buy both food and fuel at discount stores.*

dis|cour|age /dɪskɜrɪdʒ/ (**discourages, discouraging, discouraged**) **VERB** If someone or something **discourages** you, they make you feel that you do not want to do a particular activity any more. ❍ *Learning a language is difficult at first but don't let this discourage you.*

dis|cov|er /dɪskʌvər/

1 VERB If you **discover** something that you did not know about before, you become aware of it. ❍ *Their goal is to listen more closely to customers in order to discover how to improve their service.*

2 VERB If something **is discovered**, someone finds it. ❍ *Gold was discovered on their land in 1987.*

3 VERB When someone **discovers** a new place, substance, or method, they are the first person to find it or use it. ❍ *Who was the first European to discover America?*

dis|cov|ery /dɪskʌvəri/ (**discoveries**) **NOUN** the act of discovering something, or the thing that is discovered ❍ *They announced the discovery of oil off the coast.* ❍ *In that year, two important discoveries were made.*

dis|cre|tion|ary trust /dɪskrɛʃənɛri trʌst/ (**discretionary trusts**) **NOUN** a trust where the amounts paid to the people named are not fixed but are decided by the trustees [FINANCE]

dis|crimi|nate /dɪskrɪmɪneɪt/ (**discriminates, discriminating, discriminated**) **VERB** To **discriminate against** a group of people means to treat them unfairly. ❍ *They believe the law discriminates against women.*

dis|crimi|nat|ing /dɪskrɪmɪneɪtɪŋ/

1 ADJ having the ability to recognize things that are of good quality ❍ *More discriminating visitors now tend to shun the area.*

2 ADJ Discriminating tariffs or duties are charged at different rates to encourage or discourage imports or exports.

dis|crimi|na|tion /dɪskrɪmɪneɪʃən/ **NONCOUNT NOUN Discrimination** is the practice of treating one person or group unfairly. ❍ *Many companies are breaking age discrimination laws.*

dis|cuss /dɪskʌs/ **VERB** If people **discuss** something, they talk about it in detail. ❍ *We are meeting next week to discuss plans for the future.*

dis|cus|sion /dɪskʌʃən/ **NOUN** a conversation in which a subject is talked about in detail ❍ *Managers are having informal discussions later today.*

dis|ease /dɪziz/ **NOUN** an illness ❍ *There are no drugs available to treat this disease.* ❍ *heart disease*

dis|en|fran|chise /dɪsɪnfræntʃaɪz/ (**disenfranchises, disenfranchising, disenfranchised**) or **disfranchise VERB** To **disenfranchise** a group of people means to take away their right to vote or other rights that most other people have. ❍ *fears of an organized attempt to disenfranchise supporters of Father Aristide*

dis|equi|lib|rium /dɪsikwɪlɪbriəm/ **NONCOUNT NOUN Disequilibrium** is a state in which things are not stable or certain, but are likely to change suddenly. [FORMAL]

dis|grace /dɪsgreɪs/ **NOUN** If something is **a disgrace**, it is very bad or wrong. ❍ *His behavior was a disgrace.*

dis|guise /dɪsgaɪz/ (**disguises, disguising, disguised**)

1 NOUN something you wear or a change you make to your appearance so that people will not recognize you ❍ *He traveled in disguise.* ❍ *He was wearing a ridiculous disguise.*

2 VERB To **disguise** something means to hide it or make it appear different so that people will not recognize it. ❍ *I tried to disguise the fact that the meeting had been unsuccessful.*

● **dis|guised ADJ** ❍ *The robber was disguised as a medical worker.*

dis|gust /dɪsgʌst/ **NONCOUNT NOUN Disgust** is a feeling of very strong dislike or disapproval. ❍ *George watched in disgust.*

dis|gust|ing /dɪsgʌstɪŋ/ **ADJ** extremely unpleasant or unacceptable ❍ *The food tasted disgusting.*

dish /dɪʃ/ (**dishes**)

1 NOUN a shallow container for cooking or serving food ❍ *Pour the mixture into a square glass dish.*

2 NOUN food that is prepared in a particular way ❍ *There are plenty of delicious dishes to choose from.*

dis|in|fect /dɪsɪnfɛkt/ **VERB** If you **disinfect** something, you clean it using a substance that kills bacteria. ❍ *Chlorine is used for disinfecting water.*

dis|in|fla|tion /dɪsɪnfleɪʃən/ **NONCOUNT NOUN Disinflation** is a reduction in the rate of inflation. [ECONOMICS] ❍ *The 1990s was a period of disinflation, when companies lost much of their power to raise prices.*

dis|in|vest /dɪsɪnvɛst/

1 VERB To **disinvest in** a firm is to remove investment from it. [FINANCE] ❍ *Are there strong reasons for the government to disinvest in your company?*

2 VERB To **disinvest** is to reduce the capital stock of an economy or a firm. [FINANCE] ❍ *The area and buildings of the Management Development Centre were part of the assets to be disinvested.* ● **dis|in|vest|ment** /dɪsɪnvɛstmənt/ **NONCOUNT NOUN** ❍ *U.S. capital investment growth recovered significantly from the decade of disinvestment.*

disk /dɪsk/ also **disc**

1 NOUN a flat, circular object ❍ *The food processor has three slicing disks.*

2 NOUN in a computer, the part where information is stored ❍ *The program uses 2.5 megabytes of disk space.*

disk drive (**disk drives**) **NOUN** on a computer, the part that holds a disk

dis|like /dɪslaɪk/ (**dislikes, disliking, disliked**)

1 VERB If you **dislike** someone or something, you think they are unpleasant and you do not like them. ❍ *People generally dislike advertising.*

2 NOUN Your **dislikes** are the things that you do not like. ❍ *information about customers' likes and dislikes*

dis|miss /dɪsmɪs/

1 VERB If you **dismiss** something, you say that

d

it is not important enough for you to consider. ❍ *Perry dismissed the suggestion as nonsense.*

2 VERB If you **are dismissed** by someone in authority, they tell you to leave. ❍ *Two more witnesses were heard, and dismissed.*

3 VERB If you **are dismissed** from your job, you are told to leave. [HR] ❍ *A few low-ranking officials were arrested or dismissed.*

D

dis|mis|sal /dɪsmɪsəl/

1 NOUN An employee's **dismissal** is when they are told to leave their job. [HR] ❍ *Mr. Low's dismissal from his post at the head of the commission*

2 NONCOUNT NOUN Dismissal of something means deciding or saying that it is not important. ❍ *high-handed dismissal of public opinion*

dis|play /dɪspleɪ/

1 VERB If you **display** something, you put it in a place where people can see it. ❍ *Old soldiers proudly displayed their medals.*

2 NONCOUNT NOUN Display is also a noun. ❍ *The artist's work is on display in New York next month.*

3 NOUN an arrangement of things that have been put in a particular place, so that people can see them easily ❍ *In the second gallery, there was a display of World War II aircraft.*

dis|pos|able /dɪspoʊzəbəl/

1 ADJ designed to be thrown away after being used ❍ *disposable diapers*

2 ADJ available to be used if needed ❍ *disposable assets*

dis|pos|able goods or **disposables**

PL NOUN Disposable goods are goods such as food and newspapers that are used up soon after they are purchased. Compare with **durable goods**. [ECONOMICS] ❍ *A third of their income is spent on disposable goods.*

dis|pos|al /dɪspoʊzəl/ **NONCOUNT NOUN Disposal** is when you get rid of something that you no longer want or need. ❍ *waste disposal*

dis|pose /dɪspoʊz/ (**disposes, disposing, disposed**)

▸ **dispose of** If you **dispose of** something, you get rid of it. ❍ *How do they dispose of nuclear waste?*

dis|pute /dɪspyut/ **NOUN** an argument ❍ *a legal dispute over ownership*

dis|quali|fy /dɪskwɒlɪfaɪ/ (**disqualifies, disqualifying, disqualified**) **VERB** When someone **is disqualified**, they are stopped from taking part in a competition. ❍ *Thomson was disqualified from the race.*

dis|rupt /dɪsrʌpt/ **VERB** If someone or something **disrupts** an event, they cause difficulties that prevent it from continuing. ❍ *The strike has disrupted services.*

• **dis|rup|tion NOUN** ❍ *The bad weather caused disruption at many airports.*

dis|rup|tive /dɪsrʌptɪv/ **ADJ** causing problems and preventing something from continuing in a normal way ❍ *We must minimize the disruptive effects of the change.*

dis|rup|tive tech|nol|ogy (**disruptive technologies**) **NOUN** a new technology, such as computers and the Internet, which has a sudden and major effect on technologies that existed before [TECHNOLOGY] ❍ *the other great disruptive technologies of the 20th century, such as electricity, the telephone, and the car*

dis|solve /dɪzɒlv/ (**dissolves, dissolving, dissolved**) **VERB** If you **dissolve** a substance in a liquid, or if the substance **dissolves**, it becomes mixed with the liquid and disappears. ❍ *Heat the mixture gently until the sugar dissolves.*

dis|tance /dɪstəns/

1 NOUN The **distance between** two places is the amount of space between them. ❍ *We must take into account the distance between residential areas and stores.*

2 Something that is **in the distance** is a long way away from you. ❍ *We could even see the mountains in the distance.*

3 If you see something **from a distance**, you see it from a long way away. ❍ *From a distance, the lake looked beautiful.*

dis|tant /dɪstənt/

1 ADJ far away ❍ *The mountains were on the distant horizon.*

2 ADJ A **distant** relative is one who you are not

closely related to. ❍ *I received a letter from a distant cousin.*

dis|tinct /dɪstɪŋkt/
1 ADJ If something is **distinct from** something else, it is different from it. ❍ *Quebec is quite distinct from the rest of Canada.*
2 ADJ If something is **distinct**, you can hear, see, or taste it clearly. ❍ *Each brand of coffee has its own distinct flavor.*

dis|tinc|tion /dɪstɪŋkʃən/ If you **draw a distinction** or **make a distinction**, you say that two things are different. ❍ *He makes a distinction between art and culture.*

dis|tin|guish /dɪstɪŋgwɪʃ/ (**distinguishes, distinguishing, distinguished**) **VERB** If you can **distinguish between** two things, you can see or understand how they are different. ❍ *Customers find it difficult to distinguish between the two products.*

dis|tort /dɪstɔrt/
1 VERB If you **distort** something, you change it so that it is no longer correct or true. ❍ *The media distorts reality.* ● **dis|tort|ed ADJ** ❍ *These figures give a distorted view of the situation.* ● **dis|tor|tion NOUN** ❍ *a gross distortion of reality*
2 VERB If you **distort** the appearance or sound of something, you change it so that it looks or sounds very different. ❍ *An artist may distort shapes in a painting.* ● **dis|tort|ed ADJ** ❍ *The sound was becoming distorted.*

dis|tract /dɪstrækt/ **VERB** If something **distracts** you, it takes your attention away from what you are doing. ❍ *I'm easily distracted by noise.*

dis|trac|tion /dɪstrækʃən/ **NOUN** something that takes your attention away from what you are doing ❍ *DVD players in cars are a dangerous distraction for drivers.*

dis|tress /dɪstrɛs/ **NONCOUNT NOUN** **Distress** is a strong feeling of sadness or pain. ❍ *The condition can cause great distress in young people.* ● **dis|tress|ing ADJ** ❍ *It is very distressing when you lose your job.*

dis|tress mer|chan|dise or **distressed merchandise** **NONCOUNT NOUN** **Distress merchandise** is goods that are sold cheaply to pay late debts. [MARKETING AND SALES] ❍ *Our business is buying up distress merchandise and selling it at auction.*

dis|trib|ute /dɪstrɪbyut/ (**distributes, distributing, distributed**)
1 VERB If you **distribute** things, you give them to a number of people. [LOGISTICS AND DISTRIBUTION] ❍ *They distributed free tickets to young people.*
2 VERB When a firm **distributes** goods, it supplies them to the stores or businesses that sell them. [LOGISTICS AND DISTRIBUTION] ❍ *We didn't understand how difficult it was to distribute a national paper.*

dis|trib|ut|ed /dɪstrɪbyʊtɪd/ **ADJ** existing throughout an area, object, or group [LOGISTICS AND DISTRIBUTION] ❍ *These cells are widely distributed throughout the body.*

dis|tri|bu|tion /dɪstrɪbyuʃən/
1 NONCOUNT NOUN The **distribution** of things involves giving them to a number of people or places. [LOGISTICS AND DISTRIBUTION] ❍ *the council which controls the distribution of foreign aid*
2 NONCOUNT NOUN The **distribution** of goods involves delivering them to the stores where they will be sold. [LOGISTICS AND DISTRIBUTION] ❍ *Clorox introduced a laundry detergent on the West Coast last year, and has since expanded distribution to cover about 45% of the country.*
3 NONCOUNT NOUN The **distribution** of something is how much of it there is in each place or at each time, or how much of it each person has. ❍ *Mr. Roh's economic planners sought to achieve a more equitable distribution of wealth.*
4 NOUN an amount that is paid to stockholders or investors [FINANCE] ❍ *These funds claim to pay out annual distributions of more than 11%.*

dis|tri|bu|tion chain (**distribution chains**) **NOUN** all the stages that goods pass through between leaving a factory and arriving at a retailer [MARKETING AND SALES, LOGISTICS AND DISTRIBUTION] ❍ *all the companies in the distribution chain involved in bringing the mussels to Montreal*

d

dis|tri|bu|tion chan|nel (**distribution channels**) NOUN a method of distributing goods [MARKETING AND SALES, LOGISTICS AND DISTRIBUTION] ❍ *Mitel is looking to acquire a distributor to strengthen its U.S. distribution channels.*

dis|tri|bu|tion net|work (**distribution networks**) NOUN A company's **distribution network** is all the methods it uses to distribute its goods. [MARKETING AND SALES, LOGISTICS AND DISTRIBUTION] ❍ *Cadbury has widened its European distribution network.*

dis|tribu|tor /dɪstrɪbyətər/ NOUN a firm that supplies goods to stores or businesses [MARKETING AND SALES, ADMINISTRATION] ❍ *Spain's largest distributor of petroleum products*

dis|tribu|tor|ship /dɪstrɪbyətərʃɪp/ NOUN a firm that supplies goods to stores or other businesses, or the right to supply goods to stores and businesses [MARKETING AND SALES, ADMINISTRATION] ❍ *the general manager of an automobile distributorship*

dis|trict /dɪstrɪkt/ NOUN a particular area of a city or country ❍ *I drove around the business district.*

dis|turb /dɪstɜrb/

1 VERB If you **disturb** someone, you interrupt what they are doing or interrupt their peace. ❍ *Sorry, am I disturbing you?*

2 VERB If something **disturbs** you, it makes you feel upset or worried. ❍ *He was disturbed by the news of the attack.*

dis|turb|ance /dɪstɜrbəns/ NOUN an event in which people behave violently in public ❍ *During the disturbance, three men were hurt.*

dis|turb|ing /dɪstɜrbɪŋ/ ADJ making you feel worried or upset ❍ *We've received some disturbing news.*

ditch /dɪtʃ/ (**ditches**) NOUN a deep, long, narrow hole that carries water away from a road or a field ❍ *Both vehicles landed in a ditch.*

dive /daɪv/ (**dives, diving, dived** or **dove, dived**)

1 VERB If you **dive into** water, you jump in so that your arms and your head go in first. ❍ *Ben dove into a river.*

2 NOUN **Dive** is also a noun. ❍ *Pam walked out and did another perfect dive.* ● **div|ing** NONCOUNT NOUN ❍ *Shaun won medals in diving and swimming.*

3 VERB If prices, amounts, or values **dive**, they decrease very quickly. ❍ *Earnings before interest and tax from brewing dived 50% to $123.8 million.* NOUN **Dive** is also a noun. ❍ *a 43% earnings dive*

di|verse /dɪvɜrs, daɪ-/ ADJ made up of many different people or things ❍ *We have a very diverse group of shareholders.*

di|ver|si|fi|ca|tion /dɪvɜrsɪfɪkeɪʃən, daɪ-/

1 NONCOUNT NOUN **Diversification** is when a firm starts to produce new and different goods or services. [ECONOMICS] ❍ *He was the driving force behind diversification into areas such as water and sewerage projects in the Far East and Mexico.*

2 NONCOUNT NOUN **Diversification** is when people start to invest their money in more than one place or type of product. [ECONOMICS] ❍ *a simple illustration of how portfolio diversification works*

di|ver|si|fy /dɪvɜrsɪfaɪ/ (**diversifies, diversifying, diversified**)

1 VERB When a firm **diversifies**, it starts to produce new and different goods or services. [ECONOMICS] ❍ *The firm's troubles started only when it diversified into new products.*

2 VERB When an investor **diversifies**, they start to invest their money in more than one place or type of product. [ECONOMICS] ❍ *Many Japanese institutions are diversifying their equity investments away from Wall Street.*

di|vert /dɪvɜrt, daɪ-/ VERB To **divert** vehicles or travelers means to make them go a different route. ❍ *The plane was diverted to Boston's Logan International Airport.*

di|vest /dɪvɛst, daɪ-/ VERB If you **divest** or **divest yourself of** an asset, you get rid of it, usually by selling it. [FINANCE, ADMINISTRATION] ❍ *The company divested itself of its oil interests.* ● **di|vest|ment** NONCOUNT NOUN ❍ *A deficit in the current account must be financed by borrowing from abroad or by divestment of foreign assets.*

di|vide /dɪvaɪd/ (**divides, dividing, divided**)
1 VERB When people or things **are divided** or **divide into** smaller groups or parts, they become separated into smaller parts. ❍ *The cash was evenly divided.* ❍ *Participants were divided into two groups of six.*
2 VERB If you **divide** one number **by** another number, you find out how many times the second number can fit into the first number. ❍ *Divide total income by the beginning price of the stock.*
3 VERB If a line **divides** two areas, it makes the two areas separate. ❍ *A 1969-mile border divides Mexico from the United States.*
▶ **divide up** If you **divide** something **up**, you separate it into smaller or more useful groups. ❍ *They divided the country up into four areas.*

divi|dend /dɪvɪdɛnd/
1 NOUN an amount of a firm's profits that is paid to people who own shares in the firm [FINANCE] ❍ *The first quarter dividend has been increased by nearly 4 percent.*
2 If something **pays dividends**, it brings advantages at a later date. ❍ *Steps taken now to maximize your health will pay dividends later on.*

divi|dend cov|er NONCOUNT NOUN A firm's **dividend cover** is the number of times that its dividends could be paid out of its annual profits after tax. [FINANCE] ❍ *With falling profits, analysts worry that the firm's dividend cover is slim.*

di|vi|sion /dɪvɪʒᵊn/
1 NONCOUNT NOUN The **division of** something is when someone or something separates it into parts. ❍ *the division of land after the war*
2 NONCOUNT NOUN Division is the process of dividing one number by another number. ❍ *The program performs simple functions such as multiplication and division.*
3 NOUN in a large organization, a group of departments with similar tasks ❍ *She manages the bank's Latin American division.*

di|vi|sion of la|bor NONCOUNT NOUN **Division of labor** is a system of making products where different workers do different parts of the process. [ECONOMICS] ❍ *The extensive division of labor in the factory made much of the work so routine and simple that untrained women and children could do it.*

di|vorce /dɪvɔrs/ (**divorces, divorcing, divorced**)
1 NOUN the legal ending of a marriage ❍ *Many marriages end in divorce.*
2 VERB If a man and woman **get divorced** or if one of them **divorces** the other, their marriage is legally ended. ❍ *My parents got divorced in 2006.* ❍ *She divorced him after a year.*

di|vorced /dɪvɔrst/ ADJ no longer legally married ❍ *He's divorced, with a young son.*

div|vy /dɪvi/ (**divvies**) or **divi** NOUN **Divvy** is an abbreviation for **dividend**, especially one paid by a cooperative society in the past. [FINANCE, BRIT, INFORMAL]

Di|wa|li /dɪwɑli/ also **Divali** NONCOUNT NOUN **Diwali** is a Hindu festival celebrated in October or November with the lighting of lamps in homes and temples.

DIY /di aɪ waɪ/ NONCOUNT NOUN **DIY** is the activity of making or repairing things yourself, especially in your home. **DIY** is short for "do-it-yourself." ❍ *a DIY project*

diz|zy /dɪzi/ (**dizzier, dizziest**) ADJ feeling that you are losing your balance and that you are going to fall ❍ *Her head hurt, and she felt slightly dizzy.* ● **diz|zi|ness** NONCOUNT NOUN ❍ *Thankfully, the dizziness has gone.*

do
❶ AUXILIARY VERB USES
❷ OTHER VERB USES

❶ **do** /də, STRONG du/ (**does, doing, did, done**)
1 AUX Do is used with "not" to form the negative of main verbs. ❍ *They don't work very hard.* ❍ *I didn't know about the meeting.*
2 AUX Do is used with another verb to form questions. ❍ *Do you usually work late?* ❍ *What did he say?*
3 AUX You use **do** instead of repeating a verb when you are answering a question. ❍ *"Do you think he's telling the truth?"—"Yes, I do."*

❷ **do** /du/
1 VERB When you **do** something, you take

some action or perform an activity or task. ❍ *I was trying to do some work.* ❍ *In the evening I did the accounts.*
2 VERB If you ask someone what they **do**, you want to know what their job is. ❍ *"What does your father do?"—"He's a doctor."*
3 VERB If something **will do**, it is good enough. ❍ *It doesn't matter what you say—anything will do.*
4 If one thing **has** or **is** something **to do with** another thing, the two things are connected. ❍ *Clarke insists all this has nothing to do with him.*
▸ **do up** If you **do** something **up**, you fasten it. ❍ *Marie did up the zip.*

dock /dɒk/
1 NOUN an area of water next to land where ships go so that people can get on or off them
2 VERB When a ship **docks**, it is brought into a dock. ❍ *The crash happened as the ferry tried to dock on Staten Island.*

dock|er /dɒkər/ [BRIT] → **longshoreman**

dock|et /dɒkɪt/
1 NOUN a list of cases waiting for trial in a law court
2 NOUN a piece of paper that comes with a package and gives details of contents, price, etc. [mainly BRIT]

doc|tor /dɒktər/
1 NOUN a person whose job is to treat people who are sick or injured ❍ *Be sure to speak to your doctor before planning your trip.*
2 NOUN a person who has been awarded the highest academic degree by a university ❍ *a doctor of philosophy*

docu|ment /dɒkyəmənt/
1 NOUN an official piece of paper with important information on it ❍ *a legal document*
2 NOUN a piece of text that is stored on a computer ❍ *Did you save the document?*

docu|men|tary /dɒkyəmɛntəri, -tri/ (**documentaries**) **NOUN** a television program or a movie that provides information about a particular subject ❍ *a documentary on eating disorders*

dodge /dɒdʒ/ (**dodges, dodging, dodged**)
1 VERB If you **dodge**, you move suddenly, especially to avoid something. ❍ *I dodged back behind the tree and waited.*
2 VERB If you **dodge** something, you avoid it by moving. ❍ *He dodged a speeding car.*

does /dəz, STRONG dʌz/ **Does** is a form of the verb **do**.

doesn't /dʌzᵊnt/ **Doesn't** is short for "does not."

dog /dɔg/ **NOUN** an animal that is often kept by people as a pet ❍ *He was walking his dog.*

doll /dɒl/ **NOUN** a child's toy that looks like a small person or baby

dol|lar /dɒlər/ **NOUN** The **dollar** ($) is the unit of money that is used in the U.S., Canada, and some other countries. There are 100 **cents** in a **dollar**. ❍ *She earns twelve dollars an hour.*

do|main /doʊmeɪn/ **NOUN** a particular area of study or activity [FORMAL] ❍ *This theory is gaining acceptance in the domain of science.*

do|main name (**domain names**) **NOUN** the main part of a website address that tells you who the website belongs to ❍ *I've just bought the domain name "AdamWilson.com"*

dome /doʊm/ **NOUN** a round roof ❍ *Kiev is known as "the city of golden domes."*

do|mes|tic /dəmɛstɪk/
1 ADJ happening or existing within one particular country ❍ *domestic flights*
2 ADJ relating to the home and family ❍ *Most women spend over three hours a day on domestic chores.*

do|mes|tic mar|ket (**domestic markets**) **NOUN** a market that exists within a particular country [MARKETING AND SALES] ❍ *Mr. Davern said the domestic market was worth 24 percent of tourism earnings.*

domi|cile /dɒmɪsaɪl/ also **domicil** **NOUN** Your **domicile** is the place where you live. [FORMAL]

domi|nate /dɒmɪneɪt/ (**dominates, dominating, dominated**) **VERB** If a person or organization **dominates** a particular thing, they are the most successful and important person or thing in it. ❍ *GE is aiming to dominate the market for clean technologies such as wind and solar power.*

do|nate /doʊneɪt, doʊneɪt/ (**donates, donating, donated**)
1 VERB If you **donate** something **to** an organization, you give it to them. ❍ *He donates large amounts of money to charity.*
2 VERB If you **donate** your blood or a part of your body, you allow doctors to use it to help someone who is sick.

do|na|tion /doʊneɪʃən/ **NOUN** money or goods that are given to an organization, especially one that needs help ❍ *Employees make regular donations to charity.*

done /dʌn/
1 Done is a form of the verb **do**.
2 People say "**done**" when they are agreeing to a deal. ❍ *"I'll give you fifty dollars for it."—"Done!"*

dông /dɒŋ/ (**dông**) **NOUN** the unit of money that is used in Vietnam [ECONOMICS]

don|key /dɒŋki/ **NOUN** an animal like a small horse with long ears

do|nor /doʊnər/ **NOUN** a person who gives blood or a part of their body so that doctors can use them to help someone who is sick ❍ *a blood donor*

don't /doʊnt/ **Don't** is short for "do not."

door /dɔr/
1 NOUN a flat, usually rectangular, object that you pull open or push shut when entering or leaving a building, room, or vehicle ❍ *I knocked at her office door, but there was no answer.*
2 When you **answer the door**, you open a door because someone has knocked on it or rung a bell. ❍ *Carol answered the door as soon as I knocked.*

door|way /dɔrweɪ/ **NOUN** a space in a wall where a door opens and closes ❍ *David was standing in the doorway.*

dose /doʊs/ **NOUN** A **dose of** medicine or a drug is an amount you take at one time. ❍ *You can treat the infection with one big dose of antibiotics.*

dot /dɒt/ **NOUN** a very small round mark, like the one on the letter "i," or in the names of websites

dotcom /dɒtkɒm/ also **dot-com NOUN** a firm that does all or most of its business on the Internet [TECHNOLOGY] ❍ *In 1999, dotcoms spent more than $1 billion on TV spots.*

dot|com|mer /dɒtkɒmər/ **NOUN** a person who does their business on the Internet [TECHNOLOGY]

dou|ble /dʌbᵊl/ (**doubles, doubling, doubled**)
1 ADJ with two parts ❍ *This room has double doors opening on to a balcony.*
2 ADJ twice the normal size ❍ *Shareholders want to avoid double taxation.*
3 ADJ A **double** room or bed is intended for two people, usually a couple. ❍ *The hotel charges $180 for a double room.*
4 VERB If something **doubles**, or if you **double** something, it becomes twice as big. ❍ *Prices have doubled since January.*

double-click (**double-clicks, double-clicking, double-clicked**) **VERB** If you **double-click on** an area of a computer screen, you press a button on the mouse twice quickly in order to make something happen. ❍ *Double-click on a file to start the application.*

dou|ble dip (**double dips**) also **double-dip NOUN** a period when an economy goes into recession, then briefly recovers, but then goes into another recession [ECONOMICS] ❍ *Dismal economic findings have analysts fearing a double dip.* ❍ *a double-dip recession*

double-entry ADJ Double-entry book-keeping is a system of book-keeping in which each transaction appears as a debit in one account and as a credit in another. Compare with **single-entry**. [FINANCE] ❍ *a double-entry account*

dou|ble in|dem|ni|ty NONCOUNT NOUN Double indemnity is when a person with life assurance has a clause saying that they will get double the value of the policy in the case of their accidental death. [BANKING]

dou|ble time NONCOUNT NOUN If someone is paid **double time**, they get twice as much money as usual, for example for working on a public holiday.

doubt /daʊt/
1 NOUN a feeling that you are uncertain about

whether something is true or possible ❍ *Rendell had doubts about the plan.* ❍ *There is no doubt that the Earth's climate is changing.*
2 VERB If you **doubt** something, you think that it is probably not true. ❍ *I doubt if their figures are accurate.*
3 VERB If you **doubt** someone, you think that they may be saying something that is not true. ❍ *No one doubted him.*
4 If you are **in doubt** about something, you are not sure about it. ❍ *He is in no doubt about what to do.*
5 You use **no doubt** to show that you feel certain about something. ❍ *She'll no doubt be here soon.*

D

doubt|ful /daʊtfəl/ **ADJ** not likely ❍ *It's doubtful whether they will meet their target.*

dough /doʊ/ **NONCOUNT NOUN** **Dough** is a mixture of flour, water, and other things that is cooked to make bread and cookies. ❍ *cookie dough*

Dow Jones av|er|age /daʊ dʒoʊnz ævərɪdʒ, ævrɪdʒ/ or **Dow Jones industrial average** **NONCOUNT NOUN** **The Dow Jones average** is a daily index of stock-exchange prices based on the average price of a selected number of securities. [ECONOMICS]

down /daʊn/
1 PREP toward a lower level, or in a lower place ❍ *She came down the stairs to meet them.* ❍ *He was halfway down the hill.*
2 ADV **Down** is also an adverb. ❍ *I bent down and picked it up.* ❍ *She was looking down at her papers.*
3 PREP If you go **down** a road or a river, you go along it. ❍ *They walked quickly down the street.*
4 ADV If you put something **down**, you put it onto a surface. ❍ *Danny put down his glass.*
5 ADV If an amount goes **down**, it decreases. ❍ *The price has gone down.*
6 ADJ **Down** is also an adjective. ❍ *Oil is down $2 per barrel.*
7 ADJ unhappy [INFORMAL] ❍ *He sounded really down.*
8 ADJ If a computer system is **down**, it is not working. ❍ *The computer's down again.*

down|grade /daʊngreɪd/ (**downgrades, downgrading, downgraded**)
1 VERB If something **is downgraded**, it is given less importance than it used to have or than you think it should have. ❍ *The boy's condition has been downgraded from critical to serious.*
2 VERB If someone **is downgraded**, their job or status is changed so that they become less important or receive less money. [HR] ❍ *There was no criticism of her work until after she was downgraded.*

down|load /daʊnloʊd/
1 VERB If you **download** information, you move it to your computer from a bigger computer or network. [TECHNOLOGY] ❍ *You can download the software from the Internet.*
2 NOUN the process of downloading information [TECHNOLOGY] ❍ *SpeedBit has managed to slash download times for a full-length feature film to 40 minutes.*
3 NOUN a computer file that has been downloaded [TECHNOLOGY] ❍ *The Adobe ActiveShare software is also available as a free download.*

down|load|able /daʊnloʊdəbᵊl/ **ADJ** able to be copied to another computer [TECHNOLOGY] ❍ *a downloadable file*

down|market /daʊnmɑrkɪt/ also **down-market** [ECONOMICS, BRIT] → **downscale**

down pay|ment (**down payments**) also **downpayment** **NOUN** If you make a **down payment on** something, you pay part of the total cost when you buy it and the rest in regular payments later. [PURCHASING] ❍ *Celeste asked for the money as a down payment on an old farmhouse.*

down|scale /daʊnskeɪl/
1 ADJ **Downscale** products or services are designed to appeal to poorer people. Compare with **upscale**.
2 ADV If a product or service moves **downscale**, it tries to appeal to poorer people. Compare with **upscale**. ❍ *Department stores are now figuring how to go downscale.*

down|shift|ing /daʊnʃɪftɪŋ/ **NONCOUNT NOUN** **Downshifting** is the act of changing to a more simple life with an easier job and less money.

down|size /daʊnsaɪz/ (**downsizes, downsizing, downsized**) VERB To **downsize** something such as a business or industry means to make it smaller. [ADMINISTRATION, ECONOMICS] ❍ *American manufacturing organizations have been downsizing their factories.* ❍ *today's downsized economy*
● **down|siz|ing** NONCOUNT NOUN ❍ *a trend toward downsizing in the personal computer market*

down|stairs /daʊnstɛərz/
1 ADV to or on a lower floor or the first floor of a building ❍ *Denise went downstairs to meet the clients.* ❍ *He was downstairs in the lobby.*
2 ADJ **Downstairs** rooms are on the ground floor of a building. ❍ *The downstairs rooms are being decorated.*

down|stream /daʊnstrim/ ADJ **Downstream** business activity refers to the distribution of a commodity as opposed to its extraction and production. Compare with **upstream**. [LOGISTICS AND DISTRIBUTION] ❍ *Departments need to have information about their upstream suppliers and downstream customers.*

down|time /daʊntaɪm/
1 NONCOUNT NOUN In industry, **downtime** is the time during which machinery or equipment is not operating. [PRODUCTION] ❍ *On the production line, downtime has been reduced from 55% to 26%.*
2 NONCOUNT NOUN In computing, **downtime** is time when a computer is not working. ❍ *Downtime due to worm removal from networks cost close to $450 million.*
3 NONCOUNT NOUN **Downtime** is time when people are relaxing or not working. ❍ *Downtime in Hollywood can cost a lot of money.*

down|town /daʊntaʊn/ ADJ or ADV in or toward the center of a city ❍ *He works in an office in downtown Chicago.* ❍ *She worked downtown for an insurance firm.*

down|turn /daʊntɜrn/ NOUN If there is a **downturn** in the economy or in a firm or industry, it becomes worse or less successful than it had been. [ECONOMICS] ❍ *They predicted a severe economic downturn.*

COLLOCATIONS
an *economic* downturn
a *sharp* downturn
a *severe* downturn
a downturn *in business*
a downturn *in demand*

down|ward /daʊnwərd/ ADJ or ADV toward the ground or a lower level ❍ *a downward motion* ❍ *She looked downward.* ❍ *Inflation is moving downward.*

down|wards /daʊnwərdz/ [BRIT] → **downward**

doze /doʊz/ (**dozes, dozing, dozed**) VERB When you **doze**, you sleep lightly or for a short period. ❍ *She dozed for a while in the cabin.*
▸ **doze off** If you **doze off**, you fall into a light sleep. ❍ *I closed my eyes and dozed off.*

doz|en /dʌzᵊn/

The plural form is **dozen** after a number.

1 **A dozen** means twelve. ❍ *a dozen eggs*
2 **Dozens of** things or people means a lot of them. ❍ *The storm destroyed dozens of buildings.*

Dr. (**Drs.**) **Dr.** is short for **Doctor**. ❍ *Dr. John Hardy of Vanderbilt Hospital*

draft /dræft/
1 NOUN a piece of writing that you have not finished working on ❍ *I emailed a first draft of the proposal to him.*
2 NOUN cold air that comes into a room ❍ *Block drafts around doors and windows.*
3 NOUN A **draft** is the same as a **bill of exchange**.

drafts|man /dræftsmən/ (**draftsmen**) NOUN someone whose job is to prepare very detailed drawings of machinery, equipment, or buildings [TECHNOLOGY]

drag /dræg/ (**drags, dragging, dragged**) VERB If you **drag** something, you pull it along the ground. ❍ *He dragged his chair toward the table.*

drag and drop (**drags and drops, dragging and dropping, dragged and**

dropped) also **drag-and-drop** VERB If you **drag and drop** computer files or images, you move them from one place to another on the computer screen. ❍ *Drag and drop the folder to the hard drive.*

drain /dreɪn/
1 VERB If you **drain** something or if something drains, liquid flows out of it or off it. ❍ *They built the tunnel to drain water out of the mines.* ❍ *Drain the pasta well.*
2 NOUN a pipe or an opening that carries a liquid away from a place ❍ *A piece of soap was clogging the drain.*

D

dra|ma /drɑmə, dræmə/
1 NOUN a serious play or movie ❍ *a new TV drama*
2 NONCOUNT NOUN plays and the theater in general ❍ *She studied drama at college.*

dra|mat|ic /drəmætɪk/
1 ADJ happening suddenly and very noticeable ❍ *There's been a dramatic change in the way we shop.* ● **dra|mati|cal|ly** /drəmætɪkli/ ADV ❍ *The climate has changed dramatically.*
2 ADJ exciting, often involving danger ❍ *We watched dramatic scenes of the rescue on TV.*

drank /dræŋk/ **Drank** is a form of the verb **drink**.

dras|tic /dræstɪk/ ADJ A **drastic** action has a very big effect. ❍ *Drastic measures are needed to improve the situation.*

draught /drɑft, dræft/ [BRIT] → **draft 2**

draughts|man /dræftsmən/ [TECHNOLOGY, BRIT] → **draftsman**

draw /drɔ/ (**draws, drawing, drew, drawn**)
1 VERB When you **draw** or **draw** something, you use a pencil or pen to make a picture. ❍ *I've drawn a graph showing changes in sales.*
2 VERB If a vehicle **draws** somewhere, it moves there. ❍ *The train was drawing into the station.*
3 VERB If you **draw** something or someone somewhere, you move them there. ❍ *He drew his chair up to my desk.*
4 VERB When you **draw** the drapes (= long pieces of cloth that cover a window), you pull them across a window.
5 VERB If you **draw** a financial document, you write it out. [FINANCE, BANKING] ❍ *to draw a check*
6 NOUN a sum of money that is given to someone for things they will need to buy in future
▶ **draw on**
1 If you **draw on** a resource, you use some of it. ❍ *to draw on one's experience*
2 If you **draw on** an account, you take money out of it. [BANKING]
▶ **draw out**
1 If you **draw out** an event or an activity, you make it last longer. ❍ *He drew out his stay.*
2 If you **draw** someone **out**, you make them speak more freely. [BANKING] ❍ *She's been quiet all evening—see if you can draw her out.*
3 If you **draw out** money from an account or a business, you take it from there. [BANKING] ❍ *She drew out all her savings.*
▶ **draw up** If you **draw up** a list or a plan, you write it or type it. ❍ *They drew up a formal agreement.*

draw|back /drɔbæk/ NOUN a part of something that makes it less useful ❍ *A major drawback of these methods is that they require a lot of additional technology.*

drawer /drɔr/ NOUN a part of a desk or other piece of furniture that you can pull out and put things in ❍ *She opened her desk drawer and took out the report.*

draw|ing /drɔɪŋ/
1 NOUN a picture made with a pencil or pen ❍ *She did a drawing of the building.*
2 NONCOUNT NOUN the activity of creating pictures with a pencil or pen

dread /drɛd/ VERB If you **dread** something, you feel very anxious because you think it will be unpleasant or upsetting. ❍ *I'm dreading the interview.*

dread|ful /drɛdfəl/ ADJ very unpleasant, or very poor in quality ❍ *dreadful news* ❍ *These are dreadful figures.*

dream /drim/ (**dreams, dreaming, dreamed** or **dreamt**)
1 NOUN a series of events that you see in your

mind while you are asleep ❍ *He had a dream about Claire.*
2 NOUN something good that you often think about because you would like it to happen ❍ *After all these years, my dream has finally come true.*
3 VERB When you **dream**, you see events in your mind while you are asleep. ❍ *I dreamed that I was on a bus.* ❍ *She dreamed about her baby.*
4 VERB If you **dream of** something, you often think about it because you would like it to happen. ❍ *ordinary workers who dream of a better life*

dress /drɛs/
1 NOUN a piece of woman's or girl's clothing that covers the body and part of the legs ❍ *She was wearing a short black dress.*
2 NONCOUNT NOUN **Dress** refers to a particular type of clothing. ❍ *He wore formal evening dress.*
3 VERB When you **dress** or **dress yourself**, you put on clothes. ❍ *Sarah waited while he dressed.*
▸ **dress up**
1 If you **dress up**, you put on formal clothes. ❍ *You don't need to dress up for dinner.*
2 If you **dress up**, you put on clothes that make you look like someone else for fun. ❍ *He was dressed up like a cowboy.*

dress code (**dress codes**) **NOUN** The **dress code** of a place is the rules about what kind of clothes people are allowed to wear there. ❍ *There was a rigid dress code (jeans, no short hair).*

COLLOCATIONS
a *strict* dress code
a *relaxed* dress code
to *adhere to* a dress code

dress-down Fri|day (**dress-down Fridays**) **NOUN** If an organization has **dress-down Friday**, its employees are allowed to wear less smart clothes on Fridays.

drew /dru/ **Drew** is a form of the verb **draw**.

drib|ble /drɪbᵊl/ (**dribbles, dribbling, dribbled**)
1 VERB If a liquid **dribbles** somewhere, it flows there in a thin stream. ❍ *Blood dribbled down Harry's face.*
2 VERB When players **dribble** the ball in a game, they keep it moving by using their hand or foot. ❍ *Owen dribbled the ball toward Ferris.*

drift /drɪft/
1 VERB When something **drifts** somewhere, it is carried there by wind or water. ❍ *We drifted up the river.*
2 NONCOUNT NOUN **Drift** is when firms move their manufacturing operations to places where costs are lower. [PRODUCTION] ❍ *The government is tackling the consequences of the drift of manufacturing to the Far East.*
▸ **drift off** If you **drift off** to sleep, you gradually fall asleep.

d

drill /drɪl/
1 NOUN a tool for making holes ❍ *an electric drill*
2 VERB When you **drill** or **drill** a hole in something, you make a hole using a drill. ❍ *You'll need to drill a hole in the wall.*

drink /drɪŋk/ (**drinks, drinking, drank, drunk**)
1 VERB When you **drink** a liquid, you take it into your mouth and swallow it. ❍ *He drank his cup of coffee.* ● **drink|er NOUN** ❍ *We're all coffee drinkers.*
2 VERB To **drink** means to drink alcohol. ❍ *He drinks too much.* ● **drink|er NOUN** ❍ *I'm not a heavy drinker.*
3 NOUN an amount of a liquid that you drink ❍ *a drink of water*

drip /drɪp/ (**drips, dripping, dripped**)
1 VERB When liquid **drips** somewhere, it falls in drops. ❍ *The rain dripped down my face.*
2 VERB When something that contains a liquid **drips**, drops of liquid escape from it. ❍ *A faucet in the kitchen was dripping.*

drip-feed (**drip-feeds, drip-feeding, drip-fed**) also **drip feed VERB** If you **drip-feed** money **into** something, you pay the money a little at a time rather than paying it all at once. ❍ *investors who adopt the sensible policy of drip feeding money into shares*

drive /draɪv/ (**drives, driving, drove, driven**)
1 VERB When you **drive**, you control the movement and direction of a car or other

vehicle. ❍ *I drove into town.* ❍ *What car does he drive?* ● **driv|ing** NONCOUNT NOUN ❍ *a driving instructor*
2 VERB If you **drive** someone somewhere, you take them there in a car. ❍ *She drove him to the train station.*
3 NOUN a trip in a car ❍ *Let's go for a drive on Sunday.*
4 NOUN the part of a computer that reads and stores information [TECHNOLOGY]

D

driven /drɪvᵊn/ **Driven** is a form of the verb **drive**.

driv|er /draɪvər/ NOUN a person who drives a car, bus, or other vehicle ❍ *The driver got out of his truck.* ❍ *a taxi driver*

driv|er's li|cense (**driver's licenses**) NOUN a card that shows that you have passed a driving test and that you are allowed to drive

drive|way /draɪvweɪ/ NOUN a small road that leads from the street to the front of a building ❍ *There is a driveway at the front of the house.*

driv|ing li|cence /draɪvɪŋ laɪsᵊns/ (**driving licences**) [BRIT] → **driver's license**

drop /drɒp/ (**drops, dropping, dropped**)
1 VERB If a level or an amount **drops**, it quickly becomes less. ❍ *Temperatures can drop to freezing at night.*
2 NOUN **Drop** is also a noun. ❍ *There was a sudden drop in the number of visitors to the site.*
3 VERB If you **drop** something or if something **drops**, it falls straight down. ❍ *I dropped my glasses and broke them.*
4 VERB If you **drop** someone somewhere, you take them there in a car and leave them there. ❍ *He dropped me outside the hotel.*
5 **Drop off** means the same as **drop**. ❍ *Dad dropped me off at school on his way to work.*
6 NOUN A **drop of** a liquid is a very small amount of it shaped like a little ball. ❍ *a drop of water*
▸ **drop by** If you **drop by**, you visit someone informally. ❍ *I'll drop by later.*
▸ **drop in** If you **drop in**, or **drop in on** someone, you visit them informally. ❍ *Why not drop in for a chat?*
▸ **drop off** If you **drop off** to sleep, you go to sleep.
▸ **drop out** If someone **drops out of** school or a competition, they leave it without finishing. [INFORMAL] ❍ *He dropped out of high school at the age of 16.*

COLLOCATIONS
to drop *sharply*
a *significant* drop
to drop *dramatically*
a *dramatic* drop

drop-dead fee (**drop-dead fees**) NOUN A fee paid to an organization lending money to a firm hoping to use it to pay for a takeover bid. The fee is paid if the takeover fails. [ECONOMICS]

drop-down menu (**drop-down menus**) NOUN on a computer screen, a list of choices that appears, usually when you click on a small arrow [TECHNOLOGY]

drought /draʊt/ NOUN a long period of time with no rain ❍ *The drought has killed all their crops.*

drove /droʊv/ **Drove** is a form of the verb **drive**.

drown /draʊn/ VERB When someone **drowns**, they die under water because they cannot breathe. ❍ *A child can drown in only a few inches of water.*

drug /drʌg/
1 NOUN a chemical that is used as a medicine ❍ *The new drug is too expensive for most African countries.*
2 NOUN an illegal substance that some people take because they enjoy its effects

drug ad|dict (**drug addicts**) NOUN someone who cannot stop using illegal drugs

drug|store /drʌgstɔr/ NOUN a store where medicines, make-up, and some other things are sold

drum /drʌm/ NOUN a simple musical instrument that you hit with sticks or with your hands

drunk /drʌŋk/
1 ADJ having drunk too much alcohol
2 Drunk is a form of the verb **drink**.

dry /draɪ/ (**dry-cleans, dry-cleaning, dry-cleaned**)
1 ADJ having no water on the surface ❍ *Clean the metal with a soft dry cloth.*
2 ADJ without rain ❍ *The Sahara is one of the driest places in Africa.*
3 VERB When something **dries**, it becomes dry and when you **dry** something, you make it dry. ❍ *Put the glue on a surface where it can dry.* ❍ *Next, the wood is dried and heated.*
▶ **dry up** If something **dries up**, it becomes completely dry. ❍ *The river had dried up long ago.*

dry-clean (**dry-cleans, dry-cleaning, dry-cleaned**) **VERB** When clothes **are dry-cleaned**, they are cleaned with a chemical rather than with water.

duck /dʌk/
1 NOUN a bird with short legs that lives near water, or the meat from this bird
2 VERB If you **duck**, you move your head quickly downward so that something does not hit you, or so that someone does not see you. ❍ *There was a loud noise and I ducked.*

due /du/
1 If a situation is **due to** something, it exists as a result of that thing. ❍ *The factory is operating short weeks due to a drop in car sales.*
2 ADJ If something is **due** at a particular time, it is expected to happen or arrive at that time. ❍ *The results are due at the end of the month.*
3 ADJ Money that is **due** is owed to someone. ❍ *When is the next payment due?*

due bill (**due bills**) **NOUN** a document that shows that you are owed something, and that can be exchanged for goods or services [ECONOMICS] ❍ *These due bills could be sold at established prices to persons who wanted accommodations.*

dug /dʌg/ **Dug** is a form of the verb **dig**.

dull /dʌl/
1 ADJ boring ❍ *a fairly dull debate*
2 ADJ not bright ❍ *the dull gray sky of London*

dumb /dʌm/
1 ADJ unable to speak ❍ *He was born deaf and dumb.*
2 ADJ not intelligent [INFORMAL] ❍ *He was a brilliant guy and he made me feel really dumb.*
3 ADJ silly and annoying [INFORMAL] ❍ *He had this dumb idea.*

dum|my /dʌmi/ (**dummies**)
1 NOUN a model of a person, often used in safety tests ❍ *a crash-test dummy*
2 NOUN If you call a person a **dummy**, you are rudely saying that they are stupid. [INFORMAL]

dump /dʌmp/
1 VERB If you **dump** something somewhere, you leave it there quickly and without being careful. [INFORMAL] ❍ *We dumped our bags at the hotel and went to the market.*
2 VERB If something **is dumped** somewhere, it is put or left there because it is no longer wanted. [INFORMAL] ❍ *The car had been dumped near the freeway.*
3 VERB If someone **dumps** their girlfriend or boyfriend, they end their relationship. [INFORMAL] ❍ *My boyfriend dumped me last night.*
4 VERB If one country **dumps** goods in another country, the first country exports a very large quantity of cheap goods to the second country. [MARKETING AND SALES, ECONOMICS] ❍ *The Commerce Department has ruled that the companies have been dumping minivans at unfairly low prices in the U.S.*
● **dump|ing NONCOUNT NOUN** ❍ *The company overstated the prices of its steel imports to avoid charges of dumping.*
5 NOUN a place where you can take garbage ❍ *He took his trash to the dump.*
6 NOUN an ugly and unpleasant place [INFORMAL] ❍ *"What a dump!" Christabel said, looking at the house.*

dump bin (**dump bins**) **NOUN** a unit used for displaying products such as books and DVDs in a store [MARKETING AND SALES, BRIT] ❍ *The book's promotional campaign will include national advertising, full-color posters and 12-copy dump bins.*

duo|po|ly /duɒpəli/ (**duopolies**)
1 NOUN If two firms or people have a **duopoly**

on something such as an industry, they share complete control over it. [ECONOMICS] ❍ *they are no longer part of a duopoly on overseas routes*
2 NOUN a group of two firms that are the only ones that provide a particular product or service, and that therefore have complete control over an industry [ECONOMICS]

D

du|rable /dʊərəbᵊl/ **ADJ** strong and lasting a long time ❍ *a durable material*

du|rable goods also **durables PL NOUN** **Durable goods** are goods such as televisions or cars that are expected to last a long time. Compare with **disposable goods**. [MARKETING AND SALES] ❍ *a 2.6% rise in orders for durable goods in January*

du|ra|tion /dʊəreɪʃən/ **NONCOUNT NOUN** The **duration of** something is the length of time it happens or exists. ❍ *We will meet once a week for the duration of the project.*

dur|ing /dʊərɪŋ/ **PREP** between the beginning and the end of a period of time ❍ *Inflation increased during the second quarter.* ❍ *During the conference, several topics were discussed.*

dusk /dʌsk/ **NONCOUNT NOUN** **Dusk** is the time just before night when it is not completely dark. ❍ *We arrived home at dusk.*

dust /dʌst/
1 NONCOUNT NOUN **Dust** is a fine powder of dry earth or dirt. ❍ *I could see a thick layer of dust on the stairs.*
2 VERB When you **dust** or **dust** furniture, you remove dust from it with a cloth. ❍ *I dusted and polished the furniture in the living room.*

dust|bin /dʌstbɪn/ (**dustbins**) [BRIT] → **garbage can**

dusty /dʌsti/ (**dustier, dustiest**) **ADJ** covered with dust ❍ *dusty shelves*

Dutch auc|tion /dʌtʃ ɔkʃən/ (**Dutch auctions**) **NOUN** an auction in which the prices of items are gradually reduced until someone buys them [ECONOMICS] ❍ *The Dutch auction it is setting up could prove somewhat confusing to small shareholders, however.*

du|ti|able /dutiəbᵊl/ **ADJ** **Dutiable** goods must have duty paid on them. [FINANCE] ❍ *The average rate on dutiable goods rose from 40 percent to 48.*

duty /duti/ (**duties**)
1 NOUN work that you have to do ❍ *I did my duties without complaining.*
2 NOUN something that you feel you have to do ❍ *It is a manufacturer's duty to warn customers of any dangers related to a product.*
3 NOUN a tax imposed by a government [FINANCE] ❍ *Proton pays only half the normal excise duty on imported components.*
4 If someone is **off duty**, they are not working. If someone is **on duty**, they are working. ❍ *The two police officers were off duty when the accident happened.*

duty-free ADJ **Duty-free** goods are sold at airports or on airplanes at a cheaper price than usual. [FINANCE] ❍ *duty-free perfume*

duty-free store (**duty-free stores**) **NOUN** a store, for example at an airport, where you can buy goods at a cheaper price than usual, because no tax is paid on them [FINANCE]

du|vet day /duveɪ deɪ/ (**duvet days**) [BRIT, INFORMAL] → **personal day**

DVD /di vi di/ (**DVDs**) **NOUN** A **DVD** is a disk on which a movie or music is recorded. **DVD** is short for "digital video disk." ❍ *a DVD player*

DVD burn|er (**DVD burners**) /di vi di bɜrnər/ or **DVD writer NOUN** a piece of computer equipment that you use for putting information onto a DVD

DVD play|er (**DVD players**) **NOUN** a machine for showing movies that are stored on a DVD

dwell /dwɛl/ (**dwells, dwelling, dwelt** or **dwelled**) **VERB** If you **dwell on** something, you think, speak, or write about it a lot or for quite a long time. ❍ *I'd rather not dwell on the past.*

dwell time (**dwell times**) **NONCOUNT NOUN** **Dwell time** is the amount of time that a customer spends in a store, either browsing or waiting in line. ❍ *Holidaymakers' dwell time in airport shops can be anything up to 60 minutes.*

dye /daɪ/ (**dyes, dyeing, dyed**)

1 VERB If you **dye** something, you change its color by putting it in a special liquid. ❍ *The workers dye wool and other fabrics.*

2 NOUN a substance that is used for changing the color of cloth or hair ❍ *a bottle of hair dye*

dy|nam|ic /daɪnæmɪk/ **ADJ** full of energy and often having new and exciting ideas ❍ *He was a dynamic and energetic leader.*

dy|nam|ic pric|ing **NONCOUNT NOUN** **Dynamic pricing** is a method of setting prices so that they change according to a range of factors. [MARKETING AND SALES, ECONOMICS] ❍ *They tried using technology to create dynamic pricing with vending machines that could adjust the price based on outside temperature, charging more on a hot day.*

Ee

each /i̲tʃ/

1 ADJ or **PRON** **Each** person or thing in a group is every one of them. ❍ *Each item must be given an appropriate discount.* ❍ *We buy 2,000 books each year.* ❍ *We each have different interests and skills.*

2 ADV **Each** is also an adverb. ❍ *Tickets are six dollars each.*

3 **Each of** means every one of. ❍ *I made sure that each of them was assigned a responsibility.* ❍ *Each of these exercises takes one or two minutes to do.*

4 PRON You use **each other** to show that each member of a group does something to or for the other members. ❍ *Of course, banks borrow from each other, if necessary.*

eager /i̲gər/ **ADJ** wanting very much to do something ❍ *Banks remain eager to lend for large projects.* ● **eager|ly ADV** ❍ *"So what do you think will happen?" he asked eagerly.*

ear /ɪ̲ər/ **NOUN** one of the two parts of the body on the side of the head, with which you hear sounds ❍ *He whispered something in her ear.*

ear|ly /ɜ̲rli/ **(earlier, earliest)**

1 ADV before the usual time ❍ *I got to the office early this morning.* ❍ *She arrived early.*

2 ADJ **Early** is also an adjective. ❍ *I want to get an early start in the morning.*

ear|ly clo̲sing NONCOUNT NOUN **Early closing** is the shutting of most stores in a town on one afternoon each week. [BRIT] ❍ *From Monday to Saturday the store is open from 9am to 5:30pm; it closes at 1pm on Wednesdays, which is early closing day.*

earn /ɜ̲rn/

1 VERB If you **earn** money, you receive money for work that you do. ❍ *She earns $37,000 a year.*

2 VERB If you **earn** something, you get it because you deserve it. ❍ *A good manager, he quickly earned the respect of his team.*

ea̲rned i̲n|come NONCOUNT NOUN **Earned income** is the money you get for work that you do. [FINANCE] ❍ *In cases of long-term disability, there is a substantial loss of earned income.*

earn|er /ɜ̲rnər/ **NOUN** someone or something that earns money or produces profit [FINANCE] ❍ *a typical wage earner* ❍ *Sugar is Fiji's second biggest export earner.*

earn|ings /ɜ̲rnɪŋz/ **PL NOUN** Your **earnings** are the sums of money that you earn by working. [FINANCE] ❍ *Average weekly earnings rose by 1.5% in July.*

ear|ring /ɪ̲ərɪŋ/ **NOUN** a piece of jewelry that you wear on your ear ❍ *She wore large, gold earrings.*

earth /ɜ̲rθ/

1 NOUN **Earth** or **the Earth** is the planet that we live on. ❍ *The space shuttle Atlantis returned safely to Earth today.*

2 NONCOUNT NOUN **Earth** is the substance on the surface of the Earth, in which plants grow. ❍ *a huge pile of earth*

3 You use **on earth** in questions that begin with "how," "why," "what," or "where," to show great surprise. ❍ *Why on earth wasn't she invited to the meeting?*

earth|quake /ɜ̲rθkweɪk/ **NOUN** an occasion when the ground shakes because the Earth's surface is moving ❍ *The earthquake struck early in the morning.*

ease /i̲z/

1 If you do something **with ease**, you do it without difficulty or effort. ❍ *The government still raises money with ease from the capital markets.*

2 If you are **at ease**, you feel relaxed. ❍ *I never feel at ease with my boss.*

east /i̲st/ also **East**

1 NONCOUNT NOUN The **east** is the direction that is in front of you when you look at the sun in the morning. ❍ *The city lies to the east of the river.*

2 ADJ East is also an adjective. ❍ *the east coast*

3 ADV If you go **east**, you travel toward the east. ❍ *Go east on Route 9.*

4 ADJ An **east** wind is a wind that blows from the east.

5 NONCOUNT NOUN The East is the southern and eastern part of Asia, including India, China, and Japan.

East|er /i̲stər/ **NOUN** a Christian festival in March or April when Jesus Christ's return to life is celebrated

east|ern /i̲stərn/ also **Eastern**

1 ADJ in or from the east of a place ❍ *Eastern Europe*

2 ADJ relating to things or ideas that come from the countries of the East, such as India, China, or Japan ❍ *Exports to Eastern countries have gone down.*

easy /i̲zi/ (**easier, easiest**)

1 ADJ If something is **easy**, you can do it without difficulty. ❍ *They've insisted that the plastic parts will be easy to fix.* ❍ *Is the software easy to use?* • **easi|ly ADV** ❍ *Mr. Davis, with a reported net worth of $1.6 billion, could easily finance the purchase.*

2 If someone tells you to **take it easy**, they mean that you should relax and not worry. [INFORMAL] ❍ *I suggest you take it easy for a week or two.*

ea̲sy mo̲n|ey

1 NONCOUNT NOUN Easy money is money that you make without trying very hard. ❍ *Don't dream of taking home any easy money before a year (at the least).*

2 NONCOUNT NOUN Easy money is money that you can borrow at a low interest rate. ❍ *The Fed already is experiencing political pressure to supply lower interest rates and easy money.*

eat /i̲t/ (**eats, eating, ate, eaten**) **VERB** When you **eat** something, you put it into your mouth and swallow it. ❍ *I ate my sandwich at my desk.* ❍ *What time do you eat in the evening?*

EBITDA /i̲bɪtdɑ̲/ **NONCOUNT NOUN EBITDA** is a company's earnings before any necessary deductions are made. **EBITDA** is short for "earnings before interest, tax, depreciation, and amortization." [FINANCE] ❍ *Now, we had an EBITDA profit of 60 million and a net profit of 10 million.*

EBRD /i̲ bi̲ ɑ̲r di̲/ **NONCOUNT NOUN EBRD** is an organization that invests in projects that encourage the development of open market economies across central and eastern Europe and central Asia. **EBRD** is short for "European Bank for Reconstruction and Development." [ECONOMICS, BANKING] ❍ *The IMF, the World Bank, and the EBRD have their own capital, and so are less accountable to national governments.*

e-business /i̲bɪznɪs/ (**e-businesses**)

1 NOUN a business that uses the Internet to sell goods or services [E-COMMERCE] ❍ *JSL Trading, an e-business in Vancouver*

2 [E-COMMERCE] → **e-commerce**

ECB /i̲ si bi̲/ **ECB** is an abbreviation for **European Central Bank**. [ECONOMICS, BANKING]

ec|cen|tric /ɪksɛ̲ntrɪk/ **ADJ** unusual, and behaving in a way that is different from most people ❍ *Sometimes arguments broke out among the company's eccentric and strong-willed personalities.*

echo /ɛ̲koʊ/ (**echoes, echoing, echoed**)

1 NOUN a sound that you hear again because it hits a surface and then comes back ❍ *I heard the echo of someone laughing across the hall.*

2 VERB If a sound **echoes**, you hear it again because it hits a surface and then comes back. ❍ *His footsteps echoed on the stone floor.*

eclipse /ɪklɪ̲ps/ **NOUN** a short period when the light from the sun or the moon is blocked because of the position of the sun, the moon, and the Earth ❍ *a solar eclipse*

eco-friendly /i̲koʊfrɛ̲ndli/ **ADJ** less harmful to the environment ❍ *They sell eco-friendly cleaning products.*

ecol|ogy /ɪkɒ̲lədʒi/ **NONCOUNT NOUN Ecology** is the study of the relationships between living things and their environment. • **ecolo|gist NOUN** ❍ *Ecologists are concerned*

e

that these chemicals will pollute lakes. **• eco|logi|cal** /ɛkəlɒdʒɪkᵊl, ɪk-/ ADJ ❍ *How can we save the Earth from ecological disaster?*

e-commerce /ɪkɒmɜrs/ or **e-business** NONCOUNT NOUN **E-commerce** is the buying, selling, and ordering of goods and services using the Internet. [E-COMMERCE] ❍ *proven e-commerce solutions*

E

eco|nom|ic /ɛkənɒmɪk, ɪk-/ ADJ connected with the organization of the money and industry of a country [ECONOMICS] ❍ *The economic situation is very bad.*

eco|nomi|cal /ɛkənɒmɪkᵊl, ɪk-/
1 ADJ not requiring a lot of money ❍ *plans to trade in their car for something smaller and more economical* **• eco|nomi|cal|ly** ADV ❍ *Services could be operated more efficiently and economically.*
2 ADJ not spending money wastefully ❍ *ideas for economical housekeeping*

eco|nom|ic in|di|ca|tor /ɛkənɒmɪk ɪndɪkeɪtər, ɪkə-/ (**economic indicators**) NOUN a statistic that shows how well or badly the economy is doing [ECONOMICS] ❍ *Two relatively minor economic indicators are U.S. new home sales and factory orders.*

eco|nom|ics /ɛkənɒmɪks, ɪk-/ NONCOUNT NOUN **Economics** is the study of the way in which money and industry are organized in a society. ❍ *His sister is studying economics.*

eco|nom|ic zone (**economic zones**) NOUN An **economic zone** is the same as an **exclusive economic zone**. [ECONOMICS]

econo|mies of scale PL NOUN **Economies of scale** are the financial advantages of producing large quantities of products. [ECONOMICS] ❍ *Some companies are simply trying to get bigger to achieve economies of scale.*

econo|mist /ɪkɒnəmɪst/ NOUN a person who studies economics

econo|my /ɪkɒnəmi/ (**economies**) NOUN the system for organizing the money and industry of the world, a country, or local government ❍ *The Indian economy is changing fast.*

eco-tourism /ɛkoʊtʊərɪzəm/ NONCOUNT NOUN **Eco-tourism** is the business of providing vacations that are not harmful to the environment of the area. ❍ *Eco-tourism is a good way of improving the quality of life for people living along the rivers here.*

eco-tourist /ɛkoʊtʊərɪst/ (**eco-tourists**) NOUN a tourist who buys holidays and related services that are not harmful to the environment of the area ❍ *Perhaps the most popular eco-tourist destination is the Brazilian rainforest.*

e-CRM /i si ɑr ɛm/ NONCOUNT NOUN **e-CRM** is customer relationship management that is carried out on the Internet. [MARKETING AND SALES, TECHNOLOGY]

edge /ɛdʒ/
1 NOUN the part of something that is farthest from the middle ❍ *We lived in an apartment block on the edge of town.* ❍ *She was standing at the water's edge.*
2 NOUN the sharp side of a knife or other cutting tool

EDI /i di aɪ/ NONCOUNT NOUN **EDI** is an electronic system that a supplier and customer can use to communicate easily. **EDI** is short for "electronic data interchange." [TECHNOLOGY] ❍ *The growing use of EDI for financial payments is increasing the emphasis on security.*

edit /ɛdɪt/ VERB If you **edit** a text, you check it and correct the mistakes in it. ❍ *She helped him edit the report.*

edi|tion /ɪdɪʃən/ NOUN a number of books, magazines, or newspapers that are printed at one time ❍ *The second edition was published in Canada.*

edi|tor /ɛdɪtər/ NOUN a person who checks and corrects texts ❍ *a script editor*

edu|cate /ɛdʒʊkeɪt/ (**educates, educating, educated**)
1 VERB When someone **is educated**, he or she is taught at a school or college. ❍ *He was educated at Yale and Stanford.*
2 VERB To **educate** people means to teach them better ways of doing something. ❍ *We need to educate people about healthy eating.*

edu|cat|ed /ɛdʒʊkeɪtɪd/ ADJ having had a good education ❍ *educated, professional people*

edu|ca|tion /ɛdʒʊkeɪʃən/ NONCOUNT NOUN **Education** means teaching and learning. ❍ *It gave the federal government a crucial role in education.* ❍ *We need better health education.* ● **edu|ca|tion|al** /ɛdʒʊkeɪʃənᵊl/ ADJ ❍ *the American educational system*

EEA /i i eɪ/ **EEA** is an abbreviation for **European Economic Area**. [ECONOMICS]

ef|fect /ɪfɛkt/ NOUN a change or reaction that is the result of something ❍ *Strong overseas sales helped the two auto makers overcome the effects of slower production.*

ef|fec|tive /ɪfɛktɪv/ ADJ producing the intended result ❍ *He wrote a book on effective management.* ● **ef|fec|tive|ly** ADV ❍ *This helps it to compete effectively with other financial centers in the region.*

ef|fi|cient /ɪfɪʃənt/ ADJ able to do tasks successfully, without wasting time or energy ❍ *efficient market trading* ❍ *an efficient worker* ● **ef|fi|cien|cy** /ɪfɪʃənsi/ NONCOUNT NOUN ❍ *We must think of ways to improve efficiency.* ● **ef|fi|cient|ly** ADV ❍ *This would allow companies to manage their business more efficiently.*

ef|fort /ɛfərt/ NOUN an attempt to do something, or the physical or mental energy that is needed to do something ❍ *We have made an effort to use clear language in our reports.* ❍ *He stood up slowly and with great effort.*

EFTA /ɛftə/ NOUN **EFTA** is an abbreviation for **European Free Trade Association**. [ECONOMICS] ❍ *EFTA countries are heavily dependent on the EC for trade.*

e.g. /i dʒi/ **e.g.** means "for example." ❍ *By this we mean technologies and business models that improve everyday lives (e.g. microcredit).*

egg /ɛg/

1 NOUN a round object produced by a female bird, reptile, fish, and insect, from which a baby creature later comes out

2 NOUN a hen's egg, eaten as food ❍ *Break the eggs into a bowl.*

EGM /i dʒi ɛm/ (**EGMs**) NOUN **EGM** is an abbreviation for **extraordinary general meeting**. [BUSINESS MANAGEMENT, ADMINISTRATION]

eight /eɪt/ the number 8

eight|een /eɪtin/ the number 18

eight|eenth /eɪtinθ/ ADJ or ADV The **eighteenth** item in a series is the one that you count as number eighteen. ❍ *the Industrial Revolution in the eighteenth century*

eighth /eɪtθ/

1 ADJ or ADV The **eighth** item in a series is the one that you count as number eight. ❍ *Shekhar was the eighth prime minister of India.*

2 NOUN one of eight equal parts of something (⅛) ❍ *The ring was an eighth of an inch thick.*

eighti|eth /eɪtiəθ/ ADJ or ADV The **eightieth** item in a series is the one that you count as number eighty.

eighty /eɪti/ the number 80

either /iðər, aɪðər/

1 You use **either ... or ...** to show that there are two possibilities to choose from. ❍ *Either she goes or I go.* ❍ *I'll either call him or email him.* ❍ *You can contact him either by phone or by email.*

2 PRON **Either** is also a pronoun. ❍ *She wants money and status. I don't want either.*

3 ADJ **Either** means each. ❍ *The two groups waited at either end of the room.* ❍ *He couldn't remember either man's name.*

4 Either of means each of. ❍ *There are no simple answers to either of those questions.*

5 ADJ **Either** means one of two things or people. ❍ *You can choose either date.*

6 ADV You use **either** in negative sentences to mean also. ❍ *He said nothing, and she didn't speak either.*

elas|tic /ɪlæstɪk/ NONCOUNT NOUN **Elastic** is a rubber material that stretches when you pull it, and returns to its original shape when you let it go. ❍ *a piece of elastic*

elas|tici|ty /ilæstɪsɪti, ɪlæst-/ NONCOUNT NOUN The **elasticity** of supply or demand is a measure of how much the demand or supply of a product is affected by a change in its cost. [MARKETING AND SALES] ❍ *Apple's attempts to predict elasticity of demand for its products had suggested that price cuts would spur sales across its entire range.*

el|bow /ɛlboʊ/ NOUN the part in the middle of the arm, where the arm bends ❍ *She leaned forward, with her elbows on the table.*

E

el|der|ly /ɛldərli/
1 ADJ used for politely saying that someone is old ❍ *An elderly couple live next door.*
2 PL NOUN **The elderly** are people who are old. ❍ *care of the elderly*

elect /ɪlɛkt/ VERB When people **elect** someone, they choose that person to represent them, by voting for them. ❍ *We had just elected a new president.*

elec|tion /ɪlɛkʃən/ NOUN a process in which people vote to choose a person who will hold an official position ❍ *She won her first election in 2000.*

elec|tric /ɪlɛktrɪk/ ADJ using or providing electricity ❍ *an electric guitar* ❍ *electric power lines*

elec|tri|cal /ɪlɛktrɪkᵊl/ ADJ working using electricity ❍ *an electrical appliance*

elec|tri|cian /ɪlɛktrɪʃən, ilɛk-/ NOUN a person whose job is to install and repair electrical equipment

elec|tric|ity /ɪlɛktrɪsɪti, ilɛk-/ NONCOUNT NOUN **Electricity** is energy that is used for heating and lighting, and to provide power for machines.

elec|tron|ic /ɪlɛktrɒnɪk, ilɛk-/ ADJ **Electronic** equipment has small electrical parts that make it work. • **elec|troni|cal|ly** ADV ❍ *The gates are operated electronically.*

elec|tron|ic point of sale NONCOUNT NOUN **Electronic point of sale** is a computerized system for recording sales in retail stores that uses a scanner to read the barcode on a product. [TECHNOLOGY, MARKETING AND SALES] ❍ *Electronic point of sale, laser scanning, and bar coding are widespread at retail level.*

elec|tron|ic trad|ing NONCOUNT NOUN **Electronic trading** is the buying or selling of stocks and shares using the Internet. Compare with **floor trading**. [TECHNOLOGY, FINANCE]

elec|tron|ic trans|fer of funds NONCOUNT NOUN The **electronic transfer of funds** is the computerized transfer of money from one bank account to another. [TECHNOLOGY, BANKING] ❍ *If e-commerce is to take off in a big way, electronic transfer of funds has to be possible.*

el|egant /ɛlɪgənt/ ADJ attractive in a simple way ❍ *an elegant woman*

el|ement /ɛlɪmənt/
1 NOUN a part of something that combines with other parts to make a whole ❍ *This is one of the key elements of the plan.*
2 NOUN a basic chemical substance such as gold, oxygen, or carbon

el|emen|ta|ry /ɛlɪmɛntəri, -tri/ ADJ very easy and basic ❍ *elementary economics*

el|ephant /ɛlɪfənt/ NOUN a very large gray animal with a long nose called a trunk

el|eva|tor /ɛlɪveɪtər/ NOUN a machine that carries people or things up and down inside tall buildings ❍ *We took the elevator to the fourteenth floor.*

elev|en /ɪlɛvᵊn/ the number 11

elev|enth /ɪlɛvᵊnθ/ ADJ or ADV The **eleventh** item in a series is the one that you count as number eleven. ❍ *James Polk was the eleventh president of the United States.*

eli|gible /ɛlɪdʒɪbᵊl/ ADJ Someone who is **eligible to** do something is allowed to do it. ❍ *Almost half the population are eligible to vote.*

elimi|nate /ɪlɪmɪneɪt/ (**eliminates, eliminating, eliminated**) VERB To **eliminate** something means to remove it completely. [FORMAL] ❍ *The touch screen eliminates the need for a keyboard.*

else /ɛls/ ADJ or ADV used after words such as "someone" and "everyone," and after question words like "what" to talk about another person, place, or thing ❍ *Jan's not here but is* *everyone else here?* ❍ *What else did she say at the meeting?*

else|where /ɛlswɛər/ **ADV** in or to another place ❍ *80 percent of the state's residents were born elsewhere.*

email /imeɪl/ also **e-mail**
1 NONCOUNT NOUN **Email** is a system of sending written messages from one computer to another. **Email** is short for "electronic mail." [TECHNOLOGY] ❍ *You can contact us by email.*
2 NOUN a message sent from one computer to another [TECHNOLOGY] ❍ *I got an email from Paul Cassidy this morning.*
3 VERB If you **email** someone, you send them an email. [TECHNOLOGY] ❍ *Jamie emailed me to say he couldn't come.*

e-marketing /imarkɪtɪŋ/ **NONCOUNT NOUN** **E-marketing** is marketing by means of the Internet. [MARKETING AND SALES, E-COMMERCE] ❍ *The seminar will include advice on e-marketing, effective use of a website, and other aspects of e-commerce.*

em|bar|rass /ɪmbærəs/ **VERB** If something or someone **embarrasses** you, they make you feel shy or ashamed. ❍ *I hope I didn't embarrass you in front of your colleagues.*

em|bar|rassed /ɪmbærəst/ **ADJ** feeling shy or ashamed about something ❍ *I pointed out his mistake and he looked a bit embarrassed.*

em|bar|rass|ing /ɪmbærəsɪŋ/ **ADJ** making you feel shy or ashamed ❍ *The bank has recovered after an embarrassing corporate scandal two years ago.*

em|bar|rass|ment /ɪmbærəsmənt/ **NONCOUNT NOUN** **Embarrassment** is the feeling you have when you are embarrassed.

> **BUSINESS ETIQUETTE**
> Remember that hand gestures can be interpreted in very different ways by different cultures. When you are dealing with business associates abroad, avoid pointing in particular.

em|bas|sy /ɛmbəsi/ (**embassies**) **NOUN** a group of people who represent their government in a foreign country, or the building in which they work ❍ *The embassy advised British nationals to leave the country immediately.* ❍ *The embassy was surrounded by the FBI.*

em|brace /ɪmbreɪs/ (**embraces, embracing, embraced**) **VERB** If you **embrace** someone, you put your arms around them. ❍ *People were crying with joy and embracing.*

e

emerge /ɪmɜrdʒ/ (**emerges, emerging, emerged**) **VERB** To **emerge** means to come out from a place. ❍ *Finally, she emerged from her house.*

emer|gen|cy /ɪmɜrdʒᵊnsi/ (**emergencies**)
1 NOUN a serious situation, such as an accident, when people need help quickly ❍ *Come quickly. This is an emergency!*
2 ADJ done or arranged quickly, because an emergency has happened ❍ *The board held an emergency meeting.*

emer|gen|cy room (**emergency rooms**) **NOUN** The **emergency room** is the part of a hospital where people who have serious injuries or sudden illnesses are treated. The abbreviation **ER** is often used.

emerg|ing in|dus|try (**emerging industries**) **NOUN** a new industry that is growing fast [ECONOMICS] ❍ *Anyone who thinks he can make profits in an emerging industry in the first 4 years is crazy.*

emerg|ing mar|ket (**emerging markets**) **NOUN** a financial or consumer market in a newly developing country or former communist country [ECONOMICS] ❍ *Many emerging markets have outpaced more mature markets, such as the U.S. and Japan.*

emis|sion /ɪmɪʃən/ **NOUN** An **emission of** something such as gas or radiation is the release of it into the atmosphere. [FORMAL] ❍ *The emission of gases such as carbon dioxide should be stabilized at their present level.* ❍ *New vehicle technology has a very strong potential to bring down emissions.*

emit /ɪmɪt/ (**emits, emitting, emitted**) **VERB** If something **emits** heat, light, gas, a smell, or a sound, it produces it. [FORMAL] ❍ *The new device emits a powerful circular column* *of light.* ❍ *The four-by-four-inch device emits a tone and gives the caller five seconds to key in the code.* ❍ *A car emits its own weight in carbon each year.*

e-money /iːmʌni/ **NONCOUNT NOUN** **E-money** is money that is exchanged electronically. [TECHNOLOGY, E-COMMERCE] ❍ *Japanese cell phones are increasingly equipped with "e-money" devices that allow them to be used to purchase small items.*

E

emo|tion /ɪmoʊʃən/ **NOUN** a strong feeling such as love or fear ❍ *Andrew never shows his emotions in public.* ❍ *Her voice was full of emotion.*

emo|tion|al /ɪmoʊʃənəl/
1 ADJ concerned with feelings ❍ *After my wife's death, I needed emotional support from my colleagues.* ● **emo|tion|al|ly ADV** ❍ *By the end of the show, I was physically and emotionally exhausted.*
2 ADJ often showing your feelings, especially when upset ❍ *He's a very emotional man.*

emo|tion|al capi|tal NONCOUNT NOUN When people refer to the **emotional capital** of a firm, they mean all the psychological assets and resources of the firm, such as how the employees feel about the firm. [BUSINESS MANAGEMENT] ❍ *U.K. organizations are not nourishing their intellectual and emotional capital.*

em|pha|sis /ɛmfəsɪs/ **(emphases** /ɛmfəsiz/**)**
1 NOUN special importance that is given to something ❍ *The plan places more emphasis on cutting back debt and interest payments.*
2 NOUN extra force that you put on a word or part of a word when you are speaking ❍ *The emphasis is on the first syllable of the word "elephant."*

em|pha|sise /ɛmfəsaɪz/ [BRIT] → **emphasize**

em|pha|size /ɛmfəsaɪz/ **(emphasizes, emphasizing, emphasized) VERB** To **emphasize** something means to show that it is especially important. ❍ *He emphasizes the need for better training.*

em|pire /ɛmpaɪər/ **NOUN** a number of separate nations that are all controlled by the ruler of one particular country ❍ *the Roman Empire*

em|piri|cal /ɪmpɪrɪkəl/ **ADJ** based on practical experience and scientific experiments, and not based on theory ❍ *There is no empirical evidence to support his thesis.* ● **em|piri|cal|ly ADV** ❍ *Scientific knowledge is empirically based: it depends on observations and experiments.*

em|ploy /ɪmplɔɪ/ **VERB** If a person or a firm **employs** you, they pay you to work for them. [BUSINESS MANAGEMENT] ❍ *The company employs 18 workers.*

em|ployee /ɪmplɔɪi/ **NOUN** a person who is paid to work for another person or a firm [BUSINESS MANAGEMENT] ❍ *90% of the company's employees are women.* ❍ *He is an employee of Fuji Bank.*

em|ployee as|so|cia|tion (employee associations) NOUN an organization of people who work for a single employer ❍ *Unions may find themselves replaced by new forms of employee associations.*

em|ploy|er /ɪmplɔɪər/ **NOUN** the person or the firm that you work for ❍ *Your employer should agree to pay you for this work.*

em|ploy|ers' as|so|cia|tion (employers' associations) NOUN an organization of employers, usually from the same sector of the economy [HR] ❍ *The plant is not a member of the federal employers' association.*

em|ploy|er's lia|bil|ity NONCOUNT NOUN **Employer's liability** is the responsibility an employer has if workers are injured or become sick as a result of their employment. [LEGAL] ❍ *Employer's liability insurance covers employers against lawsuits by employees who are injured in the course of employment.*

em|ploy|ment /ɪmplɔɪmənt/ **NONCOUNT NOUN** **Employment** is work that you are paid for. ❍ *She was unable to find employment.*

em|ploy|ment agen|cy (employment agencies) NOUN a firm whose business is to help people to find work and help employers to find the workers they need ❍ *Most* *employment agencies wait for job seekers to come in and ask for help in finding a job.*

em|po|rium /ɛmpɔriəm/ (**emporiums** or **emporia** /ɛmpɔriə/) NOUN a store or large shop [FORMAL] ❍ *The space is part Wall Street trading room, part newsroom, part fast-food emporium.*

em|power /ɪmpaʊər/

1 VERB If someone **is empowered to** do something, they have the authority or power to do it. [FORMAL] ❍ *The army is now empowered to operate on a shoot-to-kill basis.*

2 VERB To **empower** someone means to make them stronger or more successful. [BUSINESS MANAGEMENT] ❍ *You must delegate effectively and empower people to carry out their roles with your full support.* ● **em|power|ment** NONCOUNT NOUN ❍ *This government believes very strongly in the empowerment of women.*

emp|ty /ɛmpti/ (**emptier, emptiest, empties, emptying, emptied**)

1 ADJ having no people or things inside ❍ *an empty office* ❍ *an empty glass*

2 VERB If you **empty** a container, you remove its contents. ❍ *I emptied the garbage can.* ❍ *Empty the noodles into a bowl.*

en|able /ɪneɪbᵊl/ (**enables, enabling, enabled**) VERB If someone or something **enables** you **to** do something, they make it possible for you to do it. ❍ *The increased cash flow would enable the company to reduce debt more quickly.*

en|close /ɪnkloʊz/ (**encloses, enclosing, enclosed**)

1 VERB If a place or an object **is enclosed** by something, the place or object is completely surrounded by it. ❍ *The park is enclosed by a wooden fence.*

2 VERB If you **enclose** something with a letter, you put it in the same envelope as the letter. ❍ *I have enclosed a check for $100.*

en|coun|ter /ɪnkaʊntər/

1 VERB If you **encounter** problems or difficulties, you experience them. ❍ *Most people encounter stress at work.*

2 VERB If you **encounter** someone, you meet them, usually unexpectedly.

3 NOUN **Encounter** is also a noun. [FORMAL] ❍ *a romantic encounter*

en|cour|age /ɪnkɜrɪdʒ/ (**encourages, encouraging, encouraged**)

1 VERB If you **encourage** someone, you give them hope or confidence. ❍ *When things aren't going well, he encourages me.*

2 VERB If you **encourage** someone **to** do something, you try to persuade them to do it. ❍ *The plan is to encourage people to sell their assets and pay taxes at the lower rate.*

en|cour|age|ment /ɪnkɜrɪdʒmənt/ NONCOUNT NOUN **Encouragement** is the act of encouraging someone. ❍ *Friends and colleagues gave me a lot of encouragement.*

en|cour|ag|ing /ɪnkɜrɪdʒɪŋ/ ADJ giving you hope or confidence ❍ *These are very encouraging sales figures.*

end /ɛnd/

1 NOUN the final point in a period of time or a story ❍ *He's leaving his job at the end of August.* ❍ *Don't tell me the end of the story!*

2 NOUN the farthest part of a long object ❍ *Both ends of the tunnel were blocked.*

3 VERB When an activity **ends**, or when you end an activity, it reaches its final point and stops. ❍ *The meeting ended with Chatterjee instructing Garg to speed things up.*

4 When something happens for hours, days, weeks, or years **on end**, it happens continuously and without stopping for that amount of time. ❍ *We can talk for hours on end.*

▶ **end up** If you **end up** in a particular place, you are in that place after a series of events. ❍ *We ended up back at the office again.*

end|ing /ɛndɪŋ/ NOUN the last part of a book or a movie ❍ *a happy ending*

end|less /ɛndlɪs/ ADJ lasting for a very long time ❍ *There was a seemingly endless series of financial scandals during his government.* ● **end|less|ly** ADV ❍ *We discussed the matter endlessly.*

en|dorse /ɪndɔrs/ (**endorses, endorsing, endorsed**) VERB If you **endorse** a product or firm, you appear in advertisements for it. [MARKETING AND SALES] ❍ *The twins endorsed a line of household cleaning products.*

en|dorse|ment /ɪndɔrsmənt/ NOUN An **endorsement for** a product or firm involves appearing in advertisements for it or showing support for it. [MARKETING AND SALES] ❍ *His commercial endorsements for everything from running shoes to breakfast cereals will take his earnings to more than ten million dollars a year.*

en|dow /ɪndaʊ/ VERB If someone **endows** an institution or project, they provide a large amount of money that will produce the income needed to pay for it. [ECONOMICS] ❍ *The ambassador has endowed a $1 million public-service fellowships program.*

en|dur|ance /ɪndʊərəns/ NONCOUNT NOUN **Endurance** is the ability to continue with a difficult activity over a long period of time. ❍ *The exercise will improve strength and endurance.*

en|dure /ɪndʊər/ (**endures, enduring, endured**) VERB If a person or an organization **endures** a difficult situation, they experience it. ❍ *The company endured heavy financial losses.*

end user (**end users**) NOUN the user that a piece of equipment has been designed for, rather than the person who installs or maintains it ❍ *You have to be able to describe things in a form that the end user can understand.*

en|emy /ɛnəmi/ (**enemies**)
1 NOUN someone who dislikes you and wants to harm you ❍ *He had made a few enemies during his time in office.*
2 NOUN **The enemy** is an army that is fighting against you in a war. ❍ *The enemy would fight back.*

en|er|get|ic /ɛnərdʒɛtɪk/ ADJ having a lot of energy ❍ *Mr. Jones was an inspired and energetic leader.*

en|er|gy /ɛnərdʒi/
1 NONCOUNT NOUN **Energy** is the ability and strength to do active physical things. ❍ *Save your energy for next week's race.*
2 NONCOUNT NOUN **Energy** is the power from electricity or the sun, for example, that makes machines work or provides heat. ❍ *solar energy*

en|force /ɪnfɔrs/ (**enforces, enforcing, enforced**) VERB If people in authority **enforce** a law, they make sure that it is obeyed, usually by punishing people who do not obey it. ❍ *Many states enforce drug laws.*
● **en|force|ment** /ɪnfɔrsmənt/ NONCOUNT NOUN ❍ *What we need is stricter enforcement of existing laws.*

en|gage /ɪngeɪdʒ/ (**engages, engaging, engaged**) VERB If you **engage in** an activity, you do it. [FORMAL] ❍ *He has never engaged in criminal activities.*

en|gaged /ɪngeɪdʒd/ ADJ When two people are **engaged**, they have agreed to marry each other. ❍ *We got engaged on my 26th birthday.*

en|gage|ment /ɪngeɪdʒmənt/
1 NOUN an agreement that two people have made with each other to get married ❍ *We announced our engagement in November.*
2 NOUN a period of employment

en|gine /ɛndʒɪn/
1 NOUN the part of a vehicle that produces the power to make the vehicle move ❍ *He started the engine.*
2 NOUN the front part of a train that pulls it ❍ *a steam engine*

en|gi|neer /ɛndʒɪnɪər/
1 NOUN a person who designs, builds, and repairs machines, or structures such as roads, railroads, and bridges
2 NOUN a person who repairs mechanical or electrical machines

en|gi|neer|ing /ɛndʒɪnɪərɪŋ/ NONCOUNT NOUN **Engineering** is the work of designing and constructing machines or structures such as roads and bridges.

Eng|lish /ɪŋglɪʃ/
1 NONCOUNT NOUN **English** is the language spoken by people who live in Great Britain and Ireland, the United States, Canada, Australia, and many other countries. ❍ *Do you speak English?*
2 ADJ belonging to or relating to England ❍ *the English way of life*

en|hance /ɪnhæns/ (**enhances, enhancing, enhanced**) VERB To **enhance** something means to improve its quality. ❍ *The provision of such a plan enhances the employer's image.*

en|joy /ɪndʒɔɪ/
1 VERB If you **enjoy** something, you like doing it. ❍ *I enjoyed working for them.*
2 VERB If you **enjoy yourself**, you have a good time doing something. ❍ *I'm really enjoying myself at college.*

en|joy|able /ɪndʒɔɪəbᵊl/ ADJ giving you pleasure ❍ *The whole conference was much more enjoyable than I expected.*

en|joy|ment /ɪndʒɔɪmənt/ NONCOUNT NOUN **Enjoyment** is the feeling of pleasure that you have when you do something that you like. ❍ *I think he gets a lot of enjoyment from his work.*

en|large /ɪnlɑrdʒ/ (**enlarges, enlarging, enlarged**) VERB When you **enlarge** something, you make it bigger. ❍ *Could you enlarge the image?*

enor|mous /ɪnɔrməs/ ADJ extremely large ❍ *They have an enormous office.* ● **enor|mous|ly** ADV ❍ *I admired him enormously.*

enough /ɪnʌf/
1 ADJ as much as you need ❍ *We don't have enough money in the budget.*
2 ADV **Enough** is also an adverb. ❍ *I was old enough to work and earn money.*
3 PRON **Enough** is also a pronoun. ❍ *They're not doing enough to solve the problem.*

en|quire /ɪnkwaɪər/ [mainly BRIT] → **inquire**

en|quiry /ɪnkwaɪəri/ [mainly BRIT] → **inquiry**

en|roll /ɪnroʊl/ VERB If you **enroll** in a class, you officially join it. ❍ *He has already enrolled at medical college.*

en|sure /ɪnʃʊər/ (**ensures, ensuring, ensured**) VERB To **ensure** something means to make sure that it happens. [FORMAL] ❍ *We will work hard to ensure that this doesn't happen again.*

en|ter /ɛntər/
1 VERB When you **enter** a place such as a room or a building, you go into it. [FORMAL] ❍ *He entered the room and stood near the door.*
2 VERB If you **enter** a competition or a race, you state that you will be a part of it. ❍ *To enter the competition, simply go to our website and fill in the details.*
3 VERB If you **enter** information, you write or type it in a form or a book, or into a computer. ❍ *They enter the addresses into the computer.*

en|ter|prise /ɛntərpraɪz/ NOUN a firm or a business [ECONOMICS] ❍ *We provide help for small and medium-sized enterprises.*

en|ter|prise zone (**enterprise zones**) NOUN an area where the government offers advantages in order to attract new businesses [ECONOMICS] ❍ *Because it is in an enterprise zone, taxes on non-food items are 3.5% instead of the usual 7%.*

e

en|ter|tain /ɛntərteɪn/
1 VERB If you **entertain** people, you do something that amuses or interests them. ❍ *We were entertained by singers as we dined.* ● **en|ter|tain|ing** ADJ ❍ *an entertaining show*
2 VERB If you **entertain** guests, you invite them to your home and give them food and drink. ❍ *He was entertaining clients.*

en|ter|tain|ment /ɛntərteɪnmənt/ NONCOUNT NOUN **Entertainment** is anything that people watch for pleasure, such as shows and movies. ❍ *He works in the entertainment industry.*

en|thu|si|asm /ɪnθuziæzəm/ NONCOUNT NOUN **Enthusiasm** is the feeling that you have when you really enjoy something or want to do something. ❍ *This probably reflects our enthusiasm for foreign cars and continuing dissatisfaction with American vehicles.*

en|thu|si|as|tic /ɪnθuziæstɪk/ ADJ showing great interest and pleasure in something ❍ *Tom wasn't very enthusiastic about the idea.*

en|tire /ɪntaɪər/ ADJ whole ❍ *I've read the entire document.*

en|tire|ly /ɪntaɪərli/ ADV completely and not just partly ❍ *I agree entirely.* ❍ *I'm not entirely sure what I'm supposed to do.*

en|ti|tle /ɪntaɪtᵊl/ (**entitles, entitling, entitled**) VERB If you **are entitled to** something, you are allowed to have it or do it. ❍ *They are entitled to first class travel.*

en|tity /ɛntɪti/ (**entities**) NOUN something that exists separately from other things, with its own particular qualities or features [FORMAL] ❍ *The earth is a living entity.*

en|trance /ɛntrəns/

1 NOUN the door or gate where you go into a place ❍ *He came out of a side entrance.*

2 NOUN the arrival of someone in a room ❍ *She didn't notice her father's entrance.*

E

en|trée /ɒntreɪ/ also **entree** NOUN If you have an **entrée** to a particular group, you are accepted and made to feel welcome. ❍ *She had an entree into the city's cultivated society.*

en|tre|pre|neur /ɒntrəprənɜr, -nʊər/ NOUN a person who sets up businesses and business deals [BUSINESS MANAGEMENT] ❍ *Lower capital rates help encourage entrepreneurs to commit their resources to newer, risky ventures that may fail.*

en|tre|pre|neur|ial /ɒntrəprənɜriəl, -nʊər-/ ADJ having the qualities that are needed to succeed as an entrepreneur [BUSINESS MANAGEMENT] ❍ *We feel that we have the entrepreneurial skills to build a major business in this area.*

COLLOCATIONS

entrepreneurial *spirit*
entrepreneurial *skills*
entrepreneurial *culture*
entrepreneurial *activity*

en|try /ɛntri/ (**entries**)

1 NONCOUNT NOUN **Entry to** a particular place is when you go into it. ❍ *Entry to the museum is free.*

2 NOUN an item that is recorded, for example in a journal or account

3 **No Entry** is used on signs to show that you are not allowed to go into a particular area.

entry-level

1 ADJ **Entry-level** is used to describe basic low-cost versions of products such as cars or computers that are suitable for people who have no previous experience or knowledge of them. ❍ *Several companies are offering new, entry-level models in hopes of attracting more buyers.*

2 ADJ **Entry-level** jobs are suitable for people who do not have previous experience or qualifications in a particular area of work. [HR] ❍ *Many entry-level jobs were filled by high school grads.*

en|velope /ɛnvəloʊp, ɒn-/ NOUN a paper cover in which you put a letter before you send it to someone

en|vi|ron|ment /ɪnvaɪrənmənt, -vaɪərn-/

1 NOUN the conditions in which someone lives or works ❍ *It's a very pleasant working environment.*

2 NOUN **The environment** is the natural world of land, the oceans, the air, plants, and animals. ❍ *Please respect the environment by recycling.*

en|vi|ron|men|tal /ɪnvaɪrənmɛntᵊl, -vaɪərn-/ ADJ connected or concerned with the environment [BUSINESS MANAGEMENT] ❍ *Environmental groups protested loudly during the conference.* ● **en|vi|ron|men|tal|ly** ADV ❍ *environmentally friendly cleaning products*

en|vi|ron|men|tal im|pact NONCOUNT NOUN The **environmental impact** of a scheme or product is the effect that it is likely to have on the environment. [BUSINESS MANAGEMENT] ❍ *That there would be some environmental impact in the form of traffic congestion was undeniable.*

en|vi|ron|men|tally dam|aging ADJ causing harm to the environment [BUSINESS MANAGEMENT] ❍ *The main environmentally damaging emissions from aircraft are carbon dioxide, water vapour, and nitrogen oxides.*

envy /ɛnvi/ (**envies, envying, envied**)

1 VERB If you **envy** someone, you wish that you had the same things that they have. ❍ *I don't envy young people these days.*

2 NONCOUNT NOUN **Envy** is also a noun. ❍ *She was full of envy when she heard their news.*

e.o.m. /i oʊ ɛm/ **e.o.m.** is an abbreviation for "end of the month." [ADMINISTRATION]

e-payment /ipeɪmənt/ (**e-payments**) NOUN a payment for a transaction made on the Internet [TECHNOLOGY, E-COMMERCE] ❍ *The university's new e-payment system is* *designed to make the payment of fees a more efficient process.*

epi|dem|ic /ɛpɪdɛmɪk/ **NOUN** a time when a very large number of people suffer from the same disease ❍ *a flu epidemic*

epi|sode /ɛpɪsoʊd/ **NOUN** one of the parts of a story on television or radio ❍ *The final episode will be shown next Sunday.*

EPOS /ipɒs/ **EPOS** is an abbreviation for **electronic point of sale**. [TECHNOLOGY, MARKETING AND SALES] ❍ *EPOS is increasingly being used in retail outlets such as supermarkets.*

e-procurement /iprəkyʊərmənt/ **NONCOUNT NOUN E-procurement** is the process by which businesses use the Internet to obtain the materials and services that they need. [TECHNOLOGY, PURCHASING, E-COMMERCE] ❍ *Growing use of e-procurement will quickly enable customers to find the cheapest supplier.*

eps /i pi ɛs/ **eps** is an abbreviation for "earnings per share." [ECONOMICS]

equal /ikwəl/

1 ADJ the same in size, number, or value ❍ *There are equal numbers of men and women in the company.* ● **equal|ly ADV** ❍ *If there's a loss, the loss will be divided equally between the partners.*

2 ADJ having the same rights and opportunities ❍ *All men and women are equal.* ● **equal|ly ADV** ❍ *The system should treat everyone equally.*

3 VERB If something **equals** a particular number or amount, it is the same as that amount. ❍ *9 minus 7 equals 2.*

equali|ty /ɪkwɒlɪti/ **NONCOUNT NOUN Equality** is the fair treatment of all the people in a group. ❍ *racial equality*

equal op|por|tu|nities or **equal opportunity PL NOUN Equal opportunities** refers to the policy of giving everyone the same opportunities for employment, pay, and promotion. [BUSINESS MANAGEMENT] ❍ *The profession's leaders must take action now to promote equal opportunities for all.*

COLLOCATIONS

an equal opportunities *policy*
an equal opportunities *employer*
equal opportunities *legislation*

equal op|por|tu|nities em|ploy|er (**equal opportunities employers**) **NOUN** an employer who gives people the same opportunities for employment, pay, and promotion, without discrimination against anyone ❍ *The police force is committed to being an equal opportunities employer.*

equal pay NONCOUNT NOUN Equal pay refers to the right of a man or woman to receive the same pay as a person of the opposite sex doing the same or similar work for the same or a similar employer. [BUSINESS MANAGEMENT] ❍ *A woman assembly worker sitting next to a male assembly worker, assembling similar items, would clearly be entitled to equal pay.*

equate /ɪkweɪt/ (**equates, equating, equated**) **VERB** If you **equate** one thing **with** another, you believe that they are strongly connected. ❍ *Many people equate money with success and happiness.*

equa|tion /ɪkweɪʒən/ **NOUN** a mathematical statement that two amounts or values are the same

equip /ɪkwɪp/ (**equips, equipping, equipped**) **VERB** If a person or thing **is equipped with** something, they have the things that they need to do a particular job. ❍ *The army is equipped with 5,000 tanks.* ❍ *The phone is equipped with a camera.*

equip|ment /ɪkwɪpmənt/ **NONCOUNT NOUN Equipment** is all the things that are used for a particular purpose. ❍ *They sell office equipment.*

equi|ties /ɛkwɪtiz/ **PL NOUN Equities** are the same as **common stock**. [BANKING, ECONOMICS] ❍ *Investors have poured money into U.S. equities.*

equi|ty /ɛkwɪti/ **NONCOUNT NOUN** Your **equity** is the sum of your assets once your debts have been subtracted from it. [LEGAL,

e

FINANCE] ❍ *To capture his equity, Murphy must either sell or refinance.*

equi|ty capi|tal NONCOUNT NOUN **Equity capital** is the part of the share capital of a firm that is owned by ordinary stockholders. [BANKING, ECONOMICS] ❍ *A bank with high equity capital has more to lose if it takes on risky investments.*

equiva|lent /ɪkwɪvələnt/
1 NOUN If one thing is **the equivalent of** another, they are the same, or they are used in the same way. ❍ *His pay is the equivalent of about $2,000 a month.* ❍ *The Internet has become the modern equivalent of the phone.*
2 ADJ **Equivalent** is also an adjective. ❍ *an equivalent amount*

ER /i ɑr/ (**ERs**) NOUN **ER** is short for **emergency room**.

era /ɪərə/ NOUN a period of time that is considered as a single unit ❍ *Their leader promised them a new era of peace.*

erase /ɪreɪs/ (**erases, erasing, erased**) VERB If you **erase** writing or a mark, you remove it. ❍ *She erased his name from her address book.*

erect /ɪrɛkt/ VERB If people **erect** a building or a bridge, they build it. [FORMAL] ❍ *The building was erected in 1900.*

ERM /i ɑr ɛm/ NONCOUNT NOUN **ERM** was the mechanism for maintaining currency values in the European Monetary System. **ERM** is an abbreviation for "Exchange Rate Mechanism." [ECONOMICS] ❍ *Big reductions in interest rates are possible within the ERM without putting currencies at risk.*

erode /ɪroʊd/ (**erodes, eroding, eroded**) VERB If the weather, the sea, or the wind **erodes** rock or soil, they gradually destroy it. ❍ *The sea is gradually eroding the coastline.*

er|rand /ɛrənd/ NOUN a short trip to do a job, for example, when you go to a store to buy something ❍ *We ran errands and took her meals when she was sick.*

er|ror /ɛrər/ NOUN mistake ❍ *There were a number of spelling errors in the document.*

ERS /i ɑr ɛs/ NONCOUNT NOUN **ERS** was a payment previously available to workers in Britain who became sick or unemployed. **ERS** is an abbreviation for "earnings related supplement." [ECONOMICS]

erupt /ɪrʌpt/ VERB When a volcano **erupts**, it throws out a lot of hot, melted rock (= lava). ❍ *Krakatoa erupted in 1883.* ● **erup|tion** /ɪrʌpʃən/ NOUN ❍ *a volcanic eruption*

es|ca|la|tor /ɛskəleɪtər/ NOUN a set of moving stairs ❍ *Take the escalator to the third floor.*

es|ca|la|tor clause (**escalator clauses**) NOUN a clause in a contract that allows changes in payment in certain conditions, such as a rise in the cost of living or the cost of raw materials [LEGAL] ❍ *He has proposed an escalator clause that will keep the federal contribution rising with inflation.*

es|cape /ɪskeɪp/ (**escapes, escaping, escaped**)
1 VERB If you **escape from** a place, you manage to get away from it. ❍ *A prisoner has escaped from a jail in northern Texas.*
2 NOUN **Escape** is also a noun. ❍ *He made his escape at night.*
3 VERB You **escape** when you avoid an accident. ❍ *The man's girlfriend escaped unhurt.* ❍ *The two officers escaped serious injury.*
4 NOUN **Escape** is also a noun. ❍ *I had a narrow escape on the bridge.*

es|cape clause (**escape clauses**) NOUN a clause in a contract that frees one of the parties from their obligations in certain circumstances [LEGAL] ❍ *Escape clauses allow individual countries to opt out of joint decisions.*

es|pe|cial|ly /ɪspɛʃəli/ ADV more than others ❍ *The proposed bill would restrict cigarette advertising—especially ads seen by children.*

es|say /ɛseɪ/ NOUN a short piece of writing on a subject ❍ *We asked Jason to write an essay about his hometown.*

es|sen|tial /ɪsɛnʃəl/ ADJ necessary ❍ *Productive investment is essential to future growth and prosperity.*

es|tab|lish /ɪstæblɪʃ/ (**establishes, establishing, established**)
1 VERB If someone **establishes** an organization, they create it. ❍ *He established the business in 1990.*
2 VERB If you **establish that** something is true, you discover facts that show that it is true. [FORMAL] ❍ *Before you develop a product, establish that there is a market for it.*

es|tab|lish|ment /ɪstæblɪʃmənt/
1 NOUN an organization or business [FORMAL] ❍ *an educational establishment*
2 NOUN The establishment is all the people who have power in a country. ❍ *the American establishment*

es|tate /ɪsteɪt/ **NOUN** a large house in a large area of land in the country, owned by a person or an organization ❍ *He spent the holidays at his aunt's 300-acre estate.*

es|tate agent [BRIT] → **Realtor**

es|thet|ic /ɛsθɛtɪk/ also **aesthetic ADJ** relating to beauty and art ❍ *an esthetic experience* ● **es|theti|cal|ly** /ɛsθɛtɪkli/ **ADV** ❍ *The product must be esthetically pleasing.*

es|ti|mate (**estimates, estimating, estimated**)

> Pronounce the verb /ɛstɪmeɪt/. Pronounce the noun /ɛstɪmɪt/.

1 VERB If you **estimate** an amount or a value, you say how much you think there is of it. ❍ *It's difficult to estimate how much money is involved.*
2 NOUN Estimate is also a noun. ❍ *an estimate of the cost*

e-tailing /iteɪlɪŋ/ also **etailing** or **e-tail NONCOUNT NOUN E-tailing** is the business of selling products on the Internet. [E-COMMERCE, TECHNOLOGY] ❍ *Electronic retailing has predictably become known as e-tailing.*

etc. /ɛt sɛtərə, -sɛtrə/ **etc.** is used at the end of a list to show that you have not given a full list. **etc.** is short for "etcetera." ❍ *Traders in durables (cars, household appliances, etc.) face the same problems.*

eter|nal /ɪtɜrnᵊl/ **ADJ** lasting forever ❍ *eternal life*

eth|ic /ɛθɪk/
1 PL NOUN Ethics are moral beliefs and rules about right and wrong. ❍ *There is concern about the lack of a code of ethics for brokerage firms.*
2 NOUN a basic principle or belief that influences the ideas and behavior of a group of people ❍ *the ethic of public service*

ethi|cal /ɛθɪkᵊl/
1 ADJ relating to beliefs about what is morally right and wrong ❍ *The Code of Professional Responsibility is the legal profession's ethical code.*
2 ADJ morally right or morally acceptable ❍ *ethical business practices*

ethi|cal con|sum|er (**ethical consumers**) **NOUN** a consumer who chooses not to buy products from certain firms for moral reasons ❍ *They are taking care to listen to the needs of investors and the needs of ethical consumers too.*

ethi|cal in|vest|ment NONCOUNT NOUN Ethical investment is investment in a firm whose activities or products are considered by the investor not to be morally wrong. [BANKING] ❍ *an independent financial adviser who specializes in ethical investment*

ethi|cal poli|cy (**ethical policies**) **NOUN** a policy concerning issues such as the use of child labor and matters relating to the environment [BUSINESS MANAGEMENT] ❍ *a clearly stated ethical policy that covers human rights, the arms trade, fair trade, the environment, and animal welfare* ❍ *The bank devises its ethical policies on the basis of comments from its customers.*

ethi|cal tour|ism NONCOUNT NOUN tourism that is based on ethical principles, such as a desire not to harm the environment of the place visited ❍ *Our campaign sets out to demonstrate the strength of consumer demand for ethical tourism.*

eth|nic /ɛθnɪk/ **ADJ** relating to groups of people that have the same culture or belong to the same race ❍ *Most of their friends come from other ethnic groups.*

euro /yʊəroʊ/ **NOUN** a unit of money that is used by many countries in the European Union

euro|bond /yʊəroʊbɒnd/ also **Eurobond** NOUN a bond that is issued in a eurocurrency [BANKING] ❍ *Eurobond underwriters and dealers are mainly located in London.*

euro|crat /yʊərəkræt/ also **Eurocrat** NOUN a member of the administration of the European Union [ADMINISTRATION] ❍ *A top Eurocrat is demanding Britain gives up its seat on the UN Security Council.*

euro|cur|ren|cy /yʊəroʊkɜrənsi/ (**eurocurrencies**) also **Eurocurrency** NOUN the currency of any country that is held on deposit in Europe outside its home market [ECONOMICS] ❍ *In the Eurocurrency market different currency denominations are offered in the same financial center.*

euro|de|pos|it /yʊəroʊdɪpɒzɪt/ also **Eurodeposit** NOUN a deposit of the currency of any country in the Eurocurrency market [BANKING]

Euro|pean /yʊərəpiən/

1 ADJ belonging to or coming from Europe ❍ *European countries*

2 NOUN a person who comes from Europe

Euro|pean Cen|tral Bank NOUN the central bank of the European Union [BANKING] ❍ *The European Central Bank has stopped lending banks unlimited 12-month funds.*

Euro|pean Eco|nom|ic Area NOUN a free-trade area including the European Union and members of the European Free Trade Association, excluding Switzerland [ECONOMICS]

Euro|pean Free Trade As|so|cia|tion NOUN a group of four European countries, Iceland, Lichtenstein, Norway, and Switzerland, that exists to promote free trade [ECONOMICS]

Euro|pean Un|ion NOUN an organization of European countries that have shared policies on matters such as commerce, agriculture, and finance

evacu|ate /ɪvækyueɪt/ (**evacuates, evacuating, evacuated**) VERB If people are **evacuated from** a place, they are forced to move out of it because it is dangerous. ❍ *Families were evacuated from the area because of the fighting.*

evalu|ate /ɪvælyueɪt/ (**evaluates, evaluating, evaluated**) VERB If you **evaluate** something or someone, you consider them in order to make a judgment. ❍ *We need to evaluate the situation very carefully.*
● **evalu|ation** /ɪvælyueɪʃən/ NOUN ❍ *This was revealed in a mid-year evaluation of industrial performance.*

evapo|rate /ɪvæpəreɪt/ (**evaporates, evaporating, evaporated**) VERB When a liquid **evaporates**, it changes into a gas. ❍ *Boil the sauce until most of the liquid evaporates.*

eve /iv/ NOUN the day before an event, or the period just before it ❍ *The story begins on the eve of her birthday.*

even /ivᵊn/

1 ADJ An **even** number can be divided exactly by two.

2 ADJ smooth and flat ❍ *an even surface*

3 ADV used for saying that something is somewhat surprising ❍ *Rob still seems happy, even after the bad news.*

4 ADV used for making another word stronger ❍ *Our car is big, but theirs is even bigger.*

5 You use **even if** or **even though** to show that a particular fact does not change anything. ❍ *Cynthia is never embarrassed, even if she makes a mistake.* ❍ *She wasn't sweating, even though it was extremely hot outside.*

6 PHRASE When a firm or a person running a business **breaks even**, they do not achieve a profit or a loss. ❍ *The airline hopes to break even next year and return to profit the following year.*

eve|ning /ivnɪŋ/ NOUN the part of each day between the end of the afternoon and midnight ❍ *That evening he went to see a movie.* ❍ *We usually have dinner at seven in the evening.*

event /ɪvɛnt/

1 NOUN something that happens, especially something unusual or important ❍ *recent events in Europe*

2 NOUN an organized activity or celebration ❍ *a major sports event*

even|tu|al|ly /ɪvɛntʃuəli/ **ADV** at some later time, especially after delays or problems ❍ *Eventually, the network could be extended to foreign trading centers.*

ever /ɛvər/ **ADV** at any time ❍ *I don't think I'll ever trust him again.* ❍ *Have you ever seen anything like it?*

every /ɛvri/
1 ADJ used for showing that you are talking about all the members of a group ❍ *Every room has a window facing the ocean.* ❍ *Every employee receives at least 40 hours of training each year.*
2 ADJ used for showing that something happens regularly ❍ *We had to attend meetings every day.* ❍ *I meet with him once every two weeks.*
3 If something happens **every other day**, it happens one day, then it does not happen the next day, and continues in this way. ❍ *I call her every other day.*

every|body /ɛvribɒdi, -bʌdi/ **PRON** **Everybody** means the same as **everyone**.

every|day /ɛvrideɪ/ **ADJ** normal and not unusual in any way ❍ *Computers are a central part of everyday life.*

every|one /ɛvriwʌn/ **PRON** all people, or all the people in a particular group ❍ *Everyone agreed with John's proposal.* ❍ *Not everyone thinks that the government is acting fairly.*

every|thing /ɛvriθɪŋ/ **PRON** all the parts of something or the whole of something ❍ *Everything has changed.* ❍ *We do everything together.* ❍ *Is everything all right?*

every|where /ɛvriwɛər/ or **everyplace** **ADV** in or to all places ❍ *People everywhere want the same things.* ❍ *We went everywhere together.*

evi|dence /ɛvɪdəns/ **NONCOUNT NOUN** **Evidence** is an object or a piece of information that makes you believe that something is true or has really happened. ❍ *There is no evidence that low short-term rates drove house prices upward.*

evi|dent /ɛvɪdənt/ **ADJ** able to be noticed ❍ *He was unhappy at work—that much was evident.*

evi|dent|ly /ɛvɪdəntli, -dɛnt-/ **ADV** used for saying that something is clearly true ❍ *Security is evidently not a big problem in such institutions.*

evil /iv^əl/ **ADJ** morally very bad ❍ *an evil action*

evolve /ɪvɒlv/ (**evolves, evolving, evolved**)
1 VERB When animals or plants **evolve**, they gradually change over many years and develop into different forms. ❍ *The theory is that humans evolved from apes.*
2 VERB If something **evolves**, it gradually develops over a period of time into something different. ❍ *The world economy has evolved during this time.*

ex /ɛks/
1 PREP excluding or without [FINANCE] ❍ *ex dividend*
2 PREP without charge to the buyer until removed from [LOGISTICS AND DISTRIBUTION] ❍ *ex ship*

ex|act /ɪgzækt/ **ADJ** correct and complete in every way ❍ *I don't remember the exact words.* ❍ *The exact number is not known.*

ex|act|ly /ɪgzæktli/
1 ADV used when saying facts or amounts correctly and completely ❍ *The tower was exactly a hundred meters in height.*
2 ADV in every way ❍ *You have to go into the meeting knowing exactly what you want.*
3 ADV used for agreeing strongly with someone ❍ *Eve nodded. "Exactly."*

ex|ag|ger|ate /ɪgzædʒəreɪt/ (**exaggerates, exaggerating, exaggerated**) **VERB** If you **exaggerate**, you say that something is bigger, worse, or more important than it really is. ❍ *I'm not exaggerating when I say he was the most difficult client I've ever had.* ❍ *This exaggerates the significance of the financial sector, which makes up only around 8% of the economy.*
• **ex|ag|gera|tion** /ɪgzædʒəreɪʃən/ **NOUN** ❍ *He's completely incompetent - and that's no exaggeration.*

exam /ɪgzæm/ **NOUN** a formal test that you take to show your knowledge of a subject ❍ *I don't want to take any more exams.*

ex|ami|na|tion /ɪgzæmɪneɪʃən/
1 NOUN An **examination** is the same as an **exam**. [FORMAL]

2 NOUN an occasion when a doctor looks closely at your body in order to check how healthy you are ❍ *She's waiting for the results of a medical examination.*
3 NOUN the act of looking at and considering something carefully ❍ *The government said the plan needed careful examination.*

ex|am|ine /ɪgzæmɪn/ (**examines, examining, examined**) **VERB** If you **examine** something or someone, you look at them carefully. ❍ *He examined her documents.* ❍ *A doctor examined her and could find nothing wrong.*

E

ex|am|ple /ɪgzæmpᵊl/
1 NOUN something that shows what other things in a particular group are like ❍ *Mobile phones are a good example of technology's ability to improve the lives of people in the developing world.*
2 You use **for example** to introduce an example of something. ❍ *Several times last year, for example, shares of the Fund fell.*

ex|ceed /ɪksid/ **VERB** If something **exceeds** a particular amount, it is greater than that amount. [FORMAL] ❍ *Demand for the product exceeds supply.*

ex|cel|lent /ɛksələnt/ **ADJ** extremely good ❍ *The service was excellent.*

ex|cept /ɪksɛpt/
1 PREP You use **except** or **except for** to show that you are not including a particular thing or person. ❍ *The stores are open every day except Sunday.* ❍ *The room was empty except for a television.*
2 CONJ Except is also a conjunction. ❍ *They knew little about him, except that he had managed a successful company.*

ex|cep|tion /ɪksɛpʃən/ **NOUN** a particular thing, person, or situation that is not included in what you say ❍ *In most countries, house prices have been coming down. Britain, however, is something of an exception.*

ex|cep|tion|al /ɪksɛpʃənᵊl/ **ADJ** extremely clever or skillful ❍ *He was an exceptional manager.* • **ex|cep|tion|al|ly ADV** ❍ *Ballmer was surrounded by exceptionally bright and talented people.*

ex|cess /ɛksɛs/
1 ADJ additional to what was originally proposed, planned, or taken into account [FORMAL] ❍ *a letter demanding an excess fare of £20* ❍ *Staff who have to travel farther can claim excess travel expenses.*
2 [FINANCE, BRIT] → **deductible 2**
3 In excess of means more than a particular amount. [FORMAL] ❍ *Avoid deposits in excess of $20,000 in any one account.*

ex|cess de|mand NONCOUNT NOUN Excess demand is when the price of a product rises because the market demand for it is greater than its market supply. [ECONOMICS] ❍ *Excess demand may lead the dealers to seek new sources of supply.*

ex|ces|sive /ɪksɛsɪv/ **ADJ** too great in amount or degree ❍ *It was an excessive work load.*

ex|cess sup|ply NONCOUNT NOUN Excess supply is when the price of a product falls because the market supply is greater than the market demand for it. [ECONOMICS, PRODUCTION] ❍ *The firm had to slash prices to unload the excess supply.*

ex|change /ɪkstʃeɪndʒ/ (**exchanges, exchanging, exchanged**)
1 VERB If two or more people **exchange** things, they give them to each other at the same time. ❍ *We exchanged addresses.*
2 VERB If you **exchange** something, you take it back to a store and get a different thing. ❍ *If you are unhappy with the product, we will exchange it.* → also **corn exchange, foreign exchange, stock exchange**

ex|change rate (**exchange rates**) **NOUN** the amount of one country's money that you can buy with another country's money [BANKING, ECONOMICS] ❍ *The exchange rate is around 3.7 pesos to the dollar.*

ex|cite /ɪksaɪt/ (**excites, exciting, excited**) **VERB** If something **excites** you, it makes you feel very happy or enthusiastic. ❍ *The work in itself doesn't excite me.*

ex|cit|ed /ɪksaɪtɪd/ **ADJ** very happy and enthusiastic about something ❍ *We're very excited about this product.*

ex|cite|ment /ɪksaɪtmənt/ NONCOUNT NOUN **Excitement** is the feeling you have when you are excited. ❍ *He shouted with excitement.*

ex|cit|ing /ɪksaɪtɪŋ/ ADJ making you feel very happy and enthusiastic ❍ *This is a very exciting project to be involved in.*

ex|clude /ɪksklud/ (**excludes, excluding, excluded**)
1 VERB If you **exclude** someone **from** a place or an activity, you prevent them from entering it or doing it. ❍ *The public was excluded from both meetings.*
2 VERB If you **exclude** something, you deliberately do not use it or consider it. ❍ *The price excludes taxes.*

ex|clu|sive /ɪksklusɪv/
1 ADJ available only to people who are rich or powerful ❍ *It's marketed very much as an exclusive product.*
2 ADJ If a person or firm has an **exclusive** contract or agreement with another person or firm, they only do business with that person or firm.

ex|clu|sive eco|nom|ic zone (**exclusive economic zones**) or **economic zone** NOUN the area around a country's shores, where it has fishing and exploration rights ❍ *Most of Iceland's fish are caught within its 200-mile exclusive economic zone.*

ex|clu|sive|ly /ɪksklusɪvli/ ADV used for showing that something is available to or from the place or thing mentioned only ❍ *This perfume is available exclusively from selected David Jones stores.*

ex|cuse (**excuses, excusing, excused**)

Pronounce the noun /ɪkskyus/. Pronounce the verb /ɪkskyuz/.

1 NOUN a reason that you give in order to explain why you did something ❍ *They're just trying to find excuses for their failure.*
2 VERB If you **excuse** someone **for** doing something, you forgive them for it. ❍ *I'm not excusing him for what he did.*
3 You say "**Excuse me**" when you want to politely get someone's attention. ❍ *Excuse me, but are you Mr. Hess?*

ex div|idend ADJ Investors who buy a share **ex dividend** are entitled to keep the dividend if they receive it. The short form **ex div.** is sometimes used. [FINANCE]

ex|ecute /ɛksɪkyut/ (**executes, executing, executed**) VERB To **execute** someone means to kill them as a punishment. ❍ *He was found guilty and executed.* ● **ex|ecu|tion** /ɛksɪkyuʃən/ NOUN ❍ *his execution for murder*

ex|ecu|tive /ɪgzɛkyətɪv/
1 NOUN someone who has an important job at a firm [BUSINESS MANAGEMENT] ❍ *Several top executives subsequently resigned.* ❍ *an advertising executive*
2 ADJ The **executive** sections of an organization are concerned with making decisions and making sure that decisions are carried out. [BUSINESS MANAGEMENT] ❍ *A successful job search needs to be as well organized as any other executive task.*

COLLOCATIONS
an executive *director*
an executive *officer*
an executive *chairman*
an executive *committee*

ex|ecu|tive di|rec|tor (**executive directors**) NOUN a member of the board of directors of a firm who is also an employee of that firm with an area of responsibility such as finance or production [BUSINESS MANAGEMENT, ADMINISTRATION] ❍ *He was executive director of advertising and strategic merchandising.*

ex|empt /ɪgzɛmpt/ ADJ If someone is **exempt from** a rule or a duty, they do not have to obey it or perform it. ❍ *Treasury bills are also exempt from state taxes.*

ex|er|cise /ɛksərsaɪz/ (**exercises, exercising, exercised**)
1 PL NOUN **Exercises** are a series of movements that you do in order to stay healthy and strong. ❍ *I do special neck and shoulder exercises every morning.*
2 NOUN an activity that you do in order to practice a skill ❍ *a writing exercise*

3 VERB When you **exercise**, you move your body in order to stay healthy and strong. ❍ *Try to exercise two or three times a week.*
4 NONCOUNT NOUN Exercise is also a noun. ❍ *Lack of exercise can cause sleep problems.*

ex|er|cise price (**exercise prices**) **NOUN** the price at which the holder of a traded option is allowed to buy or sell a security [FINANCE] ❍ *Investment bankers advised the company to set the exercise price at a level three times its stock price.*

E

ex|haust /ɪgzɔst/
1 VERB If something **exhausts** you, it makes you very tired. ❍ *The trip had exhausted him.*
• **ex|haust|ing ADJ** ❍ *After exhausting negotiations, the leaders finally agreed on a deal.*
• **ex|haus|tion** /ɪgzɔstʃən/ **NONCOUNT NOUN** ❍ *He collapsed with exhaustion.*
2 NONCOUNT NOUN Exhaust is the gas or steam that the engine of a vehicle produces. ❍ *exhaust fumes*

ex|hib|it /ɪgzɪbɪt/
1 VERB When an object **is exhibited**, it is put in a public place such as a museum so that people can come to look at it. ❍ *The paintings were exhibited in Paris in 1874.*
2 NOUN a public display of art or other objects ❍ *These objects are part of an exhibit at the Museum of Modern Art.*

ex|hi|bi|tion /ɛksɪbɪʃən/ **NOUN** a public event where art or other objects are shown ❍ *The Museum of the City of New York has an exhibition of photographs.*

ex|hil|ar|at|ing /ɪgzɪləreɪtɪŋ/ **ADJ** making you feel very excited and giving you energy ❍ *I find it exhilarating to cycle very quickly.*

ex|ist /ɪgzɪst/ **VERB** If something **exists**, it is a real thing or situation. ❍ *It is clear that a serious problem exists.*

ex|ist|ence /ɪgzɪstəns/ **NONCOUNT NOUN** The **existence** of something is the fact that it is a real thing or situation. ❍ *I don't doubt the existence of these attitudes.* ❍ *Is the company still in existence?*

ex|ist|ing /ɪgzɪstɪŋ/ **ADJ** in this world or available now ❍ *The existing products are simply not good enough.*

exit /ɛgzɪt, ɛksɪt/
1 NOUN the door that you use to leave a public building ❍ *He walked toward the exit.*
2 VERB If you **exit** a place, you leave it. ❍ *Exit the freeway at 128th Street Southwest.*

exit strat|egy (**exit strategies**) **NOUN** a way of ending your involvement in a situation such as a business arrangement [MARKETING AND SALES] ❍ *The exit strategy is simply how you convert your investment back into cash.*

ex|ot|ic /ɪgzɒtɪk/ **ADJ** unusual and interesting, usually coming from another country ❍ *exotic plants*

ex|pand /ɪkspænd/ **VERB** If a firm **expands** something such as its product range, it increases the number of different products that it makes. ❍ *Like the other designers, Doran moved into wallpaper as a way of expanding an existing product range.*

ex|pan|sion /ɪkspænʃən/ **NONCOUNT NOUN** The **expansion** of a product range is the act of increasing it. ❍ *The supermarket will speed up the expansion of its Internet home delivery service, creating 7,000 full-time jobs.*

ex|pan|sion strat|egy (**expansion strategies**) **NOUN** a set of plans for making a firm bigger or more successful [BUSINESS MANAGEMENT] ❍ *This confidence has enabled NWV to pursue an aggressive expansion strategy.*

ex|pect /ɪkspɛkt/
1 VERB If you **expect** something **to** happen, you believe that it will happen. ❍ *He wasn't expecting to lose his job.* ❍ *We expect the price of bananas to rise.*
2 VERB If you **are expecting** something or someone, you believe that they will arrive soon. ❍ *I'm expecting a visitor.*
3 VERB If you **expect** a person **to** do something, you believe that it is the person's duty to do it. ❍ *I expect my staff to be here on time.*
4 VERB If a woman **is expecting** a baby, she has a baby growing inside her. ❍ *She announced that she was expecting another child.*

ex|pec|ta|tion /ɛkspɛkteɪʃən/ **NOUN** A person's **expectations** are beliefs they have about how something should happen.

❍ *Young people have high expectations for the future.*

ex|pe|dit|er /ɛkspɪdaɪtər/ also **expeditor** NOUN a person who is employed in an industry to make sure that each job is done efficiently [LOGISTICS AND DISTRIBUTION] ❍ *He was more expediter than maker of decisions.*

ex|pendi|ture /ɪkspɛndɪtʃər/ NONCOUNT NOUN **Expenditure** is the spending of money on something, or the money that is spent on something. [FINANCE, FORMAL] ❍ *Policies of tax reduction must lead to reduced public expenditure.*

COLLOCATIONS

to *increase* expenditure
to *reduce* expenditure
to *cut* expenditure
to *control* expenditure

ex|pense /ɪkspɛns/

1 NONCOUNT NOUN **Expense** is the cost or price of something. ❍ *He bought a big television at great expense.*

2 PL NOUN **Expenses** are amounts of money that you spend while doing something in the course of your work, which will be paid back to you afterwards. ❍ *As a member of the International Olympic Committee, her fares and hotel expenses were paid by the IOC.* ❍ *Can you claim this back on expenses?*

ex|pense ac|count (**expense accounts**) NOUN an arrangement between an employer and an employee that allows the employee to spend the firm's money on things relating to their job, such as traveling or dealing with clients [FINANCE] ❍ *He put Elizabeth's motel bill and airfare on his expense account.*

ex|pen|sive /ɪkspɛnsɪv/ ADJ costing a lot of money ❍ *an expensive restaurant*

ex|peri|ence /ɪkspɪəriəns/ (**experiences, experiencing, experienced**)

1 NONCOUNT NOUN **Experience** is knowledge or skill in a job or an activity, which you have gained from doing that job or activity. ❍ *No teaching experience is necessary.*

2 NOUN something that you do or something that happens to you, especially something new or unusual ❍ *The funeral was a painful experience.*

3 VERB If you **experience** something, it happens to you. ❍ *I'd never experienced such pain.*

ex|pe|ri|enced /ɪkspɪəriənst/ ADJ having done something many times before ❍ *These were experienced investors.*

ex|peri|ment

Pronounce the noun /ɪkspɛrɪmənt/.
Pronounce the verb /ɪkspɛrɪmɛnt/.

1 NOUN a scientific test that you do in order to discover what happens to something ❍ *Laboratory experiments show that vitamin D slows cancer growth.*

2 VERB If you **experiment with** something or **experiment on** it, you do a scientific test on it. ❍ *They frequently experiment on mice.*

3 NOUN a test of a new idea or method ❍ *They started the magazine as an experiment.*

4 VERB To **experiment** means to test a new idea or method. ❍ *Other providers are experimenting with a range of new business loans.*

ex|peri|men|tal /ɪkspɛrɪmɛntᵊl/ ADJ new, using new ideas or methods ❍ *an experimental musician*

ex|pert /ɛkspɜrt/ NOUN a person who knows a lot about a particular subject ❍ *a computer expert*

ex|per|tise /ɛkspɜrtiz/ NONCOUNT NOUN **Expertise** is special skill or knowledge. ❍ *Mr. Teagan, however, has no special expertise in the area.*

ex|pire /ɪkspaɪər/ (**expires, expiring, expired**) VERB When a document **expires**, it cannot be used any more. ❍ *My contract expires in July.*

ex|plain /ɪkspleɪn/

1 VERB If you **explain** something to someone, you describe it so that they can understand it. ❍ *He explained the law in simple language.* ❍ *Professor Griffiths explained how the system works.*

2 VERB If you **explain** something that happened, you give reasons for it. ❍ *I asked her to explain her behavior at the meeting.*

e

ex|pla|na|tion /ɛksplən<u>eɪ</u>ʃən/ **NOUN** information that you give someone to help them to understand something ❍ *She gave no explanation for her actions.*

ex|plic|it /ɪkspl<u>ɪ</u>sɪt/ **ADJ** expressed or shown clearly, without hiding anything ❍ *Many parents worry about explicit violence on television.*

E

ex|plode /ɪkspl<u>oʊ</u>d/ (**explodes, exploding, exploded**) **VERB** If an object such as a bomb **explodes**, it bursts with great force. ❍ *A second bomb exploded in the capital yesterday.*

ex|ploit /ɪkspl<u>ɔɪ</u>t/ **VERB** If someone **exploits** you, they treat you unfairly by using your work or ideas. ❍ *It was claimed that he exploited other musicians.*

ex|ploita|tive /ɪkspl<u>ɔɪ</u>tətɪv/ **ADJ** If you describe something as **exploitative**, you disapprove of it because it treats people unfairly by using their work or ideas for its own advantage, and giving them very little in return. [FORMAL] ❍ *Success for owners and businessmen involved exploitative advantage over others.*

ex|plore /ɪkspl<u>ɔ</u>r/ (**explores, exploring, explored**) **VERB** If you **explore** a place, you travel around it to find out what it is like. ❍ *The best way to explore the area is in a boat.* ● **ex|plor|er NOUN** ❍ *Who was the U.S. explorer who discovered the Titanic shipwreck?*

ex|plo|sion /ɪkspl<u>oʊ</u>ʒᵊn/ **NOUN** an occasion when something suddenly bursts with a loud sound, often causing damage ❍ *Six soldiers were injured in the explosion.*

ex|plo|sive /ɪkspl<u>oʊ</u>sɪv/
1 NOUN a substance or an object that can cause an explosion ❍ *The 400 pounds of explosives were packaged in yellow bags.*
2 ADJ Explosive is also an adjective. ❍ *No explosive device was found.*

ex|port

Pronounce the verb /ɪksp<u>ɔ</u>rt/. Pronounce the noun /<u>ɛ</u>kspɔrt/.

1 VERB To **export** products means to sell them to another country. ❍ *They also export cotton.* ❍ *The company now exports to Japan.*
2 NONCOUNT NOUN Export is also a noun. ❍ *A lot of our land is used for growing crops for export.* ● **ex|port|er** /<u>ɛ</u>kspɔrtər, ɪksp<u>ɔ</u>rtər/ **NOUN** ❍ *Brazil is a big exporter of coffee.*
3 NOUN a product that one country sells to another country ❍ *Spain's main export is oil.*

COLLOCATIONS
exports *increase*
exports *decrease*

ex|por|ta|tion /ɛkspɔrt<u>eɪ</u>ʃən/
1 NONCOUNT NOUN the act, process, or business of exporting goods or services ❍ *They prepare coffee beans grown in Brazil for exportation to American specialty roasters.*
2 NOUN an exported product or service

ex|pose /ɪksp<u>oʊ</u>z/ (**exposes, exposing, exposed**) **VERB** To **expose** something that is usually covered means to take the cover off and show it. ❍ *Vitamin D is made when the skin is exposed to sunlight.*

ex|po|si|tion /ɛkspəz<u>ɪ</u>ʃən/ **NOUN** a large public exhibition of industrial products ❍ *The Great Exposition of 1851 in London was a trade fair celebrating the inventions of the Industrial Revolution.*

ex|po|sure /ɪksp<u>oʊ</u>ʒər/
1 NONCOUNT NOUN Exposure to something dangerous means being in a situation where it might affect you. ❍ *Exposure to lead is known to damage the brains of young children.*
2 NONCOUNT NOUN Exposure is publicity that a person, firm, or product receives. ❍ *All the candidates have been getting an enormous amount of exposure on television and in the press.*

ex|press /ɪkspr<u>ɛ</u>s/ (**expresses, expressing, expressed**)
1 VERB When you **express** an idea or feeling, you show what you think or feel. ❍ *Both parties expressed satisfaction with the agreement.*
2 NOUN An **express** or an **express train** is a fast train that stops at only a few stations.

ex|pres|sage /ɪkspr<u>ɛ</u>sɪdʒ/
1 NONCOUNT NOUN Expressage is the act or process of moving goods by express. [LOGISTICS AND DISTRIBUTION]

2 **NONCOUNT NOUN** **Expressage** is the fee charged for moving goods by express. [LOGISTICS AND DISTRIBUTION]

> **BUSINESS ETIQUETTE**
> Women travelling to Muslim countries should dress modestly. It is also a good idea for women to carry a scarf, in case they are required to cover their head at any time.

ex|pres|sion /ɪksprɛʃən/
1 **NOUN** the way that your face looks at a particular moment, showing an emotion ❍ *There was an expression of sadness on his face.*
2 **NOUN** a word or phrase ❍ *an informal expression*

ex|tend /ɪkstɛnd/ **VERB** If you **extend** something, you make it longer. ❍ *The deadline for filing Form 3115 has now been extended.*

ex|ten|sion /ɪkstɛnʃən/
1 **NOUN** an extra period of time for which something lasts ❍ *He was given a six-month extension to his visa.*
2 **NOUN** a telephone that connects to the main telephone line in a building ❍ *She can talk to me on extension 308.*

ex|ten|sive /ɪkstɛnsɪv/ **ADJ** covering a wide area ❍ *a four-bedroom house with extensive gardens*

ex|tent /ɪkstɛnt/ **NOUN** **The extent of** a situation is how important or serious it is. ❍ *We don't yet know the extent of the problem.* ❍ *He soon discovered the full extent of the damage.*

ex|te|ri|or /ɪkstɪəriər/
1 **NOUN** the outside surface of something ❍ *They're painting the exterior of the building.*
2 **ADJ** used to describe the outside part of something ❍ *exterior walls*

ex|ter|nal /ɪkstɜrnᵊl/ **ADJ** happening or existing on the outside of something ❍ *A lot of heat is lost through external walls.*

ex|tinc|tion /ɪkstɪŋkʃən/ **NONCOUNT NOUN** The **extinction** of a species of animal or plant is the death of all its living members. ❍ *We are trying to save these animals from extinction.*

ex|tin|guish /ɪkstɪŋgwɪʃ/ (**extinguishes, extinguishing, extinguished**) **VERB** If you **extinguish** a fire or a light, you stop it from burning. [FORMAL] ❍ *It took about 50 minutes to extinguish the fire.*

ex|tort /ɪkstɔrt/ **VERB** If someone **extorts** money **from** you, they get it from you using force, threats, or other unfair or illegal means. ❍ *Corrupt government officials were extorting money from him.* ❍ *Her kidnapper extorted a $175,000 ransom for her release.*

ex|tra /ɛkstrə/
1 **ADJ** more than is usual, necessary, or expected ❍ *The company now has a chance to sell an extra 40,000 cars a year.*
2 **ADV** **Extra** is also an adverb. ❍ *You may be charged $10 extra for this service.*

ex|tract /ɪkstrækt/ **VERB** If you **extract** something, you take it out or pull it out. ❍ *A dentist may decide to extract the tooth.*

extraor|di|nary /ɪkstrɔrdᵊnɛri/
1 **ADJ** having an extremely good or special quality ❍ *My advice is to work for someone who is an extraordinary leader and watch how he does it.*
2 **ADJ** very unusual or surprising ❍ *An extraordinary thing just happened.*

extraor|di|nary gen|er|al meet|ing (**extraordinary general meetings**) **NOUN** a meeting specially called to discuss a particular item of a firm's business [BUSINESS MANAGEMENT, ADMINISTRATION, BRIT] ❍ *The proposal was passed by an extraordinary general meeting in November.*

ex|trava|gant /ɪkstrævəgənt/
1 **ADJ** Someone who is **extravagant** spends more money than they can afford or uses more of something than is reasonable. ❍ *We are not extravagant; restaurant meals are a luxury and designer clothes are out.*
● **ex|trava|gant|ly** **ADV** ❍ *The day before they left Jeff had shopped extravagantly for presents for the whole family.*
2 **ADJ** Something that is **extravagant** costs more money than you can afford or uses more of something than is reasonable. ❍ *The royal family's lifestyle looks extravagant in a country where most people are dirt-poor.*

e

E

• **ex|trava|gant|ly** ADV ❍ *By supercar standards, though, it is not extravagantly priced for a beautifully engineered machine.*

ex|treme /ɪkstri̲m/ ADJ very great in degree ❍ *Dealers said London showed signs of extreme nervousness, particularly in the later stages of the session.* • **ex|treme|ly** ADV ❍ *My cellphone is extremely useful.*

eye /aɪ̲/

1 NOUN one of the two parts of your body with which you see ❍ *She has beautiful blue eyes.*

2 If something **catches** your **eye**, you suddenly notice it. ❍ *A dark-haired man suddenly caught her eye.*

3 If you **have** your **eye on** something, you want to have it. [INFORMAL] ❍ *I've had my eye on that dress for a while now.*

eye|ball /a̲ɪbɔl/ NOUN the round white ball that is the whole of the eye

eye|brow /a̲ɪbraʊ/ NOUN the line of hair that grows above the eye

eye|glasses /a̲ɪglæsɪz/ PL NOUN **Eyeglasses** are two pieces of glass or plastic (= lenses) in a frame, that some people wear in front of their eyes to help them to see better. ❍ *a pair of eyeglasses*

eye|lash /a̲ɪlæʃ/ (**eyelashes**) NOUN one of the many hairs that grows on the edges of the eye

eye|lid /a̲ɪlɪd/ NOUN the piece of skin that covers the eye when it is closed

eye|sight /a̲ɪsaɪt/ NONCOUNT NOUN Your **eyesight** is your ability to see. ❍ *He has poor eyesight.*

e-zine /i̲zin/ (**e-zines**) NOUN a website that contains the kind of articles, pictures, and advertisements that you would find in a magazine [TECHNOLOGY]

Ff

fab|ric /fæbrɪk/ **NOUN** cloth that you use for making things like clothes and bags ❍ *Wickes makes wall coverings and decorative fabrics.*

fabu|lous /fæbyələs/ **ADJ** very good [INFORMAL] ❍ *The apartment offers fabulous views of the city.*

face /feɪs/ (**faces, facing, faced**)
1 NOUN the front part of the head where the eyes, nose, and mouth are ❍ *She had a beautiful face.*
2 NOUN a surface or side of something ❍ *the south face of Mount Everest* ❍ *a clock face*
3 VERB To **face** a particular direction or thing means to look in that direction or at that thing. ❍ *Our house faces south.* ❍ *They stood facing each other.*
4 VERB If you **face** something unpleasant, you have to deal with it. ❍ *They now face a tough couple of years.* ❍ *I can't face telling my colleagues.*
5 If you are **face to face** with someone, you look at them directly. ❍ *I got off the bus and came face to face with my teacher.*
6 If you **make a face** or **pull a face**, you change your face into an ugly expression. ❍ *She made a face at the smell.*

face|lift /feɪslɪft/ also **face-lift NOUN** If you give something **a facelift**, you do something to make it look better. ❍ *For the first time in years the factory is getting a facelift.* ❍ *All the petrol stations were given a facelift.*

face value (**face values**) **NOUN** the amount of money that a coin, piece of paper money, or document is worth [ECONOMICS] ❍ *Tickets were selling at twice their face value.* ❍ *The company's bonds have fallen to 28% of their face value.*

fa|cili|tate /fəsɪlɪteɪt/ (**facilitates, facilitating, facilitated**) **VERB** If you **facilitate** an action, you help it to happen. [FORMAL] ❍ *The new airport will facilitate the development of tourism.* ❍ *The economic recovery was facilitated by his tough policies.*

fa|cil|ity /fəsɪlɪti/ (**facilities**) **NOUN** a room, building, or piece of equipment that is used for a particular purpose ❍ *The hotel has no conference facilities.*

fact /fækt/
1 NOUN a piece of information that is true or something that has certainly happened ❍ *I don't know all the facts and figures relating to the case.* ❍ *This doesn't change the fact that he was wrong.*
2 You use **in fact** when you are giving more information about something that you have just said. ❍ *There has, in fact, been a sharp fall in stocks of oil at sea.*

fac|tor /fæktər/ **NOUN** something that helps to produce a result ❍ *Investment flows are the most important factor in the stock market.*

fac|tor|ing /fæktərɪŋ/ **NONCOUNT NOUN** **Factoring** is the business of buying debts from a firm and making a profit by collecting the money owed. [ECONOMICS] ❍ *ABC sold its sales invoices to a factoring company.*

fac|tors of pro|duc|tion PL NOUN **Factors of production** are the things such as land, labor, and capital that an industry needs in order to produce a particular product. [PRODUCTION] ❍ *The rate of output depends on the supply of factors of production.*

fac|to|ry /fæktəri, -tri/ (**factories**) **NOUN** a large building where people use machines to make goods [PRODUCTION] ❍ *He owned furniture factories in New York State.*

fac|to|ry out|let (**factory outlets**) or **factory store NOUN** a store that sells goods made by a particular manufacturer at a low price [PRODUCTION, MARKETING AND SALES]

fac|to|ry shop (**factory shops**) [PRODUCTION, MARKETING AND SALES, BRIT] → **factory outlet**

fade /feɪd/ (**fades, fading, faded**) VERB When something **fades**, it slowly becomes lighter in color or less bright. ❍ *The light was fading.* ● **fad|ed** ADJ ❍ *faded jeans*

Fahr|en|heit /færənhaɪt/ NONCOUNT NOUN **Fahrenheit** is a way of measuring how hot something is. It is shown by the symbol °F. Water freezes at 32°F (0°C) and boils at 212°F (100°C). ❍ *The temperature was above 100°F.*

F

fail /feɪl/

1 VERB If you **fail** an exam or a test, you do not pass it. ❍ *75 percent of high school students failed the exam.*

2 VERB If you **fail** to do something, you do not succeed when you try to do it. ❍ *The Republicans failed to get the 60 votes they needed.*

3 VERB If a business or bank **fails**, it goes bankrupt or stops operating. ❍ *So far this year, 104 banks have failed.* ❍ *Who wants to buy a computer from a failing company?*

4 If you do something **without fail**, you always do it. ❍ *Andrew attended every board meeting without fail.*

fail|ure /feɪlyər/

1 NONCOUNT NOUN **Failure** is when you do not succeed in doing something. ❍ *The project had ended in failure.*

2 NOUN something that does not succeed ❍ *His first novel was a failure.*

3 NOUN If there is a **failure** of a business or bank, it goes bankrupt or stops operating. ❍ *Business failures rose 16% last month.*

faint /feɪnt/

1 ADJ not strong or clear ❍ *I could hear the faint sound of traffic in the distance.* ● **faint|ly** ADV ❍ *The room smelled faintly of paint.*

2 ADJ feeling weak, as if you might become unconscious ❍ *Ryan was unsteady on his feet and felt faint.*

3 VERB If you **faint**, you become unconscious for a short time.

fair /fɛər/

1 ADJ treating everyone equally ❍ *Many workers feel that they aren't getting a fair share in the nation's prosperity.* ❍ *Everyone has a right to a fair trial.* ● **fair|ness** NONCOUNT NOUN ❍ *There were concerns about the fairness of the election campaign.*

2 ADJ not bad, but not very good ❍ *"What did you think of the presentation?"—"Hmm. Fair."*

3 ADJ having light-colored hair or skin ❍ *My mother was very fair.* ❍ *Eric had thick fair hair.*

4 NOUN a place where you can play games to win prizes, and you can ride on special, big machines for fun

5 NOUN an event at which people show or sell goods, or share information ❍ *a job fair*

fair|ly /fɛərli/

1 ADV quite ❍ *Its share price has held up fairly well despite stockmarket turmoil.* ❍ *By European standards, its public finances are in fairly good shape.*

2 ADV in a way that treats everyone equally ❍ *We solved the problem quickly and fairly.*

fairly-traded ADJ bought from producers in developing countries at a fair price [ECONOMICS] ❍ *Oxfam's food and handicrafts have always been fairly-traded.*

fair trade NONCOUNT NOUN also **fairtrade** **Fair trade** is the practice of buying goods directly from producers in developing countries at a fair price. [ECONOMICS] ❍ *fair trade bananas* ❍ *More than five percent of all coffee sold in Britain is now fair trade.*

Fair|trade mark /fɛərtreɪd mɑrk/ (**Fairtrade marks**) NOUN a sign on packaging that shows that a product was fairly-traded [ECONOMICS, MARKETING AND SALES] ❍ *If you see the Fairtrade mark on a product you will know that a reasonable price has been paid to the people producing it.*

fairy /fɛəri/ (**fairies**) NOUN in children's stories, a very small creature with wings, that can do magic

faith /feɪθ/

1 NONCOUNT NOUN **Faith** is a feeling of trust and confidence in something or someone. ❍ *Have people lost their faith in politicians?*

2 NOUN a particular religion ❍ *students of all faiths and nationalities*

faith|ful /feɪθfəl/ **ADJ** loyal to someone or something and always supporting them ❍ *a faithful friend* ● **faith|ful|ly** **ADV** ❍ *She supported him faithfully over the years.*

fake /feɪk/
1 ADJ used to describe a copy of something, especially of something valuable ❍ *The market used to be Shanghai's center for fake goods.*
2 NOUN a copy of something valuable ❍ *Art experts think that the painting is a fake.*

fall /fɔl/ (**falls, falling, fell, fallen**)
1 VERB If someone or something **falls**, they move quickly downward, often by accident. ❍ *He lost his balance and fell.* ❍ *Bombs were falling all around us.*
2 NOUN an occasion when you fall to the ground ❍ *He broke his leg in a fall.*
3 Fall down means the same as **fall**. ❍ *John fell down and hurt his knee.*
4 VERB When rain or snow **falls**, it comes down from the sky. ❍ *More than 30 inches of rain fell in 6 days.*
5 NOUN the season between summer and winter, when the leaves start to fall off the trees ❍ *The launch is scheduled for the fall of 2013.*
6 VERB If something **falls**, it becomes less or lower. ❍ *Unemployment fell to 4.6 percent in May.* ❍ *Sales fell below 50,000 a year.*
7 NOUN an occasion when something becomes less or lower ❍ *There has been a sharp fall in the value of the dollar.*
8 VERB If you **fall** asleep or if you **fall** ill, you start to sleep or you become ill. ❍ *Emily suddenly fell ill and was rushed to hospital.*
▸ **fall apart** If something **falls apart**, it breaks into pieces. ❍ *My bag is so old it's falling apart.*
▸ **fall behind** If you **fall behind**, you do not make progress as fast as other people. ❍ *The company fell behind in its payments.* ❍ *The project is falling behind schedule.*
▸ **fall out**
1 If your hair or your tooth **falls out**, it comes out.
2 If you **fall out** with someone, you have an argument and stop being friendly with them. ❍ *Ashley has fallen out with Mike.*

COLLOCATIONS
to fall *sharply*
a *significant* fall
to fall *dramatically*
a *dramatic* fall

false /fɔls/
1 ADJ not true or not correct ❍ *He gave a false name.*
2 ADJ not real or not natural ❍ *false teeth*

fame /feɪm/ **NONCOUNT NOUN** **Fame** is when you are very well known by a lot of people. ❍ *Connery gained fame as Agent 007 in the Bond movies.*

fa|mili|ar /fəmɪlyər/ **ADJ** If someone or something is **familiar**, you have seem them or heard of them before. ❍ *His face looks familiar.* ❍ *The slogan may sound familiar to consumers with long memories.*

fami|ly /fæmɪli, fæmli/ (**families**) **NOUN** a group of people who are related to each other, usually parents and their children ❍ *William and his family live in Hawaii.* ❍ *A ticket for a family of four costs $68.*

fami|ly leave **NONCOUNT NOUN** **Family leave** is the time that a person spends away from work to look after a member of their family. [HR] ❍ *workplace improvements such as on-site child care, family leave, and flexible work schedules*

fami|ly name (**family names**) **NOUN** the name that you share with other members of your family ❍ *"What is your family name?"—"O'Neill."*

fam|ine /fæmɪn/ **NOUN** a time when there is not enough food for people to eat, and many people die ❍ *Their country is suffering from famine and war.*

fa|mous /feɪməs/ **ADJ** very well known by a lot of people ❍ *a famous actor* ❍ *The famous mail-order company prides itself on its service.*

fan /fæn/ (**fans, fanning, fanned**)
1 NOUN a person who likes someone or something very much ❍ *Fans of electric cars say they are clean, quiet, and economical.*
2 NOUN a piece of equipment that moves the air around a room to make you cooler

3 NOUN a flat object that you move backward and forward in front of your face to make you cooler

4 VERB If you **fan** yourself, you move a fan or another flat object around in front of yourself, to make yourself cooler. ❍ *People at the back of the room were fanning themselves with papers.*

fa|nat|ic /fənætɪk/ **NOUN** someone whose behavior or opinions are very extreme ❍ *a religious fanatic*

F

fan|cy /fænsi/ (**fancier, fanciest**) **ADJ** not simple or ordinary ❍ *fancy jewelry*

fan|tas|tic /fæntæstɪk/ **ADJ** very good [INFORMAL] ❍ *Their managers enjoy fantastic salaries.*

fan|ta|sy /fæntəsi/ (**fantasies**) **NOUN** an imaginary story or thought that is very different from real life ❍ *Everyone has had a fantasy about winning the lottery.* ❍ *a fantasy novel*

FAQ /fæk/ (**FAQs**) **NOUN** The **FAQ** is a section on a website that answers questions about a particular topic. **FAQ** is an abbreviation of "frequently asked questions."

far /fɑr/ (**farther**)

1 ADV If something is **far** from other things, there is a great distance or time between them. ❍ *They live not far from here.* ❍ *My sister moved even farther away from home.*

2 ADV used in questions and statements about distances ❍ *How far is it to the office?*

3 So far means up until now. ❍ *So far, they have failed.*

4 ADV Far means "very much" when you are comparing things. ❍ *A deal would be far better than a continued stand-off.*

5 You use **by far** to say that someone or something is the biggest, the best, or the most important. ❍ *Unemployment is by far the most important issue.*

fare /fɛər/ **NOUN** the money that you pay for a trip in a bus or other vehicle ❍ *The fare is $11 one way.*

farm /fɑrm/ **NOUN** a piece of land where people grow crops and keep animals, and the buildings on it

▶ **farm out** If you **farm out** work, you send it to be done by another person or firm. ❍ *Many firms are already farming out production to distant factories.*

farm|er /fɑrmər/ **NOUN** a person who owns or works on a farm

far|ther /fɑrðər/ **ADV** in or to a more distant place ❍ *We walked a little farther along the river.*

far|thest /fɑrðɪst/

1 ADJ most distant ❍ *Mahmoud sat at the farthest end of the table.*

2 ADV in or to the most distant place ❍ *Boston is the farthest north I've been.*

f.a.s. /ɛf eɪ ɛs/ **f.a.s.** is an abbreviation of **free alongside ship**. [LOGISTICS AND DISTRIBUTION]

fas|ci|nate /fæsɪneɪt/ (**fascinates, fascinating, fascinated**) **VERB** If something **fascinates** you, you find it extremely interesting. ❍ *American history fascinates me.*

fas|ci|nat|ing /fæsɪneɪtɪŋ/ **ADJ** very interesting ❍ *Madagascar is a fascinating place.*

fash|ion /fæʃən/

1 NONCOUNT NOUN Fashion is the activity or business that involves styles of clothing, hair, and make-up. ❍ *a career in fashion*

2 NOUN a style of clothing that is popular at a particular time ❍ *the latest fashions*

3 If something is **in fashion**, it is popular at a particular time. If it is **out of fashion**, it is not popular. ❍ *Long dresses were in fashion back then.*

fash|ion|able /fæʃənəbᵊl/ **ADJ** popular and considered attractive at a particular time ❍ *Long hair on men is very fashionable again.*

• **fash|ion|ably ADV** ❍ *Brianna is always fashionably dressed.*

fast /fæst/

1 ADJ quick ❍ *fast cars* ❍ *a fast reader* ❍ *This is one of the world's fastest growing markets.*

2 ADV quickly ❍ *They expanded too fast.*

3 VERB If you **fast**, you do not eat any food for a period of time.

4 NOUN a period of time when you do not eat food ❍ *The fast ends at sunset.*

5 Someone who is **fast asleep** is deeply asleep.

fas|ten /fæsᵊn/
1 VERB When you **fasten** something, you join the two sides of it together so that it is closed. ❍ *She got into her car and fastened the seat-belt.*
2 VERB If you **fasten** one thing **to** another, you attach the first thing to the second. ❍ *Many stores are now empty, with "For Rent" signs fastened to them.*

fast food **NONCOUNT NOUN** **Fast food** is hot food that is served quickly in a restaurant. ❍ *fast food, such as hamburgers and pizza*

fast track manu|fac|turing
NONCOUNT NOUN **Fast track manufacturing** is a system that aims to speed up manufacturing times. [PRODUCTION] ❍ *Our fast track manufacturing facility can build complete turn-key systems in a few weeks.*

fat /fæt/ (**fatter, fattest**)
1 ADJ weighing too much ❍ *I ate too much and I began to get fat.*
2 ADJ thick or wide ❍ *Emily picked up a fat book and handed it to me.*
3 NONCOUNT NOUN **Fat** is a substance containing oil that is found in some foods. ❍ *Cream contains a lot of fat.*
4 NONCOUNT NOUN **Fat** is the soft substance that people and animals have under their skin.

fa|tal /feɪtᵊl/
1 ADJ having very bad results ❍ *He made the fatal mistake of announcing the plan before getting final agreement for it.*
2 ADJ causing someone's death ❍ *a fatal accident* ● **fa|tal|ly** **ADV** ❍ *The soldier was fatally wounded.*

fat cat (**fat cats**) **NOUN** If you refer to someone as a **fat cat**, you are showing that you disapprove of the way they use their wealth and power. [BANKING, INFORMAL] ❍ *the fat cats who run the bank*

fate /feɪt/
1 NONCOUNT NOUN **Fate** is a power that some people believe controls everything that happens in the world. ❍ *I think it was fate that Andy and I met.*
2 NOUN Someone's or something's **fate** is what happens to them. ❍ *The trial also may determine the fates of three small companies.*

fa|ther /fɑðər/ **NOUN** a male parent ❍ *His father was an artist.*

father-in-law (**fathers-in-law**) **NOUN** the father of your husband or wife

fa|tigue /fətig/ **NONCOUNT NOUN** **Fatigue** is a feeling of being extremely tired. ❍ *He was taken to hospital suffering from extreme fatigue.*

fat|ten /fætᵊn/
1 VERB If you say that someone **is fattening** a business, you mean that they are increasing its value, in a way that you disapprove of. ❍ *They have kept the price of sugar artificially high and so fattened the company's profits.*
2 Fatten up means the same as **fatten**. ❍ *The taxpayer is paying to fatten up a public sector business for private sale.*

fault /fɔlt/
1 NOUN If something bad is your **fault**, you made it happen. ❍ *I wasn't my fault she didn't receive the document!*
2 NOUN something bad in someone's character ❍ *Brandon's worst fault is his temper.*

faulty /fɔlti/ **ADJ** not working well ❍ *The car had worn tires and faulty brakes.*

fa|vor /feɪvər/
1 NOUN If you **do** someone **a favor**, you do something to help them. ❍ *Please would you do me a favor and give David a message for me?*
2 If you are **in favor of** something, you think that it is a good thing. ❍ *I'm certainly in favor of income tax cuts.*

fa|vor|able /feɪvərəbᵊl/
1 ADJ positive ❍ *The president's speech received favorable reviews.*
2 ADJ **Favorable** conditions are good. ❍ *favorable repayment terms*

fa|vor|ite /feɪvərɪt, feɪvrɪt/
1 ADJ used to describe the one that you like more than all the others ❍ *What's your favorite movie?*
2 NOUN the person or thing that you like more than all the others ❍ *Of all the seasons, fall is my favorite.*

fa|vour /feɪvər/ [BRIT] → **favor**

fa|vour|ite /feɪvərɪt, feɪvrɪt/ [BRIT] → **favorite**

fax /fæks/ (**faxes, faxing, faxed**)
1 NOUN A **fax** or a **fax machine** is a special machine, joined to a telephone line, that you use to send and receive documents.
2 NOUN a copy of a document that you send or receive using a fax machine
3 VERB If you **fax** a document to someone, you send it to their fax machine. ❍ *I faxed a copy of the letter to my boss.*

fear /fɪər/
1 NONCOUNT NOUN Fear is the unpleasant feeling you have when you think that you are in danger. ❍ *My whole body was shaking with fear.*
2 NOUN something bad that you think might happen ❍ *fears of an imminent recession*
3 VERB If you **fear** someone or something, you are very afraid of them. ❍ *Many people fear public speaking.*

fear|ful /fɪərfəl/ **ADJ** afraid of something [FORMAL] ❍ *They were all fearful of losing their jobs.*

fear|less /fɪərlɪs/ **ADJ** afraid of nothing ❍ *In battle, he was fearless.*

feast /fist/ **NOUN** a large and special meal for a lot of people ❍ *a wedding feast*

feath|er /fɛðər/ **NOUN** one of the light, soft things that cover a bird's body ❍ *peacock feathers*

feather|bedding /fɛðərbɛdɪŋ/ **NONCOUNT NOUN Featherbedding** is the practice of producing goods slowly, or keeping more staff than necessary, in order to prevent redundancies or create jobs. [PRODUCTION] ❍ *They have argued against featherbedding and waste.*

fea|ture /fitʃər/
1 NOUN an important part of something ❍ *Release 2.2 includes improved graphics and better database features.*
2 NOUN a special story in a newspaper or magazine ❍ *There was a feature on Tom Cruise in the New York Times.*
3 PL NOUN Your **features** are your eyes, nose, mouth, and other parts of your face. ❍ *Emily's best feature is her dark eyes.*

Feb|ru|ary /fɛbyuɛri, fɛbru-/ **NOUN** the second month of the year ❍ *The meeting is scheduled for February 7.*

fed /fɛd/ **Fed** is a form of the verb **feed**.

Fed /fɛd/ **Fed** is an abbreviation for **Federal Reserve System**. [BANKING, ECONOMICS] ❍ *The Fed is pushing up interest rates.*

fed|er|al /fɛdərəl/
1 ADJ In a **federal** country or system, a group of states is controlled by a central government.
2 ADJ relating to the national government of a federal country ❍ *The federal government moved to Washington in the fall of 1800.*

Fed|er|al Re|serve note (**Federal Reserve notes**) **NOUN** the main type of paper money in the United States [ECONOMICS]

Fed|er|al Re|serve Sys|tem NOUN the central banking system in the United States [BANKING, ECONOMICS] ❍ *the Federal Reserve's influence on the American economy*

fed up ADJ unhappy or bored [INFORMAL] ❍ *She soon became fed up with the job.*

fee /fi/
1 NOUN money that you pay to be allowed to do something ❍ *a small entrance fee*
2 NOUN money that you pay a person or an organization for advice or for a service ❍ *We had to pay the legal fees ourselves.*

feed /fid/ (**feeds, feeding, fed**) **VERB** If you **feed** a person or an animal, you give them food. ❍ *She was feeding the baby.* ❍ *Feed a small dog twice a day.*

feed|back /fidbæk/ **NONCOUNT NOUN Feedback** is written or spoken remarks on how well you do something. ❍ *He said the company was encouraged by feedback it received from selected customers.*

feed|stock /fidstɒk/ **NONCOUNT NOUN Feedstock** is the main raw material used in the manufacture of a product. [PRODUCTION] ❍ *We use as much recycled material for feedstock as possible.*

feel /fil/ (**feels, feeling, felt**)
1 VERB If you **feel** a particular emotion or a physical feeling, you experience it. ❍ *I feel much more confident in this role.* ❍ *I felt a sharp*

pain in my shoulder. ❍ *How do you feel?*

2 VERB If something **feels** a particular way, that is the way it seems when you touch it or experience it. ❍ *The blanket felt soft.* ❍ *The sun felt hot on my back.* ❍ *The room felt cold.*

3 VERB If you **feel** something, you touch it with your hand, so that you can find out what it is like. ❍ *The doctor felt my pulse.* ❍ *Feel how soft this leather is.*

4 VERB If you **feel** something, you are aware of it because you touch it or it touches you. ❍ *Anna felt something touching her face.*

5 VERB If you **feel** a particular thing, that is your opinion. ❍ *We feel that this decision is unfair.*

6 VERB If you **feel like** doing something, you want to do it. ❍ *"I just don't feel like going out tonight," Rose said quietly.*

feel|ing /fi̲lɪŋ/

1 NOUN an emotion ❍ *feelings of sadness and despair*

2 NOUN something that you feel in your body ❍ *I had a strange feeling in my neck.*

3 NOUN a belief about something, especially based on an idea and not a certain fact ❍ *I have a feeling that she won't stay long in this company.*

4 PL NOUN Feelings are emotions or attitudes. ❍ *I have mixed feelings about her as a boss.* ❍ *The subject arouses strong feelings.*

feet /fi̲t/ **Feet** is the plural of **foot**.

fell /fɛ̲l/ **Fell** is a form of the verb **fall**.

fel|low /fɛ̲loʊ/

1 NOUN a man ❍ *Chris was a cheerful fellow.*

2 ADJ used for describing people who are like you or from the same place as you ❍ *Richard was just 18 when he married fellow student Barbara.*

felt /fɛ̲lt/

1 Felt is a form of the verb **feel**.

2 NONCOUNT NOUN Felt is a type of soft thick cloth. ❍ *a felt hat*

fe|male /fi̲meɪl/

1 NOUN any animal, including humans, that can give birth to babies or lay eggs ❍ *Each female will lay just one egg.*

2 ADJ Female is also an adjective. ❍ *female gorillas*

3 NOUN a woman or a girl ❍ *A labor shortage has forced companies to be more receptive to hiring females.*

4 ADJ Female is also an adjective. ❍ *female employees*

femi|nine /fɛ̲mɪnɪn/

1 ADJ having qualities and things that are considered to be typical of women ❍ *I love feminine clothes, like skirts and dresses.*

2 ADJ In some languages, a **feminine** noun, pronoun, or adjective is one that has a different form from other forms (such as "masculine" forms). Compare with **masculine**.

femi|nism /fɛ̲mɪnɪzəm/ **NONCOUNT NOUN Feminism** is the belief that women should have the same rights and opportunities as men.

femi|nist /fɛ̲mɪnɪst/

1 NOUN a person who believes in feminism ❍ *Feminists argue that women should not have to choose between children and a career.*

2 ADJ believing in or connected with feminism ❍ *feminist writer Simone de Beauvoir*

fence /fɛ̲ns/ **NOUN** a wooden or metal wall around a piece of land

fer|tile /fɜ̲rtᵊl/

1 ADJ If land or soil is **fertile**, plants grow very well in it.

2 ADJ able to produce babies • **fer|til|ity NONCOUNT NOUN** ❍ *Smoking and drinking alcohol both affect fertility.*

fer|ti|liz|er /fɜ̲rtᵊlaɪzər/ **NOUN** a substance that you put on soil to make plants grow better

fes|ti|val /fɛ̲stɪvᵊl/

1 NOUN a series of special events such as concerts or plays ❍ *Rome's film festival*

2 NOUN a time when people celebrate a special event ❍ *Shavuot is a two-day festival for Jews.*

fetch /fɛ̲tʃ/ (**fetches, fetching, fetched**)

VERB If you **fetch** something or someone, you go somewhere and bring them back. ❍ *Sylvia fetched a chair from her office.* ❍ *Please could you fetch me a glass of water?*

fe|ver /fi̲vər/ **NOUN** a medical condition in which the body is too hot ❍ *Jim had a high fever.*

few /fyu/
1 ADJ **A few** means some, but not many. ❍ *America's financial system is now dominated by a few dozen firms.* ❍ *Here are a few ideas that might help you.*
2 PRON **A few** is also a pronoun. ❍ *Most were American but a few were British.*
3 A few of means some, but not many. ❍ *I met a few of her colleagues at the party.*
4 ADJ **Few** means not many. ❍ *She had few friends.*
5 Few of means not many. ❍ *Few of the parties involved are willing to discuss the affair.*

F

fi|an|cé /fiɑnseɪ, fiɑnseɪ/ NOUN A woman's **fiancé** is the man that she is going to marry.

fi|an|cée /fiɑnseɪ, fiɑnseɪ/ NOUN A man's **fiancée** is the woman that he is going to marry.

fiat mon|ey /faɪət mʌni/ NONCOUNT NOUN **Fiat money** is paper money that is officially used in a country. It cannot be converted into coins or gold. [ECONOMICS]

fi|ber /faɪbər/
1 NOUN a thin thread that is used for making cloth or rope ❍ *We only sell clothing made from natural fibers.*
2 NONCOUNT NOUN **Fiber** is the part of a fruit or a vegetable that helps all the food you eat to move through your body. ❍ *Most vegetables contain fiber.*

fi|bre /faɪbər/ [mainly BRIT] → **fiber**

fic|tion /fɪkʃən/ NONCOUNT NOUN **Fiction** is books and stories about people and events that are not real. • **fictional** ADJ ❍ *the fictional hero of J.K. Rowling's books*

fid|uci|ary issue /fɪduʃiɛri ɪʃu/ (**fiduciary issues**) NOUN an issue of paper money that cannot be converted into gold [ECONOMICS]

field /fild/
1 NOUN a piece of land where crops are grown, or where animals are kept ❍ *We drove past fields of sunflowers.*
2 NOUN a piece of land where sports are played ❍ *a baseball field*
3 VERB In a game of baseball, the team that **is fielding** is trying to catch the ball. ❍ *The Tigers were pitching and fielding superbly.*
4 NOUN a subject that someone knows a lot about ❍ *Professor Greenwood is an expert in the field of international law.*

field re|search NONCOUNT NOUN **Field research** is research that is done in a real environment, for example by interviewing people. Compare with **desk research**. [R & D] ❍ *We must ensure that field research is used within American industry and commerce.*

fierce /fɪərs/ (**fiercer, fiercest**)
1 ADJ angry and likely to attack or shout ❍ *a fierce dog* • **fierce|ly** ADV ❍ *"Go away!" she said fiercely.*
2 ADJ **Fierce** feelings or actions are very strong or enthusiastic. ❍ *Fierce competition has driven down the cost of cellphone calls.* • **fierce|ly** ADV ❍ *Amanda is fiercely ambitious.*

FIFO /faɪfoʊ/ **FIFO** is a method of accounting that assumes that the oldest stock is sold first. **FIFO** is an abbreviation of "First in, first out." Compare with **LIFO**. [FINANCE] ❍ *Using FIFO, the oldest purchase costs of goods are recognized as costs first.*

fif|teen /fɪftin/ the number 15

fif|teenth /fɪftinθ/ ADJ or ADV The **fifteenth** item in a series is the one that you count as number fifteen. ❍ *her fifteenth birthday*

fifth /fɪfθ/
1 ADJ or ADV The **fifth** item in a series is the one that you count as number five. ❍ *This is his fifth trip to Australia.*
2 NOUN one of five equal parts of something (⅕) ❍ *We did the job in a fifth of the usual time.*

fif|ti|eth /fɪftiəθ/ ADJ or ADV The **fiftieth** item in a series is the one that you count as number fifty. ❍ *his fiftieth birthday*

fif|ty /fɪfti/ the number 50

fight /faɪt/ (**fights, fighting, fought**)
1 VERB When people **fight**, they try to hurt each other with physical force and sometimes weapons. ❍ *The two boys were always fighting.* ❍ *He fought in the First World War.*
2 NOUN a situation in which people try to hurt each other by hitting and kicking ❍ *He tried to stop the fight.*

3 VERB If you **fight** something unpleasant, you try very hard to stop it. ❍ *It is very hard to fight forest fires.*
4 VERB If you **fight for** something, you try very hard to get it. ❍ *Strikes continued for a second day as union leaders vowed to fight for better wage increases.*
5 VERB When people **fight**, they argue. [INFORMAL] ❍ *Robert's parents fight all the time.*

fig|ure /fɪgyər/ (**figures, figuring, figured**)
1 NOUN one of the symbols from 0 to 9 that you use to write numbers ❍ *They've put the figures in the wrong column.*
2 NOUN an amount expressed as a number ❍ *Can I see your latest sales figures?*
3 NOUN the shape of a person you cannot see clearly ❍ *Two figures moved behind the thin curtain.*
4 NOUN the shape of your body ❍ *Lauren has a very good figure.*
▸**figure out** If you **figure out** a solution to a problem, you succeed in solving it. [INFORMAL] ❍ *We couldn't figure out how to use the equipment.*

file /faɪl/ (**files, filing, filed**)
1 NOUN a box or a type of envelope that you keep papers in ❍ *The file contained letters and reports.*
2 NOUN a collection of information that you keep on your computer ❍ *I deleted the file by mistake.*
3 NOUN a tool that you use for rubbing rough objects to make them smooth ❍ *a nail file*
4 VERB If you **file** a document, you put it in the correct envelope. ❍ *The letters are all filed alphabetically.*
5 VERB If you **file** something, you make it smooth. ❍ *Mom was filing her nails.*
6 VERB If people **file** somewhere, they walk there in a line, one behind the other. ❍ *More than 10,000 people filed past the dead President's coffin.*
7 A group of people who are walking or standing **in single file** are in a line, one behind the other.

file|name /faɪlneɪm/ **NOUN** a name that you give to a particular computer file

file-sharing also **file sharing NONCOUNT NOUN File-sharing** is a way of sharing computer files among a large number of users.

fil|ing cabi|net (**filing cabinets**) **NOUN** a piece of office furniture that has drawers in which files are kept

fill /fɪl/
1 VERB If you **fill** a container with something, it becomes full of it. ❍ *She filled a glass with water.*
2 If a place **fills up**, it becomes full. ❍ *The theater was filling up quickly.*
3 VERB If something **fills** a space, the space is full of it. ❍ *Rows of desks filled the office.*
4 Fill up means the same as **fill**. ❍ *Filling up your car's gas tank these days is very expensive.*
5 VERB If you **fill** a hole, you put a substance into it to make the surface smooth again. ❍ *Fill the cracks between walls and window frames.*
6 Fill in means the same as **fill**. ❍ *Start by filling in any cracks.*
▸**fill in** If you **fill in** or **fill out** a form, you write information in the spaces. ❍ *When you have filled in the form, send it to your employer.*

film /fɪlm/
1 NOUN a movie ❍ *I'm going to see a film tonight.*
2 VERB If you **film** someone or something, you use a camera to take moving pictures of them. ❍ *A camera crew was filming her for French TV.*

fil|ter /fɪltər/
1 NOUN an object that only allows liquid or air to pass through it, and that holds back solid parts such as dirt or dust ❍ *a water filter*
2 VERB If you **filter** a liquid or air, you clean it by passing it through a filter. ❍ *The device cleans and filters the air.*

filthy /fɪlθi/ (**filthier, filthiest**) **ADJ** very dirty ❍ *He was wearing a filthy old jacket.*

fi|nal /faɪnᵊl/
1 ADJ used to describe the last one ❍ *There was a big rise in stocks in the final half-hour of trading.*
2 ADJ If a decision is **final**, it cannot be changed. ❍ *The judges' decision is final.*
3 NOUN the last game or race in a series, that decides who is the winner ❍ *Williams played in*

the final of the U.S. Open in 1997.

4 PL NOUN When you take your **finals** or your **final exams**, you take the last and most important exams in a class. ❍ *Anna took her finals in the summer.*

fi|nal|ist /faɪnᵊlɪst/ **NOUN** someone who reaches the final of a competition ❍ *an Olympic finalist*

fi|nal|ly /faɪnᵊli/

1 ADV after a long time ❍ *Confidence is finally returning to the saleroom, after the fallout from the financial crisis.*

2 ADV used before saying the last thing in a list ❍ *Combine the flour and the cheese, and finally, add the cream.*

fi|nance /faɪnæns, fɪnæns/ (**finances, financing, financed**)

1 VERB When someone **finances** something, they provide the money to pay for it. ❍ *They borrowed $10 million to finance the acquisition.*

2 NONCOUNT NOUN Finance is the management of large amounts of money. ❍ *She teaches finance and law at Princeton University.* ❍ *He is responsible for all European corporate finance within the company.*

3 PL NOUN Your **finances** are the money that you have. ❍ *Take control of your finances now and save thousands of dollars.*

fi|nance bill (**finance bills**) **NOUN** a proposal for a law that will provide money for the public treasury [ECONOMICS]

fi|nance com|pa|ny (**finance companies**) **NOUN** a business that lends money to people and charges them interest while they pay it back [BANKING]

fi|nan|cial /faɪnænʃᵊl, fɪn-/ **ADJ** relating to money ❍ *The company is in financial difficulties.*

fi|nan|cial ad|vis|er (**financial advisers**) **NOUN** someone whose job is to advise people or firms about financial products and services [BANKING, ADMINISTRATION] ❍ *The board will meet with financial advisers to evaluate the offer.*

fi|nan|cial con|sult|ant (**financial consultants**) **NOUN** A **financial consultant** is the same as a **financial adviser**. [BANKING, ADMINISTRATION] ❍ *A financial consultant can help you analyze your pension, mortgage, and insurance needs.*

fi|na|ncial fu|tures **PL NOUN** **Financial futures** are a contract to buy or sell a financial asset at a later date. [BANKING] ❍ *Institutions also use financial futures to guarantee the cost of funds.*

Fi|nan|cial Om|buds|man (**Financial Ombudsmen**) **NOUN** a British government official who investigates complaints about financial institutions and products [BANKING, ECONOMICS] ❍ *If you are unhappy with the response, contact the Financial Ombudsman.*

fi|nan|cial prod|uct (**financial products**) **NOUN** a product such as an investment, a pension, or a mortgage [BANKING] ❍ *This website allows consumers to compare financial products from several different companies.*

fi|nan|cial sec|tor (**financial sectors**) **NOUN** the part of a country's economy that provides financial services [ECONOMICS, BANKING] ❍ *An efficient financial sector is vital to a country's economy.*

fi|nan|cial ser|vices

> The form **financial service** is used as a modifier.

PL NOUN An organization that provides **financial services** can help you do things such as make investments or get a mortgage. [BANKING] ❍ *Many customers use the Internet to shop for financial services.* ❍ *financial service companies*

Fi|nan|cial Ser|vices Author|ity **NOUN** an organization that regulates financial markets in the United Kingdom [BANKING, ECONOMICS] ❍ *The Financial Services Authority is investigating the share collapse.*

fi|nan|cial ser|vices pro|vider (**financial services providers**) **NOUN** a firm or organization that offers financial services [BANKING] ❍ *It is one of the fastest-growing financial services providers in the country.*

Fi|nan|cial Times In|dus|trial Or|di|nary Share In|dex **NOUN** an index of share prices based on the average price of thirty British shares [ECONOMICS]

Fi|nan|cial Times Stock Ex|change 100 In|dex NOUN an index of share prices based on the average price of 100 British shares [ECONOMICS]

fi|nan|cial year (**financial years**) [FINANCE, BRIT] → **fiscal year**

fi|nan|ci|er /fɪnənsɪər, faɪn-/ NOUN a person or organization that provides money for projects or businesses [BANKING, ADMINISTRATION] ❍ *The film company is controlled by Italian financier Giancarlo Parretti.*

fi|nan|cing /fɪnænsɪŋ, faɪnæn-/ NONCOUNT NOUN **Financing** is the money that is needed for a venture or loan, and the way in which this money is provided. [BANKING] ❍ *Salesmen can arrange financing for home improvement loans.*

find /faɪnd/ (**finds, finding, found**)
1 VERB If you **find** something or someone, you see them after looking for them. ❍ *Did you find that document you were looking for?*
2 VERB If you **find** something that you want, you succeed in getting it. ❍ *David has finally found a job.*
3 VERB When a court **finds** someone guilty or not guilty, it says that they are guilty or not guilty of a crime. ❍ *He was found guilty of conspiring to defraud the government.*
4 VERB If you **find** something or someone boring, interesting, funny, etc. you think they are boring, interesting, funny, etc. ❍ *I found the work quite interesting.*
▸ **find out** If you **find** something **out**, you discover something. ❍ *Make sure you find out about the training available.*

fine /faɪn/ (**fines, fining, fined, finer, finest**)
1 ADJ very good ❍ *She's one of our finest actresses.*
2 ADJ well or happy ❍ *Lina is fine and sends you her love.*
3 ADJ satisfactory or acceptable ❍ *My hotel is fine.*
4 ADJ very thin ❍ *fine hairs*
5 ADJ When the weather is **fine**, the sun is shining and it is not raining.
6 NOUN money that someone has to pay because they have done something wrong
7 VERB If someone **is fined**, they have to pay some money because they have done something wrong. ❍ *Each airline was fined $2,000.*

fin|ger /fɪŋgər/
1 NOUN one of the long thin parts at the end of each hand with which you hold things ❍ *Amber had a huge diamond ring on her finger.*
2 If you **cross** your **fingers**, you put one finger on top of another and hope for good luck.

finger|nail /fɪŋgərneɪl/ NOUN one of the thin hard parts at the end of each of your fingers

finger|print /fɪŋgərprɪnt/ NOUN a mark that your finger makes when it touches something ❍ *His fingerprints were found on the gun.*

finger|tip /fɪŋgərtɪp/ also **finger-tip** NOUN the end of your finger

fin|ish /fɪnɪʃ/ (**finishes, finishing, finished**)
1 VERB When you **finish** doing something, you stop doing it. ❍ *He finished writing the report.*
2 Finish up means the same as **finish**. ❍ *We waited outside while Nick finished up his meeting.*
3 VERB When something **finishes**, it ends. ❍ *The talk finished at 4 o'clock.*
4 NOUN the end of something or the last part of it ❍ *There was an exciting finish to the women's 800-meter race.*

fin|ished /fɪnɪʃt/ ADJ If you are **finished with** something, you are no longer using it. ❍ *Could I borrow your book when you're finished with it?*

fin|ished goods PL NOUN **Finished goods** are goods that have completed the manufacturing process. [PRODUCTION] ❍ *Countries that mainly export raw materials are poorer, while countries that convert them into finished goods are richer.*

fire /faɪər/ (**fires, firing, fired**)
1 NONCOUNT NOUN **Fire** is the flames produced when something burns. ❍ *We learned how to make fire and hunt for fish.*
2 NOUN **Fire** or **a fire** is flames that destroy buildings or forests. ❍ *87 people died in a fire at the factory.* ❍ *a forest fire*
3 NOUN a burning pile of wood or coal that you make ❍ *There was a fire in the fireplace.*

4 VERB If someone **fires** a gun or a bullet, they shoot it. ❍ *Have you ever fired a gun before?*
5 VERB If an employer **fires** you, he or she tells you to leave your job. [HR] ❍ *She was fired from her job in August.*
6 If something **catches fire**, it starts burning. ❍ *Several buildings caught fire in the explosion.*
7 If something is **on fire**, it is burning and being damaged by a fire. ❍ *Quick! My car's on fire!*
8 If you **set fire to** something or if you **set** it **on fire**, you make it start to burn.

F

fire alarm (**fire alarms**) **NOUN** a piece of equipment that makes a loud noise to warn people when there is a fire

fire en|gine (**fire engines**) **NOUN** a large vehicle that carries people and equipment for putting out fires

fire ex|tin|guish|er /faɪər ɪkstɪŋgwɪʃər/ (**fire extinguishers**) **NOUN** a metal container with water or chemicals inside for stopping fires

fire|fight|er /faɪərfaɪtər/ **NOUN** a person whose job is to stop fires

fire|fighting /faɪərfaɪtɪŋ/
1 NONCOUNT NOUN Firefighting is the work of putting out fires. ❍ *There was no firefighting equipment.*
2 NONCOUNT NOUN Firefighting is the practice of dealing with problems immediately, rather than planning for the future. ❍ *We need to change emphasis from firefighting to working out how the company should be restructured.*

fire in|sur|ance NONCOUNT NOUN Fire insurance is insurance that pays money if your possessions are destroyed or damaged in a fire. [FINANCE] ❍ *Most homeowners have fire insurance.*

fire|place /faɪərpleɪs/ **NOUN** in a room, a place made out of brick or stone where you can light a fire

fire sale (**fire sales**)
1 NOUN an event in which goods are sold cheaply because the place they were stored in was damaged by fire [MARKETING AND SALES]
2 NOUN any sale in which everything is sold very cheaply [MARKETING AND SALES] ❍ *They're likely to hold big fire sales to liquidate their inventory.*

fire|work /faɪərwɜrk/ **NOUN** a small object that flies up into the air and explodes, making bright colors in the sky ❍ *We watched the fireworks from the balcony.*

firm /fɜrm/
1 NOUN a company ❍ *Kevin works for a Chicago law firm.*
2 ADJ quite hard, not changing shape when pressed ❍ *a firm mattress*
3 ADJ A **firm** physical action is strong and controlled. ❍ *a firm handshake* • **firm|ly ADV** ❍ *She held me firmly by the elbow.*
4 ADJ A **firm** person is confident when telling people what to do and does not let other people change their mind. ❍ *She was firm with him. "The report is due Wednesday at the latest."* • **firm|ly ADV** ❍ *They firmly rejected the proposal.*
5 ADJ If prices or markets are **firm**, they are rising. ❍ *Banking shares rose sharply Monday, and auto shares were also firm.*

first /fɜrst/
1 ADJ or **ADV** happening, coming, or done before all others of the same type ❍ *the first week of June* ❍ *Aaron came first in the junior competition.* ❍ *Camille arrived first.*
2 ADV before doing anything else ❍ *First I emailed the Spanish office.*
3 You use **first of all** to introduce the first thing that you want to say. ❍ *First of all, I'd like to thank you for coming.*
4 You use **at first** when you are talking about what happened at the beginning of an event. ❍ *At first, he seemed surprised.*

first aid NONCOUNT NOUN First aid is simple medical treatment that you give to a sick or injured person. ❍ *Each group leader does a course in basic first aid.*

first-class also **first class**
1 ADJ of the highest quality ❍ *The service was first class.*
2 ADJ used to describe the most expensive seats on a train or airplane ❍ *He won two first-class tickets to fly to Dublin.*
3 ADV First class is also an adverb. ❍ *The company directors always travel first-class.*

4 ADJ used to describe the quickest and most expensive form of mail ❍ *a first-class letter*

first mort|gage (**first mortgages**) **NOUN** A **first mortgage** is a mortgage that must be paid before any other mortgages on the same property. Compare with **second mortgage**. [BANKING] ❍ *Most loans are first mortgages to owners of single homes.*

first name (**first names**) **NOUN** the name that comes before a family name ❍ *"What's Dr. Garcia's first name?"—"It's Maria. Maria Garcia."*

First World **NONCOUNT NOUN** The richest and most industrialized parts of the world are sometimes called **the First World**. Compare with **Third World**. [ECONOMICS] ❍ *South Africa has many of the attributes of the First World.*

fis|cal year (**fiscal years**) **NOUN** a period of twelve months, used by organizations in order to calculate their budgets, profits, and losses [FINANCE, ECONOMICS] ❍ *the budget for the coming fiscal year*

fish /fɪʃ/ (**fish** or **fishes, fishes, fishing, fished**)
1 NOUN an animal that lives and swims in water and that people eat as food ❍ *He caught a 3-pound fish.* ❍ *This fish is delicious.*
2 VERB If you **fish**, you try to catch fish. ❍ *Brian learned to fish in the Colorado River.*

fisher|man /fɪʃərmən/ (**fishermen**) **NOUN** a person who catches fish as a job or for sport

fish|ing /fɪʃɪŋ/ **NONCOUNT NOUN** **Fishing** is the sport or business of catching fish.

fist /fɪst/ **NOUN** a hand with the fingers closed tightly together ❍ *He shook his fist at Patrick.*

fit

❶ BEING RIGHT OR GOING IN THE RIGHT PLACE
❷ HEALTHY
❸ UNCONTROLLABLE MOVEMENTS

❶ **fit** /fɪt/ (**fits, fitting, fitted** or **fit**)
1 VERB If something **fits**, it is the right shape or size for someone or something. ❍ *Did the jacket fit?* ❍ *The game is small enough to fit into your pocket.*
2 VERB If you **fit** a piece of equipment somewhere, you attach it to something. ❍ *You need to fit a lock on that door.*
3 ADJ good enough or suitable for a particular purpose ❍ *All goods sold by a business must be fit for sale.*
▸ **fit in** If you **fit** someone or something **in**, you manage to find time or space for them. ❍ *I can probably fit in a client just after lunch.* ❍ *We can't fit anyone else in the taxi.*

❷ **fit** /fɪt/ (**fitter, fittest**) **ADJ** healthy and strong ❍ *He's very fit—he jogs every morning.*

❸ **fit** /fɪt/
1 NOUN A **fit of** coughing or laughter is when you suddenly start coughing or laughing. ❍ *I had a fit of coughing in the middle of the presentation.*
2 NOUN If someone has a **fit** they suddenly become unconscious and their body makes violent movements.

fit|ness /fɪtnɪs/ **NONCOUNT NOUN** the state of being healthy, strong, and able to do physical exercise ❍ *a fitness instructor*

five /faɪv/ the number 5

five-spot (**five-spots**) **NOUN** a five-dollar bill [ECONOMICS, INFORMAL] ❍ *This beer is well worth a hard-earned five-spot.*

fix /fɪks/ (**fixes, fixing, fixed**)
1 VERB If you **fix** something, you repair it. ❍ *A man came to fix the photocopier.*
2 VERB If you **fix** a meal, you prepare it. ❍ *Everyone helped to fix dinner.*
3 VERB If you say that someone **fixes** prices, you accuse them of unfairly charging a particular price for something. ❍ *Several supermarkets were charged with fixing milk prices and had to pay fines of $116m.*

fixed as|sets **PL NOUN** **Fixed assets** are a firm's permanent assets, such as buildings, equipment, and technology. [FINANCE] ❍ *There has been a drop in spending on fixed assets such as software.*

fixed charge (**fixed charges**)
1 NOUN an expense that is paid regularly, such as rent [FINANCE] ❍ *The company's earnings were*

insufficient to cover its fixed charges.
2 NOUN a legal charge on specific assets of a property [FINANCE]

fixed costs **PL NOUN** In accounting, **fixed costs** are costs that do not vary depending on how much of a product is made. Compare with **variable costs**. [FINANCE]

flag /flæg/ **NOUN** a piece of colored cloth with a pattern on it that is used as a symbol for a country or an organization ○ *The crowd was shouting and waving American flags.*

F

flag|ship /flægʃɪp/ **NOUN** the most important thing in a group of things that a firm owns or produces ○ *The company plans to open a flagship store in New York this month.*

flag|ship brand (**flagship brands**) **NOUN** the brand that a firm considers most important [MARKETING AND SALES] ○ *They make the company's flagship brands, including Pepsi and 7UP.*

flair /flɛər/
1 NOUN If you have **a flair for** something, you have a natural ability to do it well. ○ *He showed a flair for business.*
2 NONCOUNT NOUN If you have **flair**, you do things in an original, interesting, and stylish way. ○ *They need to inject new management flair into the business.*

flake /fleɪk/ (**flakes, flaking, flaked**)
1 NOUN a small thin piece of something ○ *Large flakes of snow began to fall.*
2 VERB If paint **flakes** or **flakes off**, small thin pieces of it come off.

flame /fleɪm/
1 NOUN a hot, bright stream of gas that comes from something that is burning ○ *The flames almost burned her fingers.*
2 If something **bursts into flames**, it suddenly starts burning strongly. ○ *The plane crashed and burst into flames.*
3 Something that is **in flames** is burning. ○ *The whole building was in flames.*

flap /flæp/ (**flaps, flapping, flapped**)
1 VERB If something **flaps**, it moves quickly up and down or from side to side. ○ *Sheets flapped on the clothes line.*
2 VERB If a bird **flaps** its wings, it moves its wings up and down quickly. ○ *The birds flapped their wings and flew across the lake.*
3 NOUN a flat piece of something that can move up and down or from side to side ○ *I opened the flap of the envelope and took out the letter.*

flash /flæʃ/ (**flashes, flashing, flashed**)
1 NOUN a sudden bright light ○ *There was a flash of lightning.*
2 VERB If a light **flashes**, it shines on and off very quickly. ○ *They could see a lighthouse flashing through the fog.*

flash drive (**flash drives**) **NOUN** a small object for storing computer information that you can carry with you and use in different computers [TECHNOLOGY]

flash|light /flæʃlaɪt/ **NOUN** a small electric light that you can carry in your hand ○ *Adam shone a flashlight into the backyard but he couldn't see anyone.*

flat /flæt/ (**flatter, flattest**)
1 ADJ level or smooth ○ *Tiles can be fixed to any flat surface.* ○ *a flat roof*
2 ADJ A **flat** tire or ball does not have enough air in it.
3 ADJ A B **flat** or an E **flat**, for example, is a note that is slightly lower than B or E. Compare with **sharp**.
4 ADJ If the structure of a firm is **flat**, there are few different ranks and most employees have a similar status. ○ *The management structure is flat rather than hierarchical, and everyone has an important role to play.*

flat|ter /flætər/ **VERB** If you **flatter** someone, you say nice things to them because you want them to like you. ○ *Everyone likes to be flattered, to be told that they're clever.*

fla|vor /fleɪvər/
1 NOUN the taste of a food or drink ○ *I added some pepper for extra flavor.*
2 VERB If you **flavor** food or drink, you add something to it to give it a particular taste. ○ *strawberry-flavored candies*

fla|vour /fleɪvər/ [BRIT] → **flavor**

flaw /flɔ/ **NOUN** a mistake in a theory or argument ○ *There are a number of flaws in his theory.*

flee /fli/ (**flees, fleeing, fled**) VERB If you **flee from** something or someone, you run away from them. [FORMAL] ❍ *He slammed the door behind him and fled.*

fleece /flis/
1 NOUN the wool that covers a sheep
2 NOUN a jacket or a sweater made from a soft warm cloth ❍ *He was wearing track pants and a dark blue fleece.*

fleet /flit/ NOUN a large group of boats, aircraft, or cars ❍ *a fleet of ships*

flesh /flɛʃ/
1 NONCOUNT NOUN **Flesh** is the soft part of your body that is between your bones and your skin. ❍ *The bullet went straight through the flesh of his arm.*
2 NONCOUNT NOUN The **flesh** of a fruit or a vegetable is the soft part that is inside it.

flew /flu/ **Flew** is a form of the verb **fly**.

flex|ible /flɛksɪbᵊl/
1 ADJ bending easily without breaking ❍ *These children's books have flexible plastic covers.*
2 ADJ able to change easily for different situations ❍ *I'm very lucky to have flexible working hours.* ❍ *These flexible production lines can make whichever versions of our products are selling best.* ● **flexi|bil|ity** NONCOUNT NOUN ❍ *Working for myself gives me greater flexibility.*

COLLOCATIONS
flexible *working arrangements*
flexible *working hours*
flexible *working practices*
flexible *hours*
flexible *work schedule*

flex|ible wor|king pat|terns PL NOUN **Flexible working patterns** are arrangements in which employees are allowed to vary the hours that they work. [HR, mainly BRIT]

flexi|time /flɛksitaɪm/ [HR, mainly BRIT] → **flextime**

flex|time /flɛkstaɪm/ NONCOUNT NOUN **Flextime** is a system that allows employees to vary the time that they start or finish work. [HR] ❍ *They promote family-friendly policies such as job-sharing and flextime.* ❍ *The company has a 6am to 8pm flextime arrangement, where employees may select any eight-hour period during those hours to go to work.*

flight /flaɪt/
1 NOUN a trip in an aircraft ❍ *Our flight was two hours late.*
2 NOUN A **flight of** stairs is a set of stairs that go from one level to another. ❍ *You have to walk up a short flight of steps to get to the office.*
3 NONCOUNT NOUN **Flight** is the action of flying. ❍ *The photograph showed an eagle in flight.*

flight at|tend|ant (**flight attendants**) NOUN someone whose job is to take care of passengers on an airplane

flight of capi|tal NONCOUNT NOUN **Flight of capital** is when people lose confidence in a particular economy or market, and start to remove their money from it. [BANKING, ECONOMICS] ❍ *TI has seen its shares suffer because of a flight of capital to Internet-related businesses.*

flip /flɪp/ (**flips, flipping, flipped**)
1 VERB If you **flip** through the pages of a book, you turn the pages quickly. ❍ *He was sitting at his desk, flipping through a catalog.*
2 VERB If something **flips** over, it turns over quickly so that it is on its other side. ❍ *The car flipped over and burst into flames.*

flip chart (**flip charts**) NOUN a stand with large sheets of paper which is used when presenting information at a meeting ❍ *Each conference room is equipped with a screen, flipchart, and audio visual equipment.*

flirt /flɜrt/
1 VERB If you **flirt**, you behave toward someone in a way that shows that you think they are attractive. ❍ *My brother was flirting with all the girls.*
2 NOUN someone who flirts a lot

float /floʊt/
1 VERB If something **floats**, it stays on the surface of a liquid, and does not sink. ❍ *A plastic bottle was floating in the water.*
2 VERB If something **floats** in the air, it moves

slowly and gently through it. ❍ *A yellow balloon floated past.*
3 NOUN an object that stays on the surface of the water and supports your body while you are learning to swim
4 VERB If you **float** a firm, you sell shares in it to the public. [FINANCE] ❍ *He floated his firm on the stock market.*
5 NOUN **Float** is also a noun. ❍ *They reported a successful float of 20% of the company last month.*
6 VERB If a government **floats** its country's currency or allows it to **float**, it allows the currency's value to change freely in relation to other currencies. [ECONOMICS] ❍ *59 percent of people believed the pound should be allowed to float freely.*
7 NOUN **Float** is also a noun. ❍ *The float of the rupee is the right policy.*
8 NOUN a sum of money that is used for small expenses [BUSINESS MANAGEMENT] ❍ *The store was carrying a larger float of cash than usual.*
▶ **float off** If a firm **floats off** shares in a subsidiary firm, it sells them separately from the main firm. [FINANCE] ❍ *The group plans to raise money by floating off part of its market-research business.*

flood /flʌd/
1 NOUN an occasion when a lot of water covers land that is usually dry ❍ *More than 70 people died in the floods.*
2 VERB If water **floods** an area, the area becomes covered with water. ❍ *The water tank burst and flooded the building.* ● **flood|ing** NONCOUNT NOUN ❍ *This is the worst flooding in sixty-five years.*

floor /flɔr/
1 NOUN the part of a room that you walk on ❍ *There were no seats, so we sat on the floor.*
2 NOUN one of the levels of a building ❍ *Their offices are on the seventh floor.*
3 NOUN the room in a stock exchange where trading takes place [FINANCE] ❍ *The Chicago Mercantile Exchange restricted most reporters' access to its trading floor that day.*
4 NOUN a minimum price charged or paid ❍ *a wage floor*

floor trad|ing NONCOUNT NOUN **Floor trading** is trading by personal contact on the floor of a market. Compare with **electronic trading**. [FINANCE] ❍ *Some exchanges have added electronic trading systems to supplement floor trading.*

floor|walker /flɔrwɔkər/ NOUN a person whose job is to supervise staff and assist customers in a department store [MARKETING AND SALES]

flop|py /flɒpi/ ADJ loose and tending to hang downward ❍ *the girl with the floppy hat and glasses*

flop|py disk (**floppy disks**) NOUN a small plastic computer disk that is used for storing information

flo|ta|tion /floʊteɪʃən/ NOUN the selling of shares in a firm to the public [ADMINISTRATION, FINANCE] ❍ *Prudential's flotation will be the third largest this year.*

flour /flaʊər/ NONCOUNT NOUN **Flour** is a fine powder that is used for making bread, cakes, and pastry.

flow /floʊ/
1 VERB If something **flows** somewhere, it moves there in a steady and continuous way. ❍ *A stream flowed gently down into the valley.*
2 NONCOUNT NOUN A **flow** is a steady, continuous movement in a particular direction. ❍ *the flow of blood around the body* ❍ *The new tunnel will speed up traffic flow.*

flow|er /flaʊər/
1 NOUN the brightly colored part of a plant ❍ *a bunch of flowers*
2 VERB When a plant or a tree **flowers**, its flowers appear. ❍ *They flower in spring.*

flown /floʊn/ **Flown** is a form of the verb **fly**.

flow pro|duc|tion NONCOUNT NOUN In **flow production**, a very large number of goods are produced on a production line. Compare with **batch production** and **job production**. [PRODUCTION]

flu /flu/ NONCOUNT NOUN **Flu** is an illness that is like a very bad cold. **Flu** is short for "influenza."

fluc|tu|ate /flʌktʃueɪt/ (**fluctuates, fluctuating, fluctuated**) VERB If something **fluctuates**, it changes repeatedly, in a way that is not regular. ❍ *In the past, airline profits have fluctuated wildly.* ● **fluc|tua|tion** /flʌktʃueɪʃən/ **NOUN** ❍ *Currency fluctuations and inflation also drove up the cost of materials.*

flu|ent /fluənt/ **ADJ** If you are **fluent in** a particular language, you can speak it easily and correctly. ❍ *Jose is fluent in Spanish and English.* ● **flu|ent|ly ADV** ❍ *He spoke three languages fluently.*

flu|id /fluɪd/ **NOUN** a liquid [FORMAL] ❍ *Make sure that you drink plenty of fluids.*

flush /flʌʃ/ (**flushes, flushing, flushed**)
1 VERB If you **flush**, your face becomes red because you are hot, embarrassed, or angry. ❍ *Amanda flushed with embarrassment.*
2 VERB If you **flush** a toilet, you clean it by making water pass through it.

fly /flaɪ/ (**flies, flying, flew, flown**)
1 NOUN a small insect with two wings
2 VERB When something **flies**, it moves through the air. ❍ *The planes flew through the clouds.* ❍ *The bird flew away.*
3 VERB If you **fly** somewhere, you travel there in an aircraft. ❍ *Jerry flew to Los Angeles this morning.*
4 VERB When someone **flies** an aircraft, they make it move through the air. ❍ *He flew a small plane to Cuba.* ❍ *I learned to fly in Vietnam.*

FMCG /ɛf ɛm si dʒi/ **NOUN FMCGs** are inexpensive products that people buy regularly, such as food and toiletries. **FMCG** is an abbreviation of "fast-moving consumer goods." [ECONOMICS] ❍ *FMCG spending is continuing to grow.*

foam /foʊm/ **NONCOUNT NOUN Foam** is a mass of small bubbles on the surface of a liquid. ❍ *He drank his cappuccino, and wiped the foam off his mustache.*

f.o.b. /ɛf oʊ bi/ also **FOB f.o.b. is an abbreviation of free on board**. [LOGISTICS AND DISTRIBUTION]

fo|cus /foʊkəs/ (**focuses, focusing, focused**)
1 VERB If you **focus on** something, you give all your attention to it. ❍ *These hearings have focused on specific instances of bad judgment and possible criminal wrongdoing.*
2 VERB If you **focus** a camera, you make changes to it so that you can see clearly through it.
3 NOUN The focus of something is the thing that receives most attention. ❍ *Suddenly, media departments are the focus of attention.*

fo|cus group (**focus groups**) **NOUN** a group of people who give their opinions about products as a form of market research [MARKETING AND SALES] ❍ *The market research company BMRB conducted 12 focus groups for the project.*

fog /fɒg/ **NONCOUNT NOUN Fog** is thick cloud that is close to the ground. ❍ *The car crash happened in thick fog.*

foil /fɔɪl/ **NONCOUNT NOUN Foil** is very thin metal sheets that you use for wrapping food in. ❍ *Cover the turkey with foil and cook it for another 20 minutes.*

fold /foʊld/
1 VERB If you **fold** a piece of paper or cloth, you bend it so that one part covers another part. ❍ *I folded the memos and put them in my desk.*
2 VERB If a piece of furniture **folds**, you can make it smaller by bending parts of it. ❍ *The car has folding rear seats.*
3 Fold up means the same as **fold**. ❍ *When you don't need to use it, the table folds up.*
4 VERB When you **fold** your arms, you put one arm under the other and hold them over your chest.
5 NOUN a line in a piece of paper or cloth that you make by folding ❍ *Make another fold down the middle of the paper.*
6 VERB If a business or organization **folds**, it is unsuccessful and has to close. [BUSINESS MANAGEMENT] ❍ *2,500 small businesses were folding each week.*

fold|er /foʊldər/
1 NOUN a folded piece of cardboard or plastic that you keep papers in
2 NOUN a group of files that are stored together on a computer

folk /foʊk/

Folk can also be the plural for meaning **1**.

1 PL NOUN Folk or **folks** are people. ❍ *Most folks around here think she's a bit crazy.*

f

2 PL NOUN Your **folks** are your mother and father. [INFORMAL] ❍ *I'll introduce you to my folks.*
3 ADJ **Folk** art and music are traditional and belong to a particular group of people. ❍ *traditional folk music*

fol|low /fɒloʊ/
1 VERB If you **follow** someone, you move along behind them. ❍ *We followed him down a long corridor.*
2 VERB If you **follow** a route or sign, you go somewhere using that route or sign to direct you. ❍ *All we had to do was follow the road.*
3 VERB If you **follow** an instruction or advice, you do what the instruction or advice says. ❍ *Follow the instructions carefully.*
4 VERB If you **follow** an explanation or a movie, you understand it. ❍ *Did you follow what he was saying?*
5 You use **as follows** to introduce a list or an explanation. ❍ *The winners are as follows: E. Walker; R. Foster; R. Gates.*

fol|low|ing /fɒloʊɪŋ/ **ADJ** next ❍ *The announcement nudged the Nikkei up a fraction the following day.*

fond /fɒnd/ **(fonder, fondest) ADJ** If you are **fond of** someone or something, you like them very much. ❍ *I'm very fond of Michael.*

food /fud/ **NONCOUNT NOUN** **Food** is what people and animals eat. ❍ *We had really good food.*

food mile **(food miles) NOUN** a measure of the distance that food travels from where it is produced to where it is sold [PRODUCTION] ❍ *We must reduce food miles and increase home production.*

fool /ful/
1 NOUN a stupid person ❍ *I didn't understand anything and felt like a fool.*
2 VERB If you **fool** someone, you make them believe something that is not true. ❍ *Harris fooled people into believing she was a doctor.*
▸ **fool around** If you **fool around**, you behave in a silly way. ❍ *They fool around and get into trouble at school.*

fool|ish /fulɪʃ/ **ADJ** stupid or silly ❍ *It would be foolish to ignore the risks.* ● **fool|ish|ly ADV** ❍ *He knows that he acted foolishly.*

foot /fʊt/ **(feet)**
1 NOUN one of the parts of your body that are at the ends of your legs, and that you stand on ❍ *We danced until our feet were sore.*
2 NOUN A **foot** is a unit for measuring length. A foot is equal to 30.48 centimeters and there are 12 inches in a foot. The plural form is **feet** or **foot**. ❍ *We were six thousand feet above sea level.*
3 NOUN **The foot of** something is the part that is farthest from its top. ❍ *He was waiting at the foot of the stairs.*
4 If you go somewhere **on foot**, you walk there. ❍ *We explored the island on foot.*
5 If you **put** your **feet up**, you have a rest. ❍ *I'll do the chores - you go and put your feet up.*

foot|ball /fʊtbɔl/
1 NONCOUNT NOUN **Football** is a game for two teams of eleven players, in which the teams win points by kicking, carrying, or throwing a ball into an area at the end of the field. ❍ *Paul loves playing football.*
2 NOUN a ball that is used for playing football

foot|print /fʊtprɪnt/ **NOUN** a mark that a foot makes on the ground

Foot|sie /fʊtsi/ **NOUN** The **Footsie** is an informal name for the **Financial Times Stock Exchange 100 Index**. [ECONOMICS]

foot|step /fʊtstɛp/ **NOUN** the sound that you make each time your foot touches the ground when you walk ❍ *I heard footsteps outside.*

foot traf|fic **NONCOUNT NOUN** **Foot traffic** is the activity of pedestrians in a particular area. ❍ *Malls are great locations for gift shops because they generate heavy foot traffic.*

for /fər, STRONG fɔr/
1 PREP used for saying who something is to be given to ❍ *I've got that report for you.* ❍ *The book is for Justine.*
2 PREP used for saying who employs you ❍ *He works for a bank.*
3 PREP in order to help ❍ *I held the door open for the next person.*
4 PREP used for saying what meaning a word represents ❍ *In French, the word for "love" is "amour."*
5 PREP used for saying the purpose of

something ❍ *There are no standardized machines for making brake-linings.*

6 PREP used for saying where a public vehicle goes ❍ *They took the train for Rio early the next morning.*

7 PREP used for saying how long something lasts or how far something goes ❍ *We talked for over an hour.* ❍ *We continued to drive for a few miles.*

8 PREP used for saying the price of something ❍ *Quaker sold the company for $300 million to Triarc Companies.*

9 PREP agreeing with someone or supporting them ❍ *Are you for us or against us?*

10 PREP used for saying which team you are in ❍ *Kristy plays hockey for the high-school team.*

f.o.r. /ɛf oʊ ɑr/ also **FOR** **ADJ** If goods are **f.o.r.**, they are delivered and loaded onto a train without charge to the buyer. **f.o.r.** is an abbreviation of "free on rail." [LOGISTICS AND DISTRIBUTION]

for|bid /fərbɪd, fɔr-/ (**forbids, forbidding, forbade, forbidden**) **VERB** If you **forbid** someone **to** do something, you tell them that they must not do it. ❍ *My boss has forbidden me to travel.*

for|bid|den /fərbɪdᵊn, fɔr-/ **ADJ** not allowed ❍ *Smoking is forbidden here.*

force /fɔrs/ (**forces, forcing, forced**)

1 VERB If someone **forces** you **to** do something, they make you do it when you do not want to. ❍ *He was forced to leave the company.*

2 VERB If someone **forces** a lock or a door, they break the lock in order to enter. ❍ *Police forced the door of the apartment and arrested him.*

3 NONCOUNT NOUN If someone uses **force** to do something, they use their strength to do it. ❍ *Police used force to break up the fight.*

4 NONCOUNT NOUN **Force** is the power or strength that something has. ❍ *The force of the explosion destroyed the building.*

5 NOUN a group of people, for example soldiers or police officers, that does a particular job ❍ *Russian forces entered the region in 1994.*

6 If you **join forces with** someone, you work together in order to achieve something. ❍ *William joined forces with businessman Nicholas Court to launch the new vehicle.*

fore|cast /fɔrkæst/ (**forecasts, forecasting, forecast, forecasted**)

1 NOUN something that someone expects will happen in the future [BUSINESS MANAGEMENT] ❍ *the weather forecast* ❍ *Industry forecasts suggest that by 2020 about 10% of new cars will be electric.*

2 VERB If you **forecast** something, you say it will happen in the future. [BUSINESS MANAGEMENT] ❍ *Economists were forecasting higher oil prices.*

fore|close /fɔrkloʊz/ (**forecloses, foreclosing, foreclosed**) **VERB** If a lender **forecloses**, they take a person's property because that person did not pay back the money they borrowed to buy it. [ECONOMICS] ❍ *The bank foreclosed on the mortgage for his previous home.*

fore|clo|sure /fɔrkloʊʒər/ **NOUN** an occasion when a lender takes a person's property because that person did not pay back the money they borrowed to buy it [ECONOMICS] ❍ *If homeowners can't keep up the payments, they face foreclosure.*

fore|ground /fɔrgraʊnd/ **NOUN** **The foreground** of a picture is the part that seems nearest to you. Compare with **background**. ❍ *There are five people and a dog in the foreground of the painting.*

fore|head /fɒrhɛd, fɔrɪd/ **NOUN** the part of your face between your eyebrows and your hair

for|eign /fɔrɪn/ **ADJ** coming from a country that is not your own ❍ *Foreign companies operating in the region have been quick to see this potential.*

for|eign bill (**foreign bills**) or **foreign draft** **NOUN** a bill of exchange that is drawn in one country and made payable in another country [BANKING]

for|eign|er /fɔrɪnər/ **NOUN** someone who comes from a different country

for|eign ex|change

1 PL NOUN **Foreign exchanges** are the

institutions or systems involved with changing one currency into another. [BANKING] ❍ *On the foreign exchanges, the U.S. dollar is up point forty-five.*
2 NONCOUNT NOUN Foreign exchange is foreign currency that is obtained through the foreign exchange system. [BANKING] ❍ *an important source of foreign exchange*

fore|man /fɔ̲rmən/ (**foremen**) **NOUN** a person who is in charge of a group of workers [BUSINESS MANAGEMENT, ADMINISTRATION] ❍ *The foreman assigned duties on the assembly line.*

F

fo|ren|sic ac|count|ant /fərɛ̲nsɪk əka̲ʊntənt/ (**forensic accountants**) **NOUN** an accountant whose work relates to the law [FINANCE, ADMINISTRATION]

for|est /fɔ̲rɪst/ **NOUN** a large area where trees grow close together ❍ *a forest fire*

fore|stall /fɔrstɔ̲l/
1 VERB If you **forestall** something, you do something in order to prevent it from happening. ❍ *Governments must step in to forestall a financial collapse.*
2 VERB If you **forestall** goods or a market, you prevent sales by buying goods in advance.

for|ever /fɔrɛ̲vər, fər-/ **ADV** for all the time that is to come ❍ *I won't work here forever.*

forex /fɒ̲rɛks/ **Forex** is an abbreviation of **foreign exchange**. [BANKING, ECONOMICS] ❍ *the forex market*

for|get /fərgɛ̲t/ (**forgets, forgetting, forgot, forgotten**)
1 VERB If you **forget** something, you cannot remember it. ❍ *She forgot where she left the car.* ❍ *I forgot her name.*
2 VERB If you **forget to do** something, you do not remember to do it. ❍ *I forgot to copy Paul in on the email.*

for|give /fərgɪ̲v/ (**forgives, forgiving, forgave, forgiven**) **VERB** If you **forgive** someone who has done something bad to you, you stop being angry with them. ❍ *Eventually I forgave them for not giving me the job.*

for|got /fərgɒ̲t/ **Forgot** is a form of the verb **forget**.

for|got|ten /fərgɒ̲tᵊn/ **Forgotten** is a form of the verb **forget**.

fork /fɔ̲rk/ **NOUN** a tool with long metal points, used for eating food ❍ *a knife and fork*

form /fɔ̲rm/
1 NOUN A **form of** something is a type of it. ❍ *She has a rare form of the disease.*
2 NOUN The **form** of something is its shape. ❍ *The dress fits the form of the body exactly.*
3 NOUN a piece of paper with questions on it and spaces where you write the answers ❍ *Please fill in this form and sign it at the bottom.*
4 VERB When a group of people **form** a particular shape, they make that shape. ❍ *She asked us to form a circle.*
5 VERB Things or people **form** something when they are all parts of it. ❍ *These articles formed the basis of Randolph's book.*
6 VERB If you **form** an organization, you start it. ❍ *The league was formed in 1959.*
7 NOUN In grammar, the **form** of a noun or a verb is the way that it is spelled or spoken when it is used to talk about the plural, the past, or the present, for example.

for|mal /fɔ̲rmᵊl/ **ADJ** correct and serious rather than relaxed or friendly ❍ *We received a formal letter of apology from the company director.* ❍ *formal language* ● **for|mal|ly ADV** ❍ *He dresses more formally for work.* ● **for|mal|ity NONCOUNT NOUN** ❍ *A certain level of formality is appropriate at work.*

for|mat /fɔ̲rmæt/ (**formats, formatting, formatted**)
1 NOUN the way in which the text is arranged in a computer document ❍ *I changed the format of the document from two columns to three.*
2 VERB You **format** a document when you arrange the design of its text.

for|ma|tion /fɔrme̲ɪʃən/ **NONCOUNT NOUN** **The formation of** something is the beginning of its existence. ❍ *The vitamin is essential for the formation of red blood cells.*

for|mer /fɔ̲rmər/
1 ADJ used for showing what someone or something was in the past ❍ *Alan Greenspan, the former chairman of America's Federal Reserve*
2 PRON the first of two people or things that

you have just mentioned ❍ *Both women attended the conference—the former in her capacity as spokesperson for the organization.*

for|mer|ly /fo̲rmərli/ **ADV** in the past ❍ *Reece was formerly a group vice president.*

for|mu|la /fo̲rmyələ/ (**formulae** /fo̲rmyəli/ or **formulas**)
1 NOUN a group of letters, numbers, or other symbols that represents a scientific rule ❍ *This mathematical formula describes the distances of the planets from the Sun.*
2 NOUN a description of the chemical elements that a substance contains ❍ *Glucose and fructose have the same chemical formula.*

BUSINESS ETIQUETTE
In Japan, people around a table pour each other's drinks, so it is important to pay attention to the glass of the person sitting next to you. When their glass is nearly empty, you should top it up for them.

fort /fo̲rt/ **NOUN** a strong building that is used as a military base

for|ti|eth /fo̲rtiəθ/ **ADJ** or **ADV** The **fortieth** item in a series is the one that you count as number forty. ❍ *her fortieth birthday*

fort|night /fo̲rtnaɪt/ **NOUN** a period of two weeks [mainly BRIT] ❍ *I hope to be back in a fortnight.*

for|tu|nate /fo̲rtʃənɪt/ **ADJ** lucky ❍ *She's in the fortunate position of being able to choose which company to work for.*

for|tu|nate|ly /fo̲rtʃənɪtli/ **ADV** used before talking about a good event or situation ❍ *Fortunately, inflation continues to decline and exports remain relatively strong.*

for|tune /fo̲rtʃən/
1 NOUN a very large amount of money ❍ *He made a fortune buying and selling houses.*
2 NONCOUNT NOUN **Fortune** or good **fortune** is good luck. ❍ *Patrick still can't believe his good fortune at getting the job.*

for|ty /fo̲rti/ the number 40

for|ward /fo̲rwərd/
1 ADV toward the direction that is in front of you ❍ *He leaned forward.*
2 ADV in a position near the front of something ❍ *Try to get a seat as far forward as possible.*
3 VERB If you **forward** a letter or an email **to** someone, you send it to them after you have received it.

fo̲r|ward de|li̲v|ery **NONCOUNT NOUN** **Forward delivery** is an arrangement to deliver an asset at a time in the future. [ECONOMICS]

for|ward|ing /fo̲rwərdɪŋ/ **NONCOUNT NOUN** **Forwarding** is the collection, transportation, and delivery of goods. [LOGISTICS AND DISTRIBUTION] ❍ *Montreal is the forwarding center for wheat and flour.*

fo̲r|ward|ing agent (**forwarding agents**) **NOUN** a person or firm that is involved in the forwarding of goods [LOGISTICS AND DISTRIBUTION] ❍ *Federal Express will act as a forwarding agent for you.*

fo̲r|ward mar|ket (**forward markets**) **NOUN** a market in which contracts are made to buy or sell things at a future date [ECONOMICS] ❍ *The forward market plays an important role in avoiding foreign exchange risk.*

fo̲r|ward slash (**forward slashes**) **NOUN** the sloping line / that separates letters, words, or numbers

fos|sil /fo̲səl/ **NOUN** a plant or an animal that died a long time ago and has turned into rock

fo̲s|sil fu̲el (**fossil fuels**) **NOUN** a substance such as coal or oil that is found in the ground and used for producing power

fos|ter /fo̲stər/ **ADJ** A **foster** parent is someone who is paid by the government to take care of someone else's child for a period of time.

fought /fo̲t/ **Fought** is a form of the verb **fight**.

foul /fa̲ʊ̲l/ (**fouler, foulest**)
1 ADJ dirty and smelling or tasting unpleasant ❍ *foul, polluted water*
2 ADJ **Foul** language is offensive and contains rude words.
3 NOUN in a game or sport, an action that is not allowed according to the rules ❍ *Why did the referee not call a foul?*

found /faʊnd/
1 **Found** is a form of the verb **find**.
2 VERB When an organization **is founded**, it is started. ❍ *The New York Free-Loan Society was founded in 1892.*

foun|da|tion /faʊndeɪʃən/
1 PL NOUN The **foundations** of a building are the bricks, stones, or concrete that it is built on.
2 NOUN a sum of money that has been given to support an institution such as a school or hospital
3 NOUN an organization that provides money for a special purpose ❍ *the National Foundation for Educational Research*

found|er /faʊndər/
1 NOUN someone who starts an organization ❍ *Levine, one of the company's founders, plans to retire next year.*
2 VERB If a plan or project **founders**, it fails because of a particular problem. ❍ *Negotiations foundered on the difficulties of setting a purchase price.*

foun|tain /faʊntɪn/ NOUN a structure in a pool or a lake where water is forced up into the air and falls down again

four /fɔr/ the number 4

four|teen /fɔrtin/ the number 14

four|teenth /fɔrtinθ/ ADJ or ADV The **fourteenth** item in a series is the one that you count as number fourteen. ❍ *I rented an apartment on the fourteenth floor.*

fourth /fɔrθ/
1 ADJ or ADV The **fourth** item in a series is the one that you count as number four. ❍ *James finished the race in fourth place.*
2 NOUN one of four equal parts of something (¼) ❍ *A fourth of the public want a national vote on the new tax.*

Fourth World NONCOUNT NOUN The poorest countries in the most undeveloped parts of the world are sometimes called **the Fourth World**. Compare with **Third World** and **First World**. [ECONOMICS]

fox /fɒks/ (**foxes**) NOUN a wild animal that looks like a dog and has red fur and a thick tail

frac|tion /frækʃən/
1 NOUN a part of a whole number, for example ½ and ⅓
2 NOUN A **fraction of** something is a very small amount of it. ❍ *She hesitated for a fraction of a second.*

frac|ture /fræktʃər/ (**fractures, fracturing, fractured**)
1 NOUN a break in something, especially a bone ❍ *She suffered a hip fracture.*
2 VERB If a bone **is fractured**, it has a crack or a break in it. ❍ *Several of his ribs were fractured in the fall.*

frag|ile /frædʒəl/ ADJ easily broken or damaged ❍ *a butterfly's fragile wings* ❍ *the country's fragile economy*

frag|ment /frægmənt/ NOUN a small piece of something ❍ *tiny fragments of glass*

frail /freɪl/ ADJ Someone who is **frail** is weak and not healthy. ❍ *He looked very frail in his hospital bed.*

frame /freɪm/ (**frames, framing, framed**)
1 NOUN the structure surrounding a door, window, or picture ❍ *She had a photograph of her mother in a silver frame.*
2 VERB When a picture **is framed**, it is put in a frame.

frame|work /freɪmwɜrk/ NOUN a structure that forms a support for something ❍ *The wooden shelves sit on a steel framework.*

franc /fræŋk/ NOUN the unit of money that is used in Switzerland and some other countries [ECONOMICS]

fran|chise /fræntʃaɪz/ (**franchises, franchising, franchised**)
1 NOUN an authority that a firm gives for someone to sell its goods or services [ECONOMICS, ADMINISTRATION] ❍ *fast-food franchises* ❍ *the franchise to build and operate the tunnel*
2 VERB If a firm **franchises** its business, it allows other firms to sell its goods or services. [ECONOMICS, ADMINISTRATION] ❍ *She has recently franchised her business.*

fran|chi|see /fræntʃaɪzi/ NOUN a person or group of people who buy a particular franchise [ECONOMICS, ADMINISTRATION] ❍ *National Restaurants, a New York franchisee for Pizza Hut*

fran|chi|ser /fræntʃaɪzər/ **NOUN** an organization that sells franchises [ECONOMICS, ADMINISTRATION] ❍ *Coca-Cola, Pepsi, and Cadbury use franchisers to manufacture and distribute their products.*

fran|chi|sing /fræntʃaɪzɪŋ/ **NONCOUNT NOUN** **Franchising** is the act of selling franchises in a business. [ECONOMICS, ADMINISTRATION] ❍ *One of the most important aspects of franchising is that it reduces the risk of business failure.*

frank /fræŋk/
1 ADJ honest ❍ *I'll be frank with you, Emma.*
2 NOUN a long thin sausage ❍ *franks and beans*

fraud /frɔd/ **NONCOUNT NOUN** **Fraud** is the crime of getting money by not telling the truth. ❍ *He was jailed for two years for fraud.*

freak /frik/
1 ADJ A **freak** event or action is one that is very unusual. ❍ *James broke his leg in a freak accident playing golf.*
2 NOUN someone whose behavior or appearance is very unusual ❍ *I'm not a freak—I'm just like you guys.*

free /fri/ (**freer, freest, frees, freeing, freed**)
1 ADJ not costing money ❍ *The talks are all free.*
2 ADJ not controlled or limited ❍ *free elections* ❍ *They are free to bring their friends home at any time.* ● **free|ly ADV** ❍ *Twelve percent thought that younger people spend too freely and don't value money enough.*
3 ADJ not in prison ❍ *He walked from the court house a free man.*
4 ADJ **Free** time is time when you do not have any work to do. ❍ *She spent her free time shopping.*
5 ADJ If a seat or table is **free**, it is not being used by anyone.
6 VERB If you **free** someone or something, you help them to get out of a place. ❍ *Rescue workers freed him by cutting away part of the car.*

free along|side ship ADV If goods are delivered **free alongside ship**, they are delivered to the dock without charge, but the buyer has to pay for loading them onto the ship. Compare with **free on board**. [LOGISTICS AND DISTRIBUTION]

free|dom /fridəm/ **NONCOUNT NOUN** **Freedom** is the state of being allowed to do what you want to do. ❍ *freedom of speech* ❍ *They were given complete freedom to go wherever they liked.*

free en|ter|prise NONCOUNT NOUN **Free enterprise** is an economic system in which businesses compete for profit without government control. [ECONOMICS] ❍ *a believer in democracy and free enterprise*

free gift (**free gifts**) **NOUN** an item that is given away in order to encourage people to buy something ❍ *The book came as a free gift with a copy of The Ecologist magazine.*

free la|bor NONCOUNT NOUN **Free labor** is the labor of workers who do not belong to trade unions. [ECONOMICS]

free|lance /frilæns/
1 ADJ Someone who does **freelance** work is not employed by one organization, but is paid for each piece of work by the organization they do it for. ❍ *Michael Cross is a freelance journalist.*
2 ADV **Freelance** is also an adverb. ❍ *He is now working freelance from his home in New Hampshire.*

COLLOCATIONS
to *go* freelance
to *work on a* freelance *basis*

free|lancer /frilænsər/ **NOUN** someone who does freelance work

free mar|ket (**free markets**) **NOUN** an economic system in which businesses decide things such as prices and wages, and are not controlled by the government [ECONOMICS] ❍ *the creation of a free market*

free-marketeer (**free-marketeers**) **NOUN** a politician who is in favor of letting market forces control the economy [ECONOMICS] ❍ *Free-marketeers argue that governments do not need to intervene in the interest rate process.*

free on board ADV If goods are delivered **free on board**, they are delivered and loaded on board a ship without charge to the buyer. Compare with **free alongside ship**. [LOGISTICS AND DISTRIBUTION]

free port (**free ports**) NOUN a port or airport where tax is not paid on imported goods if they are going to be exported again [LOGISTICS AND DISTRIBUTION]

free trade NONCOUNT NOUN **Free trade** is a system that allows trade between countries without restrictions such as taxes. [ECONOMICS] ○ *They discussed a free trade pact between the U.S. and Mexico.*

F

COLLOCATIONS
a free trade *agreement*
a free trade *area*
a free trade *zone*

free-trader (**free-traders**) NOUN a person who supports free trade [ECONOMICS]

free|way /friweɪ/ NOUN a main road that has been specially built for fast travel over long distances

freeze /friz/ (**freezes, freezing, froze, frozen**)
1 VERB If a liquid **freezes**, it becomes solid because the temperature is low. ○ *If the temperature drops below 32°F, water freezes.*
2 VERB If you **freeze** food or drink, you make it very cold in order to preserve it.
3 VERB If you **freeze**, you stand completely still. ○ *"Freeze," shouted the police officer.*
4 VERB If the government or a firm **freezes** prices or wages, they do not allow them to increase for a fixed period of time. ○ *They want the government to freeze prices.*
5 NOUN **Freeze** is also a noun. ○ *A wage freeze was imposed on all staff.*
6 VERB If someone **freezes** a bank account or possession, they get a legal order which states that it cannot be used or sold for a fixed period of time. [LEGAL] ○ *The governor's action freezes 300,000 accounts.*
7 NOUN **Freeze** is also a noun. ○ *There has been a freeze on private savings.*

freez|er /frizər/ NOUN a large container or part of a refrigerator used for freezing food

freez|ing /frizɪŋ/ ADJ very cold ○ *The movie theater was freezing.* ○ *"You must be freezing," she said.*

free zone (**free zones**) NOUN A **free zone** is the same as a **free port**. [ECONOMICS]

freight /freɪt/
1 NONCOUNT NOUN **Freight** is the movement of goods by trucks, trains, ships, or airplanes. [LOGISTICS AND DISTRIBUTION] ○ *France derives 16% of revenue from air freight.*
2 NONCOUNT NOUN **Freight** is goods that are moved by trucks, trains, ships, or airplanes. [LOGISTICS AND DISTRIBUTION] ○ *a freight train* ○ *Managers wanted to see more freight carried by rail.*

freight|age /freɪtɪdʒ/
1 NONCOUNT NOUN **Freightage** is the movement of goods by trucks, trains, ships, or airplanes. [LOGISTICS AND DISTRIBUTION] ○ *A further $25,000 was paid for freightage.*
2 NONCOUNT NOUN **Freightage** is the price charged for moving goods by trucks, trains, ships, or airplanes. [LOGISTICS AND DISTRIBUTION] ○ *There's no customs-house duty, and no freightage to pay.*
3 NONCOUNT NOUN **Freightage** is goods that are moved by trucks, trains, ships, or airplanes. [LOGISTICS AND DISTRIBUTION]

freight|er /freɪtər/ NOUN a large ship or airplane that is designed for carrying freight [LOGISTICS AND DISTRIBUTION]

freight for|war|der (**freight forwarders**) NOUN A **freight forwarder** is the same as a **forwarding agent**. [LOGISTICS AND DISTRIBUTION] ○ *If a freight forwarder requests information from an airline, the airline's computer can immediately reply to the request.*

freight for|war|ding NONCOUNT NOUN **Freight forwarding** is the same as **forwarding**. [LOGISTICS AND DISTRIBUTION] ○ *Costs for freight forwarding to Moscow are around $4 a kilo.*

French fries /frɛntʃ fraɪz/ PL NOUN **French fries** are long, thin pieces of potato that are cooked in hot oil.

fre|quen|cy /frikwənsi/ (**frequencies**)
1 NONCOUNT NOUN The **frequency** of an event

is the number of times it happens. ❍ *The frequency of Kara's phone calls increased.*
2 NOUN The **frequency** of a sound wave or a radio wave is the number of times it vibrates (= moves quickly up and down) within a period of time.

fre|quent /fri̲kwənt/ **ADJ** happening often ❍ *Ms. Dean had frequent dealings with Mr. Smith's real estate organization.* **• fre|quent|ly ADV** ❍ *The two have frequently done business together.*

fresh /frɛ̲ʃ/
1 ADJ Fresh food has been picked or produced recently. ❍ *fresh fish* ❍ *fresh fruit and vegetables* **• fresh|ly ADV** ❍ *We bought some freshly-baked bread.*
2 ADJ new, sometimes replacing the thing or things before ❍ *There were fresh car tracks in the snow.* ❍ *The waiter gave her a fresh glass.*
3 ADJ smelling, tasting, or feeling clean or cool ❍ *The fresh air made her feel better.*

Fri|day /fra̲ɪdeɪ, -di/ **NOUN** the day after Thursday and before Saturday ❍ *He's going home on Friday.* ❍ *Friday November 6*

fridge /frɪ̲dʒ/ **NOUN** A **fridge** is the same as a **refrigerator**. [INFORMAL, BRIT]

fried /fra̲ɪd/ **ADJ** having been cooked in hot oil ❍ *fried eggs*

friend /frɛ̲nd/
1 NOUN someone who you like and know well ❍ *She's my best friend.* ❍ *a close friend of mine*
2 PL NOUN If you are **friends with** someone, you are their friend and they are yours. ❍ *I still wanted to be friends with Alison.*
3 If you **make friends with** someone, you meet them and become their friend. ❍ *He's made friends with the kids on the street.*

friend|ly /frɛ̲ndli/ (**friendlier, friendliest**) **ADJ** behaving in a kind, pleasant way ❍ *friendly neighbors*

frie̲nd|ly so|ci|ety (**friendly societies**) **NOUN** a group of people who pay regular amounts of money in return for pensions and other benefits [ADMINISTRATION, BRIT]

friend|ship /frɛ̲ndʃɪp/ **NOUN** a relationship between two friends ❍ *Their friendship has lasted more than sixty years.*

fries /fra̲ɪz/ **PL NOUN Fries** are the same as **French fries**.

fright|en /fra̲ɪtᵊn/ **VERB** If something or someone **frightens** you, they make you suddenly feel afraid or worried. ❍ *The thing that most frightens and angers workers is the risk of losing their jobs.*

fright|ened /fra̲ɪtᵊnd/ **ADJ** afraid or worried ❍ *She was frightened of making a mistake.*

fright|en|ing /fra̲ɪtᵊnɪŋ/ **ADJ** making you feel afraid ❍ *a frightening experience*

fri̲nge be̲n|efit (**fringe benefits**) **NOUN** a thing you get in addition to your salary, for example, a car [HR] ❍ *The job is badly paid and does not have any fringe benefits such as healthcare.*

frog /frɔ̲g/ **NOUN** a small animal with smooth skin, big eyes, and long back legs that it uses for jumping

from /frəm, STRONG frʌm/
1 PREP used for saying who gave or sent you something ❍ *I got an email from Jacob telling me the news.* ❍ *The watch was a present from his wife.*
2 PREP used for saying where someone lives or was born ❍ *I come from New Zealand.*
3 PREP used for saying the place that someone leaves ❍ *She ran from the room.* ❍ *We traveled from Washington to London for the meeting.*
4 PREP used for saying how far away something is ❍ *His office is only a hundred yards from the center of town.*
5 PREP used for saying what was used to make something ❍ *Cans are made from steel.*
6 PREP If something changes **from** one thing **to** another, it stops being the first thing and becomes the second thing. ❍ *Unemployment fell from 7.5 to 7.2%.*
7 PREP used for saying the beginning of a period of time ❍ *Breakfast is available from 6 a.m.*

front /frʌ̲nt/
1 NOUN The front of something is the part of it that faces forward. ❍ *The windows at the front of the building need replacing.*
2 A person or thing that is **in front** is ahead of

others in a moving group. ❍ *Don't drive too close to the car in front.*
3 Someone or something that is **in front of** a particular thing is facing it, ahead of it, or close to the front part of it. ❍ *She sat down in front of her mirror.* ❍ *A child ran in front of my car.*
4 If you do or say something **in front of** someone else, you do or say it when they are present. ❍ *I wouldn't say these things in front of my boss.*
▸**front up** If you **front up** money, you pay it at the beginning of a business arrangement.

F

front-end also **front end** ADJ **Front-end** costs are paid or charged before a project begins. [FINANCE] ❍ *These investments are not subject to a front-end sales charge.*

front-end load (**front-end loads**) NOUN A **front-end load** is a large early payment in an insurance policy or investment. Compare with **back-end load**. [BANKING] ❍ *They are adding a 5.75 percent front-end load for new investors.*

fron|tier /frʌntɪər, frɒn-/
1 NOUN an area of land where people are just starting to live ❍ *a frontier town*
2 NOUN In the western part of America before the twentieth century, the **frontier** was the part that Europeans had reached.

front|run|ning /frʌntrʌnɪŋ/ NONCOUNT NOUN **Frontrunning** is the practice of using information provided by investment analysts before it has been given to clients.

frown /fraʊn/
1 VERB When someone **frowns**, their eyebrows move together because they are annoyed, worried, or confused, or because they are concentrating. ❍ *Nancy shook her head, frowning.*
2 NOUN **Frown** is also a noun. ❍ *There was a frown on his face.*

froze /froʊz/ **Froze** is a form of the verb **freeze**.

fro|zen /froʊzᵊn/
1 **Frozen** is a form of the verb **freeze**.
2 ADJ If the ground is **frozen** it has become hard because the weather is very cold. ❍ *The ground was frozen hard.*
3 ADJ **Frozen** food has been stored at a very low temperature. ❍ *Birdseye launched his first range of frozen foods in 1930.*
4 ADJ If you are **frozen**, you are very cold. ❍ *I'm frozen out here.*

fruit /frut/ (**fruit**)

The plural can also be **fruits**.

NOUN **Fruit** is the part of a tree that contains seeds, covered with a substance that you can eat. ❍ *fresh fruit and vegetables* ❍ *They grow bananas and other tropical fruits for export.*

frus|trate /frʌstreɪt/ (**frustrates, frustrating, frustrated**) VERB If a problem **frustrates** you, it upsets or makes you angry because you cannot do anything about it. ❍ *His lack of ambition frustrated me.*
• **frus|trat|ing** ADJ ❍ *This situation is very frustrating for us.* • **frus|tra|tion** /frʌstreɪʃən/ NONCOUNT NOUN ❍ *Many CEOs express frustration that they have so little time to devote to long term planning.*

frus|trat|ed /frʌstreɪtɪd/ ADJ upset or angry because you cannot do what you want to do ❍ *I was so frustrated at not being able to change the situation.*

fry /fraɪ/ (**fries, frying, fried**)
1 VERB When you **fry** food, you cook it in hot fat or oil. ❍ *Fry the onions until brown.*
2 PL NOUN **Fries** are the same as **French fries**.

FSA /ɛf ɛs eɪ/ **FSA** is an abbreviation of **Financial Services Authority**. [FINANCE, LEGAL]

ft. **ft.** is a written abbreviation for **feet** or **foot**. ❍ *We flew at 1,000 ft.*

FT-SE 100 Index /fʊtsi wʌn hʌndrɪd ɪndɛks/ or **FT-SE 100** **FT-SE 100 Index** is an abbreviation of **Financial Times Stock Exchange 100 Index**. [ECONOMICS] ❍ *The FT-SE 100 closed at 2419.2, up 11.7 points.*

fuel /fyuəl/ NONCOUNT NOUN **Fuel** is a substance such as coal or oil that is burned to provide heat or power. ❍ *a tax on fuel*

ful|fil /fʊlfɪl/ [BRIT] → **fulfill**

ful|fill /fʊlfɪl/ VERB If you **fulfill** a promise or a dream, you manage to do what you said or hoped you would do. ❍ *She fulfilled her dream of starting her own company.*

full /fʊl/

1 ADJ containing as much liquid or as many people or things as possible ❍ *a full gas tank* ❍ *Her bag was full of samples.* ❍ *The room was full.*

2 ADJ feeling that you do not want any more food ❍ *Stop eating when you're full.*

3 ADJ complete or whole ❍ *For full details of the event, visit our website.* ❍ *"May I have your full name?"—"Yes, it's Patricia Mary White."*

4 ADJ used for saying that something is as loud, strong, fast, etc. as possible ❍ *The car crashed into the wall at full speed.*

5 ADJ When there is a **full** moon, the moon is a bright, complete circle.

full ca|pac|ity NONCOUNT NOUN If a factory or industry is working at **full capacity**, it is using all its available resources. [PRODUCTION] ❍ *Bread factories are working at full capacity.*

full em|ploy|ment NONCOUNT NOUN If there is **full employment** in a country, everyone who is able to work has a job. [ECONOMICS] ❍ *A major objective of the government is to achieve full employment.*

full stop [BRIT] → **period 2**

full-time also **full time**

1 ADJ **Full-time** work or study involves working or studying for all of each normal working week. ❍ *I'm looking for a full-time job.*

2 ADV **Full-time** is also an adverb. ❍ *Deirdre works full-time.*

ful|ly /fʊli/ ADV completely ❍ *We are fully aware of the problem.*

fun /fʌn/

1 NONCOUNT NOUN **Fun** is pleasure and enjoyment. ❍ *The party was great - we had a lot of fun.* ❍ *We worked hard but we had some fun in the evenings.*

2 NONCOUNT NOUN If someone or something is **fun**, you enjoy being with them or you enjoy doing it. ❍ *Liz was always so much fun.* ❍ *Work can be fun.*

3 If you **make fun of** someone or something, you make jokes about them in a way that is not kind. ❍ *Don't make fun of me.*

func|tion /fʌŋkʃən/

1 NOUN The **function** of something or someone is the useful thing that they do. ❍ *the stock market's basic function of raising capital*

2 VERB If a machine or a system **is functioning**, it is working well. ❍ *Domestic plants have been functioning at 60% of capacity.*

func|tion|al /fʌŋkʃənᵊl/

1 ADJ useful rather than decorative ❍ *Office furniture tends to be functional rather than stylish.*

2 ADJ working in the way that is intended ❍ *We have fully functional smoke alarms on all staircases.*

fund /fʌnd/

1 PL NOUN **Funds** are amounts of money that are available to be spent. ❍ *Investor interest in mutual funds is likely to increase over time.*

2 NOUN an amount of money that people save for a particular purpose ❍ *There is a scholarship fund for engineering students.*

3 VERB When a person or an organization **funds** something, they provide money for it. ❍ *The Foundation has funded a variety of programs.*

fun|da|men|tal /fʌndəmɛntᵊl/ ADJ very important and necessary ❍ *There was at a fundamental change in the economy.*

• **fun|da|men|tal|ly** ADV ❍ *He claims there's nothing fundamentally wrong with the market.*

fund|ing /fʌndɪŋ/ NONCOUNT NOUN **Funding** is money that a government or organization provides for a particular purpose. ❍ *They are hoping to get government funding for the program.*

fund|ing op|era|tions PL NOUN **Funding operations** are the conversion of short-term government bonds into long-term bonds that have a fixed rate of interest. [ECONOMICS]

fund man|ag|er (**fund managers**) NOUN a person whose job is to manage a firm's fund of investments [BANKING] ❍ *She is a leading City fund manager.*

fund-raising also **fundraising**

NONCOUNT NOUN **Fund-raising** is the activity of collecting money for a particular use. ❍ *Both candidates have a lot of fund-raising ahead of them.* ❍ *a fund-raising dinner*

f

funds /fʌndz/

1 PL NOUN Funds are money that is readily available.

2 PL NOUN Funds are British government securities that represent national debt. [FINANCE]

fu|ner|al /fyunərəl/ **NOUN** a ceremony that takes place when the body of someone who has died is buried or cremated (= burned) ❍ *The funeral will be in Joplin, Missouri.*

F

fun|ny /fʌni/ (**funnier, funniest**)

1 ADJ amusing and making you smile or laugh ❍ *A funny thing happened at work today.*

2 ADJ strange and surprising ❍ *It was a funny thing to say.*

3 ADJ If you feel **funny**, you feel slightly ill. [INFORMAL] ❍ *My stomach feels funny.*

fur /fɜr/ **NONCOUNT NOUN Fur** is the thick hair that grows on the bodies of many animals. ❍ *the bear's thick fur*

fu|ri|ous /fyʊəriəs/ **ADJ** extremely angry ❍ *He is furious at the way he has been treated.*

fur|lough /fɜrloʊ/

1 NOUN If workers are given **furlough**, they are told to stay away from work for a certain period because there is not enough for them to do. ❍ *This could mean a massive furlough of government workers.*

2 VERB If people who work for a particular organization **are furloughed**, they are given a furlough. ❍ *We regret to inform you that you are being furloughed indefinitely.*

fur|ni|ture /fɜrnɪtʃər/ **NONCOUNT NOUN Furniture** is large objects such as tables, chairs, or beds. ❍ *office furniture*

fur|ther /fɜrðər/ [BRIT] → **farther**

further|more /fɜrðərmɔr/ **ADV** used for introducing a second piece of information that adds to your first statement [FORMAL] ❍ *It's extremely hard work and, furthermore, it doesn't pay well.*

fur|thest /fɜrðɪst/ [BRIT] → **farthest**

fuse /fyuz/ **NOUN** a small wire in a piece of electrical equipment that melts when too much electricity passes through it ❍ *The fuse blew as he pressed the button to start the motor.*

fuss /fʌs/ **NONCOUNT NOUN Fuss** is anxious or excited behavior that is not useful. ❍ *I don't know what all the fuss is about.*

fu|ture /fyutʃər/

1 NOUN The future is the time that will come after now. ❍ *He's making plans for the future.*

2 ADJ happening or existing after the present time ❍ *future generations*

3 NOUN Someone's **future** is what will happen to them after the present time. ❍ *His future depends on the result of the interview.*

4 You say **in the future** when you are talking about what will happen after now. ❍ *I asked her to be more careful in the future.*

fu|tures /fyutʃərz/ **PL NOUN** When people trade in **futures**, they agree on a price for something that will be delivered in the future. [FINANCE] ❍ *This report could encourage buying in corn futures when the market opens today.* ❍ *Futures prices recovered from sharp early declines.*

fu|ture value (**future values**) **NOUN** the value that a sum of money will have after a particular period of time [FINANCE] ❍ *The worth of the contract depends on the uncertain future value of the assets.*

FX /ɛf ɛks/ **FX** is an abbreviation of **foreign exchange**. [ECONOMICS]

Gg

G7 /dʒi sɛvən/ **G7** is an abbreviation for **Group of Seven**. [ECONOMICS] ❍ *The recession lasted six quarters, longer than in any other G7 economy.*

G8 /dʒi eɪt/ **G8** is an abbreviation for **Group of Eight**. [ECONOMICS] ❍ *He will host a G8 summit of rich-country leaders which will focus on tackling poverty.*

G10 /dʒi tɛn/ **G10** is an abbreviation for **Group of Ten**. [ECONOMICS] ❍ *He accused the banks of being the slowest of the G10 major economic nations to process payments to customers.*

GAAP /gæp/ **GAAP** is an abbreviation for **generally accepted accounting principles**. [FINANCE] ❍ *Many insurance companies, particularly mutuals, do not report their data in GAAP terms.*

gadg|et /gædʒɪt/ **NOUN** a small machine or useful object ❍ *electronic gadgets*

gage /geɪdʒ/ **NOUN** something that is kept as security until you do something that you have promised, such as pay a debt [BANKING]

gain /geɪn/

1 VERB If you **gain** something that you want, you get it. ❍ *You can gain access to the website for $14 a month.* ❍ *Students can gain valuable experience by working during their vacations.*

2 VERB To **gain** something means to increase. ❍ *The index gained 445.57 points Tuesday.* ❍ *The car was gaining speed as it came toward us.*

3 NOUN Gain is also a noun. ❍ *Sales showed a gain of nearly 8% last month.*

gal|axy /gæləksi/ (**galaxies**) also **Galaxy NOUN** a very large group of stars and planets ❍ *a distant galaxy*

gale /geɪl/ **NOUN** a very strong wind ❍ *A gale was blowing outside.*

gal|lery /gæləri/ (**galleries**) **NOUN** a place where people go to look at art ❍ *an art gallery*

gal|lon /gælən/ **NOUN** A **gallon** is a unit for measuring liquids. A **gallon** is equal to 3.785 liters, and there are eight pints in a gallon. ❍ *The tank holds 1,000 gallons of water.*

gal|lop /gæləp/ **VERB** When a horse **gallops**, it runs very fast.

gam|ble /gæmbᵊl/ (**gambles, gambling, gambled**)

1 NOUN a risk that you take because you hope that something good will happen ❍ *She took a gamble and started up her own business.*

2 VERB If you **gamble on** something, you take a risk because you hope that something good will happen. ❍ *Companies sometimes have to gamble on new products.*

3 VERB If you **gamble**, you risk money in a game or on the result of a race or competition. ❍ *John gambled heavily on horse racing.*

gam|bler /gæmblər/ **NOUN** someone who risks money regularly, for example in card games or horse racing ❍ *a heavy gambler*

gam|bling /gæmblɪŋ/ **NONCOUNT NOUN Gambling** is the act or activity of risking money, for example in card games or horse racing. ❍ *The gambling laws are quite tough.*

game /geɪm/

1 NOUN an activity or a sport in which you try to win against someone ❍ *the game of football* ❍ *We played a game of cards.*

2 NOUN one particular occasion when you play a game ❍ *It was the first game of the season.*

gang /gæŋ/

1 NOUN a group of people, especially young people, who go around together and often deliberately cause trouble ❍ *street gangs*

2 NOUN an organized group of criminals ❍ *an armed gang*

Gantt chart /gænt tʃɑrt/ **NOUN** a chart that shows, in horizontal lines, activity that is planned for particular periods, which are shown in vertical bands ❍ *A project such as buying a house can be depicted in a Gantt chart.*

gap /gæp/ **NOUN** a space between two things or a hole in something ❍ *The earnings gap between women with and without disabilities has increased.* ❍ *His horse escaped through a gap in the fence.* ❍ *Hearst was a businessman who detected and exploited a gap in the market.*

G

gar|age /gərɑʒ/
1 NOUN a building where you keep a car ❍ *The house has a large garage.*
2 NOUN a place where you can have your car repaired

gar|bage /gɑrbɪdʒ/
1 NONCOUNT NOUN Garbage is things such as old papers, empty cans, and old food that you do not want anymore. ❍ *They take the trash to a garbage dump.*
2 NONCOUNT NOUN If you say that an idea or opinion is **garbage**, you mean that it is not true or not important. [INFORMAL] ❍ *His theory is total garbage.*

gar|bage can (**garbage cans**) **NOUN** a container for garbage

gar|den /gɑrdᵊn/
1 NOUN the part of a yard where you grow flowers and vegetables ❍ *She has a beautiful garden.*
2 VERB If you **garden**, you do work in your garden. ❍ *Jim gardened on weekends.*
3 PL NOUN Gardens are places with plants, trees, and grass that people can visit.

gar|den|ing /gɑrdᵊnɪŋ/ **NONCOUNT NOUN** the activity of working in a garden ❍ *My favorite hobby is gardening.*

gar|dening leave NONCOUNT NOUN If someone who leaves their job is given **gardening leave**, they continue to receive their salary and in return they agree not to work for anyone else for a period of time. [HR, BRIT] ❍ *The settlement means that the three executives can return from gardening leave and start their new jobs.*

gar|lic /gɑrlɪk/ **NONCOUNT NOUN Garlic** is a plant like a small onion with a strong flavor, which is used in cooking. ❍ *a clove of garlic*

gas /gæs/ (**gases**)
1 NOUN any substance that is not a liquid or a solid ❍ *Hydrogen is a gas, not a metal.*
2 NONCOUNT NOUN Gas is a liquid that you put into a car or other vehicle to make it work. **Gas** is short for **gasoline**. ❍ *The car has a full tank of gas.*

gaso|line /gæsəlin/ **NONCOUNT NOUN Gasoline** is a liquid that you put into a car or other vehicle to make it work.

gasp /gæsp/
1 NOUN a short, quick breath of air that you take in through your mouth ❍ *There was a gasp from the crowd as he scored the goal.*
2 VERB When you **gasp**, you take a short, quick breath through your mouth. ❍ *The entire country gasped at the finance ministry's announcement.*

gas sta|tion (**gas stations**) **NOUN** a place where you can buy gas for your car

gate /geɪt/
1 NOUN a structure like a door that you use to enter a field, or the area around a building ❍ *He opened the gate and walked up to the house.*
2 NOUN in an airport, a place where passengers leave the airport and get on an airplane ❍ *Please go to gate 15.*

gate|keeper /geɪtkipər/ **NOUN** a manager in a large organization who controls how much information is released about its activities ❍ *Companies are appointing "gatekeepers" to keep people up-to-date with what is going on in the industry.*

gath|er /gæðər/
1 VERB If people **gather** somewhere, they come together in a group. ❍ *A crowd had gathered in the square.*
2 VERB If you **gather** things, you collect them together so that you can use them. ❍ *They were gathering firewood.* ❍ *How did he gather the data?*

gath|er|ing /gæðərɪŋ/ **NOUN** a group of people meeting together for a particular purpose ❍ *a family gathering*

gave /geɪv/ **Gave** is a form of the verb **give**.

gay /geɪ/ ADJ attracted to people of the same sex ❍ *gay men and women*

gaze /geɪz/ (**gazes, gazing, gazed**) VERB If you **gaze at** someone or something, you look steadily at them for a long time. ❍ *She was gazing at herself in the mirror.* ❍ *He gazed out of the window.*

ga|zump /gəzʌmp/ VERB To **gazump** means to raise the price of something, especially a house, after agreeing a price verbally with the buyer. [ECONOMICS, BRIT] ❍ *The opportunity to gazump arises in the time between the handshake and the binding exchange of contracts.* ❍ *We were gazumped four times.*

ga|zund|er /gəzʌndər/ VERB To **gazunder** means to reduce an offer on a property immediately before exchanging contracts, having previously agreed a higher price with the seller. [ECONOMICS, BRIT] ❍ *I was gazumped and gazundered in the space of a week.*

GDP /dʒi di pi/ (**GDPs**) NOUN In economics, a country's **GDP** is the total value of goods and services produced within a country in a year, not including its income from investments in other countries. **GDP** is an abbreviation for **gross domestic product**. Compare with **GNP**. [ECONOMICS] ❍ *The deficit is projected to reach 10.6% of GDP this year.*

gear /gɪər/

1 NOUN a piece of machinery, especially in a car or on a bicycle, that turns engine power into movement ❍ *On a hill, use low gears.* ❍ *The car was in fourth gear.*

2 NONCOUNT NOUN The **gear** involved in a particular activity is the equipment or clothes that you use to do it. ❍ *lifting gear* ❍ *camping gear*

gearing /gɪərɪŋ/ [ECONOMICS, BANKING, mainly BRIT] → **leverage 3**

geese /gis/ **Geese** is the plural of **goose**.

gel /dʒɛl/ NONCOUNT NOUN **Gel** is a thick substance like jelly, especially one that you use to keep your hair in a particular style.

gem /dʒɛm/ NOUN a valuable stone that is used in jewelry ❍ *precious gems*

gen|der /dʒɛndər/ NOUN the fact of being male or female ❍ *We do not know the children's ages and genders.*

gene /dʒin/ NOUN the part of a cell that controls a person's, animal's, or plant's physical characteristics, growth, and development ❍ *They have isolated a gene that plays a key role in the ripening of fruits and vegetables.*

BUSINESS ETIQUETTE

If you are in a pub with business colleagues in the UK, it is good manners to offer to buy a 'round' of drinks (= a drink for every person in the group). Try to ensure that you reach the bar counter before your colleagues, so that you can buy the first round of drinks.

gen|er|al /dʒɛnərəl/

1 ADJ relating to the whole of something or to most things in a group ❍ *His firm took over the planting and general maintenance of the park last March.*

2 ADJ If you talk about the **general** situation, you are describing the situation as a whole rather than considering its details. ❍ *The figures represent a general decline in employment.*

3 ADJ A **general** business offers a variety of services or goods. ❍ *They ran the general store and the farm dairy.*

4 ADJ **General** is used to describe a person's job, to indicate that they have complete responsibility for the administration of an organization or business. ❍ *He then moved on to become General Manager.*

5 ADJ **General** workers do a variety of jobs which require no special skill or training. ❍ *The farm employed a tractor driver and two general laborers.*

6 You use **in general** to talk about something as a whole, rather than part of it. ❍ *We need to improve our educational system in general.*

gen|er|al elec|tion (**general elections**) NOUN A **general election** is a time when people choose a new government. Compare with **primary**.

gen|er|al|ise /dʒɛnrəlaɪz/ [BRIT] → **generalize**

gen|er|al|ize /dʒɛnrəlaɪz/ (**generalizes, generalizing, generalized**) VERB If you **generalize**, you say something that is usually, but not always, true. ❍ *You can't generalize – not all men are like that.*

gen|er|al|ly /dʒɛnrəli/ ADV usually or mainly ❍ *The reports were generally in line with what economists had expected.* ❍ *It is generally true that darker fruits contain more iron.*

gen|er|ate /dʒɛnəreɪt/ (**generates, generating, generated**)
1 VERB To **generate** something means to cause it to exist. ❍ *The reforms will generate new jobs.*
2 VERB To **generate** a form of energy or power means to produce it. ❍ *We use oil to generate electricity.*

gen|era|tion /dʒɛnəreɪʃən/ NOUN all the people in a group or country who are of a similar age ❍ *the younger generation*

Gen|era|tion X /dʒɛnəreɪʃən ɛks/ NOUN the generation of people who were born between the mid-1960s and the mid-1970s ❍ *Insecurity about jobs is a defining characteristic of Generation X.*

gen|era|tor /dʒɛnəreɪtər/ NOUN a machine that produces electricity ❍ *The building has its own power generators.*

ge|ner|ic /dʒɪnɛrɪk/
1 ADJ relating to a whole class of similar things ❍ *Parmesan is a generic term used to describe a family of hard Italian cheeses.*
2 ADJ A **generic** drug is one that does not have a trademark and that is known by a general name, rather than the manufacturer's name. ❍ *Doctors sometimes prescribe cheaper generic drugs instead of more expensive brand names.*
3 NOUN **Generic** is also a noun. ❍ *The program saved $11 million in 1988 by substituting generics for brand-name drugs.*

gen|er|ous /dʒɛnərəs/ ADJ giving a lot of something, especially money ❍ *He's very generous with his money.* ● **gen|er|os|ity** /dʒɛnərɒsɪti/ NONCOUNT NOUN ❍ *Diana was surprised by his kindness and generosity.* ● **gen|er|ous|ly** ADV ❍ *We would like to thank everyone who generously gave their time.*

ge|net|ic /dʒɪnɛtɪk/ ADJ related to genetics or genes ❍ *a rare genetic disease*

ge|neti|cal|ly modi|fied /dʒɪnɛtɪkli mɒdɪfaɪd/ ADJ **Genetically modified** plants and animals have had their genetic structure (= pattern of chemicals in cells) changed in order to make them more suitable for a particular purpose. The short form **GM** is also used.

ge|ni|us /dʒinyəs/ (**geniuses**) NOUN a very skilled or intelligent person ❍ *He was one of the greatest political geniuses of all time.*

gen|tle /dʒɛntᵊl/ (**gentler, gentlest**) ADJ kind and calm, not violent or rough ❍ *a gentle manner* ❍ *a gentle breeze* ● **gen|tly** ADV ❍ *She gently stroked his head.*

gentle|man /dʒɛntᵊlmən/ (**gentlemen**)
1 NOUN a man who is polite, educated, and kind to other people ❍ *He was always such a gentleman.*
2 PL NOUN You can use **gentlemen** to talk to a group of men politely. ❍ *This way, please, ladies and gentlemen.*

gents' /dʒɛntz/ [BRIT] → **men's room**

genu|ine /dʒɛnyuɪn/ ADJ true and real ❍ *a genuine American hero*

ge|og|ra|phy /dʒiɒgrəfi/ NONCOUNT NOUN **Geography** is the study of the countries of the world and things such as the land, oceans, weather, towns, and population.

germ /dʒɜrm/ NOUN a very small living thing that can cause disease or illness ❍ *This chemical is used for killing germs.*

ges|ture /dʒɛstʃər/ NOUN something that you say or do in order to express your attitude or intentions, often something that you know will not have much effect ❍ *As a gesture to security, cars were fitted with special locks.* ❍ *For three days this month, in an unusual gesture of openness, he allowed a correspondent to attend his meetings.*

get /gɛt/ (**gets, getting, got, gotten** or **got**)
1 VERB You use **get** with adjectives to mean "become." ❍ *Employees get excited about*

learning new skills. ❍ *Things will get better.*
2 VERB If you **get** someone **to** do something, you make them do it. ❍ *I'll get him to call you.*
3 VERB If you **get** something done, someone does it for you. ❍ *I must get the car fixed.*
4 VERB If you **get** somewhere, you arrive there. ❍ *He got home at 4 a.m.*
5 AUX You sometimes use **get** with another verb when you are talking about something that happens to someone. [INFORMAL] ❍ *He got arrested for possession of drugs.*
6 VERB If you **get** something, you buy it or obtain it. ❍ *I got a birthday present for Mom.* ❍ *You could get a job at the local store.*
7 VERB If you **get** something, you receive it. ❍ *He gets a lot of letters from fans.*
8 VERB If you **get** someone or something, you go and bring them to a particular place. ❍ *It's time to get the results back.*
9 VERB If you **get** a joke, you understand it. ❍ *I don't get it – what's funny?.*
10 VERB If you **get** an illness, you become sick with it. ❍ *I got flu while we were away.*
11 VERB When you **get** a train, bus, airplane, or boat, you leave a place on a particular train, bus, airplane, or boat. ❍ *I got the train home at 10.45 p.m.*

▸ **get along** If people **get along**, they have a friendly relationship. ❍ *We all get along well.*

▸ **get away with** If you **get away with** doing something wrong, you are not punished for it. ❍ *These people are stealing our money and getting away with it.*

▸ **get back** If you **get back** somewhere, you return there. ❍ *I'll call you when we get back from Scotland.*

▸ **get in** When a train, bus, or airplane **gets in**, it arrives. ❍ *Our flight got in two hours late.*

▸ **get off** If you **get off** a bus, train, or bicycle, you leave it. ❍ *He got off the train at Central Station.*

▸ **get on** If you **get on with** something, you continue doing it or start doing it. ❍ *Jane got on with her work.*

▸ **get over** If you **get over** an unhappy experience or an illness, you become happy or well again. ❍ *He seemed confident that we would get over our problems.*

▸ **get through** If you **get through** a task or an amount of work, you complete it. ❍ *We got through a lot of work today.*

▸ **get together** When people **get together**, they meet in order to talk together. ❍ *Thanksgiving is a time for families to get together.*

▸ **get up**
1 When someone who is sitting or lying down **gets up**, they move their body so that they are standing. ❍ *I got up and walked over to the window.*
2 When you **get up**, you get out of bed. ❍ *I have to get up early in the morning.*

ghet|to /gɛtoʊ/ (**ghettos** or **ghettoes**)
NOUN a part of a city where many poor people live ❍ *an inner-city ghetto*

ghost /goʊst/ **NOUN** a spirit of a dead person that someone believes they can see or feel ❍ *the ghost of his father*

gi|ant /dʒaɪənt/
1 ADJ very large or important ❍ *a giant corporation*
2 NOUN an imaginary person who is very big and strong, especially one that appears in children's stories

gift /gɪft/
1 NOUN something that you give to someone as a present ❍ *He brought gifts for the children.*
2 NOUN a natural ability to do something ❍ *He found he had a gift for marketing.*

gi|ga|byte /gɪgəbaɪt/ **NOUN** one thousand and twenty-four megabytes (= a unit for measuring the size of a computer's memory) [TECHNOLOGY]

gi|gan|tic /dʒaɪgæntɪk/ **ADJ** extremely large ❍ *Plastic buckets rolled into gigantic storage units.*

gig|gle /gɪgᵊl/ (**giggles, giggling, giggled**)
1 VERB If you **giggle**, you laugh in a silly way, like a child. ❍ *The girls began to giggle.*
2 NOUN **Giggle** is also a noun. ❍ *He gave a little giggle.*

gilt /gɪlt/ **NOUN** a gilt-edged security [BANKING] ❍ *The report was one factor that pushed gilt prices moderately lower.*

gilt-edged ADJ **Gilt-edged** stocks or securities are issued by the government for people to invest in for a fixed period of time at a fixed rate of interest. [BANKING]

girl /gɜrl/ NOUN a female child ❍ *They have two girls and a boy.*

girl|friend /gɜrlfrɛnd/
1 NOUN a girl or woman who someone is having a romantic relationship with ❍ *Does he have a girlfriend?*
2 NOUN a female friend ❍ *I had lunch with my girlfriends.*

G

give /gɪv/ (**gives, giving, gave, given**)
1 VERB If you **give** someone something, you let them have it. ❍ *My parents gave me a watch for my birthday.* ❍ *I gave him my phone number.*
2 VERB If you **give** someone an object, you pass it to them, so that they can take it. ❍ *Could you give me that pencil?*
3 VERB You can use **give** with nouns when you are talking about physical actions. For example, "She gave a smile" means "She smiled." ❍ *She gave me an angry look.*
4 VERB If you **give** a party, you organize it. ❍ *I gave a dinner party for a few friends.*
▶ **give away**
1 If you **give away** something that you own, you give it to someone. ❍ *They give away little pencils with names printed on them.*
2 If you **give** something **away**, you sell it very cheaply. [MARKETING AND SALES] ❍ *Dealers were giving it away for under $900.*
▶ **give back** If you **give** something **back**, you return it to the person who gave it to you. ❍ *I gave the book back to him.*
▶ **give in** If you **give in**, you agree to do something although you do not really want to do it. ❍ *After saying "no" a hundred times, I finally gave in and let him go.*
▶ **give out** If you **give out** a number of things, you give one to each person in a group of people. ❍ *The teacher gave out papers, pencils, and calculators for the math test.*
▶ **give up**
1 If you **give up** something, you stop doing it or having it. ❍ *They do not want to give up the fight against inflation.*
2 If you **give up**, you decide that you cannot do something and you stop trying to do it. ❍ *I give up. I'll never understand this.*

give|away /gɪvəweɪ/
1 NOUN something that a firm gives to someone in order to encourage people to buy a particular product ❍ *Next week we are celebrating with a great giveaway of free garden seeds.*
2 ADJ very cheap ❍ *Wine and food of superlative quality are available everywhere at giveaway prices.*
3 ADJ free ❍ *a giveaway property magazine*

giv|en /gɪvᵊn/ **Given** is a form of the verb **give**.

glaci|er /gleɪʃər/ NOUN a very large amount of ice that moves very slowly, usually down a mountain

glad /glæd/ ADJ pleased about something ❍ *I'm glad you came.* ● **glad|ly** ADV ❍ *I'll gladly help you on the day.*

glam|or|ous /glæmərəs/ ADJ very attractive in a way that gets attention ❍ *Melissa looked very glamorous in her white dress.*

glance /glæns/ (**glances, glancing, glanced**)
1 VERB If you **glance at** something or someone, you look at them very quickly. ❍ *He glanced at his watch.*
2 NOUN a quick look at someone or something ❍ *Trevor and I exchanged a glance.*

glass /glɑs, glæs/ (**glasses**)
1 NONCOUNT NOUN **Glass** is a hard, transparent substance that is used for making things such as windows and bottles. ❍ *a glass bowl*
2 NOUN a container made from glass, that you can drink from ❍ *He picked up his glass and drank.*
3 PL NOUN **Glasses** are two pieces of glass or plastic (= lenses) in a frame, that some people wear in front of their eyes to help them to see better. ❍ *He wears glasses.*

glimpse /glɪmps/ (**glimpses, glimpsing, glimpsed**)
1 NOUN a brief sight of someone or something

❍ *Fans waited outside the hotel to catch a glimpse of the star.*

2 VERB If you **glimpse** someone or something, you see them for a very short amount of time. ❍ *She glimpsed a poster through the car window.*

glob|al /gloʊbᵊl/ **ADJ** relating to the whole world [BUSINESS MANAGEMENT] ❍ *the global economy* ● **glob|al|ly ADV** ❍ *The company employs 5,800 people globally.*

glob|al brand (**global brands**) **NOUN** a brand that is sold and recognized throughout the world [MARKETING AND SALES] ❍ *We are already familiar with global brands such as Coca-Cola, McDonald's, and Microsoft.*

glob|al busi|ness (**global businesses**) or **global enterprise NOUN** a firm or industry that sells its products or services in many different parts of the world [ECONOMICS] ❍ *Telecommunications is one of the most profitable global businesses.* ❍ *global enterprises based in the advanced industrial nations*

glob|al|ise /gloʊbəlaɪz/ [ECONOMICS, BRIT] → **globalize**

glob|al|ize /gloʊbəlaɪz/ (**globalizes, globalizing, globalized**) **VERB** When industry **globalizes** or **is globalized**, firms from one country link with firms from another country in order to do business with them. [ECONOMICS] ❍ *One way to lower costs is to forge alliances with foreign companies or to expand internationally – in short, to "globalize."* ● **glob|ali|za|tion** /gloʊbəlɪzeɪʃən/ **NONCOUNT NOUN** ❍ *Trends toward the globalization of industry have dramatically affected food production in California.*

glob|al mar|ket (**global markets**) or **global marketplace NOUN** a market for something that exists throughout the world [ECONOMICS] ❍ *Producers are giving a high priority to efforts to build cars which can meet the needs of a global market.*

glob|al prod|uct (**global products**) **NOUN** a product that is marketed throughout the world under the same brand name [ECONOMICS] ❍ *Cultural difference is central to the development of new markets for global products.*

glob|al reach NONCOUNT NOUN When people talk about the **global reach** of a firm or industry, they mean its ability to have customers in many different parts of the world. [ECONOMICS] ❍ *The company does not yet have the global reach of its bigger competitors.*

glob|al tour|ism NONCOUNT NOUN Global tourism is tourism considered as a global industry. [ECONOMICS] ❍ *By the mid-1980s, the global tourism business employed more people than the oil industry.*

glob|al warm|ing NONCOUNT NOUN Global warming is the gradual rise in the Earth's temperature caused by high levels of certain gases.

globe /gloʊb/

1 NOUN an object shaped like a ball with a map of the world on it

2 NOUN The globe is the world. ❍ *Thousands of people across the globe took part in the survey.*

gloomy /glumi/ (**gloomier, gloomiest**)

1 ADJ fairly dark ❍ *It's gloomy in here – I'll put a light on.*

2 ADJ unhappy and without hope, or making you feel unhappy and without hope ❍ *He's gloomy about the future of the country.* ❍ *The economic prospects for next year are gloomy.*

glo|ri|ous /glɔriəs/

1 ADJ very beautiful ❍ *We saw a glorious sunset.*

2 ADJ involving great fame or success ❍ *He had a glorious career as a broadcaster and writer.*

glo|ry /glɔri/ **NONCOUNT NOUN Glory** is the fame and admiration from other people that you gain by doing something great. ❍ *He was sure there was little glory in war.*

glossy /glɔsi/ (**glossier, glossiest**) **ADJ** smooth and shiny ❍ *She had glossy black hair.*

glove /glʌv/ **NOUN** a piece of clothing that you wear on your hand, with separate parts for each finger

glow /gloʊ/

1 NOUN a soft, steady light ❍ *Inside she saw the red glow of a fire.*

2 VERB If something **glows**, it makes a soft, steady light. ❍ *The green light on the computer will glow and you may proceed.*

glue /glu/ (**glues, glueing** or **gluing, glued**)
1 NONCOUNT NOUN Glue is a sticky substance used for joining things together. ❍ *You will need scissors and a tube of glue.*
2 VERB If you **glue** one object to another, you stick them together with glue. ❍ *She glued the pieces of newspaper together.*

glut /glʌt/ **NOUN** so much of something that it cannot all be sold or used [ECONOMICS] ❍ *Exports have become increasingly important to wineries as they battle a global wine glut.*

GM /dʒi ɛm/ **ADJ GM** crops have had one or more genes changed to make them stronger or to help them grow. **GM** is short for **genetically modified**. ❍ *They are growing large-scale GM food crops, like soybeans.*

G

GmbH In German-speaking countries **GmbH** is used after the names of limited companies. **GmbH** is short for "Gesellschaft mit beschränkter Haftung." [ADMINISTRATION] ❍ *Schwitz Insurance GmbH*

GMO /dʒi ɛm oʊ/ (**GMOs**) **NOUN** A **GMO** is an animal, plant, or other organism whose genetic structure has been changed by genetic engineering. **GMO** is an abbreviation for "genetically modified organism." [TECHNOLOGY] ❍ *the presence of GMOs in many processed foods*

gnome /noʊm/ **NOUN** an international banker [BANKING, INFORMAL] ❍ *All three events were blamed on speculators, which at that time meant the "gnomes of Zurich."*

GNP /dʒi ɛn pi/ (**GNPs**) **NOUN** A country's **GNP** is the total value of all the goods produced and services provided by that country in one year. **GNP** is an abbreviation for **gross national product**. Compare with **GDP**. [ECONOMICS] ❍ *By 1973 the government deficit equalled thirty percent of GNP.*

go /goʊ/ (**goes, going, went, gone**)
1 VERB When you **go** somewhere, you move or travel there. ❍ *We went to Rome on vacation.* ❍ *I went home for the weekend.*
2 VERB When you **go**, you leave the place where you are. ❍ *It's time to go.*
3 VERB If you **go to** work, you do a job somewhere as part of your normal life. ❍ *Employees may select any eight-hour period during those hours to go to work.*
4 VERB You use **go** to talk about the way that something happens. ❍ *How's your job going?* ❍ *Everything's going wrong.*
5 VERB If someone **goes**, they leave their job, usually because they are forced to. ❍ *He had made a humiliating tactical error and he had to go.*
6 VERB If a machine **is going**, it is working. ❍ *Can you get my car going again?*
7 VERB If you say where money **goes**, you are saying what it is spent on. ❍ *Most of my money goes to bills.*
8 In a restaurant, you ask for food **to go** when you want to take it with you and eat it somewhere else. ❍ *She ordered coffee to go.*

▶**go ahead** If an event **goes ahead**, it takes place. ❍ *The wedding went ahead as planned.*

▶**go away**
1 If you **go away**, you leave a place or a person. ❍ *Just go away and leave me alone!*
2 If you **go away**, you leave a place and spend time somewhere else, especially as a vacation. ❍ *Why don't we go away this weekend?*

▶**go back** If you **go back** somewhere, you return there. ❍ *He'll be going back to college soon.*

▶**go by** When time **goes by**, it passes. ❍ *The week went by so quickly.*

▶**go down**
1 If an amount **goes down**, it becomes less. ❍ *House prices went down last month.*
2 When the sun **goes down**, it goes below the line between the land and the sky.

▶**go off** If a bomb **goes off**, it explodes. ❍ *A bomb went off, destroying the vehicle.*

▶**go on**
1 If you **go on** doing something, you continue to do it. ❍ *She just went on laughing.*
2 If something **is going on**, it is happening. ❍ *While this conversation was going on, I just listened.*

▶**go out**
1 If you **go out**, you leave your home to do something enjoyable. ❍ *I'm going out tonight.*
2 If you **go out with** someone, you have a romantic relationship with them. ❍ *I've been going out with my girlfriend for three months.*

3 If a light **goes out**, it stops shining.
4 If a fire **goes out**, it stops burning. ❍ *The fire went out and the room became cold.*
▶ **go over** If you **go over** something, you look at it or think about it very carefully. ❍ *We went over the details again.*
▶ **go through** If you **go through** a difficult experience, you experience it. ❍ *He went through a difficult time when his wife died.*
▶ **go up** If an amount **goes up**, it becomes greater. ❍ *The cost of calls went up to $1.95 a minute.*

goal /goʊl/
1 NOUN In games such as soccer, the **goal** is the place where the players try to get the ball, in order to win a point. ❍ *The ball went straight into the goal.*
2 NOUN in games such as soccer, a point that is scored when the ball goes into the goal ❍ *He scored five goals in one playoff game.*
3 NOUN an aim or purpose ❍ *Our goal is to make patients comfortable.*

goat /goʊt/ **NOUN** an animal similar to a sheep, with horns and long hairs on the chin

god /gɒd/
1 NOUN In many religions, **God** is the name given to the spirit that people believe created the world. ❍ *Do you believe in God?*
2 NOUN in many religions, a spirit that people believe has power over a particular part of the world or nature ❍ *Poseidon was the Greek god of the sea.*

god|dess /gɒdɪs/ (**goddesses**) **NOUN** in many religions, a female spirit that people believe has power over a particular part of the world or nature ❍ *There was a statue of a goddess in the temple.*

go-go
1 ADJ A **go-go** period of time is a time when people make a lot of money and businesses are growing. [ECONOMICS] ❍ *Current economic activity is markedly slower than during the go-go years of the mid to late 1980s.*
2 ADJ A **go-go** firm is growing fast. [ECONOMICS] ❍ *It will be a go-go business with pre-tax profits forecast to climb from $152 million last year to $200 million.*

going /goʊɪŋ/ **ADJ** The **going** rate or the **going** salary is the usual amount of money that you expect to pay or receive for something. [FINANCE, PURCHASING] ❍ *That's about half the going price on world oil markets.*

gold /goʊld/
1 NONCOUNT NOUN Gold is a valuable, yellow-colored metal that is used for making jewelry, ornaments, and coins. ❍ *a gold ring* ❍ *The price of gold was going up.*
2 ADJ Something that is **gold** is bright-yellow in color, and is often shiny. ❍ *She wore a black and gold shirt.*

gold card (**gold cards**) **NOUN** A **gold card** is a special type of credit card that gives you extra benefits such as a higher spending limit. [BANKING] ❍ *They offer gold cards as the top-of-the-line product.*

gold cer|tifi|cate (**gold certificates**)
1 NOUN a currency note that is only issued to the Federal Reserve Banks by the U.S. Treasury [ECONOMICS]
2 NOUN a currency note that was issued in the past by the U.S. Treasury to the public, that could be exchanged for gold [ECONOMICS]

gold|en /goʊldᵊn/ **ADJ** having a bright yellow color ❍ *sweet green apples and golden apricots*

gold|en good|bye (**golden goodbyes**) [HR, BRIT] → **golden handshake**

gold|en hand|cuffs PL NOUN Golden handcuffs are payments that are made to an employee over a number of years that encourage them to stay with a particular firm or in a particular job. [HR, INFORMAL] ❍ *Companies have devised various forms of "golden handcuffs" to stop employees from defecting to competitors.*

gold|en hand|shake (**golden handshakes**) or **golden goodbye NOUN** a large sum of money that a firm gives to an employee when he or she leaves, as a reward for long service or good work [HR] ❍ *And if Mr. Pell, 49, is axed following a takeover, he would be in line to collect a golden handshake of $1 million.*

gold|en hel|lo (**golden hellos**) **NOUN** a sum of money that a firm offers to a person in order to persuade them to join the firm [HR, BRIT] ❍ *Most people recognize the need to pay a golden hello to attract the best.*

gold|en para|chute (**golden parachutes**) NOUN an agreement to pay a large amount of money to a senior executive of a firm if they are forced to leave [HR] ❍ *Golden parachutes entitle them to a full year's salary if they get booted out of the company.*

gold|en share (**golden shares**) NOUN a share in a firm that controls at least 51% of the voting rights [ADMINISTRATION] ❍ *The government will retain "golden shares" in companies it wants to keep in French hands.*

G

gold-exchange stand|ard NONCOUNT NOUN The **gold-exchange standard** is a monetary system by which a currency not based on the gold standard is kept at a par with another currency that is based on the gold standard. [ECONOMICS]

gold re|serve (**gold reserves**) NOUN the gold that is reserved by a central bank to support domestic credit expansion, to cover balance of payments deficits and to protect currency [BANKING, ECONOMICS] ❍ *Foreign exchange is the balance of liquid assets such as cash and gold reserves that can be used to make international payments.*

gold|smith /goʊldsmɪθ/ NOUN a person whose job is making jewelry and other objects using gold

gold stand|ard (**gold standards**) NOUN a monetary system in which the value of the unit of currency is based on the value of gold ❍ *Back in the 1930s many countries had to choose whether or not to abandon the gold standard.*

golf /gɒlf/ NONCOUNT NOUN **Golf** is a game in which you use long sticks (= golf clubs) to hit a small, hard ball into holes. ❍ *Do you play golf?*

gon|do|la /gɒndᵊlə/ NOUN an island of shelves for displaying goods in a self-service store

gone /gɔn/ **Gone** is a form of the verb **go**.

good /gʊd/ (**better, best**)
1 ADJ pleasant or enjoyable ❍ *I had a really good time.*
2 ADJ of a high quality ❍ *We had very good food.*
3 ADJ A **good** place or time for an activity is a suitable place or time for it. ❍ *What's a good time to meet?*
4 ADJ sensible, showing good judgment ❍ *It was a good decision.*
5 ADJ If you are **good at** something, you are skillful at doing it. ❍ *I think he'll be very good at that job.*
6 ADJ A child who is **good** behaves well. ❍ *Be good!*
7 ADJ kind ❍ *You're good to me!*
8 NONCOUNT NOUN **Good** is what people consider to be morally right. ❍ *the forces of good and evil*
9 NOUN If something is **no good**, it will not bring success. ❍ *It's no good worrying about it now.*
10 If something disappears **for good**, it never comes back. ❍ *Oil ministers now hope to solve the issue for good.*

good after|noon You say "**Good afternoon**" when you see or speak to someone in the afternoon. [FORMAL]

good|bye /gʊdbaɪ/ also **good-bye** You say "**Goodbye**" to someone when you or they are leaving a place, or at the end of a telephone conversation.

good eve|ning You say "**Good evening**" the first time you see or speak to someone in the evening. [FORMAL]

good-looking (**better-looking, best-looking**) ADJ Someone who is **good-looking** has an attractive face. ❍ *Katy noticed him because he was good-looking.*

good morn|ing You say "**Good morning**" the first time you see or speak to someone in the morning. [FORMAL]

good night You say "**Good night**" to someone late in the evening before you go home or go to bed.

goods /gʊdz/ PL NOUN **Goods** are things that are made to be sold. ❍ *Money can be exchanged for goods or services.*

good|will /gʊdwɪl/
1 NONCOUNT NOUN The **goodwill** of a business is something such as its good reputation, which increases the value of the business. [BUSINESS MANAGEMENT] ❍ *We do not want to lose the goodwill built up over 175 years.*
2 NONCOUNT NOUN **Goodwill** is an intangible asset that is taken into account when the value of an enterprise is calculated, reflecting the firm's reputation and its relationship with its customers. [BUSINESS MANAGEMENT] ❍ *A major factor in the third-quarter loss was the write-down of $143.6 million of goodwill.*

Google /gugᵊl/ (**Googles, Googling, Googled**) also **google**
1 NONCOUNT NOUN **Google** is a computer program that you can use to search for information on the Internet. [TRADEMARK, TECHNOLOGY] ❍ *Why don't you look him up on Google?*
2 VERB If you **Google** information, you search for it on the Internet using Google. [TRADEMARK, TECHNOLOGY] ❍ *We googled her name, and found her website.*

goose /gus/ (**geese**) **NOUN** a large water bird with a long neck

gor|geous /gɔrdʒəs/ **ADJ** very attractive or pleasant [INFORMAL] ❍ *You look gorgeous!* ❍ *It's a gorgeous day.*

go|ril|la /gərɪlə/ **NOUN** a very large animal with long arms, black fur, and a black face

go-slow (**go-slows**) [PRODUCTION, BRIT] → **slowdown 2**

gos|sip /gɒsɪp/
1 NONCOUNT NOUN **Gossip** is informal conversation about other people. ❍ *Erika told me an interesting piece of gossip about Taylor.*
2 VERB If you **gossip**, you talk in an informal way, especially about other people or local events. ❍ *They sat at the table gossiping.*

got /gɒt/
1 Got is a form of the verb **get**.
2 You use **have got** to say that you possess a particular thing. [SPOKEN] ❍ *We've got thousands of investments that we've made over the last 10 years.*
3 You use **have got to** when you are saying that something must happen. [SPOKEN] ❍ *I've got to accept that he's not coming back.*

got|ten /gɒtᵊn/ **Gotten** is a form of the verb **get**.

gov|ern /gʌvərn/ **VERB** To **govern** a country means to officially control and organize it. ❍ *The people choose who they want to govern their country.*

gov|ern|ment /gʌvərnmənt/ **NOUN** the group of people who control and organize a country, a state, or a city ❍ *The government has decided to make changes.*

gov|ern|ment bor|row|ing **NONCOUNT NOUN** **Government borrowing** is all the money that a government owes to anyone at home and abroad in the short and long term. [ECONOMICS] ❍ *Government borrowing has helped maintain living standards, so a sharp rise in poverty is not the cause.*

gov|er|nor /gʌvərnər/ **NOUN** a person who is in charge of part of a country ❍ *He was governor of Iowa.*

gown /gaʊn/
1 NOUN a long dress that a woman wears on formal occasions ❍ *a ball gown*
2 NOUN a loose black piece of clothing that a student wears at their graduation ceremony (= the ceremony where they receive their degree)

grab /græb/ (**grabs, grabbing, grabbed**) **VERB** If you **grab** something, you take something suddenly and roughly. ❍ *I grabbed my coat.*

grace|ful /greɪsfəl/ **ADJ** moving in a smooth and attractive way ❍ *She was graceful, like a dancer.* • **grace|ful|ly** **ADV** ❍ *She stepped gracefully onto the stage.*

grad /græd/ **NOUN** A **grad** is a **graduate**. [INFORMAL]

grade /greɪd/ (**grades, grading, graded**)
1 NOUN a group of classes in a school where all the children are a similar age ❍ *Mr. White teaches first grade.*
2 NOUN a mark that a teacher gives you to show how good your work is ❍ *The best grade you can get is an A.*

g

3 VERB If you **grade** something, you judge its quality. ❍ *Teachers grade the students' work from A to F.*

grad|ual /grædʒuəl/ **ADJ** happening slowly, over a period of time ❍ *The gradual improvement is likely to continue.*

gradu|al|ly /grædʒuəli/ **ADV** slowly, over a period of time ❍ *I'm gradually learning to use the new system.*

gradu|ate (**graduates, graduating, graduated**)

Pronounce the noun /grædʒuɪt/. Pronounce the verb /grædʒueɪt/.

1 NOUN a student who has completed a course at a high school, college, or university ❍ *college graduates*

2 VERB When a student **graduates**, they complete their studies at a school or university. ❍ *Her son just graduated from high school.*

gradua|tion /grædʒueɪʃən/ **NOUN** a special ceremony for students when they have completed their studies at a university, college, or school ❍ *Her parents came to her graduation.*

grain /greɪn/

1 NOUN a single seed from a plant such as wheat or rice ❍ *a few grains of rice*

2 NOUN a tiny, hard piece of sand or salt ❍ *How many grains of sand are there in the desert?*

gram /græm/ **NOUN** A **gram** is a unit of weight. There are one thousand grams in a kilogram.

gram|mar /græmər/ **NONCOUNT NOUN** **Grammar** is a set of rules for a language that describes how words go together to form sentences. ❍ *the basic rules of grammar*

grand /grænd/ **ADJ** very large, attractive, and looking important ❍ *The hotel is a very grand building in the center of town.*

grand|child /græntʃaɪld/ (**grandchildren**) **NOUN** the child of your son or daughter ❍ *I was my grandma's favorite grandchild.*

grand|daughter /grændɔtər/ **NOUN** the daughter of your son or daughter ❍ *This is my granddaughter, Amelia.*

grand|father /grænfɑðər/ **NOUN** the father of your father or mother ❍ *His grandfather founded the company.*

grand|ma /grænmɑ/ **NOUN** a grandmother [INFORMAL] ❍ *Grandma was from Scotland.*

grand|mother /grænmʌðər/ **NOUN** the mother of your father or mother ❍ *My grandmothers were both teachers.*

grand|parent /grænpɛərənt, -pær-/ **NOUN** a parent of your father or mother ❍ *Parents buy more toys and bicycles than grandparents.*

grand|son /grænsʌn/ **NOUN** the son of your son or daughter ❍ *He is the firm's president and a grandson of its founder.*

grant /grænt/

1 NOUN an amount of money that a government gives to a person or to an organization for a special purpose ❍ *They got a grant to research the disease.*

2 VERB If someone **grants** you something, they allow you to have it. [FORMAL] ❍ *France granted him political asylum.*

3 If someone **takes** you **for granted**, they do not show that they are grateful for anything that you do. ❍ *She feels that her partners take her for granted.*

grape /greɪp/ **NOUN** a small green or purple fruit, eaten raw or used to make wine ❍ *a bunch of grapes*

grape|fruit /greɪpfrut/ (**grapefruit**)

The plural can also be **grapefruits**.

NOUN a large, round, yellow fruit that has a slightly sour taste

graph /græf/ **NOUN** a picture that shows the relationship between sets of numbers or measurements ❍ *The graph shows that prices went up about 20 percent last year.*

graph|ics /græfɪks/ **PL NOUN** **Graphics** are drawings, pictures, or symbols, especially when they are produced by a computer.

grasp /græsp/

1 VERB If you **grasp** something, you take it in your hand and hold it very firmly. ❍ *He grasped*

both my hands.
2 NOUN a very firm hold or grip ❍ *He took her hand in a firm grasp.*
3 VERB If you **grasp** something that is complicated, you understand it. ❍ *The concepts are difficult to grasp.*
4 NOUN A **grasp of** a subject is an understanding of it. ❍ *He had a good, technical grasp of finance.*

grass /græs/ **NONCOUNT NOUN** **Grass** is a plant with thin, green leaves that cover the surface of the ground. ❍ *We sat on the grass and ate our picnic.*

grate|ful /greɪtfəl/ **ADJ** pleased with someone who has helped you and wanting to thank them ❍ *We're very grateful to you for all your help.* • **grate|ful|ly ADV** ❍ *Any help would be gratefully received.*

gra|tis /grætɪs, grɑ-/
1 ADV If something is done or provided **gratis**, it does not have to be paid for. ❍ *David gives the first consultation gratis.*
2 ADJ **Gratis** is also an adjective. ❍ *What I did for you was free, gratis, you understand?*

grati|tude /grætɪtud/ **NONCOUNT NOUN** **Gratitude** is the feeling of wanting to thank someone. ❍ *He expressed gratitude to everyone for their help.*

gra|tu|ity /grətuɪti/ (**gratuities**)
1 NOUN a gift of money to someone who has done something for you [FORMAL] ❍ *The porter expects a gratuity.*
2 NOUN something that is freely given away ❍ *A taxpayer who extends credit with knowledge that he will not be paid is considered to have made a gratuity and not to have created a debt.*

grave /greɪv/ (**graver, gravest**)
1 NOUN a place where a dead person is buried ❍ *They visit her grave twice a year.*
2 ADJ serious and important ❍ *This is a grave error.*

grave|yard /greɪvyɑrd/ **NOUN** an area of land where dead people are buried ❍ *They went to the graveyard to put flowers on her grave.*

grave|yard shift (**graveyard shifts**) **NOUN** the shift between midnight and morning [PRODUCTION, INFORMAL]

grav|ity /grævɪti/ **NONCOUNT NOUN** **Gravity** is the force that makes things fall to the ground. ❍ *the force of gravity*

gra|vy /greɪvi/ **NONCOUNT NOUN** **Gravy** is a sauce made from the juices that come from meat when it cooks.

gray /greɪ/
1 ADJ having the color of black and white mixed together, like the color of clouds on a rainy day ❍ *a gray suit*
2 NOUN **Gray** is also a noun.

gray knight (**gray knights**) **NOUN** someone who enters a takeover battle without making their intentions clear [FINANCE]

gray mar|ket (**gray markets**) **NOUN** If something is bought or sold **on the gray market**, it is bought or sold secretly, but not illegally. Compare with **black market**. [ECONOMICS] ❍ *Indian PC business is still dominated by the gray market.*

gray pan|ther (**gray panthers**) **NOUN** a wealthy, older consumer, with an active and sociable lifestyle [ECONOMICS] ❍ *Gray panthers seem to like nothing better than spending their kids' inheritances.*

grease /gris/
1 NONCOUNT NOUN **Grease** is a thick substance like oil. ❍ *His hands were covered in grease.*
2 NONCOUNT NOUN **Grease** is animal fat that is produced when you cook meat.

great /greɪt/
1 ADJ very good ❍ *It's a great idea.*
2 ADJ **Great** or **great big** describes something that is very large. ❍ *She had a great big smile on her face.*
3 ADJ large in amount or degree ❍ *Some are now in positions of great responsibility.* • **great|ly ADV** [FORMAL] ❍ *He will be greatly missed.*
4 ADJ very important ❍ *great scientific discoveries* ❍ *Mr. Masson described himself as "the greatest analyst who ever lived."* • **great|ness NONCOUNT NOUN** ❍ *She dreamed of achieving greatness.*

greed /grid/ **NONCOUNT NOUN** **Greed** is the feeling that you want to have more of

g

something than you need. ❍ *People say that the world economy is based on greed.*

greedy /gridi/ (**greedier, greediest**) ADJ wanting to have more of something than you need ❍ *They want more money? I think that's a bit greedy.* ● **greedi|ly** ADV ❍ *He raised the bottle to his lips and drank greedily.*

green /grin/

1 ADJ having the color of grass or leaves ❍ *a green dress*

2 NOUN **Green** is also a noun.

3 ADJ relating to the protection of the environment ❍ *the Green Party* ❍ *The power of the Green movement in Germany has made that country a leader in the drive to recycle more waste materials.*

green|back /grinbæk/ NOUN a United States banknote [ECONOMICS, INFORMAL] ❍ *He documents the greenback's gradual rise as an international currency after the creation of the Federal Reserve in 1913.*

green card (**green cards**) NOUN a document showing that someone who is not a citizen of the United States has permission to live and work there [ADMINISTRATION] ❍ *Nicollette married Harry so she could get a green card.*

green-collar ADJ **Green-collar** workers have jobs that benefit the environment. [INFORMAL] ❍ *Mrs. Clinton wants to generate green-collar jobs in hard-hit states.*

green|field site /grinfild saɪt/ (**greenfield sites**) NOUN an area of land that has not been built on before [PRODUCTION, BRIT] ❍ *The company's factories were built on greenfield sites with the most modern capital equipment.*

green|house ef|fect NOUN **The greenhouse effect** is the problem of the Earth's temperature getting higher because of the gases that go into the air. ❍ *Carbon dioxide is one of the gases that contribute to the greenhouse effect.*

green is|sues PL NOUN **Green issues** are matters relating to the care of the environment and the world's natural resources. [BUSINESS MANAGEMENT] ❍ *Green issues, he argues, boil down to "a question of whether you want life on this planet."*

green light (**green lights**) NOUN If someone in authority **gives the green light** to a project, they formally approve of its development. ❍ *A falling headline inflation rate gives the green light for the central banks to cut interest rates.*

green|mail /grinmeɪl/ NONCOUNT NOUN **Greenmail** is when a firm buys enough shares in another firm to threaten a takeover and makes a profit if the other firm buys back its shares at a higher price. ❍ *Family control would prevent any hostile takeover or greenmail attempt.*

green shoots PL NOUN **Green shoots** are the first signs of economic growth after a recession. [ECONOMICS, INFORMAL] ❍ *Despite some sightings of green shoots, an early global recovery remains unlikely.*

greet /grit/ VERB When you **greet** someone, you say "Hello" or shake hands with them. ❍ *She went to greet her visitors.*

greet|ing /gritɪŋ/ NOUN something friendly that you say or do when you meet someone ❍ *We exchanged greetings.*

grew /gru/ **Grew** is a form of the verb **grow**.

grey /greɪ/ [BRIT] → **gray**

grief /grif/ NONCOUNT NOUN **Grief** is a feeling of great sadness. ❍ *The grief she felt when her brother died was terrible.*

griev|ance /grivᵊns/ NOUN If you have a **grievance** about something that has happened or been done, you believe that it was unfair. [HR] ❍ *They had a legitimate grievance.* ❍ *The main grievance of the drivers is the imposition of higher fees for driver's licenses.*

griev|ance pro|cedure (**grievance procedures**) NOUN a set of guidelines produced by a firm or organization, that explains how to make a formal complaint against them [HR] ❍ *One of their biggest mistakes is failing to put a formal grievance procedure in place to deal with staff complaints.*

grieve /griv/ (**grieves, grieving, grieved**) VERB If you **grieve over** or **for** someone or something, especially someone's death, you feel very sad about it. ❍ *He was still grieving for his son.*

grill /grɪl/
1 NOUN a flat frame of metal bars that you use to cook food over a fire
2 VERB When you **grill** food, or when it **grills**, you cook it on metal bars above a fire or barbecue. ❍ *Grill the steaks for about 5 minutes each side.*

grin /grɪn/ (**grins, grinning, grinned**)
1 VERB When you **grin**, you have a big smile on your face. ❍ *He grinned with pleasure.* ❍ *Phillip grinned at her.*
2 NOUN a big smile ❍ *She had a big grin on her face.*

grind /graɪnd/ (**grinds, grinding, ground**)
VERB If you **grind** a substance, you rub it against something hard until it becomes a fine powder. ❍ *It's the kind of coffee maker that actually grinds the beans as well as brewing the coffee.*

grip /grɪp/ (**grips, gripping, gripped**)
1 VERB If you **grip** something, you take it with your hand and hold it firmly. ❍ *She gripped the desk with both hands.*
2 NOUN a firm, strong hold on something ❍ *Keep a tight grip on your purse.*

groan /groʊn/
1 VERB If you **groan**, you make a long, low sound because you are in pain or unhappy. ❍ *He was groaning with pain.*
2 NOUN **Groan** is also a noun. ❍ *I heard a groan from the crowd.*

gro|cer /groʊsər/ [BRIT] → **grocery**

gro|ceries /groʊsəriz, groʊsriz/ **PL NOUN** **Groceries** are the things that you buy at a grocery or at a supermarket. ❍ *Gas stations often sell groceries.*

gro|cery /groʊsəri, groʊsri/ (**groceries**)
NOUN A **grocery** or a **grocery store** is a store that sells food.

groom /grum/
1 NOUN a person whose job is to look after horses
2 VERB If you **groom** an animal, you clean its fur, usually by brushing it. ❍ *She groomed the horses regularly.*

groove /gruv/ **NOUN** a deep line that is cut into a surface ❍ *He found ways to cut the grooves in records finer and finer.*

gross /groʊs/ (**grosses, grossing, grossed**)
1 ADJ **Gross** refers the total amount of something, especially money, before any has been taken away. Compare with **net**. ❍ *a fixed rate account guaranteeing 10.4% gross interest or 7.8% net*
2 ADV If a sum of money is paid **gross**, it is paid before any money has been subtracted from it. ❍ *Interest is paid gross, rather than having tax deducted.* ❍ *a father earning £20,000 gross a year*
▸ **gross up** If a sum is **grossed up**, it is increased to take into account the fact that a deduction, such as tax, will be made on it. ❍ *The money will be grossed up so that the payout is the same as at present.*

COLLOCATIONS
gross *income*
gross *profit*
gross *sales*
gross *earnings*
gross *revenues*

gross do|mes|tic prod|uct (**gross domestic products**) **NOUN** The **gross domestic product** is the total value of all the goods that a country has produced and the services it has provided in a particular year, not including its income from investments in other countries. Compare with **gross national product** and **net domestic product**. [ECONOMICS] ❍ *In the first quarter, the gross domestic product grew at an annual rate of more than 5 percent.*

gross mar|gin (**gross margins**) **NOUN** the difference between the selling price of a product and the cost of producing it, excluding overheads [FINANCE] ❍ *Overall sales rose 11 percent, while gross margins improved 2.7 percent.*

gross na|tion|al prod|uct (**gross national products**) **NOUN** The **gross national product** is the total value of all the goods that a country has produced and the services it has provided in a particular year, including its income from investments in other countries. Compare with **gross domestic product** and **net national product**. [ECONOMICS] ❍ *The preliminary estimate of the second-quarter gross national product showed moderate economic growth.*

gross prof|it (**gross profits**) NOUN A firm's **gross profit** is the difference between its total income from sales and its total production costs. Compare with **net profit**. [FINANCE] ❍ *He set high goals, demanding a doubling of gross profit.*

G

gross weight NONCOUNT NOUN **Gross weight** is the total weight of an article including the weight of its packaging.

group /grup/

1 NOUN a set of people who have the same interests or aims, and who organize themselves to work or act together ❍ *Members of an environmental group are staging a protest inside a chemical plant.*

2 NOUN a number of separate commercial or industrial firms that all have the same owner ❍ *The group made a pre-tax profit of $1.05 million.*

Group of Eight NOUN the Group of Seven nations and Russia, whose heads of government meet to discuss economic matters and international relations [ECONOMICS] ❍ *The argument is set to continue at the Group of Eight summit.*

Group of Sev|en NOUN the seven traditional leading industrial nations, Canada, France, Germany, Italy, Japan, the U.K., and the U.S., whose heads of government and finance ministers meet regularly [ECONOMICS] ❍ *The dollar sell-off was planned by the Group of Seven at its meeting Saturday.*

Group of Ten NOUN the ten nations who met in Paris in 1961 to discuss the IMF: Belgium, Canada, France, Italy, Japan, Netherlands, Sweden, the U.K., the U.S., and West Germany [ECONOMICS] ❍ *The Basle Committee was established by the central bank Governors of the Group of Ten countries in 1975.*

grow /groʊ/ (**grows, growing, grew, grown**)

1 VERB When someone or something **grows**, they gradually become bigger. ❍ *All children grow at different rates.*

2 VERB If a plant or tree **grows** somewhere, it lives there. ❍ *There were roses growing by the side of the door.*

3 VERB If you **grow** a particular type of plant, you put seeds or young plants in the ground and take care of them. ❍ *I always grow a few red onions.* ● **grow|er** NOUN ❍ *apple growers*

4 VERB If an amount or problem **grows**, it becomes greater. ❍ *Opposition grew and the government agreed to negotiate.* ❍ *a growing number of immigrants*

5 VERB If the economy or a business **grows**, it increases in wealth, size, or importance. ❍ *The economy continues to grow.*

6 VERB If someone **grows** a business, they take actions that will cause it to increase in wealth, size, or importance. [BUSINESS MANAGEMENT] ❍ *To grow the business, she needs to develop management expertise and innovation across her team.*

▸ **grow into** If one thing **grows into** another, it develops or changes until it becomes that thing. ❍ *This political debate threatens to grow into a full blown crisis.*

▸ **grow out of**

1 If you **grow out of** a type of behavior, you stop behaving in that way as you get older. ❍ *Most children who bite their nails grow out of it.*

2 When a child **grows out of** a piece of clothing, he or she becomes too big to wear it. ❍ *You've grown out of your shoes again.*

▸ **grow up** When someone **grows up**, they gradually change from being a child into being an adult. ❍ *She grew up in Tokyo.*

grown-up (**grown-ups**) also **grownup**

1 NOUN a child's word for an adult ❍ *I have to ask a grown-up.*

2 ADJ used to describe an adult, no longer depending on parents ❍ *She has two grown-up children.*

growth /groʊθ/

1 NONCOUNT NOUN The **growth of** something is its development. ❍ *population growth* ❍ *The government expects strong economic growth.* ❍ *high growth rates.*

2 NONCOUNT NOUN A **growth** in something is an increase in it. ❍ *The market has shown annual growth of 20 percent for several years.* ❍ *His business has had a growth in turnover of 15–20% since the 1980s.*
3 ADJ A **growth** industry, area, or market is one which is increasing in size or activity. ❍ *Computers and electronics are growth industries and need skilled technicians.* ❍ *Real estate lending has become the biggest growth area for American banks.*

GST /dʒi ɛs ti/ **NOUN** **GST** is an abbreviation for "goods and services tax." ❍ *This party supports the GST, but insists that food and books be exempt.*

guan|xi /gwɑnʃi, kwɑn-/ **NONCOUNT NOUN** **Guanxi** is a Chinese social concept that is based on the exchange of favors to form important personal relationships. [BUSINESS MANAGEMENT] ❍ *The chief asset of most companies is their guanxi, or connections.*

guar|an|tee /gærənti/
1 VERB If you **guarantee** something, you promise that it will definitely happen, or that you will do or provide it for someone. ❍ *We guarantee to refund your money if you are not delighted with your purchase.*
2 NOUN a written promise by a firm to repair a product or give you a new one if it has a fault [LEGAL] ❍ *Keep the guarantee in case something goes wrong.* ❍ *It was still under guarantee.*
3 VERB If a firm **guarantees** its product or work, they provide a guarantee for it. [LEGAL] ❍ *All our computers are guaranteed for 12 months.* ❍ *Some builders guarantee their work.*

guar|an|ty /gærənti/ (**guaranties**)
1 NOUN a promise to pay another person's debt if they do not pay it themselves [LEGAL]
2 NOUN a person who promises to pay another person's debt if they do not pay it themselves [LEGAL]

guard /gɑrd/
1 VERB If you **guard** a person, object, or place, you watch them carefully, either to protect someone or something, or to stop someone from escaping. ❍ *The details of the design have been a closely guarded secret.*
2 NOUN a person whose job is to guard a particular place or person ❍ *The security guard let them pass.*

guess /gɛs/
1 VERB If you **guess** something, you give an answer or provide an opinion when you do not know if it is true. ❍ *I would guess he's around 40 years old.* ❍ *Guess what I just did!*
2 NOUN an attempt to give an answer or provide an opinion when you do not know if it is true ❍ *If you don't know, just have a guess.*

guest /gɛst/
1 NOUN someone who you invite to your home or to an event ❍ *some very important guests*
2 NOUN someone who is staying in a hotel ❍ *We seemed to be the only guests.*

guest|house /gɛsthaʊs/ **NOUN** a private home where visitors can live ❍ *A room had been reserved for him at a guesthouse.*

gues|ti|mate /gɛstəmɪt/ **NOUN** an estimate that is based on guesswork, rather than accurate information [INFORMAL] ❍ *Two weeks ago he revised his initial guestimate.*

guid|ance /gaɪdᵊns/ **NONCOUNT NOUN** **Guidance** is help and advice. ❍ *My technique improved under his guidance.*

guide /gaɪd/ (**guides, guiding, guided**)
1 NOUN a book or website that gives information about a particular place or subject ❍ *a guide to Paris* ❍ *Our guide to doing business in Beijing.*
2 NOUN someone who shows tourists around places such as museums or cities ❍ *a tour guide*
3 VERB If you **guide** someone somewhere, you go there with them to show them the way. ❍ *He guided her toward the door.*

guide|line /gaɪdlaɪn/ **NOUN** a piece of official advice about how to do something ❍ *The government has issued new guidelines on health education.*

guide price (**guide prices**) **NOUN** a price that an agent quotes as a guide to buyers when they are considering the purchase of a property [BRIT] ❍ *Guide prices are supposed to be within 15% of a property's anticipated sale price.*

guilt /gɪlt/
1 NONCOUNT NOUN **Guilt** is an unhappy feeling of having done something wrong. ❍ *When they*

g

fall into debt they often feel guilt, failure, and shame very deeply indeed.

2 NONCOUNT NOUN Guilt is the fact that you have done something wrong or illegal. ❍ *The jury was convinced of his guilt.*

guilty /gɪlti/ (**guiltier, guiltiest**)

1 ADJ feeling unhappy because you have done something wrong ❍ *I feel so guilty, leaving all this work to you.* ● **guilti|ly ADV** ❍ *He looked up guiltily when I walked in.*

2 ADJ If someone is **guilty of** a crime or offense, they have done it. ❍ *They were found guilty of murder.*

G

gui|tar /gɪtɑr/ **NOUN** a musical instrument with six strings

gulf /gʌlf/ **NOUN** a large area of ocean that has land almost all the way around it ❍ *the Gulf of Mexico*

gum /gʌm/

1 NONCOUNT NOUN Gum is a sweet sticky substance that you keep in your mouth for a long time but do not swallow. ❍ *He always chews gum.*

2 NOUN the firm, pink flesh inside your mouth, where your teeth grow ❍ *Gently brush your teeth and gums.*

gun /gʌn/ **NOUN** a weapon that shoots bullets ❍ *The shootings led to tougher laws on gun ownership.*

guru /guru/ **NOUN** a person who some people regard as an expert or leader ❍ *Management gurus are among the most powerful opinion formers of the modern age.*

COLLOCATIONS

a *design* guru
an *advertising* guru
an *investment* guru
a *marketing* guru

gust /gʌst/ **NOUN** a short, strong, sudden rush of wind ❍ *A gust of wind came down the valley.*

gut /gʌt/

1 NOUN the tube inside the body of a person or animal that food passes through after it has been in the stomach ❍ *The food then passes into the gut.*

2 NONCOUNT NOUN If you have the **guts** to do something that is difficult or unpleasant, you have the courage to do it. [INFORMAL] ❍ *She has the guts to say what she thinks.*

guy /gaɪ/ **NOUN** a man [INFORMAL] ❍ *I was working with a guy from Milwaukee.*

gym /dʒɪm/ **NOUN** a club, a building, or a large room with equipment for doing physical exercises ❍ *I go to the gym twice a week.*

gym|nas|tics /dʒɪmnæstɪks/ **NONCOUNT NOUN Gymnastics** is a sport that consists of physical exercises that develop your strength and your ability to move easily. ❍ *the women's gymnastics team*

Hh

hab|it /hæbɪt/
1 NOUN something that you regularly do ❍ *Consumers still believe that advertising has no effect on their buying habits.*
2 If you **are in the habit of** doing something, you do it regularly. ❍ *He has never been in the habit of sharing his thoughts.*

hack /hæk/
1 VERB If you **hack** something or **hack at** it, you cut it with strong, rough strokes using a sharp tool such as an ax or a knife. ❍ *An armed gang barged onto the train and began hacking and shooting anyone in sight.* ❍ *Matthew desperately hacked through the leather.*
2 VERB If someone **hacks into** a computer system, they break into the system in order to get secret information. [TECHNOLOGY] ❍ *The saboteurs had demanded money in return for revealing how they hacked into the systems.* • **hack|er NOUN** ❍ *a hacker who steals credit card numbers* • **hack|ing NONCOUNT NOUN** ❍ *the common and often illegal art of computer hacking*
3 NOUN a politician you disapprove of because they are too loyal to their party and do not deserve the position they have ❍ *Far too many party hacks from the old days still hold influential jobs.*
4 NOUN a professional writer you disapprove of because they write for money without worrying about the quality of their writing ❍ *tabloid hacks, always eager to find victims in order to sell newspapers*

had /hæd/ **Had** is a form of the verb **have**.

hadn't /hædᵊnt/ **Hadn't** is short for "had not."

hag|gle /hægᵊl/ (**haggles, haggling, haggled**) **VERB** If you **haggle**, you argue about the cost of something that you are buying before reaching an agreement. ❍ *Ella showed her the best places to go for a good buy, and taught her how to haggle with used furniture dealers.* ❍ *Of course he'll still haggle over the price.* • **hag|gling NONCOUNT NOUN** ❍ *After months of haggling, they recovered only three-quarters of what they had lent.*

hail /heɪl/ **NONCOUNT NOUN Hail** is small balls of ice that fall like rain from the sky.

hair /hɛər/
1 NONCOUNT NOUN Your **hair** is the fine threads that grow on your head. ❍ *I wash my hair every night.*
2 NOUN Hair is the short threads that grow on the bodies of humans and animals. ❍ *The quicker, cleaner way to deal with unwanted hair.* ❍ *There were dog hairs all over the sofa.*

hair|cut /hɛərkʌt/ **NOUN** an occasion when someone cuts your hair ❍ *I need a haircut.*

hair|dresser /hɛərdrɛsər/ **NOUN** a person whose job is to cut people's hair

hair|style /hɛərstaɪl/ **NOUN** the style in which your hair has been cut or arranged ❍ *Have you seen her new hairstyle?*

hairy /hɛəri/ (**hairier, hairiest**) **ADJ** covered with hairs ❍ *hairy legs*

half /hæf/ (**halves** /hævz/)
1 Half of a number, an amount, or an object is one of two equal parts. ❍ *More than half of all U.S. houses are heated with gas.*
2 You use **half a**, **half an**, or **half the** to talk about one of two equal parts of the thing mentioned. ❍ *We talked for half an hour.* ❍ *They only received half the money.*
3 ADJ Half is also an adjective. ❍ *I'll stay with you for the first half hour.*
4 ADV You use **half** to say that something is only partly in the state that you are describing. ❍ *The hotels are less than half full.*

half-h<u>ou</u>r (**half-hours**) **NOUN** a period of thirty minutes ❍ *The talk was followed by a half-hour of discussion.*

half|time /h<u>æ</u>ft<u>aɪ</u>m/ **NONCOUNT NOUN** **Halftime** is the period between the two parts of a sports event, when the players take a short rest. ❍ *We bought something to eat during halftime.*

half|way /h<u>æ</u>fw<u>eɪ</u>/

1 ADV in the middle of a place or between two points ❍ *Lukow is a small market town halfway between Warsaw and Poland's border with Belarus.*

2 ADV in the middle of an event or period of time ❍ *We were more than halfway through our tour.*

H

hall /h<u>ɔ</u>l/

1 NOUN the area in a house or apartment that connects one room to another ❍ *The hall leads to a large living room.*

2 NOUN a large room or a building that is used for public events such as concerts and meetings ❍ *a conference hall*

Hal|low|een /h<u>æ</u>loʊw<u>i</u>n/ also **Hallowe'en** **NONCOUNT NOUN** **Halloween** is the night of October 31st when children wear special clothes, and walk from house to house asking for candy.

hall|way /h<u>ɔ</u>lweɪ/ **NOUN** an area in a building with doors that lead into other rooms ❍ *They walked along the quiet hallway.*

halo /h<u>eɪ</u>loʊ/ (**haloes**) **NOUN** a circle of light around the head of a holy figure

h<u>a</u>lo ef|fect **NONCOUNT NOUN** The **halo effect** is the positive impact on sales of a firm's range of products produced by the popularity of one particular product. [HR] ❍ *Charitable events are often used to create a halo effect of positive feeling toward a corporation.*

halt /h<u>ɔ</u>lt/

1 VERB When someone **halts** something, they stop it. ❍ *The company has now halted production.*

2 If someone or something **comes to a halt**, they stop moving. ❍ *The elevator came to a halt at the first floor.*

ham /h<u>æ</u>m/ **NONCOUNT NOUN** **Ham** is meat from a pig that has been prepared with salt and spices.

ham|burg|er /h<u>æ</u>mbɜrgər/ **NOUN** a type of food made from small pieces of meat that have been shaped into a flat circle, often eaten in a round piece of bread

ham|mer /h<u>æ</u>mər/

1 NOUN a tool consisting of a heavy piece of metal at the end of a handle, used for hitting nails into wood

2 VERB If you **hammer** an object such as a nail, you hit it with a hammer. ❍ *She hammered a nail into the window frame.*

hand /h<u>æ</u>nd/

1 NOUN the part of your body at the end of your arm, that you use for holding things ❍ *I put my hand into my pocket and took out the letter.*

2 NOUN If you give someone **a hand** with something, you help them. ❍ *Can I give you a hand with the mail?*

3 NOUN one of the long thin parts on a clock or watch that move to show the time

4 VERB If you **hand** something **to** someone, you put it into their hand. ❍ *He handed me a piece of paper.*

5 If you do something **by hand**, you do it using your hands rather than a machine. ❍ *The letter was delivered by hand.*

6 If two people are **walking hand in hand**, they are holding each other by the hand.

7 If someone or something is **on hand**, they are near and ready to be used. ❍ *There are experts on hand to give you all the help you need.*

8 You use **on the one hand ... on the other hand** to talk about two different ways of looking at something. ❍ *On the one hand, the body cannot survive without fat. On the other hand, if the body has too much fat, our health starts to suffer.*

9 If a person or a situation **gets out of hand**, they can no longer be controlled. ❍ *What started as an argument had gotten out of hand.*

▸**hand in** If you **hand in** something, you take it to someone and give it to them. ❍ *I need to hand in my expenses form today.*

▸**hand out** If you **hand** things **out**, you give one to each person in a group. ❍ *My job was to hand out the leaflets.*

hand|bag /hændbæg/ **NOUN** a small bag that a woman uses for carrying things such as money and keys

hand|cuff /hændkʌf/
1 PL NOUN Handcuffs are two connected metal rings that can be locked around someone's wrists. ❍ *He was taken to prison in handcuffs.*
2 VERB If you **handcuff** someone, you put handcuffs around their wrists. ❍ *Police had to handcuff him.*

hand|ful /hændfʊl/
1 NOUN a small number of people or things ❍ *Only a handful of people know his secret.*
2 NOUN the amount of something that you can hold in your hand ❍ *Only a handful of shirts were returned following the recall.*

handi|capped /hændikæpt/ **ADJ** having a physical or mental condition that makes you unable to do particular things ❍ *Some employers are reluctant to hire handicapped workers.*

han|dle /hænd^əl/ (**handles, handling, handled**)
1 NOUN an object that is attached to a door or drawer, used for opening and closing it ❍ *I turned the handle and the door opened.*
2 NOUN the part of a tool, a bag, or a cup that you hold ❍ *a knife handle*
3 VERB If you **handle** a particular area of work, you have responsibility for it. ❍ *a secretary must be able to handle clients* ❍ *She handled travel arrangements for the press corps during the presidential campaign.*
4 VERB If you **handle** a situation in a particular way, you deal with it in that way. ❍ *He handled the meeting very badly.*
5 VERB When you **handle** something, you hold it or move it with your hands. ❍ *Always wash your hands before handling food.*
6 VERB When you **handle** a specific type of merchandise, you trade or deal it.
• **han|dling NONCOUNT NOUN** ❍ *handling charges* ❍ *shipping and handling*

hand|out /hændaʊt/
1 NOUN a gift of money, clothing, or food that is given free to poor people ❍ *Each family is being given a cash handout of six thousand dollars.*
2 NOUN money given to someone that you believe has done nothing to deserve it ❍ *the tendency of politicians to use money on vote-buying handouts rather than on investment in the future*
3 NOUN a paper given out at meetings that contains a summary of the information or topics that will be dealt with ❍ *Many trainers are opting for group discussions instead of handouts.*

hand|shake /hændʃeɪk/ **NOUN** the act of holding someone's hand and moving it up and down, for example as a greeting ❍ *a firm handshake*

h

hand|some /hænsəm/ **ADJ** A **handsome** man has an attractive face. ❍ *The ad showed a tall, handsome soldier.*

hand|writing /hændraɪtɪŋ/ **NONCOUNT NOUN** Your **handwriting** is your style of writing with a pen or a pencil. ❍ *The address was in neat handwriting.*

handy /hændi/ (**handier, handiest**)
1 ADJ useful ❍ *The book gives handy hints on writing reports.*
2 ADJ near to you and easy to reach ❍ *Make sure you have a pencil and paper handy.*

hang /hæŋ/ (**hangs, hanging, hung** or **hanged**)

Use **hangs**, **hanging**, **hanged** for meaning **3**.

1 VERB If something **hangs** somewhere, it is attached there so that it does not touch the ground. ❍ *Flags hang at every entrance.*
2 VERB If you **hang** something somewhere, you attach it there so that it does not touch the ground. ❍ *She hung her clothes up to dry.*
3 VERB If someone **is hanged**, they are killed by having a rope tied around their neck.
▸**hang on**
1 If you ask someone to **hang on**, you want them to wait. [INFORMAL] ❍ *Can you hang on for a minute?*
2 If you **hang on to** or **hang onto** something,

you hold it very tightly. ❍ *He hung on to the rail as he went downstairs.*

▸**hang out** If you **hang out** in a particular place or area, you spend a lot of time there. [INFORMAL] ❍ *They hang out by the coffee machine.*

▸**hang up** If you **hang up**, you end a phone call. ❍ *Don't hang up on me!*

Hang Seng In|dex /hæŋ sɛŋ ɪndɛks/ NONCOUNT NOUN The **Hang Seng Index** is an index of share prices on the Hong Kong Stock Exchange. [ECONOMICS]

Ha|nuk|kah /hɑnəkə/ also **Hanukah, Chanukah** NONCOUNT NOUN **Hanukkah** is a Jewish festival that begins in November or December and lasts for eight days.

H

hap|pen /hæpən/

1 VERB When something **happens**, it takes place. ❍ *What will happen when he finds out?* ❍ *What's the worst thing that's ever happened to you?*

2 VERB If you **happen to** do something, you do it by chance. ❍ *I happened to be at the airport at the same time as Jim.*

hap|pi|ly /hæpɪli/

1 ADV used to show that you are glad about a fact ❍ *Happily, no one was hurt.*

2 ADV in a happy way ❍ *These restaurants have happily been doing business for generations.*

hap|py /hæpi/ (**happier, happiest**)

1 ADJ feeling pleased and satisfied ❍ *Are you happy about the new arrangements?*

• **hap|pi|ness** NONCOUNT NOUN ❍ *They say business brings much money but little happiness.*

2 ADJ full of happy feelings and pleasant experiences ❍ *It was the happiest time of my life.* ❍ *Happy Birthday!*

3 ADJ If you are **happy to** do something, you are willing to do it. ❍ *I'm happy to answer any questions.*

har|bor /hɑrbər/ NOUN an area of water next to the land where boats can safely stay

har|bour /hɑrbər/ [BRIT] → **harbor**

hard /hɑrd/

1 ADJ firm, and not easily bent or broken ❍ *a hard wooden floor*

2 ADJ difficult to do or deal with ❍ *That's a very hard question.* ❍ *She's had a hard life.*

3 ADV If you work **hard**, you work with a lot of effort. ❍ *If I work hard, I'll finish the job tomorrow.*

4 ADJ **Hard** is also an adjective. ❍ *He's certainly a hard worker.*

5 ADJ **Hard** cash is money in the form of coins and bills, or money that will definitely be paid. ❍ *If the company falls on hard times, it can hand over low-priced bonds instead of hard cash.*

6 ADJ A **hard** currency is one that is valuable because it comes from a country with a strong economy. [ECONOMICS] ❍ *The government doles out hard currency only for essential imports.*

7 ADJ If credit is **hard**, it is difficult to obtain.

hard disk (**hard disks**) NOUN A computer's **hard disk** is a stiff magnetic disk on which data and programs can be stored. [TECHNOLOGY]

hard drive (**hard drives**) NOUN the part of a computer that contains the hard disk [TECHNOLOGY] ❍ *You can download the file to your hard drive.*

hard|ly /hɑrdli/

1 ADV almost not, or not quite ❍ *He could hardly believe what he saw.* ❍ *I've hardly been home for three days.*

2 ADV used in expressions such as **hardly ever** and **hardly any** to mean almost never or almost none ❍ *The motel is hardly ever full.* ❍ *She has hardly any experience.*

hard sell (**hard sells**)

1 NONCOUNT NOUN A **hard sell** is a method of selling in which the salesperson puts a lot of pressure on someone to make them buy something. Compare with **soft sell**. [MARKETING AND SALES] ❍ *The clerk's hard sell made the product seem like a great deal.*

2 NOUN a product that is difficult to sell [MARKETING AND SALES] ❍ *The computer was a hard sell because of its high price.*

hard|ware /hɑrdwɛər/

1 NONCOUNT NOUN In computer systems, **hardware** is things such as the computer, the keyboard, and the screen, rather than the software programs that tell the computer what to do. Compare with **software**. [TECHNOLOGY]

2 NONCOUNT NOUN **Hardware** is tools and

equipment that are used in the home and garden. ❍ *a hardware store*

harm /hɑrm/

1 VERB To **harm** someone or something means to injure or damage them. ❍ *He didn't mean to harm anyone.* ❍ *This product may harm the environment.*

2 NONCOUNT NOUN Harm is injury or damage to a person or thing. ❍ *Don't worry. He won't do you any harm.* ❍ *It does no harm to talk.*

harm|ful /hɑrmfəl/ **ADJ** having a bad effect on someone or something ❍ *People should know about the harmful effects of the drug.*

harm|less /hɑrmlɪs/ **ADJ** not having bad effects ❍ *Lightning strikes on passenger jets are common and usually harmless.*

har|mo|ni|sa|tion /hɑrmənaɪzeɪʃən/ [BRIT] → **harmonization**

har|mo|ni|za|tion /hɑrmənaɪzeɪʃən/ **NONCOUNT NOUN Harmonization** is a system in the European Union where the blue-collar workers and the white-collar workers in an organization have similar status and any former differences in terms and conditions of employment are made equal. [ECONOMICS] ❍ *fiscal harmonization*

har|mo|ny /hɑrməni/ **NONCOUNT NOUN** If things are **in harmony**, they are arranged in a pleasant way. ❍ *Marketing management is most effective when it operates in harmony with the rest of the firm's operational areas.*

harsh /hɑrʃ/

1 ADJ severe and unpleasant ❍ *harsh weather conditions*

2 ADJ unkind and showing no sympathy ❍ *She said some harsh things.* ● **harsh|ly ADV** ❍ *He was harshly treated.*

har|vest /hɑrvɪst/

1 NOUN The harvest is the gathering of a farm crop. ❍ *Wheat harvests were poor in both Europe and America last year.*

2 VERB When you **harvest** a crop, you gather it in. ❍ *Farmers here still plant and harvest their crops by hand.*

has /hæz/ **Has** is a form of the verb **have**.

hasn't /hæzᵊnt/ **Hasn't** is short for "has not."

has|ty /heɪsti/ (**hastier, hastiest**) **ADJ** done too quickly, without enough thought ❍ *a hasty decision*

hat /hæt/ **NOUN** a covering for the head ❍ *Look for a woman in a red hat.*

hatch /hætʃ/ (**hatches, hatching, hatched**) **VERB** When an egg hatches, or when a bird, reptile, or another animal **hatches**, the egg breaks open and the young creature comes out. ❍ *The eggs hatch after a week.*

hate /heɪt/ (**hates, hating, hated**)

1 VERB If you **hate** someone or something, you have a strong feeling of dislike for them. ❍ *She thinks that everyone hates her.* ❍ *He hates losing.*

2 NONCOUNT NOUN Hate is also a noun. ❍ *He spoke of the hate that he felt for his father.*

haul /hɔl/ **VERB** If you **haul** something heavy somewhere, you move it using a lot of effort. ❍ *I hauled my luggage up the steps.*

haul|er /hɔlər/ **NOUN** a firm or a person that transports goods by road [LOGISTICS AND DISTRIBUTION]

haul|ier /hɔlyər/ [LOGISTICS AND DISTRIBUTION, BRIT] → **hauler**

have

❶ AUXILIARY VERB USES
❷ USED WITH NOUNS DESCRIBING ACTIONS
❸ OTHER VERB USES AND PHRASES
❸ MODAL PHRASES

❶ **have** /həv, STRONG hæv/ (**has, having, had**) **AUX** You use **have** and **has** with another verb to form the present perfect. ❍ *Alex hasn't left yet.* ❍ *What have you found?* ❍ *Frankie hasn't been feeling well today.*

❷ **have** /hæv/ (**has, having, had**) **VERB** You can use **have** with a noun to talk about an action or an event. ❍ *Come and have a look at this!* ❍ *We had a long discussion.* ❍ *I had an accident.*

❸ **have** /hæv/ (**has, having, had**)

1 VERB You use **have** to say that someone or

something owns something. ❍ *Bill has a new computer.*
2 VERB You use **have** to talk about people's relationships. ❍ *Do you have any brothers or sisters?*
3 VERB You use **have** when you are talking about a person's appearance or character. ❍ *She has blue eyes.* ❍ *George has a terrible temper.*
4 VERB If you **have** something done, someone does it for you. ❍ *He had his hair cut.*

❹ **have** /hæv, hæf/ (**has, having, had**) You use **have to** when you are saying that someone must do something, or that something must happen. If you do not **have to** do something, it is not necessary for you to do it. ❍ *I have to go to the airport now.* ❍ *You don't have to go.*

H

haven't /hævᵊnt/ **Haven't** is short for "have not."

hay /heɪ/ **NONCOUNT NOUN** **Hay** is grass that has been cut and dried so that it can be used for feeding animals.

haz|ard /hæzərd/ **NOUN** something that could be dangerous ❍ *a health hazard*

he /hi, i, STRONG hi/ **PRON** used for talking about a man, a boy, or a male animal ❍ *John was my boss, but he couldn't remember my name.*

head /hɛd/
1 NOUN the top part of your body that has your eyes, mouth, and brain in it ❍ *She sat with her head in her hands and looked at the telephone.*
2 NOUN your mind ❍ *I just said the first thing that came into my head.*
3 NOUN a person who is in charge of a country or organization ❍ *I spoke to the head of the department.*
4 NOUN The **head** of something is the top or front of it, or the most important end of it. ❍ *The chief executive sat at the head of the table.*
5 VERB If you **head** a department, a firm, or an organization, you are the person who is in charge of it. ❍ *Michael Williams heads the department's Office of Civil Rights.*
6 VERB If you **are heading** for a particular place, you are going toward that place. ❍ *We're heading back to Washington tomorrow.*
7 The cost or amount **a head** or **per head** is the cost or amount for one person. ❍ *This simple meal costs less than $3 a head.*

head|ache /hɛdeɪk/ **NOUN** If you have a **headache**, you have a pain in your head.

head|hunt /hɛdhʌnt/ **VERB** If someone who works for a particular firm **is headhunted**, they leave that firm because another firm has offered them another job with better pay and higher status. ❍ *He was headhunted by the firm last October to build an advertising team.* ● **head|hunt|ing** **NONCOUNT NOUN** ❍ *Headhunting is a boom industry.*

head|light /hɛdlaɪt/ **NOUN** A vehicle's **headlights** are the large lights at the front.

head|line /hɛdlaɪn/
1 NOUN the title of a newspaper story, printed in large letters ❍ *The headline said: "New Government Plans."*
2 PL NOUN **The headlines** are the important parts of the news that you hear first on radio or television news reports. ❍ *the news headlines*

head of de|part|ment (**heads of departments**) [ADMINISTRATION, mainly BRIT] → **department head**

head of|fice (**head offices**) **NOUN** the headquarters of a firm or organization [ADMINISTRATION]

head|quarters /hɛdkwɔrtərz/ **NOUN** The **headquarters** of an organization is its main office. [ADMINISTRATION] ❍ *Chicago's police headquarters*

heal /hil/ **VERB** When a broken bone or other injury **heals**, it becomes healthy again. ❍ *It took six months for her injuries to heal.*

health /hɛlθ/ **NONCOUNT NOUN** A person's **health** is the condition of their body. ❍ *Too much fatty food is bad for your health.*

health care also **healthcare** **NONCOUNT NOUN** **Health care** is services for preventing and treating illnesses and injuries.

healthy /hɛlθi/ (**healthier, healthiest**)
1 ADJ well and not often sick ❍ *a healthy child*

2 ADJ good for your health ❍ *Try to eat a healthy diet.*

heap /hip/

1 NOUN A **heap of** things is a messy pile of them. ❍ *a heap of papers*

2 VERB If you **heap** things somewhere, you put them in a large pile. ❍ *The large desk was heaped with papers.*

hear /hɪər/ (**hears, hearing, heard** /hɜrd/)

1 VERB When you **hear** a sound, you become aware of it through your ears. ❍ *She could hear music in the distance.* ❍ *I didn't hear what he said.*

2 VERB If you **hear from** someone, you receive a letter, an email, or a telephone call from them. ❍ *It's always great to hear from our customers.*

3 VERB If you **hear** information, someone tells you about it. ❍ *I heard about the plan from Karen.* ❍ *I hear that Clea is leaving.*

hear|ing /hɪərɪŋ/ **NONCOUNT NOUN** **Hearing** is the sense that makes it possible for you to be aware of sounds. ❍ *Even at 65, his hearing is excellent.*

heart /hɑrt/

1 NOUN the part inside your chest that makes the blood move around your body ❍ *His heart was beating fast.*

2 NOUN used for talking about emotions, especially love ❍ *His words filled her heart with joy.*

3 NOUN **The heart of** a place is the middle part of it. ❍ *They own a busy hotel in the heart of the city.*

4 NOUN the shape ♥

5 If someone **breaks** your **heart**, they make you very sad. ❍ *The assassination of the president broke our hearts.*

6 If you know a poem, a song, or the words of something **by heart**, you can remember all of it. ❍ *Mike knew his speech by heart.*

heart at|tack (**heart attacks**) **NOUN** an occasion when someone's heart suddenly stops working ❍ *He died of a heart attack.*

heat /hit/

1 VERB When you **heat** something, you make it hot. ❍ *The cereal's box includes directions for heating it with milk in a microwave oven.*

2 NONCOUNT NOUN **Heat** is warmth or the feeling of being hot. ❍ *Our clothes dried quickly in the heat of the sun.*

heat|er /hitər/ **NOUN** a piece of equipment that is used for making a room warm ❍ *an electric heater*

heav|en /hɛvən/ **NONCOUNT NOUN** **Heaven** is the place where some people believe good people go when they die.

heavy /hɛvi/ (**heavier, heaviest**)

1 ADJ weighing a lot ❍ *This bag is very heavy.*

2 ADJ used for talking about how much someone or something weighs ❍ *How heavy is your suitcase?*

3 ADJ great in amount ❍ *heavy traffic*

• **heavi|ly ADV** ❍ *It rained heavily all day.*

4 ADJ **Heavy** industry is firms that produce large, bulky goods.

heavy-duty ADJ very strong and able to be used a lot ❍ *a heavy-duty plastic bag*

he'd /hid, id, STRONG hid/

1 He'd is short for "he had." ❍ *He'd seen her before.*

2 He'd is short for "he would." ❍ *He'd like to come with us.*

hedge /hɛdʒ/ (**hedges, hedging, hedged**)

1 NOUN a row of bushes or small trees, usually along the edge of a lawn, garden, field, or road

2 VERB If you **hedge against** something unpleasant or unwanted that might affect you, you do something that will protect you from it. ❍ *You can hedge against illness with insurance.*

3 NOUN something that will protect you from something unpleasant or unwanted ❍ *Gold is traditionally a hedge against inflation.*

4 If you **hedge** your **bets**, you reduce the risk of losing a lot by supporting more than one person or thing in a situation where they are opposed to each other. ❍ *The company tried to hedge its bets by diversifying into other fields.*

hedge fund (**hedge funds**) **NOUN** an investment fund that invests large amounts of money using methods that involve a lot of risk [BANKING]

heel /hil/

1 NOUN the back part of your foot, just below your ankle ❍ *I have a big blister on my heel.*

2 NOUN the raised part on the bottom of a shoe at the back ❍ *She always wears shoes with high heels.*

height /haɪt/
1 NOUN The **height** of a person or thing is their size from the bottom to the top. ❍ *Her weight is normal for her height.*
2 NOUN The **height** of something is its distance above the ground. ❍ *You can change the height of the seat.*

heir /ɛər/ **NOUN** someone who will receive a person's money or property when that person dies

held /hɛld/ **Held** is a form of the verb **hold**.

H

heli|cop|ter /hɛlikɒptər/ **NOUN** an aircraft with long blades on top that go around very fast

hell /hɛl/ **NONCOUNT NOUN Hell** is the place where people believe bad people go when they die.

he'll /hɪl, il, STRONG hil/ **He'll** is short for "he will." ❍ *He'll be very successful, I'm sure.*

hel|lo /hɛloʊ/ also **hullo**
1 You say "**Hello**" to someone when you meet them. ❍ *Hello, Trish. How are you?*
2 You say "**Hello**" when you answer the phone.

hel|met /hɛlmɪt/ **NOUN** a hat made of a hard material, that you wear to protect your head

help /hɛlp/
1 VERB If you **help** someone, you do something for them. ❍ *Let me help you with the door.* ❍ *You can help by giving money.*
2 NONCOUNT NOUN Help is also a noun. ❍ *Thanks for your help.*
3 VERB If you **help yourself to** something, you take what you want. ❍ *There are biscuits on the table. Help yourself.*
4 If you **can't help** feeling or behaving in a particular way, you cannot stop yourself from feeling or doing it. ❍ *I couldn't help laughing when I saw her face.*

help desk (**help desks**) **NOUN** a special service that you can telephone or e-mail in order to get information about a particular product or subject ❍ *Call the help desk for a status on the loans.*

help|ful /hɛlpfəl/ **ADJ** giving help ❍ *The hotel staff were very helpful.*

help|less /hɛlpləs/ **ADJ** not able to do anything useful ❍ *Honest citizens feel helpless in the face of these criminals.* ● **help|less|ly ADV** ❍ *They watched helplessly as the house burned to the ground.*

hemi|sphere /hɛmɪsfɪər/ **NOUN** one half of the Earth ❍ *These animals live in the northern hemisphere.*

hen /hɛn/ **NOUN** a female chicken

her /hər, ər, STRONG hɜr/
1 PRON used for talking about a woman, a girl, or a female animal that has already been mentioned ❍ *I told her that we'd met before.*
2 ADJ used for showing that something belongs or relates to a woman, a girl, or a female animal that has already been mentioned ❍ *Isabel was there with her team.*

herb /ɜrb/ **NOUN** a plant whose leaves are used in cooking to add flavor to food, or as a medicine ❍ *Fry the mushrooms in a little olive oil and add the chopped herbs.*

herb|al /ɜrbᵊl/ **ADJ** using herbs ❍ *herbal remedies*

herd /hɜrd/ **NOUN** a large group of one type of animal that lives together ❍ *Farmers will look for increased production from their herds.*

here /hɪər/
1 ADV used for talking about the place where you are ❍ *I can't stay here all day.* ❍ *Come here.*
2 ADV said when you are offering or giving something to someone ❍ *Here is your coffee.*

here's /hɪərz/ **Here's** is short for "here is." ❍ *Here's Annie!*

hero /hɪəroʊ/ (**heroes**)
1 NOUN the main male character of a story ❍ *Radcliffe plays the hero in the Harry Potter movies.*
2 NOUN someone who has done something very brave or good ❍ *Mr. Mandela is a hero who has inspired millions.*

hero|ine /hɛroʊɪn/
1 NOUN the main female character of a story

❍ *The heroine of the book is a young doctor.*
2 NOUN a woman who has done something very brave or good ❍ *France's first gold medal winner became a national heroine.*

hers /hɜrz/ **PRON** used for showing that something belongs to a woman or a girl ❍ *I thought the bag was hers.*

her|self /hərsɛlf/
1 PRON used for showing that a woman or a girl who performs an action is also the person that the action happens to ❍ *She looked at herself in the mirror.* ❍ *If she's not careful, she'll hurt herself.*
2 PRON If a woman or a girl does something **herself**, she, and not anyone else, does it. ❍ *She meant to deal with it herself.*

he's /hiz, iz, STRONG hiz/ **He's** is short for "he is" or "he has." ❍ *He's coming tomorrow.*

hesi|tate /hɛzɪteɪt/ (**hesitates, hesitating, hesitated**) **VERB** If you **hesitate**, you do not speak or act quickly, usually because you are not sure what to say or do. ❍ *Catherine hesitated before answering.*

hey /heɪ/
1 in informal situations, used for attracting someone's attention ❍ *Hey! Be careful!*
2 in informal situations, used for greeting someone ❍ *Hey, Kate! How're you doing?*

hi /haɪ/ in informal situations, used for greeting someone ❍ *"Hi, Liz," she said.*

hid|den /hɪdən/
1 Hidden is a form of the verb **hide**.
2 ADJ not easy to see or know about ❍ *Certain assets were hidden and others undervalued.*

hid|den agen|da (**hidden agendas**) **NOUN** an objective that someone pursues while they appear to be doing something else ❍ *He accused foreign nations of having a hidden agenda to harm French influence.*

hide /haɪd/ (**hides, hiding, hid, hidden**)
1 VERB If you **hide** something or someone, you put them in a place where they cannot easily be seen or found. ❍ *Their accounting methods hid losses.*
2 VERB If you **hide**, you go somewhere where people cannot easily find you. ❍ *The little boy hid in the closet.*
3 VERB If you **hide** a feeling, you do not let people know about it. ❍ *Lee tried to hide his excitement.*

hi|er|ar|chy /haɪərɑrki/ (**hierarchies**)
1 NOUN a system of organizing people into different ranks or levels of importance, for example in society or in a firm [ADMINISTRATION, BUSINESS MANAGEMENT] ❍ *Like most other American companies with a rigid hierarchy, workers and managers had strictly defined duties.* ● **hi|er|ar|chi|cal ADJ** ❍ *The hierarchical structure of the workplace gives everyone a role to play.*
2 NOUN the group of people who manage and control an organization [ADMINISTRATION, BUSINESS MANAGEMENT] ❍ *The church hierarchy today feels the church should reflect the social and political realities of the country.*

COLLOCATIONS
corporate hierarchy
a *strict* hierarchy
a *rigid* hierarchy

h

high /haɪ/
1 ADJ tall or a long way above the ground ❍ *the high walls of the prison* ❍ *Mount Marcy is the highest mountain in the Adirondacks.*
2 ADV High is also an adverb. ❍ *She can jump higher than anyone else.*
3 ADJ used for talking or asking about how much something measures from the top to the bottom ❍ *The grass in the yard was a foot high.*
4 ADJ great in amount or strength ❍ *High winds destroyed many trees and buildings.* ❍ *The number of people injured was high.*
5 ADJ A **high** sound or voice is not deep. ❍ *a child's high voice*

higher-rate ADJ In Britain, **higher-rate** income tax is a rate of income tax that is higher than the basic rate and becomes payable on taxable income over a specified limit. [ECONOMICS] ❍ *We have seen a big jump in the number of higher-rate taxpayers under this government.*

high|light /haɪlaɪt/
1 VERB If someone or something **highlights** a

point or problem, they show that it is important. ❍ *Her talk highlighted the problems we face.*
2 NOUN the most interesting part of an event ❍ *That visit was one of the highlights of the tour.*

high|ly /haɪli/ **ADV** very ❍ *Mr. Singh was a highly successful salesman.*

high|ly lev|er|aged ADJ having a high ratio of debt to equity [BANKING] ❍ *a private bank would not be allowed to have such a highly leveraged balance sheet*

high school (high schools) NOUN a school for children usually aged between fourteen and eighteen

H

high-tech /haɪ tɛk/ also **high tech, hi tech ADJ High-tech** equipment uses modern methods and computers. ❍ *high-tech camera equipment*

high-tech sec|tor NONCOUNT NOUN The **high-tech sector** is the group of businesses that develop advanced technologies, such as computers and cellphones. [TECHNOLOGY] ❍ *Growth in the high-tech sector has resulted in price declines for the newer technologies.*

high|way /haɪweɪ/ **NOUN** a main road that connects towns or cities ❍ *The accident happened on the highway between Chicago and Madison.*

hi|jack /haɪdʒæk/
1 VERB If someone **hijacks** an airplane or other vehicle, they illegally take control of it while it is traveling from one place to another. ❍ *Two men hijacked the plane.*
2 NOUN Hijack is also a noun. ❍ *Finally, six months after the hijack, he was arrested.*

hike /haɪk/ **(hikes, hiking, hiked)**
1 NOUN a long walk, especially in the countryside ❍ *You can go for a hike up Mount Desmond.*
2 VERB If you **hike**, you go for a long walk. ❍ *We hiked through the Fish River Canyon.*
● **hik|er NOUN** ❍ *The hikers spent the night in the mountains.* ● **hik|ing NONCOUNT NOUN** ❍ *We could go hiking in the mountains.*

hi|lari|ous /hɪlɛəriəs/ **ADJ** very funny ❍ *It was a hilarious story.*

hill /hɪl/ **NOUN** an area of land that is higher than the land around it ❍ *The castle is on a hill above the old town.*

him /hɪm/ **PRON** used for talking about a man, a boy, or a male animal that has already been mentioned ❍ *Elaine met him at the railroad station.* ❍ *Is Sam there? Let me talk to him.*

him|self /hɪmsɛlf/
1 PRON used for showing that a man or a boy who performs an action is also the person that the action happens to ❍ *He poured himself a cup of coffee.* ❍ *He was talking to himself.*
2 PRON If a man or a boy does something **himself**, he, and not anyone else, does it. ❍ *He'll tell you about it himself.*

Hin|du /hɪndu/
1 NOUN a person who believes in Hinduism
2 ADJ belonging or relating to Hinduism ❍ *We visited a Hindu temple.*

Hin|du|ism /hɪnduɪzəm/ **NONCOUNT NOUN Hinduism** is an Indian religion. It has many gods and teaches that people have another life on Earth after they die.

hint /hɪnt/
1 NOUN a suggestion that is not made directly ❍ *Has he given you any hints about a promotion?*
2 VERB If you **hint at** something, you suggest it in a way that is not direct. ❍ *She has hinted at the possibility of retiring soon.*
3 NOUN a helpful piece of advice ❍ *Here are some helpful hints to make your trip easier.*

hip /hɪp/ **NOUN** Your **hips** are the two areas or bones at the sides of your body between the tops of your legs and your waist. ❍ *She put her hands on her hips and laughed.*

hire /haɪər/ **(hires, hiring, hired) VERB** If you **hire** someone, you pay them to do a job for you. [HR] ❍ *He just hired a new secretary.*

hire-purchase [PURCHASING, BRIT] → **installment plan**

his

Pronounce the adjective /hɪz/. Pronounce the pronoun /hɪz/.

1 ADJ used for showing that something belongs or relates to a man, a boy, or a male animal ❍ *He spent part of his career in Hollywood.*

2 PRON His is also a pronoun. ❍ *Henry said the decision was his.*

BUSINESS ETIQUETTE
In Brazil, business associates spend a lot of time establishing strong relationships.

his|tori|cal /hɪstɔrɪkᵊl/ **ADJ** existing in the past ❍ *an important historical figure*

historical-cost ac|count|ing **NONCOUNT NOUN Historical-cost accounting** is a method of accounting that values assets at the original cost. [FINANCE]

his|to|ry /hɪstəri, -tri/ **NONCOUNT NOUN History** is events that happened in the past, or the study of those events. ❍ *The film showed great moments in the our history.* ❍ *He studied history at Indiana University.*

hit /hɪt/ (**hits, hitting, hit**)

1 VERB If you **hit** someone or something, you strike them with force, using your hand or an object that you are holding. ❍ *She hit the 'delete' key.*

2 VERB When a moving object **hits** another object, it strikes it with force. ❍ *The car hit a traffic sign.*

3 NOUN Hit is also a noun. ❍ *The building took a direct hit from the bomb.*

4 VERB If something **hits** a person, a place, or a thing, it affects them very badly. ❍ *Mr. Bush had promised to cut taxes long before the recession hit.*

5 NOUN something that is very popular and successful, especially something such as a movie, play, or piece of music ❍ *The song was a big hit in Japan.*

6 NOUN a single visit to a web page ❍ *The company has had 78,000 hits on its website.*

7 NOUN If someone who is searching for information on the Internet gets a **hit**, they find a website that contains that information.

hitch|hike /hɪtʃhaɪk/ (**hitchhikes, hitchhiking, hitchhiked**) **VERB** If you **hitchhike**, you travel by getting rides from passing vehicles without paying. ❍ *Neil hitchhiked to New York during his vacation.*

• **hitch|hiker NOUN** ❍ *On my way to Vancouver I picked up a hitchhiker.*

HIV /eɪtʃ aɪ vi/

1 NONCOUNT NOUN HIV is a virus (= a harmful thing that can make you sick) that reduces the ability of people's bodies to fight illness and that can cause **AIDS**.

2 If someone is **HIV positive**, they are infected with the HIV virus, and may develop AIDS. If someone is **HIV negative**, they are not infected with this virus.

hoard|ing /hɔrdɪŋ/ [BRIT] → **billboard**

hob|by /hɒbi/ (**hobbies**) **NOUN** an activity that you enjoy doing in your free time ❍ *My hobbies are music and tennis.*

hock|ey /hɒki/ **NONCOUNT NOUN Hockey** is a game that is played on ice between two teams who try to score goals using long curved sticks to hit a small rubber disk.

hold /hoʊld/ (**holds, holding, held**)

1 VERB When you **hold** something, you have it in your hands or your arms. ❍ *She held the phone tightly.* ❍ *She held the baby in her arms.*

2 NOUN Hold is also a noun. ❍ *Cooper took hold of the wheel.*

3 VERB When you **hold** something in a particular position, you put it into that position and keep it there. ❍ *Hold your hands up.* ❍ *Hold the camera steady.*

4 NOUN in a ship or an airplane, the place where goods or luggage are stored

5 VERB If something **holds** a particular amount of something, it can contain that amount. ❍ *One CD-ROM disk can hold over 100,000 pages of text.*

6 VERB You can use **hold** with nouns such as "party," and "meeting," to talk about particular activities that people are organizing. ❍ *The country will hold elections within a year.*

7 VERB If someone asks you to **hold**, or to **hold the line**, when you are making a telephone call, they are asking you to wait for a short time. ❍ *Please can you hold, sir?*

8 If you **get hold of** something, you find it, usually after some difficulty. ❍ *It is hard to get hold of medicines in some areas of the country.*

9 If you **get hold of** someone, you succeed in speaking to them. ❍ *I've called him several times but I can't get hold of him.*

▶ **hold back** When you **hold** someone or

h

something **back**, you stop them from moving forward or from doing something. ❍ *The police held back the crowd.*

▶ **hold on** or **hold onto** If you **hold on** or **hold onto** something, you keep your hand on it or around it. ❍ *He pushed me away but I held onto my microphone.*

▶ **hold up** If someone or something **holds** you **up**, they make you late. ❍ *I won't hold you up—I just have one quick question.*

hold|ing /hoʊldɪŋ/ **NOUN** the amount of a firm's stock owned by a person or an organization [ADMINISTRATION] ❍ *That would increase Olympia & York's holding to 35%.*

hold|ing com|pa|ny (**holding companies**) **NOUN** a company that has enough stock in one or more other companies to be able to control the other companies [ADMINISTRATION] ❍ *a Montreal-based holding company with interests in natural resources*

hole /hoʊl/ **NOUN** an opening or an empty space in something ❍ *He dug a hole 45 feet wide and 15 feet deep.* ❍ *I've got a hole in my sock.*

holi|day /hɒlɪdeɪ/ **NOUN** a day when people do not go to work or school because of a religious or national celebration ❍ *the Jewish holiday of Passover*

hol|low /hɒloʊ/ **ADJ** having an empty space inside ❍ *a hollow tree*

holy /hoʊli/ (**holier, holiest**) **ADJ** connected with God or a particular religion ❍ *a holy place*

home /hoʊm/

1 NOUN the house or apartment where someone lives ❍ *I called her at home.*

2 ADV to or at the place where you live ❍ *I'm going to go home now.*

3 NOUN a building where people who cannot care for themselves live and are cared for ❍ *It's a home for elderly people.*

4 ADV When a sports team plays **at home**, it plays on its own ground. Compare with **away**. ❍ *The Red Sox are playing at home tonight.*

5 ADJ Home is also an adjective. ❍ *a home game*

home bank|ing **NONCOUNT NOUN** a system in which a person can monitor and transfer funds electronically [BANKING]

home|less /hoʊmlɪs/

1 ADJ having nowhere to live ❍ *There are a lot of homeless families in the city.*

2 PL NOUN The homeless are people who are homeless. ❍ *We're collecting money for the homeless.*

home loan (**home loans**) **NOUN** A **home loan** is the same as a **mortgage**. [BANKING]

home|made /hoʊmmeɪd/ **ADJ** made in someone's home, rather than in a store or factory ❍ *I miss my mother's homemade bread.*

home page (**home pages**) **NOUN** the main page of a person's or an organization's website ❍ *The company offers a number of services on its home page.*

home shop|ping **NONCOUNT NOUN** **Home shopping** is shopping that people do by ordering products they see online, in catalogs, or on television channels. [PURCHASING] ❍ *America's most successful home-shopping channel*

home|sick /hoʊmsɪk/ **ADJ** sad because you are away from home and you are missing your family and friends ❍ *He was homesick for his family.*

home|work /hoʊmwɜrk/ **NONCOUNT NOUN** **Homework** is work that teachers give to students to do at home. ❍ *Have you done your homework, Gemma?*

home|worker /hoʊmwɜrkər/ **NOUN** a person who works from home [BUSINESS MANAGEMENT] ❍ *the freedom and flexibility of homeworkers*

hon|est /ɒnɪst/ **ADJ** always telling the truth and not stealing or cheating ❍ *She's honest, and I trust her.* ● **hon|est|ly** **ADV** ❍ *Please try to answer these questions honestly.* ❍ *Honestly, I don't know anything about it.*

hon|es|ty /ɒnɪsti/ **NONCOUNT NOUN** **Honesty** is the quality of being honest. ❍ *I admire his courage and honesty.*

hon|es|ty box (**honesty boxes**) **NOUN** an unattended container into which people are trusted to place payments [BRIT]

hon|ey /hʌni/

1 NONCOUNT NOUN a sweet, sticky food that

is made by bees

2 NOUN You call someone **honey** as a sign of affection. ❍ *Honey, I don't think that's a good idea.*

honey|moon /hʌnimun/ **NOUN** a vacation taken by a man and a woman who have just gotten married ❍ *They went to Florida on their honeymoon.*

hon|or /ɒnər/

1 NOUN a special award that is given to someone ❍ *He won many honors—among them an award for his movie performance.*

2 VERB If someone **is honored**, they are given public praise for something they have done. ❍ *The star citizens were honored at a meeting in the Great Hall of the People.*

3 VERB If someone **honors** a check, they accept it and pay the money that is due. [BANKING]

hon|or|able /ɒnərəbᵊl/ **ADJ** If people or actions are **honorable**, they are good, and the person has a right to be respected. ❍ *I'm sure his intentions were perfectly honorable.*

hon|our /ɒnər/ [BRIT] → **honor**

hon|our|able /ɒnərəbᵊl/ [BRIT] → **honorable**

hood /hʊd/

1 NOUN the part of a coat that you can pull up to cover your head ❍ *Put up your hood—it's starting to rain.*

2 NOUN the metal cover over the engine of a car ❍ *He raised the hood of the truck.*

hook /hʊk/

1 NOUN a curved piece of metal or plastic that you use for hanging things on ❍ *His jacket hung from a hook.*

2 NOUN a curved piece of metal with a sharp point that you use for catching fish ❍ *He removed the hook from the fish's mouth.*

hop /hɒp/ (**hops, hopping, hopped**)

1 VERB If you **hop**, you move by jumping on one foot. ❍ *The children were seeing how far they could hop.*

2 VERB When birds and animals **hop**, they move by jumping on both or all four of their feet together. ❍ *A small brown bird hopped in front of me.*

3 VERB If you **hop** somewhere, you move there quickly or suddenly. [INFORMAL] ❍ *We hopped on the train.*

hope /hoʊp/ (**hopes, hoping, hoped**)

1 VERB If you **hope** that something is true, or that something will happen, you want it to be true or you want it to happen. ❍ *They hope to advance in the world-wide market by providing better services.* ❍ *I hope that you get better soon.* ❍ *We're all hoping for some good weather.*

2 NOUN the feeling of wanting something good to happen, and believing that it will happen ❍ *What are your hopes for the future?* ❍ *As time passes, rescuers are losing hope of finding the men alive.*

hope|ful /hoʊpfəl/ **ADJ** thinking that something you want will probably happen ❍ *The doctors seem hopeful that she'll recover.*

hope|ful|ly /hoʊpfəli/ **ADV** used when you are talking about something that you hope will happen ❍ *Hopefully, you won't have any more problems.*

hope|less /hoʊplɪs/

1 ADJ having no chance of success ❍ *I don't believe the situation is hopeless.* ● **hope|less|ly ADV** ❍ *Harry realized that he was hopelessly late.*

2 ADJ very bad at something ❍ *I'm hopeless at spelling.*

ho|ri|zon /həraɪzᵊn/ **NOUN The horizon** is the line that appears between the sky and the land or the ocean. ❍ *A small boat appeared on the horizon.*

hori|zon|tal /hɔrɪzɒntᵊl/ **ADJ** flat and level with the ground ❍ *She was wearing a gray sweater with black horizontal stripes.*

hori|zon|tal in|te|gra|tion /hɔrɪzɒntᵊl ɪntɪgreɪʃən/ **NONCOUNT NOUN Horizontal integration** is the merging of firms involved in the same stage of business activity. Compare with **vertical integration**. [ADMINISTRATION]

horn /hɔrn/

1 NOUN a hard pointed thing that grows from an animal's head

2 NOUN an object in a car or another vehicle that makes a loud noise, and that you use as a warning of danger ❍ *I could hear the sound of a car horn outside.*

3 NOUN a musical instrument with a long metal tube that you play by blowing into it

hor|ri|ble /hɒrɪbᵊl, hɒr-/ **ADJ** very unpleasant [INFORMAL] ❍ *The smell was horrible.* ❍ *Stop being horrible to me!* ● **hor|ri|bly** /hɒrɪbli, hɒr-/ **ADV** ❍ *Sam was feeling horribly ill.*

hor|ror /hɒrər, hɒr-/

1 NONCOUNT NOUN **Horror** is a feeling of great shock and fear when you see or experience something very unpleasant. ❍ *I felt sick with horror.*

2 ADJ A **horror** movie is a very frightening movie that you watch for entertainment.

H

horse /hɒrs/ **NOUN** a large animal that people can ride ❍ *Have you ever ridden a horse?*

hose /hoʊz/ **NOUN** a long rubber or plastic pipe that you use to put water on plants or on a fire

hos|pi|tal /hɒspɪtᵊl/ **NOUN** a place where doctors and nurses care for people who are sick or injured ❍ *Both men were taken to the hospital.*

host /hoʊst/

1 NOUN The **host** at a party is the person who has invited the guests. ❍ *I didn't know anyone at the party, except the host.*

2 VERB If a firm **hosts** a website for another person or firm, it provides the hardware and software needed to keep it available on the Internet.

hos|tage /hɒstɪdʒ/

1 NOUN someone who is kept as a prisoner by people until the people get what they want ❍ *The two hostages were freed yesterday.*

2 If someone **is taken hostage** or **is held hostage**, they are taken and kept as a hostage. ❍ *He was taken hostage on his first trip to the country.*

hos|tile /hɒstᵊl/

1 ADJ not friendly to someone or wanting to harm them ❍ *a hostile corporate culture*

2 ADJ A **hostile** takeover bid is one that is opposed by the firm that is being bid for. [ADMINISTRATION, ECONOMICS] ❍ *friendly and hostile counterbids*

hot /hɒt/ (**hotter, hottest**)

1 ADJ having a high temperature ❍ *Attendants offered us tea and hot towels.* ❍ *I was too hot and tired to eat.*

2 ADJ used for describing the weather when the temperature is high ❍ *It's too hot to work.*

3 ADJ **Hot** food has a strong, slightly burning taste. ❍ *I love eating hot curries.*

hot-desk (**hot-desks, hot-desking, hot-desked**) **VERB** If employees **hot-desk**, they are not assigned particular desks and work at any desk that is available. ❍ *Some employees will have to hot-desk until more accommodation can be found.* ● **hot-desking** **NONCOUNT NOUN** ❍ *Very few employees prefer hot-desking to having a fixed desk.*

hot dog (**hot dogs**) **NOUN** a long piece of bread with a hot sausage inside it

ho|tel /hoʊtɛl/ **NOUN** a building where people pay to sleep and eat meals ❍ *Janet stayed the night in a small hotel near the harbor.*

ho|tel|ier /oʊtɛlyeɪ/ **NOUN** a person who owns or manages a hotel

hour /aʊər/ **NOUN** a period of sixty minutes ❍ *We waited for two hours.* ❍ *I waited about half an hour.*

house /haʊs/

1 NOUN a building where people live ❍ *Amy's invited me to her house for dinner.*

2 NOUN You can call one of the two parts of the U.S. Congress a **House**. The House of Representatives is sometimes called **the House**. ❍ *Some members of the House and Senate worked all day yesterday.*

house|hold /haʊshoʊld/ **NOUN** all the people who live together in a house ❍ *I grew up in a large household with five brothers.*

house|hold sec|tor **NONCOUNT NOUN** The **household sector** is the part of a country's economy that is made up of private households. [ECONOMICS] ❍ *We need to create the confidence in both the household sector and the business sector that this recovery is real.*

house|keep|ing /haʊskipɪŋ/

1 NONCOUNT NOUN **Housekeeping** is the work and organization involved in running

a home. ❍ *I thought that cooking and housekeeping were unimportant, easy tasks.*
2 NONCOUNT NOUN Housekeeping is organization and tidiness of a place such as an office, shop, or computer. ❍ *an operating system that manages the computer's internal housekeeping*

house|wife /haʊswaɪf/ **NOUN** a woman who does not have a paid job, but spends most of her time looking after her house and family ❍ *Sarah's a housewife and mother of four children.*

house|work /haʊswɜrk/ **NONCOUNT NOUN Housework** is the work that you do to keep a house clean and neat. ❍ *Men are doing more housework nowadays.*

hov|er /hɒvər/ **VERB** If something **hovers**, it stays in one place in the air, and does not move forward or backward. ❍ *Helicopters hovered overhead.*

how /haʊ/
1 ADV used for asking about the way that something happens or is done ❍ *How do you spell his name?* ❍ *"How do you get to work?"—"By bus."*
2 ADV used for asking questions about time, or the amount or age of something ❍ *How much money do we have?* ❍ *How long will it take?* ❍ *How old is this machine?*
3 ADV used for asking someone whether something was good ❍ *How was your trip to Orlando?*
4 ADV used for asking if someone is well ❍ *Hi! How are you doing?* ❍ *How's Rosie?*
5 ADV You say "**How about ...**" when you are suggesting something to someone. ❍ *How about a cup of coffee?*
6 You say "**How do you do?**" when you meet someone for the first time in a formal situation. They answer by saying "**How do you do?**" also.

how|ever /haʊɛvər/
1 ADV used when you are adding a comment that is surprising after what you have just said ❍ *The office is rather small. It is, however, much brighter than the last one.*
2 CONJ in any way ❍ *Wear your hair however you want.*

HR /eɪtʃ ɑr/ **HR** is an abbreviation for **human resources**. [HR]

HRM /eɪtʒ ɑr ɛm/ **HRM** is an abbreviation for **human resource management**. [HR] ❍ *Management wants the HRM to focus on people-related business issues.*

HRP /eɪtʒ ɑr pi/ **HRP** is an abbreviation for **human resource planning**. [HR] ❍ *HRP is an effort to anticipate future business and environmental demands on an organization.*

HTML /eɪtʃ ti ɛm ɛl/ **NONCOUNT NOUN HTML** is the standard way of preparing documents so that people can read them on the Internet. **HTML** is short for "hypertext markup language." [TECHNOLOGY]

hub /hʌb/
1 NOUN a place that is a very important center for an activity ❍ *a manufacturing hub*
2 NOUN the part of a wheel at the center
3 NOUN a large airport from which you can travel to many other airports ❍ *a campaign to secure O'Hare Airport's place as America's main international hub*
4 NOUN a device for connecting computers in a network [TECHNOLOGY]

huck|ster /hʌkstər/ **NOUN** someone who sells useless or worthless things in a dishonest or aggressive way

hug /hʌg/ (**hugs, hugging, hugged**)
1 VERB When you **hug** someone, you put your arms around them and hold them tightly, to show your love or friendship. ❍ *Crystal hugged him and invited him to dinner the next day.*
2 NOUN Hug is also a noun. ❍ *She gave him a hug.*

huge /hyudʒ/ (**huger, hugest**) **ADJ** very large ❍ *The country faces huge increases in energy costs.* ● **huge|ly ADV** ❍ *This hotel is hugely popular.*

hum /hʌm/ (**hums, humming, hummed**)
1 VERB If something **hums**, it makes a low continuous noise. ❍ *The generator hummed faintly.*
2 NOUN Hum is also a noun. ❍ *I could hear the distant hum of traffic.*
3 VERB When you **hum** a tune, you sing a tune with your lips closed. ❍ *Barbara began humming a song.*

h

hu|man /hyu̲mən/
1 ADJ relating to people, and not to animals or machines ❍ *the human body*
2 NOUN a person, rather than an animal or a machine ❍ *Pollution affects animals as well as humans.*

hu̲|man be̲|ing (**human beings**) **NOUN** a man, a woman, or a child ❍ *A robot must obey orders given to it by human beings.*

hu|man ca̲p|ital **NONCOUNT NOUN** In a firm or organization, the **human capital** is the abilities and skills of any individual that may increase its revenue. [HR, ECONOMICS] ❍ *Investing in human capital helps to ensure a town's economic future.*

H

hu|man|ity /hyumæ̲nɪti/
1 NONCOUNT NOUN **Humanity** is all the people in the world. ❍ *Humanity spends over 1 trillion minutes a month on cellphones.*
2 NONCOUNT NOUN **Humanity** is the quality of being kind and thoughtful. ❍ *a woman of great humanity*

hu̲|man ra̲ce **NOUN** **The human race** means all the people living in the world.

hu̲|man re̲|source ma̲n|age|ment **NONCOUNT NOUN** **Human resource management** is the work within a firm that involves the recruitment, training, and welfare of staff. [HR] ❍ *Before this time supervisors handled nearly all aspects of human resource management.*

hu̲|man re̲|source pla̲n|ning **NONCOUNT NOUN** **Human resource planning** is the work within a firm that involves identifying the future employment needs of the firm and recruiting the staff to meet those needs. [HR] ❍ *A realistic understanding of current workforce capabilities is essential for effective human resource planning.*

hu̲|man re̲|sources **NONCOUNT NOUN** In a firm or other organization, the department of **human resources** is the department with responsibility for the recruiting, training, and welfare of the staff. The abbreviation **HR** is often used. [HR] ❍ *The firm's head of human resources is on vacation.*

hum|ble /hʌ̲mbᵊl/ (**humbler, humblest**)
1 ADJ not believing that you are better than other people ❍ *He remains humble about his achievements.*
2 ADJ ordinary and not special in any way ❍ *He comes from a very humble background.*

hu|mid|ity /hyumɪ̲dɪti/ **NONCOUNT NOUN** **Humidity** is the amount of water in the air. ❍ *low humidity*

hu|mor /hyu̲mər/ **NONCOUNT NOUN** **Humor** is the quality of being funny. ❍ *He failed to see the humor of the situation.*

hu|mour /hyu̲mər/ [BRIT] → **humor**

hun|dred /hʌ̲ndrɪd/

The plural form is **hundred** after a number.

1 A hundred or **one hundred** is the number 100. ❍ *More than a hundred people were there.*
2 Hundreds of things or people means a lot of them. ❍ *He received hundreds of letters.*

hun|dredth /hʌ̲ndrɪdθ, -drɪtθ/
1 ADJ or **ADV** The **hundredth** item in a series is the one that you count as number one hundred. ❍ *The bank's hundredth anniversary is in December.*
2 NOUN A **hundredth of** something is one of a hundred equal parts of it. ❍ *The holes are less than a hundredth of a millimeter across.*

hung /hʌ̲ŋ/ **Hung** is a form of the verb **hang**.

hun|ger /hʌ̲ŋgər/ **NONCOUNT NOUN** **Hunger** is the feeling that you get when you need something to eat. ❍ *Infection progresses more quickly in a body that is weak from hunger.*

hun|gry /hʌ̲ŋgri/ (**hungrier, hungriest**) **ADJ** wanting to eat ❍ *I hadn't eaten all day and was very hungry.* ● **hun|gri|ly** /hʌ̲ŋgrɪli/ **ADV** ❍ *James ate hungrily.*

hunt /hʌ̲nt/
1 VERB When people or animals **hunt**, they chase and kill wild animals for food or as a sport. ❍ *It's illegal to hunt elephants in Kenya.*
2 NOUN an occasion when people chase and kill wild animals for food or as a sport ❍ *Ben went on a moose hunt last year.* ● **hunt|ing** **NONCOUNT NOUN** ❍ *deer hunting*
3 VERB If you **hunt for** something or someone, you try to find them by searching carefully. ❍ *This may be a good time to hunt for bargains.*
4 NOUN a careful search for something ❍ *I was*

now on a serious job hunt. ● **hunt|ing** NONCOUNT NOUN ❍ *job hunting*

hur|ri|cane /hɜrɪkeɪn, hʌr-/ NOUN a storm with very strong winds and rain

hur|ry /hɜri, hʌr-/ (**hurries, hurrying, hurried**)

1 VERB If you **hurry**, you move or do something as quickly as you can. ❍ *Claire hurried along the road.* ❍ *Everyone hurried to find a seat.*

2 NOUN If you are **in a hurry**, you need or want to do something quickly. ❍ *I'm in a hurry because I have to leave in half an hour.*

▶ **hurry up** If you tell someone to **hurry up**, you are telling them to do something more quickly. ❍ *Hurry up, or you'll miss the opening speeches.*

hurt /hɜrt/

1 VERB If you **hurt** a person or animal, you make them feel pain. ❍ *She was frightened she would have an accident and hurt someone.* ❍ *I fell over and hurt my leg yesterday.*

2 VERB If a part of your body **hurts**, you feel pain there. ❍ *His arm hurt.*

3 ADJ injured ❍ *How badly are you hurt?*

4 VERB If you **hurt** someone, you say or do something that makes them unhappy. ❍ *I'm really sorry if I hurt your feelings.*

5 ADJ upset because of something that someone has said or done ❍ *She felt hurt by all the lies he had told her.*

hus|band /hʌzbənd/ NOUN A woman's **husband** is the man she is married to. ❍ *I'll just call my husband.*

hut /hʌt/ NOUN a small simple building, especially one made of wood

hy|brid /haɪbrɪd/

1 NOUN an animal or a plant that is produced from two different types of animal or plant ❍ *A mule is a hybrid of a horse and a donkey.*

2 ADJ **Hybrid** is also an adjective. ❍ *The hybrid seed produces larger flowers.*

3 NOUN A **hybrid** or a **hybrid car** is a car that can use either gasoline or electricity as its power. ❍ *Hybrid cars can go almost 600 miles between refueling.*

hype /haɪp/ (**hypes, hyping, hyped**)

1 NONCOUNT NOUN **Hype** is the use of a lot of publicity and advertising to make people interested in something such as a product. ❍ *We are certainly seeing a lot of hype by some companies.*

2 VERB To **hype** a product means to advertise or praise it a lot. ❍ *We had to hype the film to attract the investors.*

3 Hype up means the same as **hype**. ❍ *The media seems obsessed with hyping up individuals or groups.*

hyper|in|fla|tion /haɪpərɪnfleɪʃən/ NONCOUNT NOUN **Hyperinflation** is very severe inflation. [ECONOMICS] ❍ *The hyperinflation in 1923 was so extreme that it was cheaper to burn money than to buy fuel.*

hyper|mar|ket /haɪpərmɑrkɪt/ NOUN a very large supermarket [MARKETING AND SALES]

hype|ster /haɪpstər/ NOUN a person or organization that gives a product intense publicity in order to promote it [MARKETING AND SALES] ❍ *The film's hypesters are using words like "amazing," "astounding," and "jaw-dropping."*

hy|phen /haɪfᵊn/ NOUN the punctuation sign (-) that you use to join two words together or to show that a word continues on the next line

hy|poth|esis /haɪpɒθɪsɪs/ (**hypotheses**) NOUN an idea that is suggested as a possible explanation for something, but that has not been proved to be correct [FORMAL] ❍ *We tested the hypothesis that exercise relieves stress.*

Ii

I /aɪ/ **PRON** used to mean yourself when you are the subject of the verb ❍ *I live in Arizona.* ❍ *Jim and I will be at the meeting.*

IBRD /aɪ bi ɑr di/ **IBRD** is an abbreviation for **International Bank for Reconstruction and Development**. [BANKING, ECONOMICS]

ice /aɪs/ **NONCOUNT NOUN Ice** is frozen water. ❍ *The ground was covered with ice.* ❍ *Do you want ice in your soda?*

I

ice cream **NONCOUNT NOUN Ice cream** is a cold sweet food that is made from frozen cream. ❍ *vanilla ice cream*

icon /aɪkɒn/ **NOUN** a picture on a computer screen that you can choose using a mouse, in order to open a particular program ❍ *Click on the mail icon.*

ICT /aɪ si ti/ **NONCOUNT NOUN ICT** refers to activities or studies involving computers and other electronic technology. **ICT** is an abbreviation for "Information and Communications Technology." [TECHNOLOGY, BRIT] ❍ *ICT allows small firms to access international markets without the need for a global marketing network.*

icy /aɪsi/ (**icier, iciest**)

1 ADJ extremely cold ❍ *An icy wind was blowing.*

2 ADJ covered in ice ❍ *icy roads*

I'd /aɪd/

1 I'd is short for "I had." ❍ *I'd seen her before.*

2 I'd is short for "I would." ❍ *I'd like to come.*

ID /aɪ di/ **NONCOUNT NOUN ID** is a document, such as a passport, that shows who you are. ❍ *I had no ID so I couldn't prove that it was my car.*

idea /aɪdiə/

1 NOUN a possible plan, especially a new one ❍ *She has some interesting ideas.* ❍ *"Let's have something to eat."—"Good idea."*

2 NOUN If you have an **idea** of something, you know something about it. ❍ *We had no idea what was happening.*

3 NOUN The idea of something is its purpose. ❍ *The idea is to reduce costs.*

ideal /aɪdiəl/

1 ADJ used to describe the best person or thing for a particular purpose ❍ *He's the ideal person for the job.*

2 ADJ An **ideal** situation is a perfect one. ❍ *Imagine for a moment that you're living in an ideal world.*

3 NOUN a principle or idea that people try to achieve ❍ *We must defend the ideals of liberty and freedom.*

iden|ti|cal /aɪdɛntɪkᵊl/ **ADJ** exactly the same ❍ *The products were almost identical.*

iden|ti|fi|ca|tion /aɪdɛntɪfɪkeɪʃən/

1 NONCOUNT NOUN Identification is a document, such as a passport, that proves who you are. ❍ *The police asked him to show some identification.*

2 NONCOUNT NOUN Identification is the process of saying who or what someone or something is. ❍ *Early identification of problems is important.*

iden|ti|fy /aɪdɛntɪfaɪ/ (**identifies, identifying, identified**) **VERB** If you **identify** someone or something, you say who or what they are. ❍ *We have identified several areas where we can improve market performance.*

iden|tity /aɪdɛntɪti/ (**identities**) **NOUN** Your **identity** is who you are. ❍ *He had concealed his real identity for all those years.*

iden|tity theft **NONCOUNT NOUN Identity theft** is the crime of getting personal information about another person without their knowledge, for example, in order to gain access to their bank account. [TECHNOLOGY]

❍ *Protecting yourself from identity theft is a matter of treating all your personal and financial documents as top secret information.*

id|iot /ɪdiət/ **NOUN** a stupid person ❍ *I felt like an idiot.*

idle /aɪdᵊl/ (**idles, idling, idled**)
1 ADJ If people who were working are **idle**, they have no jobs or work. ❍ *4,000 workers have been idle for 12 of the first 27 weeks of this year.*
2 ADJ If machines or factories are **idle**, they are not working or being used. ❍ *Now the machine is lying idle.*
3 VERB To **idle** a factory means to close it down because there is no work to do or because the workers are on strike. [BUSINESS MANAGEMENT, PRODUCTION] ❍ *idled assembly plants*
4 VERB To **idle** workers means to stop them working. [BUSINESS MANAGEMENT, PRODUCTION] ❍ *The strike has idled about 55,000 machinists.*
5 ADJ Idle money is not being used to earn interest or dividends. ❍ *Since banks need to make money on deposits to be able to pay interest on them, idle money could force them to lobby for further cuts in deposit rates.*

idol /aɪdᵊl/ **NOUN** a famous person who is greatly admired or loved ❍ *a pop idol*

i.e. /aɪ i/ used to introduce a word or sentence that makes what you have just said clearer or gives details ❍ *an artificial intelligence system, i.e. a computer program*

if /ɪf/
1 CONJ used for introducing a situation in which something might happen ❍ *If you go, I'll come with you.* ❍ *You'll get there on time if you run.*
2 CONJ used for reporting a question that someone has asked ❍ *He asked if I wanted some water.*
3 You use **if only** to express a strong wish. ❍ *If only I had more time to finish this report.*

ig|no|rance /ɪgnərəns/ **NONCOUNT NOUN Ignorance of** something is lack of knowledge about it. ❍ *I feel embarrassed by my complete ignorance of the stock market.*

ig|no|rant /ɪgnərənt/ **ADJ** not knowing anything ❍ *People don't want to appear ignorant.* ❍ *Most people are ignorant of these facts.*

ig|nore /ɪgnɔr/ (**ignores, ignoring, ignored**) **VERB** If you **ignore** someone or something, you do not pay any attention to them. ❍ *We can't ignore the facts.*

ill /ɪl/ **ADJ** sick ❍ *He's seriously ill with cancer.*

I'll /aɪl/ **I'll** is short for "I will" or "I shall." ❍ *I'll go there tomorrow.*

il|legal /ɪligᵊl/ **ADJ** not allowed by law ❍ *It is illegal for the interviewer to ask your age.*
● **il|legal|ly ADV** ❍ *firms that illegally solicited funds from investors*

ill|ness /ɪlnɪs/ (**illnesses**)
1 NOUN a particular disease or a period of bad health ❍ *She's recovering from a serious illness.*
2 NONCOUNT NOUN Illness is the fact of being ill. ❍ *He was away from work because of illness.*

il|lus|trate /ɪləstreɪt/ (**illustrates, illustrating, illustrated**) **VERB** If you **illustrate** a book, you put pictures into it. ❍ *She illustrates children's books.*

il|lus|tra|tion /ɪləstreɪʃən/ **NOUN** a picture in a book ❍ *The book uses plain language and clear illustrations.*

IM /aɪ ɛm/ **NOUN IM** is short for **instant messaging**. [TECHNOLOGY] ❍ *The device lets you chat via IM.*

I'm /aɪm/ **I'm** is short for "I am." ❍ *I'm sorry.*

im|age /ɪmɪdʒ/
1 NOUN a picture of someone or something [FORMAL] ❍ *The image on screen changes every 10 seconds.*
2 NOUN a picture in your mind of someone or something ❍ *When you say "California," people have an image of sunny blue skies.*
3 NOUN the way that a person or a group appears to other people ❍ *The company is trying to improve its public image.*

im|agi|nary /ɪmædʒɪnɛri/ **ADJ** existing only in your mind or in a story, and not in real life ❍ *Lots of children have imaginary friends.*

im|agi|na|tion /ɪmædʒɪneɪʃən/ **NOUN** Your **imagination** is your ability to invent pictures or ideas in your mind. ❍ *Designers need to use creativity and imagination.*

im|ag|ine /ɪmædʒɪn/ (**imagines, imagining, imagined**)
1 VERB If you **imagine** something, you form a picture or idea of it in your mind. ❍ *I can't imagine doing my job without the Internet.*
2 VERB If you **imagine** something, you think that you have seen or heard that thing, but in fact you have not. ❍ *I must have imagined the whole thing.*

IMF /aɪ ɛm ɛf/ **IMF** is an abbreviation for **International Monetary Fund**. [BANKING, ECONOMICS]

imi|tate /ɪmɪteɪt/ (**imitates, imitating, imitated**) **VERB** If you **imitate** someone or something, you copy them. ❍ *He was imitating my voice.*

I

imi|ta|tion /ɪmɪteɪʃən/
1 NOUN a copy of someone or something ❍ *He tried to do an imitation of an English accent.* ❍ *Rival companies immediately started producing cheap imitations.*
2 ADJ made to look like a more expensive product ❍ *The books are covered in imitation leather.*

im|ma|ture /ɪmətʃʊər, -tʊər/ **ADJ** behaving or having the character of a younger person ❍ *He seemed a little immature for a man of 21.*

im|medi|ate /ɪmidiɪt/ **ADJ** happening now or very soon ❍ *Our immediate task is to find out which brands are a success.*

im|medi|ate an|nu|ity (**immediate annuities**) **NOUN** an annuity that starts less than a year after the final amount has been paid for it [BANKING]

im|medi|ate|ly /ɪmidiɪtli/ **ADV** now, without any delay ❍ *I answered his email immediately.*

im|mense /ɪmɛns/ **ADJ** extremely large ❍ *We still need to do an immense amount of work.*

im|mi|grant /ɪmɪgrənt/ **NOUN** a person who comes to live in a country from another country ❍ *The company employs several immigrant workers.*

im|mi|gra|tion /ɪmɪgreɪʃən/ **NONCOUNT NOUN** **Immigration** is when people come into a country to live and work there. ❍ *immigration laws*

im|mor|al /ɪmɔrəl/ **ADJ** bad and morally wrong ❍ *Many people believe that testing cosmetics on animals is immoral.*

im|mune /ɪmyun/ **ADJ** If you are **immune to** a particular disease, you cannot get the disease. ❍ *Some people are naturally immune to measles.*

im|pact /ɪmpækt/
1 NOUN a strong effect ❍ *The protests could have a significant impact on tourism.*
2 NOUN the action of one object hitting another ❍ *The impact of the crash turned the truck over.*

im|pa|tient /ɪmpeɪʃənt/
1 ADJ annoyed because you do not want to wait for something ❍ *People are impatient for the war to be over.* ● **im|pa|tient|ly ADV** ❍ *She waited impatiently for the mail to arrive.*
2 ADJ often annoyed by people making mistakes or by things happening too slowly ❍ *Try not to be impatient with your staff.* ● **im|pa|tience NONCOUNT NOUN** ❍ *She tried to hide her growing impatience.*

im|ple|ment

> Pronounce the verb /ɪmplɪmɛnt/ or /ɪmplɪmənt/. Pronounce the noun /ɪmplɪmənt/.

1 VERB If you **implement** a plan, system, or law, you start to use it. ❍ *The government will begin to implement the plan in September.* ● **im|ple|men|ta|tion** /ɪmplɪmənteɪʃən, -mɛn-/ **NONCOUNT NOUN** ❍ *the implementation of the peace agreement*
2 NOUN a tool or other piece of equipment [FORMAL] ❍ *agricultural implements*

im|ply /ɪmplaɪ/ (**implies, implying, implied**) **VERB** If you **imply that** something is true, you suggest it in a way that is not direct. ❍ *Are you implying that this is my fault?* ● **im|pli|ca|tion NOUN** ❍ *The implication was that she wasn't happy with his work.*

im|port

Pronounce the verb /ɪmpɔ̲rt/ or /ɪ̲mpɔrt/.
Pronounce the noun /ɪ̲mpɔrt/.

1 VERB To **import** goods means to buy them from another country for use in your own country. ❍ *The U.S. imports over half of its oil.*
2 NOUN Import is also a noun. ❍ *Cheap imports are adding to the problems of our farmers.*

COLLOCATIONS
a ban on imports
imports *increase*
imports *decrease*

im|por|tant /ɪmpɔ̲rtᵊnt/
1 ADJ valuable or necessary ❍ *The most important thing in my life is my career.* ❍ *It's important to answer her questions honestly.* ● **im|por|tance NONCOUNT NOUN** ❍ *His experience in the military taught him the importance of teamwork.* ● **im|por|tant|ly ADV** ❍ *Training is needed to update old skills and, more importantly, to learn new ones.*
2 ADJ having influence and power ❍ *She's an important person in the world of television.*

im|pose /ɪmpoʊ̲z/ (**imposes, imposing, imposed**)
1 VERB If you **impose** something **on** people, you force them to accept it. ❍ *Fines are imposed on drivers who break the speed limit.* ❍ *He tries to impose his beliefs on all of us.* ● **im|po|si|tion** /ɪ̲mpəzɪ̲ʃən/ **NONCOUNT NOUN** ❍ *the imposition of a new property tax*
2 VERB If someone **imposes on** you, they expect you to do something for them that you do not want to do. ❍ *I won't stay long—I don't want to impose on you.* ● **im|po|si|tion NOUN** ❍ *I know this is a terrible imposition, but could I possibly borrow your car?*

im|pos|sible /ɪmpɒ̲sɪbᵊl/ **ADJ** not possible to do ❍ *It's impossible for me to get another job at my age.*

im|prac|ti|cal /ɪmpræ̲ktɪkᵊl/ **ADJ** not sensible or realistic ❍ *It's an interesting idea but it's rather impractical.*

im|press /ɪmprɛ̲s/ **VERB** If something **impresses** you, you feel great admiration for it. ❍ *Their results impressed everyone.*

im|pressed /ɪmprɛ̲sd/ **ADJ** feeling admiration for someone or something ❍ *I was very impressed by his proposal.*

im|pres|sion /ɪmprɛ̲ʃən/
1 NOUN Your **impression** of a person or thing is what you feel or think about them. ❍ *What were your first impressions of your boss?*
2 If someone or something **makes an impression**, they have a strong effect on you. ❍ *It's her first day at work and she's already made an impression.*
3 If you are **under the impression that** something is true, you believe that it is true. ❍ *I was under the impression that you were moving to New York.*

im|pres|sive /ɪmprɛ̲sɪv/ **ADJ** making you feel strong admiration ❍ *They collected an impressive amount of cash: $390.8 million.*

im|prove /ɪmpru̲v/ (**improves, improving, improved**) **VERB** If something **improves** or if you **improve** it, it gets better. ❍ *The euro's rate against the dollar will also improve.* ❍ *We are trying to improve our services to customers.*

im|prove|ment /ɪmpru̲vmənt/ **NOUN** the process of getting better, or something that has got better ❍ *There has been a big improvement in his work recently.* ❍ *They were warned they were in danger of losing their franchises unless they made vast improvements to services.*

im|pulse /ɪ̲mpʌls/
1 NOUN a sudden feeling that you must do something ❍ *I felt a sudden impulse to tell her what had happened.*
2 If you do something **on impulse**, you suddenly decide to do it. ❍ *Younger shoppers are more likely to buy on impulse.*

in

Pronounce the preposition /ɪn/. Pronounce the adverb /ɪ̲n/.

1 PREP used for saying where someone or something is ❍ *Let's have the meeting in my office.* ❍ *Mark now lives in Singapore.* ❍ *I put the file in my drawer.*
2 ADV If you **are in**, you are at your home or the place where you work. ❍ *Maria isn't in just now.*

i

3 PREP used for saying what someone is wearing ❍ *Who's the woman in the red dress?*
4 PREP used for saying what job someone does ❍ *Rob was in the navy for twenty years.* ❍ *He works in the music industry.*
5 PREP used for saying the period of time when something happens ❍ *He was born in 1996.* ❍ *Sales improved in April.*
6 PREP used for saying how long something takes ❍ *We sold $60,000 worth of goods in five hours.*
7 PREP used for talking about a state or situation ❍ *Dave was in a hurry to get back to work.* ❍ *The economy is in a mess.*
8 PREP used for talking about the way that something is done or said ❍ *Please do not write in pencil.* ❍ *They were speaking in Russian.*

I

in|abil|ity /ɪnəbɪlɪti/ **NONCOUNT NOUN** Someone's **inability to** do something is the fact that they cannot do it. ❍ *She remarked on Jake's inability to concentrate.*

in|ap|pro|pri|ate /ɪnəproʊpriɪt/ **ADJ** wrong in a particular situation ❍ *The movie is clearly inappropriate for young children.*

in|box /ɪnbɒks/ (**inboxes**) also **in-box** **NOUN** the place where a computer stores emails that have arrived for you ❍ *I checked my inbox.*

Inc. **Inc.** is an abbreviation for **Incorporated**. [ADMINISTRATION] ❍ *BP America Inc*

in|ca|pable /ɪnkeɪpəbᵊl/ **ADJ** not able to do something ❍ *She's incapable of making sensible decisions.*

in|cen|tive /ɪnsɛntɪv/ **NOUN** something that makes you want to do something [HR] ❍ *We want to give our employees an incentive to work hard.*

inch /ɪntʃ/ (**inches**) **NOUN** An **inch** is a unit for measuring length. There are 2.54 centimeters in an inch, and twelve inches in a foot. ❍ *These devices are only ten inches long and four inches wide.*

in|ci|dent /ɪnsɪdənt/ **NOUN** something unpleasant that happens [FORMAL] ❍ *The incident happened in the early hours of Sunday morning.*

in|clined /ɪnklaɪnd/ **ADJ** If you are **inclined to** have a particular opinion, you mean that you have this opinion, but you do not feel strongly about it. ❍ *I'm inclined to agree with Alan.*

in|clude /ɪnklud/ (**includes, including, included**) **VERB** If something **includes** another thing, it has that thing as one of its parts. ❍ *The price includes a five-year guarantee.*

in|clud|ing /ɪnkludɪŋ/ **PREP** used for talking about people or things that are part of a particular group ❍ *Many industries, including tourism and restaurant businesses, will be affected by the tax.*

in|come /ɪnkʌm/ **NOUN** the money that a person or firm earns or receives [FINANCE] ❍ *Many of the families here are on low incomes.* ❍ *Average income is now higher here than in most of Europe.*

in|come bond (**income bonds**) **NOUN** a bond that pays interest at a rate in direct proportion to the earnings of the firm that makes it available [BANKING] ❍ *The terms of income bonds can be tailored to the advantage of both the borrower and the lender.*

in|come dis|tri|bu|tion **NONCOUNT NOUN** The **income distribution** in a particular country or area is the way in which the amount of money being earned varies between different groups of people. [FINANCE] ❍ *Research confirms a change in income distribution in which the rich have become richer, while the poor have become poorer.*

in|come state|ment (**income statements**) **NOUN** a document showing the money received by a person or organization over a period of time [FINANCE] ❍ *If the firm has a deficit in its income statement, it must borrow, raise more equity, or divest itself of assets purchased in the past.*

in|come tax (**income taxes**) **NOUN** a part of your income that you have to pay regularly to the government [FINANCE] ❍ *You pay income tax every month.*

in|com|ing /ɪnkʌmɪŋ/
1 ADJ An **incoming** message or phone call is

one that you receive. ❍ *Incoming calls can be picked up later from voicemail.*

2 ADJ **Incoming** goods are arriving at a place. ❍ *The organization of the warehouse needed to take into account both the incoming parts from suppliers and the outgoing parts to customers.*

in|com|pe|tent /ɪnkɒmpɪtənt/ ADJ without the skill to do a job or task ❍ *an incompetent employee*

in|com|plete /ɪnkəmplit/ ADJ not yet finished, or missing a part ❍ *incomplete data*

in|con|sid|er|ate /ɪnkənsɪdərɪt/ ADJ not thinking enough about how your behavior affects other people ❍ *It's very inconsiderate to walk into someone's office without knocking.*

in|con|ven|ient /ɪnkənvinyənt/ ADJ causing difficulties for someone ❍ *If this is an inconvenient time, I'll call you later.*

in|cor|po|rate /ɪnkɔrpəreɪt/ **(incorporates, incorporating, incorporated)**

1 VERB If one thing **incorporates** another thing, it includes it. [FORMAL] ❍ *The new cars will incorporate a number of major improvements.*

2 VERB If someone or something **is incorporated into** a large group, system, or area, they become a part of it. [ADMINISTRATION, FORMAL] ❍ *All of these companies are to be incorporated into the food distributor PDL.*

In|cor|po|rated /ɪnkɔrpəreɪtɪd/ ADJ **Incorporated** is used after a firm's name to show that it is a legally established firm in the United States. [ADMINISTRATION] ❍ *MCA Incorporated*

in|cor|rect /ɪnkərɛkt/ ADJ wrong or not true ❍ *an incorrect answer* • **in|cor|rect|ly** ADV ❍ *The article suggested, incorrectly, that there were plans for a merger.*

In|co|terms /ɪnkoʊtɜrmz/ PL NOUN **Incoterms** consist of a glossary of terms used in international commerce, published by the International Chamber of Commerce. [ECONOMICS]

in|crease **(increases, increasing, increased)**

> Pronounce the verb /ɪnkris/. Pronounce the noun /ɪnkris/.

1 VERB If something **increases** or you **increase** it, it gets bigger. ❍ *The population continues to increase.* ❍ *The company has increased the price of its cars.*

2 NOUN If there is an **increase in** the number, level, or amount of something, it becomes greater. ❍ *There was a sudden increase in the cost of oil.*

> **COLLOCATIONS**
> to increase *sharply*
> to *significantly* increase
> a *marked* increase
> a *dramatic* increase
> a *significant* increase

in|creas|ing|ly /ɪnkrisɪŋli/ ADV more and more ❍ *He was finding it increasingly difficult to make decisions.*

in|cred|ible /ɪnkrɛdɪbᵊl/

1 ADJ very good, or very large in amount ❍ *The food was incredible.* ❍ *He works an incredible number of hours.* • **in|cred|ibly** ADV ❍ *It was incredibly hard work.*

2 ADJ impossible to believe ❍ *It seems incredible that nobody predicted the effects of the takeover.*

in|debt|ed /ɪndɛtɪd/ ADJ owing money to other people, organizations, or countries ❍ *the most heavily indebted countries*

in|deed /ɪndid/

1 ADV used for emphasizing what you are saying ❍ *He admitted that he had indeed paid him.*

2 ADV used for making the word "very" stronger ❍ *The results were very bad indeed.*

in|dem|nity /ɪndɛmnɪti/

1 NONCOUNT NOUN If something provides **indemnity**, it provides insurance or protection against damage or loss. [LEGAL, FORMAL] ❍ *Political exiles had not been given indemnity from prosecution.*

2 NONCOUNT NOUN If something provides **indemnity**, it provides compensation for damage or loss. [BANKING, FORMAL] ❍ *The President repeated this week his decision to reject the application for indemnity made by 3,500 police officers.*

i

in|de|pend|ence /ɪndɪpɛndəns/
1 NONCOUNT NOUN If a country has **independence**, it is not ruled by another country. ❍ *In 1816, Argentina declared its independence from Spain.*
2 NONCOUNT NOUN Someone's **independence** is the fact that they do not need help from other people. ❍ *He was afraid of losing his independence.*

in|de|pend|ent /ɪndɪpɛndənt/
1 ADJ separate from, and not affected by, other people or things ❍ *We need an independent review.* ● **in|de|pen|dent|ly ADV** ❍ *We all work independently.*
2 ADJ not needing help or money from other people ❍ *Now that the children are older, they're more independent.* ● **in|de|pen|dent|ly ADV** ❍ *We want to help disabled students to live independently.*
3 ADJ not ruled by another country ❍ *Papua New Guinea became independent from Australia in 1975.*

in|dex /ɪndɛks/ (**indexes**) **NOUN** a list at the back of a book that tells you what is included in the book and on which pages you can find each item

in|dexa|tion /ɪndɛkseɪʃən/ or **index-linking NONCOUNT NOUN Indexation** is the act of making wages, interest rates, etc. index-linked. [ECONOMICS] ❍ *Wage indexation has made businesses uncompetitive.*

in|dex fund (**index funds**) **NOUN** an investment in which shares in different firms are bought and sold so that the value of the shares held always matches the average value of shares in a stock market [FINANCE]

in|dex fu|tures PL NOUN Index futures are a form of financial futures based on how a share price index is expected to change. [BANKING] ❍ *Much of the instability in stock prices lately has been blamed on arbitrage trading, designed to profit from differences in prices between stocks and index futures.*

index-linked ADJ If wages, interest rates, etc. are **index-linked**, they are directly related to the cost-of-living index, and rise or fall accordingly. [ECONOMICS] ❍ *Inflation matters little to the many elderly people who currently live off index-linked pensions.*

in|di|cate /ɪndɪkeɪt/ (**indicates, indicating, indicated**) **VERB** If one thing **indicates** another thing, the first thing shows that the second is true. ❍ *The report indicates that most people agree.*

in|di|ca|tion /ɪndɪkeɪʃən/ **NOUN** something that suggests something is true ❍ *This statement is a strong indication that the government is changing its mind.*

in|dif|fer|ent /ɪndɪfərənt/ **ADJ** not at all interested in something ❍ *We have become indifferent to the suffering of other people.*

in|di|ges|tion /ɪndɪdʒɛstʃən, -daɪ-/ **NONCOUNT NOUN** If you have **indigestion**, you have pains in your stomach because of something that you have eaten.

in|di|rect /ɪndaɪrɛkt, -dɪr-/ **ADJ** not caused immediately and obviously, but happening because of something else ❍ *Businesses are feeling the indirect effects from the recession that's going on elsewhere.*

in|di|rect costs PL NOUN Indirect costs are the same as **overheads**. Compare with **direct costs**. [FINANCE] ❍ *Revised working practices need to be implemented as a way to improve the quality of care and reduce direct and indirect costs.*

in|di|rect la|bor NONCOUNT NOUN Indirect labor is work done in administration and sales rather than in the manufacturing of a product. Compare with **direct labor**. [FINANCE] ❍ *Also the plan may require high indirect labor costs in clerical and related staff to keep all the records that it requires.*

in|di|rect tax (**indirect taxes**) **NOUN** An **indirect tax** is a tax on goods and services that is added to their price before they reach the consumer. Compare with **direct tax**. [FINANCE] ❍ *The main indirect tax in the UK is the Value-Added Tax.*

in|di|vid|ual /ɪndɪvɪdʒuəl/
1 ADJ relating to one person or thing, rather than to a large group ❍ *We ask each individual customer for suggestions.* ● **in|di|vid|ual|ly ADV**

❍ *I spoke to each member of staff individually.*
2 NOUN a separate person ❍ *We recognise that everyone is an individual.*

in|door /ɪndɔr/ **ADJ** happening or existing inside a building and not outside ❍ *The hotel has an indoor pool.*

in|doors /ɪndɔrz/ **ADV** inside a building ❍ *They warned us to close the windows and stay indoors.*

in|duc|tion /ɪndʌkʃən/ **NONCOUNT NOUN** **Induction** is a procedure for introducing someone to a new job or organization. [HR] ❍ *In our induction program, we mix graduates who will work in different disciplines to encourage them to work as a team.*

in|dus|trial /ɪndʌstriəl/ **ADJ** connected with or having a lot of industry ❍ *industrial machinery and equipment* ❍ *Western industrial countries*

in|dus|tri|al ac|tion [HR, BRIT] → **job action**

in|dus|tri|al de|sign **NONCOUNT NOUN** **Industrial design** is the art or practice of designing any object for manufacture. [TECHNOLOGY] ❍ *Computer-aided industrial design shortens development cycles for automobiles, electronics, and other products.*

in|dus|tri|al es|pion|age **NONCOUNT NOUN** **Industrial espionage** is attempting to obtain trade secrets by dishonest means. ❍ *White collar crime, excluding computer and industrial espionage crimes currently costs this country nearly $70 billion a year.*

in|dus|tri|al|ise /ɪndʌstriəlaɪz/ [BRIT] → **industrialize**

in|dus|tri|al|ist /ɪndʌstriəlɪst/ **NOUN** a powerful businessperson who owns or controls large industrial firms or factories [ECONOMICS] ❍ *prominent Japanese industrialists*

in|dus|tri|al|ize /ɪndʌstriəlaɪz/ (**industrializes, industrializing, industrialized**) **VERB** When a country **industrializes** or **is industrialized**, it develops a lot of industries. [ECONOMICS] ❍ *Energy consumption rises as countries industrialize.*

• **in|dus|tri|ali|za|tion** **NONCOUNT NOUN** ❍ *Industrialization began early in Spain.*

in|dus|trial re|la|tions **PL NOUN** **Industrial relations** refers to the relationship between employers and employees in industry, and the political decisions and laws that affect it. [HR] ❍ *The offer is seen as an attempt to improve industrial relations.*

in|dus|tri|als /ɪndʌstriəlz/ **PL NOUN** **Industrials** are stocks, shares, and bonds of industrial organizations. [ECONOMICS] ❍ *A comparison with the Dow Jones industrials sheds light on which stocks have been rising and why.*

in|dus|trial sec|tor (**industrial sectors**) **NOUN** The **industrial sector** consists of industries that produce things from raw materials, for example manufacturing and construction. Compare with **service sector**. [PRODUCTION, ECONOMICS] ❍ *The average Irish woman working in the industrial sector is paid 65% less than her male counterpart.*

in|dus|try /ɪndəstri/ (**industries**)
1 NONCOUNT NOUN **Industry** is the work of making things in factories. ❍ *The meeting was for leaders in banking and industry.*
2 NOUN all the people and activities involved in making a particular product or providing a particular service ❍ *The country depends on its tourism industry.*

in|dus|try|wide /ɪndəstriwaɪd/ **ADJ** covering or available to all parts of an industry ❍ *Analysts now say that industrywide earnings growth of about 15% is likely.*

> **BUSINESS ETIQUETTE**
> In France, people do business during any meal, but lunch is preferred for this purpose.

in|ef|fi|cient /ɪnɪfɪʃənt/ **ADJ** not using time or energy in the best way ❍ *inefficient work methods*

in|equal|ity /ɪnɪkwɒlɪti/ **NONCOUNT NOUN** **Inequality** is when people do not have the same social position, wealth, or chances. ❍ *Now there is even greater inequality in society.*

in|evi|table /ɪnɛvɪtəbᵊl/ **ADJ** not able to be prevented or avoided ❍ *Suffering is an inevitable* *part of life.* ● **in|evi|tably** /ɪnɛvɪtəbli/ **ADV** ❍ *Advances in technology will inevitably lead to unemployment.*

in|fant /ɪnfənt/ **NOUN** a baby or very young child [FORMAL] ❍ *He held the infant in his arms.*

in|fect /ɪnfɛkt/ **VERB** To **infect** a person or animal means to give them a disease or an illness. ❍ *A single mosquito can infect a large number of people.*

in|fec|tion /ɪnfɛkʃən/
1 NOUN an illness that is caused by bacteria ❍ *an ear infection*
2 NONCOUNT NOUN Infection is the process of getting a disease. ❍ *Even a small cut can lead to infection.*

in|fec|tious /ɪnfɛkʃəs/ **ADJ** A disease that is **infectious** can be passed easily from one person to another. ❍ *The disease is highly infectious.*

in|fe|ri|or /ɪnfɪəriər/ **ADJ** not as good as something else that is similar ❍ *an inferior product*

in|fer|tile /ɪnfɜrtᵊl/
1 ADJ unable to produce babies ❍ *Ten percent of couples are infertile.*
2 ADJ Infertile soil is of poor quality. ❍ *Nothing grew on the land, which was poor and infertile.*

in|fill /ɪnfɪl/
1 VERB To **infill** a hollow place or gap means to fill it. [mainly BRIT] ❍ *Most of the recent work is infilling: adding to existing infrastructure.*
2 NONCOUNT NOUN Infill is something that fills a hollow place or gap. [mainly BRIT] ❍ *There is room for infill between the new outer suburbs.*

in|fi|nite /ɪnfɪnɪt/ **ADJ** having no limit, end, or edge ❍ *There is an infinite number of stars.*

in|fini|tive /ɪnfɪnɪtɪv/ **NOUN** The **infinitive** of a verb is the basic form, for example, "do," "be," "take," and "eat." The infinitive is often used with "to" before it.

in|flate /ɪnfleɪt/ **VERB** If you **inflate** something, you fill it with air. ❍ *Inflate tires to the level recommended by the manufacturer.*

in|fla|tion /ɪnfleɪʃən/ **NONCOUNT NOUN Inflation** is a general increase in the prices of goods and services in a country. [ECONOMICS] ❍ *rising unemployment and high inflation* ❍ *an inflation rate of only 2.2%*

COLLOCATIONS
to *control* inflation
to *reduce* inflation
high/low inflation
inflation *fears*
an *increase in* inflation
the inflation *rate*

in|fla|tion|ary /ɪnfleɪʃənɛri/ **ADJ** connected with inflation or causing inflation [ECONOMICS] ❍ *The bank is worried about mounting inflationary pressures.*

in|fla|tion|ary gap (**inflationary gaps**) **NOUN** the amount by which total spending in an economy exceeds output [ECONOMICS] ❍ *A high level of credit expansion, in the context of a lower than targeted rate of economic growth, led to a widening of the inflationary gap.*

in|flu|ence /ɪnfluəns/ (**influences, influencing, influenced**)
1 NONCOUNT NOUN Influence is the power to make other people do what you want. ❍ *He used his influence to block the reforms.*
2 VERB If you **influence** someone or something, you have an effect on them. ❍ *The newspapers tried to influence public opinion.*
3 NOUN To have an **influence on** people or situations means to affect what they do or what happens. ❍ *Alan had a big influence on my career.*

in|flu|en|tial /ɪnfluɛnʃᵊl/ **ADJ** having a lot of influence over people or events ❍ *He was influential in changing the law.*

info /ɪnfoʊ/ **NONCOUNT NOUN Info** is information. [INFORMAL] ❍ *For more info call 414-3935.*

in|fo|mer|cial /ɪnfoʊmɜrʃᵊl/ **NOUN** An **infomercial** is a television program that gives detailed information about a firm's products or services. The word is formed from "information" and "commercial." [MARKETING AND SALES]

in|form /ɪnf<u>ɔ</u>rm/ **VERB** If you **inform** someone **of** something, you tell them about it. ❍ *We will inform you of any changes.*

in|for|mal /ɪnf<u>ɔ</u>rm^əl/ **ADJ** relaxed and friendly, rather than serious or official ❍ *Her style of writing is very informal.* • **in|for|mal|ly** **ADV** ❍ *They discussed the plans informally, over lunch.*

in|for|ma|tion /ɪnfərm<u>eɪ</u>ʃən/
1 NONCOUNT NOUN **Information** about someone or something is facts about them. ❍ *Consumers want to be given more information about products.* ❍ *We can provide information on training.*
2 NONCOUNT NOUN **Information** is a service that you can telephone to find out someone's telephone number. ❍ *He called information, and they gave him the number.*

in|for|ma|tion tech|nol|ogy **NONCOUNT NOUN** **Information technology** is the theory and practice of using computers. The short form **I.T.** is often used. [TECHNOLOGY] ❍ *the information technology industry*

in|forma|tive /ɪnf<u>ɔ</u>rmətɪv/ **ADJ** giving you useful information ❍ *The meeting was friendly and informative.*

infra|struc|ture /ɪnfrəstrʌktʃər/ **NOUN** The **infrastructure** of a country or organization is the systems and buildings that allow it to operate, such as transportation and power supplies. ❍ *They promised to make improvements to the country's infrastructure.*

COLLOCATIONS
an infrastructure *project*
infrastructure *investment*
infrastructure *spending*
infrastructure *development*
transportation infrastructure
telecommunications infrastructure
information infrastructure
an infrastructure *project*

in|gre|di|ent /ɪngr<u>i</u>diənt/ **NOUN** one of the things that you use to make something, especially when you are cooking ❍ *Mix together all the ingredients.*

in|hab|it /ɪnh<u>æ</u>bɪt/ **VERB** If a group of people **inhabit** a place, they live there. ❍ *The people who inhabit these islands do not use money.*

in|hab|it|ant /ɪnh<u>æ</u>bɪtənt/ **NOUN** a person who lives in a place ❍ *The inhabitants of the town wrote a letter to the president.*

in|hale /ɪnh<u>eɪ</u>l/ (**inhales, inhaling, inhaled**) **VERB** When you **inhale**, you breathe air or another substance into your lungs. ❍ *He took a long slow breath, inhaling deeply.* ❍ *They inhaled the poisonous gas.*

in|her|it /ɪnh<u>ɛ</u>rɪt/
1 VERB If you **inherit** money or property, you receive it from someone who has died. ❍ *He has no child to inherit his house.*
2 VERB If you **inherit** a personal quality from a parent, you are born with it. ❍ *Her children have inherited her love of sports.*

in|her|it|ance tax /ɪnh<u>ɛ</u>rɪt^əns t<u>æ</u>ks/ (**inheritance taxes**) **NOUN** In Britain, **inheritance tax** is the tax you pay on things that you inherit. [FINANCE]

in-house
1 ADJ **In-house** work or activities are done by employees of an organization or firm, rather than by workers outside the organization or firm. ❍ *A lot of companies do in-house training.*
2 ADV **In-house** is also an adverb. ❍ *The magazine is still produced in-house.*

in-house train|ing **NONCOUNT NOUN** **In-house training** is training of employees that is done within an organization or firm. [HR] ❍ *When you do in-house training for a business, make sure you know their technical language.*

ini|tial /ɪn<u>ɪ</u>ʃ^əl/
1 ADJ happening at the beginning of a process ❍ *The initial reaction has been excellent.*
2 NOUN the first letter of your name ❍ *She drove a silver car with her initials on the side.*

ini|tial|ly /ɪn<u>ɪ</u>ʃəli/ **ADV** at first ❍ *The plant will initially hire about 50 workers.*

in|ject /ɪndʒ<u>ɛ</u>kt/
1 VERB To **inject** a medicine or other substance into someone means to put it into their body using a special type of needle. ❍ *The drug was*

injected into patients four times a week.

2 VERB If you **inject** money or resources **into** an organization, you provide more money or resources for it. ❍ *He has injected £5.6 billion into the health service.*

> **COLLOCATIONS**
> to inject *money*
> to inject *cash*

in|jec|tion /ɪndʒɛkʃən/

1 NOUN a medicine that is put into your body using a special type of needle ❍ *They gave me an injection to help me sleep.*

2 NOUN An **injection of** money or resources into an organization is the act of providing it with more money or resources. ❍ *An injection of cash is needed to fund some of these projects.* ❍ *The company is hoping to obtain a £250 million cash injection from the government.*

in|jure /ɪndʒər/ (**injures, injuring, injured**) **VERB** If you **injure** a person or animal, you damage part of their body. ❍ *The bomb seriously injured five people.*

in|jured /ɪndʒərd/

1 ADJ having suffered damage to part of your body ❍ *Nurses helped the injured man.*

2 PL NOUN **The injured** are people who are injured. ❍ *Army helicopters moved the injured.*

in|ju|ry /ɪndʒəri/ (**injuries**) **NOUN** damage to someone's body ❍ *He was suffering from serious head injuries.*

ink /ɪŋk/ **NONCOUNT NOUN** **Ink** is the colored liquid that you use for writing or printing. ❍ *The letter was written in blue ink.*

in|land

> Pronounce the adverb /ɪnlænd, -lənd/.
> Pronounce the adjective /ɪnlənd/.

ADV or **ADJ** in or near the middle of a country, not next to the ocean ❍ *Most of the population lives inland.* ❍ *The town is about 15 minutes' drive inland from Pensacola.* ❍ *inland lakes*

in|ner /ɪnər/ **ADJ** on the inside, or near the center ❍ *James has an infection of the inner ear.*

in|no|cence /ɪnəsəns/

1 NONCOUNT NOUN **Innocence** is the quality of having no experience or knowledge of the bad things in life. ❍ *We promote family values such as parental love and the innocence of children.*

2 NONCOUNT NOUN **Innocence** is the state of not being guilty of a crime. ❍ *This information could prove your brother's innocence.*

in|no|cent /ɪnəsənt/

1 ADJ not guilty of a crime ❍ *The jury found him innocent of murder.*

2 ADJ having no experience or knowledge of the bad things in life ❍ *They seemed so young and innocent.*

in|no|va|tion /ɪnəveɪʃən/ **NOUN** a new thing or a new way of doing something [R & D] ❍ *They showed us some of their latest technological innovations.* ❍ *We must promote originality, inspire creativity, and encourage innovation.*

in|no|va|tive /ɪnəveɪtɪv/

1 ADJ new and different ❍ *The company produces innovative car designs.*

2 ADJ having new, different ideas ❍ *He's one of America's most innovative film-makers.*

in|put /ɪnpʊt/ (**inputs, inputting, input**)

1 NONCOUNT NOUN **Input** is the help, information, or advice that one person gives to another person. ❍ *There has been a lot of input from the public.*

2 NONCOUNT NOUN **Input** is information that you type into a computer. ❍ *Who is responsible for data input here?*

3 VERB If you **input** information into a computer, you type it using a keyboard. ❍ *We need more staff to input the data.*

in|quire /ɪnkwaɪər/ (**inquires, inquiring, inquired**) **VERB** If you **inquire** about something, you ask for information about it. [FORMAL] ❍ *He called the company to inquire about a job.*

in|quiry /ɪnkwaɪəri, ɪŋkwɪri/ (**inquiries**)

1 NOUN a question that you ask in order to get information ❍ *My secretary made some inquiries and found her address.*

2 NOUN an official examination of an event in order to find out the truth about it ❍ *Pike is leading the inquiry into the shooting.*

in|sane /ɪnseɪn/

1 ADJ seriously mentally ill ❍ *For a while,*

I thought I was going insane.
2 ADJ very foolish ❍ *I thought the idea was completely insane.*

in|sect /ɪnsɛkt/ **NOUN** a very small animal that has six legs and often wings

in|sert /ɪnsɜrt/ **VERB** If you **insert** an object **into** something, you put the object inside it. ❍ *All you have to do is insert a disk into the hard drive and click a button.*

in-service ADJ If people working in a particular profession are given **in-service** training, they attend special courses to improve their skills or to learn about new developments in their field. [HR] ❍ *in-service courses for people such as doctors, teachers, and civil servants*

in|side /ɪnsaɪd/

Pronounce the preposition and the adverb /ɪnsaɪd/. Pronounce the adjective and the noun /ɪnsaɪd/.

1 PREP Something or someone that is **inside** or **inside of** something, is in it. ❍ *Inside the envelope was a photograph.*
2 ADJ Inside is also an adjective. ❍ *Josh took his cellphone from the inside pocket of his jacket.*
3 ADV If you go **inside**, you go into a building. ❍ *It's raining—let's go inside.*
4 NOUN the inner part of something ❍ *The inside of the building is being painted.*
5 If a piece of clothing is **inside out**, the part that is normally inside is on the outside. ❍ *I didn't realize that my shirt was inside out.*

in|sid|er trad|ing /ɪnsaɪdər treɪdɪŋ/ or **insider dealing NONCOUNT NOUN Insider trading** is the illegal buying or selling of a firm's stock by someone who has secret or private information about the firm. [BANKING] ❍ *The investigation has found evidence of possible insider trading by four unidentified buyers.*

in|sight /ɪnsaɪt/ **NOUN** an opportunity to understand something ❍ *This report provides fascinating insights into the way the company works.*

in|sig|nifi|cant /ɪnsɪgnɪfɪkənt/ **ADJ** not important ❍ *a fiscally insignificant increase in the top rate of income tax from 40% to 45%*

in|sist /ɪnsɪst/
1 VERB If you **insist**, you say firmly that something must happen. ❍ *Rob insisted on driving them to the station.* ❍ *He insisted that I stay for dinner.*
2 VERB If you **insist** that something is true, you say so very firmly. ❍ *Clarke insisted that he was telling the truth.*

in|sol|ven|cy /ɪnsɒlvᵊnsi/ (**insolvencies**) **NOUN** the state of not having enough money to pay your debts [FINANCE, ECONOMICS, FORMAL] ❍ *eight mortgage companies, seven of which are on the brink of insolvency* ❍ *The economy has entered a sharp downturn, and unemployment and insolvencies can be expected to increase.*

in|sol|vent /ɪnsɒlvᵊnt/ **ADJ** not having enough money to pay your debts [FINANCE, ECONOMICS, FORMAL] ❍ *The bank was declared insolvent.*

in|spect /ɪnspɛkt/
1 VERB If you **inspect** something, you look at it very carefully. ❍ *Dad inspected the car carefully before he bought it.*
2 VERB When officials **inspect** a place or a group of people, they visit it and check it carefully. [BUSINESS MANAGEMENT] ❍ *The Public Utilities Commission inspects us once a year.* ❍ *Each hotel is inspected and, if it fulfills certain criteria, is recommended.*

in|spec|tion /ɪnspɛkʃən/ **NOUN** an occasion when someone looks at something very carefully [BUSINESS MANAGEMENT] ❍ *Dixon still makes weekly inspections of all his stores.* ❍ *The plant never had a safety inspection in the 11 years it was in operation.*

in|spec|tor /ɪnspɛktər/
1 NOUN a person whose job is to check that people do things correctly ❍ *a fire inspector*
2 NOUN an officer in the police ❍ *Police Inspector John Taylor*

in|spi|ra|tion /ɪnspɪreɪʃən/ **NONCOUNT NOUN Inspiration** is a feeling of enthusiasm and new ideas that you get from someone or something. ❍ *My inspiration as a writer comes from poets like Walt Whitman.*

in|spire /ɪnspaɪər/ **(inspires, inspiring, inspired)**
1 VERB If someone or something **inspires** you, they give you new ideas and a strong feeling of enthusiasm. ❍ *Good leaders inspire people to accomplish goals.* ● **in|spir|ing ADJ** ❍ *She was one of the most inspiring people I ever met.*
2 VERB If someone or something **inspires** a particular feeling in people, it makes them feel that way. ❍ *A manager has to inspire confidence in the staff.*

in|stall /ɪnstɔl/ **VERB** If you **install** something, you put it somewhere so that it is ready to be used. ❍ *They installed a new telephone line in the office.* ● **in|stal|la|tion NONCOUNT NOUN** ❍ *the installation of smoke alarms*

in|stall|ment /ɪnstɔlmənt/
1 NOUN one of many small regular payments ❍ *She is repaying the loan in monthly installments of $300.*
2 NOUN one part of a story in a magazine, or on TV or radio ❍ *Dickens' fourth novel was published in 1840-41, in weekly installments.*

in|stall|ment plan (installment plans) NOUN a way of buying products gradually, in which you make regular payments to the seller until, after some time, you have paid the full price [PURCHASING] ❍ *Some pay by check or credit card, but no one buys on the installment plan.*

in|stance /ɪnstəns/ You say **for instance** when you are giving an example of what you are talking about. ❍ *There have been continuing efforts to trim costs, for instance cutting managers' bonuses.*

in|stant /ɪnstənt/
1 NOUN a very short period of time ❍ *For an instant, I forgot what I was going to say.*
2 ADJ immediate ❍ *The product was an instant success.* ● **in|stant|ly ADV** ❍ *The man was killed instantly.*
3 ADJ Instant food or drink can be prepared very quickly and easily. ❍ *instant coffee*

in|stant mes|sag|ing NONCOUNT NOUN **Instant messaging** is the activity of sending written messages between computers that appear immediately. [TECHNOLOGY]

in|stead /ɪnstɛd/
1 If you do one thing **instead of** another, you do the first thing and not the second thing. ❍ *Why don't you walk to work, instead of driving?*
2 ADV If you do not do something, but do something else **instead**, you do the second thing and not the first thing. ❍ *If the price of one product rises, many customers will choose to buy a rival product instead.*

in|stinct /ɪnstɪŋkt/ **NOUN** a natural tendency to react in a particular way, sometimes without thinking ❍ *My first instinct was to laugh.*

in|sti|tute /ɪnstɪtut/ **NOUN** an organization or a place where people study a particular subject in detail ❍ *Clive works at the National Cancer Institute.*

in|sti|tu|tion /ɪnstɪtuʃən/
1 NOUN a large organization such as a school, a bank, or a church ❍ *financial institutions*
2 NOUN An **institution** or an **institutional investor** is a large organization such as an insurance firm or a bank that has large sums of money to invest on a stock exchange.

in-store also **instore**
1 ADJ available within a department store, supermarket, or other large store ❍ *in-store banking* ❍ *an instore bakery*
2 ADV In-store is also an adverb. ❍ *Ask in-store for details.*

in|struct /ɪnstrʌkt/ **VERB** If you **instruct** someone **to** do something, you formally tell them to do it. [FORMAL] ❍ *Managers instructed employees to notify security about any unusual calls.*

in|struc|tion /ɪnstrʌkʃən/
1 NOUN something that someone tells you to do ❍ *We had instructions from management not to give out details.*
2 PL NOUN Instructions are information on how to do something. ❍ *The manual uses simple instructions and photographs.*

in|struc|tor /ɪnstrʌktər/ **NOUN** someone whose job is to teach a skill or an activity ❍ *a swimming instructor*

in|stru|ment /ɪnstrəmənt/
1 NOUN a tool that you use for doing a

particular job ❍ *scientific instruments*
2 NOUN A musical **instrument** is an object that you use for making music. ❍ *Tim plays four musical instruments, including piano and guitar.*

in|su|late /ɪnsəleɪt/ (**insulates, insulating, insulated**) **VERB** If something **is insulated from** something, it is protected against the harmful effects of that thing. ❍ *Service firms were still insulated from foreign competition.*

in|sult

Pronounce the verb /ɪnsʌlt/. Pronounce the noun /ɪnsʌlt/.

1 VERB If someone **insults** you, they say or do something to you that is rude or offensive. ❍ *I'm sorry. I didn't mean to insult you.*
• **in|sult|ed ADJ** ❍ *I was really insulted by the way he spoke to me.* • **in|sult|ing ADJ** ❍ *Don't use insulting language.*
2 NOUN something rude that a person says or does ❍ *The boys shouted insults at each other.*

in|sur|ance /ɪnʃʊərəns/ **NONCOUNT NOUN** **Insurance** is an agreement that you make with a firm in which you pay money to them regularly, and they pay you if something bad happens to you or your property. [BANKING] ❍ *I pay about $100 per month for auto insurance.*

in|sur|ance ad|just|er (**insurance adjusters**) **NOUN** An **insurance adjuster** is the same as a **claims adjuster**. [BANKING]

in|sure /ɪnʃʊər/ (**insures, insuring, insured**) **VERB** If you **insure** yourself or your property, you pay money regularly to a firm so that, if you become ill, or if your property is damaged or stolen, the firm will pay you an amount of money. [BANKING] ❍ *It costs a lot of money to insure a car.*

in|sured /ɪnʃʊərd/ (**insured**)
1 ADJ covered by insurance [BANKING] ❍ *The bonds are insured and triple-A-rated.*
2 NOUN **The insured** is the person or organization that is insured by a particular policy. [BANKING] ❍ *Once the insured has sold his policy, he naturally loses all rights to it.*

in|sur|er /ɪnʃʊərər/ **NOUN** a firm that sells insurance [BANKING] ❍ *He has filed his own workers' compensation claim with his insurer, citing stress.*

in|tan|gi|ble /ɪntændʒɪbᵊl/ **ADJ** A business asset that is **intangible** is not physical but it has a value, such as a trademark or copyright ownership. Compare with **tangible**. [PRODUCTION] ❍ *A good reputation is an intangible asset of immense financial worth.*

in|te|grat|ed /ɪntɪgreɪtɪd/ **ADJ** An **integrated** works combines various processes normally carried out at different locations. [PRODUCTION] ❍ *an integrated steelworks*

in|teg|rity /ɪntɛgrɪti/ **NONCOUNT NOUN** **Integrity** is the quality of always being honest and behaving in a way that is morally good. ❍ *Most people believe that he is a man of integrity.*

in|tel|lec|tual /ɪntɪlɛktʃuəl/ **ADJ** involving a person's ability to think and to understand ideas and information ❍ *the intellectual development of children*

in|tel|lec|tual prop|er|ty NONCOUNT NOUN **Intellectual property** is something such as an invention or a copyright that is officially owned by someone. [LEGAL] ❍ *If there is to be innovation, the firm insists, intellectual property must be protected.*

in|tel|lec|tual prop|er|ty rights **PL NOUN** If someone has the **intellectual property rights** to an idea or invention, they are legally allowed to develop it, and nobody else can do so without their permission. [LEGAL] ❍ *The company said that it has retained the intellectual property rights to its latest light commercial vehicle.*

in|tel|li|gence /ɪntɛlɪdʒᵊns/
1 NONCOUNT NOUN **Intelligence** is the ability to understand and learn things quickly and well. ❍ *She was a woman of great intelligence.*
2 NONCOUNT NOUN **Intelligence** is information that is collected by the government or the army about other countries' activities. ❍ *military intelligence*

in|tel|li|gent /ɪntɛlɪdʒᵊnt/ **ADJ** able to think, understand, and learn things quickly and well ❍ *Sara's a very intelligent woman.*

• **in|tel|li|gent|ly** ADV ❍ *William can talk intelligently on a variety of subjects.*

in|tend /ɪntɛnd/

1 VERB If you **intend** to do something, you have decided to do it. ❍ *The company intends to sell off its real estate services.*

2 VERB If something **is intended** for a particular purpose or person, it has been planned or made for that purpose. ❍ *This money is intended for training.*

in|tense /ɪntɛns/ ADJ very great ❍ *He was under intense pressure to resign.* • **in|tense|ly** ADV ❍ *The fast-food business is intensely competitive.*

in|ten|sive /ɪntɛnsɪv/ ADJ involving a lot of effort, often over a short time ❍ *The program begins with six weeks of intensive training.* • **in|ten|sive|ly** ADV ❍ *Dan is working intensively on his new book.*

in|ten|tion /ɪntɛnʃən/ NOUN something that you plan to do ❍ *It's my intention to retire later this year.* ❍ *We have no intention of taking over the company.*

in|ten|tion|al /ɪntɛnʃənᵊl/ ADJ done on purpose, and not by mistake ❍ *I'm sorry if I hurt him—it wasn't intentional.* • **in|ten|tion|al|ly** ADV ❍ *He intentionally crashed his car to collect insurance money.*

inter|act /ɪntərækt/

1 VERB When people **interact**, they communicate with each other. ❍ *They are not in the same unit and have little reason to interact.* • **inter|ac|tion** /ɪntərækʃən/ NOUN ❍ *social interaction*

2 VERB If things **interact**, they have an effect on each other. ❍ *You have to understand how cells interact.* • **inter|ac|tion** NOUN ❍ *the interaction between the mind and the body*

inter|ac|tive /ɪntəræktɪv/ ADJ An **interactive** piece of equipment allows direct communication between itself and the user. ❍ *These services can be ordered on the Internet or through interactive TV.*

inter|bank /ɪntərbæŋk/ ADJ conducted between or involving two or more banks [BANKING] ❍ *A sudden withdrawal of interbank loans could cause the collapse of a debtor country's banking system.*

in|ter|est /ɪntrɪst, -tərɪst/

1 NOUN **Interest in** something is a feeling of wanting to know more about something or be involved in something. ❍ *There's a lot of interest in the new product.*

2 NOUN something that you like doing ❍ *"What are your interests?"—"I enjoy riding horses and I also play tennis."*

3 VERB If something **interests** you, you want to know more about it or be involved in it. ❍ *The takeover bid doesn't interest us.*

4 NONCOUNT NOUN **Interest** is the extra money that you pay if you have borrowed money, or the extra money that you receive if you have money in some types of bank account. [BANKING] ❍ *Do you earn interest on your checking account?* ❍ *How much interest do you have to pay on the loan?*

5 NOUN A person or organization that has **interests** in a firm or in a particular type of business owns shares in it. [FINANCE] ❍ *Her other business interests include a theme park in Scandinavia and hotels in the West Country.* ❍ *Disney will retain a 51 percent controlling interest in the venture.*

in|ter|est|ed /ɪntərɛstɪd, -trɪstɪd/ ADJ If you are **interested in** something, you want to know more about it or be involved in it. ❍ *I thought you might be interested in this article in the newspaper.*

in|ter|est|ing /ɪntərɛstɪŋ, -trɪstɪŋ/ ADJ If something is **interesting**, you want to know more about it or be involved in it. ❍ *It sounds like an interesting job.*

in|ter|est rate (**interest rates**) NOUN the amount of interest that must be paid on a loan or investment, expressed as a percentage of the amount that is borrowed or gained as profit [ECONOMICS, BANKING] ❍ *The Federal Reserve lowered interest rates by half a point.*

COLLOCATIONS

an interest rate *rise/fall*
a *cut in* interest rates
rising/falling interest rates
interest rates *go up/come down*
an *increase in* interest rates

interest-rate fu|tures PL NOUN **Interest-rate futures** are a form of financial futures based on how interest rates are expected to change. [BANKING] ○ *As in the bond market, purchases of interest-rate futures provide a profit when interest rates fall, and sales provide a profit when interest rates rise.*

inter|fere /ɪntərfɪər/ (**interferes, interfering, interfered**)
1 VERB If you **interfere**, you get involved in a situation when other people do not want you to. ○ *I wish everyone would stop interfering and just leave me alone.* ● **inter|fer|ence** /ɪntərfɪərəns/ NONCOUNT NOUN ○ *government interference in global trade*
2 VERB Something that **interferes with** an activity stops it from going well. ○ *Cellphones can interfere with aircraft equipment.*

in|ter|im /ɪntərɪm/ ADJ intended to be used until something permanent is done or established ○ *She was sworn in as head of an interim government.*

in|ter|im re|sults PL NOUN A firm's **interim results** are the set of figures, published outside the regular times, that show whether it has achieved a profit or a loss. [FINANCE] ○ *Interim results released last month showed a 6% rise to £256m.*

in|te|ri|or /ɪntɪəriər/
1 NOUN the inside part of something, especially a building ○ *The interior of the house was dark and old-fashioned.*
2 Interior is also an adjective. ADJ ○ *the interior walls*

in|ter|medi|ary /ɪntərmidiɛri/ (**intermediaries**) NOUN a person or organization that provides a link between two other people or organizations ○ *It will act as a non-profit intermediary putting buyers in touch with a participating dealer.*

inter|medi|ate /ɪntərmidiɪt/ ADJ in the middle level, between two other levels ○ *We teach beginner, intermediate, and advanced level students.*

in|tern

> Pronounce the verb /ɪntɜrn/. Pronounce the noun /ɪntɜrn/.

1 NOUN an advanced student or a recent graduate who is being given practical training under supervision ○ *a summer intern at a New York industrial design firm*
2 VERB **Intern** is also a verb. ○ *He will intern with a company interested in international timber ventures.*

in|ter|nal /ɪntɜrnᵊl/ ADJ existing or happening on the inside of something ○ *internal bleeding*

in|ter|nal mar|ket (**internal markets**) NOUN a system in which goods and services are sold by the provider to a range of purchasers within the same organization [BUSINESS MANAGEMENT] ○ *He commended the scrapping of the internal market in the Scottish NHS.*

inter|na|tion|al /ɪntərnæʃənᵊl/ ADJ involving different countries ○ *international trade* ● **inter|na|tion|al|ly** ADV ○ *The company wants to expand internationally.*

inter|na|tion|al ac|count|ing stan|dards PL NOUN **International accounting standards** are a set of internationally-agreed principles and procedures relating to the way that firms present their accounts. The abbreviation **IAS** is also used. [FINANCE] ○ *The World Bank is making its loans to some companies conditional on their adoption of international accounting standards.*

Inter|na|tion|al Bank for Re|con|struc|tion and De|vel|op|ment /ɪntərnæʃənᵊl bæŋk fər rikənstrʌkʃən ən dɪvɛləpmənt/ NOUN The **International Bank for Reconstruction and Development** is the official name for the **World Bank**. [BANKING]

Inter|na|tion|al Fi|nance Cor|po|ra|tion NOUN The **International Finance Corporation** is an organization that invests directly in private firms and makes or guarantees loans to private investors. [BANKING]

Inter|na|tion|al Mon|etary Fund NOUN an international agency that tries to promote trade and improve economic conditions in poorer countries [BANKING, ECONOMICS]

inter|na|tion|al stand|ard ac|count (**international standard accounts**) NOUN an account that follows international accounting standards [FINANCE] ❍ *Quoted companies now understand that if they don't produce international standard accounts, they won't find support from foreign investors.*

In|ter|net /ɪntərnɛt/ also **internet** NOUN **The Internet** is the network that allows computer users to connect with computers all over the world, and that carries email. [TECHNOLOGY] ❍ *Opportunities exist, and are being exploited, in selling fast-moving consumer goods over the Internet.*

COLLOCATIONS
to *browse* the Internet
to *buy something over* the Internet
to *sell something over* the Internet
to *publish something on* the Internet
to *post something on* the Internet

In|ter|net ac|cess also **internet access** NONCOUNT NOUN If you have **Internet access**, you are able to use a computer that allows you to use the Internet. [TECHNOLOGY] ❍ *A key part of our strategy must be getting rid of all barriers to e-commerce and making sure that we have the fastest and cheapest Internet access in the world.*

In|ter|net se|cur|ity also **internet security** NONCOUNT NOUN **Internet security** is the use of measures to improve the security of a website, in order to safeguard personal and financial information. [TECHNOLOGY] ❍ *a breach of Internet security*

In|ter|net ser|vice pro|vid|er /ɪntərnɛt sɜrvɪs prəvaɪdər/ (**Internet service providers**) also **internet service provider** NOUN A firm that provides Internet and email services. The abbreviation **ISP** is also used. [TECHNOLOGY] ❍ *The committee's hearings will examine concentration and competition in the Internet service provider market.*

in|tern|ship /ɪntɜrnʃɪp/ NOUN the position held by an intern, or the period of time when someone is an intern ❍ *The high internship success rate has led to a number of job offers.*

in|ter|pret /ɪntɜrprɪt/
1 VERB If you **interpret** something in a particular way, you decide that is what it means. ❍ *You can interpret the data in different ways.*
2 VERB If you **interpret** what someone is saying, you put the words that they are saying into another language. ● **in|ter|pret|er** /ɪntɜrprɪtər/ NOUN ❍ *He spoke through an interpreter.*

in|ter|ro|gate /ɪntɛrəgeɪt/ (**interrogates, interrogating, interrogated**) VERB If a police officer **interrogates** someone, they ask them a lot of questions in order to get information from them. ❍ *Wright was interrogated by police for eight hours.* ● **in|ter|ro|ga|tion** /ɪntɛrəgeɪʃən/ NOUN ❍ *He confessed during an interrogation by police.*

in|ter|rupt /ɪntərʌpt/
1 VERB If you **interrupt** someone, you say or do something that causes them to stop what they are doing. ❍ *Please don't interrupt me while I'm working.*
2 VERB If something **interrupts** an activity, it causes it to stop for a period of time. ❍ *The meeting was interrupted by a phone call.*

in|ter|rup|tion /ɪntərʌpʃən/
1 NOUN something that someone says or does that causes someone to stop what they are doing ❍ *I can't concentrate on my work—there are too many interruptions.*
2 NONCOUNT NOUN **Interruption** is the stopping of an activity for a period of time. ❍ *The meeting continued without interruption.*

in|ter|val /ɪntərvᵊl/ NOUN a period of time between two events ❍ *We met again after an interval of 12 years.*

inter|vene /ɪntərvin/ (**intervenes, intervening, intervened**) VERB If you **intervene in** a situation, you become involved in it and try to change it. ❍ *The situation calmed down when police intervened.* ❍ *Currency traders expect the Federal Reserve to intervene to keep the dollar from rising sharply.* ● **inter|ven|tion** /ɪntərvɛnʃən/ **NOUN** ❍ *Government intervention in the banking crisis came too late.*

inter|ven|tion /ɪntərvɛnʃən/ **NOUN** the action of a central bank in supporting the international value of a currency by buying large quantities of the currency to keep the price up [ECONOMICS] ❍ *massive intervention in the currency markets*

inter|view /ɪntərvyu/
1 NOUN a formal meeting in which someone asks you questions to find out if you are the right person for a job ❍ *The interview went well.* ❍ *Applicants should be prepared to come for an interview in London or New York, at their own expense.*
2 VERB If you **are interviewed** for a job, someone asks you questions to find out if you are the right person for it. ❍ *Anna was interviewed for a job at The New York Times yesterday.*

inter|view|er /ɪntərvyuər/ **NOUN** someone who asks you questions in a formal meeting to find out if you are the right person for a job ❍ *The interviewer asked me why I wanted the job.*

in|ti|mate /ɪntɪmɪt/ **ADJ** An **intimate** friend is someone you know well and like a lot. ❍ *I told my intimate friends I wanted to have a baby.* ● **in|ti|mate|ly** **ADV** ❍ *He knew the family intimately.*

in|timi|date /ɪntɪmɪdeɪt/ (**intimidates, intimidating, intimidated**) **VERB** If you **intimidate** someone, you frighten them, in order to make them do what you want. ❍ *He claimed he had been intimidated by his boss.* ● **in|timi|da|tion** /ɪntɪmɪdeɪʃən/ **NONCOUNT NOUN** ❍ *Witnesses are often afraid of intimidation.*

into /ɪntu/
1 PREP If you put one thing **into** another thing, you put the first thing inside the second thing. ❍ *Put the apples into a dish.*
2 PREP If you go **into** a place or a vehicle, you go inside it. ❍ *I got into the car and started the engine.*
3 PREP If you crash **into** something, you hit it accidentally. ❍ *A train crashed into the barrier at the end of the track.*
4 PREP When you change **into** a piece of clothing, you put a different piece of clothing on. ❍ *I'm cold—I'll change into some warmer clothes.*
5 PREP If one thing changes **into** another thing, it becomes that thing. ❍ *The book has been made into a movie.*
6 PREP used for talking about how something is divided ❍ *The project was divided into five stages.*
7 PREP used for talking about dividing one number by another ❍ *5 into 15 is 3.*

in|tra|net /ɪntrənɛt/ **NOUN** a network of computers in a particular organization [TECHNOLOGY]

in|tri|guing /ɪntrigɪŋ/ **ADJ** very interesting and slightly strange, making you want to know more ❍ *an intriguing story*

intro|duce /ɪntrədus/ (**introduces, introducing, introduced**)
1 VERB If you **introduce** people, you tell them each other's names so that they can get to know each other. If you **introduce yourself** to someone, you tell them your name. ❍ *Tim, may I introduce you to my wife, Jennifer?* ❍ *Before the meeting, we all introduced ourselves.*
2 VERB If you **introduce** something new, you bring it to a place or make it exist for the first time. ❍ *The airline introduced a new direct service from Houston last month.*

intro|duc|tion /ɪntrədʌkʃən/
1 NOUN the process of telling a person another person's name so that they can get to know each other ❍ *Elaine, the hostess, made the introductions.*
2 NONCOUNT NOUN the process of bringing something new to a place or making it exist for the first time ❍ *Did the introduction of the euro affect prices?*
3 NOUN the part at the beginning of a book that tells you what the book is about ❍ *J.D. Salinger wrote the introduction to the book.*

intro|duc|tory /ɪntrədʌktəri/ **ADJ** An **introductory** offer or price on a new product is something such as a free gift or a low price that is meant to attract new customers. [MARKETING AND SALES] ○ *a special introductory offer*

in|trud|er /ɪntrudər/ **NOUN** a person who goes into a place without permission ○ *Mrs. Baker called 911 when an intruder entered her home.*

in|tui|tion /ɪntuɪʃən/ **NONCOUNT NOUN** **Intuition** is an ability to know or understand something through your feelings. ○ *My intuition told me that I could trust him.*

in|vade /ɪnveɪd/ (**invades, invading, invaded**) **VERB** If an army **invades** a country, it enters and attacks it. ○ *In 1944 the Allies invaded the Italian mainland.*

I

in|va|lid

> Pronounce the noun /ɪnvəlɪd/. Pronounce the adjective /ɪnvælɪd/.

1 NOUN someone who needs to be cared for by another person because they are very sick or injured ○ *Both of Mary's parents are invalids.*

2 ADJ If a document is **invalid**, it cannot be accepted, because it breaks an official rule. ○ *an invalid passport*

in|va|sion /ɪnveɪʒən/ **NOUN** an occasion when an army from one country enters another country and attacks it

in|vent /ɪnvɛnt/

1 VERB If you **invent** something, you are the first person to think of it or make it. [R & D] ○ *The ballpoint pen was invented by the Hungarian, Laszlo Biro.* ● **in|ven|tor NOUN** ○ *the inventor of the telephone*

2 VERB If you **invent** a story or excuse that is not true, you make it up and pretend it is true. ○ *Heather invented an excuse not to attend the meeting.*

in|ven|tion /ɪnvɛnʃən/

1 NOUN something that has been invented by someone [R & D] ○ *Paper was a Chinese invention.*

2 NONCOUNT NOUN **Invention** is when something that has never been made or used before is invented. [R & D] ○ *the invention of the telescope*

in|ven|tory /ɪnvəntɔri/ (**inventories**) **NOUN** The **inventory** of a business is the amount or value of its raw materials, work in progress, and finished goods. [PRODUCTION] ○ *Second-quarter growth slowed because distributors had too much inventory.* ○ *Business inventories rose at a $22 billion annual rate.*

in|ven|tory con|trol **NONCOUNT NOUN** **Inventory control** is the activity of making sure that a firm always has exactly the right amount of goods available to sell. ○ *Better inventory control helped Wal-Mart to reduce its expenses by $2 billion.*

in|vest /ɪnvɛst/ **VERB** If you **invest** your money, you put it into a business or a bank, to try to make a profit from it. [FINANCE] ○ *He invested millions of dollars in the business.*

in|ves|ti|gate /ɪnvɛstɪgeɪt/ (**investigates, investigating, investigated**) **VERB** If you **investigate** something, you try to find out what happened. ○ *Police are investigating how the accident happened.*

in|ves|ti|ga|tion /ɪnvɛstɪgeɪʃən/ **NOUN** the process of trying to find out what happened in a situation such as a crime or an accident ○ *We have begun an investigation into the alleged fraud.*

in|ves|ti|ga|tor /ɪnvɛstɪgeɪtər/ **NOUN** someone whose job it is to find out about something ○ *Investigators have been questioning the survivors.*

in|vest|ment /ɪnvɛstmənt/

1 NONCOUNT NOUN **Investment** is the activity of investing money. [FINANCE] ○ *an investment advisor*

2 NOUN an amount of money that you invest, or the thing that you invest it in [FINANCE] ○ *Anthony made a $1 million investment in the company.*

in|vest|ment an|alyst /ɪnvɛstmənt ænəlɪst/ (**investment analysts**) **NOUN** a specialist in forecasting the prices of stocks and shares [BANKING, FINANCE] ○ *Competition among investment analysts will lead to a stock* *market in which prices at all times reflect true value.*

in|vest|ment bank (**investment banks**) NOUN a bank that deals mainly with firms and investments [BANKING, FINANCE]

in|vest|ment bank|er (**investment bankers**) NOUN someone who works for an investment bank [BANKING, FINANCE]

in|vest|ment trust (**investment trusts**) NOUN a financial enterprise that invests money in securities for its investors [BANKING, FINANCE, BRIT] ❍ *He decided to take out an investment trust for his son two years ago.*

in|ves|tor /ɪnvɛstər/ NOUN a person or organization that buys securities or property or pays money into a bank in order to receive a profit [BANKING, FINANCE] ❍ *The main investor in the project is the French bank Credit National.*

in|vis|ible /ɪnvɪzɪbᵊl/

1 ADJ impossible to see ❍ *The belt is invisible even under the thinnest garments.*

2 ADJ **Invisible** earnings are the money that a country makes as a result of services such as banking and tourism, rather than by producing goods. [FINANCE, ECONOMICS] ❍ *The revenue from tourism is the biggest single item in the country's invisible earnings.*

in|vis|ible ex|port (**invisible exports**) NOUN An **invisible export** is an export of services such as banking, insurance, and tourism rather than goods. Compare with **visible export**. [ECONOMICS] ❍ *Tourism is Britain's single biggest invisible export.*

in|vis|ible im|port (**invisible imports**) NOUN An **invisible import** is an import of services such as banking, insurance, and tourism rather than goods. Compare with **visible import**. [ECONOMICS] ❍ *A record of the overall results of a country's trading activity with the rest of the world includes both visible and invisible imports and exports and flows of capital between countries.*

in|vi|ta|tion /ɪnvɪteɪʃən/ NOUN a request to come to an event such as a party ❍ *I accepted Sarah's invitation to dinner.*

in|vite /ɪnvaɪt/ (**invites, inviting, invited**) VERB If you **invite** someone to an event, you ask them to come to it. ❍ *She invited him to her 26th birthday party.*

in|voice /ɪnvɔɪs/ (**invoices, invoicing, invoiced**)

1 NOUN a document that lists goods that have been supplied or services that have been done, and says how much money you owe for them [FINANCE] ❍ *We will then send you an invoice for the total course fees.*

2 VERB If you **invoice** someone, you send them a bill for goods or services you have provided them with. [FINANCE] ❍ *The agency invoices the client who then pays.*

in|voic|ing /ɪnvɔɪsɪŋ/ NONCOUNT NOUN **Invoicing** is the process of preparing and sending someone an invoice. [FINANCE] ❍ *a machine capable of carrying out sales invoicing, letter writing, and payroll applications*

in|volve /ɪnvɒlv/ (**involves, involving, involved**)

1 VERB If an activity **involves** something, that thing is a necessary part of it. ❍ *Setting up your own business involves taking some risks.*

2 VERB If an activity **involves** someone, they take part in it. ❍ *The scandal involved a former senator.*

3 VERB If you **involve** someone **in** something, you get them to take part in it. ❍ *We involved the whole team in the decision.*

in|volved /ɪnvɒlvd/ ADJ If you are **involved in** something, you take part in it. ❍ *All of their children are involved in the family business.*

in|volve|ment /ɪnvɒlvmənt/ NONCOUNT NOUN **Involvement in** something is the act of taking part in it. ❍ *Edwards has always denied any involvement in the crime.*

in|ward in|vest|ment /ɪnwərd invɛstmənt/ NONCOUNT NOUN **Inward investment** is the investment of money in a country by firms from outside that country. [ECONOMICS] ❍ *The UK is the main location in Europe for inward investment and the third largest recipient of inward investment in the world.*

IPO /aɪ pi oʊ/ NOUN An **IPO** is the first sale of a company's stock to the public. **IPO** is short for "initial public offering." [ECONOMICS] ❍ *Analysts say there are all sorts of reasons why the IPOs on one market might outperform those on another over a particular period.*

iPod /aɪpɒd/ **NOUN** a small piece of electronic equipment that stores music, photos, and movies and that you can carry with you [TRADEMARK, TECHNOLOGY]

iron /aɪrɒn/

1 NONCOUNT NOUN Iron is a hard, dark gray metal. ❍ *iron gates*

2 NOUN a piece of electrical equipment with a flat metal base that you heat and move over clothes to make them smooth

3 VERB If you **iron** clothes, you make them smooth using an iron. ❍ *I began to iron some shirts.* ● **iron|ing NONCOUNT NOUN** ❍ *I was doing the ironing when she called.*

I

iron|ic /aɪrɒnɪk/ or **ironical** /aɪrɒnɪkəl/ **ADJ** An **ironic** fact or situation is strange or funny because it is very different from what people expect. ❍ *The sun ages our skin so it's ironic that we lie in the sun to make ourselves look more attractive.* ● **ironi|cal|ly** /aɪrɒnɪkli/ **ADV** ❍ *His enormous dog is ironically called "Tiny."*

iro|ny /aɪrəni, aɪər-/ **NONCOUNT NOUN Irony** is a type of humor where you say the opposite of what you really mean. ❍ *"You're early!" he said, as we arrived two hours late, his voice full of irony.*

ir|ra|tion|al /ɪræʃənəl/ **ADJ Irrational** behavior is not based on sensible, clear thinking. ❍ *I think hatred is often irrational.* ● **ir|ra|tion|al|ly ADV** ❍ *My husband is irrationally jealous of my ex-boyfriends.*

ir|regu|lar /ɪrɛgyələr/

1 ADJ separated by periods of time of different lengths ❍ *an irregular heartbeat*

2 ADJ An **irregular** noun or verb does not follow the usual rules of grammar. For example, "run" is an irregular verb, because the past form is "ran" (and not "runned.") Compare with **regular**.

3 ADJ Irregular merchandise is not in perfect condition.

ir|rel|evant /ɪrɛlɪvənt/ **ADJ** not connected with what you are talking about or doing ❍ *Remove any irrelevant details from your résumé.*

ir|re|sist|ible /ɪrɪzɪstɪbəl/

1 ADJ An **irresistible** desire to do something is so strong that you cannot control it. ❍ *He had an irresistible desire to yawn.* ● **ir|re|sist|ibly** / ɪrɪzɪstɪbli/ **ADV** ❍ *I found myself irresistibly attracted to Steve.*

2 ADJ extremely good or attractive and impossible not to like [INFORMAL] ❍ *The music is irresistible.* ● **ir|re|sist|ibly ADV** ❍ *She had a charm that men found irresistibly attractive.*

ir|re|spon|sible /ɪrɪspɒnsɪbəl/ **ADJ** not thinking about the possible results of your actions ❍ *There are still too many irresponsible drivers who use their cellphones while driving.*

ir|ri|tate /ɪrɪteɪt/ (**irritates, irritating, irritated**)

1 VERB If something **irritates** you, it keeps annoying you. ❍ *His voice really irritates me.* ● **ir|ri|tat|ed ADJ** ❍ *He's become increasingly irritated by questions about his retirement.* ● **ir|ri|tat|ing ADJ** ❍ *He has an irritating habit of leaving the door open.*

2 VERB If something **irritates** a part of your body, it makes it slightly painful. ❍ *The smoke from the fire irritated his eyes and throat.*

ir|ri|ta|tion /ɪrɪteɪʃən/

1 NONCOUNT NOUN Irritation is the feeling you have when you are annoyed. ❍ *David tried not to show his irritation.*

2 NOUN a feeling of slight pain in a part of your body ❍ *These oils may cause irritation to sensitive skins.*

is /ɪz/ **Is** is a form of the verb **be**.

IS ac|count /aɪ ɛs əkaʊnt/ (**IS accounts**) **NOUN IS account** is an abbreviation for **international standard account**. [FINANCE]

Is|lam /ɪslɑm/ **NONCOUNT NOUN Islam** is the religion that was started by Muhammed. ● **Is|lam|ic** /ɪslæmɪk, -lɑ-/ **ADJ** ❍ *He's an expert in Islamic law.*

is|land /aɪlənd/ **NOUN** a piece of land that is completely surrounded by water ❍ *the Caribbean island of Barbados*

isle /aɪl/ **NOUN** an island ❍ *Ireland is sometimes called "the emerald isle."*

isn't /ɪzᵊnt/ **Isn't** is short for "is not."

iso|late /aɪsəleɪt/ (**isolates, isolating, isolated**) VERB If you **isolate** someone, you keep them away from other people. ❍ *Julie was quickly isolated from other patients in the hospital.*

iso|lat|ed /aɪsəleɪtɪd/

1 ADJ far away from other places ❍ *Commuters moving to scenic, isolated areas will change the local way of life with big-city expectations.*

2 ADJ An **isolated** example is an example of something that is not very common. ❍ *Except for isolated cases, venture capital has more or less ignored the Indian software industry.*

ISP /aɪ ɛs pi/ (**ISPs**) NOUN **ISP** is an abbreviation for **Internet service provider**. [TECHNOLOGY] ❍ *Dixons was the natural company to launch an ISP because it led the market in selling personal computers.*

is|sue /ɪʃu/ (**issues, issuing, issued**)

1 NOUN an important subject that people are talking about ❍ *Climate change is a major environmental issue.*

2 NOUN a copy of a magazine or a newspaper that is published in a particular month or on a particular day ❍ *Have you read the latest issue of the "Scientific American?"*

3 VERB If you **issue** something, you officially say it or give it. ❍ *The government issued a warning of possible attacks.* ❍ *The embassy has stopped issuing visas to journalists.*

4 NOUN the number of identical items, such as banknotes or shares in a firm, that become available at a particular time [ECONOMICS] ❍ *Any time you bring out a new issue, you have an issue that comes a little cheap to the market.*

5 VERB **Issue** is also a verb. ❍ *For the second consecutive week, newly issued U.S. Treasury bills were sold with higher yields.*

is|sue price (**issue prices**) NOUN the price at which shares are offered for sale when they first become available to the public [FINANCE, ECONOMICS] ❍ *Shares in the company slipped below their issue price on their first day of trading.*

is|suing house (**issuing houses**) NOUN a financial institution that finds capital for firms by issuing shares on their behalf [ECONOMICS, BANKING] ❍ *New share capital is most frequently raised through issuing houses or merchant banks which arrange for the sale of shares on behalf of client companies.*

it /ɪt/

1 PRON used for talking about something that you have already mentioned ❍ *I worked in a factory until it closed a few months ago.* ❍ *I'll tell you about the plan once I know more about it.*

2 PRON used before certain nouns, adjectives, and verbs to talk about your feelings ❍ *It was nice to see Steve again.* ❍ *It's a pity you can't come to the conference, Sarah.*

3 PRON used for talking about the time, the date, the weather, or the distance to a place ❍ *It's three o'clock.* ❍ *It was Saturday.* ❍ *It was snowing yesterday.* ❍ *It's ten miles to the next gas station.*

4 PRON used for saying who someone is ❍ *"Who's that on the phone?"—"It's Mrs. Williams."*

I.T. /aɪ ti/ **I.T.** is an abbreviation for **information technology**. [TECHNOLOGY] ❍ *The I.T. market is growing in Britain at a faster rate than in any other country in Europe.*

itch /ɪtʃ/ (**itches, itching, itched**)

1 VERB When a part of your body **itches**, the skin there is uncomfortable and makes you want to scratch it. ❍ *Her perfume made my eyes itch.*

2 NOUN **Itch** is also a noun. [FINANCE] ❍ *Can you scratch my back? I've got an itch.* ● **itchy** ADJ ❍ *My eyes feel itchy and sore.*

it'd /ɪtəd/

1 **It'd** is short for "it would." ❍ *It'd be better to keep quiet.*

2 **It'd** is short for "it had." ❍ *Marcie was watching a movie. It'd just started.*

item /aɪtəm/

1 NOUN one thing in a list or a group of things ❍ *The most valuable item in the sale was a Picasso drawing.*

2 NOUN an entry in an account [FINANCE] ❍ *Feed was the largest single cost item last year at $17.9 billion, accounting for 15.1% of total costs.*

it'll /ɪtᵊl/ **It'll** is short for "it will." ❍ *It'll cost a lot, but it'll be worth it.*

i

its /ɪts/ **ADJ** used for showing that something belongs or relates to a thing, a place, or an animal that has just been mentioned ○ *The company was failing, and many of its employees were looking for work elsewhere.*

it's /ɪts/ **It's** is short for "it is" or "it has."

it|self /ɪtsɛlf/

1 PRON used as the object of a verb or preposition when an animal or thing is both the subject and the object of the verb ○ *The airline plans to turn itself into a low-cost operation.*

2 PRON used for emphasizing a word ○ *There are lots of good restaurants on the road to Wilmington, and in Wilmington itself.*

3 PRON If an animal or a thing does something **by itself**, it does it without any help. ○ *The company is working on a car that can drive by itself.*

I've /aɪv/ **I've** is short for "I have." ○ *I've been working on this report for weeks.*

I

jack /dʒæk/
▸**jack up** PHRASAL VERB If prices or levels are **jacked up**, they are increased. ❍ *The quickest way of getting the cash was to jack up interest rates.*

jack|et /dʒækɪt/ NOUN a short coat with long sleeves ❍ *He wore a black leather jacket.*

jail /dʒeɪl/ NOUN a place where criminals have to stay as a punishment ❍ *He went to jail for 15 years.* ❍ *Three prisoners escaped from a jail.*

jam /dʒæm/ (**jams, jamming, jammed**)
1 VERB If you **jam** something into a place, you push it there hard. ❍ *He jammed the key in the lock.*
2 NONCOUNT NOUN **Jam** is a sweet food that contains soft fruit and sugar. ❍ *strawberry jam on toast*
3 NOUN If there is a traffic **jam** on a road, there are so many vehicles there that they cannot move. ❍ *The trucks sat in a traffic jam for ten hours.*
4 NONCOUNT NOUN **Jam** is the same as **jelly**. [mainly BRIT]

Janu|ary /dʒænyuɛri/ NOUN the first month of the year ❍ *There has been a 20% price rise since January.*

> **BUSINESS ETIQUETTE**
> German men often address each other as *Herr [surname]*, even when they know each other well.

jar /dʒɑr/ NOUN a glass container with a lid that is used for storing food ❍ *There were several glass jars filled with candy.*

jaw /dʒɔ/ NOUN the part of your face below your mouth ❍ *Andrew broke his jaw in the accident.*

jeal|ous /dʒɛləs/
1 ADJ angry because you think that another person is trying to take away someone that you love ❍ *He got jealous and there was a fight.*
2 ADJ If you are **jealous of** another person's possessions or qualities, you feel angry because you do not have them. ❍ *She was jealous of her colleague's success.* • **jeal|ous|ly** ADV ❍ *Gloria looked jealously at his new car.*

jeal|ousy /dʒɛləsi/ NONCOUNT NOUN **Jealousy** is the feeling of anger that someone has when they think that another person is trying to take away someone that they love. ❍ *He couldn't control his jealousy when he saw her new husband.*

jeans /dʒinz/ PL NOUN **Jeans** are pants that are made of strong cotton cloth. ❍ *We saw a young man in jeans and a T-shirt.*

jel|ly /dʒɛli/ NONCOUNT NOUN **Jelly** is a sweet food that contains soft fruit and sugar. ❍ *peanut butter and jelly sandwiches*

jerk /dʒɜrk/
1 VERB If you **jerk** something, you move it a short distance very suddenly and quickly. ❍ *Sam jerked his head in my direction.*
2 NOUN **Jerk** is also a noun. ❍ *He gave a jerk of his head to the other two men.*
3 NOUN a stupid person [INFORMAL]

jet /dʒɛt/
1 NOUN an aircraft that is powered by jet engines ❍ *He arrived from Key West by jet.*
2 NOUN A **jet** of liquid or gas is a strong, fast, thin stream of it. ❍ *A jet of water poured through the windows.*

jet lag /dʒɛt læg/ NONCOUNT NOUN If you have **jet lag**, you feel tired after a long trip by airplane. ❍ *We were tired because we still had jet lag.*

Jew /dʒu/ **NOUN** a person who practices the religion of Judaism or who is part of the race of people who lived in Israel in ancient times

jew|el /dʒuəl/ **NOUN** a valuable stone, such as a diamond ❍ *The box was filled with precious jewels and gold.*

jew|el|lery /dʒuəlri/ [BRIT] → **jewelry**

jew|el|ry /dʒuəlri/ **NONCOUNT NOUN** **Jewelry** is decorations that you wear on your body, such as a ring that you wear on your finger. ❍ *gold jewelry*

Jew|ish /dʒuɪʃ/

1 ADJ belonging or relating to the religion of Judaism ❍ *the Jewish festival of Passover*

2 ADJ practicing the religion of Judaism or being part of the race of people who lived in Israel in ancient times ❍ *She was from a traditional Jewish family.*

J

JIT manu|fac|turing /dʒeɪ aɪ ti mænyəfæktʃərɪŋ/ or **JIT production** **NONCOUNT NOUN** [PRODUCTION] → **just-in-time manufacturing**

job /dʒɒb/

1 NOUN the work that someone does to earn money ❍ *Terry was looking for a new job.*

2 NOUN a particular task ❍ *I have some jobs to do in the office today.*

3 If someone is **doing a good job**, they are doing something well. ❍ *Most of our sales staff are doing a good job.*

job ac|tion **NONCOUNT NOUN** If workers take **job action**, they join together and do something to show that they are unhappy with their pay or working conditions, for example refusing to work. ❍ *Prison officers will decide next week whether to take job action over staffing levels.*

job analy|sis (**job analyses**) **NOUN** a description of every part of a job ❍ *Critical job elements are identified through a job analysis.*

job de|scrip|tion (**job descriptions**) **NOUN** a written statement of all the duties involved in a particular job ❍ *This is the job description for the position of division general manager.*

job evalu|ation (**job evaluations**) **NOUN** a comparison of jobs in an organization to see how much each person should be paid ❍ *Your job evaluation is concerned with the job and not your performance.*

job in|secu|rity **NONCOUNT NOUN** **Job insecurity** is the feeling that you might lose your job. [HR] ❍ *The changing employment pattern has created job insecurity for the urban working class.*

job|less /dʒɒblɪs/ **ADJ** not having a job ❍ *The number of jobless people went up last month.*

job pro|duc|tion **NONCOUNT NOUN** **Job production** is the production of a small number of goods for one particular customer. Compare with **batch production** and **flow production**. [PRODUCTION]

job ro|ta|tion **NONCOUNT NOUN** **Job rotation** is the practice of moving staff from one activity to another. [HR] ❍ *Job rotation results in a more flexible workforce.*

job sat|is|fac|tion **NONCOUNT NOUN** **Job satisfaction** is the pleasure that you get from doing your job. [HR] ❍ *I doubt I'll ever get rich, but I get job satisfaction.*

job share (**job shares, job sharing, job shared**) **VERB** If two people **job share**, they share the same job by working part-time, for example, one person working in the mornings and the other in the afternoons. [HR] ❍ *They both want to job share.* • **job shar|ing** **NONCOUNT NOUN** ❍ *The company offers flexible working options, including job sharing.*

jog /dʒɒg/ (**jogs, jogging, jogged**)

1 VERB If you **jog**, you run slowly, often as a form of exercise. ❍ *She jogs around the park every morning.*

2 NOUN **Jog** is also a noun. ❍ *He went for an early morning jog.* • **jog|ger** **NOUN** ❍ *The park was full of joggers.* • **jog|ging** **NONCOUNT NOUN** ❍ *They went jogging every morning.*

join /dʒɔɪn/

1 VERB If you **join** an organization, you become a member of it. ❍ *He joined the* *company five years ago.*

2 VERB If you **join** a line, you stand at the end of it so that you are part of it. ❍ *He joined the line of people waiting to get on the bus.*

3 VERB To **join** two things means to attach or fasten them together. ❍ *Join the two squares of fabric to make a bag.*

joint /dʒɔɪnt/

1 NOUN a part of your body such as your knee where two bones meet and are able to move together ❍ *Her joints ache if she exercises.*

2 ADJ shared by two or more people or groups ❍ *a joint bank account* ❍ *a joint venture*

● **joint|ly ADV** ❍ *The two companies plan to jointly develop several new services.*

joint ac|count (**joint accounts**) **NOUN** a bank account that is controlled and used by two or more people [BANKING] ❍ *Both our salaries are paid into the joint account.*

joint stock NONCOUNT NOUN Joint stock is capital funds owned by several people who all own shares. [ECONOMICS]

joint-stock com|pany (**joint-stock companies**) **NOUN** a company that is owned by the people who have shares in that company and who are responsible for its debts [ECONOMICS]

joint ven|ture (**joint ventures**) **NOUN** a business set up by two or more companies or people [ECONOMICS] ❍ *It will be sold to a joint venture created by Dow Jones and Westinghouse Broadcasting.*

joke /dʒoʊk/ (**jokes, joking, joked**)

1 NOUN something that someone says to make you laugh ❍ *He made a joke about it.*

2 VERB If you **joke**, you say amusing things, or say something that is not true for fun. ❍ *She often joked about her big feet.* ❍ *I was only joking!*

jour|nal /dʒɜrnᵊl/

1 NOUN a notebook or diary ❍ *Sara wrote her private thoughts in her journal.*

2 NOUN a book in which transactions are recorded before they are entered into a ledger [FINANCE] ❍ *a journal showing all purchases, sales, receipts, and deliveries of securities and all other debits and credits*

jour|nal|ist /dʒɜrnəlɪst/ **NOUN** a person whose job is to collect news stories and write about them for newspapers, magazines, television, or radio ❍ *The president spoke to an audience of two hundred journalists.*

● **jour|nal|ism NONCOUNT NOUN** ❍ *a career in journalism*

jour|ney /dʒɜrni/ **NOUN** an occasion when you travel from one place to another ❍ *Their journey took them from New York to San Francisco.*

joy /dʒɔɪ/ **NONCOUNT NOUN Joy** is a feeling of great happiness. ❍ *She shouted with joy.*

Ju|da|ism /dʒudiɪzəm, -deɪ-/ **NONCOUNT NOUN Judaism** is the religion of the Jewish people.

judge /dʒʌdʒ/ (**judges, judging, judged**)

1 NOUN the person in a court of law who decides how a criminal should be punished [LEGAL] ❍ *The judge sent him to jail for 100 days.*

2 VERB If you **judge** something or someone, you form an opinion about them. ❍ *People should wait, and judge the movie when they see it.*

judg|ment /dʒʌdʒmənt/

1 NONCOUNT NOUN Judgment is the ability to make sensible decisions about what to do. ❍ *I respect his judgment, and I'll follow his advice.*

2 NOUN a decision made by a judge or by a court of law ❍ *We are waiting for a judgment from the Supreme Court.*

BUSINESS ETIQUETTE

In China, Japan, and other Asia-Pacific countries, you should not place your chopsticks straight up in your bowl. Doing this reminds people of death, because they look like special sticks (called joss sticks) that are burnt at funerals to give a particular sweet smell.

jug /dʒʌg/ **NOUN** a container with a handle used for holding and pouring liquids

jug|gle /dʒʌgᵊl/ (**juggles, juggling, juggled**) **VERB** If you **juggle**, you throw and catch several things repeatedly and try to keep them in the air. ❍ *She was juggling five balls.*

juice /dʒus/ **NONCOUNT NOUN** **Juice** is the liquid from a fruit or vegetable. ❍ *fresh orange juice*

juicy /dʒusi/ (**juicier, juiciest**) **ADJ** **Juicy** food contains a lot of liquid and is good to eat. ❍ *a thick, juicy steak*

July /dʒʊlaɪ/ **NOUN** the seventh month of the year ❍ *Our annual meeting will be held in Atlanta in July.*

jump /dʒʌmp/

1 VERB If you **jump**, you push your feet against the ground and move quickly upward into the air. ❍ *I jumped over the fence.*

2 NOUN **Jump** is also a noun. ❍ *She set a world record for the longest jump by a woman.*

3 VERB If you **jump** somewhere, you move there quickly and suddenly. ❍ *Adam jumped up when the manager walked in.*

4 VERB If something **makes** you **jump**, it makes you move suddenly because you are frightened or surprised. ❍ *The phone rang and made her jump.*

5 VERB If you **jump at** an offer or an opportunity, you accept it quickly and with enthusiasm. ❍ *She jumped at the chance to set up her own company.*

jump|er /dʒʌmpər/ [BRIT] → **sweater**

June /dʒun/ **NOUN** the sixth month of the year ❍ *He spent two weeks with us in June 2006.*

jun|gle /dʒʌŋgᵊl/ **NOUN** a forest in a tropical country where large numbers of tall trees and plants grow very close together ❍ *The trail led them deeper into the jungle.*

jun|ior /dʒunyər/

1 NOUN a student in the third year of high school or college ❍ *Her son is a junior in high school.*

2 ADJ having a low position in an organization ❍ *a junior officer in the army*

junk /dʒʌŋk/ **NONCOUNT NOUN** **Junk** is old and useless things that you do not want or need. [INFORMAL] ❍ *What are you going to do with all that junk, Larry?*

junk bond (**junk bonds**) **NOUN** a bond that gives a high rate of interest because it is very risky [BANKING] ❍ *Many junk bond investors seek yields above 12%.*

junk mail **NONCOUNT NOUN** **Junk mail** is publicity materials in your mail that you have not asked for. [MARKETING AND SALES] ❍ *We still get junk mail for the previous occupants.*

ju|rist /dʒʊərɪst/ **NOUN** an expert in law [LEGAL, FORMAL]

ju|ry /dʒʊəri/ (**juries**) **NOUN** in a court of law, a group of people who listen to the facts about a crime and decide if a person is guilty or not [LEGAL] ❍ *The jury decided she was not guilty of murder.*

just

❶ ADVERB USES
❷ ADJECTIVE USE

❶ **just** /dʒʌst/

1 ADV a very short time ago ❍ *I just got a call from John.*

2 ADV now ❍ *I'm just making some coffee.*

3 ADV only ❍ *It costs just a few dollars.*

4 ADV used for emphasizing the following verb ❍ *Just stop talking and listen to me!*

5 ADV exactly ❍ *It works just like a normal printer, but it's faster.*

6 Just about means almost. ❍ *All our money is just about gone.*

7 You say **just a minute**, **just a moment**, or **just a second** when you are asking someone to wait for a short time. ❍ *Just a moment. What did you say?*

❷ **just** /dʒʌst/ **ADJ** fair or right [FORMAL] ❍ *He got his just reward.*

jus|tice /dʒʌstɪs/

1 NONCOUNT NOUN **Justice** is the fair treatment of people. ❍ *We want freedom, justice, and equality.*

2 NOUN a judge ❍ *He is a justice on the Supreme Court.*

jus|ti|fy /dʒʌstɪfaɪ/ (**justifies, justifying, justified**) **VERB** To **justify** a decision or an action means to show that it is reasonable or necessary. ❍ *We need to justify the additional costs.*

just-in-time **ADJ** In business, **just-in-time** methods avoid waste by producing or sending goods as they are needed rather than holding large stocks. [PRODUCTION] ○ *Just-in-time delivery saves warehousing costs.*

just-in-time manu|fac|turing or **just-in-time production** NONCOUNT NOUN **Just-in-time manufacturing** or **just-in-time production** is a method of producing goods only when they are needed rather than holding large stocks. [PRODUCTION] ○ *The current trend towards just-in-time manufacturing has led to stock reductions in many manufacturing companies.*

j

Kk

K also **k** /keɪ/ **NOUN** **K** means one thousand. ❍ *He earns 50K a year.*

kai|zen /kaɪzɛn/ **NONCOUNT NOUN** **Kaizen** is a business strategy in which many small improvements are made in order to improve overall performance. [BUSINESS MANAGEMENT] ❍ *Workers must adopt a policy of kaizen, which is the practice of continually seeking improvement.*

kan|ban /kɑnbɑn, kænbæn/ **NONCOUNT NOUN** **Kanban** is a manufacturing process in which special cards are used to record the movement of materials through a process. [PRODUCTION] ❍ *Delivery is controlled by the kanban process.*

K

kan|ga|roo /kæŋgəru/ **NOUN** a large Australian animal, the female of which carries her baby in a pocket on her stomach

ka|ra|te /kərɑti/ **NONCOUNT NOUN** **Karate** is a Japanese sport in which people fight using their hands and feet.

kar|oshi /kæroʊʃi/ **NONCOUNT NOUN** In Japan, **karoshi** is death caused by working too much.

keen /kin/ **(keener, keenest)** **ADJ** wanting to do something, or very interested in something ❍ *They are keen to acquire the remaining shares.* ❍ *She is a keen supporter of indirect taxes.*

keep /kip/ **(keeps, keeping, kept)**

1 VERB If someone **keeps** in a particular state or place, they remain in it. ❍ *Keep away from the doors while the train is moving.* ❍ *We burned wood to keep warm.* ❍ *"Keep still!"*

2 VERB If someone or something **keeps** a person or thing in a particular state or place, they make them stay in it. ❍ *The noise kept him awake.* ❍ *He kept his head down.*

3 VERB If you **keep** doing something, you do it many times or you continue to do it. ❍ *I keep forgetting my password.* ❍ *She kept working although she was exhausted.*

4 VERB If you **keep** something, you continue to have it, and if you **keep** something somewhere, you store it there. ❍ *I want to keep these clothes, and I'm giving these away.* ❍ *She kept her diary on her desk.*

5 VERB When you **keep** a promise, you do what you said you would do. ❍ *He kept his promise to give us a bonus.*

▸ **keep up**

1 If you **keep up with** someone or something, you move as fast as they do so that you are moving together. ❍ *Sam walked faster to keep up with his father.*

2 If you **keep** something **up**, you continue to do it. ❍ *They intend to keep up economic sanctions.*

ken|nel /kɛnᵊl/ **NOUN** a place where a dog can be cared for when the owner goes away

kept /kɛpt/ **Kept** is a form of the verb **keep**.

kerb /kɜrb/ [BRIT] → **curb**

ket|tle /kɛtᵊl/ **NOUN** a metal container with a lid and a handle, that you use for boiling water ❍ *I'll put the kettle on and make us some tea.*

key /ki/

1 NOUN a specially shaped piece of metal that opens or closes a lock ❍ *He put the key in the door and entered.*

2 NOUN on a computer keyboard, one of the buttons that you press in order to operate it ❍ *Now press the "Delete" key.*

3 NOUN on a piano, one of the white and black bars that you press in order to play it

4 NOUN in music, a particular scale of musical notes ❍ *the key of A minor*

5 ADJ most important ❍ *He's a key member of the team.*

key|board /ki̲bɔrd/

1 NOUN a set of keys on a computer that you press in order to operate it [TECHNOLOGY] ❍ *Users can connect a keyboard and mouse directly to the monitor.*

2 NOUN a set of keys on a piano that you press in order to play it

ke̲y pla̲y|er (**key players**) **NOUN** the most important person or thing in a particular organization or situation ❍ *The chairman was a key player in the deals.* ❍ *Try to identify the key players in your office.*

key|word /ki̲wɜrd/ also **key word NOUN** a word or phrase that you can use when you are searching for a particular document in an Internet search ❍ *Users can search by title, by author, by subject, and by keyword.*

kg kg is short for **kilogram** or **kilograms**.

kick /kɪ̲k/

1 VERB If you **kick** someone or something, you hit them with your foot. ❍ *He kicked the door hard.* ❍ *She kicked the ball.*

2 NOUN Kick is also a noun. ❍ *Johnson scored in the fifth minute with a free kick.*

3 VERB If you **kick**, you move your legs up and down quickly. ❍ *The baby smiled and kicked her legs.*

4 NOUN A kick is a feeling of pleasure or excitement. [INFORMAL] ❍ *I love acting. I get a big kick out of it.*

kid /kɪ̲d/ (**kids, kidding, kidded**)

1 NOUN a child [INFORMAL] ❍ *They have three kids.*

2 VERB If you **are kidding**, you are saying something that is not really true, as a joke. [INFORMAL] ❍ *I'm just kidding.*

kid|nap /kɪ̲dnæp/ (**kidnaps, kidnapping** or **kidnaping, kidnapped** or **kidnaped**) **VERB** If someone **is kidnapped**, they are taken away by force and kept as a prisoner, often until someone pays a large amount of money. ❍ *The tourists were kidnapped by a group of men with guns.* ● **kid|nap|per NOUN** ❍ *His kidnappers have threatened to kill him.* ● **kid|nap|ping NOUN** ❍ *Williams was jailed for eight years for the kidnapping.*

kid|ney /kɪ̲dni/ **NOUN** one of the two organs in your body that remove waste liquid from your blood ❍ *a kidney transplant*

kill /kɪ̲l/ **VERB** If someone or something **kills** a person, animal, or plant, they cause them to die. ❍ *More than 1,000 people have been killed by the armed forces.* ❍ *Drugs can kill.* ● **kill|ing NOUN** ❍ *The TV news reported the killing of seven people.*

kill|er /kɪ̲lər/

1 NOUN a person who has killed someone ❍ *The police are searching for the killers.*

2 NOUN something that causes death, especially a disease ❍ *Heart disease is the biggest killer of men in some countries.*

kilo /ki̲loʊ/ **NOUN** A **kilo** is the same as a **kilogram**. ❍ *He's lost ten kilos in weight.*

kilo|gram /kɪ̲ləgræm/ **NOUN** A **kilogram** is a unit for measuring weight. One kilogram is equal to 2.2 pounds, and there are one thousand grams in a kilogram. ❍ *The box weighs 4.5 kilograms.*

kilo|meter /kɪ̲ləmitər, kɪlɒ̲mɪtər/ **NOUN** A **kilometer** is a unit for measuring distance. One kilometer is equal to 0.62 miles, and there are one thousand meters in a kilometer. ❍ *We're now only one kilometer from the border.*

kilo|metre /kɪ̲ləmitər, kɪlɒ̲mɪtər/ [BRIT] → **kilometer**

k

kind

❶ NOUN USE AND PHRASE
❷ ADJECTIVE USE

❶ **kind** /ka̲ɪnd/

1 NOUN A particular **kind of** thing is a type of that thing. ❍ *The question now is: what kind of recession will this be?* ❍ *He travels a lot, and sees all kinds of interesting things.*

2 Kind of means "a little" or "in some way." [INFORMAL, SPOKEN] ❍ *When I was new at school, some girls were kind of mean to me.*

❷ **kind** /ka̲ɪnd/ **ADJ** friendly and helpful ❍ *Thank you for being so kind to me.* ● **kind|ness NONCOUNT NOUN** ❍ *I'll never forget his kindness.*

kin|der|gar|ten /kɪ̲ndərgɑrtᵊn/ **NONCOUNT NOUN Kindergarten** is a class for children aged 4 to 6 years old. ❍ *She's in kindergarten now.*

kind|ly /kaɪndli/ (**kindlier, kindliest**)
1 ADJ kind and caring ❍ *He gave her a kindly smile.*
2 ADV in a thoughtful and helpful way ❍ *Alec very kindly let me borrow his book.*

king /kɪŋ/ NOUN a male ruler in some countries ❍ *the king and queen of Spain*

king|dom /kɪŋdəm/ NOUN a country that is ruled by a king or a queen ❍ *the Kingdom of Denmark*

ki|osk /kiɒsk/ NOUN a small building with a window where people can buy things like newspapers

kip /kɪp/ (**kip**) NOUN the unit of money that is used in Laos [ECONOMICS]

kiss /kɪs/ (**kisses, kissing, kissed**)
1 VERB If you **kiss** someone, you touch them with your lips to show love, or to greet them. ❍ *She smiled and kissed him on the cheek.* ❍ *We kissed goodbye at the airport.*
2 NOUN **Kiss** is also a noun. ❍ *I put my arms around her and gave her a kiss.*

K

kit /kɪt/
1 NOUN a group of items that are kept and used together for a particular purpose ❍ *a first aid kit* ❍ *a drum kit*
2 NOUN a set of parts that you put together in order to make something ❍ *a model airplane kit*

kitch|en /kɪtʃən/ NOUN a room that is used for cooking

kit|ten /kɪtᵊn/ NOUN a very young cat

km (**kms**) **km** is short for **kilometer**.

KM /keɪ ɛm/ **KM** is short for **knowledge management**. [BUSINESS MANAGEMENT]

knee /ni/ (**knees**) NOUN the part in the middle of your leg where it bends ❍ *Lie down and bring your knees up toward your chest.*

kneel /nil/ (**kneels, kneeling, kneeled** or **knelt**)
1 VERB When you **kneel**, you bend your legs and rest with one or both of your knees on the ground. ❍ *She knelt by the bed and prayed.*
2 **Kneel down** means the same as **kneel**. ❍ *She kneeled down beside him.*

knew /nu/ **Knew** is a form of the verb **know**.

knick|ers /nɪkərz/ [BRIT] → **panties**

knife /naɪf/ (**knives**) NOUN a sharp flat piece of metal with a handle, that you use to cut things or as a weapon ❍ *a knife and fork*

knight /naɪt/ NOUN in the past, a special type of soldier who rode a horse ❍ *King Arthur's knights*

knit /nɪt/ (**knits, knitting, knitted**) VERB If you **knit** a piece of clothing, you make it from wool by using two long needles (= sticks). ❍ *I've already started knitting baby clothes.*
● **knit|ting** NONCOUNT NOUN ❍ *My favorite hobbies are knitting and reading.*

knives /naɪvz/ **Knives** is the plural of **knife**.

knob /nɒb/ NOUN a round handle or switch ❍ *He turned the knob and pushed the door.* ❍ *a volume knob*

knock /nɒk/
1 VERB If you **knock on** something, you hit it in order to make a noise. ❍ *She went to Simon's apartment and knocked on the door.*
2 NOUN **Knock** is also a noun. ❍ *They heard a knock at the front door.* ● **knock|ing** NONCOUNT NOUN ❍ *There was a loud knocking at the door.*
3 VERB If you **knock** something, you touch or hit it roughly. ❍ *She accidentally knocked the glass and it fell off the shelf.*
4 To **knock** someone or something **over** means to hit them so that they fall over. ❍ *The third wave was so strong it knocked me over.*
▸ **knock down** To **knock down** a building or part of a building means to destroy it. ❍ *Their homes are being knocked down to make way for high-rise buildings.*
▸ **knock out** To **knock** someone **out** means to hit them hard on the head so that they fall and cannot get up again. ❍ *He was knocked out in a fight.*

knot /nɒt/ (**knots, knotting, knotted**)
1 VERB If you **knot** two pieces of string or rope, you tie them together. ❍ *He knotted the laces securely together.*
2 NOUN **Knot** is also a noun. ❍ *Tony wore a bright red scarf tied in a knot around his neck.*

know /noʊ/ (**knows, knowing, knew, known**)
1 VERB If you **know** a fact or an answer, you

have that information in your mind. ❍ *You should know the answer to that question.* ❍ *"What's his name?"—"I don't know."*
2 VERB If you **know** a person or a place, you are familiar with them. ❍ *I've known him for years.* ❍ *I know Chicago well. I used to live there.*
3 VERB If you **know** something, you understand it. ❍ *I know how you feel.*
4 You say **I know** when you are agreeing with what someone has just said. ❍ *"She's a great manager."—"I know."*
5 You use **you know** when you want someone to listen to what you are saying. [INFORMAL, SPOKEN] ❍ *I'm doing this for you, you know.*

knowl|edge /nɒlɪdʒ/ **NONCOUNT NOUN** **Knowledge** is information and understanding about a subject. ❍ *We want to enhance our knowledge of the marketplace.*

knowl|edge econo|my (**knowledge economies**) **NOUN** an economy in which information services are very important [ECONOMICS] ❍ *In today's knowledge economy, it is essential to protect data.*

> **BUSINESS ETIQUETTE**
> In China and Japan, you should never write on a business card or put it in your wallet or pocket. Carry a small card case.

knowl|edge man|age|ment **NONCOUNT NOUN** **Knowledge management** is the business practice of identifying and using ideas and information.

knowl|edge work|er (**knowledge workers**) **NOUN** a person whose job is to produce or analyze ideas and information ❍ *Knowledge workers do not produce a "thing." They produce ideas, information, and concepts.*

known /noʊn/
1 Known is a form of the verb **know**.
2 ADJ famous ❍ *Goldman is known for its stock research and trading.*

knuck|le /nʌkəl/ **NOUN** one of the parts where your fingers join your hands, and where your fingers bend ❍ *She tapped on the door with her knuckles.*

Ko|ran /kɔran, -ræn/ **NOUN** **The Koran** is the most important book in the religion of Islam.

ko|ru|na /kərunə/ (**korunas** or **koruna**) **NOUN** the unit of money that is used in the Czech Republic and Slovakia [ECONOMICS] ❍ *Last year, the firm lost 175 million koruna.*

kro|na /kroʊnə/ (**kroner**) **NOUN** the unit of money that is used in Sweden [ECONOMICS] ❍ *There was a 22% drop in the krona against the euro this year.*

kro|ne /kroʊnə/ (**kroner**) **NOUN** the unit of money that is used in Norway, Denmark, the Faeroe Islands and Greenland [ECONOMICS] ❍ *They made a profit of 3.7 million kroner.*

Kru|ger|rand /krugərænd/ **NOUN** a South African coin that is used only for investment [ECONOMICS]

ku|na /kunə/ (**kune**) **NOUN** the unit of money that is used in Croatia [ECONOMICS]

Ll

lab /læb/ NOUN A **lab** is the same as a **laboratory**.

la|bel /leɪbəl/

1 NOUN a piece of paper or plastic that is attached to an object to give information about it ❍ *Always read the label on the bottle.*

2 VERB If something **is labeled**, it has a label on it. ❍ *All foods must be clearly labeled.*

la|bor /leɪbər/

1 NOUN **Labor** is very hard work, usually physical work. ❍ *the labor of hauling the rocks away* ❍ *The chef looked up from his labors and we could see he was sweating.*

L

2 VERB Someone who **labors** works hard using their hands. ❍ *He will be laboring 14 hundred yards below ground.*

3 VERB If you **labor to** do something, you do it with difficulty. ❍ *Scientists labored for months to unravel the mysteries of Neptune and still remain baffled.*

4 NONCOUNT NOUN **Labor** is all the workers of a country or industry, considered as a group. [BUSINESS MANAGEMENT] ❍ *Latin America lacked skilled labor.* ❍ *Employers want cheap labor and consumers want cheap houses.*

5 NONCOUNT NOUN **Labor** is the work done by a group of workers or by a particular worker for pay. [BUSINESS MANAGEMENT] ❍ *He exhibits a profound humility in the low rates he pays himself for his labor.*

6 NONCOUNT NOUN **Labor** is the last stage of pregnancy, in which the mother gradually pushes the baby out of the womb. ❍ *Her labor lasted ten hours.*

la|bora|tory /læbrətɔri/ (**laboratories**) NOUN a building or room where scientific work is done ❍ *He works in a research laboratory at Columbia University.*

la|bor costs PL NOUN A company's **labor costs** are the money it spends on wages and benefits for its employees. [FINANCE, ECONOMICS] ❍ *America's companies are watching their profits shrivel in the face of a slowing economy and rising labor costs.*

COLLOCATIONS
low labor costs
high labor costs
rising labor costs
to *hold down* labor costs
to *drive down* labor costs
to *keep down* labor costs

La|bor Day NONCOUNT NOUN In the United States, **Labor Day** is a national holiday to celebrate working people, on the first Monday in September.

la|bor|er /leɪbərər/ NOUN a person who does a job that involves a lot of hard physical work ❍ *She still lives on the farm where he worked as a laborer.*

la|bor force (**labor forces**) NOUN **The labor force** is all the people who are able to work in a country or area, or all the people who work for a particular company. [ECONOMICS] ❍ *Unemployment rose to 8.1% of the labor force.*

labor-intensive ADJ **Labor-intensive** industries or methods of producing things involve a lot of workers. Compare with **capital-intensive**. ❍ *Construction remains a relatively labor-intensive industry.*

la|bor law NONCOUNT NOUN **Labor law** is the areas of law that are about the relationship between companies and workers or companies and labor unions. [ECONOMICS, LEGAL]

la|bor mar|ket (**labor markets**) NOUN **The labor market** is all the people who want jobs in a country or area, in relation to the number of jobs there are available. [ECONOMICS] ❍ *The longer people have been unemployed, the harder it is for them to compete in the labor market.*

la|bor re|la|tions PL NOUN **Labor relations** are the relations between companies and workers or companies and labor unions. [HR, LEGAL] ❍ *Improved labor relations were reported by 80.6 percent of the companies.*

la|bor un|ion (**labor unions**) NOUN a workers' organization that tries to improve working conditions [HR]

la|bour /leɪbər/ [BRIT] → **labor**

la|bour|er /leɪbərər/ [BRIT] → **laborer**

lace /leɪs/ (**laces, lacing, laced**)
1 NONCOUNT NOUN **Lace** is a delicate cloth with a design made of fine threads. ❍ *She wore a blue dress with a lace collar.*
2 NOUN one of two thin pieces of material used for fastening shoes ❍ *Barry put on his shoes and tied the laces.*
3 VERB If you **lace** a pair of shoes, you pull the laces through the holes and tie them together. ❍ *I laced my shoes tightly.*

lack /læk/
1 NONCOUNT NOUN If there is a **lack of** something, there is not enough of it or it does not exist. ❍ *The industry suffers from a lack of investment.*
2 VERB If someone or something **lacks** or **is lacking in** a particular quality, they do not have that quality or they do not have enough of it. ❍ *They still lack the technical expertise of Western manufacturers.*

lad|der /lædər/ NOUN a piece of equipment used for reaching high places that consists of two long pieces of wood or metal with short steps between them ❍ *He climbed the ladder so he could see over the wall.*

ladies' /leɪdiz/ [BRIT] → **women's room**

lady /leɪdi/ (**ladies**) NOUN used for talking about a woman in a polite way ❍ *She's a very sweet old lady.*

laid /leɪd/ **Laid** is a form of the verb **lay**.

laid-back ADJ calm and relaxed [INFORMAL] ❍ *Everyone here is really laid-back.*

lain /leɪn/ **Lain** is a form of the verb **lie**.

laissez-faire /leɪseɪ fɛər, lɛs-/
1 NONCOUNT NOUN **Laissez-faire** is a policy where government interferes as little as possible with businesses or the economy. [BUSINESS MANAGEMENT] ❍ *the doctrine of laissez-faire and unbridled individualism*
2 ADJ **Laissez-faire** is also an adjective. ❍ *the Government's laissez-faire attitude toward the use of motor vehicles*

lake /leɪk/ NOUN a large area of water with land around it ❍ *They went fishing in the lake.*

lamb /læm/
1 NOUN a young sheep
2 NONCOUNT NOUN **Lamb** is the flesh of a lamb eaten as food.

lame /leɪm/ (**lamer, lamest**)
1 ADJ A **lame** animal cannot walk well. ❍ *The horses were lame and the men were tired.*
2 ADJ A **lame** excuse is one that is difficult to believe. ❍ *He gave me some lame excuse about being too busy to call me.*

lame duck (**lame ducks**)
1 NOUN a politician who has little real power, usually because their period of office is coming to an end ❍ *It would be wrong for a lame duck in Washington to tie the hands of the next administration on such matters.* ❍ *a lame-duck president*
2 NOUN If you describe someone or something as a **lame duck**, you are critical of them because they are not successful and need a lot of help. ❍ *lame-duck industries*

lamp /læmp/ NOUN a light that works using electricity or by burning oil or gas ❍ *She switched on the lamp by her desk.*

land /lænd/
1 NONCOUNT NOUN **Land** is an area of ground. ❍ *farm land*
2 VERB When someone or something **lands**, they come down to the ground after moving through the air. ❍ *The ball landed 20 feet away.*
3 VERB When an airplane **lands** or when someone **lands** it, it comes down to the ground. ❍ *The plane landed just after 10 pm.*

land|ing /lændɪŋ/
1 NOUN in a house or other building, the flat

area at the top of the stairs

2 NOUN the process of bringing an airplane down to the ground ❍ *The pilot made an emergency landing into the ocean.*

land|lord /lændlɔrd/ **NOUN** a man who owns a building and allows people to live there in return for rent ❍ *His landlord doubled the rent.*

land|mark /lændmɑrk/ **NOUN** a building or other object that helps people to know where they are ❍ *The Empire State Building is a New York landmark.*

land|scape /lændskeɪp/

1 NOUN The **landscape** is everything you can see when you look across an area of land. ❍ *We traveled through the beautiful landscape of eastern Idaho.*

2 NOUN a painting that shows a scene in the countryside ❍ *She paints landscapes of hills and river valleys.*

lane /leɪn/

1 NOUN a narrow road, especially in the countryside ❍ *Our house was on a quiet country lane.*

2 NOUN a part of a road that is marked by a painted line ❍ *The truck was traveling at 20 mph in the slow lane.*

lan|guage /læŋgwɪdʒ/

1 NOUN a system of sounds and written symbols that people of a particular country or region use in talking or writing ❍ *the English language* ❍ *Students must learn to speak a second language.*

2 NONCOUNT NOUN Language is the use of a system of communication that has a set of sounds or written symbols. ❍ *Some children develop language more quickly than others.*

lap /læp/ **(laps, lapping, lapped)**

1 NOUN Your **lap** is the flat area formed by the tops of your legs when you are sitting down. ❍ *Anthony was sitting on his dad's lap.*

2 NOUN in a race, the distance around a course one time ❍ *He fell on the last lap of the race.*

3 VERB When an animal **laps** a liquid, it uses short quick movements of its tongue to drink. ❍ *The cat lapped milk from a dish.*

lap|top /læptɒp/ **NOUN** a small computer that you can carry with you ❍ *She was working at her laptop.*

large /lɑrdʒ/ **(larger, largest)**

1 ADJ greater in size than most other things of the same type ❍ *Most large banks have slightly increased their deposit rates.* ❍ *McKinsey was the world's third largest consulting firm last year.*

2 ADJ more than the average amount or number ❍ *The rest of their shares are spread over a large number of investors.* ❍ *The company has paid back large amounts of debt.*

large|ly /lɑrdʒli/ **ADV** used for saying that something is mostly true ❍ *The program is largely paid for by taxes.*

large-scale

1 ADJ happening over a very wide area, or involving a lot of people or things ❍ *Spurred by waves of large-scale buying in blue-chip stocks, the Dow Jones Industrial Average rallied yesterday.*

2 ADJ A **large-scale** map or drawing is large enough to show a lot of details. ❍ *a large-scale map of the county*

la|ser /leɪzər/ **NOUN** a strong light that is produced by a special machine ❍ *Doctors are trying new laser technology to help patients.*

la|ser print|er (laser printers) NOUN a computer printer that produces clear words and pictures on paper using laser beams (= strong lines of light)

last /læst/

1 ADJ used for talking about the most recent thing or event ❍ *I started this job last July.* ❍ *He worked late last night.* ❍ *A lot has changed since my last visit.*

2 ADJ happening or coming after all others of the same type ❍ *I read the last three pages of the report.* ❍ *He was the last person to arrive.*

3 ADV If you do something **last**, you do it at the end, or after everyone else. ❍ *I arrived home last.*

4 PRON If you are **the last to** do something, everyone else does it before you. ❍ *Rosa was the last to finish her work.*

5 ADJ only remaining ❍ *Can I have the last piece of pizza?*

6 VERB If a situation **lasts** for a particular

length of time, it continues to exist for that time. ❍ *The partnership lasted for less than two years.*

7 VERB If something **lasts** for a particular length of time, it can be used for that time. ❍ *One tube of glue lasts for a long time.*

8 If something happens **at last**, it happens after you have been hoping for it for a long time. ❍ *I'm so glad that we've met at last!*

last|ing /lǽstɪŋ/ **ADJ** permanent ❍ *Everyone wants lasting peace.*

last name (**last names**) **NOUN** Your **last name** is the name of your family. In English, your last name comes after all your other names. ❍ *"What is your last name?"—"Garcia."*

> **BUSINESS ETIQUETTE**
> In many countries of Asia, it is polite to leave some food on your plate. If you eat all of your meal, you may give the impression that you have not had enough, and that you are still hungry. Note, however, that in Japan, it is considered good manners to empty your plate completely.

late /leɪt/ (**later, latest**)

1 ADV near the end of a period of time ❍ *It was late in the afternoon.* ❍ *He found success late in his career.*

2 ADJ **Late** is also an adjective. ❍ *He was in his late 20s.*

3 ADJ If **it is late**, it is near the end of the day. ❍ *It was late and the streets were empty.*

4 ADV after the time that something should start or happen ❍ *Steve arrived late for his meeting.*

5 ADJ **Late** is also an adjective. ❍ *The train was 40 minutes late.*

late|ly /leɪtli/ **ADV** recently ❍ *The regulators have gotten extremely tough lately.*

lat|er /leɪtər/

1 **Later** is a form of the adjective **late**.

2 ADV used for talking about a time that is after the one that you have mentioned ❍ *He joined the company in 1990 and left his job ten years later.*

lat|est /leɪtɪst/

1 **Latest** is a form of the adjective **late**.

2 ADJ most recent ❍ *I really liked her latest book.*

3 ADJ new and modern ❍ *That store sells only the latest fashions.*

lat|ter /lætər/

1 PRON **The latter** is the second of two people or things that have just been mentioned. The first of them is **the former**. ❍ *He found his cousin and uncle. The latter was sick.*

2 ADJ **Latter** is also an adjective. ❍ *Some people like speaking in public and some don't. Mike belongs in the latter group.*

laugh /læf/

1 VERB When you **laugh**, you make a sound while smiling because you find something funny. ❍ *Some of the staff laughed at his jokes.*

2 NOUN **Laugh** is also a noun. ❍ *Len gave a loud laugh.*

3 VERB If people **laugh at** someone or something, they make jokes about them. ❍ *People used to laugh at me because I was so small.*

laugh|ter /læftər/ **NONCOUNT NOUN** **Laughter** is the sound of people laughing. ❍ *Their laughter filled the room.*

launch /lɔntʃ/ (**launches, launching, launched**)

1 VERB To **launch** a spacecraft (= a vehicle that goes into space) means to send it away from Earth, and to launch a ship means to put it into water. ❍ *NASA plans to launch a new satellite.* ❍ *The Titanic was launched in 1911.*

2 VERB To **launch** a large and important activity means to start it. ❍ *Launching an aggressive diversification program, it swallowed up resort hotels on the Pacific coast.*

3 VERB If a company **launches** a new product or service, it makes it available to the public. [MARKETING AND SALES] ❍ *Amtrak launched its new train service from Atlantic City to Philadelphia, New York, and Washington on May 23.*

4 NOUN **Launch** is also a noun. ❍ *the most important product launch from Microsoft in six years*

> **COLLOCATIONS**
> a launch *party*
> an *official* launch
> a *product* launch

l

launch stra|te|gy (**launch strategies**) **NOUN** a general plan that is intended to organize the launch of a new product or service [MARKETING AND SALES] ❍ *Could you devise a launch strategy for a new chain of student bars?*

laun|dry /lɔndri/ (**laundries**)
1 NONCOUNT NOUN Laundry is clothes and other things that are going to be washed. ❍ *I'll do your laundry.*
2 NOUN a business that washes and irons clothes and other things for people ❍ *He takes his shirts to the laundry.*

lava|tory /lævətɔri/ (**lavatories**) **NOUN** a room with toilets and sinks in a public building ❍ *The ladies' lavatory is over there, on the left.*

law /lɔ/
1 NONCOUNT NOUN The law is a system of rules that a society or a government develops to deal with crime, business agreements, and social relationships. ❍ *Driving too fast is against the law.* ❍ *These companies are breaking the law.*
2 NOUN one of the rules in a system of law ❍ *The government has introduced a new law to protect young people.*

L

COLLOCATIONS
to *change* a law
to *become* law
to *pass* a law
to *break* the law
law-*abiding*
by law
law *enforcement*
against the law

lawn /lɔn/ **NOUN** an area of short grass around a house or other building ❍ *They were sitting on the lawn.*

law of sup|ply and de|mand
NONCOUNT NOUN The law of supply and demand is the theory that prices are set by the relationship between the amount of goods that are available and the amount of goods that people want to buy. [ECONOMICS] ❍ *Under the law of supply and demand, the greater the supply of a product, the lower the price you can charge for it.*

law|suit /lɔsut/ **NOUN** a case that a court of law deals with [FORMAL] ❍ *The lawsuit claims more than $500 million in damages.*

law|yer /lɔɪər, lɔyər/ **NOUN** a person who advises people about the law and represents them in court [LEGAL] ❍ *His lawyers say that he is not guilty.*

lay /leɪ/ (**lays, laying, laid**)
1 VERB If you **lay** something somewhere, you put it there carefully. ❍ *She gently laid the baby in her crib.*
2 VERB When a female bird **lays** an egg, it pushes an egg out of its body.
▸**lay off** If workers **are laid off**, they are told by their company to leave their job, usually because there is no more work for them to do. [HR] ❍ *100,000 federal workers will be laid off to reduce the deficit.* ❍ *They did not sell a single car for a month and had to lay off workers.*
▸**lay out** If you **lay out** money **for** something, you spend a large amount of money on it. [INFORMAL] ❍ *You won't have to lay out a fortune for this dining table.*

lay|er /leɪər/ **NOUN** a substance or a material that covers a surface, or that lies between two other things ❍ *A fresh layer of snow covered the street.*

lay|off /leɪɔf/
1 NOUN a situation when a company tells its workers to leave their job, usually because there is no more work for them to do [HR] ❍ *It will close more than 200 stores nationwide resulting in the layoffs of an estimated 2,000 employees.*
2 NOUN a period of time when you do not work, or do not do your normal activities ❍ *They both made full recoveries after lengthy injury layoffs.*

lay|out /leɪaʊt/ **NOUN** The **layout** of a place is the way the parts of it are arranged. ❍ *He tried to remember the layout of the factory.*

lazy /leɪzi/ (**lazier, laziest**) **ADJ** not liking to work or use any effort ❍ *I'm not lazy; I like to be busy.* ● **la|zi|ness NONCOUNT NOUN** ❍ *Too much TV encourages laziness.*

lb. **lb.** is short for **pound**, when you are talking about weight. ❍ *The baby weighed 8 lbs. 5 oz.*

LBO /ɛl bi oʊ/ **NOUN** **LBO** is the abbreviation for **leveraged buyout**. [FINANCE] ❍ *Some bankers and businessmen think Germany could be ripe for hostile takeovers and even LBOs.*

lead
❶ BEING AHEAD OR TAKING SOMEONE SOMEWHERE
❷ SUBSTANCES

❶ **lead** /lid/ (**leads, leading, led**)
1 VERB If you **lead** a group of people, you go in front of them. ❍ *A jazz band led the parade.*
2 VERB If you **lead** someone to a place, you take them there. ❍ *I took his hand and led him into the house.*
3 VERB If a road or a path **leads** somewhere, it goes there. ❍ *This path leads down to the beach.*
4 VERB If you **lead** or **are leading** in a competition, you are winning. ❍ *The Eagles led by three points at half-time.*
5 NOUN If you are **in the lead** in a race or a competition, you are winning. ❍ *Harvard were already in the lead after ten minutes.*
6 VERB If you **lead** a group of people, you are in control of them. ❍ *Chris leads a large team of salespeople.*
7 VERB If you **lead** a particular type of life, you live that way. ❍ *She led a normal, happy life.*
8 VERB If something **leads to** a situation, it causes that situation. ❍ *Every time we talk about money it leads to an argument.*

❷ **lead** /lɛd/
1 NONCOUNT NOUN **Lead** is a soft, gray, heavy metal. ❍ *In the past, most water pipes were made of lead.*
2 NOUN the gray part in the middle of a pencil that makes a mark on paper

lead|er /lidər/
1 NOUN the person who is in charge of a group of people or an organization [BUSINESS MANAGEMENT] ❍ *the leader of a great marketing team*
2 NOUN the person who is winning a race or competition ❍ *The leader came in two minutes before the other runners.*

lead|er|ship /lidərʃɪp/ **NONCOUNT NOUN** **Leadership** is the position of being in control of a group of people or an organization, or the qualities needed for this. [BUSINESS MANAGEMENT, HR] ❍ *The company doubled in size under her leadership.*

lead|ing /lidɪŋ/
1 ADJ most important or successful ❍ *They are among the country's leading businessmen.*
2 ADJ winning ❍ *It always feels good to be in the leading team.*

lead|ing edge (**leading edges**)
1 NOUN **The leading edge of** an area of research or development is the most advanced area of it. ❍ *I think Israel tends to be at the leading edge of technological development.*
2 ADJ **Leading-edge** is also an adjective. ❍ *We can do more to help leading-edge industries.*

lead time (**lead times**)
1 NOUN the time between the original design or idea for a product and its actual production [PRODUCTION] ❍ *They aim to cut production lead times to under 18 months.* ❍ *Besides, a change like this needs significant lead time.*
2 NOUN the period of time that it takes for goods to be delivered after someone has ordered them [PRODUCTION] ❍ *Lead times on new equipment orders can run as long as three years.* ❍ *Orders have remained small with short lead time.*

leaf /lif/ (**leaves** or **leafs**) **NOUN** one of the parts of a tree or plant that is flat, thin, and usually green ❍ *an oak leaf*

leaf|let /liflɪt/ **NOUN** a piece of paper containing information about a particular subject ❍ *My doctor gave me a leaflet about healthy eating.*

league /lig/
1 NOUN a group of people, clubs, or countries that have joined together for a particular purpose ❍ *The League of Nations was formed after World War I.*
2 NOUN a group of teams that play against each other ❍ *The Boston Red Sox won the American League series.*

leak /lik/
1 VERB If a container **leaks**, water or gas escapes through a hole in it. ❍ *The roof leaks every time it rains.*

2 VERB If liquid or gas **leaks** from a container, it escapes through a hole in it. ❍ *The water is leaking out from the bottom of the bucket.*
3 NOUN Leak is also a noun. ❍ *A gas leak caused the explosion.*

lean /li̲n/
1 VERB When you **lean**, you bend your body from your waist in a particular direction. ❍ *The driver leaned across and opened the passenger door.*
2 VERB If you **lean on** or **against** someone or something, you rest on them. ❍ *She was feeling tired and leaned against him.*
3 ADJ If meat is **lean**, it has little or no fat.
4 ADJ A **lean** organization does not waste money and does not have any more workers than it needs. ❍ *The value of the pound will force British companies to be leaner and fitter.*

lean manu|fac|tur|ing or **lean production NONCOUNT NOUN Lean manufacturing** or **lean production** is a method that businesses use to reduce waste in the manufacturing process. [PRODUCTION] ❍ *With mass production and then lean manufacturing, the auto industry has twice changed the way producers in most other businesses organize their factories.*

leap /li̲p/ (**leaps, leaping, leaped** or **leapt**)
1 VERB If you **leap**, you jump high in the air or you jump a long distance. ❍ *He leaped in the air and waved his hands.*
2 NOUN Leap is also a noun. ❍ *Powell won the long jump with a leap of 8 meters 95 centimeters.*
3 VERB To **leap** somewhere means to move there suddenly and quickly. ❍ *The two men leaped into the car and drove away.*

learn /lɜ̲rn/ (**learns, learning, learned** or **learnt**) **VERB** If you **learn** something, you get knowledge or a skill by studying, training, or through experience. ❍ *Where did you learn English?* ❍ *He's learning to play the piano.*

lease /li̲s/ (**leases, leasing, leased**)
1 NOUN a legal agreement that allows someone to pay money so that they can use something for a particular period of time ❍ *She signed a three-year lease on the premises.*
2 VERB If you **lease** something or **lease** something **from** someone, you pay them, and they allow you to use it. ❍ *They run 2,200 stores, primarily in leased facilities.*
3 VERB If you **lease** something **to** someone, they pay you, and you allow them to use it. ❍ *She's going to lease the building to students.*

least /li̲st/
1 At least means not less than a particular number or amount. ❍ *These people all have deposits of at least $1 million.*
2 ADJ You use **the least** to mean a smaller amount than anyone or anything else, or the smallest amount possible. ❍ *This portfolio consists of stocks with the least amount of uncertainty.*
3 PRON Least is also a pronoun. ❍ *Airlines charge the least for tickets purchased substantially in advance.*
4 ADV Least is also an adverb. ❍ *These stores are the least likely to accept credit cards.*

leath|er /lɛ̲ðər/ **NONCOUNT NOUN Leather** is animal skin that is used for making shoes, clothes, bags, and furniture. ❍ *a leather jacket*

leave /li̲v/ (**leaves, leaving, left**)
1 VERB If you **leave** or **leave** a place or person, you go away from a place or person. ❍ *He left the country yesterday.* ❍ *My flight leaves in less than an hour.*
2 VERB If you **leave** something in a particular place, you do not bring it with you. ❍ *I left my laptop in the car.*
3 VERB If you **leave** part of something, you do not use it and it remains. ❍ *Please leave some cake for me!*
4 VERB If you **leave** something **to** someone, you give it to them when you die. ❍ *He left everything to his wife when he died.*
5 VERB If you **leave** something in a place, you forget to bring it with you. ❍ *I left my purse in the gas station.*
6 If you **leave** someone **alone**, you do not speak to them or annoy them. ❍ *Please just leave me alone!*
7 NONCOUNT NOUN Leave is a period of time when you are away from work. ❍ *Why don't you take a few days' leave?*
8 NONCOUNT NOUN If you are **on leave**, you are not working at your job. ❍ *She has gone on leave for a week.*

▸ **leave out** If you **leave** someone or something **out**, you do not include them. ❍ *Why did they leave her out of the team?*

leave of ab|sence (**leaves of absence**) NOUN permission to be away from work for a certain period [HR]

leaves /livz/ **Leaves** is a plural form of **leaf**, and a form of the verb **leave**.

lec|ture /lɛktʃər/ (**lectures, lecturing, lectured**)
1 NOUN a talk that someone gives in order to teach people about a particular subject ❍ *We attended a lecture by Professor Eric Robinson.*
2 VERB If you **lecture on** a particular subject, you give a lecture about it. ❍ *She invited him to Atlanta to lecture on the history of art.*

led /lɛd/ **Led** is a form of the verb **lead**.

ledg|er /lɛdʒər/ NOUN a book in which a company or organization writes down the amounts of money it spends and receives [FINANCE]

left
❶ REMAINING
❷ DIRECTION

❶ **left** /lɛft/
1 **Left** is a form of the verb **leave**.
2 ADJ remaining ❍ *Is there any milk left?*

❷ **left** /lɛft/
1 NOUN **The left** is the side or direction that is the same side as your heart. ❍ *The bank is on the left at the end of the road.* ❍ *There is a high brick wall to the left of the building.*
2 ADV **Left** is also an adverb. ❍ *Turn left at the corner.*
3 ADJ Your **left** arm, hand, or leg is the one that is opposite the side that most people write with.

left-handed ADJ using your left hand rather than your right hand for activities such as writing and sports ❍ *a left-handed tennis player*

left|over /lɛftoʊvər/
1 PL NOUN **Leftovers** means food that remains when a meal has been eaten. ❍ *Put any leftovers in the refrigerator.*
2 ADJ remaining ❍ *If you have any leftover chicken, use it to make this delicious pie.*

leg /lɛg/
1 NOUN one of the parts of the body used for walking and standing ❍ *He broke his right leg in a motorcycle accident.*
2 NOUN one of the two parts of a pair of pants that cover your legs ❍ *Anthony dried his hands on the legs of his jeans.*
3 NOUN one of the long parts of a table or chair that it stands on ❍ *a broken chair leg*

le|gal /ligᵊl/
1 ADJ relating to the law ❍ *He promised to take legal action.* ❍ *the legal system*
2 ADJ allowed by law ❍ *My actions were completely legal.*

le|gal|ise /ligəlaɪz/ [BRIT] → **legalize**

le|gal|ize /ligəlaɪz/ (**legalizes, legalizing, legalized**) VERB If something **is legalized**, it is made legal by a law being passed. ❍ *Divorce was legalized in 1981.*

le|gal ten|der NONCOUNT NOUN **Legal tender** is money that is officially part of a country's currency at a particular time. [ECONOMICS] ❍ *The French franc was no longer legal tender after midnight last night.*

leg|end /lɛdʒᵊnd/ NOUN a very old and popular story ❍ *an ancient Greek legend*

leg|is|la|tor /lɛdʒɪsleɪtər/ NOUN a person who is involved in making or passing laws [LEGAL] ❍ *an attempt to get U.S. legislators to change the system*

lei|sure /liʒər, lɛʒ-/ NONCOUNT NOUN **Leisure** is the time when you are not working, when you can relax and do things that you enjoy. ❍ *They spend their leisure time painting or drawing.*

lei|sure rev|olu|tion NONCOUNT NOUN People use **the leisure revolution** to mean an increase in activities that people do to relax and enjoy themselves. ❍ *The BBC has been slow to respond to the leisure revolution, relying on tried and tested subjects like cooking and gardening.*

lem|on /lɛmən/ NOUN a yellow fruit with very sour juice ❍ *I like a slice of lemon in my tea.*

lem|on|ade /lɛmənеɪd/ **NONCOUNT NOUN** **Lemonade** is a drink that is made from lemons, sugar, and water. ❍ *a glass of lemonade*

lend /lɛnd/ (**lends, lending, lent**)
1 VERB When a person or an institution such as a bank **lends** you money, they give it to you and you agree to pay it back later. ❍ *The government will lend you money at very good interest rates.*
2 VERB If you **lend** something that you own, you allow someone to use it for a period of time. ❍ *Will you lend me your pen?*

lend|er /lɛndər/ **NOUN** a person or an institution that lends money to people ❍ *the six leading mortgage lenders*

lend|er of last re|sort (**lenders of last resort**) **NOUN** a financial institution, usually a country's central bank, that lends money to businesses that are in financial trouble [BANKING, ECONOMICS] ❍ *As the lender of last resort, only the Fed can inject money into virtually any type of firm.*

L

lend|ing **NONCOUNT NOUN**
1 Lending is the activity of lending money to businesses or individuals who agree to pay it back later. ❍ *a slump in bank lending*
2 Lending is the amount of money that is lent. ❍ *Mexico also will get some new lending.*

lend|ing rate (**lending rates**) **NOUN** the rate of interest that you have to pay when a financial institution lends you money [BANKING, ECONOMICS] ❍ *The bank left its lending rates unchanged.*

length /lɛŋθ/
1 NOUN The **length** of something is its measurement from one end to the other. ❍ *The table is about a meter in length.*
2 NOUN The **length** of an event is how long it lasts. ❍ *Funds would have to disclose the person's length of time in the fund business.*
3 If someone does something **at length**, they do it for a long time or in great detail. ❍ *They spoke at length about the business.*

lengthy /lɛŋθi/ (**lengthier, lengthiest**)
1 ADJ lasting for a long time ❍ *a lengthy meeting*
2 ADJ containing a lot of words ❍ *a lengthy report*

lens /lɛnz/ (**lenses**) **NOUN** a thin, curved piece of glass or plastic that is used in things such as cameras and glasses, making things look larger, smaller, or clearer ❍ *I bought a powerful lens for my camera.*

lent /lɛnt/ **Lent** is a form of the verb **lend**.

less /lɛs/
1 ADJ a smaller amount of something ❍ *These securities are perceived as having less risk.* ❍ *He earns less money than his brother.*
2 PRON **Less** is also a pronoun. ❍ *He thinks people should spend less and save more.*
3 You use **less than** to talk about a smaller amount of something than the amount mentioned. ❍ *The population of the country is less than 12 million.*

les|son /lɛsən/ **NOUN** a time when you learn about a particular subject ❍ *Johanna has started taking Spanish lessons.*

let /lɛt/ (**lets, letting, let**)
1 VERB If you **let** something happen, you do not try to stop it. ❍ *I just let him sleep.*
2 VERB If you **let** someone do something, you give them your permission to do it. ❍ *I love candy but Mom doesn't let me eat it very often.*
3 VERB If you **let** someone into or out of a place, you allow them to enter or leave. ❍ *I went down and let them into the building.*
4 VERB If you **let** an apartment to someone, you rent it to them. [mainly BRIT] ❍ *When I moved to London, I let my house in Canterbury.*
5 VERB You use **let me** when you are offering to do something. ❍ *Let me hang up your coat.*
6 VERB You say **let's** (short for **let us**) when you are making a suggestion. ❍ *I'm bored. Let's go home.*
7 If you **let go of** someone or something, you stop holding them. ❍ *She let go of Mona's hand.*
8 If you **let** someone **know** something, you tell them about it. ❍ *I want to let them know that I'm safe.*
▸ **let off** If you **let** someone **off**, you give them a smaller punishment than they expect or no punishment at all. ❍ *He thought that if he said he was sorry, the judge would let him off.*

le|thal /li̲θəl/ **ADJ** able to kill a person ❍ *She swallowed a lethal dose of sleeping pills.*

let's /lɛ̲ts/ **Let's** is short for "let us."

let|ter /lɛ̲tər/

1 NOUN a message written on paper and sent to someone ❍ *I received a letter from a client.* ❍ *Mrs. Franklin sent a letter offering me the job.*

2 NOUN one of the written symbols that represent the sounds in a language ❍ *the letters of the alphabet*

le̲t|ter of ad|vi̲ce (**letters of advice**) **NOUN** a business letter giving specific information about goods that were shipped

le̲t|ter of cre̲d|it (**letters of credit**)

1 NOUN a letter written by a bank authorizing another bank to pay someone a sum of money [BANKING] ❍ *The organization has yet to secure any of the required £250,000 that must be deposited by letter of credit to secure the deal.*

2 NOUN a written promise from a bank stating that they will repay bonds to lenders if the borrowers are unable to pay them [BANKING] ❍ *The project is being backed by a letter of credit from Lasalle Bank.*

let|tuce /lɛ̲tɪs/ **NOUN** a vegetable with large green leaves that is eaten mainly in salads

leu /le̲ɪu/ (**leis**) **NOUN** the basic unit of money that is used in Romania and Moldova [ECONOMICS]

lev /lɛ̲f/ (**leva**) **NOUN** the basic unit of money that is used in Bulgaria [ECONOMICS]

lev|el /lɛ̲vəl/

1 NOUN the amount of something ❍ *We have the lowest level of inflation since 1986.*

2 NOUN how high or low something is ❍ *The water level is 6.5 feet below normal.*

3 ADJ at the same height as something ❍ *He sat down so his face was level with the boy's.*

4 ADJ completely flat ❍ *Make sure the ground is level before you start building.*

▸ **level off** If a changing number or amount **levels off**, it stops increasing or decreasing at such a fast speed. ❍ *There are predictions that prices will level off in the new year.*

lev|er|age /lɛ̲vərɪdʒ, lɛ̲vrɪdʒ/

1 NONCOUNT NOUN Leverage is the ability to influence situations or people so that you can control what happens. ❍ *His job as mayor affords him the leverage to get things done by attending committee meetings.*

2 NONCOUNT NOUN Leverage is the use of borrowed money to increase your profit from a small investment. [ECONOMICS, BANKING]

3 NONCOUNT NOUN Leverage is the amount of borrowed money that a company uses to run its business. [ECONOMICS, BANKING]

4 VERB To **leverage** an investment means to use borrowed money in order to pay for it. [ECONOMICS, BANKING] ❍ *You can leverage your investments if you happen to be a long-term investor and need some funds for a short period.*

5 VERB To **leverage** a company is to lend the company money in order to increase its profit from an investment. [ECONOMICS, BANKING] ❍ *He might feel that leveraging the company at a time when he sees tremendous growth opportunities would be a mistake.*

le̲v|er|aged bu̲y|out (**leveraged buyouts**) **NOUN** A **leveraged buyout** is when an individual or a group buys a company with borrowed money that they will pay back by selling the company's assets. [ECONOMICS, BANKING] ❍ *The buyers are struggling to finance the leveraged buyout.*

levy /lɛ̲vi/ (**levies, levying, levied**)

1 NOUN a sum of money that you have to pay, for example, as a tax to the government ❍ *an annual levy on all drivers*

2 VERB If a government or an organization **levies** a tax or other sum of money, it demands it from people or organizations. ❍ *They levied religious taxes on Christian commercial transactions.*

lia|bil|ity /la̲ɪəbɪ̲lɪti/ (**liabilities**)

1 NOUN If you say that someone or something is **a liability**, you mean that they cause a lot of problems or embarrassment. ❍ *As the president's prestige continues to fall, they're clearly beginning to consider him a liability.*

2 NOUN A company's or organization's **liabilities** are the sums of money that it owes. [FINANCE] ❍ *The company had assets of $138 million and liabilities of $120.5 million.* ❍ *U.S. investors can credit this against their tax liability.*

lia|ble /laɪəbᵊl/ If something **is liable to** happen, it is very likely to happen. ❍ *Old equipment is liable to break down.*

liar /laɪər/ NOUN someone who tells lies ❍ *He's a liar and a cheat.*

lib|er|al /lɪbərəl, lɪbrəl/ ADJ understanding and accepting that other people have different ideas, beliefs, and ways of behaving ❍ *My colleagues are very liberal and relaxed.*

lib|er|al|ise /lɪbərəlaɪz, lɪbrəl-/ [ECONOMICS, BRIT] → **liberalize**

lib|er|al|ize /lɪbərəlaɪz, lɪbrəl-/ (**liberalizes, liberalizing, liberalized**) VERB When a country or government **liberalizes**, or **liberalizes** its laws or its attitudes, it becomes less strict and allows people more freedom. [ECONOMICS] ❍ *authoritarian states that have only now begun to liberalize* • **lib|er|ali|za|tion** /lɪbərəlɪzeɪʃən, lɪbrəl-/ NONCOUNT NOUN ❍ *the liberalization of divorce laws in the late 1960s*

L

COLLOCATIONS

to liberalize *trade*
to liberalize *prices*
to liberalize *an economy*

lib|er|ty /lɪbərti/ NONCOUNT NOUN **Liberty** is the freedom to live in the way that you want to. ❍ *We must do all we can to defend liberty and justice.*

li|brary /laɪbrɛri/ (**libraries**) NOUN a building where books, newspapers, DVDs, and music are kept for people to use or borrow ❍ *I found the book I needed at the local library.*

li|cence /laɪsᵊns/ [LEGAL, BRIT] → **license**

li|cense /laɪsᵊns/ (**licenses**)
1 NOUN an official document that gives you permission to do, use, or own something [LEGAL] ❍ *You need a license to drive a car.*
2 If someone does something **under license**, they get special permission to do it. [LEGAL] ❍ *The company manufactures Marlboro under license from Philip Morris.*

li|cense plate (**license plates**) NOUN a metal sign on the back of a vehicle that shows its official number ❍ *She drives a car with California license plates.*

lick /lɪk/
1 VERB When you **lick** something, you move your tongue across its surface. ❍ *She licked the stamp and pressed it onto the envelope.*
2 NOUN **Lick** is also a noun. ❍ *Can I have a lick of your ice cream?*

lid /lɪd/ NOUN the top of a container that can be removed ❍ *She lifted the lid of the box.*

lie

❶ POSITION OR SITUATION
❷ THINGS THAT ARE NOT TRUE

❶ **lie** /laɪ/ (**lies, lying, lay, lain**)
1 VERB If you **are lying** somewhere, your body is flat, and you are not standing or sitting. ❍ *There was a man lying on the ground.*
2 VERB If an object **lies** in a particular place, it is in a flat position there. ❍ *His clothes were lying on the floor by the bed.*
▶ **lie down** When you **lie down**, you move your body so that it is flat on something, usually when you want to rest or sleep. ❍ *Why don't you go upstairs and lie down?*

❷ **lie** /laɪ/ (**lies, lying, lied**)
1 NOUN something that someone says or writes that they know is not true ❍ *You told me a lie!*
2 VERB If someone **lies**, they say something that they know is not true. ❍ *I know he's lying.* ❍ *Never lie to me again.*

life /laɪf/ (**lives**)
1 NOUN the state of being alive, or the period of time that someone is alive ❍ *A nurse tried to save his life.* ❍ *He spent the last fourteen years of his life in France.*
2 NONCOUNT NOUN **Life** is activity, interest, and energy. ❍ *The town was full of life.*

life as|sur|ance [BANKING, BRIT] → **life insurance**

life coach (**life coaches**) NOUN someone whose job involves helping people to improve their lives and achieve their goals

• **life coach|ing** NONCOUNT NOUN ❍ *life-coaching workshops*

life cy|cle (**life cycles**)
1 NOUN the series of changes and developments that an animal or plant passes through from the beginning of its life until its death ❍ *a plant that completes its life cycle in a single season*
2 NOUN the series of developments that take place in an idea, product, or organization from its beginning until the end of its usefulness ❍ *Each new product would have a relatively long life cycle.*

life in|sur|ance NONCOUNT NOUN **Life insurance** is insurance that pays a sum of money to you after a period of time, or to your family when you die. [BANKING] ❍ *I have also taken out a life insurance policy on him just in case.*

life in|te|rest
1 NONCOUNT NOUN **Life interest** is income from property that is paid to you during your life but ends when you die. [BANKING]
2 NOUN A **life interest** is the right to use property or receive income from it while you are living. [BANKING] ❍ *In order to settle the matter, he agreed to relinquish his life interest in a trust account.*

life|style /laɪfstaɪl/ also **life-style, life style** NOUN the way that someone lives, for example the place where they live, their hobbies, and the hours they work ❍ *a healthy lifestyle*

life|style busi|ness (**lifestyle businesses**) NOUN a small business that allows the owner to pursue his or her interests or to maintain a certain style of living

life|style gu|ru (**lifestyle gurus**) NOUN a person you hire to give you advice on your life, work, and relationships

life|time /laɪftaɪm/ NOUN the length of time that someone is alive ❍ *He traveled a lot during his lifetime.*

LIFO /laɪfoʊ/ **LIFO** is a method of accounting which assumes that the newest stock is sold first. **LIFO** is an abbreviation of "last in, first out." Compare with **FIFO**. [FINANCE]

lift /lɪft/
1 VERB If you **lift** something, you take it and move it upward. ❍ *He lifted the bag onto his shoulder.*
2 Lift up means the same as **lift**. ❍ *She lifted the baby up and gave him to me.*
3 NOUN If you give someone a **lift**, you take them somewhere in your car. ❍ *He often gave me a lift home.*

light
❶ BRIGHTNESS
❷ NOT GREAT IN WEIGHT OR AMOUNT

❶ **light** /laɪt/ (**lights, lighting, lit** or **lighted, lighter, lightest**)
1 NONCOUNT NOUN **Light** is the energy that comes from the sun, that lets you see things. ❍ *He opened the curtains, and suddenly the room was filled with light.*
2 NOUN an electric lamp that produces light ❍ *Remember to turn the lights out when you leave.*
3 VERB If a place or an object **is lit** by something, it has light shining in or on it from that thing. ❍ *The room was lit by only one light.*
4 ADJ If it is **light**, there is enough light from the sun to see things. ❍ *Here it gets light at about 6 a.m.*
5 VERB If you **light** a candle or a fire, you make it start burning. ❍ *Stephen took a match and lit the candle.*

❷ **light** /laɪt/
1 ADJ not heavy and easy to lift or move ❍ *The printer is quite light, so it's easy to move around.*
2 ADJ not great in amount or power ❍ *We had a light lunch of salad and fruit.* ❍ *There was a light wind that day.*
3 ADJ pale in color ❍ *He was wearing a light-blue shirt.*
4 ADJ **Light** industry is firms that produce small goods.

light bulb (**light bulbs**) NOUN a glass object that you put in an electric light to make light

light|en /laɪtᵊn/ VERB When you **lighten** something, you make it less dark. ❍ *She lightens her hair.*

▶ **lighten up** If you say that someone should **lighten up**, you mean that they should be more relaxed or less serious. ❍ *You should lighten up and enjoy yourself a bit more.*

light|er /laɪtər/ **NOUN** a small object that produces a flame and is used for lighting things such as candles or fires

light|ing /laɪtɪŋ/ **NONCOUNT NOUN** The **lighting** in a place is the way that it is lit. ❍ *The kitchen had bright overhead lighting.*

light|ning /laɪtnɪŋ/ **NONCOUNT NOUN** **Lightning** is the very bright flashes of light in the sky that happen during a storm. ❍ *One man died when he was struck by lightning.*

lik|able /laɪkəbᵊl/ also **likeable** **ADJ** pleasant and easy to be with ❍ *He was a clever and likable guy.*

like
❶ PREPOSITION USES
❷ VERB USES

L

❶ **like** /laɪk, laɪk/

1 PREP similar to ❍ *He looks like my uncle.* ❍ *His house is just like yours.*

2 PREP If you ask what someone or something **is like**, you are asking about their qualities. ❍ *"What was her presentation like?"—"Great!"* ❍ *What's Maria like?*

3 PREP used for giving an example ❍ *large cities like New York and Chicago*

❷ **like** /laɪk/ (**likes, liking, liked**)

1 VERB If you **like** something or someone, you think they are interesting, enjoyable, or attractive. ❍ *He likes his new boss.* ❍ *Do you like staying in hotels?*

2 VERB If you say that you **would like** something, you are saying politely that you want it. ❍ *I'd like to ask you a few questions.* ❍ *Would you like some coffee?*

3 You say **if you like** when you are suggesting something to someone, in an informal way. ❍ *You can stay here if you like.*

like|able /laɪkəbᵊl/ → **likable**

like-for-like **ADJ** **Like-for-like** sales figures are based on a comparison with sales in the same period in another year. ❍ *It expects like-for-like sales to be 9% lower in the six months to February than a year earlier.*

like|li|hood /laɪklihʊd/ **NONCOUNT NOUN** The **likelihood of** something happening is how probable it is. ❍ *The likelihood of winning the contract is small.*

like|ly /laɪkli/ (**likelier, likeliest**) **ADJ** Something that is **likely** is probably true or will probably happen. ❍ *He would not comment on the likely outcome of the negotiations.* ❍ *Eric is a bright young man who is likely to succeed in life.*

like|wise /laɪkwaɪz/ **ADV** in a similar way ❍ *He gave money to charity and encouraged others to do likewise.*

lik|ing /laɪkɪŋ/ If something is **to** your **liking**, you like it. ❍ *London was more to his liking than Rome.*

limb /lɪm/ **NOUN** an arm or a leg ❍ *She stretched out her aching limbs.*

lime /laɪm/ **NOUN** a round, green fruit that tastes like a lemon ❍ *Use fresh lime juice and fresh herbs in modern Asian cooking.*

lim|it /lɪmɪt/

1 NOUN the greatest amount or degree of something ❍ *There is no limit to how much you can invest.*

2 NOUN the largest or smallest amount of something that is allowed ❍ *He was driving 40 miles per hour over the speed limit.*

3 VERB If you **limit** something, you stop it from becoming greater than a particular amount. ❍ *Try to limit the amount of time you spend on the Internet.*

lim|it|ed /lɪmɪtɪd/

1 ADJ Something that is **limited** is not very great in amount, range, or degree. ❍ *They may only have a limited amount of time to get their points across.*

2 ADJ **Limited** is used after a company's name to show that it is a limited company. [ECONOMICS, BRIT] ❍ *Ace Limited*

lim|it|ed com|pa|ny (**limited companies**) **NOUN** a company whose owners are legally responsible for only a part of any money that it may owe if it goes bankrupt [ECONOMICS, BRIT]

lim|it|ed li|abil|ity NONCOUNT NOUN **Limited liability** is legal or financial responsibility that is limited by a contract or law. [ECONOMICS] ❍ *Shareholders with limited liability if the business venture failed could participate in profits.*

lim|it|ed li|abil|ity com|pa|ny (**limited liability companies**) NOUN A **limited liability company** is the same as a **limited company**. [ECONOMICS, BRIT]

lim|it|ed part|ner (**limited partners**) NOUN a business partner who has no management authority and is legally responsible for only a part of any money that the company may owe if it goes bankrupt [ECONOMICS]

lim|ou|sine /lɪməzin/ NOUN A **limousine** is a large and very comfortable car. **Limo** is an informal word for **limousine**. ❍ *As the president's limousine approached, the crowd began to cheer.*

limp /lɪmp/
1 VERB If a person or animal **limps**, they walk with difficulty because they have hurt one of their legs or feet. ❍ *James limps because of a hip injury.*
2 NOUN **Limp** is also a noun. ❍ *Anne walks with a limp.*
3 ADJ soft and weak ❍ *Her body was limp and she was too weak to move.*

line /laɪn/ (**lines, lining, lined**)
1 NOUN a long, thin mark on something ❍ *Draw a line at the bottom of the page.*
2 NOUN A **line** of people or vehicles is a number of them that are waiting one behind the other. ❍ *There was a line of people waiting to go into the movie theater.*
3 NOUN a long piece of string that you use for a particular purpose ❍ *Melissa was outside, hanging the clothes on the line.*
4 NOUN a route that trains move along ❍ *We stayed on the train to the end of the line.*
5 NOUN a very long wire for telephones or electricity ❍ *Suddenly the telephone line went dead.*
6 NOUN Your **line of** business or work is the kind of work that you do. ❍ *In my line of work I often get home too late for dinner.*
7 NOUN a particular type of product that a company makes or sells [MARKETING AND SALES] ❍ *His best selling line is the cheapest lager at £1.99.*
8 NOUN an arrangement of workers or machines where a product passes from one worker to another until it is finished [BUSINESS MANAGEMENT] ❍ *The production line is capable of producing three different products.*
9 VERB If people or things **line** a road, they stand in lines along it. ❍ *Thousands of local people lined the streets to welcome the president.*
10 VERB If you **line** a container, you cover the inside of it with something. ❍ *Line the box with newspaper.*
11 If a machine or piece of equipment comes **on line**, it starts operating. If it is **off line**, it is not operating. ❍ *The new machine will go on line in 2012.*
12 When people **stand in line** or **wait in line**, they stand one behind the other in a line, waiting for something. ❍ *For the homeless, standing in line for meals is part of the daily routine.*

line man|age|ment NONCOUNT NOUN **Line management** is the people in an organization who are in charge of a department, group, or project. [BUSINESS MANAGEMENT, mainly BRIT]

line man|ag|er (**line managers**) NOUN Your **line manager** is the person at work who is in charge of your department, group or project. [BUSINESS MANAGEMENT, mainly BRIT] ❍ *He claimed his line manager had bullied him.*

line of cred|it (**lines of credit**) NOUN A **line of credit** is the same as a **credit line**. [BANKING]

link /lɪŋk/
1 NOUN If there is a **link between** two things, there is a connection between them, often because one of them causes the other. ❍ *They analyzed the link between the dollar's value and inflation.*
2 VERB **Link** is also a verb. ❍ *Directors' pay is linked to performance.*
3 NOUN in computing, an area on the screen that allows you to move from one web page or

website to another ❍ *The website has links to other tourism sites.*
4 NOUN one of the rings in a chain

lion /laɪən/ **NOUN** a large wild cat that lives in Africa, the male of which has long hair on its head and neck (= a mane)

lip /lɪp/ **NOUN** one of the two outer parts that form the edge of the mouth ❍ *He kissed her gently on the lips.*

lip|stick /lɪpstɪk/ **NOUN** **Lipstick** is a colored substance that women sometimes put on their lips. ❍ *She was wearing red lipstick.*

liq|uid /lɪkwɪd/ **NOUN**
1 A **Liquid** is a substance, such as water, that is not a solid or a gas. **liquids** flow and can be poured. ❍ *She took out a small bottle of clear liquid.* ❍ *Solids turn to liquids at certain temperatures.*
2 ADJ A **liquid** substance is in the form of a liquid. ❍ *Wash in warm water with liquid detergent.*
3 ADJ **Liquid** assets are the things that a person or company owns that can be quickly turned into cash if necessary. ❍ *The bank had sufficient liquid assets to continue operations.*

liq|ui|date /lɪkwɪdeɪt/ (**liquidates, liquidating, liquidated**)
1 VERB To **liquidate** a company is to close it down and sell all its assets, usually because it owes a lot of money. [BUSINESS MANAGEMENT] ❍ *A unanimous vote was taken to liquidate the company.* ● **liq|ui|da|tion** /lɪkwɪdeɪʃən/ **NOUN** ❍ *The company went into liquidation.* ❍ *Liquidations of insolvent insurance companies generally are handled under state statutes.*
● **liq|ui|da|tor** **NOUN** ❍ *the failed company's liquidators*
2 VERB If a company **liquidates** its assets, its property is sold in order to get money. [BUSINESS MANAGEMENT] ❍ *The company closed down operations and began liquidating its assets in January.*

li|quid|ity /lɪkwɪdɪti/ **NONCOUNT NOUN** A company's **liquidity** is its ability to turn its assets into cash. [FINANCE] ❍ *The company maintains a high degree of liquidity.*

li|quid|ity ra|tio (**liquidity ratios**) **NOUN** the relationship between an organization's total assets and the amount of cash it holds [FINANCE] ❍ *The volume of such trading is limited due to various statutory liquidity ratios.*

liq|uor /lɪkər/ **NONCOUNT NOUN** **Liquor** is strong alcoholic drink.

liq|uor store (**liquor stores**) **NOUN** a store that sells beer, wine, and other alcoholic drinks

list /lɪst/
1 NOUN a set of names or other things that are written or printed one below the other ❍ *I added coffee to my shopping list.* ❍ *There were six names on the list.*
2 VERB If you **list** names or other things, you write or say them one after another. ❍ *The students listed the sports they liked best.*
3 VERB If a company **is listed**, or if it **lists** on a stock exchange, it gets an official price for its shares so that people can buy and sell them. ❍ *It will list on the London Stock Exchange next week with a value of 130 million pounds.*
4 VERB If a product **lists at** a certain price, that price is its list price.

list|ed com|pa|ny (**listed companies**) **NOUN** a company whose shares are traded on a stock exchange [ECONOMICS] ❍ *Some of Australia's largest listed companies are expected to announce huge interim earnings this week.*

lis|ten /lɪsᵊn/
1 VERB If you **listen to** something or someone, you give your attention to a sound, or to what someone is saying. ❍ *He spends his time listening to the radio.*
2 You say **listen** when you want someone to pay attention to you because you are going to say something. [SPOKEN] ❍ *Listen, there's something I should warn you about.*

lis|ten|er /lɪsənər, lɪsnər/ **NOUN** someone who is listening to a speaker ❍ *When he finished talking, his listeners applauded loudly.*

list price (**list prices**) **NOUN** the price that the manufacturer of an item suggests that a store should charge for it ❍ *a small car with a list price of $18,000*

lit /lɪt/ **Lit** is a form of the verb **light**.

li|ter /li̲tər/ **NOUN** A **liter** is a unit for measuring liquid. There are 1,000 milliliters in a liter. ❍ *Adults should drink about two liters of water each day.*

lit|era|cy /lɪ̲tərəsi/ **NONCOUNT NOUN** **Literacy** is the ability to read and write. ❍ *an adult literacy program*

lit|er|al|ly /lɪ̲tərəli/
1 ADV If you translate something from another language **literally**, you say what each word means in another language. ❍ *Volkswagen literally means "people's car."*
2 ADV used for emphasizing what you are saying ❍ *The view is literally breathtaking.*

lit|era|ture /lɪ̲tərətʃər, -tʃʊər/ **NONCOUNT NOUN** **Literature** is books, plays, and poetry that most people consider to be of high quality. ❍ *Chris is studying English literature at Columbia University.*

liti|gant /lɪ̲tɪgənt/ **NOUN** a person who is involved in a legal case because they are making a formal complaint about someone, or because a complaint is being made about them [LEGAL]

liti|gate /lɪ̲tɪgeɪt/ (**litigates, litigating, litigated**) **VERB** To **litigate** means to take legal action. [LEGAL] ❍ *the cost of litigating personal injury claims in the county court* ❍ *If we have to litigate, we will.*

li|ti|gious /lɪtɪ̲dʒəs/ **ADJ** Someone who is **litigious** often makes formal complaints about people to a court of law. [LEGAL, FORMAL]

li|tre /li̲tər/ [BRIT] → **liter**

lit|ter /lɪ̲tər/
1 NONCOUNT NOUN **Litter** is paper or garbage that people leave on the ground in public places. ❍ *I hate it when I see people dropping litter.*
2 VERB If things **litter** a place, they are lying around it or over it in a messy way. ❍ *Broken glass littered the sidewalk.*
3 NOUN all the babies that are born to an animal at the same time ❍ *Our cat has just given birth to a litter of three kittens.*

little
❶ ADJECTIVE, PRONOUN, AND ADVERB USES
❷ ADJECTIVE USES

❶ **lit|tle** /lɪ̲tᵊl/
1 ADJ not much ❍ *The firm makes very little money from discount brokerage.*
2 PRON **Little** is also a pronoun. ❍ *These firms contribute very little to the economy.*
3 ADV not often or not much ❍ *They spoke very little.*
4 **A little** is a small amount of something. ❍ *I need a little help sometimes.*
5 ADV **A little** or **a little bit** means rather, or to a small degree. ❍ *Prices need to increase a little bit.*

❷ **lit|tle** /lɪ̲tᵊl/ (**littler, littlest**)
1 ADJ small ❍ *We all sat in a little office.*
2 ADJ short in time or distance ❍ *Go down the road a little way and then turn left.* ❍ *We waited for a little while, and then we went home.*

live
❶ VERB USES
❷ ADJECTIVE AND ADVERB USES

❶ **live** /lɪ̲v/ (**lives, living, lived**)
1 VERB If you **live** in a particular place, your home is there. ❍ *She lived in New York for 10 years.* ❍ *Where do you live?*
2 VERB If someone **lives** in a particular way, they have that type of life. ❍ *Nash lives a quiet life in Princeton.*
3 VERB To **live** means to be alive. ❍ *We all need water to live.*
4 VERB If someone **lives to** a particular age, they stay alive until they are that age. ❍ *He lived to 103.*
▸ **live on** If an animal **lives on** a particular food, it eats this type of food. ❍ *Sheep live mainly on grass.*

❷ **live** /la̲ɪv/
1 ADJ **Live** animals or plants are not dead. ❍ *The local market sells live animals.*
2 ADJ A **live** television or radio program is one

that you watch at the same time that it happens. ❍ *a live football game*

3 ADV Live is also an adverb. ❍ *The president's speech was broadcast live.*

live|ly /laɪvli/ (**livelier, liveliest**) **ADJ** cheerful and with a lot of energy ❍ *Amy is a lively, sociable little girl.*

liv|er /lɪvər/

1 NOUN a large organ in the body that cleans the blood ❍ *liver disease*

2 NONCOUNT NOUN Liver is the liver of some animals eaten as food.

lives

Pronounce meaning **1** /laɪvz/. Pronounce meaning **2** /lɪvz/.

1 Lives is the plural of **life**.

2 Lives is a form of the verb **live**.

liv|ing /lɪvɪŋ/

1 ADJ alive, not dead ❍ *He is perhaps the world's most famous living artist.*

2 NOUN money that you earn and use for all the things you need ❍ *What does she do for a living?* ❍ *Scott earns a living as a lawyer.*

L

liv|ing room (**living rooms**) also **living-room NOUN** the room in a house where people sit together and talk or watch television

liv|ing wage (**living wages**) **NOUN** a wage that is just enough to allow you to buy food, clothing, and other necessary things [ECONOMICS] ❍ *Many farmers have to depend on subsidies to make a living wage.*

liz|ard /lɪzərd/ **NOUN** a small animal with a long tail, rough skin, and four short legs

load /loʊd/

1 VERB If you **load** a vehicle or a container, you put a large amount of things into it. ❍ *The men finished loading the truck.*

2 NOUN something heavy that is being carried ❍ *This truck can take a big load.*

loaf /loʊf/ (**loaves**) **NOUN** A **loaf** or a **loaf of bread** is bread that has been shaped and baked in one piece.

loan /loʊn/

1 NOUN an amount of money that you borrow [BANKING] ❍ *Right now it's very difficult to get a loan from a bank.*

2 VERB If you **loan** something to someone, you lend it to them. [BANKING] ❍ *Brandon loaned his girlfriend $6,000.*

loan of|fic|er (**loan officers**) **NOUN** a person whose job is to arrange loans from a bank [BANKING]

loan shark (**loan sharks**) **NOUN** someone who lends money to people and charges them very high rates of interest [BANKING, INFORMAL]

loan-to-value also **loan to value NOUN** the sum of money that a bank lends in a mortgage, divided by the value of the property as determined by the bank [BANKING] ❍ *The going rate in the market now is about 75% or 80% loan to value.*

loaves /loʊvz/ **Loaves** is the plural of **loaf**.

lob|by /lɒbi/ (**lobbies, lobbying, lobbied**)

1 VERB If you **lobby** someone in government or an organization, you try to persuade them that a particular law should be changed or that a particular thing should be done.

❍ *The Wilderness Society lobbied Congress to authorize the Endangered Species Act.*

2 NOUN a group of people who represent a particular organization or issue, and try to persuade powerful people to help or support them ❍ *Agricultural interests are some of the most powerful lobbies in Washington.*

3 NOUN the large area that is just inside the entrance of a public building ❍ *I met her in the lobby of the museum.*

lob|by|ist /lɒbiɪst/ **NOUN** someone who tries to persuade someone in government or an organization that a particular law should be changed or that a particular thing should be done

lo|cal /loʊkəl/ **ADJ** in or relating to the area where you live ❍ *the local paper* ● **lo|cal|ly ADV** ❍ *I prefer to shop locally.*

lo|cal part|ner (**local partners**) **NOUN** A company's **local partners** are companies based in a foreign country who help them start to do business in that country. ❍ *Online* *banking services were already popular in the U.S. and Microsoft would seek local partners to develop the service in Australia.*

lo|cate /loʊkeɪt/ (**locates, locating, located**)
1 VERB If you **locate** something or someone, you find out where they are. ❍ *They couldn't locate the missing ship.*
2 VERB If you **locate** something in a particular place, you put it there or build it there. ❍ *Business people voted Atlanta the best city in which to locate a business.* ● **lo|cat|ed** ADJ ❍ *A beauty salon is located in the hotel.*
3 VERB If you **locate** in a particular place, you move there or open a business there. ❍ *There are tax breaks for businesses that locate in run-down neighborhoods.*

lo|ca|tion /loʊkeɪʃən/ **NOUN** the place where something is ❍ *For dates and locations of the meetings, call this number.*

lock /lɒk/
1 VERB When you **lock** a door or a container, you close it with a key. ❍ *Are you sure you locked the front door?*
2 NOUN a device that prevents something from being opened except with a particular key ❍ *She turned the key in the lock and opened the door.*
3 VERB If you **lock** something or someone in a place, you put them there and close the door or the lid with a key. ❍ *She locked the case in the closet.*
▸ **lock away** If you **lock** something **away** in a place, you put it there and close it with a key. ❍ *She cleaned her jewelry and locked it away in a case.*
▸ **lock up** If you **lock up**, you lock all the windows and doors of a house or a car. ❍ *Don't forget to lock up before you leave.*
▸ **lock out** In an industrial dispute, if a company **locks** its workers **out**, it closes the factory or office and prevents the workers from coming to work. ❍ *The company locked out the workers, and then the rest of the work force went on strike.*

lock|er /lɒkər/ **NOUN** a small cupboard with a lock, that you keep things in at a school or at a sports club

lock|out /lɒkaʊt/ also **lock-out** **NOUN** a situation when a company closes the factory or office until the workers accept the company's proposals on working conditions such as pay

log /lɔg/ (**logs, logging, logged**)
1 NOUN a thick piece of wood that has been cut from a tree ❍ *a log fire*
2 NOUN a written record of the things that happen each day
3 VERB If you **log** something that happens, you write it down as a record of the event. ❍ *They log everything that comes in and out of the warehouse.*
▸ **log in** or **log on** If you **log in** or **log on**, you type a secret word so that you can start using a computer or a website. ❍ *She turned on her computer and logged in.*
▸ **log out** or **log off** If you **log out** or **log off**, you stop using a computer or a website by clicking on an instruction.

log|ic /lɒdʒɪk/ **NONCOUNT NOUN** **Logic** is a way of working things out, by saying that one fact must be true if another fact is true. ❍ *The students study philosophy and logic.*

logi|cal /lɒdʒɪkᵊl/ **ADJ** reasonable or sensible ❍ *There must be a logical explanation for his behavior.*

lo|gis|tic /loʊdʒɪstɪk/ or **logistical** /loʊdʒɪstɪkᵊl/ **ADJ** **Logistic** problems relate to the planning of a complicated activity that involves a lot of people or equipment. [LOGISTICS AND DISTRIBUTION] ❍ *A lack of a waterside location created logistic difficulties in relation to the transportation of the assembled product.* ● **lo|gis|ti|cal|ly** /loʊdʒɪstɪkli/ **ADV** ❍ *Some women find breast-feeding logistically difficult because of work.* ❍ *It is about time that the U.N. considers logistically deploying additional military resources.*

lo|gis|tics /loʊdʒɪstɪks/
1 PL NOUN The **logistics of** a complicated activity are the detailed plans that you must make so that it is successful. [LOGISTICS AND DISTRIBUTION] ❍ *The logistics of getting such a big show on the road pose enormous practical problems.*

2 NOUN the detailed planning of a complicated activity [LOGISTICS AND DISTRIBUTION] ❍ *Logistics is important to any company.*

LOL **LOL** is short for "laughing out loud" or "lots of love," and is often used in email and text messages.

lone|ly /loʊnli/ (**lonelier, loneliest**)
1 ADJ unhappy because you are alone ❍ *Mr. Garcia has been very lonely since his wife died.* ● **lone|li|ness NONCOUNT NOUN** ❍ *I have a fear of loneliness.*
2 ADJ A **lonely** place is a place where very few people go. ❍ *Her car broke down on a lonely country road.*

long
❶ TIME AND DISTANCE USES
❷ VERB USE

❶ **long** /lɔŋ/ (**longer** /lɔŋgər/, **longest** /lɔŋgɪst/)
1 ADJ or **ADV** continuing for a lot of time ❍ *a long meeting* ❍ *a long vacation* ❍ *Have you been waiting long?* ❍ *How long is the meeting?*
2 ADJ great in length or distance ❍ *Lucy had long dark hair.* ❍ *The long trip made him tired.*
3 ADJ If an investor takes a **long** position in particular securities, they buy them expecting their value to rise in the future.
4 As long as or **so long as** means "if." ❍ *They can do what they want as long as they're not breaking the law.*

❷ **long** /lɔŋ/ **VERB** If you **long for** something or **long to do** something, you want it very much. ❍ *I'm longing to meet her.* ● **long|ing NONCOUNT NOUN** ❍ *She still feels a longing for her own home and country.*

long-distance ADJ traveling or covering large distances ❍ *The company also owns a regional long-distance carrier.* ❍ *Stacey makes a lot of long-distance calls on her cellphone.*

long-hours cul|ture NONCOUNT NOUN The **long-hours culture** is the way in which some workers feel that they are expected to work longer hours than they are paid to do. [HR] ❍ *Our research confirms that Britain's long-hours culture is seriously undermining the quality of life.*

long list (**long lists**) **NOUN** A **long list** is a list of all the people who have applied for a job and are suitable for that job. Compare with **shortlist**. [HR, BRIT]

long|shore|man /lɔŋʃɔrmən/ (**longshoremen**) **NOUN** a person who works on the docks, loading and unloading ships [LOGISTICS AND DISTRIBUTION]

long-term (**longer-term**)
1 ADJ Something that is **long-term** has continued for a long time or will continue for a long time in the future. ❍ *They want their parents to have access to affordable long-term care.* ❍ *Accessibility to low cost, long term loans has changed things.*
2 NOUN When you talk about what happens in **the long term**, you are talking about what happens over a long period of time or in the future. ❍ *In the long term the company hopes to open in Moscow and other major cities.* ❍ *We constantly are being accused of not planning or thinking for the long term.*

long-term li|abil|ities PL NOUN **Long-term liabilities** are debts that a company does not have to pay back for a year or more. Compare with **short-term liabilities**. [FINANCE] ❍ *On the right-hand side of the balance sheet, we find total long-term liabilities of $694 billion.*

loo /lu/ [BRIT] → **bathroom**

look /lʊk/
1 VERB If you **look** in a particular direction, you turn your eyes so that you can see what is there. ❍ *I looked out of the window.*
2 NOUN **Look** is also a noun. ❍ *Lucille took a last look in the mirror.*
3 VERB If you **look for** something or someone, you try to find them. ❍ *I looked everywhere for his business card.*
4 You say **look** when you want someone to pay attention to you. ❍ *Look, I'm sorry. I didn't mean it.*
5 EXCLAM If you say or shout "**look out!**" to someone, you are warning them that they are in danger. ❍ *"Look out!" somebody shouted,*

as the truck started to move toward us.

6 VERB You use **look** when you are describing the way that a person seems to be. ❍ *"You look lovely, Marcia!"* ❍ *Sheila was looking sad.*

7 NOUN an expression on the face ❍ *He saw the look of surprise on her face.*

▶ **look after** If you **look after** someone or something, you take care of them. ❍ *Maria looks after the kids while I'm at work.*

▶ **look forward to** If you **look forward to** something that is going to happen, you think about it with pleasure. ❍ *She's looking forward to her new job.*

▶ **look up** If you **look up** a fact or a piece of information, you find it by looking in a book or on a computer. ❍ *I looked up your number in my address book.*

loop /lup/ **NOUN** a shape like a circle in a piece of string or rope ❍ *On the ground beside them was a loop of rope.*

loose /lus/ (**looser, loosest**)

1 ADJ not firmly fixed ❍ *One of Hannah's top front teeth is loose.* ● **loose|ly ADV** ❍ *He held the gun loosely in his hand.*

2 ADJ If an animal is **loose**, it has escaped from somewhere and is moving around freely. ❍ *Our dog got loose and ran away yesterday.*

3 ADJ Loose clothes do not fit closely. ❍ *Wear loose, comfortable clothing when exercising.* ● **loose|ly ADV** ❍ *A scarf hung loosely around his neck.*

loos|en /lusᵊn/ **VERB** If you **loosen** something, you make it less tight. ❍ *He loosened his tie around his neck.*

lord /lɔrd/

1 NOUN a man with a high position in society ❍ *Lord Cavendish*

2 NOUN In some religions, the **Lord** is God or Jesus Christ.

lor|ry /lɔri/ [BRIT] → **truck**

lose /luz/ (**loses, losing, lost**)

1 VERB If you **lose** a game, you do not win it. ❍ *Our team lost the game by one point.* ❍ *No one likes to lose.*

2 VERB If you **lose** something, you are not able to find it. ❍ *I've lost my keys.*

3 VERB If you **lose** something, you do not have it anymore because someone has taken it away from you. ❍ *I lost my job when the company shut down.*

4 VERB If you **lose** weight, you become less heavy. ❍ *His doctor told him to lose weight.*

5 VERB If a business **loses** money, it earns less money than it spends. ❍ *The company has been losing money for the last three years.*

los|er /luzər/ **NOUN** a person who does not win a game ❍ *In any game, there's always a winner and a loser.*

loss /lɔs/

1 NOUN the fact of not having something that you used to have, or having less of it than before ❍ *The first symptoms are a slight fever and a loss of appetite.* ❍ *The job losses will reduce the total workforce to 7,000.*

2 NOUN If a business reports a **loss**, it earns less money than it spends. ❍ *The company suffered a loss of $270 million.* ❍ *The effects of the approach on profit and loss must be considered.*

COLLOCATIONS

to operate at a loss
to take a loss
to post a loss
to incur a loss

loss ad|just|er (**loss adjusters**) also **loss adjustor NOUN** [BANKING, BRIT] → **claims adjuster**

loss lead|er (**loss leaders**) also **loss-leader NOUN** an item that a store sells at a price lower than its cost in order to attract customers to buy other products at the store [MARKETING AND SALES] ❍ *Hoskins does not expect a huge profit from the cookies, viewing them more as a loss leader.*

loss-maker (**loss-makers**) also **loss maker, lossmaker NOUN** an organization, industry, or business activity that does not make a profit [BRIT] ❍ *The factory was a loss-maker and in a pitiful state.*

loss-making also **lossmaking ADJ** losing money or not making a profit [BRIT] ❍ *The loss-making company hopes to move into the black next year.*

loss ra|tio **(loss ratios)** NOUN the amount of money that an insurance company pays out in one year, divided by the amount of money in premiums that it receives [BANKING, FINANCE] ❍ *States with regulated auto insurance rates had higher loss ratios than did states with competitive pricing.*

lost /lɔst/
1 **Lost** is a form of the verb **lose**.
2 ADJ not knowing where you are and unable to find your way ❍ *I realized I was lost.*
3 ADJ If something is **lost**, you cannot find it. ❍ *We complained to the airline about our lost luggage.*

lot /lɒt/
1 **A lot of** something or **lots of** something is a large amount of it. ❍ *Manchester has attracted a lot of investment in the past few years.* ❍ *Japan has lots of private-equity funds.*
2 PRON **Lot** is also a pronoun. ❍ *I learned a lot from him.*
3 ADV **A lot** means very much or often. ❍ *The smart money moves around a lot.*
4 NOUN an item or set of items for sale in an auction

lot|tery /lɒtəri/ **(lotteries)** NOUN a game in which many people buy tickets with numbers on them and the person whose number is later chosen wins a prize ❍ *the national lottery*

loud /laʊd/
1 ADJ If a noise is **loud**, the level of sound is very high. ❍ *The music was so loud that I couldn't hear what she was saying.* ● **loud|ly** ADV ❍ *The cat rolled onto its back, purring loudly.*
2 If you say something or laugh **out loud**, you say it or laugh so that other people can hear it. ❍ *Parts of the book made me laugh out loud.*

lounge /laʊndʒ/ NOUN a room in a hotel or an airport where people can sit ❍ *an airport lounge*

lov|able /lʌvəbᵊl/ ADJ easy to love ❍ *He is a sweet, lovable dog.*

love /lʌv/ **(loves, loving, loved)**
1 VERB If you **love** someone, you care very much about them, or you have strong romantic feelings for them. ❍ *Oh, Amy, I love you.* ❍ *You will love your baby from the moment she's born.*
2 NONCOUNT NOUN **Love** is the very strong warm feeling that you have when you care very much about someone, or you have strong romantic feelings for them. ❍ *In the four years since we married, our love has grown stronger.* ❍ *a love story*
3 VERB If you **love** something, you like it very much. ❍ *I love food, I love cooking, and I love eating.* ❍ *Sophie loves to play the piano.*
4 You can write **love**, **love from**, and **all my love**, before your name, at the end of a letter to a friend or a relative. ❍ *The letter ended, "With all my love, Anna."*
5 If you **fall in love with** someone, you start to love them in a romantic way. ❍ *Maria fell in love with Danny as soon as she met him.*

love|ly /lʌvli/ **(lovelier, loveliest)** ADJ beautiful, very nice, or very enjoyable ❍ *You look lovely, Marcia.* ❍ *Thank you for a lovely evening!*

lov|er /lʌvər/
1 NOUN a person who is having a sexual relationship with someone, especially someone they are not married to
2 NOUN someone who likes something very much ❍ *a website for music lovers*

lov|ing /lʌvɪŋ/ ADJ feeling or showing love for other people ❍ *My parents had a loving relationship.* ● **lov|ing|ly** ADV ❍ *Brian looked lovingly at Mary.*

low /loʊ/
1 ADJ close to the ground ❍ *It was late afternoon and the sun was low in the sky.*
2 ADV **Low** is also an adverb. ❍ *An airplane flew low over the beach.*
3 ADJ small in amount ❍ *House prices are still very low.*
4 ADJ If the quality of something is **low**, it is bad. ❍ *The hospital was criticized for its low standards of care.*
5 ADJ A **low** sound or noise is deep or quiet. ❍ *He has a very low voice.*

low-cost cen|ter **(low-cost centers)** NOUN a country or region where business costs are lower [ECONOMICS] ❍ *Over the past* *decade, the region has established itself as a viable, low-cost center for manufacturing.*

low|er /loʊər/

1 ADJ under another thing of the same type ❍ *Emily bit her lower lip nervously.*

2 VERB If you **lower** something, you move it down. ❍ *They lowered the coffin into the grave.*

3 VERB If you **lower** something, you make it less. ❍ *The Central Bank lowered interest rates yesterday.*

low|er case **NONCOUNT NOUN** If you write or type something **in lower case**, you write or type it using small letters, not capital letters. Compare with **upper case**.

low-hanging fruit **(low-hanging fruit)**

1 NONCOUNT NOUN **The low-hanging fruit** is something that you can do or achieve quickly and easily as part of a larger goal or solution. [BUSINESS MANAGEMENT] ❍ *With the low-hanging fruit plucked, the hope is that smaller companies will come in to pursue modest new discoveries.*

2 NOUN a company that is suitable to buy as a small investment [FINANCE]

loy|al /lɔɪəl/ **ADJ** always being a friend to or supporting someone or something, even when this is difficult ❍ *They have always stayed loyal to the Republican party.* ❍ *A company that deals with loyal customers knows a good deal about them and about how to get in touch with them.* ● **loy|al|ly** **ADV** ❍ *The staff loyally supported their boss.*

loy|al|ty card **(loyalty cards)** **NOUN** a card that stores give to regular customers who can use it to get lower prices and other benefits [MARKETING AND SALES, mainly BRIT]

Ltd **Ltd** is used after the names of limited companies. **Ltd** is a written abbreviation for **Limited**. [ECONOMICS] ❍ *J Walter Thompson Company Ltd*

luck /lʌk/

1 NONCOUNT NOUN **Luck** or **good luck** is the good things that happen to you, that have not been caused by yourself or other people. ❍ *Before the interview, we shook hands and wished each other luck.*

2 NONCOUNT NOUN **Bad luck** is the bad things that happen to you, that have not been caused by yourself or other people. ❍ *We had a lot of bad luck during the first half of this season.*

3 If you say "**Good luck**" to someone, you are telling them that you hope they will be successful in what they are doing. [INFORMAL]

lucki|ly /lʌkɪli/ **ADV** used for saying that it is good that something happened ❍ *Luckily, nobody was seriously injured in the accident.*

lucky /lʌki/ **(luckier, luckiest)**

1 ADJ always having good things happen to you and avoiding bad things ❍ *I am luckier than most people here. I have a job.* ❍ *Rob is lucky to be alive after that accident.*

2 ADJ used to describe something that brings you good luck ❍ *I'm wearing my lucky shirt. How can I lose?*

lug|gage /lʌgɪdʒ/ **NONCOUNT NOUN** **Luggage** is the bags that you take with you when you travel. ❍ *"Do you have any luggage?"—"Just my briefcase."*

lump /lʌmp/

1 NOUN a solid piece of something ❍ *a lump of coal*

2 NOUN a small, hard part in or on the body ❍ *I've got a painful lump in my mouth.*

lump sum **(lump sums)** **NOUN** an amount of money that is paid as a large amount at one time rather than as smaller amounts at separate times ❍ *a tax-free lump sum of $50,000*

> **BUSINESS ETIQUETTE**
> In Japan, people drink soup by lifting the bowl to their mouth with both hands. However, in Korea, China, Thailand, and Indonesia, people use soup spoons.

lunch /lʌntʃ/ **NOUN** the meal that you have in the middle of the day ❍ *Are you free for lunch?* ❍ *business lunches*

lunch break **(lunch breaks)** also **lunchbreak** **NOUN** the period in the middle of the day when you stop work in order to have a meal

lunch|time /lʌntʃtaɪm/ **NONCOUNT NOUN** **Lunchtime** is the time of the day when people have their lunch. ❍ *Could we meet at lunchtime?*

lung /lʌŋ/ **NOUN** one of the two large organs inside your chest that you use for breathing ❍ *lung cancer*

luxu|ry /lʌkʃəri, lʌgʒə-/ (**luxuries**)

1 NONCOUNT NOUN **Luxury** is a way of living when you are able to buy all the beautiful and expensive things that you want. ❍ *He leads a life of luxury.*

2 NOUN something pleasant and expensive that people want but do not need ❍ *Having a vacation is a luxury they can no longer afford.*

ly|ing /laɪɪŋ/ **Lying** is a form of the verb **lie**.

L

Mm

ma'am /mæm/ NOUN used as a polite way of talking to a woman ❍ *Would you repeat that please, ma'am?*

ma|chine /məʃin/ NOUN a piece of equipment that uses electricity or an engine to do a particular job ❍ *a coffee machine*

ma|chin|ery /məʃinəri/ NONCOUNT NOUN **Machinery** is machines in general. ❍ *We need new machinery for our factories.*

macro|eco|nom|ics /mækroʊɛkənɒmɪks, -ikə-/ also **macro-economics** NONCOUNT NOUN **Macroeconomics** is the study of the whole of a country's economy. Compare with **microeconomics**. [ECONOMICS] ❍ *Too many politicians forget the importance of macroeconomics.* ● **ma|cro|ec|o|nom|ic** /mækroʊɛkənɒmɪk, -ikə-/ ADJ ❍ *The country has implemented better macroeconomic policies.*

mad /mæd/ (**madder, maddest**)
1 ADJ very angry [INFORMAL] ❍ *You're just mad at me because I'm late.*
2 ADJ Someone who is **mad** has a mental illness that makes them behave in a strange way. [INFORMAL] ❍ *She was afraid of going mad.*
3 ADJ If you are **mad about** something or someone, you like them very much. [INFORMAL] ❍ *I'm mad about sports.*
4 ADJ **Mad** behavior is not controlled. ❍ *There was a mad rush to buy shares.*

mad|am /mædəm/ also **Madam** NOUN used as a polite way of talking to a woman ❍ *Good morning, madam.*

made /meɪd/
1 Made is a form of the verb **make**.
2 ADJ If something is **made of** a particular substance, that substance was used to make it. ❍ *The top of the table is made of glass.*

maga|zine /mægəzin, -zin/ NOUN a thin book with stories and pictures that you can buy every week or every month ❍ *a fashion magazine*

mag|ic /mædʒɪk/
1 NONCOUNT NOUN **Magic** is a special power that seems to make impossible things happen. ❍ *Most children believe in magic.*
2 NONCOUNT NOUN **Magic** is tricks that a person performs in order to entertain people. ❍ *His stage act combines magic, music, and humor.*

mag|net /mægnɪt/ NOUN a piece of special metal that attracts iron toward it

mag|nifi|cent /mægnɪfɪsənt/ ADJ extremely good or beautiful ❍ *a magnificent country house*

mag|ni|fy /mægnɪfaɪ/ (**magnifies, magnifying, magnified**) VERB If you **magnify** something, you make it look larger than it really is. ❍ *This telescope magnifies objects 11 times.*

maid /meɪd/ NOUN a woman whose job is to cook or clean rooms in a hotel or a private house

mail /meɪl/
1 NONCOUNT NOUN **The mail** is the system used for sending and receiving letters and packages. ❍ *Your check is in the mail.*
2 NONCOUNT NOUN **Mail** is the letters and packages or email that you receive. ❍ *There was no mail this morning.*
3 VERB If you **mail** something to someone, you send it to them by mail. ❍ *He mailed me the contract.*
4 NONCOUNT NOUN **Mail** is **email**. ❍ *I need to check my mail.*

mail|box /meɪlbɒks/ (**mailboxes**)
1 NOUN a box outside your home where letters

are delivered ❍ *There was a letter in her mailbox.*
2 NOUN a box in a public place where you put letters that you want to send ❍ *He dropped the letters into the mailbox.*
3 NOUN On a computer, your **mailbox** is the file where your email is stored. ❍ *There were 30 new messages in his mailbox.*

mail|man /meɪlmæn/ (**mailmen**) **NOUN** a man whose job is to collect and deliver letters and parcels that are sent by mail

mail or|der **NONCOUNT NOUN** **Mail order** is a system of buying goods by mail. [MARKETING AND SALES] ❍ *The toys are available by mail order.* ❍ *Many of them also offer a mail-order service.*

COLLOCATIONS
a mail order *catalog*
a mail order *service*
a mail order *company*
a mail order *business*
a mail order *firm*
available by mail order

mail|shot /meɪlʃɒt/ **NOUN** an advertisement that a company sends by post to a lot of people at the same time [MARKETING AND SALES, BRIT] ❍ *Advertisers are using narrower marketing techniques, such as mailshots and promotions, rather than newspapers and television.*

main /meɪn/ **ADJ** most important ❍ *He explained the main differences between companies and partnerships.*

main|land /meɪnlænd/ **NONCOUNT NOUN** **The mainland** is the largest piece of land in a country, not including any smaller islands. ❍ *They go to school on the mainland.*

main|ly /meɪnli/ **ADV** Used for saying that a statement is mostly true. ❍ *These people are mainly from Senegal.*

main mar|ket **NOUN** the market for larger companies on the London Stock Exchange [MARKETING AND SALES]

main|tain /meɪnteɪn/
1 VERB If you **maintain** something, you make it continue at the same level. ❍ *They are under steady pressure to keep prices down while maintaining quality.*
2 VERB If you **maintain** something, you keep it in good condition. ❍ *The refineries have been poorly maintained.*

main|te|nance /meɪntɪnəns/ **NONCOUNT NOUN** The **maintenance** of something is the process of keeping it in good condition. ❍ *Maintenance work starts next week.*

maître d'hô|tel /meɪtrə doʊtɛl, meɪtər/ (**maîtres d'hôtel**)
1 NOUN a head waiter or steward
2 NOUN the manager or owner of a hotel ❍ *We asked the maître d'hôtel for a table by the window.*

maize /meɪz/ → **corn**

maj|es|ty /mædʒɪsti/ (**majesties**) **NOUN** People use **Your Majesty** when they are talking to a king or a queen, or **Her Majesty** or **His Majesty** when they are talking about a king or a queen. ❍ *His Majesty would like to see you now.*

ma|jor /meɪdʒər/
1 ADJ more important than other things ❍ *Homelessness is a major problem here.*
2 NOUN the main subject that a student is studying ❍ *"What's your major?"—"Chemistry."*
3 VERB If a student **majors in** a particular subject, that subject is the main one they study. ❍ *He majored in finance at Claremont College.*
4 NOUN an officer of high rank in the army ❍ *Major Wayne Rollings*
5 NOUN a large or important company ❍ *Oil majors are worried about being unable to sell their crude oil.*

ma|jor|ity /mədʒɔrɪti/ (**majorities**) **NOUN** The **majority** of people or things in a group is more than half of them. ❍ *The majority of my patients are women.*

make /meɪk/ (**makes, making, made**)
1 VERB If you **make** something, you produce it, build it, or create it. ❍ *She makes all her own clothes.* ❍ *All our furniture is made from solid wood.*
2 VERB You can use **make** with nouns to show that someone does or says something. ❍ *I'd just like to make a comment.* ❍ *I made a few phone calls.*

3 VERB If something **makes** you do, feel or be something, it causes you to do, feel or be it. ❍ *Falling prices made them unprofitable.* ❍ *My boss's behavior makes me so angry!*
4 VERB If you **make** someone do something, you force them to do it. ❍ *Mom made me apologize to him.*
5 VERB If you **make** money, you earn it. ❍ *He makes lots of money.*
6 NOUN The **make** of something is the name of the company that made it. ❍ *What make of car do you drive?*
▸ **make out** If you **make** something **out**, you can see, hear or understand it. ❍ *I could just make out a tall figure of a man.* ❍ *I couldn't make out what he was saying.*
▸ **make up**
1 If you **make up** a story or excuse, you invent it. ❍ *It was all lies. I made it all up.*
2 If two people **make up** after an argument, they become friends again. ❍ *You two are always fighting and then making up again.*

mak|er /meɪkər/ **NOUN** the person or company that makes something ❍ *car makers*

make|up /meɪkʌp/ or **make-up** **NONCOUNT NOUN** **Makeup** is the creams and powders that people put on their face to make themselves look more attractive. Actors also wear makeup. ❍ *I don't wear much makeup.*

male /meɪl/
1 NOUN a person or an animal that belongs to the sex that does not have babies ❍ *Two 17-year-old males were arrested.*
2 ADJ relating to men or animals of the sex that does not have babies ❍ *male unemployment*

mall /mɔl/ **NOUN** a large shopping area [MARKETING AND SALES]

mam|mal /mæməl/ **NOUN** **Mammals** are animals that feed their babies with milk.

man /mæn/ (**men**)
1 NOUN an adult male human ❍ *Both men and women are paid the same salary.*
2 NOUN People sometimes use **Man** and **men** to talk about all humans. ❍ *Man first arrived in the Americas thousands of years ago.*

man|age /mænɪdʒ/ (**manages, managing, managed**)
1 VERB If you **manage to** do something, you succeed in doing it. ❍ *Three girls managed to escape the fire.*
2 VERB If you **manage** a business or organization, you control it. ❍ *He manages a clothing store.*

man|aged bonds **PL NOUN** **Managed bonds** are a combination of types of investment, controlled by an investment manager. [BANKING, mainly BRIT]

man|aged cur|ren|cy (**managed currencies**) **NOUN** a currency that is controlled by the government [BANKING, ECONOMICS]

man|age|ment /mænɪdʒmənt/
1 NONCOUNT NOUN **Management** is the control of a business or another organization. [BUSINESS MANAGEMENT] ❍ *The zoo needed better management.*
2 NONCOUNT NOUN The people who control a business are the **management**. [BUSINESS MANAGEMENT] ❍ *The management is trying hard to keep employees happy.* ❍ *A change of management would help.*

COLLOCATIONS
business management
management *skills*
management *style*
senior management
new management

m

man|age|ment abil|ity (**management abilities**) **NOUN** the qualities that a person has as a manager [BUSINESS MANAGEMENT] ❍ *Taylor has demonstrated outstanding management abilities.*

man|age|ment ac|count|ing **NONCOUNT NOUN** **Management accounting** is the same as **cost accounting**. [FINANCE]

man|age|ment buy|out (**management buyouts**) **NOUN** A **management buyout** is the buying of a company by its managers. The abbreviation **MBO** is also used. [BUSINESS MANAGEMENT] ❍ *It is thought that a management buyout is one option.*

man|age|ment com|pa|ny (**management companies**) **NOUN** a company that manages a unit trust [BUSINESS MANAGEMENT]

man|age|ment con|sult|ant (**management consultants**) **NOUN** someone whose job is to advise companies on the most efficient ways to run their business [BUSINESS MANAGEMENT] ❍ *After a management consultant visited the office, a solution to the problem was found.*

man|age|ment lay|ers **PL NOUN** **Management layers** are the different levels of managers in a company. [BUSINESS MANAGEMENT, ADMINISTRATION] ❍ *The company plans to reduce management layers as a way of cutting costs.*

man|age|ment phi|loso|phy (**management philosophies**) **NOUN** the set of ideas that a company has about how it should be run [BUSINESS MANAGEMENT] ❍ *His management philosophy is that managers should run their parts of the business independently.*

M

man|age|ment style (**management styles**) **NOUN** the way a person behaves as a manager [BUSINESS MANAGEMENT] ❍ *Ware was unhappy about the new management style and he left the company.*

man|age|ment un|ion (**management unions**) **NOUN** an organization that represents managers to improve working conditions [BUSINESS MANAGEMENT]

man|ag|er /mænɪdʒər/ **NOUN** a person who controls all or part of a business or an organization [BUSINESS MANAGEMENT] ❍ *department managers* ❍ *Linda Emery, marketing manager for Wall's sausages*

mana|gerial /mænɪdʒɪəriəl/ **ADJ** relating to the work of a manager [BUSINESS MANAGEMENT] ❍ *his managerial skills* ❍ *a managerial career*

man|ag|ing /mænədʒɪŋ/ **ADJ** having control or authority [BUSINESS MANAGEMENT] ❍ *Eric Shaw, the law firm's managing partner*

man|ag|ing di|rec|tor (**managing directors**) **NOUN** the most important working director of a company [BUSINESS MANAGEMENT, ADMINISTRATION, mainly BRIT] ❍ *Nick Webb, managing director of Simon & Schuster UK*

ma|neu|ver /mənuvər/

1 VERB If you **maneuver** something into or out of a difficult position, you skillfully move it there. ❍ *He maneuvered the car through the narrow gate.*

2 NOUN **Maneuver** is also a noun. ❍ *The airplanes performed some difficult maneuvers.*

ma|nipu|late /mənɪpyəleɪt/ (**manipulates, manipulating, manipulated**) **VERB** If you **manipulate** people or events, you control them for your own benefit. ❍ *The defendants allegedly manipulated the stock prices of six companies.*

man|kind /mænkaɪnd/ **NONCOUNT NOUN** People sometimes use **mankind** to talk about all humans. ❍ *We hope for a better future for all mankind.*

man man|age|ment **NONCOUNT NOUN** **Man management** is the work of controlling and organizing staff. [mainly BRIT] ❍ *Team leaders need to have effective man-management skills.*

man|ner /mænər/

1 NOUN The **manner** in which you do something is the way that you do it. ❍ *She smiled in a friendly manner.*

2 PL NOUN Your **manners** are how polite you are. ❍ *He had perfect manners.*

ma|noeu|vre /mənuvər/ [BRIT] → **maneuver**

man|power /mænpaʊər/ **NONCOUNT NOUN** Workers are sometimes referred to as **manpower**. [BUSINESS MANAGEMENT] ❍ *the shortage of skilled manpower in the industry*

man|power plan|ning **NONCOUNT NOUN** **Manpower planning** is the process of working out what employees will be needed in the future. [BUSINESS MANAGEMENT, HR]

man|sion /mænʃən/ **NOUN** a very large, expensive house ❍ *an eighteenth-century mansion*

manu|al /mæ̲nyuəl/

1 ADJ Manual work is work in which you use your hands or your physical strength. ❍ *a manual worker*

2 ADJ Manual equipment is operated by hand, rather than by electricity or a motor. ❍ *We used a manual pump.*

3 NOUN a book that tells you how to do something ❍ *an instruction manual*

manuf. or **manufac. Manuf.** is an abbreviation for **manufacture** or **manufactured**. [PRODUCTION]

manu|fac|ture /mæ̲nyəfæ̲ktʃər/ (**manufactures, manufacturing, manufactured**)

1 VERB To **manufacture** something means to make it in a factory. [PRODUCTION] ❍ *The company manufactures plastics.*

2 NONCOUNT NOUN The **manufacture** of a product is the work involved in making it. [PRODUCTION] ❍ *Coal is used in the manufacture of steel.*

3 PL NOUN Manufactures are products that have been made in a factory. [PRODUCTION] ❍ *The growth of trade in manufactures was most rapid when the world economy was growing rapidly.*

manu|fac|tur|er /mæ̲nyəfæ̲ktʃərər/ **NOUN** a company that makes large amounts of things [PRODUCTION] ❍ *the world's largest doll manufacturer*

manu|fac|turing /mæ̲nyəfæ̲ktʃərɪŋ/ **NONCOUNT NOUN Manufacturing** is the business of making things in factories. [PRODUCTION] ❍ *the manufacturing industry*

manu|fa̲c|turing base (**manufacturing bases**) **NOUN** all the factories or companies that produce goods in a particular place [PRODUCTION, ECONOMICS] ❍ *Working with foreign investors, they were beginning to rebuild the country's manufacturing base.*

manu|fa̲c|turing fa|cil|ity (**manufacturing facilities**) **NOUN** a factory [PRODUCTION, FORMAL] ❍ *Last week the company closed down its San Jose manufacturing facilities.*

many /mɛ̲ni/

1 ADJ or **PRON** You use **many** to talk about a large number of people or things. ❍ *Federal employment seems to be an attractive option for many people.* ❍ *He made a list of his friends. There weren't many.* ❍ *"How many units have they sold?"—"Not very many."*

2 You use **many of** for talking about a large number of people or things. ❍ *They privatized over 100 industries, many of them highly profitable.*

map /mæ̲p/ **NOUN** a drawing of an area that shows things like mountains, rivers, and roads ❍ *a tourist map*

ma|ple /meɪ̲pəl/

1 NOUN a tree with leaves that turn a bright red or gold color in the fall

2 NONCOUNT NOUN Maple is the wood of this tree. ❍ *a maple table*

mara|thon /mæ̲rəθɒn/ **NOUN** a race in which people run a distance of 26 miles (about 42 km) ❍ *He is running in his first marathon next weekend.*

mar|ble /mɑ̲rbəl/ **NONCOUNT NOUN** a type of very hard, cold stone that people use to make parts of buildings or statues (= models of people)

march /mɑ̲rtʃ/ (**marches, marching, marched**)

1 VERB When soldiers **march** somewhere, they walk there with regular steps, as a group. ❍ *Some soldiers were marching down the street.*

2 NOUN March is also a noun. ❍ *After a short march, the soldiers entered the village.*

3 VERB When a large group of people **march**, they walk through the streets together in order to show that they disagree with something. ❍ *They marched through the city to protest against the war.*

4 NOUN March is also a noun. ❍ *Organizers expect 300,000 protesters to join the march.*

5 VERB If someone **marches** somewhere, they walk there quickly, often because they are angry. ❍ *He marched into my office without knocking.*

March /mɑrtʃ/ **NOUN** the third month of the year ❍ *I flew to Milwaukee in March.* ❍ *She was born on March 6, 1920.*

mar|ga|rine /mɑrdʒərɪn/ **NONCOUNT NOUN** **Margarine** is a yellow substance that is made from vegetable oil, and is similar to butter.

mar|gin /mɑrdʒɪn/
1 NOUN the difference between two amounts ❍ *Carter won by a narrow margin.*
2 NOUN the empty space down the side of a page ❍ *She wrote comments in the margin.*
3 NOUN the profit on a transaction [FINANCE] ❍ *Net profit margins have slipped to 1.4%.*

mar|gin|al /mɑrdʒɪnᵊl/
1 ADJ small or not very important ❍ *This is a marginal improvement on last month's figures.*
2 ADJ **Marginal** costs or revenues are costs or revenues that arise from a very small change in production. ❍ *Marginal costs declined due to improvements in operating efficiency.*

mar|gin|al cos|ting **NONCOUNT NOUN** **Marginal costing** is a type of cost accounting in which marginal costs are charged to cost units and fixed costs are treated as a lump sum. [FINANCE]

M

ma|rine /mərin/
1 NOUN a soldier who is trained to fight at sea as well as on land ❍ *A few Marines were wounded.*
2 ADJ relating to the ocean ❍ *marine life*

ma|rine in|sur|ance **NONCOUNT NOUN** **Marine insurance** is insurance that covers damage caused by the sea. [BANKING]

mark /mɑrk/
1 NOUN a small area of dirt or damage on something ❍ *There was a red paint mark on the wall.*
2 NOUN a written or printed symbol ❍ *a question mark*
3 VERB When a teacher **marks** a student's work, they write a number or a letter on it to show how good it is. ❍ *The teacher was marking essays after class.*
4 VERB If something **marks** a place, it shows where a particular thing is. ❍ *A big hole in the road marks the place where the bomb landed.*

mark|down /mɑrkdaʊn/ **NOUN** a reduction in the price of something [MARKETING AND SALES] ❍ *Customers know that our sales offer genuine markdowns across the store.*

mar|ket /mɑrkɪt/
1 NOUN a place where people buy and sell products ❍ *They buy their fruit and vegetables at the market.*
2 NOUN The **market** for a particular product is the people who want to buy it. [ECONOMICS] ❍ *The market for organic wines is growing.*
3 VERB If you **market** a product you advertise it and sell it. [MARKETING AND SALES] ❍ *The products were marketed under a different brand name in Europe.*
4 NOUN The **market** refers to the total amount of a product that is sold each year. [ECONOMICS] ❍ *The two big companies control 72% of the market.*
5 NOUN **The job market** or **the labor market** refers to the people who are looking for work and the jobs available for them to do. [ECONOMICS] ❍ *Every year, 250,000 people enter the job market.*
6 NOUN The stock market is sometimes referred to as **the market**. [FINANCE] ❍ *The market collapsed last October.*
7 PHRASE If something is **on the market**, it is available for people to buy. ❍ *The house has been on the market for six months.*
8 PHRASE If you **price** yourself **out of the market**, you try to sell things at a higher price than other people, with the result that no one buys them from you. ❍ *At £150,000 for a season, he really is pricing himself out of the market.*

COLLOCATIONS
to *enter* a market
an *emerging* market

mar|ket|able /mɑrkɪtəbᵊl/ **ADJ** able to be sold because people want to buy it [ECONOMICS] ❍ *What began as an attempt at artistic creation has turned into a marketable commodity.*

mar|ket con|di|tions **PL NOUN** The **market conditions** are the state of a particular market at a particular time. [ECONOMICS] ❍ *Business schools must be responsive to market conditions.*

mar|ket econo|my (**market economies**) NOUN an economic system in which the prices of things depend on how many are available and how many people want to buy them, rather than prices being fixed by governments [ECONOMICS] ❍ *Their ultimate aim was a market economy for Hungary.*

mar|ket|eer /mɑrkɪtɪər/ NOUN A **marketeer** is the same as a **marketer**. [MARKETING AND SALES] → also **free-marketeer**

mar|ket en|try NONCOUNT NOUN **Market entry** is when a company starts doing business in a particular market. [ECONOMICS] ❍ *Digital delivery will lower the cost of market entry.*

mar|ket|er /mɑrkɪtər/ NOUN someone whose job involves marketing [MARKETING AND SALES] ❍ *As a marketer I understood what makes people buy things.*

mar|ket forces PL NOUN **Market forces** are things that affect the availability of goods and the demand for them, without any help or control by governments. [ECONOMICS] ❍ *The country is opening the economy to market forces and increasing the role of private enterprise.*

mar|ket|ing /mɑrkɪtɪŋ/ NONCOUNT NOUN **Marketing** is the activity of advertising and selling products. [ECONOMICS] ❍ *She works in the marketing department.* ❍ *They were given expert advice on production and marketing.*

mar|ket|ing mix NOUN the combination of marketing activities that a company uses in order to promote a particular product or service [MARKETING AND SALES, ECONOMICS] ❍ *The key focus of the marketing mix will be on price and distribution.*

mar|ket|ing strat|egy (**marketing strategies**) NOUN a plan for the sale of a product, for example deciding on its price and how it should be advertised [MARKETING AND SALES] ❍ *Keeping an up-to-date customer database is vital to our marketing strategy.*

mar|ket lead|er (**market leaders**) NOUN a company that sells more of a particular product or service than most of its competitors do [MARKETING AND SALES, ECONOMICS] ❍ *We are becoming one of the market leaders in the fashion industry.*

mar|ket mak|er (**market makers**) NOUN a person who buys and sells shares on the London Stock Exchange [BANKING]

market-oriented or **market-led, market-orientated** ADJ aiming to develop products or services in order to fill gaps in the market [ECONOMICS, BUSINESS MANAGEMENT] ❍ *Service industries like banking and insurance have also become more market-oriented.*

market-oriented pric|ing NONCOUNT NOUN **Market-oriented pricing** is the policy of setting the price of a product based on the market and consumer requirements. Compare with **competition-based pricing**, **cost-based pricing**, and **penetration pricing**. [BUSINESS MANAGEMENT]

market|place /mɑrkɪtpleɪs/ NOUN the activity of buying and selling products [ECONOMICS] ❍ *We hope to play a greater role in the marketplace and, therefore, supply more jobs.*

mar|ket price (**market prices**) NOUN the price of an item, determined by how many of the items are available and how many people want to buy them [BUSINESS MANAGEMENT] ❍ *the market price of cocoa*

mar|ket re|search NONCOUNT NOUN **Market research** is the activity of collecting and studying information about what people want, need, and buy. [MARKETING AND SALES] ❍ *Market research showed that customers want both online and telephone banking.*

COLLOCATIONS

to *conduct* market research
to *do* market research
to *carry out* market research
a market research *company*
a market research *firm*

m

mar|ket sec|tor (**market sectors**) NOUN one part of a market consisting of related products or services [ECONOMICS] ❍ *It achieved this growth by identifying a market sector, and moving quickly to become the leader in that sector.*

mar|ket seg|ment (**market segments**) NOUN a part of a market that has particular customers who buy particular things [ECONOMICS] ❍ *The older market segments look for comfort, quality, and durability.*

mar|ket seg|men|ta|tion /mɑrkɪt sɛgmənteɪʃən/ NONCOUNT NOUN **Market segmentation** is the division of a market into separate parts. [ECONOMICS] ❍ *There has been increasing market segmentation, with specialist builders designing houses aimed at the young singles market and elderly people.*

mar|ket share NONCOUNT NOUN A company's **market share** in a product is the proportion of the total sales of that product that is produced by that company. [ECONOMICS] ❍ *Ford has been gaining market share this year at the expense of GM.*

M

COLLOCATIONS

to *lose* market share
to *gain* market share
to *increase* market share
to *grab* market share

mar|ket test (**market tests**)
1 NOUN a trial of a new product or service by people who then give their opinions on it [ECONOMICS] ❍ *Results from market tests show little enthusiasm for the product.*
2 VERB If a new product or service **is market tested**, a group of people are asked to try it and give their opinions on it. [ECONOMICS] ❍ *These nuts have been market tested. We found that Australians rated them highest.* ● **mar|ket test|ing** NONCOUNT NOUN ❍ *They learned a lot from the initial market testing exercise.*

mar|ket value (**market values**) NOUN the value of an item that depends on how many of the items are available and how many people want to buy them [ECONOMICS] ❍ *He must sell the house for the current market value.*

mark-up NOUN a percentage added to the cost of a product, in order to cover costs and provide profit ❍ *The firm imports cement and sells it at a 10% mark-up.*

mar|ma|lade /mɑrməleɪd/ NONCOUNT NOUN **Marmalade** is a food like jelly that is usually made from oranges.

mar|riage /mærɪdʒ/
1 NOUN the relationship between a husband and a wife ❍ *a happy marriage*
2 NOUN the act of getting married ❍ *a marriage ceremony*

mar|ried /mærid/ ADJ If you are **married**, you have a husband or a wife. ❍ *She is married to an Englishman.*

mar|ry /mæri/ (**marries, marrying, married**) VERB When two people **get married** or **marry**, they legally become husband and wife. ❍ *They married a month after they met.*

mar|shal /mɑrʃᵊl/ (**marshals, marshaling** or **marshalling, marshaled** or **marshalled**)
1 VERB If you **marshal** people or things, you gather them together and arrange them for a particular purpose. ❍ *The company turned its attention to marshaling its creditors' approval.*
2 VERB If you **marshal** assets or mortgages, you arrange them in order of priority.
3 NOUN an official who helps to supervise a public event ❍ *The tournament is controlled by well-trained marshals.*
4 NOUN a police officer who is responsible for a particular area ❍ *A federal marshal was killed in a shoot-out.*

mart /mɑrt/ NOUN a place such as a market where things are bought and sold [MARKETING AND SALES] ❍ *the flower mart*

mar|vel|lous /mɑrvələs/ [BRIT] → **marvelous**

mar|vel|ous /mɑrvələs/ ADJ excellent ❍ *Shareholders haven't complained, because they've had marvelous performance.*

mas|cu|line /mæskyəlɪn/
1 ADJ **Masculine** qualities are typical of men. ❍ *She has a deep, rather masculine voice.*
2 ADJ In some languages, a **masculine** noun, pronoun, or adjective has a different form

from other forms (such as "feminine" forms). Compare with **feminine**.

> **BUSINESS ETIQUETTE**
> In many cultures, particularly the Indian subcontinent, Asia Pacific, and sometimes the UK, the word 'no' is considered to be very strong, and people often avoid using it because they do not want to offend or disappoint you.

mask /mæsk/ **NOUN** something that you wear over your face to protect it or to hide it ❍ *Wear a mask to protect yourself from the smoke.*

mass /mæs/
1 NOUN A **mass of** something is a large amount of it. ❍ *She had a mass of black hair.*
2 Masses of something is a large amount of it. [INFORMAL] ❍ *I have masses of work to do.*
3 Mass is the amount of physical matter that something contains. ❍ *Pluto and Triton have nearly the same size, mass, and density.*
4 NONCOUNT NOUN Mass is a Christian church ceremony, especially in a Roman Catholic church. ❍ *She went to Mass each day.*

mas|sa|cre /mæsəkər/ (**massacres, massacring, massacred**)
1 NOUN A **massacre** happens when a large number of people are killed at the same time in a violent and cruel way. ❍ *Her mother died in the massacre.*
2 VERB If people **are massacred**, a large number of them are killed in a violent and cruel way. ❍ *Three hundred people were massacred by the soldiers.*

mas|sage /məsɑʒ/ (**massages, massaging, massaged**)
1 NOUN Massage is the activity of rubbing someone's body to make them relax or to reduce their pain. ❍ *Alex asked me if I wanted a massage.*
2 VERB If you **massage** a part of someone's body, you rub it in order to make them relax or reduce their pain. ❍ *She massaged her right foot.*

mas|sive /mæsɪv/ **ADJ** very big ❍ *He said the process wouldn't entail massive layoffs.*

mass mar|ket (**mass markets**)
1 NOUN the large numbers of people who want to buy a particular product [ECONOMICS, BUSINESS MANAGEMENT] ❍ *They now have access to the mass markets of Japan and the U.K.*
2 ADJ designed for selling to large numbers of people [ECONOMICS, BUSINESS MANAGEMENT] ❍ *mass-market paperbacks*

mass-produce (**mass-produces, mass-producing, mass-produced**) **VERB** If someone **mass-produces** something, they make it in large quantities by machine. [PRODUCTION] ❍ *the invention of machinery to mass-produce footwear* ● **mass-produced ADJ** ❍ *In 1981 it launched the first mass-produced mountain bike.*

mass pro|duc|tion **NONCOUNT NOUN** **Mass production** is the production of something in large quantities by machine. [PRODUCTION] ❍ *This equipment will allow the mass production of baby food.*

mass|tige /mæstiʒ/ **NONCOUNT NOUN** **Masstige** is the technique of creating goods that seem exclusive although many people can afford them. [MARKETING AND SALES] ❍ *Masstige goods appeal most to consumers that earn $50,000 and above.*

mass tour|ism **NONCOUNT NOUN** **Mass tourism** is tourism that involves very large numbers of people. [ECONOMICS] ❍ *Mass tourism has caused immense damage to the environment.*

mas|ter /mæstər/
1 NOUN a man who controls and owns or employs a person or animal ❍ *He was working for his masters in Paris.*
2 VERB If you **master** something, you learn how to do it well. ❍ *They need to master the arts of hiring, firing, and appraisals.*

master|piece /mæstərpis/ **NOUN** an extremely good painting, novel, movie, or other work of art ❍ *His book is a masterpiece.*

mas|ter's de|gree (**master's degrees**) **NOUN** a university qualification that is of a higher level than an ordinary degree

mat /mæt/
1 NOUN a small piece of cloth, wood, or plastic

that you put on a table to protect it ❍ *a set of red and white check place mats*
2 NOUN a piece of thick material that you put on the floor ❍ *There was a letter on the doormat.*

match /mætʃ/ (**matches, matching, matched**)
1 NOUN a small wooden or paper stick that produces a flame when you move it along a rough surface ❍ *Kate lit a match.*
2 NOUN an organized sporting contest ❍ *He was watching a tennis match.*
3 VERB If something **matches** another thing, they have the same color or design, or they look good together. ❍ *Do these shoes match my dress?* ● **match|ing ADJ** ❍ *She wore a hat and a matching scarf.*

mate /meɪt/ (**mates, mating, mated**)
1 NOUN An animal's **mate** is its sexual partner. ❍ *The male bird wants to attract a mate.*
2 VERB When animals **mate**, a male and a female have sex in order to produce babies. ❍ *After mating, the female does not eat.*

ma|terial /mətɪəriəl/
1 NONCOUNT NOUN Material is cloth. ❍ *The thick material of her skirt was too warm for summer.*
2 PL NOUN Materials are the things that you need for a particular activity. ❍ *building materials*

ma|ter|nity leave /mətɜrnɪti liv/ **NONCOUNT NOUN Maternity leave** is a period of time when a woman can be away from work before and after the birth of her child. [HR] ❍ *The company has introduced flexible working hours and extended paid maternity leave.*

math /mæθ/ **NONCOUNT NOUN Math** is the same as **mathematics**. ❍ *He studied math in college.*

math|emat|ics /mæθəmætɪks/ **NONCOUNT NOUN Mathematics** is the study of numbers, quantities, or shapes. ❍ *He is a professor of mathematics.*

maths /mæθs/ [BRIT] → **math**

mat|ter /mætər/
1 NOUN something that you must talk about or do ❍ *She wanted to discuss a private matter with me.*
2 You say "**What's the matter?**" when you think that someone has a problem and you want to know what it is. ❍ *Carol, what's the matter? You don't seem happy.*
3 VERB If you say that something does not **matter**, you mean that it is not important to you. ❍ *A lot of the food goes on the floor but that doesn't matter.*
4 NONCOUNT NOUN Matter is a type of substance. ❍ *vegetable matter*

mat|ters aris|ing PL NOUN Matters arising are subjects that need to be discussed. [ADMINISTRATION] ❍ *We will discuss other matters arising from the meeting.*

mat|tress /mætrɪs/ **NOUN** the thick, soft part of a bed that you lie on

ma|ture /mətyʊər, -tʊər, -tʃʊər/ (**matures, maturing, matured, maturer, maturest**)
1 VERB When a child or a young animal **matures**, it becomes an adult. ❍ *The children will face many challenges as they mature into adulthood.*
2 ADJ A **mature** person or animal is fully grown.
3 ADJ If someone is **mature**, their behavior is responsible and sensible. ❍ *Fiona was mature for her age.*
4 VERB When an investment **matures**, you stop paying money and the company pays you back the money you have saved, with interest. ❍ *These bonuses will be paid when your savings plan matures in ten years' time.*

ma|tur|ity /mətyʊərɪti, -tʊər-, -tʃʊər-/ (**maturities**)
1 NONCOUNT NOUN Maturity is the state of being fully developed. ❍ *The market will have reached maturity within two or three years.*
2 NONCOUNT NOUN Maturity is the quality of being responsible and sensible. ❍ *Her speech showed great maturity.*
3 NONCOUNT NOUN When an investment reaches **maturity**, the company pays you back the money you have saved, with interest. ❍ *Customers are told what their policies will be worth on maturity.*
4 NOUN the length of time between investment and repayment of money and

interest ❍ *Most of these loans have maturities of one to eight years.*

maxi|mi|sa|tion /mæksəməzeɪʃən/ [BRIT] → **maximization**

max|im|ise /mæksɪmaɪz/ [BRIT] → **maximize**

maxi|mi|za|tion /mæksəməzeɪʃən/ NONCOUNT NOUN The **maximization** of something is the act of making it as great in amount or importance as possible. ❍ *Profit maximization is one of the major objectives of a business.*

max|im|ize /mæksɪmaɪz/ (**maximizes, maximizing, maximized**) VERB If you **maximize** something, you make it as big as possible. ❍ *They want to maximize profit.*

maxi|mum /mæksɪməm/
1 ADJ The **maximum** amount is the largest amount possible. ❍ *Maximum sales charges are included in the returns.*
2 NOUN **Maximum** is also a noun. ❍ *The rate then would rise to a maximum of 28%.*

may /meɪ/
1 MODAL You use **may** to show that there is a possibility that something will happen or that something is true. ❍ *Prices may rise.*
2 MODAL You use **may** to say that someone is allowed to do something. ❍ *May we come in?*

May /meɪ/ NOUN the fifth month of the year ❍ *We signed the contract in May.*

may|be /meɪbi/
1 ADV used when you are uncertain about something ❍ *Maybe there's a new product out there that's taking some of your market share.*
2 ADV used for making suggestions or giving advice ❍ *Maybe we can try selling at a higher price.* ❍ *Maybe you should leave the company name off the package.*

may|on|naise /meɪəneɪz/ NONCOUNT NOUN **Mayonnaise** is a cold, thick sauce made from eggs and oil.

mayor /meɪər, mɛər/ NOUN a person who is responsible for the government of a town or city ❍ *the mayor of New York*

MBO /ɛm bi oʊ/ NOUN **MBO** is an abbreviation for **management buyout**. [BUSINESS MANAGEMENT] ❍ *She joined the company in 1978, and following an MBO in 1989 she became joint managing director.*

m-commerce /ɛmkɒmərs/
NONCOUNT NOUN **M-commerce** refers to business that is done on the Internet using a mobile phone. [E-COMMERCE] ❍ *M-commerce is seen as an important revenue earner for the networks.*

MD /ɛm di/ NOUN **MD** is an abbreviation for **managing director**. [ADMINISTRATION, BUSINESS MANAGEMENT, mainly BRIT]

me /mi, STRONG mi/ PRON used to talk about yourself ❍ *He asked me to go to California with him.*

meal /mil/ NOUN an occasion when people eat, or the food that they eat at that time ❍ *She sat next to him during the meal.* ❍ *Logan finished his meal in silence.*

mean
❶ VERB USES
❷ ADJECTIVE USE
❷ NOUN USE

❶ **mean** /min/ (**means, meaning, meant**)
1 VERB If something **means** something, it has that meaning. ❍ *"Unable" means "not able."*
2 VERB If something **means** a lot **to** you, it is very important to you. ❍ *It's just a day off but means a lot to the employee.*
3 VERB If one thing **means** another, the second thing will happen because of the first thing. ❍ *The new factory means more jobs for people.*
4 VERB If you **mean** what you are saying, you are serious about it. ❍ *He set out the case for low inflation as though he really meant it.*
5 VERB If someone **meant to** do something, they did it deliberately. ❍ *I'm so sorry. I didn't mean to hurt you.*

❷ **mean** /min/ ADJ unkind or cruel ❍ *He appears even-tempered and controlled, but he has a mean streak.*

❸ **mean** /min/ NOUN In math, the **mean** is the amount that you get if you add a set of numbers together and divide them by the number of things that you originally added together.

mean|ing /minɪŋ/ **NOUN** the idea that a word or expression represents ❍ *Do you know the meaning of the words you're singing?*

mean|ing|less /minɪŋlɪs/ **ADJ** without meaning or purpose ❍ *He felt that his life was meaningless.*

means /minz/ **NOUN** A **means** of doing something is a way to do it. **Means** is both the singular and the plural form for this use. ❍ *People are questioning corporate profits as a means of support for stock prices.*

meant /mɛnt/
1 Meant is a form of the verb **mean**.
2 ADJ used for saying that something or someone was intended to be or do a particular thing ❍ *It was meant to be India's biggest-ever foreign investment.* ❍ *He was meant to arrange the meeting.*

mean|time /mintaɪm/ used for talking about the period of time between two events ❍ *This panic will soon be over but in the meantime investors have become very sensitive to risk.*

mean|while /minwaɪl/ **ADV** used for talking about the period of time between two events or what happens while another thing is happening ❍ *I'll be ready to meet them tomorrow. Meanwhile, I'm going to talk to Karen.* ❍ *Many hospitals have been hit by strikes. Meanwhile, investment projects have been postponed.*

meas|ure /mɛʒər/ (**measures, measuring, measured**)
1 VERB If you **measure** something, you find out its size. ❍ *Measure the length of the table.*
2 VERB If something **measures** a particular length or amount, that is its size. ❍ *The desk measures three feet by five feet.*
3 NOUN When someone takes **measures** to do something, they act in a particular way to try to do it. [FORMAL] ❍ *Some companies are taking measures to curb the cost of retirement plans.*

meas|ure|ment /mɛʒərmənt/ **NOUN** the number that you get when you measure something ❍ *You'll need to take the measurements of the room.*

meat /mit/ **NONCOUNT NOUN Meat** is the part of an animal that people cook and eat. ❍ *I don't eat meat or fish.*

mec|ca /mɛkə/ **NOUN** If you describe a place as a **mecca** for a particular thing, you mean that many people who are interested in it go there. ❍ *Thailand has become the tourist mecca of Asia.*

me|chan|ic /mɪkænɪk/ **NOUN** a person whose job is to repair machines and engines [TECHNOLOGY] ❍ *Ask your mechanic to check the brakes.*

me|chani|cal /mɪkænɪkəl/ **ADJ** relating to machines and engines ❍ *a mechanical clock*

mecha|nism /mɛkənɪzəm/ **NOUN** a part of a machine ❍ *the locking mechanism*

med|al /mɛdəl/ **NOUN** a small metal disk that you get as a prize ❍ *a gold medal*

me|dia /midiə/
1 NOUN You can call television, radio, newspapers, and magazines **the media**. ❍ *They told their story to the news media.*
2 Media is a plural of **medium**.

me|dia|gen|ic /midɪədʒɛnɪk/ **ADJ** presenting an attractive image when shown in the media ❍ *The company has had great success in producing mediagenic collections of luxury goods.*

me|di|ate /midieɪt/ (**mediates, mediating, mediated**) **VERB** If someone **mediates between** two groups of people, they try to settle an argument between them by finding things that they can both agree to. ❍ *Officials have mediated a series of meetings between the two sides.*
• **me|di|ator NOUN** ❍ *An archbishop has been acting as mediator between the rebels and the authorities.*

me|dia|tion /midieɪʃən/
1 NONCOUNT NOUN Mediation is the activity of trying to settle a disagreement between two people or groups. [LEGAL] ❍ *The two sides could reach an agreement through the mediation of a third party.*
2 NONCOUNT NOUN Mediation is a method of resolving a disagreement between

M

workers and a company. [LEGAL] ❍ *The unions and the company agreed to mediation.*

med|ic /mɛ̲dɪk/
1 NOUN a doctor or medical student [INFORMAL]
2 NOUN a doctor who works with the armed forces ❍ *A navy medic was wounded by gunshot.*

medi|cal /mɛ̲dɪkᵊl/ **ADJ** relating to illness and injuries and how to treat or prevent them ❍ *They received medical treatment.*

medi|ca|tion /mɛ̲dɪke̲ɪʃən/ **NONCOUNT NOUN** **Medication** is medicine that is used for treating and curing illness. ❍ *Are you taking any medication?*

medi|cine /mɛ̲dɪsɪn/
1 NONCOUNT NOUN **Medicine** is the treatment of illness and injuries by doctors and nurses. ❍ *a career in medicine*
2 NOUN a substance that you use to treat or cure an illness ❍ *The medicine saved his life.*

me|dium /mi̲diəm/ (**mediums** or **media**) **ADJ** If something is of **medium** size, it is neither large nor small. ❍ *Many small and medium-sized businesses are outsourcing their IT.*

meet /mi̲t/ (**meets, meeting, met**)
1 VERB If you **meet** someone who you know, you see them by chance and you speak to them. ❍ *I met Shona in town today.*
2 VERB If you **meet** someone who you do not know, you see them and speak to them for the first time. ❍ *I have just met an amazing man.*
3 VERB If two or more people **meet**, they go somewhere because they have planned to be there together. ❍ *We could meet for a game of tennis after work.*
4 VERB If you **meet** someone at a place, you go there and wait for them to arrive. ❍ *A colleague met me at the airport.*
5 VERB The place where two lines **meet** is the place where they join. ❍ *This is the point where the two rivers meet.*
6 NOUN a sports competition ❍ *He never misses swim meets or baseball games.*

meet|ing /mi̲tɪŋ/ **NOUN** an event in which a group of people come together to discuss things or to make decisions [ADMINISTRATION] ❍ *Can we have a meeting to discuss that?*

mega|buck /mɛ̲gəbʌk/ **NOUN** a million dollars [ECONOMICS, INFORMAL] ❍ *I.T. is where the megabucks are coming from.*

mega|byte /mɛ̲gəba̲ɪt/ **NOUN** In computing, a **megabyte** is a unit for measuring information. There are one million bytes in a megabyte. ❍ *The hard drive has 256 megabytes of memory.*

melo|dy /mɛ̲lədi/ (**melodies**) **NOUN** a group of musical notes that sound pleasant together ❍ *a beautiful melody*

mel|on /mɛ̲lən/ **NOUN** a large fruit with soft, sweet flesh and a hard green or yellow skin ❍ *slices of melon*

melt /mɛ̲lt/ **VERB** When a solid substance **melts**, it changes to a liquid because it has become warm. ❍ *The snow melted.* ❍ *Melt the chocolate in a bowl.*

melt|down /mɛ̲ltdaʊn/ **NONCOUNT NOUN** The **meltdown** of a company or system is its sudden and complete failure. ❍ *There have been urgent talks to prevent the market going into financial meltdown.*

mem|ber /mɛ̲mbər/ **NOUN** someone or something that belongs to a group or organization ❍ *Joe is a member of our sales staff.*

mem|ber|ship /mɛ̲mbərʃɪp/
1 NONCOUNT NOUN **Membership** in an organization means being a member of it. ❍ *Employees have free membership at the gym.*
2 NOUN The **membership** of an organization is the people who belong to it. ❍ *The organization has a membership of 409,000.*

memo /mɛ̲moʊ/ **NOUN** a short note that you send to a person who works with you ❍ *He sent a memo to everyone in his department.*

memo|rable /mɛ̲mərəbᵊl/ **ADJ** easy to remember because of being special or very enjoyable ❍ *They created many memorable advertising campaigns.*

me|mo|rial /mɪmɔ̲riəl/ **NOUN** something that you build in order to remind people of a famous person or event ❍ *a memorial to Columbus*

memo|rise /mɛ̲məraɪz/ [BRIT] → **memorize**

memo|rize /mɛ̲məraɪz/ (**memorizes, memorizing, memorized**) VERB If you **memorize** something, you learn it so that you can remember it exactly. ○ *He tried to memorize the sales figures.*

memo|ry /mɛ̲məri/ (**memories**)
1 NONCOUNT NOUN Your **memory** is your ability to remember things. ○ *All the details are clear in my memory.*
2 NOUN something that you remember from the past ○ *happy memories*
3 NOUN A computer's **memory** is the part where it stores information. ○ *The data is stored in the computer's memory.*

me̲mo|ry card (**memory cards**) NOUN a small part that stores information inside a piece of electronic equipment such as a camera

me̲mo|ry stick (**memory sticks**) NOUN a small object for storing computer information that you can carry with you and use in different computers

men /mɛ̲n/ **Men** is the plural of **man**.

M

mend /mɛ̲nd/ VERB If you **mend** something that is broken, you repair it. ○ *He earns money by mending clothes.*

me̲n's room NOUN **The men's room** is a bathroom for men in a public building.

men|tal /mɛ̲ntᵊl/ ADJ relating to the mind ○ *mental illness* • **men|tal|ly** ADV ○ *mentally tired*

mental-he̲alth day (**mental-health days**) NOUN A **mental-health day** is the same as a **personal day**.

men|tion /mɛ̲nʃən/ VERB If you **mention** something, you say something about it, without giving much information. ○ *She mentioned the new contract.*

men|tor /mɛ̲ntɔr/
1 NOUN someone who gives you help and advice about your job over a period of time [HR] ○ *To get your career back on track, seek help from a mentor or a career coach.*
2 VERB To **mentor** someone means to give them help and advice about their job over a period of time. [HR] ○ *He had mentored many younger doctors.*

men|tor|ing /mɛ̲ntərɪŋ/ NONCOUNT NOUN **Mentoring** is a situation where an experienced member of staff helps and advises a more junior member of staff over a period of time. [HR] ○ *There will be a system of mentoring where successful business people will become the applicants' mentors.*

menu /mɛ̲nyu/
1 NOUN a list of the food and drink that you can have in a restaurant ○ *A waiter offered him the menu.*
2 NOUN a list of choices on a computer screen ○ *Press F7 to show the print menu.*

mer|can|tile /mɜ̲rkəntaɪl/ ADJ relating to or involved in trade [ECONOMICS, FORMAL] ○ *the emergence of a new mercantile class*

me̲r|can|tile agen|cy (**mercantile agencies**) NOUN an organization that collects and supplies information about the financial reliability of people and companies [ECONOMICS]

mer|chan|dise /mɜ̲rtʃəndaɪz, -daɪs/ NONCOUNT NOUN **Merchandise** is products that are bought, sold, or traded. [MARKETING AND SALES, FORMAL] ○ *Several stores have reported running out of merchandise.*

mer|chan|dis|er /mɜ̲rtʃəndaɪzər/ NOUN a person or company that sells products to the public [MARKETING AND SALES] ○ *These products were sold by leading U.S. merchandisers.*

mer|chan|dis|ing /mɜ̲rtʃəndaɪzɪŋ/
1 NONCOUNT NOUN **Merchandising** is the way stores and businesses organize the sale of their products, for example the way they are displayed and the prices that are chosen. [MARKETING AND SALES] ○ *The company has lost money every year because of its poor merchandising strategy.*
2 NONCOUNT NOUN **Merchandising** consists of goods that are linked with something such as a movie, sports team, or pop group. [MARKETING AND SALES] ○ *We are selling the full range of World Cup merchandising.*

mer|chant /mɜ̲rtʃənt/
1 NOUN a person who buys or sells goods in large quantities ○ *Any knowledgeable wine merchant would be able to advise you.*

2 NOUN a person who owns or runs a store ○ *The family was forced to live on credit from local merchants.*

3 ADJ Merchant seamen or ships are involved in carrying goods for trade. ○ *There's been a big reduction in the size of the merchant fleet in recent years.*

mer|chant bank [BANKING, BRIT] → **investment bank**

mer|chant bank|er [BANKING, BRIT] → **investment banker**

mer|chant navy or **merchant marine** NONCOUNT NOUN The **merchant navy** is the ships and crew that are involved in a country's commercial shipping.

mer|cy /mɜrsi/ **NONCOUNT NOUN** If someone shows **mercy**, they choose not to harm or punish someone. ○ *His life was now at the mercy of a judge.*

mere /mɪər/ **ADJ** used for saying that something is small or not important ○ *Exports grew by a mere 6.8%.*

mere|ly /mɪərli/ **ADV** used to emphasize that something is only the thing you are describing ○ *What we have here is merely a bailout, not a fix.*

merge /mɜrdʒ/ (**merges, merging, merged**) **VERB** If one thing **merges with** another, or **is merged with** another, they combine to make one whole thing. You can also say that two things **merge**, or **are merged**. [FINANCE] ○ *Bank of America merged with a rival bank.* ○ *The two countries merged into one.*

mer|ger /mɜrdʒər/ **NOUN** the joining together of two separate companies or organizations so that they become one [FINANCE] ○ *a merger between two of America's biggest trade unions*

mess /mɛs/

1 NOUN If something is **a mess**, it is not neat. ○ *After the party, the house was a mess.*

2 NOUN If a situation is **a mess**, it is full of problems. ○ *I've made such a mess of this project.*

▸ **mess around** If you **mess around**, you spend time doing silly things or things with no purpose. ○ *We were just messing around playing with paint.*

▸ **mess up**

1 If you **mess** something **up**, you make something go wrong. [INFORMAL] ○ *This has messed up our plans.*

2 If you **mess up** a place or a thing, you make it dirty or not neat. [INFORMAL] ○ *He didn't want to mess up his neat hair.*

mes|sage /mɛsɪdʒ/ (**messages, messaging, messaged**)

1 NOUN a piece of information that you send to someone ○ *I got messages from friends all over the world.*

2 VERB If you **message** someone, you send them an electronic message using a computer. ○ *I messaged her yesterday but she didn't reply.*

mes|sage board (**message boards**) **NOUN** a system that allows users to send and receive messages on the Internet

mes|sen|ger /mɛsɪndʒər/ **NOUN** a person whose job is to take messages or packages to people ○ *A messenger delivered a large envelope to his office.*

messy /mɛsi/ (**messier, messiest**) **ADJ** dirty or not neat, or making things dirty or not neat ○ *His writing is rather messy.* ○ *She's a terribly messy cook.*

met /mɛt/ **Met** is a form of the verb **meet**.

met|al /mɛtᵊl/ **NOUN Metal** is a hard substance such as iron, steel, or gold. ○ *The tin agreement controlled prices when demand for the metal was strong.*

meta|phor /mɛtəfɔr/ **NOUN** A **metaphor** is a way of describing someone or something by showing how they are like something else. For example, the metaphor "a shining light" describes a person who is very skillful or intelligent. ○ *religious metaphors*

me|ter /mitər/

1 NOUN an instrument that measures and records something ○ *A man came to read the electricity meter.*

2 NOUN A **meter** is a unit for measuring

length. There are 100 centimeters in a meter. ❍ *Storage space should be no less than 6,500 square meters.*

meth|od /mɛθəd/ **NOUN** a particular way of doing something ❍ *teaching methods*

me|tre /mitər/ [BRIT] → **meter 2**

met|ric /mɛtrɪk/ **ADJ** A **metric** measurement is given in meters, grams, or liters. ❍ *the metric system*

mez|za|nine /mɛzənin/ **ADJ** The **mezzanine** stage in a financial process is the intermediate stage. ❍ *Capital stopped going into early-stage deals and went instead into mezzanine financing, the stage before the company went public.*

mice /maɪs/ **Mice** is the plural of **mouse**.

micro|chip /maɪkroʊtʃɪp/ **NOUN** a very small part inside a computer that makes it work

micro|cred|it /maɪkroʊkrɛdɪt/ also **micro-credit NONCOUNT NOUN** **Microcredit** is small loans offered to local businesses, especially in developing countries. [BANKING, ECONOMICS] ❍ *One tool to fight poverty is the use of microcredit loans.*

M

micro|eco|nom|ics /maɪkroʊɛkənɒmɪks, -ikə-/ also **micro-economics NONCOUNT NOUN** **Microeconomics** is the study of small units of economic activity. Compare with **macroeconomics**. [ECONOMICS] ❍ *He has 250 students in his microeconomics module.*
• **micro|eco|nom|ic** /maɪkroʊɛkənɒmɪk, -ik-/ **ADJ** ❍ *a textbook on microeconomic theory*

micro|elec|tron|ics /maɪkroʊɪlɛktrɒnɪks/

The form **microelectronic** is used as a modifier.

NONCOUNT NOUN **Microelectronics** is the branch of electronics that deals with miniature electronic circuits. [TECHNOLOGY]

micro|phone /maɪkrəfoʊn/ **NOUN** a piece of electronic equipment that you use to make sounds louder or to record them onto a machine

micro|scope /maɪkrəskoʊp/ **NOUN** a scientific instrument that makes very small objects look bigger

micro|wave /maɪkroʊweɪv/ **NOUN** an oven that cooks food very quickly using electric waves

mid|day /mɪddeɪ/ **NONCOUNT NOUN** **Midday** is twelve o'clock in the middle of the day. ❍ *At midday everyone had lunch.*

mid|dle /mɪdᵊl/

1 NOUN **The middle of** something is the part of it that is farthest from its edges. ❍ *Howard stood in the middle of the room.*

2 ADJ The **middle** object in a series of objects is the one that has an equal number of objects on each side. ❍ *The middle button of his uniform jacket was missing.*

3 NOUN **The middle of** a period of time is the part between the beginning and the end.
❍ *I woke up in the middle of the night and heard a noise outside.*

mid|dle age NONCOUNT NOUN **Middle age** is the time in your life when you are between the ages of about 40 and 65. ❍ *Men often gain weight in middle age.*

middle-aged ADJ A **middle-aged** person is between the ages of about 40 and 65.
❍ *a middle-aged woman*

mid|dle class (**middle classes**)

1 NOUN **The middle class** or **middle classes** are the people in a society who are not very rich and not very poor, for example business people, doctors, and teachers. ❍ *Most of our clients come from the middle class.*

2 ADJ **Middle class** is also an adjective.
❍ *They live in a very middle class area.*

middle|man /mɪdᵊlmæn/ (**middlemen**)

1 NOUN a person or company that buys things from the people who produce them and sells them to the people who want to buy them [ECONOMICS] ❍ *Why don't they cut out the middleman and let us do it ourselves?*

2 NOUN a person who helps in negotiations between people who do not want to meet each other directly ❍ *The two sides would only meet indirectly, through middlemen.*

mid|dle man|age|ment NONCOUNT NOUN **Middle management** refers to managers who are below the top level of management. [ADMINISTRATION, BUSINESS MANAGEMENT] ❍ *The proportion of women in middle management has risen to 40%.*

mid|night /mɪdnaɪt/ NONCOUNT NOUN **Midnight** is twelve o'clock in the middle of the night. ❍ *It was well after midnight.*

mid|way /mɪdweɪ/
1 ADV If something is **midway between** two places, it is the same distance from each of them. ❍ *The studio is midway between his office and his home.*
2 ADJ **Midway** is also an adjective. ❍ *the midway point between Los Angeles and San Francisco*
3 ADV If something happens **midway through** a period of time, it happens during the middle part of it. ❍ *The index was down 59.72 points midway through the morning session.*

might
❶ MODAL USE
❷ NOUN USE

❶ **might** /maɪt/ MODAL You use **might** when something is possible. ❍ *They indicated that they might accept that bid.* ❍ *Yesterday's dollar weakness might be short-lived.*

❷ **might** /maɪt/ NONCOUNT NOUN **Might** is power or strength. ❍ *I pulled with all my might.*

mighty /maɪti/ (**mightier, mightiest**) ADJ very large or powerful ❍ *The company must fight off some mighty rivals.*

mike /maɪk/ NOUN A **mike** is the same as a **microphone**. [INFORMAL]

mild /maɪld/ (**milder, mildest**) ADJ not very strong or severe ❍ *Analysts are predicting only a relatively mild recession.* ❍ *We like the area because it has very mild winters.*

mile /maɪl/ NOUN A **mile** is a unit for measuring distance. A **mile** is equal to 1.6 kilometers. There are 5,280 feet in a mile. ❍ *They drove 600 miles across the desert.*

mili|tary /mɪlɪtɛri/
1 ADJ relating to the armed forces of a country ❍ *military leaders*
2 NONCOUNT NOUN **The military** are the armed forces of a country. ❍ *The military have said very little about the attacks.*

milk /mɪlk/
1 NONCOUNT NOUN **Milk** is the white liquid that cows and some other animals produce, which people drink. ❍ *He went out to buy a quart of milk.*
2 VERB If someone **milks** a cow or another animal, they take milk from it. ❍ *Farm workers milk the cows in the morning.*

mil|len|nium /mɪlɛniəm/ (**millenniums** or **millennia**) NOUN a period of one thousand years [FORMAL]

mil|li|meter /mɪlɪmitər/ NOUN A **millimeter** is a unit for measuring length. There are ten millimeters in a centimeter. ❍ *The creature is just 10 millimeters long.*

mil|li|metre /mɪlɪmitər/ [BRIT] → **millimeter**

mil|lion /mɪlyən/

The plural form is **million** after a number.

A **million** or one **million** is the number 1,000,000. ❍ *They will receive $32.8 million in financing and advisory fees.*

mil|lion|aire /mɪlyənɛər/ NOUN a person who has more than a million dollars ❍ *He was a millionaire.*

mil|lionth /mɪlyənθ/ ADJ or ADV The **millionth** item in a series is the one you count as number one million. ❍ *Two years into production, the millionth Mustang rolled off the production line.*

mim|ic /mɪmɪk/ (**mimics, mimicking, mimicked**) VERB If you **mimic** the way someone moves or speaks, you copy them in an amusing way. ❍ *He could mimic anybody.*

mind /maɪnd/
1 NOUN Your **mind** is all your thoughts and the way that you think about things. ❍ *She is a bit deaf, but her mind is still sharp.*
2 If you **change** your **mind**, you change a decision or an opinion. ❍ *I was going to vote for him, but I changed my mind.*

3 If you **make up** your **mind**, you decide something. ❍ *He made up his mind to sack Kathy.*
4 If something is **on** your **mind**, you are worried about it and you think about it a lot. ❍ *I don't sleep well. I've got a lot on my mind.*
5 VERB If you do not **mind** something, you do not feel annoyed or upset about it. ❍ *It was hard work but she didn't mind.*
6 VERB If you have a choice, and you say that you do not **mind**, you mean that you are happy to do or have either thing. ❍ *"Would you rather play tennis or baseball?"—"I don't mind."*
7 You say **never mind** when something is not important. ❍ *"He's going to be late."—"Oh, never mind, we'll start the meeting without him."*
8 If you **wouldn't mind** something, you would like it. ❍ *I wouldn't mind a cup of coffee.*

mind|share /maɪndʃeər/ **NONCOUNT NOUN** **Mindshare** refers to how aware consumers are of a particular product. ❍ *This new product has been a great success in achieving mindshare and establishing our brand.*

mine
❶ PRONOUN USE
❷ NOUN AND VERBS USES

❶ **mine** /maɪn/ **PRON** **Mine** means belonging to me. ❍ *That isn't your bag, it's mine.*

❷ **mine** /maɪn/ (**mines, mining, mined**)
1 NOUN a deep hole in the ground from which people dig coal, diamonds, or gold ❍ *The company owns gold and silver mines.*
2 VERB When people **mine**, they dig deep holes and tunnels into the ground to remove coal, diamonds, or gold. ❍ *Diamonds are mined in South Africa.* • **min|er NOUN** ❍ *My father was a miner.*
3 NOUN a bomb that is hidden under the ground

min|er|al /mɪnərəl/ **NOUN** a natural substance such as gold, salt, or coal that comes from the ground

min|er|al wa|ter NONCOUNT NOUN **Mineral water** is water that comes from the ground that contains substances that are good for your health.

minia|ture /mɪniətʃər, -tʃʊər/ **ADJ** very small, or much smaller than usual ❍ *The toy house was filled with miniature chairs and tables.*

mini|mal /mɪnɪməl/ **ADJ** If an effect is **minimal**, it is very small. ❍ *There is minimal risk of inflation.*

mini|mise /mɪnɪmaɪz/ [BRIT] → **minimize**

mini|mize /mɪnɪmaɪz/ (**minimizes, minimizing, minimized**)
1 VERB If you **minimize** something, you make it as small as possible. ❍ *Minimize the window if you're not working in it.*
2 VERB If you **minimize** something harmful or unpleasant, you reduce it as much as possible. ❍ *The government wants to minimize the effects of this legislation on small businesses.*
3 VERB If you **minimize** something, you make it seem less important than it really is. ❍ *I am not minimizing the importance of your work.*

mini|mum /mɪnɪməm/
1 ADJ The **minimum** amount is the smallest amount possible. ❍ *the minimum wage*
2 NOUN **Minimum** is also a noun. ❍ *Investors must put in a minimum of $3,000.*

mini|mum len|ding rate NONCOUNT NOUN The **minimum lending rate** is the lowest interest rate at which a bank will lend money. [BANKING]

mini|mum wage (**minimum wages**) **NOUN** the lowest wage that an employer is allowed to pay an employee [ECONOMICS] ❍ *Some of them earn below the minimum wage.*

min|is|ter /mɪnɪstər/
1 NOUN a religious leader in some types of church ❍ *Thirty priests and ministers attended the meeting.*
2 NOUN a person in charge of a government department ❍ *He was finance minister.*

min|is|try /mɪnɪstri/ (**ministries**) **NOUN** a government department that deals with one particular thing ❍ *the ministry of education*

mi|nor /maɪnər/ **ADJ** not very important or serious ❍ *They made some minor modifications to their product.*

mi|nor|ity /mɪnɔrɪti, maɪ-/ (**minorities**) **NOUN** A **minority** of people or things is fewer than half of them. ❍ *Only a minority of these women go out to work.*

M

mi|nor|ity in|ter|est (**minority interests**) **NOUN** a share held in a subsidiary company by stockholders other than the parent company ❍ *There have been negotiations involving Mr. Rodale's acquisition of a minority interest in the store.*

mint /mɪnt/
1 NONCOUNT NOUN **Mint** is a plant that has leaves with a fresh, strong taste and smell. ❍ *mint tea*
2 NOUN a candy with this flavor

mi|nus /maɪnəs/
1 CONJ You use **minus** when you are taking one number away from another number. ❍ *One minus one is zero.*
2 ADJ You use **minus** before a number or an amount to show that it is less than zero. ❍ *minus 20 degrees F*

minute
❶ NOUN USES
❷ ADJECTIVE USES

❶ **mi|nute** /mɪnɪt/
1 NOUN a unit for measuring time, equal to sixty seconds ❍ *We will have ten minutes for questions at the end.*
2 NOUN a short period of time ❍ *I will give you the full sales figures in a minute.* ❍ *Wait a minute, something is wrong here.*
3 PL NOUN The **minutes** of a meeting are the written records of the things that are discussed at it. [ADMINISTRATION] ❍ *He read the minutes of the last meeting.*

❷ **mi|nute** /maɪnut/ **ADJ** extremely small ❍ *You only need a minute amount of glue.*

mira|cle /mɪrəkᵊl/ **NOUN** a surprising and lucky event that you cannot explain ❍ *It's a miracle that he survived.*

mir|ror /mɪrər/ **NOUN** a flat piece of special glass that you can see yourself in ❍ *Dan looked at himself in the mirror.*

mis|cel|la|neous /mɪsəleɪniəs/ **ADJ** consisting of many different kinds of things or people that are difficult to put into a particular category ❍ *They questioned the rise in the company's miscellaneous expenses.*

mis|er|able /mɪzərəbᵊl/ **ADJ** very unhappy, or making you feel unhappy ❍ *My job was making me miserable.* ❍ *It was a gray, wet, miserable day.* ● **mis|er|ably** /mɪzərəbli/ **ADV** ❍ *"I feel so guilty," Diane said miserably.*

mis|ery /mɪzəri/ **NONCOUNT NOUN** **Misery** is great unhappiness. ❍ *the misery of war*

mis|lead /mɪslid/ (**misleads, misleading, misled**) **VERB** If you **mislead** someone, you make them believe something that is not true. ❍ *The firm's auditors misled investors.*

mis|lead|ing /mɪslidɪŋ/ **ADJ** making you believe something that is not true ❍ *Their advertisements are misleading.*

miss
❶ VERB USES
❷ AS PART OF A WOMAN'S NAME

❶ **miss** /mɪs/ (**misses, missing, missed**)
1 VERB If you **miss** something that you are trying to hit or catch, you do not manage to hit it or catch it. ❍ *His first shot missed the goal completely.*
2 VERB If you **miss** something, you do not notice it. ❍ *What did he say? I missed it.*
3 VERB If you **miss** someone, you feel sad that they are not with you. ❍ *I miss my family terribly.*
4 VERB If you **miss** something, you feel sad because you no longer have it. ❍ *I love my new apartment, but I miss my garden.*
5 VERB If you **miss** an airplane or a train, you arrive too late to get on it. ❍ *He missed the last bus home.*
6 VERB If you **miss** a meeting or an activity, you do not take part in it. ❍ *He missed the meeting because he was in Berlin.*
▸ **miss out** If you **miss out on** something, you do not have the chance take part in it. ❍ *You missed out on all the fun yesterday.*

❷ **Miss** /mɪs/ **NOUN** You use **Miss** in front of the name of a girl or a woman who is not married. [FORMAL] ❍ *It was nice talking to you, Miss Ellis.*

m

mis-sell /mɪss<u>ɛ</u>l/ (**mis-sells, mis-selling, mis-sold**) VERB To **mis-sell** a financial product means to sell it to someone even though you know that it is not suitable for them. [MARKETING AND SALES] ○ *The company has been accused of mis-selling policies to thousands of elderly investors.* ● **mis-selling** NONCOUNT NOUN ○ *the scandal of pensions mis-selling*

mis|sile /m<u>ɪ</u>s^{ə}l/
1 NOUN a weapon that flies through the air and explodes when it hits something ○ *The army fired missiles at the building.*
2 NOUN any object that is thrown as a weapon ○ *They were throwing missiles at the police.*

miss|ing /m<u>ɪ</u>sɪŋ/ ADJ If someone or something is **missing**, you cannot find them. ○ *Police are hunting for the missing girl.*

mis|sion /m<u>ɪ</u>ʃən/ NOUN an important job that someone has to do ○ *He was sent on a mission to North America.*

m<u>i</u>s|sion state|ment (**mission statements**) NOUN a document that states what a company aims to achieve and the kind of service it intends to provide [ADMINISTRATION, BUSINESS MANAGEMENT] ○ *Our mission statement is to be the best design firm in the world.*

M

mist /m<u>ɪ</u>st/ NONCOUNT NOUN **Mist** is a lot of tiny drops of water in the air, that make it difficult to see. ○ *The mist did not lift until midday.* ● **misty** ADJ ○ *Charlie looked across the misty valley.*

mis|take /mɪst<u>eɪ</u>k/ (**mistakes, mistaking, mistook, mistaken**)
1 NOUN something that is not correct ○ *a spelling mistake*
2 If you do something **by mistake**, you do something that you did not want or plan to do. ○ *They gave us the wrong figures by mistake.*
3 VERB If you **mistake** one person **for** another person, you wrongly think that they are the other person. ○ *People are always mistaking Lauren for her sister.*

mis|tak|en /mɪst<u>eɪ</u>kən/ ADJ If you are **mistaken about** something, you are wrong about it. ○ *I think that you must be mistaken—Jackie wouldn't do a thing like that.* ● **mis|tak|en|ly** ADV ○ *Investors may mistakenly assume that the bank is guaranteeing the securities.*

mis|took /mɪst<u>ʊ</u>k/ **Mistook** is a form of the verb **mistake**.

mis|under|stand /m<u>ɪ</u>sʌndərst<u>æ</u>nd/ (**misunderstands, misunderstanding, misunderstood**) VERB If you **misunderstand** someone or something, you do not understand them correctly. ○ *I think you've misunderstood me.*

mis|under|stand|ing /m<u>ɪ</u>sʌndərst<u>æ</u>ndɪŋ/ NOUN a situation where someone does not understand something correctly ○ *Make your plans clear to avoid misunderstandings.*

mix /m<u>ɪ</u>ks/ (**mixes, mixing, mixed**)
1 VERB If you **mix** things, you put different things together. ○ *Mix the sugar with the butter.*
2 VERB If two substances **mix**, they join together. ○ *Oil and water don't mix.*
▸ **mix up** If you **mix up** two things or people, you think that one of them is the other one. ○ *People often mix me up with my brother.*

mixed /m<u>ɪ</u>kst/ ADJ including different types of things or people ○ *a mixed salad*

m<u>i</u>xed ec<u>o</u>no|my (**mixed economies**) NOUN an economic system in which some companies are owned by the state and some are not [ECONOMICS] ○ *Britain is a mixed economy in which both the state and private enterprise are directly involved in the marketing process.*

mix|ture /m<u>ɪ</u>kstʃər/ NOUN a substance that you make by mixing different substances together ○ *The money is a mixture of grants and tax breaks.*

mm **mm** is short for **millimeter** or **millimeters**. ○ *a 135 mm lens*

moan /m<u>oʊ</u>n/
1 VERB If you **moan**, you make a low sound because you are unhappy or in pain. ○ *She was moaning in pain.*
2 NOUN **Moan** is also a noun. ○ *She gave a soft moan.*

mo|bile /moʊbᵊl/
1 ADJ able to move or be moved easily ❍ *a mobile home*
2 NOUN an abbreviation for **mobile phone** [BRIT] ❍ *He left a message on my mobile.*

mo|bile phone (**mobile phones**) [TECHNOLOGY, BRIT] → **cellphone**

mock /mɒk/ **VERB** If you **mock** someone, you laugh at them and try to make them feel foolish. ❍ *My friends mocked me because I didn't have a girlfriend.*

mod|al /moʊdᵊl/ **NOUN** a word such as "can" or "would" that you use with another verb to express ideas such as possibility, intention, or necessity

mode /moʊd/ **NOUN** a particular style or way of doing something [FORMAL] ❍ *It is futile to expect any mode of safe investment to fetch 18 percent of return.* ❍ *the capitalist mode of production*

mod|el /mɒdᵊl/
1 NOUN a small copy of something ❍ *The architects brought a model of the proposed business park.*
2 ADJ Model is also an adjective. ❍ *model aircraft*
3 NOUN a particular design of a vehicle or a machine ❍ *You don't need an expensive computer, just a basic model.*
4 NOUN a person who sits or stands in front of an artist so that they can draw or paint them ❍ *The model for his painting was his sister.*
5 NOUN a person whose job is to wear and show new clothes in photographs and at fashion shows ❍ *a fashion model*
6 VERB If you **model**, you wear clothes as a model. ❍ *Nicole began modeling at age 15.*

mo|dem /moʊdəm, -dɛm/ **NOUN** a piece of equipment that uses a telephone line to connect computers [TECHNOLOGY] ❍ *a cellphone with a built-in modem*

mod|er|ate /mɒdərɪt/ **ADJ** If an amount or level is **moderate**, it is not too much or too little. ❍ *Temperatures are moderate between October and March.* ● **mod|er|ate|ly ADV** ❍ *Prices rose moderately after recent declines.*

mod|ern /mɒdərn/ **ADJ** new or relating to the present time ❍ *We use modern production methods.* ❍ *Modern business trends are likely to make human rights a bigger issue.*

mod|ern|ise /mɒdərnaɪz/ [BRIT] → **modernize**

mod|ern|ize /mɒdərnaɪz/ (**modernizes, modernizing, modernized**) **VERB** To **modernize** a system or a factory means to change it by introducing new equipment, methods, or ideas. ❍ *We need to modernize our factories.*

mod|est /mɒdɪst/ **ADJ** If you are **modest**, you do not talk much about your abilities or success. ❍ *He's modest, as well as being a great player.* ● **mod|est|ly ADV** ❍ *"I was just lucky," Hughes said modestly.*

modi|fy /mɒdɪfaɪ/ (**modifies, modifying, modified**) **VERB** If you **modify** something, you change it slightly in order to improve it. ❍ *They modified the design of the equipment.* ● **modi|fi|ca|tion** /mɒdɪfɪkeɪʃən/ **NOUN** ❍ *They made a few small modifications to the plan.*

moist /mɔɪst/ **ADJ** slightly wet ❍ *The soil was moist after the rain.*

mois|ture /mɔɪstʃər/ **NONCOUNT NOUN** **Moisture** is small drops of water in the air, on a surface, or in the ground. ❍ *Keep the food covered so that it doesn't lose moisture.*

mold /moʊld/
1 NOUN a hollow container that you pour a liquid substance into and leave until it becomes a solid shape ❍ *Pour the mixture into molds and place them in the refrigerator.*
2 VERB If you **mold** a soft substance, you make it into a particular shape. ❍ *The mixture is heated then molded.*
3 NONCOUNT NOUN Mold is a soft gray, green, or blue substance that grows on old food or on damp surfaces. ❍ *There was mold growing in her bedroom closet.*

mol|ecule /mɒlɪkyul/ **NOUN** the smallest amount of a chemical substance that can exist by itself ❍ *hydrogen and oxygen molecules*

mom /mɒm/ **NOUN** Your **mom** is your mother. [INFORMAL] ❍ *We waited for my mom and dad to get home.* ❍ *Bye, Mom. Love you.*

mom and pop store (**mom and pop stores**) NOUN a business that is owned independently and is not part of a chain [MARKETING AND SALES]

mo|ment /moʊmənt/
1 NOUN a very short period of time ❍ *In a moment he was gone.* ❍ *"Please take a seat. Mr. Garcia will see you in a moment."*
2 NOUN A particular **moment** is the time when something happens. ❍ *At that moment a car stopped at the house.*
3 If something is happening **at the moment**, it is happening now. ❍ *No one wants to sell shares at the moment.*

mon|ar|chy /mɒnərki/ (**monarchies**) NOUN A **monarchy** is a system in which a country has a king or a queen. ❍ *Greece abolished the monarchy in 1974.*

Mon|day /mʌndeɪ, -di/ NOUN the day after Sunday and before Tuesday ❍ *I went back to work on Monday.*

mon|etar|ism /mɑnɪtərɪzəm/ NONCOUNT NOUN **Monetarism** is an economic policy that involves controlling the amount of money that is in use in a country. [ECONOMICS] • **mon|etar|ist** NOUN ❍ *This policy, monetarists claim, encourages steady growth and price stability.*

mon|etary /mɑnɪtɛri/ ADJ relating to the total amount of money in a country [ECONOMICS] ❍ *Some countries tighten monetary policy to avoid inflation.*

mon|etary unit (**monetary units**) NOUN a country's standard unit of money [ECONOMICS] ❍ *The dollar was established as the monetary unit of the United States in 1792.*

mon|ey /mʌni/ NONCOUNT NOUN **Money** is the coins or bills that you use to buy things. [ECONOMICS] ❍ *Cars cost a lot of money.*

money|lender /mʌnilɛndər/ NOUN a person who lends money that has to be paid back at a high rate of interest [BANKING]

money-maker NOUN a business or product that makes a lot of money [BANKING] ❍ *This car is the group's biggest money-maker.*

mon|ey mar|ket (**money markets**) NOUN A **money market** is all the organizations in a country that deal with short-term loans, capital, and foreign exchange. Compare with **capital market**. [ECONOMICS] ❍ *On the money markets the dollar was weaker against European currencies.*

mon|ey or|der (**money orders**) NOUN a piece of paper representing a sum of money that you can buy at a post office or a bank and send to someone [BANKING] ❍ *I sent them a money order for $40.*

mon|ey sup|ply NONCOUNT NOUN **The money supply** is the total amount of money in a country's economy at any one time. [ECONOMICS] ❍ *They believed that controlling the money supply would reduce inflation.*

mon|ied /mʌnid/ also **moneyed** ADJ having a lot of money ❍ *A small monied elite can afford these holidays.*

moni|tor /mɒnɪtər/ VERB If you **monitor** something, you regularly check how it is developing or progressing. [BUSINESS MANAGEMENT] ❍ *Our prices are determined by local markets and we monitor prices carefully.*

moni|toring /mɒnɪtərɪŋ/ NONCOUNT NOUN **Monitoring** is the process of checking the development or progress of something. [BUSINESS MANAGEMENT] ❍ *The managers have called for better training and monitoring of staff.*

mon|key /mʌŋki/ NOUN an animal that has a long tail and climbs trees

mo|nopo|lise /mənɒpəlaɪz/ [ECONOMICS, BRIT] → **monopolize**

mo|nopo|lize /mənɒpəlaɪz/ (**monopolizes, monopolizing, monopolized**) VERB If someone **monopolizes** something, they have a very large share of it and prevent other people from having a share. [ECONOMICS] ❍ *They are controlling so much cocoa that they are almost monopolizing the market.* • **mo|nopo|li|za|tion** /mənɒpəlaɪzeɪʃən/ NONCOUNT NOUN ❍ *the monopolization of a market by a single supplier*

mo|nopo|ly /mənɒpəli/ (**monopolies**)
1 NOUN If a company, person, or state has a

M

monopoly on something such as an industry, they have complete control over it, so that it is impossible for others to become involved in it. [ECONOMICS] ❍ *Russia plans to end a state monopoly on land ownership.*
2 NOUN a company that is the only one providing a particular product or service [ECONOMICS] ❍ *a state-owned monopoly*

COLLOCATIONS
a *near* monopoly
to *break* a monopoly
a *virtual* monopoly
to *end* a monopoly

mon|ster /mɒnstər/ **NOUN** a big, frightening creature in stories ❍ *The movie is about a monster in the bedroom closet.*

month /mʌnθ/ **NOUN** one of the twelve parts that a year is divided into ❍ *September is the ninth month of the year.*

month|ly /mʌnθli/
1 ADJ happening or appearing every month ❍ *Monthly payments will be $143.47.*
2 ADV Monthly is also an adverb. ❍ *The magazine is published monthly.*

monu|ment /mɒnyəmənt/ **NOUN** something that you build to help people remember an important event or person ❍ *a monument in memory of the soldiers who died in the war*

mood /mud/ **NOUN** the way you are feeling at a particular time ❍ *Dad is in a very good mood today.*

moo|lah /mulɑ/ **NONCOUNT NOUN Moolah** is money. [ECONOMICS, INFORMAL] ❍ *Is your moolah safe on the Internet?*

moon /mun/ **NOUN The moon** is the large object that shines in the sky at night. ❍ *The first man on the moon was an American, Neil Armstrong.*

moon|light /munlaɪt/ **VERB** If someone **moonlights**, they have a second job in addition to their main job, often without informing their main employers or the tax authorities. ❍ *an engineer who was moonlighting as a taxi driver* ● **moon|lighting NONCOUNT NOUN** ❍ *He was fired for moonlighting.*

mor|al /mɔrᵊl/
1 PL NOUN Your **morals** are your ideas and beliefs about right and wrong behavior. ❍ *Amy has strong morals.*
2 ADJ relating to people's beliefs about what is right or wrong ❍ *We all have a moral duty to stop racism.* ● **mor|al|ly ADV** ❍ *It is morally wrong to kill a person.*

mo|rale /məræl/ **NONCOUNT NOUN Morale** is the amount of confidence and hope that a group of people has. ❍ *Many of the workers are suffering from low morale.*

COLLOCATIONS
low morale
to *boost* morale
staff morale

more /mɔr/
1 ADJ or **PRON** You use **more** to talk about a greater amount of something. ❍ *More people are investing in green technology.* ❍ *We should be doing more to help these people.*
2 ADV More shows that something continues to happen. ❍ *You should talk about your problems more.*
3 More of something means a greater amount of it than before, or than usual. ❍ *They're doing more of their own work.*
4 You use **more than** to talk about a greater amount of something than the amount mentioned. ❍ *The airport had been closed for more than a year.*
5 You can use **more and more** to show that something is becoming greater all the time. ❍ *She began eating more and more.*

more|over /mɔroʊvər/ **ADV** used for adding more information about something [FORMAL] ❍ *They struggled with high production costs. Moreover, the price of raw materials continued to rise.*

morn|ing /mɔrnɪŋ/
1 NOUN the part of each day between the time that people usually wake up and noon ❍ *Tomorrow morning we will visit the production plant.*
2 If you say that something will happen **in the morning**, you mean that it will happen during the morning of the following day. ❍ *I'm flying to St. Louis in the morning.*

mort|gage /mɔrgɪdʒ/
1 NOUN a loan of money that you get from a bank in order to buy a house [BANKING] ❍ *I couldn't afford the mortgage payments.*
2 NOUN the amount of money that you borrow in order to buy a house [BANKING] ❍ *a mortgage of £48,000*
3 NOUN the amount of money that you pay back each month when you have borrowed money to buy a house [BANKING] ❍ *a mortgage of £247 per month*

mort|gage rate (**mortgage rates**) **NOUN** the level of interest that a bank charges people who borrow money to buy a house [BANKING] ❍ *The bank has cut its variable mortgage rate by 0.14%.*

Mos|lem /mʌzlɪm, mʊs-/ → **Muslim**

mosque /mɒsk/ (**mosques**) **NOUN** a building where Muslims go to pray

mos|qui|to /məskitoʊ/ (**mosquitoes** or **mosquitos**) **NOUN** **Mosquitos** are small flying insects that bite people and animals.

M

most /moʊst/
1 used to talk about the largest quantity of people or things ❍ *Most of the workers here are women.* ❍ *I was away from home most of the time.*
2 ADJ or **PRON** used to talk about the largest amount of people or things ❍ *Most people think he is a great actor.* ❍ *Seventeen people were hurt. Most were students.*
3 ADV used to show that something is true or happens more than anything else ❍ *What do you like most about your job?*
4 If you **make the most of** something, you use it in the best possible way. ❍ *You should make the most of what you have if you want to be happy.*

most|ly /moʊstli/ **ADV** used to show that something is almost always true ❍ *Cars are made mostly of metal.*

mo|tel /moʊtɛl/ **NOUN** a hotel for people who are traveling by car

moth /mɔθ/ **NOUN** an insect that has large wings and is attracted by lights at night

moth|er /mʌðər/ **NOUN** Your **mother** is your female parent. ❍ *She's a mother of two children.*

mother-in-law (**mothers-in-law**) **NOUN** the mother of your husband or wife

mo|tion /moʊʃən/ **NONCOUNT NOUN** **Motion** is movement. ❍ *The doors will not open when the elevator is in motion.*

mo|ti|vate /moʊtɪveɪt/ (**motivates, motivating, motivated**) **VERB** If someone **motivates** you to do something, they make you feel determined to do it. [BUSINESS MANAGEMENT] ❍ *How do you motivate people to work hard?* ● **mo|ti|vat|ed ADJ** ❍ *We are looking for a highly motivated professional.*
● **mo|ti|va|tion** /moʊtɪveɪʃən/ **NONCOUNT NOUN** ❍ *His poor performance is caused by lack of motivation.*

COLLOCATIONS
self-motivation
lack of motivation
the motivation *behind* something

mo|tive /moʊtɪv/ **NOUN** a reason for doing something ❍ *They had a strong motive to try to prop up the stock price.*

mo|tor /moʊtər/ **NOUN** the part of a machine that makes it move or work ❍ *She got in the boat and started the motor.*

motor|bike /moʊtərbaɪk/ [mainly BRIT] → **motorcycle**

motor|cycle /moʊtərsaɪkᵊl/ **NOUN** a vehicle with two wheels and an engine

mo|tor|ist /moʊtərɪst/ **NOUN** a person who drives a car ❍ *Motorists should take extra care when it is raining.*

motor|way /moʊtərweɪ/ [BRIT] → **freeway**

mot|to /mɒtoʊ/ (**mottoes** or **mottos**) **NOUN** a short sentence or phrase that gives a rule for sensible behavior ❍ *My motto is "Don't start what you can't finish."*

moun|tain /maʊntᵊn/ **NOUN** a very high area of land with steep sides ❍ *Mt. McKinley is the highest mountain in North America.*

mourn /mɔrn/ **VERB** If you **mourn for** someone who has died, you show your deep sadness. ❍ *He mourned for his dead son.*

mouse /maʊs/ (**mice**)

Mouses is the usual plural form for meaning **2**.

1 NOUN a small animal with a long tail ❍ *The product was tested on rats and mice.*
2 NOUN an object that you move with your hand to do things on a computer without using the keyboard [TECHNOLOGY] ❍ *I clicked the mouse and the message appeared on the screen.*

mouse pad (**mouse pads**) also **mousepad NOUN** a flat piece of soft material that you move a computer mouse on

mous|tache /mʊstæʃ/ [BRIT] → **mustache**

mouth /maʊθ/
1 NOUN Your **mouth** is the part of your face that you use for eating or speaking. ❍ *When you cough, please cover your mouth.*
2 NOUN The **mouth** of a river is the place where it goes into the ocean.

move /muv/ (**moves, moving, moved**)
1 VERB When you **move** something, you put it in a different place. ❍ *A police officer asked him to move his car.*
2 VERB When someone or something **moves**, they change their position or go to a different place. ❍ *The train began to move.* ❍ *She waited for him to get up, but he didn't move.*
3 NOUN Move is also a noun. ❍ *The doctor made a move toward the door.*
4 VERB If you **move**, you go to live in a different place. ❍ *She's moving to Seattle next month.*
5 NOUN Move is also a noun. ❍ *After his move to New York, he got a job as an actor.*
6 VERB If something **moves** you, it makes you have strong emotional feelings. ❍ *The story surprised and moved me.*
7 VERB If you **move** goods, you sell them.
▸**move in** When you **move in** somewhere, you begin to live there. ❍ *A new family has moved in next door.*
▸**move out** If you **move out**, you stop living in a particular place. ❍ *I decided to move out.*

move|ment /muvmənt/
1 NONCOUNT NOUN Movement means changing position, or going from one place to another. ❍ *He has limited movement in his left arm.*
2 NOUN a group of people who have the same beliefs or ideas ❍ *a political movement*

mov|er /muvər/ **Movers and shakers** are the people who have the most power or influence. ❍ *It is the movers and shakers of the record industry who will decide which bands make it.*

movie /muvi/
1 NOUN a story that is shown in a series of moving pictures ❍ *Matton made a movie about Rembrandt.*
2 PL NOUN If you go to **the movies**, you go to see a movie in a movie theater. ❍ *Sam took her to the movies last week.*

movie star (**movie stars**) **NOUN** a famous actor or actress who acts in movies

movie thea|ter (**movie theaters**) **NOUN** a place where people go to watch movies

mov|ing /muvɪŋ/ **ADJ** making you feel a strong emotion such as sadness, pity, or sympathy ❍ *a moving story*

MP3 /ɛm pi θri/ (**MP3s**) **NOUN** a type of computer file that contains music

MP3 play|er (**MP3 players**) **NOUN** a small machine for listening to music that is stored on computer files

m-payment /ɛmpeɪmənt/ **NOUN** a payment made through a wireless device such as a cellphone [E-COMMERCE]

mph also **m.p.h. mph** shows the speed of a vehicle. **mph** is short for "miles per hour." ❍ *On this road, you must not drive faster than 20 mph.*

Mr. /mɪstər/ **NOUN** used before a man's name when you want to be polite or formal ❍ *Could I please speak to Mr. Johnson?*

Mrs. /mɪsɪz/ **NOUN** used before the name of a married woman when you want to be polite or formal ❍ *Hello, Mrs. Morley. How are you?*

Ms. /mɪz/ **NOUN** used before a woman's name, instead of **Mrs.** or **Miss**. ❍ *Ms. Kennedy refused to speak to reporters after the meeting.*

much /mʌtʃ/
1 ADJ or **PRON** You use **much** to talk about the large amount of something. ❍ *They put too much emphasis on advertising brand names.* ❍ *Our workers do not need much supervision.* ❍ *I paid too much.*
2 ADV If something does not happen **much**, it does not happen very often. ❍ *Gwen did not see her father very much.*
3 ADV **Much** means a lot. ❍ *The commercial-computer market is much bigger than the scientific one.* ❍ *Thank you very much.* ❍ *He doesn't like jazz much.*
4 ADJ You use **how much** to ask questions about amounts. ❍ *How much money did you spend?*

mud /mʌd/ **NONCOUNT NOUN** **Mud** is a sticky mixture of earth and water. ❍ *Andy's clothes were covered with mud.*

mud|dy /mʌdi/ (**muddier, muddiest**) **ADJ** covered in mud ❍ *Philip left his muddy boots at the kitchen door.*

mug /mʌg/ (**mugs, mugging, mugged**)
1 NOUN a deep cup with straight sides ❍ *He poured tea into the mugs.*
2 VERB If someone **mugs** you, they attack you and steal your money. ❍ *This guy tried to mug me.* ● **mug|ging NOUN** ❍ *Muggings are unusual in this neighborhood.* ● **mug|ger NOUN** ❍ *The mugger grabbed her purse.*

multi|media /mʌltimidiə/ **NONCOUNT NOUN** **Multimedia** computer programs have sound, pictures, and film, as well as text. ❍ *Most of his teachers use multimedia in the classroom.*

multi|millionaire /mʌltimɪliənɛər/ **NOUN** a very rich person who has money or property worth several million dollars [ECONOMICS] ❍ *He became a multimillionaire in the business of reselling oil.*

multi|na|tion|al /mʌltinæʃənəl/
1 ADJ A **multinational** company has branches in many different countries. [ECONOMICS] ❍ *It is a multinational company with operations in several countries and tens of thousands of employees.*
2 NOUN **Multinational** is also a noun. ❍ *multinationals such as Ford and IBM*

COLLOCATIONS
a multinational *corporation*
a multinational *firm*
a multinational *enterprise*
a multinational *company*

multi|pack /mʌltipæk, mʌltaɪ-/ **NOUN** a package that contains several items of a product and is sold at a lower price than the same number of units sold individually [MARKETING AND SALES] ❍ *You can save money by buying multipacks of chips or chocolate bars.*

multi|ple /mʌltɪpəl/ **ADJ** used for talking about things that consist of many parts, involve many people, or have many uses ❍ *He died of multiple injuries.*

multi|plex (**multiplexes** /mʌltiplɛks/) **NOUN** a movie theater complex with several screens

multi|pli|ca|tion /mʌltɪplɪkeɪʃən/ **NONCOUNT NOUN** **Multiplication** is when you add a number to itself a certain number of times. ❍ *a multiplication sum*

multi|ply /mʌltɪplaɪ/ (**multiplies, multiplying, multiplied**) **VERB** If you **multiply** a number, you add it to itself a certain number of times. ❍ *What do you get if you multiply six by nine?*

multi-skilled /mʌltiskɪld, mʌltaɪ-/ **ADJ** having a number of different skills [HR] ❍ *Employers are seeking multi-skilled graduates.*

multi-skilled work|force (**multi-skilled workforces**) **NOUN** a workforce that has many different skills [HR] ❍ *The importance of a highly trained, multi-skilled workforce is crucial to the survival of the industry.*

multi-skilling /mʌltiskɪlɪŋ, mʌltaɪ-/ **NONCOUNT NOUN** **Multi-skilling** is the practice of training employees to do a number of different tasks. [HR] ❍ *Restructuring will lead to increased multi-skilling among staff.*

multi|story /mʌltistɔri/ also **multistoried ADJ** A **multistory** building has several levels. ❍ *The store is in a big multistory building.*

mum /mʌm/ [BRIT] → **mom**

mum|ble /mʌmbᵊl/ (**mumbles, mumbling, mumbled**) VERB If you **mumble**, you speak quietly and not clearly. ○ *The boy blushed and mumbled a few words.*

mum|my /mʌmi/ (**mummies**) NOUN a dead body that was preserved long ago by being rubbed with special oils and wrapped in cloth ○ *an Ancient Egyptian mummy*

mu|nici|pal /myunɪsɪpᵊl/ ADJ relating to a city or a town and its local government ○ *a municipal building*

mur|der /mɜrdər/
1 NOUN the crime of deliberately killing a person ○ *The jury found him guilty of murder.*
2 VERB If someone **murders** another person, they commit the crime of killing them deliberately. ○ *She murdered her husband.*
● **mur|der|er** /mɜrdərər/ NOUN ○ *One of these men is the murderer.*

mur|mur /mɜrmər/ VERB If you **murmur** something, you say it very quietly. ○ *He turned and murmured something to Karen.*

mus|cle /mʌsᵊl/ NOUN Your **muscles** are the parts inside your body that connect your bones, and that help you to move. ○ *Exercise helps to keep your muscles strong.*

mus|cu|lar /mʌskyələr/ ADJ having strong, firm muscles ○ *Jordan was tall and muscular.*

mu|seum /myuziəm/ NOUN a building where you can look at interesting and valuable objects

mush|room /mʌʃrum/ NOUN a plant with a short stem and a round top that you can eat ○ *wild mushrooms*

mu|sic /myuzɪk/
1 NONCOUNT NOUN **Music** is the pleasant sound that you make when you sing or play instruments. ○ *Diane is studying classical music.*
2 NONCOUNT NOUN **Music** is the symbols that you write on paper to tell people what to sing or play. ○ *He can't read music.*

mu|si|cal /myuzɪkᵊl/
1 ADJ relating to playing or studying music ○ *musical talent*
2 NOUN a play or a movie that uses singing and dancing in the story
3 ADJ having a natural ability and interest in music ○ *I come from a musical family.*

mu|si|cal in|stru|ment (**musical instruments**) NOUN an object such as a piano or a violin that you play in order to produce music ○ *The drum is one of the oldest musical instruments.*

mu|si|cian /myuzɪʃən/ NOUN a person who plays a musical instrument ○ *Michael is a brilliant musician.*

Mus|lim /mʌzlɪm, muzlɪm/
1 NOUN someone who believes in the religion of Islam and lives according to its rules
2 ADJ relating to Islam or Muslims ○ *an ancient Muslim mosque*

must /məst, STRONG mʌst/
1 MODAL used for showing that you think something is very important or necessary ○ *Cutbacks must be made in factory subsidies.* ○ *Managers must take action to achieve results.*
2 MODAL used for showing that you are almost sure that something is true ○ *Claire's car isn't there, so she must be at work.*

mus|tache /mʌstæʃ/ NOUN the hair that grows on a man's upper lip ○ *David has a black mustache and beard.*

mus|tard /mʌstərd/ NONCOUNT NOUN **Mustard** is a spicy yellow or brown sauce that you eat with meat. ○ *roast beef and mustard*

mustn't /mʌsᵊnt/ **Mustn't** is short for "must not."

must've /mʌstəv/ **Must've** is short for "must have."

mut|ter /mʌtər/ VERB If you **mutter**, you speak in quiet, often angry way. ○ *"He's crazy," she muttered.*

mu|tu|al /myutʃuəl/
1 ADJ If a feeling or an action is **mutual**, it is felt or done by two people or groups. ○ *a mutual decision* ○ *The East and the West can work together for their mutual benefit and progress.*
● **mu|tu|al|ly** ADV ○ *A meeting would take place at a mutually convenient time.*
2 ADJ If a savings and loan association or an insurance company has **mutual** status, it is

owned by its customers. [BRIT] ❍ *Britain's third-largest savings and loan association abandoned its mutual status and became a bank.*

mu|tu|al fund (**mutual funds**) NOUN an organization that invests money in many different kinds of business and sells units to the public [BANKING]

mu|tu|al in|sur|ance NONCOUNT NOUN **Mutual insurance** is a system of insurance in which policyholders are company members. [BANKING] ❍ *a mutual insurance company*

mu|tu|al|ise /myutʃuəlaɪz/ [BANKING, ECONOMICS, BRIT] → **mutualize**

mu|tu|al|ize /myutʃuəlaɪz/ (**mutualizes, mutualizing, mutualized**) VERB If a business **is mutualized**, it is organized so that customers or employees own a majority of shares. [BANKING, ECONOMICS]

mu|tu|al sav|ings bank (**mutual savings banks**) NOUN a savings bank that is owned by its customers [BANKING]

M

my /maɪ/ ADJ You use **my** to show that something belongs or relates to yourself. ❍ *We can eat at my apartment tonight.*

my|self /maɪsɛlf/

1 PRON used when the person speaking or writing is both the subject and the object of the verb ❍ *I asked myself what I should do.*

2 PRON used for saying that you do something alone without help from anyone else ❍ *"Where did you get that dress?"—"I made it myself."*

mys|teri|ous /mɪstɪəriəs/ ADJ strange and not understood ❍ *A mysterious illness made him sick.* ● **mys|teri|ous|ly** ADV ❍ *The evidence mysteriously disappeared.*

mys|tery /mɪstəri, mɪstri/ (**mysteries**)

1 NOUN something that you cannot explain or understand ❍ *Why he behaved in this way is a mystery.*

2 NOUN a story or a movie about a crime or strange events that are only explained at the end ❍ *a murder mystery*

myth /mɪθ/

1 NOUN an ancient story about gods and magic

2 NOUN If a belief or an explanation is a **myth**, it is not true. ❍ *This story is a myth.*

Nn

NAFTA /næftə/ NONCOUNT NOUN **NAFTA** is the abbreviation for **North American Free Trade Agreement**. [ECONOMICS]

nail /neɪl/
1 NOUN a thin, pointed piece of metal that you hit with a hammer in order to fasten things such as pieces of wood together ❍ *A mirror hung on a nail above the sink.*
2 VERB If you **nail** something somewhere, you fasten it there using nails. ❍ *A sign was nailed to the gate.*
3 NOUN one of the thin, hard parts that grow at the end of your fingers and toes ❍ *Try to keep your nails short.*

nai|ra /naɪrə/ NOUN the unit of money used in Nigeria [ECONOMICS]

na|ive /naɪiv/ also **naïve** ADJ If someone is **naive**, they do not have a lot of experience of the world. ❍ *I was naive to think they would agree.*

na|ked /neɪkɪd/ ADJ not wearing any clothes ❍ *She held the naked baby in her arms.*

name /neɪm/ (**names, naming, named**)
1 NOUN a word that you use to show who or what you are talking about ❍ *"What's his name?"—"Peter."* ❍ *They changed the name of the company.*
2 VERB When you **name** someone or something, you give them a name. ❍ *The most important decision you will ever make is what to name your product.*

nan|ny /næni/ (**nannies**) NOUN a person whose job is to take care of children

nap /næp/ NOUN a short sleep, usually during the day ❍ *We had a nap after lunch.*

nap|kin /næpkɪn/ NOUN a square of cloth or paper that you use when you are eating to protect your clothes

nar|ra|tor /næreɪtər/ NOUN the person who tells the story in a book or a movie

nar|row /nærou/ (**narrower, narrowest**) ADJ Something that is **narrow** is a small distance from one side to the other. ❍ *narrow streets*

NASDAQ /næzdæk/ NONCOUNT NOUN The **NASDAQ** is a stock exchange on which many technology companies are listed. **NASDAQ** is short for "National Association of Securities Dealers Automated Quotations System." [ECONOMICS]

nas|ty /næsti/ (**nastier, nastiest**) ADJ very unpleasant ❍ *a nasty surprise* ❍ *The consequences of cutting costs can be nasty.*

na|tion /neɪʃən/ NOUN an individual country ❍ *the United States and other nations*

na|tion|al /næʃənᵊl/
1 ADJ relating to the whole of a country ❍ *the national newspapers*
2 ADJ typical of a particular country ❍ *Baseball is the national pastime.*

na|tion|al a|gree|ment (**national agreements**) NOUN a nationwide agreement between a labor union and a company about terms and conditions of employment

na|tion|al bank (**national banks**) also **National Bank**
1 NOUN In the United States, a **national bank** is a commercial bank established under a Federal charter. National banks are legally required to be members of the Federal Reserve System. Compare with **state bank**. [BANKING] ❍ *First National Bank of Chicago*
2 NOUN a bank which is owned and operated by a government [BANKING] ❍ *the National Bank of Greece*

na|tion|al debt [ECONOMICS, BRIT]
→ **public debt**

na|tion|al holi|day (**national holidays**) NOUN a day when people do not go to work or to school, in order to celebrate a special event

na|tion|al in|sur|ance NONCOUNT NOUN In Britain, **national insurance** is the government system of collecting money from workers and employers and making payments to people who are sick, unemployed, or retired. Compare with **social security**. [BANKING]

na|tion|al|ise /næʃənᵊlaɪz/ [BRIT] → **nationalize**

na|tion|al|ity /næʃənælɪti/ (**nationalities**) NOUN If you have the **nationality** of a particular country, you are a legal citizen of that country. ❍ *I'm not sure of her nationality, but I think she's Canadian.*

na|tion|al|ize /næʃənᵊlaɪz/ (**nationalizes, nationalizing, nationalized**) VERB If a government **nationalizes** a private company or industry, that company or industry becomes owned by the state and controlled by the government. [ECONOMICS] ❍ *In 1987, Garcia introduced legislation to nationalize Peru's banking and financial systems.*
● **na|tion|ali|za|tion** /næʃənᵊlɪzeɪʃən/ NONCOUNT NOUN ❍ *a campaign for the nationalization of the coal mines*

Na|tion|al Sav|ings and In|vest|ments NOUN In Britain, **National Savings and Investments** is a government-owned savings bank that offers most of its services at post offices. [BANKING]

nation|wide /neɪʃənwaɪd/ ADJ happening or existing in all parts of a country ❍ *Car crime is a nationwide problem.* ❍ *a nationwide network of wholesalers*

na|tive /neɪtɪv/
1 ADJ Your **native** country, region, or town is where you were born.
2 NOUN A **native of** a particular place is someone who was born there. ❍ *Dr. Aubin is a native of St. Louis.*
3 ADJ Your **native** language is the first language that you learned to speak. ❍ *Her native language was Swedish.*

natu|ral /nætʃərəl, nætʃrəl/
1 ADJ normal ❍ *It is natural for investors to want questions answered before they make business choices.*
2 ADJ **Natural** things exist in nature and were not created by people. ❍ *Natural resources account for most of the country's exports.*
● **natu|ral|ly** ADV ❍ *a protein which occurs naturally in the human body*

natu|ral|ly /nætʃərəli, nætʃrəli/ ADV used for showing that something is not surprising ❍ *When things go wrong, we naturally feel disappointed.*

natu|ral re|sources PL NOUN **Natural resources** are all the land, energy sources, and minerals existing naturally in a place that can be used by people. [ECONOMICS] ❍ *The country is rich in natural resources.*

natu|ral wast|age NONCOUNT NOUN [HR, mainly BRIT] → **attrition**

na|ture /neɪtʃər/
1 NONCOUNT NOUN **Nature** is all the animals, plants, and other things in the world that are not made by people. ❍ *the relationship between humans and nature*
2 NOUN Someone's **nature** is their character. ❍ *She has a friendly nature.*

naugh|ty /nɔti/ (**naughtier, naughtiest**) ADJ A **naughty** child behaves badly. ❍ *He spoke to me as if I was a naughty child.*

nau|sea /nɔziə, -ʒə, -siə, -ʃə/ NONCOUNT NOUN **Nausea** is a feeling that you are going to vomit. ❍ *The symptoms include headaches and nausea.*

NAV /næv/ NOUN **NAV** is an abbreviation for **net asset value**. [FINANCE]

navi|gate /nævɪgeɪt/ (**navigates, navigating, navigated**)
1 VERB You **navigate** when you find the direction that you need to travel in, using a map or the sun, for example. ❍ *We navigated using the sun.*
2 VERB If you **navigate** a website, you move around it to find the information you need. ❍ *The site is easy to navigate.* ● **navi|ga|tion** /nævɪgeɪʃən/ NONCOUNT NOUN ❍ *navigation lights*

navy /neɪvi/ (**navies**) **NOUN** A country's **navy** is the military force that can fight at sea, and the ships they use. ❍ *Alfred was in the navy for thirty years.*

near /nɪər/

1 PREP If something is **near** a place, a thing, or a person, it is a short distance from them. ❍ *I sat near the door.* ❍ *Our headquarters are near the station in Edmonton.*

2 If something will happen **in the near future**, it will happen very soon. ❍ *I hope I'll be able to meet her sometime in the near future.*

near|by /nɪərbaɪ/

1 ADV a short distance away ❍ *The new airport will have a serious effect on people living nearby.*

2 ADJ **Nearby** is also an adjective. ❍ *He sat at a nearby table.*

near|ly /nɪərli/ **ADV** not completely but almost ❍ *He has worked for the company for nearly 20 years.* ❍ *I've nearly finished.*

near mon|ey **NONCOUNT NOUN** **Near money** is assets that can be sold quickly to get cash. [FINANCE, ECONOMICS, mainly BRIT]

near-sighted **ADJ** Someone who is **near-sighted** cannot clearly see things that are far away.

neat /nit/

1 ADJ well organized, with everything in the correct place ❍ *The office was clean and neat.* ● **neat|ly** **ADV** ❍ *He folded his newspaper neatly.*

2 ADJ If you say that someone or something is **neat**, you mean that you like them a lot. [INFORMAL] ❍ *He thought Mike was a really neat guy.*

nec|es|sary /nɛsɪsɛri/ **ADJ** needed ❍ *I'm sure I've got the necessary skills for this job.*

ne|ces|sity /nɪsɛsɪti/ (**necessities**) **NOUN** **Necessities** are things that you must have to live. ❍ *Water is a basic necessity of life.*

neck /nɛk/ **NOUN** the part of your body between your head and the rest of your body

neck|lace /nɛklɪs/ **NOUN** a piece of jewelry that you wear around your neck ❍ *She was wearing a diamond necklace.*

need /nid/

1 VERB If you **need** something, you must have it. ❍ *He desperately needed money.*

2 VERB If you **need to** do something, you must do it. ❍ *I need to make a phone call.* ❍ *The company needs to cut costs.*

3 NOUN If there is a **need for** something, it is necessary to have or to do that thing. ❍ *There is a growing need for faster PCs.*

4 NOUN Your **needs** are the things that are necessary for you to live or to succeed in life. ❍ *physical and emotional needs*

nee|dle /nidᵊl/

1 NOUN a small, thin metal tool with a sharp point that you use for sewing ❍ *a needle and thread*

2 NOUN a thin hollow metal tube with a sharp point that is used for putting a drug into someone's body ❍ *Dirty needles spread disease.*

3 NOUN the long strip of metal or plastic that shows a measurement on an instrument that measures something such as speed or weight ❍ *The needle is pointing to 200 degrees.*

need|less /nidlɪs/ **ADJ** not necessary ❍ *We want to avoid needless paperwork.* ● **need|less|ly** **ADV** ❍ *The whole plan seems to be needlessly expensive.*

needy /nidi/ (**needier, neediest**)

1 ADJ **Needy** people do not have enough money. ❍ *housing for needy families*

2 PL NOUN **The needy** are people who are needy. ❍ *We are trying to get food to the needy.*

> **BUSINESS ETIQUETTE**
> In France, cultural and intellectual interests are admired. Gifts relating to music and literature are well received.

nega|tive /nɛgətɪv/

1 ADJ unpleasant or harmful ❍ *the negative impact of inflation*

2 ADJ If someone is **negative** they consider only the bad parts of a situation. ❍ *Don't be so negative.* ● **nega|tive|ly** **ADV** ❍ *Why do so many people think negatively?*

3 ADJ A **negative** reply or decision is the answer "no." ❍ *Dr. Velayati gave a negative response.* ● **nega|tive|ly** **ADV** ❍ *Sixty percent of*

people answered negatively.
4 ADJ A **negative** number is less than zero. Compare with **positive**.
5 ADJ In grammar, a **negative** form or word expresses the meaning "no" or "not." For example, "don't" and "haven't" are negative forms.

neg|a|tive equi|ty NONCOUNT NOUN If someone who has borrowed money to buy a house has **negative equity**, the amount of money they owe is greater than the present value of their home. [ECONOMICS] ❍ *Some investors were deeply in debt, the victims of negative equity.*

neg|a|tive prof|it (**negative profits**) NOUN a financial loss [FINANCE]

ne|glect /nɪglɛkt/
1 VERB If you **neglect** someone or something, you do not take care of them. ❍ *The neighbors claim that she is neglecting her children.*
2 NONCOUNT NOUN Neglect is also a noun. ❍ *The house is being repaired after years of neglect.*

ne|go|tiable /nɪgoʊʃiəbᵊl, -ʃəbᵊl/
1 ADJ able to be talked about before reaching an agreement or decision ❍ *He warned that his economic program for the country was not negotiable.*
2 ADJ A **negotiable** asset is able to be transferred legally from one owner to another. ❍ *negotiable securities*

COLLOCATIONS
negotiable *certificates of deposit*
negotiable *bonds*
negotiable *currency*

ne|go|tiable in|stru|ment (**negotiable instruments**) NOUN a legal document, such as a check, that can be transferred legally from one owner to another [BANKING]

ne|go|ti|ate /nɪgoʊʃieɪt/ (**negotiates, negotiating, negotiated**) VERB If people **negotiate with** each other, they talk about a problem or a situation in order to reach an agreement. [BUSINESS MANAGEMENT] ❍ *He is willing to negotiate with the Democrats.*

ne|go|tia|tion /nɪgoʊʃieɪʃən/ NOUN **Negotiations** are discussions between people, during which they try to reach an agreement. ❍ *The negotiations were successful.*

neigh|bor /neɪbər/ NOUN a person who lives near you ❍ *Sometimes we invite the neighbors over for dinner.*

neigh|bor|hood /neɪbərhʊd/ NOUN one of the parts of a town where people live ❍ *He's from a rich Los Angeles neighborhood.*

neigh|bour /neɪbər/ [BRIT] → **neighbor**

neigh|bour|hood /neɪbərhʊd/ [BRIT] → **neighborhood**

nei|ther /niðər, naɪ-/
1 ADJ not one or the other of two things or people ❍ *Neither company would benefit from a merger.*
2 Neither of means not one or the other of two things or people. ❍ *Neither of us felt like going out.*
3 You use **neither…nor…** when you are talking about two or more things that are not true or that do not happen. ❍ *Professor Hisamatsu spoke neither English nor German.*
4 ADV also not ❍ *I hadn't read the report and neither had they.*

neo|lib|er|al|ism /nioʊlɪbərəlɪzəm, -lɪbrə-/ NONCOUNT NOUN **Neoliberalism** is a theory that favors free trade, reduced government interference in business, and reduced government spending [ECONOMICS]
● **neoliberal** NOUN ❍ *Conservative support for this simple proposition still is a mystery to neoliberals.*

neph|ew /nɛfyu/ NOUN the son of your sister or brother

nerve /nɜrv/
1 NOUN one of the long thin threads in your body that send messages between your brain and other parts of your body ❍ *pain from a damaged nerve*
2 PL NOUN Someone's **nerves** are their feelings of worry or fear. ❍ *Before a presentation, take deep breaths to calm your nerves.*
3 If someone or something **gets on** your **nerves**, they annoy you. [INFORMAL] ❍ *The constant interruptions were getting on his nerves.*

nerv|ous /nɜrvəs/ **ADJ** frightened or worried ❍ *I was very nervous during the job interview.* ● **nerv|ous|ly** **ADV** ❍ *Beth stood up nervously when her boss came into the room.* ● **nerv|ous|ness** **NONCOUNT NOUN** ❍ *I smiled warmly so he wouldn't see my nervousness.*

nest /nɛst/ **NOUN** the place where a bird, a small animal, or an insect keeps its eggs or its babies

net /nɛt/
1 ADJ The **net** amount of something is the amount that remains after subtracting taxes, expenses, losses, and costs. Compare with **gross**. → also **net profit**
2 ADJ The **net** weight of something is its weight without its wrapping or container. ❍ *the net weight of a can of beans*
3 NONCOUNT NOUN **Net** is a material made of threads or wire with spaces in between.
4 NOUN a piece of net that you use for a particular purpose ❍ *a fishing net*
5 NONCOUNT NOUN **The Net** is the same as the **Internet**. ❍ *We've been on the Net since 1993.*

COLLOCATIONS
net *income*
net *assets*
net *earnings*

net as|set value (**net asset values**) **NOUN** the total value of a company's assets, after subtracting any money it still owes [FINANCE] ❍ *It is not just the net asset value that determines the valuation of your company; factors such as goodwill are also considered.*

net do|mes|tic prod|uct **NONCOUNT NOUN** The **net domestic product** is the value of all goods and services produced by a country in one year, after subtracting the depreciation of its capital goods. It does not include payments on foreign investments. Compare with **net national product** and **gross domestic product**. [ECONOMICS]

net na|tion|al prod|uct **NONCOUNT NOUN** The **net national product** is the value of all goods and services produced by a country in one year, after subtracting the depreciation of its capital goods. It includes payments on foreign investments. Compare with **net domestic product** and **gross national product**. [ECONOMICS]

net pres|ent value (**net present values**) **NOUN** The **net present value** of an investment is all the income it can be expected to produce minus all the costs. If the **net present value** is above zero, the investment is likely to be profitable. The abbreviation **NPV** is also used. [FINANCE] ❍ *Losses or negative returns must get subtracted from future profits or gains to calculate the net present value of the company to investors.*

net prof|it (**net profits**) **NOUN** A company's **net profit** is its profit after subtracting all costs. Compare with **gross profit**. [FINANCE]

net re|al|iz|able value /nɛt riəlaɪzəbəl vælyu/ (**net realizable values**) **NOUN** the value of an asset if it is sold, after subtracting all the costs connected with the sale [FINANCE]

net|work /nɛtwɜrk/
1 NOUN a company that broadcasts television or radio programs in a particular area ❍ *a local TV network*
2 NOUN a large number of people or things that have a connection with each other and that work together [BUSINESS MANAGEMENT] ❍ *a network of business consultants* ❍ *a wireless network*

net|work|ing /nɛtwɜrkɪŋ/ **NONCOUNT NOUN** **Networking** is the process of trying to meet new people who might be useful to you in your job, often through social activities. [BUSINESS MANAGEMENT] ❍ *If executives fail to exploit the opportunities of networking they risk being left behind.*

neuro|mar|ket|ing /nʊəroʊmɑrkɪtɪŋ/ **NONCOUNT NOUN** **Neuromarketing** is the process of researching the brain patterns of consumers in order to discover their responses to particular advertisements and products. [MARKETING AND SALES] ❍ *Neuromarketing can help companies find out more about our shopping decisions.*

neu|tral /nutrəl/
1 ADJ A **neutral** person or country does not

support either side in an argument or a war. ❍ *Let's meet on neutral territory.*

2 ADJ If you have a **neutral** expression or a **neutral** voice, you do not show what you are thinking or feeling.

3 NONCOUNT NOUN **Neutral** is the position between the gears of a vehicle, in which the gears are not connected to the engine. ❍ *She put the truck in neutral and started it again.*

nev|er /nɛvər/ ADV at no time ❍ *I have never been abroad before.* ❍ *That was a mistake. I'll never do it again.*

never|the|less /nɛvərðəlɛs/ ADV used for saying that although one thing is true, something else is also true [FORMAL] ❍ *The report showed a drop in productivity. Nevertheless, managers are optimistic about the next quarter.*

new /nu/

1 ADJ recently made or invented ❍ *They've just opened a new hotel.* ❍ *These ideas are not new.*

2 ADJ not used or owned by anyone before ❍ *New cars are expensive, and many people are buying used ones instead.*

3 ADJ different ❍ *I'm looking for a new job.*

N

new|born /nubɔrn/ ADJ A **newborn** baby or animal has just been born.

new is|sue (**new issues**) NOUN a security that is being offered to the public for the first time [ECONOMICS] ❍ *Prices on new issues tend to vary less from dealer to dealer than do prices on older bonds.*

new|ly /nuli/ ADV used for showing that an action or a situation is very recent ❍ *a newly formed company*

new mar|ket (**new markets**) NOUN a group of people that has not previously bought a company's products ❍ *The lack of national boundaries on the Internet offers a huge opportunity to reach new markets.*

COLLOCATIONS

to *open up* new markets
to *break into* new markets
to *expand into* new markets
to *move into* new markets
to *find* new markets
to *develop* new markets

news /nuz/

1 NONCOUNT NOUN **News** is information about recent events. ❍ *I've just had some bad news.*

2 NONCOUNT NOUN **News** is information about recent events that is reported in newspapers, or on the radio, television, or Internet. ❍ *Here are some of the top stories in the news.*

news|letter /nuzlɛtər/ NOUN a report giving information about an organization that is sent regularly to its members ❍ *All members receive a free monthly newsletter.*

new sol /nu sɒl/ NOUN the unit of money used in Peru [ECONOMICS]

news|paper /nuzpeɪpər, nus-/ NOUN a number of large sheets of folded paper with news, advertisements, and other information printed on them ❍ *They read about it in the newspaper.*

New Year's Day NONCOUNT NOUN **New Year's Day** is the time when people celebrate the start of a year.

New Year's Eve NONCOUNT NOUN **New Year's Eve** is the day before New Year's Day. ❍ *a New Year's Eve party*

next /nɛkst/

1 ADJ The **next** thing, person, or event is the one that comes immediately after this one or after the one before. ❍ *I got up early the next morning.* ❍ *Who will be the next chairman?*

2 ADJ used for talking about the first day, week, or year that comes after this one or the one before ❍ *Let's meet again next week to discuss these issues.* ❍ *He retires next January.*

3 ADJ **The next** place is the one that is nearest to you. ❍ *There was a meeting going on in the next room.*

4 ADV The thing that happens **next** is the thing that happens immediately after something else. ❍ *I don't know what to do next.*

5 If one thing is **next to** another, it is at the side of it. ❍ *She sat down next to him.*

nib|ble /nɪbəl/ (**nibbles, nibbling, nibbled**) VERB If you **nibble** food, you eat it by biting very small pieces of it. ❍ *She nibbled at a piece of bread.*

nice /naɪs/ (**nicer, nicest**) ADJ attractive, pleasant, or enjoyable ❍ *The chocolate-chip cookies were nice.* ❍ *It's nice to see you again.* ❍ *They were extremely nice to me.* ● **nice|ly** ADV ❍ *The book is nicely illustrated.*

niche /nɪtʃ, niʃ/
1 NOUN a specific area of marketing which has its own particular requirements, customers, and products [MARKETING AND SALES] ❍ *Domestic firms that understand their customers and identify profitable niches can still prosper.*
2 NOUN Your **niche** is the job or activity which is exactly suitable for you. ❍ *He quickly found his niche as a busy freelance editor.*

niche mar|ket (**niche markets**) NOUN a specialized area for which particular products are made [MARKETING AND SALES] ❍ *In soft drink niche markets, being second is being nowhere.*

niche mar|ket|ing NONCOUNT NOUN **Niche** marketing is the practice of dividing the market into specialized areas for which particular products are made. ❍ *Many media experts see such all-news channels as part of a general move towards niche marketing.*

nick|el /nɪkᵊl/
1 NONCOUNT NOUN **Nickel** is a silver-colored metal that is used in making steel.
2 NOUN In the United States and Canada, a **nickel** is a coin worth five cents. [ECONOMICS] ❍ *a large glass jar filled with pennies, nickels, dimes, and quarters*

nick|name /nɪkneɪm/ NOUN an informal name for someone or something ❍ *Red got his nickname for his red hair.*

niece /nis/ NOUN the daughter of your sister or brother ❍ *He bought a present for his niece.*

night /naɪt/
1 NOUN the time when it is dark outside, and most people sleep ❍ *The rain continued all night.* ❍ *It was a dark, cold night.*
2 NOUN the period of time between the end of the afternoon and the time that you go to bed ❍ *Did you work late last night?*

night|club /naɪtklʌb/ NOUN a place where people go late in the evening to drink and dance

night|ly /naɪtli/
1 ADJ A **nightly** event happens every night. ❍ *We watched the nightly news.*
2 ADV **Nightly** is also an adverb. ❍ *She appears nightly on the television news.*

night|mare /naɪtmɛər/
1 NOUN a very frightening dream ❍ *She had nightmares for weeks after seeing that movie.*
2 NOUN a very unpleasant situation ❍ *New York traffic is a nightmare.*

night safe (**night safes**) NOUN a safe that is built into the outside wall of a bank, in which customers can deposit money at times when the bank is closed [BANKING]

night shift (**night shifts**)
1 NOUN the group of workers that work during the night in a factory or other business [HR]
2 NOUN the period of time that these workers work [HR]

NIH syn|drome /ɛn aɪ eɪtʃ sɪndroʊm/ NONCOUNT NOUN **NIH syndrome** is an abbreviation for **not-invented-here syndrome**.

Nik|kei Stock Av|er|age /nikeɪ stɒk ævərɪdʒ, ævrɪdʒ/ NONCOUNT NOUN **The Nikkei Stock Average** is an index of prices on the Tokyo Stock Exchange. [ECONOMICS]

nil /nɪl/
1 NONCOUNT NOUN If something **is nil**, it does not exist at all. ❍ *Their legal rights are almost nil.*
2 In sports scores, **nil** means "zero." [BRIT] ❍ *They lost two nil to Italy.*

nine /naɪn/
1 the number 9
2 If you work **nine to five**, you work normal office hours. ❍ *He works nine to five.* ❍ *a nine to five job*

nine|teen /naɪntin/ the number 19 ❍ *He was a senior manager for nineteen years.*

nine|teenth /naɪntinθ/ ADJ or ADV The **nineteenth** item in a series is the one that you count as number nineteen. ❍ *The museum was built in the late nineteenth century*

nine|ti|eth /naɪntiɪθ/ ADJ or ADV The **ninetieth** item in a series is the one that you

n

count as number ninety. ❍ *He celebrates his ninetieth birthday on Friday.*

nine-to-five job **(nine-to-five jobs)** NOUN a job in which the working day lasts from nine o'clock in the morning to five o'clock in the evening [HR]

nine|ty /naɪnti/ the number 90

ninth /naɪnθ/

1 ADJ or ADV The **ninth** item in a series is the one that you count as number nine. ❍ *January the ninth* ❍ *the ninth largest bank in the world*

2 NOUN one of nine equal parts of something (⅑) ❍ *The area covers one-ninth of the Earth's surface.*

no /noʊ/

1 used for giving a negative response to a question ❍ *"Are you having any problems?"—"No, I'm O.K."* ❍ *"Would you like another coffee?"—"No thanks, I've had enough."*

2 EXCLAM used when you are shocked or disappointed about something ❍ *Oh no, not again.*

3 ADJ not any or not one person or thing ❍ *There are no plans to change management.*

4 ADJ used in notices to say that something is not allowed ❍ *no parking*

No. **(Nos)** **No.** is short for **number**. ❍ *It was named the nation's No.1 car rental company.*

no|body /noʊbɒdi, -bʌdi/ PRON not a single person ❍ *For a long time nobody spoke.*

no-claims bo|nus or **no-claim bonus** **(no-claims bonuses)** NOUN a reduction on an insurance premium if no claims have been made within a specified period of time [BANKING, BRIT] ❍ *As for retail customers, they are happy paying more for their car insurance while building a no-claims bonus.*

nod /nɒd/ **(nods, nodding, nodded)**

1 VERB If you **nod**, you move your head downward and upward to show that you agree. ❍ *"Are you okay?" I asked. She nodded and smiled.*

2 NOUN **Nod** is also a noun. ❍ *She gave a nod and said, "I see."*

no-frills ADJ offering only the most basic features or services ❍ *The airline specializes in no-frills, low-cost flights over short distances.*

noise /nɔɪz/

1 NONCOUNT NOUN **Noise** is loud sound. ❍ *People are concerned about the increase in noise and air pollution.*

2 NOUN a sound that someone or something makes ❍ *a noise like thunder*

noisy /nɔɪzi/ **(noisier, noisiest)** ADJ making a lot of noise or full of noise ❍ *It was a car with a particularly noisy engine.* ❍ *The airport was crowded and noisy.* • **noisi|ly** ADV ❍ *The students cheered noisily.*

nom|inal value /nɒmənᵊl vælyu/ NONCOUNT NOUN [ECONOMICS] → **par value**

nomi|nate /nɒmɪneɪt/ **(nominates, nominating, nominated)** VERB If you **nominate** someone, you formally suggest their name for a job, a position, or a prize. ❍ *He was nominated for the presidency.*

nomi|na|tion /nɒmɪneɪʃən/ NOUN an official suggestion that someone should be considered for a job, a position, or a prize ❍ *a nomination for best actor*

non|con|tribu|tory /nɒnkəntrɪbyətɔri/ ADJ If you have a **noncontributory** pension plan, your employer pays the entire cost of it. ❍ *All our American employees are covered by a noncontributory plan.*

none /nʌn/

1 **None of** something means not one or not any. ❍ *None of us knew her.*

2 PRON **None** is also a pronoun. ❍ *I searched the Internet for information, but found none.*

none|the|less /nʌnðəlɛs/ ADV **Nonetheless** means "although something is true." [FORMAL] ❍ *There is still a long way to go. Nonetheless, some progress has been made.*

non|ex|ecu|tive /nɒnɪgzɛkyətɪv/ ADJ If someone has a **nonexecutive** position in an organization, they give advice but do not make decisions. [ADMINISTRATION] ❍ *The issue is whether he should leave altogether or remain as chairman in a nonexecutive role.*

COLLOCATIONS

a nonexecutive *officer*
a nonexecutive *chairman*

N

non|ex|ecu|tive di|rec|tor (**nonexecutive directors**) NOUN one of the directors of a company who gives advice to the other directors but is not an employee [ADMINISTRATION]

non|fat /nɒnfæt/ ADJ **Nonfat** food and drinks have very little or no fat in them. ❍ *nonfat milk*

non|fic|tion /nɒnfɪkʃən/ NONCOUNT NOUN **Nonfiction** is writing that is about real people and events.

non|prof|it /nɒnprɒfɪt/
1 ADJ A **nonprofit** organization aims to help people or to provide a public service rather than to make a profit for its owners. Compare with **profit-making**. [BUSINESS MANAGEMENT]
2 NOUN **Nonprofit** is also a noun. ❍ *And with money always in short supply, the nonprofits cannot add paid staff.*

non-profit-making ADJ [BUSINESS MANAGEMENT, BRIT] → **nonprofit**

non|re|fund|able /nɒnrifʌndəbᵊl/ ADJ If you pay for something that is **nonrefundable**, you will not get your money back if you want to cancel the purchase. ❍ *Tickets must be purchased by August 11 and are nonrefundable.*

non|resi|dent /nɒnrɛzɪdənt/
1 NOUN someone who is visiting a place but not living or staying there permanently
2 ADJ **Nonresident** is also an adjective. ❍ *The paper said that 100,000 nonresident workers would be sent back to their home villages.*

non|re|turn|able /nɒnritɜrnəbᵊl/ ADJ
1 If a container is **nonreturnable**, you cannot return it to the store to be used again. ❍ *nonreturnable soda bottles*
2 If you buy something that is **nonreturnable**, you cannot return it to the store to get your money back. ❍ *Those gloves are nonreturnable.*

non|sense /nɒnsɛns, -səns/ NONCOUNT NOUN If something is **nonsense**, it is not true or it is silly. ❍ *Peter said I was talking nonsense.*

non|stop /nɒnstɒp/
1 ADJ continuing without stopping ❍ *a nonstop flight*
2 ADV **Nonstop** is also an adverb. ❍ *We drove nonstop from New York to Miami.*

non|tax|able /nɒntæksəbᵊl/ ADJ not able to be taxed [FINANCE] ❍ *Many job benefits are nontaxable to the employee.*

non|un|ion /nɒnyunyən/ ADJ **Nonunion** workers do not belong to a labor union. A **nonunion** company does not employ workers who belong to a labor union.

noo|dle /nudᵊl/ NOUN **Noodles** are long, thin strips of pasta (= a type of food made from eggs, flour, and water).

noon /nun/ NONCOUNT NOUN **Noon** is twelve o'clock in the middle of the day. ❍ *The meeting started at noon.*

no one or **no-one** PRON not a single person, or not a single member of a particular group or set ❍ *No one will be made redundant.*

nor /nɔr/ CONJ used after "neither" to introduce the second of two negative things ❍ *Neither Mr. Baker nor Ms. Simms were able to attend.*

norm /nɔrm/ NOUN If a situation is **the norm**, it is usual and expected. ❍ *Families of six or seven are the norm in here.*

n

nor|mal /nɔrmᵊl/ ADJ usual and ordinary ❍ *Interest rates have returned to normal levels.*

nor|mal|ly /nɔrməli/
1 ADV If something **normally** happens, it usually happens. ❍ *I normally get up at 7 a.m. for work.*
2 ADV in the usual or ordinary way ❍ *Despite problems, operations are working normally.*

north /nɔrθ/ also **North**
1 NONCOUNT NOUN The **north** is the direction that is on your left when you are looking at the sun in the morning. ❍ *He lives in the north of Canada.*
2 ADV toward the north ❍ *Anita drove north up Pacific Highway.*
3 ADJ relating to the north ❍ *North America*

North Ameri|can Free Trade Agree|ment NONCOUNT NOUN The **North American Free Trade Agreement** is an international trade agreement between the United States, Canada, and Mexico.

The abbreviation **NAFTA** is often used. [ECONOMICS]

north|east /nɔ̲rθi̲st/
1 NONCOUNT NOUN The **northeast** is the direction that is between north and east. ❍ *They live in Jerusalem, more than 250 miles to the northeast.*
2 ADJ relating to the northeast ❍ *northeast Louisiana*

north|ern /nɔ̲rðərn/ also **Northern ADJ** relating to the north of a place ❍ *Northern Ireland*

north|west /nɔ̲rθwɛ̲st/
1 NONCOUNT NOUN The **northwest** is the direction that is between north and west.
2 ADJ relating to the northwest

nose /noʊ̲z/ **NOUN** the part of your face that sticks out above your mouth and is used for smelling and breathing ❍ *She wiped her nose with a tissue.*

not /nɒ̲t/
1 ADV used to form negative sentences ❍ *Their plan was not working.* ❍ *I don't have his email address.*
2 Not at all is a strong way of saying "No" or of agreeing that the answer to a question is "No." ❍ *"Sorry, am I bothering you?"—"No. Not at all."*

N

note /noʊ̲t/
1 NOUN a short letter ❍ *Steven wrote her a note.*
2 NOUN something that you write down to remind yourself of something ❍ *I made a note to call him later.*
3 NOUN a particular sound in music, or a symbol that represents this sound ❍ *high notes*
4 NOUN Note is short for **banknote**.

note|book /noʊ̲tbʊk/
1 NOUN a small book for writing notes in
2 NOUN a small personal computer that you can carry with you

no̲t-for-pro̲fit ADJ [BUSINESS MANAGEMENT, BRIT] → **nonprofit**

noth|ing /nʌ̲θɪŋ/ **PRON** not a single thing, or not a single part of something ❍ *There is nothing wrong with the car.* ❍ *Nothing in the memo was surprising.*

no|tice /noʊ̲tɪs/ (**notices, noticing, noticed**)
1 VERB If you **notice** something or someone, you become aware of them. ❍ *Did you notice anything unusual about him?*
2 NOUN a piece of writing that gives information in a place where everyone can read it ❍ *The notice said "USED FURNITURE FOR SALE."*
3 NOUN a formal announcement in a newspaper or magazine about something that has happened or is going to happen ❍ *This notice is published in local papers and filed in public records.*
4 NONCOUNT NOUN If you give **notice** about something that is going to happen, you give a warning in advance. ❍ *Unions are required to give seven days' notice of industrial action.* ❍ *Three months' notice is required for withdrawals from your account.* ❍ *His was dismissed without notice.*
5 If your employer **gives** you **notice**, you must leave your job soon. [HR] ❍ *The next morning I called him and gave him notice.*
6 If you **hand in** your **notice** or **give in** your **notice**, you tell your employer that you will leave your job soon. [HR] ❍ *He handed in his notice at the bank.*

no|tice|able /noʊ̲tɪsəbᵊl/ **ADJ** obvious and easy to see ❍ *The difference in quality is noticeable.*

no|ti|fy /noʊ̲tɪfaɪ/ (**notifies, notifying, notified**) **VERB** If you **notify** someone of something, you officially tell them about it. [FORMAL] ❍ *We have notified the police.*

no̲t-invented-he̲re syn|drome
NONCOUNT NOUN People sometimes use **not-invented-here syndrome** to refer to the resistance within a company toward accepting ideas or products that were developed by other companies. ❍ *Software developers tend to suffer from the not-invented-here syndrome.*

no|tion /noʊ̲ʃən/ **NOUN** an idea or belief ❍ *We each have a notion of what kind of brand image we want to have.*

nought /nɔ̲t/ [mainly BRIT] → **zero**

noun /naʊn/ **NOUN** a word such as "car," "love," or "Anne" that is used for talking about a person or a thing

nov|el /nɒvᵊl/ **NOUN** a long written story about imaginary people and events ❍ *a novel by Herman Hesse*

nov|el|ist /nɒvəlɪst/ **NOUN** a person who writes novels (= long written stories about imaginary people and events)

No|vem|ber /noʊvɛmbər/ **NOUN** the eleventh month of the year ❍ *He came to New York in November 1939.*

now /naʊ/

1 ADV used for talking about the present time ❍ *I must go now.*

2 PRON Now is also a pronoun. ❍ *Now is your chance to talk to him.*

3 CONJ You use **now** or **now that** to show that something has happened, and as a result something else will happen. ❍ *Now that we've come to an agreement, let's discuss costs.*

4 If something happens **now and then**, it happens sometimes but not very often or regularly. ❍ *Now and then they heard the sound of a heavy truck outside.*

nowa|days /naʊədeɪz/ **ADV** at the present time, and not in the past ❍ *Nowadays almost all children play electronic games.*

no|where /noʊwɛər/ **ADV** not anywhere ❍ *I have nowhere else to go.*

nu|clear /nukliər/ **ADJ Nuclear** describes the energy that is released when the central parts (= nuclei) of atoms are split or combined. ❍ *a nuclear power station*

nu|cleus /nukliəs/ (**nuclei** /nukliaɪ/) **NOUN** the central part of an atom or cell

nude /nud/ **ADJ** not wearing any clothes ❍ *She came into the room, almost completely nude.*

nui|sance /nusᵊns/ **NOUN** If someone or something is a **nuisance**, they annoy you. ❍ *He can be a bit of a nuisance sometimes.*

numb /nʌm/ **ADJ** If a part of your body is **numb**, you cannot feel anything there. ❍ *His fingers were numb.*

num|ber /nʌmbər/

1 NOUN a word or symbol such as "two," "nine," or "47," that is used in counting ❍ *What's your phone number?*

2 NOUN used with words such as "large" or "small" to say approximately how many things or people there are ❍ *I received a large number of emails on the subject.*

3 PL NOUN In business, **numbers** are statistics showing the amount of money earned, or the amount of money that was spent or will be spent. ❍ *Let's look at last year's numbers.*

4 VERB If you **number** things, you write a series of numbers on them, usually starting at 1. ❍ *He numbered the pages.*

num|ber crunch|er /nʌmbər krʌntʃər/ (**number crunchers**) also **number-cruncher**

1 NOUN someone whose job is working with numbers or with data in the form of numbers [TECHNOLOGY, INFORMAL] ❍ *Accounting is the land of number-crunchers.* ● **number crunching NONCOUNT NOUN** ❍ *the number crunching done by Wall Street analysts*

2 NOUN a powerful computer [TECHNOLOGY, INFORMAL]

num|bered ac|count (**numbered accounts**) **NOUN** a bank account identified by a number rather than a name, to protect the identity of the account owner [BANKING]

nu|mer|ous /numərəs/ **ADJ** existing in large numbers ❍ *The company has been sued on numerous occasions.*

> **BUSINESS ETIQUETTE**
> In Brazil, handshaking is common. People often shake hands with each other for quite a long time.

nurse /nɜrs/ (**nurses, nursing, nursed**)

1 NOUN a person whose job is to care for people who are sick

2 VERB If you **nurse** someone, you care for them when they are sick. ❍ *My mother has nursed him for the last ten years.*

nurse|ry /nɜrsəri/ (**nurseries**)

1 NOUN a place where people grow and sell plants ❍ *Buy your plants at the local nursery.*

2 NOUN a room in a family home in which young children sleep or play

nut /nʌt/

1 NOUN a dry fruit with a hard shell ○ *Nuts and seeds are very good for you.*

2 NOUN If someone is a baseball **nut** or a health **nut**, for example, they are very enthusiastic about that activity. [INFORMAL]

3 ADJ If you are **nuts about** something or someone, you like them very much. [INFORMAL] ○ *She's nuts about cars.*

nu|tri|ent /nutriənt/ **NOUN Nutrients** are substances that help plants and animals to grow and stay healthy. ○ *The juice contains vitamins, minerals, and other essential nutrients.*

nu|tri|tion /nutrɪʃən/ **NONCOUNT NOUN Nutrition** is the way that the body uses the food that it needs to grow and stay healthy. ○ *He talked about the importance of good nutrition.*

ny|lon /naɪlɒn/ **NONCOUNT NOUN Nylon** is a strong artificial material. ○ *nylon rope*

NYSE /ɛn waɪ ɛs i/ **NYSE** is short for "New York Stock Exchange." [ECONOMICS]

Oo

O & M /oʊ ənd ɛm/ **NONCOUNT NOUN** In studies of working methods, **O & M** is an abbreviation for "organization and method." [BUSINESS MANAGEMENT]

obese /oʊbis/ **ADJ** very fat ❍ *Obese people often have health problems.*

obey /oʊbeɪ/ **VERB** If you **obey** a person or a command, you do what you are told to do. ❍ *Most people obey the law.*

ob|ject

Pronounce the noun /ɒbdʒɪkt/. Pronounce the verb /əbdʒɛkt/.

1 NOUN a thing that has a shape and is not alive ❍ *I can't see distant objects clearly.*
2 NOUN an aim or purpose ❍ *The object of the event is to raise money.*
3 NOUN In grammar, the **object** of a verb is the person or thing that is affected by the action.
4 VERB If you **object** to something, you say that you do not like it or agree with it. ❍ *A lot of people objected to the book.*

ob|jec|tion /əbdʒɛkʃən/ **NOUN** If you have an **objection**, you do not like or agree with something. ❍ *I don't have any objection to people making money.*

ob|jec|tive /əbdʒɛktɪv/ **NOUN** the thing you are trying to achieve [BUSINESS MANAGEMENT] ❍ *Our main objective is cost-reduction.*

ob|li|ga|tion /ɒblɪgeɪʃən/ **NOUN** If you have an **obligation to** do something, you should do it. ❍ *Directors do not have an obligation to present alternatives to shareholders.*

oblige /əblaɪdʒ/ (**obliges, obliging, obliged**) **VERB** If you **are obliged to** do something, a situation or law makes it necessary for you to do it. ❍ *Private utilities are obliged to buy electricity at government-fixed prices.*

OBO /oʊ bi oʊ/ also **o.b.o. OBO** is used in advertisements to say that the seller will accept slightly less than the price stated. **OBO** is short for "or best offer." ❍ *Aquarium for sale. $50 OBO.*

ob|scene /əbsin/ **ADJ** Something that is **obscene** relates to sex or violence in an offensive way. ❍ *obscene photographs*

ob|serve /əbzɜrv/ (**observes, observing, observed**) **VERB** If you **observe** a person or thing, you watch them carefully. ❍ *Olson observed the behavior of babies.*

ob|ses|sion /əbsɛʃən/ **NOUN** If someone has an **obsession** with a person or thing, they spend too much time thinking about them. ❍ *We do not serve the customer best by an obsession with costs, stocks, and product flow.*

ob|so|lete /ɒbsəlit/ **ADJ** no longer needed because something better has been invented ❍ *So much equipment becomes obsolete almost as soon as it's made.*

ob|sta|cle /ɒbstəkəl/ **NOUN** something that makes it difficult for you to do what you want to do ❍ *We had to overcome two major obstacles.*

ob|struct /əbstrʌkt/ **VERB** If someone or something **obstructs** a place, they block it. ❍ *A group of cars obstructed the road.*

ob|tain /əbteɪn/ **VERB** To **obtain** something means to get it. [FORMAL] ❍ *It can still take years for foreigners to obtain work permits.*

ob|vi|ous /ɒbviəs/ **ADJ** easy to see or understand ❍ *It is obvious that marketing includes more than simply selling the product.*

ob|vi|ous|ly /ɒbviəsli/ **ADV** in a way that is easy to see or understand ❍ *There is obviously a need for more revenue for the industry.*

oc|ca|sion /əkeɪʒən/
1 NOUN a time when something happens

○ *His colleagues complained about him on several occasions.*

2 NOUN an important event or celebration ○ *The wedding was a happy occasion.*

oc|ca|sion|al /əkeɪʒənəl/ **ADJ** happening sometimes but not often ○ *I get occasional headaches.* ● **oc|ca|sion|al|ly ADV** ○ *Importers have occasionally rejected their shipments.*

oc|cu|pant /ɒkyəpənt/ **NOUN** The **occupants** of a building or a room are the people who live or work there.

oc|cu|pa|tion /ɒkyəpeɪʃən/

1 NOUN Your **occupation** is your job.

2 NOUN something that you spend time doing ○ *Cooking was his favorite occupation.*

oc|cu|pa|tion|al pen|sion /ɒkyəpeɪʃənəl pɛnʃən/ (**occupational pensions**) **NOUN** a pension provided for the members of a particular occupation or by a specific employer [BANKING, mainly BRIT] ○ *The retirement age for men and women in occupational pension plans must be the same.*

oc|cu|py /ɒkyəpaɪ/ (**occupies, occupying, occupied**)

1 VERB The people who **occupy** a place are the people who live or work there. ○ *The company occupies the top floor of the building.*

2 VERB If a room or a seat **is occupied**, someone is using it. ○ *The chair was occupied by his wife.*

3 VERB If something **occupies** you, you are busy with it. ○ *Her career occupies all of her time.* ● **oc|cu|pied ADJ** ○ *Keep your brain occupied.*

oc|cur /əkɜr/ (**occurs, occurring, occurred**)

1 VERB When something **occurs**, it happens. ○ *When financial crises occur, the public wants someone to blame.*

2 VERB If a thought or an idea **occurs to** you, you suddenly think of it. ○ *Suddenly it occurred to her that this could be a sales opportunity.*

oc|cur|rence /əkɜrəns/ **NOUN** something that happens [FORMAL] ○ *Complaints against the company were an everyday occurrence.*

ocean /oʊʃən/

1 NOUN The ocean is the salty water that covers much of the Earth's surface. ○ *The house is on a cliff overlooking the ocean.*

2 NOUN one of the five very large areas of salt water on the Earth's surface ○ *the Pacific Ocean*

o'clock /əklɒk/ **ADV** used after numbers to say what time it is ○ *ten o'clock*

Oc|to|ber /ɒktoʊbər/ **NOUN** the tenth month of the year ○ *They left on October 2.*

odd /ɒd/

1 ADJ strange or unusual ○ *His behavior was odd.* ● **odd|ly ADV** ○ *He dresses rather oddly.*

2 ADJ Odd numbers are numbers that cannot be divided exactly by two.

3 ADJ You say that two things are **odd** when they do not belong to the same set or pair. ○ *odd socks*

odor /oʊdər/ **NOUN** a smell ○ *an unpleasant odor*

odour /oʊdər/ [BRIT] → **odor**

OECD /oʊ i si di/ **NONCOUNT NOUN** The **OECD** is an organization of countries set up to encourage trade and economic growth. **OECD** is short for "Organization for Economic Cooperation and Development."

of /əv, STRONG ʌv/

1 PREP belonging to or connected with ○ *Police searched the homes of the criminals.* ○ *the head of their New York division*

2 PREP consisting of ○ *He was trying to hide his feelings of anger.*

3 PREP used for talking about someone or something else who is involved in an action ○ *He was dreaming of her.*

4 PREP forming part of a larger group or thing ○ *She is the youngest child of three.*

5 PREP used for talking about amounts or contents ○ *The boy was drinking a glass of milk.*

6 PREP Of describes someone's behavior. ○ *It's very kind of you to help.*

of course

1 ADV used for suggesting that something is not surprising [SPOKEN] ○ *Of course there was a lot of opposition from staff.*

2 used as a polite way of giving permission [SPOKEN] ○ *"Can I ask you something?"—"Yes, of course."*

off /ɔf/

1 PREP or ADV not on something or not connected to something ❍ *He took his feet off the desk.* ❍ *I broke off a piece of chocolate and ate it.*

2 PREP or ADV out of a vehicle ❍ *Don't get off a moving train!* ❍ *At the next station, the man got off.*

3 PREP or ADV away from an area or not on an area ❍ *The police told visitors to keep off the beach.* ❍ *He was just about to drive off.*

4 ADV or PREP If you have time **off**, you do not go to work or school. ❍ *She had the day off.* ❍ *I'm off work tomorrow.*

5 ADV If something is a long time **off**, it will not happen for a long time. ❍ *An agreement is still a long way off.*

6 ADV If an event is **off**, it is canceled. ❍ *The meeting is off.*

7 ADV When a piece of electrical equipment is **off**, it is not being used. ❍ *Her bedroom light was off.*

of|fence /əfɛns/ [BRIT] → **offense**

of|fend /əfɛnd/ VERB If you **offend** someone, you say or do something that upsets them. ❍ *I'm sorry if I offended you.*

of|fense /əfɛns/

Pronounce meaning **3** /ɔfɛns/.

1 NOUN a crime ❍ *There is a fine of $1,000 for a first offense.*

2 NONCOUNT NOUN **Offense** is behavior that upsets people. ❍ *He didn't mean to cause offense.*

3 NOUN In sports such as football or basketball, **the offense** is the team that has the ball and is trying to score.

of|fen|sive /əfɛnsɪv/ ADJ rude or insulting ❍ *an offensive remark*

of|fer /ɔfər/

1 VERB If you **offer** something to someone, you ask them if they would like to have it. ❍ *She offered him a cup of coffee.*

2 VERB If you **offer to** do something, you say that you are willing to do it. ❍ *They offered to buy the company for $110 a share.*

3 NOUN something that someone says they will give you or do for you ❍ *The company accepted a takeover offer of $29.835 a share.*

4 VERB If you **offer** goods, you present them for sale. ❍ *The paintings were initially offered as three separate lots.*

5 VERB If you **offer** something, you propose to give it as payment. ❍ *They offered $21.50 a share in cash for 49.5 million shares.*

6 NOUN **Offer** is short for **offer price**.

7 If goods are **on offer**, they are for sale at a reduced price. [BRIT] ❍ *Over 40 new books are on offer at 25% off their normal retail price.*

of|fer price (**offer prices**) NOUN The **offer price** is the price that the person selling a particular stock or share says that they want for it. Compare with **bid price**. ❍ *The company increased its offer price to $26.*

of|fice /ɔfɪs/

1 NOUN a room where people work sitting at a desk ❍ *I work in an office with about 25 people.*

2 NOUN a department of an organization, especially the government ❍ *the Congressional Budget Office*

of|fice hours PL NOUN **Office hours** are the times when an office or similar place is open for business. For example, office hours in the United States and Britain are usually between 9 o'clock and 5 o'clock from Monday to Friday. ❍ *If you have any questions, please call Anne Fisher at 555-6203 during office hours.*

of|fice jun|ior (**office juniors**) NOUN a young person employed in an office for running errands and doing other minor jobs [ADMINISTRATION, mainly BRIT]

of|fic|er /ɔfɪsər/ NOUN a person who is in charge of other people in the armed forces, the police, or a government ❍ *an army officer*

of|fi|cial /əfɪʃᵊl/

1 ADJ approved by the government or by someone in power ❍ *They destroyed all the official documents.* ● **of|fi|cial|ly** ADV ❍ *The results have not been officially announced.*

2 ADJ done by a person in power as part of their job ❍ *The president is in Brazil for an official visit.*

3 NOUN a person who holds a position of power in an organization ❍ *White House officials*

of|fi|cial strike (**official strikes**) NOUN a time when some or all of the workers in an organization stop work with the approval of a labor union [BUSINESS MANAGEMENT] ❍ *An official strike cannot occur until a secret ballot of the workforce has been carried out.* [mainly BRIT]

off|line /ɒflaɪn/ also **off-line**
1 ADJ If a computer is **offline**, it is not connected to the Internet. Compare with **online**. ❍ *Initially the system was offline for a number of days.*
2 ADV **Offline** is also an adverb. ❍ *Most software programs allow you to compose emails offline.*

off|set /ɔfsɛt/ (**offsets, offsetting, offset**) VERB If one thing **is offset** by another, the effect of the first thing is reduced by the second. ❍ *The increase in costs was offset by higher sales.*

off|shore /ɔfʃɔr/ also **off-shore**
1 ADJ situated or happening in the sea, near to the coast, rather than on land ❍ *the offshore oil industry*
2 ADV **Offshore** is also an adverb. ❍ *One day a larger ship anchored offshore.*
3 ADJ **Offshore** investments or companies are located in a place, usually an island, that has fewer tax regulations than most other countries. [ECONOMICS] ❍ *The island offers a wide range of offshore banking facilities.*

O

COLLOCATIONS
offshore *banking*
an offshore *company*
an offshore *fund*

off|shor|ing /ɒfʃɔrɪŋ, ɔf-/ NONCOUNT NOUN **Offshoring** is the practice of moving a company's work to a foreign country where labor costs are cheaper. [ECONOMICS] ❍ *Offshoring provides an opportunity to obtain I.T. services at low cost.*

off-the-job train|ing NONCOUNT NOUN **Off-the-job training** is training that takes place outside the workplace. [HR] ❍ *A quarter had received off-the-job training in their jobs.*

of|ten /ɔfᵊn/
1 ADV many times or much of the time ❍ *Investors often borrow heavily to buy their holdings.* ❍ *That doesn't happen very often.*
2 ADV used for asking questions about the number of times something happens ❍ *How often do you communicate with your clients?*

oh /oʊ/ EXCLAM used for expressing a feeling such as surprise, pain, annoyance, or happiness [SPOKEN] ❍ *"Oh!" Kenny said. "Has everyone gone?"*

oil /ɔɪl/
1 NONCOUNT NOUN **Oil** is a smooth, thick liquid that is used for making machines work. ❍ *a barrel of oil*
2 VERB If you **oil** something, you put oil onto or into it. ❍ *He oiled the lock on the door.*
3 NOUN a smooth, thick liquid that is used for cooking ❍ *olive oil*

okay /oʊkeɪ/ also **OK, O.K., ok**
1 ADJ or ADV If something is **okay**, it is acceptable. [INFORMAL] ❍ *Is it okay if I go by myself?* ❍ *We seemed to manage okay.*
2 ADJ If someone is **okay**, they are safe and well. [INFORMAL] ❍ *Check that the baby's okay.*
3 used for showing that you agree to something [INFORMAL] ❍ *"Just tell him I would like to talk to him."—"OK."*

old /oʊld/
1 ADJ Someone or something who is **old** has lived or existed for a long time. ❍ *Mr. Kaufmann was a small old man with a beard.* ❍ *These books look very old.*
2 ADJ used to talk or ask about the age of someone or something ❍ *He is three months old.*
3 ADJ no longer used, or replaced by something else ❍ *I still remember my old school.*

old-fashioned ADJ no longer used, done, or believed by most people ❍ *The kitchen was old-fashioned.*

oli|go|po|ly /ɒlɪgɒpəli/ (**oligopolies**) NOUN a market situation in which control over the supply of a commodity is held by a small number of producers [ECONOMICS] ❍ *With the increased number of take-overs and mergers in recent years, a considerable number of markets operate as an oligopoly.*

omit /oʊmɪt/ (**omits, omitting, omitted**) VERB If you **omit** something, you do not include it. ❍ *The fund omitted information regarding risks of international investing.*

on /ɒn/
1 PREP supported by or attached to a surface ❍ *There was a large box on the table.* ❍ *We hung some paintings on the walls.*
2 ADV When you **put** a piece of clothing **on** or **have** it **on**, you wear it. ❍ *He put his coat on.* ❍ *I can't go out. I don't have any shoes on.*
3 PREP getting into or traveling on a vehicle ❍ *We got on the plane.*
4 PREP using a piece of equipment or an object ❍ *I played these songs on the piano.* ❍ *My dad called me on my cellphone.*
5 PREP If something is **on** television or **on** the radio, it is being broadcast. ❍ *What's on TV tonight?*
6 PREP If something happens **on** a particular day or date, that is when it happens. ❍ *This year's event will be on June 19th.* ❍ *We'll see you on Tuesday.*
7 PREP about a subject ❍ *a book on the history of Russian ballet*
8 ADJ When a machine or an electric light is **on**, it is being used. ❍ *The lights were on, but nobody was at home.*

once /wʌns/
1 ADV If something happens **once**, it happens one time only. ❍ *I met Miquela once, at a conference.*
2 ADV If something was **once** true, it was true at some time in the past, but is no longer true. ❍ *Her parents once owned a store.*
3 CONJ If something happens **once** another thing has happened, it happens immediately afterward. ❍ *The decision was easy once he read the letter.*
4 If you do something **at once**, you do it immediately. ❍ *I have to go at once.*
5 **For once** is used for emphasizing that something happens on this particular occasion only. ❍ *For once, Dad is not complaining.*

one /wʌn/
1 the number 1 ❍ *They have one daughter.*
2 PRON used instead of the name of a person or thing ❍ *"Which dress do you prefer?"—"I like the red one."*
3 ADJ used for talking about a time in the past or in the future ❍ *Would you like to go out one night?*
4 PRON **One** means people in general. [FORMAL] ❍ *One can get very tired on these long flights.*

one's /wʌnz/
1 ADJ used to show that something belongs to or relates to people in general [FORMAL] ❍ *It is natural to want to progress in one's career.*
2 **One's** is a spoken form of "one is" or "one has." ❍ *No one's going to hurt you.* ❍ *This one's been broken too.*

one|self /wʌnsɛlf/ PRON Speakers or writers use **oneself** to make statements about themselves and people in general. [FORMAL] ❍ *To work, one must have time to oneself.*

on|going /ɒngoʊɪŋ/ ADJ still continuing ❍ *There is an ongoing debate on the issue.*

on|ion /ʌnyən/ NOUN a round vegetable with many layers and a strong, sharp taste

on|line /ɒnlaɪn/ also **on-line**
1 ADJ using the Internet or connected to the Internet ❍ *an online bookstore* ❍ *You can chat to other people who are online.* ❍ *the first bank to go online*
2 ADV **Online** is also an adverb. ❍ *I buy most of my clothes online.*

on|line bank|ing NONCOUNT NOUN **Online banking** is a system allowing people to perform banking activities via the Internet. [BANKING, TECHNOLOGY] ❍ *Online banking is well established, so buying financial services via the web comes naturally.*

on|line book|ing NONCOUNT NOUN **Online booking** is the activity of booking services such as train tickets or vacations via the Internet. [E-COMMERCE] ❍ *Travel agency Flightbookers was the first to offer online booking.*

on|line re|tail|ing NONCOUNT NOUN **Online retailing** is the business or activity of selling goods or services via the Internet. [E-COMMERCE] ❍ *Good old-fashioned marketing* *principles apply as much to online retailing as to conventional retailing.*

on|line shop|ping NONCOUNT NOUN
Online shopping is the activity of buying goods and services via the Internet. [E-COMMERCE] ❍ *Flextech owns a string of websites and provides interactive services such as online shopping.*

only /oʊnli/
1 ADV **Only** means "and nobody or nothing else." ❍ *Only one person knew the answer.* ❍ *We have only twelve employees.*
2 ADJ **The only** person or thing is the one person or thing of a particular type. ❍ *She's the only woman on the board.*
3 ADJ An **only** child is a child who has no brothers or sisters.
4 ADV used for saying how small or unimportant something is ❍ *Their offices are only a few miles from here.*
5 CONJ but [INFORMAL] ❍ *It's like my house, only it's nicer.*

o.n.o. /oʊ ɛn oʊ/ **o.n.o.** is used in advertisements to say that the seller will accept slightly less than the price stated. **o.n.o.** is short for "or nearest offer." [BRIT]

on-the-job trai|ning NONCOUNT NOUN
On-the-job training is training that is given to employees while they are at work. [HR] ❍ *Japanese companies provide on-the-job training as well as access to technical education.*

onto /ɒntu/
1 PREP If something moves **onto** a surface, it moves to a position on that surface. ❍ *The cat climbed onto her lap.*
2 PREP When you get **onto** a bus, train, or plane, you enter it. ❍ *He got onto the plane.*

oops /ups/ EXCLAM You say **oops!** when a small mistake or accident has happened. ❍ *Oops! Sorry. Are you all right?*

open /oʊpən/
1 VERB If you **open** something, you move it so that it is no longer closed. ❍ *He opened the window.*
2 ADJ **Open** is also an adjective. ❍ *His eyes were open and he was smiling.*
3 VERB If you **open** a container, you remove part of it so that you can take out what is inside. ❍ *Nicole opened the silver box on the table.*
4 VERB If you **open** a computer file, you give the computer an instruction to show it on the screen. ❍ *To open a file, go to the File menu.*
5 VERB When a store, office, or public building **opens**, people can go into it. ❍ *The banks will open again on Monday morning.*
6 ADJ **Open** is also an adjective. ❍ *The store is open Monday through Friday, 9 a.m. to 6 p.m.*
7 ADJ If a person is **open**, they are honest about their thoughts and feelings. ❍ *He was always open with her.*
8 ADJ If you are **open to** suggestions or ideas, you are ready and willing to consider or accept them. ❍ *We are always open to suggestions.*
9 VERB On the stock exchange, the price at which currencies, shares, or commodities **open** is their value at the start of that day's trading. ❍ *Gold declined $2 in Zurich to open at 385.50.*

open door (**open doors**) also **open-door**
1 NOUN a policy by which a nation gives opportunities for trade to all other nations equally ❍ *He convinced world leaders not to restrict trade through colonization, but rather to keep an open door.*
2 ADJ If an organization has an **open-door** policy, management is prepared to talk to workers in the office at any time. ❍ *With very good intentions some senior managers maintain an "open-door" policy.*

open|er /oʊpənər/ NOUN a tool that is used for opening cans or bottles ❍ *a can opener*

open|ing /oʊpənɪŋ/
1 ADJ The **opening** event, day, or week in a series is the first one. ❍ *The team lost the opening game.*
2 NOUN a hole that things or people can pass through ❍ *He managed to get through a narrow opening in the fence.*

open mar|ket (**open markets**) NOUN
Goods that are bought and sold on **the open market** are advertised and sold to anyone who wants to buy them. [ECONOMICS] ❍ *On the open market, this would be worth much more.*

open shop (**open shops**) NOUN an organization that employs people whether or not they belong to a labor union

op|era /ɒpərə, ɒprə/ NOUN a play in which the words are sung ❍ *an opera singer*

op|er|ate /ɒpəreɪt/ (**operates, operating, operated**)
1 VERB If an organization **operates**, it does its work. ❍ *The organization has been operating in the area for some time.*
2 VERB When you **operate** a machine, you make it work. ❍ *Weston showed him how to operate the machine.*
3 VERB When doctors **operate on** a patient, they cut them open in order to remove or repair a part.

> **BUSINESS ETIQUETTE**
> In the UK, a firm handshake is expected from both men and women in business contexts.

op|er|at|ing /ɒpəreɪtɪŋ/ ADJ **Operating** profits and costs are the money that a company earns and spends in carrying out its ordinary trading activities. ❍ *The group made operating profits of $80M before interest.*

op|er|at|ing budg|et (**operating budgets**) NOUN a forecast of the costs and profits of an organization, used to monitor its trading activities, usually for one year [FINANCE] ❍ *The division's annual operating budget of about $245 million is under constant strain.*

op|era|tion /ɒpəreɪʃən/
1 NOUN an organized activity that involves many people doing different things ❍ *a rescue operation*
2 NOUN When a patient has an **operation**, a doctor cuts open their body in order to remove, replace, or repair a part. ❍ *Charles had an operation on his arm.*
3 NOUN a business or company [BUSINESS MANAGEMENT] ❍ *Thorn's electronics operation employs around 5,000 people.*

op|era|tion|al /ɒpəreɪʃənᵊl/ ADJ in use or is ready for use ❍ *The whole system will be fully operational by December.*

op|era|tions re|search NONCOUNT NOUN **Operations research** is the analysis of problems in business and industry. [R & D] ❍ *Other approaches are based on the use of models and statistical techniques, such as forecasting methods, operations research, and ratio analysis.*

op|era|tive /ɒpərətɪv, -əreɪtɪv/
1 ADJ working or having an effect [FORMAL] ❍ *The commercial telephone service was no longer operative.*
2 NOUN a worker, especially one who does work with their hands [FORMAL] ❍ *In an automated car plant there is not a human operative to be seen.*
3 NOUN someone who works for a government agency such as the intelligence service ❍ *Naturally the CIA wants to protect its operatives.*

op|era|tor /ɒpəreɪtər/
1 NOUN a person who connects telephone calls in a place such as an office or hotel ❍ *He called the operator.*
2 NOUN a person who is employed to operate a machine ❍ *a crane operator*
3 NOUN a person or a company that runs a business [ADMINISTRATION] ❍ *Tele-Communications, the nation's largest cable TV operator*

opin|ion /əpɪnyən/ NOUN a belief or view ❍ *I didn't ask for your opinion.* ❍ *I don't have a very high opinion of Thomas.*

op|po|nent /əpoʊnənt/ NOUN the person who is against you in a fight or a competition ❍ *She'll face six opponents in today's race.*

op|por|tu|nity /ɒpərtunɪti/ (**opportunities**) NOUN a chance to do or have something that you want ❍ *This is an opportunity to buy shares without taking too great a risk.*

op|pose /əpoʊz/ (**opposes, opposing, opposed**) VERB If you **oppose** something, you disagree with it and try to stop it. ❍ *He will oppose any tax increase.*

op|posed /əpoʊzd/ ADJ If you **are opposed to** something, you disagree with it. ❍ *I am opposed to any form of terrorism.*

op|po|site /ɒpəzɪt/
1 PREP or **ADV** If one person or thing is **opposite** another, it is across from it. ❍ *Jennie sat opposite Sam at breakfast.* ❍ *He looked at the buildings opposite.*
2 ADJ completely different ❍ *We watched the cars driving in the opposite direction.*
3 NOUN **The opposite of** someone or something is the person or thing that is most different from them. ❍ *Whatever he says, he's probably thinking the opposite.*

op|po|si|tion /ɒpəzɪʃən/ **NONCOUNT NOUN** **Opposition** is strong disagreement. ❍ *There is strong opposition to the plan.*

opt /ɒpt/
1 VERB If you **opt** to do something, you choose to do it. ❍ *He wavered, but sensibly opted to say very little.*
2 ▸**opt in** If you **opt in** to a scheme, you choose to be involved in or part of it. ❍ *Previously, corporate customers had to opt in to enable the banking group to share client information.*

op|ti|mise /ɒptɪmaɪz/ [BUSINESS MANAGEMENT, BRIT] → **optimize**

op|ti|mism /ɒptɪmɪzəm/ **NONCOUNT NOUN** **Optimism** is a feeling of hope about the future. ❍ *Shares rose steadily on a wave of optimism about technology stocks.* • **op|ti|mist NOUN** ❍ *He is an optimist about the company's future.*

op|ti|mis|tic /ɒptɪmɪstɪk/ **ADJ** hopeful about the future ❍ *She is optimistic that they can reach an agreement.*

op|ti|mize /ɒptɪmaɪz/ (**optimizes, optimizing, optimized**) **VERB** To **optimize** a plan, system, or machine means to arrange or design it so that it operates as smoothly and efficiently as possible. [BUSINESS MANAGEMENT, FORMAL] ❍ *The new systems have been optimized for running Microsoft Windows.* • **op|ti|mi|za|tion** /ɒptəməzeɪʃən/ **NONCOUNT NOUN** ❍ *The optimization of such benefits is best achieved by conditions of free trade.*

op|tion /ɒpʃən/
1 NOUN a choice between two or more things ❍ *We will consider all options before making a decision.*
2 NOUN an agreement or contract that gives someone the right to buy or sell a property or shares at a future date ❍ *Each bank has granted the other an option on 19.9% of its shares.*

op|tion|al /ɒpʃənəl/ **ADJ** If something is **optional**, you can choose whether or not you do it or have it. ❍ *Insurance is optional.*

or /ər, STRONG ɔr/
1 CONJ used for showing choices or possibilities ❍ *"Do you want tea or coffee?" John asked.*
2 CONJ used between two numbers to show that you are giving an approximate amount ❍ *You should only drink one or two cups of coffee a day.*
3 CONJ used to introduce a warning that something bad could happen ❍ *She has to have the operation, or she will die.*

oral /ɔrəl/
1 ADJ **Oral** communication is spoken rather than written. ❍ *The English test includes written and oral examinations.*
2 ADJ relating to your mouth ❍ *good oral hygiene*

or|ange /ɔrɪndʒ/
1 ADJ having a color between red and yellow
2 NOUN **Orange** is also a noun. ❍ *His supporters were dressed in orange.*
3 NOUN a round, juicy fruit with a thick, orange-colored skin

or|bit /ɔrbɪt/ **NOUN** the path of an object that goes around a planet, a moon, or the sun

or|ches|tra /ɔrkɪstrə/ **NOUN** a large group of musicians who play different instruments together

or|deal /ɔrdil/ **NOUN** a very unpleasant experience ❍ *The attack was a terrifying ordeal for both victims.*

order
❶ IN ORDER TO
❷ COMMANDS AND REQUESTS
❸ THE WAY THINGS ARE ARRANGED

❶ **or|der** /ɔrdər/ If you do something **in order to** achieve something, you do it because you want to achieve that thing. ❍ *The operation was necessary in order to save the baby's life.*

❷ **or|der** /ɔrdər/

1 VERB If you **order** someone **to** do something, you tell them to do it. ❍ *Williams ordered him to leave.*

2 NOUN If someone gives you an **order**, they tell you to do something. ❍ *The commander gave his men orders to move out of the camp.*

3 VERB When you **order** something you are going to pay for, you ask for it to be brought or sent to you. ❍ *They ordered a new washing machine on the Internet.* ❍ *The waitress asked, "Are you ready to order?"*

4 NOUN Someone's **order** is what they have asked for in return for money. ❍ *He's just placed an order for a new car.*

5 Something that is **on order** at a store or factory has been asked for but has not yet been supplied. ❍ *The airlines still have 2,500 new airplanes on order.*

❸ **or|der** /ɔrdər/

1 NONCOUNT NOUN If you arrange things **in** a particular **order**, you put one thing first, another thing second, and so on. ❍ *The books are all arranged in alphabetical order.*

2 NONCOUNT NOUN **Order** is the situation that exists when everything is in the correct place, or happens at the correct time. ❍ *Everything on the desk is in order.*

3 A machine or piece of equipment that is **out of order** does not work. ❍ *The photocopier is out of order.*

or|der book (**order books**) **NOUN** When you talk about the state of a company's **order book** or **order books**, you are talking about how many orders for their goods the company has. [PRODUCTION, BRIT] ❍ *He has a full order book for his boat-building yard on the Thames.*

or|der|ly /ɔrdərli/ **ADJ** neat and with everything done or happening correctly ❍ *It's a clean and orderly city.*

or|di|nary /ɔrdᵊnɛri/ **ADJ** not special or different ❍ *ordinary people*

or|di|nary shares **PL NOUN** **Ordinary shares** are the same as **common stock**. Compare with **preference shares**. [FINANCE, BRIT]

or|gan /ɔrgən/

1 NOUN a part of your body that has a particular purpose ❍ *The brain is the most powerful organ in the body.*

2 NOUN a large musical instrument that is like a piano ❍ *a church organ*

or|gan|ic /ɔrgænɪk/ **ADJ** **Organic** food is grown without using chemicals. ❍ *organic fruits and vegetables*

or|gani|sa|tion /ɔrgənɪzeɪʃən/ [BRIT] → **organization**

or|gan|ise /ɔrgənaɪz/ [BRIT] → **organize**

or|gani|za|tion /ɔrgənɪzeɪʃən/

1 NOUN an official group of people such as a business or a club ❍ *She worked for the same organization for six years.*

2 NONCOUNT NOUN The **organization** of something is the act of planning or arranging it. ❍ *I helped in the organization of the concert.*

or|gani|za|tion|al cul|ture /ɔrgənəzeɪʃənᵊl kʌltʃər/ (**organizational cultures**) **NOUN** the customs, beliefs, and values shared by the members of an organization that have to be accepted by new members [HR] ❍ *For some organizations, appraisal is a central process, and a mechanism through which they promote the organizational culture.*

or|gani|za|tion chart (**organization charts**) **NOUN** a diagram showing the management structure of an organization and the responsibilities of each department [ADMINISTRATION] ❍ *AT&T only last week put out an organization chart showing who reports to whom under a new structure announced last spring.*

or|gan|ize /ɔrgənaɪz/ (**organizes, organizing, organized**)

1 VERB If you **organize** an activity, you plan or arrange it. ❍ *The company organized several training seminars.* ● **or|gan|iz|er** **NOUN** ❍ *Organizers are hoping to raise $65,000 from the concert.*

2 VERB If you **organize** things, you arrange them in a particular way. ❍ *He began to organize his papers.*

or|gan|ized /ɔrgənaɪzd/ **ADJ** Someone who is **organized** plans their work and activities well. ❍ *Managers need to be very organized.*

or|gano|gram /ɔrgænəgræm/ [ADMINISTRATION, BRIT] → **organization chart**

ori|ent /ɔriənt, -ɛnt/
1 VERB If something is **oriented to** or **toward** a particular person or subject, that person or subject is its aim or area of concentration. ❍ *The company is oriented to customer satisfaction.*
2 VERB When you **orient yourself**, you find out where you are and where you need to go. ❍ *I found the map and compass and oriented myself.*
3 VERB When you **orient yourself to** a new situation, you learn about it and prepare to deal with it. [FORMAL] ❍ *You will need to orient yourself to eating different types of food.*

ori|gin /ɔrɪdʒɪn/ **NOUN** where or how something or someone started ❍ *Scientists study the origin of life on Earth.* ❍ *Americans of Hispanic origin*

O

origi|nal /ərɪdʒɪnᵊl/
1 ADJ used for talking about something that existed at the beginning ❍ *Under the original plan, they paid a deposit of $1.2 billion.*
● **origi|nal|ly ADV** ❍ *The issue size was increased from the originally planned $50 million.*
2 NOUN something that is not a copy ❍ *Make a copy of the document and send the original to your employer.*
3 ADJ using imagination and new ideas ❍ *He is the most original painter of the past 100 years.*

or|na|ment /ɔrnəmənt/ **NOUN** an attractive object that you use to decorate your home

or|phan /ɔrfən/ **NOUN** a child whose parents are dead

OSHA /oʊ ɛs eɪtʃ eɪ/ **NOUN OSHA** is a government agency in the United States that is responsible for maintaining standards of health and safety in workplaces. **OSHA** is short for "Occupational Safety and Health Administration." ❍ *Fuller says OSHA must target its resources as effectively as possible.*

oth|er /ʌðər/
1 ADJ used for talking about more things or people of the same type ❍ *Other industries are better at recycling.*
2 PRON Other is also a pronoun. ❍ *He had a pen in one hand and a book in the other.*
3 ADJ used for talking about a thing or a person that is different from the thing or person you have mentioned ❍ *He will have to accept it; there is no other way.* ❍ *William was at the other end of the room.*
4 ADJ The other day means a recent day. ❍ *I called her the other day.*

other|wise /ʌðərwaɪz/
1 ADV used for saying what the result would be if the situation was different ❍ *I really enjoy this job, otherwise I would not be here.*
2 ADV used when you mention a different state or situation ❍ *He was very tired but otherwise happy.*

ouch /aʊtʃ/ **EXCLAM** People say **"ouch!"** when they suddenly feel pain.

ought /ɔt/
1 If someone **ought to** do something, it is the right thing to do. ❍ *You ought to look for another job.*
2 used for saying that you think something will be true or will happen ❍ *"This party ought to be fun," he told Alex.*

ounce /aʊns/ **NOUN** An **ounce** is a unit for measuring weight. There are sixteen ounces in a pound and one ounce is equal to 28.35 grams.

our /aʊər/ **ADJ** used to show that something belongs or relates both to you and to one or more other people ❍ *We've increased our forecasts.*

ours /aʊərz/ **PRON** used for talking about something that belongs to you and one or more other people ❍ *That car is ours.*

our|selves /aʊərsɛlvz/
1 PRON used for talking about yourself and one or more other people ❍ *We sat by the fire to keep ourselves warm.*
2 PRON used for saying that you and one or more other people do something alone,

without help from anyone else ❍ *We built the house ourselves.*

out /aʊt/

1 ADV towards the outside of a place ❍ *She ran out of the house.*

2 ADV When you take something **out**, you remove it from a place. ❍ *He took out his notebook.* ❍ *I took the key out of my purse.*

3 ADV If you are **out**, you are not at home. ❍ *I called you yesterday, but you were out.*

4 ADJ no longer shining or burning ❍ *All the lights were out in the house.* ❍ *Please don't let the fire go out.*

5 ADJ If a product is **out**, it is in stores and people can buy it. ❍ *Their new CD is out now.*

6 ADV Out is also an adverb. ❍ *The book came out in 2006.*

7 If something is made **out of** a particular material, it has been produced from it. ❍ *The house is made out of wood.*

out|age /aʊtɪdʒ/ **NOUN** a period of time when the electricity supply to a building or area is interrupted [TECHNOLOGY] ❍ *A windstorm in Washington is causing power outages throughout the region.*

out-box (**out-boxes**) **NOUN** a place for putting letters and documents that are waiting to be sent

out|break /aʊtbreɪk/ **NOUN** If there is an **outbreak of** violence or a disease, it suddenly starts to happen.

out|come /aʊtkʌm/ **NOUN** The **outcome** of an activity is the result of it. ❍ *It's too early to know the outcome of the election.*

out|door /aʊtdɔr/ **ADJ Outdoor** activities happen outside and not in a building.

out|doors /aʊtdɔrz/ **ADV** outside rather than in a building ❍ *It was warm enough to play outdoors.*

out|er /aʊtər/ **ADJ** The **outer** parts of something are the parts furthest from the center. ❍ *the hard outer surface of a tooth*

out|fit /aʊtfɪt/ **NOUN** a set of clothes ❍ *I need a new outfit for the wedding.*

out|go|ings /aʊtgoʊɪŋz/ **PL NOUN** Your **outgoings** are the regular amounts of money that you have to spend every week or every month, for example, in order to pay your rent or bills. [FINANCE, BRIT] ❍ *Many consumers are looking for savings and reassessing their outgoings.*

out|ing /aʊtɪŋ/ **NOUN** a short trip for pleasure ❍ *We went on an outing to the local movie theater.*

out|let /aʊtlɛt, -lɪt/

1 NOUN a store that sells the goods made by a particular manufacturer at a low price [MARKETING AND SALES] ❍ *a factory outlet*

2 NOUN If someone has an **outlet for** their feelings or ideas, they have a way to express them. ❍ *He found another outlet for his anger.*

3 NOUN a place in a wall where you can connect electrical equipment to the electricity supply

4 NOUN a market for a product or service [MARKETING AND SALES] ❍ *He took a new tack to find outlets for the computers he was selling.*

out|line /aʊtlaɪn/ (**outlines, outlining, outlined**)

1 NOUN a general explanation or description of something ❍ *an outline of the plan*

2 VERB Outline is also a verb. ❍ *The report outlined some possible changes to the rules.*

3 NOUN The **outline** of an object or person is the shape of its edges. ❍ *the dark outline of a man*

out|look /aʊtlʊk/

1 NOUN The **outlook** for something is whether or not it is going to be successful. ❍ *The economic outlook is not good.*

2 NOUN Your **outlook** is your general feeling about life. ❍ *He had a positive outlook on life.*

out|place|ment /aʊtpleɪsmənt/ **NONCOUNT NOUN** An **outplacement** agency gives advice to professional people who have recently become unemployed, and helps them find new jobs. ❍ *an outplacement firm in Denver*

COLLOCATIONS

an outplacement *agency*
an outplacement *consultancy*
an outplacement *firm*
an outplacement *group*

out|put /aʊtpʊt/
1 NONCOUNT NOUN **Output** is the amount of something that a person or thing produces. [PRODUCTION] ❍ *a large fall in industrial output*
2 NONCOUNT NOUN **Output** is information produced by a computer. ❍ *You run the software, then look at the output.*

out|rage /aʊtreɪdʒ/ (**outrages, outraging, outraged**)
1 VERB If you **are outraged** by something, it shocks you or makes you very angry. ❍ *Many people were outraged by his comments.*
2 NONCOUNT NOUN **Outrage** is an intense feeling of anger and shock. ❍ *Several teachers wrote to express their outrage.*

out|ra|geous /aʊtreɪdʒəs/ **ADJ** Something that is **outrageous** shocks you or makes you very angry. ❍ *outrageous behavior*

out|sell /aʊtsɛl/ (**outsells, outselling, outsold**) **VERB** If one product **outsells** another product, the first product is sold more quickly or in larger quantities than the second. [MARKETING AND SALES] ❍ *The team's products easily outsell those of other American baseball teams overseas.*

out|side /aʊtsaɪd/
1 NOUN The **outside** of something is the part that surrounds or covers the rest of it. ❍ *The outside of the building was recently painted.*
2 ADJ **Outside** is also an adjective. ❍ *The outside walls are white.*
3 ADV or **PREP** not in a building but close to it ❍ *She went outside to look for Sam.* ❍ *She found him standing outside the classroom.*

out|skirts /aʊtskɜrts/ **PL NOUN** **The outskirts of** a city or a town are the parts that are farthest away from its center. ❍ *I live on the outskirts of the city.*

out|source /aʊtsɔrs/ (**outsources, outsourcing, outsourced**) **VERB** If a company **outsources** work or things, it pays workers from outside the company and often outside the country to do the work or supply the things. [BUSINESS MANAGEMENT] ❍ *companies that outsource I.T. functions* ❍ *The company began looking for ways to cut costs, which led to the decision to outsource.*
● **out|sourc|ing NONCOUNT NOUN** ❍ *The difficulties of outsourcing have been compounded by the increasing resistance of labor unions.*

out|stand|ing /aʊtstændɪŋ/
1 ADJ extremely good ❍ *She is an outstanding athlete.*
2 ADJ Money that is **outstanding** has not yet been paid and is still owed to someone. ❍ *The total debt outstanding is $70 billion.*
3 ADJ Shares that are **outstanding** are owned by a company's shareholders. ❍ *The company had 140.9 million shares outstanding in the latest quarter.*
4 ADJ **Outstanding** issues or problems have not yet been resolved. ❍ *We still have some outstanding issues to resolve before we'll have a contract that is ready to sign.*
5 ADJ very important or obvious ❍ *The company is an outstanding example of a small business that grew into a big one.*

out-tray [BRIT] → **out-box**

oval /oʊvᵊl/ **ADJ** having a shape like an egg ❍ *an oval face*

oven /ʌvᵊn/ **NOUN** a piece of equipment for cooking that is like a large metal box with a door

over /oʊvər/
1 PREP above or higher than ❍ *There was a gold mirror over the fireplace.* ❍ *I heard some planes flying over the house.*
2 PREP covering part or all of something ❍ *He lay down and pulled the blanket over himself.*
3 PREP to the other side of something ❍ *They jumped over the wall.*
4 ADV used for talking about a short distance ❍ *Come over here!* ❍ *The café is just over there.*
5 ADV If something turns **over**, the part that was facing up is now facing down. ❍ *His car rolled over on an icy road.*
6 PREP more than an amount ❍ *The house cost over $1 million.*
7 ADV If you do something **over**, you do it again. ❍ *If you don't like it, you can just do it over.*
8 ADJ completely finished ❍ *The war is over.*

over|all
1 ADJ /oʊvərɔl/ used for talking about a

situation in general or about the whole of something ❍ *We are very happy with the company's overall performance.*
2 PL NOUN Overalls are pants with a piece of cloth that covers your chest.

over|came /oʊvərkeɪm/ **Overcame** is a form of the verb **overcome**.

over|ca|pac|ity /oʊvərkəpæsɪti/ **NONCOUNT NOUN** If there is **overcapacity** in a particular industry or area, more goods have been produced than are needed. [PRODUCTION] ❍ *There is huge overcapacity in the world car industry.*

over|charge /oʊvərtʃɑrdʒ/ (**overcharges, overcharging, overcharged**) **VERB** If someone **overcharges** you, they charge you too much for their goods or services. ❍ *If you feel a taxi driver has overcharged you, say so.*

over|come /oʊvərkʌm/ (**overcomes, overcoming, overcame, overcome**) **VERB** If you **overcome** a problem or a feeling, you successfully deal with it and control it. ❍ *Strong overseas results helped the two auto makers overcome the effects of slower production, weaker sales and heavier incentives in the U.S.*

over|crowd|ed /oʊvərkraʊdɪd/ **ADJ** An **overcrowded** place has too many people in it. ❍ *We sat on the overcrowded beach.*

over|draft /oʊvərdræft/ **NOUN** If you have an **overdraft**, you have spent more money than you have in your bank account. [BANKING] ❍ *Her bank warned that unless she repaid the overdraft she could face legal action.*

> **BUSINESS ETIQUETTE**
> In Japan, you should give gifts at the end of a visit.

over|draw /oʊvərdrɔ/ (**overdraws, overdrawing, overdrew, overdrawn**) **VERB** If you **overdraw** or **overdraw** a bank account, you spend more money than you have in your bank account. [BANKING] ❍ *to overdraw an account by $200 million* ❍ *These consumers overdraw every quarter, and so always pay bank charges.* ❍ *Only a quarter of customers go overdrawn each year.*

over|due /oʊvərdu/ **ADJ** If something is **overdue**, it should have happened or arrived before now. ❍ *Your tax payment is overdue.*

over|flow /oʊvərfloʊ/ **VERB** If a container **overflows**, the liquid that is in it flows over the edges. ❍ *The sink overflowed.*

over|head

> Pronounce the adjective and noun /oʊvərhɛd/. Pronounce the adverb /oʊvərhɛd/.

1 ADJ or **ADV** above you ❍ *She turned on the overhead light.* ❍ *Planes passed overhead.*
2 NONCOUNT NOUN Overhead is the regular and essential expenses of running a business, such as salaries, rent, and bills. ❍ *We had to reduce overhead to remain competitive.*

over|head costs [FINANCE] → **overhead 2**

over|head pro|jec|tor NOUN a machine that has a light inside it and makes the writing or pictures on a sheet of plastic appear on a screen or wall [TECHNOLOGY]

over|heads /oʊvərhedz/ [FINANCE, BRIT] → **overhead 2**

over|hear /oʊvərhɪər/ (**overhears, overhearing, overheard**) **VERB** If you **overhear** someone, you hear what they are saying when they are not talking to you. ❍ *I overheard two doctors discussing me.*

over|heat /oʊvərhit/
1 VERB If something **overheats**, it becomes too hot. ❍ *The car's engine was overheating.*
2 VERB If a country's economy **overheats** or if conditions **overheat** it, it grows so rapidly that inflation and interest rates rise very quickly. [ECONOMICS] ❍ *The private sector is increasing its spending so sharply that the economy is overheating.* ❍ *Their prime consideration has been not to overheat the economy.*

over|lap (**overlaps, overlapping, overlapped**)

> Pronounce the noun /oʊvərlæp/. Pronounce the verb /oʊvərlæp/.

1 VERB If two things **overlap**, a part of one thing covers a part of the other. ❍ *The* *companies' operations don't overlap in most markets, and the corporate staffs of both have already been pared considerably.*

2 NOUN Overlap is also a noun. ❍ *There is little overlap in the companies' product lines world-wide or in geographical strength.*

over-leveraged also **overleveraged**
ADJ If an organization is **over-leveraged**, it has borrowed more money than it can pay back. [ECONOMICS, BANKING] ❍ *The company's troubles began with the collapse of an over-leveraged banking system.*

over|look /oʊvərlʊk/
1 VERB If you **overlook** a fact or a problem, you do not notice it. ❍ *We cannot overlook this important fact.*
2 VERB If a building or window **overlooks** a place, you can see the place from it. ❍ *The rooms overlook a beautiful garden.*

over|night /oʊvərnaɪt/ **ADV** or **ADJ** through the whole night or at some point during the night ❍ *The decision was made overnight.* ❍ *He decided to take an overnight fishing trip.*

over|pro|duc|tion /oʊvərprədʌkʃən/
NONCOUNT NOUN Overproduction is the production of more of a product than can be used or sold. [PRODUCTION] ❍ *The price of cocoa has been depressed by five seasons of overproduction.*

O

over|quali|fied /oʊvərkwɒlɪfaɪd/ **ADJ** having more experience or qualifications than are needed for a particular job ❍ *Many of those employed in India's remote-services business would be deemed overqualified in the West.*

over|run /oʊvərrʌn/ (**overruns, overrunning, overran**)
1 VERB If costs **overrun**, they are higher than was planned or expected. ❍ *We should stop the nonsense of taxpayers trying to finance new weapons whose costs always overrun hugely.* ❍ *Costs overran the budget by about 30%.*
2 NOUN Overrun is also a noun. ❍ *He was stunned to discover cost overruns of at least $1 billion.*
3 VERB If an event or meeting **overruns** by, for example, ten minutes, it continues for ten minutes longer than it was intended to. [BRIT] ❍ *This fee would be fairly flexible should a meeting overrun by a few minutes.*

over|seas /oʊvərsiz/ **ADJ** or **ADV** happening or existing abroad ❍ *He enjoyed his overseas trip.* ❍ *He's now working overseas.*

over|sell /oʊvərsɛl/ (**oversells, overselling, oversold**) **VERB** If you **oversell** a product, you sell more of it than can be supplied. [MARKETING AND SALES] ❍ *The company oversold crop insurance before and during last summer's drought.*

over|sleep /oʊvərslip/ (**oversleeps, oversleeping, overslept**) **VERB** If you **oversleep**, you sleep longer than you should. ❍ *I forgot to set my alarm and I overslept.*

over|spend (**overspends, overspending, overspent**)

> Pronounce the verb /oʊvərspɛnd/.
> Pronounce the noun /oʊvərspɛnd/.

1 VERB If you **overspend**, you spend more money than you can afford to. ❍ *Don't overspend on your home and expect to get the money back when you sell.*
2 NOUN If an organization has an **overspend**, it spends more money than was planned or allowed in its budget. [BRIT] ❍ *The National Audit Office identified an overspend of £4.1bn on four projects last year.*

over|staffed /oʊvərstæft/ **ADJ** If a company or an organization is **overstaffed**, too many staff have been employed to work there. [HR] ❍ *The personnel department is grossly overstaffed.*

over|sub|scribed /oʊvərsəbscraɪbd/ **ADJ** If shares are **oversubscribed**, people want to buy more of them than there are available. ❍ *If the share issue is oversubscribed, then the firm must use some formula to allocate shares between applicants.*

over-the-counter
1 ADJ Over-the-counter shares are not bought and sold on a stock exchange, but directly with a broker. [FINANCE] ❍ *The announcement sent the stock tumbling $2.75 a share, or 23%, to close at $9.125 in national over-the-counter trading.*

2 ADV **Over the counter** is also an adverb. ❍ *a real-estate investment trust that has traded over the counter*

3 ADJ **Over-the-counter** medicines are able to be sold without a prescription. ❍ *The company has large interests in over-the-counter drugs.*

over|time /oʊvərtaɪm/

1 NONCOUNT NOUN **Overtime** is extra time that you spend doing your job. [HR] ❍ *You can earn 1.5 times your regular pay for up to 8 hours of overtime.*

2 ADV **Overtime** is also an adverb. ❍ *He worked overtime to finish the job.*

over|weight /oʊvərweɪt/ ADJ Someone who is **overweight** is heavier than they should be.

over|whelm|ing /oʊvərwɛlmɪŋ/ ADJ An **overwhelming** feeling affects you very strongly. ❍ *an overwhelming feeling of guilt*

owe /oʊ/ (**owes, owing, owed**)

1 VERB If you **owe** money **to** someone, you have to pay money to them. [FINANCE] ❍ *Blake owed him $50.*

2 VERB If you **owe** someone something, you want to do it for them because you are grateful. ❍ *She thought Will owed her a favor.*

owl /aʊl/ NOUN a bird with large eyes that is active at night

own /oʊn/

1 ADJ or PRON If something is your **own**, it belongs to you. ❍ *I wanted to have my own business.* ❍ *Jennifer wanted her own office.* ❍ *The man's face was a few inches from my own.*

2 VERB If you **own** something, it belongs to you. ❍ *His father owns a local computer store.*

3 When you are **on** your **own**, you are alone. ❍ *He lives on his own.*

4 If you do something **on** your **own**, you do it without any help. ❍ *I work best on my own.*

own brand or **own label** [MARKETING AND SALES, BRIT] → **store brand**

own|er /oʊnər/ NOUN If you are the **owner** of something, it belongs to you. ❍ *My brother is the owner of the store.*

own|er|ship /oʊnərʃɪp/ NONCOUNT NOUN **Ownership** of something is when you own it. ❍ *The industry was transferred to private ownership.*

oxy|gen /ɒksɪdʒən/ NONCOUNT NOUN **Oxygen** is a gas in the air that is needed by all plants and animals.

oys|ter /ɔɪstər/ NOUN a small flat ocean animal that has a hard shell, is eaten as food and can produce pearls (= small round white objects used for making jewelry)

oz. **Oz.** is short for **ounce**. ❍ *1 oz. of butter*

ozone lay|er /oʊzoʊn leɪər/ NOUN **The ozone layer** is the area high above the Earth's surface that protects living things from the harmful effects of the sun.

Pp

p.a. **p.a.** is a written abbreviation for **per annum**.

PA /pi̲ eɪ/ (**PAs**) NOUN **PA** is an abbreviation for **personal assistant**. [HR]

pace /peɪs/ (**paces, pacing, paced**)
1 NOUN The **pace** of something is the speed at which it happens. ❍ *She is taking life at a slower pace now.*
2 NOUN the distance that you move when you take one step ❍ *We walked a few paces behind the guide.*
3 VERB If you **pace** a small area, you keep walking around in it because you are worried. ❍ *As they waited, Kravis paced the room nervously.*

Pacific Rim /pəsɪfɪk rɪm/ NOUN the areas and countries around the Pacific Ocean [ECONOMICS] ❍ *They plan to sell their products into new markets, such as Latin America and Pacific Rim countries.*

P

pack /pæk/
1 VERB When you **pack** a bag, you put clothes and other things into it, because you are going away. ❍ *When I was 17, I packed my bags and left home.* ❍ *I began to pack for the trip.*
2 NOUN A **pack of** things is a collection of them together in a container. ❍ *a pack of playing cards*

pack|age /pækɪdʒ/ (**packages, packaging, packaged**)
1 NOUN something wrapped in paper, or in a box or an envelope in order to be sent somewhere ❍ *I tore open the package.*
2 VERB If you **package** goods, you design and produce wrapping or a box for them. [MARKETING AND SALES] ❍ *The plant will produce film used to package products such as snack foods and tobacco.*

pack|ag|er /pækɪdʒər/ NOUN a firm that designs and produces books or television programs which are sold to publishers or television companies as finished products [MARKETING AND SALES] ❍ *The company is America's largest independent producer and packager of children's books.*

pack|ag|ing /pækɪdʒɪŋ/ NONCOUNT NOUN **Packaging** is the paper or plastic that something is in when you buy it. [MARKETING AND SALES] ❍ *plastic packaging*

pack|et /pækɪt/
1 NOUN a set of information about a particular subject ❍ *Call us for a free information packet.*
2 NOUN a small box, bag, or envelope in which an amount of something is sold ❍ *a packet of cookies*

pack|ing /pækɪŋ/ NONCOUNT NOUN **Packing** is the paper, plastic, or other material that is put around things that are being sent somewhere to protect them. [MARKETING AND SALES] ❍ *My fingers shook as I pulled the packing from the box.*

pack shot NOUN a large photograph of a product that is being advertised [MARKETING AND SALES] ❍ *Its universal logo does away with the need for different pack shots for each country.*

pad /pæd/
1 NOUN a thick, flat piece of soft material ❍ *elbow pads*
2 NOUN a number of pieces of paper attached together along one side ❍ *Have a pad ready and write down the information.*

pad|ded /pædɪd/ ADJ Something that is **padded** has soft material in it. ❍ *a padded jacket*

pad|ding /pædɪŋ/
1 NONCOUNT NOUN **Padding** is soft material in something that makes it softer or warmer. ❍ *These headphones have foam rubber padding.*
2 NONCOUNT NOUN **Padding** is false

information that is shown in a financial account, especially in an expense account.

page /peɪdʒ/ **NOUN** one side of a piece of paper in a book, a magazine, or a newspaper ○ *Turn to page 4.*

page traf|fic **NONCOUNT NOUN** **Page traffic** refers to the number of times a web page is accessed. [TECHNOLOGY]

page view (**page views**) **NOUN** an instance of someone visiting a page on the World Wide Web [TECHNOLOGY] ○ *The new company hopes to create the world's largest Chinese-language portal with about 65 million page views per month.*

paid /peɪd/
1 **Paid** is a form of the verb **pay**.
2 **ADJ** A **paid** worker receives money for their work. ○ *A team of paid staff manages the company.*

pain /peɪn/
1 **NOUN** **Pain** is the feeling of being hurt that is caused by illness or an injury. ○ *Six out of ten of the subjects suffered from pain in the lower back.*
2 **NONCOUNT NOUN** **Pain** is the sadness that you feel when something upsets you. ○ *My words caused him great pain.*

pain|ful /peɪnfəl/ **ADJ** causing physical or emotional pain ○ *Her toe was swollen and painful.*

pain|killer /peɪnkɪlər/ **NOUN** a drug that reduces or stops pain

pain|less /peɪnlɪs/ **ADJ** causing no pain ○ *The operation is a quick, painless procedure.*

paint /peɪnt/
1 **NONCOUNT NOUN** **Paint** is a colored liquid that you put onto a surface with a brush. ○ *We'll need about three cans of red paint.*
2 **VERB** If you **paint** a wall or an object, you cover it with paint.
3 **VERB** If you **paint** something or **paint** a picture of it, you produce a picture of it using paint. ○ *He is very good at painting flowers.*

paint|er /peɪntər/ **NOUN** an artist who paints pictures

paint|ing /peɪntɪŋ/ **NOUN** a picture that someone has painted ○ *She hung a large painting on the wall.*

pair /pɛər/
1 **NOUN** A **pair of** things is two things of the same size and shape that are used together. ○ *a pair of shoes*
2 **NOUN** You can call some objects that have two main parts of the same size and shape a **pair**. ○ *a pair of jeans*

pa|jam|as /pədʒɑməz, -dʒæm-/ **PL NOUN** **Pajamas** are loose pants and a top that people wear in bed.

pal /pæl/ **NOUN** Your **pals** are your friends. [INFORMAL] ○ *They talked like old pals.*

pal|ace /pælɪs/ **NOUN** a large, grand building where a king or queen lives ○ *We visited Buckingham Palace.*

pale /peɪl/ (**paler, palest**)
1 **ADJ** A **pale** color is not strong or bright. ○ *a pale blue dress*
2 **ADJ** If someone looks **pale**, their face is a lighter color than usual. ○ *She looked pale and tired.*

pal|let /pælɪt/ **NOUN** a flat wooden or metal platform on which goods are stored in a warehouse [PRODUCTION] ○ *The warehouse will hold more than 90,000 pallets storing 30 million Easter eggs.*

palm /pɑm/
1 **NOUN** a tree that grows in hot countries with long leaves at the top and no branches ○ *white sand and palm trees*
2 **NOUN** The **palm of** your hand is the inside part of your hand, between your fingers and your wrist.

pam|phlet /pæmflɪt/ **NOUN** a thin book with a paper cover that gives information about something ○ *There are numerous pamphlets on how to deal with interviews.*

pan /pæn/ **NOUN** a round metal container with a long handle, used for cooking things in ○ *Heat the butter and oil in a large pan.*

P & L /pi ən el/ **P & L** is an abbreviation for **profit and loss**. [FINANCE]

p & p /pi ən pi/ **p & p** is an abbreviation for "postage and packing." [LOGISTICS AND DISTRIBUTION, BRIT] ○ *The cost is £10 plus £3.50 p&p.*

pan|el /pæ̲nᵊl/
1 NOUN a small group of people who discuss something, give advice, or make a decision ❍ *a panel of experts*
2 NOUN a flat piece of wood or other material that forms part of a larger object such as a door ❍ *a glass panel*

pan|ic /pæ̲nɪk/ (**panics, panicking, panicked**)
1 NONCOUNT NOUN Panic is a strong feeling of fear that makes you act without thinking carefully. ❍ *As panic spread, speculators began to sell blue-chip stocks to offset their losses.*
2 VERB If you **panic**, you suddenly feel afraid, and act without thinking carefully. ❍ *Guests panicked and screamed when the bomb exploded.*

pan|ties /pæ̲ntiz/ **PL NOUN Panties** are underwear for women or girls that covers the lower part of the body, but not the legs.

pants /pæ̲nts/ **PL NOUN Pants** are a piece of clothing that covers your legs. ❍ *He wore brown corduroy pants.*

pa|per /peɪ̲pər/
1 NONCOUNT NOUN Paper is a material that you write on or wrap things with. ❍ *a piece of paper* ❍ *a paper bag*
2 NOUN a newspaper ❍ *I got a paper when I went downtown.*
3 PL NOUN Papers are sheets of paper with information on them. ❍ *The briefcase contained important official papers.*

paper|back /peɪ̲pərbæk/ **NOUN** a book with a thin cardboard cover

paper|work /peɪ̲pərwɜrk/ **NONCOUNT NOUN Paperwork** is work that involves dealing with letters, reports, and records.

par /pɑ̲r/
1 If you say that two people or things are **on a par with** each other, you mean that they are equally good or bad, or equally important. ❍ *They hope to transform Brazil into an oil power on a par with Venezuela or Saudi Arabia.*
2 If someone or something is **below par** or **under par**, they are below the standard you expected. ❍ *These targets are difficult to meet when growth is below par.*
3 If someone or something is **up to par**, they are as good as the standard you expected. ❍ *He is counting on a changing market to bring his firm's performance up to par.*

para|chute /pæ̲rəʃut/ **NOUN** a large piece of thin cloth that a person attaches to their body when they jump from an aircraft to help them float safely to the ground ❍ *They fell 41,000 feet before opening their parachutes.*

pa|rade /pəreɪ̲d/ **NOUN** a line of people or vehicles moving through a public place in order to celebrate an important event ❍ *a military parade*

para|dise /pæ̲rədaɪs/
1 NOUN In some religions, **paradise** is a beautiful place where good people go after they die.
2 NOUN a beautiful or perfect place ❍ *The island really is a tropical paradise.*

para|graph /pæ̲rəgræf/ **NOUN** a section of a piece of writing which begins on a new line ❍ *a short introductory paragraph*

par|al|lel /pæ̲rəlɛl/ **ADJ** If two lines are **parallel**, they are the same distance apart along their whole length. ❍ *Remsen Street is parallel with Montague Street.*

pa̲r|al|lel i̲m|port|ing NONCOUNT NOUN Parallel importing is the practice of importing products such as medicines that are then sold more cheaply than products produced locally.

para|lyse /pæ̲rəlaɪz/ [BRIT] → **paralyze**

para|lyze /pæ̲rəlaɪz/ (**paralyzes, paralyzing, paralyzed**) **VERB** If someone **is paralyzed**, they are unable to move all or part of their body. ❍ *She is paralyzed from the waist down.*

par|cel /pɑ̲rsᵊl/ **NOUN** something that is wrapped in paper so that it can be sent by mail ❍ *They sent parcels of food and clothing.*

par|don /pɑ̲rdᵊn/
1 You say "**Pardon?**," "**I beg your pardon?**," or "**Pardon me?**" when you want someone to repeat what they have just said. [SPOKEN]
2 You say "**I beg your pardon**" as a way of apologizing for making a small mistake.

[SPOKEN] ❍ *I beg your pardon. I thought you were someone else.*

par|ent /pɛərənt, pær-/ **NOUN** Your **parents** are your mother and father.
● **pa|ren|tal** /pərɛntᵊl/ **ADJ** ❍ *Nordic countries have a generous system of paid parental leave.*

pa|ren|tal leave **NONCOUNT NOUN** **Parental leave** is time away from work, usually without pay, that parents are allowed in order to care for their children. [HR] ❍ *Parents are entitled to 13 weeks' parental leave.*

par|ent com|pa|ny (**parent companies**) **NOUN** a company that owns more than half the shares of another company [ADMINISTRATION, ECONOMICS] ❍ *Workers fear that the job cuts announced by its American parent company may hit Scotland.*

par|ent|hood /pɛərənthʊd, pær-/ **NONCOUNT NOUN** **Parenthood** is the state of being a parent.

par|ity /pærɪti/ **NONCOUNT NOUN** If there is **parity** between two things, they are equal. [FORMAL] ❍ *Women have yet to achieve wage or occupational parity in many fields.*

park /pɑrk/
1 NOUN a public area of land with grass and trees ❍ *Central Park*
2 NOUN a place where people play baseball ❍ *We played baseball in that park every summer.*
3 VERB When you **park** somewhere, you drive a vehicle into a position and leave it there. ❍ *They parked in the street outside the house.* ❍ *He found a place to park the car.*

park|ing lot (**parking lots**) **NOUN** an area of ground where people can leave their cars ❍ *I found a parking lot one block up the street.*

par|lia|ment /pɑrləmənt/ also **Parliament** **NOUN** the people who make the laws of some countries ❍ *The German Parliament today approved the policy.*

part /pɑrt/
1 NOUN **Part of** something is a piece of it. ❍ *This is the second part of a two-step action.*
2 NOUN a piece of a machine ❍ *The company makes small parts for airplanes.*
3 NOUN one character's words and actions in a play or movie ❍ *He played the part of Hamlet.*
4 If you **take part in** an activity, you do it together with other people. ❍ *Thousands of patients took part in the study.*

part ex|change **NONCOUNT NOUN** **Part exchange** is a method of payment where used goods are taken as part of the payment for more expensive goods of the same type. [MARKETING AND SALES] ❍ *They offer part exchange deals on all their new cars.*

par|tial /pɑrʃᵊl/ **ADJ** not complete or whole ❍ *These plants prefer to grow in partial shade.*
● **par|tial|ly** **ADV** ❍ *Lisa is partially blind.*

par|tici|pant /pɑrtɪsɪpənt/ **NOUN** a person who takes part in an activity ❍ *Participants in the course will learn techniques to improve their memory.*

par|tici|pate /pɑrtɪsɪpeɪt/ (**participates, participating, participated**) **VERB** If you **participate in** an activity, you take part in it. ❍ *About 30,000 employees are eligible to participate in the plan.* ● **par|tici|pa|tion** /pɑrtɪsɪpeɪʃən/ **NONCOUNT NOUN** ❍ *Doctors recommend exercise or participation in sport at least two times a week.*

par|ti|ci|ple /pɑrtɪsɪpᵊl/ **NOUN** In grammar, a **participle** is a form of the verb that usually ends in "-ed" or "-ing."

P

par|ticu|lar /pərtɪkyələr/
1 ADJ used for showing that you are talking about one thing or one type of thing rather than other similar ones ❍ *Where did you hear that particular story?*
2 ADJ used for showing that something is greater or stronger than usual ❍ *We place particular importance on language training.*

par|ticu|lar|ly /pərtɪkyələrli/ **ADV** especially ❍ *I particularly liked the wooden chairs.*

part|ly /pɑrtli/ **ADV** not completely, but a little ❍ *It's partly my fault.*

part|ner /pɑrtnər/
1 NOUN your husband or wife or your boyfriend or girlfriend ❍ *Len's partner died four years ago.*

2 NOUN the person you are doing something with, for example dancing, playing a sport or running a business [ADMINISTRATION] ❍ *One business partner can insure the life of the other partner.*

part|ner|ship /pɑrtnərʃɪp/

1 NOUN a relationship in which two or more people or groups work together ❍ *We want to develop a closer partnership between the two schools.*

2 NOUN a relationship in which two or more people, businesses or industries work together as partners [ADMINISTRATION] ❍ *Alex and Mikhail were in partnership then: Mikhail handled the creative side; Alex was the financier.*

3 NOUN a company that is owned by two or more people [ADMINISTRATION] ❍ *They formed a partnership with a franchise owner.*

part-time

The adverb is spelled **part time**.

ADJ or ADV If you work **part time**, you work for only part of each day or week. [HR] ❍ *She has a part-time job.* ❍ *I want to work part time.*

part-time job (**part-time jobs**) NOUN a job in which you work for only part of each day or week [HR] ❍ *Many professionals juggle part-time jobs.*

P

par|ty /pɑrti/ (**parties**)

1 NOUN a social event, often to celebrate something ❍ *a birthday party*

2 NOUN a political organization whose members have similar aims and beliefs ❍ *He is a member of the Republican Party.*

3 NOUN a group of people doing something together ❍ *We passed by a party of tourists.*

par value (**par values**) NOUN the value printed on the face of a share certificate

pass /pæs/

1 VERB When you **pass** someone or something, you go past them. ❍ *When she passed the door, the telephone began to ring.* ❍ *Jane stood aside to let her pass.*

2 VERB When someone or something **passes** in a particular direction, they move in that direction. ❍ *A helicopter passed overhead.*

3 VERB If you **pass** an object **to** someone, you give it to them. ❍ *Pam passed the books to Dr. Wong.*

4 VERB If you **pass** something **on to** someone, you give them some information. ❍ *Mary Hayes passed on the news to McEvoy.*

5 VERB When time **passes**, it goes by.

6 VERB If you **pass** time in a particular way, you spend it in that way. ❍ *A relatively small number of people pass the time in a job for life.*

7 VERB If you **pass** an examination, you succeed in it. ❍ *Tina passed her driving test last week.*

8 VERB When a government **passes** a new law, they formally agree to it.

▶ **pass out** If you **pass out**, you suddenly become unconscious. ❍ *He felt sick and then passed out.*

pas|sage /pæsɪdʒ/

1 NOUN a long narrow space that connects two places ❍ *A narrow passage leads to the kitchen.*

2 NOUN a short part of a book ❍ *He read a passage to her from one of Max's books.*

pas|sen|ger /pæsɪndʒər/ NOUN a person traveling in a vehicle but not driving it

pas|sion /pæʃən/ NONCOUNT NOUN **Passion** is a very strong feeling of interest or attraction. ❍ *She has a passion for music.*

pas|sion|ate /pæʃənɪt/ ADJ If you are **passionate about** something, you have very strong feelings about it or a strong belief in it. ❍ *He is very passionate about the project.*

pas|sive /pæsɪv/

1 ADJ A **passive** person allows things to happen without taking action. ❍ *I disliked his passive attitude.*

2 NOUN In grammar, **the passive** is the form of a verb that you use to show that the subject does not perform the action but is affected by it. For example, in "He's been murdered," the verb "murder" is in the passive. Compare with **active**.

Pass|over /pæsoʊvər/ NONCOUNT NOUN **Passover** is a Jewish festival in March or April.

pass|port /pæspɔrt/ NOUN an official document that you have to show when you enter or leave a country ❍ *You should take your passport with you when you change your money.*

pass|word /pæswɜrd/ **NOUN** a secret word or phrase that allows you to enter a place or to use a computer system

past /pæst/

1 NOUN The past is the time before the present. ○ *In the past, most babies with this disease died.*

2 PREP used for talking about a time that is thirty minutes or less after an hour ○ *It's ten past eleven.*

3 PREP or **ADV** If you go **past** someone or something, you pass them. ○ *I walked past him.* ○ *An ambulance drove past.*

pas|ta /pɑstə/ **NONCOUNT NOUN Pasta** is a type of food made from a mixture of flour, eggs, and water that is made into different shapes and then boiled.

paste /peɪst/ (**pastes, pasting, pasted**)

1 VERB If you **paste** something onto a surface, you stick it there with glue. ○ *He pasted labels onto the bottles.*

2 VERB If you **paste** text or images into a computer document, you copy them there. ○ *The text can be copied and pasted into your email program.*

pas|try /peɪstri/ (**pastries**)

1 NONCOUNT NOUN Pastry is a food made from flour, fat, and water that is often used for making pies (= a dish of meat, vegetables or fruit with a cover made of pastry).

2 NOUN a small cake made with sweet pastry ○ *The bakery sells delicious cakes and pastries.*

pat /pæt/ (**pats, patting, patted**)

1 VERB If you **pat** something or someone, you touch them lightly with your flat hand. ○ *The woman patted her hair nervously.*

2 NOUN Pat is also a noun. ○ *He gave her a friendly pat on the shoulder.*

patch /pætʃ/

1 NOUN a part on a surface that is different in appearance from the area around it ○ *There was a small patch of blue in the gray clouds.*

2 NOUN a piece of cloth that you use to cover a hole in a piece of clothing ○ *His jacket had leather patches on the elbows.*

pa|tent /pætᵊnt/

1 NOUN an official right to be the only person or company allowed to make or sell a new product for a certain period of time [BUSINESS MANAGEMENT] ○ *P&G applied for a patent on its cookies.*

2 VERB If you **patent** something, you obtain a patent for it. [BUSINESS MANAGEMENT] ○ *The invention has been patented by the university.*

COLLOCATIONS

to *file* a patent *on/for* something
to *grant* somebody a patent *on/for* something
to *have* a patent *on/for* something
to *obtain* a patent *on/for* something
patent *infringement*

pa|ter|nity leave /pətɜrnɪti liv/ **NONCOUNT NOUN** If a man has **paternity leave**, his employer allows him some time off work because his child has just been born. [HR] ○ *Paternity leave is rare and, where it does exist, it's unlikely to be for any longer than two weeks.*

path /pæθ/ **NOUN** a long, narrow piece of ground that people walk along ○ *We followed the path along the cliff.*

pa|thet|ic /pəθɛtɪk/ **ADJ** weak or not very good ○ *What a pathetic attempt to hide the truth.*

pa|tience /peɪʃəns/ **NONCOUNT NOUN** If you have **patience**, you are able to stay calm when something is annoying or takes a long time. ○ *He doesn't have the patience to wait.*

pa|tient /peɪʃənt/

1 NOUN a person who is receiving medical treatment ○ *The patient was suffering from heart problems.*

2 ADJ able to stay calm when something is annoying or takes a long time ○ *Please be patient—your check will arrive soon.*

• **pa|tient|ly ADV** ○ *She waited patiently for Frances to finish talking.*

pat. pend. pat. pend. is a written abbreviation for "patent pending." [LEGAL, BUSINESS MANAGEMENT]

pa|trol /pətroʊl/ (**patrols, patrolling, patrolled**)

1 VERB When soldiers, police, or guards **patrol** an area, they go around it to make sure that there is no trouble there. ❍ *Prison officers continued to patrol the grounds.*

2 NOUN a group of soldiers or vehicles that go around an area in order to make sure that there is no trouble there ❍ *The three men attacked a border patrol last night.*

pa|tron /peɪtrən/

1 NOUN a person who supports and gives money to artists, writers, or musicians ❍ *Catherine the Great was a patron of the arts and sciences.*

2 NOUN The **patron** of a charity, group, or campaign is an important person who allows his or her name to be used for publicity. ❍ *He has now become one of the patrons of the association.*

3 NOUN The **patrons** of a place such as a bar or hotel are its customers. ❍ *Few patrons of a high-priced hotel can be led to expect anything other than luxury service.*

pat|tern /pætərn/

1 NOUN the way in which something often happens or is done ❍ *This small gain contrasts with the usual pattern of bigger increases at this time of year.*

2 NOUN an arrangement of lines or shapes that form a design ❍ *The carpet had a pattern of light and dark stripes.*

P

pause /pɔz/ (**pauses, pausing, paused**)

1 VERB If you **pause** while you are doing something, you stop for a short time and then continue. ❍ *She started speaking when I paused for breath.*

2 NOUN a short period of time when you stop doing something ❍ *After a pause Al said: "I'm sorry."*

pave|ment /peɪvmənt/

1 NOUN the hard surface of a road ❍ *It can be difficult to control the car on a wet pavement.*

2 NOUN A **pavement** is the same as a **sidewalk**. [BRIT]

paw /pɔ/ **NOUN** The **paws** of an animal such as a dog are its feet. ❍ *The kitten was black with white paws.*

pawn /pɔn/ **VERB** If you **pawn** something that you own, you leave it with a person who gives you money for it and who can sell it if you do not pay back the money before a certain time. ❍ *He is thinking of pawning his watch.*

pawn|broker /pɔnbroʊkər/ **NOUN** a person who lends people money in return for something they own, which can be sold if the money is not paid back before a certain time

pay /peɪ/ (**pays, paying, paid**)

1 VERB When you **pay for** something, you give someone an amount of money for it. ❍ *Can I pay for my ticket with a credit card?*

2 VERB When you **pay** a bill or a debt, you give someone the money you owe. ❍ *She paid the hotel bill before she left.*

3 VERB When you **are paid**, you get your salary from your employer. ❍ *I get paid monthly.*

4 NONCOUNT NOUN **Pay** is also a noun. ❍ *They complained about their pay and working conditions.*

▸ **pay back** If you **pay back** money that you have borrowed from someone, you give them the money you owe. ❍ *He promised to pay the money back as soon as he could.*

▸ **pay down**

1 If you **pay down**, you pay a sum of money at the time when you buy something as the first of a series of payments.

2 If you **pay down** a debt, you pay money to reduce the amount of your debt. ❍ *If the tire business were sold, the proceeds could pay down a significant portion of their debt.*

▸ **pay in** If you **pay in** money or checks, you take them to a bank to be put in a bank account. ❍ *I paid in the checks from last week's sales.*

▸ **pay off**

1 If you **pay off** a debt, you pay the complete amount of money you owe. ❍ *Such losses could impair any airline's ability to pay off their debts.*

2 If you **pay** someone **off**, you give them all the money you owe them and stop employing them.

▸ **pay out** If you **pay out** money, you distribute it. ❍ *The company pays out about 25% of its earnings in dividends.*

COLLOCATIONS

a pay *rise*
a pay *cut*
a *rate of* pay
a pay *increase*

pay|able /peɪəbᵊl/
1 ADJ If an amount of money is **payable**, it has to be paid or it can be paid. ❍ *The money is not payable until January 31.*
2 ADJ If a check or money order is made **payable to** you, it has your name written on it to show that you are the person who will receive the money. ❍ *Make your check payable to "Stanford Alumni Association."*

pay-as-you-go also **pay as you go ADJ** **Pay-as-you-go** services are ones where you pay for something when you use it rather than before or afterward. ❍ *a new pay-as-you-go telephone service*

pay|check /peɪtʃɛk/ **NOUN** the money that your employer gives you for your work ❍ *I get a small paycheck every month.*

pay|day /peɪdeɪ/ **NOUN** the day of the week or month on which you receive your wages or salary ❍ *Until next payday, I was literally without any money.*

PAYE /piː eɪ waɪ iː/ **NONCOUNT NOUN** In Britain, **PAYE** is a system of paying income tax in which your employer pays your tax directly to the government. **PAYE** is short for "pay as you earn." [FINANCE, ECONOMICS]

payee /peɪi/ **NOUN** a person who is to receive money [FORMAL] ❍ *On the check, write the name of the payee and then sign your name.*

paying-in slip (**paying-in slips**) **NOUN** a small piece of paper on which you write information when you are paying in a check by giving it to a person who works in a bank [BANKING, BRIT]

pay|load /peɪloʊd/
1 NOUN The **payload** of an aircraft or spacecraft is the amount or weight of things or people that it is carrying. ❍ *With these very large passenger payloads one question looms above all others – safety.*
2 NOUN The **payload** of a missile is the quantity of explosives it contains. ❍ *The missile can carry a 1000kg payload up to 1300 miles.*

pay|ment /peɪmənt/
1 NOUN an amount of money that is paid to someone ❍ *You will receive 13 monthly payments.*
2 NONCOUNT NOUN Payment is the act of paying money. ❍ *Players now expect payment for interviews.*

pay-per-click NONCOUNT NOUN Pay-per-click is a system of payment used on the Internet in which an advertiser on a website pays the website owner according to the number of people who visit the advertiser's website. [E-COMMERCE] ❍ *The company launched a pay-per-click listing service last month.*

pay|roll /peɪroʊl/ **NOUN** The people **on** the **payroll** of a company are the people who work for it and are paid by it. [ADMINISTRATION] ❍ *They had 87,000 employees on the payroll.*

PC /pi si/ (**PCs**) **NOUN** A **PC** is a computer that people use at school, at home, or in an office. **PC** is short for **personal computer**.

PDF /pi di ɛf/ **NONCOUNT NOUN PDF** files are computer documents that look exactly like the original documents. **PDF** is short for "Portable Document Format."

pea /pi/ **NOUN Peas** are very small, round, green vegetables.

peace /pis/
1 NONCOUNT NOUN When there is **peace** in a country, there is not a war. ❍ *The two countries signed a peace agreement.*
2 NONCOUNT NOUN Peace is the state of being quiet and calm. ❍ *I just want some peace and quiet.*

peace|ful /pisfəl/
1 ADJ not involving war or violence ❍ *a peaceful solution to the conflict* • **peace|ful|ly ADV** ❍ *The governor asked the protestors to leave peacefully.*
2 ADJ quiet and calm ❍ *the peaceful waters of the Indian Ocean*

peach /pitʃ/ (**peaches**) **NOUN** a round fruit with a soft red and orange skin

peak /pik/
1 NOUN The **peak** of a process or an activity is the point at which it is at its strongest or most successful. ❍ *His career was at its peak when he died.*
2 NOUN a mountain or the top of a mountain ❍ *They could see the snowy peaks of the Canadian Rockies.*

pea|nut /pinʌt, -nət/ **NOUN Peanuts** are small nuts that you can eat.

pear /pɛər/ **NOUN** a juicy fruit with white flesh and green skin that is narrow at the top and wider at the bottom

pearl /pɜrl/ **NOUN** a hard, white jewel that grows inside the shell of an oyster (= a water creature) ❍ *She wore a string of pearls.*

peas|ant /pɛzᵊnt/ **NOUN** a person who works on the land, especially in poor countries

pe|cu|liar /pɪkyulyər/ **ADJ** strange or unusual ❍ *Mr. Kennet has a rather peculiar sense of humor.*

ped|al /pɛdᵊl/

1 NOUN The **pedals** on a bicycle are the two parts that you push with your feet.

2 VERB When you **pedal** a bicycle, you push the pedals around with your feet. ❍ *We pedaled slowly through the city streets.*

3 NOUN a part of a car or machine that you press with your foot ❍ *the brake pedal*

pe|des|trian /pɪdɛstriən/ **NOUN** a person who is walking ❍ *The sidewalks were busy with pedestrians.*

peel /pil/

1 NONCOUNT NOUN The **peel** of a fruit is its skin. ❍ *Add in the grated lemon peel.*

2 VERB When you **peel** fruit or vegetables, you remove their skins. ❍ *She began peeling potatoes.*

3 VERB If something **peels off** a surface, it comes away from it. ❍ *Paint was peeling off the walls.* ❍ *It took me two days to peel off the labels.*

peer /pɪər/ **VERB** If you **peer at** something, you look at it very closely, usually because it is difficult to see. ❍ *He found her peering at a computer print-out.*

peg /pɛg/ (**pegs, pegging, pegged**)

1 NOUN a small piece of wood or metal that you use for attaching one thing to another thing ❍ *Before they began to use copper nails, they used oak pegs.*

2 NOUN a small hook on a wall that you hang things on ❍ *The hall had a row of pegs on one wall with some coats hanging on it.*

3 VERB If you **peg** the price of something, you set it at a fixed value. ❍ *The government announced efforts to peg the currency to the euro, despite lacking the reserves to defend it.*

pen /pɛn/ **NOUN** an object that you use for writing with ink (= a colored liquid)

pen|al|ty /pɛnᵊlti/ (**penalties**) **NOUN** a punishment for doing something that is against a law or rule ❍ *The maximum penalty for dangerous driving is five years in prison.*

pen|cil /pɛnsᵊl/ **NOUN** a thin piece of wood with a substance through the middle that you use to write or draw with

pend|ing /pɛndɪŋ/ **ADJ** If something is **pending**, it is due to be dealt with or granted. [FORMAL] ❍ *The company has ten patents pending in foreign countries.*

pen|etrate /pɛnɪtreɪt/ (**penetrates, penetrating, penetrated**)

1 VERB If something **penetrates** an object, it gets into it or passes through it. ❍ *X-rays can penetrate many objects.*

2 VERB If a company **penetrates** a market, it becomes successful in that market. [MARKETING AND SALES] ❍ *Manufacturing companies have been successful in penetrating overseas markets in recent years.*

pen|etra|tion /pɛnɪtreɪʃən/

1 NONCOUNT NOUN Penetration is the act of getting into or passing through an object. ❍ *The angle of penetration showed that the blade had been pushed towards the heart.*

2 NONCOUNT NOUN Penetration is the number of people who know about a product or who buy it. [MARKETING AND SALES] ❍ *They looked at new technologies that had achieved a penetration of at least 5% in the developed world.*

3 NONCOUNT NOUN The **penetration** of a market by a company is when that company starts being successful in that market. [MARKETING AND SALES] ❍ *These factors were major elements in the successful foreign penetration of the UK market.*

pen|etra|tion pric|ing NONCOUNT NOUN Penetration pricing is the policy of setting a low price for goods or services in order to encourage sales. Compare with **competition-based pricing**, **cost-based pricing**, and

market-oriented pricing. [MARKETING AND SALES] ❍ *A policy of penetration pricing was adopted to achieve maximum penetration in this sector.*

pen|ny /pɛni/ (**pennies**) **NOUN** one cent [INFORMAL] ❍ *The price of gasoline rose by more than a penny a gallon.*

pen|ny share (**penny shares**) **NOUN** a share that is offered for sale at a low price [BANKING]

pen|sion /pɛnʃən/ **NOUN** the money that you regularly receive after you stop working [HR] ❍ *He gets a $35,000 a year pension.*

pen|sion plan (**pension plans**) or **pension scheme** **NOUN** an arrangement to receive a pension from an organization in return for making regular payments to them over a number of years [HR] ❍ *I would have been much wiser to start my own pension plan when I was younger.*

peo|ple /pipᵊl/ **PL NOUN** **People** are men, women, and children. ❍ *Millions of people have lost their homes.*

peo|ple skills **PL NOUN** **People skills** are the ability to deal with, influence, and communicate effectively with other people. [HR] ❍ *She has very good people skills and is able to manage a team.*

pep|per /pɛpər/
1 NONCOUNT NOUN **Pepper** is a spice with a hot taste that you put on food. ❍ *Season with salt and pepper.*
2 NOUN a hollow green, red, or yellow vegetable with seeds inside it ❍ *Thinly slice two red or green peppers.*

per /pər, STRONG pɜr/ **PREP** each ❍ *Average earnings per hour have not improved.*

per an|num /pər ænəm/ **ADV** A particular amount **per annum** means that amount each year. ❍ *a fee of $35 per annum*

per capi|ta /pər kæpɪtə/
1 ADJ The **per capita** amount of something is the total amount of it in a country or area divided by the number of people in that country or area. [ECONOMICS] ❍ *They have the world's largest per capita income.*
2 ADV **Per capita** is also an adverb. ❍ *Ethiopia has almost the lowest oil consumption per capita in the world.*

COLLOCATIONS
per capita *spending*
per capita *consumption*
to *do* something *on a* per capita *basis*

per|ceive /pərsiv/ (**perceives, perceiving, perceived**)
1 VERB If you **perceive** something, you notice or realize it. ❍ *A great artist teaches us to perceive reality in a different way.*
2 VERB If something is **perceived as** a particular thing, people believe it is that thing. ❍ *Stress is widely perceived as a cause of heart disease.*

percent /pərsɛnt/ (**percent**) also **per cent** **NOUN** You use **percent** to talk about amounts as parts of a hundred. One hundred percent (100%) is all of something, and 50 percent (50%) is half. ❍ *Only ten percent of our customers live in this city.*

per|cent|age /pərsɛntɪdʒ/ **NOUN** an amount of something expressed as a number of hundredths ❍ *Only a small percentage of merchandise is returned because of defects.*

per|cep|tual map|ping /pərsɛptʃuəl mæpɪŋ/ **NONCOUNT NOUN** **Perceptual mapping** is the use of a graph or map to present the findings of market research showing what people think about a product that is being developed. ❍ *The investigation used perceptual mapping techniques to develop an understanding of which aspects of the ICT service users value most.*

per|fect /pɜrfɪkt/ **ADJ** Something that is **perfect** is as good as it could possibly be. ❍ *He spoke perfect English.* ● **per|fect|ly** **ADV** ❍ *The system worked perfectly.*

per|fec|tion /pərfɛkʃən/ **NONCOUNT NOUN** **Perfection** is the quality of being as good as possible. ❍ *The technology is still years away from perfection.*

per|form /pərfɔrm/
1 VERB When you **perform** a task or an action,

you do it. ❍ *You must perform this exercise correctly to avoid back pain.*
2 VERB If you **perform** a play, a piece of music, or a dance, you do it in front of an audience. ❍ *They will be performing works by Bach and Scarlatti.*

per|for|mance /pərfɔrməns/
1 NOUN If you give a **performance**, you entertain an audience by singing, dancing, or acting. ❍ *They were giving a performance of Bizet's "Carmen."*
2 NONCOUNT NOUN Someone's or something's **performance** is how successful they are or how well they do something. [BUSINESS MANAGEMENT] ❍ *He spoke about the poor performance of the economy.*

per|for|mance ap|prais|al NONCOUNT NOUN **Performance appraisal** is the process of judging the quality of an employee's work. [HR] ❍ *They improved productivity through employee involvement and meaningful performance appraisal.*

per|for|mance cul|ture NONCOUNT NOUN A **performance culture** in a company is where the emphasis is on being successful and achieving results. [HR] ❍ *Mr. Brookes said that the group's performance culture is putting intense pressure on staff.*

P

performance-related pay NONCOUNT NOUN **Performance-related pay** is a rate of pay which is based on how well someone does their job. [BUSINESS MANAGEMENT] ❍ *plans to introduce performance-related pay for teachers*

per|for|mer /pərfɔrmər/ **NOUN** someone who entertains an audience by singing, dancing, or acting ❍ *She was one of the top jazz performers in New York City.*

per|fume /pɜrfyum, pərfyum/ **NOUN** a liquid with a pleasant smell that you put on your skin

per|haps /pərhæps, præps/ **ADV** used for showing that you are not sure whether something is true or possible ❍ *Perhaps, in time, they will understand.*

pe|ri|od /pɪəriəd/
1 NOUN a length of time ❍ *He couldn't work for a long period of time.*
2 NOUN the punctuation mark (.) that you use at the end of a sentence
3 NOUN the time each month when a woman loses blood from her body

perk /pɜrk/ **NOUN** **Perks** are special benefits that are given to people who have a particular job or belong to a particular group. [HR] ❍ *We get a company car, health insurance and other perks.*
▸ **perk up**
1 If something or someone **perks up** or if you **perk** them **up**, they become more interesting, cheerful or lively. ❍ *He perks up and jokes with them.* ❍ *To make the dish taste more interesting, the locals began perking it up with local produce.*
2 If sales, prices, or economies **perk up**, or if something **perks** them **up**, they begin to increase or improve. ❍ *House prices could perk up during the fall.*

per|ma|nent /pɜrmənənt/ **ADJ** existing or continuing forever ❍ *Some ear infections can cause permanent damage.* ❍ *a permanent job*
● **per|ma|nent|ly ADV** ❍ *His confidence has been permanently affected.*

per|mis|sion /pərmɪʃən/ **NONCOUNT NOUN** If you give someone **permission to** do something, you allow them to do it. ❍ *He asked permission to leave the room.*

per|mit (**permits, permitting, permitted**)

Pronounce the verb /pərmɪt/. Pronounce the noun /pɜrmɪt/.

1 VERB If someone **permits** you **to** do something, they allow you to do it. [FORMAL] ❍ *The guards permitted me to bring my camera.*
2 NOUN an official document that allows you to do something ❍ *a work permit*

per|pe|tu|ity /pɜrpɪtuɪti/ (**perpetuities**) **NOUN** an annuity which has no date at which it ends, and which continues to be paid for a period without limits ❍ *The return on a perpetuity is equal to the yearly cash flow divided by the present value.*

per|sist /pərsɪst/
1 VERB If something unpleasant **persists**, it continues to exist. ❍ *Contact your doctor if the cough persists.*
2 VERB If you **persist in** doing something, you

continue to do it, even if it is difficult or annoys other people. ❍ *Why do people persist in ignoring the problem?*

per|son /pɜrsᵊn/ (**people** or **persons**) **NOUN** a man, a woman, or a child ❍ *We spend eight cents per person for research on crime control.* ❍ *They were both lovely, friendly people.*

per|son|al /pɜrsənᵊl/
1 ADJ belonging or relating to a particular person ❍ *The story is based on his own personal experience.*
2 ADJ relating to your private life ❍ *Did he have any personal problems?*

per|son|al as|sis|tant (**personal assistants**) **NOUN** A **personal assistant** is a person who does office work and administrative work for someone. The abbreviation **PA** is also used. [ADMINISTRATION] ❍ *She was a busy personal assistant to a company chairman.*

per|son|al bank|ing **NONCOUNT NOUN** **Personal banking** is the part of a bank's activities that is for individual customers rather than businesses. [BANKING] ❍ *Services are confined to a range of personal banking products, such as mortgages.*

per|son|al com|put|er (**personal computers**) **NOUN** a computer that you use at work, school, or home [TECHNOLOGY]

per|son|al day (**personal days**) **NOUN** a day when an employee decides to stay at home rather than go to work

per|son|al|ity /pɜrsənælɪti/ (**personalities**) **NOUN** your character ❍ *She has a friendly personality.*

per|son|al|ly /pɜrsənəli/
1 ADV used to emphasize that you are giving your own opinion ❍ *Personally I think it's a waste of time.*
2 ADV If you do something **personally**, you do it yourself. ❍ *He wrote to them personally.*

per|son|al sec|tor (**personal sectors**) **NOUN** the part of the market that is made up of private individuals [ECONOMICS] ❍ *In the days when the personal sector saved more than it borrowed, falling inflation and high real interest rates meant people had more money.*

per|son|al sell|ing **NONCOUNT NOUN** **Personal selling** is the selling of goods or services by means of direct contact between sales staff and possible customers. [MARKETING AND SALES] ❍ *Avon concentrates on personal selling in the home.*

per|son|al shop|per (**personal shoppers**) **NOUN** a person whose job is to help people to choose their purchases, or to buy things for them [MARKETING AND SALES] ❍ *If you aren't confident about trying new fashions, consult a personal shopper.*

per|son|nel /pɜrsənɛl/ **PL NOUN** The **personnel** of an organization are the people who work for it. [HR] ❍ *military personnel*

BUSINESS ETIQUETTE
In Brazil, good conversation topics include football, family, and children.

per|spec|tive /pərspɛktɪv/
1 NOUN a way of thinking about something ❍ *This is not an adequate bid from our perspective.*
2 NOUN In art, **perspective** is a way of making some parts of a picture seem further away than others.

per|suade /pərsweɪd/ (**persuades, persuading, persuaded**) **VERB** If you **persuade** someone **to** do something, you make them do it or believe it by giving them reasons. ❍ *He intends to try to persuade them to cut their emissions of toxic chemicals.*

peso /peɪsoʊ/ (**pesos**) **NOUN** The **peso** is the unit of money that is used in Argentina, Colombia, Cuba, the Dominican Republic, Mexico, the Philippines, and Uruguay. [ECONOMICS]

pet /pɛt/ **NOUN** an animal that you keep in your home ❍ *This woman raises rabbits to sell as pets.*

pet|ro|dol|lar /pɛtroʊdɒlər/ **NOUN** a dollar earned by a country for exporting petroleum [ECONOMICS] ❍ *The flow of petrodollars is fanning a massive consumption boom.*

pet|rol /pɛtrəl/ [BRIT] → **gasoline**

P

[TECHNOLOGY] ❍ *To use the service you'll need a PIN.*

pinch /pɪntʃ/ (**pinches, pinching, pinched**)
1 VERB If you **pinch** someone, you press their skin between your thumb and first finger. ❍ *She pinched his arm as hard as she could.*
2 NOUN a very small amount of something such as salt or pepper ❍ *Add a pinch of cinnamon to the apples.*

pine|apple /paɪnæpəl/ **NOUN** a large fruit with sweet yellow flesh and thick brown skin

pink /pɪŋk/
1 ADJ having the color between red and white ❍ *pink lipstick*
2 NOUN Pink is also a noun. ❍ *I prefer pale pinks and blues.*

pink slip (**pink slips**) **NOUN** a form given to employees to inform them that they are no longer needed to do the job that they have been doing [HR, INFORMAL] ❍ *It was his fourth pink slip in two years.*

pint /paɪnt/ **NOUN** a unit for measuring liquids that is equal to 0.57 liters ❍ *a pint of ice cream*

pipe /paɪp/
1 NOUN a long tube through which a liquid or a gas can flow ❍ *water pipes*
2 NOUN an object that is used for smoking tobacco (= the dried leaves that are used for making cigarettes)

P

pi|rate /paɪrɪt/ (**pirates, pirating, pirated**)
1 NOUN Pirates are people who attack ships and steal property from them.
2 VERB Someone who **pirates** things like movies or computer programs copies them and sells them illegally.

pis|tol /pɪstəl/ **NOUN** a small gun

pit /pɪt/
1 NOUN a large hole that is dug in the ground ❍ *It takes ten people two years to fill one pit.*
2 NOUN the part of a coal mine that is under the ground
3 NOUN the large hard seed of a fruit ❍ *cherry pits*

pitch /pɪtʃ/ (**pitches, pitching, pitched**)
1 VERB If you **pitch** something somewhere, you throw it. ❍ *We spent long, hot afternoons pitching a baseball.*
2 NONCOUNT NOUN The **pitch** of a sound is how high or low it is.
3 NOUN a speech aimed at persuading people to buy something ❍ *The Office of Fair Trading is thinking of requiring all salesmen to disclose their commissions when they make their sales pitch.*

pity /pɪti/ (**pities, pitying, pitied**)
1 VERB If you **pity** someone, you feel sorry for them. ❍ *I pity him.*
2 NONCOUNT NOUN Pity is also a noun. ❍ *He felt pity for her.*
3 NOUN If you say that something is **a pity**, you mean that you feel disappointed about it. ❍ *It's a pity you arrived so late.*

piz|za /pitsə/ **NOUN** a flat, round piece of bread that is covered with tomatoes, cheese, and sometimes other foods, and then baked in an oven

place /pleɪs/ (**places, placing, placed**)
1 NOUN a building, area, town, or country ❍ *Keep your dog on a leash in public places.* ❍ *your place of birth*
2 NOUN the right or usual position for something ❍ *He returned the photo to its place on the shelf.*
3 NOUN a seat for one person ❍ *This girl was sitting in my place.*
4 NOUN your position in a race or competition ❍ *Victoria is in third place with 22 points.*
5 VERB If you **place** something somewhere, you put it there. ❍ *Brand placed the letter in his pocket.*
6 In place of means "instead of" something or someone. ❍ *Try using herbs and spices in place of salt.*
7 When something **takes place**, it happens. ❍ *The discussions took place in Paris.*

plain /pleɪn/
1 ADJ simple in style, or all the same color and with no pattern or decoration ❍ *A plain carpet makes a room look bigger.* ❍ *a plain, gray stone house*
2 ADJ obvious or easy to understand ❍ *It was plain to him what he had to do.*
3 ADJ Someone who is **plain** is not beautiful. ❍ *She was a shy, rather plain girl.*

plain|ly /pleɪnli/ **ADV** clearly ❍ *I could plainly see him turning his head.*

plan /plæn/ (**plans, planning, planned**)
1 NOUN a method for doing something that you think about in advance ❍ *They are meeting to discuss the peace plan.*
2 VERB If you **plan** what you are going to do, you decide what you are going to do. ❍ *He plans to leave Berlin on Monday.*
3 PL NOUN If you have **plans**, you are intending to do something. ❍ *He added that the company didn't have plans to sell the chain.*
4 NOUN a detailed drawing of something ❍ *Draw a plan of the garden before you start planting.*

plane /pleɪn/ **NOUN** a vehicle with wings and engines that can fly ❍ *He had plenty of time to catch his plane.*

plan|et /plænɪt/ **NOUN** a large, round object in space that moves around a star ❍ *We study the planets in the solar system.*

planned ex|pen|di|ture NONCOUNT NOUN A company's **planned expenditure** is the amount of money it expects to spend over a particular period of time. [FINANCE] ❍ *This 2.4 percent planned expenditure for capital may be too high.*

plan|ner /plænər/ **NOUN** a person whose job is to make decisions about something that is going to be done in the future ❍ *city planners*

plan|ning /plænɪŋ/ **NONCOUNT NOUN** **Planning** is the process of deciding in detail how to do something. [BUSINESS MANAGEMENT] ❍ *The advertising campaign needs careful planning.*

plant /plænt/
1 NOUN a living thing that grows in the earth ❍ *Water each plant daily.*
2 VERB When you **plant** something, you put it into the ground so that it will grow. ❍ *He plans to plant fruit trees.*
3 NOUN a factory, or a place where power is produced [PRODUCTION] ❍ *a car assembly plant*

plas|ma screen /plæzmə skrin/ (**plasma screens**) or **plasma display NOUN** a type of thin television or computer screen with good quality images

plas|tic /plæstɪk/ **NONCOUNT NOUN** **Plastic** is a light but strong material that is produced by a chemical process. ❍ *The windows are made from sheets of plastic.* ❍ *a plastic bag*

plas|tic sur|gery NONCOUNT NOUN **Plastic surgery** is operations to improve someone's appearance. ❍ *She needed several major operations, plastic surgery, and rehabilitation.*

plate /pleɪt/ **NOUN** a flat dish that is used for holding food ❍ *He ate a huge plate of bacon and eggs.*

plat|form /plætfɔrm/
1 NOUN a flat raised structure on which someone or something can stand ❍ *He walked toward the platform to begin his speech.*
2 NOUN the area in a station where you wait for a train ❍ *a subway platform*

play /pleɪ/
1 VERB When children **play**, they use toys or take part in games. ❍ *Polly was playing with her dolls.*
2 NONCOUNT NOUN **Play** is also a noun. ❍ *Children learn mainly through play.*
3 VERB When you **play** a game or a sport, you take part in it. ❍ *The twins played cards.* ❍ *I used to play basketball.*
4 VERB When one person or team **plays** another, they compete against them in a sport or a game. ❍ *Dallas will play Green Bay today.*
5 VERB If you **play** a joke or a trick on someone, you deceive them, often for fun. ❍ *She wanted to play a trick on her friends.*
6 NOUN a piece of writing performed in a theater, on the radio, or on television ❍ *"Hamlet" is my favorite play.*
7 VERB If an actor **plays** a character in a play or movie, he or she performs that part. ❍ *He played Mr. Hyde in the movie.*
8 VERB If you **play** a musical instrument, you produce music from it. ❍ *Nina was playing the piano.* ❍ *He played for me.*
9 VERB If you **play** a CD, you put it into a machine and listen to it. ❍ *She played her CDs too loudly.*
10 VERB If you **play** a market, you buy and sell in order to make a profit. ❍ *Looser margin rules allowed individual investors to play the market with borrowed funds.*

play|er /pleɪər/ **NOUN** a person who takes part in a sport or game ❍ *She was a good tennis player.*

play|ful /pleɪfəl/ **ADJ** not intended to be serious ❍ *She gave him a playful kiss.*

play|ground /pleɪgraʊnd/ **NOUN** a piece of land where children can play ❍ *playground equipment*

play|wright /pleɪraɪt/ **NOUN** a person who writes plays

pla|za /plɑzə, plæzə/
1 NOUN an open square in a city
2 NOUN a group of stores or buildings in the same area ❍ *a shopping plaza*

plc /pi ɛl si/ also **PLC NOUN** In Britain, **plc** is short for **public limited company**. [ADMINISTRATION, ECONOMICS] ❍ *British Telecommunications plc.*

plea /pli/ **NOUN** an emotional request ❍ *Their president made a desperate plea for international help.*

plead /plid/ (**pleads, pleading, pleaded, pled**)
1 VERB If you **plead with** someone to do something, you ask them in an emotional way to do it. ❍ *She pleaded with her daughter to come back home.*
2 VERB When someone **pleads guilty** or **not guilty** in a court of law, they officially say that they are guilty or not guilty of the crime. ❍ *Morris pleaded guilty to robbery.*

pleas|ant /plɛzᵊnt/
1 ADJ enjoyable or attractive ❍ *I have many pleasant memories of this place.*
2 ADJ nice and friendly ❍ *The doctor was a pleasant young man.*

please /pliz/ (**pleases, pleasing, pleased**)
1 ADV used for politely asking someone for something or to do something ❍ *Can you help us, please?* ❍ *Please come in.* ❍ *Can we have the bill, please?*
2 ADV You say **yes, please** when you are accepting something politely. ❍ *"Tea?"—"Yes, please."*
3 VERB If someone or something **pleases** you, they make you feel happy and satisfied. ❍ *The show has greatly pleased audiences in London and New York.*

pleased /plizd/
1 ADJ happy about something or satisfied with something ❍ *I'm so pleased that we solved the problem.* ❍ *I'm pleased with the way things have been going.*
2 "**Pleased to meet you**" is a polite way of saying hello to someone that you are meeting for the first time.

pleas|ure /plɛʒər/
1 NONCOUNT NOUN Something that gives you **pleasure** makes you feel happy and satisfied. ❍ *Watching sports gave him great pleasure.*
2 NOUN an activity or an experience that you find enjoyable ❍ *Watching TV is their only pleasure.*

pledge /plɛdʒ/ (**pledges, pledging, pledged**)
1 NOUN a serious promise ❍ *The meeting ended with a pledge to step up cooperation between the six states of the region.*
2 VERB When someone **pledges to** do something, they promise in a serious way to do it. When they **pledge** something, they promise to give it. ❍ *The group has pledged to support the opposition's motion.* ❍ *Philip pledges support and offers to help in any way that he can.*
3 VERB If you **pledge** a sum of money to an organization or activity, you promise to pay that amount of money to it. ❍ *The French president is pledging $150 million in French aid next year.*
4 NOUN Pledge is also a noun. ❍ *a pledge of forty two million dollars a month*
5 VERB If you **pledge** something such as a valuable possession, you officially agree that someone can have it if you do not repay money that you have borrowed. ❍ *He asked her to pledge the house as security for a loan.*

plen|ty /plɛnti/ **PRON** If there is **plenty of** something, there is a lot of it. ❍ *Don't worry. There's still plenty of time.* ❍ *I don't like long interviews. Fifteen minutes is plenty.*

plot /plɒt/ (**plots, plotting, plotted**)
1 VERB If people **plot to** do something, they plan secretly to do it. ❍ *They plotted to merge their firms and thus create the world's largest*

P

advertising group.
2 NOUN **Plot** is also a noun. ❍ *a plot to kill the president*
3 NOUN the story of a movie or a movie ❍ *He told me the plot of his new book.*

plough /plaʊ/ [BRIT] → **plow**

plow /plaʊ/
1 NOUN a large farming tool that is pulled across the soil to turn it over
2 VERB When someone **plows** land, they turn over the soil using a plow.
▸ **plow back** If you **plow back** profits into a business, you spend that money developing the business. ❍ *Earnings not paid out as dividends are plowed back into the business.*

plug /plʌg/ (**plugs, plugging, plugged**)
1 NOUN a piece of electrical equipment with metal pins that connect it to the electricity supply ❍ *Remove the power plug when you have finished.*
2 NOUN a round object that you use to block the hole in a bathtub or a sink ❍ *She pulled out the plug.*
▸ **plug in** If you **plug** a piece of electrical equipment **in**, you connect it to the electricity supply. ❍ *If you have a TV, you need a place to plug it in.*

plum /plʌm/ **NOUN** a small, sweet fruit with a smooth purple, red, or yellow skin and a large seed (= a pit) in the middle

plumb|er /plʌmər/ **NOUN** a person whose job is to put in and repair water and gas pipes

plump /plʌmp/ **ADJ** rather fat ❍ *Maria was small and plump.*

plunge /plʌndʒ/ (**plunges, plunging, plunged**)
1 VERB If something or someone **plunges** into water, they fall into it. ❍ *The bus plunged into a river.*
2 VERB If you **plunge** an object **into** something, you push it violently into it. ❍ *He plunged a fork into his dinner.*

plu|ral /plʊərəl/
1 NOUN The **plural** of a noun is the form of it that is used for talking about more than one person or thing. ❍ *"People" is the plural of "person."*
2 ADJ **Plural** is also an adjective. ❍ *"Men" is the plural form of "man."*

plus /plʌs/ **CONJ** used for showing that one number is being added to another ❍ *Two plus two equals four.*

p.m. /pi ɛm/ also **pm** **ADV** You use **p.m.** after a number when you are talking about a particular time between 12 noon and 12 midnight. Compare with **a.m.** ❍ *The building is open from 7:00 a.m. to 9:00 p.m.*

pock|et /pɒkɪt/
1 NOUN a small bag that forms part of a piece of clothing and is used for carrying things ❍ *He put the key in his jacket pocket.*
2 If you are **in pocket** after a transaction, you have made a profit. ❍ *It could lower land prices a bit, and yet leave both parties still well in pocket.*
3 If you are **out of pocket** after a transaction, you have lost money. ❍ *Public bodies may be left even more out of pocket if receipts from the sale of land and buildings after the games are lower than expected.*

pod|cast /pɒdkæst/ **NOUN** a file containing a radio show or something similar, that you can listen to on a computer or an MP3 player (= a small piece of electrical equipment for listening to music)

poem /poʊəm/ **NOUN** a piece of writing, usually in short lines, in which the words are chosen for their beauty and sound ❍ *a book of love poems*

poet /poʊɪt/ **NOUN** a person who writes poems

po|et|ry /poʊɪtri/ **NONCOUNT NOUN** **Poetry** is the form of literature that consists of poems. ❍ *She received her first U.S. paycheck for proofreading a book of Polish poetry.*

point /pɔɪnt/
1 NOUN an opinion or a fact ❍ *We disagreed with every point she made.*
2 NOUN **The point of** something is its purpose. ❍ *There's no point in fighting.*
3 NOUN a particular position or time ❍ *We're all going to die at some point.*
4 NOUN the thin, sharp end of something such as a knife
5 NOUN the small dot that separates whole numbers from parts of numbers ❍ *The highest*

temperature today was 98.5° (ninety-eight point five degrees).

6 NOUN a mark that you win in a game or a sport ❍ *Chamberlain scored 50 points.*

7 VERB If you **point at** a person or a thing, you use your finger to show where they are. ❍ *He stood and pointed at a map of the world.*

8 VERB If you **point** something **at** someone, you hold it toward them. ❍ *She smiled when Laura pointed a camera at her.*

9 NOUN an amount that is expressed as a percentage or a fraction of a percentage ❍ *The additional points can equal significantly higher charges for those seeking small loans.*

10 ▸ point out If you **point out** something, you tell someone about it or show it to them. ❍ *He pointed out the errors in the book.*

point|ed /pɔɪntɪd/ **ADJ** having a point at one end ❍ *pointed shoes*

point|less /pɔɪntlɪs/ **ADJ** having no purpose ❍ *Without an audience the performance is pointless.*

point of sale **(points of sale)**

1 NOUN The **point of sale** is the place in a store where a product is passed from the seller to the customer. The abbreviation **POS** is also used. [MARKETING AND SALES] ❍ *This technology gives us information on consumer behavior at the point of sale.*

2 NONCOUNT NOUN **Point-of-sale** is used to describe things that occur or are used at the place where you buy something. The abbreviation **POS** is also used. [MARKETING AND SALES] ❍ *Introduction of electronic point-of-sale systems is improving efficiency.*

point-of-sale ter|min|al **(point-of-sale terminals)** **NOUN** a device that is used to record information relating to the act of paying for an item in a store [MARKETING AND SALES]

point of view **(points of view)** **NOUN** Your **point of view** is your opinion on a subject. ❍ *Thanks for your point of view, John.*

poi|son /pɔɪzᵊn/

1 NONCOUNT NOUN **Poison** is a substance that harms or kills people or animals if they swallow or touch it. ❍ *Poison from the factory is causing the fish to die.*

2 VERB To **poison** someone or something means to harm them by giving them poison. ❍ *They say that she poisoned her husband.*

poi|son|ous /pɔɪzᵊnəs/ **ADJ** Something that is **poisonous** will kill you or harm you if you swallow or touch it. ❍ *All parts of this tree are poisonous.*

poi|son pill **(poison pills)** **NOUN** a way of trying to stop a takeover by doing something to make the company worth much less if the takeover were successful [FINANCE] ❍ *Some believe this level of compensation is essentially a poison pill to put off any rival bidders.*

poke /poʊk/ **(pokes, poking, poked)**

1 VERB If you **poke** someone or something, you quickly push them with your finger or with a sharp object. ❍ *Lindy poked him in the ribs.*

2 VERB If you **poke** one thing **into** another, you push the first thing into the second thing. ❍ *He poked his finger into the hole.*

pok|er /poʊkər/ **NONCOUNT NOUN** **Poker** is a card game, usually played for money.

po|lar /poʊlər/ **ADJ** relating to the North Pole or South Pole ❍ *the polar regions*

pole /poʊl/

1 NOUN a long thin piece of wood or metal, used especially for supporting things ❍ *a telephone pole*

2 NOUN The Earth's **poles** are its most northern and southern points.

po|lice /pəlis/

1 PL NOUN The **police** is the organization that is responsible for making sure that people obey the law. ❍ *The police are looking for the car.*

2 PL NOUN **Police** are men and women who are members of the police. ❍ *More than one hundred police are in the area.*

police|man /pəlismən/ **(policemen)** **NOUN** a man who is a member of the police

po|lice of|fic|er **NOUN** a member of the police ❍ *a senior police officer*

police|woman /pəliswʊmən/ **(policewomen)** **NOUN** a woman who is a member of the police

poli|cy /pɒlɪsi/ **(policies)**

1 NOUN a set of ideas or plans, especially in politics or business [BUSINESS MANAGEMENT] ❍ *The company seems to have a policy of not responding to emails.*
2 NOUN a document that shows the agreement that you have made with an insurance company [BANKING] ❍ *You are advised to read the small print of household and motor insurance policies.*

policy|holder /pɒlɪsihoʊldər/ **NOUN** a person who has an insurance policy with an insurance company [BANKING] ❍ *The first 10 percent of legal fees will be paid by the policyholder.*

pol|ish /pɒlɪʃ/ (**polishes, polishing, polished**)
1 NONCOUNT NOUN **Polish** is a substance that you put on a surface in order to clean it and make it shine. ❍ *furniture polish*
2 VERB If you **polish** something, you rub it to make it shine. ❍ *He polished his shoes.*

po|lite /pəlaɪt/ **ADJ** having or showing good manners ❍ *He seemed a polite young man.* ● **po|lite|ly** **ADV** ❍ *"Your home is beautiful," I said politely.* ● **po|lite|ness** **NONCOUNT NOUN** ❍ *She listened to him out of politeness.*

po|liti|cal /pəlɪtɪkᵊl/ **ADJ** relating to politics ❍ *I am not a member of any political party.* ● **po|liti|cal|ly** /pəlɪtɪkli/ **ADV** ❍ *Politically, this is a very risky move.*

po|liti|cal econo|my **NONCOUNT NOUN** **Political economy** is the study of the way in which a government influences or organizes a nation's wealth. [ECONOMICS]

po|liti|cal sta|bil|ity **NONCOUNT NOUN** If there is **political stability** in a country, there is a stable government or political system. [ECONOMICS] ❍ *Even though political stability is a major factor in attracting investment, politicians never get any credit.*

poli|ti|cian /pɒlɪtɪʃən/ **NOUN** a person who works in politics, especially a member of a government

poli|tics /pɒlɪtɪks/ **NONCOUNT NOUN** **Politics** is the activities and ideas that are concerned with government. ❍ *He was involved in local politics.*

poll /poʊl/ **NOUN** a way of discovering what people think about something by asking many of them questions about it ❍ *The polls are showing that women are very involved in this campaign.*

pol|len /pɒlən/ **NONCOUNT NOUN** **Pollen** is a powder that is produced by flowers.

pol|lute /pəlut/ (**pollutes, polluting, polluted**) **VERB** To **pollute** water, air, or land means to make it dirty. ❍ *Industry pollutes our rivers with chemicals.* ● **pol|lut|ed** **ADJ** ❍ *Fish are dying in the polluted rivers.*

pol|lu|tion /pəluʃən/
1 NONCOUNT NOUN **Pollution** is the process of making water, air, or land dirty. ❍ *The government announced plans for reducing pollution.*
2 NONCOUNT NOUN **Pollution** is poisonous substances that pollute water, air, or land. ❍ *The level of pollution in the river was falling.*

poly|es|ter /pɒliɛstər/ **NONCOUNT NOUN** **Polyester** is a type of artificial cloth that is mainly used for making clothes. ❍ *a green polyester shirt*

pond /pɒnd/ **NOUN** a small area of water ❍ *a duck pond*

pony /poʊni/ (**ponies**) **NOUN** a small or young horse

Pon|zi scheme /pɒnzi skim/ (**Ponzi schemes**) **NOUN** A **Ponzi scheme** is a type of illegal investment scheme. The early investors make quick profits from the money from later investors, who lose their investment. [ECONOMICS]

pool /pul/
1 NOUN A **pool** is the same as a **swimming pool**. ❍ *a heated indoor pool*
2 NONCOUNT NOUN **Pool** is a game that is played on a special table on which players try to hit balls into holes with a long stick.

poor /pʊər/
1 ADJ having very little money ❍ *"We were very poor in those days," he says.*
2 PL NOUN **The poor** are people who are poor.
3 ADJ used for showing that you are sorry for someone ❍ *I feel sorry for that poor child.*

4 ADJ of low quality ❍ *The firm has brought this problem on itself through poor management.* ● **poor|ly ADV** ❍ *"We played poorly in the first game," Mendez said.*

pop /pɒp/ (**pops, popping, popped**)
1 NONCOUNT NOUN Pop is modern music that usually has a strong rhythm. ❍ *pop stars*
2 VERB If something **pops**, it makes a short sharp sound. ❍ *He heard a balloon pop behind his head.*
3 NOUN Pop is also a noun. ❍ *Each piece of corn will make a loud pop when it is cooked.*
4 NOUN Some people call their father **Pop**. [INFORMAL]

popu|lar /pɒpyələr/ **ADJ** liked by a lot of people ❍ *Chocolate sauce is always popular with kids.* ● **popu|lar|ity** /pɒpyəlærɪti/ **NONCOUNT NOUN** ❍ *Her popularity grew.*

popu|la|tion /pɒpyəleɪʃən/ **NOUN** The **population** of a country or an area is the number of people who live in it.

pop-up store (**pop-up stores**) **NOUN** a store that is set up quickly in a temporary location [ECONOMICS] ❍ *Pop-up stores reflect a weak economy; otherwise landlords would have those spaces rented to the hilt.*

porch /pɔrtʃ/ (**porches**) **NOUN** a raised structure with a roof that is built along the outside wall of a house

P

pore /pɔr/ **NOUN** Your **pores** are the very small holes in your skin. ❍ *Warm up the skin with steam to allow the pores to open.*

pork /pɔrk/ **NONCOUNT NOUN Pork** is meat from a pig. ❍ *Foods to be sent include beef, pork, corn, butter, and rice.*

port /pɔrt/
1 NOUN a town by the sea where ships arrive and leave ❍ *the Mediterranean port of Marseilles*
2 NOUN a place on a computer where you can attach another piece of equipment ❍ *The scanner plugs into the printer port.*

port|able /pɔrtəbᵊl/ **ADJ** designed to be carried or moved around ❍ *a portable storage device*

port|age /pɔrtɪdʒ, pɔrtɑʒ/ **NONCOUNT NOUN** In business, **portage** is the cost of transporting something. [LOGISTICS AND DISTRIBUTION]

por|ter /pɔrtər/ **NOUN** a person whose job is to carry people's baggage

port|fo|lio /pɔrtfoʊlioʊ/
1 NOUN a collection of examples of someone's work ❍ *After dinner that evening, Edith showed them a portfolio of her own political cartoons.*
2 NOUN In finance, a **portfolio** is the combination of investments that a particular person or company owns. ❍ *Roger Early, a portfolio manager at Federated Investors Corp*
3 NOUN a range of products or designs ❍ *The company has continued to invest heavily in a strong portfolio of products.*

port|fo|lio work|er (**portfolio workers**) **NOUN** someone who works for several employers at the same time ❍ *More and more people are becoming portfolio workers, hopping from job to job.*

por|tion /pɔrʃən/
1 NOUN a part of something ❍ *I have spent a large portion of my life here.*
2 NOUN the amount of food that is given to one person at a meal ❍ *The portions were huge.*

por|trait /pɔrtrɪt, -treɪt/ **NOUN** a painting, a drawing, or a photograph of a person ❍ *family portraits*

por|tray /pɔrtreɪ/ **VERB** To **portray** someone or something means to represent them, for example in a book or a movie. ❍ *The film portrays a group of young people who live in lower Manhattan.*

POS /pi oʊ ɛs/ **POS** is an abbreviation for **point of sale**. [MARKETING AND SALES] ❍ *a POS system that doubles as an inventory and sales control system*

pose /poʊz/ (**poses, posing, posed**)
1 VERB If you **pose for** a photograph or a painting, you stay in one position so that someone can photograph you or paint you.
2 NOUN a way of standing, sitting, or lying ❍ *In one pose he is laughing as a baby tries to push food into his mouth.*
3 VERB If you **pose** a question, you ask it. [FORMAL] ❍ *I finally posed the question, "Why?"*
4 VERB If you **pose as** someone, you pretend

to be that person. ❍ *Many stores employ detectives who pose as customers.*

BUSINESS ETIQUETTE
When you are addressing people in Japan, you should use the person's surname followed by the word *san*, which means *Mr.* or *Ms*. Japanese business associates may feel uncomfortable using first names.

po|si|tion /pəzɪʃən/
1 NOUN the place where someone or something is ❍ *Mark the position of the handle on the door.*
2 NOUN Your **position** is the way you are sitting, lying, or standing. ❍ *Mr. Dambar raised himself to a sitting position.*
3 NOUN A **position** in a company or organization is a job. [FORMAL] ❍ *He left to take a position with IBM.*
4 NOUN Your **position** is the situation you are in. ❍ *He's in a very difficult position.*

po|si|tion|ing /pəzɪʃənɪŋ/ **NONCOUNT NOUN** A product's **positioning** is its position in the opinion of consumers, compared to other brands. [MARKETING AND SALES]

posi|tive /pɒzɪtɪv/
1 ADJ hopeful and confident ❍ *Be positive about your future.* ● **posi|tive|ly ADV** ❍ *You must try to start thinking positively.*
2 ADJ A **positive** experience or effect is pleasant and encouraging. ❍ *I want to have a positive effect on the company.*
3 ADJ If you are **positive** about something, you are completely sure about it. ❍ *"Are you sure she said eight?"—"Positive."*
4 ADJ If a medical or scientific test is **positive**, it shows that something has happened or is present.
5 ADJ A **positive** number is higher than zero. Compare with **negative**.

posi|tive dis|crimi|na|tion or **positive action** [HR, BRIT] → **affirmative action**

pos|sess /pəzɛs/ (**possesses, possessing, possessed**) **VERB** If you **possess** something, you own it. ❍ *They sold everything they possessed.*

pos|ses|sion /pəzɛʃən/
1 NONCOUNT NOUN If you are **in possession of** something, you have it. [FORMAL] ❍ *Those documents are now in the possession of the Washington Post.*
2 NOUN Your **possessions** are the things that you own. ❍ *People have lost their homes and all their possessions.*

pos|sibil|ity /pɒsɪbɪlɪti/ (**possibilities**) **NOUN** If there is a **possibility that** something will happen or be true, it might happen or be true. ❍ *The possibility of a loss cannot be ruled out.*

pos|sible /pɒsɪbᵊl/
1 ADJ If it is **possible** to do something, that thing can be done. ❍ *It is never possible to predict with any certainty what will happen.*
2 ADJ If something is **possible**, it might happen or be true. ❍ *It is possible that he's telling the truth.*
3 ADJ If you do something **as** soon **as possible**, you do it as soon as you can. ❍ *Please make your decision as soon as possible.*

pos|sibly /pɒsɪbli/
1 ADV used when you think something might be true or might happen, but you are not sure ❍ *Exercise will possibly protect against heart attacks.*
2 ADV used to emphasize what you are saying ❍ *They've done everything they can possibly think of.*

post /poʊst/
1 VERB If you **post** signs on a wall, you put them there so that everyone can see them. ❍ *Officials began posting warning notices.*
2 VERB If you **post** information on the Internet, you put it on a website. ❍ *The statement was posted on the Internet.*
3 NOUN an important job in an organization [FORMAL] ❍ *She accepted the post of the director's assistant.*
4 NOUN a strong piece of wood or metal that is fixed into the ground ❍ *a fence post*

post|age /poʊstɪdʒ/ **NONCOUNT NOUN** **Postage** is the money that you pay for sending mail. ❍ *All prices include postage.*

post|card /poʊstkɑrd/ also **post card** **NOUN** a thin card, often with a picture on one

P

side, that you mail to someone without an envelope

post|er /poʊstər/ **NOUN** a large notice or picture that you stick on a wall ❍ *We used a poster for the jazz festival in Monterey.*

post of|fice (**post offices**)
1 NOUN a building where you can buy stamps and send mail
2 NOUN You can use **the post office** to talk about the U.S. Postal Service.

post|pone /poʊstpoʊn, poʊspoʊn/ (**postpones, postponing, postponed**) **VERB** If you **postpone** an event, you arrange for it to happen at a later time. ❍ *He postponed the trip until the next day.*

pot /pɒt/
1 NOUN a deep round container used for cooking food ❍ *metal cooking pots*
2 NOUN a round container ❍ *a coffee pot* ❍ *a pot of paint*

po|ta|to /pəteɪtoʊ/ (**potatoes**) **NOUN** a white vegetables with brown or red skin that grows under the ground

po|ta|to chip (**potato chips**) **NOUN** **Potato chips** are very thin slices of potato that have been cooked in oil.

po|ten|tial /pətɛnʃᵊl/
1 ADJ used to say that someone or something could become a particular type of person or thing ❍ *The company has identified 60 potential customers.* ● **po|ten|tial|ly ADV** ❍ *The cable TV system potentially could serve 1.5 million households.*
2 NONCOUNT NOUN If someone or something has **potential**, they could become successful or useful in the future. ❍ *The boy has great potential.*

pot|tery /pɒtəri/ **NONCOUNT NOUN** **Pottery** is pots, dishes, and other objects made from clay.

poul|try /poʊltri/ **PL NOUN** **Poultry** is birds such as chickens, that are kept for their eggs and meat.

pound /paʊnd/
1 NOUN a unit of weight that is used in the U.S., Britain, and some other countries, equal to 0.454 kilograms ❍ *a pound of cheese*
2 NOUN The **pound** (£) is the unit of money used in Britain. [ECONOMICS]

pound ster|ling (**pounds sterling**) **NOUN** the official name of unit of money of the United Kingdom [ECONOMICS]

pour /pɔr/
1 VERB If you **pour** a liquid or other substance, you make it flow out of a container. ❍ *She poured some water into a bowl.* ❍ *She asked Tillie to pour her a cup of coffee.*
2 VERB When a liquid **pours** somewhere, it flows there in large amounts. ❍ *Tears poured down our faces.*
3 VERB When it rains a lot, you can say that **it is pouring**.

pov|er|ty /pɒvərti/ **NONCOUNT NOUN** **Poverty** is the state of being very poor. ❍ *These people are living in poverty.*

pow|der /paʊdər/ **NONCOUNT NOUN** **Powder** is a substance made of extremely small, dry parts. ❍ *cocoa powder*

pow|er /paʊər/
1 NONCOUNT NOUN If someone has **power**, they have control over people. ❍ *When children are young, parents still have a lot of power.*
2 NONCOUNT NOUN Your **power to** do something is your ability or right to do it. ❍ *She has the power to charm anyone.* ❍ *The police have the power to arrest people who carry knives.*
3 NONCOUNT NOUN If people are **in power**, they are in charge of a country or an organization. ❍ *He was in power for eight years.*
4 NONCOUNT NOUN The **power** of something is its physical strength or the ability that it has to affect things. ❍ *This vehicle has more power and better brakes.*
5 NONCOUNT NOUN **Power** is energy that can be used for making electricity or for making machines work. ❍ *nuclear power*
▸ **power ahead** If an economy or company **powers ahead** it becomes stronger and more successful. ❍ *The most widely held view is the market will continue to power ahead.*

pow|er brand (**power brands**) **NOUN** a brand of a product that is made by a very successful company [MARKETING AND SALES]

pow|er|ful /paʊərfəl/
1 ADJ able to control people and events ❍ *They are both large, powerful companies.*
2 ADJ very strong ❍ *powerful muscles* ❍ *a powerful smell*

power|house /paʊərhaʊs/ NOUN a person, country, or organization that has a lot of power or influence ❍ *Nigeria is an economic powerhouse for the continent.*

pow|er|less /paʊrlɪs/ ADJ unable to do anything to control a situation ❍ *Radio stations are powerless to refuse to run the commercials or censor them in any way.*

pp **pp** is written before a person's name at the bottom of a business letter to show that they have signed the letter on behalf of the person whose name appears before theirs. ❍ *J.R. Adams, pp D. Philips*

PR /pi ɑr/ NONCOUNT NOUN **PR** is an abbreviation for **public relations**. [MARKETING AND SALES] ❍ *It will be good PR.*

COLLOCATIONS
a PR *firm*
a PR *campaign*
a PR *exercise*
a PR *consultant*
a PR *coup*
a PR *offensive*
a PR *stunt*
a PR *disaster*

prac|ti|cal /præktɪkᵊl/
1 ADJ involving real situations and events, rather than ideas and theories ❍ *This is a practical way of preventing crime.*
2 ADJ If someone is **practical**, they make sensible decisions and deal effectively with problems. ❍ *You were always so practical, Maria.*
3 ADJ **Practical** clothes are useful and suitable for a situation.

prac|ti|cal|ly /præktɪkli/ ADV almost ❍ *He's known the old man practically all his life.*

prac|tice /præktɪs/ (**practices, practicing, practiced**)
1 NOUN A **practice** is something that people do regularly. ❍ *They campaign against the practice of using animals for experiments.*
2 NONCOUNT NOUN **Practice** is the act of doing something regularly in order to improve. ❍ *It takes practice to do this analysis well.*
3 VERB If you **practice** something, you do it regularly in order to improve. ❍ *She practiced the piano in the school basement.*

prac|tise /præktɪs/ [BRIT] → **practice 3**

praise /preɪz/ (**praises, praising, praised**)
1 VERB If you **praise** someone or something, you say that you admire them or that they are good. ❍ *He praised the company for releasing the bad news quickly.*
2 NONCOUNT NOUN **Praise** is also a noun. ❍ *They were full of praise for the staff.*

pray /preɪ/
1 VERB When people **pray**, they speak to God or a god. ❍ *We pray that Billy's family will now find peace.*
2 VERB If you **are praying** that something will happen, you are hoping for it very much. ❍ *We are praying that everything is going to be okay.*

prayer /prɛər/
1 NOUN the words that a person says when they speak to God or a god ❍ *They should say a prayer for her.*
2 NONCOUNT NOUN **Prayer** is the activity of speaking to God or a god. ❍ *The monks give their lives to prayer.*

pre|cau|tion /prɪkɔʃən/ NOUN A **precaution** is an action that is intended to prevent something bad from happening. ❍ *She says that there were no safety precautions at all at the site.*

pre|cede /prɪsid/ (**precedes, preceding, preceded**) VERB If one thing **precedes** another, it comes before it. [FORMAL] ❍ *The group meeting preceded the annual meeting of the World Bank.*

pre|cious /prɛʃəs/ ADJ valuable or important to you ❍ *precious metals*

pre|cise /prɪsaɪs/ ADJ exact and accurate ❍ *I can remember the precise moment when I heard the news.*

pre|cise|ly /prɪsaɪsli/ ADV accurately and exactly ❍ *Nobody knows precisely how many people died.*

pre|ci|sion /prɪsɪʒən/ NONCOUNT NOUN If you do something **with precision**, you do it exactly as it should be done. ❍ *The machines were capable of greater precision than human beings.*

preda|tory pric|ing /prɛdətɔri praɪsɪŋ/ NONCOUNT NOUN If a company practices **predatory pricing**, it charges a much lower price for its products or services than its competitors in order to force them out of the market. [MARKETING AND SALES] ❍ *Predatory pricing by large supermarkets was threatening the livelihood of smaller businesses.*

pre|dict /prɪdɪkt/ VERB If you **predict** an event, you say that it will happen. ❍ *He correctly predicted the results of fifteen matches.*

pre|dict|able /prɪdɪktəbəl/ ADJ If something or someone is **predictable**, they happen or behave in a way that everyone expects. ❍ *This was a predictable reaction.*

pre|dic|tion /prɪdɪkʃən/ NOUN If you make a **prediction**, you say what you think will happen.

pre|fer /prɪfɜr/ (**prefers, preferring, preferred**) VERB If you **prefer** someone or something, you like that person or thing better than another. ❍ *I preferred books and people to politics.* ❍ *He would prefer to be in Philadelphia.*

pref|er|able /prɛfərəbəl, prɛfrə-, prɪfɜrə-/ ADJ When one thing is **preferable to** another, it is better or more suitable. ❍ *For many, a trip to the supermarket is preferable to buying food on the Internet.* • **pref|er|ably** /prɛfərəbli, prɛfrə-, prɪfɜrə-/ ADV ❍ *Get exercise, preferably in the fresh air.*

pref|er|ence /prɛfərəns/ NOUN If you have a **preference for** something, you prefer it. ❍ *Customers have shown a preference for salty snacks.*

pref|er|ence shares PL NOUN **Preference shares** are the same as **preferred stock**. Compare with **ordinary shares**. [BANKING, BRIT]

pref|erred stock NONCOUNT NOUN **Preferred stock** is the shares in a company that are owned by people who have the right to receive part of the company's profits before the holders of common stock. Compare with **common stock**. [BANKING]

preg|nant /prɛgnənt/ ADJ If a woman or animal is **pregnant**, she has a baby developing in her body. ❍ *I'm seven months pregnant.* • **preg|nan|cy** /prɛgnənsi/ (**pregnancies**) NOUN ❍ *We keep a record of your weight gain during pregnancy.*

preju|dice /prɛdʒədɪs/ NONCOUNT NOUN **Prejudice** is an unreasonable dislike of someone or something. ❍ *racial prejudice*

preju|diced /prɛdʒədɪst/ ADJ having an unreasonable dislike of someone or something ❍ *They complained that she was racially prejudiced.*

pre|limi|nary /prɪlɪmɪnɛri/ ADJ **Preliminary** activities or discussions take place at the beginning of an event, often as a form of preparation. ❍ *Preliminary results show the Republican Party are ahead.*

prema|ture /primətʃʊər/ ADJ Something that is **premature** happens earlier than it should. ❍ *Heart disease is a common cause of premature death.* ❍ *a premature baby*

prem|ises /prɛmɪsɪz/ PL NOUN A company's **premises** are the land and buildings where its work takes place. ❍ *The company offers a gym and aerobics classes on its premises.*

pre|mium /primiəm/

1 NOUN a sum of money that you pay regularly to an insurance company for an insurance policy ❍ *It is too early to say whether insurance premiums will be affected.*

2 NOUN a sum of money that you have to pay for something in addition to the normal cost ❍ *Even if customers want "solutions," most are not willing to pay a premium for them.*

3 ADJ **Premium** products are of a higher than usual quality and are often expensive. ❍ *At the premium end of the market, business is booming.*

4 If something is **at a premium**, it is wanted or needed, but is difficult to get or achieve. ❍ *If space is at a premium, choose adaptable furniture that won't fill the room.*

P

5 If you buy or sell something **at a premium**, you buy or sell it at a higher price than usual. ❍ *He eventually sold the shares back to the bank at a premium.*

prepa|ra|tion /prɛpəreɪʃən/
1 NONCOUNT NOUN **Preparation** is the process of getting something ready. ❍ *Todd packed the papers in preparation for the meeting.*
2 PL NOUN **Preparations** are all the arrangements that are made for an event. ❍ *We were making preparations for the takeover.*

pre|pare /prɪpɛər/ (**prepares, preparing, prepared**)
1 VERB If you **prepare** something, you make it ready. ❍ *We will need several weeks to prepare the report.* ❍ *She started preparing dinner.*
2 VERB If you **prepare for** something, you get ready for it. ❍ *You should begin to prepare for the cost of your child's education.*

pre|pared /prɪpɛərd/
1 ADJ If you are **prepared to** do something, you are willing to do it. ❍ *Are you prepared to help if we need you?*
2 ADJ If you are **prepared for** something, you are ready for it. ❍ *The dollar rose as traders prepared for the release of today's employment figures.*

prepo|si|tion /prɛpəzɪʃən/ **NOUN** a word such as "by" or "with" that usually comes before a noun

pre|scribe /prɪskraɪb/ (**prescribes, prescribing, prescribed**) **VERB** If a doctor **prescribes** medicine or treatment for you, he or she tells you what medicine or treatment to have.

pre|scrip|tion /prɪskrɪpʃən/ **NOUN** a piece of paper on which a doctor writes an order for medicine ❍ *He gave me a prescription for some cream.*

pre|sell /prisɛl/ (**presells, preselling, presold**) **VERB** When a company **presells** a product, it advertises it before it is available to be bought. [MARKETING AND SALES] ❍ *This weekend is Microsoft's last chance to presell Xbox before the official launch next Thursday.*

pres|ence /prɛzᵊns/
1 NOUN Someone's **presence** in a place is the fact that they are there. ❍ *His presence always causes trouble.*
2 If you are **in** someone's **presence**, you are in the same place as that person. ❍ *Children should do their homework in the presence of their parents.*

present
❶ ADJECTIVE AND NOUN USES
❷ VERB USE

❶ **pres|ent** /prɛzᵊnt/
1 ADJ used to talk about things and people that exist now ❍ *The present situation is very difficult for us.*
2 A situation that exists **at present** exists now. ❍ *At present, we do not know the cause of the disease.*
3 ADJ If someone is **present at** an event, they are there. ❍ *Nearly 85 percent of men are present at the birth of their children.*
4 NOUN something that you give to someone, for example, on their birthday ❍ *a birthday present*

❷ **pres|ent** /prɪzɛnt/ **VERB** If you **present** something, you formally give it to someone. ❍ *The mayor presented him with a gold medal.*

pres|en|ta|tion /prizɛnteɪʃən/
1 NOUN an event at which someone is given an award ❍ *He received his award at a presentation in Kansas City.*
2 NONCOUNT NOUN **Presentation** is the act of formally giving someone something. ❍ *The evening began with the presentation of awards.*
3 NOUN a talk that gives information about something ❍ *Philip and I gave a short presentation.*

pre|serva|tive /prɪzɜrvətɪv/ **NOUN** a chemical that keeps something in good condition

pre|serve /prɪzɜrv/ (**preserves, preserving, preserved**) **VERB** If you **preserve** something, you protect it or keep it in a good condition. ❍ *We need to preserve the forest.*
• **pres|er|va|tion** **NONCOUNT NOUN** ❍ *the preservation of historic buildings*

P

presi|dent /prɛzɪdənt/
1 NOUN the person with the highest political position in some countries ❍ *The president must act quickly.*
2 NOUN the person with the highest position in a company or other organization [ADMINISTRATION] ❍ *He is the national president of the Screen Actors Guild.*

press /prɛs/ (**presses, pressing, pressed**)
1 VERB If you **press** something, you push it or push it firmly against something else. ❍ *David pressed a button and the door closed.* ❍ *He pressed his back against the door.*
2 VERB If you **press** clothes, you iron them. ❍ *Vera pressed his shirt.*
3 NOUN The press consists of newspapers and magazines, and the people who write for them. ❍ *She gave several interviews to the local press.*

press con|fer|ence (**press conferences**) **NOUN** a meeting held by a famous or important person in which they answer reporters' questions ❍ *She gave her reaction to his release at a press conference.*

press re|lease (**press releases**) **NOUN** a written statement about a matter of public interest that is given to the press ❍ *Fox issued a press release saying the show had sold out in 24 hours.*

P

pres|sure /prɛʃər/
1 NONCOUNT NOUN Pressure is force that you produce when you press hard on something. ❍ *The pressure of his fingers on her arm relaxed.*
2 NONCOUNT NOUN The **pressure** in a place or a container is the force produced by the gas or liquid in it. ❍ *If the pressure falls in the cabin, an oxygen mask will drop in front of you.*
3 NONCOUNT NOUN If you are experiencing **pressure**, you feel that you have too much to do or are in a difficult situation. ❍ *Can you work under pressure?*

pres|tige pric|ing /prestiʒ praɪsɪŋ/ **NONCOUNT NOUN** In marketing, **prestige pricing** is the practice of giving a product a high price, in order to give the impression that it must be of high quality. [MARKETING AND SALES] ❍ *There's always prestige pricing in the market; some rich kids will buy the most expensive pair of shoes, no matter what.*

pre|sum|ably /prɪzuməbli/ **ADV** If you say that something is **presumably** true, you think it is true. ❍ *He's not going this year, presumably because of his age.*

pre|sume /prɪzum/ (**presumes, presuming, presumed**) **VERB** If you **presume that** something is true, you think that it is true. ❍ *I presume that you're here on business.*

pre-tax /pritæks/
1 ADJ Pre-tax profits or losses are the total profits or losses made by a company before tax has been taken away. [FINANCE] ❍ *Storehouse made pre-tax profits of £3.1m.*
2 ADV Pre-tax is also an adverb. ❍ *Last year it made £2.5m pre-tax.*

pre|tend /prɪtɛnd/
1 VERB If you **pretend that** something is true, you try to make people believe that it is true, although it is not. ❍ *He pretended to be asleep.*
2 VERB If you **pretend that** you are doing something, you imagine that you are doing it. ❍ *She can sunbathe and pretend she's in Cancun.*

pret|ty /prɪti/ (**prettier, prettiest**)
1 ADJ attractive and pleasant ❍ *a pretty girl* ❍ *a very pretty little town*
2 ADV used before an adjective or adverb to mean "fairly" [INFORMAL] ❍ *I had a pretty good idea what she was going to do.*

pre|vent /prɪvɛnt/ **VERB** To **prevent** something means to make sure that it does not happen. ❍ *The best way to prevent injury is to wear a seat belt.*

pre|ven|tion /prɪvɛnʃən/ **NONCOUNT NOUN Prevention** is making sure that something does not happen. ❍ *the prevention of heart disease*

pre|vi|ous /priviəs/ **ADJ** happening or existing before the thing that you are talking about ❍ *In the previous quarter growth had been nil.*

pre|vi|ous|ly /priviəsli/
1 ADV at some time before the period that you are talking about ❍ *The railroads were previously owned by private companies.*
2 ADV used to say how much earlier one event

was than another ❍ *Ingrid had moved to San Diego two weeks previously.*

prey /preɪ/ **NONCOUNT NOUN** An animal's **prey** is the animals that it hunts and eats.

price /praɪs/ **NOUN** the amount of money that you have to pay in order to buy something ❍ *the price of gas*

COLLOCATIONS

a *market* price
a *purchase* price
cut price
a price *tag*
a price *rise*

price con|trol **NONCOUNT NOUN** **Price control** is the control of prices for basic goods and services by a government. ❍ *The government imposed price control on privately owned public utilities.*

price cut|ting **NONCOUNT NOUN** **Price cutting** is when a company reduces the price of its products or services in order to try to sell more of them. [MARKETING AND SALES] ❍ *a price-cutting campaign*

price dis|crim|ina|tion **NONCOUNT NOUN** **Price discrimination** is the practice of charging different prices to different consumers or in different markets for the same products or services. [MARKETING AND SALES] ❍ *the government's past efforts to prevent price discrimination*

price-divi|dend ra|tio (**price-dividend ratios**) **NOUN** the ratio of the price of a share on the stock exchange to the dividends per share paid in the previous year [BUSINESS MANAGEMENT]

price-earn|ings ra|tio (**price-earnings ratios**) **NOUN** the ratio of the price of a share on the stock exchange to the earnings per share [BUSINESS MANAGEMENT]

price fix|ing also **price-fixing** **NONCOUNT NOUN** **Price fixing** is the setting of prices by groups of producers so that none of them sell their product or service at a lower price. [MARKETING AND SALES, ECONOMICS] ❍ *The new system provides strong measures to discourage companies from price fixing.*

price|less /praɪslɪs/ **ADJ** extremely useful or valuable ❍ *Our national parks are priceless treasures.*

price point (**price points**) **NOUN** the standard price that is set for a product [MARKETING AND SALES] ❍ *No price point exists for the machine yet.*

price-sensitive

1 ADJ **Price-sensitive** information or activity is likely to affect the price of something, especially shares. [MARKETING AND SALES] ❍ *The company was judged to have withheld price-sensitive information.*

2 ADJ A **price-sensitive** buyer is someone who is likely to stop buying a particular product if they think it is too expensive. [MARKETING AND SALES] ❍ *This is going to push our prices up, and the most price-sensitive passengers won't travel any more.*

price tag (**price tags**)

1 NOUN a small piece of card or paper attached to the article in a store with the price written on it [MARKETING AND SALES]

2 NOUN the amount that you must pay in order to buy something ❍ *The monorail can be completed at the price tag of $1.7 billion.*

price war (**price wars**) **NOUN** a competitive situation in which companies each try to gain an advantage by lowering their prices as much as possible [MARKETING AND SALES, ECONOMICS] ❍ *Their loss was partly due to a vicious price war between manufacturers that has cut margins to the bone.*

pricey /praɪsi/ (**pricier, priciest**) also **pricy** **ADJ** expensive [INFORMAL] ❍ *Medical insurance is very pricey.*

pric|ing /praɪsɪŋ/ **NONCOUNT NOUN** The **pricing** of a product or service is the decision about how much to charge for it. ❍ *Pricing was also a problem. Every time the competition raised their prices, Remington followed suit.*

pric|ing strat|egy (**pricing strategies**) **NOUN** the system of prices a company sets for the goods it produces or the service it provides [MARKETING AND SALES] ❍ *This leads us to the conclusion that The Economist has different pricing strategies in different markets.*

prick /prɪk/ **VERB** If a person or a sharp object **pricks** something, they make a small hole in it with a sharp point. ❍ *Prick the potatoes and rub the skins with salt.*

pride /praɪd/
1 NONCOUNT NOUN Pride is a feeling of satisfaction that you have because you have done something well. ❍ *We all felt the sense of pride when we finished early.*
2 NONCOUNT NOUN Pride is a sense of self-respect. ❍ *His pride wouldn't allow him to ask for help.*

priest /prist/ **NOUN** a religious leader or official ❍ *a Catholic priest*

pri|mari|ly /praɪmɛrɪli/ **ADV** used to say what is mainly true in a situation ❍ *These reports come primarily from passengers on the plane.*

pri|ma|ry /praɪmɛri, -məri/ (**primaries**)
1 ADJ most important [FORMAL] ❍ *Language difficulties were the primary cause of his problems.*
2 ADJ Primary education is the first few years of formal. ❍ *Most primary students now have experience with computers.*
3 NOUN A **primary** is an election in a state in the U.S. in which people vote for someone to represent a political party. Compare with **general election**. ❍ *He won the 1968 New Hampshire primary.*
4 ADJ A **primary** product consists of a natural raw material. Compare with **secondary** and **tertiary**. ❍ *Already, production shortfalls are bumping up primary product prices.*

P

pri|ma|ry data NONCOUNT NOUN Primary data is information about a subject that is collected directly from people, for example by interviews. Compare with **secondary data**. ❍ *A large number of published books and articles, plus various newspaper reports, are used to supplement his primary data.*

pri|ma|ry school (**primary schools**) **NOUN** a school for children aged about 5–11 [mainly BRIT]

pri|ma|ry sec|tor (**primary sectors**) **NOUN** The **primary sector** is the part of a country's economy that consists of industries which produce raw materials. Compare with **secondary sector** and **tertiary sector**. [ECONOMICS] ❍ *Developing countries are characterized by very large primary sectors and small industrial and service sectors.*

prime /praɪm/ (**primes, priming, primed**)
1 ADJ most important ❍ *Safety of facilities is a prime concern.*
2 ADJ of the best possible quality ❍ *These beaches are prime sites for development.*
3 NONCOUNT NOUN Your **prime** is the best or most successful stage in your life. ❍ *I'm just coming into my prime now.*
4 ADJ having a very good credit rating ❍ *prime investments*

prime cost (**prime costs**) **NOUN** The **prime cost** of a product is the part of the cost which varies according to the amount produced. [FINANCE]

prime min|is|ter (**prime ministers**) **NOUN** the leader of the government in some countries ❍ *the former prime minister of St. Lucia*

prime rate (**prime rates**) **NOUN** A bank's **prime rate** is the lowest rate of interest that it charges at a particular time and that is offered only to certain customers. [BANKING] ❍ *At least one bank cut its prime rate today.*

primi|tive /prɪmɪtɪv/
1 ADJ belonging to or relating to a society that has not developed much ❍ *primitive man*
2 ADJ very basic and not modern ❍ *Even the most primitive computer chips were useful.*

prince /prɪns/ **NOUN** a male member of a royal family, especially the son of the king or queen

prin|cess /prɪnsɪs, -sɛs/ (**princesses**) **NOUN** a female member of a royal family, especially the daughter of a king or queen

prin|ci|pal /prɪnsɪpᵊl/
1 ADJ main or most important ❍ *Money was not the principal reason for his action.*
2 NOUN the person in charge of a school

prin|ci|ple /prɪnsɪpᵊl/
1 NOUN Your **principles** are the beliefs that you have about how you should behave. ❍ *It's against my principles to be dishonest.*

2 NOUN a rule about how something works or happens ❍ *Some people hold tight to the principle that all income should be taxed alike.*

print /prɪnt/

1 VERB If you **print** something like a book or a newspaper, you use a machine to produce it. ❍ *The publishers have printed 40,000 copies of the novel.*

2 NONCOUNT NOUN Print is all the letters and numbers in a printed document. ❍ *I can't read this—the print is too small.*

3 VERB If you **print** a document or **print** it **out**, you use a machine to produce a copy of it on paper. ❍ *I printed out a copy of the letter.*

print|er /prɪntər/

1 NOUN a machine for printing copies of computer documents

2 NOUN a person or a company whose job is printing things such as books

pri|or /praɪər/ **Prior to** a particular time or event means before it. [FORMAL] ❍ *Prior to his trip to Japan, Steven was in New York.*

pri|or|ity /praɪɒrɪti/ **(priorities) NOUN** something that is more important that everything else or needs to be dealt with before everything else ❍ *Her children are her first priority.* ❍ *The government's priority is to build more schools.*

pris|on /prɪzᵊn/ **NOUN** a building where criminals are kept as punishment ❍ *He was sent to prison for five years.*

pris|on|er /prɪzənər/ **NOUN** a person who is in prison ❍ *More than 30,000 Australians were taken prisoner in World War II.*

pri|va|cy /praɪvəsi/ **NONCOUNT NOUN Privacy** is the freedom to do things without other people knowing what you are doing. ❍ *We have changed the names to protect the privacy of those involved.*

pri|vate /praɪvɪt/

1 ADJ Private companies are not owned by the government. ❍ *a private hospital*

2 ADJ only for one particular person or group, and not for everyone ❍ *The door was marked "Private."*

3 ADJ taking place between a small number of people and kept secret from others ❍ *a private conversation* • **pri|vate|ly ADV** ❍ *We need to talk privately.*

4 ADJ Your **private life** is the part of your life that concerns your personal relationships and activities.

5 If you do something **in private**, you do it without other people being there. ❍ *Mark asked to talk to his boss in private.*

pri|vate com|pa|ny (private companies) NOUN A **private company** is a limited company that does not issue shares for the public to buy. Compare with **public company**. [ECONOMICS] ❍ *It is Jamaica's largest private company and the country's biggest earner of foreign exchange.*

pri|vate eye (private eyes) NOUN You can refer to a private detective as a **private eye**, especially when he or she is a character in a movie or story. [INFORMAL]

pri|vate sec|tor (private sectors) NOUN The private sector is the part of a country's economy that consists of industries and commercial companies that are not owned or controlled by the government. Compare with **public sector**. [ECONOMICS] ❍ *small firms in the private sector*

pri|vat|ise /praɪvətaɪz/ [BRIT] → **privatize**

pri|vati|za|tion is|sue (privatization issues) NOUN an issue of shares that is available for the public to buy when a publicly owned organization becomes a private company [ECONOMICS]

pri|vat|ize /praɪvətaɪz/ **(privatizes, privatizing, privatized) VERB** If a company, industry, or service that is owned by the state **is privatized**, the government sells it and makes it a private company. [ECONOMICS] ❍ *Many state-owned companies were privatized.* • **pri|vati|za|tion** /praɪvətɪzeɪʃən/ **NONCOUNT NOUN** ❍ *the privatization of government services*

privi|lege /prɪvɪlɪdʒ, prɪvlɪdʒ/ **NOUN** a special advantage that only one person or group has ❍ *We are not asking for special privileges.*

prize /praɪz/ **NOUN** something that is given to the person who wins a game, or a

P

competition ❍ *He won first prize in the golf tournament.*

PRO /pi ɑr oʊ/ **PRO** is an abbreviation for **public relations officer**. [ADMINISTRATION]

prob|able /prɒbəbᵊl/ **ADJ** likely to be true or likely to happen ❍ *It was clear back in October that this would be the probable outcome.*

prob|ably /prɒbəbli/ **ADV** Something that is **probably** true is likely to be true. ❍ *I will probably go home on Tuesday.*

pro|ba|tion|ary /proʊbeɪʃənɛri/ **ADJ** A **probationary** period is a period after someone starts a job, during which their employer can decide whether the person is suitable and should be allowed to continue. [HR] ❍ *Teachers should have a probationary period of two years.*

prob|lem /prɒbləm/ **NOUN** A **problem** is something or someone that causes difficulties. ❍ *Pollution is a problem in this city.*

pro|cedure /prəsidʒər/ **NOUN** the usual or correct way of doing something ❍ *If your car is stolen, the correct procedure is to report the theft to the local police.*

pro|ceed /prəsid/

1 VERB If you **proceed to** do something, you do it after doing something else. ❍ *He picked up a book, which he proceeded to read.*

2 VERB If something **proceeds**, it continues. [FORMAL] ❍ *The building work is proceeding very slowly.*

pro|ceeds /proʊsidz/ **PL NOUN** **The proceeds** of an activity or the sale of something is the money that is made from it. ❍ *He uses the proceeds from his photographs to finance his productions.*

pro|cess /prɒsɛs/ **(processes) NOUN** a series of actions that have a particular result [PRODUCTION, BUSINESS MANAGEMENT] ❍ *They began the long process of returning to normal life.*

pro|ces|sor /prɒsɛsər/ **NOUN** the part of a computer that performs the tasks that the user has requested

pro|cure|ment /prəkyʊərmənt/ **NONCOUNT NOUN** **Procurement** is the act of obtaining something such as supplies for an army or other organization. [PURCHASING, FORMAL] ❍ *Russia was cutting procurement of new weapons "by about 80 percent," he said.*

pro|duce **(produces, producing, produced)**

> Pronounce the verb /prədus/. Pronounce the noun /prɒdus/ or /proʊdus/.

1 VERB If you **produce** something, you make it, grow it, or cause it to happen. [PRODUCTION] ❍ *The company produces about 2.3 million tons of steel a year.* ❍ *The talks failed to produce results.*

2 VERB If you **produce** a play or a movie, you organize it and decide how it should be made. ❍ *The movie was produced and directed by Johnny White.*

3 NONCOUNT NOUN **Produce** is fruit and vegetables that are grown to be sold. ❍ *The restaurant uses local produce.*

pro|duc|er /prədusər/

1 NOUN a company that makes or grows something [PRODUCTION] ❍ *the world's leading oil producer*

2 NOUN someone who organizes a play or a movie and decides how it should be made ❍ *The movie was created by producer Alison Millar.*

prod|uct /prɒdʌkt/ **NOUN** something that you make or grow, in order to sell it [PRODUCTION] ❍ *This cellphone is one of the company's most successful products.*

prod|uct dif|fer|en|tia|tion /prɒdʌkt dɪfərɛnʃieɪʃən/ **NONCOUNT NOUN** **Product differentiation** is the way that a particular product is presented to the public in order to distinguish it from other, similar products. [MARKETING AND SALES] ❍ *They cannot seize a significant part of the market unless they achieve product differentiation.*

pro|duc|tion /prədʌkʃən/

1 NONCOUNT NOUN **Production** is the process of making or growing something in large amounts, or the amount of goods that you make or grow. [PRODUCTION] ❍ *This car went into production last year.* ❍ *The factory needs to increase production.*

2 NOUN a play or other show that is performed

in a theater ❍ *Tonight our class is going to see a production of "Othello."*

pro|duc|tion line (**production lines**) NOUN an arrangement of machines in a factory where the products pass from machine to machine until they are finished [PRODUCTION] ❍ *Honda added a production line this year, hoping to boost domestic sales.*

pro|duc|tive /prədʌktɪv/ ADJ producing or doing a lot ❍ *Training makes workers more productive.*

pro|duc|tive sec|tor (**productive sectors**) NOUN the part of a country's economy consisting of industries and companies which produce goods that can be sold [ECONOMICS] ❍ *goods that are required by the productive sector*

prod|uc|tiv|ity /prɒdʊktɪvɪti/ NONCOUNT NOUN **Productivity** is the rate at which goods are produced. [PRODUCTION] ❍ *The third-quarter results reflect continued improvements in productivity.*

product-led ADJ A company that is **product-led** aims to develop new products and then create a market for them. [BUSINESS MANAGEMENT] ❍ *The new S-Type represents the first stage of a dramatic product-led expansion of the company.*

prod|uct lia|bil|ity NONCOUNT NOUN **Product liability** is the liability to the public that a manufacturer or seller has for selling a faulty product. [LEGAL]

prod|uct life cy|cle (**product life cycles**) NOUN the four stages (introduction, growth, maturity, and decline) into which the sales of a product fall during its market life [MARKETING AND SALES] ❍ *Product life cycles have shortened, leading to the need for more frequent changes to product features.*

prod|uct line (**product lines**) NOUN a group of related products produced by one manufacturer [MARKETING AND SALES] ❍ *the company's most successful product lines*

prod|uct mix (**product mixes**) NOUN the range of products that a company produces [MARKETING AND SALES] ❍ *The high costs of change or modification make firms reluctant to revise their product mix for each market.*

product-orien|ted or **product-orientated** ADJ A company that is **product-oriented** aims to develop new products and then create a market for them. [BUSINESS MANAGEMENT] ❍ *I feel that we need to become a little more product-oriented.*

prod|uct place|ment NONCOUNT NOUN **Product placement** is a form of advertising in which a company has its product placed where it can be clearly seen during a movie or television program. [MARKETING AND SALES] ❍ *It was the first movie to feature onscreen product placement for its own merchandise.*

prod|uct range (**product ranges**) or **product portfolio** NOUN all the products sold by a particular company [MARKETING AND SALES] ❍ *Unilever's product range spans food, teas, detergents, deodorants, soaps, and hair-care.* ❍ *We intend to position Kambrook as a value brand within our current product portfolio.*

pro|fes|sion /prəfɛʃən/ NOUN a type of job for which you need special education or training ❍ *Ava was a doctor by profession.*

pro|fes|sion|al /prəfɛʃənᵊl/
1 ADJ relating to a person's work ❍ *Get professional advice from your accountant first.*
2 ADJ used to describe people who do something for money rather than as a hobby ❍ *professional musicians*
3 NOUN **Professional** is also a noun. ❍ *The competition is open to both professionals and amateurs.* ● **pro|fes|sion|al|ly** ADV ❍ *I've been singing professionally for 10 years.*
4 NOUN a person who does a job for which you need special education or training ❍ *investment professionals*

pro|fes|sor /prəfɛsər/ NOUN a teacher at a university or a college ❍ *a professor of history*

pro|file /proʊfaɪl/ NOUN the shape of your face when people see it from the side ❍ *He was slim, with black hair and a handsome profile.*

prof|it /prɒfɪt/ NOUN the amount of money that you gain when you sell something for more than you paid for it [FINANCE,

ECONOMICS] ❍ *When he sold the house, Chris made a profit of about $50,000.*

COLLOCATIONS
interim profits
pre-tax profits
record profits
an *operating* profit
annual profits

prof|it|abil|ity /prɒfɪtəbɪlɪti/ NONCOUNT NOUN A company's **profitability** is its ability to make a profit. [FINANCE, ECONOMICS] ❍ *Changes were made in operating methods in an effort to increase profitability.*

prof|it|able /prɒfɪtəbᵊl/ ADJ making a profit [FINANCE] ❍ *The business started to be profitable in its second year.*

prof|it and loss or **profit and loss account** NOUN an account that is created at the end of a financial year which shows that year's income and expenditure and indicates a company's profit or loss [FINANCE] ❍ *Salaries go into your profit and loss as operating expenses.*

prof|it cen|ter (**profit centers**) NOUN a part of a company that is responsible for its own costs and profits [ADMINISTRATION, FINANCE] ❍ *Now that each profit center has to pay salaries, managers aren't so happy to take more workers than they need.*

P

prof|it|eer|ing /prɒfɪtɪərɪŋ/ NONCOUNT NOUN **Profiteering** is the making of large profits by charging high prices for goods that are hard to get. [ECONOMICS] ❍ *There's been a wave of profiteering and corruption.*

prof|it fore|cast (**profit forecasts**) NOUN a statement of what the profits of a company are likely to be [FINANCE] ❍ *Even an upbeat profit forecast for next year did not cheer investors much.*

profit-making ADJ A **profit-making** business or organization makes a profit. Compare with **nonprofit**. [FINANCE] ❍ *He wants to set up a profit-making company, owned mostly by the university.*

prof|it mar|gin (**profit margins**) NOUN the difference between the selling price of a product and the cost of producing and marketing it [FINANCE] ❍ *The group had a net profit margin of 30% last year.*

profit-sharing NONCOUNT NOUN **Profit-sharing** is a system by which all the people who work in a company have a share in its profits. [ECONOMICS] ❍ *the bank's profit-sharing plan*

profit-taking NONCOUNT NOUN **Profit-taking** is the selling of stocks and shares at a profit after their value has risen or just before their value falls. [ECONOMICS] ❍ *The market was held down by profit-taking in the banking sector yesterday.*

prof|it warn|ing (**profit warnings**) NOUN an announcement by a company that its profits will be much lower than had been expected [FINANCE] ❍ *Siemens issued a surprise profit warning because of delays to projects.*

pro for|ma /proʊ fɔrmə/
1 ADJ In banking, a company's **pro forma** balance or earnings is their expected balance or earnings.
2 ADJ A **pro forma** invoice is one that is issued before the goods are delivered, giving all the details and costs.

pro|gram /proʊgræm, -grəm/ (**programs, programming, programmed**)
1 NOUN a television or radio show ❍ *a network television program*
2 NOUN a set of instructions that a computer uses to do a particular task ❍ *Ada Lovelace wrote the world's first computer program in 1842.*
3 VERB When you **program** a computer or a machine, you give it a set of instructions so that it can do a particular task. ❍ *They can teach you how to program a computer in two weeks.* ● **pro|gram|ming** NONCOUNT NOUN ❍ *a programming language*
4 NOUN a planned series of events ❍ *the art gallery's education program*
5 NOUN a small book or sheet of paper that tells you about a play or concert ❍ *When you go to concerts, it's helpful to read the program.*

pro|gramme /proʊgræm/ [mainly BRIT] → **program**

pro|gram|mer /proʊgræmər/ NOUN someone whose job is to write computer programs ❍ *a computer programmer*

pro|gress (**progresses, progressing, progressed**)

Pronounce the noun /prɒgrɛs/ or /proʊgrɛs/. Pronounce the verb /prəgrɛs/.

1 NONCOUNT NOUN Progress is the process of gradually improving or getting nearer to achieving something. ❍ *Some of these banks have made progress in cutting costs and recovering loans.*

2 VERB If you **progress**, you improve or become more developed or successful. ❍ *All our trainees are progressing well.*

3 VERB If events **progress**, they continue to happen. ❍ *As the evening progressed, Leila grew tired.*

4 If something is **in progress**, it has started and is still happening. ❍ *The meeting was already in progress when we arrived.*

pro|hib|it /proʊhɪbɪt/ **VERB** If a rule or a law **prohibits** something, it makes it illegal. [FORMAL] ❍ *Smoking is prohibited here.*

pro|hi|bi|tion /proʊɪbɪʃən/

1 NOUN a law that says you must not do something ❍ *The government intends to remove the prohibition on exporting live horses.*

2 NONCOUNT NOUN In the United States, **Prohibition** was the period between 1920 and 1933 when it was illegal to make or sell alcoholic drinks.

proj|ect /prɒdʒɛkt/ **NOUN** an activity that takes a lot of time and effort ❍ *The charity is funding a housing project in India.*

pro|long /prəlɔŋ/ **VERB** If you **prolong** something, you make it last longer. ❍ *I did not wish to prolong the process.* ● **prolonged ADJ** ❍ *a prolonged period of wet weather*

promi|nent /prɒmɪnənt/

1 ADJ A **prominent** person is important and well-known. ❍ *She is a prominent lawyer.*

2 ADJ easy to see or notice ❍ *a prominent nose*

prom|ise /prɒmɪs/ (**promises, promising, promised**)

1 VERB If you **promise that** you will do something, you say that you will certainly do it. ❍ *They have promised to invest $45 million over five years in the three companies.* ❍ *Promise me you'll come to the party.*

2 NOUN Promise is also a noun. ❍ *James broke every promise he made.*

prom|is|sory note /prɒmɪsɔri noʊt/ (**promissory notes**) **NOUN** a written, dated promise to pay a specific sum of money to a particular person [BANKING] ❍ *a $36.4 million, five-year promissory note*

pro|mo /proʊmoʊ/ **NOUN** something such as a short video film that promotes a product [MARKETING AND SALES, INFORMAL] ❍ *He races his cars, and rents them out for film, TV, and promo videos.*

pro|mote /prəmoʊt/ (**promotes, promoting, promoted**)

1 VERB If you **promote** something, you advertise it. [MARKETING AND SALES] ❍ *There will be a new TV campaign to promote the products.*

2 VERB If someone **is promoted**, they are given a more important job. [HR] ❍ *Richard has just been promoted to general manager.*

pro|mo|tion /prəmoʊʃən/

1 NOUN when someone is given a more important job [HR] ❍ *We went out for dinner to celebrate Dad's promotion.*

2 NONCOUNT NOUN Promotion is a company's attempts to make a product or event successful by advertising. [MARKETING AND SALES] ❍ *During 1984, Remington spent a lot of money on advertising and promotion.*

3 NOUN something that advertises a product or that helps to sell more of it [MARKETING AND SALES] ❍ *Ask about special promotions and weekend deals too.*

prompt /prɒmpt/ **ADJ** A **prompt** action is done without waiting. ❍ *These questions require prompt answers from the government.*

prompt|ly /prɒmptli/

1 ADV immediately ❍ *They announced an investment plan which promptly pushed the company's share price up 7%.*

2 ADV If you do something **promptly at** a particular time, you do it at exactly that time. ❍ *Promptly at seven o'clock, we left the hotel.*

pro|noun /proʊnaʊn/ **NOUN** A **pronoun** is a word that you use instead of a noun when you are talking about someone or something. "It," "she," "something," and "myself" are pronouns.

pro|nounce /prənaʊns/ (**pronounces, pronouncing, pronounced**) VERB When you **pronounce** a word, you make its sound. ❍ *Have I pronounced your name correctly?*

proof /pruf/ NONCOUNT NOUN **Proof** is something that shows that something else is true or exists. ❍ *The scientists hope to find proof that there is water on Mars.*

prop|er /prɒpər/ ADJ correct, real, or satisfactory ❍ *The book is intended as a guide to proper behavior.*

prop|er|ty /prɒpərti/ (**properties**)
1 NONCOUNT NOUN Your **property** is anything that belongs to you. [FORMAL] ❍ *"That's my property. You can't just take it."*
2 NOUN a building and the land around it [FORMAL] ❍ *In the past year property prices have surged to new highs.*

pro|por|tion /prəpɔrʃən/
1 NOUN a part of an amount or number when compared to the total [FORMAL] ❍ *The proportion of the population using cellphones is 80-85%.*
2 NONCOUNT NOUN **Proportion** is the correct relationship between the size of objects in a piece of art. ❍ *the symmetry and proportion of classical Greek and Roman architecture*

P

pro|po|sal /prəpoʊzᵊl/
1 NOUN a suggestion or a plan ❍ *The president has announced new proposals for a peace agreement.*
2 NOUN the act of asking someone to marry you ❍ *Pam accepted Randy's proposal of marriage.*

pro|pose /prəpoʊz/ (**proposes, proposing, proposed**)
1 VERB If you **propose** a plan or an idea, you suggest it. ❍ *The minister has proposed a change in the law.*
2 VERB If you **propose to** someone, you ask them to marry you. ❍ *David proposed to his girlfriend.*

pro|pri|et|ary name /prəpraɪɪtɛri neɪm/ (**proprietary names**) NOUN a name that is a trademark [LEGAL]

pro|pri|etor /prəpraɪətər/ NOUN The **proprietor** of a hotel, store, newspaper, or other business is the person who owns it. [ADMINISTRATION, FORMAL] ❍ *the proprietor of a local restaurant*

pros|ecute /prɒsɪkyut/ (**prosecutes, prosecuting, prosecuted**) VERB If the police **prosecute** a person, they say formally that the person has committed a crime and that person must go to court. ❍ *A senior official has successfully been prosecuted for corruption.*
● **pros|ecu|tion** NOUN ❍ *This evidence led to the prosecution of the former leader.*

pros|pect /prɑspɛkt/
1 NOUN the possibility of something happening ❍ *The prospects for peace are becoming brighter.*
2 PL NOUN Someone's **prospects** are their chances of being successful. ❍ *I chose to work abroad to improve my career prospects.*

pro|tect /prətɛkt/ VERB If you **protect** someone or something, you keep them safe. ❍ *Make sure you protect your children from the sun.*

pro|tec|tion /prətɛkʃən/ NONCOUNT NOUN If something gives you **protection** against something unpleasant, it stops you from being harmed by it. ❍ *Long-sleeved t-shirts offer greater protection against the sun.*

pro|tec|tion|ism /prətɛkʃənɪzəm/ NONCOUNT NOUN **Protectionism** is the policy some countries have of helping their own industries by putting a large tax on imported goods or by restricting imports in some other way. [ECONOMICS] ❍ *The aim of the current round of talks is to promote free trade and to avert the threat of increasing protectionism.*

pro|tec|tion|ist /prətɛkʃənɪst/
1 NOUN A **protectionist** is someone who agrees with and supports protectionism. [ECONOMICS] ❍ *Trade frictions between the two countries had been caused by trade protectionists.*
2 ADJ **Protectionist** policies, measures, and laws are meant to stop or reduce imports. [ECONOMICS] ❍ *The administration may be moving away from free trade and toward more protectionist policies.*

pro|tec|tive /prətɛktɪv/

1 ADJ intended to protect you from harm ❍ *protective gloves*

2 ADJ If someone is **protective toward** you, they look after you and try to keep you safe. ❍ *Ben is very protective toward his staff.*

pro|tein /proʊtin/ **NONCOUNT NOUN** **Protein** is a substance that found in foods like meat, eggs, and fish, that the body needs in order to grow. ❍ *Fish is a major source of protein.*

pro|test

Pronounce the verb /prətɛst/ and /proʊtɛst/. Pronounce the noun /proʊtɛst/.

1 VERB If you **protest**, you say or show publicly that you do not approve of something. ❍ *The students were protesting against the arrest of one of their teachers.* ● **pro|test|er** also **protestor** **NOUN** ❍ *The protesters say that the government is corrupt.*

2 NOUN the act of showing publicly that you do not approve of something ❍ *I took part in a protest against the war.*

Prot|es|tant /prɒtɪstənt/ **NOUN** a Christian who is not a Catholic

proto|type /proʊtətaɪp/ **NOUN** a new type of machine or device that is not yet ready to be made in large numbers and sold ❍ *Chris Retzler has built a prototype of a machine called the wave rotor.*

proud /praʊd/

1 ADJ pleased and satisfied about something good that you or people close to you have done ❍ *She was very proud of her students' success.* ● **proud|ly** **ADV** ❍ *He says proudly that there hasn't been a single complaint.*

2 ADJ thinking that you are better or more important than other people ❍ *He described his boss as "proud and selfish."*

prove /pruv/ (**proves, proving, proved**) **VERB** If you **prove** something, you show that it is true. ❍ *These results prove that we were right.*

pro|vide /prəvaɪd/ (**provides, providing, provided**) **VERB** If you **provide** something that someone needs or wants, you give it to them. ❍ *The company's website provides lots of useful information.*

pro|vid|ed /prəvaɪdɪd/ **CONJ** If something will happen **provided** that something else happens, the first thing will happen only if the second thing also happens. ❍ *He can go running at his age, provided that he is sensible.*

prov|ince /prɒvɪns/ **NOUN** a large area of a country that has its own local government ❍ *the Canadian province of British Columbia*

pro|vi|sion /prəvɪʒən/ **NONCOUNT NOUN** The **provision of** something is the act of giving it to people who need or want it. ❍ *This department is responsible for the provision of legal services.*

pro|vi|sion|al /prəvɪʒənəl/ **ADJ** Something that is **provisional** exists now, but may be changed or taken away in the future. ❍ *Your provisional driver's license is valid for 18 months.* ● **pro|vi|sion|al|ly** **ADV** ❍ *She provisionally accepted the job offer.*

pro|voke /prəvoʊk/ (**provokes, provoking, provoked**) **VERB** If you **provoke** someone, you deliberately annoy them. ❍ *The demonstrators did not provoke the police.*

prowl /praʊl/ **VERB** If an animal or a person **prowls around**, they move around quietly, waiting to do something. ❍ *Gangs of youths prowled the area.*

psy|chia|trist /sɪkaɪətrɪst/ **NOUN** a doctor who treats illnesses of the mind

psycho|graph|ics /saɪkoʊgræfɪks/ **NONCOUNT NOUN** In marketing, **psychographics** is the study and grouping of people according to their attitudes and tastes, especially for market research. ❍ *While most people are familiar with demographics, it is often psychographics that drive product definition and marketing decisions.*

psycho|logi|cal /saɪkəlɒdʒɪkəl/ **ADJ** relating to a person's mind and thoughts ❍ *psychological illness*

psy|chol|ogy /saɪkɒlədʒi/ **NONCOUNT NOUN** the study of the human mind and people's behavior ❍ *a professor of educational psychology* ● **psy|cholo|gist** **NOUN** ❍ *Amy is seeing a psychologist.*

Pty In Australia and New Zealand **Pty** is used after the names of private limited companies. **Pty** is short for "proprietary." [ADMINISTRATION]

pub /pʌb/ [mainly BRIT] → **bar 3**

pub|lic /pʌblɪk/
1 NOUN **The public** is all ordinary people. ❍ *The exhibition is open to the public from tomorrow.*
2 ADJ relating to or intended for all the people in a country ❍ *Their policies have strong public support.* ❍ *public transportation*
3 If a company **goes public**, it starts selling its shares on the stock exchange. [ECONOMICS] ❍ *In 1951 AC went public, having achieved an average annual profit of more than £50,000.*
4 If you do something **in public**, you do it when other people are there. ❍ *He hasn't performed in public in more than 40 years.*

pub|li|ca|tion /pʌblɪkeɪʃən/
1 NONCOUNT NOUN The **publication** of a book or a magazine is the act of printing it and sending it to stores to be sold. ❍ *The store stayed open late to celebrate the book's publication.*
2 NOUN a book or a magazine ❍ *It has earned favorable reviews in several publications.*

pub|lic com|pa|ny (**public companies**) NOUN A **public company** is a company whose shares can be bought by the general public. Compare with **private company**. [ECONOMICS]

pub|lic debt NONCOUNT NOUN A country's **public debt** is all the money that is owed by its government. [ECONOMICS]

pub|lic im|age (**public images**) NOUN The **public image** of a company, product, or person is the opinion that the public has of them. ❍ *It would be in the banks' best interests to participate in the scheme because it might help to improve their public image.*

pub|li|cise /pʌblɪsaɪz/ [BRIT] → **publicize**

pub|lic|ity /pʌblɪsɪti/ NONCOUNT NOUN **Publicity** means advertising or information about a person, or a product. ❍ *A lot of publicity was given to the talks.* ❍ *a publicity campaign*

pub|lic|ity man|ag|er (**publicity managers**) or **publicity officer** NOUN a person whose job is to make sure that a large number of people know about a company's activities [MARKETING AND SALES, ADMINISTRATION] ❍ *Bob Deuel, Disney's publicity manager* ❍ *a publicity officer for Granada TV*

pub|li|cize /pʌblɪsaɪz/ (**publicizes, publicizing, publicized**) VERB If you **publicize** something, you advertise it or give people information about it. ❍ *The author appeared on television to publicize her latest book.*

pub|lic lim|it|ed com|pa|ny (**public limited companies**) NOUN A **public limited company** is a company whose shares can be bought by the general public. The abbreviation **plc** is used after such companies' names. [ECONOMICS, BRIT]

pub|lic of|fer|ing (**public offerings**) NOUN a time when shares in a company are made available for people to buy [ECONOMICS] ❍ *The electric-utility sale will mark the world's largest public offering.*

pub|lic re|la|tions
1 NONCOUNT NOUN **Public relations** is the part of an organization's work that is concerned with obtaining the public's approval for what it does. The abbreviation **PR** is often used. [BUSINESS MANAGEMENT] ❍ *The move was good public relations.*
2 PL NOUN You can refer to the opinion that the public has of an organization as **public relations**. [BUSINESS MANAGEMENT] ❍ *Limiting casualties is important for public relations.*

COLLOCATIONS
a public relations *firm*
a public relations *campaign*
a public relations *exercise*
a public relations *consultant*
a public relations *coup*
a public relations *offensive*
a public relations *stunt*
a public relations *disaster*

pub|lic re|la|tions of|fic|er (**public relations officers**) NOUN An organization's

public relations officer is someone who is responsible for obtaining the public's approval for what it does. The abbreviation **PRO** is sometimes used. [ADMINISTRATION]

pub|lic sec|tor (**public sectors**) NOUN **The public sector** is the part of a country's economy which is controlled or supported financially by the government. Compare with **private sector**. [ECONOMICS] ❍ *Menem's policy of reducing the public sector and opening up the economy to free-market forces*

COLLOCATIONS

a public sector *worker*
public sector *borrowing*
a public sector *employee*
public sector *pay*
a public sector *union*
a public sector *organization*

pub|lic sec|tor en|ter|prise (**public sector enterprises**) NOUN a commercial venture that is controlled or supported financially by the government [ECONOMICS] ❍ *Investment Corporation of Pakistan, another public sector enterprise, held 5.86% of the company's stock.*

public-service cor|po|ra|tion (**public-service corporations**) NOUN a private corporation that provides services such as transportation and communications to the public [ECONOMICS]

pub|lish /pʌblɪʃ/ (**publishes, publishing, published**) VERB When a company **publishes** a book, a magazine, or a newspaper, it prepares and prints copies of it. ❍ *HarperCollins will publish his new novel on March 4.*

pub|lish|er /pʌblɪʃər/ NOUN a person or a company that publishes books, newspapers, or magazines ❍ *She sent the book to a publisher.*

pud|ding /pʊdɪŋ/ NOUN a soft, sweet food made from eggs and milk and eaten at the end of a meal ❍ *chocolate pudding*

pud|dle /pʌdᵊl/ NOUN a small pool of water on the ground ❍ *Young children love splashing in puddles.*

puff /pʌf/

1 NONCOUNT NOUN In marketing, **puff** is exaggerated praise of a product, especially in an advertisement. [MARKETING AND SALES] ❍ *The author should not be blamed for the publisher's puff.*

2 VERB When people **puff** a product, they praise it in an exaggerated way, often in advertising. [MARKETING AND SALES] ❍ *The publishers had trouble finding anyone to read the book, let alone puff it.*

pull /pʊl/

1 VERB When you **pull** something, you hold it firmly and move it somewhere. ❍ *I helped to pull the boy out of the water.* ❍ *Someone pulled her hair.*

2 NOUN **Pull** is also a noun. ❍ *He felt a pull on the fishing line.*

▶ **pull away** When a vehicle or a driver **pulls away**, the vehicle starts moving forward. ❍ *I watched the car back out of the driveway and pull away.*

▶ **pull down** If you **pull down** a building, you deliberately destroy it. ❍ *They pulled the offices down, leaving a large open space.*

▶ **pull in** If a vehicle or a driver **pulls in** somewhere, the vehicle stops there. ❍ *The bus pulled in at the side of the road.*

▶ **pull out** When a vehicle or a driver **pulls out**, the vehicle moves out into the road or nearer the center of the road. ❍ *I pulled out into the street.*

▶ **pull over** When a vehicle or driver **pulls over**, the vehicle moves closer to the side of the road and stops there. ❍ *I pulled over to let the police car pass.*

▶ **pull up** When a vehicle or driver **pulls up**, the vehicle slows down and stops. ❍ *The cab pulled up and the driver jumped out.*

pull date (**pull dates**) NOUN a date printed on a food container indicating the date by which the food should be sold or eaten before it starts to decay ❍ *a piece of cheese four weeks past its pull date*

pulse /pʌls/ NOUN Your **pulse** is the regular beat of your heart that you can feel when you touch your wrist. ❍ *Dr. Garcia checked her pulse.*

pump /pʌmp/

1 NOUN a machine that makes a liquid or gas

flow in a particular direction ❍ *A pump brings water from the well.*

2 VERB If something **pumps** a liquid or a gas in a particular direction, it makes it flow in that direction using a pump. ❍ *Many members continue to pump oil in excess of their quotas.*

pump|kin /pʌmpkɪn/ **NOUN** a large, round, orange vegetable with a thick skin ❍ *pumpkin pie*

pump prim|ing /pʌmp praɪmɪŋ/ **NONCOUNT NOUN** **Pump priming** is spending by the government that is intended to improve the economy when it is doing badly. [ECONOMICS] ❍ *The new government resorted to pump priming to jump-start economic activity.*

punch /pʌntʃ/ (**punches, punching, punched**)

1 VERB If you **punch** someone or something, you hit them hard with your closed hand. ❍ *The singer punched a photographer.*

2 NOUN **Punch** is also a noun. ❍ *My brother gave me a punch in the nose.*

punc|tu|al /pʌŋktʃuəl/ **ADJ** doing something or arriving somewhere at the right time ❍ *He's always very punctual. I'll see if he's here yet.* ● **punc|tu|al|ity** /pʌŋktʃuælɪti/ **NONCOUNT NOUN** ❍ *The airline hopes to improve punctuality next year.*

P

punc|tua|tion /pʌŋktʃueɪʃən/ **NONCOUNT NOUN** **Punctuation** is signs such as ( ), !, or ? that you use to divide writing into sentences and phrases.

punc|tua|tion mark (**punctuation marks**) **NOUN** a symbol such as ( ), !, or ?

punc|ture /pʌŋktʃər/ (**punctures, puncturing, punctured**)

1 NOUN a small hole that has been made by a sharp object ❍ *I repaired the puncture in my front tire.*

2 VERB If a sharp object **punctures** something, it makes a hole in it. ❍ *The bullet punctured his left lung.*

pun|ish /pʌnɪʃ/ (**punishes, punishing, punished**) **VERB** If you **punish** someone, you make them suffer because they have done something wrong. ❍ *The firm was punished for refusing to co-operate.*

pun|ish|ment /pʌnɪʃmənt/ **NOUN** a particular way of punishing someone ❍ *There will be tougher punishments for violent crimes.*

pu|pil /pyupɪl/

1 NOUN a child who goes to an elementary school ❍ *Around 270 pupils attend this school.*

2 NOUN Your **pupils** are the small, round, black holes in the center of your eyes.

pup|pet /pʌpɪt/ **NOUN** a small model of a person or animal that you can move

pup|py /pʌpi/ (**puppies**) **NOUN** a young dog

pur|chase /pɜrtʃɪs/ (**purchases, purchasing, purchased**)

1 VERB If you **purchase** something, you buy it. [PURCHASING, FORMAL] ❍ *He purchased a ticket for the concert.*

2 NONCOUNT NOUN The **purchase of** something is the act of buying it. [PURCHASING, FORMAL] ❍ *The Canadian company announced the purchase of 1,663 stores in the U.S.*

3 NOUN something that you have bought [PURCHASING, FORMAL] ❍ *Her latest purchase is a shiny, black motorcycle.*

pur|chas|ing de|part|ment (**purchasing departments**) **NOUN** the section of a company that is responsible for buying materials used by the company [PURCHASING, ADMINISTRATION] ❍ *Company policy on raw materials must be flexible enough to enable the purchasing department to exploit price opportunities.*

pur|chas|ing pow|er

1 NONCOUNT NOUN The **purchasing power** of a currency is the amount of goods or services that you can buy with it. [ECONOMICS] ❍ *The real purchasing power of the rouble has plummeted.*

2 NONCOUNT NOUN The **purchasing power** of a person or group of people is the amount of goods or services that they can afford to buy. [ECONOMICS] ❍ *Wage rates must be maintained in order to maintain the purchasing power of the consumer.*

pure /pyʊər/ (**purer, purest**)

1 ADJ not mixed with anything else ❍ *pure orange juice*

2 ADJ clean and not containing any harmful substances ❍ *The water is very pure.*
3 ADJ complete and total ❍ *a look of pure surprise*

pure|ly /pyʊərli/ **ADV** only or completely ❍ *This car is designed purely for speed.*

pur|ple /pɜrpəl/
1 ADJ having a red-blue color ❍ *She wore a purple dress.*
2 NOUN **Purple** is also a noun. ❍ *I love the purples and grays of the Scottish mountains.*

pur|pose /pɜrpəs/
1 NOUN the reason for something ❍ *The purpose of the occasion was to raise money for charity.*
2 If you do something **on purpose**, you do it deliberately. ❍ *A management group bid low on purpose, knowing the board would ask a few dollars more.*

purse /pɜrs/ **NOUN** a small bag that women use to carry money and other things ❍ *Lauren reached in her purse for her keys.*

purse strings **PL NOUN** If you say that someone holds or controls **the purse strings**, you mean that they control the way that money is spent in a particular family, group, or country. ❍ *Women control the purse strings of most families.*

pur|sue /pərsu/ (**pursues, pursuing, pursued**) **VERB** If you **pursue** someone or something, you follow them because you want to catch them. [FORMAL] ❍ *Police pursued the driver for two miles.*

pur|suit /pərsut/ **NONCOUNT NOUN** If you are **in pursuit of** someone or something, you are trying to catch them or get them. ❍ *He has traveled the world in pursuit of his dream.*

push /pʊʃ/ (**pushes, pushing, pushed**)
1 VERB If you **push** something, you move it by pressing with your hands or body. ❍ *The men pushed him into the car and locked the door.* ❍ *Justin put both hands on the door and pushed hard.*
2 NOUN **Push** is also a noun. ❍ *Laura gave me a sharp push and I fell to the ground.*

push-up **NOUN** **Push-ups** are exercises in which you lie on your front and push your body up with your hands.

put /pʊt/ (**puts, putting, put**)
1 VERB If you **put** something somewhere, you move it into that place or position. ❍ *Steven put the photograph on the desk.* ❍ *She put her hand on Grace's arm.*
2 VERB If you **put** someone or something in a particular state or situation, you cause them to be in that state or situation. ❍ *This has put us in direct competition with firms that already offer this service.*
3 NOUN an option to sell securities at a specified price during a specified limited period ❍ *A higher interest rate increases the market value of a call and reduces the market value of a put.*
▸ **put away** If you **put** something **away**, you put it back in the place where it is usually kept. ❍ *Kyle put the milk away in the refrigerator.*
▸ **put down** If you **put** something **down** somewhere, you stop holding it and place it on a surface. ❍ *The woman put down her phone and looked at me.*
▸ **put into** If you **put** money **into** a business, etc., you invest in it. ❍ *There was no chance of getting anyone to put money into the airline in its current form.*
▸ **put off** If you **put** something **off**, you delay doing it. ❍ *Tony always puts off making difficult decisions.*
▸ **put on**
1 If you **put on** clothing or make-up, you place it on your body. ❍ *She put her coat on and went out.*
2 If you **put on** weight, you become heavier.
3 If you **put on** a piece of electrical equipment, you make it start working. ❍ *Maria put on the light.*
▸ **put out** If you **put out** a fire, you make it stop burning.
▸ **put through** If you **put** someone **through to** someone else, you connect them by telephone. ❍ *I'll put you through to our sales department.*
▸ **put up**
1 If you **put up** a building or other structure, you build it. ❍ *The Smiths have put up electric fences on their farm.*
2 If you **put up** prices, you increase them. ❍ *He warned stores not to put their prices up.*

3 If you **put up** the money for something, you provide the money for it. ❍ *Vale has put up $4.8 billion for two recent purchases.*
4 If you **put** something **up for sale**, you make it available to be bought. ❍ *The first of such transactions could be Bloomingdale's, which Mr. Campeau put up for sale last week.*
▶ **put up with** If you **put up with** someone or something unpleasant, you accept them without complaining. ❍ *I won't put up with this poor performance any longer.*

puz|zle /pʌzᵊl/ (**puzzles, puzzling, puzzled**)
1 VERB If something **puzzles** you, you do not understand it. ❍ *Many other traders seemed puzzled by the sudden turnaround in bond prices.*
• **puz|zling ADJ** ❍ *Michael's comments are very puzzling.*
2 NOUN a question, a game, or a toy that is difficult to answer, do, or put together correctly ❍ *Mom loves doing word puzzles.*

py|ja|mas /pɪdʒɑməz/ [mainly BRIT]
→ **pajamas**

pyra|mid /pɪrəmɪd/
1 NOUN a solid shape with a flat base and flat sides that form a point where they meet at the top ❍ *the Egyptian Pyramids*
2 NOUN In business, a **pyramid** is a group of enterprises containing a series of holding companies structured so that the top holding company controls the entire group with a relatively small proportion of the total capital invested. [ECONOMICS] ❍ *Pinnacle West Capital Corp. is at the peak of the energy pyramid in Arizona. It is the holding company for the state's largest electric utility.*

pyra|mid sell|ing NONCOUNT NOUN
Pyramid selling is a sales method where a manufacturer sells goods to sellers who each sell them to more sellers. This continues until the goods can only be sold at a loss. [ECONOMICS, MARKETING AND SALES] ❍ *The Commission needs to examine whether these practices are adequately distinguished from pyramid selling, an activity which is not allowed in many countries.*

P

Qq

qt. **qt.** is short for **quart**.

quali|fi|ca|tion /kwɒlɪfɪkeɪʃən/ **NOUN** **Qualifications** are the examinations you have passed or the skills that you have. ❍ *All our workers have professional qualifications in electronics.*

quali|fied /kwɒlɪfaɪd/ **ADJ** having the right skills or training to do something ❍ *Blake is qualified in both U.K. and U.S. law.*

quali|fy /kwɒlɪfaɪ/ (**qualifies, qualifying, qualified**)
1 VERB If you **qualify** for something, you have the right to do it or have it. ❍ *You qualify for a discount.*
2 VERB When someone **qualifies**, they pass their examinations for a particular job. ❍ *I qualified, and started teaching last year.*

qual|ity /kwɒlɪti/ (**qualities**)
1 NONCOUNT NOUN The **quality** of something is how good or bad it is. [PRODUCTION] ❍ *The quality of their work is excellent.*
2 NOUN a characteristic ❍ *Poland has many attractive qualities for foreign investors.*

qual|ity cir|cle (**quality circles**) **NOUN** a small group of workers and managers who meet to solve problems and improve the quality of the organization's products or services [PRODUCTION] ❍ *Flexible work hours, quality circles, and various innovative approaches to productivity have arisen outside the United States.*

qual|ity con|trol or **quality assurance** **NONCOUNT NOUN** **Quality control** is the activity of checking that goods or services are of an acceptable standard. [PRODUCTION] ❍ *The message is you need better quality control.* ❍ *The report also calls for national standards of quality assurance for all X-ray units.*

qual|ity of life **NOUN** the extent to which your life is comfortable or satisfying [BUSINESS MANAGEMENT] ❍ *"Would you go back to England?"—"Never, the quality of life is so much better here."* ❍ *A vibrant and growing economy does not improve everyone's quality of life.*

quan|tity /kwɒntɪti/ (**quantities**) **NOUN** an amount ❍ *It was prohibited for us to sell that quantity of gas.*

quar|rel /kwɔrəl/
1 NOUN an argument ❍ *I had a terrible quarrel with my colleague.*
2 VERB When people **quarrel**, they have an argument. ❍ *Yes, we quarreled over something silly.*

quart /kwɔrt/ **NOUN** a unit for measuring liquid that is equal to two pints ❍ *a quart of milk*

quar|ter /kwɔrtər/
1 NOUN one of four equal parts of something ❍ *Each director controls roughly a quarter of the firm's shares.* ❍ *I'll be with you in a quarter of an hour.*
2 NOUN an American or Canadian coin that is worth 25 cents
3 NOUN a period of three months ❍ *We will send you a bill every quarter.*
4 NONCOUNT NOUN **Quarter** is used when telling the time to talk about the fifteen minutes before or after an hour. ❍ *We arrived at quarter of nine that night.*

quar|ter|ly /kwɔrtərli/
1 ADJ happening four times a year, at intervals of three months ❍ *the latest Bank of Japan quarterly survey of 5,000 companies*
2 ADV **Quarterly** is also an adverb. ❍ *It makes no difference whether dividends are paid quarterly or annually.*

quar|tet /kwɔrtɛt/ **NOUN** a group of four musicians or a piece of music for four instruments or singers

queen /kwin/ NOUN a woman ruler in some countries, or a woman who is married to a king ❍ *Queen Elizabeth*

ques|tion /kwɛstʃən/
1 NOUN something that you say or write in order to ask a person about something ❍ *They asked a lot of questions about her health.*
2 VERB If you **question** someone, you ask them a lot of questions. ❍ *The panel questioned him about his business experience.*
● **ques|tion|ing** NONCOUNT NOUN ❍ *The police want thirty-two people for questioning.*
3 VERB If you **question** something, you express doubts about it. ❍ *They never question the director's decisions.*
4 NOUN a subject that needs to be considered ❍ *The question of nuclear energy is complex.*

ques|tion mark (**question marks**) NOUN the punctuation mark (?) that is used in writing at the end of a question

ques|tion|naire /kwɛstʃənɛər/ NOUN a written list of questions which are answered by a lot of people in order to provide information for a report or a survey ❍ *Employers will be asked to fill in a questionnaire.*

queue /kyu/ [BRIT] → **line 2**

quick /kwik/
1 ADJ moving or doing things with great speed ❍ *You'll have to be quick.* ● **quick|ly** ADV ❍ *Cussane worked quickly.*
2 ADJ lasting only a short time or happening in a short time ❍ *He took a quick look around the room.* ❍ *We are hoping for a quick end to the strike.*
● **quick|ly** ADV ❍ *They are likely to recoup their investments quickly.* ❍ *Their job is to bring this information to the market as quickly as possible.*

qui|et /kwaɪɪt/
1 ADJ making very little noise ❍ *The car has an extremely quiet engine.* ● **qui|et|ly** ADV ❍ *She spoke very quietly.*
2 ADJ If a place is **quiet**, there is no activity or trouble there. ❍ *It's a quiet little village.*
3 ADJ If you are **quiet**, you are not saying anything. ❍ *Be quiet and go to sleep.* ● **qui|et|ly** ADV ❍ *Amy stood quietly in the doorway.*

quit /kwit/ (**quits, quitting, quit**) VERB If you **quit** something, you stop doing it. [INFORMAL] ❍ *Quit talking now and do some work.* ❍ *That's enough! I quit!*

quite /kwaɪt/
1 ADV very but not extremely ❍ *Gross investment has been quite strong for the past five years.* ❍ *I think the market is holding up quite well.*
2 ADV completely ❍ *My position is quite different.*

quiz /kwiz/ (**quizzes**) NOUN a competition in which someone tests your knowledge by asking you questions ❍ *We'll have a quiz after we visit the museum.*

quo|ta /kwoʊtə/
1 NOUN the limited number or quantity of something which is officially allowed ❍ *Farmers are given a set quota of sheep to produce in return for a subsidy.* ❍ *Sometimes it's cod we're throwing back into the water because we can't exceed our quota, other times it's plaice or haddock.*
2 NOUN a fixed maximum or minimum proportion of people from a particular group who are allowed to do something, such as come and live in a country or work for the government ❍ *The bill would force employers to adopt a quota system when recruiting workers.*

quo|ta samp|ling /kwoʊtə sæmplɪŋ/ NONCOUNT NOUN In marketing, **quota sampling** is a method of carrying out market research, in which the sample of people is selected according to, for example, their age, sex or social class. [MARKETING AND SALES] ❍ *Opinion pollsters use the simple and cheap method of quota sampling.*

quo|ta|tion /kwoʊteɪʃən/
1 NOUN a sentence from a book, a poem, a speech, or a play ❍ *He used quotations from Martin Luther King Jr.*
2 NOUN a statement of how much it will cost to do a particular piece of work ❍ *Get several written quotations and check exactly what's included in the cost.*
3 NOUN a statement of the current market price of a security or commodity ❍ *Money is moved at lightning speed in response to the tiniest differences in price quotations.*
4 NOUN a registration on the stock exchange, which enables a company's shares to be officially listed and traded ❍ *an American-*

dominated investment manager with a quotation on the London stock market

> **BUSINESS ETIQUETTE**
> In the UK and Germany, punctuality is considered to be very important.

quo|ta|tion mark (**quotation marks**)
NOUN **Quotation marks** are used in writing to show where speech begins and ends. They are usually written or printed as **"..."**.

quote /kwoʊt/ (**quotes, quoting, quoted**)
1 VERB If you **quote** someone, you repeat what they have written or said. ❍ *I gave the letter to the reporter and he quoted from it.*
2 NOUN A **quote from** a book, a poem, a play, or a speech is a sentence from it. ❍ *The article starts with a quote from an unnamed member of the Cabinet.*
3 VERB If someone **quotes** a price **for** doing something, they say how much money they would charge you for a service they are offering or a for a job that you want them to do. ❍ *He quoted a price for the repairs.*
4 NOUN A **quote for** a piece of work is the price that someone says they will charge you to do the work. ❍ *Always get a written quote for any repairs needed.*
5 VERB If a company's shares, a substance, or a currency **is quoted** at a particular price, that is its current market price. ❍ *In early trading in Hong Kong yesterday, gold was quoted at $368.20 an ounce.*
6 PL NOUN **Quotes** are the same as **quotation marks**. [INFORMAL] ❍ *The word "remembered" is in quotes here.*

quot|ed com|pa|ny [ECONOMICS, BRIT]
→ **listed company**

q

Rr

rab|bi /ræbaɪ/ **NOUN** a Jewish religious leader

rab|bit /ræbɪt/ **NOUN** a small animal that has long ears and lives in a hole in the ground

race /reɪs/ (**races, racing, raced**)
1 NOUN a competition to see who is the fastest ❍ *Mark easily won the race.*
2 VERB If you **race**, you take part in a race. ❍ *Leo started racing in the early 1950s.* ❍ *We raced them to the top of the hill.*
3 NOUN one of the major groups that humans can be divided into according to their physical features ❍ *The college welcomes students of all races.*
4 VERB If you **race** somewhere, you go there as quickly as possible. ❍ *He raced across town to the hospital.*

ra|cial /reɪʃᵊl/ **ADJ** relating to people's race ❍ *racial equality* ● **ra|cial|ly ADV** ❍ *a racially mixed community*

ra|cial dis|crimi|na|tion NONCOUNT NOUN Racial discrimination is the practice of treating the members of one race less fairly or less well than those of the other race. [HR] ❍ *Of 37,000 complaints received, there were only 16 alleged cases of racial discrimination in real estate lending.*

rac|ing /reɪsɪŋ/ **NONCOUNT NOUN Racing** is the sport of competing in races. ❍ *a racing car*

rac|ism /reɪsɪzəm/ **NONCOUNT NOUN Racism** is the belief that people of some races are not as good as others. ❍ *Many of these children experienced racism.*

rac|ist /reɪsɪst/
1 ADJ influenced by the belief that people of some races are better than others ❍ *We live in a racist society.*
2 NOUN Racist is also a noun. ❍ *He was attacked by a gang of racists.*

rack /ræk/ **NOUN** a frame or shelf that is used for holding things ❍ *a luggage rack*

rack|et /rækɪt/ **NOUN** an illegal activity that is done to make money [INFORMAL] ❍ *He admitted he had been in the drug racket.*

ra|dar /reɪdɑr/ **NONCOUNT NOUN Radar** is a way of discovering the position of objects when they cannot be seen, by using radio signals. ❍ *They saw the submarine on the ship's radar screen.*

ra|dia|tion /reɪdieɪʃən/ **NONCOUNT NOUN Radiation** is a type of energy that comes from some substances, and that can be harmful. ❍ *The gas protects the Earth against radiation from the sun.*

ra|dia|tor /reɪdieɪtər/
1 NOUN a metal object that is filled with hot water to heat a room
2 NOUN the part of a car's engine that is filled with water in order to cool it

radi|cal /rædɪkᵊl/ **ADJ Radical** changes and differences are very big and important. ❍ *radical economic reforms* ● **radi|cal|ly** /rædɪkli/ **ADV** ❍ *people with radically different beliefs*

ra|dio /reɪdioʊ/
1 NOUN a piece of equipment that you use in order to listen to radio programs ❍ *He turned on the radio.*
2 NONCOUNT NOUN Radio is a system of sending and receiving sound through the air. ❍ *They are in radio contact with the leader.*
3 NOUN a piece of equipment that is used for sending and receiving spoken messages ❍ *The police officer called for extra help on his radio.*

radio|ac|tive /reɪdioʊæktɪv/ **ADJ** containing a substance that produces a type of energy that can be harmful to living things ❍ *radioactive waste products*

raft /ræft/ **NOUN** a flat boat made from large pieces of wood that are tied together

rag /ræg/
1 NOUN a piece of old cloth ❍ *an oily rag*
2 PL NOUN **Rags** are old torn clothes. ❍ *children dressed in rags*

rage /reɪdʒ/ **NONCOUNT NOUN** **Rage** is very strong anger. ❍ *His face was red with rage.*

raid /reɪd/
1 VERB If police officers or soldiers **raid** a building, they enter it suddenly in order to look for someone or something. ❍ *Police raided the company's offices.*
2 NOUN **Raid** is also a noun. ❍ *They were arrested after a raid on a house by police.*

rail /reɪl/
1 NOUN a horizontal bar that use for support or to hang things on ❍ *a hand rail* ❍ *a curtain rail*
2 NOUN **Rails** are the steel bars that trains run on. ❍ *The train left the rails.*
3 NONCOUNT NOUN If you travel **by rail**, you travel on a train.

rail|ing /reɪlɪŋ/ **NOUN** a fence that is made from metal bars ❍ *He jumped over the railing.*

rail|road /reɪlroʊd/ **NOUN** a route between two places that trains travel along ❍ *railroad tracks*

rail|way /reɪlweɪ/ [BRIT] → **railroad**

rain /reɪn/
1 NONCOUNT NOUN **Rain** is water that falls from the clouds. ❍ *We got very wet in the rain.*
2 VERB When rain falls, you can say that **it is raining**.

rain|bow /reɪnboʊ/ **NOUN** a half circle of different colors, made when sun shines through rain

rain|coat /reɪnkoʊt/ **NOUN** a coat that you can wear to keep dry when it rains

rain|drop /reɪndrɒp/ **NOUN** a single drop of rain

rain|fall /reɪnfɔl/ **NONCOUNT NOUN** **Rainfall** is the amount of rain that falls during a particular period. ❍ *below average rainfall*

rain|for|est /reɪnfɔrɪst/ **NOUN** a thick forest of tall trees that grows in tropical areas ❍ *the Amazon Rainforest*

rainy /reɪni/ (**rainier, rainiest**) **ADJ** raining a lot ❍ *a rainy day*

raise /reɪz/ (**raises, raising, raised**)
1 VERB If you **raise** something, you move it upward. ❍ *He raised his hand to wave.*
2 VERB If you **raise** the rate or level of something, you increase it. ❍ *Many stores have raised their prices.*
3 NOUN an increase in the amount of money that you are paid for your work ❍ *Kelly got a raise of $100.*
4 VERB If you **raise** money **for** a particular purpose, you get it from other people. ❍ *The event is to raise money for the school.*
5 VERB If you **raise** a subject, you start to talk about it. ❍ *The matter will be raised at our annual meeting.*

rake /reɪk/ (**rakes, raking, raked**)
1 NOUN a garden tool with a long handle, used for collecting loose grass or leaves
2 VERB If you **rake** leaves, you move them using a rake. ❍ *We raked the leaves into piles.*

ral|ly /ræli/ (**rallies, rallying, rallied**)
1 VERB When something, for example the price of shares, **rallies**, it begins to recover or improve. ❍ *Markets began to rally worldwide.*
2 NOUN **Rally** is also a noun. ❍ *After a brief rally the shares returned to 30 cents.*

COLLOCATIONS
a *strong* rally
a *powerful* rally

RAM /ræm/ **NONCOUNT NOUN** **RAM** is the part of a computer where information is stored while you are using it. **RAM** is short for "Random Access Memory."

Rama|dan /ræmədɑn/ **NONCOUNT NOUN** **Ramadan** is the ninth month of the Muslim year, when Muslims do not eat or drink during the day.

ramp /ræmp/ **NOUN** a slope between two places that are at different levels ❍ *a wheelchair ramp*

ran /ræn/ **Ran** is a form of the verb **run**.

ranch /ræntʃ/ (**ranches**) NOUN a large farm used for keeping animals ❍ *a cattle ranch*

ranch|er /ræntʃər/ NOUN a person who owns or manages a large farm, especially one used for raising cattle, horses, or sheep ❍ *a cattle rancher*

R & D /ɑr ən di/ also **R and D** NONCOUNT NOUN **R & D** is an abbreviation for **Research and Development**. [R & D] ❍ *Businesses need to train their workers better, and spend more on R&D.*

ran|dom /rændəm/ ADJ without a plan or a pattern ❍ *a random sample of two thousand people* ❍ *We have seen random violence against innocent victims.*

rang /ræŋ/ **Rang** is a form of the verb **ring**.

range /reɪndʒ/ (**ranges, ranging, ranged**)
1 NOUN a number of different things of the same type ❍ *The product is available in a wide range of colors.*
2 NOUN a group that is included between two points on a scale ❍ *The average age range is between 35 and 55.*
3 NOUN The **range of** something is the largest area in which it can reach things. ❍ *This electric car has a range of 100 miles.*
4 VERB If things **range from** one point on a scale **to** another point, they are between these two fixed points. ❍ *These companies have market values ranging from $50 million to $300 million.*
5 NOUN the total products of a manufacturer, designer, or store [MARKETING AND SALES] ❍ *the new Autumn range*

rang|er /reɪndʒər/ NOUN a person whose job is to take care of a forest or large park ❍ *Bill Justice is a park ranger at the Carlsbad Caverns National Park.*

rank /ræŋk/ NOUN the position that someone has in an organization ❍ *He holds the rank of colonel in the U.S. Army.*

rap /ræp/ (**raps, rapping, rapped**) NONCOUNT NOUN **Rap** is a type of modern music in which the words are spoken. ❍ *a rap group* ● **rap|per** NOUN ❍ *He's a singer and a talented rapper.*

R

rape /reɪp/ (**rapes, raping, raped**)
1 VERB If someone **is raped**, they are forced to have sex when they do not want to. ● **rapist** NOUN ❍ *The information led to the rapist's arrest.*
2 NOUN the crime of forcing someone to have sex

rap|id /ræpɪd/ ADJ very quick ❍ *rapid economic growth* ❍ *He walked at a rapid pace.* ● **rap|id|ly** ADV ❍ *The firm continues to grow rapidly.* ❍ *He was moving rapidly around the room.*

rare /rɛər/ (**rarer, rarest**)
1 ADJ not happening or existing very often ❍ *Investment-grade bonds are relatively rare.*
2 ADJ **Rare** meat is cooked very lightly.

rare|ly /rɛərli/ ADV not very often

rash /ræʃ/
1 ADJ acting without thinking carefully ❍ *Don't make any rash decisions.*
2 NOUN an area of red spots on your skin ❍ *I always get a rash when I eat nuts.*

rasp|berry /ræzbɛri/ (**raspberries**) NOUN a small, soft, red fruit that grows on bushes

rat /ræt/ NOUN an animal with a long tail that looks like a large mouse

rate /reɪt/
1 NOUN how fast or how often something happens ❍ *An adult's heart rate is about 72 beats per minute.* ❍ *Spain has the lowest birth rate in Europe.*
2 NOUN the amount of money that goods or services cost ❍ *The hotel offers a special weekend rate.*
3 NOUN the amount of tax or interest that needs to be paid on money that is earned or borrowed ❍ *The government insisted that it would not be panicked into interest rate cuts.*

rate of re|turn (**rates of return**) NOUN the amount of profit that an investment makes [FINANCE] ❍ *High rates of return can be earned on these investments.*

ra|ther /ræðər/
1 **Rather than** means "instead of." ❍ *The new advertisements will focus on product and features, rather than image.* ❍ *The cash is being reinvested rather than being handed to shareholders as dividends.*

2 If you **would rather** do or have something, you would prefer to do or have it. ❍ *OPEC members would rather boost export volumes at low prices than force price increases.*
3 ADV slightly ❍ *The firm's performance last year was rather disappointing.*

rat|ing /reɪtɪŋ/
1 NOUN a measurement of how good or popular something is ❍ *The president's popularity rating is at its lowest point.*
2 NOUN the estimated financial standing of a business or individual ❍ *The rating reflects the risks of a new company in a highly competitive industry.*

ra|tio /reɪʃoʊ, -ʃioʊ/ **NOUN** a relationship in size or amount between two things, expressed in numbers ❍ *The adult to child ratio is one to six.*

ra|tion|al /ræʃənəl/ **ADJ** based on reason rather than emotion ❍ *Rational behavior for the employee is clearly to maximize wage and salary income.* ● **ra|tion|al|ly ADV** ❍ *It is difficult to think rationally when you're worried.*

ra|tion|al|ise /ræʃənəlaɪz/ [BRIT] → **rationalize**

ra|tion|al|ize /ræʃənəlaɪz/ (**rationalizes, rationalizing, rationalized**) **VERB** If you **rationalize** an operation or a business, you remove unnecessary equipment, personnel, or processes from it in order to make it more efficient. [BUSINESS MANAGEMENT] ❍ *Savings and general improvements could best be achieved from rationalizing the distribution activities of the group.*

BUSINESS ETIQUETTE
In Germany and Scandinavian countries, people do not often make much small talk at the beginning of a meeting. They usually prefer to get straight down to business.

rat|tle /rætəl/ (**rattles, rattling, rattled**)
1 VERB When something **rattles**, it makes short, sharp, knocking sounds. ❍ *The windows rattled in the wind.*
2 NOUN a baby's toy that make a noise when the baby shakes it

rave /reɪv/ (**raves, raving, raved**) **VERB** If you **rave about** something, you speak or write about it with great enthusiasm. ❍ *Rachel raved about the movie.*

raw /rɔ/
1 ADJ Raw materials or substances are in their natural state. ❍ *raw sugar*
2 ADJ not cooked ❍ *raw fish*

raw ma|terials PL NOUN Raw materials are materials that are in their natural state, before they are processed or used in manufacturing. [PRODUCTION] ❍ *ships bringing the raw materials for the ever-expanding textile industry* ❍ *Villages became associated with different trades, depending on the availability of raw materials in the area.*

ray /reɪ/ **NOUN** A **ray** of light is a narrow line of light. ❍ *Protect your eyes against the sun's rays.*

ra|zor /reɪzər/ **NOUN** a tool that people use for shaving

reach /ritʃ/ (**reaches, reaching, reached**)
1 VERB When someone or something **reaches** a place, they arrive there. ❍ *He did not stop until he reached the door.*
2 VERB If someone or something has **reached** a certain level or amount, they are at that level or amount. ❍ *The number of unemployed could reach 3 million next year.*
3 VERB If you **reach** somewhere, you move your arm to take or touch something. ❍ *Judy reached into her bag.*
4 VERB If you can **reach** something, you are able to touch it. ❍ *Can you reach your toes with your fingertips?*
5 NONCOUNT NOUN The **reach** of a marketing campaign is the proportion of a market that an advertiser hopes to contact. ❍ *There was a reduction in the value and reach of traditional media as the market became more diverse.*

re|act /riækt/
1 VERB When you **react to** something, you behave in a particular way because of it. ❍ *Investors react violently to any cuts in dividends.*
2 VERB When two chemical substances **react**, they combine and change to form another substance. ❍ *Calcium reacts with water.*

re|ac|tion /riækʃən/
1 NOUN Your **reaction to** something is how you behave because of it. ❍ *Try to predict the trainees' reactions before reading their feedback.*
2 NOUN a process in which two chemical substances combine and change to form another substance ❍ *a chemical reaction between oxygen and hydrogen*

read (**reads, reading, read**)

Pronounce the present tense /rid/. Pronounce the past tense and the past participle /rɛd/.

1 VERB When you **read** something, you look at its written words and understand them. ❍ *Have you read this book?* ❍ *I read about it in the paper.*
2 VERB When you **read** words that you can see, you say them aloud. ❍ *He read a statement to his staff.*

read|ily /rɛdɪli/ **ADV** willingly ❍ *I asked her to help, and she readily agreed.*

read|ing /ridɪŋ/ **NONCOUNT NOUN Reading** is the activity of reading books. ❍ *I love reading.*

ready /rɛdi/ (**readier, readiest**)
1 ADJ If someone is **ready**, they are prepared for something. ❍ *Their management is not ready for the challenges involved in building an international business.*
2 ADJ If something is **ready**, it has been prepared. ❍ *These products will not be ready for delivery for several months.*
3 ADJ If you are **ready to** do something, you are willing to do it. ❍ *They were ready to help.*

R

ready mon|ey or **ready cash NONCOUNT NOUN Ready money** is cash that can be used immediately. [ECONOMICS] ❍ *As a retail bank customer, I want to lay my hands on ready money when I need it.* ❍ *To give themselves ready cash, some airlines want to keep a 10% ticket tax for up to a year before handing it over to the government.*

real /ril/
1 ADJ existing and not invented ❍ *No, it wasn't a dream. It was real.*
2 ADJ not artificial ❍ *I love the smell of real leather.*
3 ADJ true and not pretended ❍ *This is the real reason why pension costs have not been curbed.*
4 ADV very [INFORMAL] ❍ *He is finding prison life real tough.*

real es|tate NONCOUNT NOUN Real estate is property in the form of land and buildings.

re|al|ise /riəlaɪz/ [BRIT] → **realize**

re|al|is|tic /riəlɪstɪk/
1 ADJ If you are **realistic** about a situation, you recognize and accept its true nature. ❍ *She is realistic about markets: sometimes they do fail.*
2 ADJ representing things in a way that is like real life

re|al|ity /riælɪti/ (**realities**) **NOUN Reality** is the way things really are rather than how someone imagines them or hopes them to be. ❍ *The firm was, in reality, bankrupt.* ❍ *The system does not reflect the realities of the modern market.*

re|al|ize /riəlaɪz/ (**realizes, realizing, realized**)
1 VERB If you **realize** something, you become aware of it or understand it. ❍ *Bankers have realized that they will face a lot of loan defaults.* ❍ *People don't realize how serious the situation is.*
● **re|a|li|za|tion NOUN** ❍ *There's a growing realization that to fuel growth, they must broaden their customer base.*
2 VERB If goods, property, etc. **realize** a particular sum, they sell for or make that sum. ❍ *This table realized £800.*

re|al|ly /riəli/
1 ADV used to give a sentence a stronger meaning [SPOKEN] ❍ *I'm very sorry. I really am.*
2 ADV used when you are talking about the real facts about something ❍ *The firm's problems really began in the 1990s.*
3 EXCLAM used to express surprise at what someone has said [SPOKEN] ❍ *"I once met the president."—"Really?"*

Real|tor /riəltər, -tɔr/ **NOUN** a person whose job is to sell houses, buildings, and land [ECONOMICS, TRADEMARK] ❍ *The U.S. National Association of Realtors reported yesterday that sales of previously owned homes rose in January.*

rear /rɪər/
1 NOUN the back part of something ❍ *The car hit the rear of the truck.*

2 ADJ Rear is also an adjective. ○ *You must fasten all rear seat belts.*
3 VERB If you **rear** children or animals, you take care of them until they are adults. ○ *I was reared in Texas.*
4 VERB When a horse **rears**, it stands on its back legs. ○ *The horse reared and threw off its rider.*

rea|son /rizən/
1 NOUN a fact that explains why something has happened ○ *There is a reason for every important thing that happens.*
2 NONCOUNT NOUN Reason is the ability that people have to think and to make sensible judgments. ○ *He was more interested in emotion than reason.*

rea|son|able /rizənəbəl/
1 ADJ fair and sensible ○ *She seems to be a reasonable person.* ○ *The current offer is way below reasonable value.*
2 ADJ fairly good ○ *He spoke reasonable French.* • **rea|son|ably ADV** ○ *Their investments performed reasonably well.*

re|assure /riəʃʊər/ (**reassures, reassuring, reassured**) **VERB** If you **reassure** someone, you say or do things to make them stop worrying. • **re|assur|ance NONCOUNT NOUN** ○ *Suppliers need reassurance that they will be paid.*

re|bal|ancing /ribælənsɪŋ/ **NONCOUNT NOUN Rebalancing** is the process of returning an investment portfolio to carry the level of risk originally required by the investor. [BUSINESS MANAGEMENT] ○ *Without such a rebalancing, inflation or a property boom and bust could destroy growth.*

re|bate /ribeɪt/ **NOUN** an amount of money which is returned to you after you have paid for goods or services or after you have paid tax or rent [FINANCE] ○ *Citicorp will guarantee its credit card customers a rebate on a number of products.*

re|bel (**rebels, rebelling, rebelled**)

Pronounce the noun /rɛbəl/. Pronounce the verb /rɪbɛl/.

1 NOUN someone who is fighting against the people who are in charge somewhere, for example the government ○ *There is still heavy fighting between rebels and government forces.*
2 VERB When someone **rebels**, they fight against the people who are in charge. ○ *Teenagers often rebel against their parents.*

re|boot /ribut/ **VERB** If you **reboot** a computer, you turn it off and start it again.

re|brand /ribrænd/ **VERB** To **rebrand** a product or organization means to present it to the public in a new way, for example by changing its name or appearance. [MARKETING AND SALES] ○ *There are plans to rebrand many Texas stores.* • **re|brand|ing NONCOUNT NOUN** ○ *A complete rebranding of the school is expected within two years.*

re|call /rɪkɔl/ **VERB** When you **recall** something, you remember it. ○ *He recalled meeting Pollard during a business trip.*

re|capi|tal|ise /rikæpɪtəlaɪz/ [BRIT] → **recapitalize**

re|capi|tal|ize /rikæpɪtəlaɪz/ (**recapitalizes, recapitalizing, recapitalized**) **VERB** If a company **recapitalizes**, it changes the way it manages its financial affairs, for example by borrowing money or reissuing shares. [ECONOMICS] ○ *Mr. Warnock resigned as the company abandoned a plan to recapitalize.* ○ *He plans to recapitalize the insurance fund.* • **re|capi|tali|za|tion** /rikæpɪtəlɪzeɪʃən/ **NOUN** ○ *The new management is to explore a recapitalization of the company.*

re|ceipt /rɪsit/ **NOUN** a piece of paper that shows that you have received goods or money ○ *I gave her a receipt for the money.*

re|ceive /rɪsiv/ (**receives, receiving, received**) **VERB** When you **receive** something, you get it. ○ *Some suppliers won't release goods until they receive cash payment.*

re|ceiv|er /rɪsivər/ **NOUN** a person who is appointed by a court of law to manage the affairs of a business, usually when it is failing financially [LEGAL] ○ *Between July and September, a total of 1,059 firms called in the receiver.*

re|ceiv|er|ship /rɪsivərʃɪp/ **NOUN** the administration of a business by the receiver [LEGAL] ○ *The company has now gone into* *receivership with debts of several million.* ❍ *Insolvency practitioners who earn fees overseeing administrations and receiverships.*

re|cent /rɪsᵊnt/ **ADJ** happening only a short time ago ❍ *There was additional interest expense resulting from recent acquisitions.*

re|cent|ly /rɪsᵊntli/ **ADV** only a short time ago ❍ *The bank recently opened a branch in Miami.*

re|cep|tion /rɪsɛpʃən/

1 NOUN is a formal party that is given to welcome someone, or to celebrate a special event ❍ *a wedding reception*

2 NONCOUNT NOUN Reception in a hotel or a business is the place that you go to when you arrive. ❍ *She was waiting at reception.*

re|cep|tion|ist /rɪsɛpʃənɪst/ **NOUN** a person in a hotel or a business whose job is to answer the telephone and deal with visitors

re|ces|sion /rɪsɛʃən/ **NOUN** a period when the economy of a country is not performing well [ECONOMICS] ❍ *The oil price increases sent Europe into recession.*

COLLOCATIONS

a *deep* recession
to *sink into* a recession
a *severe* recession
to *come out of* a recession
a *global* recession
to *emerge from* a recession
recession-*proof*
recession-*hit*

R

reci|pe /rɛsɪpi/ **NOUN** a list of food and a set of instructions telling you how to cook something ❍ *Do you have a recipe for chocolate cake?*

reck|less /rɛklɪs/ **ADJ** not caring about the risks of something ❍ *The company took reckless gambles with other people's money.*

rec|og|nise /rɛkəgnaɪz/ [BRIT] → **recognize**

rec|og|ni|tion /rɛkəgnɪʃən/ **NONCOUNT NOUN Recognition** is the ability to know who a person is or what something is. ❍ *There was no sign of recognition on her face.*

rec|og|nize /rɛkəgnaɪz/ (**recognizes, recognizing, recognized**) **VERB** If you **recognize** someone or something, you know who or what they are. ❍ *She recognized him immediately.*

rec|ol|lec|tion /rɛkəlɛkʃən/ **NOUN** a memory ❍ *Pat has few recollections of the trip.*

rec|om|mend /rɛkəmɛnd/ **VERB** If someone **recommends** a person or thing to you, they suggest that you would find them good or useful. ❍ *The committee recommended disciplinary action.* ❍ *I'll recommend you for the job.*

rec|om|men|da|tion /rɛkəmɛndeɪʃən/ **NOUN** when someone suggests that you would find something good or useful ❍ *People who acted on his recommendations lost most of their money.*

rec|ord

Pronounce the noun /rɛkərd/. Pronounce the verb /rɪkɔrd/.

1 NOUN information that is stored about something ❍ *Keep a record of all the payments.*

2 VERB If you **record** information or an event, you write it down or photograph it. ❍ *Her letters record the details of her life in China.*

3 VERB If you **record** sounds or pictures, you store them using electronic equipment so that they can be heard or seen again. ❍ *The phone calls were recorded.*

4 NOUN the best result ever in a particular activity ❍ *Sales increased 15%, to 334.56 billion yen, setting a record for any six-month period.*

re|cord|er /rɪkɔrdər/ **NOUN** a wooden or plastic musical instrument that you play by blowing down it and covering holes with your fingers

re|cord|ing /rɪkɔrdɪŋ/

1 NOUN sounds or pictures that have been recorded ❍ *There is a video recording of his police interview.*

2 NONCOUNT NOUN Recording is the process of storing moving pictures and sounds. ❍ *the recording industry*

re|cov|er /rɪkʌvər/ **VERB** When the economy or a currency **recovers**, it begins to improve after having been weak. ❍ *The spokesperson told businessmen that the economy would recover in the second half of the year.*

re|cov|ery /rɪkʌvəri/ (**recoveries**) **NOUN** If a sick person makes a **recovery**, he or she becomes well again. ❍ *Natalie is making an excellent recovery.*

rec|rea|tion /rɛkrieɪʃən/ **NONCOUNT NOUN** **Recreation** is things that you do in your spare time to relax. ❍ *Saturday afternoon is for recreation.*

re|cruit /rɪkrut/ **VERB** If you **recruit** people for an organization, you ask them to join it. [HR] ❍ *We need to recruit and train more skilled workers.* ● **re|cruit|ment** **NONCOUNT NOUN** ❍ *There has been a drop in the recruitment of soldiers.*

re|cruit|ment con|sult|ant (**recruitment consultants**) **NOUN** a person or service that helps professional people to find work [HR] ❍ *You should look out for appointment ads and also send your résumé to leading recruitment consultants.*

re|cruit|ment poli|cy (**recruitment policies**) **NOUN** the set of attitudes and actions that an organization uses when selecting new staff [HR] ❍ *The council has set up an inquiry into its recruitment policy.*

rec|tan|gle /rɛktæŋgᵊl/ **NOUN** a shape with four straight sides and 90 degree corners ● **rec|tan|gu|lar** /rɛktæŋgyələr/ **ADJ** ❍ *The room contains a rectangular table.*

re|cur /rɪkɜr/ (**recurs, recurring, recurred**) **VERB** Something that **recurs** happens more than once. ❍ *a recurring dream*

re|cy|cle /risaɪkᵊl/ (**recycles, recycling, recycled**) **VERB** If you **recycle** things such as paper or bottles, you put them through a process so that they can be used again. [BANKING]

red /rɛd/ (**redder, reddest**)

1 ADJ having the color of blood or of a tomato ❍ *a bunch of red roses*

2 NOUN **Red** is also a noun. ❍ *She was dressed in red.*

3 ADJ **Red** hair is between red and brown in color.

4 If you are **in the red**, you are in debit or owing money. [BANKING] ❍ *Last year, the team ended up $2 million in the red on $30 million in revenue.*

re|deem /rɪdim/ **VERB** If you **redeem** a debt or money that you have promised to someone, you pay money that you owe or that you promised to pay. [FORMAL] ❍ *The amount required to redeem the mortgage was $358,587.*

re|deploy /ridɪplɔɪ/ **VERB** If resources or workers **are redeployed**, they are used for a different purpose or task. ❍ *Some of the workers there will be redeployed to other sites.* ❍ *It would give us an opportunity to redeploy our resources.*

red ink **NONCOUNT NOUN** **Red ink** is a state of financial loss. [ECONOMICS, INFORMAL] ❍ *After years of red ink, the corporation will soon report a net profit for its second quarter.*

red tape **NONCOUNT NOUN** You refer to official rules and procedures as **red tape** when they seem unnecessary and cause delay. [ADMINISTRATION] ❍ *The little money that was available was tied up in bureaucratic red tape.*

re|duce /rɪdus/ (**reduces, reducing, reduced**) **VERB** If you **reduce** something, you make it smaller. ❍ *They took steps to reduce the risk of takeover.*

re|duc|tion /rɪdʌkʃən/ **NOUN** When there is a **reduction in** something, it is made smaller. ❍ *a reduction in prices*

r

re|dun|dan|cy /rɪdʌndənsi/ [HR, BRIT] → **layoff 1**

re|dun|dan|cy pay|ment [HR, FINANCE, BRIT] → **severance pay**

re|dun|dant /rɪdʌndənt/ **ADJ** If you are made **redundant**, your employer tells you to leave because your job is no longer necessary or because your employer cannot afford to keep paying you. [HR, BRIT] ❍ *My husband was made redundant late last year.* ❍ *a redundant miner*

re-evaluate /riɪvælyueɪt/ (**re-evaluates, re-evaluating, re-evaluated**) **VERB** If you

re-evaluate a plan or an idea, you consider it again in order to decide how good or bad it is. ❍ *We are currently re-evaluating our strategy to increase the profile of this campaign.*

Ref. /rɛf/ also **ref. Ref.** is written in front of a code at the top of business letters and documents. **Ref.** is an abbreviation for **reference**. ❍ *Our Ref.: JAH/JW.*

re|fer /rɪfɜr/ (**refers, referring, referred**)
1 VERB If you **refer to** a subject, you mention it. ❍ *He referred to his trip to Canada.*
2 VERB If a word **refers to** a particular thing, it describes it. ❍ *The word "man" refers to an adult male.*
3 VERB If you **refer to** something for information, you look there in order to find something out. ❍ *He referred briefly to his notebook.*

ref|eree /rɛfəri/ [HR, BRIT] → **reference 3**

ref|er|ence /rɛfərəns, rɛfrəns/
1 NOUN a number or a name that tells you where you can obtain the information you want ❍ *Make a note of the reference number shown on the form.*
2 NOUN a letter written by someone who knows you, describing your character and your abilities [HR] ❍ *My boss gave me a good reference.*
3 NOUN a person who gives you a reference, for example when you are applying for a job [HR]

R

re|fi|nanc|ing /rifənænsɪŋ, rifaɪnæn-/ **NONCOUNT NOUN Refinancing** is the act or process of paying a debt by borrowing money from another lender. [BANKING] ❍ *The proceeds will be used for general corporate purposes, which may include refinancing existing debt.*

re|fine /rɪfaɪn/ (**refines, refining, refined**)
1 VERB When a substance **is refined**, it is made pure by having other substances removed from it. ❍ *Oil is refined to remove impurities.*
2 VERB If a method or a system **is refined**, it is improved by having small changes made to it. ❍ *Medical techniques are constantly being refined.*

re|fin|ery /rɪfaɪnəri/ (**refineries**) **NOUN** a factory where a substance such as oil or sugar is purified [PRODUCTION] ❍ *an oil refinery*

re|flate /rifleɪt/ (**reflates, reflating, reflated**) **VERB** If a government tries to **reflate** its country's economy, it increases the amount of money that is available in order to encourage more economic activity. [ECONOMICS] ❍ *The administration may try to reflate the economy next year.* ● **re|fla|tion** /rifleɪʃən/ **NONCOUNT NOUN** ❍ *They're talking about reflation and price controls.*

re|flect /rɪflɛkt/
1 VERB If something **reflects** an opinion or a situation, it shows what it is. ❍ *The report reflects the views of both students and teachers.*
2 VERB When light or heat **reflects** off a surface, it is sent back from the surface. ❍ *The sun reflected off the snow-covered mountains.*
3 VERB When something **is reflected** in a mirror or in water, you can see its image there. ❍ *His face was reflected in the mirror.*

re|flec|tion /rɪflɛkʃən/
1 NOUN an image that you can see in a mirror or in glass or water ❍ *Meg stared at her reflection in the mirror.*
2 NOUN If something is a **reflection of** a person's opinion or of a situation, it shows what that opinion or situation is like. ❍ *Its ability to attract staff is a reflection of the agency's reputation.*

re|form /rɪfɔrm/
1 NOUN a change to a law, an organization, or a system, that is intended to improve it ❍ *tax reforms* ❍ *We will introduce a program of economic reform.*
2 VERB If someone **reforms** a law, an organization, or a system, they change it to try to improve it. ❍ *He has plans to reform the country's economy.*

re|fresh /rɪfrɛʃ/ (**refreshes, refreshing, refreshed**) **VERB** If something **refreshes** you when you are hot, tired, or thirsty, it makes you feel better. ❍ *The water refreshed them.* ● **re|freshed ADJ** ❍ *He awoke feeling completely refreshed.*

re|frig|era|tor /rɪfrɪdʒəreɪtər/ **NOUN** a large electric container that is used for keeping food cool

ref|uge /rɛfyudʒ/
1 NONCOUNT NOUN If you take **refuge** somewhere, you go there to try to protect yourself. ❍ *They took refuge in a shelter.*
2 NOUN a place where you go for safety and protection ❍ *a refuge for homeless people*

refu|gee /rɛfyudʒi/ **NOUN** someone who has been forced to leave their country, because it is too dangerous ❍ *a refugee camp*

re|fund

> Pronounce the noun /rifʌnd/. Pronounce the verb /rɪfʌnd/.

1 NOUN an amount of money that is returned to you, for example because you have returned goods to a store ❍ *He asked for a refund.*
2 VERB If someone **refunds** your money, they return what you have paid them. ❍ *We will refund your delivery costs if the items arrive later than 12 noon.*

re|fus|al /rɪfyuzᵊl/ **NOUN** when someone says that they will not do something, allow someting, or accept something ❍ *The workers have repeated their refusal to take part in the program.*

re|fuse /rɪfyuz/ (**refuses, refusing, refused**)
1 VERB If you **refuse to** do something, you say that you will not do it. ❍ *He refused to comment.*
2 VERB If someone **refuses** you something, they say that you cannot have it. ❍ *The United States has refused him a visa.*
3 VERB If you **refuse** something that is offered to you, you do not accept it. ❍ *The patient has the right to refuse treatment.*

re|gard /rɪgard/
1 VERB If you **regard** someone or something **as** being a particular thing, you believe that they are that thing. ❍ *He was regarded as the most successful president of modern times.*
2 NONCOUNT NOUN Regard is respect and admiration. ❍ *I have a very high regard for him.*

re|gard|ing /rɪgardɪŋ/ **PREP** used to say what subject is being talked or written about ❍ *He refused to give any information regarding the man's financial situation.*

re|gard|less /rɪgardlɪs/ If something happens **regardless of** something else, the first thing is not affected at all by the second thing. ❍ *The organization helps anyone regardless of their age.*

re|gime /rəʒim, reɪ-/ **NOUN** a government that many people do not approve of ❍ *the collapse of the old regime*

re|gion /ridʒᵊn/ **NOUN** an area of a country or of the world ❍ *the coastal region of South Carolina* ● **re|gion|al ADJ** ❍ *Hawaiian regional cooking*

reg|is|ter /rɛdʒɪstər/
1 NOUN an official list of people or things ❍ *the register of births, deaths, and marriages*
2 VERB If you **register** to do something, you put your name on an official list, in order to be able to do it. ❍ *Thousands of people registered to vote.* ● **regi|stra|tion** /rɛdʒɪstreɪʃən/ **NONCOUNT NOUN** ❍ *The website is free, but it asks for registration from users.*
3 VERB When something **registers on** a scale, it shows a particular value. ❍ *The earthquake registered 5.7 on the Richter scale.*

reg|is|tered trade|mark (**registered trademarks**) **NOUN** a trademark that is legally protected [LEGAL] ❍ *All other names are trademarks and/or registered trademarks of their respective owners.* → also **trademark**

reg|is|trant /rɛdʒɪstrənt/ **NOUN** a person who registers a trademark or patent

re|gret /rɪgrɛt/ (**regrets, regretting, regretted**)
1 VERB If you **regret** something that you did, you feel sorry that you did it. ❍ *I regret my decision to leave my job.*
2 NOUN Regret is a feeling of being sorry that you did something. ❍ *He had no regrets about leaving.*

regu|lar /rɛgyələr/
1 ADJ Regular events have equal amounts of time between them. ❍ *Get regular exercise.*
2 ADJ Regular events happen often. ❍ *I get regular feedback from my supervisor.*
● **regu|lar|ly ADV** ❍ *He writes regularly for the magazine.*

3 ADJ **Regular** customers or visitors often go a store or a place. ❍ *She was a regular visitor to the museum.*
4 ADJ normal or ordinary ❍ *Fred is just a regular guy.*
5 ADJ If something has a **regular** shape, both halves are the same and it has straight or smooth edges. ❍ *He has regular features.*
6 ADJ A **regular** noun or verb follows the usual rules of grammar. Compare with **irregular**. ❍ *The past tense of English regular verbs ends in -ed.*

regu|late /rɛgyəleɪt/ (**regulates, regulating, regulated**) VERB To **regulate** an activity or organization means to control it with rules. ❍ *The government introduced new laws to regulate the food industry.*

regu|la|tion /rɛgyəleɪʃən/
1 NOUN a rule for controlling the way something is done or the way people behave [LEGAL] ❍ *Here are the new safety regulations.*
2 NONCOUNT NOUN **Regulation** is the controlling of an activity or process, usually by means of rules. [LEGAL] ❍ *AGT opposed the application and claimed immunity from federal regulation.*

regu|la|tor /rɛgyəleɪtər/ NOUN a person or organization appointed by a government to regulate an area of activity [LEGAL] ❍ *An independent regulator will be appointed to ensure fair competition.* ● **regu|la|tory** /rɛgyələtɔri/ ADJ ❍ *the United States' financial regulatory system*

R

re|hears|al /rɪhɜrsᵊl/ NOUN a practice of a performance ❍ *Tomorrow we start rehearsals for the concert.*

re|hearse /rɪhɜrs/ (**rehearses, rehearsing, rehearsed**) VERB When people **rehearse** a performance, they practice it. ❍ *The actors are rehearsing a play.*

reign /reɪn/
1 VERB When a king or queen **reigns**, he or she rules a country. ❍ *Henry II reigned in England from 1154 to 1189.*
2 NOUN **Reign** is also a noun. ❍ *Queen Victoria's reign*

re|inforce /riɪnfɔrs/ (**reinforces, reinforcing, reinforced**)
1 VERB If something **reinforces** a feeling or a belief, it makes it stronger. ❍ *This reinforced our determination to deal with the problem.*
2 VERB If you **reinforce** an object, you make it stronger. ❍ *They had to reinforce the floor with concrete.*

re|ject /rɪdʒɛkt/ VERB If you **reject** something or someone, you do not accept them. ❍ *The president rejected the offer.* ❍ *He was rejected by several universities.* ● **re|jec|tion** NOUN ❍ *Be prepared for lots of rejections before you get a job.*

re|ju|venate /rɪdʒuvəneɪt/ (**rejuvenates, rejuvenating, rejuvenated**) VERB If you **rejuvenate** an organization or system, you make it more lively and more efficient, for example by introducing new ideas. ❍ *The government pushed through plans to rejuvenate the inner cities.*

re|late /rɪleɪt/ (**relates, relating, related**)
1 VERB If something **relates to** a particular subject, it is about that subject. ❍ *The document provides general information relating to share capital, directors, and auditors.*
2 VERB The way that two things **relate** is the connection that exists between them. ❍ *There is new thinking about how the two sciences relate.*

re|lat|ed /rɪleɪtɪd/
1 ADJ connected in some way ❍ *They are restricted to owning businesses that are closely related to banking.*
2 ADJ belonging to the same family ❍ *The boys have the same last name but they are not related.*

re|la|tion /rɪleɪʃən/
1 PL NOUN **Relations** between people are their feelings and behavior toward each other. ❍ *The country has good relations with Israel.*
2 NOUN a connection between two things ❍ *They will not reveal the relation between their charges and their costs.*
3 NOUN a member of your family ❍ *We make frequent visits to friends and relations.*

re|la|tion|ship /rɪleɪʃənʃɪp/
1 NOUN The **relationship** between two people or groups is the way they feel and behave toward each other. ❍ *a friendly relationship*
2 NOUN a close friendship between two

people, especially involving romantic feelings ❍ *She could not accept that their relationship was over.*

3 NOUN the way in which two things are connected ❍ *There is a relationship between the strength of the economy and interest rates.*

re|la|tion|ship mar|ket|ing NONCOUNT NOUN **Relationship marketing** is a strategy in which a company tries to build long-term relationships with its customers by ensuring that they are always satisfied. [MARKETING AND SALES] ❍ *All this relationship marketing is aimed at getting the company's message across to the 30-something career person earning $70,000-plus.*

rela|tive /rɛlətɪv/ **NOUN** a member of your family ❍ *Ask a relative to look after the children.*

re|lax /rɪlæks/ (**relaxes, relaxing, relaxed**) **VERB** If you **relax**, you feel more calm and less worried. ❍ *You should relax and stop worrying.* • **re|laxa|tion** /rilækseɪʃən/ **NONCOUNT NOUN** ❍ *Try learning some relaxation techniques.* • **re|laxed ADJ** ❍ *The atmosphere at lunch was relaxed.*

re|lax|ing /rɪlæksɪŋ/ **ADJ** causing you to relax ❍ *I find cooking very relaxing.*

re|lease /rɪlis/ (**releases, releasing, released**)

1 VERB If a person or an animal **is released**, they are allowed to go free. ❍ *He was released from prison the next day.*

2 VERB If you **release** someone or something, you stop holding them. [FORMAL] ❍ *He released her hand.*

3 VERB When a company **releases** a new CD, DVD, or movie, it becomes available so that people can buy it or see it. ❍ *He is releasing a CD of love songs.*

rel|evant /rɛləvᵊnt/ **ADJ** useful and interesting for someone or connnected to a subject that is being talked about ❍ *Include any other information that is relevant to your application.*

re|li|able /rɪlaɪəbᵊl/ **ADJ** able to be trusted ❍ *She was efficient and reliable.* ❍ *The ratings are not always a reliable guide for consumers.* • **re|li|ably ADV** ❍ *We are reliably informed that he is here.* • **re|li|a|bi|li|ty NONCOUNT NOUN** ❍ *We have serious doubts about the reliability of this information.*

re|lief /rɪlif/

1 NONCOUNT NOUN **Relief** is the feeling of being happy because something unpleasant has stopped or not happened. ❍ *I breathed a sigh of relief.*

2 NONCOUNT NOUN **Relief** is money, food, or clothing that is provided for people who suddenly need it. ❍ *Relief agencies are providing food and shelter.*

re|lieve /rɪliv/ (**relieves, relieving, relieved**)

1 VERB If something **relieves** an unpleasant feeling or situation, it makes it better. ❍ *Drugs can relieve the pain.*

2 VERB If someone or something **relieves** you **of** an unpleasant feeling or task, they take it from you. ❍ *Receiving the check relieved me of a lot of worry.*

3 VERB If you **relieve** someone, you take their place and continue to do their work. ❍ *At seven o'clock another nurse arrived to relieve her.*

re|lieved /rɪlivd/ **ADJ** feeling happy because something unpleasant has stopped or not happened ❍ *Officials are relieved that the rise in prices has slowed.*

re|li|gion /rɪlɪdʒᵊn/

1 NONCOUNT NOUN **Religion** is belief in a god or gods. ❍ *organized religion*

2 NOUN a particular system of religious beliefs ❍ *the Christian religion*

re|li|gious /rɪlɪdʒəs/

1 ADJ connected with religion ❍ *Religious groups are able to meet quite freely.*

2 ADJ having a strong belief in a god or gods

re|lo|cate /riloʊkeɪt/ (**relocates, relocating, relocated**) **VERB** If people or businesses **relocate** or if someone **relocates** them, they move to a different place. ❍ *If the company was to relocate, most employees would move.* ❍ *The real estate investment trust relocated its principal office to downtown Austin, Texas.* • **re|lo|ca|tion** /riloʊkeɪʃən/ **NONCOUNT NOUN** ❍ *The company says the cost of relocation will be negligible.*

r

COLLOCATIONS
relocation *costs*
relocation *expenses*
a relocation *package*
forced *relocation*
proposed *relocation*

re|lo|ca|tion ex|penses or **relocation costs** PL NOUN **Relocation expenses** are a sum of money that a company pays to someone who moves to a new area in order to work for the company. [FINANCE] ○ *Relocation expenses were paid to encourage senior staff to move to the region.*

re|luc|tant /rɪlʌktənt/ ADJ If you are **reluctant to** do something, you are unwilling to do it. ○ *Bankers were reluctant to finance the project.* ● **re|luc|tant|ly** ADV ○ *The company reluctantly agreed to the takeover.*
● **re|luc|tance** NONCOUNT NOUN ○ *There is a reluctance to sell aggressively.*

rely /rɪlaɪ/ (**relies, relying, relied**)
1 VERB If you **rely on** someone or something, you need them in order to live or do something. ○ *They relied heavily on our advice.*
2 VERB If you can **rely on** someone, you can trust them. ○ *I know I can rely on you to deal with the problem.*

re|main /rɪmeɪn/
1 VERB To **remain** in a state or condition means to stay in that state or condition. ○ *The economy remains strong.* ○ *Banks remain eager to lend for large projects.*
2 VERB If you **remain** in a place, you stay there. ○ *Police asked people to remain in their homes.*
3 PL NOUN **The remains of** something are the parts of it that are left after most of it has been taken away or destroyed. ○ *They were cleaning up the remains of their picnic.*

re|main|der /rɪmeɪndər/ NOUN **The remainder of** something is the part that is still there after the first part has gone. ○ *He predicts record results for the remainder of the year.*

re|main|ing /rɪmeɪnɪŋ/ ADJ The **remaining** things or people are the things or people that are still there. ○ *The remaining shares were sold to outside investors.*

R

re|mark /rɪmɑrk/
1 VERB If you **remark** that something is true, you say that it is true. ○ *He remarked that it was very cold.*
2 NOUN something that you say ○ *She made some positive remarks about the company's finances.*

re|mark|able /rɪmɑrkəbᵊl/ ADJ very unusual or surprising in a good way ○ *They encouraged the growth of private businesses, with remarkable success.* ● **re|mark|ably** /rɪmɑrkəbli/ ADV ○ *The company was remarkably successful.*

rem|edy /rɛmədi/ (**remedies**) NOUN something that cures an illness or deals with a problem ○ *natural remedies for infections* ○ *The government's remedy involved tax increases.*

re|mem|ber /rɪmɛmbər/
1 VERB If you **remember** people or events from the past, you still have an idea of them in your mind. ○ *I remember the first time I met him.* ○ *The weather was terrible; do you remember?*
2 VERB If you **remember** something, you become aware of it again after forgetting it for a time. ○ *She remembered that she was going to the club that evening.*
3 VERB If you **remember to** do something, you do not forget to do it. ○ *Please remember to mail the letter.*

re|mind /rɪmaɪnd/
1 VERB If someone **reminds** you **of** something or **reminds** you **to** do something, they say something that makes you think about it or remember to do it. ○ *She reminded Tim of the last time they met.* ○ *Can you remind me to call Jim?*
2 VERB If someone or something **reminds** you **of** another person or thing, they are similar to them and they make you think about them. ○ *She reminds me of your sister.*

re|mind|er /rɪmaɪndər/ NOUN something that makes you think about a thing again ○ *The scar on her hand was a constant reminder of the accident.*

re|mit|tance /rɪmɪtᵊns/ NOUN a sum of money that you send to someone [FORMAL]

❍ *Please enclose your remittance, making checks payable to Valley Technology Services.*

re|mort|gage /rimɔrgɪdʒ/ (**remortgages, remortgaging, remortgaged**) VERB If you **remortgage** a property, you take out a new or different mortgage on it. [BANKING] ❍ *There are no legal fees if you are remortgaging your property.*

re|mote /rɪmoʊt/ ADJ far away from cities and places where most people live ❍ *remote areas*

re|mote con|trol (**remote controls**) NOUN a piece of equipment that you use to control a machine such as a television from a distance

re|mote|ly /rɪmoʊtli/ ADV used to emphasize the negative meaning of a sentence ❍ *He wasn't remotely interested in her.*

re|mov|al /rɪmuvᵊl/ NONCOUNT NOUN The **removal** of something is the act of removing it. ❍ *She had surgery for the removal of a tumor.*

re|move /rɪmuv/ (**removes, removing, removed**) VERB If you **remove** something, you take it away or take it off. [FORMAL] ❍ *Remove the cake from the oven when it is cooked.* ❍ *They are committed to removing barriers to trade.*

re|mu|nera|tion /rɪmyunəreɪʃən/ NONCOUNT NOUN **Remuneration** is the amount of money that a person is paid for the work that they do. [BUSINESS MANAGEMENT, FORMAL] ❍ *the continuing marked increases in the remuneration of the company's directors*

COLLOCATIONS

a *rate of* remuneration
a remuneration *package*
a remuneration *policy*

re|new /rɪnu/ VERB When you **renew** something, you get a new one to replace the old one, or you arrange for the old one to continue. ❍ *Larry's landlord refused to renew his lease.*

re|new|able /rɪnuəbᵊl/ ADJ **Renewable** resources are natural ones such as wind, water, and sunlight that are always available. ❍ *renewable energy sources*

ren|min|bi /rɛnmɪnbi/ or **renminbi yuan** [ECONOMICS] → **yuan**

rent /rɛnt/

1 VERB If you **rent** something, you pay its owner in order to be able to use it yourself. ❍ *She rents a house with three other women.*

2 VERB If you **rent** something **to** someone, or if you **rent** it **out**, you let them use it in exchange for money. ❍ *She rented rooms to university students.* ❍ *Last summer Brian rented out his house and went camping.*

3 NONCOUNT NOUN **Rent** is the amount of money that you pay to use something that belongs to someone else. ❍ *She worked hard to pay the rent on the apartment.*

re-order /riɔrdər/ VERB If you **re-order** goods, you order more of them from a supplier.

re-order lev|el (**re-order levels**) NOUN the point at which existing stock becomes so low that new stock needs to be ordered [PRODUCTION] ❍ *The re-order level will depend upon the rate of usage of the stock, how frequently new stock can be brought in and the lead time.*

rep /rɛp/

1 NOUN A **rep** is a person whose job is to sell a company's products or services, especially by traveling around and visiting other companies. **Rep** is short for "representative." [MARKETING AND SALES] ❍ *I'd been working as a sales rep for a photographic company.*

2 NOUN a person who acts as a representative for a group of people ❍ *Contact the health and safety rep at your union.*

re|pair /rɪpɛər/

1 VERB If you **repair** something that is damaged, you fix it. ❍ *Goldman has repaired the roof.*

2 NOUN something that you do to fix something that is damaged ❍ *Repairs were made to the roof.*

re|pay /rɪpeɪ/ (**repays, repaying, repaid**) VERB If you **repay** a debt, you pay back the money that you borrowed.

r

re|pay|ment /rɪpe̲ɪmənt/ **NONCOUNT NOUN** The **repayment of** money is the act or process of paying it back to the person you borrowed it from. ❍ *The bank will expect the repayment of the $114 million loan.* ❍ *He took a loan with small, frequent repayments.*

re|peat /rɪpi̲t/

1 VERB If you **repeat** something, you say it, write it, or do it again. ❍ *She repeated her request for more money.* ❍ *He repeated that he did not intend to resign.* ❍ *Such gains may not be repeated for a while.*

2 VERB If you **repeat** something that someone else has said or written, you say or write the same thing. ❍ *She had a habit of repeating everything I said to her.*

re|pe̲at bu̲si|ness NONCOUNT NOUN If a company gets **repeat business**, people who have already bought their goods and services buy them again. ❍ *Nearly 60% of our bookings come from repeat business and personal recommendation.*

rep|e̲at cu̲s|tom|er (repeat customers) NOUN someone who buys from a company having bought or used their goods or services before ❍ *Our quality craftsmanship has seen many repeat customers.*

re|peat|ed /rɪpi̲tɪd/ **ADJ** happening many times ❍ *He did not return the money, despite repeated reminders.* ● **re|peat|ed|ly ADV** ❍ *I asked him repeatedly to help me.*

R

rep|eti|tion /rɛ̲pɪtɪ̲ʃən/ **NOUN** If there is a **repetition of** something, it happens again. ❍ *They want to prevent a repetition of last year's violence.*

re|place /rɪple̲ɪs/ **(replaces, replacing, replaced)**

1 VERB If one person or thing **replaces** another, they do the job of the other person or thing. ❍ *During the war, many women replaced male workers.*

2 VERB If you **replace** something that is damaged or lost, you get a new one. ❍ *The shower broke so we have to replace it.*

3 VERB If you **replace** something, you put it back where it was before. ❍ *Replace the caps on the bottles.*

re|place|ment /rɪple̲ɪsmənt/ **NOUN** a person or thing that replaces another person or thing ❍ *It won't be easy to find a replacement for Grace.*

re|play /ri̲pleɪ/ **NOUN** when an action on television is broadcast again ❍ *We watched the replay of the game.*

re|ply /rɪpla̲ɪ/ **(replies, replying, replied)**

1 VERB When you **reply**, you say or write something as an answer to someone. ❍ *He never replied to my letters.*

2 NOUN something that you say or write when you answer someone ❍ *Give a specific example in your reply if you can.*

re|port /rɪpɔ̲rt/

1 VERB If you **report** that something has happened, you tell people about it. ❍ *I reported the crime to the police.*

2 NOUN an account of an event, a situation or an investigation ❍ *a newspaper report* ❍ *After an inspection, the inspectors must publish a report.* ❍ *She came back to give us a progress report on how the project is going.*

3 VERB If you **report to** a person or place, you go to that person or place and say that you are ready to start work. ❍ *He first reported to the Director of the hospital.* ❍ *None of the men had reported for duty.*

4 VERB If you say that one employee **reports to** another, you mean that the first employee is told what to do by the second one. [FORMAL] ❍ *He reported to a section chief, who reported to a division chief, and so on up the line.*

re|port|er /rɪpɔ̲rtər/ **NOUN** someone who writes newspaper articles or broadcasts the news ❍ *a TV reporter*

re|po|si|tion /ri̲pəzɪ̲ʃən/ **VERB** When a company **repositions** a product or brand, it tries to interest more people or different people in it by changing its image. ❍ *The agency's mission was to reposition the company to appeal to people planning vacations.*

re|posi|tory /rɪpɒ̲zɪtɔri/ **(repositories) NOUN** a place where something is kept safely [FORMAL] ❍ *So far, no country has succeeded in building a permanent geological repository for high-level nuclear waste.*

rep|re|sent /rɛprɪzɛnt/
1 VERB If someone **represents** you, they act for you or make decisions for you. ❍ *We vote for politicians to represent us.*
2 VERB If a sign **represents** something, it means that thing. ❍ *The red line on the map represents a wall.*

rep|re|sen|ta|tion /rɛprɪzɛnteɪʃən/ **NONCOUNT NOUN** If you have **representation** on a committee, someone on the committee supports you. ❍ *These people have no representation in Congress.*

rep|re|senta|tive /rɛprɪzɛntətɪv/ **NOUN** a person who acts or makes decisions for another person or group ❍ *The mediator talked to union and company representatives separately.*

re|pro|duce /riprədus/ (**reproduces, reproducing, reproduced**)
1 VERB If you **reproduce** something, you copy it. ❍ *The effect was hard to reproduce.*
2 VERB When people, animals, or plants **reproduce**, they produce babies, eggs, or seeds. ● **re|pro|duc|tion** /riprədʌkʃən/ **NONCOUNT NOUN** ❍ *human reproduction*

rep|tile /rɛptaɪl, -tɪl/ **NOUN** one of a group of animals that lay eggs and have cold blood

re|pub|lic /rɪpʌblɪk/ **NOUN** a country where the people choose their government and there is no king or queen ❍ *In 1918, Austria became a republic.*

repu|ta|tion /rɛpyəteɪʃən/ **NOUN** the opinion that people have about someone or something ❍ *They have a good reputation for managing other people's money.*

re|quest /rɪkwɛst/
1 VERB If you **request** something, you ask for it. [FORMAL] ❍ *To request more information, please check this box.*
2 NOUN If you **make** a **request**, you ask for something. ❍ *They agreed to his request for more money.*

re|quire /rɪkwaɪər/ (**requires, requiring, required**)
1 VERB If you **require** something, you need it. [FORMAL] ❍ *If you require more information, please write to this address.*
2 VERB If a law or a rule **requires** you **to** do something, you must do it. [FORMAL] ❍ *The rules require employers to provide safety training.*

re|quire|ment /rɪkwaɪərmənt/ **NOUN** something that you must have or must do ❍ *Our products meet all legal requirements.*

re|sale /riseɪl/ **NONCOUNT NOUN** The **resale** price of something that you own is the amount of money that you would get if you sold it. ❍ *a well-maintained used car with a good resale value*

re|sched|ule /riʃkɛdʒul, -dʒuəl/ (**reschedules, rescheduling, rescheduled**)
1 VERB If someone **reschedules** an event, they change the time at which it is supposed to happen. ❍ *Since I'll be away, I'd like to reschedule the meeting.*
2 VERB To **reschedule** a debt means to arrange for it to be paid back over a longer period of time. ❍ *companies that have gone bust or had to reschedule their debts*

res|cue /rɛskyu/ (**rescues, rescuing, rescued**)
1 VERB If you **rescue** someone, you save them from a dangerous situation. ❍ *They rescued 20 people from the roof of the building.*
2 NOUN an attempt to save someone from a dangerous situation ❍ *a rescue operation* ❍ *A neighbor came to her rescue.*

re|search /risɜrtʃ, rɪsɜrtʃ/ (**researches, researching, researched**)
1 NONCOUNT NOUN **Research** involves studying something and trying to discover facts about it. [R & D] ❍ *scientific research*
2 VERB If you **research** something, you try to discover facts about it. [R & D] ❍ *She spent two years researching the subject.*

re|search and de|vel|op|ment **NONCOUNT NOUN** **Research and development** is work that applies scientific research to the development of new products. [R & D] ❍ *The organization is encouraging companies to group together to finance research and development projects.*

re|searcher /risɜrtʃər, rɪsɜr-/ **NOUN** a person whose work involves studying

r

something in order to discover facts about it [R & D] ❍ *the country's leading researcher into breast cancer*

re|sem|blance /rɪzɛmbləns/ **NOUN** If there is a **resemblance** between two people or things, they are similar to each other. ❍ *There was a strong resemblance between the two girls.*

re|sem|ble /rɪzɛmbᵊl/ (**resembles, resembling, resembled**) **VERB** If one person or thing **resembles** another, they look similar to each other. ❍ *She resembles her mother.*

re|sent /rɪzɛnt/ **VERB** If you **resent** something, you feel angry about it because you think it is not fair. ❍ *Certain people resented my success.*

res|er|va|tion /rɛzərveɪʃən/ **NOUN** If you **make** a **reservation**, you ask a hotel or a restaurant to keep a room or a table for you. ❍ *Have you canceled our reservation?*

re|serve /rɪzɜrv/ (**reserves, reserving, reserved**)

1 NOUN a supply of something that is available for use when it is needed ❍ *The Gulf has 65 percent of the world's oil reserves.*

2 VERB If something **is reserved for** a particular person or purpose, it is kept for them. ❍ *A room was reserved for him.*

re|serve price (**reserve prices**) **NOUN** the lowest price which is acceptable to the owner of property being auctioned or sold ❍ *Eventually the auctioneer has to withdraw many items, when bids fail to reach the reserve price.*

R

res|er|voir /rɛzərvwɑr/ **NOUN** a lake that is used for storing water

re|side /rɪzaɪd/ (**resides, residing, resided**) **VERB** If someone **resides** somewhere, they live there. [FORMAL] ❍ *Margaret resides with her mother.*

resi|dence /rɛzɪdəns/ **NOUN** the place where someone lives [FORMAL] ❍ *the president's official residence*

resi|dent /rɛzɪdənt/ **NOUN** The **residents** of a house or an area are the people who live there. ❍ *Local residents complained that the road was dangerous.*

resi|den|tial /rɛzɪdɛnʃᵊl/ **ADJ** A **residential** area contains houses rather than offices or stores.

re|sign /rɪzaɪn/ **VERB** If you **resign** from a job, you tell your employer that you are leaving it. [HR] ❍ *He was forced to resign.*

res|ig|na|tion /rɛzɪgneɪʃən/ **NOUN** Your **resignation** is when you tell your employer that you are leaving your job. ❍ *Barbara offered her resignation this morning.*

re|sist /rɪzɪst/

1 VERB If you **resist** a force or a change, you fight against it. ❍ *There are people in the organization who resist change.*

2 VERB If you **resist** a feeling that you want to do something, you stop yourself from doing it. ❍ *Resist the temptation to help your child too much.*

re|sist|ance /rɪzɪstəns/ **NONCOUNT NOUN** **Resistance** to a force or a change is when you fight back against it. ❍ *The soldiers are facing strong resistance.*

re|skill /riskɪl/ [HR, BRIT] → **retrain**

reso|lu|tion /rɛzəluʃən/

1 NOUN the final solving of a problem or difficulty [FORMAL] ❍ *The President said that he didn't expect a quick resolution of the hostage crisis.*

2 NOUN a formal decision taken at a meeting by means of a vote ❍ *The purchase follows a board resolution authorizing the purchase of as many as 300,000 shares.*

re|solve /rɪzɒlv/ (**resolves, resolving, resolved**)

1 VERB If you **resolve** a problem, you find a solution to it. [FORMAL] ❍ *We must resolve these problems.*

2 VERB If you **resolve to** do something, you make a decision to do it. [FORMAL] ❍ *When the group meets again on December 17th, it will resolve to cut its production further.*

re|sort /rɪzɔrt/

1 NOUN a place where people stay for a vacation ❍ *a ski resort*

2 If you do something **as a last resort**, you do it because you can find no other solution. ❍ *As a last resort, we hired an expert.*

re|source /rɪ̱sɔrs/ **NOUN** The **resources** of a country, an organization, or a person are the money and other things that they have and can use. ❍ *We must protect the country's natural resources.*

re|spect /rɪspɛ̱kt/

1 VERB If you **respect** someone, you admire them. ❍ *I want people to respect me for my work.*

2 NONCOUNT NOUN If you have **respect for** someone, you admire them and are polite to them. ❍ *I have great respect for Tom.*

re|spect|able /rɪspɛ̱ktəbᵊl/ **ADJ** If someone or something is **respectable**, people have a good opinion of them, and think they are morally correct. ❍ *He comes from a respectable family.*

re|spect|ful /rɪspɛ̱ktfəl/ **ADJ** showing respect ❍ *He is always respectful to his clients.*

re|spond /rɪspɒ̱nd/ **VERB** When you **respond** to something that someone does or says, you react to it by doing or saying something. ❍ *They responded to the president's request for financial help.*

re|spond|ent /rɪspɒ̱ndənt/ **NOUN** a person who replies to something such as a survey ❍ *Sixty percent of the respondents said they disapproved of the president's performance.*

re|sponse /rɪspɒ̱ns/ **NOUN** something that someone does or says as a reaction to something ❍ *There was no response to his remarks.*

re|spon|sibil|ity /rɪspɒ̱nsɪbɪ̱lɪti/ (**responsibilities**)

1 NONCOUNT NOUN If you have **responsibility** for something or someone, it is your job or duty to deal with them or look after them. ❍ *Each manager had responsibility for ten people.*

2 NONCOUNT NOUN If you accept **responsibility for** something, you agree that it was your fault. ❍ *Someone had to give orders and take responsibility for mistakes.*

3 PL NOUN Your **responsibilities** are the duties that you have because of your job or position. ❍ *programs to help employees balance work and family responsibilities*

re|spon|sible /rɪspɒ̱nsɪbᵊl/

1 ADJ If you are **responsible for** something or someone, it is your job or duty to deal with them or look after them. ❍ *I met the people who are responsible for sales and advertising.*

2 ADJ If someone or something is **responsible for** a particular event or situation, they caused it. ❍ *He still felt responsible for the failure of the business.*

rest /rɛ̱st/

1 VERB If you **rest**, you spend some time relaxing. ❍ *The doctor advised him to rest.*

2 NOUN If you have a **rest**, you spend some time relaxing. ❍ *You're exhausted—go home and get some rest.*

3 VERB If you **rest** something somewhere, you put it on another thing. ❍ *He rested his arms on the table.*

4 NOUN The rest is the parts of something that are left. ❍ *It was an experience I will remember for the rest of my life.* ❍ *I ate two cakes and saved the rest.*

res|tau|rant /rɛ̱stərənt, -tərɑnt, -trɑnt/ **NOUN** a place where you can buy and eat a meal ❍ *an Italian restaurant*

rest|less /rɛ̱stlɪs/ **ADJ** not relaxed and wanting to move around ❍ *My father seemed very restless and excited.*

re|store /rɪstɔ̱r/ (**restores, restoring, restored**) **VERB** To **restore** someone or something **to** a former condition means to put them in that condition again. ❍ *They are experts in restoring old buildings.*

re|strict /rɪstrɪ̱kt/

1 VERB If you **restrict** something, you prevent it from becoming too big. ❍ *The school is restricting the number of students it accepts this year.*

2 VERB To **restrict** the actions of someone or something means to prevent them from acting freely. ❍ *They want to remove legislation that restricts competition.*

re|stric|tion /rɪstrɪ̱kʃən/ **NOUN** something that prevents someone from acting freely ❍ *There are a number of restrictions on employee benefits.*

re|stric|tive prac|tice /rɪstrɪ̱ktɪv præ̱ktɪs/ (**restrictive practices**)

1 NOUN a trading agreement that is not in the public interest [LEGAL, BRIT] ❍ *The Government*

r

should tackle restrictive practices in order to enhance a competitive economy.

2 NOUN a practice of a union or other group that limits the freedom of other workers or employees [LEGAL] ❍ *The reforms range from reducing import protection to ending restrictive practices in the ports.*

rest|room /rɛstrum/ also **rest room** **NOUN** a public room with toilets for people to use

re|sult /rɪzʌlt/

1 NOUN something that happens or exists because something else has happened ❍ *People developed the disease as a direct result of their work.*

2 VERB If something **results in** a situation or event, it causes that situation or event. ❍ *Their acquisitions will eventually result in higher dividends.*

3 VERB If something **results from** a particular event or action, it is caused by that event or action. ❍ *Further business opportunities resulted from the sale.*

4 PL NOUN A company's **results** are the set of figures that show whether it has achieved a profit or a loss. ❍ *CGU is due to report its annual results to shareholders this week.*

5 PL NOUN **Results** are the score that you get at the end of a competition or a test. ❍ *election results*

re|sume /rɪzum/ (**resumes, resuming, resumed**) **VERB** If you **resume** an activity, you begin it again. [FORMAL] ❍ *After the war he resumed his job at Wellesley College.* ❍ *The talks will resume on Tuesday.*

ré|su|mé /rɛzʊmeɪ/ also **resume** **NOUN** a short description of your education and the jobs you have had [HR]

re|tail /riteɪl/ **NONCOUNT NOUN** **Retail** is the activity of selling goods directly to the public. Compare with **wholesale**. [MARKETING AND SALES, ECONOMICS] ❍ *My sister works in retail.* ❍ *Retail sales grew just 3.8 percent last year.*

re|tail|er /riteɪlər/ **NOUN** a person or business that sells goods directly to the public [MARKETING AND SALES] ❍ *a furniture retailer*

re|tail|ing /riteɪlɪŋ/ **NONCOUNT NOUN** **Retailing** is the activity of selling products direct to the public, usually in small quantities. Compare with **wholesaling**. [MARKETING AND SALES] ❍ *She spent fourteen years in retailing.*

re|tail out|let (**retail outlets**) **NOUN** a store or other place that sells goods direct to the public [MARKETING AND SALES] ❍ *the largest retail outlet in the city*

re|tail park [MARKETING AND SALES, BRIT] → **shopping mall**

re|tail price in|dex [ECONOMICS, BRIT] → **consumer price index**

re|tain /rɪteɪn/ **VERB** To **retain** something means to continue to have it. [FORMAL] ❍ *He was looking for a way to retain control of his company.*

re|tained earn|ings **PL NOUN** **Retained earnings** are the profit that a company does not pay out in dividends, but keeps in order to reinvest in itself. [FINANCE] ❍ *Dividends and retained earnings come from after-tax income.*

retd **retd** is an abbreviation for **retired**. [HR]

re|think /riθɪŋk/ (**rethinks, rethinking, rethought**) **VERB** If you **rethink** something, you change your opinions or plans. ❍ *Many banks are rethinking their strategy.*

re|tire /rɪtaɪər/ (**retires, retiring, retired**) **VERB** When people **retire**, they stop working. [HR] ❍ *He planned to retire at age 65.*

re|tired /rɪtaɪərd/ **ADJ** having stopped work [HR] ❍ *I am a retired teacher.*

re|tire|ment /rɪtaɪərmənt/ **NONCOUNT NOUN** A person's **retirement** is the period in their life after they stop working. [HR] ❍ *What do you plan to do during retirement?*

re|tire|ment fund (**retirement funds**) **NOUN** a fund of money set aside to pay for a pension

re|train /ritreɪn/ If you **retrain**, or if someone **retrains** you, you learn new skills, so that you can do a different job or do your old job in a different way. [HR] ❍ *The Government also might help with retraining any workers who* *lose their jobs.* • **re|train|ing** NONCOUNT NOUN ❍ *The unemployed must be offered retraining instead of long term unemployment.*

re|treat /rɪtri̲t/ VERB If you **retreat**, you move away from something or someone. ❍ *I retreated from the room.* ❍ *The soldiers were forced to retreat.*

re|trench /rɪtrɛ̲ntʃ/ (**retrenches, retrenching, retrenched**) VERB If a person or organization **retrenches**, they spend less money. [FORMAL] ❍ *Shortly afterwards, cuts in defense spending forced the aerospace industry to retrench.*

re|turn /rɪtɜ̲rn/

1 VERB When you **return to** a place, you go back there. ❍ *He will return to Moscow tomorrow.*

2 NOUN Your **return** is when you arrive back at a place. ❍ *Kenny explained the reason for his return to Dallas.*

3 VERB If you **return** something, you give it back or put it back. ❍ *They will return the money later.*

4 NOUN **Return** is also a noun. ❍ *They demanded the return of the stolen money.*

5 NOUN the profit that you get from an investment ❍ *Profits have picked up but the return on capital remains tiny.* ❍ *Higher returns and higher risk usually go hand in hand.*

re|union /riyu̲niən/ NOUN a meeting between people who have not seen each other for a long time ❍ *a family reunion*

re|unite /riyuna̲ɪt/ (**reunites, reuniting, reunited**) VERB If people **are reunited**, they see each other again after a long time. ❍ *She was finally reunited with her family.*

re|veal /rɪvi̲l/

1 VERB To **reveal** something means to tell people something that they do not know already. ❍ *She has refused to reveal any more details.*

2 VERB If you **reveal** something, you show it by removing the thing that was covering it. ❍ *She smiled, revealing small white teeth.*

re|venge /rɪvɛ̲ndʒ/ NONCOUNT NOUN **Revenge** involves hurting or punishing someone who has hurt or harmed you. ❍ *He wanted revenge for the way they treated his mother.*

rev|enue /rɛ̲vənyu/ NONCOUNT NOUN **Revenue** is money that a company, an organization, or a government receives. [FINANCE] ❍ *The company gets 98% of its revenue from Internet advertising.*

re̲v|enue stream (**revenue streams**) NOUN the money that a company receives from selling a particular product or service [FINANCE] ❍ *The events business, she said, was crucial to the group in that it provides a constant revenue stream.*

re|verse /rɪvɜ̲rs/ (**reverses, reversing, reversed**)

1 VERB To **reverse** a decision or a situation means to change it to its opposite. ❍ *They will not reverse the decision to increase prices.*

2 VERB If you **reverse** the order of a group of things, you arrange them in the opposite order. ❍ *You need to reverse the "i" and the "e."*

3 NONCOUNT NOUN If your car is **in reverse**, you can drive it backward.

re|ve̲rse en|gi|ne̲e̲r|ing NONCOUNT NOUN **Reverse engineering** is a process in which a product or system is analyzed in order to see how it works, so that a similar version of the product or system can be produced more cheaply. [BUSINESS MANAGEMENT] ❍ *Reverse engineering strives to economize on development costs and is quite legal.*

re|ve̲rse ta̲ke|over (**reverse takeovers**) NOUN the purchase of a larger company by a smaller company [ECONOMICS] ❍ *A British supermarket group announced a reverse takeover of an ailing food distributor.*

re|view /rɪvyu̲/

1 NOUN the process of considering something to see if it needs changes [BUSINESS MANAGEMENT] ❍ *The president ordered a review of the situation.*

2 VERB If you **review** something, you consider it to see if it needs changes. [BUSINESS MANAGEMENT] ❍ *The new plan will be reviewed by the city council.*

re|vise /rɪva̲ɪz/ (**revises, revising, revised**) VERB If you **revise** something, you change it in

r

order to make it better or more correct. ❍ *We are revising the rules.*

re|vive /rɪvaɪv/ (**revives, reviving, revived**) VERB If you **revive** someone who has fainted, you make them become conscious again. ❍ *A doctor revived the patient.*

re|volt|ing /rɪvoʊltɪŋ/ ADJ extremely unpleasant ❍ *The smell was revolting.*

revo|lu|tion /rɛvəluʃən/
1 NOUN an attempt by a group of people to change their country's government by force ❍ *The period since the revolution has been peaceful.*
2 NOUN a very big change ❍ *a revolution in ship design*

revo|lu|tion|ary /rɛvəluʃənɛri/
1 ADJ trying to cause a revolution ❍ *a revolutionary movement*
2 ADJ causing very big changes ❍ *It is a revolutionary new product.*

re|volve /rɪvɒlv/ (**revolves, revolving, revolved**)
1 VERB If your life **revolves around** a particular thing, that is the most important thing to you. ❍ *Her life has revolved around sports.*
2 VERB When something **revolves**, it turns in a circle. ❍ *The Earth revolves around the sun.*

re|volv|er /rɪvɒlvər/ NOUN a type of small gun

re|ward /rɪwɔrd/
1 NOUN something that you are given for doing something good ❍ *The school gives rewards for good behavior.*
2 VERB If you **are rewarded** for doing something good, you get something for it. ❍ *She was rewarded for her years of hard work.*

re|ward|ing /rɪwɔrdɪŋ/ ADJ giving you satisfaction ❍ *I have a job that is very rewarding.*

re|work /riwɜrk/ VERB If you **rework** an idea or a piece of writing, you make changes in order to improve it or bring it up to date. ❍ *Keep reworking your résumé until you can't improve it anymore.*

re|write /riraɪt/ (**rewrites, rewriting, rewrote, rewritten**) VERB If someone **rewrites** something, they write it in a different way in order to improve it. ❍ *She decided to rewrite her article.*

rhyme /raɪm/ (**rhymes, rhyming, rhymed**)
1 VERB If words **rhyme**, they have a very similar sound. ❍ *June rhymes with moon.*
2 NOUN a poem that has words that rhyme at the ends of its lines

rhythm /rɪðəm/ NOUN a regular pattern of sounds or movements ❍ *Listen to the rhythms of jazz.*

rial /rial, -ɔl/ NOUN the unit of money of Iran and Oman [ECONOMICS]

rib /rɪb/ NOUN one of the 12 pairs of curved bones that surround your chest ❍ *Her heart was beating hard against her ribs.*

rib|bon /rɪbən/ NOUN a long, narrow piece of cloth that you use to tie things together, or as a decoration ❍ *She tied her hair with a ribbon.*

rice /raɪs/ NONCOUNT NOUN **Rice** is white or brown grains from a plant that grows in wet areas. ❍ *The meal consisted of chicken, rice, and vegetables.*

rich /rɪtʃ/
1 ADJ having a lot of money ❍ *He was a very rich man.*
2 PL NOUN **The rich** are rich people. ❍ *Only the rich can afford to live there.*

rid /rɪd/ (**rids, ridding, rid**) When you **get rid of** something or someone, you remove them completely or make them leave. ❍ *Our industry didn't want to get rid of purchase orders.*

rid|den /rɪdᵊn/ **Ridden** is a form of the verb **ride**.

rid|dle /rɪdᵊl/ NOUN a strange, difficult question has a clever answer

ride /raɪd/ (**rides, riding, rode, ridden**)
1 VERB When you **ride** a bicycle or a horse, you sit on it, and control it as it moves. ❍ *Riding a bike is great exercise.* ❍ *We passed three men riding on motorcycles.*
2 VERB When you **ride in** a vehicle, you travel in it. ❍ *He rode in the bus to the hotel.*
3 NOUN A **ride** is a trip on a horse or a bicycle, or in a vehicle. ❍ *She took some friends for a ride in the car.*

R

rid|er /raɪdər/ **NOUN** someone who rides a horse, a bicycle, or a motorcycle ❍ *She is a very good rider.*

ridge /rɪdʒ/ **NOUN** a long, narrow part of something that is higher than the rest ❍ *a mountain ridge*

ri|dicu|lous /rɪdɪkyələs/ **ADJ** very silly ❍ *a ridiculous idea*

ri|fle /raɪfᵊl/ **NOUN** a long gun

right
❶ CORRECT
❷ DIRECTION
❸ LAW
❹ EXACTLY OR IMMEDIATELY

❶ **right** /raɪt/
1 ADJ correct ❍ *Ron was right about the result of the election.* ❍ *"C" is the right answer.*
2 ADV Right is also an adverb. ❍ *If I'm going to do something, I want to do it right.*
3 ADJ The **right** action is the best one. ❍ *You made the right choice in taking that job.*
4 NONCOUNT NOUN You use **right** to talk about actions that are morally good. ❍ *He knew right from wrong.*
5 ADJ Right is also an adjective. ❍ *It's not right to leave the children here alone.*

❷ **right** /raɪt/
1 NOUN the side that is toward the east when you look north ❍ *On the right is a vegetable garden.*
2 ADV Right is also an adverb. ❍ *Turn right into the street.*
3 ADJ on the right side of your body

❸ **right** /raɪt/
1 NOUN Your **rights** are the things that you are allowed to do morally, or by law. ❍ *Make sure you know your rights.*
2 NOUN Rights are the privilege of a company's stockholders to apply to buy new issues of the its shares on special terms. ❍ *The board adopted a stock-purchase rights plan intended to deter any hostile takeover attempts.*

❹ **right** /raɪt/
1 ADV used to say that something happens exactly in a particular place or at a particular time ❍ *A car appeared right in front of him.* ❍ *Liz arrived right on time.*
2 I'll be right back means that you will get back to a place in a very short time. [SPOKEN]

right-handed ADJ Someone who is **right-handed** uses their right hand for activities such as writing and sports.

rights is|sue (**rights issues**) **NOUN** an offer of shares at a reduced price to people who already have shares in that company [BANKING, ECONOMICS] ❍ *The acquisition will be financed mainly by a rights issue raising £354 million.*

rig|id /rɪdʒɪd/
1 ADJ Laws or systems that are **rigid** cannot be changed. ❍ *Staff were given narrow jobs in a rigid hierarchy.*
2 ADJ A **rigid** substance or object does not bend. ❍ *Use rigid plastic containers.*

ring /rɪŋ/ (**rings, ringing, rang, rung**)
1 VERB When a bell **rings**, it makes its sound. ❍ *The school bell rang.* ❍ *They rang the bell but nobody came to the door.*
2 NOUN Ring is also a noun. ❍ *There was a ring at the door.*
3 NOUN a small circle of metal that you wear on your finger ❍ *a gold wedding ring*
4 NOUN something in the shape of a circle ❍ *a ring of stones*
▸ **ring up**
1 If a store worker **rings up** a sale on a cash register, he or she presses the keys in order to record the amount that is being spent. ❍ *She was ringing up her sale on an ancient cash register.*
2 If a company **rings up** an amount of money, it makes that amount of money in sales or profits. ❍ *The advertising agency rang up 1.4 billion dollars in yearly sales.*

ring-fence (**ring-fences, ring-fencing, ring-fenced**) **VERB** To **ring-fence** money means to decide that it can only be used for a particular purpose. ❍ *There should be ring-fenced funding for local crime prevention initiatives.*

ring|tone /rɪŋtoʊn/ **NOUN** the sound made by your cellphone when someone calls you

rinse /rɪns/ (**rinses, rinsing, rinsed**) VERB When you **rinse** something, you wash it in clean water. ○ *Make sure you rinse all the shampoo out of your hair.*

riot /raɪət/

1 NOUN violent behavior by a group of people in a public place ○ *Twelve people were injured during a riot at the prison.*

2 VERB If people **riot**, they behave violently in a public place. ○ *They rioted against the government.*

rip /rɪp/ (**rips, ripping, ripped**) VERB When you **rip** something, you tear it. ○ *I ripped my pants when I fell.*

▶ **rip up** If you **rip** something **up**, you tear it into small pieces. ○ *He ripped up the letter and threw it in the fire.*

ripe /raɪp/ (**riper, ripest**) ADJ ready to eat ○ *ripe fruit*

rip|ple /rɪpᵊl/ (**ripples, rippling, rippled**) NOUN a small wave on the surface of water

rise /raɪz/ (**rises, rising, rose, risen**)

1 VERB If something **rises**, it moves upward. ○ *We could see black smoke rising from the chimney.* ○ *He rose slowly from the chair.*

2 VERB If an amount or a number **rises**, it increases. ○ *His income rose by $5,000.*

3 NOUN **Rise** is also a noun. ○ *There's been a rise in the price of oil.*

COLLOCATIONS

to rise *sharply*
to rise *rapidly*
to rise *dramatically*

R

risk /rɪsk/

1 NOUN a possibility that something bad may happen ○ *There is a small risk of damage.* ○ *He also thought the risks far outweighed the advantages.*

2 NOUN If something involves **risk**, or is a **risk**, it may not be safe. ○ *Seeking a higher rate of return automatically involves accepting a higher degree of risk.* ○ *Firms take great risks, spending money on projects they have no certainty will ever pan out.*

3 VERB If you **risk** something bad, you do something knowing that it might happen. ○ *Your product had better become a global brand or you risk losing out altogether.*

4 VERB If you **risk** something important, you behave in a way that might result in it being lost. ○ *She risked her own life to help him.*

risk capi|tal [ECONOMICS, mainly BRIT] → **venture capital**

risky /rɪski/ (**riskier, riskiest**) ADJ dangerous or likely to fail ○ *Not all investments are equally risky.*

ritu|al /rɪtʃuəl/ NOUN a series of actions that people always perform in the same way ○ *Every religion has rituals such as baptism.*

ri|val /raɪvᵊl/ NOUN a person, business, or organization that you are competing against in the same area or for the same things [MARKETING AND SALES] ○ *He was accused of spying on his business rivals.*

riv|er /rɪvər/ NOUN a long line of water that flows into an ocean

road /roʊd/ NOUN a long piece of hard ground that vehicles travel on ○ *There was very little traffic on the roads.*

roam /roʊm/ VERB If you **roam** an area, you move around it without planning where exactly you are going. ○ *Children roamed the streets in groups.*

roar /rɔr/

1 VERB If a person, an animal, or a thing **roars**, they make a very loud noise. ○ *The engine roared, and the vehicle moved forward.*

2 NOUN **Roar** is also a noun. ○ *Who could forget the first time they heard the roar of a lion?*

roast /roʊst/

1 VERB When you **roast** meat or other food, you cook it in an oven or over a fire. ○ *He roasted the chicken.*

2 ADJ **Roast** meat or other food is cooked in an oven or over a fire. ○ *We had roast beef.*

rob /rɒb/ (**robs, robbing, robbed**) VERB If a person **is robbed**, someone steals something from them. ○ *She was robbed of her watch.*

• **rob|ber** NOUN ○ *a bank robber*

rob|bery /rɒbəri/ (**robberies**) NOUN when a person steals something ○ *There have been several robberies in the area.*

ro|bot /roʊbət, -bɒt/ **NOUN** a machine that can move and perform tasks automatically [TECHNOLOGY] ❍ *We have robots that we could send to the moon.*

ro|bot|ics /roʊbɒtɪks/ **NONCOUNT NOUN** **Robotics** is the science of designing and building robots. [TECHNOLOGY] ❍ *You could use robotics to reduce labor costs.*

ROCE /ɑr oʊ si i/ **ROCE** is an abbreviation for "Return on Capital Employed." [FINANCE] ❍ *A company's ROCE target is often accompanied by a growth target for either profit or sales.*

rock /rɒk/
1 NONCOUNT NOUN **Rock** is the hard substance forms part of the Earth's surface. ❍ *The ground was solid rock.*
2 NOUN a large piece of rock ❍ *She sat on a rock and looked out across the ocean.*
3 VERB When something **rocks**, it moves slowly backward and forward. ❍ *His body rocked gently in the chair.* ❍ *She rocked the baby in her arms.*
4 NONCOUNT NOUN **Rock** is loud music with a strong beat that you play on electric instruments. ❍ *a rock concert*

rock and roll also **rock'n'roll** **NONCOUNT NOUN** **Rock and roll** is a type of music that was popular in the 1950s. ❍ *Elvis Presley was known as the King of Rock and Roll.*

rock|et /rɒkɪt/
1 NOUN a vehicle that people use to travel into space
2 NOUN A **rocket** is the same as a **missile**. ❍ *a rocket attack*

rocky /rɒki/ (**rockier, rockiest**) **ADJ** having a lot of rocks ❍ *The paths are very rocky.*

rod /rɒd/ **NOUN** a long, thin metal or wooden bar ❍ *The roof was supported with steel rods.*

rode /roʊd/ **Rode** is a form of the verb **ride**.

rogue trad|er /roʊg treɪdər/ (**rogue traders**) **NOUN** an employee of a financial institution who carries out business without the knowledge or approval of his or her company [ECONOMICS] ❍ *the unauthorized dealings by a rogue trader which brought down the bank*

ROI /ɑr oʊ aɪ/ **ROI** is an abbreviation for "return on investment." [FINANCE] ❍ *ROI analyses should be part of any assessment of human resources programs.*

role /roʊl/
1 NOUN the purpose of someone or something in a situation or what they do in that situation ❍ *The proposal would reduce the role of the Securities and Exchange Commission.*
2 NOUN the character that an actor plays in a movie or a play ❍ *Who plays the role of the doctor?*

roll /roʊl/
1 VERB When something **rolls**, it moves along a surface, turning over many times. ❍ *The pencil rolled off the desk.* ❍ *I rolled a ball to the baby.*
2 NOUN a long piece of something such as cloth or paper that had been rolled into the shape of a tube ❍ *There are twelve rolls of cloth here.*
3 NOUN a small, round piece of bread ❍ *He spread some butter on a roll.*
4 NOUN an amount of money, especially a wad of paper money ❍ *She reached into her jacket pocket and pulled out a roll of dollars.*
▸ **roll out** When a company **rolls out** a new product, it gradually increases the number of outlets in which it is sold. ❍ *Kellogg said it would roll out the product this fall with its largest cereal advertising and promotion budget ever.*
▸ **roll up** If you **roll up** something, you form it into the shape of a tube. ❍ *Steve rolled up the paper bag.*

Ro|man Catho|lic /roʊmən kæθəlɪk/ (**Roman Catholics**)
1 ADJ The **Roman Catholic** Church is the branch of the Christian Church based at the Vatican in Rome. ❍ *I am a Roman Catholic priest.*
2 NOUN A **Roman Catholic** is a member of this Church. ❍ *Maria was a Roman Catholic.*

ro|mance /roʊmæns, roʊmæns/
1 NOUN a relationship between two people who love each other ❍ *After a short romance they got married.*
2 NOUN a book or a movie about a romantic relationship ❍ *Claire writes romances.*

ro|man|tic /roʊmæntɪk/ ADJ relating to loving relationships ❍ *It is a lovely romantic movie.*

roof /ruf/ (**roofs** or **rooves**)

Pronounce the plural /rufs/ or /ruvz/.

NOUN the top surface of a building or a vehicle ❍ *The house has a red roof.*

room /rum/

1 NOUN a separate area inside a building that has its own walls ❍ *A minute later he left the room.*

2 NONCOUNT NOUN If there is **room** for something, there is enough space for it. ❍ *There is room for 80 guests.*

room|mate /rummeɪt/ NOUN the person you share a room or an apartment with ❍ *We were roommates in college.*

root /rut/ NOUN the part of a plant that grows under the ground ❍ *the roots of an apple tree*

rope /roʊp/ NOUN very thick string ❍ *He tied the rope around his waist.*

rose /roʊz/

1 **Rose** is a form of the verb **rise**.

2 NOUN a flower with a pleasant smell and sharp points (= thorns) on its stems

rot /rɒt/ (**rots, rotting, rotted**) VERB When a substance **rots**, it decays, and sometimes smells bad. ❍ *The grain will start to rot after the rain.*

R

Ro|ta|ry Club /roʊtəri klʌb/ NOUN an association of professional and businessmen that works for the benefit of the community ❍ *In San Antonio, Texas, the Rotary Club pays $50 a month to children who are at risk of dropping out of high school for financial reasons.*

ro|tate /roʊteɪt/ (**rotates, rotating, rotated**) VERB When something **rotates**, it turns in a circle. ❍ *The Earth rotates every 24 hours.* ● **ro|ta|tion** /roʊteɪʃən/ NOUN ❍ *We learned about the daily rotation of the Earth.*

rot|ten /rɒtᵊn/

1 ADJ decayed and often smelling bad ❍ *rotten eggs*

2 ADJ very unpleasant or bad [INFORMAL] ❍ *I think it's a rotten idea.*

rou|ble /rubᵊl/ [ECONOMICS] → **ruble**

rough /rʌf/

1 ADJ not smooth or even ❍ *His hands were rough.*

2 ADJ using too much force ❍ *Football's a rough game.* ● **rough|ly** ADV ❍ *They roughly pushed past him.*

3 ADJ not exact ❍ *He gave us a rough estimate of the amount of capital needed.* ● **rough|ly** ADV ❍ *Their stake in the company is valued at roughly $130 million.*

round /raʊnd/

1 ADJ shaped like a circle or ball ❍ *She has a round face.*

2 NOUN one game or a part of a competition ❍ *The team went through to the fifth round of the competition.* ❍ *a round of golf*

round|ed /raʊndɪd/ ADJ curved in shape ❍ *We came to a low, rounded hill.*

Round Ta|ble NOUN an organization of young business and professional men who meet for social and business activities and charitable work ❍ *He's chairman of the Chamber of Commerce and the Round Table.*

round trip (**round trips**) NOUN a journey to a place and back again ❍ *The train makes the 2,400-mile round trip every week.*

route /rut, raʊt/ NOUN a way from one place to another ❍ *Which is the most direct route to the center of the town?*

rou|tine /rutin/

1 NOUN the usual series of things that you do at a particular time ❍ *He followed the same routine he'd used on the previous Wednesday.*

2 ADJ done as a normal part of a job or process [BUSINESS MANAGEMENT] ❍ *The operator has to be able to carry out routine maintenance of the machine.*

rou|tine check (**routine checks**) NOUN an examination of a product, place, or piece of equipment as part of a regular checking procedure [BUSINESS MANAGEMENT] ❍ *The museum said that it came across the asbestos during routine checks on its premises.*

row /roʊ/

1 NOUN a line of things or people ❍ *a row of houses*

2 VERB When you **row**, you make a boat move through the water by using oars (= long pieces of wood with flat ends). ❍ *We rowed across the lake.*

roy|al /rɔɪəl/ **ADJ** relating to a king or queen ❍ *We have an invitation to a royal garden party.*

Roy|al Mint NOUN the place where all British coins are made [ECONOMICS] ❍ *The Royal Mint introduced a smaller 10-pence coin.*

roy|al|ty /rɔɪəlti/ (**royalties**)

1 NONCOUNT NOUN Royalty means members of royal families. ❍ *He met royalty and government leaders from around the world.*

2 PL NOUN Royalties are payments made to authors and musicians when their work is sold or performed. ❍ *I lived on about £3,000 a year from the royalties on my book.*

rub /rʌb/ (**rubs, rubbing, rubbed**)

1 VERB If you **rub** something, you move a cloth or your fingers backward and forward over it. ❍ *He rubbed his stiff legs.*

2 VERB If you **rub** a substance **into** a surface, you spread it over the surface using your hand. ❍ *He rubbed oil into my back.*

rub|ber /rʌbər/ **NONCOUNT NOUN Rubber** is a strong substance used for making tires, boots, and other products. ❍ *The agreement sets a target price for rubber.*

rub|bish /rʌbɪʃ/ [BRIT] → **trash**

ru|ble /rubᵊl/ also **rouble NOUN** the unit of money of Russia and some other countries that used to be part of the Soviet Union [ECONOMICS]

ruby /rubi/ (**rubies**) **NOUN** a dark red stone that is used in jewelry ❍ *a ruby ring*

rude /rud/ (**ruder, rudest**) **ADJ** not polite ❍ *He's so rude to her friends.* ❍ *Fred keeps telling rude jokes.* ● **rude|ly ADV** ❍ *Some hotel guests treat our employees rudely.* ● **rude|ness NONCOUNT NOUN** ❍ *Mom was annoyed at Cathy's rudeness.*

rug /rʌg/ **NOUN** a piece of thick cloth that you put on a floor ❍ *There was a beautiful red rug on the floor.*

rug|by /rʌgbi/ **NONCOUNT NOUN Rugby** or **rugby football** is a game that is played by two teams who try to get a ball past a line at the end of the field.

ruin /ruɪn/

1 VERB To **ruin** something means to destroy it or spoil it completely. ❍ *The incident ruined his company's reputation.*

2 PL NOUN The ruins of a building are the parts of it that remain after something destroys the rest. ❍ *Police found two bodies in the ruins of the house.*

rule /rul/ (**rules, ruling, ruled**)

1 NOUN an instruction that tells you what you must do or must not do ❍ *They pushed through tough rules on hedge funds.*

2 VERB The person or group that **rules** a country controls it. ❍ *King Hussein ruled for 46 years.*

3 If you **rule out** something, you decide that it is not possible or not suitable.

rul|er /rulər/

1 NOUN the person who rules a country ❍ *He was the ruler of France at that time.*

2 NOUN a long, flat object that you use for measuring things

rum|ble /rʌmbᵊl/ (**rumbles, rumbling, rumbled**)

1 NOUN a low, continuous noise ❍ *We could hear the distant rumble of traffic.*

2 VERB If something **rumbles**, it makes a low, continuous noise. ❍ *Her stomach was rumbling because she did not eat breakfast.*

ru|mor /rumər/ **NOUN** something that someone says, that may not be true ❍ *There's a rumor that you're leaving.*

ru|mour /rumər/ [BRIT] → **rumor**

run /rʌn/ (**runs, running, ran, run**)

1 VERB When you **run**, you move very quickly on your legs. ❍ *It's very dangerous to run across the road.*

2 NOUN Run is also a noun. ❍ *After a six-mile run, Jackie went home for breakfast.* ● **run|ning NONCOUNT NOUN** ❍ *He goes running every morning.*

3 VERB If you **run** a business or an activity, you are in charge of it. ❍ *She runs a restaurant in San Francisco.*

4 VERB When a machine **is running**, it is switched on and is working. ❍ *Sam waited in* *the car, with the engine running.*

5 VERB If a liquid **runs** in a particular direction, it flows in that direction. ❍ *Tears were running down her cheeks.*

6 used to talk about what will happen over a long period of time ❍ *Spending more on education now will save money in the long run.*

▸ **run away** If you **run away**, you leave a place suddenly or secretly.

▸ **run into**

1 If you **run into** someone, you meet them unexpectedly. ❍ *He ran into William in the supermarket.*

2 If a vehicle **runs into** something, it hits it. ❍ *The driver was going too fast and ran into a tree.*

▸ **run off** If someone **runs off**, they go away from a place when they should stay there. ❍ *Our dog is always running off.*

▸ **run out** If you **run out of** something, you have no more of it left. ❍ *We ran out of milk this morning.*

▸ **run over** If a vehicle **runs** someone **over**, it hits them and they fall to the ground. ❍ *A police car ran her over.*

rung /rʌŋ/ **Rung** is a form of the verb **ring**.

run|ner /rʌnər/ **NOUN** a person who runs, especially in a competition ❍ *He is the oldest runner in the race.*

runner-up (**runners-up**) **NOUN** the person who comes second in a competition ❍ *The runner-up will receive $500.*

R

run|ning cost (**running costs**)

1 NOUN the amount of money that you spend on the gas, electricity, or other type of energy that a device uses [FINANCE] ❍ *The biggest problem with this printer is the running cost.*

2 PL NOUN Running costs are the same as **overheads**. [FINANCE, BRIT]

run|way /rʌnweɪ/ **NOUN** a long road that an aircraft uses at the beginning or end of a flight

ru|pee /rupi/ **NOUN** a unit of money that is used in India, Pakistan, and some other countries [ECONOMICS] ❍ *He earns 20 rupees a day.*

ru|piah /rupiə/ **NOUN** the unit of money of Indonesia [ECONOMICS]

ru|ral /rʊərəl/ **ADJ** not near cities or large towns ❍ *rural areas*

rush /rʌʃ/ (**rushes, rushing, rushed**)

1 VERB If you **rush** somewhere, you go there quickly. ❍ *Emma rushed into the room.*

2 VERB If people **rush to** do something, they do it quickly. ❍ *Foreign banks rushed to buy as many dollars as they could.*

3 If you do something **in a rush**, you do it quickly. ❍ *The men left in a rush.*

rush hour (**rush hours**) **NOUN** a period of the day when many people are traveling to or from their job ❍ *the evening rush hour*

rust /rʌst/

1 NONCOUNT NOUN Rust is a red-brown substance that forms on iron or steel. ❍ *The old car was red with rust.*

2 VERB When a metal object **rusts**, rust starts to appear on it. ❍ *Iron rusts.*

ruth|less /ruθlɪs/ **ADJ** determined to do something and not caring if you harm other people ❍ *They undertook a ruthless cost-cutting exercise.*

Ss

SA /ɛs eɪ/
1 In Spanish-speaking countries **SA** is used after the names of public companies. **SA** is short for "Sociedad Anónima." [ADMINISTRATION] ❍ *Soria Natural SA*
2 In French-speaking countries **SA** is used after the names of public companies. **SA** is short for "Société Anonyme." [ADMINISTRATION] ❍ *Rhone-Poulenc SA*

sab|bati|cal /səbætɪkᵊl/ **NOUN** a period of time during which someone can leave their ordinary work and travel or study [HR] ❍ *He took a year's sabbatical from teaching to write a book.*

sack /sæk/
1 NOUN a large bag made of thick paper or rough material ❍ *a sack of potatoes*
2 VERB If you **sack** someone, you tell them that they can no longer work for you. [HR, mainly BRIT, INFORMAL] ❍ *Earlier today the Prime Minister sacked 18 government officials for corruption.*
3 If someone is **given the sack**, or if they **get the sack**, they are sacked. [HR, INFORMAL, mainly BRIT] ❍ *People who make mistakes can be given the sack the same day.* ❍ *52 managers got the sack in one year.*

sack|able /sækəbᵊl/
1 ADJ A **sackable** offense is serious enough to cause someone to be sacked. [HR, mainly BRIT] ❍ *Several companies have also warned employees that accessing Facebook during office hours is a sackable offense.*
2 ADJ A **sackable** employee is able to be sacked. [HR, mainly BRIT] ❍ *Board directors are sackable only for criminal or scandalous behavior.*

sack|ing /sækɪŋ/ **NOUN** a situation in which an employer tells a worker to leave their job [HR, mainly BRIT, INFORMAL] ❍ *Until his sacking last month, he remained deputy head of finance in the party's ruling Politburo.*

sa|cred /seɪkrɪd/ **ADJ** having a special religious meaning ❍ *The eagle is sacred to Native Americans.*

sac|ri|fice /sækrɪfaɪs/ (**sacrifices, sacrificing, sacrificed**)
1 VERB If you **sacrifice** something that is valuable or important, you give it up in order to get something else. ❍ *Many of the early companies sacrificed quality for speed.*
2 NOUN Sacrifice is also a noun. ❍ *The family made many sacrifices so that they could send the children to a good school.*
3 VERB To **sacrifice** an animal or a person means to kill them in a special religious ceremony. ❍ *The priest sacrificed a chicken.*

sad /sæd/ (**sadder, saddest**)
1 ADJ unhappy ❍ *I'm sad that Jason's leaving.*
● **sad|ness NONCOUNT NOUN** ❍ *I left with a mixture of sadness and joy.*
2 ADJ making you feel unhappy ❍ *I have some sad news for you.*

sad|dle /sædᵊl/
1 NOUN a leather seat that you put on the back of a horse
2 NOUN a seat on a bicycle or a motorcycle

sad|ly /sædli/
1 ADV in a sad way ❍ *"My girlfriend is moving away," he said sadly.*
2 ADV used to show that you are sorry about something ❍ *Sadly, he came to a very tragic end*

sa|fa|ri /səfɑri/ **NOUN** a trip to look at or hunt wild animals ❍ *She went on a seven-day African safari.*

safe /seɪf/ (**safer, safest**)
1 ADJ not dangerous ❍ *We must try to make our roads safer.*
2 ADJ not in danger ❍ *Where's Sophie? Is she safe?*
● **safe|ly ADV** ❍ *"Drive safely," he said, waving goodbye.*

3 NOUN a strong metal box with a lock, where you keep valuable things ❍ *Who has the key to the safe?*

safe|ty /seɪfti/

1 NONCOUNT NOUN Safety is the state of not being in danger. ❍ *We need to improve safety on our building sites.*

2 ADJ intended to make something less dangerous ❍ *There are child safety locks on all the gates.*

said /sɛd/ **Said** is a form of the verb **say**.

sail /seɪl/

1 NOUN a large piece of cloth on a boat, that catches the wind and moves the boat along

2 VERB A boat **sails** when it moves over water. ❍ *The ferry sails between Seattle and Bremerton.*

3 VERB If you **sail** a boat, you use its sails to move it across water. ❍ *I'd like to buy a big boat and sail around the world.*

sail|ing /seɪlɪŋ/ **NONCOUNT NOUN Sailing** is the activity or sport of sailing boats. ❍ *There was swimming and sailing on the lake.*

sail|or /seɪlər/ **NOUN** someone who sails ships or boats as a job or for sport

saint /seɪnt/ **NOUN** a dead person who has been officially honoured by the Christian church for living in a very holy way ❍ *Every church here was named after a saint.*

sake /seɪk/

1 If you do something **for** someone's **sake**, you do it to help them or please them. ❍ *They stayed together for the sake of the children.*

2 If you do something **for** something's **sake**, you do it for that purpose or reason. ❍ *If you're investing for safety's sake, stick with open-end mutual funds!* ❍ *For the sake of peace, I am willing to forgive them.*

sal|able /seɪləbᵊl/ [MARKETING AND SALES] → **saleable**

sal|ad /sæləd/ **NOUN** a mixture of cold foods, especially vegetables ❍ *She ordered pasta and a green salad.*

sala|ry /sæləri/ (**salaries**) **NOUN** the money that you earn from your employer [ADMINISTRATION, ECONOMICS] ❍ *The lawyer was paid a huge salary.*

S

sale /seɪl/

1 NOUN the act of selling something ❍ *He made a lot of money from the sale of the business.*

2 NOUN an amount sold ❍ *The two groups had combined sales of $71.6 million.*

3 NOUN a time when a store sells things at less than their normal price ❍ *Did you know the book store was having a sale?*

4 NOUN the rate of selling or being sold ❍ *a slow sale of synthetic fabrics*

5 If something is **for sale**, it is available for people to buy. ❍ *The house had a "For Sale" sign in the yard.*

6 Products that are **on sale** are available for less than their normal price. ❍ *She bought the coat on sale at a department store.*

sale|able /seɪləbᵊl/ also **salable ADJ** easy to sell to people [MARKETING AND SALES] ❍ *The Salvation Army stores depend on regular supplies of saleable items.*

sale or re|turn or **sale and return NONCOUNT NOUN Sale or return** is an arrangement by which a retailer pays only for goods sold, returning those that are unsold to the wholesaler or manufacturer. [MARKETING AND SALES, mainly BRIT] ❍ *No goods are supplied on a sale or return basis.*

sales /seɪlz/ **PL NOUN** The **sales** of a product are the quantity of it that is sold. [MARKETING AND SALES] ❍ *The newspaper has sales of 1.72 million.* ❍ *the huge Christmas sales of computer games* ❍ *retail sales figures*

sales ex|ecu|tive (**sales executives**) **NOUN** a senior member of a sales team [MARKETING AND SALES, ADMINISTRATION] ❍ *an advertising sales executive*

sales fig|ures PL NOUN Sales figures are the numbers of a product or products that have been sold and the money resulting from these sales. [FINANCE] ❍ *He pointed to disappointing sales figures in Poland.*

sales force (**sales forces**) also **salesforce NOUN** all the people that work for a company selling its products [MARKETING AND SALES] ❍ *His sales force is signing up schools at the rate of 25 a day.*

sales fore|cast (**sales forecasts**) **NOUN** a prediction of future sales of a product

[BUSINESS MANAGEMENT] ❍ *Despite the revised sales forecast, the company's shares were up 1.87%.*

sales|man /seɪlzmən/ (**salesmen**) NOUN a man whose job is to sell things [MARKETING AND SALES, ADMINISTRATION] ❍ *He's an insurance salesman.*

sales mana|ger (**sales managers**) NOUN a senior member of a sales team [MARKETING AND SALES, ADMINISTRATION] ❍ *The sales effort is handled through a sales manager with three full-time salesmen.*

sales|man|ship /seɪlzmənʃɪp/ NONCOUNT NOUN **Salesmanship** is the skill of persuading people to buy things. [MARKETING AND SALES] ❍ *I was captured by his brilliant salesmanship.*

sales ob|jec|tives PL NOUN A company's **sales objectives** are the number of sales that it is trying to achieve. [MARKETING AND SALES] ❍ *Sales objectives have surpassed expectations.*

sales|person /seɪlzpɜrsᵊn/ (**salespeople** or **salespersons**) NOUN a person whose job is to sell things [MARKETING AND SALES, ADMINISTRATION] ❍ *They will usually send a salesperson out to measure your bathroom.*

sales pitch (**sales pitches**) or **sales talk** NOUN the speech that a salesperson uses in order to persuade someone to buy something from them [MARKETING AND SALES] ❍ *His sales pitch was smooth and convincing.*

sales pro|mo|tion (**sales promotions**) NOUN any activity that is intended to create consumer demand for a product or service [MARKETING AND SALES] ❍ *The business center did not have any formal budget in 2010 for advertising or sales promotion.* ❍ *Sales for the year to date are down 6.5% from a year earlier in spite of expensive sales promotions.*

sales rep (**sales reps**) NOUN a member of a company's sales team [MARKETING AND SALES, ADMINISTRATION] ❍ *I'd been working as a sales rep for a photographic company.*

sales rev|enue NONCOUNT NOUN **Sales revenue** is money that a company or organization receives from sales of its goods and services. [FINANCE] ❍ *They estimate that sales revenue will rise to $134 million.*

sales tax (**sales taxes**) NOUN the percentage of money that you pay to the local or state government when you buy things [FINANCE, ECONOMICS] ❍ *The state's unpopular sales tax on snacks has ended.*

sales team (**sales teams**) NOUN all the people that work for a company selling its products [MARKETING AND SALES, ADMINISTRATION] ❍ *He is responsible for leading and controlling a highly motivated sales team.*

sales terr|it|ory (**sales territories**) NOUN the area or areas where a salesperson tries to sell the company's products [MARKETING AND SALES] ❍ *He was responsible for a six-state sales territory.*

sales|wom|an /seɪlzwʊmən/ (**saleswomen**) NOUN a woman whose job is to sell things [MARKETING AND SALES, ADMINISTRATION] ❍ *an insurance saleswoman*

salm|on /sæmən/ (**salmon**)
1 NOUN a large fish with silver skin
2 NONCOUNT NOUN **Salmon** is the pink flesh of this fish that you can eat. ❍ *He gave them a plate of salmon.*

sa|lon /səlɑn/ NOUN a place where you go to have your hair cut, or to have beauty treatments ❍ *The club has a beauty salon.*

salt /sɔlt/ NONCOUNT NOUN **Salt** is a white substance that you use to improve the flavor of food. ❍ *Now add salt and pepper.*

salty /sɔlti/ (**saltier, saltiest**) ADJ containing salt or tasting of salt ❍ *Ham and bacon are salty foods.*

same /seɪm/
1 ADJ very similar or exactly alike ❍ *The houses are all the same.*
2 ADJ You use **the same** to show that you are talking about only one thing, and not two different ones. ❍ *Jayden works at the same office as Gabrielle.* ❍ *He gets up at the same time every day.*

sam|ple /sæmpᵊl/ NOUN a small amount of something that shows you what the rest of it is like ❍ *We're giving away 2,000 free samples.*

sam|ple bag (**sample bags**) NOUN a bag containing samples of a company's products or promotional material, given out at trade fairs and other events ❍ *Visitors leave exhibitions with a sample bag bulging with brochures.*

sand /sænd/ NONCOUNT NOUN **Sand** is a powder made of very small pieces of stone. ❍ *They walked across the sand to the water's edge.*

san|dal /sændᵊl/ NOUN **Sandals** are light shoes that you wear in warm weather. ❍ *He put on a pair of old sandals.*

S & L /ɛs ən ɛl/ NOUN **S & L** is an abbreviation for **savings and loan**. [BANKING]

sand|wich /sænwɪtʃ, sænd-/ (**sandwiches**) NOUN two slices of bread with another food such as cheese or meat between them ❍ *a ham sandwich*

sane /seɪn/ (**saner, sanest**) ADJ not mad ❍ *He seemed perfectly sane.*

sang /sæŋ/ **Sang** is a form of the verb **sing**.

sank /sæŋk/ **Sank** is a form of the verb **sink**.

sat /sæt/ **Sat** is a form of the verb **sit**.

sat|el|lite /sætᵊlaɪt/ NOUN a piece of electronic equipment that is sent into space in order to receive and send back information ❍ *The rocket carried two communications satellites.*

sat|el|lite dish (**satellite dishes**) NOUN a piece of equipment that people put on their house in order to receive television signals from a satellite

S

sat|el|lite tele|vi|sion NONCOUNT NOUN **Satellite television** is a system of broadcasting television programs using a satellite. ❍ *We have access to 49 satellite television channels.*

sat|is|fac|tion /sætɪsfækʃən/ NONCOUNT NOUN If you feel **satisfaction**, you feel pleased to do or get something. ❍ *It gives me a real sense of satisfaction when I close a deal.*

sat|is|fac|tory /sætɪsfæktəri/ ADJ good enough ❍ *I never got a satisfactory answer.*

sat|is|fied /sætɪsfaɪd/ ADJ happy with what has happened or what you have received or achieved ❍ *Most customers were satisfied with the service they received.*

sat|is|fy /sætɪsfaɪ/ (**satisfies, satisfying, satisfied**) VERB If someone or something **satisfies** you, they give you enough of what you want or need. ❍ *They have been successful in satisfying customer demands for increased choice.*

sat|is|fy|ing /sætɪsfaɪɪŋ/ ADJ making you feel pleased or happy ❍ *I find my work very satisfying.*

satu|rate /sætʃəreɪt/ (**saturates, saturating, saturated**) VERB If a market **is saturated**, so many similar products are already available that any new products are unlikely to sell well. [MARKETING AND SALES] ❍ *The car market is saturated in rich countries.*
● **satu|rat|ed** ADJ ❍ *As the market became more saturated, firms began to export the product.*

satu|ra|tion /sætʃəreɪʃən/
1 NONCOUNT NOUN The **saturation** of a market is the process or state that occurs when so many similar products are already available that any new products are unlikely to sell well. [MARKETING AND SALES] ❍ *Car makers have been equally blind to the saturation of their markets at home and abroad.*
2 ADJ used for describing a campaign or other activity that is carried out very thoroughly, so that nothing is missed [MARKETING AND SALES] ❍ *The concept of saturation marketing makes perfect sense.*

Sat|ur|day /sætərdeɪ, -di/ NOUN the day after Friday and before Sunday ❍ *He called her on Saturday morning.*

sauce /sɔs/ NOUN a thick liquid that you eat with other food ❍ *a garlic and tomato sauce*

sauce|pan /sɔspæn/ NOUN a deep metal cooking pot, with a long handle ❍ *Place the potatoes in a saucepan.*

sau|cer /sɔsər/ NOUN a small curved plate that you put under a cup

sau|sage /sɔsɪdʒ/ NOUN a mixture of very small pieces of meat, spices, and other foods, inside a long thin skin ❍ *They ate sausages for breakfast.*

save /seɪv/ (**saves, saving, saved**)
1 VERB If you **save** someone or something, you help them to escape from a dangerous or bad situation. ❍ *We must save these children from disease and death.*
2 VERB If you **save**, you gradually collect money by spending less than you get. ❍ *Tim and Barbara are now saving for a house.* ❍ *I was saving money to go to college.*
3 Save up means the same as **save**. ❍ *Taylor was saving up for something special.*
4 VERB If you **save** something such as time or money, you use less of it. ❍ *Going through the city by bike saves time.*
5 VERB If you **save** something, you keep it to use later. ❍ *Save the vegetable water for making the sauce.*
6 VERB If you **save** information in a computer, you store it there. ❍ *It's important to save frequently when you are working on a document.*
7 NOUN In a sports game, if you make a **save**, you stop someone from scoring a goal. ❍ *The goalkeeper made some great saves.*

sav|ings /seɪvɪŋz/ **PL NOUN** Your **savings** are the money that you have saved. ❍ *Her savings were in the First National Bank.*

sav|ings acc|ount (**savings accounts**) **NOUN** an account at a bank that accumulates interest [BANKING] ❍ *Balances above a certain amount in a checking account are automatically transferred into a savings account that pays interest.*

sav|ings and loan (**savings and loans**) or **savings and loan association** **NOUN** A **savings and loan** is a business where people save money to earn interest, and that lends money to savers to buy houses. [ECONOMICS] ❍ *new capital standards for savings and loans* ❍ *The nation's savings and loan associations continued to liquidate large amounts of the securities.*

sav|ings bank (**savings banks**) **NOUN** a bank that accepts people's savings and pays interest on them [BANKING]

saw /sɔ/ (**saws, sawing, sawed, sawed** or **sawn**)
1 Saw is a form of the verb **see**.
2 NOUN a metal tool for cutting wood
3 VERB If you **saw** something, you cut it with a saw. ❍ *I sawed the dead branches off the tree.*

say /seɪ/ (**says** /sɛz/, **saying, said** /sɛd/)
1 VERB When you **say** something, you speak. ❍ *She said that they were very pleased.* ❍ *I packed and said goodbye to Charlie.*
2 VERB If a notice or a clock **says** something, it gives information. ❍ *The clock said four minutes past eleven.*

say|ing /seɪɪŋ/ **NOUN** something that people often say, that gives advice about life ❍ *Remember that old saying: "Forgive and forget."*

scab /skæb/ **NOUN** a layer of dry blood that forms over the surface of a wound

scale /skeɪl/
1 NOUN a machine that you use for weighing people or things ❍ *a bathroom scale*
2 NOUN The **scale** of something is the size or level of it. ❍ *He doesn't realize the scale of the problem.*
3 NOUN a set of levels or numbers that you use to measure things ❍ *The earthquake measured 5.5 on the Richter scale.*
4 NOUN Scales are small, flat pieces of hard skin that cover the body of animals like fish and snakes.
5 NOUN a set of musical notes that are played in a fixed order ❍ *the scale of F major*

scalp|er **NOUN** someone who sells tickets for events for which all the tickets have sold out, at much higher prices than the official ticket prices

scan /skæn/ (**scans, scanning, scanned**)
1 VERB When you **scan** a piece of writing, you look through it quickly. ❍ *She scanned the front page of the newspaper.*
2 VERB If you **scan** a picture or a document, you make an electronic copy of it using a special piece of equipment (= a scanner). ❍ *She scanned the images into her computer.*

scan|dal /skændᵊl/ **NOUN** a situation or an event that people think is shocking ❍ *a financial scandal*

> **BUSINESS ETIQUETTE**
> In the US and the UK, many companies discourage the giving of gifts.

S

scan|ner /sk<u>æ</u>nər/
1 NOUN a machine that makes electronic copies of pictures or documents [TECHNOLOGY] ❍ *Scan your photos using any desktop scanner.*
2 NOUN a machine that gives a picture of the inside of something [TECHNOLOGY] ❍ *His bag was passed through the airport X-ray scanner.*

scar /sk<u>ɑ</u>r/ (**scars, scarring, scarred**)
1 NOUN a mark that is left on the skin by an old wound ❍ *He had a scar on his forehead.*
2 VERB If your skin **is scarred**, it is marked because of an old wound. ❍ *He was scarred for life during a fight.*

scarce /sk<u>ɛə</u>rs/ (**scarcer, scarcest**) **ADJ** If something is **scarce**, there is not much of it. ❍ *Jobs remain scarce.*

scarce|ly /sk<u>ɛə</u>rsli/ **ADV** hardly ❍ *The concept of manufacturing for export scarcely exists here.*

scare /sk<u>ɛə</u>r/ (**scares, scaring, scared**)
1 VERB If something or someone **scares** you, they frighten you. ❍ *The thought of failure scares me.*
2 NOUN If something or someone gives you a **scare**, they frighten you. ❍ *You gave us a terrible scare!*

scared /sk<u>ɛə</u>rd/ **ADJ** If you are **scared of** someone or something, you are frightened of them. ❍ *Bankers will now be scared of extreme leverage.*

scarf /sk<u>ɑ</u>rf/ (**scarfs** or **scarves**) **NOUN** a piece of cloth that you wear around your neck or head ❍ *He loosened the scarf around his neck.*

S

scary /sk<u>ɛə</u>ri/ (**scarier, scariest**) **ADJ** frightening [INFORMAL] ❍ *The movie is too scary for children.*

scat|ter /sk<u>æ</u>tər/ **VERB** If you **scatter** things over an area, you throw them so that they spread over it. ❍ *She scattered the flowers over the grave.*

sce|nario /sɪn<u>ɛə</u>rioʊ/ **NOUN** a situation, or the way in which a situation may develop ❍ *The only reasonable scenario is that he will resign.*

scene /s<u>i</u>n/
1 NOUN a part of a play, a movie, or a book that happens in the same place ❍ *This is the opening scene of "Tom Sawyer."*
2 NOUN something that you can see or a picture of something ❍ *The photographs show scenes of everyday life in the village.*
3 NOUN a place where something has happened ❍ *Firefighters rushed to the scene of the car accident.*

scent /s<u>ɛ</u>nt/ **NOUN** a pleasant smell ❍ *This perfume gives off a heavy scent of roses.*
● **scent|ed** **ADJ** ❍ *scented soap*

scep|ti|cal /sk<u>ɛ</u>ptɪkəl/ [mainly BRIT] → **skeptical**

sched|ule /sk<u>ɛ</u>dʒul, -uəl/ (**schedules, scheduling, scheduled**)
1 NOUN a plan that gives a list of the times when things will happen [BUSINESS MANAGEMENT] ❍ *a training schedule*
2 NONCOUNT NOUN You can use **schedule** to refer to the time or way something is planned to be done. For example, if something is completed **on schedule**, it is completed at the time planned. [BUSINESS MANAGEMENT] ❍ *Building work was finished one month ahead of schedule.* ❍ *Everything went according to schedule.*
3 VERB If something **is scheduled** to happen at a particular time, arrangements are made for it to happen at that time. [BUSINESS MANAGEMENT] ❍ *The new tax rules are scheduled to take effect in October.*

scheme /sk<u>i</u>m/ (**schemes, scheming, schemed**)
1 VERB If people **are scheming**, they are making secret, dishonest plans. ❍ *The family was scheming to stop the wedding.*
2 NOUN a secret plan ❍ *a scheme for making money*
3 NOUN a plan formally adopted by a business or government body [BRIT] ❍ *Most companies already have two types of pension scheme.*

schol|ar|ship /sk<u>ɒ</u>lərʃɪp/ **NOUN** an amount of money that is given to a student to pay for their education ❍ *He got a scholarship to the Pratt Institute of Art.*

school /skul/
1 NOUN a place where people go to learn ❍ *The school was built in the 1960s.*
2 NONCOUNT NOUN You can use **school** to talk about your time in school or college. ❍ *Parents want their kids to do well in school.*

sci|ence /saɪəns/ **NONCOUNT NOUN** **Science** is the study of natural things. ❍ *He studied plant science in college.*

sci|en|tif|ic /saɪəntɪfɪk/ **ADJ** relating to science ❍ *scientific research*

sci|en|tist /saɪəntɪst/ **NOUN** someone whose job is to do research in science ❍ *Scientists have discovered a new gene.*

scis|sors /sɪzərz/ **PL NOUN** **Scissors** are a small tool for cutting with two sharp parts that are joined together. ❍ *Cut the card using scissors.*

scope /skoʊp/
1 NONCOUNT NOUN If there is **scope for** something, there is an opportunity for it to exist or happen. ❍ *There's not a lot of scope for change here.*
2 NOUN The **scope of** something is the things it deals with or includes. ❍ *This merger falls within the scope of the legislation.*

scorched earth pol|icy /skɔrtʃt ɜrθ pɒlɪsi/ (**scorched earth policies**) **NOUN** a policy of greatly reducing the profitability of a company in order to deter an unwelcome takeover bid

score /skɔr/ (**scores, scoring, scored**)
1 VERB In a sport or a game, if a player **scores**, they get a goal or a point. ❍ *Patten scored his second goal of the game.*
2 VERB If you **score** a particular amount on a test, you achieve that amount. ❍ *Kelly scored 88 on the test.*
3 NOUN Someone's **score** in a game or on a test is the number of points they have won. ❍ *Hogan won, with a score of 287.*

scowl /skaʊl/ **VERB** If you **scowl**, you make an angry face. ❍ *He scowled, and slammed the door.*

scram|ble /skræmbᵊl/ (**scrambles, scrambling, scrambled**)
1 VERB If you **scramble** over rocks or up a hill, you climb quickly, using your hands. ❍ *Tourists were scrambling over the rocks.*
2 VERB If you **scramble** eggs, you break them, mix them together, and then cook them. ❍ *Make the toast and scramble the eggs.*
● **scram|bled ADJ** ❍ *We're having scrambled eggs and bacon.*

scrap /skræp/ (**scraps, scrapping, scrapped**)
1 NOUN a very small piece or amount of something ❍ *a scrap of paper*
2 VERB If you **scrap** something, you get rid of it or cancel it. ❍ *The government has scrapped plans to build a new airport.*

scrape /skreɪp/ (**scrapes, scraping, scraped**)
1 VERB If you **scrape** something, you damage its surface by rubbing it against something sharp or rough. ❍ *She fell, scraping her hands and knees.*
2 VERB If you **scrape** something from a surface, you remove it by moving a sharp object over the surface. ❍ *She scraped the frost off the car windows.*

scratch /skrætʃ/ (**scratches, scratching, scratched**)
1 VERB If you **scratch** part of your body, you rub your fingernails against your skin. ❍ *He scratched his head thoughtfully.*
2 VERB If a sharp object **scratches** someone or something, it makes small cuts on their skin or on its surface. ❍ *The branches scratched my face.*
3 NOUN a small cut made by a sharp object ❍ *He had scratches on his face and neck.*

scream /skrim/
1 VERB When you **scream**, you give a very loud, high cry. ❍ *Women were screaming in the houses nearest the fire.*
2 NOUN **Scream** is also a noun. ❍ *Rose gave a loud scream.*

screen /skrin/
1 NOUN a flat surface on a piece of electronic equipment, where you see pictures or words [TECHNOLOGY] ❍ *Traders can deal on both exchanges from a single computer screen.*
2 NOUN a flat area on the wall of a movie

theater, where you see the movie ❍ *The theater has 20 screens.*

screen|saver /skrinseɪvər/ **NOUN** a moving picture that appears on a computer screen when the computer is not being used

screw /skru/

1 NOUN a small metal object with a sharp end, that you use to join things together ❍ *Each shelf is attached to the wall with screws.*

2 VERB If you **screw** something somewhere, you join it to another thing using a screw. ❍ *I screwed the shelf on the wall myself.*

scrib|ble /skrɪbᵊl/ (**scribbles, scribbling, scribbled**) **VERB** If you **scribble** something, you write or draw it quickly and roughly. ❍ *She scribbled a note to Mom.*

scrip /skrɪp/ **NOUN** a certificate that shows that an investor owns part of a share of stock [BANKING] ❍ *The cash or scrip would be offered as part of a pro rata return of capital to shareholders.*

scrip is|sue (**scrip issues**) **NOUN** A **scrip issue** is the same as a **bonus issue**.

script /skrɪpt/ **NOUN** the written words that actors speak ❍ *Jenny's writing a movie script.*

scroll /skroʊl/ **VERB** If you **scroll** through text on a computer screen, you move the text up or down to find the information that you need. ❍ *I scrolled down to find "United States of America."*

scrub /skrʌb/ (**scrubs, scrubbing, scrubbed**) **VERB** If you **scrub** something, you rub it hard in order to clean it. ❍ *Surgeons must scrub their hands and arms with soap and water.*

S

sculp|tor /skʌlptər/ **NOUN** an artist who makes solid objects out of stone, metal, or wood

sculp|ture /skʌlptʃər/

1 NOUN a piece of art that is made into a shape from a material like stone or wood ❍ *There were stone sculptures of different animals.*

2 NONCOUNT NOUN Sculpture is the art of making sculptures. ❍ *Both of them studied sculpture.*

sea /si/ **NOUN** a large area of salty water ❍ *They swam in the warm Caribbean Sea.*

sea|food /sifud/ **NONCOUNT NOUN Seafood** is fish and other small animals from the ocean that you can eat. ❍ *Let's find a seafood restaurant.*

seal /sil/

1 VERB When you **seal** an envelope, you close it by sticking it down. ❍ *He sealed the envelope and put on a stamp.*

2 NOUN a large animal with a rounded body and short fur that eats fish and lives near the ocean

seam /sim/ **NOUN** a line where two pieces of cloth are joined together

search /sɜrtʃ/ (**searches, searching, searched**)

1 VERB If you **search for** something or someone, you look for them. ❍ *Police are already searching for the men.*

2 VERB If you **search** a place, you look carefully for something or someone there. ❍ *The police are searching the town for the missing men.*

3 NOUN an attempt to find something or someone ❍ *The search was stopped because of the heavy snow.*

search en|gine (**search engines**) **NOUN** a computer program that you use to search for information on the Internet [TECHNOLOGY]

sea|son /sizᵊn/

1 NOUN one of the four parts of a year that have their own typical weather conditions ❍ *Fall is my favorite season.*

2 NOUN a time each year when something happens ❍ *the baseball season*

seat /sit/ **NOUN** something that you can sit on ❍ *The car has comfortable leather seats.*

seat belt (**seat belts**) **NOUN** a long thin belt that you fasten around your body in a vehicle to keep you safe ❍ *Please fasten your seat belts.*

SEC /ɛs i si/ **NOUN SEC** is an abbreviation for **Securities and Exchange Commission**. [ECONOMICS]

sec|ond

> Pronounce the noun, adjective, and adverb /sɛkənd/. Pronounce the verb /sɪkɒnd/.

1 NOUN A **second** is a measurement of time. There are sixty seconds in one minute. ❍ *For a few seconds, nobody spoke.*

2 ADJ The **second** thing in a series is the one that you count as number two. ❍ *It was the second day of his visit to Florida.*
3 ADV Second is also an adverb. ❍ *Emma came in second in the race.*
4 PL NOUN Seconds are goods of inferior quality. ❍ *The manufacturer operates an outlet store, selling seconds and excess merchandise.*
5 VERB If you **second** an employee, you transfer them temporarily to another part of the organization. [BRIT] ❍ *The head of the pension fund is usually seconded from the finance department.*

sec|ond|ary /sɛkəndɛri/
1 ADJ less important than something else ❍ *Money is of secondary importance to them.*
2 ADJ Secondary education is given to students between the ages of 11 and 18. ❍ *They take examinations after five years of secondary education.*
3 ADJ A **secondary** product is manufactured from raw materials. Compare with **primary** and **tertiary**. ❍ *They import scrap and manufacture secondary products.*

sec|ond|ary da|ta **NONCOUNT NOUN** **Secondary data** is information about a subject that has already been written or published. Compare with **primary data**. ❍ *Secondary data sources were used to supplement the main body of information.*

sec|ond|ary school **(secondary schools)** **NOUN** a school for students aged about 11–18 [BRIT] ❍ *She taught history at a secondary school.*

sec|ond|ary sec|tor **(secondary sectors)** **NOUN** The **secondary sector** consists of industries that produce things from raw materials, for example manufacturing and construction. Compare with **primary sector** and **tertiary sector**. [ECONOMICS] ❍ *In 1930 a third of all women in the secondary sector worked in the textile industry.*

second-class also **second class** **ADJ** not as good or important as other things or people of the same type ❍ *Many local trains have only second-class seats.*

second-hand **ADJ** or **ADV** **Second-hand** things have been used by another person. ❍ *a second-hand car* ❍ *They bought the furniture second-hand.*

sec|ond|ly /sɛkəndli/ **ADV** used to talk about a second thing, or give a second reason for something ❍ *Firstly, this is a far more efficient way of running IT systems. Secondly, many firms will find they have no choice.*

se|cond|ment /sɪkɒndmənt/ **NOUN** a temporary transfer to another post within the same organization [BRIT] ❍ *In his eight years with us, he has had responsibility for our largest brands and a one-year secondment to our strategic partner's operations in West Asia.* ❍ *Its 400 staff include 170 on secondment from member firms.*

sec|ond mort|gage **(second mortgages)** **NOUN** A **second mortgage** is a mortgage that is taken out in addition to a first mortgage on a property, usually at a higher interest rate. Compare with **first mortgage**. [BANKING] ❍ *She took out a second mortgage on her house to pay for improvements.*

se|cre|cy /sikrəsi/ **NONCOUNT NOUN** **Secrecy** is a situation in which you do not tell anyone about something. ❍ *They met in complete secrecy.*

se|cret /sikrɪt/
1 ADJ known by only one person or a small number of people ❍ *The management demanded that details of the offer be kept secret.*
2 NOUN something that only one person or a small number of people knows ❍ *Can you keep a secret?*

sec|re|tary /sɛkrɪtɛri/ **(secretaries)**
1 NOUN a person whose job is to do office work such as typing letters and answering the telephone
2 NOUN a person with an important position in the government ❍ *the defense secretary*

sec|tion /sɛkʃən/ **NOUN** a part of something ❍ *It is wrong to blame one section of society.*

sec|tor /sɛktər/
1 NOUN one part of a country's business activity ❍ *the manufacturing sector*
2 NOUN a group that is part of a larger group ❍ *These workers came from the poorest sectors of society.*

S

se|cure /sɪkyʊər/ (**secures, securing, secured**)
1 ADJ A **secure** place is well protected or locked. ❍ *We'll make our home as secure as possible.* ● **se|cure|ly** ADV ❍ *He locked the heavy door securely.*
2 ADJ firmly fixed in position ❍ *The farmer made sure that the fence was always secure.* ● **se|cure|ly** ADV ❍ *He fastened his belt securely.*
3 ADJ If a job is **secure**, it will not end soon. ❍ *For the moment, his job is secure.*
4 ADJ If you feel **secure**, you feel safe and not worried. ❍ *She felt secure when she was with him.*
5 VERB If a loan **is secured**, the person who lends the money may take property from the person who borrows the money if they fail to repay it. [BANKING] ❍ *The loan is secured against your home.*

Se|cu|ri|ties and Ex|change Com|mis|sion NOUN The **Securities and Exchange Commission** is a government agency in the United States that regulates the buying and selling of securities. [ECONOMICS] ❍ *The Securities and Exchange Commission has filed fraud charges and is launching an investigation.*

se|cu|ri|ti|sa|tion /sɪkyʊərɪtɪzeɪʃən/ [ECONOMICS, BRIT] → **securitization**

se|cu|ri|ti|za|tion /sɪkyʊərɪtɪzeɪʃən/ NONCOUNT NOUN **Securitization** is the use of securities to enable investors to lend directly to borrowers with a minimum of risk. [ECONOMICS] ❍ *The company ranked first in home equity securitization.*

S

se|cu|rity /sɪkyʊərɪti/ (**securities**)
1 NONCOUNT NOUN **Security** is everything that you do to protect a place. ❍ *They are improving airport security.*
2 NONCOUNT NOUN A feeling of **security** is a feeling of being safe and not worried. ❍ *He loves the security of a happy home life.*
3 NONCOUNT NOUN If something is **security** for a loan, you promise to give that thing to the person who lends you money, if you fail to pay the money back. ❍ *The central bank will provide special loans, and the banks will pledge the land as security.*
4 PL NOUN **Securities** are stocks, bonds, or other certificates that you buy in order to earn regular interest from them or to sell them later for a profit. [BANKING] ❍ *National banks can package their own mortgages and underwrite them as securities.*

see /si/ (**sees, seeing, saw, seen**)
1 VERB When you **see** something, you notice it using your eyes. ❍ *The fog was so thick we couldn't see anything.* ❍ *Have you seen my keys?*
2 VERB If you **see** someone, you visit or meet them. ❍ *I saw him yesterday.*
3 VERB If you **see** a play, a movie, or a sports game, you watch it. ❍ *Let's go see a movie tonight.*
4 VERB If you **see** something, you understand it. ❍ *Oh, I see what you're saying.*
5 used to show that someone will decide something later ❍ *"Can we go swimming tomorrow?"—"We'll see."*
6 used to say goodbye to someone [INFORMAL, SPOKEN] ❍ *"Talk to you later."—"All right. See you."*
▶ **see off** When you **see** someone **off**, you go somewhere with someone who is going on a journey to say goodbye to them. ❍ *Ben saw Jackie off on her plane.*

seed /sid/ NOUN a small, hard part of a plant from which a new plant grows ❍ *Plant the seeds in small plastic pots.*

seed capi|tal NONCOUNT NOUN **Seed capital** is an amount of money that a new company needs to pay for the costs of producing a business plan so that they can raise further capital to develop the company. [FINANCE, ECONOMICS] ❍ *I am negotiating with financiers to raise seed capital for my latest venture.*

seed corn [FINANCE, ECONOMICS, mainly BRIT] → **seed money**

seed mon|ey NONCOUNT NOUN **Seed money** is money that is given to someone to help them start a new business or project. [FINANCE, ECONOMICS] ❍ *The government will give seed money to the project.*

seek /sik/ (**seeks, seeking, sought**) VERB If you **seek** something, you try to find it or get it. [FORMAL] ❍ *They are seeking work in hotels and bars.*

seem /siːm/ VERB If someone or something **seems** a particular way, they appear to be that way. ❍ *Unemployment seems stuck at close to 10%.*

seen /siːn/ **Seen** is a form of the verb **see**.

seg|ment

Pronounce the noun /sɛgmənt/. Pronounce the verb /sɛgmɛnt/.

1 NOUN one part of something ❍ *These people come from the poorer segments of society.*
2 NOUN one part of a market considered separately from the rest ❍ *Three-to-five day cruises are the fastest-growing segment of the market.*
3 VERB If a company **segments** a market, it divides it into separate parts, usually in order to improve marketing opportunities. ❍ *The big six record companies are multinational, and thus can segment the world market into national ones.*

seize /siːz/ (**seizes, seizing, seized**) VERB If you **seize** something, you take hold of it quickly and firmly. ❍ *He seized my arm and pulled me closer.*

sel|dom /sɛldəm/ ADV not often ❍ *They seldom speak to each other.*

se|lect /sɪlɛkt/ VERB If you **select** someone or something, you choose them. ❍ *Select "Save" from the File menu.*

se|lec|tion /sɪlɛkʃən/ NOUN a set of people or things that someone has chosen, or that you can choose from ❍ *They will be able to provide customers with as good a selection of goods and services as before.* ❍ *Choose from our selection of fine wines.*

self /sɛlf/ (**selves**) NOUN your own personality or nature ❍ *You're looking like your usual self again.*

self-as|sess|ment NONCOUNT NOUN In Britain, **self-assessment** is a system that enables taxpayers to assess their own tax liabilities. [HR] ❍ *You have two weeks to complete and return your self-assessment form.*

self-defense NONCOUNT NOUN **Self-defense** is the use of force to protect yourself against an attack. ❍ *Use your weapon only in self-defense.*

self-employed ADJ working for yourself, rather than for a company [ECONOMICS] ❍ *There are no paid holidays or sick leave if you are self-employed.* ❍ *a self-employed builder*

self|ish /sɛlfɪʃ/ ADJ caring only about yourself ❍ *I think I've been very selfish.*
● **self|ish|ly** ADV ❍ *Someone has selfishly emptied the cookie jar.* ● **self|ish|ness** NONCOUNT NOUN ❍ *Julie's selfishness shocked us.*

self-respect NONCOUNT NOUN If you have **self-respect** you feel sure about your own ability and value. ❍ *They have lost their jobs, their homes, and their self-respect.*

self-standing ADJ A company or organization that is **self-standing** is independent of other companies or organizations. ❍ *Five separate companies, all operating as self-standing units, are now one.*

sell /sɛl/ (**sells, selling, sold**)
1 VERB If you **sell** something, you let someone have it in return for money. ❍ *They announced plans to sell 1.5 million shares.* ● **sell|er** NOUN ❍ *The buyer should ask the seller to have a test carried out.*
2 VERB If a store **sells** a particular thing, people can buy it there. ❍ *The store sells newspapers and candy bars.* ● **sell|er** NOUN ❍ *a flower seller*
▶ **sell off** If you **sell off** remaining or unprofitable items, you sell them at low prices. [MARKETING AND SALES] ❍ *A provisional liquidator can either restructure the company or sell off its assets.*
▶ **sell out**
1 If a store **sells out of** something, it has sold it all. ❍ *One branch of Bank of America sold out of dollars completely.*
2 If products **sell out**, all of them that are available are sold. ❍ *Sleeping bags sold out almost immediately.*
3 If you **sell out** or **sell up**, you sell everything you have, such as your house or your business, because you need the money. ❍ *Several franchisees now want to sell out because they don't think the business has a future.*

sell-by date [MARKETING AND SALES, mainly BRIT] → **pull date**

sell|er's mar|ket NOUN When there is a **seller's market** for a particular product, there are fewer products for sale than there are people who want to buy them. In a **seller's market**, buyers have little choice and can make prices go up. [MARKETING AND SALES] ❍ *It's a seller's market, and no one is forced to discount to remain competitive.*

sell|ing point (**selling points**) NOUN a desirable quality or feature that something has that makes it likely that people will want to buy it [MARKETING AND SALES] ❍ *A garden is one of the biggest selling points with house-hunters.*

sell|ing price (**selling prices**) NOUN the price for which something is sold [MARKETING AND SALES] ❍ *The average selling price of its devices was $183.*

sell-off also **selloff**

1 NOUN the selling of unwanted items at low prices [MARKETING AND SALES]

2 NOUN the selling of shares in an industry that is owned by the state [ECONOMICS, BRIT] ❍ *The privatization of the electricity industry was the biggest sell-off of them all.*

se|mes|ter /sɪmɛstər/ NOUN a half of a school or college year ❍ *the spring semester*

semi|fi|nal /sɛmifaɪnᵊl, sɛmaɪ-/ or **semi-final** NOUN one of the two games in a competition that decide who will play in the final game ❍ *The basketball team lost in their semifinal yesterday.*

S

semi|nar /sɛmɪnɑr/

1 NOUN a class at a college or university in which the teacher and a small group of students discuss a topic ❍ *Students are asked to prepare material for the weekly seminars.*

2 NOUN any group or meeting for holding discussions or exchanging information [HR] ❍ *She spoke at a seminar on investment opportunities in Malaysia.*

semi-skilled /sɛmiskɪld, sɛmaɪ-/ also **semiskilled** ADJ A **semi-skilled** worker has some training and skills, but not enough to do specialized work. [HR] ❍ *The region's advantage in semi-skilled and unskilled labor costs will continue for an indefinite period.*

send /sɛnd/ (**sends, sending, sent**)

1 VERB When you **send** someone something, you arrange for it to be delivered to them. ❍ *I sent her an email this morning.* ❍ *Hannah sent me a letter last week.*

2 VERB If you **send** someone somewhere, you make them go there. ❍ *His parents sent him to business school.*

▶ **send for** If you **send for** someone, you send them a message asking them to come to you. ❍ *When he arrived in Portland, he sent for his wife and children.*

sen|ior /sinyər/

1 ADJ having the most important job in an organization ❍ *Each group presents its findings to senior managers.*

2 NOUN a student in the final year of study ❍ *high school seniors*

sen|ior citi|zen (**senior citizens**) NOUN an older person, especially someone over 65

sen|ior man|age|ment NONCOUNT NOUN **Senior management** are the most senior staff of an organization. [ADMINISTRATION, BUSINESS MANAGEMENT] ❍ *Senior management has changed its way of running the business as a result of being accountable to their employees as stockholders.*

sen|sa|tion /sɛnseɪʃən/ NOUN a physical feeling ❍ *Floating can be a pleasant sensation.*

sen|sa|tion|al /sɛnseɪʃənᵊl/ ADJ very exciting or good ❍ *a sensational victory*

sense /sɛns/

1 NOUN Your **senses** are the ability to see, smell, hear, touch, and taste. ❍ *Foxes have a strong sense of smell.*

2 NOUN If you have a **sense of** something, you feel it. ❍ *Many younger adults lack a sense of fiscal responsibility.*

3 NONCOUNT NOUN **Sense** is the ability to think carefully about something and do the right thing. ❍ *Now that he's older, he has a bit more sense.*

4 NOUN a meaning of a word ❍ *This noun has four senses.*

5 If something **makes sense**, you can understand it. ❍ *Do these figures make sense to you?*

sense of hu|mor (**senses of humor**) **NOUN** the ability to make jokes and find things funny ❍ *She has a good sense of humor.*

sen|sible /sɛnsɪbᵊl/ **ADJ** based on good reasons or showing good judgment ❍ *It might be sensible to get a lawyer.* ● **sen|sibly** /sɛnsɪbli/ **ADV** ❍ *Mr. Streiff sensibly gave himself time to get to know the business.*

sen|si|tive /sɛnsɪtɪv/
1 ADJ easily affected by something ❍ *We know that manufacturing is very sensitive to recessions.*
2 ADJ able to understand people's feelings and not upset them ❍ *The classroom teacher must be sensitive to a child's needs.*
3 ADJ easily worried or upset ❍ *Young people are sensitive about their appearance.*
4 ADJ If a stock market or prices are sensitive, they tend to go up and down a lot in response to outside influences. ❍ *Insurance company stocks, also sensitive to interest rates, fell as well.*

sent /sɛnt/ **Sent** is a form of the verb **send**.

sen|tence /sɛntəns/ (**sentences, sentencing, sentenced**)
1 NOUN a group of words that tells you something or asks a question, written with a capital letter at the beginning and a period at the end ❍ *After I've written each sentence, I read it aloud.*
2 NOUN a punishment that someone is given in a court ❍ *He was given a four-year sentence.*
3 VERB When a judge **sentences** someone, he or she tells the court what their punishment will be. ❍ *The court sentenced him to five years in prison.*

sen|ti|ment|al /sɛntɪmɛntᵊl/ **ADJ** feeling or showing too much pity or love ❍ *I'm trying not to be sentimental about the past.*

sepa|rate (**separates, separating, separated**)

Pronounce the adjective /sɛpərɪt/. Pronounce the verb /sɛpəreɪt/.

1 ADJ not connected or the same ❍ *The entire reserve is held in a separate account.* ● **sepa|rate|ly** /sɛpərɪtli/ **ADV** ❍ *The two companies will be sold separately.*
2 VERB If you **separate** people or things, you move them apart. ❍ *He favored eliminating the rules separating commercial banking and investment banking.*
3 VERB If a couple **separate**, they decide to live apart. ❍ *Her parents separated when she was very young.* ● **sepa|rat|ed** /sɛpəreɪtɪd/ **ADJ** ❍ *Rachel's parents are separated.*

Sep|tem|ber /sɛptɛmbər/ **NOUN** the ninth month of the year ❍ *Her son was born in September.*

se|quence /sikwəns/ **NOUN** a number of events or things that come one after another ❍ *The solid arrows trace the sequence of events in a typical financial crisis.*

se|rial /sɪəriəl/ **NOUN** a story that is told in a number of separate parts ❍ *The book was filmed as a six-part TV serial.*

se|ries /sɪəriz/ (**series**)
1 NOUN a number of events or things that come one after another ❍ *There will be a series of meetings with political leaders.*
2 NOUN a set of radio or television programs ❍ *a long-running TV series*

se|ri|ous /sɪəriəs/
1 ADJ very bad and causing worry ❍ *He doesn't think quotas will pose a serious problem.* ● **se|ri|ous|ness NONCOUNT NOUN** ❍ *They don't realize the seriousness of the crisis.*
2 ADJ important and needing careful thought ❍ *This is a very serious matter.*
3 ADJ If you are **serious about** something, you really mean what you say. ❍ *You really are serious about this, aren't you?*

se|ri|ous|ly /sɪəriəsli/
1 ADV in a very bad way ❍ *This law could seriously damage my business.*
2 If you **take** someone or something **seriously**, you believe that they are important and deserve attention. ❍ *The company takes all complaints seriously.*
3 ADV used to show that you really mean what you say ❍ *"I followed him home," he said. "Seriously?"*

serv|ant /sɜrvᵊnt/ **NOUN** someone who does work like cooking and cleaning at another person's home ❍ *The family employed several servants.*

serve /sɜ̲rv/ (**serves, serving, served**)
1 VERB When you **serve** food and drinks, you give people food and drinks. ❍ *The restaurant serves breakfast, lunch, and dinner.*
2 VERB Someone who **serves** in a store helps customers buy the things they want. ❍ *Auntie and Uncle suggested she serve in the store.*
3 VERB If you **serve** your country, an organization, or a person, you do useful work for them. ❍ *He spoke of the fine character of those who serve their country.*
4 VERB When you **serve** in a game such as tennis, you throw up the ball and hit it to start to play. ❍ *She served again and won the game.*
5 VERB If something **serves** people or an area, it provides them with something that they need. ❍ *This could mean the closure of thousands of small businesses which serve the community.*

serv|er /sɜ̲rvər/
1 NOUN a computer that stores information and supplies it to other computers on a network ❍ *The mail server was down.*
2 NOUN a person whose job is to serve food and drink in a restaurant ❍ *A server came by with a tray of coffee cups.*

ser|vice /sɜrvɪs/ (**services, servicing, serviced**)
1 NOUN a system that supplies something that the public needs, such as transportation or energy ❍ *There is a regular local bus service to Yorkdale.*
2 NONCOUNT NOUN Service is the help that people in a restaurant or a store give you. ❍ *We always receive good service in that restaurant.*
3 NONCOUNT NOUN Service is the time that you spend working for someone. ❍ *Most employees had long service with the company.* ❍ *He has been in the service of our firm for ten years.*
4 NOUN a religious ceremony ❍ *After the service, his body was taken to a cemetery.*
5 NOUN If an organization or company provides a particular **service**, they can do a particular job for you. ❍ *Our main objective is to provide an excellent service to our customers.* ❍ *a twenty-four hour service*
6 NONCOUNT NOUN The level or standard of **service** provided by an organization or a company is the amount or quality of the work it can do for you. ❍ *First Technology is proud of its commitment to excellence and its high standard of service.*
7 VERB If you **service** a debt, you pay interest on it. ❍ *The nation's meager exports are inadequate to service its foreign debt of $39 billion.*
8 VERB If you have a vehicle or machine **serviced**, you arrange for someone to examine, adjust, and clean it so that it will keep working well. ❍ *I had my car serviced at the local garage.* ❍ *Make sure that all gas fires and central heating boilers are serviced annually.*

COLLOCATIONS
to *provide* a service
to *offer* a service
a *mail-order* service
to service *equipment*
to service a *car*
to service an *appliance*

ser|vice busi|ness (**service businesses**)
NOUN a business that provides a service but does not produce anything [ECONOMICS] ❍ *Still more significant was the formal announcement on June 25th that service businesses such as retailing, transportation, and banking will be opened to foreign investors.*

ser|vice in|dus|try (**service industries**)
NOUN an industry such as banking or insurance that provides a service but does not produce anything [ECONOMICS] ❍ *Seventy-two percent of people now work in service industries.*

ser|vice|man /sɜ̲rvɪsmən/ (**servicemen**)
NOUN a man whose job is to service and maintain equipment

ser|vice or|ga|ni|za|tion (**service organizations**) **NOUN** an organization that provides a service but does not produce anything [ECONOMICS] ❍ *service organizations that deliver repeated services of a common kind, such as car-hire businesses, transportation companies, restaurants, and so on*

ser|vice pro|vid|er (**service providers**)
NOUN a company that provides a service, especially an Internet service [ECONOMICS]

❍ *Just under 50 percent of all home users switched to another service provider last year, compared to 24 percent of business users.*

ser|vice qual|ity NONCOUNT NOUN **Service quality** is the level or standard of service provided by an organization or company. ❍ *Improvements in efficiency and in service quality may well require substantial changes.*

ser|vices /sɜrvɪsɪz/ PL NOUN **Services** are activities such as tourism, banking, and selling things that are part of a country's economy, but are not concerned with producing or manufacturing goods. ❍ *Mining rose by 9.1%, manufacturing by 9.4% and services by 4.3%.*

COLLOCATIONS
goods and services
public services
financial services

ser|vice sec|tor NOUN The **service sector** consists of industries that provide a service, such as transportation and finance. Compare with **industrial sector**. [ECONOMICS] ❍ *Industries in the service sector that employ any number of low-paid workers would be especially hit by the implementation of a minimum wage.*

ses|sion /sɛʃən/ NOUN a period of doing a particular activity ❍ *a photo session*

set /sɛt/ (**sets, setting, set**)
1 NOUN a number of things that belong together ❍ *a chess set*
2 NOUN A television **set** is a television.
3 VERB If you **set** something somewhere, you put it there carefully. ❍ *She set the vase down on the table.*
4 VERB When you **set** a clock or a control, you adjust it so that it will work in a particular way or at a particular time. ❍ *I set my alarm clock for seven o'clock every morning.*
5 VERB If you **set** a date or a price, you decide what it will be. ❍ *They have finally set a date for the product launch.*
6 VERB When the sun **sets**, it goes down. ❍ *They watched the sun set behind the hills.*
7 VERB When someone **sets** the table, they prepare it for a meal.
8 ADJ A **set** time is fixed and cannot be changed.
9 ADJ If a story is **set** in a particular place or time, the events in it happen in that place or at that time. ❍ *The play is set in a small Midwestern town.*
10 If you **set fire to** something or **set** something **on fire**, you make it burn. ❍ *Angry protestors threw stones and set cars on fire.*
11 If you **set** someone **free**, you cause them to be free. ❍ *They agreed to set the prisoners free.*
▸ **set off**
1 When you **set off**, you start going somewhere. ❍ *Nick set off for his farmhouse in Connecticut.*
2 In accounting, if you **set off** an amount, you cancel a credit on one account against a debit on another. [FINANCE] ❍ *A number of consumer credit laws give debtors the right to set off certain amounts owed on credit cards, thereby reducing the outstanding balance.*
▸ **set out** If you **set out to** do something, you try to do it. ❍ *He did what he set out to do.*
▸ **set up** If you **set** something **up**, you start or arrange it. ❍ *He plans to set up his own business.*

set|tle /sɛtᵊl/ (**settles, settling, settled**)
1 VERB If people **settle** an argument or a problem, they decide what to do about it. ❍ *They agreed to try to settle the dispute.*
2 VERB If something **is settled**, it has been decided and arranged. ❍ *We feel the matter is now settled.*
3 VERB When people **settle** in a place, they start living there. ❍ *He visited Paris and eventually settled there.*
4 VERB If you **settle** somewhere, you sit down and make yourself comfortable. ❍ *Brandon settled in front of the television.*
5 VERB If you **settle** a debt, you pay it off. ❍ *The creditors may accept a partial payment to settle the debt.*
▸ **settle down** If a person **settles down**, they become calm. ❍ *Time to settle down and go to sleep now.*
▸ **settle in** If you **settle in**, you become used to a new place. ❍ *I enjoyed school once I settled in.*

set|tle|ment /sɛtᵊlmənt/
1 NOUN an official agreement between two

people or groups after they have disagreed about something ❍ *The firm reached a settlement with the Federal Trade Commission over its sales practices.*

2 NOUN a place where people have come to live and have built homes ❍ *The village is a settlement of just fifty houses.*

sev|en /sɛvᵊn/ the number 7

sev|en|teen /sɛvᵊntin/ the number 17

sev|en|teenth /sɛvᵊntinθ/ **ADJ** or **ADV** The **seventeenth** item in a series is the one that you count as number seventeen. ❍ *The book was written in the seventeenth century*

sev|enth /sɛvᵊnθ/

1 ADJ or **ADV** The **seventh** item in a series is the one that you count as number seven. ❍ *I was the seventh child in the family.*

2 NOUN one of seven equal parts of something (1/7)

sev|en|ti|eth /sɛvᵊntiəθ/ **ADJ** or **ADV** The **seventieth** item in a series is the one that you count as number seventy. ❍ *It was her seventieth birthday last week.*

sev|en|ty /sɛvᵊnti/ the number 70 ❍ *All the guests were over seventy.*

sev|er|al /sɛvrəlʃ/ **ADJ** or **PRON** some, but not very many ❍ *Several countries have high deficits.* ❍ *The cakes were delicious, and we ate several.*

sev|er|ance pay /sɛvrəns peɪ, -ərəns/ **NONCOUNT NOUN** **Severance pay** is a sum of money that a company gives to its employees when it has to stop employing them. [HR] ❍ *We were offered 13 weeks' severance pay.*

se|vere /sɪvɪər/ **(severer, severest)**

1 ADJ very bad ❍ *severe financial problems*
● **se|vere|ly** **ADV** ❍ *Credit in Mexico has been severely restricted.*

2 ADJ **Severe** punishments or criticisms are very hard or strong. ❍ *A severe sentence is necessary for this type of crime.* ● **se|vere|ly** **ADV** ❍ *They want to punish dangerous drivers more severely.*

sew /soʊ/ **(sews, sewing, sewed, sewn)** **VERB** When you **sew** things together, you join them using thread. ❍ *Anyone can sew a button onto a shirt.* ● **sew|ing** **NONCOUNT NOUN** ❍ *She lists her hobbies as cooking, sewing, and going to the movies.*

sew|er /suər/ **NOUN** a large pipe under the ground that carries away water and waste from people's bodies

sex /sɛks/ **(sexes)**

1 NOUN one of the two groups, male and female, into which you can divide people and animals ❍ *This movie appeals to both sexes.*

2 NOUN The **sex** of a person or an animal is whether it is male or female. ❍ *We can identify the sex of your unborn baby.*

3 NONCOUNT NOUN **Sex** is the physical activity by which people can produce children. ❍ *He was very open in his attitudes about sex.*

sex dis|crimi|na|tion or **sexual discrimination** **NONCOUNT NOUN** **Sex discrimination** is the practice of treating the members of one sex, usually women, less fairly or less well than those of the other sex. [HR] ❍ *Women's groups denounced sex discrimination.*

sex|ual /sɛkʃuəl/

1 ADJ relating to the act of sex ❍ *sexual health*

2 ADJ relating to the differences between men and women ❍ *sexual discrimination*

sex|ual har|ass|ment **NONCOUNT NOUN** **Sexual harassment** is repeated and unwelcome sexual comments, looks, or physical contact at work, usually a man's actions that offend a woman. [HR] ❍ *Sexual harassment of women workers by their bosses is believed to be widespread.*

sexy /sɛksi/ **(sexier, sexiest)** **ADJ** sexually attractive ❍ *She is the sexiest woman I have ever seen.*

shade /ʃeɪd/

1 NOUN a particular form of a color ❍ *The walls were painted in two shades of green.*

2 NONCOUNT NOUN **Shade** is an area where sunlight does not reach. ❍ *Alexis was reading in the shade of a tree.*

3 NOUN a piece of material that you can pull down over a window ❍ *Nancy left the shades down.*

shad|ow /ʃædoʊ/ **NOUN** a dark shape on a surface that is made when something blocks the light ❍ *The long shadows of the trees fell across their path.*

shake /ʃeɪk/ (**shakes, shaking, shook, shaken**)
1 VERB If someone or something **shakes**, they make quick, small movements. ❍ *My whole body was shaking with fear.*
2 VERB If you **shake** something, you hold it and move it quickly up and down. ❍ *Always shake the bottle before you pour out the medicine.*
3 NOUN Shake is also a noun. ❍ *We gave the children a gentle shake to wake them.*
4 VERB If you **shake** your **head**, you move it from side to side to say "no." ❍ *Kathryn shook her head.*
5 If you **shake hands with** someone, you hold their hand and move it up and down. ❍ *Michael shook hands with Burke.*

shaky /ʃeɪki/ (**shakier, shakiest**)
1 ADJ unlikely to be successful ❍ *The economic recovery is shaky.*
2 ADJ weak and not well controlled ❍ *Her voice was shaky and she was close to tears.* ● **shak|ily ADV** ❍ *"I don't feel well," she said shakily.*

shall /ʃəl, STRONG ʃæl/
1 MODAL used to make offers or suggestions ❍ *Shall I get the keys?* ❍ *Well, shall we go?*
2 MODAL used for talking about something that will happen to you in the future [FORMAL] ❍ *We shall be landing in Paris in sixteen minutes.* ❍ *I shall know more tomorrow.*

shal|low /ʃæloʊ/ **ADJ** not deep ❍ *The river is very shallow here.*

shame /ʃeɪm/
1 NONCOUNT NOUN Shame is the unpleasant feeling that you have when you have done something wrong or stupid. ❍ *I was filled with shame.*
2 NOUN If you say that something is **a shame**, you feel sad or disappointed about it. ❍ *It's a shame about the weather.*

sham|poo /ʃæmpu/ **NONCOUNT NOUN Shampoo** is a liquid soap that you use for washing your hair. ❍ *Don't forget to pack a towel, soap, and shampoo.*

shape /ʃeɪp/ (**shapes, shaping, shaped**)
1 NOUN the form of the outside edges of something ❍ *Pasta comes in all different shapes and sizes.*
2 NOUN a form such as a circle, a square, or a triangle
3 VERB If you **shape** something, you give it a particular shape. ❍ *Shape the dough into a ball and place it in the bowl.*
4 If someone or something is **in good shape**, they are in a good state of health or in a good condition. ❍ *He's 76 and still in good shape.*
5 If you are **out of shape**, your body is not in a good condition. ❍ *I weighed 245 pounds and I was out of shape.*

share /ʃɛər/ (**shares, sharing, shared**)
1 VERB If you **share** something **with** another person, you both use it or both have part of it. ❍ *Jose shares an apartment with six other students.* ❍ *Maria and I shared a dessert.*
2 NOUN the part of something that you do or have ❍ *I need my share of the money now.*
3 NOUN one of the equal parts that the value of a company is divided into and that you can buy [FINANCE] ❍ *I've bought shares in my brother's new company.*

share capi|tal [FINANCE, BRIT] → **capital stock**

share cer|tifi|cate (**share certificates**) [FINANCE, BRIT] → **stock certificate**

share flo|ta|tion (**share flotations**) [ECONOMICS, BRIT] → **stock flotation**

share|holder /ʃɛərhoʊldər/ **NOUN** A **shareholder** is the same as a **stockholder**. [ECONOMICS]

share|holding /ʃɛərhoʊldɪŋ/ **NOUN** If you have a **shareholding** in a company, you own some of its shares. [ECONOMICS] ❍ *She will retain her very significant shareholding in the company.*

share in|dex [ECONOMICS, BRIT] → **stock index**

share is|sue [ECONOMICS, BRIT] → **stock issue**

share mar|ket [ECONOMICS, BRIT] → **stock market**

S

share of|fer|ing [ECONOMICS, BRIT] → **stock offering**

share op|tion [ECONOMICS, BRIT] → **stock option**

share price (**share prices**) NOUN the price at which a company's shares are bought and sold [ECONOMICS] ❍ *The impact is reflected in the company's share price, which has slumped to $10.13.*

share shop (**share shops**) NOUN a store or website where members of the public can buy shares in companies [ECONOMICS, BRIT]

sharia-compliant /ʃəriəkəmplaɪənt/ ADJ If a product or service is **sharia-compliant**, it is produced or offered in accordance with Islamic law. [ECONOMICS] ❍ *The number of sharia-compliant financial packages has grown in response to Muslims' beliefs about interest.*

shark /ʃɑrk/ NOUN a large, dangerous fish with sharp teeth

shark re|pell|ents /ʃɑrk rɪpɛlənts/ PL NOUN **Shark repellents** are arrangements made in the rules of a company to deter takeover bids.

sharp /ʃɑrp/
1 ADJ having a thin point or edge that can cut things ❍ *a sharp knife*
2 ADJ A **sharp** bend or turn changes direction suddenly.
3 ADV **Sharp** is also an adverb. ❍ *Turn sharp left.* ● **sharp|ly** ADV ❍ *After a mile, the road turns sharply to the right.*
4 ADJ good at noticing and understanding things ❍ *Dan's very sharp.*
5 ADJ showing that you are annoyed ❍ *His sharp reply surprised me.* ● **sharp|ly** ADV ❍ *"Why didn't you tell me?" she asked sharply.*
6 ADJ A **sharp** change is sudden and very big. ❍ *There's been a sharp rise in oil prices.* ● **sharp|ly** ADV ❍ *Unemployment rose sharply last year.*
7 ADJ A **sharp** pain is sudden and strong. ❍ *I felt a sharp pain in my right leg.*
8 ADJ A **sharp** image is very clear. ❍ *Digital TV offers sharper images.*
9 ADJ An F **sharp** or a G **sharp**, for example, is a note that is slightly higher than F or G. Compare with **flat**.

S

sharp|en /ʃɑrpən/ VERB If you **sharpen** something, you make its edge very thin or its end pointed. ❍ *Mike had to sharpen the pencils every morning.*

shat|ter /ʃætər/ VERB If something **shatters**, it breaks into small pieces. ❍ *The glass shattered on the floor.*

shave /ʃeɪv/ (**shaves, shaving, shaved**)
1 VERB If you **shave**, you remove hair from your face or body using a special knife (= a razor) or a piece of electric equipment (= a shaver). ❍ *Samuel took a bath and shaved.*
2 NOUN **Shave** is also a noun. ❍ *I need a shave.*

she /ʃɪ, STRONG ʃi/ PRON used to talk about a female person or animal when they are the subject of a sentence ❍ *She's seventeen years old.*

shed /ʃɛd/ (**sheds, shedding, shed**)
1 NOUN a small building where you store things ❍ *The house has a large shed in the backyard.*
2 NOUN a large retail outlet in the style of a warehouse ❍ *What happens when an entrepreneur needs to procure land or a shed in an industrial area?*
3 VERB If a company **sheds** jobs or workers, it abolishes or gets rid of them. ❍ *The company may need to shed about 100 of its 365 dealers.*

she'd /ʃid, ʃɪd/
1 **She'd** is short for "she had." ❍ *She'd been all over the world.*
2 **She'd** is short for "she would." ❍ *She'd do anything for a bit of money.*

sheep /ʃip/ (**sheep**) NOUN a farm animal with thick hair called wool

sheet /ʃit/
1 NOUN a large piece of cloth that you put on a bed ❍ *Once a week, we change the sheets.*
2 NOUN a flat piece of something such as paper or glass ❍ *Sean folded the sheets of paper.*

shelf /ʃɛlf/ (**shelves**)
1 NOUN a long flat piece of wood that you can keep things on ❍ *Dad took a book from the shelf.*
2 If you buy something **off the shelf**, you buy it from the stock of goods available in the store. ❍ *You can have this model off the shelf.* ❍ *an off-the-shelf model*

shell /ʃɛl/ **NOUN** the hard outer part of a nut, an egg, or some creatures ❍ *They cracked the nuts and removed their shells.* ❍ *I have gathered shells since I was a child.*

she'll /ʃil, ʃɪl/ **She'll** is short for "she will."

shell com|pa|ny (**shell companies**)
1 NOUN a company that another company takes over in order to use its name to gain an advantage [ECONOMICS] ❍ *The U.S. shell company was set up to mount a bid for Kingston Communications.*
2 NOUN a company that has been officially registered so that it can be used for fraud [ECONOMICS]

shel|ter /ʃɛltər/
1 NOUN a place that protects you from bad weather or danger ❍ *a bus shelter*
2 NONCOUNT NOUN Shelter is protection from bad weather or danger. ❍ *They took shelter under a tree.*

sher|iff /ʃɛrɪf/ **NOUN** a person who is elected to make sure that the law is obeyed in a particular county of the United States ❍ *the local sheriff*

she's /ʃiz, ʃɪz/
1 She's is short for "she is." ❍ *She's a really good boss.*
2 She's is short for "she has." ❍ *She's been in the post for seven years.*

shield /ʃild/
1 VERB If something or someone **shields** you **from** something, they protect you from it. ❍ *I shielded my eyes from the sun with my hands.*
2 NOUN a large object used by police and soldiers to protect their bodies

shift /ʃɪft/
1 VERB If you **shift** something, you move it to another place. ❍ *Please would you help me shift the table over to the window?*
2 NOUN a fixed period of work in a factory or a hospital [HR, PRODUCTION] ❍ *Nick works night shifts at the hospital.*

shift|work /ʃɪftwɜrk/ **NONCOUNT NOUN Shiftwork** is a system of employment where someone's hours of work may be in the evening or at night and may follow a different pattern in different weeks. [HR, PRODUCTION] ❍ *He loves shiftwork because he sees more of his infant children.*

shin /ʃɪn/ **NOUN** the front part of your leg between your knee and your ankle ❍ *Ken suffered a bruised left shin.*

shine /ʃaɪn/ (**shines, shining, shined** or **shone**)
1 VERB When the sun or a light **shines**, it gives out bright light. ❍ *Today it's warm and the sun is shining.*
2 VERB If you **shine** a light somewhere, you point it there. ❍ *The guard shone a light in his face.*

shiny /ʃaɪni/ (**shinier, shiniest**) **ADJ** If a surface is **shiny**, it is bright and reflects light. ❍ *Her blonde hair was shiny and clean.*

ship /ʃɪp/ (**ships, shipping, shipped**)
1 NOUN a large boat that carries people or goods ❍ *The ship was ready to sail.*
2 VERB If goods **are shipped** somewhere, they are sent there. ❍ *Our company ships orders worldwide.*

ship|builder /ʃɪpbɪldər/ **NOUN** a company or a person that builds ships

ship|ping ag|ent (**shipping agents**)
NOUN a person or a company whose business is to make arrangements to send goods on a ship or by some other means of transportation [ADMINISTRATION]

shirt /ʃɜrt/ **NOUN** a piece of clothing with a collar and buttons, that you wear on the top part of your body

shiv|er /ʃɪvər/
1 VERB If you **shiver**, your body shakes because you are cold, frightened, or sick. ❍ *She shivered with cold and fear.*
2 NOUN Shiver is also a noun. ❍ *She gave a small shiver.*

shock /ʃɒk/
1 NOUN a feeling of being very surprised and upset because something bad has happened ❍ *The shock of another steep plunge in stock prices will shake many investors' confidence.*
2 VERB If something **shocks** you, it surprises you and upsets you. ❍ *Some Wall Street observers were shocked by the charges.*

S

shock|ing /ʃɒkɪŋ/ ADJ making you feel very surprised and upset ❍ *The pound's sudden fall against the dollar has been shocking.*

shoe /ʃu/ NOUN **Shoes** are things that you wear on your feet. ❍ *I need a new pair of shoes.*

shone /ʃoʊn/ **Shone** is a form of the verb **shine**.

shook /ʃʊk/ **Shook** is a form of the verb **shake**.

shoot /ʃut/ (**shoots, shooting, shot**)
1 VERB If someone **shoots** a person or an animal, they kill them or injure them by firing a gun at them. ❍ *A man was shot dead during the robbery.*
2 VERB If someone **shoots**, they fire a bullet from a gun. ❍ *He shouted, "Don't shoot!"*
3 VERB When people **shoot** a movie, they make a movie. ❍ *Tim wants to shoot his new movie in Mexico.*
4 NOUN a new part that is growing from a plant ❍ *It was spring, and new shoots began to appear.*
5 VERB In soccer or basketball, when you **shoot**, you kick or throw the ball toward the goal or net. ❍ *Brennan shot and missed.*

shop /ʃɒp/ (**shops, shopping, shopped**)
1 NOUN a small store ❍ *Paul and his wife run a flower shop.*
2 VERB When you **shop**, you go to stores or shops and buy things. ❍ *He always shops on Saturday mornings.* ● **shop|per** NOUN ❍ *The streets were filled with crowds of shoppers.*

S

shop|keep|er /ʃɒpkipər/ [mainly BRIT] → **storekeeper**

shop|lift|ing /ʃɒplɪftɪŋ/ NONCOUNT NOUN **Shoplifting** is stealing from a store by hiding things in a bag or in your clothes. [LEGAL] ❍ *The grocer accused her of shoplifting and demanded to look in her bag.*

shop|ping /ʃɒpɪŋ/ NONCOUNT NOUN When you do **the shopping**, you go to stores or shops and buy things. ❍ *I'll do the shopping this afternoon.*

shop|ping cen|ter (**shopping centers**) NOUN a specially built area containing a lot of different stores [MARKETING AND SALES] ❍ *The new shopping center was constructed at a cost of $1.1 million.*

shop|ping chan|nel (**shopping channels**) NOUN a television channel that broadcasts programs showing products that you can buy over the phone or online [MARKETING AND SALES]

shop|ping mall (**shopping malls**) NOUN A **shopping mall** is the same as a **mall**.

shop stew|ard /ʃɒp stuərd/ (**shop stewards**) NOUN a labor union member who is elected by the other members in a factory or office to speak for them at official meetings

shop|walker /ʃɒpwɔkər/ [BRIT] → **floorwalker**

shore /ʃɔr/ NOUN the land along the edge of an ocean or lake ❍ *They walked slowly down to the shore.*

short /ʃɔrt/
1 ADJ not lasting very long ❍ *They lost 50% of their equity in a short period.*
2 ADJ not tall ❍ *She's a short woman with gray hair.*
3 ADJ not long ❍ *The restaurant is only a short distance away.* ❍ *She has short, curly hair.*
4 ADJ If you are **short of** something, you do not have enough of it. ❍ *His family is very short of money.*
5 ADJ A word that is **short for** another word is a shorter way of saying it. ❍ *Her name's Jo—it's short for Josephine.*
6 ADJ If an investor takes a **short** position in particular securities, they sell stocks they do not own expecting their value to fall in the future.
7 PL NOUN **Shorts** are pants with very short legs. ❍ *She was wearing pink shorts.*

short|age /ʃɔrtɪdʒ/ NOUN If there is a **shortage of** something, there is not enough of it. ❍ *There is not likely to be a shortage of buyers.*

short|en /ʃɔrtᵊn/ VERB If you **shorten** something, you make it shorter. ❍ *Such steps may help to shorten the recession.*

short-handed also **shorthanded** ADJ If a company or an organization is **short-**

handed, it does not have enough people to work on a particular job or for a particular purpose. ❍ *We're actually a bit short-handed at the moment.*

short|list /ʃɔrtlɪst/ also **short list**
1 NOUN A **shortlist** is a list of a few suitable applicants for a job from which the successful person will be chosen. Compare with **long list**. [HR] ❍ *If you've been asked for an interview you are probably on a shortlist of no more than six.*
2 VERB If someone or something **is shortlisted for** a job, they are put on a shortlist. [HR] ❍ *He was shortlisted for the job.*

short|ly /ʃɔrtli/ **ADV** soon ❍ *"Please take a seat. Dr. Garcia will see you shortly."*

short sell|ing **NONCOUNT NOUN** **Short selling** is the practice of selling stocks and currencies that you do not have, hoping that falling prices will enable you to buy them back at a profit before they have to be returned to their owner. [ECONOMICS] ❍ *Regulatory action is needed to limit the use of short selling in these markets.*

short-staffed **ADJ** A company or place that is **short-staffed** does not have enough people working there. ❍ *The hospital is desperately short-staffed.*

short-term **ADJ** lasting for a short period of time ❍ *The company has 90 staff, almost all on short-term contracts.*

COLLOCATIONS
a short-term *investment*
a short-term *rate*

short-term li|abil|ities **PL NOUN** **Short-term liabilities** are debts that a company has to pay back in less than a year. Compare with **long-term liabilities**.

short time or **short-time working** **NONCOUNT NOUN** **Short time** is a temporary system of working when employees are required to work and be paid for fewer than their normal hours per week due to a shortage of work. ❍ *Germany's workforce is either unemployed or on short-time working.*

shot /ʃɒt/
1 Shot is a form of the verb **shoot**.
2 NOUN an act of firing a gun ❍ *The man was killed with a single shot.*
3 NOUN an act of kicking, hitting, or throwing the ball, to try to score a point ❍ *Grant missed two shots at the goal.*
4 NOUN a photograph ❍ *The photographer got some great shots of the bride.*

shot|gun wed|ding /ʃɒtgʌn wɛdɪŋ/ (**shotgun weddings**)
1 NOUN a wedding that has to take place quickly, often because the woman is pregnant
2 NOUN a merger between two companies that takes place in a hurry because one or both of the companies is having difficulties ❍ *Two of the world's top four computer manufacturers have announced a shotgun wedding prompted by slumping sales and disastrous financial losses.*

should /ʃəd, STRONG ʃʊd/
1 MODAL used for saying what is the right thing to do ❍ *You should take on more staff.*
2 MODAL used for saying that something is probably true or will probably happen ❍ *You should have no problems with this exercise.*
3 MODAL used for asking for advice ❍ *What should I do?*

shoul|der /ʃoʊldər/ **NOUN** one of the two parts of your body between your neck and the tops of your arms ❍ *She put her arm around his shoulders.*

shouldn't /ʃʊdᵊnt/ **Shouldn't** is short for "should not."

should've /ʃʊdəv/ **Should've** is short for "should have."

shout /ʃaʊt/
1 VERB If you **shout**, you say something very loudly. ❍ *"She's alive!" he shouted.*
2 NOUN **Shout** is also a noun. ❍ *There were angry shouts from the crowd.*

shove /ʃʌv/ (**shoves, shoving, shoved**)
VERB If you **shove** someone or something, you push them roughly. ❍ *The woman shoved the other customers out of the way.*

shov|el /ʃʌvᵊl/ **NOUN** a flat tool with a handle that is used for moving earth or snow ❍ *I'll need the coal shovel.*

show /ʃoʊ/ (**shows, showing, showed, shown**)
1 VERB If information or a fact **shows that** a situation exists, it proves it. ❍ *The setback in gold shows that the metal is still in a downward trend.*
2 VERB If you **show** someone something, you let them see it. ❍ *She showed me her sales forecast.*
3 VERB If you **show** someone how to do something, you teach them how to do it. ❍ *Claire showed us how to extract the data we needed.*
4 VERB If something **shows**, it is easy to notice. ❍ *When I feel angry, it shows.*
5 NOUN a television or radio program, or a theater performance ❍ *I never missed his TV show when I was a kid.*
▸**show off** If someone **is showing off**, they are trying to make people admire them. ❍ *He spent the entire evening showing off.*
▸**show up** If a person **shows up**, they arrive at a place. ❍ *We waited until five, but he didn't show up.*

show bag (**show bags**) NOUN A **show bag** is the same as a **sample bag**.

show|er /ʃaʊər/
1 NOUN a device that you stand under to wash yourself ❍ *I was in the shower when the phone rang.*
2 NOUN If you take a **shower**, you wash yourself under a shower. ❍ *I think I'll take a shower.*
3 VERB If you **shower**, you wash yourself under a shower. ❍ *I was late and there wasn't time to shower.*
4 NOUN a short period of rain ❍ *A few showers are expected Saturday.*
5 NOUN a party for a woman who is getting married or having a baby ❍ *Kelly's baby shower is on Thursday night.*

S

shown /ʃoʊn/ **Shown** is a form of the verb **show**.

show|room /ʃoʊrum/ NOUN a store in which goods such as cars or domestic appliances are displayed for sale [MARKETING AND SALES] ❍ *a car showroom*

shrimp /ʃrɪmp/ (**shrimp**)

The plural can also be **shrimps**.

NOUN a small pink or gray sea animal, with a long tail that you can eat ❍ *Add the shrimp and cook for 30 seconds.*

shrink /ʃrɪŋk/ (**shrinks, shrinking, shrank** or **shrunk, shrunk**) VERB If something **shrinks**, it becomes smaller. ❍ *Dad's pants shrank after just one wash.*

shrub /ʃrʌb/ NOUN a small bush

shrug /ʃrʌg/ (**shrugs, shrugging, shrugged**)
1 VERB If you **shrug**, you move your shoulders up to show that you do not know or care about something. ❍ *Melissa just shrugged and replied, "I don't know."*
2 NOUN **Shrug** is also a noun. ❍ *"Who cares?" said Anna with a shrug.*

shrunk /ʃrʌŋk/ **Shrunk** is a form of the verb **shrink**.

shud|der /ʃʌdər/ VERB If you **shudder**, your body shakes because you feel disgust or fear. ❍ *Some people shudder at the idea of injections.*

shuf|fle /ʃʌfᵊl/ (**shuffles, shuffling, shuffled**)
1 VERB If you **shuffle**, you walk without lifting your feet off the ground. ❍ *Moira shuffled across the kitchen.*
2 VERB If you **shuffle** playing cards, you mix them up. ❍ *Aunt Mary shuffled the cards.*

shut /ʃʌt/ (**shuts, shutting, shut**)
1 VERB If you **shut** something, you close it, and if it shuts, it closes. ❍ *Please shut the gate.* ❍ *Lucy shut her eyes and fell asleep at once.*
2 ADJ **Shut** is also an adjective. ❍ *The police have told us to keep our doors and windows shut.* ❍ *Her eyes were shut and she seemed to be asleep.*
▸**shut down** If a business **shuts down**, it closes. ❍ *The factory was shut down last month.*
▸**shut up** If you tell someone to **shut up**, you are telling them, in a rude way, to be quiet. ❍ *Just shut up, will you?*

shut|down /ʃʌtdaʊn/ NOUN the closing of a factory, store, or other business ❍ *The shutdown is the latest in a series of painful budget measures.*

shut|ter /ʃʌtər/ NOUN a wooden or metal cover on the outside of a window ❍ *She opened the shutters and looked out of the window.*

shut|tle /ʃʌtᵊl/ NOUN a plane, a bus, or a train that makes regular trips between two places ❍ *There is a free shuttle between the airport terminals.*

shy /ʃaɪ/ ADJ nervous about talking to people that you do not know well ❍ *I was too shy to say anything.* ● **shy|ly** ADV ❍ *The children smiled shyly.* ● **shy|ness** NONCOUNT NOUN ❍ *His shyness made it difficult for him to make friends.*

sib|ling /sɪblɪŋ/ NOUN a brother or sister [FORMAL] ❍ *I often had to take care of my five younger siblings.*

sick /sɪk/

1 ADJ If you are **sick**, you are not well. ❍ *He's very sick. He needs a doctor.*

2 ADJ If you are **sick of** something, you are very annoyed by it and want it to stop. [INFORMAL] ❍ *I am sick of all your complaints!*

3 If you are **out sick**, you are not at work because you are sick. ❍ *Tom is out sick today.*

sick leave NONCOUNT NOUN **Sick leave** is the time that a person spends away from work because of illness or injury. [HR] ❍ *I have been on sick leave for seven months with depression.*

sick|ness /sɪknɪs/ NONCOUNT NOUN **Sickness** is the state of not being well. ❍ *Grandpa had only one week of sickness in fifty-two years.*

sick pay NONCOUNT NOUN When you are ill and unable to work, **sick pay** is the money that you get from your employer instead of your normal wages. [HR] ❍ *They are not eligible for sick pay.*

BUSINESS ETIQUETTE
In Japan and Hong Kong, it is normal to noisily suck your noodles into your mouth. This will show others that you are enjoying your food.

side /saɪd/

1 NOUN a position to the left or right of something ❍ *On the left side of the door there's a door bell.*

2 NOUN a surface or edge of an object that is not its front, back, top, or bottom ❍ *He took me along the side of the house.* ❍ *We parked on the side of the road.*

3 NOUN one of the two surfaces of something thin ❍ *You should write on both sides of the paper.*

4 NOUN one of the groups of people who are fighting or playing against each other ❍ *Both sides want the dispute to end.*

5 If you are **on** someone's **side**, you are supporting them in an argument. ❍ *Whose side are you on?*

6 If two people or things are **side by side**, they are next to each other. ❍ *The children were sitting side by side on the sofa.*

side deal (**side deals**) NOUN a transaction between two people for their private benefit, that is separate from a contract negotiated by them on behalf of the organizations they represent ❍ *Our attorney suggests our buyers do a side deal with us outside of the contract.*

side|walk /saɪdwɔk/ NOUN a path with a hard surface by the side of a road ❍ *She was walking down the sidewalk toward him.*

side|ways /saɪdweɪz/ ADV or ADJ from or toward the side ❍ *Pete looked sideways at her.* ❍ *Alfred gave him a sideways look.*

sigh /saɪ/

1 VERB If you **sigh**, you let out a deep breath. ❍ *Roberta sighed with relief.*

2 NOUN **Sigh** is also a noun. ❍ *Maria sat down with a sigh.*

sight /saɪt/

1 NONCOUNT NOUN Your **sight** is your ability to see. ❍ *Grandpa has lost the sight in his right eye.*

2 NOUN something you see or the act of seeing it ❍ *Liz can't bear the sight of blood.*

3 PL NOUN **The sights** are interesting places that tourists visit. ❍ *We saw the sights of Paris.*

4 If you **catch sight of** someone or something, you suddenly see them for a short time. ❍ *He caught sight of Helen in the crowd.*

5 If something is **in sight**, you can see it. If it is **out of sight**, you cannot see it. ❍ *At last the town was in sight.*

sight bill (**sight bills**) or **sight draft** NOUN A **sight bill** or **sight draft** is the same as a **demand bill**. [BANKING]

sight|see|ing /saɪtsiɪŋ/ NONCOUNT NOUN **Sightseeing** is visiting places that tourists usually go to. ❍ *We had a day's sightseeing in Venice.*

sign /saɪn/
1 NOUN a mark, a shape, or a movement that has a particular meaning ❍ *In math, + is a plus sign.* ❍ *They gave me a sign to show that everything was OK.*
2 NOUN a board with words or pictures that give information or instructions ❍ *road signs*
3 NOUN something that shows that something exists or is happening ❍ *Matthew showed no sign of fear.*
4 VERB When you **sign** a document, you write your name on it. ❍ *I signed the contracct.*

sig|nal /sɪgnəl/
1 NOUN a movement, a sound, or a piece of equipment that gives a message to the person who sees or hears it ❍ *The captain gave the signal for the soldiers to attack.*
2 VERB If you **signal to** someone, you make a movement or sound to give them a message. ❍ *Mandy signaled to Jesse to follow her.*

sig|na|ture /sɪgnətʃər, -tʃʊər/ **NOUN** your name, written by you [ADMINISTRATION] ❍ *I put my signature at the bottom of the page.*

sign|board /saɪnbɔrd/ **NOUN** a board carrying a sign or notice, used to advertise a product, event, etc. [MARKETING AND SALES]

sig|nifi|cance /sɪgnɪfɪkəns/ **NONCOUNT NOUN** The **significance** of something is its importance or meaning. ❍ *What do you think is the significance of this event?*

sig|nifi|cant /sɪgnɪfɪkənt/ **ADJ** important or large ❍ *There has been a significant increase in the price of oil.* ● **sig|nifi|cant|ly ADV** ❍ *The firm expects significantly lower earnings for the year.*

S

Sikh /sik/ **NOUN** a person who follows the Indian religion called **Sikhism** ❍ *a Sikh temple*

si|lence /saɪləns/ **NONCOUNT NOUN** If there is **silence**, no one is speaking and there is no sound. ❍ *They stood in silence.* ❍ *There was a long silence before Sarah replied.*

si|lent /saɪlənt/
1 ADJ If you are **silent**, you are not speaking. ❍ *Jessica was silent.* ● **si|lent|ly ADV** ❍ *She and Ned sat silently, enjoying the peace.*
2 ADJ completely quiet or making no sound ❍ *The room was silent except for the TV.* ● **si|lent|ly ADV** ❍ *The thief moved silently across the room.*

si|lent part|ner (**silent partners**) **NOUN** a person who provides some of the capital for a business but who does not take an active part in managing the business ❍ *firms run by his friends in which he was a silent partner*

silk /sɪlk/ **NONCOUNT NOUN** **Silk** is a smooth, shiny, thin cloth. ❍ *Pauline was wearing a beautiful silk dress.*

sil|ly /sɪli/ (**sillier, silliest**) **ADJ** not sensible or serious ❍ *"Don't be so silly, darling!"*

sil|ver /sɪlvər/
1 NONCOUNT NOUN **Silver** is a valuable pale gray metal that is used for making jewelry. ❍ *He bought her a bracelet made from silver.*
2 ADJ the color of silver ❍ *He had thick silver hair.*

SIM card /sɪm kɑrd/ **NOUN** a small electronic part in a cellphone that contains information about you

simi|lar /sɪmɪlər/ **ADJ** the same in some ways but not in every way ❍ *ECB will cut rates soon, as it did in similar circumstances in 2001.*

simi|lar|ity /sɪmɪlærɪti/ (**similarities**) **NOUN** one of the things that are the same about two people or things ❍ *There are many similarities between their products.*

sim|ple /sɪmpᵊl/ (**simpler, simplest**)
1 ADJ easy to understand ❍ *Just follow the simple instructions below.*
2 ADJ plain in style ❍ *Amanda was wearing a simple black silk dress.*

sim|ple in|ter|est **NONCOUNT NOUN** **Simple interest** is interest that is calculated only on an original sum of money. Compare with **compound interest**. [BANKING] ❍ *an investment that pays only simple interest*

sim|plic|ity /sɪmplɪsɪti/ **NONCOUNT NOUN** **Simplicity** is the quality of being simple. ❍ *I love the simplicity of his designs.*

sim|pli|fy /sɪmplɪfaɪ/ (**simplifies, simplifying, simplified**) **VERB** If you **simplify** something, you make it easier to understand or to do. ❍ *This program simplifies the task of searching for information.* ● **sim|pli|fied ADJ**

❍ *Key managers have adopted a simplified model of what works in the market.*

simp|ly /sɪmpli/
1 ADV in a way that is easy to understand ❍ *He explained his views simply and clearly.*
2 ADV used to emphasize what you are saying ❍ *Your behavior is simply unacceptable.*
3 ADV in a plain style ❍ *Her house is decorated simply.*

sin /sɪn/ (**sins, sinning, sinned**)
1 NOUN an action that breaks a religious law ❍ *They believe that lying is a sin.*
2 VERB If you **sin**, you do something that breaks a religious law. ❍ *The Bible says that we have all sinned.* ● **sin|ner** /sɪnər/ **NOUN** ❍ *Is she a sinner or a saint?*

since /sɪns/
1 PREP or **ADV** or **CONJ** from a time in the past until now ❍ *Yields have dropped below 9% for the first time since February.* ❍ *They worked together in the 1980s, and have been friends ever since.* ❍ *I've lived here since I was six years old.*
2 CONJ because ❍ *Harvard does not like to reveal how much he earns, since financial salaries are so much higher than academic salaries.*

sin|cere /sɪnsɪər/ **ADJ** honest and really meaning what you say ❍ *Do you think Ryan's being sincere?*

sin|cere|ly /sɪnsɪərli/
1 ADV in a sincere way ❍ *"Well done!" he said sincerely.*
2 You write "**Sincerely yours**" or "**Sincerely**" before your signature at the end of a formal letter. ❍ *Sincerely yours, Robbie Weinz.*

sing /sɪŋ/ (**sings, singing, sang, sung**) **VERB** When you **sing**, you make music with your voice. ❍ *I love singing.* ❍ *My brother and I used to sing this song.*

sing|er /sɪŋər/ **NOUN** a person who sings, especially as a job ❍ *My mother was a singer in a band.*

sin|gle /sɪŋgᵊl/
1 ADJ only one ❍ *We sold over two hundred pizzas in a single day.*
2 ADJ not married ❍ *Joseph is a single man.*
3 ADJ intended for one person only ❍ *Would you like a single or a double room?*

single-entry ADJ **Single-entry** bookkeeping is a system of bookkeeping in which transactions are entered in one account only. Compare with **double-entry**. ❍ *a single-entry account*

sin|gu|lar /sɪŋgyələr/
1 ADJ The **singular** form of a word is the form that you use to talk about one person or thing. ❍ *The singular form of "mice" is "mouse."*
2 NOUN **The singular** is the singular form of a word. ❍ *What is the singular of "geese?"*

sink /sɪŋk/ (**sinks, sinking, sank, sunk**)
1 NOUN a large bowl that is fixed to a wall in a kitchen or bathroom and has parts that supply water ❍ *The sink was filled with dirty dishes.*
2 VERB If a boat **sinks**, it goes under the water. ❍ *The boat hit the rocks and began to sink.*
3 VERB If something **sinks** to a lower level or standard, it falls to that level or standard. ❍ *Pay increases have sunk to around seven percent.* ❍ *The pound had sunk 10% against the schilling.*
4 VERB If you **sink** money into something, you invest money in it. ❍ *The defense contractor has sunk more than $1 billion of its own money into developing the company.*

sip /sɪp/ (**sips, sipping, sipped**)
1 VERB If you **sip** a drink, you drink it slowly, taking a small amount at a time. ❍ *Jessica sipped her drink.*
2 NOUN a small amount of drink that you take into your mouth ❍ *Harry took a sip of tea.*

sir /sɜr/
1 NOUN used as a polite way of talking to a man ❍ *Excuse me sir, is this your car?*
2 You write "**Dear Sir**" at the beginning of a formal letter when you are writing to a man. ❍ *Dear Sir, Thank you for your letter.*

si|ren /saɪrən/ **NOUN** a piece of equipment that makes a long, loud noise to warn people about something ❍ *In the distance I could hear a siren.*

sis|ter /sɪstər/ **NOUN** a girl or woman who has the same parents as you ❍ *This is my sister Sarah.*

sis|ter com|pany (**sister companies**) **NOUN** **Sister companies** are companies that are owned by the same parent organization. [ECONOMICS] ❍ *As its reputation spreads it has increasing potential to grow into a brand as strong as that of its advertising sister company.*

sister-in-law (**sisters-in-law**) NOUN the sister of your husband or wife, or the woman who is married to their brother

sit /sɪt/ (**sits, sitting, sat**) VERB If you **are sitting** somewhere, your bottom is resting on something and the upper part of your body is straight. ❍ *Dan was sitting at his desk, reading.*
▸ **sit down** If you **sit down**, you move your body down until you are sitting on something. ❍ *Kath sat down beside me.*
▸ **sit up** If you **sit up**, you change the position of your body, so that you are sitting instead of lying down. ❍ *She felt dizzy when she sat up.*

sit-down strike (**sit-down strikes**) NOUN a strike in which workers refuse to leave their place of employment until an agreement is reached ❍ *A long strike by members of the local branch has led to attacks on replacement workers and sit-down strikes by both sides.*

site /saɪt/
1 NOUN a place where a particular thing happens or exists ❍ *Dad works on a building site.*
2 NOUN A **site** is the same as a **website**. ❍ *The site earns its revenue from advertisers.*

sit-in NOUN a protest in which people go to a public place and stay there for a long time ❍ *The campaigners held a sit-in outside the Supreme Court.*

S

situ|at|ed /sɪtʃueɪtɪd/ ADJ If something is **situated** in a particular place, it is in that place. ❍ *Their office is situated in the center of Berlin.*

situa|tion /sɪtʃueɪʃən/ NOUN the things that are happening and the way things are in a particular place at a particular time ❍ *There has been a huge improvement in the economic situation.*

six /sɪks/ the number 6

six|teen /sɪkstin/ the number 16

six|teenth /sɪkstinθ/ ADJ or ADV The **sixteenth** item in a series is the one that you count as number sixteen. ❍ *the sixteenth century*

sixth /sɪksθ/
1 ADJ or ADV The **sixth** item in a series is the one that you count as number six. ❍ *The sixth round of the competition begins tomorrow.* ❍ *Brad came sixth in the swimming race.*
2 NOUN one of six equal parts of something (⅙)

six|ti|eth /sɪkstiəθ/ ADJ or ADV The **sixtieth** item in a series is the one that you count as number sixty. ❍ *his sixtieth birthday*

six|ty /sɪksti/ the number 60 ❍ *We rode sixty miles on our bikes.*

size /saɪz/
1 NOUN how big or small something is ❍ *The size of the room is about 10 feet by 15 feet.* ❍ *The shelves contain books of various sizes.* ● **-sized** ADJ ❍ *I work for a medium-sized company in Chicago.*
2 NOUN one of a series of measurements for clothes and shoes ❍ *My sister is a size 12.*

skate /skeɪt/ (**skates, skating, skated**)
1 NOUN **Skates** (or **ice-skates**) are boots with a long, sharp piece of metal on the bottom for moving on ice.
2 NOUN **Skates** (or **roller-skates**) are boots with wheels on the bottom.
3 VERB If you **skate**, you move around wearing skates. ❍ *When the pond froze, we skated on it.* ● **skat|ing** NONCOUNT NOUN ❍ *They all went skating together in the winter.* ● **skat|er** NOUN ❍ *The ice-rink was full of skaters.*

skel|eton /skɛlɪtᵊn/ NOUN all the bones in a person's or an animal's body ❍ *a human skeleton*

skep|ti|cal /skɛptɪkᵊl/ ADJ If you are **skeptical about** something, you have doubts about it. ❍ *Many analysts are highly skeptical of the firm's prospects.*

sketch /skɛtʃ/ (**sketches, sketching, sketched**)
1 NOUN a drawing that you do quickly, without a lot of details ❍ *He did a quick sketch of the building.*
2 VERB If you **sketch** something, you make a quick drawing of it. ❍ *She started sketching designs.*

ski /ski/ (**skis, skiing, skied**)
1 NOUN Skis are long, flat, narrow objects that you fasten to your boots so that you can move easily on snow.
2 VERB When you **ski**, you move over snow on skis. ❍ *They tried to ski down Mount Everest.*
● **ski|er** /skiər/ **NOUN** ❍ *My dad's a very good skier.* ● **ski|ing NONCOUNT NOUN** ❍ *My hobbies are skiing and swimming.*

skid /skɪd/ (**skids, skidding, skidded**) **VERB** If a vehicle **skids**, it slides in a way that is not controlled. ❍ *The car skidded on the icy road.*

skil|ful /skɪlfəl/ [mainly BRIT] → **skillful**

skill /skɪl/
1 NOUN a job or an activity that needs special training and practice [BUSINESS MANAGEMENT] ❍ *You're never too old to learn new skills.*
2 NONCOUNT NOUN Skill is the ability to do something well. ❍ *Last year's IT installation problems raise questions about the quality and depth of management skill.*

skilled /skɪld/ **ADJ** having the knowledge and ability to do something well [BUSINESS MANAGEMENT] ❍ *skilled workers*

skill|ful /skɪlfəl/ **ADJ** able to do something very well ❍ *We need skillful, hands-on managers.* ● **skill|ful|ly ADV** ❍ *Murthy has skillfully steered the company through a difficult time.*

skin /skɪn/
1 NONCOUNT NOUN Skin is the substance that covers the outside of a person's or an animal's body. ❍ *His skin is pale and smooth.* ❍ *a crocodile skin handbag*
2 NOUN The **skin** of a fruit or a vegetable is its outer layer. ❍ *a banana skin*

skin|ny /skɪni/ (**skinnier, skinniest**) **ADJ** very thin [INFORMAL] ❍ *He was a skinny little boy.*

skip /skɪp/ (**skips, skipping, skipped**)
1 VERB If you **skip** somewhere, you move quickly, jumping from one foot to the other. ❍ *We skipped down the street.*
2 VERB If you **skip** something, you decide not to do it or have it. ❍ *Don't skip breakfast.*

skirt /skɜrt/ **NOUN** a piece of clothing for women and girls that hangs down from the waist

skull /skʌl/ **NOUN** the bones in your head that protect your brain ❍ *After the accident, they X-rayed his skull.*

sky /skaɪ/ (**skies**) **NOUN** the space above the Earth that you can see when you stand outside and look upward ❍ *The sun was shining in the sky.*

slab /slæb/ **NOUN** a thick, flat piece of something ❍ *slabs of stone*

slack /slæk/
1 ADJ loose ❍ *Suddenly, the rope went slack.*
2 ADJ A **slack** period is a time when you are not busy. ❍ *The store has busy times and slack periods.*

slam /slæm/ (**slams, slamming, slammed**)
1 VERB If you **slam** a door, you shut it very noisily and roughly. ❍ *She slammed the door behind her.*
2 VERB If you **slam** something **down**, you put it there noisily and roughly. ❍ *Lauren slammed the phone down.*

slang /slæŋ/ **NONCOUNT NOUN Slang** is very informal words. ❍ *The slang word for "money" is "dough."*

slant /slænt/ **VERB** If something **slants**, it has one side higher than the other. ❍ *The roof of the house slants sharply.*

slap /slæp/ (**slaps, slapping, slapped**)
1 VERB If you **slap** someone, you hit them with the flat inside part of your hand. ❍ *I slapped him hard across the face.*
2 NOUN Slap is also a noun. ❍ *She gave him a slap on the face.*

slash /slæʃ/
1 VERB If you **slash** something, you make a long, deep cut in it. ❍ *Someone slashed my car tires in the night.*
2 VERB If you **slash** prices, you reduce them by a large amount. ❍ *The store yesterday slashed the price of nearly every book in stock by 25%.*
3 NOUN a line (/) that separates numbers, letters, or words

slaugh|ter /slɔtər/
1 VERB If people or animals **are slaughtered**,

they are killed. ❍ *So many innocent people have been slaughtered.* ❍ *The farmers here slaughter their own cows.*

2 NONCOUNT NOUN Slaughter is also a noun. ❍ *The slaughter of women and children was common.*

slave /sleɪv/ (**slaves, slaving, slaved**)

1 NOUN a person who belongs to another person and has to work for them

2 VERB If you **slave**, you work very hard. ❍ *He was slaving away in the hot kitchen.*

sleep /slip/ (**sleeps, sleeping, slept**)

1 NONCOUNT NOUN Sleep is a person's or an animal's state of rest when their eyes are closed, and their body is not active. ❍ *Try to get as much sleep as possible.*

2 VERB When you **are sleeping**, your eyes are closed and your mind and body are not active. ❍ *I didn't sleep well last night.*

3 NOUN a period of sleeping ❍ *Good morning, Pete. Did you have a good sleep?*

4 When you **go to sleep**, you start sleeping. ❍ *Be quiet and go to sleep!*

sleep|ing part|ner [ECONOMICS, BRIT] → **silent partner**

sleepy /slipi/ (**sleepier, sleepiest**) **ADJ** very tired and almost asleep ❍ *The pills made me sleepy.*

sleeve /sliv/ **NOUN** the part of a piece of clothing that covers your arm ❍ *a blue dress with long sleeves*

slen|der /slɛndər/

1 ADJ thin in an attractive, graceful way ❍ *She was tall and slender, like a dancer.*

2 ADJ very small or inadequate in amount, size, etc ❍ *Lightly processed or generic products tend to have slender margins.*

slept /slɛpt/ **Slept** is a form of the verb **sleep**.

slice /slaɪs/ (**slices, slicing, sliced**)

1 NOUN a thin piece that you cut from a larger amount of something ❍ *a large slice of chocolate cake*

2 VERB If you **slice** food, you cut it into thin pieces. ❍ *I blew out the candles and Mom sliced the cake.*

slide /slaɪd/ (**slides, sliding, slid**)

1 VERB When someone or something **slides**, they move quickly and smoothly over a surface. ❍ *She slid across the ice on her stomach.*

2 VERB When something **slides**, it slowly becomes worse or lower in value. ❍ *After-tax profits slid 1.4%, to $136 million from $138 million a year earlier.* ❍ *Exports will continue to slide this year.*

3 NOUN a large metal frame with a smooth slope that children can slide down

slid|ing scale (**sliding scales**) **NOUN** Payments that are calculated **on a sliding scale** are higher or lower depending on various different factors. ❍ *Many practitioners have a sliding scale of fees.*

slight /slaɪt/

1 ADJ small and not important or serious ❍ *a slight increase in sales*

2 ADJ thin and not strong looking ❍ *She had a slight build.*

slight|ly /slaɪtli/ **ADV** just a little ❍ *They bought the shares at slightly higher prices.*

slim /slɪm/ (**slimmer, slimmest, slims, slimming, slimmed**)

1 ADJ thin in an attractive way ❍ *The young woman was tall and slim.*

2 VERB If an organization **slims** its products or workers, it reduces the number of them that it has. [BUSINESS MANAGEMENT] ❍ *The company recently slimmed its product line.*

▸ **slim down**

1 If you **slim down**, you become thinner. ❍ *I've slimmed down a size or two.*

2 If an organization **slims down** or **is slimmed down**, it employs fewer people, in order to save money or become more efficient. [BUSINESS MANAGEMENT] ❍ *Many firms have had little choice but to slim down.* ❍ *Pension reform will help slim down the civil service.*

slip /slɪp/ (**slips, slipping, slipped**)

1 VERB If you **slip**, you accidentally slide and fall. ❍ *He slipped on the wet grass.*

2 VERB If something **slips**, it slides out of position. ❍ *Grandpa's glasses slipped down his nose.*

3 VERB If you **slip** somewhere, you go there quickly and quietly. ❍ *She quietly slipped out of the house.*

4 VERB If you **slip** something somewhere, you put it there quickly and quietly. ❍ *I slipped the letter into my pocket.*
5 NOUN a small mistake ❍ *Even a tiny slip could ruin everything.*
6 NOUN A **slip of** paper is a small piece of paper.
▸ **slip up** If you **slip up**, you make a mistake. ❍ *We slipped up a few times, but no-one noticed.*

slip|per /slɪpər/ **NOUN** a soft shoe that you wear indoors ❍ *She put on a pair of slippers and went downstairs.*

slip|pery /slɪpəri/ **ADJ** smooth or wet, and difficult to walk on or to hold ❍ *Be careful—the floor is slippery.*

slo|gan /sloʊgən/ **NOUN** a short phrase that is used in advertisements or by political parties ❍ *His campaign slogan was "Time for Action."*

slo|gan|eer /sloʊgənɪər/
1 NOUN a person who invents slogans, or uses them frequently ❍ *Wall Street's sloganeers advised us to "sell in May and go away."*
2 VERB When a company **sloganeers**, it invents or uses slogans in order to sway opinion. [MARKETING AND SALES] ❍ *"It's time to put people in front of profits," sloganeered the president of the city's Central Labor Council.*

slope /sloʊp/ (**slopes, sloping, sloped**)
1 NOUN a flat surface with one end higher than the other ❍ *A steep slope leads to the beach.*
2 VERB If a surface **slopes**, one end of it is higher than the other. ❍ *The land sloped down sharply to the river.*

slop|py /slɒpi/ (**sloppier, sloppiest**) **ADJ** done in a careless and lazy way ❍ *I hate sloppy work from my team.*

slot /slɒt/ **NOUN** a long, narrow hole ❍ *Please place your credit card in the slot.*

slow /sloʊ/
1 ADJ not moving or happening quickly ❍ *His bike was heavy and slow.* ❍ *The investigation was a long and slow process.* ● **slow|ly ADV** ❍ *He spoke slowly and clearly.*
2 ADJ If a clock or a watch is **slow**, it shows a time that is earlier than the correct time. ❍ *The clock is five minutes slow.*
▸ **slow down** If something **slows down**, it starts to move or happen more slowly. ❍ *The bus slowed down for the next stop.*

slow|down /sloʊdaʊn/
1 NOUN a reduction in speed or activity [ECONOMICS] ❍ *a slowdown in economic growth*
2 NOUN a protest in which workers deliberately work slowly and cause problems for their employers [HR] ❍ *It's impossible to assess how many officers are participating in the slowdown.*

slow mo|tion also **slow-motion**
NONCOUNT NOUN When film or television pictures are shown **in slow motion**, they are shown much more slowly than normal. ❍ *They played it again in slow motion.*

slum /slʌm/ **NOUN** an area of a city where the buildings are in a bad condition and the people are very poor ❍ *More than 2.4 million people live in the city's slums.*

slump /slʌmp/
1 VERB If the value or quantity of something **slumps**, it falls suddenly. [ECONOMICS] ❍ *The company's profits slumped by 41% in a single year.* ❍ *In the same period, productivity slumped and labor costs climbed.*
2 NOUN Slump is also a noun. ❍ *There has been a slump in house prices.*
3 VERB If you **slump** somewhere, you fall or sit down suddenly and heavily. ❍ *She slumped into a chair and burst into tears.*

COLLOCATIONS
an *economic* slump
a *market* slump
a slump *in sales*
a slump *in profits*
a slump *in demand*

smack /smæk/
1 VERB If you **smack** someone, you hit them with the inside part of your hand. ❍ *She smacked me on the side of the head.*
2 NOUN Smack is also a noun. ❍ *She gave him a smack.*

small /smɔl/
1 ADJ not large ❍ *My daughter is small for her age.* ❍ *He runs a small construction business.*

S

2 ADJ A **small** child is a young child. ❍ *I have two small children.*

3 ADJ not very serious or important ❍ *It's a small problem, and we can easily solve it.*

small busi|ness (**small businesses**) NOUN a business that does not employ many people and earns relatively little money [ECONOMICS] ❍ *The move could finally reduce borrowing costs for consumers and small businesses.*

small-scale ADJ limited in extent ❍ *the small-scale production of farmhouse cheeses in Vermont*

smart /smart/ ADJ intelligent ❍ *He's a very smart guy.*

smart|phone /smartfoʊn/ NOUN a type of cellphone that can do many of the things that a computer does

smash /smæʃ/ (**smashes, smashing, smashed**)

1 VERB If you **smash** something, you break it into many pieces. ❍ *The gang started smashing windows in the street.* ❍ *I dropped the bottle and it smashed on the floor.*

2 VERB If you **smash** a business or a person, you make them bankrupt. ❍ *With this power he was able to smash most of his competitors.*

smell /smɛl/

1 NOUN a quality that you notice when you use your nose ❍ *the smell of freshly baked bread*

2 VERB If something **smells** a particular way, it has a quality that you notice when you use your nose. ❍ *The room smelled of lemons.* ❍ *The soup smells delicious!*

3 VERB If something **smells**, it smells unpleasant. ❍ *My girlfriend says my feet smell.*

4 VERB If you **smell** something, you notice it when you use your nose. ❍ *We could smell smoke.*

smile /smaɪl/ (**smiles, smiling, smiled**)

1 VERB If you **smile**, the corners of your mouth curve up because you are happy or you think that something is funny. ❍ *When he saw me, he smiled.*

2 NOUN the expression that you have on your face when you smile ❍ *She gave a little smile.*

smoke /smoʊk/ (**smokes, smoking, smoked**)

1 NONCOUNT NOUN **Smoke** is the gray or white gas that forms in the air when something burns. ❍ *Thick black smoke blew over the city.*

2 VERB If you **smoke** a cigarette, you suck the smoke from it and blow it out again. ❍ *He smokes 20 cigarettes a day.*

3 VERB If you **smoke**, you regularly smoke cigarettes. ❍ *You must quit smoking.* • **smok|er** NOUN ❍ *Smokers have a much higher risk of developing this disease.* • **smok|ing** NONCOUNT NOUN ❍ *Smoking is banned in many restaurants.*

smooth /smuð/

1 ADJ having no rough parts or lumps ❍ *The baby's skin was soft and smooth.* ❍ *Stir the mixture until it is smooth.*

2 ADJ well controlled and with no sudden movements or changes ❍ *The pilot made a very smooth landing.* • **smooth|ly** ADV ❍ *The boat was traveling smoothly through the water.*

3 ADJ successful and without problems ❍ *We hope for a smooth changeover to the new system.* • **smooth|ly** ADV ❍ *I hope your trip goes smoothly.*

smoth|er /smʌðər/

1 VERB If you **smother** a fire, you cover it in order to stop it burning. ❍ *She tried to smother the flames with a blanket.*

2 VERB If you **smother** someone, you kill them by covering their face with something. ❍ *She tried to smother him with a pillow.*

smug|gle /smʌgᵊl/ (**smuggles, smuggling, smuggled**) VERB If you **smuggle** things or people into or out of a place, you take them there illegally or secretly. ❍ *They smuggled goods into the country.* • **smug|gler** NOUN ❍ *diamond smugglers* • **smug|gling** NONCOUNT NOUN ❍ *A pilot was arrested and charged with smuggling.*

snack /snæk/

1 NOUN a small amount of food eaten between meals ❍ *The kids have a snack when they come in from school.*

2 VERB If you **snack**, you eat a small amount of food between meals. ❍ *During the day, I snack on fruit.*

snail /sneɪl/ NOUN a small animal with a long, soft body, no legs, and a round shell

snake /sneɪk/ **NOUN** a long, thin animal with no legs, that slides along the ground

snap /snæp/ (**snaps, snapping, snapped**)
1 VERB If something **snaps**, or if you snap it, it breaks with a short, loud noise. ❍ *Angrily, Matthew snapped the plastic pen in two.*
2 VERB If you **snap at** someone, you speak to them in a sharp, angry way. ❍ *Sorry, I didn't mean to snap at you.*

snatch /snætʃ/ (**snatches, snatching, snatched**) **VERB** If you **snatch** something, you take it quickly and roughly. ❍ *Michael snatched the key from Archie's hand.*

sneak /snik/ (**sneaks, sneaking, sneaked** or **snuck**)

The form **snuck** is informal.

1 VERB If you **sneak** somewhere, you go there quietly and secretly. ❍ *He sneaked out of his house late at night.*
2 VERB If you **sneak** a look at something, you quickly and secretly look at it. ❍ *She sneaked a look at her watch.*

sneak|er /snikər/ **NOUN Sneakers** are shoes that people wear for sports. ❍ *a pair of sneakers*

sneeze /sniz/ (**sneezes, sneezing, sneezed**)
1 VERB When you **sneeze**, air suddenly comes down your nose with force, usually because you have a cold. ❍ *Cover your nose and mouth when you sneeze.*
2 NOUN Sneeze is also a noun. ❍ *The disease is passed from person to person by a sneeze.*

sniff /snɪf/
1 VERB When you **sniff**, you suddenly and quickly breathe in air through your nose. ❍ *She dried her eyes and sniffed.*
2 NOUN Sniff is also a noun. ❍ *I could hear quiet sobs and sniffs.*

snob /snɒb/ **NOUN** someone who feels that they are better than other people because of their social class

snore /snɔr/ (**snores, snoring, snored**)
1 VERB When someone **snores**, they make a loud noise in their nose when they are asleep. ❍ *His mouth was open, and he was snoring.*
2 NOUN Snore is also a noun. ❍ *We heard loud snores coming from the next room.*

snow /snoʊ/
1 NONCOUNT NOUN Snow is soft white frozen water that falls from the sky. ❍ *Six inches of snow fell.*
2 VERB When **it snows**, snow falls from the sky. ❍ *It snowed all night.*

snowed un|der **ADJ** having a lot of work or other things to deal with [INFORMAL] ❍ *The director of operations was snowed under by complaints from clients of the company's Integrated Building Management Systems.*

snuck /snʌk/ **Snuck** is a form of the verb **sneak**. [INFORMAL]

so /soʊ/
1 ADV used to talk about something that has just been mentioned ❍ *"Do you think the partnership will last?"—"I hope so."* ❍ *If you don't like it, then say so.*
2 ADV used for saying that something is also true ❍ *As the futures price fell, so did the cash value of shares.*
3 CONJ used to talk about the result of a situation ❍ *I am shy and so I find it hard to talk to people.*
4 CONJ used to talk about the reason for something ❍ *Investment banks make bridge loans so that a client can complete a major takeover quickly.*
5 ADV used before adjectives and adverbs to make them stronger ❍ *How could I have been so stupid?*
6 You use **or so** when you are giving an approximate amount. ❍ *A ticket will cost you $20 or so.*

soak /soʊk/
1 VERB If you **soak** something, you put it into a liquid and leave it there. ❍ *Soak the beans for 2 hours.*
2 VERB If a liquid **soaks** something, it makes that thing very wet. ❍ *The water soaked his jacket.* ● **soak|ing** **ADJ** ❍ *My raincoat was soaking wet.*
3 VERB If a liquid **soaks through** something, it passes through it. ❍ *Blood soaked through the bandages.*
▶ **soak up** If a soft or dry material **soaks up**

a liquid, the liquid goes into it. ❍ *Use a towel to soak up the water.*

soap /soʊp/ **NONCOUNT NOUN** **Soap** is a substance that you use with water for washing yourself. ❍ *a bar of soap*

soar /sɔr/
1 VERB If the amount or level of something **soars**, it quickly increases. ❍ *Prices soared in the first half of the year.*
2 VERB If a bird or an aircraft **soars**, it flies high in the air or goes quickly upward. ❍ *A golden eagle soared overhead.*

sob /sɒb/ (**sobs, sobbing, sobbed**)
1 VERB When someone **sobs**, they cry in a noisy way. ❍ *She began to sob.*
2 NOUN a noise that you make when you are crying ❍ *She heard quiet sobs from the next room.*

so|ber /soʊbər/ **ADJ** not drunk ❍ *He was completely sober.*

so-called also **so called** **ADJ** used to show that you think a word or an expression is wrong ❍ *Companies with annual sales between $1 million and $100 million are in the so-called middle market.*

soc|cer /sɒkər/ **NONCOUNT NOUN** **Soccer** is a game played by two teams of eleven players who kick a ball and try to score goals. ❍ *She plays soccer.*

so|cial /soʊʃᵊl/
1 ADJ relating to society ❍ *We support social entrepreneurs - people with ideas for solving social problems.* ● **so|cial|ly** **ADV** ❍ *It wasn't socially acceptable to eat in the street.*
2 ADJ relating to enjoyable activities that involve meeting other people ❍ *We organize social events.* ● **so|cial|ly** **ADV** ❍ *We have known each other socially for a long time.*

so|cial aud|it (**social audits**) **NOUN** If a company carries out a **social audit**, it analyzes the social costs and social benefits of its operations in order to measure their success. ❍ *Some argue that banks should be forced to offer services to poor people and carry out a social audit before closing a branch.*

so|cial bene|fit (**social benefits**) **NOUN** a desirable effect that a policy is likely to have on society, such as a reduction in crime, unemployment, or pollution [ECONOMICS] ❍ *the social benefits of transportation investment*

so|cial change (**social changes**) **NOUN** a change in the way people interact with each other [ECONOMICS] ❍ *The winners of the future will adapt and innovate to exploit emerging technological and social changes.*

so|cial chap|ter **NONCOUNT NOUN** The **social chapter** is an agreement between countries in the European Union concerning workers' rights and working conditions. ❍ *Britain's rejection of the social chapter of the Maastricht treaty preserves employers' freedom from over-regulation and under-flexibility of labor.*

so|cial cost (**social costs**) **NOUN** an undesirable effect that a policy is likely to have on society, such as an increase in crime, unemployment, or pollution [ECONOMICS] ❍ *There are heavy social costs to neglecting the countryside, including crowded, car-clogged cities and high urban unemployment.*

so|cial dump|ing **NONCOUNT NOUN** **Social dumping** is the practice of allowing employers to lower wages and reduce employees' benefits in order to attract and keep jobs and investment. [ECONOMICS] ❍ *When Britain goes on to attract industrial jobs from the continent because of the relatively low social costs it imposes on industry, cries of social dumping ring out.*

so|cial|ise /soʊʃəlaɪz/ [BRIT] → **socialize**

so|cial|ism /soʊʃəlɪzəm/ **NONCOUNT NOUN** **Socialism** is a set of political principles whose general aim is to create a system in which everyone has equal chances to gain wealth and to own the country's main industries.

so|cial|ist /soʊʃəlɪst/
1 ADJ based on socialism or relating to socialism ❍ *He's a member of the Socialist Party.*
2 NOUN a person who believes in socialism ❍ *His grandparents were socialists.*

so|cial|ize /soʊʃəlaɪz/ (**socializes, socializing, socialized**) **VERB** If you **socialize**, you meet other people for social events. ❍ *I like socializing and making new friends.*

so|cial life (**social lives**) NOUN the time you spend with your friends ❍ *I was popular and had a busy social life.*

so|cial|ly re|spon|sible ADJ involving correct and proper behavior toward workers and the local community [BUSINESS MANAGEMENT] ❍ *$1 out of every $9 under professional management in America now involves an element of socially responsible investment.*

so|cial net|working NONCOUNT NOUN **Social networking** is the activity of using websites to make social contacts. ❍ *Have you used a social networking site such as Facebook?*

so|cial re|spon|sibil|ity NONCOUNT NOUN **Social responsibility** is the duty that some people feel companies have to behave in a correct and proper way toward their workers and the local community. [ECONOMICS, BUSINESS MANAGEMENT] ❍ *All businesses have a wider social responsibility and are answerable to more than just their shareholders.*

so|cial se|cu|rity NONCOUNT NOUN **Social security** is money provided by a government for people who are retired, disabled, unemployed, etc. [ECONOMICS] ❍ *Europe's spending on social security is nearly twice as high as Japan's.*

so|ciet|al mar|ket|ing /səsaɪɪtəl mɑrkɪtɪŋ/ NONCOUNT NOUN **Societal marketing** is marketing that involves social responsibility. [MARKETING AND SALES] ❍ *Societal marketing recognizes all the stakeholders in a transaction rather than a narrow focus on the company bottom line.*

so|ci|ety /səsaɪɪti/ (**societies**)
1 NOUN all the people in a country or area ❍ *These are common problems in today's society.*
2 NOUN an organization for people who have the same interest or aim ❍ *He's a member of the American Historical Society.*

so|cio|cul|tur|al /soʊsioʊkʌltʃərəl, soʊʃi-/ ADJ involving a combination of social and cultural factors [HR] ❍ *Various sociocultural constraints on female entrepreneurship can explain these figures.*

so|cio|eco|nom|ic /soʊsioʊɛkənɒmɪk, -ikə-/ ADJ involving a combination of social and economic factors [ECONOMICS] ❍ *The age, education, and socioeconomic status of these young mothers led to less satisfactory child care.*

sock /sɒk/ NOUN a piece of clothing that covers your foot and is worn inside shoes ❍ *a pair of red socks*

sock|et /sɒkɪt/ NOUN a device where you connect a piece of equipment to a supply of electricity ❍ *There's an electric socket by every seat on the train.*

soda /soʊdə/ NONCOUNT NOUN **Soda** is a sweet drink that contains bubbles. ❍ *a glass of soda*

so|dium /soʊdiəm/ NONCOUNT NOUN **Sodium** is a silvery white chemical element.

sofa /soʊfə/ NOUN a long, comfortable seat with a back and arms, that two or more people can sit on

soft /sɔft/
1 ADJ smooth and pleasant to touch ❍ *Body lotion will keep your skin soft.*
2 ADJ not hard, and easy to shape or press ❍ *Sales of soft cheeses dropped by 2%.*
3 ADJ gentle and not loud or bright ❍ *There was a soft tapping on my door.* ● **soft|ly** ADV ❍ *She walked into the softly lit room.*
4 ADJ **Soft** prices or markets are unstable and tending to decline. ❍ *The large semiconductor maker has been plagued recently by soft sales and dwindling margins.*

soft com|mod|ities PL NOUN **Soft commodities** are nonmetal commodities such as cocoa, sugar, and grains. [ECONOMICS] ❍ *Supplies of soft commodities are very low so a bumper crop is needed.*

soft drink (**soft drinks**) NOUN A **soft drink** is a soda. ❍ *Can I get you some tea or coffee, or a soft drink?*

sof|ten /sɔfᵊn/ VERB If you **soften** something, you make it less hard. ❍ *Soften the butter in a small saucepan.* ❍ *This tactic was designed to soften the blow of declining stock prices.*

soft goods PL NOUN **Soft goods** are things that are made of cloth, such as cushions, curtains, and furniture covers. ❍ *About two-thirds of its merchandise consists of hard goods such as furniture and appliances, rather than clothing and other soft goods.*

soft loan (**soft loans**) **NOUN** a loan with a very low interest rate [BANKING] ❍ *A donor conference recently pledged $2.6 billion, half in grants and the rest in soft loans.*

soft sell also **soft-sell** **NONCOUNT NOUN** A **soft sell** is a method of selling that involves persuading people in a gentle way rather than putting a lot of pressure on people to buy things. Compare with **hard sell**. [MARKETING AND SALES] ❍ *I think more customers probably prefer a soft sell.*

soft skills **PL NOUN** **Soft skills** are interpersonal skills such as the ability to communicate well with other people and to work on a team. [HR] ❍ *To develop their employees' soft skills, companies are investing in training programs and team-building activities.*

soft|ware /sɔftwɛər/ **NONCOUNT NOUN** Computer programs are called **software**. Compare with **hardware**. [TECHNOLOGY] ❍ *He writes computer software.*

soil /sɔɪl/ **NONCOUNT NOUN** **Soil** is the substance on the surface of the Earth in which plants grow. ❍ *The soil here is good for growing vegetables.*

so|lar /soʊlər/ **ADJ** relating to or using energy from the sun

sold /soʊld/ **Sold** is a form of the verb **sell**.

S

sol|dier /soʊldʒər/ **NOUN** a member of an army

sole /soʊl/

1 ADJ The **sole** thing or person of a particular type is the only one of that type. ❍ *Their sole aim is to win.* ● **sole|ly** **ADV** ❍ *The money you earn belongs solely to you.*

2 NOUN the underneath surface of your foot or a shoe ❍ *Wear shoes with thick soles.*

sol|emn /sɒləm/ **ADJ** very serious ❍ *His face looked solemn.* ● **sol|emn|ly** **ADV** ❍ *Her listeners nodded solemnly.*

sole pro|pri|etor (**sole proprietors**) **NOUN** the owner of a business, when it is owned by only one person [ECONOMICS] ❍ *a law firm of which he was the sole proprietor*

sole trad|er [ECONOMICS, BRIT] → **sole proprietor**

sol|id /sɒlɪd/

1 ADJ A **solid** substance is hard or firm and is not a liquid or a gas. ❍ *The walls are made from solid concrete blocks.* ❍ *The lake was frozen solid.*

2 NOUN a hard substance ❍ *Solids turn to liquids at certain temperatures.*

3 ADJ A **solid** object has no space inside it. ❍ *They had to cut through 50 feet of solid rock.*

4 ADJ financially sound or solvent ❍ *This is one of the most solid companies in the world.*

soli|tary /sɒlɪtɛri/

1 ADJ spending a lot of time alone ❍ *Paul was a shy, solitary man.*

2 ADJ A **solitary** activity is done alone. ❍ *He spent his evenings in solitary reading.*

solo /soʊloʊ/

1 ADJ or **ADV** used to describe someone who does something alone rather than with other people ❍ *He has just recorded his first solo album.* ❍ *Lindbergh flew solo across the Atlantic.*

2 NOUN a piece of music or a dance performed by one person ❍ *She asked me to sing a solo.*

sol|us /soʊləs/

1 ADJ **Solus** posters or press advertisements are separated physically from competing advertisements. [MARKETING AND SALES] ❍ *Front page solus advertisement (6 in. x 10 in.): $1446.00.*

2 ADJ **Solus** retail outlets sell the products of one company only. [MARKETING AND SALES] ❍ *the company's new solus retail franchise*

so|lu|tion /səluʃən/ **NOUN** a way of dealing with a problem ❍ *A number of businesses have discovered an innovative solution.*

solve /sɒlv/ (**solves, solving, solved**) **VERB** If you **solve** a problem or a question, you find an answer to it. ❍ *They have not solved the problem of unemployment.*

sol|ven|cy /sɒlvᵊnsi/ **NONCOUNT NOUN** A person's or organization's **solvency** is their ability to pay their debts. [ECONOMICS] ❍ *unsound investments that could threaten the company's solvency*

sol|vent /sɒlvᵊnt/ **ADJ** having enough money to pay all your debts [ECONOMICS] ❍ *They're going to have to show that the company is now solvent.*

some /səm, STRONG sʌm/
1 ADJ or **PRON** used to talk about an amount of something or a number of people or things ❍ *Would you like some orange juice?* ❍ *The apples are ripe, and we picked some today.* ❍ *We have seen some economic growth.*
2 ADJ used to mean that you do not know exactly which person or thing ❍ *She wanted to talk to him about some problem she was having.*

some|body /sʌmbɒdi, -bʌdi/ **PRON** **Somebody** means the same as **someone**.

some|how /sʌmhaʊ/ **ADV** used to say that you do not know how something was done or will be done ❍ *We'll manage somehow, I know we will.* ❍ *Somehow investment has been enough to keep output growing.*

some|one /sʌmwʌn/

The form **somebody** is also used.

PRON used to talk about a person without saying exactly who you mean ❍ *I need someone to help me.*

some|place /sʌmpleɪs/ **ADV** **Someplace** means the same as **somewhere**. ❍ *Maybe we could go someplace together.*

some|thing /sʌmθɪŋ/ **PRON** used to talk about a thing or a situation, without saying exactly what it is ❍ *He knew that there was something wrong.*

some|time /sʌmtaɪm/ **ADV** used to talk about a time without saying exactly when it is ❍ *We will finish sometime next month.*

some|times /sʌmtaɪmz/ **ADV** on some occasions but not all the time ❍ *I sometimes sit out in the garden and read.*

some|what /sʌmwʌt, -wɒt/ **ADV** slightly [FORMAL] ❍ *She behaved somewhat differently when he was there.*

some|where /sʌmwɛər/ **ADV** used to talk about a place without saying exactly where it is ❍ *I needed somewhere to live.*

son /sʌn/ **NOUN** Someone's **son** is their male child. ❍ *Sam is the seven-year-old son of Eric Davies.*

song /sɔŋ/
1 NOUN a piece of music with words that are sung ❍ *She sang a Spanish song.*
2 If you buy something **for a song**, you buy it at a bargain price. ❍ *If anyone has spotted an opportunity to buy the entire firm for a song, they have yet to reveal themselves.*

son-in-law (**sons-in-law**) **NOUN** the husband of your daughter

soon /sun/
1 ADV after a short time ❍ *I'll call you soon.*
2 If something happens **as soon as** something else happens, it happens immediately after it. ❍ *The insiders sold the holdings as soon as they were able to.*

soothe /suð/ (**soothes, soothing, soothed**)
1 VERB If you **soothe** someone who is angry or upset, you make them feel calmer. ❍ *He sang to her to soothe her.*
2 VERB Something that **soothes** a part of your body where there is pain makes it feel better. ❍ *Use this lotion to soothe dry skin.*

so|phis|ti|cat|ed /səfɪstɪkeɪtɪd/
1 ADJ A **sophisticated** machine or system is complicated and highly developed. ❍ *The 70 employees are aided by sophisticated computer systems.*
2 ADJ A **sophisticated** person knows about things like culture and fashion. ❍ *Claude was a charming, sophisticated man.*

sore /sɔr/ (**sorer, sorest**) **ADJ** painful and uncomfortable ❍ *I had a sore throat and a cough.*

sor|row /sɒroʊ/ **NONCOUNT NOUN** **Sorrow** is a feeling of deep sadness. ❍ *Words cannot express my sorrow.*

sor|ry /sɒri/ (**sorrier, sorriest**)
1 You say "**Sorry**" to apologize for something that you have done. ❍ *"You're making too much noise."—"Sorry."* ❍ *Sorry I took so long.*
2 ADJ If you are **sorry** about a situation, you feel sadness or disappointment about it. ❍ *I'm sorry he's gone.*
3 You say "**I'm sorry**" to express your sympathy. ❍ *"Robert's sick today."—"I'm sorry to hear that."*

4 ADJ If you feel **sorry for** someone, you feel sympathy for them. ❍ *I felt sorry for him because nobody listened to him.*

sort /sɔrt/

1 NOUN A particular **sort of** thing is a type of thing. ❍ *What sort of school did you go to?*

2 VERB If you **sort** things or **sort** them **out**, you separate them into different groups. ❍ *He sorted the materials into their folders.*

3 You use **sort of** when your description of something is not very accurate. [INFORMAL] ❍ *"What's a sub?"—"Well, it's sort of a sandwich."*

▸**sort out** If you **sort out** a problem, you deal with it successfully. ❍ *The two companies have sorted out their disagreement.*

sort code (**sort codes**) **NOUN** a sequence of numbers printed on a check or bank card that identifies the branch holding the account [BANKING] ❍ *You need to quote your sort code and account number for paying money into your current account from an external source.*

sought /sɔt/ **Sought** is a form of the verb **seek**.

soul /soʊl/ **NOUN** a person's spirit, that some people believe continues to exist when you are dead ❍ *She prayed for the soul of her dead husband.*

sound
❶ NOUN AND VERB USES
❷ ADJECTIVE AND ADVERB USES

❶ sound /saʊnd/

1 NOUN something that you hear ❍ *Peter heard the sound of a car engine outside.*

2 VERB When you are describing a noise, you can talk about the way it **sounds**. ❍ *They heard what sounded like a huge explosion.*

3 VERB The way someone **sounds** is how they seem when they speak. ❍ *She sounds very angry.*

4 VERB When you are describing your opinion of something you have heard about, you can talk about the way it **sounds**. ❍ *It sounds like a wonderful idea to me.*

❷ sound /saʊnd/

1 ADJ in good condition ❍ *The building is perfectly sound.*

2 ADJ **Sound** advice is sensible, and can be trusted. ❍ *Our experts will give you sound advice.*

3 ADV If someone is **sound** asleep, they are in a deep sleep. ❍ *He was lying in bed, sound asleep.*

soup /sup/ **NONCOUNT NOUN** **Soup** is liquid food made by boiling meat, fish, or vegetables in water. ❍ *homemade chicken soup*

sour /saʊər/ **ADJ** having a sharp, unpleasant taste like a lemon ❍ *The stewed apple was sour.*

source /sɔrs/ (**sources, sourcing, sourced**)

1 NOUN where something comes from ❍ *We are developing new sources of energy.*

2 VERB If a person or company **sources** a product or a raw material, they find someone who will supply it. ❍ *Together they travel the world, sourcing clothes for the small, privately owned company.*

south /saʊθ/ also **South**

1 NONCOUNT NOUN The **south** is the direction that is on your right when you are looking at the sun in the morning. ❍ *The town lies ten miles to the south.*

2 ADV toward the south ❍ *I drove south on Highway 9.*

3 ADJ relating to the south ❍ *We live on the south coast of Long Island.*

south|east /saʊθist/

1 NONCOUNT NOUN The **southeast** is the direction that is between south and east. ❍ *The train left Colombo for Galle, 70 miles to the southeast.*

2 ADJ relating to the southeast ❍ *Southeast Asia*

south|ern /sʌðərn/ also **Southern** **ADJ** relating to the south of a place ❍ *southern Florida*

south|west /saʊθwɛst/

1 NONCOUNT NOUN The **southwest** is the direction that is between south and west. ❍ *He lives about 500 miles to the southwest of Johannesburg.*

2 ADJ relating to the southwest ❍ *southwest Louisiana*

sou|venir /suvənɪər/ **NOUN** something that you buy or keep to remind you of a place or event ❍ *The cup was a souvenir of the summer of 1992.*

sov|er|eign /sɒvrɪn/ **NOUN** a king, queen, or other royal ruler of a country ❍ *In March 1889, she became the first British sovereign to set foot on Spanish soil.*

spa /spɑ/
1 NOUN a place with a natural supply of water that people drink and wash in because they think it is healthy ❍ *a spa town*
2 NOUN a place where people go to exercise and have beauty treatments ❍ *Hotel guests may use the health spa.*

space /speɪs/ (**spaces, spacing, spaced**)
1 NOUN an area that is empty or available ❍ *The space under the stairs could be used as a storage area.*
2 NOUN A **space of** time is a period of time. ❍ *They've come a long way in a short space of time.*
3 NONCOUNT NOUN Space is the area beyond the Earth's atmosphere, where the stars and planets are. ❍ *The astronauts will spend ten days in space.*

spa|ghet|ti /spəgɛti/ **NONCOUNT NOUN Spaghetti** is a type of pasta (= a food made from flour and water) in long, thin pieces.

spam /spæm/ **NONCOUNT NOUN Spam** is advertising messages that are sent by email to large numbers of people. [MARKETING AND SALES] ❍ *As much as 42% of all e-mail whizzing around the world today may be spam.*

span /spæn/ (**spans, spanning, spanned**)
1 NOUN a period of time ❍ *The batteries had a life span of six hours.*
2 VERB If something **spans** a long period of time, it lasts for that period of time. ❍ *His professional career spanned 16 years.*
3 VERB A bridge that **spans** a river or a road, stretches right across it.

spare /spɛər/ (**spares, sparing, spared**)
1 ADJ Spare things are extra things that you keep in case you need them. ❍ *I'll give you the spare key.*
2 VERB If you **spare** time or money, you make it available. ❍ *I can only spare 35 minutes for this meeting.*

spare ca|pac|ity **NONCOUNT NOUN** If there is **spare capacity** within a factory or industry, it is not using all its available resources. [PRODUCTION] ❍ *Building the new model at one of its American factories with spare capacity would have been cheaper.*

spark /spɑrk/
1 NOUN a very small piece of burning material ❍ *Sparks flew out of the fire.*
2 NOUN a flash of light caused by electricity ❍ *I saw a spark when I connected the wires.*

spar|kle /spɑrkəl/ (**sparkles, sparkling, sparkled**) **VERB** If something **sparkles**, it shines with a lot of very small points of light. ❍ *The jewels on her fingers sparkled.*

spar|kling /spɑrklɪŋ/
1 ADJ Sparkling drinks are slightly carbonated. ❍ *a glass of sparkling wine*
2 ADJ If a company has **sparkling** figures or **sparkling** results, it has performed very well and made a lot of money. [BRIT] ❍ *The top retailer has romped in with another set of sparkling results.*

speak /spik/ (**speaks, speaking, spoke, spoken**)
1 VERB When you **speak**, you use your voice to say something. ❍ *I called the hotel and spoke to Louie.* ❍ *He often speaks about retirement.*
2 VERB When someone **speaks**, they make a speech. ❍ *He will speak at the Democratic Convention.*
3 VERB If you **speak** a foreign language, you know the language. ❍ *He speaks English.*

speak|er /spikər/
1 NOUN a person who is speaking ❍ *You can understand a lot from the speaker's tone of voice.*
2 NOUN someone who is giving a speech ❍ *a guest speaker*
3 NOUN a piece of electrical equipment that sound comes out of ❍ *I bought a pair of speakers for my computer.*

spe|cial /spɛʃəl/
1 ADJ better or more important than normal people or things ❍ *My special guest will be Zac Efron.*
2 ADJ different from normal ❍ *In special cases, a child can be educated at home.*

spe|cial|ise /spɛʃəlaɪz/ [BRIT] → **specialize**

spe|cial|ist /spɛʃəlɪst/ **NOUN** a person who knows a lot about a particular subject ❍ *a cancer specialist*

spe|ci|al|ity /spɛʃiælɪti/ [BRIT] → **specialty**

spe|cial|ize /spɛʃəlaɪz/ (**specializes, specializing, specialized**) VERB If you **specialize in** something, you spend most of your time studying it or doing it. ❍ *They work for banks or law firms that specialize in business.*

spe|cial|ly /spɛʃəli/
1 ADV for a particular purpose ❍ *This soap is specially designed for sensitive skin.*
2 ADV more than usual [INFORMAL] ❍ *On his birthday I got up specially early.*

spe|cial|ty /spɛʃᵊlti/ (**specialties**) NOUN something that someone does particularly well, or a subject that they know a lot about ❍ *His specialty is international law.*

spe|cies /spiʃiz/ (**species**) NOUN a related group of plants or animals ❍ *Many species could disappear from our Earth.*

spe|cif|ic /spɪsɪfɪk/
1 ADJ used to talk about one particular thing or several particular things ❍ *Traditionally, companies hire people with specific skills for specific jobs.*
2 ADJ exact and clear ❍ *She refused to be more specific about her plans.*

spe|cifi|cal|ly /spɪsɪfɪkli/ ADV for one particular thing or type of thing ❍ *The show is specifically for children.*

speci|fy /spɛsɪfaɪ/ (**specifies, specifying, specified**) VERB If you **specify** something, you explain it in a detailed way. ❍ *Does the recipe specify the size of egg to be used?*

S

speci|men /spɛsɪmɪn/ NOUN an example of something or a small amount of something that is used for a test ❍ *Job applicants have to give a specimen of handwriting.*

spec sheet /spɛk ʃit/ (**spec sheets**) NOUN a list describing the specifications of a product or property that is for sale ❍ *All 600 salespeople received high-performance laptops with access to spec sheets and technical information on 170,000 parts.*

spec|ta|cle /spɛktəkᵊl/ NOUN a big, wonderful sight or event ❍ *The fireworks were an amazing spectacle.*

spec|tacu|lar /spɛktækyələr/ ADJ big and dramatic ❍ *We had spectacular views of Sugar Loaf Mountain.* ● **spec|tacu|lar|ly** ADV ❍ *Our sales increased spectacularly.*

specu|late /spɛkyəleɪt/ (**speculates, speculating, speculated**)
1 VERB If you **speculate** about something, you make guesses about it. ❍ *Everyone has been speculating about why she left.* ● **specu|la|tion** /spɛkyəleɪʃən/ NONCOUNT NOUN ❍ *There has been a lot of speculation about the future of the band.*
2 VERB If you **speculate**, you buy or sell securities or property in the hope of making a profit. [ECONOMICS] ❍ *He survives comfortably by speculating on the financial markets.*

specu|la|tion /spɛkyəleɪʃən/ NONCOUNT NOUN **Speculation** is investment involving high risk but also the possibility of high profits. [ECONOMICS] ❍ *The latest outburst of takeover speculation in media and airline stocks sent those sectors higher.*

specu|la|tive /spɛkyəleɪtɪv, -lətɪv/
1 ADJ A piece of information that is **speculative** is based on guesses rather than knowledge. ❍ *The papers ran speculative stories about the collapse of the company.*
2 ADJ **Speculative** investment involves buying goods or shares in the hope of being able to sell them again at a higher price and make a profit. [ECONOMICS] ❍ *Thousands of retirees were persuaded to mortgage their homes to invest in speculative bonds.*

sped /spɛd/ **Sped** is a form of the verb **speed**.

speech /spitʃ/ (**speeches**)
1 NONCOUNT NOUN **Speech** is the ability to speak or the act of speaking. ❍ *The medicine can affect speech.*
2 NOUN a formal talk given to a group of people ❍ *The president gave a speech to the nation.*

speed /spid/ (**speeds, speeding, sped** or **speeded**)

> Use **sped** in meaning **3** and **speeded** for the phrasal verb.

1 NOUN The **speed** of something is how fast it

moves or is done. ❍ *He drove off at high speed.*
2 NONCOUNT NOUN **Speed** is very fast movement, travel, or action. ❍ *Few computer networks need this sort of speed at the moment.*
3 VERB If you **speed** somewhere, you go there quickly. ❍ *Trains speed through the tunnel at 186 mph.*
4 VERB Someone who **is speeding** is driving a vehicle faster than the legal speed limit. ❍ *Police stopped him because he was speeding.*
● **speed|ing** NONCOUNT NOUN ❍ *He was fined for speeding.*
▶ **speed up** When something **speeds up**, it happens more quickly than before. ❍ *The plan would speed up the collection of payroll taxes from large companies.*

speedy /spidi/ (**speedier, speediest**) ADJ quick ❍ *We wish Bill a speedy recovery.*

spell /spɛl/
1 VERB When you **spell** a word, you write or say each letter in the correct order. ❍ *How do you spell "potato?"*
2 NOUN a set of magic words ❍ *They say a witch cast a spell on her.*

spell|ing /spɛlɪŋ/
1 NOUN the correct order of the letters in a word ❍ *I'm not sure about the spelling of his name.*
2 NONCOUNT NOUN **Spelling** is the ability to spell words correctly. ❍ *His spelling is very bad.*

spend /spɛnd/ (**spends, spending, spent**)
1 VERB When you **spend** money, you use it to pay for something. [ECONOMICS] ❍ *We have spent all our budget.*
2 VERB If you **spend** time doing something, you use your time doing it. ❍ *She spends hours surfing the Internet.*
3 NOUN an amount of money that is spent on something, or that will be spent [ECONOMICS] ❍ *Their sales and marketing spend dwarfs the software revenue of whole continents.*

spend|er /spɛndər/ NOUN someone who spends money [ECONOMICS] ❍ *The Swiss are Europe's biggest spenders on food.*

spend|ing mon|ey NONCOUNT NOUN **Spending money** is money that you have or are given to spend on personal things for pleasure, especially when you are on vacation. [ECONOMICS] ❍ *Jo will use her winnings as spending money on her vacation to the Costa Brava.*

spend|thrift /spɛndθrɪft/
1 NOUN a person who spends too much money [ECONOMICS]
2 ADJ **Spendthrift** is also an adjective. ❍ *The country's financial systems were plagued by reckless lending and spendthrift consumers.*

spent /spɛnt/ **Spent** is a form of the verb **spend**.

sphere /sfɪər/ NOUN a round shape, like a ball

spice /spaɪs/ NOUN a powder or seeds from a plant that you add to food to give it flavor ❍ *herbs and spices*

spicy /spaɪsi/ (**spicier, spiciest**) ADJ strongly flavored with spices ❍ *Thai food is hot and spicy.*

spi|der /spaɪdər/ NOUN a small animal with eight legs

spike /spaɪk/
1 NOUN a long piece of metal with a sharp point ❍ *iron spikes*
2 NOUN a sudden increase in the price, volume, or amount of something ❍ *Economists said forecasts of a 1% to 1.5% seasonally adjusted spike in sales for December were "not unreasonable."*

spill /spɪl/ (**spills, spilling, spilled** or **spilt**) VERB If you **spill** a liquid, you accidentally make it flow over the edge of a container. ❍ *He always spilled the drinks.*

spill|over /spɪloʊvər/ NOUN any indirect effect of public spending ❍ *the spillover effect of spending cuts*

spin /spɪn/ (**spins, spinning, spun**)
1 VERB If something **spins**, it turns quickly around a central point. ❍ *The disk spins 3,600 times a minute.*
2 NOUN a sudden downward trend in prices, values, etc. ❍ *Either strike or resignation could have sent the currency and the financial markets into a spin.*
▶ **spin off** or **spin out** To **spin off** or **spin out** something such as a company means to

create a new company that is separate from the original organization. ❍ *He rescued the company and later spun off its textile division into a separate company.* ❍ *Corven plans to help large companies spin out smaller, entrepreneurial firms.*

spine /spaɪn/ **NOUN** the row of bones down your back ❍ *He suffered injuries to his spine.*

spi|ral /spaɪrəl/ (**spirals, spiraling** or **spiralling, spiraled** or **spiralled**)
1 NOUN a shape that winds around and around, with each curve above or outside the previous one ❍ *The maze is actually two interlocking spirals.*
2 VERB If an amount or level **spirals**, it rises or falls quickly and at an increasing rate. ❍ *Production costs began to spiral.* ❍ *spiraling health care costs*
3 NONCOUNT NOUN **Spiral** is also a noun. ❍ *an inflationary spiral* ❍ *a spiral of debt*

spir|it /spɪrɪt/
1 NOUN the part of you that is not physical and that consists of your character and feelings ❍ *The human spirit is hard to destroy.*
2 NOUN the part of you that some people believe remains alive after you die ❍ *He is gone, but his spirit is still with us.*
3 PL NOUN Your **spirits** are your feelings of happiness or unhappiness. ❍ *After the meeting, everyone was in high spirits.*

spir|itu|al /spɪrɪtʃuəl/ **ADJ** relating to people's feelings and religious beliefs ❍ *He is their spiritual leader.*

spit /spɪt/ (**spits, spitting, spit** or **spat**) **VERB** If you **spit** liquid or food somewhere, you force it out of your mouth. ❍ *Spit out that gum.*

S

spite /spaɪt/
1 You use **in spite of** to introduce a fact that makes the rest of what you are saying seem surprising. ❍ *He hired her in spite of her lack of experience.*
2 NONCOUNT NOUN **Spite** is a feeling of wanting to hurt or upset someone. ❍ *I didn't help him, out of spite I suppose.*

splash /splæʃ/ (**splashes, splashing, splashed**)
1 VERB If you **splash** in water, you move in it in a noisy way. ❍ *People were splashing around in the water.*
2 VERB If a liquid **splashes**, drops of it hit somewhere. ❍ *The icy water splashed over her boots.*
3 NOUN the sound of something hitting water
▸ **splash out** If you **splash out**, you spend money freely on something. [BRIT] ❍ *People are starting to splash out on everything from new homes to cars to computers.*

splen|did /splɛndɪd/ **ADJ** very good ❍ *The book includes some splendid photographs.*

splin|ter /splɪntər/ **NOUN** a thin, sharp piece of wood or glass that has broken off a larger piece ❍ *We found splinters of the glass in our clothes.*

split /splɪt/ (**splits, splitting, split**)
1 VERB If something **splits**, it breaks into two or more parts, and if you **split** something, you divide it into two or more parts. ❍ *The ship split in two during a storm.* ❍ *In 1974, they split the company into two firms.*
2 VERB If something **splits**, a long crack or tear appears in it. ❍ *My pants split while I was climbing over the wall.*
3 VERB If two or more people **split** something, they share it. ❍ *Their financial advisers split a $100 million success fee.*
▸ **split up** If two people **split up**, they end their relationship. ❍ *His parents split up when he was ten.*

split shift (**split shifts**) **NOUN** a work period divided into two parts that are separated by an interval longer than a normal rest period [PRODUCTION]

spoil /spɔɪl/ (**spoils, spoiling, spoiled** or **spoilt**)
1 VERB If you **spoil** something, you stop it being good or successful. ❍ *Don't let mistakes spoil your life.*
2 VERB If you **spoil** children, you let them have or do everything they want. ❍ *Grandparents often like to spoil their grandchildren.*

spoke /spoʊk/ **Spoke** is a form of the verb **speak**.

spo|ken /spoʊkən/
1 Spoken is a form of the verb **speak**.
2 ADJ said rather than written ❍ *They took tests in written and spoken English.*

spokes|man /spoʊksmən/ (**spokesmen**) **NOUN** a man who speaks as the representative of a group ❍ *A spokesman refused to comment on speculation about the future of the bank.*

spokes|person /spoʊkspɜrsᵊn/ (**spokespersons** or **spokespeople**) **NOUN** a person who speaks as the representative of a group ❍ *a White House spokesperson*

spokes|woman /spoʊkswʊmən/ (**spokeswomen**) **NOUN** a woman who speaks as a representative of a group ❍ *A hospital spokeswoman said he was recovering well.*

sponge /spʌndʒ/ **NOUN** a piece of a very light material with lots of little holes in it, used for washing things ❍ *He wiped the table with a sponge.*

spon|sor /spɒnsər/

1 VERB If an organization or a person **sponsors** an event, they pay for it. [BUSINESS MANAGEMENT] ❍ *A local bank is sponsoring the race.*

2 NOUN Sponsor is also a noun. ❍ *The sponsors of the plan report that training time was halved and training costs reduced by two-thirds as a result of this approach.*

3 VERB If you **sponsor** someone who is doing something to raise money, you agree to give them money if they succeed in doing it. ❍ *The children asked friends and family to sponsor them.*

4 NOUN Sponsor is also a noun. ❍ *He may well surprise his sponsors by his powers of endurance.*

spon|sor|ship /spɒnsərʃɪp/ **NONCOUNT NOUN Sponsorship** is financial support given by a sponsor. [BUSINESS MANAGEMENT] ❍ *Campbell is one of an ever-growing number of skiers in need of sponsorship.*

spon|ta|neous /spɒnteɪniəs/ **ADJ** done suddenly and without being planned ❍ *The audience broke into spontaneous applause.*
• **spon|ta|neous|ly ADV** ❍ *People spontaneously stood up and cheered.*

spoon /spun/ **NOUN** a long object with a round end that is used for eating, serving, or mixing food ❍ *He stirred his coffee with a spoon.*

sport /spɔrt/ **NOUN** a game and other activity that need physical effort and skill ❍ *Basketball is my favorite sport.*

spot /spɒt/ (**spots, spotting, spotted**)

1 NOUN a small, round, colored area on a surface ❍ *The leaves are yellow with orange spots.*

2 NOUN a particular place ❍ *This is one of the country's top tourist spots.*

3 VERB If you **spot** something or someone, you notice them. ❍ *I didn't spot the mistake in his memo.*

spot de|liv|ery NONCOUNT NOUN Spot delivery is an arrangement to deliver a commodity for immediate cash payment. [LOGISTICS AND DISTRIBUTION]

spot|light /spɒtlaɪt/ **NOUN** a powerful light that shines on a small area

spot mar|ket NOUN a market in which commodities are traded for immediate delivery and payment [LOGISTICS AND DISTRIBUTION] ❍ *The shutdown will reduce the amount of products sold on the spot market.*

spot price (**spot prices**) **NOUN** the price of goods, currencies, or securities that are offered for immediate delivery and payment [LOGISTICS AND DISTRIBUTION] ❍ *When the futures contract expires, its price will be equivalent to the spot price of silver.*

spouse /spaʊs/ **NOUN** your husband or wife ❍ *You and your spouse must both sign the contract.*

sprang /spræŋ/ **Sprang** is a form of the verb **spring**.

spray /spreɪ/

1 NONCOUNT NOUN Spray is a lot of small drops of liquid. ❍ *We were hit by spray from the waterfall.*

2 VERB If you **spray** a liquid somewhere, drops of the liquid cover a place. ❍ *Firefighters sprayed water on the fire.*

spread /sprɛd/ (**spreads, spreading, spread**)

1 VERB If you **spread** something somewhere or **spread** it **out**, you open it or arrange it over a surface. ❍ *She spread a towel on the sand.* ❍ *He spread the papers out on a table.*

2 VERB If you **spread** a substance on a surface, you put it all over the surface. ❍ *She was spreading butter on the bread.*

3 VERB If something **spreads**, it gradually reaches a larger area. ❍ *Information technology has spread across the world.*
4 NOUN **Spread** is also a noun. ❍ *We closed schools to stop the spread of the disease.*
5 NONCOUNT NOUN **The spread** is the difference between the price that a seller wants someone to pay for a particular stock and the price that the buyer is willing to pay.
▸**spread out** If people **spread out**, they move apart from each other. ❍ *They spread out to search the area.*

spread|sheet /sprɛdʃit/ **NOUN** a computer program that arranges numbers and information in rows and can be used for calculating and planning

spring /sprɪŋ/ (**springs, springing, sprang, sprung**)
1 NOUN the season between winter and summer ❍ *They are getting married next spring.*
2 NOUN a long thin piece of metal that goes round and round and quickly goes back to its original shape after you press or pull it ❍ *The springs in the bed were old and soft.*
3 NOUN a place where water comes up through the ground ❍ *The town is famous for its hot springs.*
4 VERB When a person or an animal **springs** up or forward, they jump suddenly. ❍ *He sprang to his feet.*

sprin|kle /sprɪŋkᵊl/ (**sprinkles, sprinkling, sprinkled**) **VERB** If you **sprinkle** something **with** a substance, you drop small amounts of it over the surface. ❍ *Sprinkle the meat with salt before you cook it.*

S

sprint /sprɪnt/
1 NOUN a short, fast race ❍ *Rob Harmeling won the sprint.*
2 VERB If you **sprint**, you run very fast. ❍ *Sergeant Adams sprinted to the car.*

sprung /sprʌŋ/ **Sprung** is a form of the verb **spring**.

spun /spʌn/ **Spun** is a form of the verb **spin**.

spy /spaɪ/ (**spies, spying, spied**)
1 NOUN a person whose job is to find out secret information about another country or organization ❍ *He used to be a spy.*
2 VERB Someone who **spies** tries to find out secret information about another country or organization.
3 VERB If you **spy on** someone, you watch them secretly. ❍ *The security manager says the company isn't spying on workers.*

squad /skwɒd/
1 NOUN a section of a police force that is responsible for a particular type of crime ❍ *Someone called the bomb squad.*
2 NOUN a group of players from which a sports team will be chosen ❍ *There have been a lot of injuries in the squad.*

square /skwɛər/ (**squares, squarer, squarest**)
1 NOUN a shape with four straight sides that are all the same length and four 90 degree angles ❍ *Cut the cake in squares.*
2 NOUN is an open area in a town or city with buildings around it ❍ *The restaurant is in the town square.*
3 ADJ having the shape of a square ❍ *They sat at a square table.*
4 ADJ used for talking about the area of something ❍ *3,000 square feet*
5 NOUN The **square of** a number is the number you get when you multiply that number by itself. ❍ *The square of 4 is 16.*

squash /skwɒʃ/ (**squashes, squashing, squashed**)
1 VERB If someone or something **is squashed**, they are pressed hard. ❍ *Robert was squashed against a fence by a car.*
2 NONCOUNT NOUN **Squash** is a game in which two players hit a small rubber ball against the walls of a court. ❍ *I play squash once a week.*
3 NOUN a large vegetable with a thick skin

squeak /skwik/
1 VERB If something or someone **squeaks**, they make a short, high sound. ❍ *My boots squeaked as I walked.*
2 NOUN **Squeak** is also a noun. ❍ *I heard a squeak, like a mouse.*

squeeze /skwiz/ (**squeezes, squeezing, squeezed**)
1 VERB If you **squeeze** something, you press it firmly from two sides. ❍ *He squeezed her arm*

gently. ❍ *Joe squeezed some toothpaste out of the tube.*
2 NOUN Squeeze is also a noun. ❍ *She took my hand and gave it a squeeze.*
3 NOUN a condition of restricted credit imposed by a government to counteract price inflation [ECONOMICS] ❍ *A new fiscal squeeze looms and export growth is likely to stay sluggish.*

squid /skwɪd/

The plural can be **squid** or **squids**.

1 NOUN a sea animal that has a long soft body and many soft arms called tentacles
2 NONCOUNT NOUN Squid is pieces of this creature eaten as food. ❍ *Cook the squid for 2 minutes.*

squir|rel /skwɜrəl/ **NOUN** a small animal with a long thick tail that lives mainly in trees

stab /stæb/ (**stabs, stabbing, stabbed**) **VERB** If someone **stabs** you, they push a knife into your body. ❍ *Someone stabbed him in the stomach.*

sta|bi|lise /steɪbɪlaɪz/ [ECONOMICS, BRIT] → **stabilize**

sta|bi|lize /steɪbɪlaɪz/ (**stabilizes, stabilizing, stabilized**) **VERB** If something **stabilizes**, or **is stabilized**, it becomes stable. [ECONOMICS] ❍ *The inflation rate will stabilize at around 3% this year.* ❍ *Officials hope the move will stabilize exchange rates.* ● **sta|bi|li|za|tion** /steɪbɪlɪzeɪʃən/ **NONCOUNT NOUN** ❍ *the stabilization of property prices*

sta|ble /steɪbᵊl/ (**stabler, stablest**)
1 ADJ not likely to change suddenly [ECONOMICS] ❍ *The price of oil has remained stable.* ● **sta|bil|ity** /stəbɪlɪti/ **NONCOUNT NOUN** ❍ *It was a time of political stability.*
2 ADJ firmly fixed in position ❍ *Make sure the ladder is stable.*
3 NOUN a building in which horses are kept

stack /stæk/
1 NOUN a pile of things on top of each other ❍ *There were stacks of books on the floor.*
2 VERB If you **stack** things, you arrange them in piles. ❍ *Soap sales climbed 5% when bars were neatly stacked on shelves.*

sta|dium /steɪdiəm/ **NOUN** a large sports field with seats around it ❍ *a baseball stadium*

staff /stæf/ **NOUN** the people who work for an organization [HR, BUSINESS MANAGEMENT] ❍ *The outpatient program has a staff of six people.* ❍ *members of staff*

staff de|vel|op|ment NONCOUNT NOUN Staff development is the process of teaching the employees of a company new skills that will help them to advance in their job. [HR] ❍ *a program of systematic staff development*

staff|ing /stæfɪŋ/ **NONCOUNT NOUN Staffing** refers to the number of workers employed to work in a particular organization or building. [HR] ❍ *Staffing levels in prisons are too low.*

staff rep|re|sen|ta|tive (**staff representatives**) **NOUN** a worker who is elected by other workers to represent their interests to management [ADMINISTRATION] ❍ *He called for staff representatives on the committees that control directors' earnings.*

staff sug|ges|tion scheme (**staff suggestion schemes**) **NOUN** a program in which the employees of a company are encouraged to suggest ways of improving the company's performance or its working conditions [BRIT] ❍ *a staff suggestion scheme that offers good rewards for viable suggestions*

staff train|ing NONCOUNT NOUN Staff training is the process of teaching the employees of a company the skills they need for their job. [HR] ❍ *The industry is anxious to improve staff training.*

stage /steɪdʒ/
1 NOUN one part of an activity or a process ❍ *We are completing the first stage of the plan.*
2 NOUN the area where people perform in a theater ❍ *The band walked onto the stage.*

stag|fla|tion /stægfleɪʃən/ **NONCOUNT NOUN** If an economy is suffering from **stagflation**, inflation is high but there is no increase in the demand for goods or in the number of people who have jobs. [ECONOMICS] ❍ *Many of the industrialized economies would be pushed into a cycle of stagflation.*

stain /steɪn/
1 NOUN a mark on something that is difficult to remove ❍ *How do you remove tea stains?*
2 VERB If a liquid **stains** something, it makes a mark on it. ❍ *Some foods can stain the teeth.*

stair /stɛər/
1 PL NOUN **Stairs** are steps inside a building that go from one level to another. ❍ *Nancy began to climb the stairs.*
2 NOUN one of the steps in a set of stairs ❍ *Terry was sitting on the bottom stair.*

stair|case /stɛərkeɪs/ **NOUN** a set of stairs inside a building ❍ *They walked down the staircase together.*

stake /steɪk/
1 If something is **at stake**, it might be lost if you are not successful. ❍ *It demanded money from the government, claiming that up to 133,000 jobs were at stake.*
2 NOUN a pointed wooden pole that you push into the ground, for example in order to support a young tree

stake|hold|er /steɪkhoʊldər/
1 NOUN a person who has an interest in a company's or organization's affairs [ECONOMICS] ❍ *The stakeholders in the workers' compensation system all have strong opinions.*
2 NOUN a person or group owning a significant percentage of a company's shares [ECONOMICS] ❍ *Deregulation is beginning to loosen the ties between firms and their financial stakeholders, such as banks and insurance firms.*

S

stake|hold|er pen|sion (**stakeholder pensions**) **NOUN** a flexible pension plan with low charges, to which both employees and the government contribute [ECONOMICS, BANKING, BRIT] ❍ *New stakeholder pensions will aim to give all workers a retirement pension they can live on.*

stalk /stɔk/ **NOUN** the thin part that joins a flower, a leaf, or a fruit to a plant or tree ❍ *A single flower grows on each long stalk.*

stall|hold|er /stɔlhoʊldər/ **NOUN** a person who sells goods at a market stall [BRIT]

stamp /stæmp/
1 NOUN a small piece of paper that you stick on an envelope before you mail it ❍ *She put a stamp on the corner of the envelope.*
2 NOUN an object that you press onto something to make a special mark, often using ink ❍ *a date stamp*
3 VERB If you **stamp** a mark or a word on an object, you press the mark or word onto it using a stamp. ❍ *They stamp a special number on new cars.*

stamp duty or **stamp tax** **NONCOUNT NOUN** **Stamp duty** is a tax on legal documents, publications, etc. [BRIT, FINANCE] ❍ *A purchaser now pays 1% stamp duty on houses above £60,000.*

stand /stænd/ (**stands, standing, stood**)
1 VERB When you **are standing**, you are on your feet. ❍ *She was standing beside my desk.*
2 VERB When someone **stands** or **stands up**, they move so that they are on their feet. ❍ *Becker stood and shook hands with Ben.* ❍ *When I walked in, they all stood up.*
3 VERB If you **stand aside** or **stand back**, you move a short distance away. ❍ *I stood aside to let her pass me.*
4 VERB If something **stands** somewhere, it is in that place. ❍ *The house stands alone on top of a hill.*
5 VERB If you cannot **stand** someone or something, you dislike them very strongly. [INFORMAL] ❍ *I can't stand that awful man.*
6 NOUN a small structure where you can buy things like food, drink, and newspapers ❍ *I bought a magazine from a newspaper stand.*
7 NOUN a small piece of furniture that you use to hold a particular thing ❍ *Take the television set off the stand.*
8 NOUN an exhibition area in a trade fair ❍ *We need to build an exhibition stand which attracts customers, allows the firm to display its products and meets safety standards.*
▸ **stand for** Letters that **stand for** a particular word are a short form of that word. ❍ *U.S. stands for United States.*
▸ **stand out** If someone or something **stands out**, they are very easy to see. ❍ *We needed a message that stood out.*
▸ **stand up for** If you **stand up for** a person or a belief, you support them. ❍ *We have to learn to stand up for ourselves.*

stand-alone
1 ADJ A **stand-alone** business or organization is independent and does not receive financial support from another organization. ❍ *They plan to relaunch it as a stand-alone company.*
2 ADJ A **stand-alone** computer is one that can operate on its own and does not have to be part of a network. ❍ *an operating system that can work on networks and stand-alone machines*

stand|ard /stændərd/
1 NOUN a level of quality ❍ *The standard of his work is very low.*
2 PL NOUN **Standards** are moral principles. ❍ *My father always had high moral standards.*
3 ADJ usual and normal ❍ *It's just a standard size car.*

stand|ard cost (**standard costs**) NOUN the budgeted cost of a regular manufacturing process against which actual costs are compared ❍ *Of course, if a new product, service or process is to be carried out, the initial standard costs will have to be estimated.*

stand|ard|ise /stændərdaɪz/ [ECONOMICS, BRIT] → **standardize**

stand|ard|ize /stændərdaɪz/ (**standardizes, standardizing, standardized**) VERB To **standardize** things means to change them so that they all have the same features. [ECONOMICS] ❍ *There is a drive both to standardize components and to reduce the number of models.*
● **stand|ardi|za|tion** /stændərdɪzeɪʃən/ NONCOUNT NOUN ❍ *the standardization of working hours* ● **stand|ard|ized** ADJ ❍ *People prefer differentiated products to standardized products.*

stand|ard of liv|ing (**standards of living**) NOUN the quality of life and the amount of money that you have ❍ *We're all trying to improve our standard of living.*

stand|ing or|der (**standing orders**) NOUN A **standing order** is an instruction to a bank by a depositor to pay a stated sum at regular intervals. Compare with **direct debit**. [BANKING] ❍ *More people are being encouraged to pay their bills automatically by standing order or direct debit.*

stand|off /stændɔf/ also **stand-off** NOUN a situation in which neither of two opposing groups or forces will make a move until the other one does something ❍ *After he said he was unwilling to shoulder the increased taxes, a standoff ensued, and the deal fell apart late Monday.*

sta|ple /steɪpᵊl/ (**staples, stapling, stapled**)
1 ADJ A **staple** food or product is one that is important in people's lives. ❍ *Rice is the staple food of the region.*
2 NOUN a small piece of bent wire that holds sheets of paper together
3 VERB If you **staple** something, you fix it in place using staples. ❍ *Staple some sheets of paper together.*

sta|pler /steɪplər/ NOUN a piece of equipment that is used for fastening sheets of paper together with small pieces of bent wire

star /stɑr/ (**stars, starring, starred**)
1 NOUN a large ball of burning gas in space, that looks like a light in the sky at night ❍ *Stars lit the sky.*
2 NOUN a shape that has five or more points sticking out of it in a regular pattern ❍ *How many stars are there on the American flag?*
3 NOUN a famous actor, musician, or sports player ❍ *He's one of the stars of the TV series "Friends."*
4 VERB If someone **stars in** a play or a movie, or if a play or a movie **stars** that person, he or she has one of the most important parts in it. ❍ *Meryl Streep stars in the movie "The Devil Wears Prada."*

stare /stɛər/ (**stares, staring, stared**)
1 VERB If you **stare at** someone or something, you look at them for a long time. ❍ *We all spend too much time staring at computer screens.*
2 NOUN **Stare** is also a noun. ❍ *Harry gave him a long stare.*

start /stɑrt/
1 VERB If you **start doing** something, you begin doing it. ❍ *Susanna started working in TV in 2005.*
2 VERB When something **starts**, it begins to happen or exist. ❍ *The program started three years ago.*

3 NOUN Start is also a noun. ❍ *It was 1918, four years after the start of the Great War.*
4 VERB When someone **starts** something, they create it or cause it to begin. ❍ *She has started a child care center in Ohio.*
5 VERB If you **start** an engine or a machine, you make it begin to work. ❍ *He started the car and drove off.*
▶ **start over** If you **start over**, you begin something again from the beginning. ❍ *I did it all wrong and had to start over.*

star|tle /stɑrtᵊl/ (**startles, startling, startled**) **VERB** If something **startles** you, it suddenly surprises and frightens you slightly. ❍ *The telephone startled him.*

start-up
1 ADJ A **start-up** company is a small business that has recently been started by someone. [ECONOMICS] ❍ *Thousands of start-up firms have entered the computer market.*
2 NOUN a small business that has recently been started by someone [ECONOMICS] ❍ *For now the only bright spots in the labor market are small businesses and high-tech start-ups.*
3 ADJ Start-up capital is money spent to establish a new project or business. [ECONOMICS] ❍ *They blamed the loss on increased competition in certain markets and start-up costs of new facilities.*

COLLOCATIONS
a *business* start-up
an *Internet* start-up
start-up *costs*
start-up *capital*
a start-up *company*
a start-up *firm*

starve /stɑrv/ (**starves, starving, starved**)
1 VERB If people **starve**, they suffer or die because of lack of food. ❍ *All these people are now in danger of starving.* ● **star|va|tion** /stɑrveɪʃən/ **NONCOUNT NOUN** ❍ *Over three hundred people died of starvation.*
2 VERB To **starve** someone means not to give them any food. ❍ *He was starving himself.*

starv|ing /stɑrvɪŋ/ **ADJ** very hungry [INFORMAL] ❍ *Does anyone have any food? I'm starving.*

state /steɪt/ (**states, stating, stated**)
1 NOUN a country ❍ *a socialist state*
2 NOUN an area of some large countries such as the U.S. ❍ *the Southern states*
3 NOUN Some people say **the States** when they mean the U.S. [INFORMAL] ❍ *She bought it in the States.*
4 NOUN The state is the government of a country. ❍ *In Sweden, child care is provided by the state.*
5 NOUN the condition that someone or something is in ❍ *After Daniel died, I was in a state of shock.*
6 VERB If you **state** something, you say it or write it in a formal or definite way. ❍ *Clearly state your address and telephone number.*

state bank (**state banks**) **NOUN** In the United States, a **state bank** is a commercial bank established under a State charter. State banks are not legally required to be members of the Federal Reserve System. Compare with **national bank**. [BANKING] ❍ *California State Bank*

state|ment /steɪtmənt/
1 NOUN something that you say or write that gives information in a formal way ❍ *I was very angry when I made that statement.*
2 NOUN a printed document containing a summary of bills or invoices and displaying the total amount due ❍ *At the end of each billing cycle you will receive a statement.*
3 NOUN a printed document showing how much money has been paid into and taken out of a bank account over a particular period of time ❍ *Transactions and interest payments are recorded in a monthly statement or in a small book held by the owner of the account.*

state-of-the-art ADJ If something is **state-of-the-art**, it is the best available because it has been made using the most modern techniques and technology. ❍ *the production of state-of-the-art military equipment*

stat|ic /stætɪk/
1 ADJ not moving or changing ❍ *House prices were static last month.*
2 NONCOUNT NOUN Static or **static electricity** is electricity that collects on things such as your body or metal objects.

sta|tion /steɪʃən/
1 NOUN a place where trains stop so that people can get on or off ❍ *Ingrid went with him to the train station.*
2 NOUN A bus **station** is a place where buses start or end their journey. ❍ *I walked to the bus station and bought a ticket.*
3 NOUN A radio or television **station** is a company that broadcasts programs. ❍ *a local radio station*

sta|tion|ery /steɪʃənɛri/ **NONCOUNT NOUN** **Stationery** is paper, envelopes, and other materials or equipment used for writing. ❍ *envelopes and other office stationery*

sta|tis|tic /stətɪstɪk/ **NOUN** **Statistics** are facts that are expressed in numbers. ❍ *Statistics show that wages are rising.*

statue /stætʃu/ **NOUN** a large model of a person or an animal, made of stone or metal ❍ *She gave me a stone statue of a horse.*

sta|tus /steɪtəs, stæt-/ **NONCOUNT NOUN** The **status** of someone or something is the importance that people give them. ❍ *There are some jobs that are more attractive and carry higher status than others.*

statu|tory /stætʃʊtɔri/ **ADJ** relating to written rules or laws [LEGAL, FORMAL] ❍ *The FCC has no statutory authority to regulate the Internet.*

stay /steɪ/
1 VERB If you **stay** where you are, you continue to be there and do not leave. ❍ *"Stay here," Trish said.*
2 VERB If you **stay** somewhere, you live there for a short time. ❍ *Gordon stayed at The Park Hotel, Milan.*
3 NOUN **Stay** is also a noun. ❍ *Please contact the hotel reception if you have any problems during your stay.*
4 VERB If someone or something **stays** in a particular state or situation, they continue to be in it. ❍ *Exercise is one of the best ways to stay healthy.*
▶ **stay in** If you **stay in**, you remain at home. ❍ *We decided to stay in and have dinner at home.*
▶ **stay up** If you **stay up**, you do not go to bed at your usual time. ❍ *I need to stay up late and finish this report.*

steady /stɛdi/ (**steadier, steadiest**)
1 ADJ developing in a gradual, regular way ❍ *Despite these problems there has been steady progress.* ● **steadi|ly** /stɛdɪli/ **ADV** ❍ *Prices have been rising steadily.*
2 ADJ not moving around ❍ *Hold the camera steady.*

steak /steɪk/ **NOUN** a large flat piece of meat or fish ❍ *There was a steak cooking on the grill.*

steal /stil/ (**steals, stealing, stole, stolen**) **VERB** If you **steal** something, you take it without their permission. ❍ *They said he stole money from the till.* ❍ *It's wrong to steal.*

steam /stim/
1 NONCOUNT NOUN **Steam** is the hot gas that forms when water boils. ❍ *The heat converts water into steam.*
2 VERB If you **steam** food, you cook it in steam. ❍ *Steam the carrots.*
▶ **steam ahead** If an economy or company **steams ahead** it becomes stronger and more successful. ❍ *The latest figures show industrial production steaming ahead at an 8.8 percent annual rate.*

steel /stil/ **NONCOUNT NOUN** **Steel** is a very strong metal that is made mainly from iron.

steep /stip/
1 ADJ A **steep** slope rises at a very sharp angle. ❍ *Some of the hills in San Francisco are very steep.* ● **steep|ly** **ADV** ❍ *The road climbs steeply.*
2 ADJ A **steep** increase or fall in an amount is big and sudden. ❍ *There have been steep price increases.* ● **steep|ly** **ADV** ❍ *Unemployment is rising steeply.*

S

steer /stɪər/ **VERB** When you **steer** a vehicle, you control it so that it goes in the direction that you want. ❍ *What is it like to steer a big ship?*

steer|ing wheel (**steering wheels**) **NOUN** the wheel that you hold to control the direction of a vehicle

stem /stɛm/ **NOUN** the long, thin part of a plant that the flowers and leaves grow on ❍ *He cut the stem and gave her the flower.*

step /stɛp/ (**steps, stepping, stepped**)
1 NOUN a movement made by putting one

foot in front of the other ❍ *I took a step toward him.*

2 VERB If you **step on** something, you put your foot on it. ❍ *Neil Armstrong was the first man to step on the Moon.*

3 NOUN a raised flat surface, that you put your foot on in order to walk up or down stairs ❍ *We went down some steps into the yard.*

4 NOUN one of a series of actions that you take in a process ❍ *The parent company took the first step toward a possible sale of the airline.*

step|father /stɛpfɑðər/ also **step-father NOUN** the man who has married your mother but is not your father

step|mother /stɛpmʌðər/ also **step-mother NOUN** the woman who has married your father but is not your mother

ster|ile /stɛrəl/

1 ADJ completely clean ❍ *a sterile bandage*

2 ADJ unable to produce babies ❍ *The tests showed that George was sterile.*

ster|ling /stɜrlɪŋ/ **NONCOUNT NOUN** **Sterling** is the system of money used in Great Britain. [ECONOMICS] ❍ *The stamps had to be paid for in sterling.* ❍ *the pound sterling*

stern /stɜrn/ **ADJ** very severe ❍ *a stern warning* ● **stern|ly ADV** ❍ *"We will punish anyone who breaks the rules," she said sternly.*

stew /stu/ **NOUN** a meal that you make by cooking meat and vegetables in liquid ❍ *She gave him a bowl of beef stew.*

stick /stɪk/ (**sticks, sticking, stuck**)

1 NOUN a long thin piece of wood ❍ *She put some dry sticks on the fire.* ❍ *a walking stick*

2 VERB If you **stick** one thing to another, you join them with glue. ❍ *Now stick your picture on a piece of paper.*

3 VERB If you **stick** a pointed object **into** something, you push it into it. ❍ *The doctor stuck the needle into Joe's arm.*

4 VERB If one thing **sticks to** another, it becomes joined to it and is difficult to remove. ❍ *Dirt will not stick to fabric like this.*

▸ **stick by** If you **stick by** someone, you continue to give them support. ❍ *All my friends stuck by me.*

▸ **stick out** If something **sticks out**, it comes out further than the main part of something. ❍ *His two front teeth stick out slightly.*

▸ **stick to** If you **stick to** a promise or a decision, you do not change your mind. ❍ *We are waiting to see if he sticks to his promise.*

▸ **stick up for** If you **stick up for** someone or something, you support them and say that they are right. ❍ *My manager always sticks up for me.*

stick|er /stɪkər/ **NOUN** a small piece of paper with writing or a picture on one side, that you can stick onto a surface ❍ *I bought a sticker that said, "I love Florida."*

sticky /stɪki/ (**stickier, stickiest**) **ADJ** Something that is **sticky** sticks to other things. ❍ *The floor was sticky with spilled orange juice.*

stiff /stɪf/

1 ADJ firm and difficult to bend ❍ *The smartest invitations were engraved on stiff card.* ● **stiff|ly ADV** ❍ *Moira sat stiffly in her chair.*

2 ADJ If you are **stiff**, your body hurts when you move. ❍ *A hot bath is good for stiff muscles.*

still

❶ ADVERB USES
❷ ADJECTIVE USES

❶ **still** /stɪl/

1 ADV If a situation **still** exists, it continues to exist. ❍ *Do you still live in Illinois?*

2 ADV used to say that something is true, despite something else ❍ *Unemployment is below the national average, but still rather high.*

3 ADV used to make another word stronger ❍ *It's good to travel, but it's better still to come home.*

❷ **still** /stɪl/

1 ADJ not moving ❍ *Please stand still!*

2 ADJ If it is **still**, there is no wind. ❍ *It was a warm, still evening.*

stimu|late /stɪmyəleɪt/ (**stimulates, stimulating, stimulated**)

1 VERB To **stimulate** something means to make it develop more. ❍ *America is trying to stimulate its economy.*

2 VERB If you **are stimulated by** something, it makes you feel full of ideas and enthusiasm.

○ *Bill was stimulated by the challenge.*
• **stimu|lat|ing** ADJ ○ *It is a stimulating book.*
• **stimu|la|tion** NONCOUNT NOUN ○ *Her real. stimulation came from friends and the writers and artists she met.*

stimu|lus /stɪmyələs/ (**stimuli**) NOUN something that encourages activity [BUSINESS MANAGEMENT] ○ *Interest rates could fall soon and be a stimulus to the economy.*

sting /stɪŋ/ (**stings, stinging, stung**)
1 VERB If a plant, an animal, or an insect **stings** you, it gives you a sharp pain. ○ *She was stung by a bee.*
2 NOUN a sharp pain ○ *You will just feel a little sting.*
3 VERB If a part of your body **stings**, you feel a sharp pain there. ○ *His cheeks were stinging from the cold wind.*

stink /stɪŋk/ (**stinks, stinking, stank, stunk**) VERB To **stink** means to smell very bad. ○ *The kitchen stinks of fish.*

stir /stɜr/ (**stirs, stirring, stirred**)
1 VERB If you **stir** a substance, you mix it with a spoon. ○ *Stir the soup for a few seconds.*
2 VERB If someone **stirs**, they move slightly. ○ *Eileen shook him, and he started to stir.*

stitch /stɪtʃ/ (**stitches, stitching, stitched**)
1 VERB If you **stitch** cloth, you sew it. ○ *Stitch the two pieces of fabric together.*
2 NOUN one of the short lines of thread that have been sewn in a piece of cloth ○ *Sew a row of straight stitches.*
3 NOUN one of the lines of thread that has been used for sewing a wound together ○ *He had six stitches in the cut.*

stock /stɒk/
1 NOUN one of the parts or shares that the value of a company is divided into, that people can buy [FINANCE] ○ *She works for a bank, buying and selling stocks.*
2 NONCOUNT NOUN A company's **stock** is the total number of its shares. [FINANCE] ○ *Two years later, when the company went public, their stock was valued at $38 million.*
3 VERB If a store **stocks** particular products, it keeps a supply of them to sell. [MARKETING AND SALES] ○ *The store stocks everything from pens to TV sets.*
4 NONCOUNT NOUN A store's **stock** is the goods that it has available to sell. [MARKETING AND SALES] ○ *Most of the stock was destroyed in the fire.*
5 NOUN the raw materials or components that a company has ready to be made into finished goods [PRODUCTION] ○ *That buyer ordered £27,500 worth of stock.* ○ *The performance of the textiles side might have looked worse had it not been for the fact that stocks have been kept to a minimum.*
6 If goods are **in stock**, they are stored on the premises or available for sale or use. [PRODUCTION] ○ *Employees no longer have to run to the back room to print out lists of goods that are in stock.*
7 If goods are **out of stock**, they are not immediately available for sale or use. [PRODUCTION] ○ *But if their sales forecasting is not on the button, companies risk annoying consumers who cannot get hold of their products because they are out of stock.*

stock|broker /stɒkbroʊkər/ NOUN a person whose job is to buy and sell stocks for people who want to invest money [ECONOMICS]

stock|broking /stɒkbroʊkɪŋ/ NONCOUNT NOUN **Stockbroking** is the professional activity of buying and selling stocks for clients. [ECONOMICS] ○ *His stockbroking firm was hit by the 1987 crash.*

COLLOCATIONS
a stockbroking *firm*
a stockbroking *company*

S

stock cer|tifi|cate (**stock certificates**) NOUN a document issued by a company showing who owns its stock ○ *If stock certificates have been issued for shares being redeemed, they must accompany the written request.*

stock com|pany (**stock companies**) NOUN a business enterprise whose capital is divided into transferable shares of stock [ECONOMICS] ○ *Life insurance companies are organized in two forms: as stock companies or as mutuals.*

stock con|trol NONCOUNT NOUN Stock **control** is the same as **inventory control**. [PRODUCTION]

stock ex|change (**stock exchanges**)
1 NOUN a place where people buy and sell stocks [ECONOMICS] ❍ *the New York stock exchange*
2 NOUN an organization for the buying and selling of stocks [ECONOMICS] ❍ *In late trading on London's stock exchange, the shares were quoted at 833 pence.*
3 NOUN the prices or trading activity of a stock exchange [ECONOMICS] ❍ *The stock exchange fell heavily today.*

stock flo|ta|tion (**stock flotations**) NOUN an occasion when shares in a company are made available for people to buy [ECONOMICS] ❍ *a stock flotation that aims to raise $32 million*

stock|holder /stɒkhoʊldər/ NOUN a person who owns stock in a company [ECONOMICS] ❍ *He was a stockholder in a hotel corporation.*

COLLOCATIONS
a *corporation* stockholder
a *major* stockholder

stock in|dex (**stock indices** or **stock indexes**) NOUN a number that indicates the value of a stock market, based on the combined share prices of a set of companies [ECONOMICS] ❍ *The stock index was up 16.4 points to 1,599.6.*

stock|ing /stɒkɪŋ/ NOUN a piece clothing women wear over their feet and legs ❍ *a pair of nylon stockings*

S

stock in trade
1 NONCOUNT NOUN goods in stock necessary for carrying on a business ❍ *The equipment dealers coverage form covers the stock in trade of dealers in agricultural implements and construction equipment.*
2 NONCOUNT NOUN anything constantly used by someone as a part of their job ❍ *Friendliness is the salesman's stock in trade.*

stock is|sue (**stock issues**) NOUN A **stock issue** is the same as a **stock flotation**. [ECONOMICS]

stock mar|ket (**stock markets**) NOUN the activity of buying stock, or the place where this is done [ECONOMICS] ❍ *The company's shares promptly fell by 300 lire on the stock market.* ❍ *This is a practical guide to investing in the stock market.*

COLLOCATIONS
stock markets *rise*
stock markets *crash*
the stock market *closes up/down*
on the stock market

stock-market col|lapse (**stock-market collapses**)
1 NOUN a sudden decrease in value among all the stocks on a particular country's stock market [ECONOMICS] ❍ *the great stock-market collapse of the early nineties*
2 NOUN a sudden decrease in the value of the stock of a particular company [ECONOMICS] ❍ *a share support operation designed to prevent the stock market collapse of Maxwell Communication Corporation*

stock of|fer|ing (**stock offerings**) NOUN A **stock offering** is the same as a **stock flotation**. [ECONOMICS]

stock op|tion (**stock options**) NOUN an opportunity for the employees of a company to buy stock at a special price [ECONOMICS] ❍ *He made a huge profit from the sale of shares purchased in January under the company's stock-option program.*

stock split (**stock splits**) NOUN a procedure in which each share of a company's stock is replaced by several shares with the same total value [ECONOMICS]

stock|taking /stɒkteɪkɪŋ/ [PRODUCTION, mainly BRIT] → **inventory**

stole /stoʊl/ **Stole** is a form of the verb **steal**.

sto|len /stoʊlᵊn/
1 **Stolen** is a form of the verb **steal**.
2 ADJ having been taken without someone's permission ❍ *We have now found the stolen money.*

stom|ach /stʌmək/
1 NOUN the organ inside your body where food goes when you eat it ❍ *He has stomach problems.*

2 NOUN the front part of your body below your waist ❍ *The children lay down on their stomachs.*

stone /stoʊn/

1 NONCOUNT NOUN **Stone** is a hard solid substance that is found in the ground and often used for building. ❍ *a stone floor*

2 NOUN a small piece of rock ❍ *He removed a stone from his shoe.*

stood /stʊd/ **Stood** is a form of the verb **stand**.

stool /stul/ **NOUN** a seat with legs but no back or arms

stop /stɒp/ (**stops, stopping, stopped**)

1 VERB If you **stop** doing something, you do not do it anymore. ❍ *We must stop borrowing from abroad to pay for imports.* ❍ *She stopped and then continued eating.*

2 VERB If you **stop** something from happening, you prevent it. ❍ *They are trying to find a way to stop the war.*

3 VERB If an activity or a process **stops**, it does not happen anymore. ❍ *The price drop has slowed but it hasn't stopped.*

4 VERB If a machine **stops**, it is no longer working. ❍ *The clock stopped at 11:59 Saturday night.*

5 VERB When a person or vehicle **stops**, they do not move anymore. ❍ *The car failed to stop at a stoplight.*

6 NOUN If something that is moving comes **to a stop**, it no longer moves. ❍ *Do not open the door before the train comes to a stop.*

7 NOUN a place where buses or trains regularly stop ❍ *The nearest subway stop is Houston Street.*

8 VERB If you **stop** a check, you instruct a bank not to honour it. [BRIT]

9 VERB If you **stop** money from someone's pay, you deduct it. [BRIT] ❍ *Employees may have money stopped from their wages in the event of causing reckless or negligent damage to company property.*

10 If you **put a stop to** something, you prevent it from happening or continuing. ❍ *I'm going to put a stop to all this talk.*

stop|page /stɒpɪdʒ/

1 NOUN an occasion when people stop working because of a disagreement with their employers [HR] ❍ *Mineworkers in the Ukraine have voted for a one-day stoppage next month.*

2 NOUN a deduction of money from someone's pay [HR] ❍ *All workers are entitled to a payslip, which should show how much you have earned before and after stoppages.*

COLLOCATIONS
work stoppages
labor stoppages

stor|age /stɔrɪdʒ/

1 NONCOUNT NOUN **Storage** is keeping something in a special place until it is needed. ❍ *This room is used for storage.*

2 NONCOUNT NOUN **Storage** is a charge made for storing goods. [PRODUCTION] ❍ *Storage can include charges for a thirty-day period after the day of the move.*

store /stɔr/ (**stores, storing, stored**)

1 NOUN a place where things are sold ❍ *a grocery store*

2 VERB When you **store** things, you put them somewhere until they are needed. ❍ *We store the receipts in a box.*

store brand (**store brands**) **NOUN** a cheap product that has the trademark or label of the store that sells them ❍ *This range is substantially cheaper than any of the other store brands available.*

store card (**store cards**) **NOUN** a card issued by a store that enables customers to obtain goods and services for which they pay at a later date ❍ *Arrears on credit card or store card purchases are usually eventually pursued by a debt recovery agency.*

store|keeper /stɔrkipər/ **NOUN** a person who owns or manages a store [LOGISTICS AND DISTRIBUTION]

sto|rey /stɔri/ [mainly BRIT] → **story 3**

storm /stɔrm/ **NOUN** A **storm** is very bad weather, for example with heavy rain and strong winds. ❍ *There will be violent storms along the East Coast.*

sto|ry /stɔri/ (**stories**)

1 NOUN a description of imaginary people and events, that is intended to entertain people ❍ *I'm going to tell you a story about four little rabbits.*

2 NOUN a description of something that has happened ❍ *He calls the story "an absolute lie."*
3 NOUN one of the different levels of a building ❍ *Our apartment block is 25 stories high.*

stove /stoʊv/ **NOUN** a piece of equipment for cooking or for heating a room ❍ *She put the saucepan on the gas stove.*

straight /streɪt/
1 ADJ or **ADV** not bending or curving ❍ *The interstate highway is a long, straight road through the valley.* ❍ *Stand straight and hold your arms out to the side.*
2 ADV immediately ❍ *He went straight to his office.*
3 ADJ sold at a fixed unit price irrespective of the quantity sold ❍ *Ad agencies typically earned a straight 15% commission.*

straight|en /streɪtᵊn/ **VERB** If you **straighten** something, you make it straight. ❍ *She straightened a picture on the wall.*

straight|forward /streɪtfɔrwərd/
1 ADJ easy to do or understand ❍ *The computer system is straightforward to use.*
2 ADJ honest and direct ❍ *She is straightforward, and very honest.*

strain /streɪn/
1 NOUN a feeling of being anxious and having too much to do ❍ *She couldn't cope with the stresses and strains of her career.*
2 NOUN an injury to a muscle in your body ❍ *Avoid muscle strain by taking rests.*
3 VERB If you **strain** a muscle, you injure it by using it too much. ❍ *He strained his back playing tennis.*
4 VERB When you **strain** food, you separate the liquid part of it from the solid parts. ❍ *Strain the soup and put it back into the pan.*

strange /streɪndʒ/ (**stranger, strangest**)
1 ADJ unusual or unexpected ❍ *There was something strange about the way she spoke.*
● **strange|ly ADV** ❍ *She noticed he was acting strangely.*
2 ADJ A **strange** person or place is one that you do not know. ❍ *I was alone in a strange city.*

stran|ger /streɪndʒər/ **NOUN** someone that you have never met before ❍ *We don't want a complete stranger staying with us.*

S

strap /stræp/ (**straps, strapping, strapped**)
1 NOUN is a long, narrow piece of leather or other material ❍ *Nancy held the strap of her bag.*
2 VERB If you **strap** something somewhere, you fasten it there with a strap. ❍ *She strapped the baby seat into the car.*

stra|tegic /strətidʒɪk/ **ADJ** relating to the most important, general aspects of something, especially when these are decided in advance [BUSINESS MANAGEMENT] ❍ *new strategic thinking* ● **stra|tegi|cal|ly ADV** ❍ *strategically important roads, bridges, and buildings*

strat|egy /strætədʒi/ (**strategies**) **NOUN** a plan for how to achieve something [BUSINESS MANAGEMENT] ❍ *What should our marketing strategy have achieved?*

straw /strɔ/
1 NONCOUNT NOUN Straw is the dried, yellow stems of crops. ❍ *a straw hat*
2 NOUN a thin tube that you use to suck a drink into your mouth ❍ *I drank from a bottle of soda with a straw in it.*

straw|berry /strɔbɛri/ (**strawberries**) **NOUN** a small soft red fruit with a lot of very small seeds on its skin ❍ *strawberries and cream*

stray /streɪ/ **VERB** If someone **strays** somewhere, they go away from where they should be. ❍ *Be careful not to stray into dangerous parts of the city.*

streak /strik/ **NOUN** a long mark on a surface ❍ *There are dark streaks on the surface of the moon.*

stream /strim/
1 NOUN a small river ❍ *There was a small stream at the end of the garden.*
2 NOUN a large number of things that come one after another ❍ *The TV show caused a stream of complaints.*
3 VERB If something **streams** somewhere, it moves there in large amounts. ❍ *Buying orders streamed into the market from early morning.*
4 NOUN a flow of money into a business ❍ *a revenue stream*

street /strit/ **NOUN** a road in a city or a town ❍ *He lived at 66 Bingfield Street.*

strength /strɛŋkθ, strɛŋθ/
1 NONCOUNT NOUN Your **strength** is how physically strong you are. ❍ *Swimming builds up the strength of your muscles.*
2 NONCOUNT NOUN Someone's **strength** is their confidence or courage. ❍ *The appointment of a new chief financial officer will give us new strength.*
3 NOUN The **strength** of an object or a material is how strong it is. ❍ *He checked the strength of the rope.*
4 NONCOUNT NOUN The **strength of** a feeling or a belief is how deeply people feel it or believe it. ❍ *He was surprised at the strength of his own feeling.*

strength|en /strɛŋθᵊn/ **VERB** If you **strengthen** something, you make it stronger. ❍ *He said the bank has strengthened financial controls in its investment-banking unit.*

stress /strɛs/ (**stresses, stressing, stressed**)
1 VERB If you **stress** a point in a discussion, you emphasize it. ❍ *He stressed that the problem was not serious.*
2 NONCOUNT NOUN Stress is a feeling of being worried because of problems in your life. ❍ *The tests measured the ability to reason and handle stress.*
3 VERB If you **stress** a word or part of a word, you say it slightly more loudly. ❍ *She stressed the words "very important."*
4 NOUN Stress is also a noun. ❍ *The stress is on the first part of the word "animal."*
5 If you are **under stress**, you are worried because of problems in your life. ❍ *Many managers feel under stress at work.*
6 If an organization is **under stress**, it is having problems. ❍ *The company's financial position came under stress due to large losses.*

stressed /strɛst/ **ADJ** If someone is **stressed** or **stressed out**, they are very tense and anxious because of difficulties in their life. ❍ *What situations make you feel stressed?* ❍ *I can't imagine sitting in traffic, getting stressed out.*

stress|ful /strɛsfəl/ **ADJ** making you feel worried ❍ *I've got one of the most stressful jobs there is.*

stretch /strɛtʃ/ (**stretches, stretching, streched**)
1 VERB When you **stretch** something, or when it **stretches**, it becomes longer or wider. ❍ *Can you feel your leg muscles stretching?*
2 VERB Something that **stretches** over a distance covers all of it. ❍ *The line of cars stretched for several miles.*
3 NOUN a length or an area of road, water, or land ❍ *It's a very dangerous stretch of road.*
4 VERB When you **stretch** part of your body, you make it straighter and longer. ❍ *He yawned and stretched.*
▸ **stretch out** If you **stretch out** a part of your body, you hold it out toward something. ❍ *He stretched out his hand to touch the screen.*

strict /strɪkt/
1 ADJ A **strict** rule or order must be obeyed completely. ❍ *She gave them strict instructions not to remove the documents.* ❍ *The union's rules are very strict.* ● **strict|ly ADV** ❍ *The number of new members each year is strictly controlled.*
2 ADJ A **strict** person expects rules to be obeyed. ❍ *Our trainers were very strict.* ● **strict|ly ADV** ❍ *The government is strictly controlling credit expansion.*

stride /straɪd/ (**strides, striding, strode**)
1 VERB If you **stride** somewhere, you walk there with long steps. ❍ *The farmer came striding across the field.*
2 NOUN a long step ❍ *He crossed the street with long, quick strides.*

strike /straɪk/ (**strikes, striking, struck**)
1 VERB If a person or a moving object **strikes** someone or something, they hit them. [FORMAL] ❍ *She took two steps forward and struck him across the face.* ❍ *His head struck the bottom when he dived into the pool.*
2 VERB If something unpleasant **strikes**, it has a quick and violent effect. ❍ *A storm struck on Saturday.*
3 VERB If an idea **strikes** you, it suddenly comes into your mind. ❍ *A thought struck her. Was she jealous of her mother?*
4 VERB When a clock **strikes**, it makes a sound so that people know what the time is. ❍ *The clock struck nine.*
5 VERB When you **strike** a match, you make it produce a flame. ❍ *Robina struck a match and lit the fire.*

6 NOUN a period of time when workers refuse to work, usually to try to get better pay or conditions [BUSINESS MANAGEMENT] ❍ *The strike began yesterday.*

7 VERB Strike is also a verb. ❍ *Workers have the right to strike.*

8 When workers **go on strike**, they strike. [BUSINESS MANAGEMENT] ❍ *Staff at the hospital went on strike in protest at the incidents.*

9 If you **strike it rich**, you have an unexpected financial success. ❍ *When firms find the right combination of features, they will strike it rich.*

strike|bound /straɪkbaʊnd/ also **strike-bound ADJ** A **strikebound** factory is closed because of a strike. [BUSINESS MANAGEMENT] ❍ *Japan depends heavily on supplies from the strike-bound Highland Valley and Bougainville mines.*

strike|breaker /straɪkbreɪkər/ also **strike breaker NOUN** a person who continues to work during a strike, or someone who takes over the work of a person who is on strike [BUSINESS MANAGEMENT] ❍ *The company's use of strikebreakers led to a battle between workers and management forces at the plant.*

strike pay NONCOUNT NOUN Strike pay is money paid to strikers by a labor union. [BUSINESS MANAGEMENT, FINANCE] ❍ *But the confrontation is short, partly because the divided French unions cannot afford to provide members with strike pay.*

strik|er /straɪkər/ **NOUN** a person who is on strike [BUSINESS MANAGEMENT] ❍ *Strikers have rejected a pay raise offer of 10% over three years.*

string /strɪŋ/

1 NOUN String is thin rope. ❍ *The containers are made of cardboard and carefully wrapped with string.*

2 NOUN a thin piece of wire makes sounds on some musical instruments ❍ *He changed a guitar string.*

strip /strɪp/ (**strips, stripping, stripped**)

1 NOUN a long, narrow piece of something ❍ *The rugs are made from strips of fabric.* ❍ *a narrow strip of land*

2 VERB If you **strip**, you take off your clothes. ❍ *They stripped and jumped into the pool.*

stripe /straɪp/ **NOUN** a long line that is a different color from the areas next to it ❍ *She wore a blue skirt with white stripes.*

stroke /stroʊk/ (**strokes, stroking, stroked**)

1 VERB If you **stroke** someone or something, you move your hand slowly and gently over them. ❍ *Carla was stroking her cat.*

2 NOUN a medical problem that affects a person's brain, often making them unable to speak or move parts of their body ❍ *He had a stroke last year, and now he can't walk.*

strong /strɔŋ/

1 ADJ Someone who is **strong** has powerful muscles. ❍ *I'm not strong enough to carry him.*

2 ADJ confident and determined ❍ *You have to be strong and do what you believe is right.*

3 ADJ Strong objects or materials do not break easily. ❍ *This strong plastic will not crack.*
● **strong|ly ADV** ❍ *The wall was very strongly built.*

4 ADJ Strong opinions are opinions you believe in very firmly. ❍ *She has strong views on environmental issues.* ● **strong|ly ADV** ❍ *Obviously you feel very strongly about this.*

5 ADJ A **strong** drink, chemical, or drug contains a lot of the substance that makes it effective. ❍ *a cup of strong coffee*

6 ADJ very noticeable ❍ *Onions have a strong flavor.* ● **strong|ly ADV** ❍ *He smelled strongly of sweat.*

7 ADJ A **strong** industry, market or currency tends to have stable or increasing prices. ❍ *Investors were encouraged by the strong dollar.*

struck /strʌk/ **Struck** is a form of the verb **strike**.

struc|ture /strʌktʃər/

1 NOUN the way in which something is made, built, or organized ❍ *the structure of the brain*

2 NOUN something that has been built ❍ *This modern brick and glass structure was built in 1905.*

strug|gle /strʌgᵊl/ (**struggles, struggling, struggled**)

1 VERB If you **struggle to** do something, you try hard to do it, but you find it very difficult. ❍ *She struggled to find the right words.*

S

2 NOUN something that is very difficult to do ❍ *Losing weight was a terrible struggle.*
3 NOUN a long and difficult attempt to achieve something ❍ *The movie is about a young boy's struggle to survive.*
4 VERB If you **struggle** when you are being held, you move violently in order to get free. ❍ *I struggled, but she was too strong for me.*

stub|born /stʌbərn/ **ADJ** Someone who is **stubborn** is determined to do what they want. ❍ *I am a very stubborn and determined person.* ● **stub|born|ly** **ADV** ❍ *He stubbornly refused to tell her the truth.*

stuck /stʌk/
1 Stuck is a form of the verb **stick**.
2 ADJ unable to move or leave ❍ *His car got stuck in the snow.* ❍ *I don't want to get stuck in another job like that.*
3 ADJ unable to continue doing something because it is too difficult ❍ *The support desk will help if you get stuck.*

stu|dent /stuːdᵊnt/ **NOUN** a person who is studying at a school, college, or university ❍ *business school students*

stu|dio /stuːdioʊ/
1 NOUN a room where someone paints, draws, or takes photographs
2 NOUN a room where people make radio or television programs, music recordings, or movies ❍ *a recording studio*

study /stʌdi/ (**studies, studying, studied**)
1 VERB If you **study**, you spend time learning about a particular subject. ❍ *She spends most of her time studying.* ❍ *He studied History and Economics.*
2 NONCOUNT NOUN Study is the activity of studying. ❍ *What is the study of earthquakes called?*
3 VERB If you **study** something, you look at it very carefully. ❍ *Debbie studied the graph.*
4 NOUN a room in a house that is used for reading, writing, and studying ❍ *We sat together in his study.*

stuff /stʌf/
1 NONCOUNT NOUN Stuff is used to talk about things in a general way. [INFORMAL] ❍ *He pointed to a bag. "That's my stuff."*
2 VERB If you **stuff** something somewhere, you push it there quickly and roughly. ❍ *I stuffed the dollar bills into my pocket.*
3 VERB If you **stuff** something, you fill it with something. ❍ *He wanted to help the campaign by stuffing envelopes.*

stum|ble /stʌmbᵊl/ (**stumbles, stumbling, stumbled**) **VERB** If you **stumble**, you nearly fall over. ❍ *He stumbled and almost fell.*

stun /stʌn/ (**stuns, stunning, stunned**)
1 VERB If you **are stunned**, you are extremely shocked or surprised. ❍ *We're stunned by today's news.*
2 VERB If something **stuns** you, it makes you unconscious for a short time. ❍ *The blow to his head stunned him.*

stung /stʌŋ/ **Stung** is a form of the verb **sting**.

stun|ning /stʌnɪŋ/ **ADJ** extremely beautiful ❍ *a stunning woman*

stu|pid /stuːpɪd/ (**stupider, stupidest**) **ADJ** not intelligent or sensible ❍ *I made a stupid mistake.* ● **stu|pid|ly** **ADV** ❍ *I'm sorry. I behaved stupidly.* ● **stu|pid|ity** /stupɪdɪti/ **NONCOUNT NOUN** ❍ *I was surprised by his stupidity.*

style /staɪl/
1 NOUN the way in which something is done ❍ *Trading styles on Wall Street differ.*
2 NOUN the design of something ❍ *These kids want everything in the latest style.*

styl|ish /staɪlɪʃ/ **ADJ** attractive and fashionable ❍ *a stylish uniform*

sub|con|tract

Pronounce the verb /sʌbkəntrækt/. Pronounce the noun /sʌbkɒntrækt/.

1 VERB If one company **subcontracts** part of its work **to** another company, it pays the other company to do part of the work that it has been employed to do. [LEGAL, BUSINESS MANAGEMENT] ❍ *The company is subcontracting production of most of the parts.*
2 NOUN a contract between a company that is being employed to do a job and another company that agrees to do part of that job [LEGAL, BUSINESS MANAGEMENT] ❍ *IPL Systems announced today that it was awarded a subcontract by Compuwork Inc.*

S

sub|con|trac|tor /sʌbkɑntræktər/ also **sub-contractor** NOUN a person or company that has a contract to do part of a job that another company is responsible for [LEGAL, BUSINESS MANAGEMENT] ❍ *The company was considered as a possible subcontractor to build the airplane.*

sub|ject /sʌbdʒɪkt/
1 NOUN the thing that is being written or spoken about ❍ *I'd like to hear the president's own views on the subject.*
2 NOUN an area of knowledge that you study in school or college ❍ *Math is my favorite subject.*
3 NOUN In grammar, the **subject** is the noun referring to the person or thing that is doing the action expressed by the verb.

sub|limi|nal ad|ver|tis|ing /sʌblɪmɪnᵊl ædvɜrtaɪzɪŋ/ NONCOUNT NOUN **Subliminal advertising** is a form of advertising on film or television that displays images for a fraction of a second to influence the viewer unconsciously. [MARKETING AND SALES] ❍ *The advertising industry, a prominent and powerful industry, engages in deceptive subliminal advertising that most us are unaware of.*

sub|ma|rine /sʌbmərin/ NOUN a ship that can travel below the surface of the ocean ❍ *a nuclear submarine*

sub|mit /səbmɪt/ (**submits, submitting, submitted**) VERB If you **submit** a proposal, a report, or a request, you formally send it to someone. ❍ *They submitted their reports yesterday.*

sub|or|di|nate /səbɔrdᵊnɪt/
1 NOUN someone who has a less important position than someone else in an organization [ADMINISTRATION] ❍ *Haig did not ask for advice from subordinates.*
2 ADJ lower in rank, position, or importance ❍ *Sixty of his subordinate officers were with him.* ❍ *Science became subordinate to technology.*

sub|prime /sʌbpraɪm/ ADJ A **subprime** loan is made to a borrower with a poor credit rating, usually at a high rate of interest. [BANKING] ❍ *More big banks are set to reveal damage caused by their exposure to subprime mortgage lending.*

sub|scribe /səbskraɪb/ (**subscribes, subscribing, subscribed**)
1 VERB If you **subscribe to** a magazine or a newspaper, you pay to receive copies of it regularly. ❍ *My main reason for subscribing to New Scientist is to keep abreast of advances in science.*
2 VERB If you **subscribe to** an online newsgroup or service, you send a message saying that you wish to receive it or belong to it. ❍ *Usenet is a collection of discussion groups, known as newsgroups, to which anybody can subscribe.*
3 VERB If you **subscribe for** shares in a company, you apply to buy shares in that company. ❍ *Employees subscribed for far more shares than were available.*

sub|scrip|tion /səbskrɪpʃən/ NOUN an amount of money that you pay regularly in order to belong to an organization or to receive a service ❍ *Members pay a subscription every year.*

sub|se|quent /sʌbsɪkwənt/ ADJ happening or existing after the time that has just been mentioned [FORMAL] ❍ *the increase of prices in subsequent years* ● **sub|se|quent|ly** ADV ❍ *He subsequently worked in Canada.*

sub|sidi|ary /səbsɪdiɛri/ (**subsidiaries**) or **subsidiary company** NOUN a company that is part of a larger and more important company [ADMINISTRATION] ❍ *WM Financial Services is a subsidiary of Washington Mutual.*

sub|si|dise /sʌbsɪdaɪz/ [ECONOMICS, BRIT] → **subsidize**

sub|si|dize /sʌbsɪdaɪz/ (**subsidizes, subsidizing, subsidized**) VERB If a government or other authority **subsidizes** something, they pay part of the cost of it. [ECONOMICS] ❍ *Around the world, governments have subsidized the housing of middle- and upper-income groups.* ● **sub|si|dized** ADJ ❍ *heavily subsidized prices for housing, bread, and meat*

sub|si|dy /sʌbsɪdi/ (**subsidies**) NOUN money that is paid by a government or other authority in order to help an industry or business, or to pay for a public service [ECONOMICS] ❍ *European farmers are planning a massive demonstration against farm subsidy cuts.*

sub|sis|tence wage /səbsɪstəns weɪdʒ/ (**subsistence wages**) NOUN the lowest wage upon which a worker and his or her family can survive [ECONOMICS, FINANCE] ❍ *The continuing fall in world prices means that many coffee-producing countries are finding it difficult to pay growers a subsistence wage.*

sub|stance /sʌbstəns/ NOUN a solid, a powder, a liquid, or a gas ❍ *The waste contained several unpleasant substances.*

sub|stan|tial /səbstænʃəl/ ADJ large [FORMAL] ❍ *A substantial number of people disagree with the new plan.*

sub|sti|tute /sʌbstɪtut/ (**substitutes, substituting, substituted**)
1 VERB If you **substitute** one thing **for** another, you use it instead of the other thing. ❍ *She stole the money by substituting her name for theirs on checks from suppliers.*
2 NOUN A **substitute** is something that you use instead of something else. ❍ *They are using calculators as a substitute for thinking.*

sub|tle /sʌtəl/ (**subtler, subtlest**) ADJ not obvious or strong ❍ *Subtle differences in store decor also affect how shoppers feel.* ● **sub|tly** ADV ❍ *The truth is subtly different.*

sub|tract /səbtrækt/ VERB If you **subtract** one number **from** another, you take it away. ● **sub|trac|tion** /səbtrækʃən/ NONCOUNT NOUN ❍ *She's ready to learn subtraction.*

sub|urb /sʌbɜrb/ NOUN The **suburbs of** a city are the areas on the edge of it where people live. ❍ *His family lives in the suburbs.*

sub|ur|ban /səbɜrbən/ ADJ relating to the suburbs ❍ *They have a comfortable suburban home.*

sub|way /sʌbweɪ/ NOUN a railroad system that runs under the ground ❍ *I don't ride the subway late at night.*

suc|ceed /səksid/
1 VERB If you **succeed**, you get the result that you wanted. ❍ *We have already succeeded in starting our own company.*
2 VERB If you **succeed** someone, you take over a post from them. ❍ *He resigned as chairman and chief executive officer and will be succeeded by Gary Freedman.*

suc|cess /səksɛs/ (**successes**)
1 NONCOUNT NOUN **Success** is doing well and getting the result that you wanted. ❍ *We were surprised by the plan's success.*
2 NOUN someone or something that does very well, or is popular ❍ *We hope the movie will be a success.*

suc|cess|ful /səksɛsfəl/ ADJ achieving what you want [BUSINESS MANAGEMENT] ❍ *How successful will this new project be?* ● **suc|cess|ful|ly** ADV ❍ *All three laser systems have been successfully tested on the eyes of blind patients.*

suc|ces|sor /səksɛsər/ NOUN the person who takes someone's job after they have left it ❍ *He set out several principles that he hopes will guide his successors.*

such /sʌtʃ/
1 ADJ used to refer to the person or thing you have just mentioned, or to someone or something similar ❍ *How could you do such a thing?*
2 ADJ used to emphasize the degree or amount of something ❍ *These roads are not designed for such heavy traffic.* ❍ *It was such a pleasant surprise.*
3 used to introduce an example ❍ *Avoid fatty food such as butter and red meat.*

suck /sʌk/ VERB If you **suck** something, you hold it in your mouth and pull at it with your cheeks and tongue, usually in order to get liquid out of it. ❍ *They sucked their candies.* ❍ *The baby sucked the milk from his bottle.*

sud|den /sʌdən/ ADJ quick and unexpected ❍ *There has been a sudden increase in costs.* ● **sud|den|ly** ADV ❍ *Her expression suddenly changed.*

sue /su/ (**sues, suing, sued**) VERB If you **sue** someone, you start a legal case against them, usually in order to get money from them because they have harmed you. ❍ *The couple are suing the company for $4.4 million.*

suf|fer /sʌfər/ **VERB** If you **suffer**, you feel pain, or unpleasant emotions. ❍ *She was very sick, and suffering great pain.* ❍ *He was suffering from cancer.* ● **suf|fer|er** **NOUN** ❍ *asthma sufferers*

suf|fer|ing /sʌfərɪŋ/ **NONCOUNT NOUN** **Suffering** is pain, or unpleasant emotions that someone feels.

suf|fi|cient /səfɪʃənt/ **ADJ** enough ❍ *The food we have is sufficient for 12 people.* ● **suf|fi|cient|ly** **ADV** ❍ *She recovered sufficiently to go on vacation.*

sug|ar /ʃʊgər/ **NONCOUNT NOUN** **Sugar** is a sweet substance that is used for making food and drinks taste sweet. ❍ *Do you take sugar in your coffee?*

sug|gest /səgdʒɛst/ **VERB** If you **suggest** something, you tell someone an idea or plan that you have. ❍ *I suggested we postpone the meeting.*

sug|ges|tion /səgdʒɛstʃən/ **NOUN** an idea or plan that someone has ❍ *Do you have any suggestions for improving the service we provide?*

suit /sut/
1 NOUN a jacket and pants or a skirt that are made from the same cloth ❍ *a dark business suit*
2 VERB If something **suits** you, it makes you look attractive. ❍ *Green suits you.*
3 VERB If something **suits** you, it is convenient for you. ❍ *With online shopping, you can do your shopping when it suits you.*
4 NOUN a business executive or manager [INFORMAL] ❍ *I guess that the suits think that the extra cost is worth it for the certainty of a sure-fire success.*

S

suit|able /sutəbᵊl/ **ADJ** right for a particular occasion or purpose ❍ *This film would be suitable for children 8-13 years.* ● **suit|ably** **ADV** ❍ *He was suitably dressed for the occasion.*

suit|case /sutkeɪs/ **NOUN** a case for carrying your clothes when you are traveling ❍ *It did not take Andrew long to pack a suitcase.*

suite /swit/ **NOUN** a set of rooms in a hotel ❍ *They stayed in a suite at the Paris Hilton.*

suit|or /sutər/
1 NOUN A woman's **suitor** is a man who wants to marry her. [OLD-FASHIONED] ❍ *My mother had a suitor who adored her.*
2 NOUN a company or organization that wants to buy another company ❍ *The company was making little progress in trying to find a suitor.*

sum /sʌm/ (**sums, summing, summed**)
1 NOUN an amount of money ❍ *Large sums of money were lost.*
2 NOUN the total amount when two or more numbers are added together ❍ *Fourteen is the sum of eight and six.*
▶ **sum up** If you **sum up** the main points of an argument, you describe them in a few words. ❍ *We can sum up the answer in three words: supply and demand.*

sum|ma|rise /sʌməraɪz/ [BRIT] → **summarize**

sum|ma|rize /sʌməraɪz/ (**summarizes, summarizing, summarized**) **VERB** If you **summarize** something, you give the most important points about it. ❍ *The article can be summarized in three sentences.*

sum|mary /sʌməri/ (**summaries**) **NOUN** a short description that gives the main points of something ❍ *Here is a short summary of the process.*

sum|mer /sʌmər/ **NOUN** the season between spring and fall ❍ *It was a perfect summer's day.*

sum|mit /sʌmɪt/
1 NOUN a meeting between the leaders of two or more countries ❍ *The topic will be discussed at next week's Washington summit.*
2 NOUN the top of a mountain ❍ *the summit of Mount Everest*

sum|mon /sʌmən/ **VERB** If you **summon** someone, you order them to come to you. [FORMAL] ❍ *Suddenly we were summoned to his office.*

sun /sʌn/
1 NOUN the ball of fire in the sky that gives us heat and light ❍ *Suddenly, the sun came out.*
2 NONCOUNT NOUN **The sun** is the heat and light that comes from the sun. ❍ *They deserve a holiday in the sun.*

sun|bathe /sʌnbeɪð/ (**sunbathes, sunbathing, sunbathed**) **VERB** When people

sunbathe, they sit or lie in the sun. ❍ *Frank swam and sunbathed at the pool every morning.*

sun|burn /sʌnbɜrn/ NONCOUNT NOUN If someone has **sunburn**, their skin is pink and sore because they have spent too much time in the sun.

sun|burned /sʌnbɜrnd/ also **sunburnt** ADJ Someone who is **sunburned** has pink, sore skin because they have spent too much time in the sun.

Sun|day /sʌndeɪ, -di/ NOUN the day after Saturday and before Monday ❍ *We went for a drive on Sunday.*

sung /sʌŋ/ **Sung** is a form of the verb **sing**.

sun|glasses /sʌnglæsɪz/ PL NOUN **Sunglasses** are dark glasses that you wear to protect your eyes from bright light. ❍ *She put on a pair of sunglasses.*

sunk /sʌŋk/ **Sunk** is a form of the verb **sink**.

sun|light /sʌnlaɪt/ NONCOUNT NOUN **Sunlight** is light from the sun. ❍ *Sunlight filled the room.*

sun|ny /sʌni/ (**sunnier, sunniest**) ADJ bright with light from the sun ❍ *The weather was warm and sunny.*

sun|rise /sʌnraɪz/ NONCOUNT NOUN **Sunrise** is the time in the morning when the sun appears in the sky. ❍ *The rain began before sunrise.*

sun|rise ind|us|try (**sunrise industries**) NOUN any of the high-technology industries that hold promise of future development [TECHNOLOGY] ❍ *Since food-processing is a sunrise industry, we will see a lot happening in the cookie market.*

sun|screen /sʌnskrin/ NONCOUNT NOUN **Sunscreen** is a cream that protects your skin from the sun.

sun|set /sʌnsɛt/ NONCOUNT NOUN **Sunset** is the time in the evening when the sun goes down. ❍ *The party began at sunset.*

sun|shine /sʌnʃaɪn/ NONCOUNT NOUN **Sunshine** is the light and heat that comes from the sun. ❍ *She was sitting outside a cafe in bright sunshine.*

sun|tan /sʌntæn/ NOUN If you have a **suntan**, the sun has made your skin darker.

su|per /supər/ ADV used to describe things that are better, larger, or more extreme than other things ❍ *Beverly Hills, home of the rich and the super rich*

super|an|nu|ated /supərænyueɪtɪd/ ADJ discharged from your job owing to age or illness ❍ *Traditional pension systems were designed to take care of surviving widows and minor children rather than to provide the superannuated employee with a retirement pension.*

super|an|nua|tion /supərænyueɪʃən/ NONCOUNT NOUN **Superannuation** is the same as a **retirement fund**. [BANKING, mainly BRIT]

su|perb /supɜrb/ ADJ extremely good ❍ *There is a superb golf course 6 miles away.* ● **su|perb|ly** ADV ❍ *The orchestra played superbly.*

super|in|ten|dent /supərɪntɛndənt, suprɪn-/

1 NOUN a person who is responsible for a particular department in an organization ❍ *He became superintendent of the bank's East African branches.*

2 NOUN a person whose job is to take care of a large building such as an apartment building

su|peri|or /supɪəriər/

1 ADJ better than other similar people or things ❍ *superior quality coffee* ● **su|peri|or|ity** /supɪəriɔrɪti/ NONCOUNT NOUN ❍ *Belonging to a powerful organization gives them a feeling of superiority.*

2 NOUN Your **superior** at work is a person who has a higher position than you.

super|la|tive /supɜrlətɪv/ ADJ **Superlative** describes the form of an adjective or adverb that shows that something has more of a quality than anything else. For example, "biggest" and "most quickly" are superlative forms. Compare with **comparative**.

super|mar|ket /supərmarkɪt/ NOUN a large store that sells food and other products for the home [ECONOMICS, MARKETING AND SALES] ❍ *Most of us do our food shopping in the supermarket.*

COLLOCATIONS

a supermarket *chain*
a *leading* supermarket
a *local* supermarket
a *major* supermarket

super|store /su̲pərstɔr/ **NOUN** a very large store selling household goods and equipment, usually built outside a city and away from other stores [ECONOMICS, MARKETING AND SALES] ❍ *a Do-It-Yourself superstore*

super|vise /su̲pərvaɪz/ (**supervises, supervising, supervised**) **VERB** If you **supervise** an activity or a person, you make sure that things are being done correctly. ❍ *He supervises 33 people and the preparation of about 1,000 meals a day.* ● **super|vi|sion** /su̲pərvɪʒᵊn/ **NONCOUNT NOUN** ❍ *He got no supervision and was paid on a piecework basis.*

super|vi|sor /su̲pərvaɪzər/ **NOUN** someone whose job is to make sure that work is done correctly [BUSINESS MANAGEMENT, ADMINISTRATION] ❍ *He got a job as a supervisor at a factory.*

sup|per /sʌ̲pər/ **NONCOUNT NOUN** a meal that people eat in the evening ❍ *Would you like to join us for supper?*

sup|plement /sʌ̲plɪmənt/

1 VERB If you **supplement** something, you add something to it. ❍ *Some people do extra jobs to supplement their incomes.*

2 NOUN Supplement is also a noun. ❍ *These classes are a supplement to school study.*

S

sup|pli|er /səplaɪ̲ər/ **NOUN** a company that sells products to customers [LOGISTICS AND DISTRIBUTION] ❍ *We are one of the country's biggest food suppliers.*

COLLOCATIONS

a *leading* supplier
a *major* supplier
a *sole* supplier
a *preferred* supplier
a *main* supplier
an *arms* supplier
a *component* supplier
an *equipment* supplier
a *goods* supplier

sup|pli̲|er base NONCOUNT NOUN A company's **supplier base** consists of all the companies that are its suppliers. [LOGISTICS AND DISTRIBUTION] ❍ *We needed to dramatically reduce our supplier base.*

sup|pli̲|er pa̲rt|ner|ship (**supplier partnerships**) **NOUN** a relationship between a company and a supplier [LOGISTICS AND DISTRIBUTION] ❍ *Villadsen is responsible for reducing manufacturing cycle time, strengthening supplier partnerships, overseeing quality assurance and streamlining purchasing procedures.*

sup|ply /səplaɪ̲/ (**supplies, supplying, supplied**)

1 VERB If you **supply** someone with something, you provide it. [LOGISTICS AND DISTRIBUTION] ❍ *In recent years, U.S. steelmakers have supplied about 80% of the 100 million tons of steel used annually by the nation.*

2 NOUN an amount of something that is available for people to use ❍ *The brain needs a constant supply of oxygen.*

3 NONCOUNT NOUN Supply is the quantity of goods and services that can be made available for people to buy. Compare with **demand**. [ECONOMICS] ❍ *Prices change according to supply and demand.*

sup|ply̲ chain (**supply chains**) **NOUN** the various stages, in order, of a product's progress from raw materials until it reaches the consumer [LOGISTICS AND DISTRIBUTION] ❍ *"Lean" manufacturing processes aim to eliminate waste across the supply chain.*

supply̲-side eco|no̲m|ics NONCOUNT NOUN an economic theory that emphasizes the importance to a strong economy of policies that remove anything that stops supply [LOGISTICS AND DISTRIBUTION, ECONOMICS]

sup|port /səpɔ̲rt/

1 VERB If you **support** someone or their ideas, you agree with them, and want them to succeed. ❍ *He thanked everyone who had supported him during his campaign.*

2 NONCOUNT NOUN Support is also a noun. ❍ *The president gave his full support to the reforms.*

3 NONCOUNT NOUN If you give **support** to

someone, you help them. ❍ *The directors voted 7-2 to give us their support.*
4 VERB If you **support** someone, you provide them with money or the things that they need. ❍ *I have three children to support.*
5 VERB If something **supports** an object, it is holding it up. ❍ *Thick wooden posts supported the roof.*

sup|port|er /səpɔrtər/ **NOUN** someone who agrees with the ideas of a person or organization and wants them to succeed ❍ *But supporters of the World Bank contend it is constrained by the lack of economic management in the countries themselves.*

sup|port|ive /səpɔrtɪv/ **ADJ** kind and helpful to someone ❍ *They were always supportive of each other.*

sup|pose /səpoʊz/ (**supposes, supposing, supposed**)
1 VERB You can use **suppose** or **supposing** before suggesting a situation that could happen. ❍ *Suppose someone gave you a check for $6 million. What would you do with it?*
2 VERB If you **suppose that** something is true, you think that it is probably true. ❍ *I suppose you're in human resources, too?*
3 You can say "**I suppose**" when you are slightly uncertain about something. [SPOKEN] ❍ *I suppose you're right.*

sup|posed

Pronounce meanings **1** and **2** /səpoʊzd/ or /səpoʊst/ and meanings **3** and **4** /səpoʊzd/.

1 If you **are supposed to** do or have something, you should do or have it. ❍ *We are supposed to have an hour for lunch.*
2 If something **is supposed to** happen, it is planned or expected. ❍ *Mr. Stewart is supposed authorize the bank's electronic payments.*
3 If something **is supposed to** be true, many people say it is true. ❍ *"Avatar" is supposed to be a really great movie.*
4 ADJ used to suggest that something may not be what people say it is ❍ *the supposed cause of the accident* ● **sup|pos|ed|ly** /səpoʊzɪdli/ **ADV** ❍ *It was supposedly his own work.*

sur|charge /sɜrtʃɑrdʒ/ **NOUN** an extra payment of money in addition to the usual payment for something ❍ *The government introduced a 15% surcharge on imports.*

sure /ʃʊər/ (**surer, surest**)
1 ADJ certain ❍ *I'm not sure where he lives.*
2 Sure is an informal way of saying "yes." [SPOKEN] ❍ *"Do you know where she lives?"—"Sure."*
3 If you **make sure that** something is true or has happened, you check it. ❍ *He looked around to make sure that he was alone.*

sure|ly /ʃʊərli/ **ADV** used to express surprise about something ❍ *You surely haven't forgotten Dr. Walters?*

surf /sɜrf/
1 NONCOUNT NOUN Surf is the top of waves in the ocean. ❍ *We watched the surf rolling onto the white sandy beach.*
2 VERB If you **surf**, you ride on big waves in the ocean on a special board. ❍ *I'm going to buy a board and learn to surf.*
3 VERB If you **surf** the Internet, you spend time looking at different websites. [TECHNOLOGY] ❍ *It's hard to imagine doing business today without surfing the Net.*

COLLOCATIONS
to surf *the Net*
to surf *the Internet*

sur|face /sɜrfɪs/ **NOUN** the flat top part of something or the outside of it ❍ *Small waves moved on the surface of the water.*

surge /sɜrdʒ/ (**surges, surging, surged**)
1 NOUN a sudden large increase ❍ *a surge in prices*
2 VERB If a crowd of people **surge** forward, they suddenly move forward together. ❍ *The crowd surged forward into the store.*

sur|geon /sɜrdʒᵊn/ **NOUN** a doctor who performs operations ❍ *a heart surgeon*

sur|gery /sɜrdʒəri/ **NONCOUNT NOUN Surgery** is a process in which a doctor performs an operation. ❍ *His father just had heart surgery.*

sur|gi|cal /sɜrdʒɪkᵊl/ **ADJ Surgical** equipment and clothing is used for doing operations. ❍ *a collection of surgical instruments*

S

sur|name /sɜ̲rneɪm/ [BRIT] → **last name**

sur|plus /sɜ̲rplʌs, -pləs/ (**surpluses**)
1 NOUN more than you need of something ❍ *There was a surplus of food.*
2 ADJ more than is needed ❍ *Few people have large sums of surplus cash.*
3 NOUN any money that is left over at the end of an accounting period ❍ *A charity's surplus at the end of a financial year is not liable to taxation.*

sur|prise /sərpra̲ɪz/ (**surprises, surprising, surprised**)
1 NOUN an unexpected event or fact ❍ *I have a surprise for you: We are moving to Switzerland!*
2 ADJ **Surprise** is also an adjective. ❍ *a surprise visit*
3 NONCOUNT NOUN **Surprise** is the feeling that you have when something that you do not expect happens. ❍ *The Pentagon has expressed surprise at his comments.*
4 VERB If something **surprises** you, it gives you a feeling of surprise. ❍ *We'll do the job ourselves and surprise everyone.*

sur|prised /sərpra̲ɪzd/ **ADJ** having a feeling of surprise ❍ *I was surprised at how easy it was.*

sur|pris|ing /sərpra̲ɪzɪŋ/ **ADJ** making you feel surprised ❍ *The focus on health-care benefits isn't surprising.* ● **sur|pris|ing|ly** **ADV** ❍ *They have announced surprisingly weak second-quarter results.*

sur|ren|der /sərɛ̲ndər/ **VERB** If you **surrender**, you stop fighting because you cannot win. ❍ *The army finally surrendered.*

sur|re̲n|der value (**surrender values**) **NOUN** The **surrender value** of a life insurance policy is the amount of money you receive if you decide that you no longer wish to continue with the policy. [BANKING] ❍ *An ordinary life policy may have a cash surrender value of $50,000.*

sur|round /səra̲ʊnd/ **VERB** If a person or thing **is surrounded** by something, that thing is all around them. ❍ *New housing developments surround the city.*

sur|round|ings /səra̲ʊndɪŋz/ **PL NOUN** Your **surroundings** are the place where you are. ❍ *He soon felt at home in his new surroundings.*

sur|tax /sɜ̲rtæks/ **NONCOUNT NOUN** **Surtax** is an additional tax on incomes higher than the level at which ordinary tax is paid. [ECONOMICS] ❍ *a 10% surtax for Americans earning more than $250,000 a year*

sur|vey /sɜ̲rveɪ/
1 NOUN an attempt to find out information by asking people questions ❍ *According to the survey, overall world trade has also slackened.*
2 VERB If you **survey** a number of people or organizations, you try to find out information about their opinions or behavior. ❍ *Business Advisers surveyed 211 companies for the report.*

sur|viv|al /sərva̲ɪvᵊl/ **NONCOUNT NOUN** The **survival** of something or someone is the fact that they continue to live or exist. ❍ *Many of these companies are now struggling for survival.*

sur|vive /sərva̲ɪv/ (**survives, surviving, survived**) **VERB** If someone **survives** a dangerous situation, they do not die. ❍ *It's a miracle that anyone survived.* ● **sur|vi|vor** **NOUN** ❍ *There were no survivors of the plane crash.*

sus|pect

> Pronounce the verb /səspɛ̲kt/. Pronounce the noun /sʌ̲spɛkt/.

1 VERB If you **suspect** that something is true, you think that it is true but you are not certain. ❍ *He suspected that she was telling lies.*
2 VERB If you **suspect** someone **of** doing something bad, you believe that they probably did it. ❍ *The police did not suspect him of anything.*
3 NOUN a person who the police think may be guilty of a crime ❍ *Police have arrested a suspect.*

sus|pend /səspɛ̲nd/
1 VERB If you **suspend** something, you stop it for a period of time. ❍ *The company will suspend production June 1st.* ❍ *The government declared bankruptcy and suspended payment on some portion of its debt.*
2 VERB Something that **is suspended** from a high place is hanging from that place. ❍ *Three television screens were suspended from the ceiling.*

sus|pen|sion /səspɛ̲nʃən/
1 NONCOUNT NOUN The **suspension** of

something is the act of delaying or stopping it for a while or until a decision is made about it. ❍ *There's been a temporary suspension of flights out of LA.* ❍ *suspension of payments to bankrupt states*

2 NONCOUNT NOUN Suspension is the act of removing someone from their job or position for a period of time or until a decision is made about them. ❍ *The minister warned that any civil servant not at his desk faced immediate suspension.*

sus|pi|cion /səspɪʃən/ **NOUN** a belief or feeling that someone has done something wrong ❍ *Don't do anything that might cause suspicion.*

sus|pi|cious /səspɪʃəs/

1 ADJ believing that someone has done something wrong or cannot be trusted ❍ *He was suspicious of me at first.* ● **sus|pi|cious|ly ADJ** ❍ *"What is it you want me to do?" Adams asked suspiciously.*

2 ADJ If someone or something is **suspicious**, you feel that there is something bad or illegal about them. ❍ *Please contact the police if you see any suspicious person in the area.*

● **sus|pi|cious|ly ADV** ❍ *Has anyone been acting suspiciously over the last few days?*

sus|tain /səsteɪn/

1 VERB If you **sustain** something, you make it continue. ❍ *He has difficulty sustaining relationships.*

2 VERB If you **sustain** a loss or an injury, it happens to you. [FORMAL] ❍ *The company sustained a loss of about $10 million for the entire year.*

sus|tain|able /səsteɪnəbᵊl/

1 ADJ not damaging to the environment ❍ *a program of sustainable development*

● **sus|tain|abil|ity** /səsteɪnəbɪlɪti/ **NONCOUNT NOUN** ❍ *environmental sustainability*

2 ADJ A **sustainable** business is able to continue at a steady level without the need to invest more money in it or to develop new markets. [BUSINESS MANAGEMENT] ❍ *Further, operating without a domestic source of supply in a major market like the U.S.A. was not and is not a sustainable business model.*

COLLOCATIONS

ecologically sustainable
environmentally sustainable
sustainable *development*
sustainable *growth*
sustainable *agriculture*

swal|low /swɒloʊ/ **VERB** If you **swallow** something, you make it go down your throat. ❍ *Polly took a bite of the apple and swallowed it.*

swam /swæm/ **Swam** is a form of the verb **swim**.

swap /swɒp/ (**swaps, swapping, swapped**) also **swop**

1 VERB If you **swap** one thing **for** another, you replace the first thing with the second. ❍ *Next week they will swap places.* ❍ *I swapped my t-shirt for one of Karen's.*

2 NOUN In business, a **swap** is an exchange of debts according to a contract. ❍ *Interest rate swaps are very popular.*

sway /sweɪ/ **VERB** When people or things **sway**, they move slowly from one side to the other. ❍ *The people swayed back and forth singing.*

swear /swɛər/ (**swears, swearing, swore, sworn**)

1 VERB If someone **swears**, they use offensive words. ❍ *It's not helpful to swear and shout.*

2 VERB If you **swear to** do something, you promise in a serious way that you will do it. ❍ *I swear to do everything I can to help you.*

sweat /swɛt/

1 NONCOUNT NOUN Sweat is the liquid that comes out of your skin when you are hot or afraid. ❍ *Both horse and rider were dripping with sweat.*

2 VERB When you **sweat**, sweat comes out of your skin. ❍ *It's really hot. I'm sweating.*

3 PL NOUN Sweats are loose, warm, comfortable pants. [INFORMAL]

sweat|er /swɛtər/ **NOUN** a warm piece of clothing that covers the upper part of your body and your arms

sweat|shop /swɛtʃɒp/ also **sweat shop** **NOUN** a small factory in which many people work long hours in poor conditions for low pay

[ECONOMICS, PRODUCTION] ❍ *the dingy, hidden world of garment sweatshops*

sweat|shop la|bor NONCOUNT NOUN **Sweatshop labor** is work done by people for long hours in poor conditions for low pay. [ECONOMICS, PRODUCTION] ❍ *78% of those polled would avoid shopping in a store that sold garments made with sweatshop labor.*

sweaty /swɛti/ (**sweatier, sweatiest**) ADJ covered with sweat ❍ *hot, sweaty hands*

sweep /swip/ (**sweeps, sweeping, swept**)
1 VERB If you **sweep** an area, you push dirt off it with a brush. ❍ *The owner of the store was sweeping his floor.*
2 VERB If you **sweep** things somewhere, you push them there with a quick, smooth movement. ❍ *She swept the cards from the table.*

sweet /swit/
1 ADJ containing sugar or tasting like sugar ❍ *a cup of sweet tea*
2 ADJ A **sweet** smell or sound is pleasant. ❍ *I recognized the sweet smell of her perfume.*
3 ADJ If someone is **sweet**, they are kind, gentle, and pleasant. ❍ *He was a sweet man.* ● **sweet|ly** ADV ❍ *I just smiled sweetly and said no.*
4 ADJ If a small person or thing is **sweet**, they are attractive. [INFORMAL] ❍ *a sweet little baby*
5 PL NOUN **Sweets** are small pieces of sweet food made with sugar.
6 NOUN A **sweet** is the same as **candy** or a **dessert**. [BRIT]

sweet|en|er /swit^ənər/
1 NOUN an artificial substance that can be used in drinks instead of sugar
2 NOUN something that you give or offer someone in order to persuade them to accept an offer or business deal ❍ *A corporation can buy back its bonds by paying investors the face value (plus a sweetener).*

swell /swɛl/ (**swells, swelling, swelled, swollen**) VERB If a part of your body **swells** or **swells up**, it becomes larger than normal. ❍ *The skin around the area injected will swell up, and may redden slightly.*

swept /swɛpt/ **Swept** is a form of the verb **sweep**.

swerve /swɜrv/ (**swerves, swerving, swerved**) VERB If a vehicle or other moving thing **swerves**, it suddenly changes direction. ❍ *Her car swerved off the road.*

swift /swɪft/ ADJ very quick ❍ *We need to make a swift decision.* ● **swift|ly** ADV ❍ *The law school reacted swiftly, and the firm was banned from campus.*

swim /swɪm/ (**swims, swimming, swam, swum**)
1 VERB When you **swim**, you move through water by making movements with your arms and legs. ❍ *She learned to swim when she was 10.*
2 NOUN **Swim** is also a noun. ❍ *When can we go for a swim?* ● **swim|mer** NOUN ❍ *I'm a good swimmer.*

swim|ming /swɪmɪŋ/ NONCOUNT NOUN **Swimming** is the activity of swimming, especially as a sport or for pleasure. ❍ *Swimming is a great form of exercise.*

swim|ming pool (**swimming pools**) NOUN a structure filled with water that people can swim in

swim|suit /swɪmsut/ NOUN a piece of clothing that you wear for swimming

swing /swɪŋ/ (**swings, swinging, swung**)
1 VERB If something **swings**, it moves repeatedly backward and forward or from side to side. ❍ *Amber walked beside him, her arms swinging.*
2 NOUN a seat that hangs by two ropes that children sit on and move forward and backward ❍ *I took the kids to play on the swings.*
3 NOUN a fluctuation in an activity ❍ *What other country would have taken such a swing in its trade account without resorting to wholesale protectionism?*

swing shift (**swing shifts**)
1 NOUN the group of workers that work from late afternoon to midnight in a factory or other business
2 NOUN the period of time that these workers work

switch /swɪtʃ/ (**switches, switching, switched**)
1 NOUN a device for turning a machine or electricity supply on or off ❍ *She closed the scanner and pressed the switch.*

S

2 VERB If you **switch to** something different, you change to it. ❍ *Companies are switching to cleaner fuels.*
3 VERB If you **switch** two things, you replace one with the other. ❍ *They switched the keys, so Karen had the key to my office and I had the key to hers.*
▶ **switch off** If you **switch off** a light or a machine, you stop it working by pushing a switch. ❍ *She switched off the coffee machine.*
▶ **switch on** If you **switch on** a light or a machine, you make it start working by pushing a switch. ❍ *He switched on the lamp.*

swol|len /swoʊlᵊn/
1 ADJ larger than normal ❍ *My eyes were swollen and I could hardly see.*
2 Swollen is a form of the verb **swell**.

sword /sɔrd/ **NOUN** a weapon with a handle and a long sharp blade

swore /swɔr/ **Swore** is a form of the verb **swear**.

sworn /swɔrn/ **Sworn** is a form of the verb **swear**.

SWOT analy|sis /swɒt ənælɪsɪs/ **NONCOUNT NOUN SWOT analysis** is a method used for evaluating a product before it is marketed. **SWOT** is an abbreviation for "strengths, weaknesses, opportunities, and threats." [BUSINESS MANAGEMENT] ❍ *SWOT analysis is an incredibly simple, but structured, approach to evaluating a company's strategic position when planning.*

swum /swʌm/ **Swum** is a form of the verb **swim**.

swung /swʌŋ/ **Swung** is a form of the verb **swing**.

syl|la|ble /sɪləbᵊl/ **NOUN** a part of a word that contains a single vowel sound

sym|bol /sɪmbᵊl/ **NOUN** a number, a letter, or a shape that represents something ❍ *What's the chemical symbol for oxygen?*

sym|pa|thet|ic /sɪmpəθɛtɪk/ **ADJ** A **sympathetic** person is kind and tries to understand other people's feelings. ❍ *Try talking about your problem with a sympathetic coworker.* ● **sym|pa|theti|cal|ly** /sɪmpəθɛtɪkli/ **ADV** ❍ *She nodded sympathetically.*

sym|pa|thy /sɪmpəθi/ **NONCOUNT NOUN** If you have **sympathy** for someone who is in a bad situation, you are sorry for them. ❍ *I get no sympathy from my family when I'm sick.*

sym|pho|ny /sɪmfəni/ (**symphonies**) **NOUN** a piece of music that has been written to be played by an orchestra ❍ *Beethoven's Ninth Symphony*

symp|tom /sɪmptəm/ **NOUN** A **symptom** of an illness a sign that you have an illness. ❍ *All these patients have flu symptoms.*

syna|gogue /sɪnəgɒg/ **NOUN** a building where Jewish people go to pray

syn|di|cate /sɪndɪkɪt/ **NOUN** an association of people or organizations that is formed for business purposes or in order to carry out a project ❍ *They formed a syndicate to buy the car in which they competed in the race.* ❍ *a syndicate of 152 banks*

syn|drome /sɪndroʊm/ **NOUN** a medical condition ❍ *Sudden Infant Death Syndrome*

syn|er|gy /sɪnərdʒi/ **NONCOUNT NOUN** If there is **synergy** between two or more organizations, they are more successful when they work together than when they work separately. [BUSINESS MANAGEMENT] ❍ *Of course, there's quite obviously a lot of synergy between the two companies.*

syn|thet|ic /sɪnθɛtɪk/ **ADJ** made from chemicals or artificial substances ❍ *synthetic rubber*

sys|tem /sɪstəm/
1 NOUN a way of doing something that follows a plan or rules ❍ *You need a better system for organizing your invoices.*
2 NOUN a set of connected pieces of equipment ❍ *a heating system*

Tt

ta|ble /teɪbᵊl/
1 NOUN a piece of furniture with a flat top that you put things on or sit at ❍ *the kitchen table*
2 NOUN a set of facts or numbers arranged in rows ❍ *See the table on page 14.*

table|cloth /teɪbᵊlklɔθ/ **NOUN** a cloth that you use to cover a table

table|spoon /teɪbᵊlspun/ **NOUN** a large spoon that you use for serving food

tab|let /tæblɪt/ **NOUN** a small solid piece of medicine that you swallow ❍ *a sleeping tablet*

tab|loid /tæblɔɪd/ **NOUN** a small newspaper, often with simple articles and many pictures ❍ *I sometimes read the tabloids.*

tack|le /tækᵊl/ (**tackles, tackling, tackled**)
1 VERB If you **tackle** a problem or a job, you deal with it. ❍ *We need to tackle the budget deficit.*
2 VERB If you **tackle** someone in a sports game, you try to take the ball away from them. ❍ *Foley tackled the quarterback.*
3 NOUN Tackle is also a noun. ❍ *A great tackle from Beckham saved the game.*

tac|tic /tæktɪk/ **NOUN** a planned way of trying to achieve something ❍ *I decided to change my tactics.*

T

tag /tæg/ **NOUN** a small piece of cardboard or other material with information on it, that is attached to something or someone ❍ *The staff all wear name tags.*

tag line (**tag lines**) also **tag-line NOUN** The **tag line** of something such as a television commercial or a joke is the phrase that comes at the end and is meant to be easy to remember.

tail /teɪl/
1 NOUN the long thin part at the end of an animal's body ❍ *The dog barked and wagged its tail.*
2 NOUN the end part of something ❍ *The plane's tail hit the runway.*

tai|lor /teɪlər/
1 NOUN a person whose job is to make and repair clothes
2 VERB If you **tailor** something such as a product or activity to someone's needs, you make it suitable for a particular person or purpose by changing parts of it. ❍ *A computer system can only answer yes or no, but we tailor our response to fit the individual customer.*

take /teɪk/ (**takes, taking, took, taken**)
1 VERB If you **take** something, you put your hand around it and move it somewhere. ❍ *Let me take your coat.* ❍ *The waitress took away the dirty dishes.*
2 VERB If you **take** something, you have it with you when you go somewhere. ❍ *Don't forget to take a map with you.*
3 VERB If a person or a vehicle **takes** someone somewhere, they transport them there. ❍ *Michael took me to the airport.*
4 VERB If you **take** something, you steal it. ❍ *They took my pocketbook.*
5 VERB If something **takes** an amount of time, it needs that time in order to happen. ❍ *The sauce takes 25 minutes to prepare.*
6 VERB If you **take** something that someone offers you, you accept it. ❍ *Sylvia has taken a job in Tokyo.*
7 VERB If you **take** a road, you choose to travel along it. ❍ *Take a right at the stop sign.*
8 VERB If you **take** a vehicle, you use it to go from one place to another. ❍ *She took the train to New York.*
9 VERB used to show the thing that is done ❍ *She was too tired to take a bath.* ❍ *She took her driving test yesterday.*

10 VERB If you **take** a subject at school, you study it. ❍ *Students can take European history and American history.*

11 VERB If someone **takes** medicine, they swallow it. ❍ *I try not to take pills of any kind.*

▸**take after** If you **take after** a member of your family, you look or behave like them. ❍ *You take after your mom.*

▸**take off**

1 When an airplane **takes off**, it leaves the ground. ❍ *We took off at 11 o'clock.*

2 If a business **takes off**, it becomes very successful, and if sales **take off**, they increase quickly. ❍ *The color-copier market may be about to take off.*

3 If you **take** clothes **off**, you remove them. ❍ *Come in and take off your coat.*

▸**take on**

1 If you **take on** staff, you start to employ them. ❍ *The right to export will encourage domestic firms to expand their capacity and take on more staff.*

2 If you **take on** work or a job, you agree to do it. ❍ *Watson then took on the job of running a company that made tabulating equipment.*

3 If you **take on** debt, you borrow an amount of money. ❍ *When Kohlberg Kravis acquired Beatrice, it took on debt totaling $7.8 billion.*

▸**take out** If you **take** someone **out**, you take them somewhere enjoyable. ❍ *Sophia took me out to lunch today.*

▸**take over** If people **take over** something, they get control of it. ❍ *I'm going to take over this company one day.*

▸**take up**

1 If you **take up** an activity, you start doing it. ❍ *Peter took up tennis at the age of eight.*

2 If something **takes up** an amount of time or space, it uses that amount. ❍ *I don't want to take up too much of your time.*

take|away /teɪkəweɪ/ [BRIT] → **takeout**

take-home pay **NONCOUNT NOUN** Your **take-home pay** is the amount of your wages or salary that is left after income tax and other payments have been subtracted. [FINANCE] ❍ *Her monthly take-home pay is $1,500 after taxes.*

tak|en /teɪkən/ **Taken** is a form of the verb **take**.

take|off /teɪkɔf/ also **take-off** **NOUN** **Takeoff** is the time when an aircraft leaves the ground. ❍ *What time is takeoff?*

take|out /teɪkaʊt/

1 NONCOUNT NOUN **Takeout** is prepared food that you buy from a store or a restaurant and take home to eat. ❍ *Let's just get a takeout pizza tonight.*

2 NOUN a store or a restaurant that sells takeout food ❍ *We took Kerry to her favorite Chinese takeout for her birthday.*

take|over /teɪkoʊvər/

1 NOUN an act of gaining control of a company by buying more of its shares than anyone else [ADMINISTRATION] ❍ *He lost his job in a corporate takeover.*

2 NOUN an act of taking control of a country, political party, or movement by force ❍ *There's been a military takeover of some kind.*

COLLOCATIONS

a *hostile* takeover
a *proposed* takeover
a takeover *offer*
a takeover *battle*
a takeover *bid*

take|over bid (**takeover bids**) **NOUN** an attempt to gain control of a company by buying more of its shares than anyone else [ADMINISTRATION, ECONOMICS] ❍ *a takeover bid for America's fifth-biggest computer-maker*

tak|ings /teɪkɪŋz/ **PL NOUN** The **takings** of a business is the amount of money that it gets from selling its goods or services during a particular period. ❍ *Their takings were fifteen to twenty thousand dollars a week.*

tale /teɪl/ **NOUN** a story ❍ *It's a tale about the friendship between two boys.*

tal|ent /tælənt/ **NONCOUNT NOUN** **Talent** is your natural ability to do something well. [HR] ❍ *He's got lots of talent.*

tal|ent|ed /tæləntɪd/ **ADJ** having a natural ability to do something well [HR] ❍ *Mr. Diefenbach is a talented executive.*

talk /tɔk/

1 VERB If you **talk**, you say things to someone. ❍ *They were all talking about the takeover bid.*

2 NOUN a conversation or discussion ❍ *I had a long talk with my line manager.*
3 NOUN an informal speech ❍ *She gave a brief talk on the new pension regulations.*
4 PL NOUN **Talks** are formal discussions between different groups. ❍ *peace talks*

tall /tɔl/
1 ADJ higher than average ❍ *John is very tall.* ❍ *The lighthouse is a tall square tower.*
2 ADJ used for asking or talking about the height of someone or something ❍ *"How tall are you?"—"I'm six foot five."*

tame /teɪm/ (**tames, taming, tamed, tamer, tamest**)
1 ADJ A **tame** animal is not afraid of humans.
2 VERB If you **tame** a wild animal, you teach it not to be afraid of humans.

tan /tæn/ (**tans, tanning, tanned**)
1 NOUN If you have a **tan**, your skin has become darker because you have spent time in the sun. ❍ *She is tall and blonde, with a tan.*
2 VERB If your skin **tans**, it becomes darker in the sun. ❍ *I have very pale skin that never tans.*

tang|ible /tændʒɪbᵊl/ **ADJ** A business asset that is **tangible** is a physical asset, such as a factory or office. Compare with **intangible**. [FINANCE] ❍ *Capital, in the form of tangible assets such as machinery or intangible assets such as money, can be a key consideration.*

tan|gle /tæŋgᵊl/ (**tangles, tangling, tangled**)
1 NOUN a mass of something that has become twisted together ❍ *A tangle of wires connected the two computers.*
2 VERB If something **is tangled** or **tangles**, it becomes twisted together. ❍ *Her hair is curly and tangles easily.*

tank /tæŋk/
1 NOUN a large container for holding liquid or gas ❍ *a fuel tank*
2 NOUN a heavy, strong military vehicle, with large guns
3 VERB If something **tanks**, it fails commercially. [INFORMAL] ❍ *Even before the economy tanked, discount stores were looking healthy.*

tank|er /tæŋkər/ **NOUN** a large ship or truck that carries large amounts of gas or liquid ❍ *an oil tanker*

tap /tæp/ (**taps, tapping, tapped**)
1 VERB If you **tap** something, you hit it quickly and lightly. ❍ *Karen tapped on his office door and went in.*
2 NOUN **Tap** is also a noun. ❍ *There was a tap on the door.*
3 NOUN an object that controls the flow of a liquid or a gas from a pipe

tape /teɪp/ (**tapes, taping, taped**)
1 NONCOUNT NOUN **Tape** is a sticky strip of cloth or plastic used for sticking things together. ❍ *sticky tape*
2 NONCOUNT NOUN **Tape** is a long narrow plastic strip that you use to record music, sounds, or moving pictures.
3 VERB If you **tape** music, sounds, or moving pictures, you record them on tape. ❍ *She taped her conversation with her boss.*
4 VERB If you **tape** one thing to another, you stick them together using tape. ❍ *I taped the envelope shut.*

tar|get /tɑrgɪt/
1 NOUN something that you try to attack or hit ❍ *One of the missiles missed its target.*
2 NOUN something that you try to achieve [BUSINESS MANAGEMENT] ❍ *sales targets*

COLLOCATIONS
to *meet* a target
to *reach* a target
to *miss* a target
to *set* a target

tar|get mar|ket (**target markets**) **NOUN** a market in which a company is trying to sell its products or services [MARKETING AND SALES] ❍ *We decided that we needed to change our target market from the over-45's to the 35-45's.*

tar|iff /tærɪf/
1 NOUN a tax that a government collects on goods coming into a country [ECONOMICS] ❍ *America wants to eliminate tariffs on items such as electronics.*
2 NOUN a price that is charged for something, especially one which varies according to the

time or day of use [ECONOMICS] ❍ *The most appropriate choice of system and tariff depends on where and how often a customer uses the phone.*

tart /tɑrt/ **NOUN** a case made of flour, fat, and water (= pastry), filled with fruit or vegetables and cooked ❍ *apple tarts*

task /tæsk/
1 NOUN a piece of work [BUSINESS MANAGEMENT] ❍ *I had the task of updating the website.*
2 VERB If you **task** someone **with** something, you give it to them as job to do. [BUSINESS MANAGEMENT] ❍ *The team was tasked by their company with generating a new strategy to gain market share.*

task|bar /tæskbɑr/ also **task bar NOUN** a narrow strip at the bottom of a computer screen that shows you which programs are open

taste /teɪst/ (**tastes, tasting, tasted**)
1 NONCOUNT NOUN Your sense of **taste** is your ability to recognize the flavor of things.
2 NOUN the flavor of something ❍ *I like the taste of chocolate.*
3 VERB If food or drink **tastes of** something, it has that flavor. ❍ *The water tasted of metal.*
4 VERB If you **taste** food or drink, you have a small amount of it in order to see what the flavor is like. ❍ *Don't add salt until you've tasted the food.*
5 VERB If you can **taste** something, you are aware of its flavor. ❍ *Can you taste the onions in this dish?*
6 NONCOUNT NOUN Your **taste** is the type of things you like. ❍ *Will's got great taste in clothes.*

taste|ful /teɪstfəl/ **ADJ** attractive, with an appropriate style ❍ *Sarah was wearing tasteful jewelry.* ● **taste|ful|ly ADV** ❍ *a tastefully decorated home*

taste|less /teɪstlɪs/
1 ADJ not attractive, and showing bad judgment about style ❍ *tasteless furniture*
2 ADJ If a remark or joke is **tasteless**, it is offensive.
3 ADJ If food or drink is **tasteless**, it has no flavor. ❍ *The fish was tasteless.*

tast|er /teɪstər/ **NOUN** a sample of a product or experience for someone who is thinking of buying a product or doing an activity ❍ *The book is essentially a taster for those unfamiliar with the subject.*

tasty /teɪsti/ (**tastier, tastiest**) **ADJ** having a good, pleasant flavor ❍ *The food here is tasty and good value.*

tat|too /tætu/
1 NOUN a design made on a person's skin with a needle and ink ❍ *He has a tattoo of three stars on his arm.*
2 VERB If something **is tattooed** on your body, it is drawn on your body with a needle and ink. ❍ *She has had a small black cat tattooed on one of her shoulders.*

taught /tɔt/ **Taught** is a form of the verb **teach**.

tax /tæks/ (**taxes, taxing, taxed**)
1 NOUN an amount of money that you have to pay to the government so that it can pay for public services such as roads and schools ❍ *The government has promised not to raise taxes.*
2 VERB When a person or company **is taxed**, they have to pay a part of their income to the government. ❍ *We are the most heavily taxed people in North America.*

tax|able /tæksəbᵊl/ **ADJ Taxable** income is income on which you have to pay tax. [ECONOMICS] ❍ *It is worth consulting the guide to see whether your income is taxable.*

taxa|tion /tækseɪʃən/
1 NONCOUNT NOUN Taxation is the system by which a government takes money from people and spends it on things such as education, health, and defense. [FINANCE, ECONOMICS] ❍ *the proposed reforms to taxation*
2 NONCOUNT NOUN Taxation is the amount of money that people have to pay in taxes. [FINANCE, ECONOMICS] ❍ *The result will be higher taxation.*

tax avoid|ance /tæks əvɔɪdəns/ **NONCOUNT NOUN Tax avoidance** is the use of legal methods to pay the smallest possible amount of tax. [ECONOMICS]

tax brack|et (**tax brackets**) **NOUN** a range of incomes at which a particular rate of tax is payable [ECONOMICS] ○ *Unlike many countries, Germany does not adjust tax brackets automatically for inflation.*

tax-deductible ADJ If an expense is **tax-deductible**, it can be paid out of the part of your income on which you do not pay tax, so that the amount of tax you pay is reduced. [FINANCE] ○ *The cost of private childcare should be made tax-deductible.*

tax eva|sion /tæks ɪveɪʒᵊn/ NONCOUNT NOUN **Tax evasion** is the use of illegal methods to avoid paying tax. [ECONOMICS]

tax-exempt

1 ADJ Income or property that is **tax-exempt** is not taxed. [FINANCE] ○ *The Trust intends to achieve a high level of tax-exempt income.*

2 ADJ In accounting, if an asset is **tax-exempt**, the income from it is not taxed. [FINANCE] ○ *tax-exempt investments*

tax-free ADJ Income that is **tax-free** is not taxed. [FINANCE] ○ *a tax-free investment plan*

tax ha|ven (**tax havens**) NOUN a country or place which has a low rate of tax so that people choose to live there or register companies there in order to avoid paying higher tax in their own countries [ECONOMICS, FINANCE] ○ *The Caribbean has become an important location for international banking because it is a tax haven.*

tax holi|day (**tax holidays**) NOUN a period during which a person or company is allowed to pay no tax or less tax than usual [ECONOMICS, FINANCE] ○ *There is a five-year tax holiday for new power plants.*

taxi /tæksi/ NOUN a car with a driver who you pay to take you somewhere ○ *We took a taxi back to our hotel.*

T

tax loss (**tax losses**) NOUN a loss made by a company that can be set against future tax payments [ECONOMICS] ○ *Firms with large accumulated tax loss carry-forwards shouldn't borrow at all.*

tax|payer /tækspeɪər/ NOUN someone who pays tax ○ *The government has wasted taxpayers' money.*

tax rate (**tax rates**) NOUN the percentage of an income or an amount of money that has to be paid as tax [ECONOMICS] ○ *These officials prefer lower tax rates on capital gains.*

tax re|lief NONCOUNT NOUN **Tax relief** is a reduction in the amount of tax that a person or company has to pay. [ECONOMICS] ○ *mortgage interest tax relief*

tax re|turn (**tax returns**) NOUN an official form that you fill in with details about your income so that the tax you owe can be calculated [ECONOMICS]

tax shel|ter (**tax shelters**) NOUN a way of arranging the finances of a business or a person so that they have to pay less tax [ECONOMICS, FINANCE]

tax year (**tax years**) NOUN a period of twelve months which is used by the government as a basis for calculating taxes [FINANCE, ECONOMICS]

tea /ti/

1 NONCOUNT NOUN **Tea** is a drink that you make by pouring boiling water on dried leaves. ○ *a cup of tea*

2 NONCOUNT NOUN **Tea** is the dried leaves of the plant that tea is made from.

teach /titʃ/ (**teaches, teaching, taught**)

1 VERB If you **teach** someone something, you give them instructions so that they know about it or know how to do it. ○ *She taught me to read.*

2 VERB If you **teach**, you give lessons in a subject. ○ *Christine teaches biology at Piper High.* ● **teach|ing** NONCOUNT NOUN ○ *The quality of teaching in the school is excellent.*

teach|er /titʃər/ NOUN someone whose job is to teach in a school or college ○ *I was a teacher for 21 years.*

team /tim/

1 NOUN a group of people who play a sport or game together against other groups ○ *Kate was on the school basketball team.*

2 NOUN a group of people who work together ○ *The government appointed a team of economic advisers.*

team|work /timwɜrk/ NONCOUNT NOUN **Teamwork** is the ability of a group of people to work well together. ○ *She knows the importance of teamwork.*

tear
❶ CRYING
❷ DAMAGING OR MOVING

❶ **tear** /tɪər/ **NOUN** a drop of liquid that comes out of your eyes when you cry ❍ *Her eyes filled with tears.*

❷ **tear** /tɛər/ (**tears, tearing, tore, torn**)
1 VERB If you **tear** something, you pull it into pieces or make a hole in it. ❍ *I tore my coat on a nail.*
2 NOUN Tear is also a noun. ❍ *I looked through a tear in the curtains.*
▸**tear up** If you **tear up** a piece of paper, you tear it into small pieces. ❍ *He tore up the letter and threw it in the fire.*

tease /tiz/ (**teases, teasing, teased**) **VERB** If you **tease** someone, you make jokes about them or embarrass them deliberately. ❍ *Amber's brothers are always teasing her.*

teas|er /tizər/ **NOUN** an advertisement that attracts people's attention by not mentioning the name of the product, and makes them curious to know what is being advertised [MARKETING AND SALES] ❍ *The company ran a teaser ad in the New York Times last Sunday.*

tea|spoon /tispun/ **NOUN** a small spoon that you use for putting sugar into tea or coffee

tech|ni|cal /tɛknɪkᵊl/ **ADJ** involving machines, processes, and materials that are used in science and industry ❍ *We still have some technical problems.* ● **tech|ni|cal|ly** /tɛknɪkli/ **ADV** ❍ *It is a very technically advanced car.*

tech|ni|cian /tɛknɪʃən/ **NOUN** someone whose job involves working with special equipment or machines ❍ *He works as a laboratory technician.*

tech|nique /tɛknik/ **NOUN** a special way of doing something ❍ *Doctors have recently developed these new techniques.*

tech|no|lo|gist /tɛknɒlədʒɪst/ **NOUN** someone whose job involves developing or using technology [TECHNOLOGY]

tech|nol|ogy /tɛknɒlədʒi/ (**technologies**) **NOUN Technology** is knowledge, equipment, and methods used in science and industry. ❍ *Computer technology has developed fast during the last 10 years.*

teen /tin/ **PL NOUN** If you are in your **teens**, you are between thirteen and nineteen years old. ❍ *I met my husband when I was in my teens.*

teen|age /tineɪdʒ/ **ADJ** between thirteen and nineteen years old ❍ *Taylor is a typical teenage girl.*

teen|ager /tineɪdʒər/ **NOUN** someone who is between thirteen and nineteen years old

teeth /tiθ/ **Teeth** is the plural of **tooth**.

tele|com /tɛlɪkɒm/ **NONCOUNT NOUN Telecom** is the same as **telecommunications**.

tele|com|mu|ni|ca|tions /tɛlɪkə myunɪkeɪʃənz/ **NONCOUNT NOUN Telecommunications** is the sending of information over long distances using equipment such as radio or telephones. [TECHNOLOGY]

tele|com|mut|er /tɛlɪkəmyutər/ **NOUN** someone who works from home using equipment such as telephones and computers to contact their colleagues and customers

tele|com|mut|ing /tɛlɪkəmyutɪŋ/ **NONCOUNT NOUN Telecommuting** is working from home using equipment such as telephones and computers to contact people. ❍ *There is also the potential to develop telecommuting and other more flexible working practices.*

tele|com rev|olu|tion NOUN The **telecom revolution** is the sudden changes in telecommunications such as the increased use of the Internet and cell phones. [TECHNOLOGY] ❍ *The telecom revolution has created a new pattern of rural working.*

tele|con|fer|ence /tɛlɪkɒnfərəns, -frə ns/ **NOUN** a meeting involving people in different places who use telephones or video links to communicate with each other [TECHNOLOGY] ❍ *Managers at their factory hold a two-hour teleconference with head office every day.* ● **tele|con|fer|enc|ing NONCOUNT NOUN** ❍ *teleconferencing facilities*

t

tele|mar|ket|ing /tɛlɪmarkɪtɪŋ/ **NONCOUNT NOUN Telemarketing** is a method of selling in which someone telephones people to try to persuade them to buy products or services. [MARKETING AND SALES, TECHNOLOGY] ❍ *As postal rates go up, many businesses have been turning to telemarketing as a way of contacting new customers.*

tele|phone /tɛlɪfoʊn/ (**telephones, telephoning, telephoned**)
1 NOUN a piece of electronic equipment that you use for speaking to someone who is in another place ❍ *He got up and answered the telephone.*
2 VERB If you **telephone** someone, you speak to them using a telephone. ❍ *I telephoned my client to say I would be late.*

tele|phone bank|ing NONCOUNT NOUN Telephone banking is banking services that are available to customers over the telephone. [BANKING, TECHNOLOGY] ❍ *Online banking is not yet much more convenient than telephone banking.*

tele|sales /tɛlɪseɪlz/ **NONCOUNT NOUN Telesales** is the selling of a company's products or services by telephone, either by phoning possible customers or by answering calls from customers. [MARKETING AND SALES, TECHNOLOGY] ❍ *Many people start their careers in telesales.*

tele|scope /tɛlɪskoʊp/ **NOUN** a piece of equipment shaped like a tube, with special glass that makes things that are far away seem bigger or closer

tele|vi|sion /tɛlɪvɪʒᵊn, -vɪʒ-/
1 NOUN a piece of equipment like a box with a screen on which you watch programs ❍ *She turned the television on.*
2 NONCOUNT NOUN Television is the programs that are shown on a television. ❍ *Michael spends too much time watching television.*

tele|work|er /tɛliwɜrkər/ **NOUN Teleworkers** are the same as **telecommuters**. [TECHNOLOGY]

tele|work|ing /tɛliwɜrkɪŋ/ **NONCOUNT NOUN Teleworking** is the same as **telecommuting**. [TECHNOLOGY]

tell /tɛl/ (**tells, telling, told**)
1 VERB If you **tell** someone something, you give them information. ❍ *I told Rachel I got the job.*
2 VERB If you **tell** someone **to** do something, you say they must do it. ❍ *The police officer told him to get out of his car.*
3 VERB If you can **tell** what is happening or what is true, you are able to judge correctly what is happening or what is true. ❍ *I could tell that Tom was tired and bored.*

tell|er /tɛlər/ **NOUN** someone who works in a bank and who customers pay money to or get money from [BANKING] ❍ *Every bank pays close attention to the speed and accuracy of its tellers.* ❍ *a bank teller*

tem|per /tɛmpər/
1 NONCOUNT NOUN If you have a **temper**, you become angry very easily. ❍ *Their mother had a terrible temper.*
2 NONCOUNT NOUN If you are **in** a bad **temper** you are feeling angry. ❍ *I was in a bad temper because I was so tired.*
3 If you **lose** your **temper**, you suddenly become angry. ❍ *Simon lost his temper and punched me.*

tem|pera|ture /tɛmprətʃər, -tʃʊər/
1 NOUN how hot or cold something or someone is ❍ *At night, the temperature drops below freezing.* ❍ *The baby's temperature continued to rise.*
2 If you **have a temperature**, your temperature is higher than it should be.

tem|ple /tɛmpᵊl/ **NOUN** a building where people of some religions go to pray ❍ *a Sikh temple*

tem|po|rary /tɛmpərɛri/ **ADJ** existing or happening for only a limited time ❍ *His job here is only temporary.* ● **tem|po|rari|ly** /tɛmpərɛərɪli/ **ADV** ❍ *Her website was temporarily shut down yesterday.*

tempt /tɛmpt/ **VERB** If something **tempts** you, it makes you want it or want to do it. ❍ *I was tempted to lie.* ● **tempt|ing ADJ** ❍ *The berries look tempting, but they're poisonous.*

temp|ta|tion /tɛmpteɪʃən/ **NONCOUNT NOUN Temptation** is the feeling that you want to do something or to have something, when you know you should not. ❍ *Try to resist the temptation to eat snacks.*

ten /tɛn/ **Ten** is the number 10.

ten|ant /tɛnənt/ **NOUN** someone who pays money to the owner for the use of an apartment or an office ❍ *Each tenant in the apartment pays $200 a week.*

tend /tɛnd/ **VERB** If something **tends to** happen, it usually happens or often happens. ❍ *Women tend to live longer than men.*

ten|den|cy /tɛndənsi/ (**tendencies**) **NOUN** A **tendency** is something that usually happens. ❍ *There is a tendency to forget what the fixed cost of debt can do in a recession.*

ten|der /tɛndər/

1 ADJ kind and gentle ❍ *Her voice was tender.*
● **ten|der|ly ADV** ❍ *He kissed her tenderly.*

2 ADJ easy to cut or bite ❍ *Cook it until the meat is tender.*

3 ADJ If part of your body is **tender**, it is painful when you touch it. ❍ *My cheek felt very tender.*

4 NOUN a formal offer to supply goods or services and a statement of the price that you or your company will charge ❍ *Builders will then be sent the specifications and asked to submit a tender for the work.*

5 If a contract is **put out to tender**, companies are invited to make an offer of a price to do the work. ❍ *Some services are now compulsorily put out to tender.*

6 If a company **wins a tender**, its offer is chosen and they get the work. ❍ *the consortium that has won the tender to build the second Severn Bridge*

7 VERB If a company **tenders for** something, it makes a formal offer to supply goods or do a job for a particular price. ❍ *The staff are forbidden to tender for private-sector work.*
● **ten|der|ing NONCOUNT NOUN** ❍ *compulsory competitive tendering for council leisure and recreation services*

8 VERB If you **tender** something such as a suggestion, your resignation, or money, you formally offer or present it. ❍ *She quickly tendered her resignation.*

ten|nis /tɛnɪs/ **NONCOUNT NOUN Tennis** is a game for two or four players, who hit a ball across a net between them.

tense /tɛns/ (**tenser, tensest**)

1 ADJ anxious and nervous ❍ *We were very tense before the meeting.*

2 ADJ If your body is **tense**, your muscles are tight. ❍ *A bath can relax tense muscles.*

3 NOUN The **tense** of a verb is the form that shows whether something is happening in the past, the present, or the future.

ten|sion /tɛnʃən/ **NONCOUNT NOUN Tension** is a feeling of worry or anxiety. ❍ *Physical exercise can reduce tension.*

tent /tɛnt/ **NOUN** a shelter made of cloth, held up by poles and ropes, that you sleep in when you go camping

tenth /tɛnθ/

1 ADJ or **ADV** The **tenth** item in a series is the one that you count as number ten. ❍ *She's having a party for her tenth birthday.*

2 NOUN one of ten equal parts of something (⅒) ❍ *She won the race by a tenth of a second.*

term /tɜrm/

1 NOUN a word or phrase that refers to a particular thing ❍ *He thinks 'venture investing' is the right term for what the fund will do.*

2 NOUN one of the periods of time that a school, college, or university year is divided into ❍ *She will retire at the end of the term.*

3 PL NOUN The **terms** of an agreement are the rules of the agreement. [LEGAL] ❍ *The terms of the agreement are quite simple.*

4 PL NOUN A company or person's **terms** is the amount of money that they charge for goods or services. [FINANCE]

ter|mi|nal /tɜrmɪnᵊl/ **NOUN** a place where vehicles and passengers begin or end a journey ❍ *a bus terminal*

term in|sur|ance NONCOUNT NOUN Term insurance is a type of life insurance which is paid only if the person dies within a particular period of time. [BANKING]

terms of trade PL NOUN A country's **terms of trade** are its ratio of export prices to import prices, used as a measure of that country's trading position. [LEGAL, ECONOMICS]

❍ *Soaring coal and iron-ore prices have improved Australia's terms of trade by 40% since 2004.*

ter|race /tɛrɪs/ **NOUN** a flat area next to a building, where people can sit

ter|ri|ble /tɛrɪbᵊl/ **ADJ** extremely bad ❍ *Their one-product policy was a terrible mistake.* ● **ter|ri|bly** **ADV** ❍ *The results were not terribly out of line with projections.*

ter|rif|ic /tərɪfɪk/ **ADJ** very good [INFORMAL] ❍ *What a terrific idea!*

ter|ri|fy /tɛrɪfaɪ/ (**terrifies, terrifying, terrified**) **VERB** If something **terrifies** you, it makes you feel extremely afraid. ❍ *Flying terrifies him.* ● **ter|ri|fied** **ADJ** ❍ *Employees are terrified of losing their jobs.*

ter|ri|fy|ing /tɛrɪfaɪɪŋ/ **ADJ** making you very afraid ❍ *a terrifying experience*

ter|ri|tory /tɛrətɔri/ (**territories**)

1 NONCOUNT NOUN **Territory** is all the land that a particular country owns. ❍ *This forest is now Indian territory.*

2 NOUN the district for which someone is responsible ❍ *a salesman's territory*

ter|ror /tɛrər/ **NONCOUNT NOUN** **Terror** is very great fear. ❍ *I shook with terror.*

ter|ror|ism /tɛrərɪzəm/ **NONCOUNT NOUN** **Terrorism** is the use of violence to try to achieve political aims. ❍ *We need new laws to fight terrorism.*

ter|ror|ist /tɛrərɪst/ **NOUN** a person who uses violence to achieve political aims ❍ *terrorist attacks*

ter|tiary /tɜrʃiɛri/

1 ADJ third in order or importance [FORMAL] ❍ *He must have come to know those philosophers through secondary or tertiary sources.*

2 ADJ **Tertiary** education is education at a university or college. [mainly BRIT]

3 ADJ **Tertiary** industries are those which provide services rather than manufacturing goods. Compare with **primary** and **secondary**. [ECONOMICS, PRODUCTION]

ter|tiary sec|tor (**tertiary sectors**) **NOUN** **The tertiary sector** consists of industries which provide a service, such as transportation and finance. Compare with **primary sector** and **secondary sector**. [ECONOMICS] ❍ *economies that are slowly increasing the proportion of their labor force in the tertiary sector*

test /tɛst/

1 VERB If you **test** something, you do something to find out what condition it is in, or how well it works. ❍ *The drug has only been tested on mice.*

2 NOUN **Test** is also a noun. ❍ *The car achieved great results in crash tests.*

3 VERB If you **test** someone, you ask them questions to find out how much they know about something. ❍ *The students were tested on grammar and spelling.*

4 NOUN **Test** is also a noun. ❍ *Only 15 students passed the test.*

test mar|ket (**test markets**) **NOUN** an area or a group of people that are used to test reactions to a new product [TECHNOLOGY] ❍ *This test market will allow the producer to carry out further market research about the product.*

test mar|ket|ing **NONCOUNT NOUN** **Test marketing** is a method for testing consumers' reactions to a new product by selling it in a small area or to a small group of customers. [TECHNOLOGY] ❍ *Test marketing is rapidly approaching the state of a science.*

text /tɛkst/

1 NONCOUNT NOUN **Text** is the words in a book, a document, a newspaper, or a magazine. ❍ *You can insert text, delete text, or move text around.*

2 NOUN A **text** is the same as a **text message**. ❍ *The new system can send a text to a cellphone.*

3 VERB If you **text** someone, you send them a text message. ❍ *Mary texted me when she got home.*

text|book /tɛkstbʊk/ also **text book** **NOUN** a book containing facts about a particular subject that is used by students ❍ *a textbook on international law*

text|ing /tɛkstɪŋ/ **NONCOUNT NOUN** **Texting** is the same as **text messaging**.

text mes|sage (**text messages**) **NOUN** a message that you write and send using a cellphone

text mes|sag|ing NONCOUNT NOUN **Text messaging** is sending messages in writing using a cellphone.

tex|ture /tɛkstʃər/ NOUN The **texture** of something is the way that it feels when you touch it. ❍ *The cheese has a soft, creamy texture.*

than /ðən, STRONG ðæn/ PREP or CONJ used when you are comparing two people or things ❍ *Levels of debt were lower than expected.* ❍ *Senior managers are earning 11 percent more than they did last year.*

thank /θæŋk/
1 You say **thank you**, or in more informal English **thanks**, to show that you are grateful for something. ❍ *Thank you very much for inviting me to your conference.* ❍ *"Tea?"—"No thanks."*
2 VERB If you **thank** someone **for** something, you tell them that you are grateful to them. ❍ *I thanked them for their help.*
3 PL NOUN If you express your **thanks** to someone, you say that you are grateful to them. ❍ *I would like to express my thanks to our wonderful team in Moscow.*
4 If something happens **thanks to** a particular person or thing, it happens because of them. ❍ *Her income had risen, thanks to high interest rates.*

thank|ful /θæŋkfəl/ ADJ grateful and glad ❍ *Policymakers should be thankful that the euro has fallen.*

Thanks|giving /θæŋksgɪvɪŋ/ NONCOUNT NOUN **Thanksgiving** is a public holiday in the United States in November, and in Canada in October, when families have a special meal together. ❍ *Dad always managed to be home for Thanksgiving.*

that /ðæt/
1 ADJ or PRON used to talk about someone or something that is a distance away from you in position or time ❍ *Look at that guy over there.* ❍ *What's that?*
2 PRON used to talk about something that you have mentioned before ❍ *They said you wanted to talk to me. Why was that?*
3 PRON used to show which person or thing you are talking about ❍ *There's the girl that I told you about.*
4 CONJ used to start the part of a sentence that says what a person says or thinks ❍ *He said that he and his wife were coming to New York.*
5 CONJ You use **so that** to talk about why something was done. ❍ *I shouted so that they could hear me.*

that's /ðæts/ **That's** is short for "that is."

the

> Pronounce **the** /ði/ before a vowel (a, e, i, o, or u). Pronounce **the** /ðə/ before a consonant (all the other letters).

1 ARTICLE used before a noun when it is clear which person or thing you are talking about ❍ *The company announced bigger than expected profits.*
2 ARTICLE used before a singular noun to talk about things of that type in general ❍ *The computer has developed very fast in recent years.*
3 ARTICLE used before adjectives and plural nouns to talk about people of a particular type ❍ *the British and the French*
4 ARTICLE used before dates ❍ *The meeting should take place on the fifth of May.*
5 ARTICLE used in front of superlative adjectives ❍ *These are some of the most successful products of AEG.*

thea|ter /θiətər/ NOUN a place where you go to see plays, shows, and movies ❍ *Yesterday, we went to the theater.* ❍ *a movie theater*

thea|tre /θiətər/ [BRIT] → **theater**

theft /θɛft/ NONCOUNT NOUN **Theft** is the crime of stealing. ❍ *He was arrested for car theft.*

their /ðɛər/
1 ADJ used to show that something belongs to or relates to the group of people, animals, or things that you are talking about ❍ *They want to recoup their investments.*
2 ADJ used instead of "his or her" to show that something belongs or relates to a person, without saying if that person is a man or a woman ❍ *Each student works at their own pace.*

theirs /ðɛərz/ PRON used to show that something belongs or relates to the group of people, animals, or things that you are talking about ❍ *Some countries would be forced to raise their rates and others to lower theirs.*

them /ðəm, STRONG ðɛm/
1 PRON used to talk about more than one person, animal, or thing ❍ *They sold securities at a loss and then repurchased them at the same price.*
2 PRON used instead of "him or her" to talk about a person without saying whether that person is a man or a woman ❍ *If anyone calls, tell them I'm out.*

theme /θim/ **NOUN** the subject of something such as a piece of writing or a discussion ❍ *Progress was the main theme of his speech.*

them|selves /ðəmsɛlvz/
1 PRON used to talk about people, animals, or things that you have just talked about ❍ *They all seemed to be enjoying themselves.*
2 PRON If people do something **themselves**, they do it without help from anyone else. ❍ *My parents designed our house themselves.*

then /ðɛn/
1 ADV at that time ❍ *I bought my shares in 2005. Since then, prices have fallen.*
2 ADV used to say what happens next ❍ *They started producing glass and then branched out into steel.*
3 ADV used to start the second part of a sentence that begins with "if" ❍ *If you are not sure about this, then you must say so.*

theo|ry /θɪəri/ (**theories**) **NOUN** an idea or a set of ideas that tries to explain something ❍ *There is one other theory as to why the index hasn't kept up.*

T

theo|ry X /θiəri ɛks/ **NONCOUNT NOUN** **Theory X** is the idea that employees work better when they are closely supervised and when their work is strictly controlled. [HR]

the|ory Y /θiəri waɪ/ **NONCOUNT NOUN** **Theory Y** is the idea that employees work better when they are given responsibility for their own work and when their personal needs are satisfied. [HR]

thera|pist /θɛrəpɪst/ **NOUN** a person whose job is to help people who have emotional or physical problems ❍ *Scott saw a therapist after his marriage ended in 2004.*

thera|py /θɛrəpi/ **NONCOUNT NOUN** **Therapy** is treatment for an emotional or physical problem. ❍ *He is still having therapy.*

there

> Pronounce meaning **1** /ðər, STRONG ðɛər/ and meanings **2** and **3** /ðɛər/.

1 PRON used with the verb "be" to say that something exists or is happening ❍ *There is a color printer in Mike's office.*
2 ADV used to talk about a place that has already been mentioned ❍ *I'm going back to California. My family have lived there for many years.*
3 ADV used to talk about a place that you are pointing to or looking at ❍ *He's sitting over there.*

there|by /ðɛərbaɪ/ **ADV** in this way [FORMAL] ❍ *They need to slash spending and thereby cut borrowing needs.*

there|fore /ðɛərfɔr/ **ADV** for this reason ❍ *They tried to show that they had corrected their billing problems and therefore should be eligible for new contracts.*

there's /ðɛərz/ **There's** is short for "there is."

ther|mom|eter /θərmɒmɪtər/ **NOUN** a piece of equipment for measuring the temperature of something or someone

these

> Pronounce the adjective /ðiz/. Pronounce the pronoun /ðiz/.

1 ADJ or **PRON** used to talk about people or things that are near you, especially when you touch them or point to them ❍ *These scissors are heavy.* ❍ *Do you like these?*
2 ADJ used to talk about people or things that you have already mentioned ❍ *Investors are not putting cash into these funds.*
3 ADJ used introduce people or things that you are going to talk about ❍ *If you're looking for a builder, these phone numbers will be useful.*

they /ðeɪ/
1 PRON used when you are talking about more than one person, animal, or thing ❍ *They are*

unwilling to incur more costs.
2 PRON used instead of "he or she" when you are talking about a person without saying whether that person is a man or a woman ❍ *"Someone phoned. They said they would call back later."*

they'd /ðeɪd/
1 They'd is short for "they had." ❍ *They'd both worked in the oil industry.*
2 They'd is short for "they would." ❍ *He agreed that they'd visit her later.*

they'll /ðeɪl/ **They'll** is short for "they will." ❍ *They'll probably be here Monday.*

they're /ðɛər/ **They're** is short for "they are." ❍ *People work better when they're happy.*

they've /ðeɪv/ **They've** is short for "they have," especially when "have" is an auxiliary verb. ❍ *They've appointed a new CEO.*

thick /θɪk/
1 ADJ having a large distance between one side and the other ❍ *a thick slice of bread*
2 ADJ used to say or ask how wide something is ❍ *How thick are these walls?* ● **thick|ness NONCOUNT NOUN** ❍ *The cooking time depends on the thickness of the steaks.*
3 ADJ growing closely together in large amounts ❍ *Jessica has thick dark curly hair.*
4 ADJ Thick smoke or cloud is difficult to see through. ❍ *The crash happened in thick fog.*
5 ADJ If a liquid is **thick**, it does not flow easily. ❍ *Cook the sauce until it is thick and creamy.*

thief /θif/ (**thieves** /θivz/) **NOUN** a person who steals something ❍ *The thieves took his camera.*

thigh /θaɪ/ **NOUN** the top part of your leg ❍ *She's broken her thigh bone.*

thin /θɪn/ (**thinner, thinnest**)
1 ADJ having a small distance between one side and the other ❍ *The book is printed on very thin paper.*
2 ADJ A **thin** person or an animal has no extra fat on their body. ❍ *Bob was a tall, thin man.*
3 ADJ If a liquid is **thin**, it flows easily. ❍ *The soup was thin and tasteless.*

thing /θɪŋ/
1 NOUN used to refer to an object without saying its name ❍ *What's that thing in the middle of the road?*
2 PL NOUN Your **things** are your possessions. ❍ *She told him to take all his things and not to return.*
3 NOUN something that happens or something that you think or talk about ❍ *We had so many things to talk about.*

think /θɪŋk/ (**thinks, thinking, thought**)
1 VERB If you **think** something, that is your opinion or belief. ❍ *Many people think that interest rates will be higher next year.*
2 VERB When you **think**, you use your mind to consider something. ❍ *She closed her eyes for a moment, trying to think.*
3 VERB If you **think of** something, it comes into your mind. ❍ *I can't think of his name.*
▶ **think over** If you **think** something **over**, you consider it carefully. ❍ *They've offered her the job but she needs time to think it over.*

third /θɜrd/
1 ADJ or **ADV** The **third** item in a series is the one that you count as number three. ❍ *My office is the third door on the right.*
2 NOUN one of three equal parts of something (⅓)

third par|ty (**third parties**)
1 NOUN someone who is not one of the main people involved in a business agreement or legal case, but who is involved in it in a minor role [LEGAL] ❍ *You can instruct your bank to allow a third party to remove money from your account.*
2 ADJ Third party insurance provides payments if you hurt someone else or damage their property. [LEGAL]

Third World NONCOUNT NOUN The poor countries of Africa, Asia, and Central and South America are sometimes referred to all together as **the Third World**. Compare with **First World**. [ECONOMICS] ❍ *development in the Third World*

thirst /θɜrst/ **NONCOUNT NOUN Thirst** is the feeling that you want to drink something. ❍ *Drink water to satisfy your thirst.*

thirsty /θɜrsti/ (**thirstier, thirstiest**) **ADJ** wanting to drink something ❍ *Drink some water whenever you feel thirsty.*

t

thir|teen /θɜrti̲n/ the number 13

thir|teenth /θɜrti̲nθ/ **ADJ** or **ADV** The **thirteenth** item in a series is the one that you count as number thirteen. ❍ *his thirteenth birthday*

thir|ti|eth /θɜrtiəθ/ **ADJ** or **ADV** The **thirtieth** item in a series is the one that you count as number thirty. ❍ *the thirtieth anniversary of my parents' wedding*

thir|ty /θɜrti/ the number 30

this

Pronounce the adjective /ðɪs/. Pronounce the pronoun /ðɪ̲s/.

1 ADJ or **PRON** used to talk about a person or a thing that is near you, especially when you touch them or point to them ❍ *I like this room much better than the other one.* ❍ *"Would you like a different one?"—"No, this is great."*

2 ADJ used to talk about someone or something that you have already mentioned ❍ *How can we solve this problem?*

3 PRON used to introduce someone or something that you are going to talk about ❍ *This is what I will do. I will telephone Anna and explain.*

4 ADJ used to talk about the next day, month, or season ❍ *The meeting will be held this summer.*

thor|ough /θɜroʊ/ **ADJ** done completely, and with great attention to detail ❍ *a thorough investigation* ● **thor|ough|ly ADV** ❍ *All their customers are thoroughly checked for creditworthiness.*

those

Pronounce the adjective /ðoʊz/. Pronounce the pronoun /ðo̲ʊ̲z/.

1 ADJ or **PRON** used to talk about people or things that are a distance away from you in position or time ❍ *What are those buildings?* ❍ *Those are nice shoes.*

2 ADJ used to talk about people or things that have already been mentioned ❍ *I don't know any of those people.*

though /ðoʊ/

1 CONJ despite the fact that ❍ *I love him though I do not know him.*

2 CONJ but ❍ *The agency stopped hiring about a week ago, though it isn't laying off employees.*

thought /θɔ̲t/

1 Thought is a form of the verb **think**.

2 NOUN an idea or an opinion ❍ *What are your thoughts about the political situation?*

3 NONCOUNT NOUN Thought is the activity of thinking. ❍ *Alice was deep in thought.*

thought|ful /θɔ̲tfəl/

1 ADJ quiet and serious because you are thinking about something ❍ *Nancy paused, looking thoughtful.* ● **thought|ful|ly ADV** ❍ *Daniel nodded thoughtfully.*

2 ADJ thinking and caring about other people's feelings ❍ *Ben is a thoughtful boy.*

thou|sand /θa̲ʊ̲zᵊnd/

The plural form is **thousand** after a number.

1 the number 1,000 ❍ *Over five thousand people attended the conference.*

2 Thousands of things or people means a very large number of them. ❍ *I have been there thousands of times.*

thou|sandth /θa̲ʊ̲zᵊnθ/ **ADJ** or **ADV** The **thousandth** item in a series is the one that you count as number one thousand. ❍ *The magazine has just published its thousandth edition.*

thread /θrɛ̲d/

1 NOUN a long, very thin piece of a material such as cotton or nylon, used for sewing ❍ *a needle and thread*

2 VERB If you **thread** a needle, you put a piece of thread through the hole in the end of it.

threat /θrɛ̲t/

1 NOUN a statement that someone will hurt or harm you if you do not do what they want ❍ *death threats*

2 NOUN something that can harm someone or something ❍ *They see imports as a threat to their livelihood.*

threat|en /θrɛ̲tᵊn/

1 VERB If you **threaten** someone, you say that you will hurt or harm them if they do not do what you want. ❍ *Unions have threatened to strike on August 27.* ● **threat|en|ing ADJ** ❍ *threatening behavior*

T

2 VERB If something **threatens** people or things, it may harm them. ❍ *The proposed bailout may threaten the euro's stability.*

three /θri/ the number 3 ❍ *We waited three months before going back.*

threw /θru/ **Threw** is a form of the verb **throw**.

thrift /θrɪft/

1 NONCOUNT NOUN **Thrift** is the quality and practice of being careful with money and not wasting things. ❍ *They were rightly praised for their thrift and enterprise.*

2 NOUN A **thrift** or a **thrift institution** is a kind of savings bank.

thrill /θrɪl/

1 NOUN a sudden feeling of great excitement ❍ *Retailers love the thrill of a good sale.*

2 VERB If something **thrills** you, it gives you a feeling of great excitement. ❍ *The Yankees thrilled the crowd with a 7-5 victory.*

thrill|er /θrɪlər/ **NOUN** an exciting book, movie, or play about a crime ❍ *a historical thriller*

thrill|ing /θrɪlɪŋ/ **ADJ** very exciting and enjoyable ❍ *It was a thrilling finish to the tournament.*

throat /θroʊt/

1 NOUN the back part of your mouth, where you swallow ❍ *a sore throat*

2 NOUN the front part of your neck ❍ *Mr. Williams grabbed him by the throat.*

throb /θrɒb/ (**throbs, throbbing, throbbed**)

1 VERB If something **throbs**, it makes a strong regular sound. ❍ *His heart throbbed with excitement.*

2 VERB If part of your body **throbs**, pain comes and goes in a regular pattern. ❍ *Kevin's head throbbed.*

through /θru/

1 PREP or **ADV** from one side of something to the other side ❍ *The bullet went through the front windshield.* ❍ *There was a hole in the wall and water was coming through.*

2 PREP from the beginning until the end of a period ❍ *She kept quiet all through breakfast.*

3 PREP If something happens from a period of time **through** another, it starts at the first period and continues until the end of the second period. ❍ *The office is open Monday through Friday from 9 to 5.*

4 PREP because of ❍ *I succeeded through hard work.*

through|out /θruaʊt/

1 PREP during all of a period of time ❍ *It rained heavily throughout the game.*

2 PREP or **ADV** in all parts of a place ❍ *Such a failure creates problems throughout the financial system.* ❍ *The apartment is painted white throughout.*

throw /θroʊ/ (**throws, throwing, threw, thrown**)

1 VERB If you **throw** an object, you move your hand quickly and let go of it, so that it moves through the air. ❍ *The crowd began throwing stones at the police.*

2 NOUN **Throw** is also a noun. ❍ *That was a good throw.*

▸ **throw away** or **throw out** If you **throw away** or **throw out** something that you do not want, you get rid of it. ❍ *I never throw anything away.* ❍ *I've decided to throw out all the clothes I never wear.*

thrown /θroʊn/ **Thrown** is a form of the verb **throw**.

thumb /θʌm/ **NOUN** the short thick finger on the side of your hand

thump /θʌmp/

1 VERB If you **thump** something, you hit it hard with your hand. ❍ *Ramon thumped the table with his fist.*

2 VERB If your heart **thumps**, it beats strongly and quickly.

thun|der /θʌndər/

1 NONCOUNT NOUN **Thunder** is the loud noise that you hear during a storm. ❍ *Last night there was thunder and lightning.*

2 VERB When **it thunders**, a loud noise comes from the sky during a storm. ❍ *It will probably thunder later.*

thunder|storm /θʌndərstɔrm/ **NOUN** a very noisy storm

Thurs|day /θɜrzdeɪ, -di/ **NOUN** the day after Wednesday and before Friday ❍ *We go to the supermarket every Thursday morning.*

tick /tɪk/ VERB When a clock **ticks**, it makes a regular series of short sounds. ❍ *An alarm clock ticked loudly.*

tick box (**tick boxes**) [BRIT] → **check box**

tick|et /tɪkɪt/ NOUN a small piece of paper that shows that you have paid to go somewhere or to do something ❍ *a first-class plane ticket*

tick|et tout (**ticket touts**) /tɪkɪt taʊt/ [MARKETING AND SALES, BRIT] → **scalper**

tick|le /tɪkᵊl/ (**tickles, tickling, tickled**) VERB If you **tickle** someone, you move your fingers lightly over a part of their body to make them laugh. ❍ *Stephanie was cuddling the baby and tickling her toes.*

tide /taɪd/ NOUN the regular change in the level of the ocean ❍ *The tide was going out.*

tidy /taɪdi/ (**tidier, tidiest, tidies, tidying, tidied**)
1 ADJ Someone who is **tidy** likes everything to be in its correct place. ❍ *I'm not a very tidy person.*
2 ADJ arranged in a neat way ❍ *The room was neat and tidy.*
▸ **tidy up** When you **tidy up** a place, you make it neat it by putting things in the correct place. ❍ *You relax while I tidy up the house.*

tie /taɪ/ (**ties, tying, tied**)
1 VERB If you **tie** something, you fasten it with a knot. ❍ *She tied the ends of the two ropes together.*
2 VERB If you **tie** something in a particular position, you fasten it using rope or string. ❍ *He tied the dog to the fence.*
3 NOUN a long narrow piece of cloth that you wear around your neck with a shirt ❍ *Jason took off his jacket and loosened his tie.*
4 NOUN **Ties** are the connections that you have with people or a place. ❍ *Quebec has close ties to France.*
5 VERB If two people or teams **tie** in a game, they have the same score at the end of the game. ❍ *The teams tied 2-2.*
6 NOUN **Tie** is also a noun. ❍ *The first game ended in a tie.*
▸ **tie up**
1 If you **tie** something **up**, you fasten it with string or rope.
2 If you **tie up** money, you invest it or keep it for a specific purpose, so that it is not available for other uses. ❍ *Savers prepared to tie up their money for three years can obtain 5.30 percent annually.*

tie-in
1 NOUN a product that is connected with a successful movie, book, TV program, etc.
2 NOUN a sales method in which one item is offered for sale, often at a reduced price, to people who also buy another item
3 NOUN an item that is sold at a reduced price to people who also buy another item

ti|ger /taɪgər/
1 NOUN a large wild animal of the cat family, with orange and black stripes
2 NOUN a country that is achieving rapid economic growth [ECONOMICS] ❍ *Many of Asia's tiger economies seem to have been hit harder than their Western counterparts.*

tight /taɪt/
1 ADJ **Tight** clothes fit very closely to your body. ❍ *Amanda was wearing a tight black dress.*
2 ADV very firmly ❍ *Just hold tight to my hand and don't let go.*
3 ADJ **Tight** is also an adjective. ❍ *He kept a tight hold of her arm.* ● **tight|ly** ADV ❍ *The children hugged me tightly.*

tight|en /taɪtᵊn/ VERB If you **tighten** something, you make it tighter. ❍ *She tightened the belt on her robe.*

tights /taɪts/ PL NOUN **Tights** are a piece women's clothing made from thin material that covers the legs.

tile /taɪl/ NOUN a flat, square object used for covering floors, walls, or roofs

till /tɪl/
1 PREP or CONJ until ❍ *They had to wait till Monday to go to the bank.* ❍ *I didn't leave home till I was nineteen.*
2 NOUN the drawer of a cash register, where the money is kept ❍ *There was money in the till.*
3 [BRIT] → **cash register**

time /taɪm/ (**times, timing, timed**)
1 NONCOUNT NOUN **Time** is something that we measure in minutes, hours, days, and years. ❍ *Listen to me. I haven't much time.*

2 NOUN used to talk about a particular point in the day ❍ *What time is it?* ❍ *Departure times are 08:15 from Baltimore, and 10:15 from Newark.*
3 NOUN used to talk about a particular period of time or occasion when something happens ❍ *He isn't alleged to have sold any stock at that time.* ❍ *Sarah and I had a great time at the party.*
4 NOUN used to talk about how often you do something ❍ *three times a week*
5 PL NOUN You use **times** after numbers to show how much bigger or smaller one thing is than another. ❍ *The sun is 400 times bigger than the moon.*
6 CONJ You can use **times** when you are multiplying numbers. ❍ *Four times six is 24.*
7 VERB If you **time** something, you measure how long it lasts. ❍ *Practice your speech and time yourself.*
8 If you are **in time for** something, you are not late. ❍ *I arrived just in time for my flight to Hawaii.*
9 If someone or something is **on time**, they are not late or early. ❍ *The train arrived on time.*

time de|pos|it (**time deposits**) **NOUN** A **time deposit** is a bank deposit from which money may be withdrawn only with advance notice or on a particular agreed date. Compare with **demand deposit**. [BANKING] ❍ *Small investors are deserting stock markets to invest in time deposit plans.*

time|line /taɪmlaɪn/ also **time line** **NOUN** a picture that shows the order of historical events

time man|age|ment **NONCOUNT NOUN** **Time management** is a method of organizing tasks to make the best use of available time. [BUSINESS MANAGEMENT] ❍ *All effective people work on their time management perpetually.*

time-share (**time-shares**) also **time share** **NOUN** If you have a **time-share**, you have the right to use a particular property as vacation accommodations for a specific amount of time each year. ❍ *Other prizes include hotel discounts and a time-share at a resort in Palm Springs.*

time sheet (**time sheets**) **NOUN** a document on which the hours worked by employees are recorded [ADMINISTRATION]

time|table /taɪmteɪbᵊl/ **NOUN** a list of the times when vehicles like trains and buses arrive and depart ❍ *Have you checked the bus timetable?*

time zone (**time zones**) **NOUN** one of the areas that the world is divided into for measuring time

tim|ing /taɪmɪŋ/ **NONCOUNT NOUN** **Timing** is the skill of judging the right time to do something. ❍ *"Am I too early?"—"No, your timing is perfect."*

tin /tɪn/
1 NONCOUNT NOUN **Tin** is a type of soft metal. ❍ *a tin can*
2 NOUN A **tin** is the same as a **can**. [BRIT]

tiny /taɪni/ (**tinier, tiniest**) **ADJ** extremely small ❍ *The funds' assets are still tiny.*

> **BUSINESS ETIQUETTE**
> In Northern European countries, people usually follow a meeting's agenda quite strictly.

tip /tɪp/ (**tips, tipping, tipped**)
1 NOUN the long, narrow end of something ❍ *He pressed the tips of his fingers together.*
2 VERB If an object **tips**, it moves so that one end is higher than the other. ❍ *The baby carriage can tip backward if you hang bags on the handles.*
3 VERB If you **tip** something somewhere, you pour it there. ❍ *I tipped the water over his head.*
4 VERB If you **tip** someone, you give them some extra money to thank them for a job they have done for you. ❍ *He tipped the waiter.*
5 NOUN **Tip** is also a noun. ❍ *I gave the barber a tip.*
6 NOUN a useful piece of advice ❍ *The article gives tips on applying for jobs.*
7 NOUN a place where garbage is dumped
▸ **tip over** If you **tip** something **over**, you make it fall over. [BRIT] ❍ *He tipped the table over.*

tire /taɪər/ (**tires, tiring, tired**)
1 NOUN a thick round piece of rubber that fits around a wheel
2 VERB If something **tires** you, it makes you

feel that you want to rest or sleep. ❍ *If driving tires you, take the train instead.*

tired /taɪərd/
1 ADJ feeling that you want to rest or sleep ❍ *Michael is tired after his long flight.*
2 ADJ If you are **tired of** something, you do not want it to continue because you are bored or annoyed by it. ❍ *They have become tired of waiting and have sold their holdings.*

tis|sue /tɪʃu/
1 NONCOUNT NOUN Tissue is the material that animals and plants are made of. ❍ *brain tissue*
2 NONCOUNT NOUN Tissue or **tissue paper** is thin paper that you use for wrapping things that break easily.
3 NOUN a piece of thin, soft paper that you use to wipe your nose ❍ *a box of tissues*

ti|tle /taɪtᵊl/
1 NOUN the name of a book, a play, a movie, or a piece of music ❍ *What is the title of the poem?*
2 NOUN a word such as "Mr." or "Dr." that is used in front of someone's name

to /tə/
1 PREP used to talk about the direction of something ❍ *Two friends and I drove to Florida.*
2 PREP When you give something **to** someone, they receive it. ❍ *He picked up the knife and gave it to me.*
3 PREP used when you are talking about how something changes ❍ *The shouts of the crowd changed to laughter.*
4 PREP To means the last thing in a range. ❍ *I worked there from 1990 to 1996.*
5 PREP used to say how many minutes there are until the next hour ❍ *twenty to six*
6 used before the infinitive (= the simple form of a verb) ❍ *We just want to help.*

toast /toʊst/
1 NONCOUNT NOUN Toast is slices of bread that you have heated until they are brown. ❍ *For breakfast, he had toast and jam.*
2 VERB If you **toast** bread, you heat it so that it becomes brown. ❍ *toasted sandwiches*
3 NOUN a time when you lift up your glass to wish someone happiness or success before you drink ❍ *We drank a toast to the bride and groom.*
4 VERB Toast is also a verb. ❍ *We all toasted the baby's health.*

T

to|bac|co /təbækoʊ/ **NONCOUNT NOUN Tobacco** is the dried leaves of a plant that people smoke.

to|day /tədeɪ/
1 ADV or **NONCOUNT NOUN** used to talk about the day on which you are speaking or writing ❍ *How are you feeling today?* ❍ *Today is Friday, September 14th.*
2 ADV in the present period ❍ *More people have cars today.*

tod|dler /tɒdlər/ **NOUN** a young child who has only just learned to walk ❍ *Toddlers love music and singing.*

toe /toʊ/ **NOUN** one of the five parts at the end of your foot ❍ *He is in the hospital with a broken toe.*

to|geth|er /təgɛðər/
1 ADV If people do something **together**, they do it with each other. ❍ *We went into business together.*
2 ADV joined to each other or mixed with each other ❍ *He announced the creation of a European group to bring together its trading interests in the region.*
3 ADV in the same place or near to each other ❍ *The trees grew close together.*
4 ADV at the same time ❍ *"Yes," they said together.*

toi|let /tɔɪlɪt/ **NOUN** a large bowl with a seat that you use when you want to get rid of waste from your body ❍ *She flushed the toilet.*

toi|let|ries /tɔɪlətriz/ **PL NOUN Toiletries** are the things that you use when you are washing or taking care of your body, such as soap and toothpaste.

to|ken /toʊkən/ **NOUN** a round, flat piece of metal or plastic that you use in a machine instead of money ❍ *The machine uses plastic tokens rather than coins.*

to|ken pay|ment (**token payments**) **NOUN** a very small payment made to acknowledge a debt

told /toʊld/ **Told** is a form of the verb **tell**.

tol|er|ate /tɒləreɪt/ (**tolerates, tolerating, tolerated**) **VERB** If you **tolerate** something or someone, you accept or allow them although you do not like them very much. ❍ *The college will not tolerate such behavior.*

to|ma|to /təmeɪtoʊ/ (**tomatoes**) NOUN a soft, red fruit that you can eat raw in salads or cook like a vegetable

to|mor|row /təmɔroʊ/
1 ADV or NONCOUNT NOUN the day after today ❍ *Bye, see you tomorrow.* ❍ *What's on your schedule for tomorrow?*
2 ADV in the future ❍ *What is the world going to be like tomorrow?*

ton /tʌn/
1 NOUN a unit of weight equal to 2,000 pounds ❍ *Hundreds of tons of oil spilled into the ocean.*
2 NOUN a unit of weight equal to 1,000 kilograms [BRIT]

tone /toʊn/
1 NOUN the particular quality of a sound ❍ *Lisa has a deep tone to her voice.*
2 NOUN the feelings that someone's words show ❍ *I didn't like his tone of voice; he sounded angry.*

tongue /tʌŋ/ NOUN the soft part inside your mouth that moves when you speak or eat

to|night /tənaɪt/ ADV or NONCOUNT NOUN the evening of today ❍ *I'm at home tonight.* ❍ *Tonight is a very important night for him.*

ton|nage /tʌnɪdʒ/
1 NONCOUNT NOUN The **tonnage** of a ship is its size or the amount of space that it has inside it for cargo.
2 NONCOUNT NOUN **Tonnage** is the total number of tons that something weighs.

too /tu/
1 ADV also ❍ *I like swimming and tennis too.*
2 ADV more than is wanted, needed, or possible ❍ *Investors should be wary about paying too much.* ❍ *Many people think companies and executives are too greedy.*

took /tʊk/ **Took** is a form of the verb **take**.

tool /tul/ NOUN a piece of equipment that you hold in your hands and use to do a particular type of work ❍ *Do you have the right tools for the job?*

tool|bar /tulbɑr/ NOUN a narrow strip across a computer screen that contains pictures (= icons) that represent different things that the computer can do

tooth /tuθ/ (**teeth**) NOUN one of the hard white objects in your mouth, that you use for biting and eating ❍ *Brush your teeth at least twice a day.*

tooth|brush /tuθbrʌʃ/ NOUN a small brush that you use for cleaning your teeth

tooth|paste /tuθpeɪst/ NONCOUNT NOUN **Toothpaste** is a thick substance that you use to clean your teeth.

top /tɒp/
1 NOUN the highest part of something ❍ *We climbed to the top of the hill.*
2 ADJ The **top** thing is the highest one. ❍ *I can't reach the top shelf.*
3 NOUN a lid ❍ *He twisted the top off the bottle.*
4 NOUN a piece of clothing that you wear on the upper half of your body [INFORMAL] ❍ *I was wearing a black skirt and a red top.*
5 If one thing is **on top** of another, it is on its highest part. ❍ *There was a clock on top of the television.*

top-end ADJ **Top-end** products are expensive and of extremely high quality. ❍ *top-end camcorders*

top-heavy
1 ADJ Something that is **top-heavy** is larger or heavier at the top than at the bottom, and might therefore fall over. ❍ *top-heavy flowers such as sunflowers*
2 ADJ A **top-heavy** business or organization has too many senior managers. ❍ *top-heavy bureaucratic structures*

top|ic /tɒpɪk/ NOUN a subject that you discuss or write about ❍ *What is the topic of your essay?*

top man|age|ment or **senior management** NONCOUNT NOUN The **top management** of an organization or business is its most senior staff. [ADMINISTRATION, BUSINESS MANAGEMENT] ❍ *He insists top management didn't exert any pressure on its researchers to cheat.*

t

torch /tɔ̲rtʃ/

1 NOUN a long stick that has a flame at one end ❍ *the Olympic Torch*

2 NOUN A **torch** is the same as a **flashlight**. [BRIT]

tore /tɔ̲r/ **Tore** is a form of the verb **tear**.

torn /tɔ̲rn/ **Torn** is a form of the verb **tear**.

tor|ture /tɔ̲rtʃər/ (**tortures, torturing, tortured**)

1 VERB If someone **tortures** another person, they deliberately cause them terrible pain.

2 NONCOUNT NOUN Torture is also a noun. ❍ *The use of torture is prohibited by international law.*

toss /tɔ̲s/ (**tosses, tossing, tossed**)

1 VERB If you **toss** something, you throw it without care. ❍ *Kate tossed the ball to Jessica.*

2 VERB If you **toss** a coin, you spin it in the air and guess which way up it will be when it comes down. ❍ *We tossed a coin to decide who should go first.*

to|tal /to̲ʊtᵊl/

1 NOUN the number that you get when you add several numbers together ❍ *The three companies have a total of 1,776 employees.*

2 ADJ Total is also an adjective. ❍ *The total cost of the project was $240 million.*

3 ADJ complete ❍ *a total failure* ● **to|tal|ly ADV** ❍ *He has vowed to transform the company totally.*

to̲|tal qua̲l|ity ma̲n|age|ment

NONCOUNT NOUN Total quality management is a set of management principles aimed at improving performance throughout a company, especially by involving employees in decision-making. The abbreviation **TQM** is also used. [PRODUCTION, BUSINESS MANAGEMENT] ❍ *He is a firm believer in total quality management.*

T

touch /tʌ̲tʃ/

1 VERB If you **touch** something, you put your hand on it. ❍ *Her hands gently touched my face.*

2 NOUN Touch is also a noun. ❍ *She felt the touch of his hand on her arm.*

3 VERB If one thing **touches** another, there is no space between them. ❍ *Their knees were touching.*

4 NONCOUNT NOUN Your sense of **touch** is your ability to tell what something is like when you feel it with your hands.

5 If you are **in touch with** someone, you write or speak to them regularly. ❍ *My brother and I keep in touch by phone.*

tough /tʌ̲f/

1 ADJ A **tough** person is strong and determined. ❍ *a tough businessman*

2 ADJ difficult ❍ *tough decisions*

3 ADJ difficult to break or cut ❍ *The meat was tough and chewy.*

tour /tʊ̲ər/

1 VERB When musicians or performers **tour**, they go to several different places, where they perform. ❍ *A few years ago the band toured Europe.*

2 NOUN Tour is also a noun. ❍ *The band is planning a national tour.*

3 NOUN a trip to an interesting place or around several interesting places ❍ *Michael took me on a tour of the nearby islands.*

4 VERB If you **tour** a place, you go on a trip around it. ❍ *Tour the museum with a guide for $5 per person.*

tour|ism /tʊ̲ərɪzəm/ **NONCOUNT NOUN Tourism** is the business of providing hotels, restaurants, trips, and activities for people who are on vacation. [ECONOMICS] ❍ *Tourism is the island's main industry.*

tou̲r|ism se|ctor (**tourism sectors**) **NOUN** A country's **tourism sector** is that part of its economy that earns money through tourism. [ECONOMICS] ❍ *a booming tourism sector*

tour|ist /tʊ̲ərɪst/ **NOUN** a person who is visiting a place on vacation ❍ *About 75,000 tourists visit the town each year.*

tou̲r op|era|tor (**tour operators**) **NOUN** a company that provides vacations in which your travel and accommodations are booked for you

to|ward /tɔ̲rd/ also **towards**

1 PREP If you move **toward** something or someone, you move in their direction. ❍ *They drove toward Lake Ladoga.*

2 PREP Your attitude **toward** something or someone is the way you feel about them. ❍ *How do you feel toward the man who stole your purse?*

3 PREP If you give money **toward** something, you give it to help pay for that thing. ❍ *They gave us $50,000 toward our first house.*

tow|el /taʊəl/ **NOUN** a piece of thick, soft cloth that you use to dry yourself ❍ *I've put clean towels in the bathroom.*

tow|er /taʊər/ **NOUN** a tall, narrow building, or a tall part of another building ❍ *a church tower*

town /taʊn/ **NOUN** a place with many streets, buildings, and stores, where people live and work ❍ *a small town near the Canadian border*

tox|ic /tɒksɪk/ **ADJ** poisonous ❍ *The leaves of the plant are highly toxic.*

toy /tɔɪ/ **NOUN** an object that children play with ❍ *Sophie went to sleep holding her favorite toy.*

toy|et|ic /tɔɪɛtɪk/ **ADJ** In marketing, a **toyetic** film or television program generates consumer interest in associated merchandise, such as toys and computer games. [MARKETING AND SALES] ❍ *Another element in Bob the Builder's American success is that he has turned out to be what media analysts now term 'toyetic'.*

TQM /ti kyu ɛm/ **TQM** is short for **total quality management**. [PRODUCTION, BUSINESS MANAGEMENT]

trace /treɪs/ (**traces, tracing, traced**) **VERB** If you **trace** someone or something, you find them. ❍ *The police quickly traced the owner of the car.*

track /træk/
1 NOUN a rough road or path ❍ *a track in the forest*
2 NOUN a piece of ground that is used for races ❍ *a running track*
3 NOUN Railroad **tracks** are the metal lines that trains travel along.
4 NOUN one of the pieces of music on a CD
5 PL NOUN Tracks are the marks that an animal leaves on the ground. ❍ *William found fresh bear tracks in the snow.*

track|er fund /trækər fʌnd/ [BANKING, BRIT] → **index fund**

trac|tor /træktər/ **NOUN** a vehicle that a farmer uses to pull farm machinery

trade /treɪd/ (**trades, trading, traded**)
1 VERB If people or countries **trade**, they buy and sell goods. ❍ *We have been trading with this company for over thirty years.*
2 NONCOUNT NOUN Trade is also a noun. ❍ *Texas has a long history of trade with Mexico.*
▸ **trade up** If you **trade up**, you sell something that you own and replace it with a better, more expensive version. [MARKETING AND SALES]

trade as|so|cia|tion (**trade associations**) **NOUN** a body representing the interests of organizations within the same trade ❍ *one of the two main trade associations for antique dealers*

trade cred|it **NONCOUNT NOUN Trade credit** is when a supplier allows a customer to pay for goods or services some time after they were supplied. [ECONOMICS] ❍ *It might be that the business is able to sell its finished goods before having to pay off the trade credit.*

trade defi|cit (**trade deficits**) **NOUN** If a country has a **trade deficit**, it imports goods worth more than the value of the goods that it exports. Compare with **trade surplus**. [ECONOMICS] ❍ *The U.S. trade deficit grew to just under $30 billion in the third quarter.*

Trade Des|crip|tions Act or **Trades Descriptions Act** **NOUN** In Britain, the **Trade Descriptions Act** is a law designed to prevent companies from presenting their goods or services in a dishonest or misleading way. [MARKETING AND SALES, LEGAL] ❍ *Last year it was convicted and fined under the Trades Descriptions Act for placing For Sale boards on empty homes in the area.*

trade dis|count (**trade discounts**) **NOUN** an amount by which the price of something is reduced for a person or business in the same trade [PURCHASING] ❍ *They can get trade discounts of up to 50%.*

trade gap (**trade gaps**) **NOUN** A **trade gap** is the same as a **trade deficit**. [ECONOMICS] ❍ *The trade gap surprised most analysts by shrinking, rather than growing.*

trade-in NOUN an arrangement in which someone buys a new car at a reduced price by giving their old one, as well as money, in payment ❍ *the trade-in value of the car*

trade jour|nal (**trade journals**) NOUN a magazine with articles about a particular trade ❍ *He did an interview with the trade journal Automotive News.*

trade|mark /treɪdmɑrk/

1 NOUN a special name or a symbol that a company owns and uses on its products [MARKETING AND SALES, LEGAL] ❍ *Kodak is a trademark of Eastman Kodak Company.*

2 VERB If a company **trademarks** the name of a product, it makes it officially illegal for another company to use the name. [MARKETING AND SALES, LEGAL] ❍ *The hope is that trademarking these regional varieties will enable farmers to demand higher prices.*

trade name (**trade names**) NOUN a name which manufacturers give to a product or to a range of products [BUSINESS MANAGEMENT] ❍ *It's marketed under the trade name "Mirage."*

trad|er /treɪdər/

1 NOUN someone whose job is to buy and sell products [MARKETING AND SALES] ❍ *Market traders display an exotic selection of the island's produce.*

2 someone who buys and sells shares or money on the stock exchange [BANKING] ❍ *Many traders feel Japan's currency could recover soon.*

Trades Des|crip|tions Act [MARKETING AND SALES, LEGAL] → **Trade Descriptions Act**

trade se|cret (**trade secrets**) NOUN a piece of information that is known, used, and kept secret by a particular company, for example, about a method of production ❍ *The nature of the polymer is currently a trade secret.*

trades|man /treɪdzmən/ (**tradesmen**) NOUN someone who is a skilled worker ❍ *tradesmen such as electricians or plumbers*

trade sur|plus (**trade surpluses**) NOUN If a country has a **trade surplus**, it exports goods worth more than the value of the goods that it imports. Compare with **trade deficit**. [ECONOMICS] ❍ *The country's trade surplus widened to 16.5 billion dollars.*

trade un|ion (**trade unions**) [ADMINISTRATION, mainly BRIT] → **labor union**

trad|ing floor (**trading floors**) NOUN the area in a bank or stock exchange where shares are bought and sold [BANKING]

trad|ing re|lation|ship (**trade relationships**) NOUN If two countries or businesses have a **trading relationship**, they trade with each other on a regular basis. [ECONOMICS] ❍ *Mr. Palaszczuk did not believe New Zealand's actions would affect the close trading relationship between the two countries.*

tra|di|tion /trədɪʃən/ NOUN an activity, event, or belief that has existed for a long time ❍ *Thanksgiving dinner is an American tradition.* ● **tra|di|tion|al** /trədɪʃənəl/ ADJ ❍ *traditional Scottish music* ● **tra|di|tion|al|ly** ADV ❍ *Christmas is traditionally a time for families.*

traf|fic /træfɪk/ (**traffics, trafficking, trafficked**)

1 NONCOUNT NOUN **Traffic** is all the vehicles that are on the roads in an area. ❍ *There was heavy traffic on the roads.* ❍ *Yesterday, traffic was light on the freeway.*

2 NONCOUNT NOUN **Traffic** is illegal trade. ❍ *drug traffic*

3 NONCOUNT NOUN **Traffic** is the number of customers that goes to a place in a given time period. ❍ *The group attributed its earnings gains to stronger traffic.*

4 VERB If you **traffic in** something, you carry on illegal trade or business. ❍ *A number of other major defense companies are suspected of trafficking in secret government documents.*

traf|fic jam (**traffic jams**) NOUN a line of vehicles that cannot move forward, or can only move very slowly

traf|fic light (**traffic lights**) NOUN **Traffic lights** are colored lights that control the flow of traffic.

trag|edy /trædʒɪdi/ (**tragedies**) NOUN an extremely sad event or situation ❍ *They have suffered a terrible personal tragedy.*

trag|ic /trædʒɪk/ ADJ extremely sad, and often involving death ❍ *a tragic accident* ● **tragi|cal|ly** /trædʒɪkli/ ADV ❍ *He died tragically in a car accident.*

trail /treɪl/
1 NOUN a rough path ❍ *He was walking along a trail through the trees.*
2 NOUN a series of marks that is left by someone or something as they move around ❍ *a sticky trail of orange juice*

trail|er /treɪlər/
1 NOUN a long narrow house that can be moved on a large vehicle
2 NOUN a vacation home with wheels that is pulled by a car
3 NOUN a large container on wheels that is pulled by a vehicle

train /treɪn/
1 NOUN a long vehicle that is pulled by an engine along a railroad ❍ *He came to New York by train.*
2 VERB If you **train** or if someone **trains** you, you learn the skills that you need in order to do something. [BUSINESS MANAGEMENT] ❍ *Stephen is training to be a teacher.* ● **train|ing** NONCOUNT NOUN ❍ *Kennedy had no formal training as an artist.*
3 VERB If you **train for** a sports competition, you prepare for it. ❍ *She spent six hours a day training for the race.* ● **train|ing** NONCOUNT NOUN ❍ *He keeps fit through exercise and training.*

COLLOCATIONS
vocational training
youth training
a training *course*
management training
a training *session*
a training *program*

train|er /treɪnər/ [BRIT] → **sneaker**

trai|tor /treɪtər/ **NOUN** someone who is not loyal to their country or to a group ❍ *Traitors among us were sending messages to the enemy.*

tram /træm/ **NOUN** a public transportation vehicle that travels along rails on a street ❍ *You can get to the beach by tram.*

tranche /trɑnʃ/ **NOUN** a part or group that forms part of a larger unit [FORMAL] ❍ *They risk losing the next tranche of funding.* ❍ *He put up for sale a second tranche of 32 state-owned companies.*

trans|ac|tion /trænzækʃən/ **NOUN** a piece of business, for example an act of buying or selling something [FORMAL] ❍ *The transaction is completed by payment of the fee.*

trans|fer (**transfers, transferring, transferred**)

Pronounce the verb /trænsfɜr/ or /trænsfər/. Pronounce the noun /trænsfər/.

1 VERB If you **transfer** something or someone **from** one place **to** another place, you move them there. ❍ *I transferred the money to a different account.*
2 NOUN Transfer is also a noun. ❍ *Arrange for the transfer of medical records to your new doctor.*

trans|fer pric|ing **NONCOUNT NOUN** **Transfer pricing** is the setting of a price for the transfer of materials, goods or services between different parts of a large organization. ❍ *He claims that foreign companies are engaged in massive tax avoidance through transfer pricing.*

trans|form /trænsfɔrm/ **VERB** To **transform** someone or something means to change them completely. ❍ *Such a tax would transform the nation's financial markets.* ● **trans|for|ma|tion** /trænsfərmeɪʃən/ **NOUN** ❍ *The industry is going through a transformation.*

trans|late /trænzleɪt/ (**translates, translating, translated**) **VERB** If you **translate** something, you write it in a different language. ❍ *His books have been translated into English.* ● **trans|la|tor** **NOUN** ❍ *She works as a translator.*

trans|la|tion /trænzleɪʃən/ **NOUN** a piece of writing or speech that has been put into a different language ❍ *a translation of the Bible*

trans|mit /trænzmɪt/ (**transmits, transmitting, transmitted**)
1 VERB When electronic signals **are transmitted**, they are sent out. ❍ *The game was transmitted live.*
2 VERB If one person or animal **transmits** a disease to another, they pass it to them. [FORMAL] ❍ *insects that transmit disease to humans*

trans|par|en|cy /trænspɛərənsi, -pær-/ (**transparencies**)
1 NOUN a small piece of photographic film with a frame around it ❍ *transparencies of masterpieces from Lizzie's art collection*
2 NONCOUNT NOUN **Transparency** is the quality that an object or substance has when you can see through it. ❍ *Cataracts affect the transparency of the eye's lenses.*
3 NONCOUNT NOUN **Transparency** is the quality of being clear and easy to understand. ❍ *Investment analysts had long complained of a lack of transparency.*

trans|par|ent /trænspɛərənt, -pær-/ **ADJ** If an object or a substance is **transparent**, you can see through it. ❍ *a sheet of transparent plastic*

trans|port /trænspɔrt/
1 VERB To **transport** people or goods somewhere is to take there in a vehicle. ❍ *Buses transported passengers to the town.*
2 NONCOUNT NOUN **Transport** is the same as **transportation**. [mainly BRIT]

trans|por|ta|tion /trænspərteɪʃən/
1 NONCOUNT NOUN **Transportation** means any type of vehicle that you can travel in or carry goods in. ❍ *The company will provide transportation.*
2 NONCOUNT NOUN **Transportation** is the activity of taking goods or people from one place to another place in a vehicle. ❍ *transportation costs*

trap /træp/ (**traps, trapping, trapped**)
1 NOUN a piece of equipment for catching animals ❍ *Nathan's dog got caught in a trap.*
2 NOUN a trick that is intended to catch or deceive someone ❍ *He wondered if there was a trap in the question.*
3 VERB If someone **traps** you, they trick you so that you do or say something that you do not want to do or say. ❍ *Were you trying to trap her into confessing?*
4 VERB If you **are trapped** somewhere, you cannot move or escape. ❍ *The car turned over, trapping both men.*

trash /træʃ/ **NONCOUNT NOUN** **Trash** consists of things that people have thrown away because they do not want them. ❍ *The yards are full of trash.*

trash can (**trash cans**) **NOUN** a large round container where people put things that they no longer want

trav|el /trævəl/
1 VERB If you **travel**, you go on a trip. ❍ *I've been traveling all day.*
2 NONCOUNT NOUN **Travel** is the activity of traveling. ❍ *He hated air travel.*

trav|el agen|cy (**travel agencies**) or **travel bureau** **NOUN** a business which makes arrangements for people's vacations and trips

trav|el|er /trævələr/ also **traveller** **NOUN** a person who is on a trip or a person who travels a lot ❍ *airline travelers*

trav|el|er's check (**traveler's checks**) **NOUN** a check that is sold to people traveling abroad and can be exchanged for cash [BANKING]

tray /treɪ/ **NOUN** a flat piece of wood, plastic, or metal that is used for carrying things, especially food and drinks

treas|ure /trɛʒər/ **NONCOUNT NOUN** In children's stories, **treasure** is a collection of valuable objects, such as gold coins and jewelry. ❍ *buried treasure*

Treas|ury bill (**Treasury bills**) **NOUN** a type of security, issued by a government, that does not pay interest and can be redeemed within a year [BANKING] ❍ *Japan's Finance Ministry has decided to issue a three-month Treasury bill.*

Treas|ury bond (**Treasury bonds**) **NOUN** a type of security, issued by the U.S. treasury, that pays interest and matures after twenty or thirty years [BANKING] ❍ *a 30-year Treasury bond*

Treas|ury note (**Treasury notes**) **NOUN** a type of security, issued by the U.S. treasury, that pays interest and matures in one to ten years [BANKING] ❍ *The yield on the five-year Treasury note is 3.45%.*

treat /trit/
1 VERB If you **treat** someone or something in a particular way, you behave toward them in that way. ❍ *Stop treating me like a child.*
2 VERB When doctors or nurses **treat** patients,

they give them medical care. ❍ *The boy was treated for a minor head wound.*

3 VERB If you **treat** someone **to** something, you buy it or arrange it for them. ❍ *She was always treating him to ice cream.*

4 NOUN **Treat** is also a noun. ❍ *a special treat*

treat|ment /tritmənt/

1 NOUN **Treatment** is medical attention given to a sick or injured person or animal. ❍ *They are not getting the medical treatment they need.*

2 NONCOUNT NOUN Your **treatment** of someone is the way you behave toward them. ❍ *We don't want any special treatment.*

trea|ty /triti/ (**treaties**) NOUN a written agreement between countries ❍ *a treaty on global warming*

tree /tri/ NOUN a tall plant with a hard central part (= a trunk), branches, and leaves ❍ *apple trees*

trem|ble /trɛmbᵊl/ (**trembles, trembling, trembled**) VERB If someone or something **trembles**, they shake slightly. ❍ *Lisa was white and trembling with anger.*

tre|men|dous /trɪmɛndəs/

1 ADJ very large in amount or level ❍ *There is tremendous pressure to keep down commercial rates.* ● **tre|men|dous|ly** ADV ❍ *The market has grown tremendously in the last few years.*

2 ADJ very good ❍ *I thought her performance was absolutely tremendous.*

trend /trɛnd/ NOUN a change or a development toward a different situation [BUSINESS MANAGEMENT] ❍ *a trend toward healthier eating*

trendy /trɛndi/ (**trendier, trendiest**) ADJ fashionable and modern [INFORMAL] ❍ *a trendy Seattle night club*

tri|al /traɪəl/

1 NOUN a process in a law court, to decide whether a person is guilty of a crime [LEGAL] ❍ *He is on trial for murder.*

2 NOUN an experiment in which you test something by using it or doing it for a period of time ❍ *The drug is being tested in clinical trials.*

3 VERB If you **trial** something, you test it to see how effective it is or what its quality is like.

tri|al bal|ance (**trial balances**) NOUN a statement of all the credits and debits in a double-entry accounting system, created to test that they are equal [FINANCE]

tri|an|gle /traɪæŋgᵊl/ NOUN a shape with three straight sides

tribe /traɪb/ NOUN a group of people of the same race, language, and culture, who live away from towns and cities ❍ *three hundred members of the Xhosa tribe* ● **trib|al** /traɪbᵊl/ ADJ ❍ *tribal lands*

tri|bu|nal /traɪbyunᵊl/ NOUN a special court or committee that is appointed to deal with particular problems [LEGAL] ❍ *His case comes before an industrial tribunal in March.*

trib|ute /trɪbyut/ NOUN something that you say, do, or make to show that you admire and respect someone ❍ *The song is a tribute to Roy Orbison.*

trick /trɪk/

1 VERB If someone **tricks** you, they do something dishonest in order to make you do or believe something. ❍ *They tricked him into signing the contract.*

2 NOUN **Trick** is also a noun. ❍ *His son loves to play tricks on him.*

3 NOUN a clever or skillful action that someone does in order to entertain people ❍ *card tricks*

trickle-down ADJ The **trickle-down** theory is the theory that benefits given to people at the top of a system will eventually be passed on to people lower down the system. ❍ *The government is not simply relying on trickle-down economics to tackle poverty.*

trig|ger /trɪgər/ NOUN the part of a gun that you pull to make it shoot ❍ *He pulled the trigger.*

trim /trɪm/ (**trims, trimming, trimmed**)

1 VERB If you **trim** something, you cut off small amounts of it in order to make it look neater. ❍ *My friend trims my hair every eight weeks.*

2 NOUN **Trim** is also a noun. ❍ *His hair needed a trim.*

trip /trɪp/ (**trips, tripping, tripped**)

1 NOUN a short journey that you make to

a particular place ❍ *She has just returned from a week-long trip to Montana.*

2 VERB If you **trip** when you are walking, you fall or nearly fall. ❍ *She tripped and broke her hip.*

tri|ple /trɪpᵊl/ (**triples, tripling, tripled**)

1 ADJ consisting of three things or parts ❍ *The property includes a triple garage.*

2 VERB Something that **triples** becomes three times as large. ❍ *My salary tripled.*

tri|plet /trɪplɪt/ **NOUN** one of three children born at the same time to the same mother

tri|umph /traɪʌmf/

1 NOUN a great success ❍ *The campaign was a triumph for the marketing people.*

2 NONCOUNT NOUN Triumph is a feeling of great satisfaction after a great success. ❍ *She felt a sense of triumph.*

triv|ial /trɪviəl/ **ADJ** not important or serious ❍ *trivial details*

trol|ley /trɒli/

1 NOUN an electric vehicle that travels on rails in the streets of a city ❍ *He took a northbound trolley on State Street.*

2 NOUN A shopping **trolley** or luggage **trolley** is the same as a **cart**. [BRIT]

tro|phy /troʊfi/ (**trophies**) **NOUN** a prize, such as a silver cup, that is given to the winner of a competition ❍ *The special trophy for the best rider went to Chris Read.*

trou|ble /trʌbᵊl/ (**troubles, troubling, troubled**)

1 NONCOUNT NOUN Trouble is problems or difficulties. ❍ *You've caused us a lot of trouble.*

2 NONCOUNT NOUN If there is **trouble**, people are arguing or fighting. ❍ *Police were sent to prevent trouble.*

3 VERB If something **troubles** you, it makes you feel worried. ❍ *Is anything troubling you?*

trouble|maker /trʌbᵊlmeɪkər/ **NOUN** someone who causes trouble ❍ *She has always been a troublemaker.*

trouble|shoot|ing /trʌbᵊlʃutɪŋ/ **NONCOUNT NOUN Troubleshooting** is the activity or process of solving major problems or difficulties that occur in a company or government. [BUSINESS MANAGEMENT] ❍ *The company provides technological inputs for troubleshooting on the suppliers' shopfloors, so that they can cut their costs.*

• **trouble|shoot|er NOUN** ❍ *Three troubleshooters are on their way to Japan to help stem heavy losses at Mazda.*

trou|sers /traʊzərz/ **PL NOUN Trousers** are a piece of clothing that covers the body from the waist downward, and that covers each leg separately. [FORMAL] ❍ *He was dressed in a shirt, dark trousers and boots.*

truck /trʌk/ **NOUN** a large vehicle that is used for transporting goods by road ❍ *a truck driver*

truck|er /trʌkər/ **NOUN** someone who drives a truck as their job [LOGISTICS AND DISTRIBUTION] ❍ *the type of place where truckers and farmers stopped for coffee and pie*

truck|ing /trʌkɪŋ/ **NONCOUNT NOUN Trucking** is the activity of transporting goods from one place to another using trucks. [LOGISTICS AND DISTRIBUTION] ❍ *the deregulation of the trucking industry*

true /tru/ (**truer, truest**)

1 ADJ based on facts, and not invented ❍ *Everything she said was true.*

2 If a dream or wish **comes true**, it actually happens. ❍ *When I was 13, my dream came true and I got my first horse.*

true and fair view NOUN If auditors say that an organization's accounts give a **true and fair view**, they believe that they give an accurate and complete picture of its financial state.

tru|ly /truli/ **ADV** really and completely ❍ *We want a truly democratic system.*

trunk /trʌŋk/

1 NOUN the large main stem of a tree ❍ *The tree trunk was more than five feet across.*

2 NOUN a covered space at the back of a car, in which you put bags or other things ❍ *She opened the trunk of the car.*

3 NOUN a large, strong box that is used for storing things ❍ *Maloney unlocked his trunk and took out some clothing.*

4 NOUN An elephant's **trunk** is its long nose.

trust /trʌst/
1 VERB If you **trust** someone, you believe that they are honest and that they will not harm you. ❍ *"I trust you completely," he said.*
2 NONCOUNT NOUN **Trust** is also a noun. ❍ *He destroyed my trust in men.*
3 VERB If you **trust** someone **to** do something, you believe that they will do it. ❍ *I trust you to keep this secret.*
4 NOUN a group of businesses that combine to control the market for any commodity [ECONOMICS]

trust ac|count (**trust accounts**) **NOUN** a savings account in the name of a trustee who controls it during their lifetime, after which the balance is payable to someone who has already been nominated [BANKING] ❍ *The funds were held in a trust account.*

trust fund (**trust funds**) **NOUN** an amount of money or property that someone owns, usually after inheriting it, but which is kept and invested for them [BANKING] ❍ *The money will be placed in a trust fund for her daughter.*

truth /truθ/ **NONCOUNT NOUN** **The truth** is the facts about something, rather than things that are imagined or invented. ❍ *Are you telling me the truth?*

try /traɪ/ (**tries, trying, tried**)
1 VERB If you **try** to do something, you make an effort to do it. ❍ *He tried to help her at work.*
2 NOUN **Try** is also a noun. ❍ *It was a good try.*
3 VERB If you **try** something, you use it or do it in order to discover what it is like. ❍ *You may choose to try something completely new.*
4 NOUN **Try** is also a noun. ❍ *All we're asking is that you give it a try.*
5 VERB When people **are tried**, they appear in a law court where it is decided if they are guilty of a crime. ❍ *They were arrested and tried for murder.*
▸ **try on** If you **try on** a piece of clothing, you put it on in order to see if it fits you or if it looks nice. ❍ *Try on the shoes to make sure they fit.*
▸ **try out** If you **try** something **out**, you test it in order to find out how useful or effective it is. ❍ *I want to try the boat out next weekend.*

T-shirt /tiʃɜrt/ also **tee-shirt** **NOUN** a simple cotton shirt with no collar and short sleeves

tub /tʌb/
1 NOUN A **tub** is the same as a **bathtub**. ❍ *I went into the bathroom to fill the tub.*
2 NOUN a deep container ❍ *a tub of ice cream*

tube /tub/
1 NOUN a long hollow object like a narrow pipe ❍ *He is fed by a tube that enters his nose.*
2 NOUN a long, thin container that you can press in order to force a substance out ❍ *a tube of toothpaste*

Tues|day /tuzdeɪ, -di/ **NOUN** the day after Monday and before Wednesday ❍ *Work on the project will start next Tuesday.*

tug /tʌg/ (**tugs, tugging, tugged**)
1 VERB If you **tug** something, you give it a quick, strong pull. ❍ *A little boy tugged at his sleeve excitedly.*
2 NOUN **Tug** is also a noun. ❍ *I felt a tug at my sleeve.*

tu|mor /tumər/ **NOUN** a lump in someone's body caused by cells that are not growing normally ❍ *a brain tumor*

tu|mour /tumər/ [BRIT] → **tumor**

tuna /tunə/

The plural can be either **tuna** or **tunas**.

NOUN a large fish that lives in warm seas, or the meat of this fish ❍ *a can of tuna*

tune /tun/ (**tunes, tuning, tuned**)
1 NOUN a series of musical notes that is pleasant to listen to ❍ *She was humming a little tune.*
2 A singer or a musical instrument that is **in tune** produces exactly the right notes. A person or a musical instrument that is **out of tune** does not produce exactly the right notes. ❍ *He sang in tune.*

tun|nel /tʌnᵊl/ **NOUN** a long passage that has been made under or through the ground

tur|key /tɜrki/ **NOUN** a large bird that is kept on a farm for its meat, or the meat of this bird

turn /tɜrn/
1 VERB If someone or something **turns** or you **turn** them, they move so that they are facing or moving in a different direction. ❍ *He turned and walked away.*

2 NOUN Turn is also a noun. ❍ *You can't do a right-hand turn here.*

3 VERB When something **turns**, it moves around in a circle. ❍ *The wheels turned very slowly.*

4 VERB If you **turn** a page in a book, you move it so that you can look at the next page.

5 VERB If something **turns into** something else, it becomes something different. ❍ *In the story, the prince turns into a frog.*

6 NOUN Your **turn to** do something is the time when you can or must do it. ❍ *Tonight it's my turn to cook.*

7 VERB If a business **turns** a profit, it earns more money than it spends. ❍ *The firm will be able to service debt and still turn a modest profit.*

▸**turn around**

1 If you **turn** something **around**, or if it **turns around**, it is moved so that it faces the opposite direction. ❍ *Bud turned the truck around, and started back for Dalton Pond.*

2 If something such as a business or economy **turns around**, or if someone **turns** it **around**, it becomes successful, after being unsuccessful for a period of time. ❍ *Turning the company around won't be easy.*

▸**turn away**

1 If you **turn** someone **away**, you do not allow them to enter your country, home, or other place. ❍ *Turning refugees away would be an inhumane action.*

2 To **turn away from** something such as a method or an idea means to stop using it or to become different from it. ❍ *Japanese corporations have been turning away from production and have diverted into finance and real estate.*

T

▸**turn down**

1 If you **turn down** an offer, you refuse it. ❍ *The company offered me a new contract, but I turned it down.*

2 When you **turn down** a piece of equipment, you make it produce less sound or heat. ❍ *Please turn the TV down!*

▸**turn off** When you **turn off** a piece of equipment, you make it stop working. ❍ *She turned off the faucet.*

▸**turn on** When you **turn on** a piece of equipment, you make it start working. ❍ *I turned on the television.*

▸**turn out** The way that something **turns out** is the way that it happens. ❍ *I didn't know my life was going to turn out like this.*

▸**turn over**

1 If you **turn** something **over**, you move it so that the top part is on the bottom. ❍ *Liz picked up the envelope and turned it over.*

2 If a company **turns over** an amount of money, that is the value of goods and services it sells in a given period. ❍ *By April 2000, staff numbers had grown to 35 people and the company turned over £4 million.*

▸**turn up**

1 If someone **turns up**, they arrive. ❍ *They finally turned up at nearly midnight.*

2 When you **turn up** a piece of equipment, you make it produce more sound or heat. ❍ *I turned the volume up.*

turn|around /tɜrnəraʊnd/

1 NOUN a complete change in opinion, attitude, or method ❍ *I have personally never done such a complete turnaround in my opinion of a person.*

2 NOUN a sudden improvement, especially in the success of a business or a country's economy ❍ *The company has been enjoying a turnaround in recent months.*

3 NOUN The **turnaround** or **turnaround time** of a task is the amount of time that it takes. ❍ *It is possible to produce a result within 34 hours but the standard turnaround is 12 days.* ❍ *The agency should reduce turnaround time by 11 percent.*

tur|nip /tɜrnɪp/ **NOUN** a round white vegetable that grows under the ground

turn|out /tɜrnaʊt/ **NOUN** the number of people who go to an event ❍ *It was a great afternoon with a huge turnout of people.*

turn|over /tɜrnoʊvər/ **NOUN** the value of the goods or services that a company sells during a particular period of time, usually a year [FINANCE, ECONOMICS] ❍ *The company had a turnover of $3.8 million.*

tu|tor /tutər/ **NOUN** someone who gives lessons to one student or a very small group of students ❍ *a math tutor*

TV /ti vi/ (**TVs**) NOUN **TV** means the same as **television**. ❍ *The TV was on.*

twelfth /twɛlfθ/ ADJ or ADV The **twelfth** item in a series is the one that you count as number twelve. ❍ *They're celebrating the twelfth anniversary of the revolution.*

twelve /twɛlv/ the number 12

twen|ti|eth /twɛntiəθ/ ADJ or ADV The **twentieth** item in a series is the one that you count as number twenty. ❍ *the twentieth century*

twen|ty /twɛnti/ the number 20

24-7 /twɛntifɔrsɛvᵊn/ also **twenty-four seven** ADV If something happens **24-7**, it happens all the time. [INFORMAL] ❍ *I worked 24-7 to build up this company.*

twice /twaɪs/ ADV two times ❍ *I phoned twice a day.* ❍ *Budapest is twice as big as my home town.*

twi|light /twaɪlaɪt/ NONCOUNT NOUN **Twilight** is the time just before night when it is getting dark.

twin /twɪn/
1 NOUN one of two people who were born at the same time to the same mother ❍ *Sarah was looking after the twins.*
2 ADJ used to describe two similar things that are a pair ❍ *twin beds*

twist /twɪst/
1 VERB If you **twist** something, you turn its ends in opposite directions or bend it into a different shape. ❍ *She sat twisting the handles of the bag.*
2 VERB If you **twist** part of your body, you turn that part while keeping the rest of your body still. ❍ *She twisted her head around to look at him.*
3 VERB If you **twist** something, you turn it around. ❍ *She was twisting the ring on her finger.*

two /tu/ the number 2

ty|coon /taɪkun/ NOUN a person who is successful in business and so has become rich and powerful [ECONOMICS] ❍ *a self-made Irish-American property tycoon*

COLLOCATIONS
a *media* tycoon
a *property* tycoon
a *business* tycoon
a *publishing* tycoon

type /taɪp/ (**types, typing, typed**)
1 NOUN a particular kind ❍ *These types of fund tend to be relatively safe.*
2 VERB If you **type** something, you write it using a machine like a computer. ❍ *I can type your essays for you.*

typi|cal /tɪpɪkᵊl/ ADJ having the normal and expected characteristics of someone or something ❍ *These products followed a typical sales pattern.*

typi|cal|ly /tɪpɪkli/
1 ADV used to say that something is a good example of a person or thing ❍ *The food is typically American.*
2 ADV usually ❍ *The fourth quarter is typically a period when borrowing is high.*

tyre /taɪər/ [mainly BRIT] → **tire 1**

Uu

ugly /ʌgli/ (**uglier, ugliest**) ADJ unpleasant to look at ❍ *an ugly scar*

ul|ti|mate /ʌltɪmɪt/ ADJ used for talking about the final result of a long series of events ❍ *The ultimate goal of any investor is to make a profit.*

ul|ti|mate|ly /ʌltɪmɪtli/ ADV finally, after a long series of events ❍ *Who, ultimately, is going to pay?*

um|brel|la /ʌmbrɛlə/ NOUN an object that you hold above your head to protect yourself from the rain

um|pire /ʌmpaɪr/ NOUN a person whose job is to watch a sports game to make sure that the rules are not broken ❍ *The umpire's decision is final.*

un|able /ʌneɪbᵊl/ ADJ If you are **unable to** do something, you are not able to do it. ❍ *They were unable to meet their interest payments.*

un|ac|cep|table /ʌnəksɛptəbᵊl/ ADJ too bad or wrong to be allowed ❍ *He took an unacceptable risk by investing so heavily in industry.*

unani|mous /yunænɪməs/ ADJ agreed by everyone ❍ *Their decision was unanimous.* • **unani|mous|ly** ADV ❍ *The board unanimously approved the project last week.*

U

un|at|trac|tive /ʌnətrӕktɪv/ ADJ not beautiful or attractive ❍ *an unattractive orange color*

un|avail|able /ʌnəveɪləbᵊl/

1 ADJ When people are **unavailable**, you cannot meet them or contact them. ❍ *She was unavailable for comment.*

2 ADJ If something is unavailable, you cannot have it or obtain it. ❍ *Figures are unavailable for the period April-June.*

un|aware /ʌnəwɛər/ ADJ If you are **unaware** of something, you do not know about it. ❍ *They are unaware of what other managers think.*

un|bear|able /ʌnbɛərəbᵊl/ ADJ too unpleasant to continue experiencing ❍ *The pain was unbearable.* • **un|bear|ably** /ʌnbɛərəbli/ ADV ❍ *In the afternoon, the sun became unbearably hot.*

un|be|liev|able /ʌnbɪlivəbᵊl/

1 ADJ very hard to believe ❍ *SSI had an almost unbelievable growth in its education business.*

2 ADJ very good or bad ❍ *He described his unbelievable luck in landing a job there.*

• **un|be|liev|ably** /ʌnbɪlivəbli/ ADV ❍ *Such clauses are unbelievably difficult to enforce.*

un|born /ʌnbɔrn/ ADJ An **unborn** child has not yet been born.

un|cer|tain /ʌnsɜrtᵊn/ ADJ not sure ❍ *If you're uncertain about anything, you must ask.*

un|cle /ʌŋkᵊl/ NOUN the brother of your mother or father, or the husband of your aunt ❍ *An email from Uncle Fred arrived.*

un|clear /ʌnklɪər/ ADJ not known or not certain ❍ *The future direction of interest rates remains unclear.* ❍ *Consumers are unclear about how the laws can be enforced.*

un|com|fort|able /ʌnkʌmftəbᵊl, -kʌmfərtə-/

1 ADJ slightly worried or embarrassed ❍ *The Bank of England was uncomfortable about sterling trading above that level.*

• **un|com|fort|ably** /ʌnkʌmftəbli, -kʌmfərtə-/ ADV ❍ *The jobless total remains uncomfortably high.*

2 ADJ not feeling comfortable or not making you feel comfortable ❍ *This is an extremely uncomfortable chair.*

un|con|scious /ʌnkɒnʃəs/ **ADJ** not awake and not aware of what is happening because of illness or injury ❍ *When the ambulance arrived, he was unconscious.*
● **un|con|scious|ness NONCOUNT NOUN** ❍ *Breathing in this toxic gas can cause unconsciousness and death.*

un|cov|er /ʌnkʌvər/
1 VERB If you **uncover** something, you take away something that is covering it. ❍ *Uncover the dish and cook the chicken for about 15 minutes.*
2 VERB If you **uncover** something secret, you find out about it. ❍ *They want to uncover the truth of what happened that night.*

un|de|cid|ed /ʌndɪsaɪdɪd/ **ADJ** not having made a decision ❍ *Mary is still undecided about her future.*

un|der /ʌndər/
1 PREP below ❍ *There are hundreds of tunnels under the ground.* ❍ *The two girls were sitting under a tree.* ❍ *There was a big splash and she disappeared under the water.*
2 PREP or **ADV** less than ❍ *Venezuelan oil had fallen to under $90 a barrel.* ❍ *Children (14 years and under) get in free.*

under|bid /ʌndərbɪd/ (**underbids, underbidding, underbid**) **VERB** If you **underbid** someone, you make an offer that is lower than their offer. ❍ *Irena underbid the other dealers.*

under|charge /ʌndərtʃɑrdʒ/ (**undercharges, undercharging, undercharged**) **VERB** If you **undercharge** someone, you do not charge them enough money. ❍ *The company miscalculated premiums and undercharged the pool by $9.4 million.*

under|cut /ʌndərkʌt/ (**undercuts, undercutting, undercut**) **VERB** If you **undercut** someone or **undercut** their prices, you sell a product more cheaply than they do. [MARKETING AND SALES] ❍ *The firm will be able to undercut its competitors while still making a profit.* ❍ *They aim to undercut fares on some routes by 40 percent.*

COLLOCATIONS
to undercut a *competitor*
to undercut a *rival*
to undercut *prices*

under|em|ployed /ʌndərɪmplɔɪd/ **ADJ** not having enough work to do, or having work that is too easy ❍ *People are looking for something better: a job, if they are unemployed; a better job, if they are underemployed.*

under|go /ʌndərgoʊ/ (**undergoes, undergoing, underwent, undergone**) **VERB** If you **undergo** something, it is done to you. ❍ *The whole city's economy has undergone a remarkable transformation.*

under|gradu|ate /ʌndərgrædʒuɪt/ **NOUN** a student in their first, second, third, or fourth year at a college ❍ *More than 55 percent of undergraduates are female.*

under|ground

Pronounce the adverb /ʌndərgraʊnd/.
Pronounce the adjective /ʌndərgraʊnd/.

ADV or **ADJ** below the surface of the ground ❍ *Much of the White House is built underground.* ❍ *an underground parking garage*

under|in|sured /ʌndərɪnʃʊərd/ **ADJ** not having enough insurance [BANKING] ❍ *If you haven't renewed your policy recently, you may be underinsured.*

under|line /ʌndərlaɪn/ (**underlines, underlining, underlined**) **VERB** If you **underline** a word or a sentence, you draw a line under it. ❍ *She underlined her name.*

under|ling /ʌndərlɪŋ/ **NOUN** someone who has lower status than someone else, and takes orders from them [BUSINESS MANAGEMENT, HR] ❍ *The speech was written by one of his underlings.*

under|ly|ing /ʌndərlaɪɪŋ/ **ADJ** The **underlying** features of something are the things that cause it, although they may not be obvious. ❍ *To stop a problem you have to understand its underlying causes.*

under|neath /ʌndərniθ/ **PREP** or **ADV** below or under ❍ *The bomb exploded underneath a van.* ❍ *He was wearing a blue sweater with a white T-shirt underneath.*

under|pants /ʌndərpænts/ **PL NOUN** **Underpants** are a short piece of underwear that covers the area between your waist and the top of your legs. ❍ *Richard packed a spare shirt, socks, and underpants.*

under|price /ʌndərpraɪs/ (**underprices, underpricing, underpriced**) VERB If you **underprice** a product, you put a price on it that is less than its actual value. [MARKETING AND SALES] ○ *The stock was underpriced.*

under|pro|duc|tion /ʌndərprədʌkʃən/ NONCOUNT NOUN If there is **underproduction**, not enough products are being made. [PRODUCTION]

under-represented ADJ If a group of people is **under-represented**, there are fewer of them in a particular group than you think there should be. ○ *Women are still under-represented in top-level jobs.*

under|sell /ʌndərsɛl/ (**undersells, underselling, undersold**) VERB **Undersell** means the same as **undercut**. [MARKETING AND SALES] ○ *John Lewis: never knowingly undersold.*

under|shirt /ʌndərʃɜrt/ NOUN a piece of clothing worn under a shirt to keep you warm ○ *Luis put on a pair of shorts and an undershirt.*

under|stand /ʌndərstænd/ (**understands, understanding, understood**)
1 VERB If you **understand** something, you know what it means, or why or how it happens. ○ *Toni can speak and understand Russian.* ○ *Nobody understands the concept better than this company.*
2 VERB If you **understand** that something is true, you believe it is true because you have been given information about it. ○ *I understand that you're leaving tomorrow.*

under|stand|ing /ʌndərstændɪŋ/
1 NOUN If you have an **understanding of** something, you know how it works or what it means. ○ *Marketing policy can only be effective if it is based on an understanding of the market.*
2 ADJ kind and sympathetic ○ *He was very understanding when we told him about our mistake.*

under|stood /ʌndərstʊd/ **Understood** is a form of the verb **understand**.

under|take /ʌndərteɪk/ (**undertakes, undertaking, undertook, undertaken**) VERB When you **undertake** some work, you start doing it. ○ *The company has undertaken two large projects in Dubai.*

under|took /ʌndərtʊk/ **Undertook** is a form of the verb **undertake**.

under|wa|ter /ʌndərwɔtər/ ADV or ADJ below the surface of the ocean, a river, or a lake ○ *Submarines are able to travel at high speeds underwater.* ○ *The divers were using underwater cameras.*

under|wear /ʌndərwɛər/ NONCOUNT NOUN **Underwear** is clothes that you wear next to your skin, under your other clothes. ○ *I bought some new underwear for the children.*

under|went /ʌndərwɛnt/ **Underwent** is a form of the verb **undergo**.

under|write /ʌndərraɪt/ (**underwrites, underwriting, underwrote, underwritten**)
1 VERB If an organization **underwrites** an activity or cost, it agrees to provide money to cover losses or buy special equipment. [BANKING] ○ *The government created a special agency to underwrite small business loans.*
2 VERB If an organization **underwrites** insurance, it decides how much to charge for insurance. [BANKING] ○ *All three firms underwrite and market specialized individual life, accident, and health insurance.*

under|writ|er /ʌndərraɪtər/
1 NOUN someone who provides money for a particular activity or pays for any losses [BANKING] ○ *If the market will not buy the shares, the underwriter buys them.*
2 NOUN someone whose job is decide how much to charge for insurance [BANKING] ○ *AIG is an organization of insurance underwriters.*

un|dis|trib|ut|ed /ʌndɪstrɪbyətɪd/ ADJ If profits are **undistributed**, they are not paid to shareholders but are reinvested into the business. [LOGISTICS AND DISTRIBUTION]

undo /ʌndu/ VERB If you **undo** something that is tied or fastened, you open it. ○ *I undid the buttons of my shirt.*

un|dress /ʌndrɛs/ VERB When you **undress**, you take off your clothes. ○ *Emily undressed, got into bed and turned off the light.* ○ *Often* *young babies don't like being undressed and bathed.* • **un|dressed** ADJ ❍ *Fifteen minutes later Brandon was undressed and in bed.*

un|earned in|come /ʌnɜrnd ɪnkʌm/ NONCOUNT NOUN **Unearned income** is money that people gain from property or investment, rather than from a job. [FINANCE] ❍ *Your IRA deduction cannot be taken from unearned income.*

un|easy /ʌnizi/ ADJ anxious ❍ *Prices have slipped, making many investors uneasy.* • **un|easi|ly** /ʌnizɪli/ ADV ❍ *Bankers are uneasily aware of the mounting burden of bad property loans.*

un|eco|nom|ic /ʌnɛkənɒmɪk, -ik-/ or **uneconomical** ADJ not producing enough profit [ECONOMICS] ❍ *the closure of uneconomic factories* ❍ *The methods employed are old-fashioned and uneconomical.*

un|em|ploya|ble /ʌnɪmplɔɪəbᵊl/ ADJ not able to get or keep a job ❍ *He admits he is unemployable and will probably never find a job.*

un|em|ployed /ʌnɪmplɔɪd/
1 ADJ without a job [ECONOMICS] ❍ *Millions of people are unemployed.*
2 PL NOUN **The unemployed** are people who are unemployed. ❍ *We want to create jobs for the unemployed.*

un|em|ploy|ment /ʌnɪmplɔɪmənt/ NONCOUNT NOUN **Unemployment** is when people do not have jobs. [ECONOMICS] ❍ *They live in an area of high unemployment.* ❍ *There are concerns that rising unemployment will lead to more crime.*

un|em|ploy|ment ben|efit [ECONOMICS, FINANCE, BRIT] → **unemployment compensation**

un|em|ploy|ment com|pen|sa|tion NONCOUNT NOUN **Unemployment compensation** is money that some people receive from the state, usually for a limited time after losing a job, when they do not have a job and are unable to find one. [ECONOMICS] ❍ *He has to get by on unemployment compensation.*

un|em|ploy|ment in|su|rance NONCOUNT NOUN **Unemployment insurance** is a system that makes payments to people if they lose their jobs. [ECONOMICS, BANKING] ❍ *Non-regular workers earn as little as 40% of the pay for the same work, and do not receive training, pensions, or unemployment insurance.*

un|ethi|cal /ʌnɛθɪkᵊl/ ADJ unacceptable according to a society's rules ❍ *Regulators have stepped up enforcement efforts in an attempt to weed out unethical operators.* • **un|ethi|cal|ly** ADV ❍ *They were accused of using the money unethically.*

un|even /ʌnivᵊn/ ADJ not flat or smooth ❍ *The ground was uneven.*

un|ex|pec|ted /ʌnɪkspɛktɪd/ ADJ If something is **unexpected**, it surprises you because you did not think that it was likely to happen. ❍ *The firm reported an unexpected loss of $23.1 million.* • **un|ex|pect|ed|ly** ADV ❍ *The pound rallied on news of an unexpectedly small trade deficit.*

un|fair /ʌnfɛər/ ADJ not treating people in a way that is equal or reasonable ❍ *They tried to stifle competition with unfair pricing.* ❍ *The tribunal held that the dismissal was unfair.* • **un|fair|ly** ADV ❍ *She feels they treated her unfairly.* • **un|fair|ness** NONCOUNT NOUN ❍ *I joined the police to tackle unfairness in society.*

un|fair dis|mis|sal NONCOUNT NOUN If an employee claims **unfair dismissal**, they claim that they were dismissed from their job unfairly. [HR, LEGAL] ❍ *He is claiming unfair dismissal on the grounds of racial discrimination.*

un|fa|mil|iar /ʌnfəmɪlyər/ ADJ not known to you ❍ *Success overseas in unfamiliar markets could be difficult.*

un|fit /ʌnfɪt/
1 ADJ not suitable ❍ *Managers who come up in the business are normally considered unfit for top jobs.*
2 ADJ If you are **unfit**, your body is not healthy or strong. ❍ *Many children are so unfit they cannot do even basic exercises.*

un|fold /ʌnfoʊld/ VERB If you **unfold** something that has been folded, you open it out. ❍ *Mom unfolded the piece of paper.*

un|for|tu|nate /ʌnfɔrtʃənɪt/
1 ADJ unlucky ○ *We were very unfortunate to lose her services.*
2 ADJ used for showing that you wish something had not happened ○ *We made some unfortunate mistakes in the past.*

un|for|tu|nate|ly /ʌnfɔrtʃənɪtli/ **ADV** used for saying that you wish something was not true ○ *Unfortunately, I don't have time to stay.*

un|friend|ly /ʌnfrɛndli/ **ADJ** not friendly ○ *The people he met there were unfriendly and rude.*

un|hap|py /ʌnhæpi/ (**unhappier, unhappiest**)
1 ADJ sad ○ *Christopher was a shy, unhappy man.* • **un|hap|pi|ly ADV** ○ *Jean shook her head unhappily.* • **un|hap|pi|ness NONCOUNT NOUN** ○ *There was a lot of unhappiness in my childhood.*
2 ADJ not pleased or satisfied ○ *The partners were unhappy with the firm's management.*

un|healthy /ʌnhɛlθi/ (**unhealthier, unhealthiest**)
1 ADJ An **unhealthy** person is not in good physical condition. ○ *A pale, unhealthy looking man walked into the store.*
2 ADJ likely to harm your health ○ *Avoid unhealthy foods such as hamburgers and fries.*
3 ADJ An **unhealthy** economy or company is financially weak and unsuccessful. ○ *A high unemployment rate is a clear sign of an unhealthy economy.*

uni|form /yunɪfɔrm/ **NOUN** the special clothes that some people wear to work in, and that some children wear in school ○ *The police wear blue uniforms.*

U

un|in|cor|po|rated busi|ness /ʌnɪnkɔrpəreɪtɪd bɪznɪs/ (**unincorporated businesses**) **NOUN** a privately owned business [ADMINISTRATION]

un|ion /yunyən/
1 NOUN a workers' organization that tries to improve working conditions [ECONOMICS] ○ *Ten new members joined the union.* ○ *Union leaders vowed to fight for better wage increases.*
2 NOUN a group of states or countries that join together ○ *The United Kingdom is a union of nations.*

un|ion card (**union cards**) **NOUN** a membership card for a labor union ○ *Only 16% of workers carry a union card.*

unique /yunik/ **ADJ** Something that is **unique** is the only one of its kind. ○ *Each person's signature is unique.*

unit /yunɪt/
1 NOUN a single, complete thing that can be part of something larger ○ *The building is divided into twelve units.*
2 NOUN a measurement ○ *An inch is a unit of measurement.*

unit cost (**unit costs**) **NOUN** the amount of money that it costs a company to produce one article [PRODUCTION] ○ *They aim to reduce unit costs through extra sales.*

unite /yunaɪt/ (**unites, uniting, united**) **VERB** If different people or things **unite**, they join together and act as a group. ○ *The world must unite to fight this disease.* ○ *Only the president can unite the people.*

un|it pri|ce (**unit prices**) **NOUN** The **unit price** of a product is the total revenue received from sales divided by the total number of items sold. [FINANCE] ○ *Packaged goods have a lower unit price compared to the price charged separately.*

un|it pri|cing NONCOUNT NOUN Unit pricing is a system of showing the cost of a single unit on the packaging of a product. [FINANCE] ○ *Unit pricing helps consumers compare packaged items of different sizes easily and quickly.*

unit sales PL NOUN The **unit sales** of a product are the numbers of that product that are sold. ○ *Unit sales of T-shirts increased 6%.*

unit trust (**unit trusts**) [BANKING, BRIT] → **mutual fund**

uni|ver|sal /yunɪvɜrsᵊl/ **ADJ** relating to everyone in the world ○ *Love is a universal emotion.* • **uni|ver|sal|ly** /yunɪvɜrsəli/ **ADV** ○ *Reading is universally accepted as being good for kids.*

uni|ver|sal bank (**universal banks**) NOUN a bank that offers both banking and stockbroking services [BANKING] ❍ *universal banks offering a wide range of services*

uni|verse /yuːnɪvɜrs/ NOUN **The universe** is everything that exists, including the Earth, the sun, the moon, the planets, and the stars. ❍ *Can you tell us how the universe began?*

uni|ver|sity /yuːnɪvɜrsɪti/ (**universities**) NOUN a place where you can study after high school ❍ *Maria goes to Duke University.*

un|known /ʌnnoʊn/
1 ADJ not known ❍ *The cost of their product is unknown.*
2 ADJ not famous ❍ *Ten years ago he was an unknown writer but now he is a celebrity.*

un|less /ʌnlɛs/ CONJ except if ❍ *Everyone will be enrolled in the plan unless they specifically opt out.*

un|like /ʌnlaɪk/ PREP not similar to ❍ *Unlike many other businesses, retail clothing hasn't been subject to federal sales tax.*

un|like|ly /ʌnlaɪkli/ (**unlikelier, unlikeliest**) ADJ not likely to happen ❍ *The economic news for the euro area seems unlikely to get better.*

BUSINESS ETIQUETTE
In Scandinavia and Japan, most people are comfortable with silence. Don't feel that you need to quickly fill silences in conversation.

un|lim|it|ed /ʌnlɪmɪtɪd/ ADJ An **unlimited** company, or a company with **unlimited** liability, is a company in which each investor can lose all the money they invest. [ADMINISTRATION] ❍ *There is unlimited liability: the owner will gain all the profits from the business but is responsible for all the debts of the business.*

un|list|ed /ʌnlɪstɪd/ ADJ An **unlisted** company or **unlisted** stock is not listed officially on a stock exchange. [ECONOMICS]

un|load /ʌnloʊd/
1 VERB If you **unload** goods from a ship or a vehicle, you take them off it. ❍ *We unloaded everything from the car.* ❍ *The men started unloading the truck.*
2 VERB If you **unload** investments, you sell them. [FINANCE] ❍ *Since March, he has unloaded 1.3 million shares.*

un|lock /ʌnlɒk/ VERB If you **unlock** something, you open it using a key. ❍ *Taylor unlocked the car.*

un|lucky /ʌnlʌki/ (**unluckier, unluckiest**)
1 ADJ An **unlucky** person has had bad luck. ❍ *Michael was very unlucky not to be given a contract.*
2 ADJ causing bad luck ❍ *Four is my unlucky number.*

un|natu|ral /ʌnnætʃərᵊl/ ADJ not normal ❍ *His eyes were an unnatural shade of blue.*

un|nec|es|sary /ʌnnɛsəsɛri/ ADJ not needed ❍ *It is unnecessary to have teams of highly paid analysts making frequent portfolio changes.*

un|of|fi|cial /ʌnəfɪʃᵊl/ ADJ not organized or approved by an official person or group ❍ *There are unofficial reports that trading losses cut their capital by half.*

un|pack /ʌnpæk/ VERB When you **unpack** a suitcase or a box, you take things out of it. ❍ *He unpacked his bag.* ❍ *Bill helped his daughter to unpack.*

un|paid /ʌnpeɪd/
1 ADJ If you do **unpaid** work, you do it without receiving any money. ❍ *Most of the work I do is unpaid.*
2 ADJ **Unpaid** taxes or bills have not been paid yet.

un|pleas|ant /ʌnplɛzᵊnt/
1 ADJ not nice or enjoyable ❍ *The plant has an unpleasant smell.* ● **un|pleas|ant|ly** ADV ❍ *unpleasantly cold*
2 ADJ An **unpleasant** person is unfriendly and rude. ❍ *He is such an unpleasant man!*

un|plug /ʌnplʌg/ (**unplugs, unplugging, unplugged**) VERB If you **unplug** electrical equipment, you take it out of its electrical supply. ❍ *Whenever there's a storm, I unplug my computer.*

un|popu|lar /ʌnpɒpyələr/ ADJ not liked by many people ❍ *an unpopular decision* ❍ *I was very unpopular in high school.*

un|pre|dict|able /ʌnprɪdɪktəbᵊl/ **ADJ** If someone or something is **unpredictable**, you do not know how they will behave or what they will do. ❍ *Many of the stocks remain volatile and unpredictable.*

un|pre|pared /ʌnprɪpɛərd/ **ADJ** not ready ❍ *We were totally unprepared for the recession.*

un|pro|duc|tive /ʌnprədʌktɪv/ **ADJ** not producing good results [PRODUCTION] ❍ *Research workers are aware that much of their time and effort is unproductive.* ❍ *If businesses want to survive, they must be prepared to cut costs and let unproductive staff go.*

un|prof|it|able /ʌnprɒfɪtəbᵊl/ **ADJ** not making enough profit [ECONOMICS, FINANCE] ❍ *unprofitable, badly-run industries* ❍ *The newspaper has been unprofitable for at least a decade.*

un|rea|son|able /ʌnrizənəbᵊl/ **ADJ** not fair or sensible ❍ *The commission voted that the charge was unreasonable and should be refunded.*

un|re|li|able /ʌnrɪlaɪəbᵊl/ **ADJ** not able to be trusted ❍ *Long-range estimates are unreliable.*

un|safe /ʌnseɪf/ **ADJ** dangerous ❍ *The building is unsafe and beyond repair.*

un|sat|is|fac|tory /ʌnsætɪsfæktəri/ **ADJ** not good enough ❍ *Their earnings are still unsatisfactory.*

un|secured /ʌnsɪkyʊərd/ **ADJ** An **unsecured** loan or debt is not guaranteed by an asset such as a person's home. [BANKING] ❍ *Sam received an unsecured loan of $282,000.*

un|skilled /ʌnskɪld/

1 ADJ without any special training ❍ *an unskilled laborer*

2 ADJ Unskilled work does not require any special training. ❍ *low-paid, unskilled jobs*

un|steady /ʌnstɛdi/ **ADJ** likely to fall ❍ *My grandma is unsteady on her feet.*

un|suc|cess|ful /ʌnsəksɛsfəl/ **ADJ** not successful ❍ *The company was subject to an unsuccessful takeover bid.*

un|suit|able /ʌnsutəbᵊl/ **ADJ** not suitable ❍ *These investments were unsuitable for their customers.*

un|sure /ʌnʃʊər/ **ADJ** not certain ❍ *They were unsure whether to invest in the region.*

un|ti|dy /ʌntaɪdi/ [mainly BRIT] → **messy**

un|til /ʌntɪl/

1 PREP or **CONJ** If something happens **until** a particular time, it happens before that time and stops at that time. ❍ *Until 2004, Julie worked in Canada.* ❍ *I waited until it got dark.*

2 PREP or **CONJ** If something does not happen **until** a particular time, it does not happen before that time. ❍ *I won't arrive in New York until Saturday.* ❍ *They won't be safe until they get out of the country.*

un|true /ʌntru/ **ADJ** not true or correct ❍ *Bryant said the story was untrue.*

un|usual /ʌnyuʒuəl/ **ADJ** not happening or existing very often ❍ *Waiting lists of a month aren't unusual for popular models.*
● **un|usu|al|ly** /ʌnyuʒuəli/ **ADV** ❍ *The industry benefited from unusually strong demand in the second quarter.*

un|waged /ʌnweɪdʒd/

1 PL NOUN The unwaged are people who do not have a paid job. [ECONOMICS, BRIT] ❍ *There are special rates for children, full-time students and the unwaged.*

2 ADJ Unwaged is also an adjective. ❍ *the effect on unwaged adults and children*

un|want|ed /ʌnwɒntɪd/ **ADJ** not wanted ❍ *These measures are designed to deter unwanted takeover attempts.*

un|will|ing /ʌnwɪlɪŋ/ **ADJ** not wanting to do something ❍ *They are unwilling to incur more costs.*

un|wind /ʌnwaɪnd/ (**unwinds, unwinding, unwound**)

1 VERB If you **unwind** something that is wrapped around something else, you make it loose and straight. ❍ *She unwound the scarf from her neck.*

2 VERB When you **unwind**, you relax. ❍ *Dad needs to unwind after a busy day at work.*

un|wise /ʌnwaɪz/ **ADJ** not sensible ❍ *Many people have taken out unwise loans in foreign currencies.* ● **un|wise|ly ADV** ❍ *She understands that she acted unwisely.*

un|wrap /ʌnræp/ (**unwraps, unwrapping, unwrapped**) VERB When you **unwrap** something, you take off the paper or plastic that is around it. ❍ *I untied the ribbon and unwrapped the small box.*

un|zip /ʌnzɪp/ (**unzips, unzipping, unzipped**)
1 VERB If you **unzip** a computer file, you make it go back to its original size after it has been zipped (= reduced using a special program). ❍ *Use the "Unzip" command to unzip the file.*
2 VERB If you **unzip** clothing, you undo the metal strip (= a zipper) that is fastening it. ❍ *Pete unzipped his leather jacket and sat down.*

up /ʌp/
1 PREP or ADV toward a higher place ❍ *They were climbing up a mountain road.* ❍ *I ran up the stairs.* ❍ *Keep your head up.*
2 ADV If someone stands **up**, they move from sitting or lying down, so that they are standing. ❍ *He stood up and went to the window.*
3 PREP If you go **up** a road, you go along it. ❍ *A dark blue truck came up the road.*
4 ADV If you go **up** to something or someone, you move toward them. ❍ *He came up to me and gave me a big hug.*
5 ADV If an amount or level goes **up**, it increases. ❍ *Gasoline prices went up in June.*
6 ADJ **Up** is also an adjective. ❍ *Coffee is up again.*
7 ADJ not in bed ❍ *They were up very early to get to the airport on time.*
8 If it is **up to** someone to do something, they must do it. ❍ *It's up to you to solve your own problems.*

up|date (**updates, updating, updated**)

Pronounce the verb /ʌpdeɪt/ or /ʌpdeɪt/. Pronounce the noun /ʌpdeɪt/.

1 VERB If you **update** something, you make it more modern or add new information to it. ❍ *We update our news reports regularly.*
2 NOUN when someone provides the most recent information about something ❍ *Now here's a weather update.*

up|front /ʌpfrʌnt/
1 ADV If money is paid **upfront**, it is paid at the beginning of a business arrangement. ❍ *Consultants usually ask for their money upfront.*
2 ADJ **Upfront** costs are paid at the beginning of a business arrangement. ❍ *Clients were faced with heavy upfront fees.*

up|grade /ʌpgreɪd, -greɪd/ (**upgrades, upgrading, upgraded**)
1 VERB If you **upgrade** something, you improve it or replace it with a better one. ❍ *The road into town is being upgraded.* ❍ *I recently upgraded my computer.*
2 NOUN **Upgrade** is also a noun. ❍ *a software upgrade*

up|hill /ʌphɪl/ ADV or ADJ up a slope ❍ *He ran uphill a long way.* ❍ *It was a long, uphill journey.*

up|lift /ʌplɪft/ NOUN an increase in value ❍ *an uplift in the stock market*

up|load /ʌploʊd/ VERB If you **upload** a document or a program, you move it from your computer to another one, often using the Internet. ❍ *Next, upload the files on to your website.*

up|market /ʌpmɑrkɪt/ also **up-market** [MARKETING AND SALES, BRIT] → **upscale**

upon /əpɒn/ PREP **Upon** means on. [FORMAL] ❍ *The decision was based upon science and fact.*

up|per /ʌpər/ ADJ **Upper** describes something that is in a higher area. ❍ *the upper floor of the building*

up|per case NONCOUNT NOUN If you write or type something **in upper case**, you write or type it using capital letters. Compare with **lower case**.

up|right /ʌpraɪt/ ADJ in a straight position ❍ *John offered Andrew a seat, but he remained upright.*

up|scale /ʌpskeɪl/
1 ADJ **Upscale** products or services are designed to appeal to people with money and education. Compare with **downscale**.
2 ADV If a product or service moves **upscale**, it tries to appeal to people with money and education. Compare with **downscale**. ❍ *A lot of our customers wanted to move upscale when the kids got older.*

up|sell /ʌpsɛl/ also **up-sell** (**upsells, upselling, upsold**) VERB If you **upsell** something, or **upsell** a customer, you try to sell another product or service in addition to the one the customer wants. [MARKETING AND SALES] ❍ *Retailers may try to upsell you additional, more expensive, goods.*

up|set /ʌpsɛt/ (**upsets, upsetting, upset**)
1 ADJ unhappy because something bad has happened ❍ *After Grandma died, I was very, very upset.* ❍ *Marta looked upset.*
2 VERB If something **upsets** you, it makes you feel unhappy. ❍ *Workers may be reluctant to do anything to upset employers.*
3 VERB If something **upsets** your plans, it makes them go wrong. ❍ *Heavy rain upset our plans for a barbecue on the beach.*
4 ADJ An **upset** stomach is a slight sickness in your stomach. ❍ *Paul was sick last night with an upset stomach.*

up|side down /ʌpsaɪd daʊn/ ADV or ADJ with the part that is usually at the bottom at the top ❍ *The painting was hanging upside down.* ❍ *Paul drew an upside-down triangle and colored it in.*

up|size /ʌpsaɪz/ (**upsizes, upsizing, upsized**)
1 VERB When a company **upsizes** a product, it produces a larger version of it. ❍ *The former metric cans of 500ml and 440ml have been upsized to create the new pint cans.*
2 VERB When a company **upsizes**, it employs more workers.

up|stairs /ʌpstɛərz/ ADV or ADJ on or to a higher floor ❍ *He went upstairs and changed his clothes.* ❍ *Mark lived in the upstairs apartment.*

U

up|stream /ʌpstrim/ ADJ **Upstream** business activity refers to the extraction and production of a commodity as opposed to its distribution. Compare with **downstream**. [PRODUCTION] ❍ *Investment in the upstream oil and gas sector has slowed.*

up|swing /ʌpswɪŋ/ NOUN a sudden improvement in an economy

up-to-date also **up to date** ADJ modern or having the most recent information ❍ *His statement had failed to include up-to-date financial information.*

up|turn /ʌptɜrn/ NOUN an improvement in the economy or in a business [BUSINESS MANAGEMENT] ❍ *They do not expect an upturn in the economy until the end of the year.*

COLLOCATIONS
an *economic* upturn
a *sharp* upturn
a *sustained* upturn
a *strong* upturn
a *slight* upturn
an upturn *in business*
an upturn *in demand*

up|ward /ʌpwərd/ ADV toward a higher place ❍ *She turned her face upward.*

up|wards /ʌpwərdz/ [BRIT] → **upward**

ur|ban /ɜrbən/ ADJ relating to a city or a town ❍ *an urban neighborhood*

urge /ɜrdʒ/ (**urges, urging, urged**)
1 VERB If you **urge** someone **to** do something, you try to persuade them to do it. ❍ *Financial planners often urge investors to diversify.*
2 NOUN a strong feeling that you want to do or have something ❍ *He felt a sudden urge to call Mary.*

ur|gent /ɜrdʒᵊnt/ ADJ needing action as soon as possible ❍ *He was summoned home on urgent business.* • **ur|gent|ly** ADV ❍ *The company urgently needs to cut costs.*

URL /yu ɑr ɛl/ (**URLs**) NOUN A **URL** is an address that shows where you can find a particular page on the World Wide Web. **URL** is short for "Uniform Resource Locator." ❍ *The URL for Collins Language is http://www.collinslanguage.com.*

us /əs, STRONG ʌs/ PRON used to talk about yourself and another person or other people ❍ *It's just the right strategy for us to pursue.* ❍ *These stocks are too pricey for us.*

USB /yu ɛs bi/ (**USBs**) NOUN A **USB** is a part of a computer where you can attach another piece of equipment. **USB** is short for "Universal Serial Bus." ❍ *The printer plugs into the computer's USB port.*

use (**uses, using, used**)

> Pronounce the verb /yuz/. Pronounce the noun /yus/.

1 VERB If you **use** something, you do something with it. ❍ *They wouldn't let him use the phone.* ❍ *She used the money to set up a business.*
2 VERB If you **use** something, you finish an amount of it. ❍ *She used all the shampoo.*
3 NONCOUNT NOUN The **use** of something is the action of using it. ❍ *We encourage the use of computers in the classroom.*
4 NOUN a way in which you can use something ❍ *Bamboo has many uses.*
5 NONCOUNT NOUN If you have the **use of** something, you are able to use it. ❍ *He has the use of an executive jet.*
6 You say **it's no use** when you stop doing something because you believe that it is impossible to succeed. ❍ *It's no use asking him what happened.*
▶ **use up** If you **use up** something, you finish all of it. ❍ *If you use up the milk, please buy some more.*

use-by date (**use-by dates**) **NOUN** the date printed on a product, which shows you when it should be used or eaten by [MARKETING AND SALES] ❍ *Any food items past their use-by date should be thrown away.*

> **used**
> ❶ MODAL USES AND PHRASES
> ❷ ADJECTIVE USE

❶ **used** /yust/
1 You use **used to** to talk about something that was true in the past but is not true now. ❍ *I used to live in Los Angeles.*
2 If you **are used to** something, you are familiar with it. ❍ *I'm used to hard work.*
3 If you **get used to** something, you become familiar with it. ❍ *This is how we do things here. You'll soon get used to it.*

❷ **used** /yuzd/ **ADJ** **Used** objects are not new. ❍ *If you are buying a used car, you will need to check it carefully.*

use|ful /yusfəl/ **ADJ** If something is **useful**, it helps you in some way. ❍ *useful advice*
● **use|ful|ly ADV** ❍ *The students used their extra time usefully, doing homework or playing sports.*

use|less /yuslɪs/ **ADJ** having no use or effect ❍ *It's useless to intervene in a market where there's a bullish mood.*

user /yuzər/ **NOUN** a person who uses something ❍ *I'm a regular user of the subway.*

user|name /yuzərneɪm/ **NOUN** the name that you type onto your screen in order open a particular computer program or website ❍ *You have to log in with a username and a password.*

USP /yu ɛs pi/ (**USPs**) **NOUN** The **USP** of a product or service is a particular feature that shows how it is better than other similar products or services. **USP** is an abbreviation of "Unique Selling Point." [MARKETING AND SALES, BUSINESS MANAGEMENT] ❍ *With Volvo, safety was always the USP.*

usu|al /yuʒuəl/
1 ADJ **Usual** describes what happens or exists most often. ❍ *It is a large city with all the usual problems.* ❍ *Trading has been heavier than usual since last Friday.*
2 If something happens **as usual**, it happens in the way that it normally does. ❍ *As usual, consumers ended up suffering.*

usu|al|ly /yuʒuəli/ **ADV** in the way that most often happens ❍ *The cost to the shareholders is usually 2-3%.*

uti|lise /yutɪlaɪz/ [BRIT] → **utilize**

util|ity /yutɪlɪti/ (**utilities**)
1 NOUN an important service such as water, electricity, or gas that is provided for everyone, and that everyone pays for ❍ *public utilities such as gas, electricity, and phones*
2 NONCOUNT NOUN A product's **utility** is its ability to provide things that people need.

uti|lize /yutɪlaɪz/ (**utilizes, utilizing, utilized**) **VERB** If you **utilize** something, you use it. ❍ *We need to utilize the talent of everyone in the company.* ● **uti|li|za|tion** /yutɪlɪzeɪʃən/ **NONCOUNT NOUN** ❍ *the best utilization of space*

ut|ter /ʌtər/

1 VERB If you **utter** sounds or words, you say them. [FORMAL] ❍ *He finally uttered the words "I'm sorry."*

2 ADJ complete ❍ *utter nonsense*

ut|ter|ly /ʌtərli/ **ADV** completely or extremely ❍ *They utterly failed to carry out their duties.*

Vv

v. **v.** is short for **versus**. ❍ *the case of United States v Robertson*

va|can|cy /veɪkənsi/ (**vacancies**)
1 NOUN a room in a hotel that is available ❍ *The hotel still has a few vacancies.*
2 NOUN a job that has not been filled ❍ *We have a vacancy for an assistant.*

va|cant /veɪkənt/ **ADJ** not being used or filled by anyone ❍ *They saw two vacant seats in the center.* ❍ *The post of governor is still vacant.*

va|ca|tion /veɪkeɪʃən/
1 NOUN a period of time when you relax and enjoy yourself away from home ❍ *They planned a vacation in Europe.*
2 NOUN a period of the year when schools, universities, and colleges are closed ❍ *During his summer vacation he visited Russia.*

vac|ci|nate /væksɪneɪt/ (**vaccinates, vaccinating, vaccinated**) **VERB** If a person or animal **is vaccinated**, they are given a substance to prevent them from getting a disease. ❍ *He thinks he can find a way to vaccinate the elephants from a safe distance.*
• **vac|ci|na|tion** /væksɪneɪʃən/ **NOUN** ❍ *I got my flu vaccination last week.*

vac|cine /væksin/ **NOUN** is a substance that is given to people to prevent them from getting a disease ❍ *The flu vaccine is free for those aged 65 years and over.*

vacuum clean|er /vækyum klinər/ (**vacuum cleaners**) **NOUN** an electric machine that cleans floors by sucking up dirt

vague /veɪg/ (**vaguer, vaguest**) **ADJ** not clear or certain ❍ *The description was pretty vague.*

vague|ly /veɪgli/ **ADV** slightly ❍ *The voice on the phone was vaguely familiar.*

vain /veɪn/
1 ADJ A **vain** attempt does not achieve what was intended.
2 ADJ too proud of the way you look ❍ *He was so vain he spent hours in front of the mirror.*
3 If you do something **in vain**, you do not succeed in doing what you want. ❍ *She tried in vain to open the door.*

val|id /vælɪd/ **ADJ** If a ticket is **valid**, it can be used and will be accepted. ❍ *All tickets are valid for two months.*

val|ley /væli/ **NOUN** a low area of land between hills ❍ *a steep mountain valley*

valu|able /vælyuəb[ə]l/ **ADJ** very useful or worth a lot of money ❍ *Television can be a valuable tool in the classroom.* ❍ *Do not leave any valuable items in your hotel room.*

value /vælyu/ (**values, valuing, valued**)
1 NONCOUNT NOUN The **value** of something is its importance or usefulness. ❍ *The value of this work experience should not be underestimated.*
2 VERB If you **value** something or someone, you think that they are important. ❍ *I've done business with Mr. Weston before. I value the work he gives me.*
3 NOUN The **value** of something is how much money it is worth. ❍ *The value of his investment rose by $50,000 in a year.*
4 VERB When experts **value** something, they decide how much money it is worth. ❍ *A surveyor valued the property.*
5 NONCOUNT NOUN If something is **good value** or **excellent value**, it is worth the money that it costs. ❍ *The restaurant is informal, stylish, and extremely good value.*
6 PL NOUN The **values** of a person or group are their moral principles and beliefs. ❍ *The countries of South Asia share many common values.*

va|lue add|ed NONCOUNT NOUN **Value-added** is the difference between the cost of goods purchased by a business and its revenues. [MARKETING AND SALES] ❍ *Sales volume is less important than value added.*

valve /vælv/ NOUN an object that controls the flow of air or liquid through a tube

van /væn/ NOUN a vehicle with space for carrying things in the back

van|dal|ism /vændᵊlɪzəm/ NONCOUNT NOUN **Vandalism** is the act of deliberately damaging property. ❍ *Since the strike began, the company has recorded 120 cases of vandalism.*

va|nil|la /vənɪlə/ NONCOUNT NOUN **Vanilla** is a flavor used in sweet food.

van|ish /vænɪʃ/ VERB If someone or something **vanishes**, they disappear. ❍ *He vanished ten years ago.*

va|por /veɪpər/ NONCOUNT NOUN **Vapor** is tiny drops of liquid in the air. ❍ *The effects of vapors from cleaning liquids are not widely understood.*

va|pour /veɪpər/ [BRIT] → **vapor**

vari|able /vɛəriəbᵊl/ ADJ changing quite often ❍ *The quality of his work is very variable.*

vari|able costs PL NOUN **Variable costs** are costs that vary depending on how much of a product is made. Compare with **fixed costs**. [FINANCE] ❍ *We managed to reduce our expenses by controlling the variable costs such as raw materials and fuel consumption.*

vari|ance /vɛəriəns/ NOUN the difference between actual and standard costs of production [PRODUCTION] ❍ *You are required to calculate the variance in respect of the following items.*

V

vari|ation /vɛərieɪʃən/
1 NOUN something that is slightly different from its usual form ❍ *This is a delicious variation on an omelet.*
2 NOUN a difference in level, amount, or quality ❍ *Can you explain the wide variation in your prices?*

var|ied /vɛərid/ ADJ consisting of different types of things ❍ *Your diet should be varied.*

va|ri|ety /vəraɪɪti/ NONCOUNT NOUN If something has **variety**, it consists of a lot of different things. ❍ *Susan wanted variety in her lifestyle.*

vari|ous /vɛəriəs/ ADJ several different ❍ *He spent the day doing various jobs around the house.*

vary /vɛəri/ (**varies, varying, varied**)
1 VERB If things **vary**, they are different from each other. ❍ *The bowls are handmade, so they vary slightly.*
2 VERB If something **varies** or if you **vary** it, it becomes different. ❍ *Be sure to vary the topics you write about.*

vase /veɪs, vɑz/ NOUN a container for holding flowers

vast /væst/ ADJ extremely large ❍ *The completed version is a vast improvement over earlier test versions.*

VAT /væt/ NONCOUNT NOUN In Britain, **VAT** is a tax on the difference between the cost of materials and the price of a product or service. **VAT** is short for "value-added tax." [FINANCE] ❍ *There have been plans to raise the VAT rate on fuel.*

veg|eta|ble /vɛdʒtəbᵊl, vɛdʒɪ-/ NOUN a plant that you can eat, for example a potato or an onion

veg|etar|ian /vɛdʒɪtɛəriən/
1 ADJ not containing meat or fish ❍ *a vegetarian diet*
2 NOUN someone who never eats meat or fish ❍ *When did you decide to become a vegetarian?*

ve|hi|cle /viɪkᵊl/ NOUN a machine such as a car that carries people or things from one place to another ❍ *There are too many vehicles on the road.*

veil /veɪl/ NOUN a piece cloth that women sometimes wear to cover their faces ❍ *She wore a veil over her face.*

vein /veɪn/ NOUN A **vein** is a thin tube in your body that carries blood to your heart. Compare with **artery**.

vel|vet /vɛlvɪt/ NONCOUNT NOUN **Velvet** is cloth that is thick and soft on one side. ❍ *red velvet drapes*

ven|dor /vɛndər/
1 NOUN someone who sells things from a small stall or cart ❍ *ice cream vendors*
2 NOUN a company or person that sells a product or service ❍ *Tour America acts as an agent for other vendors and cannot be held responsible for any delays.*

ven|dor rat|ing (**vendor ratings**) **NOUN** a measure of the performance of a supplier, based on factors such as price and flexibility ❍ *You can search the vendor ratings either by vendor's name or by category.*

vent /vɛnt/
1 NOUN a hole that allows clean air to come in, and smoke or gas to go out
2 VERB If you **vent** your feelings, you express them strongly. ❍ *She telephoned her best friend to vent her anger.*

ven|ture /vɛntʃər/ **NOUN** a business activity that may or may not be successful ❍ *He gambled his family business on a new venture.*

ven|ture capi|tal **NONCOUNT NOUN** **Venture capital** is money that is invested in projects that have a high risk of failure, but that will bring large profits if they are successful. [BANKING, FINANCE] ❍ *Successful venture capital investment is a lot harder than it sometimes looks.*

ven|ture capi|tal|ist (**venture capitalists**) **NOUN** someone who makes money by investing in very risky projects [BANKING, FINANCE] ❍ *Many venture capitalists are making investments in software and networking businesses.*

venue /vɛnyu/ **NOUN** the place where an event or activity will happen ❍ *Fenway Park will be used as a venue for the rock concert.*

verb /vɜrb/ **NOUN** a word such as "sing," "feel," or "eat" that is used for saying what someone or something does

ver|bal /vɜrbᵊl/ **ADJ** using speech ❍ *verbal abuse* • **ver|bal|ly** **ADV** ❍ *We complained both verbally and in writing.*

ver|dict /vɜrdɪkt/ **NOUN** a decision that is given in a court of law ❍ *The jury delivered a verdict of "not guilty."*

verge /vɜrdʒ/ If you are **on the verge of** something, you are going to do it or it is going to happen very soon. ❍ *Carole was on the verge of tears.*

veri|fy /vɛrɪfaɪ/ (**verifies, verifying, verified**) **VERB** If you **verify** something, you check that it is true. [FORMAL] ❍ *We haven't yet verified his information.*

verse /vɜrs/
1 NONCOUNT NOUN **Verse** is poetry. ❍ *The story is written in verse.*
2 NOUN one of the parts into which a poem or song is divided

ver|sion /vɜrʒᵊn/ **NOUN** a particular form of something ❍ *He is bringing out a new version of his book.*

ver|sus /vɜrsəs/ **PREP** **Versus** is used for showing that two teams or people are on different sides in a sports event. The short forms **vs.** and **v.** are also used. ❍ *It will be the U.S. versus Belgium in tomorrow's game.*

ver|ti|cal /vɜrtɪkᵊl/ **ADJ** standing or pointing straight up or down ❍ *These planes can even fly backwards as they maneuver for a vertical landing.*

ver|ti|cal in|te|gra|tion /vɜrtɪkᵊl ɪntɪgreɪʃən/ **NONCOUNT NOUN** **Vertical integration** is the merging of companies involved in different aspects of the same business. Compare with **horizontal integration** and **virtual integration**. [ECONOMICS] ❍ *Vertical integration may help a firm to reduce its production and distribution costs.*

very /vɛri/ **ADV** used before an adjective to make it stronger ❍ *I'm very sorry.*

vet /vɛt/ **NOUN** a person whose job is to treat sick animals [BUSINESS MANAGEMENT, INFORMAL]

vet|er|an /vɛtərən/
1 NOUN someone who has fought in a war ❍ *He's a veteran of the Vietnam War.*
2 NOUN someone who has been doing a particular activity for a long time ❍ *a veteran teacher*

vet|eri|nar|ian /vɛtərɪnɛəriən/ **NOUN** a person whose job is to treat sick animals

veto /vitoʊ/ (**vetoes, vetoing, vetoed**)
1 VERB If someone **vetoes** something, they stop it from happening. ❍ *The president vetoed the proposal.*
2 NONCOUNT NOUN **Veto** is the power that someone has to stop something from happening. ❍ *The president has power of veto over the matter.*

via /vaɪə, viə/ PREP If you go somewhere **via** a particular place, you go through that place on the way. ❍ *I'm flying to Sweden via New York.*

vi|able /vaɪəbᵊl/ ADJ Something that is **viable** is capable of doing what it is intended to do. [BUSINESS MANAGEMENT] ❍ *Cash alone will not make Eastern Europe's banks viable.*
• **vi|abil|ity** /vaɪəbɪlɪti/ NONCOUNT NOUN ❍ *the shaky financial viability of the nuclear industry*

vi|brate /vaɪbreɪt/ (**vibrates, vibrating, vibrated**) VERB If something **vibrates**, it shakes with repeated small, quick movements. ❍ *There was a loud bang and the ground seemed to vibrate.* • **vi|bra|tion** /vaɪbreɪʃən/ NOUN ❍ *Vibrations from the trains make the house shake.*

vice /vaɪs/
1 NONCOUNT NOUN **Vice** is criminal activity connected with sex and drugs.
2 NOUN a bad habit ❍ *My only vice is that I spend too much on clothes.*

vi|cious /vɪʃəs/ ADJ violent and cruel ❍ *He was a cruel and vicious man.*

vic|tim /vɪktəm/ NOUN someone who has been hurt or killed ❍ *The driver apologized to the victim's family.*

vic|to|ry /vɪktəri, vɪktri/ (**victories**) NOUN a success in a war or a competition ❍ *The Democrats are celebrating their victory.*

V

video /vɪdioʊ/
1 NOUN a movie, television program, or event that has been recorded on videotape (= a thin strip used for recording sound and moving pictures) ❍ *You could rent a video for two dollars and watch it at home.*
2 NONCOUNT NOUN **Video** is a system of recording movies and events. ❍ *She has watched the show on video.*

video-conference (**video-conferences**) also **videoconference, video conference** NOUN a meeting that takes place using video conferencing [TECHNOLOGY] ❍ *The panel will meet Monday via video-conference.*

video con|fer|enc|ing /vɪdioʊ kɒnfrənsɪŋ/ also **video-conferencing, videoconferencing** NONCOUNT NOUN **Video conferencing** is a system that allows people in different places to have a meeting by seeing and hearing each other on a screen. [TECHNOLOGY] ❍ *We also hope to use video conferencing to train and supervise staff.*

video game (**video games**) NOUN an electronic game that you play on your television or computer

view /vyu/
1 NOUN Your **views** are your opinions. ❍ *We have similar views on politics.*
2 NOUN The **view** from a place is everything that you can see from there. ❍ *There's a great view of the ocean.*
3 NOUN If you have a **view of** something, you can see it. ❍ *He stood up to get a better view of the blackboard.*

vil|lage /vɪlɪdʒ/ NOUN a small town in the countryside

vine /vaɪn/ NOUN a plant with a very long stem that grows up or over things ❍ *a grape vine*

vin|egar /vɪnɪgər/ NONCOUNT NOUN **Vinegar** is a sour liquid that is used in cooking.

vio|late /vaɪəleɪt/ (**violates, violating, violated**) VERB If someone **violates** an agreement or a law, they do not obey it. [FORMAL] ❍ *The company has violated international law.* • **vio|la|tion** /vaɪəleɪʃən/ NOUN ❍ *This is a violation of state law.*

vio|lence /vaɪələns/ NONCOUNT NOUN **Violence** is behavior that is intended to hurt or kill people. ❍ *Twenty people died in the violence.*

vio|lent /vaɪələnt/ ADJ using violence ❍ *We lost tourist earnings as a result of the violence.*
• **vio|lent|ly** ADV ❍ *The woman was violently attacked while out walking.*

vio|lin /vaɪəlɪn/ **NOUN** a musical instrument that you hold under your chin and play by moving a long stick (= a bow) across its four strings ❍ *Lizzie plays the violin.*

VIP /vi aɪ pi/ **NOUN** A **VIP** is someone who is given better treatment than ordinary people because they are famous or important. **VIP** is short for "very important person." ❍ *Everywhere we went we were treated like VIPs.*

> **BUSINESS ETIQUETTE**
> If you are doing business in a country or region that uses a different alphabet to English, such as Korea, the Middle East, or Russia, you should have your business cards printed in English on one side and in the other language on the back.

vi|ral mar|ket|ing /vaɪrəl mɑrkɪtɪŋ/
1 NONCOUNT NOUN Viral marketing is a technique in which a company encourages Internet users to forward its publicity emails to their friends, usually by including jokes, games, and video clips. [MARKETING AND SALES, TECHNOLOGY] ❍ *Using the Internet for viral marketing is a cheap, speedy way for marketers to get their message across.*
2 NONCOUNT NOUN Viral marketing is a strategy that uses unconventional techniques to create publicity for a product by word of mouth. [MARKETING AND SALES] ❍ *Viral marketing depends on the amount of "buzz" it generates.*

vir|tual /vɜrtʃuəl/
1 ADJ used to say that someone or something is almost something ❍ *The wave of airline mergers created virtual monopolies on many routes.* ● **vir|tu|al|ly** /vɜrtʃuəli/ **ADV** ❍ *The office he inherited was virtually an empty box.*
2 ADJ Virtual objects and activities are made by a computer to seem real. ❍ *the virtual world*

vir|tual com|pa|ny (**virtual companies**) **NOUN** a company that outsources all of its activities, and that uses computers to communicate with clients or customers [ADMINISTRATION, TECHNOLOGY] ❍ *It is a virtual company, outsourcing everything from manufacture to sales.*

vir|tual in|te|gra|tion /vɜrtʃuəl ɪntɪgreɪʃən/ **NONCOUNT NOUN Virtual integration** is cooperation, using information technology, between companies involved in different aspects of the same business. Compare with **vertical integration**. [ECONOMICS, TECHNOLOGY]

vir|tual re|al|ity NONCOUNT NOUN Virtual reality is images and sounds that are produced by a computer to seem real to the person experiencing it. ❍ *a virtual reality game*

vi|rus /vaɪrəs/ (**viruses**)
1 NOUN a very small living thing that causes disease
2 NOUN a computer program that enters a system and damages or destroys information [TECHNOLOGY] ❍ *You should protect your computer against viruses.*

visa /vizə/ **NOUN** an official document or mark in your passport that allows you to enter or leave a country ❍ *The firm needs visas for 150 foreign workers.*

vis|ibil|ity /vɪzɪbɪlɪti/ **NONCOUNT NOUN Visibility** means how far or how clearly you can see. ❍ *Visibility was poor.*

vis|ible /vɪzɪbəl/
1 ADJ able to be seen ❍ *The warning lights were clearly visible.*
2 ADJ Visible earnings are the money that a country makes from goods rather than services.
3 NOUN a product, rather than a service

vis|ible ex|port (**visible exports**) **NOUN** A **visible export** is an export of goods rather than services. Compare with **invisible export**. [ECONOMICS] ❍ *In the UK visible imports have traditionally been greater than visible exports.*

vis|ible im|port (**visible imports**) **NOUN** A **visible import** is an import of goods rather than services. Compare with **invisible import**. [ECONOMICS]

vi|sion /vɪʒən/
1 NOUN an idea in your mind of what something could be like ❍ *I have a vision of world peace.*

2 NONCOUNT NOUN Your **vision** is your ability to see. ❍ *He's suffering from loss of vision.* **NOUN** the stated aims and objectives of a business or other organization [BUSINESS MANAGEMENT] ❍ *He needs to focus on developing a vision for the company.*

vis|it /vɪzɪt/
1 VERB If you **visit** someone, you go to see them. ❍ *He wanted to visit his client.* ❍ *In the evenings, friends often visit.*
2 NOUN **Visit** is also a noun. ❍ *I recently had a visit from our English agent.*
3 VERB If you **visit** a place, you go there for a short time. ❍ *He'll be visiting four cities on his trip.*

visi|tor /vɪzɪtər/ **NOUN** someone who is visiting a person or place ❍ *We had some visitors from Milwaukee.*

vis|ual /vɪʒuəl/ **ADJ** relating to sight, or to things that you can see ❍ *The movie's visual effects are amazing.*

vis|ual aids **PL NOUN** **Visual aids** are items such as drawings, graphs, or maps that help people understand a topic when you are presenting or explaining it. [TECHNOLOGY] ❍ *Visual aids can give a professional touch to any presentation.*

vi|tal /vaɪtᵊl/ **ADJ** very important ❍ *El Paso lies on vital American freight routes.*

vita|min /vaɪtəmɪn/ **NOUN** a substance in food that you need in order to stay healthy ❍ *These problems are caused by lack of vitamin D.*

viv|id /vɪvɪd/
1 ADJ **Vivid** memories and descriptions are very clear and detailed. ❍ *I had a very vivid dream last night.* • **viv|id|ly** **ADV** ❍ *I can vividly remember the first time I saw him.*
2 ADJ very bright in color ❍ *a vivid pink jacket*

V

vo|cabu|lary /voʊkæbyəlɛri/ (**vocabularies**)
1 NOUN all the words you know in a language ❍ *He has a very large vocabulary.*
2 NOUN all the words in a language ❍ *English has the biggest vocabulary of any language.*

vo|cal /voʊkᵊl/
1 ADJ Someone who is **vocal** gives their opinion very strongly. ❍ *Local people were very vocal about the problem.*
2 ADJ using the human voice, especially in singing ❍ *She has an interesting vocal style.*

voice /vɔɪs/ **NOUN** the sound that comes from your mouth when you speak or sing ❍ *She spoke in a soft voice.*

void /vɔɪd/ **NOUN** an empty space or feeling ❍ *How can the huge void left by the president's death be filled?*

vol|ume /vɒlyum/ **NOUN** The **volume of** something is the amount of it that there is. [PRODUCTION] ❍ *Senior management will be discussing how the volume of sales might be increased.*

vol|un|tary /vɒlənteri/
1 ADJ **Voluntary** actions are done because you want to and not because you must. ❍ *Participation is completely voluntary.* • **vol|un|tar|ily** /vɒlənteərɪli/ **ADV** ❍ *I would never leave here voluntarily.*
2 ADJ **Voluntary** work is done by people who are not paid. ❍ *I do voluntary work with handicapped children.*

vol|un|tary liqui|da|tion **NONCOUNT NOUN** **Voluntary liquidation** is a situation where members of a company agree to sell their assets and close down the company. [ECONOMICS, ADMINISTRATION]

vol|un|teer /vɒləntɪər/
1 NOUN someone who does work without being paid for it ❍ *She helps in a local school as a volunteer.*
2 VERB If you **volunteer** to do something, you offer to do it. ❍ *Mary volunteered to make coffee for everyone.*

vote /voʊt/ (**votes, voting, voted**)
1 NOUN a choice made by a someone in an election or a meeting ❍ *Mr. Reynolds won the election by 102 votes to 60.*
2 VERB When you **vote**, you make your choice officially at a meeting or in an election. ❍ *The workers voted to strike.*

vot|er /voʊtər/ **NOUN** someone who votes in an election ❍ *The state has 2.1 million registered voters.*

vow /vaʊ/
1 VERB If you **vow** to do something, you promise that you will do it. ❍ *She vowed to continue the fight.*
2 NOUN a serious promise ❍ *I made a vow to be more careful in the future.*

voy|age /vɔɪɪdʒ/ **NOUN** a long trip on a ship or in a spacecraft ❍ *The voyages of discovery to America were entirely about money.*

vs. **vs.** is short for **versus**. ❍ *We were watching the Yankees vs. the Red Sox.*

vul|ner|able /vʌlnərəbᵊl/ **ADJ** weak and without protection ❍ *Older people are particularly vulnerable to colds and flu in cold weather.*

Ww

wag /wæg/ (**wags, wagging, wagged**) **VERB** When a dog **wags** its tail, it moves its tail from side to side.

wage /weɪdʒ/ **NOUN** the regular payment that someone receives for their work [FINANCE, ECONOMICS] ❍ *His wages have gone up.*

COLLOCATIONS
a wage *rise*
a wage *cut*
a wage *increase*
a wage *demand*

wage dif|fe|ren|tial (**wage differentials**) **NOUN** the difference in wages between workers with different skills or between those with the same skills who work in different industries [FINANCE, ECONOMICS] ❍ *Wage differentials widened in the 1980s in 12 of the 17 industrial countries studied.*

wage earn|er (**wage earners**) or **wage worker NOUN**
1 a person who works for wages, rather than a salary [FINANCE] ❍ *Nearly a third of the major household earners in India are wage earners and storekeepers.*
2 a person who earns money to support a household [FINANCE] ❍ *More and more households have two wage earners.*

wage in|cen|tive (**wage incentives**) **NOUN** an additional payment intended to encourage someone to work harder [FINANCE, HR] ❍ *Large wage incentives could not prevent worker output from slipping.*

wage slave (**wage slaves**) **NOUN** a person who depends on earning a wage [FINANCE, ECONOMICS, INFORMAL] ❍ *What turns employees into employers, wage slaves into risk-takers?*

waist /weɪst/ **NOUN** the middle part of your body, where it becomes more narrow ❍ *Ricky put his arm around her waist.*

wait /weɪt/
1 VERB When you **wait**, you spend time doing very little, before something happens. ❍ *I was waiting for my client to arrive.*
2 NOUN a period of time in which you do very little, before something happens ❍ *There was a four-hour wait at the airport.*
3 VERB If something can **wait**, it can be dealt with later. ❍ *I want to talk to you, but it can wait.*
4 If you **can't wait** to do something, you are very excited about it. [SPOKEN] ❍ *We can't wait to get started.*

wait|er /weɪtər/ **NOUN** a man whose job is to serve food in a restaurant

wait|ing room (**waiting rooms**) **NOUN** a room where people can sit down while they wait ❍ *She sat in the dentist's waiting room.*

wait|ress /weɪtrɪs/ **NOUN** a woman whose job is to serve food in a restaurant

wake /weɪk/ (**wakes, waking, woke, woken**)
1 VERB When you **wake** or **wake up**, you stop sleeping. ❍ *It was cold and dark when I woke at 6:30.*
2 VERB When someone or something **wakes** you, they make you stop sleeping. ❍ *I asked her to wake me at 7:00.*

walk /wɔk/
1 VERB When you **walk**, you move forward by putting one foot in front of the other. ❍ *I walk two miles to the office every day.*
2 NOUN a trip that you make by walking, usually for pleasure ❍ *I went for a walk after lunch.*
▶ **walk out**
1 If you **walk out of** a place, you leave it suddenly, to show that you are angry or bored.

○ *Several people walked out of the meeting in protest.*
2 When workers **walk out**, they go on strike. ○ *Within hours more than 600,000 steelworkers walked out.*

walk|ing pa|pers PL NOUN Someone's **walking papers** are a dismissal from their employment. [BRIT, INFORMAL] ○ *The department gave him his walking papers.*

wall /wɔl/
1 NOUN one of the sides of a building or a room ○ *His office walls are covered with charts.*
2 NOUN a long narrow structure made of stone or brick that divides an area of land ○ *The well is surrounded by a low wall.*
3 If a person or company **goes to the wall**, they lose all their money and their business fails. [BRIT, INFORMAL] ○ *Even quite big companies are going to the wall these days.*

wal|let /wɒlɪt/ NOUN a small case in which you can keep money and cards

Wall Street NOUN **Wall Street** is a street in New York where the Stock Exchange and important banks are. **Wall Street** is often used to refer to the financial business carried out there and to the people who work there. [ECONOMICS, BANKING] ○ *On Wall Street, stocks closed at their second highest level today.* ○ *Wall Street seems to be ignoring the fact that consumers are spending less.*

wan|der /wɒndər/ VERB If you **wander** around a place, you walk without much purpose and in no particular direction. ○ *He wandered around the park.*

want /wɒnt/ VERB If you **want** something, you would like to have it or you would like it to happen. ○ *I want a new job.*

war /wɔr/ NOUN a period of fighting between countries or groups ○ *He spent part of the war in France.*

ward /wɔrd/ NOUN a room in a hospital that has beds for many people ○ *They took her to the children's ward.*

ward|robe /wɔrdroʊb/ NOUN the clothes that someone has ○ *Ingrid bought a new wardrobe for the trip.*

ware|house /wɛərhaʊs/ NOUN a large building where goods are stored before they are sold [PRODUCTION] ○ *A big warehouse will deliver groceries to households throughout London.*

ware|hous|ing /wɛərhaʊzɪŋ/ NONCOUNT NOUN **Warehousing** is the act or process of storing large quantities of goods before they are sold. [PRODUCTION] ○ *All donations go toward the cost of warehousing.*

wares /wɛərz/ PL NOUN A person's or a company's **wares** are the things that they are selling. ○ *Many companies are choosing to display their wares online.*

warm /wɔrm/
1 ADJ having a pleasant amount of heat, but not very hot ○ *On warm summer days, she would sit outside.*
2 ADJ **Warm** clothes and blankets keep you warm. • **warm|ly** ADV ○ *I dress warmly for my walk to work.*
3 ADJ friendly ○ *She was a warm and loving mother.* • **warm|ly** ADV ○ *We warmly welcome new members.*
▸ **warm up** If you **warm** something **up**, you make it less cold. ○ *He blew on his hands to warm them up.*

warmth /wɔrmθ/
1 NONCOUNT NOUN **Warmth** is a pleasant amount of heat. ○ *Feel the warmth of the sun on your skin.*
2 NONCOUNT NOUN **Warmth** is friendly behavior. ○ *They treated us with warmth and kindness.*

warm-up NOUN a period of gentle exercise that you do to prepare yourself for a sport ○ *Training consists of a 20-minute warm-up, followed by ball practice.*

warn /wɔrn/ VERB If you **warn** someone about a possible problem or danger, you tell them about it. ○ *I warned him not to invest in them.*

warn|ing /wɔrnɪŋ/ NOUN something that tells people of a possible danger ○ *It was a warning that we should be careful.*

war|rant /wɔrənt/
1 NOUN a legal document that allows

someone to do something [LEGAL] ❍ *Police issued a warrant for his arrest.*
2 NOUN a document that certifies or guarantees something [LEGAL] ❍ *The issue also includes a warrant for a 2% stake in the airline.*

war|ran|ty /wɔrənti/ (**warranties**) **NOUN** a promise by a company that if you find a fault in something they have sold you, they will repair it or replace it ❍ *The TV comes with a twelve-month warranty.* ❍ *The equipment is still under warranty.*

wary /wɛəri/ (**warier, wariest**) **ADJ** If you are **wary of** something or someone, you are careful because you do not trust them. ❍ *A lot of consumers are still wary of the stock market.*

was /wəz, STRONG wʌz, wɒz/ **Was** is a form of the verb **be**.

wash /wɒʃ/
1 VERB If you **wash** something, you clean it using water and soap. ❍ *She finished her dinner and washed the dishes.*
2 VERB If you **wash**, you clean your body using soap and water. ❍ *I haven't washed for days.*
▸**wash up** If you **wash up**, you clean your hands and face with soap and water. ❍ *He went to the bathroom to wash up.*

wash|ing [BRIT] → **laundry 1**

wash|ing ma|chine (**washing machines**) **NOUN** a machine that you use to wash clothes

wasn't /wʌzᵊnt, wɒz-/ **Wasn't** is short for "was not."

wasp /wɒsp/ **NOUN** an insect with wings and yellow and black stripes

wast|age /weɪstɪdʒ/ **NONCOUNT NOUN** **Wastage** of something is the act of wasting it or the amount of it that is wasted. [PRODUCTION] ❍ *There was a lot of wastage and many bad decisions were taken.*

waste /weɪst/ (**wastes, wasting, wasted**)
1 VERB If you **waste** something, you use too much of it doing something that is not a good use of it. ❍ *I decided not to waste money on a hotel.*
2 NOUN **Waste** is also a noun. ❍ *It is a waste of time complaining about it.*
3 NONCOUNT NOUN **Waste** is material that is no longer wanted, especially because the useful part of it has been used. [PRODUCTION] ❍ *Waste materials such as paper and aluminum cans can be recycled.* ❍ *The money will fund research into new methods of disposing of nuclear waste.*

waste|basket /weɪstbæskɪt/ **NOUN** a container for things that you no longer want, especially paper ❍ *He emptied the wastebasket and found her letter.*

watch /wɒtʃ/ (**watches, watching, watched**)
1 VERB If you **watch** someone or something, you look at them for a period of time. ❍ *I watched him as he made the call.*
2 VERB If you **watch** someone or something, you take care of them for a period of time. ❍ *Could you watch my bags? I need to go to the bathroom.*
3 NOUN a small clock that you wear on your wrist ❍ *Dan gave me a watch for my birthday.*
▸**watch out** If you tell someone to **watch out**, you are warning them to be careful. ❍ *Police warned shoppers to watch out for thieves.*

wa|ter /wɔtər/
1 NONCOUNT NOUN **Water** is the clear liquid that falls from clouds as rain. ❍ *Get me a glass of water, please.*
2 VERB If you **water** plants, you pour water over them.
3 VERB If your eyes **water**, you have tears in them, often because they are hurting.

water|proof /wɔtərpruf/ **ADJ** not allowing water to pass through ❍ *waterproof clothing*

wave /weɪv/ (**waves, waving, waved**)
1 VERB If you **wave**, you move your hand from side to side, usually in order to say hello or goodbye. ❍ *She waved to me from the other side of the office.*
2 NOUN **Wave** is also a noun. ❍ *Steve stopped him with a wave of the hand.*
3 VERB If you **wave** something, you hold it up and move it from side to side. ❍ *More than 4,000 people waved flags and sang songs.*
4 NOUN a higher part of water on the surface of an area of water, caused by the wind ❍ *I fell asleep to the sound of waves hitting the rocks.*

5 NOUN Waves are the form in which things such as sound, light, and radio signals travel. ❍ *radio waves*

wax /wæks/ **NONCOUNT NOUN Wax** is a soft substance that is used for making candles (= sticks that you burn for light) and polish for furniture. ❍ *The candle wax melted in the heat.*

way /weɪ/

1 NOUN A **way** of doing something is how you do it or the manner in which you do it. ❍ *What is the best way of getting extra financing?* ❍ *She smiled in a friendly way.*

2 NOUN The way to a place is the route that you take in order to get there. ❍ *Do you know the way to the post office?*

3 NOUN A long way is a long distance. ❍ *It's a long way from New York to Nashville.*

4 You say **by the way** when you are going to talk about something different. [SPOKEN] ❍ *By the way, did you see Steve Trimarco's report?*

5 If someone **is in the way**, they stop you from moving freely or seeing clearly. ❍ *Please can you move? You're in the way.*

6 If someone **gets out of the way**, they move so that they are no longer stopping you from moving freely or seeing clearly. ❍ *Get out of the way of the ambulance!*

we /wɪ, STRONG wi/ **PRON** used to talk or write about yourself and one or more other people ❍ *We work together.*

weak /wik/

1 ADJ not healthy or strong ❍ *I was too weak to move.* ❍ *The Fed is worried about a weak economy.* • **weak|ly ADV** ❍ *"I'm all right," Max said weakly.*

2 ADJ A **weak** drink, chemical, or drug contains very little of a particular substance. ❍ *We sat at the table drinking weak coffee.*

3 ADJ easily influenced and not having a strong character ❍ *He proved a weak leader.*

4 ADJ A **weak** industry, market or currency tends to have unstable or falling prices. ❍ *British government bonds fell due to a weak pound.*

weak|en /wikən/ **VERB** If something **weakens** or something **weakens** it, it becomes less strong. ❍ *The economy weakened in early 2001.*

weak|ness /wiknɪs/

1 NONCOUNT NOUN Weakness is when someone does not have a strong character. ❍ *He didn't like to admit to weakness at work.*

2 NONCOUNT NOUN Weakness is the state of not being healthy or strong. ❍ *Symptoms of the disease include weakness in the arms.*

3 NOUN If you have a **weakness for** something, you like it very much. ❍ *Stephen had a weakness for chocolate.*

wealth /wɛlθ/ **NONCOUNT NOUN Wealth** is a large amount of money. ❍ *Growing businesses are crucial to the economy to generate wealth and jobs.*

wealth tax (**wealth taxes**) **NOUN** a tax on personal property [FINANCE, ECONOMICS] ❍ *The government will abolish the wealth tax on capital in family-owned companies this year.*

wealthy /wɛlθi/ (**wealthier, wealthiest**) **ADJ** rich ❍ *Their clients are mainly wealthy businessmen and women.*

weap|on /wɛpən/ **NOUN** an object such as a gun, that is used for killing or hurting people ❍ *He was charged with carrying a dangerous weapon.*

wear /wɛər/ (**wears, wearing, wore, worn**)

1 VERB When you **wear** clothes, shoes, or jewelry, you have them on your body. ❍ *She wears very smart clothes to work.*

2 NONCOUNT NOUN Wear is the damage that is caused by something being used a lot. ❍ *The suit showed signs of wear.*

▶ **wear off** If a sensation or feeling **wears off**, it disappears gradually. ❍ *The excitement of having a new job soon wore off.*

▶ **wear out** If something **wears** you **out**, it makes you feel extremely tired. [INFORMAL] ❍ *She travels a lot for work and it wears her out.*

weath|er /wɛðər/ **NONCOUNT NOUN** The **weather** is the temperature and conditions outside, for example if it is raining, hot, or windy. ❍ *I like cold weather.*

weave /wiv/ (**weaves, weaving, wove, woven**) **VERB** If you **weave** cloth, you make it by crossing threads over and under each other. ❍ *We gathered wool and learned how to weave it into cloth.*

web /wɛb/
1 NOUN The Web is system of connected websites that is used all over the world. [TECHNOLOGY] ❍ *The handbook is available on the Web.*
2 NOUN a thin net made by a spider ❍ *a spider's web*

web|cam /wɛbkæm/ **NOUN** a camera on a computer that produces images that can be seen on a website

web page (**web pages**) **NOUN** a part of a website that can be seen on a computer screen at one time

web|site /wɛbsaɪt/ also **web site NOUN** a set of information about a particular subject that is available on the Internet [TECHNOLOGY] ❍ *Every time you visit a website, you leave a record showing you were there.*

COLLOCATIONS
to *build* a website
to *visit* a website
an *official* website
to *design* a website

wed|ding /wɛdɪŋ/ **NOUN** a marriage ceremony ❍ *Many couples want a big wedding.*

Wednes|day /wɛnzdeɪ, -di/ **NOUN** the day after Tuesday and before Thursday ❍ *The meeting is on Wednesday.*

weed /wid/
1 NOUN a plant that grows where you do not want it ❍ *The garden was full of weeds.*
2 VERB If you **weed** an area, you remove the weeds from it. ❍ *Try not to walk on the flowerbeds while you are weeding.*

week /wik/ **NOUN** a period of seven days ❍ *I thought about it all week.*

week|day /wikdeɪ/ **NOUN** one of the days of the week from Monday to Friday

week|end /wikɛnd/ **NOUN** The **weekend** is Saturday and Sunday. ❍ *I had to work last weekend.*

week|ly /wikli/ **ADJ** or **ADV** happening once a week or every week ❍ *Our team has a weekly meeting.*

weep /wip/ (**weeps, weeping, wept**) **VERB** If someone **weeps**, they cry. ❍ *She was weeping at her desk.*

weigh /weɪ/
1 VERB If someone or something **weighs** a particular amount, that is how heavy they are. ❍ *She weighs nearly 120 pounds.*
2 VERB If you **weigh** something or someone, you measure how heavy they are. ❍ *Lisa weighed the boxes for postage.*

weight /weɪt/
1 NOUN how heavy someone or something is ❍ *What is your height and weight?*
2 NOUN an object that people lift as a form of exercise ❍ *I was in the gym lifting weights.*
3 If someone **loses weight**, they become thinner. If they **gain weight** or **put on weight**, they become fatter. ❍ *I'm lucky because I never put on weight.*

weight|ing /weɪtɪŋ/ **NOUN** a higher rate of pay that is intended to balance the higher cost of living and working in a particular area ❍ *a London weighting*

weird /wɪərd/ **ADJ** strange [INFORMAL] ❍ *Tim's boss is a very weird guy.*

wel|come /wɛlkəm/ (**welcomes, welcoming, welcomed**)
1 VERB If you **welcome** someone, you act in a friendly way when they arrive somewhere. ❍ *If you'll excuse me, I must go and welcome my visitors.*
2 NOUN Welcome is also a noun. ❍ *They gave him a warm welcome.*
3 You say "**You're welcome**" to someone who has thanked you for something. ❍ *"Thank you for dinner."—"You're welcome."*

wel|fare /wɛlfɛər/
1 NONCOUNT NOUN Someone's **welfare** is their health and happiness. ❍ *I don't believe he is thinking of Emma's welfare.*
2 NONCOUNT NOUN Welfare is money that the government pays to people who are poor or sick or who do not have jobs. ❍ *Some states are making cuts in welfare.*

wel|fare eco|nom|ics NONCOUNT NOUN Welfare economics is the study of how economic policies affect individuals in society.

[ECONOMICS] ❍ *Welfare economics, by itself, is not concerned with providing political tools.*

well
❶ INTRODUCING STATEMENTS
❷ ADVERB USES
❸ PHRASES
❹ ADJECTIVE USE
❺ NOUN USES

❶ **well** /wɛl/
1 ADV used before you begin to speak, or when you are surprised about something ❍ *Well, it's a pleasure to meet you.* ❍ *Well, I didn't expect to see you here!*
2 You say "**oh well**" to show that you accept a situation, even though you are not very happy about it. ❍ *Oh well, I guess the figures could be worse.*

❷ **well** /wɛl/ (**better, best**)
1 ADV in an effective or good way ❍ *I think Annette dealt with the situation very well.*
2 ADV completely or to a large degree ❍ *Mix the butter and sugar well.*
3 If you **do well**, you are successful. ❍ *She's done very well at work.*
4 You say **"well done!"** to praise someone when they have done something good. ❍ *That was a great talk, Pilar. Well done!*

❸ **well** /wɛl/
1 As well means also. ❍ *Everywhere he went, I went as well.*
2 As well as means and also. ❍ *Adults as well as children enjoy their products.*
3 If you say that you **may as well** do something, you mean that you will do it because there is nothing better to do. ❍ *Anyway, you're here now—you may as well stay.*

❹ **well** /wɛl/ **ADJ** healthy ❍ *He said he wasn't feeling well.*

❺ **well** /wɛl/ **NOUN** a deep hole in the ground from which people take water or oil ❍ *They were carrying water from the well.*

we'll /wɪl, STRONG wil/ **We'll** is short for "we shall" or "we will." ❍ *We'll call them in the morning.*

well-heeled ADJ wealthy [INFORMAL] ❍ *The small town has become a magnet for well-heeled foreign tourists.*

well-known ADJ famous ❍ *She was a very well-known author.*

well-off ADJ rich [INFORMAL]

well-to-do ADJ moderately wealthy [ECONOMICS] ❍ *a well-to-do family of diamond cutters*

went /wɛnt/ **Went** is a form of the verb **go**.

wept /wɛpt/ **Wept** is a form of the verb **weep**.

were /wər, STRONG wɜr/ **Were** is a form of the verb **be**.

we're /wɪər/ **We're** is short for "we are." ❍ *We're going to the theater tonight.*

weren't /wɜrnt, wɜrənt/ **Weren't** is short for "were not."

west /wɛst/ also **West**
1 NONCOUNT NOUN The **west** is the direction that is in front of you when you look at the sun in the evening. ❍ *I drove to Flagstaff, a hundred miles to the west.*
2 ADJ West is also an adjective. ❍ *the west coast*
3 ADV toward the west ❍ *We are going west to California.*
4 NOUN The West is the United States, Canada, and the countries of Western Europe. ❍ *relations between Japan and the West*

west|ern /wɛstərn/ also **Western**
1 ADJ relating to the west of a place ❍ *Western Europe*
2 ADJ relating to things, people, or ideas that come from the United States, Canada, and the countries of Western Europe ❍ *They need billions of dollars from Western governments.*

wet /wɛt/ (**wetter, wettest, wets, wetting, wet** or **wetted**)
1 ADJ covered in water or another liquid ❍ *He dried his wet hair with a towel.*
2 VERB To **wet** something means to put water or another liquid on it. ❍ *She wet a cloth and wiped the child's face.*
3 ADJ If the weather is **wet**, it is raining. ❍ *It's cold and wet outside.*

we've /wɪv, STRONG wiv/ **We've** is short for "we have." ❍ *We've never worked in the same office.*

whale /weɪl/ **NOUN** a very large mammal that lives in the ocean

what /wʌt, wɒt/

1 PRON or **ADJ** used in questions to ask for information about something ❍ *What do you need from me in terms of sales figures?* ❍ *What time are we meeting?*

2 PRON or **ADJ** **What** means "the thing that." ❍ *I want to know what happened to Norman.*

3 ADJ used to emphasize the next word or phrase ❍ *What a strange thing to say in a meeting!* ❍ *What pretty hair she has!*

4 You use **what about** when you make a suggestion. ❍ *What about asking Paul for his opinion?*

5 You say **what if** when you ask about something that might happen. ❍ *What if this doesn't work?*

what|ev|er /wʌtɛvər, wɒt-/

1 PRON or **ADJ** anything or everything of a particular type ❍ *Frank was his own boss and free to do whatever he wanted.* ❍ *He has to accept whatever job they give him.*

2 CONJ used to say that something is the case in all situations ❍ *I'll support you, whatever happens.*

what's /wʌts, wɒts/ **What's** is short for "what is" or "what has." ❍ *What's that?* ❍ *What's happened?*

wheat /wit/ **NONCOUNT NOUN** **Wheat** is a crop that is grown for grain that is made into flour.

wheel /wil/

1 NOUN a round object used under a vehicle to allow it to move along the ground ❍ *The car's wheels slipped on the wet road.*

2 NOUN a round object that you turn to make a vehicle go in different directions ❍ *He sat down behind the wheel and started the engine.*

3 VERB If you **wheel** an object somewhere, you push it along on its wheels. ❍ *He wheeled his bike into the alley.*

wheel|chair /wiltʃɛər/ **NOUN** a chair with wheels that you use if you cannot walk

when /wɛn/

1 ADV used to ask questions about the time something happens ❍ *When are you leaving the office tonight?* ❍ *I asked him when he was coming back.*

2 CONJ used to talk about the time something happens ❍ *When I met Jill, I was working as a lawyer.*

when|ever /wɛnɛvər/ **CONJ** any time or every time ❍ *I'm at my desk all day today so call me whenever you like.*

where /wɛər/

1 ADV used to ask questions about the place someone or something is in ❍ *Where did you meet him?*

2 CONJ used to talk about the place something or someone is in ❍ *Max knew where the file was.* ❍ *This is the room where I work.*

where's /wɛərz/ **Where's** is short for "where is."

wher|ever /wɛrɛvər/

1 CONJ in any place or situation or every place or situation ❍ *Some people enjoy themselves wherever they are.*

2 CONJ used when you say that it is not important where a person or place is ❍ *I'd like to be with my children, wherever they are.*

wheth|er /wɛðər/ **CONJ** used when you are talking about a choice between two or more things ❍ *I have to decide whether or not to take the job.*

which /wɪtʃ/

1 ADJ used to talk about a choice between two or more people or things ❍ *Which office do you work in?*

2 PRON used to show the exact thing that you are talking about ❍ *Police stopped a car which didn't stop at a red light.*

3 PRON used to talk about something that you have just said ❍ *She gave a very good talk, which didn't surprise me.*

while /waɪl/

1 CONJ at the same time as ❍ *I get up and go to work while my wife sleeps.*

2 NOUN a period of time ❍ *They worked in silence for a while.*

whip /wɪp/ (**whips, whipping, whipped**)
1 NOUN a long thin piece of material attached to a handle, used for hitting people or animals
2 VERB If someone **whips** a person or an animal, they hit them with a whip. ❍ *Mr. Melton whipped the horse several times.*

whisk /wɪsk/
1 VERB If you **whisk** someone or something somewhere, you move them there very quickly. ❍ *He whisked her across the dance floor.*
2 VERB If you **whisk** eggs or cream, you stir them very fast.
3 NOUN a kitchen tool used for whisking eggs or cream

whis|per /wɪspər/
1 VERB When you **whisper**, you say something very quietly. ❍ *She whispered something to him in the meeting.*
2 NOUN **Whisper** is also a noun. ❍ *People were talking in whispers.*

whis|tle /wɪsᵊl/ (**whistles, whistling, whistled**)
1 VERB When you **whistle**, you make musical sounds by blowing between your lips. ❍ *He was whistling softly to himself.*
2 NOUN a small tube that you blow in order to produce a loud, high sound ❍ *The guard blew his whistle.*

white /waɪt/ (**whiter, whitest**)
1 ADJ having the color of snow ❍ *He had nice white teeth.*
2 NOUN **White** is also a noun. ❍ *He was dressed in white from head to toe.*
3 ADJ A **white** person has pale skin.

white|board /waɪtbɔrd/ NOUN a white board that you can write on with a special pen to present information to a group of people

white-collar also **white collar** ADJ relating to workers who work in offices rather than doing physical work such as making things in factories or building things [ECONOMICS] ❍ *White-collar workers now work longer hours.* ❍ *a New York lawyer who specializes in white-collar crime*

white goods PL NOUN People in business sometimes refer to refrigerators, washing machines, and other large pieces of electrical household equipment as **white goods**. Compare with **brown goods**. [ECONOMICS] ❍ *The economy relies on such traditional industries as textiles, shoes, white goods and furniture.*

White House NOUN **The White House** is the official home of the president of the United States. ❍ *He drove to the White House.*

white knight (**white knights**) NOUN A **white knight** is a person or an organization that rescues a company from financial difficulties. Compare with **black knight**. [FINANCE] ❍ *They need to find a "white knight" to provide the $300m that the banks are demanding.*

who /hu/

Pronounce meaning **2** /hu/.

1 PRON used for asking about the name of a person or a group of people ❍ *Who is giving the talk this afternoon?* ❍ *Who went to the conference?*
2 PRON used in the part of a sentence before you talk about a person or a group of people ❍ *I'm not sure who told him.*

who'd /hud, hud/
1 **Who'd** is short for "who had." ❍ *I met someone who'd been waiting for three hours.*
2 **Who'd** is short for "who would." ❍ *Who'd like a coffee?*

who|ever /huɛvər/
1 PRON any person ❍ *You can have whoever you like visit you.*
2 CONJ used to say that it is not important which person does something ❍ *Whoever gets the job will have a big mess to sort out.*

whole /hoʊl/
1 **The whole of** something means all of it. ❍ *This is a problem for the whole of society.*
2 ADJ **Whole** is also an adjective. ❍ *We spent a whole year working on the project.*
3 **On the whole** means "in general." ❍ *On the whole I agree with him.*

whole|sale /hoʊlseɪl/
1 NONCOUNT NOUN **Wholesale** is the activity of buying and selling goods in large quantities and therefore at cheaper prices, usually to stores who then sell them to the public. Compare with **retail**. [MARKETING AND SALES]

○ *Warehouse clubs allow members to buy goods at wholesale prices.*
2 ADV **Wholesale** is also an adverb. ○ *The fabrics are sold wholesale to retailers, fashion houses, and other manufacturers.*
3 ADJ affecting a very large number of things or people ○ *They are only doing what is necessary to prevent wholesale destruction of vegetation.*

whole|sale price in|dex (**wholesale price indexes**) NOUN an indicator of price changes in the wholesale market [MARKETING AND SALES, BANKING] ○ *Switzerland's wholesale price index in July fell 0.3% from June, reflecting a decline in import prices.*

whole|sal|er /hoʊlseɪlər/ NOUN a person whose business is buying large quantities of goods and selling them in smaller amounts, for example, to stores [MARKETING AND SALES] ○ *Under state law, bar owners must buy their liquor from wholesalers.*

whole|sal|ing /hoʊlseɪlɪŋ/ NONCOUNT NOUN **Wholesaling** is the activity of buying or selling goods in large amounts, especially in order to sell them in stores or supermarkets. Compare with **retailing**. [MARKETING AND SALES] ○ *The business did well and he turned to wholesaling.*

who'll /hul, hul/ **Who'll** is short for "who will" or "who shall." ○ *We need someone in this role who'll coordinate the whole project.*

whol|ly /hoʊlli/ ADV You use **wholly** to emphasize the extent or degree to which something is the case. ○ *While the two are only days apart in age they seem to belong to wholly different generations.*

wholly-owned sub|sidi|ary (**wholly-owned subsidiaries**) NOUN a company whose shares are all owned by another company [ADMINISTRATION] ○ *The Boston-owned software company became a wholly-owned subsidiary of IBM.*

whom /hum/ PRON used in formal English instead of "who" when it is the object of a verb or preposition ○ *She described the company founder, Melissa Walsh, whom she met in Paris in 1994.* ○ *To whom am I speaking?*

who's /huz, huz/ **Who's** is short for "who is" or "who has." ○ *Who's going to argue with that?* ○ *Who's been using my laptop?*

whose /huz/
1 PRON or ADJ used in questions to ask who something belongs to ○ *"Whose is this?"—"It's mine."* ○ *Whose daughter is she?*
2 PRON used to talk about something that belongs to the person or thing mentioned before ○ *That's the driver whose car was blocking the street.*

who've /huv, huv/ **Who've** is short for "who have." ○ *These are people who've never used a computer before.*

why /waɪ/
1 ADV used in questions about the reasons for something ○ *Why are you laughing?*
2 ADV used when you talk about the reasons for something ○ *He wondered why she was late.* ○ *I liked him - I don't know why.*
3 ADV You use **why not** to make a suggestion. ○ *Why not give Jenny a call?*

wick|ed /wɪkɪd/ ADJ morally bad ○ *That's a wicked lie!*

wide /waɪd/ (**wider, widest**)
1 ADJ measuring a large distance from one side to the other ○ *The desk is too wide for this office.*
2 ADV If you open something **wide**, you open it as far as possible. ○ *"It was huge," he announced, spreading his arms wide.*
3 ADJ used to talk about how much something measures from one side to the other ○ *The lake was over a mile wide.*

wid|en /waɪdᵊn/ VERB If something **widens** or you **widen** it, it becomes bigger from one side to the other. ○ *They are planning to widen the road.*

wide|screen /waɪdskrin/ ADJ A **widescreen** television or computer has a very wide screen.

wide|spread /waɪdsprɛd/ ADJ happening a lot or over a large area ○ *There were widespread warnings that the nation was headed for a recession.*

wid|ow /wɪdoʊ/ NOUN a woman whose husband has died ○ *She became a widow a year ago.*

W

width /wɪdθ, wɪtθ/ **NONCOUNT NOUN** The **width** of something is the distance from one side of it to the other. ❍ *Measure the full width of the window.*

wife /waɪf/ (**wives**) **NOUN** the woman someone is married to ❍ *He runs the company with his wife, Jane.*

Wi-Fi /waɪfaɪ/ **NONCOUNT NOUN** **Wi-Fi** is a system of using the Internet without being connected with a wire.

wig /wɪg/ **NOUN** a covering of artificial hair that you wear on your head

wild /waɪld/
1 ADJ **Wild** animals or plants live in natural areas, without people taking care of them.
2 ADJ **Wild** behavior is not controlled. ❍ *The crowds went wild when they saw him.* ● **wild|ly ADV** ❍ *The crowd clapped wildly.*

wild|cat strike /waɪldkæt straɪk/ (**wildcat strikes**) **NOUN** a sudden strike that workers begin without consulting a union ❍ *The unions have as much interest as managers in preventing wildcat strikes.*

wil|der|ness /wɪldərnɛs/ (**wildernesses**) **NOUN** an area of natural land that is not used by people ❍ *There will be no wilderness left on the planet within 30 years.*

wild|life /waɪldlaɪf/ **NONCOUNT NOUN** The **wildlife** in an area is the animals, birds, and plants that live there. ❍ *The area is rich in wildlife.*

will
❶ MODAL VERB USES
❷ NOUN USES

❶ **will** /wɪl/
1 MODAL used to talk about things that are going to happen in the future ❍ *The economy will improve.* ❍ *The talk will finish at 2:30 p.m.*
2 MODAL used to ask someone to do something ❍ *Please will you be quiet?*
3 MODAL used to say that you are willing to do something ❍ *I'll send you those figures, if you like.*

❷ **will** /wɪl/
1 NOUN Your **will** is your determination to do something. ❍ *I have a strong will.*
2 NOUN a legal document that says who will receive your possessions when you die ❍ *He left $8 million in his will to the University of Alabama.*

will|ing /wɪlɪŋ/ **ADJ** happy to do something ❍ *She's willing to answer questions.* ● **willingly ADV** ❍ *Bryant talked willingly to the police.* ● **willingness NONCOUNT NOUN** ❍ *She showed her willingness to work hard.*

win /wɪn/ (**wins, winning, won**)
1 VERB If you **win** a competition, a fight, or an argument, you defeat your opponents. ❍ *The four local teams all won their games.*
2 NOUN **Win** is also a noun. ❍ *They played eight games without a win.*
3 VERB If you **win** a prize, you get it because you have been successful at something. ❍ *The first correct entry wins the prize.*

wind
❶ AIR
❷ TURNING

❶ **wind** /wɪnd/ **NONCOUNT NOUN** **Wind** is air that moves. ❍ *A strong wind was blowing from the north.*

❷ **wind** /waɪnd/ (**winds, winding, wound**)
1 VERB If a road or river **winds**, it has a lot of bends in it. ❍ *From here, the river winds through attractive countryside.*
2 VERB When you **wind** something long around something else, you wrap it around several times. ❍ *She wound the rope around her waist.*
3 VERB When you **wind** a clock or a watch, you turn part of it several times in order to make it work. ❍ *Did you remember to wind the clock?*
▸ **wind up** When a business is **wound up** it is closed down. [ADMINISTRATION, BRIT, INFORMAL] ❍ *The company will cease trading, and, when the winding up is complete, cease to exist.*

wind|fall /wɪndfɔl/ **NOUN** a sum of money that you receive unexpectedly ❍ *the man who received a $250,000 windfall after a banking error* ❍ *windfall profits*

wind|fall tax (**windfall taxes**) NOUN a tax on a company's excessively large profits [FINANCE] ❍ *They want to use the money from a windfall tax on energy companies to help poor families meet their rising fuel bills.*

winding-up NONCOUNT NOUN **Winding-up** is the process of closing down a business. [FINANCE, BRIT] ❍ *The winding-up order appointed an official liquidator to represent the interests of the workmen.*

win|dow /wɪndoʊ/
1 NOUN a space in the side of a building or a vehicle that has glass in it ❍ *He looked out of the window.*
2 NOUN one of the areas that a computer screen can be divided into ❍ *Open the document in a new window.*

window-dressing
1 NONCOUNT NOUN **Window-dressing** is the decoration of store windows.
2 NONCOUNT NOUN **Window-dressing** is the stressing of an attractive aspect of an idea in order to hide its real, less pleasant nature. ❍ *It was all true, but it was intellectual window dressing for something much deeper.*

wind|screen /wɪndskrin/ [BRIT] → **windshield**

wind|shield /wɪndʃild/ NOUN a glass window at the front of a vehicle

windy /wɪndi/ (**windier, windiest**) ADJ If it is **windy**, the wind is blowing a lot. ❍ *It was a wet and windy day.*

wine /waɪn/ NONCOUNT NOUN **Wine** is an alcoholic drink made from grapes (= small green or purple fruit). ❍ *a bottle of white wine*

wing /wɪŋ/
1 NOUN one of the two parts of a bird or insect that it uses for flying ❍ *The bird flapped its wings.*
2 NOUN one of the long flat parts at the side of an aircraft that support it while it is flying

wink /wɪŋk/
1 VERB When you **wink at** someone, you look at them and close one eye quickly.
2 NOUN **Wink** is also a noun. ❍ *I gave her a wink.*

W

win|ner /wɪnər/ NOUN a person that wins a game or a competition ❍ *She will present the prizes to the winners.*

win|ter /wɪntər/ NOUN the season between fall and spring ❍ *In winter the nights are long and cold.*

wipe /waɪp/ (**wipes, wiping, wiped**)
1 VERB If you **wipe** something, you rub its surface to remove dirt or liquid. ❍ *I'll just wipe my hands.*
2 NOUN **Wipe** is also a noun. ❍ *The table's dirty - could you give it a wipe, please?*
3 VERB If you **wipe** dirt or liquid from something, you remove it with a cloth or your hand. ❍ *Gary wiped the sweat from his face.*

wire /waɪər/ NOUN a long thin piece of metal ❍ *a telephone wire*

wire|less /waɪərlɪs/ ADJ not using wires ❍ *a wireless Internet connection*

wire trans|fer (**wire transfers**) NOUN a direct payment of money from one bank account into another

wis|dom /wɪzdəm/ NONCOUNT NOUN **Wisdom** is the ability to make sensible decisions or judgments. ❍ *Some in the firm expressed doubts about the wisdom of this plan.*

wise /waɪz/ (**wiser, wisest**) ADJ able to make sensible decisions and judgments ❍ *She knows the business better than anyone and she's very wise.* ● **wise|ly** ADV ❍ *They invested wisely.*

wish /wɪʃ/ (**wishes, wishing, wished**)
1 NOUN something that you would like ❍ *Her wish is to become a doctor.*
2 VERB If you **wish** to do something, you want to do it. [FORMAL] ❍ *I wish to leave a message.*
3 VERB If you **wish** something were true, you would like it to be true. ❍ *I wish I could do that.*
4 VERB If you **wish for** something, you say in your mind that you want that thing. ❍ *Every birthday I closed my eyes and wished for a guitar.*
5 NOUN **Wish** is also a noun. ❍ *Did you make a wish?*
6 VERB If you **wish** someone luck or happiness, you express the hope that they will be lucky or happy. ❍ *I wish you both a good trip.*
7 PL NOUN If you give your good **wishes** to someone, you express your hope that they will

be successful or happy. ❍ *Please give him my best wishes.*

wit /wɪt/ **NONCOUNT NOUN** **Wit** is the ability to use words or ideas in an amusing and clever way. ❍ *He writes with great wit.*

witch /wɪtʃ/ (**witches**) **NOUN** a woman in stories who has magic powers that she uses to do bad things

with /wɪð, wɪθ/

1 PREP together in the same place ❍ *She travels with her personal assistant.*

2 PREP If you fight, compete, or discuss something **with** someone, you are both involved in a fight, competition, or discussion. ❍ *We didn't discuss it with each other.*

3 PREP If you do something **with** a particular tool, object, or substance, you do it using that tool, object, or substance. ❍ *Turn the meat over with a fork.*

4 PREP If someone stands or goes somewhere **with** something, they are carrying it. ❍ *A woman came in with a cup of coffee.*

5 PREP Someone or something **with** a particular feature or possession has that feature or possession. ❍ *He was tall, with blue eyes.*

with|draw /wɪðdrɔ, wɪθ-/ (**withdraws, withdrawing, withdrew, withdrawn**)

1 VERB If you **withdraw** something, you remove it or take it away. ❍ *The chain stores withdrew the product or stopped advertising it.*

2 VERB If you **withdraw** money **from** a bank account, you take it out of that account. [BANKING] ❍ *They withdrew 100 dollars from a bank account after checking out of their hotel.*

3 VERB If you **withdraw from** an activity or a process, you stop taking part in it. ❍ *In some cases, U.S. concerns have withdrawn from the alternative-energy market.*

with|hold /wɪðhoʊld, wɪθ-/ (**withholds, withholding, withheld** /wɪðhɛld, wɪθ-/)

1 VERB If you **withhold** something that someone wants, you do not let them have it. [FORMAL] ❍ *Does Mr. Lewis have the legal authority to withhold payment?*

2 VERB Money that **is withheld** from wages is not paid to a worker but kept by an employer for some other purpose. ❍ *Employers that don't turn in taxes withheld from employees are major IRS targets.*

with|hold|ing tax (**withholding taxes**) **NOUN** an amount of money that is taken in advance from someone's income, in order to pay some of the tax they will owe [BANKING, FINANCE]

with|in /wɪðɪn, wɪθ-/

1 PREP in or inside [FORMAL] ❍ *The sports fields must be within the city.*

2 PREP less than a particular distance from someone or something ❍ *The man was within a few feet of him.*

3 PREP before the end of a particular length of time ❍ *Within twenty-four hours I had accepted the job.*

with|out /wɪðaʊt, wɪθ-/

1 PREP used to show that someone or something does not have or do something ❍ *I prefer tea without milk.*

2 PREP If one thing happens **without** another thing, the second thing does not happen. ❍ *They worked without stopping.*

3 PREP If you do something **without** someone else, they are not with you. ❍ *I told Frank to start the meeting without me.*

with-profits ADJ earning money for investors each year depending on how successful their investment has been [ECONOMICS, BRIT] ❍ *Returns on with-profits bonds have improved.*

wit|ness /wɪtnɪs/ (**witnesses, witnessing, witnessed**)

1 NOUN a person who saw an event such as an accident or a crime ❍ *Witnesses say they saw an explosion.*

2 VERB If you **witness** something, you see it happen. ❍ *Anyone who witnessed the attack should call the police.*

3 NOUN someone who appears in a court of law to say what they know about a crime ❍ *Eleven witnesses appeared in court.*

wit|ty /wɪti/ (**wittier, wittiest**) **ADJ** amusing in a clever way ❍ *His books were very witty.*

wives /waɪvz/ **Wives** is the plural of **wife**.

woke /woʊk/ **Woke** is a form of the verb **wake**.

wok|en /woʊkən/ **Woken** is a form of the verb **wake**.

wolf /wʊlf/ (**wolves**) NOUN a wild animal that looks like a large dog

wom|an /wʊmən/ (**women**) NOUN an adult female human being ❍ *My boss is a woman.*

wom|en /wɪmɪn/ **Women** is the plural of **woman**.

wom|en's room (**women's rooms**) NOUN a bathroom for women in a public building

won /wʌn/ **Won** is a form of the verb **win**.

won|der /wʌndər/

1 VERB If you **wonder** about something, you think about it, and try to guess or understand more about it. ❍ *I wondered for a while what she meant.*

2 NOUN If it is a **wonder that** something happened, it is very surprising. ❍ *It's a wonder that the company is still going.*

3 NONCOUNT NOUN **Wonder** is a feeling of great surprise and pleasure. ❍ *My eyes opened wide in wonder at the view.*

won|der|ful /wʌndərfəl/ ADJ extremely good ❍ *It's a wonderful achievement.*

won't /woʊnt/ **Won't** is short for "will not." ❍ *I won't tell him if you don't want me to.*

wood /wʊd/

1 NONCOUNT NOUN **Wood** is the hard material that trees are made of. ❍ *Some houses are made of wood.*

2 NOUN a large area of trees ❍ *We went for a walk in the woods.*

wood|en /wʊdᵊn/ ADJ made of wood ❍ *a wooden chair*

wool /wʊl/

1 NONCOUNT NOUN **Wool** is the hair that grows on sheep and on some other animals.

2 NONCOUNT NOUN **Wool** is a material made from animal's wool. ❍ *The socks are made of wool.*

W

word /wɜrd/

1 NOUN a unit of language with meaning ❍ *The Italian word for "love" is "amore."*

2 NOUN If you have **a word** with someone, you have a short conversation with them. [SPOKEN] ❍ *Could I have a word with you in my office, please?*

3 You say **in other words** before you repeat something in a different way. ❍ *Ray is in charge of the office. In other words, he's my boss.*

4 If news or information passes by **word of mouth**, people tell it to each other rather than it being written down. ❍ *Word of mouth can influence purchasing decisions more than advertising.*

word pro|cess|ing also **word-processing** NONCOUNT NOUN **Word processing** is the work or skill of producing printed documents using a computer. [TECHNOLOGY] ❍ *Many temp agencies offer word processing courses to those with rusty office skills.*

wore /wɔr/ **Wore** is a form of the verb **wear**.

work /wɜrk/

1 VERB People who **work** have a job. ❍ *He worked as a manager for 40 years.*

2 VERB If you **work**, you do something that uses a lot of your time or effort. ❍ *You should work harder.*

3 VERB If a machine **works**, it operates correctly. ❍ *My cellphone isn't working.*

4 VERB If something **works**, it is successful. ❍ *Our plan worked perfectly.*

5 VERB If you **work** a machine, you use or control it. ❍ *Do you know how to work the photocopier?*

6 NONCOUNT NOUN Your **work** is the job that you do to earn money. ❍ *I start work at 8:30 a.m.*

7 NONCOUNT NOUN **Work** is the place where you do your job. ❍ *I'm lucky. I can walk to work.*

8 NONCOUNT NOUN **Work** is any activity that uses a lot of your time or effort. ❍ *I did some work in the backyard this weekend.*

9 NOUN a painting, a book, or a piece of music that someone has produced ❍ *a work of art*

▸ **work out**

1 If you **work out** something, you discover the solution by thinking. ❍ *It took me some time to work out the answer.*

2 If you **work out**, you do physical exercises in order to make your body strong. ❍ *I work out at a gym twice a week.*

3 Someone who is **in work** has a job. ❍ *Even for those in work, wages are lower than in the rest of the country.*

4 Someone who is **out of work** does not have a job. ❍ *a town where half the men are usually out of work*

5 If workers **work to rule** as a form of protest, they do only the minimum that the rules of their employment require. ❍ *The 60,000 employees have so far limited themselves to holding demonstrations and working to rule.*

worka|day /wɜrkədeɪ/ or **workday** ADJ ordinary, practical, and not especially interesting or unusual ❍ *Enough of fantasy, the workaday world awaited him.*

work|day /wɜrkdeɪ/ also **work day**

1 NOUN the amount of time during a normal day that you spend doing your job

2 NOUN a day on which people go to work

3 ADJ another word for **workaday**

work|er /wɜrkər/ NOUN someone who works for a company but is not a manager ❍ *His parents were factory workers.*

work|ers' com|pen|sa|tion NONCOUNT NOUN **Workers' compensation** is money that is paid to a worker or their family if they are injured or if they die while they are working. ❍ *She can't survive on her workers' compensation.*

work|ers' co-operative (**workers' co-operatives**) NOUN **Workers' co-operative** is another word for **co-operative**. [ADMINISTRATION]

work|force /wɜrkfɔrs/

1 NOUN all the people in a country or area who are available for work [ECONOMICS] ❍ *Half the workforce is unemployed.*

2 NOUN all the people who are employed by a particular company [BUSINESS MANAGEMENT] ❍ *The company employs a very large workforce.*

work|ing capi|tal NONCOUNT NOUN **Working capital** is money available for use immediately, rather than money invested in land or equipment. [FINANCE] ❍ *He borrowed a further $1.5 m to provide working capital.*

work|ing con|di|tions PL NOUN Your **working conditions** are the environment in which you work and the rules relating to your job. ❍ *The strikers are demanding higher pay and better working conditions.*

work|ing day

1 NOUN [mainly BRIT] → **workday**

work|ing hours

1 PL NOUN Your **working hours** are the number of hours that you spend doing your job. [HR] ❍ *Some firms have cut wages and working hours, or extended vacations.*

2 PL NOUN **Working hours** are the hours during which people are working. [HR] ❍ *She runs a company that provides childcare to parents with unusual working hours.*

work|ing week [HR, mainly BRIT] → **workweek**

work-in-progress NONCOUNT NOUN In accounting, **work-in-progress** is the value of work that has begun but which has not been completed, as shown in a profit-and-loss account. ❍ *Adopting regular billing to reduce work-in-progress is likely to improve cash flow.*

work-life bal|ance NONCOUNT NOUN **Work-life balance** is the way in which you divide your time between working, and doing things you enjoy. [BUSINESS MANAGEMENT] ❍ *Do you help your employees achieve an ideal work-life balance?*

> **BUSINESS ETIQUETTE**
> In China, Japan, and Korea, most people bow or nod as a greeting. People do sometimes shake hands. You should wait to see if your Chinese associate offers his or her hand.

work|load /wɜrkloʊd/ NOUN the amount of work that has to be done by a person, machine, or organization [BUSINESS MANAGEMENT] ❍ *You need someone to share your workload.*

work|man|like /wɜrkmənlaɪk/ or **workmanly** ADJ done well and sensibly, but not in a particularly imaginative or original way ❍ *Really it's a workmanlike conference rather than a dramatic one.* ❍ *The script was workmanlike at best.*

work|mate /wɜrkmeɪt/ **NOUN** a person that you work with [mainly BRIT, INFORMAL]

work|out /wɜrkaʊt/ **NOUN** a series of physical exercises ❍ *She does a 35-minute workout every day.*

work|place /wɜrkpleɪs/ also **work place** **NOUN** the place where you work [BUSINESS MANAGEMENT] ❍ *This new law will make the workplace safer for everyone.*

works /wɜrks/ **NOUN** a place where a number of people are employed, such as a factory [PRODUCTION] ❍ *The steel works is still operating, but at half its previous capacity.*

work|safe /wɜrkseɪf/ **ADJ** suitable for viewing in the workplace ❍ *a worksafe website*

works coun|cil (**works councils**) **NOUN** a group of workers within a company who are elected to negotiate with management over things such as working conditions, vacations, and safety [HR] ❍ *a European directive calling for works councils for all companies with more than 50 employees*

work-sharing **NONCOUNT NOUN** **Work-sharing** is an arrangement in which one full-time job is done by two part-time workers. [BUSINESS MANAGEMENT] ❍ *So far, multiple production lines and strict work-sharing have done little to improve efficiency.*

work|shop /wɜrkʃɒp/

1 NOUN an event where people meet to learn about a subject by taking part in discussions and activities ❍ *They regularly organize workshops to help artists with new design ideas and new media.*

2 NOUN a place where people make or repair things [PRODUCTION] ❍ *He works as a mechanic in the workshop.*

work|station /wɜrksteɪʃən/ also **work station**

1 NOUN the desk and computer that you sit at when you are at work

2 NOUN a screen and keyboard that are part of an office computer system

work-study **NONCOUNT NOUN** **Work-study** is the investigation into how a job may done most efficiently, especially in terms of time and effort. ❍ *In many industrial corporations work-study was applied with considerable success.*

work-to-rule (**works-to-rule**) **NOUN** a form of protest that slows productivity down because workers do only the minimum that the rules of their employment require ❍ *A work-to-rule might in fact cause more damage to a company than an all-out strike.*

work|week /wɜrkwik/ **NOUN** the amount of time during a normal week that you spend doing your job [HR] ❍ *The union wanted a wage increase and a shorter workweek.*

world /wɜrld/ **NOUN** **The world** is the planet that we live on. ❍ *Scotland is a beautiful part of the world.*

World Bank **NOUN** an international organization of many member nations that assists economic development, especially in developing countries [BANKING] ❍ *The World Bank has approved $600 million worth of loans for Poland.* ❍ *World Bank debt relief*

World Bank Group **NOUN** the collective name for the International Bank, the International Finance Corporation, and the International Development Association [BANKING]

world mar|ket (**world markets**) **NOUN** all the people throughout the world who wish to buy a particular product [ECONOMICS] ❍ *steep rises in fuel prices on the world market*

world mar|ket price (**world market prices**) **NOUN** the price that is paid for something internationally [ECONOMICS] ❍ *The farmers would benefit greatly if the nuts were exported at world market prices.*

World Trade Or|gani|za|tion **NOUN** an international organization that deals with the rules concerning trade between its member states [ECONOMICS] ❍ *The United States has brought this matter to the World Trade Organization for formal dispute resolution.*

world|wide /wɜrldwaɪd/ **ADV** or **ADJ** all over the world ❍ *His books have sold more than 20 million copies worldwide.* ❍ *They made $20 billion in worldwide sales last year.*

wo̲rld|wide ma̲r|ket [MARKETING AND SALES] → **global market**

Wo̲rld Wide We̲b **NOUN** a computer system that allows you to see information from all over the world on your computer [TECHNOLOGY] ❍ *the rapid growth in the use of the World Wide Web* ❍ *Buyers spotted her ads on the Web.*

worm /wɜ̲rm/ **NOUN** a small animal with a long thin body, no bones, and no legs

worn /wɔ̲rn/

1 **Worn** is a form of the verb **wear**.

2 **ADJ** thin or damaged because of being used a lot ❍ *a worn blue carpet*

wor|ried /wɜ̲rid/

1 **ADJ** anxious ❍ *He seemed very worried.*

wor|ry /wɜ̲ri, wʌ̲ri/ (**worries, worrying, worried**)

1 **VERB** If you **worry**, you keep thinking about problems or unpleasant things that might happen. ❍ *I worry about my work all the time.*

2 **VERB** If someone or something **worries** you, they make you anxious. ❍ *"Why didn't you tell us?"—"I didn't want to worry you."*

3 **NONCOUNT NOUN** **Worry** is a feeling of anxiety. ❍ *Modern life is full of worry.*

4 **NOUN** a problem that you keep thinking about ❍ *Work worries are keeping him awake at night.*

worse /wɜ̲rs/

1 **Worse** is a form of the adjective **bad**.

2 **Worse** is a form of the adverb **badly**.

wor|ship /wɜ̲rʃɪp/

1 **VERB** If you **worship**, you show your respect to God or a god, for example by saying prayers. ❍ *He likes to worship in his own home.* ❍ *We talked about different ways of worshiping God.*

2 **NONCOUNT NOUN** **Worship** is also a noun. ❍ *This was his family's place of worship.*

3 **VERB** If you **worship** someone or something, you love them or admire them very much. ❍ *She worshiped him for many years.*

worst /wɜ̲rst/

1 **Worst** is the superlative of **bad**.

2 **Worst** is the superlative of **badly**.

3 **NOUN** **The worst** is the most unpleasant thing that could happen. ❍ *Many people still fear the worst.*

worth /wɜ̲rθ/

1 **ADJ** If something is **worth** a particular amount of money, it has that value. ❍ *The picture is worth $500.*

2 **NOUN** the value or price of something ❍ *I bought six dollars' worth of potato chips.* ❍ *Not every property will hold its worth or increase in value.*

3 **VERB** If something is **worth** having or doing, it is useful or enjoyable to have or do. ❍ *It's worth finding out what training they can offer you.*

worth|less /wɜ̲rθlɪs/ **ADJ** having no value or use ❍ *a worthless piece of paper*

worth|while /wɜ̲rθwa̲ɪl/ **ADJ** enjoyable or useful, and worth the money or effort that you spend on it ❍ *Was your trip worthwhile?*

would /wəd, STRONG wʊd/

1 **MODAL** used in questions with "like," when you are making a polite offer ❍ *Would you like a drink?*

2 **MODAL** used to talk about the result of a possible situation ❍ *Would it be all right if I opened a window?*

3 **MODAL** used to talk about the result of an unlikely situation ❍ *If I had a lot of money, I wouldn't work.*

4 **MODAL** used to talk about what someone believed, hoped, or expected to happen ❍ *We all hoped you would come.*

5 **MODAL** used to say that someone is willing to do something ❍ *He said he would help her.* ❍ *She wouldn't say where she bought her shoes.*

6 **MODAL** used to talk about something that someone often did in the past ❍ *He would sit by the window, watching people go by.*

wouldn't /wʊ̲dᵊnt/ **Wouldn't** is short for "would not." ❍ *He wouldn't tell me who was given the job.*

would've /wʊdəv/ **Would've** is short for "would have." ❍ *I would've loved the chance to work with her.*

wound

Pronounce meaning **1** /wa̲ʊnd/. Pronounce meanings **2** and **3** /wu̲nd/.

1 **Wound** is a form of the verb **wind**.

2 **NOUN** an area of damage on your body

caused by a gun or something sharp ❍ *The wound is healing nicely.*

3 VERB If a weapon or something sharp **wounds** you, it damages your body. ❍ *He killed one man and wounded five others.*

wrap /ræp/ (**wraps, wrapping, wrapped**)

1 VERB When you **wrap** something or **wrap** it **up**, you cover it with paper or cloth. ❍ *Diana is wrapping up the presents.*

2 VERB When you **wrap** a piece of paper or cloth around something, you put it around it. ❍ *She wrapped a cloth around her hand.*

▶ **wrap up** When you **wrap up** a deal or some other arrangement, you settle the final details. ❍ *Mr. Checchi expected to wrap up the acquisition as early as Friday.*

wreck /rɛk/

1 VERB To **wreck** something means to completely destroy it. ❍ *The storm wrecked the garden.*

2 NOUN a ship, a car, a plane, or a building that has been destroyed ❍ *They discovered the wreck of a sailing ship.*

wres|tle /rɛsᵊl/ (**wrestles, wrestling, wrestled**) **VERB** If you **wrestle** with someone, you fight them by trying to throw them to the ground. ❍ *My father taught me to wrestle.*

wrin|kle /rɪŋkᵊl/ **NOUN** a line that forms on your face as you grow old

wrist /rɪst/ **NOUN** the part between your hand and your arm that bends when you move your hand ❍ *She fell over and broke her wrist.*

write /raɪt/ (**writes, writing, wrote, written**)

1 VERB When you **write**, you use a pen or a pencil to produce words, letters, or numbers. ❍ *Write your name and address on the postcard.* ❍ *I'm teaching her to read and write.*

2 VERB If you **write** something like a book, a poem, or a piece of music, you create it. ❍ *She wrote articles for French newspapers.*

3 VERB When you **write to** someone, you ask or tell them something in a letter or an email. ❍ *She wrote to her aunt asking for help.*

▶ **write down**

1 When you **write** something **down**, you record it on a piece of paper using a pen or pencil. ❍ *I wrote down what I thought was good about the program.*

2 When you **write down** an asset, you decrease the value it is given in a set of accounts. [FINANCE] ❍ *Most operators have written down the value of their 3G licences.*

▶ **write off** If you **write off** an amount from your accounts, you treat it as a loss. [FINANCE] ❍ *Since December the company has written off $300 million on secret projects, reducing shareholders equity to $914 million.*

▶ **write up**

1 If you **write up** a company asset, you place an excessively high value on it. [FINANCE] ❍ *improperly writing up assets to claimed market values*

2 If you **write up** an asset, you increase its book value in order to reflect more accurately its current worth. [FINANCE] ❍ *The company must write up its assets to fair market value, which generally are greater than the historical costs.*

write|down /raɪtdaʊn/ also **write-down** **NOUN** a reduction in the value of an asset in a set of accounts [FINANCE] ❍ *The net loss in 1993 included $2,900,000 of staff reduction costs and asset write-downs.*

write-off

1 NOUN the act or process of canceling an amount from an account ❍ *There is speculation that the troubled British company plans a big write-off.*

2 NOUN an amount, such as a bad debt, that is canceled from an account and therefore regarded as a loss [FINANCE] ❍ *This quarter's loss includes $3.7 million of write-offs.*

writ|er /raɪtər/ **NOUN** a person whose job is to write books, stories, or articles

write-up (**write-ups**) also **write up**

1 NOUN an excessive or illegally high valuation of business assets [FINANCE] ❍ *the significant write-up of assets upon merger or acquisition*

2 NOUN the act or process of raising the book value of an asset [FINANCE] ❍ *A write up sometimes occurs when the asset was not initially properly valued in the company's books.*

writ|ing /raɪtɪŋ/

1 NONCOUNT NOUN **Writing** is something that

has been written or printed. ❍ *Joe tried to read the writing on the next page.*
2 NONCOUNT NOUN **Writing** is the activity of writing. ❍ *She makes her living from writing.*
3 NONCOUNT NOUN Your **writing** is the way that you write. ❍ *It's difficult to read your writing.*

writ|ten /rɪtᵊn/ **Written** is a form of the verb **write**.

wrong /rɔŋ/
1 ADJ not correct ❍ *I didn't know if Mark's answer was right or wrong.* ❍ *He called the wrong number.*
2 ADV **Wrong** is also an adverb. ❍ *I must have added it up wrong.* ● **wrong|ly** ADV ❍ *He was wrongly accused of stealing.*
3 ADJ If there is something **wrong**, there is a problem. ❍ *What's wrong with him?*
4 ADJ If a decision is **the wrong** one, it is not the best or most suitable one.
5 ADJ morally bad ❍ *She was wrong to leave the job without telling them.*
6 NONCOUNT NOUN **Wrong** is behavior that is morally bad. ❍ *He can't tell the difference between right and wrong.*
7 If a situation **goes wrong**, it starts having problems. ❍ *Everything started to go wrong when Tyler left the company.*

wrote /roʊt/ **Wrote** is a form of the verb **write**.

WTO /dʌbᵊlyu ti oʊ/ NOUN **WTO** is an abbreviation for **World Trade Organization**. [ECONOMICS]

WWW /dʌbᵊlyu dʌbᵊlyu dʌbᵊlyu/ **WWW** is an abbreviation for **World Wide Web**. It appears at the beginning of website addresses in the form **www**. [TECHNOLOGY] ❍ *Check our website at www.collinslanguage.com.*

X-ray /ɛksreɪ/ also **x-ray**

1 NOUN a picture that is made by sending a special type of light through an object or someone's body ○ *She had a chest X-ray at the hospital.*

2 VERB If someone or something **is X-rayed**, an X-ray picture is taken of them. ○ *All hand baggage must be x-rayed.*

Yy

yacht /yɒt/ **NOUN** a large boat with sails, used for racing or for pleasure trips

yard /yɑrd/

1 NOUN a unit for measuring length, equal to 91.4 centimeters ❍ *He keeps an average 200,000 yards of fabric in stock.*

2 NOUN a piece of land next to a house, with grass and plants growing in it

yarn /yɑrn/ **NONCOUNT NOUN Yarn** is thick cotton or wool thread. ❍ *She brought me a bag of yarn and some knitting needles.*

yawn /yɔn/

1 VERB If you **yawn**, you open your mouth very wide and breathe in deeply because you are tired. ❍ *She yawned, and stretched lazily.*

2 NOUN Yawn is also a noun. ❍ *Sophia woke and gave a huge yawn.*

yeah /yɛə/ yes [INFORMAL, SPOKEN] ❍ *"Don't forget your library book."—"Oh, yeah."*

year /yɪər/

1 NOUN a period of twelve months ❍ *We had an election last year.* ❍ *Graceland has more than 650,000 visitors a year.*

2 NOUN A financial or business **year** is a period of twelve months which businesses use as a basis for organizing their finances. ❍ *He announced big tax increases for the next two financial years.* ❍ *The company announced its results for the year ending September.*

year|ling /yɪərlɪŋ/ **NOUN** a bond that is intended to mature after one year [BANKING] ❍ *yearling bonds*

year|ly /yɪərli/ **ADJ** or **ADV** happening once a year or every year ❍ *The company dinner is a yearly event.* ❍ *Spending has risen by 5.8% yearly in real terms.*

yell /yɛl/

1 VERB If you **yell**, you shout loudly. ❍ *"Eva!" he yelled.*

2 NOUN A **yell** is a loud shout. ❍ *I heard a yell.*

yel|low /yɛloʊ/

1 ADJ having the color of lemons ❍ *a yellow dress*

2 NOUN Yellow is also a noun. ❍ *Her favorite color is yellow.*

yen /yɛn/ (**yen**) **NOUN** the unit of money that is used in Japan [ECONOMICS] ❍ *She earns 2000 yen a month.*

yes /yɛs/

1 used to give a positive answer to a question ❍ *"Are you a friend of Nick's?"—"Yes."*

2 used to accept an offer or a request, or to give permission ❍ *"More coffee?"—"Yes please."*

yes|ter|day /yɛstərdeɪ, -di/ **ADV** or **NONCOUNT NOUN** the day before today ❍ *She left yesterday.* ❍ *That's slightly above yesterday's closing price of $49.875.*

> **BUSINESS ETIQUETTE**
> In Muslim countries, most people do not do business on Friday. Friday is the Muslim holy day.

yet /yɛt/

1 ADV used when something has not happened up to the present time, although it probably will happen ❍ *They haven't made a profit yet.*

2 ADV used to ask if something has happened before the present time ❍ *Have they finished yet?*

3 ADV now or at this time ❍ *You can't go home just yet.*

4 CONJ used to add a fact that is surprising ❍ *He has met with nearly 250 entrepreneurs, yet he hasn't made a single investment.*

yield /yild/

1 VERB If fields, trees or plants **yield** crops,

fruit or vegetables, they produce them. ❍ *Each tree yields about 40 pounds of apples.*

2 VERB If you **yield**, you finally agree something. ❍ *Finally, he yielded to his parents' demands.*

3 VERB If a tax or investment **yields** an amount of money or profit, this money or profit is obtained from it. [BANKING] ❍ *It yielded a profit of at least $36 million.*

4 NOUN the amount of money or profit produced by an investment [BANKING] ❍ *a yield of 4%*

yoga /yoʊgə/ **NONCOUNT NOUN Yoga** is a type of exercise where you bend your body into special positions, and practice breathing methods. ❍ *I do yoga twice a week.*

yo|gurt /yoʊgərt/ also **yoghurt NOUN Yogurt** is a thick, slightly sour liquid food that is made from milk. ❍ *Frozen yogurt is $2 per cup.*

Yom Kip|pur /yɒm kɪpʊər/ **NONCOUNT NOUN Yom Kippur** is a day when Jewish people do not eat, and say prayers asking to be forgiven for the things they have done wrong.

you /yu/

1 PRON used to refer to the person or people that you are talking or writing to ❍ *I'll call you tonight.*

2 PRON people in general ❍ *Getting good results gives you confidence.*

you'd /yʊd, STRONG yud/

1 You'd is short for "you had." ❍ *I think you'd better tell us what you want.*

2 You'd is short for "you would." ❍ *You'd look good in red.*

you'll /yʊl, STRONG yul/ **You'll** is short for "you will." ❍ *Promise me you'll take care of yourself.*

young /yʌŋ/ (**younger** /yʌŋgər/, **youngest** /yʌŋgɪst/)

1 ADJ not having lived for very long ❍ *young people*

2 PL NOUN The young are people who are young. ❍ *Everyone from the young to the elderly can enjoy yoga.*

3 PL NOUN An animal's **young** are its babies. ❍ *You can watch birds feed their young.*

your /yɔr, yʊər/

1 ADJ used to show that something belongs or relates to the person or people that you are talking or writing to ❍ *I left your newspaper on your desk.*

2 ADJ used to show that something belongs to or relates to people in general ❍ *Always wash your hands after touching raw meat.*

you're /yɔr, yʊər/ **You're** is short for "you are." ❍ *Tell him you're sorry.*

yours /yɔrz, yʊərz/

1 PRON used to refer to something that belongs or relates to the person or people that you are talking to ❍ *I believe Paul is a friend of yours.*

2 People write **"yours"**, **"yours sincerely"**, or **"yours truly"** at the end of a letter before their signature. ❍ *I hope to see you soon. Yours truly, George.*

your|self /yɔrsɛlf, yʊər-, yər-/ (**yourselves**)

1 PRON used to refer to the person that you are talking or writing to ❍ *You should familiarize yourself with the report's contents.*

2 PRON used to emphasize the word "you" ❍ *You don't know anything about it—you said so yourself.*

3 PRON alone, or without help from anyone else ❍ *Don't do all of that yourself—let me help you.*

youth /yuθ/ (**youths** /yuðz/)

1 NONCOUNT NOUN Someone's **youth** is the period of their life before they become an adult. ❍ *In my youth, my ambition was to be a dancer.*

2 NONCOUNT NOUN Youth is the state of being young. ❍ *Youth is not an excuse for bad behavior.*

3 NOUN a young man ❍ *A 17-year-old youth was arrested yesterday.*

you've /yuv/ **You've** is short for "you have." ❍ *You've got to see it to believe it.*

yuan /yuɑn/ (**yuan**) **NOUN** the unit of money that is used in the People's Republic of China [ECONOMICS] ❍ *For most events, tickets cost one, two or three yuan.*

yup /yʌp/ **Yup** is a very informal word for **yes**. ❍ *"Are you ready to leave?"—"Yup!"*

Zz

zero /zɪ̲əroʊ/ (**zeros** or **zeroes**)
1 the number 0
2 NONCOUNT NOUN **Zero** is a temperature of 0° C, at which water freezes. ❍ *a few degrees above zero*

ze̲ro de̲|fects PL NOUN A policy of **zero defects** aims to remove all errors from the process of providing goods or services. ❍ *Where a zero defects policy is applied, defective products should not leave the factory.*

zip /zɪ̲p/ (**zips, zipping, zipped**)
1 VERB When you **zip** a computer file, you use a special program to reduce its size so that it is easier to send it to someone.
2 NOUN A **zip** or **zip fastener** is the same as a **zipper**.
▸ **zip up** If you **zip up** a piece of clothing, you fasten it using its zipper. [mainly BRIT] ❍ *He zipped up his bag.*

zip|per /zɪ̲pər/ NOUN a device for fastening clothes and bags, with two rows of very small metal or plastic parts that fit together

złoty /zlɔ̲ti/ (**złotys** or **złoty**) NOUN the unit of money that is used in Poland

zone /zoʊ̲n/ NOUN an area where something particular happens ❍ *The area is a disaster zone.*

> **BUSINESS ETIQUETTE**
> In Arabic countries, when you are sitting, you should keep both your feet flat on the ground. It is considered offensive to show the bottom of your feet.

zoo /zu̲/ NOUN a park where animals are kept and people can go to look at them ❍ *Berlin has an excellent zoo.*

zoom /zu̲m/ VERB If you **zoom** somewhere, you go there very quickly. [INFORMAL] ❍ *Trucks zoomed past at 70 miles per hour.*

WRITING FOR BUSINESS

General tips for writing in English at work

- Think about the reader and what they will need to know.
- Plan what you want to say before you write.
- Do not translate directly from other languages. Styles can differ greatly.
- If you are in doubt about formality levels, choose a little more formal—you are less likely to offend anyone.
- Write in plain English and avoid unnecessary jargon.
- Always check what you have written before you send it to others. You can remove errors of spelling and layout even if your writing is not perfect.
- Improve your writing by reading what others write. You can learn a lot about directness, tone, politeness, and so on from other people's writing.

Email

Emails are often fairly informal or neutral in tone, but there are still rules to follow, and a certain degree of good manners is expected between business partners, or people who do not know each other well.

If you are communicating with a company, a potential client, or a business contact for the first time, the language you use in your email should be formal. Even if you are writing to someone with whom you have already established a relationship, a formal style might be appropriate. Examples of cases where a more formal style might be preferred are: (1) if the person is much older than you, (2) if the person has a higher rank than you in the same company, or (3) if the person is from a country or culture where business relations are more formal than in your own.

Once you have built a business relationship, and you feel that it is appropriate, you can use a more informal style. It is also useful to pay attention to the style of the emails you receive in business and at work. If a business contact uses an informal style, then you can do the same in your reply. Emails to colleagues tend to be less formal, but should still be polite. If you are unsure about which style to use, keep it more formal.

Key points

It is important to keep emails clear, concise, and polite. You can do this by following the suggestions below.

- Remember that busy people receive a lot of correspondence. For this reason, you should avoid sending long emails. Try to tell them your points quickly and clearly.
- Ensure that the first sentence introduces the topic of the email clearly, and in a few words.

- Write short paragraphs. This will make the information easier to understand. Leave a space between each paragraph.
- If the email is long, consider numbering your points, using bullet points, or using headings. The reader will find this useful when responding to particular points.
- Write your emails carefully. Emails that are written very quickly and carelessly can seem unfriendly and rude.

The subject line

The subject line should clearly show the main point of your email. For example, if you are emailing a company to ask for information about a product, use the subject line to give the name of the product, and to mention the fact that you need information:

Subject: Balance bike (ref: N765) information required

Here are some more examples of subject lines:

Subject: Meeting Room changed to 307
Subject: Lunch (Fri, Oct 9) canceled
Subject: REQ: Feb sales figures
Subject: Reminder: conference agenda due

Salutations (= words or phrases for saying hello)

Formal emails are similar to formal letters, and the same salutations can be used.

If you decide to use the more formal salutation "Dear Mr. Sanchez" or "Dear Ms. Sanchez," remember to make sure that you use the title, e.g. Mr., Miss, Mrs., Ms., Dr., etc., with last names, not first names. For example:

- Dear Mr. Sanchez,
- Dear Mrs. O'Neill,
- Dear Miss Lee,
- Dear Dr. Armstrong,

In less formal emails, you can be more familiar. If the sender of the message has used his or her first name only, it is acceptable to use his or her first name when you reply. When you are communicating regularly with colleagues or business contacts, you can start with *Hello* or *Hi*.

- Hello James,
- Hi Akiko,
- Hello,
- Hi,

Ending an email

There is often a short sentence that links the main part of the email and the sign-off (= the part that says goodbye). What you write will, of course, depend on the purpose of your email, but here are a few typical sentences that are often used:

- I hope to hear from you soon.
- I look forward to hearing from you.
- Thanks again for your help.
- Thanks in advance.
- Thank you for taking the time to answer my questions.
- I hope this helps.
- Please get in touch if you have any more queries.
- Let me know what you think.

It is also polite to finish an email with a sign-off. There are no fixed rules for the type of sign-off that you use. The phrases below are some of the most common ones.

- Many thanks,
- Thank you,

- Thanks again,
- Thanks,
- Best,
- Regards,
- Best regards,
- Kind regards,
- Warm regards,
- Best wishes,
- With best wishes,

Attachments

An attachment is a document that you send with your correspondence. You can refer to attachments by using the expressions shown under "Referring to attachments" on page 9.

Language

Contractions (*I'm*, *he's*, *can't*, *we'd*, etc.) are acceptable in formal or work emails. Note, however, that in formal letters, the full form of words should be used.

Passive forms are common in more formal emails. For example, "...the sales report that you were sent in February" (passive) sounds slightly more formal than "...the sales report that I sent you in February" (active). If you are emailing a colleague that you know well, you may want to avoid the passive structure.

Indirect language: you should present your content in a careful way, paying special attention to the tone of your email, and the way the recipient will feel when he or she reads it. A very direct style can seem rude, and can cause offense. Here are some words and phrases that you can use to soften your message:

- In general .../On the whole, .../However, ...
- Usually, .../Typically, .../Often, ...

- It is possible that ...
- It is probable that ...
- It seems/appears that ...
- ... tends to be ...

- We tend to think that ...
- We feel that ...

- We would say that ...
- Taking the above into consideration ...

Key phrases for business correspondence

The phrases listed below are suitable for both business emails and business letters.

Starting your email/stating your purpose

- I recently read your ...
- I was given your name by ... who ...
- I am writing to ...

Referring to previous contact

- In response to ...
- Thank you for your letter ...

Asking for something

- Could you please send/supply/let us know ...
- I wonder if you could ...
- I would be grateful if you could ...
- I would appreciate it if you could provide/tell us/forward ...

Providing information

- I would like to inform you that ...
- I'm writing to let you know that ...
- I'm delighted to tell you that ...
- We can confirm that ...

Attachments

- Please find attached ...
- I am attaching ...
- I'm sending you a copy of my résumé.
- I am enclosing (in a letter)/attaching (in a letter or email) ...
- I've enclosed (in a letter)/attached (in a letter or email) ...
- Please find enclosed (in a letter)/attached (in a letter or email) ...

Complaining

- I am writing to complain about the quality of ...
- I am writing to express my dissatisfaction with the service I received ...
- I was very disappointed with the quality of ...
- The merchandise was damaged on arrival.
- The merchandise has still not been delivered.
- I would be grateful if you could replace the faulty merchandise as soon as possible.

Apologizing

- I was very concerned to hear that ...
- I am sorry to hear/learn that ...
- I would like to apologize for ...
- I apologize for ...
- I have looked into the matter, and ...
- I regret any inconvenience this has caused you.
- I can assure you that this will not happen again.

Thanking

- Thank you very much for ...
- I would like to thank you for ...

Asking for clarification

- It is not clear whether ....
- Could you clarify .... for us?
- Could you please explain what you mean by ...?

Giving good news

- I am happy to tell you that ...
- We are pleased to inform you that ...
- You will be delighted to hear that ...

Giving bad news

- Unfortunately, we are unable to ...
- I am sorry to tell you that ...
- I regret to tell you that ...
- I am afraid that ...
- We regret to inform you that ...

Giving reasons

- This is due to ...
- As a result of ..., we cannot ...
- Because of ..., we are unable to ...

Referring to future contact

- If you have any questions, please contact me.
- Please contact me if you would like any further assistance.
- Please do not hesitate to contact me if you need further information.

Referring to future action

- I look forward to hearing from you.
- I look forward to receiving your report.
- I am looking forward to seeing you in ....

Thanking

- Thank you once again for ....
- Thank you in advance for ...

Closing

Formal

- Yours sincerely,
- Sincerely,
- Sincerely yours,
- Yours faithfully (used in British English if you do not know the name of the person you are writing to)

Less formal

- Best regards,
- Kind regards,
- Best wishes,
- Regards,

Dealing with technical problems

- Did you get my last email, sent on ...?
- I can't open/I'm having trouble opening the attachment.
- The attachment doesn't seem to have come through. Could you possibly re-send it?

Formal email: first contact

From: "Hill, Lucy" <Lucy.Hill@bigbooks.com>
To: "Olivia Walsh"
Subject: Photography shoot for company brochure

Dear Ms. Walsh,

I am writing to ask if you would be interested in doing some photography work for our new brochure. I understand that you did some excellent photos for our associates in the Boston office, and Catherine Elliott has recommended you highly.

Please find attached a brief for you to look at. If you feel it would be helpful to speak to us about anything, please let me know and I can put you in touch with the marketing director.

I would be grateful if you could contact me this week.

I hope to hear from you soon.

Kind regards,

Lucy Hill

Less formal email

From: "Lewis, Lara" <lara.lewis@macp.com>
To: "Michael Peters"
Subject: Training courses for admin staff

Hello Michael,

It was good to meet you at the presentation last Thursday. I'm glad to hear that you found it useful.

When we talked, you expressed an interest in our IT training courses. I'm attaching descriptions of the courses we offer that you may find suitable for your admin staff. I think you were interested in starting fairly soon, and we are pretty flexible about dates and locations.

When you've had a look, give me a call and we can talk about the details.

Best wishes,
Lara

Informal email: from one colleague to another

From: "Rose, Andrew" <andrew.rose@wentworths.com>
To: "Helena Ghiotto"
Subject: Minutes of meeting January 6, 2012

Hi Helena,

I'm attaching the minutes from yesterday's meeting. Thanks very much for coming to the meeting—it was useful to have your sales perspective on the various issues.

Sophia and I agreed that it would be good to have you or Chris present at meetings in the future. Perhaps we could discuss this over coffee sometime?

Could you email me a copy of Jeanne's report? Thanks in advance.

Have a good trip. Please say hi to Carlo from me.

Best,
Andrew

Formal letters

Below are some examples of situations where a formal letter might be appropriate:

- when the recipient needs to sign a post office document to confirm that he or she has received it
- accompanying a document that needs to be signed by hand
- accompanying a résumé
- rejecting a candidate after an interview
- recommending someone for a job
- resigning from a job
- informing a customer that he or she has defaulted on payments

The layout of formal letters varies, but the format on page 16 is widely used.

Pay attention to the appearance of your letter. Present the text in short blocks and leave plenty of white space between them.

If possible, your letter should not be longer than one page.

Errors of spelling, layout, structure, opening, and closing can have a strong negative impact on the reader.

Structure

Formal letters are composed of an introduction, a main part, and a conclusion.

In your first paragraph, introduce the reason for writing. This should be brief; one or two short sentences are usually enough.

In the main part of the letter give the details of your reason for writing. Keep this as brief as you can, and present the facts in a logical order.

In the conclusion of your letter, tell the reader what you would like him or her to do as a result of your letter.

Language

Your letter should be polite, and should avoid slang or informal language and contractions, such as *I'm*, *he's*, *they've*, etc.

Make sure that you spell the name of the person that you are writing to correctly.

See "Key phrases for business correspondence" (page 8) for a wide range of expressions suitable for business correspondence.

Sample letter: giving information to a customer

[1] **ECOLOGY SYSTEMS Inc.**
1323 Washington Drive
Miami Beach, FL 33138
(305) 531-1276
www.ecosys.com

---

[2] December 21, 2011

[3] Sean Daly
Purchasing Director
Beaulieu Construction
2100 Ponce de Leon Blvd.
Coral Gables, FL 33132

[4] Dear Mr. Daly:

[5] **Change to delivery service policy**

I am writing to tell you about a change to our delivery service policy, which may affect you.

We have always provided free delivery for any orders placed with Ecology Systems, regardless of the size of the order. Unfortunately, due to increasing fuel prices we have been forced to review our policy, and will limit the free delivery service to orders over $500 starting November 1st.

If you have any questions, please contact me.

We thank you for your continued support.

[6] Yours sincerely,

S. Leon

[7] Samuel Leon

1 Most businesses write letters on headed paper that shows the company's name and address.

2 Write the date on the left, under the letterhead. Note that British style is to write the day followed by the month; American style is to write the month followed by the day. This can be confusing with a date like 12/03/12. To avoid confusion, always write the month in full as a word. For example, "12 March; 2012," or "March 12, 2012."

3 Write the address of the person that you are writing to on the left, under the date.

4 Salutations (= ways of saying hello) vary according to the level of formality and the culture of the sender. In American English, it is usual to use a period after the title, and a comma or a colon after the salutation:

- Dear Mr. Baker:

In British English, it is usual to use a comma or no punctuation after the salutation, and no period after the title.

- Dear Mr Baker

Here are some more salutations that are used in formal letters:

- *Dear Mr./Ms. [+ last name]*, (Some women prefer *Miss* or *Mrs.* depending on their marital status. If you are unsure, use *Ms.*)
- *Dear Sir or Madam*: (if you do not know the name of the person)
- *To Whom it May Concern*: (if you do not know the name of the person)
- *Ladies and Gentlemen*, (American English, addressing an organization)
- *Dear [+ first name]*, (informal only)

5 The heading goes after the salutation, in bold, giving the subject matter of the letter.

6 Write "Yours sincerely," "Sincerely yours," or just "Sincerely" at the end of the letter. Remember to start the first word with a capital letter.

7 Write your signature by hand and then type your name under it. Put your first name first and last name second. You can put your position under your name.

APPLYING FOR A JOB

When you apply for a job it is usual to submit a standard document that gives details of your work experience, education, and background. It also gives your full name and contact details. For most jobs, this document is called a résumé in American English. In British English it is called a "curriculum vitae," or a "CV." The term "CV" is also used in American English, but usually only for certain professions such as academia and medicine. In American usage, the term "CV" is used to describe a much more detailed and longer document that is presented in a different format than a résumé.

People usually send a cover letter or accompanying email with their résumé, which may be in paper or electronic form. Some organizations may ask applicants to fill in an application form, often online, instead of sending a résumé.

Writing a résumé

Remember that the reader of your résumé may have very little time, so the first impression is extremely important.

Your résumé should:

- be short; just one or two pages, no longer than three
- be relevant to the job you are applying for
- have a clear structure
- contain all the essential information, written concisely
- be attractively presented and contain plenty of white space
- be printed on good quality paper, if you are going to send it in paper form

Here is a typical layout for a résumé. The structure and layout of résumés varies but this format is widely used. Notice the clear headings and the white space around the paragraphs. If you need ideas for writing a résumé for a particular job, look at one that has been produced by someone who does the same type of work as you.

[2] 382 Danvers Court (317) 923-7102
Indianapolis, IN 46219 [3] markort@lycos.com

[1] Mark Ortega

[4] a self-motivated and efficient sales professional with a wide range of experience in the building sector

[5] Experience 2006–2010 Trellis Components Louisville, KY

National Sales Manager

Increased sales from $50 million to $100 million.
Doubled sales per representative from $5 million to $10 million.
Suggested new products that increased earnings by 23%.

2003–2006 Massey and Barrett Castings Bowling Green, KY

District Sales Manager

Increased regional sales from $25 million to $100 million.
Managed 250 sales representatives in 10 Midwestern states.
Implemented training course for new recruits.

1997–2003 Doublair Ventilation Systems Nashville, TN

Senior Sales Representative

Expanded sales team from 50 to 100 representatives.
Tripled division revenues for each sales associate.
Expanded sales to include mass market accounts.

1994–1997 DuraWare, Inc. Nashville, TN

Sales Representative

Expanded territorial sales by 400%.
Received company's highest sales award four years in a row.
Developed Excellence In Sales training course.

[6] Expertise HVAC architecture
CAD design specification
JIT inventory management systems

[7] Education 1995–1997 Phoenix University Online MBA
1991–1995 Vanderbilt University BA Economics

[8] Interests digital photography, NASCAR, soccer, genealogy

1 Give your name in full at the top of the résumé where it can easily be seen.

2 Provide your contact details prominently at the top.

3 Always provide your email address.

4 Write your personal statement at the top of your résumé. Describe your main attributes for the job, and the type of relevant experience you have in one sentence.

5 Provide details of your most recent employment first and then work backward.

6 Summarize skills that will be of interest to potential employers, and isolate these for easy reading. This is especially important for any software knowledge and other technical skills you possess.

7 Your educational background should also be listed with the most recent/ greatest accomplishments first.

8 It is not essential to list your personal interests, but for candidates who are otherwise equal, some personal information about you might make your résumé stand out and give a fuller picture of the type of person you are.

Note: It is not usual to attach a photo of yourself to your résumé in the US or the UK.

Language

When you are writing a résumé and cover letter or accompanying email, you need to highlight your strengths and your skills. Choosing suitable verbs can help you to do this effectively. Below is a selection of verbs that you can use when you are describing skills, responsibilities, and achievements in a work context. They are shown in the past simple—the form that you should use when you are writing your résumé.

Communication and teamwork skills

arranged	collaborated	communicated	developed
elicited	formulated	involved	influenced
mediated	negotiated	persuaded	resolved

Creative skills

adapted	created	customized	designed
established	initiated	instituted	introduced
modified	shaped		

Data management and financial skills

allocated	analyzed	budgeted	calculated
determined	devised	estimated	forecast(ed)
measured	managed	programmed	projected

Management skills

administered	appointed	authorized	contracted
coordinated	delegated	enhanced	expanded
headed	implemented	improved	led
planned	produced	reorganized	tripled

Research skills

collected	compared	evaluated	explored
gathered	investigated	interviewed	measured
researched	reviewed	summarized	tested

The cover letter or accompanying email

As well as a résumé, you will need to send the company a cover letter (if you are sending a paper copy of your résumé) or an accompanying email (if you are sending an electronic version). The purpose of a cover letter or accompanying email is as follows:

- It should point out the most important parts of your résumé.
- It should show a potential employer that you can write effectively.
- It should show a potential employer that you are a pleasant person.

The main part of the letter or email should consist of two or three short paragraphs only. If you are sending a letter, everything should fit on one page.

Write a cover letter or accompanying email for each different job that you apply for. Write specifically about the job that you are applying for, and keep in mind the skills and qualities that are right for that job.

Sample 1: an accompanying email

From: "Thomas Maruako " <Thomas.Maruako@globalinternet.com>
To: "Helena Sano"
Subject: [1]Editorial assistant

Dear Ms. Sano,

[2]I am writing to apply for the above post as advertised in the *Evening Sun* on October 16th. I am attaching my résumé, as requested.

[3]I am currently working at a publishing company that specializes in children's books. [4]I have been working on various aspects of publishing, including editing and checking manuscripts. In addition, I have experience organizing author events in bookstores throughout the Kansai area.

I have worked for this company for two years and have developed considerable skills in planning and organizing events. [5]I now feel that it is time to take my career to the next step. I am looking for a position that will provide new challenges and engage me more fully in the publishing process. [6]I am regarded as an organized and energetic person, and have been complimented on my ability to communicate with people from a wide variety of cultural backgrounds.

[7]I hope my application will be of interest to you. I would welcome the opportunity to discuss my skills and experience with you, and am available to come in for interview at a mutually convenient time.

I look forward to hearing from you.

Yours sincerely,

Thomas Maruako

1. Give the title of the job that you are applying for here.
2. Give details of the job that you are applying for and say how you found out about it.
3. Describe the job that you are doing now, including details of tasks and responsibilities.
4. Tell the reader what skills and knowledge you have gained in your current job.
5. Tell the reader why you want to leave your current job for the new job.
6. Describe the qualities that make you suitable for the new job.
7. Say that you would be pleased to provide the reader with more information.

The speculative letter or email

A speculative letter or email is one that you send to an organization in the hope that they will be interested in hiring you, even though they have not advertised a job vacancy.

Always address a speculative letter or email to a particular person. If you know the title of their job but not the person's name, call the company and ask for the name, or look it up online.

Sample 2: a speculative letter

Sophia Pylas

3 Victoria Street
Wellington 6011

August 6, 2011

Hotel Grand
26 Quay Street
Auckland 1021
BR2 4UT

Dear Sir or Madam:

I am writing to inquire about the possibility of work in your hotel this summer. I am especially interested in reception duties, but would seriously consider any other type of work that you could offer me.

I am a twenty-year-old student and for the last three years have spent every summer working in hotels in Wellington. I have worked as a receptionist, a waitress, and a cleaner. This summer I intend to stay in Auckland from 5 December till 31 January and am hoping to find employment for this period.

I enclose a résumé giving details of my work experience, and very much look forward to hearing from you.

With thanks

Yours faithfully

Sophia Pylas

Sophia Pylas

A job description

A job description is a document that defines a person's role in an organization.

Why is it necessary?

It is a key instrument for several reasons:

- It provides clear mutual agreement for employers and employees about responsibilities associated with a particular job.
- It is useful for employers when writing job advertisements and contracts.
- It provides a clear description for job candidates.
- It is useful for measuring employee performance.
- It is a useful tool for setting pay grades internally.
- It can be a reference tool in disputes and disciplinary situations.

What should it include?

- job title
- main purpose of the job
- position of the role in the organization, and the lines of responsibility
- location and setting
- key responsibilities/duties
- person specification*

*If a job description is for internal use only, it need not contain a person specification. If, however, it is used in the recruitment process, it is likely to include this. See page 589 for more information on person specifications.

Before writing a job description, you should:

- clarify the role with others in the organization
- read several examples of job descriptions

When you are writing a job description, remember to:

- write clearly and in plain English
- group individual tasks into main responsibility areas
- check and adhere to the employment and discrimination laws of the country you are working in

Sample job description

Job title: Web administrator

Main purpose of the job: to create and maintain content for the company website, assuring quality, and optimizing revenue-generating potential.

Reports to: Head of IT

Based at: Head Office, Peru, Illinois

Key responsibilities:

1. Design and create company web pages, including images, text, and functionality.
2. Monitor performance of company site.
3. Monitor search engine optimization performance.
4. Implement quality control for all content.
5. Maintain company intranet.
6. Advise Head of IT on new developments in technology and the Web.
7. Administrate and manage company database.
8. Ensure that site security is maintained.
9. Source and manage new online marketing opportunities.

Person specification

A job description that is sent to an applicant during the recruitment process usually includes a person specification: a description of the qualifications, skills, work experience, and qualities of the ideal candidate. It may specify what is essential and what is desirable.

Example:

	Essential	Desirable
Qualifications	• Bachelor's degree	• MA Marketing
Work experience	• 4–6 years in marketing department of international organization • effective customer care skills	• experience of working in Spanish
Skills	• excellent communication and networking skills • fluent Spanish • excellent presentation skills	• budget management skills • fluent Portuguese • good level of IT skills
Personal	• outstanding interpersonal skills • enjoyment of team working • willingness to travel in South and Central America	• interest in languages and cultures

Useful language

The main part of a job description is the section that outlines the responsibilities of the position. Many of the verbs used are common to a wide range of jobs.

Here is a list of verbs that are commonly used in job descriptions. The nouns shown in the second column are commonly used with these verbs:

adhere to	policies/regulations/laws
advise on	policies/opportunities
analyze	data/figures/statistics/markets/results
anticipate	changes/developments
approve	decisions/expenditure/requests
arrange	meetings/conferences
assist	a manager/team/team leader
attain	goals
build	relationships/business
coordinate	strategies/projects
commission	reports/surveys/research
communicate with	customers/clients/suppliers/authorities
delegate	responsibility
demonstrate	leadership skills/ability
develop	skills/contacts
drive	solutions/change
establish	a customer base/contacts/relationships
evaluate	effectiveness/success
lead	projects/teams

liaise with	teams/colleagues
measure	success/performance
meet	deadlines
maintain and develop	systems/databases
manage	people/staff/teams/processes/resources/costs
monitor	progress/implementation/performance/ development
negotiate	deals/terms/contracts
organize	events/training
plan and carry out	plans/activities/research/surveys
prepare and submit	plans/reports/documentation
prioritize	activities/tasks
recruit	staff
respond to	enquiries/developments/changes
recommend	action/changes
review	progress/contracts
support	a team
utilize	processes/tools
work closely with	the management/the Sales department

Reports

A report is a written document that presents information about a particular subject to a specific reader or group of readers. The purpose of a report may be to enable decision making, problem solving, reflection on past practice, etc.

All reports present a number of facts that the writer examines in detail. The writer then makes judgments based on those facts. Many reports also make recommendations for the future.

It is important to know the purpose of the report and who you are writing it for. You may be writing for readers with the same understanding of the subject and the same interests, or you may be writing for different types of reader. Your report will need to cover everything that your readers are expecting.

The structure of a report

The structure of your report will partly depend on what is contained in it, and the length. However, most long reports have a similar structure:

- title page
- contents list
- executive summary
- introduction
- main part of the report "Findings"
- conclusions
- recommendations
- appendices
- bibliography

A short report may not need a title page, and the conclusions and recommendations can be combined into one section. In some cases, there may be no recommendations at all. Note also that organizations sometimes have their own in-house report format. In such cases, ensure that your report follows the format precisely.

The headings and sub-headings of a long report need to be numbered. The system used by most report writers is as follows:

- Each section is numbered 1, 2, 3, etc.
- Sections within those main sections (called "subsections") are then numbered 1.1, 1.2, 1.3, 1.4, etc.
- If there are any subsections within those subsections, they appear as 1.1.1, 1.1.2, etc.

Title page

Include the following formation on your title page:

- the title of the report
- the name of the report writer
- the date
- the company or organization name

Contents list

A long report will need a contents list giving the main headings and sub-headings of the report and the page numbers.

Executive summary

The purpose of the executive summary is to focus the reader on the main conclusions of the report. It can also help the reader decide whether or not to read the rest of the report.

Introduction

This section contains:

- any background information that the reader should be aware of
- the purpose of the report
- the scope of the report

Main part of the report (also called "Findings")

This is the longest part of the report, where you present evidence and arguments. This section should not contain the opinions of the report writer. A long report is usually divided into sections and sub-sections; a short report may simply consist of bulleted or numbered points.

Conclusions

This is the part of a report where you review the evidence, data, results, etc., and reach a judgment. Present the conclusions in the order in which they appeared in the main body. Do not include any new information here.

Recommendations

Some reports include recommendations for action.

Appendices

This section contains information that is referred to in the report, but that is too detailed or complicated to include in the main part of the report. Examples of the type of information presented in the appendices are questionnaires, long, detailed tables, maps, or a glossary of technical terms used in the report, with definitions.

Note that if there is only one item, for example, a questionnaire, the singular form, "Appendix," should be used in the main heading.

Bibliography

If you refer to other people's work in your report, give the following information here:

- the author's name (or authors' names)
- the year the work was first published, or the number of the edition and the date it was published
- the work's full title
- the place of publication and the name of the publisher

For example:

Ellis, R. (1994) *The Study of Second Language Acquisition*. Oxford: Oxford University Press.

Style

Formatting and layout

- Break up your text with headings.
- Give information in the form of bullets in a short report. Bulleted lists are quick to understand, and are an effective way of presenting information.
- Clearly label tables, diagrams, charts, and other visual information.

Language

Do not use:

- informal or slang words
- contractions, such as *isn't* and *won't*
- words that suggest a moral judgment, such as *horrible* or *atrocious*
- unnecessarily long sentences and complex grammar

Try to avoid frequent use of *I*, *we*, *me*, or *my* in a formal report. In the recommendations section, however, this style is more acceptable.

Phrases and words used in reports

The words and phrases below are examples of the type of language you can use in a formal report in business and work contexts.

Introducing the topic and purpose of the report

- This report will examine/look at ...
- This report aims to/sets out to examine ...
- This report focuses on ...
- This report considers/explores ...
- The aim/purpose of this report is to assess/examine ...
- This report seeks to evaluate/examine ...

Defining key terms

Explain the meaning of key terms if you think the reader will not know them. If your report has a lot of technical terms, put them in a glossary in an appendix.

- Throughout this report, the term "x" will refer to ...
- The term "x" here refers to ...
- For the purposes of this report, the term "x" is used to mean ...

Reporting findings

- The findings/results/statistics/figures show that ...
- This has led to a situation where ...
- Several issues/problems/questions/points arise from this
- It appears that ...
- There is no evidence of ...

Referring to visual data

- This graph shows that ...
- As can be seen in figure 2, ..
- The data in table 1.2 represents/shows/indicates ...

Reasons and results

- This may be because of/caused by ...
- This may be a result/consequence of ...
- It is likely/possible that ...
- One possible explanation is that ...

- Consequently ...
- As a result/consequence ...
- The result is ...
- It follows that ...
- Therefore ...

Additional information

- In addition, ...
- What is more, ...
- Furthermore, ...
- Moreover, ...
- More importantly, ...

Discussing differences

- There is a marked/sharp contrast between x and y.
- There is a clear distinction between x and y.
- There are significant differences between x and y.
- This contrasts sharply with ...
- X differs/varies widely from y.
- By/In contrast, ...
- By/In comparison, ...
- Conversely, ...

Reporting what others have said or written

- Smith asserts/claims/proposes/suggests that ...
- Smith maintains/states that ...
- Jones comments/observes/remarks/reports/writes that ...
- Jones concludes that ...

Summarizing

- In summary, ...
- To summarize, ...
- In conclusion, ...
- To conclude, ...
- The following points summarize our key findings:
- The key findings are outlined below:

Drawing conclusions

- It can be concluded that ...
- We can therefore conclude that ...
- It is clear that ...
- No conclusions were reached regarding ...

Recommending

- We strongly recommend that ...
- It is my recommendation that ...
- It is essential that ...
- It would be advisable to ...

Passive forms

Use of the passive is common in report writing. However, if it is over-used, it can lead to a boring and repetitive style.

Examples:

- This report was compiled on the basis of ...
- Four hundred people were interviewed.
- The figures are based on ...
- The following conclusions can be drawn:
- Changes should be made ...

EFFECTIVE PRESENTATIONS

A presentation is a speech in which you provide information to an audience about a subject that you know about, that you have researched, or that you have written about. Most presentations are accompanied by visual aids such as slides.

Why write out a presentation?

The process of writing your presentation can help you to decide the key points of your material, to think of the most logical order in which to present your main points, to decide on the slides you need for your talk, and to estimate the time it will take.

Writing notes for a presentation

You may decide to write out all of your presentation during the early stages of preparation. However, once you have done this, you should make notes on prompt cards which you can then use during the presentation. Write one or two main points on each card. Alternatively, you can use your slides as your prompts.

It is not advisable to use a long written text during the presentation for these reasons:

- If you are nervous, you might be tempted to read from the text, and not speak directly to the audience.
- If you read directly from a written text, you will not make enough eye-contact with the audience, and your language may sound unnatural.
- If you read and make little eye-contact, you will lose the attention of the audience.

Preparing slides for a presentation

- Do not prepare too many slides. The audience is there to hear your presentation, not to read from slides. Try to aim for no more than one slide per minute.
- Keep the text on your slides simple and brief. Do not put too much information on a slide. Limit the amount of text on a slide to six or seven words on each line and to six or seven lines of text per slide.
- It is important that the text on your slides is large enough to be seen from the back of the room.
- Check your slides carefully for any spelling or grammar mistakes. Ask someone to read through them for you.

Preparation

While you are preparing your presentation, there are several points you should consider:

Area	**Points to consider**
Audience knowledge and expectations	Think about what the audience already knows about the topic. Try to anticipate their questions.
Content of the presentation	What should you include? How many key points will you talk about? How much time do you have?
Structure of the presentation	Organize your presentation into a clear sequence: introduction, main points, and conclusion.
Delivery	How formal or informal can you be in this context? Is your voice loud enough? Think about your body language: movement, gestures, and eye-contact. You should face the audience, and not the screen.

Visuals	Are your slides visible? Do they have too much text on them?
Equipment	Do you know how to use it? Can you try it out in advance?
Language	Check your slides for grammatical and spelling errors. Check the pronunciation of any words you are not sure about. Make sure you can pronounce the names of companies, people, and places correctly. Use "presentation language" to provide a clear structure for yourself and the audience (See "Useful phrases" section).
Practice	Apart from the content, practice is the key to a good presentation. It can be useful for checking timing; it can also calm nerves, and help you to avoid problems on the day.

Useful phrases

These phrases will help to provide a clear structure for yourself and the audience.

Introducing yourself and your presentation

- Good morning/afternoon/evening everyone.
- It's a pleasure to be here today.
- It's good to be here (*informal*).
- I'm ...
- My name's ...

Explain the structure of your talk

- What I'd like to do today is talk about/tell you something about/ outline ...

- I'm going to talk about ... today.
- First, I'll talk about ...
- Then, I'll tell you ...
- And finally, I'd like to consider ...

Referring to visuals (= charts, diagrams, images, etc.)

- If you look at this, you'll see ...
- This slide shows ...
- You can see here that ...
- This chart/diagram/table illustrates ...
- Take a look at this next set of data.

Moving through the talk

- Now let's move to ...
- I'd like to move on now to my next point.
- Now, I'm going to ...
- The next point I'd like to make is ...
- That's all I want/have to say about ...

Concluding

- I'd like to finish with ...
- That brings me to the end of what I wanted to say.
- So, to summarize, ...
- Thank you for your attention.
- Now, does anyone have any questions or comments?
- We have some time now for questions.

Handling questions and comments

- Thank you.
- An interesting question. I'll try to answer it.
- Well, if you look back at this slide, you'll see that ...
- I'm afraid I don't have an answer to your question.
- I'm afraid that's really outside the scope of this talk.
- Sorry, I'm not sure I've understood your question. Could you repeat it please?
- ... Does that answer your question?

Dealing with problems

Equipment/materials

If your equipment does not seem to be working properly, or you are having problems with your materials, don't panic! People are usually happy to wait while a problem is being fixed. Here are some phrases you can use to apologize for the delay:

- Excuse me; if you could just give me a moment ...
- Please bear with me for a couple of minutes while I figure this out.
- Apologies for the delay; we just need to get another laptop/ screen/projector.

Language

You may feel that you have not expressed an idea very clearly, or a member of the audience may ask you to repeat something that they have not understood.

- Sorry, let me rephrase that.
- What I'm trying to say is ...
- What I mean is ...

Time

Presentations are normally restricted to a particular length of time. Here are some expressions you can use if you notice that the end of the allotted time is approaching:

- I'm running out of time, so I'll just say ...
- There's just time for a couple of questions.
- I'm afraid there's no time left for questions, but if you'd like to see me during the coffee break, I'd be delighted to answer any you may have.

USEFUL PHRASES IN SPOKEN BUSINESS COMMUNICATION

This section provides you with a selection of useful phrases that you can use in the most common business situations.

Basic business communication

Note: in the UK and the US, once people have been introduced, they often use first names at work and in business dealings. If someone says "Call me [first name]," then it is fine to do so. If you are dealing with more senior people, it is better to wait until you see how other people address them.

First meeting/Introductions

- Hello/Hi. My name's [*your name*]...
- It's good to meet you.
- It's nice to meet you.
- I'm very pleased to meet you.
- May I introduce [*a third person*]?

Greeting someone you know

- It's good to see you again.
- How are you?
- How have you been?

Arriving at a company

- My name is [*your name*]. I have an appointment to see [*name*] at 10:30.
- I'm [*your name*]. I'm here to see [*name*].

Waiting to be seen

- If you just take a seat, I'll tell him/her you are here.
- Can I get you a coffee?
- Can you come with me please?

Making small talk

Small talk is important in many cultures because it helps to build relationships. It is usual to talk about your trip, the weather, family, your hotel, sports, and other relevant topics, especially while you are getting to know people better.

- So, did you have any problems getting here?
- And is your hotel OK?
- Did you see the game last night?
- So, what do you think of Osaka?
- How is your family?
- Too bad it's raining today.

Asking for something

It is important to make requests politely. It is best not to say "~~Give me ..., please~~" or "~~I want ...~~" because it sounds too direct and sometimes rude. In the UK, "please" and "thank you" are used a lot.

- Can you ....., please?
- Could you ...., please?
- Could you tell me ..., please?
- Do you think you could ...?
- Would you mind ...ing, please?
- Would it be possible for you to ...?

Making arrangements

Note that it is a good idea to check dates, times, and locations to make sure you have not misunderstood the details.

What time would you like to meet?	How about 4 o'clock tomorrow?
What are you doing this afternoon?	I'm flying to Houston.
Do you have any plans for tonight?	No, not really.
Can we meet next week?	Yes, that'd be fine/that works for me.
I'll call you tomorrow.	Great, I'll talk to you then.
So, we'll meet at the airport at 8 pm.	See you there/sounds good.

Making, accepting, and rejecting invitations

- A few of us are going out after work. Would you like to join us?
- Would you like to join us for a drink later?
- Do you want to come over Saturday evening for a barbecue?
- Do you want to play tennis with us on the weekend?

- Thanks, I'd really like that.
- I'd love to, thanks.

- Oh, thanks, but I'm already busy on Saturday.
- I can't make it on Saturday, but thank you for the invitation.
- Oh, thanks for inviting me, but I've made other plans for Friday evening.

Meetings

Formal meetings have an agenda, and a secretary takes the minutes (= notes about what was discussed and decided). Informal, everyday meetings may be less structured.

Opening

- Thank you for coming.
- We've received apologies from .... (In a formal meeting, this refers to people who have informed the chair that they will not be able to come.)
- Let's get started.

Starting the meeting

- We're here to discuss/review/decide/report on ...
- What we need to do today is ...
- The background to this is ...

Asking for and giving opinions

- I'd like to hear from ....
- What do you think?
- Anything to add to that?
- Any suggestions or comments?

- Well, I think ...
- We think/believe/agree/feel ...
- Actually, I think ...

Agreeing and disagreeing with others

- I agree with ... [name]
- Absolutely!
- I think ... [name] is right.

- I can't agree with you.
- I don't really agree.
- I'm not so sure about that.

Asking for clarification

- Sorry, I don't understand.
- I'm sorry, I just don't follow.
- What do you mean by ...?
- Can you explain that?

Checking understanding

- Is that clear?
- Is that clearer now?
- Do you follow me?
- Do you understand what I mean?

Interrupting and handling interruptions

- Excuse me, can I say something here?
- Could I come in at this point?
- Before we move on, I'd like to say ...
- Sorry to interrupt, but ...

- Sure, go ahead.
- Let me just finish this thought, and then you can make your point.
- I'll address that point/come back to that later.

Summarizing and ending

- I think we should end there. Just to summarize, ...
- So, that's all we have time for.
- Well, I think that's everything. Let's meet again on ...
- Thank you for coming. We'll be in touch.

Negotiations

A negotiation normally starts with greetings and introductions if necessary, followed by some small talk. Once people are feeling comfortable, the negotiation can begin.

Stating aims

- I'd like to begin with a few words about what we expect to do today.
- What we hope to do today is to ...
- What we'd like to achieve in this meeting is ...
- I hope that we will be able to agree on ...

Making proposals

- What I/we would like to propose is ...
- I suggest that we ...
- What we're proposing is ...

Bargaining and making concessions

- We can agree to that if ...
- We can agree to that as long as ...
- We could offer ..., if you ...
- What sort of ... could you offer us on that?
- If you could ..., we will ...
- We are not in a position to accept anything less.
- Is that your best offer/price/deal?

Accepting and rejecting

- We agree to that.
- That seems acceptable.

- We are unable to ...
- I'm not convinced.
- That's really not acceptable to us.
- I'm afraid that would be difficult/impossible for us.
- I'm sorry but there's no way we can agree to that.

Confirming

- Can we run through what we have agreed?
- I'd like to check what we have agreed so far.

Summarizing and finalizing

- So, I'd like to summarize what we have agreed.
- I'd like to summarize the main points of our agreement.

Phone calls

Before you make a call, think through what you want to say and write down the details.

Be prepared to ask people to repeat and confirm details if necessary.

Before you finish the call, confirm what you have understood if you have any doubts.

If you think you might have to leave a message on voicemail, plan what you want to say before you make the call.

Making a call

- My name is ...
- This is ... (not "~~I am~~")
- I'd like to speak to ...
- Can I speak to ...?
- I'm calling about ...

Leaving messages

- Could you give him a message, please?
- Could you ask her to call me back?

Taking a call

- Hello.
- Hello, [*name or organization/company*]
- How can I help you?
- May I ask who's calling?
- Just a moment, please.
- Can you hold on a moment, please?

- I'm afraid he's not available at the moment.
- Sorry, she's not in at the moment.

Taking messages

- Can I take a message?
- Would you like to leave a message?

Asking for repetition

- Sorry, I didn't catch your name/the number/the time ...
- Sorry, could you repeat that, please?
- Can you spell that, please?

Confirming

- So, that's ... [*names*, *arrangements*, *numbers*, *etc*.]

Ending a call

- Okay, I think that's all.
- Thank you very much for your help.
- Bye/Goodbye.

Presentations

For the language of presentations, see page 42 in 'Effective Presentations'.

Avoiding misunderstandings

Norms of communication vary greatly between cultures, within cultures, and between different sectors and companies. It is therefore very difficult to make reliable generalizations about what is most usual in global business communication.

However, one area that can cause difficulties is the notion of directness and indirectness. In some places, directness is valued, but in others it is considered rude. Becoming better prepared to work in an English-speaking context requires more than good language skills. You need to learn how to understand and use language appropriately.

Compare:

- Can I open this window?

and:

- I was wondering, would anyone mind at all if I opened this window?

In the UK, the first question is too direct, and may sound rude in a context in which you do not know the people in the room very well, and, particularly, when you are suggesting doing something that might bother them. Generally, US communication style is more direct than UK style.

Possible misunderstandings
Below are some examples of where misunderstandings can occur, and some advice on how to avoid them.

Saying "no"

One area that can cause problems is how to say "no" politely, and also how to understand when someone else has said "no" in an indirect way.

To avoid appearing too direct and causing offense, some people use longer, indirect sentences with softer words. This can cause confusion for people who come from a culture where directness is valued. Here are a few examples:

What people say	What they might mean
I'm not sure that we can take this any further at this stage.	Sorry, but no.
I hear what you're saying.	I hear you but I don't agree.
I was a bit disappointed that ...	I am annoyed that ....
With the greatest respect, ...	Actually, I completely disagree with you.
I'll bear it in mind.	I probably won't do it.

Requests

Sometimes a request may not seem like a request. In the apparently unfinished sentences below, the speaker is, in fact, asking for something:

Sentence	Meaning
If you could just let me know	Can you let me know?
If I could have your report by Friday ...	I want your report by Friday

Strategies

It is essential to check that you have understood. You can do this by using the following phrases:

- So, does this mean that you are not interested in our products?
- Am I right in thinking that you are going to call me tomorrow?
- Do you mean ...?
- Sorry; what exactly does that mean?
- Do you want the report by Friday?

CULTURAL AWARENESS

This section describes some of the cultural differences that exist in the way people approach business around the world. Note that these descriptions describe tendencies only; you will, of course, find a wide variety of behaviors within countries and between sectors. However, it is important to be aware of such tendencies while you are building relationships with overseas business partners. In this way, you are in a better position to avoid causing offense or misunderstandings.

Quantity of information

The quantity of information that you may find in communication is not the same for all cultures. In some cultures, people might expect a lot of details. In others, people assume that listeners or readers will be able to work out the full meaning of the message for themselves.

For example, a German manager might deliver a long, detailed presentation about the launch of a new product. Some of the members of the audience, especially those from the Asia Pacific region, might feel that the presenter has provided too many technical details.

In Germany, Holland, and Scandinavia, people tend to value detail, especially when making decisions. In other areas of the world, such as Asia Pacific, Southern Europe, the Middle East, Latin America, and India, you might find less detail in presentations and that people need less detail as part of the decision making process.

Complexity of communication

When you are communicating internationally, it is usually best to avoid using very complex language, so that there is a greater chance that you will be understood by everyone in your audience.

However, it is important to be aware that in some contexts, if you use very simple language, people may feel that you are not very competent, or that you do not understand the subject very well.

For example, an American marketing director might give a very informal and entertaining presentation about a new product. His European audience may not be very impressed by this, because they think that his language is too simple, and his style is too informal.

People tend to prefer a more formal communication style in Germany and the Netherlands. People tend to prefer simpler, more informal language in the US and Australia.

Showing emotions

Not all cultures have the same attitude towards the expression of feelings. Some cultures tend to display their emotions more openly and immediately. Other cultures tend to keep their emotions hidden or controlled.

So, if you come from a culture where people tend to express their feelings openly, it is important to remember that some people — who come from a different type of background — may think that you are overreacting to a situation. On the other hand, if you come from a culture where people hide or control their emotions, some people you meet on your travels may find you rather 'cold,' or think that you are not very interested in the subject being discussed.

People tend to express their feelings more openly in Southern Europe, the Middle East, Latin America, and Eastern Europe. People are more likely to hide or control their emotions in the UK, Northern Europe, and Asia Pacific.

Private life and working life

In some cultures, a person's private life is clearly separated from his or her working life. In other cultures, someone's relationship with his or her boss extends outside the walls of the office.

If you are doing business with someone from a culture where private and working life are mixed together, building up a close relationship with your business partner can be as important as the business deal itself. In cultures where private and working life are kept separate, it is the terms of the business deal that are most important in reaching agreement.

For example, a Danish manager who is spending a period of time in the Chinese subsidiary of her company might observe that Chinese managers get involved with their employees' personal lives, for example, getting a loan to buy a house, attending their weddings, or visiting their sick family members in hospital. This would be very different from her own working experience, where managers are only involved with their staff on work-related issues.

People from Germany and Scandinavia typically separate their private life from their working life. In other parts of the world, such as China, people are generally more involved in their colleagues' personal lives.

Keeping to a structured plan

Some cultures prefer a more planned approach to working, while others are comfortable with a more flexible style.

In structured cultures (particularly those in Northern European countries), rules play an important role in how people organize their lives. In a work context, for example, a job description is the basis for which tasks a person is expected to do. In more flexible cultures (for example, South America, and most cultures in Asia), there are rules, but they are not always followed.

This difference is reflected in approaches to speech and writing. In cultures that prefer rules and structure, it is important that communication follows a clear, logical development of information. In more flexible cultures, people pay more attention to building a relationship with their listeners or readers, or to provoking a reaction.

Direct or indirect communication

Some cultures prefer a direct style of communicating, focusing on the explicit meaning of words. They prefer to say exactly what they mean, to deal with conflict directly, and to tell people openly when they do not want, or do not like, something.

People from cultures that prefer indirect communication, on the other hand, do not believe that everything needs to be said. An important feature of their communication style is to maintain a harmonious relationship between members of the group. They prefer to rely on suggested meaning, to avoid conflict, and to avoid saying "no".

For example, after giving a presentation, a German presenter might ask for feedback from the audience about his presentation. He would be very interested to find out if the audience agreed with the ideas in his presentation. The Asian participants might give him positive feedback, even if they were of a different opinion, because it would not feel natural for them to disagree with someone directly.

People from Germany, Holland, and Finland typically prefer a direct style of communication. People from the UK, Asia Pacific, and the Indian subcontinent typically prefer an indirect style of communication.

Level of formality

All societies have rules, rituals, and customs. However, in certain formal cultures, breaking these rules may lead to serious social consequences. In informal cultures, social relations are more informal and casual.

For example, an Australian business traveler is likely to be comfortable in informal situations with her superiors. If she spends time working in Japan, she might need some time to get used to Japanese formal greetings, which often involve bowing, and the careful and respectful examination of business cards.

People from Asia Pacific and the Indian subcontinent typically have stricter rules. Social relations between people in the UK, the US, and Australia are typically more informal and casual.

Humor

Humor is a universal human behavior. However, something that makes people laugh in one culture is not necessarily considered to be amusing in another.

In addition, some cultures consider humor to be appropriate in certain situations and not in other situations. For example, in some contexts it might be acceptable to include one or two jokes in business communication such as a presentation. Here, the use of humor is intended to lighten the content or to stimulate the audience. In other cultural contexts, while tasteful humor is still a natural part of human interaction, the telling of jokes in a meeting or presentation may be considered inappropriate.

For example, an Australian might decide to include a number of jokes in a presentation. In the US and in most European countries, these would be generally well received. However, a German, Austrian, or Swiss audience might not appreciate this style; they might find his jokes inappropriate.

Personal space

When you are talking to someone who is not a close friend or relative, how close to them do you stand? The physical "comfort zone" between communicators varies between cultures. For example, the comfortable conversation distances for a Latin American or Arab can be too close for someone from the US, the UK, or Asia Pacific, causing a feeling of discomfort.

Note that in a French or Middle Eastern company, morning greetings might involve a lot of physical contact, including handshaking and kissing on cheeks.

Conflict

In certain cultures such as those in Asia Pacific, loyalty to groups such as family, friends, and employers play an important role in the way that people deal with disagreements. Direct confrontation, open criticism, and controversial topics are avoided. The aim of this approach is to ensure that good relationships are maintained, and that people are less likely to feel offended.

In other cultures, such as those in Germany, the Netherlands, and Scandinavia, discussion and debate are widely used to solve problems. People are encouraged to take opposite positions, and to present their side of the argument. People who are not used to this type of behavior can sometimes feel personally criticized.

Respect

In some cultures, employees are expected to show respect for their bosses simply because the bosses have a higher position in the company.

In other cultures, bosses and their subordinates are much closer together, and treat one another more as equals. As a result, employees in these cultures will be comfortable telling their bosses what they think, and even disagreeing with them.

For example, a Swedish manager working in India should realize that she might be expected to openly show respect to those above her in the company. She would also have to be aware that she needs to give clear and explicit instructions to the staff who work for her; she should not assume that they will take action without asking her first, as doing this could be seen as a sign of disrespect.

Loyalty to the company

Some cultures, particularly in the US, the UK, and Europe, focus mainly on the individual; people tend to concentrate on trying to improve their financial situation for themselves and their family.

In contrast, people in more "collective" cultures — in Asia, for example — place great emphasis on loyalty and the membership of groups. Here, harmony and loyalty within a company are very important. The wealth of the company may be viewed as more important than the wealth of the individual.

Building a relationship

In some cultures, particularly in Asia Pacific, a first business meeting is likely to include questions about your background, especially your family and your education. In this type of culture, people like to establish a sense of trust before getting down to business.

In other cultures, such as the US and Northern Europe, people like to know a little about their business partners before starting to work together. However, detailed knowledge is not as important for establishing business relations. In these cultures, people like to get straight down to business, believing that relationships can be developed later.

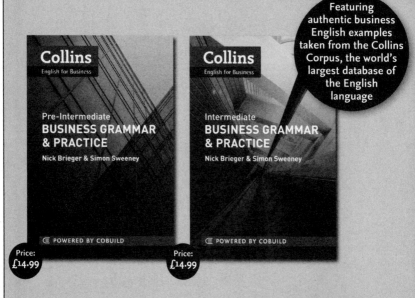